LET HISTORY JUDGE

LET HISTORY JUDGE

The Origins and Consequences of Stalinism

REVISED AND EXPANDED EDITION
EDITED AND TRANSLATED BY GEORGE SHRIVER

ROY MEDVEDEV

COLUMBIA UNIVERSITY PRESS   NEW YORK

Columbia University Press

New York
Copyright © 1989 Columbia University Press
All rights reserved

Library of Congress Cataloging-in-Publication Data

Medvedev, Roy Aleksandrovich, 1925–
    [K sudu istorii. English]
    Let history judge : the origins and consequences of Stalinism /
Roy Medvedev ; edited and translated by George Shriver. —Rev. and
expanded ed.
      p. cm.
    Includes index.
    ISBN 0-231-06350-4
    ISBN 0-231-06351-2 (pbk.)
    1. Soviet Union—Politics and government—1917–1936. 2. Soviet
Union—Politics and government—1936–1953. 3. Stalin, Joseph,
1879–1953. 4. Political atrocities—Soviet Union. I. Shriver,
George, 1936– . II. Title.
DK267.M41413   1989
947.084'2—dc19   89-758
                                             CIP

Casebound editions of Columbia University Press books are
Smyth-sewn and printed on permanent and durable acid-free paper

∞

Printed in the United States of America

c 10 9 8 7 6 5 4 3 2
p 10 9 8 7 6 5 4 3 2

Book design by Ken Venezio

CONTENTS

PART 2
STALIN'S USURPATION OF POWER, AND THE GREAT TERROR

PART 4
SOME CONSEQUENCES OF STALIN'S PERSONAL DICTATORSHIP

12. Errors in Diplomacy and War   723

13. Crimes and Mistakes in the Postwar Period   781

14. The Impact of Stalinism on Science and Art   808

AUTHOR'S PREFACE TO THE REVISED AND EXPANDED EDITION

The book that I am presenting for the reader's consideration is the main work of my life. I have been occupied with it nearly all my adult years. For approximately ten years I was preparing myself in one way or another for this task, and during the subsequent twenty-five years I worked directly on the book, gathering evidence particle by particle, sometimes by entire handfuls—testimony, facts, and documents on the history of Stalinism. I reflected deeply on these materials, discussing them with friends and co-thinkers and arguing with opponents holding the most varied ideological positions.

I met and discussed at length with many who had passed through Stalin's labor camps—Old Bolsheviks, including a few surviving adherents of Trotsky, Zinoviev, or Bukharin; former Socialist Revolutionaries (SRs), anarchists, and Mensheviks who had miraculously survived; technical specialists not belonging to any party; former military people, scientists, writers, journalists, party functionaries, and ordinary workers and peasants; people who had been labeled kulaks and those who had "de-kulakized" them; clergymen and lay people; former Chekists (members of the state security police); former Russian emigres who had returned to the USSR; and Russians, Jews, Ukrainians, and Armenians who dreamed of leaving the Soviet Union to become part of the new wave of emigration.

Only in the conditions and atmosphere of the sixties were such meetings and conversations possible—before death carried some off to a better world and before arguments and disagreements divided others into irreconcilably hostile camps. Only in the sixties could Mikhail Suslov have shaken the hand of Aleksandr Solzhenitsyn, and Andrei Sakharov have discussed problems of democratization of Soviet society with Mstislav Keldysh, president of the Soviet Academy of Sciences. Only in the sixties could I have discussed initial versions of my work with Varlam Shalamov in his tiny room, with Yuli Dombrovsky in his apartment, with Aleksandr Tvardovsky at his home, with the director of the Institute of Marxism-Leninism and the editor in chief of the Publishing House for Political Literature in their offices, and with party officials in several offices of the CPSU Central Committee. That time and that social atmosphere have gone never to return, but I am happy that I was in a position to take advantage of the situation in the sixties to pursue my work on this book.

Since the time I first began to think about the political realities in my country and the world—and in my generation such thinking began very early—I considered myself on the side of social justice and socialism. But I was never a blind supporter of any political or social doctrine. Reality was too harsh. Not only was the tragedy that befell our family in 1938 a difficult experience for me; so also were the tragic events of the war, from 1941 to 1945, in which we participated directly or indirectly. I understood that socialism as I wished to see it was still a distant ideal, while the actual life of the mass of the people remained full of injustice and suffering. It long ago became my primary aim and the driving motive of my life and work to orient myself in the contradictory reality around me and to find a way of changing it for the better, including changes in the prevailing ideological conceptions. This influenced me in choosing philosophy as my main field of specialization and in making history and education my first spheres of practical activity.

As early as the fifties I began thinking about a big book on the history of Soviet society but not until early 1962 did I make the first rough outlines. By 1964 I was able to discuss draft versions of the book with many of my friends. I worked openly, making no secret of my manuscript and taking no measures to prevent it from circulating privately. In 1969 when the eleventh version of the book had been completed I decided to publish it abroad. The real threat on the one hand of a rehabilitation of Stalin, and on the other, the no less distinct danger of repression against my twin brother, Zhores, and myself were the main considerations behind that decision. I am deeply grateful to Professor David Joravsky in the United States and Professor Georges Haupt in France, who assisted in the editing and publication of that first edition. I also wish to thank several Austrian and German Socialists, Communists, and liberals, who from 1969 to 1971 helped me maintain communication with the editors and publisher. Today I can name some of those persons — Helmut Liebknecht, Agnes Juneman, and Heinrich Böll. The first, somewhat abridged, edition of this book came out in the United States under the title *Let History Judge* (New York, 1972). In 1972 and 1973 it appeared under other titles in West Germany, France, Italy, Belgium, and Japan, and somewhat later in Spain. A more complete edition appeared in Russian in the United States in 1974 and later in Chinese in Peking.

All sections of the present edition have been enlarged, and the book has been fundamentally revised. This applies as well to the author's ideas and opinions. It is, in fact, a new book.

The appearance of this book in print was followed by the publication of many reviews, critical comments, and discussions, mainly favorable to the author. But I could not consider the subjects touched on in the book exhausted, and I continued my work as a historian and philosopher in many areas.

Several considerations prompted me to continue work on this book. First of all, its publication in many different countries and its circulation in the USSR resulted in the transmittal to the author of various kinds of documents and materials and recently written memoirs, as well as books and articles from the twenties and thirties previously unknown to me. A person who works openly on the subject of Stalin and Stalinism in the Soviet Union inevitably becomes a center of attraction for many who wish to express their opinions or impart testimony on this question, which is still a very sore subject in Soviet society.

Second, my work in other areas of Soviet history and on the structure and particular features of Soviet society enabled me to publish several books from 1972 to 1985 that helped me reach a better understanding of Stalinism, its preconditions and consequences, and the fates of various opponents of Stalin and members of his entourage.

Third, I have had the opportunity in the fifteen years since this book was published to read many studies by Western Sovietologists on Stalin and the Stalin era, on problems of Stalinism, and on Soviet history in general. Although some of these writings were published in the fifties and sixties, they were received by me and my friends only after great delay, which is understandable under Soviet conditions. I am referring to works by Robert C. Tucker, Adam Ulam, Robert Conquest, Stephen F. Cohen, Boris Souvarine, Leonard Schapiro, Jean-Jacques Marie, Harrison Salisbury, Giuseppe Boffa, Moshe Lewin, Robert V. Daniels, Wolfgang Leonhard, and several others. I also had the pleasure of meeting and talking with some of these authors in Moscow on various occasions—Tucker, Cohen, Boffa, Daniels, and Ulam.

I cannot leave unmentioned of course the larger number of books and articles published by Soviet authors and by writers who have emigrated from the USSR and several Eastern European countries. These works, written from different points of view, shed light on many little-known pages of our past and bring forward a number of theories, conceptions, and proposals, the discussion of which must surely prove useful to the historian, regardless of viewpoint. I have in mind the writings of Eugenia Ginzburg, Nadezhda Mandelstam, Lev Kopelev, Varlam Shalamov, Aleksandr Solzhenitsyn, Zhores Medvedev, Yevgeny Gnedin, Anton Antonov-Ovseyenko, Vasily Grossman, Boris Bazhanov, Mikhail Agursky, Michal Reiman, Aleksandr Nekrich, Michel Heller, Milovan Djilas, Anatoly Levitin-Krasnov, Arnost Kolman, Valery Chalidze, Lidia Chukovskaya, the memoirs of Nikita Khrushchev, and many others.

Finally, an extremely important factor promoted me to continue my work on Stalinism: the stubborn attempts to rehabilitate Stalin that have persisted since 1969. In scholarly works, novels, memoirs, films, magazines, and newspapers the image of Stalin has continually reappeared as a "wise statesmen," a "prudent manager," an "experienced politician," and an "outstanding military leader," who suffered only from some minor shortcomings. Especially strong pressure was exerted along these lines by certain highly influential forces in 1979, on the hundredth anniversary of Stalin's birth, and in 1984–1985, in connection with the fortieth anniversary of the Soviet victory over Nazi Germany. It is only natural under such conditions that opponents of Stalinism should continue their efforts to expose the monstrous crimes of Stalin and his accomplices, who victimized millions and millions of Soviet citizens and hundreds of thousands in neighboring countries. Stalinism and neo-Stalinism unfortunately remain a real danger for Soviet society and it is impossible to reduce this danger in any fundamental way if there is a refusal to make an objective, attentive, and honest study of the realities of Soviet history.

Of course Stalinism can be criticized from various points of view and various conclusions can be drawn from such criticism. The Soviet people have a very poor knowledge of their past; their collective historical memory has been attenuated to a very dangerous degree. It is not surprising therefore that even the limited revelations about Stalin's crimes made in 1956 at the Twentieth Congress of the Soviet Communist Party produced not only confusion and bewilderment but also disillusionment in socialism. Nonetheless, it would be wrong to assume that such disillusionment can be avoided by continuing to keep the Soviet people in ignorance. We live in a big world, in which many different forces contend for people's minds and hearts. If "in the interests of socialism" we refuse to make a thorough study of the Stalin era, we will not be serving those interests. Socialism cannot maintain a reputation as a scientific social doctrine if it is unable to explain the socio-historical, economic, and political processes that under specific circumstances led to the degeneration of the socialist state and to tyranny by specific individuals in socialist countries.

"What was hurt under Stalin," asked Ilya Ehrenburg in his memoirs, "the idea or people? It was not the idea that was stricken. It was people of my generation that were stricken." (*Novy Mir*, 1965, no. 5.)

Ehrenburg's answer is mistaken. The lawlessness of the Stalin era struck a terrible blow against both people and the very idea of socialism. Those to whom this idea is precious, who do not wish the deaths of millions of victims of cruel and arbitrary rule to remain as a senseless tragedy in Soviet history, those people must overcome one of the most dangerous consequences of Stalinism—fear of speaking the truth.

The author of this book has modified his views in many respects to make them more precise, but he has maintained his adherence to socialist ideals. I have had to listen to a great deal of rude and unjust criticism as well as threats from Soviet and foreign Stalinists. For example, some Italian Maoists wrote in their newspaper: "Medvedev's book, from its first page to its last, constitutes an accumulation of crude slander and obvious lies. Stalin is showered with such abuse and accused of so many things contradictory to reason that practically nothing remains of his work. Such resort to the lowest kind of mud-slinging can be explained only by the degree of degeneration typical of the revisionist intellecuals." (*Nuovo Unita* [Rome], April 3, 1973.)

I have also had occasion to hear or read rude and unjust criticism from Soviet and foreign anti-Stalinists, emigres and Sovietologists who find it difficult to pronounce the word socialism in any positive connection. A certain Joseph A. Renyansky has written about the "moral degradation of Medvedev," who swims cheerfully on a sea of blood shed by his country-men while celebrating the death and discreditment of Stalin (*National Review*, May 16, 1980).

I hope that the best answer to such accusations will be the content and conclusions of this book.

Edward Crankshaw, the prominent British Sovietologist, whose recent death was a great loss to scholarship, wrote a review of the first edition in March 1972. He likened my efforts to grapple with the history of Stalinism to the struggle of Laocoon and predicted that in the end the serpents would probably devour me. If they did not, he said, and if I were to survive and continue my study of life and thought in the West, about which I supposedly knew too little, and to look again at the question of continuity in Russian history, which—he charged—I had too lightly left out of consideration, I might some day be able to correct the insufficiencies in my work. (See *The Observer* [London], March 26, 1972.)

I will not hide the fact that I find it pleasant to read the praise as well as the critical remarks of such a scholar as Edward Crankshaw. True, he did not predict the best possible future for me, but thus far the serpents have not managed to devour me, and I am happy that during the past fifteen years I have been able to correct, if not everything in my book, at least many of its shortcomings.

I have not changed the book's general structure very much, although some readers and reviewers have criticized it for one-sidedness. I ac-knowledge this reproach but I do not consider this a serious shortcoming. My research had the aim of studying only one aspect of Soviet reality in one period of historical development. Like any other science, history has the right to make abstractions. If I may resort to a comparison, this book could be called "the history of a disease," to be precise the history of that serious and prolonged disease of Soviet society which has been given the

name Stalinism. Of course we all know very well that the Stalin era was
not only the time of the Great Terror. It was also a time of progress in
many areas, which must also be the subject of historical research. But
history cannot avoid the darker pages of the past. Unfortunately, as
Victor Hugo remarked, history does not have a wastebasket.

It is natural that the author's attention should be focused on the figure
of Stalin. But this book is not a biography of Stalin; it discusses not only
Stalin but also the socio-political and economic conditions and social
groups on which he based himself.

Over many years of work hundreds of people, holding various opinions
and points of view, have given me assistance, without which my research
could not have gone forward. This assistance took the form of documen-
tary materials, testimony, advice, and critical commentary. At this point
I would like to express my thanks for the help given me by the veteran
party members I. P. Gavrilov, Suren Gazaryan, L. M. Portnov, A. I.
Babinets, Yevgeny Frolov, A. M. Durmashkin, Pyotr Chagin, S. I.
Berdichevskaya, D. Yu. Zorina, Pavel Shabalkin, A. V. Snegov, A. Ye.
Yevstafyev, M. V. Ostrogorsky, I. M. Danishevsky, Olga Shatunovskaya,
Raisa Lert, A. P. Khosiev, M. V. Solntseva, Pavel Aksyonov, I. P.
Aleksakhin, E. G. Leikin, M. N. Averbakh, Yevgeny Gnedin, A. N.
Gramp, N. K. Ilyukhov, Ye. A. Kosareva, Sergei Pisarev, R. G. Alikhan-
ova, P. V. Rudnev, N. M. Ulanovskaya, A. I. Khankovsky, M. L.
Fishman, Ya. I. Drobinsky, A. I. Todorsky, Boris Ivanov, and S. B.
Brichkina. Participants in important events of the past have also helped
me, including Mikhail Yakubovich, Z. B. Gandlevskaya, Anna Larina,
I. N. Forshtendeker, T. S. Tretyakova, G. I. Menshikov, Ye. A. Grin,
Ye. Z. Ogorodinitskaya, and A. Z. Ogorodinitskaya. In this instance I am
naming only those who have given me permission to do so or those who
are no longer alive.

Great help with documents and materials from personal archives was
given me by the following authors: Konstantin Simonov, Aleksandr Tvar-
dovsky, Ilya Ehrenburg, Alesksandr Dementyev, Igor Sats, Veniamin
Kaverin, Yuri Trifonov, Aleksandr Bek, Vladimir Tendryakov, Kamil
Ikramov, Lev Kopelev, Boris Yampolsky, I. S. Shkapa, Vasily Akysonov,
Eugenia Ginzburg, Varlam Shalamov, S. N. Rostovsky (Ernst Henry),
A. G. Pismenny, A. G. Gladkov, V. A. Rudny, S. E. Babyonysheva,
Vladimir Dudintsev, Yelizaveta Drabkina, Yuri Karyakin, L. F. Kabo,
Ye. Yu. Maltsev, L. Ye. Pinsky, and the film director Mikhail Romm.

I also received support and assistance from scientists and scholars in various fields of knowledge—Pavel Zdrodovsky, F. F. Korolyov, Boris Astaurov, Andrei Sakharov, Aleksandr Nekrich, Mikhail Agursky, Valentin Turchin, Yuli Tuvin, A. P. Alliluyev, I. V. Nikolaev, Leonid Petrovsky, D. I. Lev, V. N. Litvinov, Lev Karpinsky, G. B. Fyodorov, Donald Maclean, I. N. Khokhlushkin, V. P. Efroimson, A. A. Shibanov, and several others who must remain unnamed.

From the very beginning and through all the stages of work on this book, from its first conception until its publication, my chief helper has been my brother, Zhores Medvedev, who also took upon himself the organization and supervision of the publication of this new edition.

This work is fundamentally the product of private research. During the past eighteen years I have not been employed by any official Soviet institution, nor have I been obliged to accommodate my methods, my timing, or the conclusions of my work to any such institutions. My collaboration with the people I have mentioned was based exclusively on personal initiative and trust. I did not make use of or have access to any closed archives, "special collections," or any other limited-access depositories and I am not familiar with any. I have not resorted to conspiratorial methods: that would have ruled out discussion of this book with my friends. I have neither asked for nor received assistance from any official body. I hope this book will be of benefit to its readers.

NOTE: The Introductory Essay, with which the book opens, was written in 1988, and takes into account recent developments under Gorbachev.

TRANSLATOR'S NOTE

By George Shriver

This is substantially a new work in comparison with the first English edition of *Let History Judge,* translated by Colleen Taylor and edited by David Joravsky and Georges Haupt (New York, 1972). Major portions of this edition, especially in the first two chapters, are entirely new, and throughout the book there are new passages, sometimes whole sections. On the other hand, the author has deleted quite a few passages that appeared in the first edition. In addition, there are many minor alterations expressing changes in the author's point of view. For example, in referring to the Soviet Communist Party he speaks of "the party" rather than "our party." Nevertheless, many parts of this edition reproduce to a greater or lesser extent the translation made by Colleen Taylor and David Joravsky, especially when the author's changes were minimal and the existing English version served the purpose perfectly well. I have also followed the first edition in paraphrasing some quotations and making some other abridgments in order to save space.

During the work on this edition, particularly in 1988, major changes occurred in the official Soviet attitude toward Stalin and the former opposition leaders in the Soviet Communist Party. Most notably Bukharin, Rykov, Zinoviev, Kamenev, Pyatakov, and Radek have now been cleared of the charges leveled against them in the Moscow trials of 1936–1938, and Bukharin's party membership has been posthumously restored. This points toward rehabilitation of all the defendants in those trials, including Leon Trotsky and his son Leon Sedov. In fact a Soviet official reportedly announced in October 1988 that works by Trotsky would be published in the Soviet Union in 1989 (for the first time since 1927). Works by Bukharin have already appeared in the official Soviet press.

In view of this flurry of rapid changes the author has not tried to rewrite and update those passages in the book which discuss the opposition leaders, their convictions, and the official attitude toward them that prevailed for so many years. That is a subject now for separate work.

The changes in the Soviet Union have affected the author himself. Instead of a persecuted dissident, he is now published in the Soviet press, was allowed to take part in a press conference for foreign reporters in June 1989 sponsored by the government news agency Novosti, and may even be appointed to an official post as a historian. These changes, too, cannot be reflected in the present edition.

In his years of work on this new edition, during the seventies and the first half of the eighties, the author worked under great restrictions. Consequently he has not always been able to cite or verify the sources of quotations. On occasion the KGB confiscated parts of his archives, making further reference or verification impossible. Some materials were passed on to him by others who copied them from the originals, not always giving full information (place and date of publication, page numbers, etc.). It was one of Stalin's common practices, according to Roy Medvedev, to make statements or issue orders verbally, without putting them in writing. Some of these statements were overheard by Old Bolsheviks or others, who told the author about them. What Stalin said became widely known, by his own intention, but there was and is no published source. In the nature of things there could not be a published source for much of the information in this book; it was passed on by the victims of repression or their friends or relatives. The police records of their cases, if they exist, have not been published. Often the author gives the names of those reporting information about Stalin, his system, and the repression, but sometimes because of conditions in the Soviet Union the name of the source is still withheld. In the light of these difficulties Roy Medvedev's accomplishment in historical research and documentation is all the more impressive.

On Transliteration. The style I have used for Russian names differs substantially from the one used in the first edition. In the text, the system most accessible to general readers has been used—that is, one with no diacritical marks and with *y* rather than *i* or *ii* in the appropriate places. For example, Vasily Aksyonov (not Vasilli Aksenev), Grigory Zinoviev (not Grigorii Zinov'ev), Yevgeny Preobrazhensky (not Evgenii Preobrazhenskii), and Yemelyan Yaroslavsky (not Emel'ian Iaroslavskii). Likewise, the *y* usually appears when that sound occurs between vowels, as in Ovseyenko and Chalmayev. In contrast, bibliographical items follow the Library of Congress transliteration system, to assist readers who might want to look them up. Names that appear in both the text and the notes are given in the more readable form. If a library user encounters difficulty locating works by an author using the text spelling, the name should be adjusted to the Library of Congress system (for example, look up Lidiia, not Lydia; and Trotskii, not Trotsky).

Whenever possible, first names have been used rather than initials, but when the first name has not been available, initials appear as in the Russian text. Some letters of the Russian alphabet are transliterated by more than one English letter. Thus Ch., Kh., Sh., Ts., and Zh. stand for certain Russian consonants, and Ya., Ye., Yo., and Yu. for the corresponding Russian vowels.

Most first names are not Westernized. The exceptions include those best known by the Westernized forms of their names. Thus, Joseph (not Iosif) Stalin, Leon (not Lev) Trotsky, Adolph and Maria Joffe (not Adol'f and Mariia Ioffe, or Yoffe), Eugenia (not Yevgeniya) Ginzburg, and Maxim Gorky (not Maksim Gor'kii).

On the Notes. Some are by the author, some by David Joravsky, editor of the first edition, and some by myself. Those by the author are unbracketed. Those retained from the first edition are in brackets followed by David Joravsky's initials. Those by me are in brackets followed by G. S.

January 1989

INTRODUCTORY ESSAY:
PERESTROIKA AND STALINISM

The period during which this new and enlarged edition was being prepared for publication has proved to be a time of great changes for the
Soviet Union. For three years now the policy of perestroika (restructuring) has been under way. There is more to this new policy than merely
the effort to accelerate scientific, technical, and economic progress; restructuring in the realm of ideology and culture is also one of its essential
components. The social sciences are faced with the task of filling in their
own "blank pages," correcting the numerous falsifications and omissions
that exist in great number in all fields of social science, especially history.
In fact, in its present form it is even rather awkward to call Soviet history
a science.

In this area a change for the better has already taken place, though no
fundamental breakthrough has yet occurred, either in the relations of

production or in the numerous superstructural aspects of life. And the possibility of reaction or retroactive motion is still quite real. In order to overcome the resistance of reactionary forces in all areas of Soviet life, it is necessary to carry out a more thoroughgoing reevaluation of the attitude of the people and the intelligentsia toward the figure of Stalin and toward everything that is customarily called Stalinism. In ideology and the social sciences the problem of Stalin and Stalinism has proved to be central and most important both for those who are struggling for the renewal of Soviet society and for those who oppose such renewal. In early 1985 new and extremely stubborn attempts were made to rehabilitate Stalin. As the fortieth anniversary of the Soviet victory in World War II drew near, the number of voices extolling Stalin multiplied. He was hailed as both a statesman and a military leader, as one who supposedly speeded up the development of our country dramatically, turning it into a superpower. It was proposed that the triumphal celebration of the fortieth anniversary of the victory over Hitler's Germany be marked by restoring Stalin's name to the city of Volgograd and to a part of Moscow called the Volgograd district. This did not happen, primarily because of the death of Chernenko and the change of party leadership at the March and April 1985 plenums of the Central Committee.

During the first half of 1986 condemnation of Stalin and Stalinism was hinted at rather than stated outright. The playwright Mikhail Shatrov, in choosing a prototype for the typical Stalinist in his play *Dictatorship of Conscience,* did not select someone from Stalin's immediate circle but rather the French Communist André Marty, a commissar of the International Brigades during the Spanish civil war, who is little known in the Soviet Union. The relaxation of censorship restrictions, changes in the personnel of the Central Committee apparatus, the leading bodies of the "creative unions" (the writers' union, cinematographers' union, and other cultural organizations), and the editorial boards of literary and sociopolitical magazines, and the first steps in applying the policy of glasnost (increased openness)—all this began to markedly alter the Soviet cultural scene. An important step forward was the publication of *The Appointment* by Aleksandr Bek.[1] In this novel, written in the early sixties (I quote from a manuscript copy of the novel in the present book), the author presents a very accurate and quite sinister portrait of Stalin, as

1. *Znamya* 1986, no. 10.

well as pointing out the defects of supercentralization and an authoritarian-despotic style of government.

The most dramatic change in the areas of ideology and culture began after the Central Committee plenum of January 1987, whose decisions were reached only after resistance and a sharp struggle. The film *Repentance* by the Georgian director Tengiz Abuladze proved to be a major event in public life. Produced several years earlier, the film aroused the ire of local Stalinists in Georgia who demanded not only that any showings be prohibited but even that the negatives be destroyed. Nevertheless, as early as the summer of 1986 the film appeared on the screen in Georgia, and in January 1987 it was screened throughout the Soviet Union. Unusual in its artistic form, employing the methods of surrealism, the grotesque, and the absurd, as well as realism, and the genres of tragedy and satire, *Repentance* struck a blow of great emotional force at the ideology of totalitarianism in general and Stalinism in particular.

At the same time the unfinished novel *The Disappearance* by the recently deceased Yuri Trifonov was published.[2] Its main theme is the repression in the thirties of many who were prominent figures in the 1917 Bolshevik revolution. Also, the Leningrad magazine *Neva* published Vladimir Dudintsev's long novel *Belye odezhdy*, which is about the ravaging of classical genetics by Stalin and Lysenko.[3] And on the same topic, the short novel *Zubr* by Danil Granin was published.[4] Almost simultaneously two Moscow magazines printed "By right of Memory," a long narrative poem by Aleksandr Tvardovsky about the tragic fate of his father, a victim of the inhuman "de-kulakization," and about many other illegalities of the Stalin era and the moral losses to society and the people.[5] In March 1987 *Requiem*, Anna Akhmatova's celebrated work about the terrible acts of repression in Leningrad that began in 1935 and did not end until Stalin's death, was finally published in the USSR.[6] Of universal interest is the short novel by Anatoly Pristavkin *Nochevala zolotaya tuchka* (A Golden Cloudlet Spent the Night), about a tragedy of the Chechen people deported in 1944 from their ancestral homeland.[7] During the winter and spring of 1987 a number of other

2. *Druzhba narodov* (1987), no. 1.
3. *Neva* (1987) nos. 1–4.
4. *Novy mir* (1987), nos. 2 and 3.
5. *Znamya* (1987), no. 2; and *Novy mir* (1987), no. 3.
6. *Oktyabr* (1987), no. 3.
7. *Znamya* (1987), nos. 3 and 4.

important short stories and novels appeared, in particular ones by Bulat Okudzhava, Fazil Iskander, and I. Gerasimov, as well as major cycles of poems by Boris Slutsky, Olga Berggolts, Nikolai Zabolotsky, Rasul Gamzatov, Varlam Shalamov, B. Chichibabin, A. Tarkovsky, A. Zhigulin, and a number of other poets. Because of the outspokenly anti-Stalinist and otherwise critical content of these works, most of them had remained in their authors' desk drawers for the past fifteen to twenty-five years.

A major event in the literary, social, and political life of the Soviet Union was the publication of Anatoly Rybakov's novel *Children of the Arbat* by the magazine *Druzhba narodov* in its April, May, and June issues for 1987. The author had finished the first part of this novel as early as the mid-sixties but was unable to have it published. Undaunted, he continued to work on the novel through the seventies and into the eighties. For the first time in Soviet literature Stalin appears not as an episodic figure but as the central character of a novel. *Children of the Arbat* has met with the warm approval of the majority and the vicious disapproval of the minority. In my view the novel is not only an excellent work of art; it also gives a psychologically and historically accurate portrait of Stalin in 1933–34, when he was already laying the basis for a series of perfidious acts of provocation, establishing a pretext for the destruction of all those he found unsuitable, and starting to organize an apparatus that would be based solely on his own totalitarian authority.

The offensive against Stalinism begun in novel, verse, and film was continued through the summer and fall of 1987 in dozens of journalistic essays, scholarly articles, reviews, and letters from readers and audiences. Partially suppressed writings from the twenties began to be reprinted, including Boris Pilnyak's celebrated *Tale of the Unextinguished Moon*, which was banned in 1926 on Stalin's personal orders.[8] It was obvious to everyone that Pilnyak's story dealt with the dubious circumstances surrounding the death of Mikhail Frunze (which I discuss in ch. 2, sec. 7). The cinema entered the fray against Stalinism with renewed force. The crimes of Stalin were taken up in two new historico-documentary films, "The Risk" and "More Light," while "The Cold Summer of Fifty-Three" deals with the touchy subject of certain events that unfolded in a northern Russian village shortly after Stalin's death.

The new year, 1988, has begun with probably an even stronger attack

8. *Znamya* (1987), no. 12.

on Stalinism than in 1987. While *Novy mir* has begun publication of Pasternak's *Doctor Zhivago*, the magazine *Oktyabr* is publishing Vasily Grossman's *Life and Fate*, which was written in the late fifties under the direct impact of the Twentieth Party Congress. In 1961, immediately after Grossman had completed his work, the novel was "arrested"—that is, all copies, including rough drafts, were taken from the author, from his friends, and from the editorial boards of the two magazines to which he had submitted it. Politburo member Mikhail Suslov told Grossman that the novel could not be printed for another two or three hundred years. Yet, wonder of wonders, we have had to wait "only" twenty-seven years for it. *Znamya* began the new year by publishing Mikhail Shatrov's new play, *Dalshe . . . Dalshe . . . Dalshe* (Further . . . Further . . . Further), in which the playwright himself goes much further in analyzing and condemning the phenomenon of Stalinism. The Latvian magazine *Daugava* is planning to publish *Journey Into the Whirlwind*, Eugenia Ginzburg's autobiographical account of Stalin's purges and prison camps. I frequently referred to the manuscript copy of her book in the present work as well as to Suren Gazaryan's *Eto ne dolzhno povtorit'sia, (This Must Never Happen Again)* which will be published by the magazine *Literaturnaya Armenia*. I consider these accounts by Ginzburg and Gazaryan, together with Varlam Shalamov's *Tales of Kolyma*, also being prepared for publication in the USSR, the best on the subject of Stalin's camps.

Most of the newly published works listed here were written in the fifties and sixties, and in most cases the authors have already died. Many other works of this kind are still waiting their turn, and we must hope that their publication is not very far off. Some writings published in the fifties and sixties that are well known to the older generation but not to younger people have been reprinted—"The Heirs of Stalin," by Yevtushenko, "One's Own Opinion" by Danil Granin, and "Levers" by Aleksandr Yashin. Only now can we appreciate what a powerful forward impulse the Twentieth and Twenty-Second party congresses gave to Soviet thought and culture. The best representatives of our culture began the attempt to grapple with the tragic lessons of our history. However, only a small part of their work saw the light of day. What an infinitely large amount was lost by those generations whose moral, intellectual, and political development occurred in the "period of stagnation" (as the Brezhnev era is now being called), the years when mediocrity and suppression of information triumphed. Fortunately that period, which in a moral sense probably did no less harm to our people than the Stalin era, is now passing away.

The present criticism of Stalin and Stalinism is linked in many ways with the anti-Stalin campaign of the early sixties. But in many ways it differs. The secret speech at the Twentieth Congress criticizing Stalin's personality cult and the anti-Stalinist thrust of the Twenty-Second Congress were, of course, primarily the result of initiatives taken by Nikita Khrushchev, who encountered open and hidden resistance from the majority of the Presidium of the Central Committee and sabotage on the part of a considerable section of the party's ideological apparatus and influential government agencies and military leaders. Many things were done only under duress. Even the decision to publish Solzhenitsyn's "One Day in the Life of Ivan Denisovich" required two sessions of the party's Presidium. Of the major magazines only Tvardovsky's *Novy mir* worked consistently and courageously for the renewal of Soviet culture on a democratic anti-Stalinist basis.

In 1987 the offensive against Stalinism was being waged on a broad front with the unquestionable support of the majority of the Political Bureau (Politburo) and the Secretariat of the party's Central Committee. As early as the summer of 1987, General Secretary Gorbachev himself began to speak about the crimes of Stalin, his mass destruction of party and government personnel. In his speech at the October 1987 Plenum of the Central Committee Gorbachev repeated his earlier remarks about the crimes of the thirties, the result of the abuse of power, and about Stalin's personal responsibility for those crimes.

"It is sometimes said," Gorbachev stated, "that Stalin did not know about many of the instances of lawlessness. Documents at our disposal show that this is not so. The guilt of Stalin and his immediate entourage before the party and the people for the wholesale repressive measures and acts of lawlessness is enormous and unforgivable. This is a lesson for all generations."[9]

Similarly at a meeting Gorbachev held at the offices of the party's Central Committee on January 8, 1988, with directors of the mass media, the "creative unions," and various agencies concerned with ideology, he stressed that the party would not tolerate any glossing over of the historical truth. "We cannot forgive those who committed lawless acts, still less those guilty of grave crimes."[10]

9. *Pravda*, November 3, 1987.
10. *Pravda*, January 13, 1988.

A consistently anti-Stalinist line is being followed today by such "thick" journals as *Novy mir, Oktyabr, Druzhba narodov, Znamya,* and *Neva.* Important material on historical subjects is also being published by the magazines *Yunost, Moskva, Don,* and even *Nash sovremennik* [which previously was noted for a strongly Russian-nationalist position, close to Stalinism]. Many weeklies have been waging an active campaign against Stalinism—*Nedelya, Literaturnaya gazeta, Literaturnaya Rossiya,* and especially *Moscow News, Argumenty i fakty,* and *Ogonyok* [which previously was notorious for its pro-Stalinist line]. Interesting material can also be found in the magazines *Nauka i zhizn, Voprosy literatury, Literaturnoe obozrenie, Mir i dvadtsatyi vek, Sovetskii ekran,* and *Iskusstvo kino* and in the newspapers *Sovetskaya kultura, Izvestia,* and *Sovetskaya Rossiya.* Of course there are many other magazines and newspapers that have taken an intermediate position, refraining from publication of any sharply controversial material on Soviet history. But only one magazine has come out openly and actively against the current criticism of Stalin: *Molodaya gvardiya,* led by such writers as A. Ivanov, P. Proskurin, and V. Gorbachev [no relation to Mikhail Gorbachev]. They have taken as their slogan two lines by the pro-Stalinist poet V. Fyodorov: "Do not disturb the graves of old. They are fraught with new disasters." Their spokesman, V. Gorbachev, cries out, "The new direction of *Ogonyok* is something far worse than the pollution of Lake Baikal!"[11]

In addressing the tragic question of Stalinism in our history, the Soviet press has usually raised the same issues that were raised in the early sixties. This is natural because two generations have grown up who do not really know Soviet history, either from their own experience or from the textbooks. Only now are these people learning from our press about the terror of the thirties, the famine of 1933, the abuse during collectivization, the assassination of Kirov, the decimation of the command personnel of the Red Army, the defeats in the first years of the war, the atmosphere of terror imposed by "the Father of the Peoples," and his disastrous interference in the natural and social sciences. Once again our newspapers and magazines are publishing articles by prominent scientists, scholars, writers, government figures, and military leaders who fell victim to Stalin's repression. Only now are the younger generations hearing something about the activities and contributions of Nikita

11. *Molodaya gvardiya* (1987), No. 7, p. 240.

Khrushchev. For twenty years Khrushchev's very name was kept out of our press. If one were to go by the history textbooks of the seventies, one might conclude that after Stalin's death the leadership of the party and the country passed directly to—Leonid Brezhnev.

Nevertheless, we are not seeing a simple repetition of what was already said in the sixties. We are learning new names and new details about the Stalinist terror. In marking the hundredth anniversary of N. I. Vavilov's birth, our press has made public many new facts about the life and tragic fate of this classic figure in Soviet natural science, together with many new details about the difficult history of the biological sciences in the Soviet Union. We have also learned more details about the fates of many writers, diplomats, and government figures who "disappeared." For example, there is new information about Mikhail Kolstov[12] and new facts about Nikolai Voznesenksy and A. Kuznetsov [victims in the "Leningrad Affair" described in chapter 13].[13]

We usually speak of both Stalin and his immediate entourage in discussing responsibility for the crimes of Stalinism. In the early sixties this referred most often to Molotov, Malenkov, Kaganovich, Voroshilov, Beria, Yagoda, and Yezhov. In 1987 the magazine *Nauka i zhizn* presented a detailed account of the sinister role played by another one of Stalin's close associates, Lev Mekhlis, in the fate that befell most Red Army commanders before the war and in the fate of the armies under Mekhlis's command during the war.[14] Similarly, *Literaturnaya gazeta* has published an essay full of detail about one of the most odious figures of the Stalin era—Andrei Vyshinsky, the chief government prosecutor in the frame-up trials of 1936, 1937, and 1938.[15]

In articles about scientists whose lives ended in positions of honor and distinction we learn about the difficult and dramatic moments they too experienced under Stalin. For example, we learn that only thanks to the intervention of Pyotr Kapitsa was the talented physicist Lev Landau saved from death during prison interrogation. Landau, of course, went on to win a Nobel Prize and become a member of the Soviet Academy of Sciences.[16] We also have new information about the years of confinement endured by the outstanding aircraft designer Andrei Tupolev and the

12. *Ogonyok* (1937), no. 4.
13. *Komsomolskaya pravda,* January 16, 1988.
14. *Nauka i zhizn* (1987), nos. 6 and 12.
15. *Literaturnaya gazeta,* January 27, 1988.
16. *Ogonyok* (1988), no. 3.

chief designer of Soviet spacecraft, S. P. Korolev. The newspaper *Moskovskaya pravda* has recounted the tragic fate of Nikolai Muralov, one of the leaders of the armed insurrection in Moscow during the Bolshevik revolution of 1917. A hero of the civil war and the first commander of the Moscow military district, Muralov belonged to the Trotskyist Opposition for several years in the twenties. In 1937 that fact cost him his life. Only now has he been rehabilitated.[17] *Literaturnaya gazeta* has informed us about the painful experiences of Isaak Moiseevich Zaltsman, former director of the Kirov Works in Leningrad, organizer of the industrial center for tank production in the Urals during the war, and people's commissar for tank production. Zaltsman was never arrested, but immediately after the war Stalin ordered him removed from all his posts simply because he was a Jew. Stalin asked, "What did Zaltsman start as?" As a foreman, he was told. "Then let him start over from the beginning," was Stalin's order. This people's commissar, who held the rank of general, who had been awarded the title Hero of Socialist Labor, and who served as a deputy to the Supreme Soviet, then began to work as a foreman at a small factory.[18] Much worse "luck" befell Academician V. V. Obolensky, one of the most prominent Soviet economists and an organizer of the statistical services. Removed from his post as head of the Central Statistical Agency, he was arrested and shot.[19]

From materials recently published, we learn quite a few new things about Stalin's mistakes and miscalculations before the war and during its first two years. Information now given in the Soviet press about the many millions of prisoners of war who perished, as well as those who died of hunger in occupied areas and in besieged Leningrad, those who simply disappeared, and those who died at slave labor in German factories, suggests that even the enormous official figure of twenty million dead proves to be greatly understated. Together with those who died in combat, the number of victims probably exceeds thirty million, both soldiers and civilians. This reaffirms more than ever my view that Stalin did not try to fight with minimal loss of life and that the Soviet victories were gained not only through military skill but through the sheer use of numbers.

17. *Moskovskaya pravda*, September 17, 1987. [Muralov is the first and, as of March 1988, the only one of the defendants in the January 1937 Moscow trial yet to be rehabilitated. There was also an article about him in *Sotsialicheskaya industriya* (1987).— [G. S.]

18. *Literaturnaya Rossiya*, August 28, 1987.

19. *Ogonyok* (1987), no. 26.

The deepening and widening criticism of Stalin and Stalinism and the filling in of the many blank pages in our history logically point toward a fundamental revision of existing textbooks on the history of the Communist Party of the Soviet Union (CPSU) and the Soviet Union itself. Students now in the universities and the higher grades in secondary school are studying these aspects of history without the textbooks. A commission has been established to work on a new textbook, Essays in the History of the CPSU, the first step toward producing textbooks that will be more long-lived. It is not easy to do such work quickly, however, because Soviet historical scholarship has seriously lagged behind the demands of the time. A decision has been made to produce a new ten-volume History of the Great Patriotic War. New encyclopedias on the October revolution and the civil war of 1918–1921 have appeared. Although they differ favorably from the previous, completely unsatisfactory ones, they are still full of omissions.

Some historians have raised the question of producing scholarly biographies of both Stalin and Khrushchev. Unfortunately, within the framework of official Soviet history such work is not yet possible.

An attempt at a partial solution to this problem on a "semiofficial" basis is a book whose publication has been announced for 1988 by the magazine Ogonyok: Triumph and Tragedy (A Political Portrait of J. V. Stalin) by Colonel-General D. A. Volkogonov. General Volkogonov holds the high post of deputy head of the Political Directorate of the Soviet Army. It is evident from the recently published preface to his book[20] that many party and government archives previously unavailable to Soviet historians have been opened to Volkogonov. One may disagree with one or another conception held by Volkogonov, who obviously seeks to minimize the extent and perfidy of Stalin's crimes and counterbalances them by stressing the gains made by the Soviet people in the thirties and forties. Even so, it is to Volkogonov's credit that he has already put into circulation for historians a number of extremely important facts and pieces of evidence from those previously inaccessible archives. We learn, for example, that Vasily Ulrikh, together with Vyshinsky, regularly reported to Stalin (and most often to Molotov and Yezhov at the same time) on the trials and sentences. In 1937 Ulrikh presented monthly reports on the total number of persons sentenced for "spying, diversion, and terrorist activity." Stalin read these reports together with ones on the harvest-

20. Literaturnaya gazeta, December 9, 1987.

ing of grain, the mining of coal, and the smelting of steel. I cannot agree with Volkogonov's conjecture that Stalin suffered from a severe mental illness that supposedly went unrecognized and undiagnosed. Yet this author gives testimony of great importance in stating that during the thirties more than twenty thousand NKVD personnel were wiped out on Stalin's orders. For some reason Volkogonov calls all of them honorable men, although among these thousands were such figures as Yagoda and Yezhov, with hundreds and hundreds of their close associates. Volkogonov is also firmly convinced that no party leader of the twenties other than Stalin could have come to power after Lenin's death and that if Trotsky, for example, had come to power, the tragedy for our people, our country, and our party would have been still more terrible. I think that on this point Volkogonov is obviously a victim of preconceived notions.

Almost daily we encounter new facts and documents of the most varied kind from Soviet history—not only from magazines and newspapers but from documentary films that have been carefully hidden from us for decades. L. Ovrutsky has justly commented, "Of all the known definitions of history today the most relevant is the one by Jules Michelet: 'History is the action of bringing things back to life.' The shrine of Clio, which only yesterday was uninhabited, is gradually filling up with people again. The cast of characters in the dramas of recent times is coming back to life, consigned until now to oblivion by the stroke of an unhesitating and authoritative pen."[21]

The main participants in this work have been writers, journalists, playwrights, poets, and film makers, not professional historians. Only a very few well-known historians, among them Yuri Afanasiev, A. M. Samsonov, and V. Polikarpov, have supported the fight against Stalinism in recent months. And these prominent scholars have not been able to publish their articles on this subject in professional historical journals; their work has appeared only in such magazines as *Ogonyok* or *Nauka i zhizn* or newspapers such as *Moscow News, Sovetskaya kultura,* and *Sotsialisticheskaya industriya.* Confusion reigns among the leaders of the historical sciences in all the chief academic institutions as well as among most social science instructors at higher educational institutions. They are used to working in the old way. They are frightened by the new approach to historical facts and events. Many of the major works of

21. *Sovetskaya kultura,* February 4, 1988.

literature and art that I have mentioned made their appearance only after
long and difficult behind-the-scenes struggles and after much resistance.
In the flood of letters now reaching the editors of Soviet newspapers and
magazines there are quite a few containing angry vicious attacks on anti-
Stalinist material and sometimes direct threats against the authors.

For example, a certain K. Kulyamova writes to the editors of *Sovetskaya kultura:*

> Come to your senses! Stop sowing confusion in our consciousness and ideology!
> With your articles you are doing harm to society, destroying the faith that people
> have, their civic awareness, depriving them of patriotism and pride in the ideals
> of socialism. Don't you really have any other problems to deal with, instead of
> rummaging around in old linen?[22]

And A. Arbuzov writes to the editors of *Ogonyok:*

> I want to express to you my indignation. In No. 48 you gave a platform to the
> wife of Bukharin. I can't describe the feeling of indignation that has overcome
> me. I am literally shaking as though I had a fever. I have lost my health from
> encephalitis precisely because of degenerates like Bukharin and his wife who for
> five years I had to guard at the Dalstroi complex. . . . In your issue No. 47 you
> published a huge amount of material praising the enemy of the people Vavi-
> lov. . . . I have come to the conclusion that your magazine is anti-Soviet, and I
> am not going to read it any more. But know this—that justice will be dealt
> to you.[23]

Fortunately, the reaction of most readers nowadays to letters like this
is to laugh. Public opinion in the last two years has passed through a
notable evolution. A year or a year and a half ago the response to anti-
Stalinist publications in our press was not particularly strong and could
be described with the formula: "The writers write and the readers read."
Gradually the interest in publications on historical subjects has grown,
and it continues to grow. Of course our public life is proceeding differently than it did twenty-five years ago. Most of those who lived through
collectivization, Stalin's terror of the thirties, and the Great Patriotic
War, have died. Even the children of the victims of the Stalin era have
grown old and are starting to leave us. The most deeply moved by the
publications of the last two years are people over fifty whom we can call
the generation of the Twentieth Congress. But for those between twenty-
five and forty-five the Stalin era is not a youthful memory but only history

22. *Sovetskaya kultura,* July 28, 1987.
23. *Ogonyok* (1988) no. 4.

—moreover, history full of blank pages. The deaths of Molotov or Malenkov mean little to them. They do not know what Molotov or Malenkov represent in Soviet history, nor Khrushchev for that matter. The problem of rehabilitating Pyatakov, Bukharin, or the other victims of the Moscow trials does not concern these people because they do not know those names.

Nevertheless, we can observe, especially in the last few months, among the young and even the not so young an awakening of interest in our history. These people are dissatisfied with the slow progress of our economy, our science, and our technology, the relatively low standard of living of our people, and the lack of ordinary decency in almost every sphere of Soviet life. Such people are becoming more and more resolutely opposed to dogmatism and the accepted attitudes of previous eras. This in turn increases their interest in history. The overwhelming majority of Soviet citizens are beginning to support the new course taken by our press, as is particularly noticeable in the changing circulation figures for the most interesting of our magazines and newspapers today. In 1988 the cautious *Pravda* lost a million subscribers, while the more daring *Izvestia* acquired two million new ones. *Literaturnaya gazeta* increased the number of its subscribers by 700,000 and the newspaper *Argumenty i fakty* raised its circulation from three to nine million! *Druzhba narodov*, the magazine that printed *Children of the Arbat* and announced the forthcoming publication of its sequel, has expanded from 150,000 to 800,000 subscribers, while *Novy mir* increased from 500,000 to 1,150,000, an unheard-of number for a Soviet "thick journal." The circulation of *Znamya, Ogonyok,* and *Oktyabr* also grew substantially. At the same time most professional historical and political journals remained at the same level or lost subscribers; so did economics journals and magazines holding to a conservative position. This is a referendum of its own kind among readers, and it serves as an important moral support for all who advocate an expansion of glasnost and reassertion of the truth about our history. The mass of readers in the Soviet Union, whose tastes were deformed during the "period of stagnation," must be and are being restored to active participation in social and political life.

It is not only the many films, novels, works of poetry, essays, and articles that are playing an exceptionally important role in exposing the truth about Stalin and Stalinism. The solidity and irreversibility of the new policy changes should also be seen as depending directly on the new wave of rehabilitations that began in the summer of 1987 and continued with the recent rehabilitation of Bukharin, Rykov, and several other once prominent party figures. These people were slanderously accused and convicted of espionage and terrorist activity fifty years ago at the 1938 Moscow trial. In accordance with the verdict of the Military Collegium of the USSR Supreme Court they were all shot.

Of course many people are asking why the rehabilitation of Bukharin, Rykov, and the others came so late. Why weren't they all rehabilitated after the Twentieth Party Congress, at which Khrushchev gave his secret speech on Stalin's crimes? After all, did not the Twentieth Congress and after it the Twenty-Second Congress pass resolutions calling for a consistent continuation of the effort to overcome all the consequences of the cult of Stalin and his crimes? Why has the rehabilitation of Bukharin and Rykov become possible only now?

Other questions are being asked: Who are Bukharin and Rykov anyway? And why is so much importance now being paid to their full rehabilitation?

It is generally known that Bukharin and Rykov were numbered among Lenin's closest associates. From 1917 on they were part of the Central Committee, which was not very numerous at that time. In mid-1918 Bukharin became the editor of *Pravda*, in 1919 a candidate (alternate) member of the Politburo, and in 1924 a full member of the Politburo. In the mid-twenties Bukharin became the chief theoretician of the New Economic Policy (NEP) and was generally recognized as the party's top theoretician and one of the leaders of the Comintern. Rykov was people's commissar of internal affairs in the first Soviet government. As early as 1921, when Lenin was ill, Rykov was appointed Lenin's deputy as chairman of the Council of People's Commissars (Sovnarkom). After Lenin's death Rykov occupied the post of head of the Soviet government. In 1923 he became a member of the Politburo. Until the end of the twenties Bukharin and Rykov defended Lenin's New Economic Policy and opposed a revival of the methods of war communism. Specifically, they argued against forced collectivization and adventuristic plans for "super-industrialization," policies that Stalin was beginning to put into practice and that led to the deaths of more than ten million peasants and to repression and death for tens of thousands of "bourgeois" specialists. In this dispute, which Stalin won, he denounced Bukharin and Rykov as leaders of a "right deviation." But even after their political defeat

Bukharin and Rykov continued to hold responsible positions and were still members of the party's Central Committee.

When, as early as the mid-thirties, Stalin began his campaign to exterminate the basic Leninist cadres of the party he could not spare the lives of Bukharin and Rykov. But in dealing with such Bolsheviks, who had been intimates of Lenin, Stalin resorted to the most refined and cynical methods. Before the whole world Stalin put on the notorious Moscow show trials, inviting not only Soviet but also Western journalists, diplomats, and intellectuals. Lion Feuchtwanger attended one of these trials; Roosevelt's ambassador, Joseph Davies, another. Broken by torture and blackmail, the defendants "confessed" to the most monstrous crimes: spying, wrecking, terrorism, plans for diversionary actions with the aim of destroying socialism in the USSR, and the creation for that purpose of a deeply underground anti-Soviet terrorist organization. Not everyone believed these confessions, either in the Soviet Union or in the West. But the majority believed them. The possibility of such a cynical and brazen provocation was too much to admit.

Only after the Twentieth Party Congress in 1956 did we learn about most of Stalin's crimes, the use of the cruelist tortures during interrogation and the physical destruction of millions of innocent persons. The "mechanism" of the show trials then became comprehensible in many respects. Even at that time Khrushchev wished to rehabilitate Bukharin, Rykov, and many other former close associates of Lenin. As we know, that did not happen. Khrushchev decided not to go all the way in exposing Stalin's crimes. As for Brezhnev, during his time in power he was more concerned with trying to rehabilitate—Stalin. He wished to reverse the decisions of the Twentieth and Twenty-Second congresses rather than carry them through consistently. The conditions for a renewed exposure of Stalin's crimes have arisen only now, one result being the rehabilitation of Bukharin and Rykov.

There are other circumstances that have obliged the new party leadership to reexamine many important questions in the history of the CPSU and the Soviet Union. Since Stalin's death every new leader has talked about restoring "the Leninist norms of party life," including democracy and the full public airing of issues and information—that is, glasnost. Only today does this "return to Lenin" provide a genuine basis for a restructuring to be carried out both in the economic sphere and in the realm of ideology and politics. Yet is is not possible to speak sincerely about a return to Lenin without reexamining the fates and reassessing accepted views of the people who were Lenin's closest associates in the party and the revolution.

In the conception advanced by the Twentieth and Twenty-Second congresses, Stalin's chief crimes began after 1934, while his policies of the late twenties and early thirties were correct. This conception is now being subjected to increasingly cogent criticism. In the first months of 1987 Soviet literature and journalism began to give special attention to the subject of collectivization and the coercion employed against the middle and better-off sections of the peasantry, to the question of the crude, abrupt, and artificial suspension of NEP, with all the consequences of that action for our economy and society.

Three new novels—V. Mozhaev's *Muzkiki i baby*, V. Belov's *Kanuny*, and Sergei Antonov's *Ovragi*[24]—present a picture of the swift and natural development of the Russian countryside on a healthy economic basis in the years 1927–1929. In them we see the policies of NEP being carried out successfully, the bond between city and countryside being strengthened, and many different forms of cooperatives, including the first steps toward producers' cooperatives, growing. The rural areas were not free of contradictions, but coercion and a "second revolution" were not required to overcome them, especially since one of the main contradictions was that between the hard-working middle peasant and his inefficient demagogue of a neighbor who shouted slogans of "class struggle" to conceal his own incompetence and reluctance to exert himself, to apply his hands to the land given to him by the Soviet revolution. The enormous potential of the Russian village, in the north, center, east, and south, was just beginning to be revealed, promising our country a previously unheard-of abundance of agricultural goods. Instead of that abundance there suddenly occurred, as these novels describe, a rude and violent interference in the natural course of development of agricultural production, destruction of the most productive farms, and unjustifiably harsh treatment of the peasant families placed with arbitrary malice and often quite senselessly in the category of "kulak." These novels further dramatize what happened in 1932–33—the massive dislocation of the rural economy and impoverishment of the Russian and Ukrainian countryside, universal famine and the death of millions. Imaginative literature is reinforced by journalism. In *Moscow News* L. Voskresensky has proposed the removal from all school curricula of Mikhail Sholokhov's novel

24. V. Mozhaev, *Muzhiki i baby*, *Don* (1987) nos. 1–3; V. Belov, *Kanuny*, *Novy mir* (1987), no. 8; and Sergei Antonov, *Ovragi*, *Druzhba narodov* (1988), nos. 1 and 2.

Virgin Soil Upturned, which presents a purely Stalinist interpretation of collectivization and dekulakization.[25]

Journalists and writers of fiction as well as scholars specializing in the agrarian question are today disputing the accuracy of the term "kulak" in the way it was used from 1929 to 1932 as a justification for the mass deportation of relatively well-to-do peasants. Academician V. A. Tikhonov has tried to show that the kulaks of the late nineteenth and early twentieth centuries, about whom Lenin wrote so bitterly (and not always rightly), almost completely disappeared during the civil war. In the late twenties the term "kulak" was applied mainly to hard-working middle peasants who by stubborn toil and effort had achieved relative prosperity during the few short years of NEP.[26]

A decisive reconsideration of previously held views regarding NEP and its potential is also evident in the statements and policies of the present leadership. The encouragement of cooperatives in all areas, of individual effort, of household plots and family farms—all this represents a partial revival of many of the methods and policies of NEP. Within this context of a reconsideration of current economic policy and of the system for managing the Soviet economy it is easier to grasp the significance of the July 1987 decision of the Soviet Supreme Court to rehabilitate a large group of prominent Soviet economists and agrarian experts, including A. V. Chayanov, N. D. Kondratiev, A. N. Chelintsev, N. P. Makarov, L. N. Yurovsky, and A. G. Doyarenko. These specialists were not party members, but they did extremely important work in studying the developmental potential of Soviet agriculture on the basis of NEP, in organizing the cooperative movement and developing everything that today is called "the agro-industrial complex." All of them were critical of Stalin's methods of forced collectivization, they were all shot or died in the camps on false charges of organizing the nonexistent Toiling Peasants' Party (TPP). Altogether more than a thousand persons have been cleared of the charges in the "case" of the TPP. Added to this number now are the party members, including some of the most prominent party leaders, who in the twenties were accused without any basis of "right deviation" and who seven or eight years later were shot on charges of spying, wrecking, and terrorism.

Of course, we all welcome the rehabilitation of Bukharin, Rykov, and the others—even if it comes many years late. This action sheds a clearer

25. *Moskovskie novosti,* August 9, 1987.
26. *Don* (1987), no. 1.

light on the crimes of Stalin and the Stalinist system. But it has also shown very graphically many of the shortcomings of our present political and governmental system. For most reasonable people the innocence of Bukharin, Rykov, and the others became obvious after the Twentieth Congress in 1956. Even then the relatives and close friends of people destroyed by Stalin began to call for their full rehabilitation. These demands were repeated many times thereafter. Ten years ago the campaign for the exoneration of Bukharin became an international one. However neither the USSR Supreme Court nor the Procuracy of the USSR dared to undertake a review of his case. For that, instructions from the highest party bodies were needed. Yet the Soviet Constitution contains a special article stating that judicial agencies are totally independent and should be guided by the law alone. The recent rehabilitation of Bukharin, Rykov, and the others shows how fully dependent the judiciary actually is on the political leaders rather than than on the law. The Soviet Supreme Court was not independent when it handed down the verdict for the execution of Bukharin, Rykov, et al.; it is not independent now in fully rehabilitating them.

Equally dependent on the highest party bodies is Soviet historical scholarship. Many people in the Soviet Union today are talking and writing about the need to fill in the numerous gaps in our history. But who prevented Soviet historians from filling in these gaps earlier, before they received "permission from above"?

On February 4, 1988, the Soviet Supreme Court reversed the verdict of its Military Collegium in the case of the "Right-Trotskyite Bloc." However, we know that in addition to the falsified trial of 1938 there were similar show trials in 1937, in 1936, and in 1935, as well as a series of such trials much earlier, from 1928 to 1932. All of these were equally criminal frame-up affairs, and each served as a pretext for the arrest and destruction of thousands, tens of thousands, eventually millions of people. When will the time come for the review of these other trials? We must assume that we will not have to wait several more decades for that.

Specifically in regard to Leon Trotsky, his activities and tragic fate require a precise and carefully weighed political and legal evaluation. At different times Trotsky appeared as a strong opponent and as a devoted supporter of Lenin. His relations with the party leadership and with Stalin also took different forms at different times. But Trotsky was never a spy for the Gestapo. And, we must remember, the death sentences passed against Trotsky in absentia at the three major Moscow trials did not remain a dead letter. The "verdict" was carried out in 1940 in Mexico by an NKVD group "for special assignments abroad."

Despite its limitations the new campaign against Stalin and Stalinism that began in the Soviet Union in late 1986 arouses feelings of hope and approval. This campaign provides me with new encouragement because it means that a new mass readership is appearing that will be receptive to the present book. The views and interests of Soviet readers were deformed during the "period of stagnation." These readers were turned away from politics; there was an attempt to make them indifferent toward the history of their own country. This readership must now be restored to active participation in social and political life. It gives me satisfaction to think that the turn toward a new critique of Stalinism was helped along, if only to a small extent, by previous editions of this book and by the other books that my brother, Zhores, and I have brought out.

Today with a policy of democratization and openness being implemented in our country, I can name more of the people who helped me greatly at various times in my work on this book, people whose names I could not give, for a number of reasons, in the first preface to this edition. First I would like to name a number of philosophers, historians, and writers who are my very close friends: N. B. Ter-Akopyan, R. G. Simongulyan, R. Blyum, A. M. Gendin, V. Ya. Lakshin, L. N. Kurchikov, and I. G. Popova. Let me also mention the historians V. P. Danilov, M. Gefter, and Ya. Drabkin and four officials of the Central Committee apparatus in the sixties: G. Kh. Shakhnazarov, Yu. P. Krasin, L. P. Delyusin, and F. M. Burlatsky. Unfortunately, this list of names is still not exhaustive. The history of the writing of this book is in many ways highly instructive; I hope to be able to tell it some day in full detail.

October 1988

A NOTE ON THE FOOTNOTES

All of the author's references to Marx and Engels *Sochineniia* (Collected Works) are to the 2d Russian edition (Moscow, 1955–1966). In some cases references have been added to English-language editions in which the quoted passages may be found.

Citations of Lenin's *Polnoe sobranie sochinenii* (Complete Collected Works), 5th ed., 55 vols. (Moscow, 1958–1965), are given as "PSS," followed by volume and page number(s) separated by a colon. Wherever possible I have cited the corresponding reference in the English-language official version of Lenin's *Collected Works* (45 vols.), issued by Progress Publishers of Moscow in the 1960s, using the abbreviation "CW," again with volume and page separated by a colon. I have not always followed the English wording of the Progress Publisher's edition, either for reasons of style or sometimes because of inadequacy in the translation. In most cases the reader who wishes to, may compare the CW version, as in the following sample note: Lenin, PSS, 48:162. [Cf. CW, 35:84.] — G. S.

STALIN'S RISE IN THE PARTY

1

STALIN AS A PARTY CHIEF

■ 1
STALIN BEFORE 1917

Western biographers of Stalin have devoted considerable attention to his childhood and youth on the valid assumption that basic personality traits are formed in the early years. As Adam Ulam observes in his book on Stalin, "The poverty and harshness of Stalin's early life left . . . indelible imprints" on him.[1] Quite early in life he became a crude, unsentimental,

1. Adam B. Ulam, *Stalin: The Man and His Era* (New York, 1973), pp. 19–20. See also Robert C. Tucker, *Stalin as Revolutionary* (New York, 1972); and Jean-Jacques Marie, *Staline* (Paris, 1967).

As far as I know, only one Western author has argued that Stalin's childhood and family environment explain nothing about his personality and later life. See Ian Grey, *Stalin: Man of History,* (London, 1979). However, a number of reviewers have convincingly rebutted Grey's arguments. See, for example, the review by L. Kelly in *Books and Bookmen,* December 1979.

and mistrustful person, tormented by an inferiority complex and very ambitious. Georgian was his native tongue, and he never learned to speak Russian well, but he had contempt for the traditions of kinship and personal friendship usually so important to Georgians.

As is generally known, the man who became Stalin was born Joseph Vissarionovich Dzhugashvili on December 9 (21), 1879, in the small Georgian town of Gori. His family was quite poor. His father, Vissarion Ivanovich Dzhugashvili, came from the peasantry but worked as a shoemaker in Gori. He was a coarse and uneducated man and could not have influenced his son in any positive way. Early in Stalin's life, his father left the family home, moving to Tiflis and taking up work in a shoe factory there. He returned to Gori quite ill and died there when Stalin was still an adolescent. In later life Stalin never referred to his father, and the date of his father's death was not even listed in the official chronology of Stalin's life and works.[2]

Stalin's mother, Yekaterina Georgievna (nee Geladze), also came from a peasant background. She earned the family's livelihood by sewing and doing laundry. Since she had no time to spend with the children, little Soso (Georgian for Joseph) was out on the streets for most of each day. He was not the only child in the family, but the others died young. In his early childhood Stalin suffered a severe case of smallpox, which left its marks on his face for the rest of his life. Among the nicknames under which Stalin later figured in police documents was Ryaboi ("pockmarked"). In an accident on the streets little Soso suffered an injury to his left arm, leaving it permanently weaker and shorter than the right. He carefully hid his withered arm, trying not to undress in the presence of others and preferring not to go swimming or be examined by doctors. Indeed, he never learned to swim, and in later life, when vacationing at his dachas on the Black Sea, he would walk along the shore fully dressed.

Although his mother lived a long life, Stalin never had close or warm relations with her. After he became involved in revolutionary activity and especially after the victory of the revolution he saw his mother only a few times. In the twenties many Georgian leaders who visited Stalin

2. Stalin, *Sochineniia* (Works), 1:415–425. There are reports that Stalin's father drank a lot, often punished his son cruelly, and often fought with his religious-minded spouse, whose modest earnings were the family's main support. The Georgian emigre literature includes assertions that Stalin's father, considered by some of his fellow countrymen to be an Ossetian, was killed in a barroom brawl in 1890.

were surprised and shocked by his rude and cynical comments about his mother, who continued to live in Tiflis, not wishing to live with her son in Moscow. For her part, his mother, an independent and defiant woman, did not have especially flattering remarks to make about her son when Georgian leaders visited her on her birthday or her son's. She died in 1936 and was buried in the small cemetery on Mamadaviti (Father David Hill) in Tbilisi, which has become a pantheon honoring the celebrities of Georgian culture. In the Caucasus the burial of friends or relatives is usually considered a matter of great importance. Many Georgians were therefore surprised that Stalin did not wish to attend his mother's funeral. In any case, we have ample grounds for the assertion that Stalin's family could not have instilled any warm human qualities in him. Undoubtedly that is one reason for Stalin's total indifference toward most of his relatives.

Even in childhood Stalin displayed a certain intractable quality and constantly strove for preeminence among his peers. He had no outstanding abilities, but he was persistent and read a great deal. Short in stature and weak physically, Soso could not expect success in boyhood tussles with others of his age, and he had a fear of being beaten physically. He became secretive and vengeful while still a child and throughout his life retained a dislike for men who were tall and strong. A longing for fame took hold of him quite early, but he was poor and non-Russian. He understood that a Georgian youth from a small town in the provinces could not achieve much in tsarist Russia.

A big impression was made on the young Stalin by the writings and life of the Georgian author Alexander Kazbegi. One of the wealthiest landowners in Georgia, Kazbegi released his peasants from their obligation to pay land redemption fees, renounced his own riches, and for nearly ten years led the life of a simple shepherd in the hills. He occupied himself as a writer for only six years, from 1880 to 1886. Depression and a serious mental illness soon led him to the grave.[3] Stalin was especially taken with Kazbegi's novel *The Patricide*, which dealt with the struggle of the peasant mountain peoples for freedom and independence. One of the heroes of the novel was the fearless Koba. Young Soso Dzhugashvili chose this character as his hero and began to call himself Koba. Later that became his first party name. In the 1930s, Old Bolsheviks often addressed Stalin as Koba (and Molotov and Mikoyan

3. Kazbegi's novels were reprinted in Georgia in the late 1940s, first in Georgian and then in Russian.

did so for even longer). Dzhugashvili had other party names, such as Ivanovich, Vasily, and Vasilyev, but Koba and Stalin remained with him all his life.

When Soso reached the age of eight his mother enrolled him in the Gori church school. It took him six years to complete the four-year course. The difficulty was that instruction was mainly in Russian. Stalin learned to write Russian well, but never spoke it with any fluency. In revolutionary circles, where oratorical ability was especially valued, Stalin always felt inadequate. Nevertheless he graduated with honors from the church school and in 1894 entered the Tiflis seminary. In both institutions obscurantism, hypocrisy, constant petty supervision, and a system of informing prevailed. The rules were very strict, with virtually a military discipline being enforced. It is not surprising that the seminaries of Russia produced revolutionaries as well as loyal servants of the church and government. Stalin himself told the German writer Emil Ludwig in 1931:

I cannot contend that I was drawn to socialism from the age of six. Or even from the age of ten or twelve. I joined the revolutionary movement at the age of fifteen, when I made contact with underground groups of Russian Marxists who were living in Transcaucasia. . . . I was ready to move on from protest against the humiliating regime and jesuitical methods in the seminary to become a revolutionary, a supporter of Marxism, and that is what I did.[4]

The Tiflis seminary gave Russia not only Stalin but such prominent revolutionaries as Mikha Tskhakaya, Noi Zhordania, Lado Ketskhoveli, Sylvester Dzhibladze, Nikolai Chkheidze, and Filipp Makharadze. The seminary in Armenia produced just as many important revolutionaries.

The seminary undoubtedly affected Stalin in another respect. It encouraged the growth of those crafty, sneaky, and nasty qualities that were characteristic of him even earlier in life. His dogmatism and intolerance as well as the catechistic style typical of his articles and speeches also took shape under the influence of his clerical education. Besides this, Stalin absolutely lacked a sense of humor even as a young man. "A strange Georgian," said his friends in the seminary. "He simply cannot take a joke. He doesn't understand joking and answers with his fists to the most innocent of jibes."[5]

Stalin's daughter, Svetlana Alliluyeva, in her book *Only One Year*,

4. Stalin, *Sochineniia*, 13:113.
5. I. Dubinsky-Mukhadze, *Ordzhonikidze* (Moscow, 1964), p. 167.

which gives a much more exact psychological portrait of her father than her first book, *Twenty Letters to a Friend,* wrote the following:

A church education was the only systematic education my father ever had. I am convinced that the parochial schools in which he spent more than ten years played an immense role, setting my father's character for the rest of his life, strengthening and intensifying inborn traits. My father never had any feeling for religion. In a young man who had never for a moment believed in the Spirit, in God, endless prayers and enforced religious training could have brought out only contrary results: extreme skepticism of everything 'heavenly,' of everything 'sublime.' The result was total materialism, the cynical realism of an 'earthly,' 'sober,' practical, and low view of life. Instead of a 'spiritual outlook,' he evolved something very different: a close acquaintance with hypocrisy, bigotry, two-facedness, typical of a goodly number among the clergy, who only believe externally—in other words, do not believe at all. . . . From his experiences at the seminary he had come to the conclusion that men were intolerant, coarse, deceiving their flocks in order to hold them in obedience; that they intrigued, lied, and as a rule possessed numerous faults and few virtues. . . . This lack of compromise, this inflexibility, this inability to agree with an opposing opinion even if it was obviously a good one, I also attribute to his experiences at the seminary, where students had been imbued with fanaticism and intolerance.[6]

As a seminary student Stalin made contact with the first Marxist circles and with the first workers' groups founded at factories in Tiflis. He became a member of the Mesame Dasi group, the first Georgian Social Democratic organization. He also read quite a few works of Russian classical literature and acquired a passion for underground literature. It was at this time that he read his first books by Marx and Engels. According to the official Soviet version, it was because of his reading of illegal literature and formation of a Social Democratic study circle that Stalin was expelled from the seminary in May 1899. He obtained a job at the Tiflis observatory and continued to be active in Georgian Social Democratic circles.

According to Adam Ulam, the young Stalin was greatly influenced by the Georgian revolutionary Sylvester Dzhibladze, one of the most prominent founders of the Mesame Dasi group and a man well known to all the Social Democrats of Georgia. The official Soviet biography of Stalin does not even mention Dzhibladze, who later joined the Mensheviks, helped to found the independent Georgian Democratic Republic in 1918, was arrested after the establishment of Soviet Georgia in 1921, and was released shortly before his death in 1922.[7]

6. Svetlana Alliluyeva, *Only One Year* (New York, 1969), pp. 361, 362, 377.
7. Noi Zhordania, *Moia zhizn'* (Stanford, 1968), p. 15.

From 1897 to 1900 Stalin was strongly influenced by Lado (Vladimir) Ketskhoveli, one of the most prominent organizers of the Social Democratic movement in Georgia and later in Baku. The compilers of the "short biography" of Stalin made the twenty-six year old Ketskhoveli out to be the "closest comrade-in-arms" of the nineteen year old Stalin. Ketskhoveli was shot to death by a prison guard at the Metekh fortress prison in September 1902.

In 1900 Stalin made the acquaintance of Viktor Kurnatovsky, a thirty-two year old professional revolutionary who arrived in Tiflis from internal exile. Not long before, Kurnatovsky had met with Lenin, who was in exile at Minusinsk. The acquaintance with Kurnatovsky, the reading of Lenin's writings, and after that, the reading of the newspaper *Iskra*, which became known in Transcaucasia in 1901, turned the young Stalin into a supporter of Lenin. After the split in the Russian Social Democratic Labor Party (RSDLP) into Bolsheviks and Mensheviks, Stalin decisively took the side of the Bolsheviks. It should be noted, however, that in Georgia the influence of the Mensheviks predominated. In 1917 the Georgian Mensheviks proved to be not only the most influential but also the best organized revolutionary force, which enabled them to take power rather quickly and remain at the head of the government of independent Georgia for three years.

As early as the spring of 1901, Stalin went underground. He helped organize strikes and demonstrations, including the famous Batumi demonstration of March 1902. In Batumi Stalin was arrested and exiled to eastern Siberia, where he spent approximately two years. Trotsky, in one of his articles, wrote about Stalin's lack of creative output from 1900 to 1910. This assertion is unjust. Stalin was not only an activist; he also aspired to the role of theoretician, at least on the Transcauscasian level. From 1900 to 1910 he wrote quite a few articles and pamphlets, but almost all were in Georgian, published in the Georgian Social Democratic press. Stalin's writings of this period make up the first two volumes of his *Works*, the greater part of them having been translated from Georgian for the first time in 1945–1946. To be sure, Stalin's creative literary output cannot be placed in the same rank either quantitatively or qualitatively with other leaders of the Social Democratic movement in the Russian empire. But it is incorrect to speak of a complete absence of creative output on Stalin's part.

Jean-Jacques Marie in his book on Stalin says the following:

When the [1905] revolution began Koba was only a regional activist. The revolution did not change anything for him. It did not "discover" him, as it did Trotsky at the other end of the empire. It passed over him like a shadow. Stalin always was a *committee man,* who shone in limited groups of leaders, be they on the top, middle, or lower level. . . . Koba did not possess any qualities enabling him to lead the mass movement, neither oratorical talent, liveliness of thought, breadth of vision, a feeling for what the next day would bring, nor enthusiasm. Last of all, in the heat and ardor of a time when in a single moment the masses transcended their everyday existence to make history Stalin, cold and secretive by nature, lost his footing. Quite capable in maneuvering behind the scenes, he was pushed into the background in 1905, when the focus of politics was in the streets. . . . Koba and the revolution did not know each other.[8]

These assertions are also unjust. It is true that Stalin was not a tribune of the revolution and did not have a quick mind, but he cannot be called a mere "regional activist." His sphere of activity was all of Transcaucasia. Besides, he took part in the All-Russian Party Conference at Tammerfors in 1905, the Fourth Party Congress in Stockholm in 1906, and the Fifth Party Congress in London in 1907. At the Fifth Congress one of the main speakers was Leon Trotsky, who later wrote that he first learned of Stalin's presence at those early party gatherings from a biography of Stalin by a "French author" (Boris Souvarine) published in Paris in 1935. Trotsky's scornful comment provides grounds for an unflattering evaluation—mainly of Trotsky himself. The number of delegates at party congresses in those years was not very great (about 150 at the Fourth Congress and about 350 at the Fifth). But the young Trotsky was already possessed of excessive haughtiness and had no desire to notice rank and file delegates who had not yet distinguished themselves, especially if they had only "consultative votes."[9]

It is also incorrect to argue that the 1905 revolution did not "discover" Stalin, that it passed over him like a shadow. The revolution did disclose many aspects of Stalin's nature, and he took part in many of its important events, although he usually preferred not to operate in the foreground. To Stalin belongs the dubious honor not only of participating in but organizing several major terrorist acts—or as they were then called,

8. Jean-Jacques Marie, *Staline,* p. 37.

9. It was possible to read about Stalin's attendance at the Fourth and Fifth congresses of the RSDLP (well before the appearance of Souvarine's book) in various publications of the twenties, which Trotsky undoubtedly read—for example, the collection of essays on Stalin's fiftieth birthday *Stalin. Sbornik statei k 50-letiiu so dnia rozhdeniia* (Moscow-Leningrad, 1929).

"expropriations" ("exes" for short). These consisted mainly of armed robberies of banks, mail coaches, and steamships. The Bolsheviks considered such actions permissible at the time as a means of replenishing the party treasury, buying weapons, and making an impact on the tsarist administration. Especially famous was the robbery of the Tiflis State Bank, which brought more than three hundred thousand rubles into the Bolshevik coffers. This "ex" was carried out by a group of fighters including Kamo (S.A. Ter-Petrosyan), but Stalin and Leonid Krasin organized and planned the operation. Krasin was the head of the Technical Combat Group, under the Central Committee. The organization of such actions required of Stalin not only cold-bloodedness, craftiness, and ruthlessness but also links with the criminal world of Georgia. Many acts of expropriation were accompanied by human losses, but these were killings "in the interest of the cause." In the thirties and forties many articles and quite a few books dealt with the early stages of Stalin's revolutionary activities in the Caucasus. These works credited Stalin with a great many services he had never performed. But all the authors, including Beria, carefully omitted mention of Stalin's terrorist activities in the Caucasus.

In 1907 Stalin transferred to the Baku organization of the RSDLP. His part in the "exes" made his continued stay in Tiflis dangerous. Moreover, in Georgia the Mensheviks dominated the Social Democratic movement, and they were firm opponents of terrorism. In Baku, Stalin took part in the organization of a number of workers' demonstrations that were very large for those days and that attracted Lenin's attention. Several times Stalin was arrested and deported but each time managed to escape and resume his activities in the Caucasus. Sergei Kavtaradze, an activist of the revolutionary movement in Transcaucasia, later recalled that the young Stalin was often crude, coarse, nasty, and unrestrained toward his comrades and often showered them with unprintable gutter language. But that was not exceptional. Examples of such rudeness and lack of restraint were fairly common in revolutionary circles.

In regard to Stalin's personal life in this period, the death (around 1909) of his first wife, Yekaterina Svanidze, should be noted. They had been married for only a few years, and Stalin was very attached to his young wife. Her death by no means helped to moderate his difficult personality. Their son, Yakov, was left to the care of relatives. Stalin was not much concerned with the boy and gave little thought to his welfare.

In 1911–1912 the scene of Stalin's activity shifted to the capital of the

Russian empire. His articles appeared frequently in the St. Petersburg paper *Zvezda* and in *Pravda* and *Sotsial-Demokrat*. Stalin's merits were duly noted. At the Sixth All-Russia Conference of the RSDLP (the so-called Prague conference) held in January 1912 Stalin was co-opted in his absence to the Central Committee and made a member of the Russian Bureau of the Central Committee together with Yakov Sverdlov, Filipp Goloshchekin, Yelena Stasova, Pyotr Petrovsky, Aleksei Badayev, and Aleksei Kiselev.

Stalin's many pretensions and at the same time his independence can be seen from the fact that he by no means agreed with Lenin on all matters, even though he belonged to the Bolshevik faction. For example, in 1905–1906 he spoke out against Lenin's program for the nationalization of the land and abolition of private land ownership. In 1909 Stalin expressed his opposition to Lenin's organizational policies (in Georgian, in Baku Bolshevik publications).[10] Unlike Lenin, Stalin advocated a boycott of the Third State Duma and considered the refusal to boycott "an accidental deviation from the old Bolshevism." As he said in one of his letters, "Does it follow from this that we should 'go all the way' with these accidental deviations, making a mountain out of a molehill? . . . Ilyich somewhat overestimates the importance of such (legal) organizations."[11] Several of Stalin's letters contain ironic comments in regard to Lenin's *Materialism and Empiriocriticism*. Stalin read Bogdanov's book replying to Lenin and agreed with some of Bogdanov's arguments. "In my opinion," he wrote in a private letter, "some of Ilyich's blunders are very tellingly and correctly noted. It is also correctly pointed out that Ilyich's materialism differs in many ways from that of Plekhanov, which, in spite of the demands of logic (and for the sake of diplomacy?) Ilyich tries to cover over."[12]

To Stalin, then, Lenin was not at all an unchallengeable authority, a fact that was noted by the six-volume *Istoriia KPSS*, the current official history of the Communist Party of the Soviet Union. In that book Stalin is reproached as follows:

At one time Stalin took an unclear position on philosophical questions. He underestimated the importance of Lenin's struggle against the Machists. . . . In one of his letters to M.G. [Mikha] Tskhakaya he declared that empiriocriticism

10. Stalin, Sochineniia, 2:168.
11. *Voprosy istorii KPSS*, 1965, no. 2, p. 39.
12. Dubinsky-Mukhadze, pp. 92–93.

also had its "good sides." "The task of the Bolsheviks," he wrote, "is to advance
the philosophy of Marx and Engels in the spirit of Dietzgen, absorbing the good
sides of Machism along the way." However, although the German Social Democrat Joseph Dietzgen, a self-educated worker, really did write valuable philosophical works, he retreated from materialism on a number of fundamental
issues, and the suggestion that Marxism be carried further in the spirit of Dietzgen, while giving consideration to the philosophy of the idealist Mach, was, of
course, incorrect.[13]

In the years 1910–1912 Stalin was not inclined, as Lenin was, to
intensify the conflict between Bolsheviks and Mensheviks. Before the
Prague conference, in a letter to Tskhakaya, Stalin referred to Lenin's
struggle to revive the party organization as a "tempest in a teapot."[14]
After the Prague conference Stalin, unlike Lenin, called for a conciliatory
attitude toward the "liquidators." In his very first article for *Pravda* he
called for unity among Social Democrats "at all costs" and "without
distinction as to factions."[15]

To be sure, Lenin himself hardly noticed these differences. Stalin first
met Lenin at the Tammerfors conference in 1905, then again at the
Fourth and Fifth congresses of the RSDLP. These meetings made a big
impression on Stalin.[16] Lenin, for his part, took little note of the young
party activist from the Caucasus. The personal acquaintance between
Lenin and Stalin began only at the end of 1912, when Koba, who was
helping to organize and edit the first legal Bolshevik paper, *Pravda*, went
to see Lenin in Krakow at a conference of the Central Committee with
party activists. It was in Poland and Austria in January–February 1913
that Stalin wrote his *Marxism and the National Question*, which Lenin
regarded favorably. In fact, Stalin made a very good impression on Lenin
at the time. In a letter to Gorky Lenin wrote: "We have a marvelous
Georgian who has sat down to write a big article for *Prosveshchenie*, for
which he has collected all the Austrian and other materials" on the
national question.[17]

In connection with the work on *Pravda* Lenin wrote to Stalin several
times. But the contacts between them were so irregular that Lenin soon

13. *Istoriia KPSS*, vol. 2 (Moscow, 1967), p. 272.
14. Stepan Shaumyan, *Izbrannye proizvedeniia*, vol. 1 (Moscow, 1957), p. 267; and
Dubinsky-Mukhadze, pp. 92–93.
15. V. T. Loginov, *Leninskaia "Pravda" (1912–1914 gg.)* (Moscow, 1962).
16. Stalin, *Sochineniia*, 6:54–57.
17. Lenin, PSS, 48:162. [Cf. CW, 35:84.]

forgot Stalin's last name. "Do you remember Koba's name?" he asked
Zinoviev in a letter of July 1915.[18] Zinoviev didn't remember, and therefore in November 1915 Lenin wrote to Vyacheslav Karpinsky. "Do me a
big favor: find out from Stepko [Kiknadze] or Mikha [Tskhakaya] the last
name of 'Koba' (Joseph Dzh——??) We have forgotten. Very important!!"[19]

Stalin spent four years (1913–1917) in Siberian exile in the remote
Turukhansk territory. In the small colony of political exiles he conducted
himself in far from the best manner. For example, R. G. Zakharova (nee
Rose Brontman), in her memoirs about her husband, the Old Bolshevik
Filipp Zakharov, recalls her husband's account of Stalin's arrival in Turu-
khansk in 1913.

"It was an unwritten law that each new arrival would report on the
situation in Russia. And whom would you expect to give a more interesting and profound elucidation of what was happening in far-off Russia, left
so long ago, then a member of the Bolshevik Central Committee? A
group of exiles, among them Yakov Sverdlov and Filipp, were at that
time working on construction [of a home] in the village of Monastyrskoe. . . . Stalin was to arrive there soon. Dubrovinsky was no longer
alive. Filipp, who was not inclined by nature to set up idols for himself
and who, moreover, had heard Dubrovinsky's unbiased evaluation of the
leading revolutionary activists of the time, was not especially delighted
by Stalin's impending arrival. Sverdlov, on the contrary, . . . tried to do
everything possible under the conditions to give Stalin a grand welcome.
They prepared a separate room for him, saved up some food for him from
their very scanty provisions. He arrived! He entered the room prepared
for him and—didn't show his face again! Nor did he deliver a report on
the situation in Russia. Sverdlov was very upset. . . . Stalin was sent to
the village assigned to him, and it soon became known that he had seized
for himself all of Dubrovinsky's books. But before his arrival, the exiles
had reached a general understanding that Dubrovinsky's library would in
his memory be considered the property of everyone, a sort of circulating
library. What right had one man to take it? Hot-tempered Filipp went to
get an explanation. Stalin 'received' him more or less as a tsarist general
would receive an ordinary soldier who dared to appear before him with a
demand. Filipp was indignant (as was everyone!), and the impression of

18. Lenin, PSS, 49:101. [Cf. CW, 43:469.]
19. Lenin, PSS, 49:161. [Cf. CW, 43:498.]

the conversation stayed with him for the rest of his life. He never changed his unflattering opinion of Stalin."[20]

Stalin behaved no better in the town of Kureika, where he was sent to serve his term of exile. He quarreled with almost all the exiled Bolsheviks, including Sverdlov. "There are two of us [in one room]," Sverdlov wrote to his wife in 1913. "With me is the Georgian Dzhugashvili, an old acquaintance. . . . He's a good guy, but too much of an egoist in everyday life."[21] After living with Stalin for a time, Sverdlov began to refer to him more critically. "With me [in Kureika] is a comrade. . . . We know each other very well. And the saddest thing is that in conditions of exile or prison a man is stripped bare before you and revealed in all petty respects. . . . Now the comrade and I are living in different quarters and rarely see each other."[22]

Stalin's conflict with Sverdlov and other Bolsheviks continued after Stalin was reassigned to Monastryskoe and even after many of the exiles were conscripted for military service. The Old Bolshevik Boris I. Ivanov, who was also in exile in Turukhansk territory, wrote the following in his memoirs in the late 1950s.

The departure of twelve wagons [of conscripts] was a great event for Monastyrskoe. Departure for the army should have made Dzhugashvili and A. A. Maslennikov reasonable, made them see the need to revive comradely relations with the majority of the colony of political exiles. This was necessary also from the point of view of party organization. But neither Dzhugashvili nor Maslennikov tried to do this, and there was no one else on their side. [Suren] Spandaryan died in the Krasnoyarsk hospital in September, and after his death Vera Schweitzer evidently lived in Krasnoyarsk, so that Dzhugasvili represented a tiny minority of the exile community, if you didn't count the Anarchists, the members of the Polish Socialist Party, and the Menshevik Toponogov, who inclined toward their side. When Dzhugashvili arrived at Monastyrskoe from Kureika, he stayed with Maslennikov and as before kept aloof from all the other political exiles. He did not resume party ties with the two members of the Russian Bureau of the Central Committee who were there, Sverdlov and Goloshchekin, or with the leading members of the party underground. . . . The necesary reconciliation did not take place. Dzhugashvili remained as proud as ever, as locked up in himself, in his own thoughts and plans. . . . As before, he was hostile to Sverdlov, and would not move toward reconciliation, although Sverdlov was prepared to extend the hand of friendship and was willing to discuss problems of the workers' movement

20. From the archives of Yuri Trifonov. Rosa Zakharova's reminiscences were published in part by Trifonov in his *Otblesk kostra* (Moscow, 1966), pp. 47–48.

21. K. T. Sverdlova, *Ya. M. Sverdlov* (Moscow, 1960), p. 199.

22. Yakov Sverdlov, *Izbrannye proizvedeniia*, vol. 1 (Moscow 1957), pp. 276–277.

in the company of the three members of the Russian Bureau of the party's Central Committee.[23]

Siberian exile, especially in Turukhansk territory, was a harsh punishment. Still, it was not hard labor, and many of the political exiles used the enforced inactivity to supplement their knowledge, exchange opinions, and engage in creative work. Stalin did not know how to work under the restrictions of exile and prison. The last piece of writing in Volume 2 of his *Works* is dated January–February 1913, and the first item in Volume 3 is dated March 1917. It cannot be said that Stalin took no part whatsoever in party life. He was present in the summer of 1915 at a conference of members of the Russian Bureau of the Central Committee and the Bolshevik Duma group, which had been denied its parliamentary rights and exiled to Siberia. In 1916, together with a group of other Bolsheviks, he signed a letter of salutations to the Bolshevik magazine *Voprosy strakhovaniya*. Stalin did, however, let most of this time pass in idleness. Trotsky, who missed no opportunity to slight his opponent, wrote in 1930:

These four years of exile should have been a time of intense intellectual activity. The exiles, under such conditions, keep diaries, write treatises, draft theses and platforms, exchange polemical letters, and so forth. It is hardly conceivable that during the four years of exile Stalin did not write anything on the basic questions of the war, the International, and the revolution. Yet one would seek in vain for any traces of Stalin's intellectual labors during those four amazing years. How could this have happened? It is all too obvious that had a single line been found in which Stalin had formulated the idea of defeatism or proclaimed the need for a new International, this line would long ago have been printed, photographed, translated into all languages, and endowed with learned commentaries by all the academies and institutes. But no such line has been found. Does this mean that Stalin wrote nothing at all. No, it means nothing of the sort. That would be utterly improbable. It does mean that among the things he wrote during those four years there turned out to be nothing, absolutely nothing, that could be utilized today to help reinforce his reputation.[24]

Stalin did send letters to Lenin from Siberian exile. These passed through illegal channels and were later lost, but a few letters Stalin sent through the regular mail were copied by the Yenisei gendarme adminis-

---

23. Ivanov's memoirs are in unpublished manuscript form in the archive of A. V. Snegov.

24. *Biulleten' oppozitsii*, no. 14, (August 1930), p. 8. [Cf. The English version, Leon Trotsky, "A Contribution to the Political Biography of Stalin," in his *Stalin School of Falsification* (New York, 1972), p. 184–185. —G. S.]

tration and have been preserved. One of them was addressed to Roman Malinovsky, the notorious Bolshevik member of the Duma, who also worked for the secret police. It was on the basis of a denunciation by Malinovsky that the gendarmes had tracked Stalin down and arrested him. At the end of November 1913 Stalin wrote:

Hello, friend! It's somehow awkward to write, but necessary. I've never been through such an awful situation, it seems. All the money's gone, some sort of suspicious cough has started because of the intense cold (thirty-seven degrees below freezing), the general situation is one of illness, there are no supplies or bread, neither sugar nor meat nor kerosene (all the money went on ordinary expense and to provide ourselves with shoes). And without supplies, everything here is expensive—rye bread is four kopeks a pound, kerosene fifteen kopeks, meat eighteen, sugar twenty-five. Milk is needed, firewood is needed, but— money, there's no money, friend. I don't know how I'll get through the winter in this condition. I don't have wealthy relatives or acquaintances; there's positively no one for me to turn to, and so I turn to you, and not only to you but also to Petrovksy and Badayev. My request is that if the Social Democratic Duma group still has a fund for "victims of repression," let it, or better the group's bureau, give me the only help I can get, even if it's just sixty rubles. Pass on my request to Chkheidze and tell him also that I ask him to take my request to heart. I ask this of him not only as a fellow countryman but mainly as chairman of the Duma group. . . . I understand that all of you, and you in particular, don't ever have time, but devil take it, there's no one else to turn to and I wouldn't want to kick off here without writing a single letter to you. This is something that has to be taken care of right away. And send the money by telegraph, because to wait longer means to starve and I'm already sick and exhausted. You know my address: Turukhanskii krai, Yenisei gubernia, village of Kostino, Joseph Dzhugashvili. Another thing. Zinoviev writes me that the articles on the national question are coming out in a separate pamphlet. Do you know anything about this? The thing is that if it's true, one chapter should be added to the articles (I could do that in a few days if you'd only let me know), and then I hope (and I have the right to hope this) that there'll be an honorarium. (In this miserable region where there's nothing but fish, money's as necessary as air.) I hope that when you get a chance you'll stand up for me and wangle an honorarium for me. . . . Well, sir, I'll be waiting for what I've asked of you and I firmly shake your hand and kiss you, devil take it. . . . Greetings to Stefania and the guys. Greetings to Badayev, Petrovksy, Samoilov, Shagov, and Mironov [Bolshevik members of the Social Democratic Duma group]. I can't believe that I've been condemned to freeze here for four years. . . . Yours, Joseph.

The other letter was addressed to T. A. Slovatinskaya, a woman who was a close acquaintance of Stalin's and who worked at the Prosevesh-chenie publishing house:

November 10. This letter has been lying here in my place for two weeks because the post road's out. Tatyana Aleksandrovna! It's somehow shameful to write but I'm forced to by need. I don't have a penny and all my supplies are gone. There was some money but it all went on warm clothing, shoes, and supplies, which are terribly expensive here. For the time being, they trust my credit, but what will happen later, God knows; I don't. . . . Wouldn't it be possible to stir up some friends and acquaintances (like Krestinsky) to get together twenty or thirty rubles or maybe more? It would be a real salvation, and the sooner the better, because winter is at its fiercest. . . . I hope that if you decide to, you'll get the money. And so to work, my dear, or else the "Caucasian from the Kalashnikov Market" will be a goner—you'll see. . . . You know my address, so send it directly to me. If necessary, you can stir up Sokolov, and then more than thirty rubles might come of it, and that would be a real holiday for me.

November 20. My dear, need is growing by the hour, and I'm in a desperate situation. On top of that I'm ill; some sort of suspicious cough has started. Milk is needed, but money—there's no money. My dear, if you can get hold of some money, send it immediately by telegraph; I haven't the strength to wait longer.

Of course, Stalin's situation was not the easiest, but in this instance he was deliberately overdramatizing. He had money and supplies, but not enough to use for the escape he was planning. He had no intention of sitting in exile for four years. The local authorities knew the exiles' material situation and guessed at Stalin's plans. In the files of the Yenisei gendarme office, together with Stalin's letters was the following official note:

January 4, 1914, Krasnoyarsk. Top Secret. In presenting reports by our agents on number 578, attached, I have the honor to inform your Highness that the author of these is Joseph Vissarionovich Dzhugashvili, an exile under surveillance in Turukhansk territory. . . . Measures to prevent Dzhugashvili's escaping have been taken by me.[25]

The measures taken were that Stalin and Sverdlov were transferred 180 versts (approximately 120 miles) farther north, to Kureika. Stalin did receive money from his friends but was not able to escape.

■ 2
STALIN IN 1917

The year 1917 culminated in the victory of the October socialist revolution in Russia and the establishment of the first proletarian state in the

25. Copies of the three documents quoted above are in the personal archives of Yuri Trifonov. The originals are in the Central State Archive of the October Revolution.
"The Caucasian" (Kavkazets) was one of Stalin's party names. The Kalashnikov Grain Market in St. Petersburg, next to the university, was a traditional spot people chose for meeting one another.

world based on workers' councils (soviets). The Bolsheviks came to power in a vast country and established a revolutionary government there. This event proved to be the most important in the twentieth century. It changed the fate of the world and the history of all humanity.

The revolutionaries of one day were transformed on the next into government officials, from whom the times and circumstances demanded new and different qualities and concerns. Still, membership in the upper echelons of the party and a position in the party or government apparatus was linked for a long time with the question of services performed and conduct displayed during the crucial year in 1917. It is natural then to review Stalin's activities in that year. In researching the subject, I have encountered two different tendencies: on the one hand, an extreme exaggeration of Stalin's role in 1917; on the other, an attempt to reduce his role to the performance of few insignificant tasks.

The beginning of 1917 found Stalin in Krasnoyarsk. Called up for military service together with a group of other exiles, Stalin did not pass examination by a medical commission. He was found unfit for military service because of his weak left arm. His term of exile was coming to an end, and he was allowed to serve the rest of it in Krasnoyarsk. He made contact with several Krasnoyarsk Bolsheviks but much of his time was spent at evening gatherings at the home of Lev Kamenev, who had also been exiled to Siberia. A political exile named A. Baikalov was sometimes invited to these evenings, and many years later, as an émigré, Baikalov described his encounter with Stalin. According to Baikalov, Stalin almost constantly smoked a pipe. His face was "marked by smallpox; he had a low forehead over which rose thick matted hair; his mouth was hidden beneath a dirty mustache. His small dark-brown, almost black eyes, looked around with a gloomy expression, beneath thick brows." Baikalov added that Stalin spoke slowly, in a heavy Georgian accent, with difficulty selecting Russian words he needed. Kamenev often interrupted Stalin with an ironic or even scornful remark, and Stalin, frowning, would return to puffing on his pipe.[26]

The revolution was a surprise for most of the population, including the political activists, although many had looked forward to it. One of the first results of the February revolution was the quick and complete collapse of the entire tsarist system of repression. The gendarmes shed their uniforms and hid. The prison gates were opened, and the system of exile and hard labor stopped functioning. Not only were political pris-

26. A. Baikalov, "Moi vstrechi s Iosifom Dzhugashvili," *Vozrozhdenie* (Paris), March–April 1950, p. 118.

oners freed; so were the vast majority of inmates who had been convicted on criminal charges.

On March 3, 1917, a soviet was established in Krasnoyarsk. It immediately took power and decreed the arrest of tsarist officials. A special train was set aside to take political exiles to Moscow and Petrograd. Together with Kemenev and Matvei Muranov, Stalin immediately left for the capital.

In the first days of March 1917 the Bolsheviks in Petrograd came out from underground and took the necessary steps to begin publication of *Pravda* and establish a party leadership. All the members of the Russian Bureau of the Central Committee, instituted at the Prague Conference in 1912, had either been sent into internal exile or had emigrated abroad. During the war a new bureau had therefore been formed, and of its members three were in Petrograd—Aleksandr Shlyapnikov, Pyotr Zalutsky, and Vyacheslav Molotov. On March 7 and 8 the Russian Bureau coopted several new members, including Mikhail Kalinin, Vladimir Zalezhsky, Maria Ulyanova, and Mikhail Olminsky. The first issue of the newly legal *Pravda* appeared on March 5, with an editorial board consisting of Kalinin, Molotov, and Konstantin Yeremeev.

With the arrival of the exiled Bolsheviks from Siberia, the question of their being added to the party's new central institutions naturally arose. The matter was not settled without difficulties and disputes. For example, on March 12, the day of Stalin, Kamenev, and Muranov's arrival in Petrograd, a meeting of the Bureau was held. The minutes of that meeting contain the following passage:

Next the question of comrades Muranov, Stalin, and Kamenev was decided. The first was invited by a unanimous vote [to join the Bureau]. Concerning Stalin, it was reported that he had been an agent of the Central Committee in 1912, and therefore it would be advisable to have him as a member of the Bureau of the Central Committee. However, in view of certain personal characteristics, the Bureau decided to give him only a consulting vote. As for Kamenev, in view of his behavior at the trial [that is, the trial of the Bolshevik deputies to the Duma, described below] and in view of the resolutions passed in Siberia and in Russia, it was decided to add him to the staff of *Pravda* if he offers his services, but to demand from him an explanation of his behavior. His articles are to be accepted for *Pravda*, but he is not to get a by-line.[27]

We do not know the details of the clash between Stalin and the new members of the Bureau, although there must have been such a conflict

27. Central Party Archive, Institute of Marxism-Leninism, collection 17, list 1, item 385, sheet 11.

after the March 12 meeting. The Bolsheviks who had returned from exile were older and more experienced. In addition, Stalin was not only an "agent" of the Central Committee but the only member in Petrograd who had been placed on it by the Prague Conference. It is not surprising that on the very next day he was made a member of the Bureau after all. On the same day the Bureau named a new editorial board of *Pravda*: Olminsky, Stalin, Yeremeev, Kalinin, and Ulyanova. Once he was on the board, Stalin in fact seized control of the paper. As early as March 15 *Pravda* announced in its ninth issue that Stalin, Kamenev, and Muranov had been added to the editorial board. The other two approved by the Bureau as members of the board were not mentioned. Stalin's actions aroused widespread protest among Petrograd Bolsheviks. On a motion by Olminsky the Bureau passed a resolution on March 17: "The Bureau of the Central Committee and the Petrograd Committee, while protesting the annexationist procedure by which Comrade Kamenev was placed on the editorial board, postpone the question of his behavior and his participation in the editorial board of *Pravda* until the next party conference."[28] Of course this resolution did not trouble Stalin.

These developments did not merely signify a change in the personnel of the editorial board but a change in its political and tactical orientation. In its first issues *Pravda* had called for a struggle against the Provisional Government and against the policies of the Mensheviks and the Socialist Revolutionaries (SRs) which were aimed at reaching agreement with the bourgeois parties and the Provisional Government. *Pravda*'s initial opposition to the Provisional Government corresponded to the first recommendations that reached Russia from Lenin. In its ninth issue and after, however, the tone and content of the main articles changed. *Pravda* came out in support of the Provisional Government "insofar as the actions of this government contribute to the development of the revolution." *Pravda* spoke up quite clearly and definitively in favor of unification with the Mensheviks in a single party within which both factions could work out their differences. While advocating peace, *Pravda* called on the Russian soldiers to firmly hold the front until the conclusion of peace became a reality.

There may have been indignation in the Petrograd organization, but the articles in *Pravda* served as a guide for all the party organizations in Russia. Until Lenin arrived in Petrograd, Stalin in effect stood at the

28. Ibid., sheet 26.

head not only of *Pravda* but of the entire party. *Pravda*'s more moderate position was greeted with satisfaction in the leading circles of the other parties. Shlyapnikov, in his memoirs published in the twenties under the title *Semnadtsatyi god* (Nineteen Seventeen), wrote:

The day of the first issue of the "transformed" *Pravda*—March 15—was a day of rejoicing for the defensists. The entire Tauride Palace, from the wheeler-dealers in the State Duma Committee to the very heart of revolutionary democracy, the Executive Committee of the Petrograd Soviet, buzzed with a single piece of news: the victory of the moderate and reasonable Bolsheviks over the extremists. In the Executive Committee itself we were met with venomous smiles. This was the first and only occasion on which *Pravda* won the approval of even the hardened defensists of the Lieber-Dan stripe. When this issue of *Pravda* reached the factories it produced utter dismay among our party members and sympathizers and sarcastic satisfaction among our opponents. Inquiries poured into the Petersburg Committee, the Bureau of the Central Committee, and the editorial board of *Pravda*—What's going on? Why has our newspaper renounced the Bolshevik line and taken the path of defensism? But the Petersburg Committee, as well as the entire organization, was caught unawares by this coup. There was general indignation and the Bureau of the Central Committee was blamed for this incident. The indignation in local districts was enormous, and when the workers found out that *Pravda* had been seized by three former editors of *Pravda* arriving from Siberia, they demanded their expulsion from the party.[29]

The leading role in formulating *Pravda*'s new line was undeniably played by Kamenev. Stalin supported him completely both as the effective editor of the paper and as author of several articles. Their line followed from the old slogans of the Bolshevik Party from the time of the revolution of 1905–1907, when the question of the stages the revolution would have to pass through was discussed. The terms of that discussion were changed by the world war and the situation of dual power that arose in Russia in 1917. Stalin and Kamenev did not understand the new possibilities that had opened before the working class and the Bolsheviks. At first only Lenin understood them. But even he had difficulty convincing the party that he was correct. In fact, the first of a series of orientational letters Lenin sent to *Pravda* was published by Stalin and Kamenev in abridged form only, and the next three were not published at all.[30]

Stalin and Kamenev defended their position at the All-Russia Conference of Party Activists held in Petrograd March 27–April 2. Even when Lenin's celebrated "April Theses" were published in *Pravda* (after his

29. Aleksandr Shlyapnikov, *Semnadtsatyi god*, vol. 1 (Moscow-Leningrad, 1925), pp. 219–220.
30. See N. Krutikova, *Na krutom povorote* (Moscow, 1965).

arrival in Russia), Kamenev on the very next day, with Stalin's support, printed an article sharply criticizing the theses.

Later on, Stalin was obliged more than once to acknowledge the erroneousness of his position in March 1917. "It was a profoundly mistaken position," he said in one of his speeches, "for it gave rise to pacifist illusions, brought grist to the mill of defensism, and hindered the revolutionary education of the masses. This mistaken position I shared at that time with other comrades in the party."[31]

At the Seventh All-Russia Conference of the Bolshevik Party (in April) a Central Committee was elected, consisting of only twelve members. Both Stalin and Kamenev became part of that Central Committee. After the First Congress of Soviets, Stalin was one of the Bolsheviks on the All-Russia Central Executive Committee of the Soviets (CEC), but it was a very large body, with more than three hundred full and candidate members, about sixty of them Bolsheviks. Stalin attended sessions of the CEC but spoke rarely, even though he belonged to the presiding committee. During the period up to August 9 his name is mentioned in the minutes of the CEC only four times, and then in passing. Irakly Tsereteli, one of the leaders of the first CEC, later wrote in his memoirs, "Stalin never took part in the meetings or in private discussions."[32]

Nikolai Sukhanov, another figure active in the CEC, gives similar testimony in his memoirs:

From the Bolsheviks at that time in addition to Kamenev there appeared in the Central Executive Committee—Stalin. . . . I do not know how Stalin was able to reach such high posts in his party. During the time of his modest activity on the CEC he gave me the impression—and not me alone—of a gray blur sometimes emitting a dim and inconsequential light. There is literally nothing more to be said about him.[33]

These comments are indicative, but they do not adequately reflect Stalin's real role in 1917.

The spring and summer of 1917 were a time of endless meetings. All the parties, and the Bolshevik Party in particular, were fighting for influence upon the masses. It was important to the Bolsheviks not only to work out political slogans in keeping with the moods of the masses but to send skilled agitators, orators, and propagandists to the factories and military units. Stalin was poorly suited for such work. From March to

31. Stalin, *Sochineniia*, 6:333.
32. Irakly Tsereteli, *Vospominaniia o fevral'skoi revoliutsii* (Paris, 1963), 1:142.
33. Nikolai Sukhanov, *Zapiski o revoliutsii* (Berlin, 1922), 2:265–266.

October 1917 he spoke only three times at public meetings. Stalin did not have the resources to become a tribune of the revolution. Even his latterday apologists recognized this. Henri Barbusse put it this way in his book on Stalin:

Let us say, if you like, that Lenin, especially because of circumstances, was more of an agitator. In the vast directing system which is now much better organized and more developed, Stalin must necessarily act far more through the medium of the Party, by the intermediary of the organization, as it were. Stalin is not, nowadays, the man of great tempestuous meetings. . . . [He] never made use of that tumultuous force of eloquence which is the great asset of upstart tyrants and the only one, very often, of successful apostles: this is a point which should be considered carefully by historians who attempt to gauge him. It is by other paths that he came into and remains in contact with the working, peasant, and intellectual population of the U.S.S.R.[34]

Barbusse's reasoning is quite superficial. First, Lenin was by no means primarily an agitator. Second, the Bolsheviks in 1917 had a great need for the "eloquence" of "apostles." Without the entire galaxy of brilliant orators who came to the fore at that time they could not have won in October or have consolidated their victory. It is also true that the party was very well organized, a factor no less important in the Bolshevik victory. The Bolsheviks were more solidly and cohesively organized than the other parties and therefore could maneuver very effectively as a political force. It is true that although he did not have oratorical abilities, Stalin undoubtedly possessed an extraordinary organizational talent. The Bolshevik Party was growing from month to month with exceptional speed. Stalin, together with the party's best organizer, Sverdlov, brought the party's ranks into military order. Stalin and Sverdlov also carried out the main work of preparing and conducting the Sixth Congress of the Bolshevik Party in August 1917, and it was Stalin who gave the political report for the Central Committee at that congress.

It should be noted that at the Sixth Congress Stalin took an insufficiently clear stand on whether Lenin should give himself up for trial before a court of the Provisional Government. Stalin considered it possible for Lenin to turn himself into the authorities if certain guarantees were provided: "If . . . a government should come to the fore that could guarantee our comrades against violence, a government that would have even some degree of honor, then they would appear."[35]

34. Henri Barbusse, *Stalin: A New World Seen Through One Man* (New York, 1935), p. 276. [The author cites the Russian edition *Stalin* (Moscow, 1936), p. 109.—G. S.]
35. *Shestoi s'ezd RSDRP (b). Avgust 1917 goda. Protokoly* (Moscow, 1958), p. 28.

At the Sixth Congress a more numerous and representative Central Committee was elected—including, for the first time, Trotsky. In the absence of Lenin and Zinoviev, Stalin's role in the direction of party organizations increased. During those months he was the de facto director of the central newspaper, which came out under various names. The opinions of Lenin, who directed the party from underground, and those of Stalin, who was still in a legal position, did not always coincide. In such cases Stalin arbitrarily edited Lenin's articles, which aroused Lenin's indignation.

Lenin was in a hurry to overthrow the Provisional Government and was extremely dissatisfied with the slowness of the Central Committee: "Delay is criminal! To wait for the Congress of Soviets would be a childish game of formalities, a shameful playing at formalities, and a betrayal of the revolution." "There is no middle course." "There can be no delay." "The revolution will perish." "The Bolsheviks, it turned out took a wrong attitude toward parliamentarism in moments of revolutionary . . . crisis." "There is not the slightest doubt that at the 'top' of our party there are noticeable vacillations that may become *ruinous*. . . . All is not well with the 'parliamentary' upper echelons of our party." "In view of the fact that the Central Committee has even left unanswered the persistent demands I have been making . . . , in view of the fact that the central organ is *deleting* from my articles all references to such glaring errors on the part of the Bolsheviks as the shameful decision to participate in the Preparliament, . . . I am compelled to regard this as a 'subtle' hint . . . that I should keep my mouth shut, and as a proposal for me to retire. I am compelled to tender my resignation [from the Central Committee], which I hereby do, reserving for myself freedom to campaign among the rank and file of the party and at the party congress."[36] The constant disagreements with the Central Committee prompted Lenin's decision to return to Petrograd to personally direct preparations for armed insurrection.

Stalin took part in the decisive Central Committee meetings of October 10 and 24, at which the decision for an armed insurrection was made on the basis of reports by Lenin. Only Kamenev and Zinoviev voted against the decision, and in violation of all conspiratorial norms they published their objections in the non-Bolshevik newspaper *Novaya zhizn.*

36. Lenin, PSS, Vol. 34, pp. 280–283, 340–341, and passim. [The quotations from Lenin are from September and October 1917. As cited by the author, they are not in chronological order. English versions are in CW, 26: 141, 48, 58, 84, and passim.—G. S.]

As is generally known, Lenin demanded that Zinoviev and Kamenev be expelled from the party. The only Central Committee member who opposed Lenin on this question was Stalin.

What was Stalin doing on October 24–26—that is, during the decisive hours of the armed insurrection in Petrograd?

It is well known that the Petrograd Soviet played the key role in the organization and preparation of the insurrection and that it was headed by Trotsky. At Lenin's suggestion a Military Revolutionary Committee was established in mid-October under the Executive Committee of the Petrograd Soviet, and it began working out all the details of the insurrection. An especially large amount of work in the directing bureau of the Military Revolutionary Committee was carried out by Vladimir Antonov-Ovseyenko and Nikolai Podvoisky. The role of other Bolshevik activists (such as Dybenko, Volodarsky, Krylenko, Raskolnikov, Bubnov, Dzerzhinsky, Boky, Avanesov, and Yeremeev) was also very important. As for Stalin, he was mainly occupied with publication of the Bolshevik paper, *Rabochy put*. He did not immediately direct any operations by Red Guards, sailors, and soldiers on the streets of Petrograd.

In fact, the entire story that Stalin played a key role in organizing the October insurrection hangs by a slender thread—a resolution of the Central Committee on October 16, calling for the formation of a "Party Center" or "Military Revolutionary Center" to lead the insurrection. It was to consist of Sverdlov, Stalin, Dzerzhinsky, Bubnov, and Uritsky. It was proposed that this center be part of the Military Revolutionary Committee and direct its work. But events in Petrograd moved at such a headlong pace, that the "Party Center," created on paper, never actually met and did not function as any sort of special agency directing the insurrection. Similarly, a decision of the Central Committee survived on paper, calling for the formation of a Political Bureau consisting of seven members. This resolution was passed as early as October 10, 1917.[37] But it was not implemented.

Although the Party Center never met and never made any decisions, many Soviet historians continue to assert that it was the "guiding nucleus" of the Military Revolutionary Committee. There is no corroboration of this in the minutes of the meetings of the Military Revolutionary Committee or in those of the Petrograd Soviet. Unquestionably, the individuals named as members of the Party Center carried out important

37. *Protokoly tsentral'nogo komiteta RSDRP (b). Avgust 1917-fevral' 1918* (Moscow, 1958), p. 86. A really functioning Politburo did not come into existence until March 1919.

assignments. For example, Bubnov was appointed commissar of all the railroad stations. Dzerzhinsky was directly in charge of the seizure of the main postal and telegraph building. Uritsky took an active part in the work of the Military Revolutionary Committee and the Committee for the Defense of Petrograd. Sverdlov's signature appears on several documents of the Military Revolutionary Committee. But Stalin neither spoke at meetings of the Military Revolutionary Committee nor signed any of its documents. He did not actually take any part in its work. It is not surprising that John Reed, in his book on the October Revolution, did not devote a single line to Stalin.[38]

In all of Lenin's pamphlets, articles, and letters, published in Volume 34 (July–October 1917) of his *Polnoe sobranie sochinenii* Stalin's name is mentioned only once, and then in connection with a mistake by Stalin, Sokolnikov, and Dzerzhinsky. The minutes of the Bolshevik Central Committee tell us that on the morning of October 24 a new session of the Central Committee was held at the Smolny Institute, at which duties were assigned to various members of the Central Committee for directing the insurrection. Stalin was not present at this meeting. As I conclude from other documents, Stalin spent the days October 24 and 25 at the editorial offices of *Rabochy put* and among the Bolshevik delegates to the Second Congress of Soviets.

The result of the victorious armed insurrection in Petrograd was the transfer of power to the Soviets. The Provisional Government was overthrown. In its place came a "provisional workers' and peasants' government" elected by the Second Congress of Soviets. It was given the name Council of People's Commissars (or Sovnarkom, to use the Soviet acronym). The chairman of the first Soviet government was Lenin, and its members—people's commissars—numbered fourteen, all Bolsheviks. Among them was Stalin, who was assigned to head the People's Commissariat for Nationalities.

One of the most important slogans of the October revolution was the call for freedom and equality for all nations and nationalities of the tsarist empire. This major plank in the Bolshevik platform determined the importance of the new Commissariat of Nationalities. It was not by

38. In a foreword to Reed's *Ten Days That Shook the World* Lenin expressed a very high opinion of it and recommended its publication in millions of copies in all languages. Stalin, on the other hand, banned the book. In the 1930s Reed's book was removed from the libraries in the Soviet Union. There were quite a few cases in which party members were sentenced to long terms in prison or the camps "for keeping and circulating John Reed's book."

accident that Stalin became the first head of this commissariat. Not only was he one of the leading figures in the Bolshevik Party but also—as non-Russian—his nomination was intended to increase confidence in the council of People's Commissars in the national regions and districts of Russia. Besides, on the basis of his articles on the national question published in 1913, Stalin was regarded in the party as an expert on nationality problems.

On November 1, 1917, Stalin, together with Lenin, signed the Declaration of the Rights of the Peoples of Russia. Drafted by Lenin, it proclaimed the basic principles of Soviet national policy: abolition of all national and religious restrictions or privileges, equality of all peoples, free development of all national and ethnic groups, and the right of self-determination up to and including separation and the formation of an independent government.

■ 3
HEAD OF THE PEOPLE'S COMMISSARIAT OF NATIONALITIES

For most of the people's commissars in the first Soviet government the main difficulty was to overcome sabotage by the bureaucrats in almost all the agencies left over from the Provisional Government and the tsarist regime. For Stalin such difficulties did not arise because tsarist Russia had no counterpart to his new commissariat. It was necessary therefore to put together at least a minimal staff. One of the first functionaries of the commissariat and the organizer of its minuscule apparatus was Stanislav Pestkovsky.[39]

Stalin's entire commissariat was accommodated in one of the rooms of the Smolny Institute not far from Lenin's office. For a long time the commissariat had no thought-out plan of work. Tasks arose of their own accord, and they were quite often unexpected and difficult. For example, from November 1917 to January 1918 Stalin took part in negotiations with the Central Rada, a grouping of several petty bourgeois nationalist parties that had come to the forefront in the Ukraine. The Rada, headed at the time by Simon Petlyura, took a hostile attitude toward the October revolution and proclaimed itself the supreme organ of the Ukrainian People's Republic. At first this People's Republic declared itself part of a federal Russia, but in late January 1918 it proclaimed its full indepen-

39. *Proletarskaia revoliutsiia*, 1930, no. 6, p. 128.

dence. Talks with the Central Rada were broken off. As a counter to the Rada, the Bolsheviks and Left SRs convoked the first All-Ukraine Congress of Soviets in Kharkov and announced the formation of the Ukrainian Socialist Soviet Republic. After the Second All-Ukraine Congress of Soviets in Yekaterinoslav in March 1918, the Bolshevik Nikolai Skrypnik became head of the People's Secretariat of the Ukraine. Almost all of the Ukraine at that time was occupied by the Germans, who installed the promonarchist government of Hetman Skoropadksy in Kiev. Nevertheless, when Lenin learned of the decision by the Second All-Ukraine Congress of Soviets to establish a soviet government in the Ukraine, he sent a statement of greetings from the Council of People's Commissars of the Russian Socialist Federated Soviet Republic (RSFSR) expressing "enthusiastic sympathy for the heroic struggle of the laboring and exploited masses of the Ukraine, who are at present one of the advanced detachments of the world socialist revolution." In contrast, on April 4 Stalin sent the following telegram to the Soviet government of the Ukraine: "Enough playing at a government and a republic. It's time to stop that game; enough is enough." In reply to this message, which was intolerable both in tone and content, Skrypnik sent the following telegram to Moscow on April 6:

> We must protest in the strongest possible way against the statement of Commissar Stalin. We must declare that the Central Executive Committee of the Ukrainian Soviets bases its actions, not on the attitude of any commissar of the Russian Federation, but on the will of the toiling masses of the Ukraine, as expressed in the decree of the Second All-Ukraine Congress of Soviets. Declarations like that of Commissar Stalin would destroy the Soviet regime in the Ukraine. . . . They are direct assistance to the enemies of the Ukrainian toiling masses.[40]

The Bolsheviks advocated the self-determination of nations up to and including their complete governmental separation from Russia as independent nation-states. This did not mean that the Bolsheviks would welcome the separation of the national regions from Russia or help them secede. The Bolsheviks were fighting for the victory of proletarian revolution throughout the former Russian empire and the formation on its territory of an alliance of free peoples and nations as the first step in a worldwide socialist revolution. It should not be forgotten that the Bolshe-

40. The documents quoted above are from the archive of A. V. Snegov, who took part in the Second All-Ukraine Congress of Soviets. See also the Central State Archives of the October Revolution, Ukrainian SSR, collection 1, list 1, file 7v, sheet 1.

vik Party was not just a Russian party; it sought to unite revolutionary socialists of all nationalities in the Russian empire.

The socialists of Poland and Finland were two exceptions. In those parts of the Russian empire independent Social Democratic parties existed, having been founded several years before the RSDLP. Moreover, the Polish and Finnish movements for independence from Russia had grown to large dimensions and won broad popular support long before 1917. Parliamentary elections in Finland in October 1917 gave a majority to the bourgeois parties. On December 6 the new Finnish parliament declared Finland an independent state. On December 31, 1917, the Sovnarkom of the RSFSR recognized Finland's independence in a decree signed by Lenin and Stalin. A few days later, after a report by Stalin, this decree was approved by the All-Russia Central Executive Committee of the Soviets of the RSFSR.

As people's commissar of nationalities Stalin gave a number of reports to sessions of the Sovnarkom and Central Executive Committee on the situation in Turkestan, the Caucasus, the Urals region, the Don region, Turkish Armenia, on the autonomous status of the Tatars, and on the federal institutions of the RSFSR.

As a member of the Bolshevik Central Committee Stalin took part in all the meetings of that body at which the Brest-Litovsk peace treaty and Russia's withdrawal from the imperialist war were discussed. The minutes of the Central Committee meetings show clearly that Stalin almost always supported Lenin's position, although in the early stages of the discussion Lenin was in the minority. The only exception was the meeting of February 1, 1918, when Stalin called for an end to the disagreements. "We must put an end to this. . . . The way out of this grave situation has been shown to us by the middle position, the position of Trotsky."[41]

In all the voting on this question in the Central Committee Stalin supported Lenin's motions. The intensity of the dispute is seen in the fact that the motion for immediate conclusion of a peace with Germany was adopted on February 18, 1918, by a majority of only one vote. Those voting for were Lenin, Smilga, Stalin, Sverdlov, Sokolnikov, Trotsky, and Zinoviev. Opposed were Uritsky, Joffe, Lomov, Bukharin, Krestinsky, and Dzerzhinsky.[42]

In April 1918 a conflict arose between Stalin and the leader of the

41. *Protokoly TsK*, p. 178.
42. Ibid., p. 204.

Menshevik Internationalists, Yuli Martov. Some biographers of Stalin attribute too much importance to this incident. Anton Antonov-Ovseyenko, for example, begins his book on Stalin with an account of this dispute.[43]

In the spring of 1918 the Bolsheviks were not the only legal party. The Left SRs, Mensheviks, Menshevik Internationalists, Anarchists, Maximalists, and several other small political parties also existed legally and published their newspapers. After the Brest-Litovsk treaty they were all in opposition to the Bolsheviks. Naturally, the Bolsheviks kept a very close eye on this opposition press. On March 31 *Vperyod* (Forward), the newspaper of the Menshevik Internationalists, ran an article by Martov in which he criticized the Bolsheviks in general for having committed excesses in carrying out "expropriations." He asserted that Stalin "at one time had been expelled from the party organization for his involvement with the expropriations." Stalin denounced this as libel and submitted a complaint to the revolutionary tribunal on the press, which had been established by a Sovnarkom decree of January 28, 1918.[44] A three-member investigative commission was set up under this tribunal. Sessions of the tribunal were supposed to be held publicly, with both accusers and defenders taking part.

It is not hard to conclude that in this case Stalin was not harmed at all by Martov's reproaches for his involvement in the "expropriations." After coming to power, the Bolsheviks could only take pride in such episodes from their revolutionary past. The SRs, who at this time were the political allies of the Mensheviks, had also frequently resorted to such actions. Stalin emphatically denied, however, that he had been expelled from a party organization. Martov had no proof or documentation of this point. He demanded that witnesses be called to the court. But Bolshevik witnesses would hardly have given evidence against one of their own leaders. As for witnesses from among the Mensheviks, such as Sylvester Dzhibladze and Noi Zhordania, in 1918 they were all in Georgia, and it was impossible to summon them to Moscow. Antonov-Ovseyenko calls Suren Spandaryan the most important witness, but he had died in Siberian exile in 1916. Apparently Martov was not aware of that fact.

Stalin demanded an immediate trial and investigation without waiting for all the witnesses named by Martov to be summoned. The decree

43. Anton Antonov-Ovseyenko, *The Time of Stalin: Portrait of a Tyranny* (New York, 1981), pp. 3–7.
44. *Dekrety Sovetskoi vlasti*, vol. 1 (Moscow, 1957), p. 434.

establishing the tribunal provided for speeded-up and simplified legal procedures in especially urgent cases, but in spite of everything, Martov was able to obtain a ruling that the case be postponed for a week for the summoning of witnesses. Stalin himself did not appear at the tribunal. His interests were represented by Lev Sosnovsky. Antonov-Ovseyenko claims that during that week the tribunal on the press was dissolved, apparently at Stalin's insistence, and the entire matter was transferred to an ordinary court in Moscow.[45] This is an obvious inaccuracy. It is true that as early as the end of March 1918 a proposal was introduced in the Sovnarkom to eliminate the revolutionary tribunals on the press because there were many Left SRs on these tribunals. But Lenin argued against the proposal, and the tribunals continued to operate with a full workload until the end of May 1918.[46]

I cannot here go into all the details of Stalin's suit against Martov. As was to be expected, Martov did not succeed in bringing his witnesses before the tribunal. In view of the general character of Martov's article, the revolutionary tribunal condemned him for undermining the authority of the government and administered a public reprimand. In evaluating this verdict, Antonov-Ovseyenko writes that Stalin had been discredited. "He had not refuted Martov's charge or removed the blot from his own reputation. He decided it would be a good idea to leave Moscow for a while. . . . He would not soon recover from the shame of the Martov case."[47]

Again, all this is plainly exaggerated. The trial was an episode of little importance for Stalin. Martov's charges could not make any impression on the Bolsheviks. Even the question of Stalin's alleged expulsion from the party in 1906 or 1907 could not trouble the Bolsheviks because the Transcaucasian Regional Committee of the RSDLP at that time had been dominated by the Mensheviks, and the Bolshevik faction did not consider the decisions of that committee binding upon them. The trial was evidently used as a pretext to close down Martov's newspaper *Vperyod*.

In the spring of 1918 the Bolsheviks were fighting fairly energetically against the entire opposition press. In May and June alone approximately sixty bourgeois, SR, and Menshevik publications were shut down, including *Drug naroda* (Friend of the People), *Narodnoye slovo* (The

---

45. Antonov-Ovseyenko, *The Time of Stalin*, p. 5.
46. A. Z. Okorokov, *Oktiabr' i krakh russkoi burzhuaznoi pressy* (Moscow, 1970), pp. 260, 283.
47. Antonov-Ovseyenko, p. 6.

People's Word), *Rodina,* and *Prizyv.* The main reason for closing Martov's paper was not so much his polemic against Stalin as a number of false reports it had carried, which under the existing conditions could have caused panic. Sverdlov spoke at a session of the Central Executive Committee on May 9, 1918, demanding that publication of *Vperyod* be stopped. On May 11 the Presidium of the Central Executive Committee, on a motion by Sverdlov, decreed that "all newspapers printing false rumors and absurdly untrue *(vzdornye)* reports be immediately shut down until this question has been reviewed by a tribunal on the press."[48] Stalin actually did leave Moscow in early June 1918, but the conflict with Martov had nothing to do with that departure.

We must violate the chronology of our account somewhat at this point in order to discuss some important changes in Stalin's personal life. A year later, in 1919, he married for the second time. His wife was the nineteen-year-old Nadezhda Alliluyeva. She kept her family name, and few of her acquaintances knew she had become Stalin's wife. Wedding ceremonies were not put on in those days. Very few Bolsheviks bothered to have their marriages registered. They simply began to live together and called themselves husband and wife. Stalin had for a long time known Nadezhda's father, Sergei Yakovlevich Alliluyev, one of the oldest Bolshevik workers. They had first met in 1900 in Tiflis. But the thirty-four-year-old Alliluyev had paid no particular attention to the twenty-year-old Stalin. They met again in Baku in 1907, where Stalin was already one of the leaders of the Bolshevik organization. Alliluyev went to see him for assistance in getting a passport under a false name. According to Alliluyev, Koba also rendered him considerable financial assistance.[49] When Stalin returned from Siberia in March 1917 he stayed with the Alliluyev family for a while. The pretty sixteen-year-old daughter of Sergei Alliluyev immediately attracted Stalin's attention. Having grown up in the family of a professional revolutionary, Nadezhda naturally sympathized with the Bolsheviks and was very much taken with the thirty-seven-year-old Stalin. The taciturn and gloomy Koba was able to restrain his rudeness and be attentive, almost tender, toward people he found useful or women he liked. When he became a commissar in the first Soviet government, Stalin offered Nadezhda a position as secretary in the small apparatus of his commissariat. She agreed and moved to Moscow with

48. Okorokov, pp. 275–277.
49. Sergei Alliluyev, *Proidennyi put'* (Moscow, 1956), pp. 132–134.

the commissariat in the spring of 1918. In 1919 she linked her fate with Stalin's and began to take up wifely duties in his simple household. Since it was inappropriate for her to be employed by a government body run by her husband, she was obliged to leave the Commissariat of Nationalities. Instead she took a job with the Sovnarkom secretariat.

In the first years of their life together Stalin loved his young wife very much, and she responded in kind. They soon had a son, Vasily (in the past that had been one of Stalin's party names). A few years later their daughter, Svetlana, was born.

I will not return again to the question of Stalin's relations with women and therefore should note at this point that Stalin was something of an ascetic and never let women affect his political activity. Before his marriage to Alliluyeva and after her death, he had some brief liaisons with several women, but he truly loved only his two wives, Yekaterina Svanidze, who died early, and Nadezhda Alliluyeva, who also suffered an early death. It is a fact that Stalin had two sons born out of wedlock, but he took no part in their upbringing. One of them lives and works in Moscow today. There is no need to give his name.

In some Western newspapers after Stalin's death as well as in the Russian emigre press of the twenties there were various speculations on the subject of Stalin and women. One author, hiding under the pseudonym Essad-Bey, claimed that Stalin, like an Oriental sheikh, kept his beautiful wife locked up at his Kremlin apartment or at his dacha and forbade her to show herself to other men, so that even his Kremlin colleagues never saw her face.[50] Others asserted that Stalin married secretly after Alliluyeva's death or that he held orgies at his dachas or in his Kremlin apartment. All this is the product of unfounded rumor or deliberate fabrication.

■ 4

STALIN IN THE CIVIL WAR

In the late twenties Stalin was frequently referred to as a top military leader of the revolution. Later, when most of the commanders and

50. Essad-Bey (real name: Nisselbaum), *Stalin: Iz zhizni sovetskogo diktatora* (Riga, 1932). [Cf. the English-language version, *Stalin: The Career of a Fanatic* (London, 1932). —G. S.] This book made use of information about Stalin published in the Soviet Union in connection with his fiftieth birthday and also drew on some emigre sources. But much of it was sheer invention.

commissars of the civil war had been killed, people began to write about Stalin as the "direct inspirer and organizer of the most important victories of the Red Army in the civil war, a man whom the party sent to every front where the fate of the revolution was being decided."[51] This myth was destroyed by Soviet historians in the early sixties. Therefore I will take up only a few episodes of Stalin's activity as military leader in the civil war.

On May 29, 1918, in connection with the increasingly grave food situation in Moscow and the central provinces of Russia, the Sovnarkom appointed Stalin general director for food supplies in the south of Russia and granted him extraordinary powers. In this capacity, on June 4 Stalin left for Tsaritsyn. There he found confusion and chaos not only in food and military matters but in transport, finance, and so on. Utilizing the authority granted him, Stalin took full power in the entire Tsaritsyn region.

There is no doubt that he did significant work in restoring order and supplying food to the industrial centers of Russia. But the main method he used to restore order was mass terror. He wrote to Lenin, "I curse and persecute everyone I have to. I hope that the situation will soon be straightened out. You can be sure I will spare no one, neither myself nor others, and we will provide bread in spite of everything."[52] Truly Stalin spared no one. He didn't hesitate to have dozens of real enemies of Soviet power shot; but he also destroyed anyone even suspected of ties with the counterrevolution. Voroshilov wrote about this at one time, without condemning Stalin for it at all.[53] Gradually Stalin assumed all the main military functions in the Northern Caucasus. He wrote to Lenin:

There's a lot of grain in the south. In order to get it, we must have a smoothly functioning apparatus that will not encounter any obstacles from trains, army commanders, etc. Also the military men have to help the food-supply people. The food question naturally gets intertwined with the military question. For the good of the cause I need military powers. I already wrote about this but received no answer. Very well, in that case I myself, without formalities, will remove those commanders and commissars who are ruining the cause. The interests of the cause prompt me to do this and the absence of any papers from Trotsky will not stop me.[54]

51. *I. V. Stalin. Kratkaia biografiia* (Stalin: A Short Biography) (Moscow, 1952), pp. 82–83.
52. Stalin, *Sochineniia*, 4:118.
53. Kliment Voroshilov, *Stalin i Vooruzhennye sily SSSR* (Moscow, 1951), p. 24.
54. Stalin, *Sochineniia*, 4:120–121.

The military specialists were among Stalin's first victims. He started to remove them from their posts, and he often had them shot. Stalin was extremely hostile and mistrustful toward Andrei Snesarev, the military man in charge of the Northern Caucasus military district.[55] A general of the old tsarist army and also an outstanding orientalist, Snesarev was one of the first to volunteer for the Red Army. His energetic leadership helped to beat back the White Cossack assault on Tsaritsyn. Nevertheless, just at that time Stalin sent a telegram to Moscow accusing the general of sabotage. Stalin declared Snesarev's plan for the defense of the city a "wrecker's" plan. In the end, Stalin arbitrarily removed Snesarev and had him arrested. Also arrested on Stalin's orders were almost all the military specialists on the staff of the military district. They were placed on a barge on the Volga. This floating prison then suddenly sank with most of its prisoners.

At Stalin's insistence a new plan for the defense of Tsaritsyn was worked out. Part of the troops on the northern sector of the front defending Tsaritsyn were removed with the aim of attacking to the west and south. The military historians V. Dudnik and D. Smirnov testify that "this disrupted the stability of the defense, which had been organized with great difficulty. . . . On August 1 the inadequately prepared offensive began, but on August 4 [Moscow's] contact with the south was broken and the city [of Tsaritsyn] was cut off from central Russia. It was necessary to hastily transfer units back to the northern part of the front."[56] Stalin tried to blame former commander Snesarev for this failure, claiming that Snesarev had left a totally unmanageable "heritage."

An inspection committee of the Supreme Military Council, headed by Aleksei Okulov, arrived in Tsaritsyn to investigate. Snesarev was immediately freed and appointed chief of defense of the western region. Later he worked as director of the Red Army's Academy of the General Staff— but was arrested again in 1930.

In mid-August 1918 a particularly grave situation developed at Tsaritsyn. The White Cossacks were able to advance to the very outskirts of the city. By the end of August, however, despite heavy losses, the Red Army managed to break the encirclement of Tsaritsyn and drive the enemy back across the Don.

On September 11, 1918, a Southern Front was organized, with Pavel Sytin as commander and Stalin, Voroshilov, Sergei Minin, and Konstan-

55. *Voenno-istoricheskii zhurnal*, 1965, no. 1.
56. *Voenno-istoricheskii zhurnal*, 1965, no. 2.

tin Mekhonoshin as members of its Revolutionary Military Council. Sharp differences arose between Stalin, Voroshilov, and Minin (old Tsaritsynites) on the one hand and Sytin and Mekhonoshin on the other. As before, the Tsaritsynites refused to trust the military specialists and tried to introduce a kind of collective leadership in directing the Soviet forces, a method the party had considered and rejected. At Stalin's insistence, the Revolutionary Military Council of the Southern Front overruled Sytin's first operational orders and then removed him from his command. At that very time the enemy's forces began a new offensive against Tsaritsyn, driving the weakened and exhausted Red Army units before them. The situation was saved by Dmitry Zhloba's Steel Division, which arrived from the Northern Caucasus and surprised the enemy from the rear.[57]

Even earlier it had been Stalin's practice to pay no attention to directives coming from the People's Commissariat of War and the Military Revolutionary Council of the Republic. On one of Trotsky's orders he wrote his own comment: "To be disregarded" (*Ne prinimat vo vnimanie*).[58] In connection with such attitudes and practices on Stalin's part, Sverdlov, the chairman of the Central Executive Committee, telegraphed Stalin in Tsaritsyn on October 1, 1919:

> All decisions of the Revolutionary Military Council are binding on the Military Councils of the fronts. Without subordination there is no unified army. Without preventing an order from being implemented, one may make a complaint about it to a higher body—to the Council of People's Commissars or the Central Executive Committee, or in an extreme case to the Central Committee of the party. We insistently urge that the decisions of the Revolutionary Military Council be put into effect. . . . There should not be any conflicts.[59]

But Stalin paid no attention to this telegram either. The conflict had a negative effect on the fighting capacity of the Southern Front. As chairman of the Revolutionary Military Council of the Republic Trotsky telegraphed Moscow:

> I categorically insist that Stalin be recalled. Things are going badly in the Tsaritsyn sector, despite superior forces. Voroshilov is capable of commanding a regiment, but not an army of 50,000. However, I will leave him in command of the Tenth Army if he will report to the commander of the front, Sytin. Up to now Tsaritsyn has not even sent operational reports. . . . I have asked that

57. *Grazhdanskaia voina v SSSR*, vol. 1 (Moscow, 1980), p. 229.
58. Kliment Voroshilov, *Stalin i Krasnaia Armiia* (Moscow, 1929), p. 27.
59. Sverdlov, *Izbrannye proizvedeniia*, vol. 3 (Moscow, 1960), p. 28.

reports on reconnaissance and operations be sent twice daily. If all this is not carried out tomorrow, I will remand Voroshilov to court martial and publish the fact in an order to the army.[60]

Stalin was removed from the Military Council of the Southern Front and recalled to Moscow. However, as Robert Tucker points out in his book on Stalin, "the inglorious ending of Stalin's mission to Tsaritsyn caused him no serious political setback."[61]

Difficulties and conflicts occurred on all the fronts of the civil war in those days. The introduction of former tsarist officers as military specialists was an extremely difficult operation. The Red Army was just being built, and a single competent command was coming into existence in the course of a painful struggle against holdovers of a guerrilla-warfare mentality. In the end the Red Army succeeded in holding Tsaritsyn, and no one thought of punishing Stalin. Moreover, at the very time that Stalin was recalled to Moscow he was, at Trotsky's suggestion, appointed a member of the Revolutionary Military Council of the Republic.

Stalin spent the last part of 1918 in Moscow, occupied mainly with the affairs of the Nationalities Commissariat. He attended the First Congress of Muslim Communists, held in Moscow, drafted a decree on the independence of Estonia, and helped organize the Byelorussian Soviet Republic. On January 1, 1918, Stalin and Dzerzhinsky were sent to the Eastern Front to investigate setbacks suffered there by the Red Army, particularly the causes of the surrender of Perm. After the situation on the Eastern Front improved, Stalin and Dzerzhinsky returned to Moscow.

The Tsaritsyn events were discussed at the Eighth Party Congress. Voroshilov and Minin openly adhered to the so-called Military Opposition which opposed the use of former Tsarist officials as military specialists. In words Stalin was against the Military Opposition, but in fact he sympathized with it. In the corridors he tried to create the impression that Lenin and the Central Committee did not understand military matters, and were placing too much confidence in Trotsky. At the party congress Avram Kamensky was reprimanded and told that there was no military policy of Trotsky's; there was only the military policy of the Central Committee, which Trotsky was carrying out. The main disagreement was over the use of military specialists in the Red Army. It can be assumed that Lenin persuaded Stalin not to speak out against Trotsky,

60. Leon Trotsky, *Kak vooruzhalas' revoliutsiia*, vol. 1 (Moscow, 1924), pp. 350–351.
61. Tucker, *Stalin as Revolutionary*, p. 196.

and in return Lenin refrained from criticizing Stalin, even approving the executions carried out in Tsaritsyn. "We have had disagreements and made mistakes," said Lenin. "No one denies this. When Stalin had people shot in Tsaritsyn I thought it was a mistake, I thought that the shootings were incorrect, but the documents Voroshilov has quoted revealed our error. My error was revealed, but still I had telegraphed: Be careful. I made a mistake. We are all human."[62]

On the main question, the use of military specialists and the observance of discipline in the army, Lenin was adamant. He severely condemned the actions of the Tsaritsyn leaders, naming Voroshilov first of all. Lenin attributed the enormous losses suffered by the Red Army at Tsaritsyn primarily to the guerrilla mentality that regarded military specialists with contempt.

At the Eighth Congress Stalin was reelected to the Central Committee. Although the Central Committee was not very large then, a decision was made to establish a smaller direct body within it—a Political Bureau (Politburo), which would decide important political issues on a day-to-day basis. The first Politburo consisted of Lenin, Kamenev, Krestinsky, Stalin, and Trotsky. The candidate members were Bukharin, Kalinin, and Zinoviev. An Organizational Bureau (Orgburo) was also established for the first time to direct the ongoing organizational work of the party. It consisted of five members: Beloborodov, Krestinsky, Serebryakov, Stalin, and Yelena Stasova. A few days later a decree of the Central Executive Committee appointed Stalin people's commissar of state control.

I will not dwell on the various assignments Stalin carried out as a representative of the Central Committee and the Military Revolutionary Council on the Petrograd, Western, and Southern fronts. These were not third-rate assignments, as Anton Antonov-Ovseyenko suggests. On the other hand, they were not so exceptionally important as Stalin's apologists later made them out to be.

It is appropriate to look more closely, however, at Stalin's activity in 1920 on the Southwestern Front, where he was sent at the end of May as a member of the Military Council of that front. The invading Polish army had been stopped by then, and after heavy fighting in the Ukraine and Byelorussia, Kiev and Minsk had been liberated.

62. *Leninskii sbornik*, no. 37 (Moscow, 1970), pp. 138–139. (Lenin's speech at the special closed session of the Eighth Congress, a session dealing with the disputes on military questions, was published here for the first time.)

Most of the Red Army's reinforcements were initially sent to the Southwestern Front. But toward the end of July a situation developed which required a rapid regroupment of forces. Facing the Western Front, which had only sixty thousand infantry and cavalry, was a Polish force more than twice the size. Opposite the Southwestern Front, on the other hand, were only three Polish divisions and some demoralized units loyal to Petlyura. In June 1920 the troops of General Wrangel emerged from the Crimea and occupied a substantial part of Northern Tauria. The forces of the Sixth and Thirteenth armies were insufficent to repel Wrangel's offensive; moreover, these two Soviet armies were under the command of the Southwestern Front, which had moved far to the west.

On August 2, 1920, the Politburo passed a resolution that all the armies in action against Poland should be united under one command, the Western Front, headed by Tukhachevsky. At the same time a decision was made to establish a separate Southern Front. It was proposed that Stalin form a Military Revolutionary Council for the Southern Front, about which Lenin informed him in the following telegram:

Urgent. In code. To Stalin. We have just passed [a resolution] in the Politburo separating the fronts, so that you can occupy yourself exclusively with Wrangel. In connection with peasant revolts, especially in the Kuban and then in Siberia, Wrangel is becoming an enormous danger, and within the Central Committee there is a growing mood in favor of an immediate peace with Poland. I ask you to consider the Wrangel situation very carefully and send your conclusions.[63]

On the basis of the same Central Committee decision, S. S. Kamenev, the Red Army commander in chief, ordered the Twelfth Army and First Cavalry Army to be transferred within a few days from the Southwestern to the Western Front in order to strengthen the main Soviet forces advancing on Warsaw.

Stalin refused to carry out the instructions of Lenin and Kamenev. On the evening of August 2 he replied to Lenin by telegram:

I received your note on the separation of the fronts. The Politburo shouldn't concern itself with trifles. I can work for the front a maximum of two more weeks. I need a rest. Find a replacement. I don't believe the promises of the commander in chief for a minute. He only lets people down with his promises. As for the mood of the Central Committee in favor of peace with Poland, it's impossible not to remark that our diplomats very successfully undermine the results of our military victories.[64]

63. Lenin, PSS, 51:247.
64. *Leninskii sbornik*, no. 36 (Moscow, 1959), p. 116.

On August 3 Lenin sent Stalin a new telegram insisting that the fronts be separated. "Our diplomats," he wrote, "are subordinate to the Central Committee and would never undermine our victories unless the Wrangel danger caused vacillation in the Central Committee."[65] Lenin did not object to Stalin taking "a rest" but asked him to find his own replacement.

On August 5 the Central Committee reaffirmed the decision to separate the fronts and resolved that the Fourteenth Army also be transferred to the Western Front. The commander in chief gave the necessary orders, but Stalin and A. I. Yegorov, the commander of the Southwestern Front, who was under Stalin's influence, did not carry them out. S. S. Kamenev repeated his command: "The Western Front is preparing to deal a decisive blow to smash the enemy and take control of the Warsaw region. In view of this it is necessary right now to abandon for the time being the idea of immediately occupying the Lvov region on your front."[66] But Stalin and Yegorov paid no attention to this order. Instead they issued the following directive to the First Cavalry Army: "In the shortest possible time destroy the enemy on the right bank of the Bug with a mighty blow, force a crossing of the river, and over the backs of the fleeing remnants of the Third and Sixth Polish armies, occupy the city of Lvov."[67] The First Cavalry Army was unable to carry out this order.

The Western Front also suffered a defeat in its drive on Warsaw. Of course a number of factors contributed to the failure of the Warsaw campaign, but not the least of them was Stalin's willfulness (samouprav-stvo). With major forces at his disposal, Stalin did not want the laurels of victory to go to the Western Front. Apparently, he himself wanted to march into Warsaw from its rear after taking Lvov. "But who in the world would march on Warsaw by way of Lvov?" Lenin asked Bonch-Bruevich when the latter reported to him about the failures on the Polish front.[68]

In view of Stalin's failure to obey the orders of the commander in chief, the Secretariat of the Central Committee sent Stalin the following telegram on August 14: "The disputes between you and the commander in chief have reached the point where . . . it is necessary to clear them up

65. Lenin, PSS, 51:248.
66. Iz istorii grazhdanskoi voiny v SSSR (Moscow, 1961), p. 348.
67. Voenno-istoricheskii zhurnal, 1962, no. 9, p. 61.
68. V. D. Bonch-Bruevich, Na boevykh postakh fevral'skoi i oktiabr'skoi revoliutsii, (Moscow, 1930), p. 283. (Lenin's remark was omitted in later editions of these memoirs by Bonch-Bruevich.)

by a joint discussion in a face-to-face meeting, and therefore we request that you come to Moscow as soon as possible."[69]

On August 17 Stalin went to Moscow and requested that he be relieved of military duties. On September 1 the Politburo relieved him of all assignments with the army.

At the Ninth Party Conference, held in late September 1920, Lenin defended the actions of Commander in Chief Kamenev and Chairman of the Military Council Trotsky, and in the summary of his report on behalf of the Central Committee he found it necessary to condemn Stalin's behavior. The next day Stalin took the floor on a point of personal privilege and stated that "parts of yesterday's speeches by comrades Lenin and Trotsky do not correspond to reality."[70] The conference paid no attention to his rebuttal.

■ 5

LENIN'S SUPPORT FOR STALIN

One may ask how Stalin managed to get away so easily with the instances of willfulness and rudeness that have been described. First, Stalin was a fairly powerful figure in the party leadership and knew how to stand up for himself. Second, many other representatives of the Central Committee at the fronts of the civil war also acted at times with excessive severity. There were quite a few complaints on this score against Trotsky, but Lenin usually defended Trotsky too. In the struggle among groupings in the party at that time Stalin took Lenin's side, and Lenin valued that. In the conditions of a fierce civil war and a critical situation Lenin was obliged to make use of every real force on the side of the revolution.

Lenin often gave Stalin direct support, as he had at Krakow when the articles on the national question were written and when he coopted Stalin onto the Central Committee and appointed him to the Russian Bureau. It was at Lenin's suggestion that Stalin was named commissar of nationalities and commissar of state control, and later commissar of the Workers' and Peasants' Inspection (or Rabkrin, to use the Soviet acronym). Although Trotsky demanded many times that Stalin be removed

69. *Kratkaia istoriia grazhdanskoi voiny v SSSR* (Moscow, 1962), p. 444.

70. *Deviataia konferentsia RKP (b). Protokoly* (Moscow, 1972), p. 82. Lenin's summary at the second session of the congress has not been published to this day—on the grounds that it was "not corrected." We know of his criticism of Stalin only from the notes on pp. 372–373 in this 1972 edition of the Ninth Conference's proceedings.

from military work, Lenin was in no hurry to take such action and sometimes supported Stalin more than he did Trotsky. On October 23, 1918, for example, Lenin sent Trotsky the following telegram:

Today Stalin arrived, bringing news of three major victories by our forces at Tsaritsyn. . . . Stalin would very much like to work on the Southern Front; he expresses great fear that people who don't know this front well will make mistakes, examples of which he cites in large numbers. Stalin hopes that in his work he will succeed in convincing people of the correctness of his approach, and does not make an ultimatum of the demand for the removal of Sytin and Mekhonoshin, agreeing to work together with them on the Revolutionary Military Council of the Southern Front, expressing also the desire to be a member of the Supreme Military Council of the Republic. . . . In informing you, Lev Davidovich, of all these statements by Stalin, I ask you to think them over and to reply, first of all, whether you agree to have a personal talk with Stalin, for which he is ready to come see you; and, second, whether you consider it possible on the basis of certain conditions to set aside the previous conflicts and arrange to work together, as Stalin so much desires.

For my part, I think it necessary to exert every effort to arrange to work together with Stalin.[71]

The personal meeting between Stalin and Trotsky did not take place, nor did Stalin return to the Southern Front. But he was appointed a member of the Supreme Military Council of the Republic.

As Trotsky wrote later:

After the conquest of power Stalin began to feel and act more confidently without ceasing to be a figure of the second rank. I soon noticed that Lenin was "pushing" Stalin. I did not pay much attention to this fact, because I never doubted for a moment that Lenin was governed not by personal preferences but by considerations of the cause. Gradually these became clear to me. What Lenin valued in Stalin was his character, firmness, tenacity, insistence, and partly also his craftiness. He valued these as indispensable qualities in a fight. Independent ideas, political initiative, or creative imagination he did not expect or demand of Stalin.

I remember during the civil war I once asked Serebryakov, a member of the Central Committee who at that time was working with Stalin on the Military Council of the Southern Front, whether the two Central Committee members were really needed there? Couldn't Serebryakov, for the sake of economizing forces, make do without Stalin? After thinking for a moment, Serebryakov answered: "No, I don't know how to exert pressure the way Stalin does. That is not my specialty." The ability to exert pressure was what Lenin valued most highly in Stalin. And Stalin felt increasingly confident, the more the state apparatus for

71. *Leninskii sbornik*, no. 37 (Moscow, 1970), p. 106.

the exertion of pressure grew and became stronger. And it must be added, the more the spirit of 1917 departed from this apparatus.[72]

There is more than a little truth in Trotsky's words. I must add, however, that Stalin not only was pushed by Lenin but also strove actively to promote himself to the first rank. Moreover, the "spirit of 1917" was not only the spirit of revolution and freedom but also the spirit of endless meetings, demonstrations, anarchy, and lack of discipline. Trotsky felt very much at home in that atmosphere. But Stalin was smart enough not to try to compete in the arena of propaganda and oratory with other revolutionaries. He waited until his ability to apply pressure and his mastery of political intrigue could best serve his purposes. Stalin was a man of few words even in a small group of friends. However, he knew how to give importance to even a brief remark. This was noticed by someone as far from politics as Fyodor Chaliapin, who had the chance to meet Stalin at the apartment of Demyan Bedny.

Stalin spoke little, and when he did it was with a fairly strong Caucasian accent. Yet everything he said had a weighty ring to it, perhaps because he spoke briefly. From his short sentences, which were not always clear to me in their meaning but energetic in tone, I went away with the impression that this was a man who did not fool around. If necessary he could easily, as easily as his light Lezghinka step in soft boots, do a dance or blow up the temple of Christ the Savior or a post office, telegraph office, what you will.[73]

Stalin left military work almost at the end of the civil war. It was neither a demotion nor a retirement. He had to concentrate his attention on work at the Commissariat of Nationalities; Soviet power had been established in almost all the national regions. Stalin traveled to the Northern Caucasus and Azerbaidzhan several times and received delegations from the various nationalities. He paid much less attention to the

72. [The author cites as his source for this quotation some "unpublished notes" by Trotsky dated January 4, 1937. These "notes" actually were published in French as part of Trotsky's *Les Crimes de Staline* (Paris, 1937). An English version of the January 4 "note" (entitled "Hatred of Stalin?") is in *Writings of Leon Trotsky, 1936–1937* (New York, 1978), pp. 67–71, where it is translated from the French with some inaccuracies. I have translated the quotation directly from Trotsky's Russian as quoted by Roy Medvedev. Copies of the Russian originals are among Trotsky's papers at Harvard Library. After 1937 Trotsky apparently adapted the material in this "note" for his biography of Stalin. The English edition of that biography, whose later chapters were pieced together after Trotsky's death with much added commentary by the edition-translator, contains two separate passages that correspond very close to the material quoted here. See Leon Trotsky, *Stalin: An Appraisal of the Man and His Influence* (New York, 1941), pp. 243, 270. —G. S.]

73. *Izvestia*, 1962, no. 249.

Commissariat of Workers' and Peasants' Inspection. He not only had to take part in the work of the Politburo and Orgburo Bureau but also served on several permanent commissions of the party's Central Committee and the government's Central Executive Committee.

In late 1920 and early 1921, when the party was feverishly caught up in the "trade union discussion," Stalin was not very active, although he supported Lenin's platform and spoke against the positions of Bukharin and Trotsky. At the Tenth Party Congress Stalin gave a report on the national question. Soon after, when the Red Army entered Georgia and the Menshevik government in that area was overthrown, Stalin went to Tiflis. With his involvement a Bolshevik government for Georgia and all of Transcaucasia was formed. However, Stalin's attempts to speak in front of meetings of workers ended miserably. He was booed off the platform at a meeting of Georgian railroad workers and left the meeting guarded by Russian Chekists. In his place a prominent Menshevik, Isidore Ramishvili, was carried to the speaker's platform by some of the crowd. This failure intensified Stalin's dislike for Georgia, and he hardly ever visited the country again. He felt more and more that his homeland was not tiny Georgia but great Russia.[74]

At the Eleventh Party Congress Preobrazhensky proposed that Stalin's powers be somewhat curtailed. He said in his speech:

Take Comrade Stalin, for example, a member of the Politburo who is, at the same time, people's commissar of two commissariats. Is it conceivable that a person could be responsible for the work of two commissariats, and in addition work in the Politburo, the Orgburo, and a dozen Central Committee subcommissions?[75]

Lenin answered Preobrazhensky as follows:

Preobrazhensky comes along and airily says that Stalin is involved in two different commissariats. Who among us has not sinned in this way? Which of us has not taken on several responsibilities at once? And how could we do otherwise? What can we do now to maintain the existing situation in the Commissariat of Nationalities, in order to sort out all the Turkestan, Caucasian, and other questions? After all, these are political questions! And these questions have to be answered. They are questions such as European states have occupied themselves with for hundred of years, and only an insignificant portion of such problems have been solved in the democratic republics. We are working to resolve them and we need a man to whom representatives of any of our different nations can

74. Tucker, *Stalin as Revolutionary*, pp. 236–238.
75. *Odinnadtsatyi s'ezd RKP(b). Stenograficheskii otchet* (Moscow, 1961), pp. 84–85.

go and discuss their difficulties in full detail. Where are we to find such a person? I think that even Preobrazhensky would be unable to name another candidate besides Comrade Stalin.

The same thing applies to the Workers' and Peasants' Inspection. This is a vast business; but to be able to handle investigations we must have someone in charge who has authority. Otherwise we'll get bogged down and drown in petty intrigues.[76]

Lenin's attitude toward Stalin was so benevolent in the years 1918–1921 that he personally concerned himself with finding a quiet apartment for him in the Kremlin. He reprimanded Ordzhonikidze for disturbing Stalin while the latter was on vacation in the Northern Caucausus. Lenin asked for a doctor to be found to treat Stalin and asked that he be sent the doctor's conclusions about Stalin's health. On one occasion, half joking and half serious, Lenin suggested that Stalin marry his younger sister, Maria Ulyanova. He was sure that Stalin was still a bachelor and was surprised when Stalin said he was married and that his wife worked in the secretariat of the Central Committee. Hostility toward Stalin arose on Lenin's part only after the Eleventh Congress.

■ 6
STALIN AS GENERAL SECRETARY

The Eleventh Congress did not reduce Stalin's powers. He was reelected to the Central Committee, and after the congress at the first plenary session of the new Central Committee a new position was introduced, that of general secretary of the Central Committee. On April 3, 1922, the plenum elected Stalin general secretary. The official "short biography" of Stalin claims that the plenum elected Stalin at Lenin's suggestion. Trotsky later asserted that Lenin was opposed to Stalin's promotion or, at any rate, "dodged" the question, merely expressing a few doubts. It was then that Lenin allegedly made the remark frequently quoted by Trotsky: "This cook will prepare only peppery dishes."

But what does it mean that Lenin "dodged" the question? Kamenev chaired the opening of the plenary session and proposed that a Secretariat consisting of all new members be elected. A new Politburo and Orgburo were also elected at the plenum. It is hard to imagine that preliminary agreement had not been reached with Lenin on the composition of the leading bodies of the Central Committee. A *Biographical*

76. Ibid., p. 143. [Cf. CW, 33: 315.—G. S.]

Chronicle of Lenin's life and work, published in recent years, gives the following account of April 3, 1922, based on materials from party archives.

> April 3. Lenin participates in the plenary session of the Central Committee, is elected a member of the Politburo, and is approved as a member of the Russian Communist Party delegation to the Comintern. During the session Lenin looks over the agenda, adds a number of points to it, and makes some comments and underlinings: he inserts a draft resolution, written by himself, on the organization of the work of the Secretariat. The plenum makes the decision to establish the position of general secretary with two Central Committee secretaries. Stalin is assigned to be general secretary; Molotov and Kuibyshev are the secretaries.[77]

At plenary sessions of the Central Committee all appointments of personnel are made by open voting, not by secret ballot, and there is no indication that Lenin, or even Trotsky, abstained when the slate of the new Secretariat was submitted for approval.

It should be noted that the post of general secretary was not then thought of as the main post in the party hierarchy, or even a very important one for that matter. The Secretariat occupied a subordinate position in relation to the Politburo and the Orgburo. The functions of the secretaries essentially differed in the early twenties from their present ones. At that time the Secretariat was mainly occupied with technical and internal party matters; it had not as yet intruded into the fundamental areas of government administration. Neither the army nor the security police, neither the Supreme Economic Council nor public education, was under the control of the Secretariat. The main commissariats were headed by prominent members of the Central Committee, and their work was discussed in the Politburo or at plenums of the Central Committee. Nor did the Secretariat concern itself with foreign policy and the Comintern.

Until the spring of 1919 the functions that later were carried out by the Orgburo and Secretariat were actually performed by Sverdlov, who had been assigned to head the Secretariat as early as the Sixth Congress. It was Sverdlov, and not Trotsky or Stalin, who was second in authority and importance as a leader of the Bolshevik party. After his death in March 1919 Lenin said:

> The work he performed as an organizer, in choosing men and appointing them to responsible posts in all the various departments, will be performed in the

77. *Vladimir Il'ich Lenin. Biograficheskaia khronika*, vol. 12 (Moscow, 1982), p. 267.

future only if we appoint whole groups of men to handle the different major departments that he had sole charge of, and if these men, following in his footsteps, come near to doing what this one man did alone.[78]

At the end of March 1919 Yelena Stasova was elected as chief secretary for the Central Committee. She encountered difficulties, and in November of the same year a Central Committee plenum elected Krestinsky to be second secretary of the Central Committee. In April 1920 a Secretariat consisting of three people—Krestinsky, Preobrazhensky, and Serebryakov—was elected. The leading figure in the Secretariat became Krestinsky, who also belonged to the Orgburo and Politburo. However, during the "trade union discussion," all of the Central Committee secretaries supported Trotsky's or Bukharin's platform and none of them were reelected at the Central Committee plenum following the Tenth Party Congress. Instead Molotov, Yemelyan Yaroslavsky, and V.M. Mikhailov were elected to the Secretariat. They were all members of the Orgburo as well.

Lenin, however, was displeased with the work of these party centers, accusing them of inadmissible red tape, delay, and bureaucratism. It was assumed, therefore, that the election of Stalin, whose organizational abilities and abrupt manner were well known in party circles, would bring order into the working bodies of the Central Committee. Thus there was nothing surprising about Stalin's placement in this new post. As Yelizaveta Drabkina has written, "This was an event of the kind to which no one attributed special importance and even in party circles no one paid any attention to it."[79] In April 1922 Lenin still stood at the head of the party and the government. He was the generally recognized leader of the revolutionary masses of Russia. Therefore the election of Stalin to the post of general secretary, despite the later legends, did not signify the advancement of the party's new leader, the successor to Lenin.

The situation changed as Lenin's illness grew worse, removing him more and more often from the administration of the country and direction of the party. Stalin was not only general secretary; he belonged to the Orgburo, the Politburo, and the Presidium of the Central Executive Committee, as well as heading two commissariats. Stalin had become a key figure in the party apparatus. With local elections to party bodies

78. Lenin, PSS, 38:79. [Cf. CW, 29:93–94.]
79. Drabkina was a secretary of Sverdlov. Later she became a writer. Her memoirs, *Zimnii pereval*, were published (Moscow, 1968), but not in full. The passage quoted here is from the unpublished part.

taking place under his direction, he was able to carry through a mass reshuffling of cadres in the provincial and regional party committees and in the central committees of the Communist parties in the non-Russian republics. Lazar Kaganovich, Sergei Syrtsov, and Andrei Bubnov, all active supporters of Stalin, were put in charge of the three main departments of the Central Committee, the Organizational and Instruction Department, the Records and Assignments Department (Uchraspred), and the Agitation and Propaganda Department (Agitprop). Stalin could also count on Molotov, Rudzutak, and Andreev, members of the Orgburo and Secretariat whom he brought under his influence. These men— together with Stalin's personal assistant, Ivan Tovstukha—constituted Stalin's first staff in the Central Committee apparatus. Stalin had other active supporters on the Central Committee, among them Valerian Kuibyshev, Grigory (Sergo) Ordzhonikidze, and Anastas Mikoyan. It was also at this time that Lev Mekhlis and Georgy Malenkov began their rise in the Central Committee apparatus.

In the first half of 1922 Lenin's illness grew worse. As the result of sclerosis in the brain his speech was impaired, and he had difficulty moving his legs. After a few weeks these symptoms disappeared, but it was not until October 1922 that Lenin was able to return to work. By this time he was obliged to consider the question of his successors.

Late in 1922 Lenin's political and personal relations with Trotsky, which had deteriorated badly during the "trade union discussion," began to mend. Lenin also showed more confidence in his former chief opponent of 1917, Lev Kamenev. Kamenev became Lenin's first deputy in the Sovnarkom, and in 1923, when Lenin's illness removed him from activity altogether, Kamenev presided at sessions of the Sovnarkom and Politburo. As for Stalin, Lenin responded more and more negatively to his activities during 1922. Lenin was extremely displeased at the attempt by Stalin, Bukharin, and Sokolnikov to weaken the state monopoly on foreign trade. Only Lenin's energetic intervention prevented a relaxation of the monopoly. Lenin also sharply criticized Stalin's policy on the national question. During Lenin's illness in 1922 Stalin carried his own proposal for "autonomization" through a Central Committee commission, a proposal that envisaged the national republics joining the RSFSR with rights of autonomy. Stalin's original draft stated:

> It is considered useful and expedient for the independent Soviet republics— the Ukraine, Byelorussia, Azerbaidzhan, Georgia, and Armenia—to formally enter the Russian Socialist Federated Soviet Republic (RSFSR). . . .

It is considered desirable that the formal powers assigned to the All-Russia Central Executive Committee, the Council of People's Commissars, and the Council of Labor and Defense of the RSFSR be extended to the corresponding central institutions of the republics named in point one. The people's commissariats of finance, food, labor, and national economy would be formally subordinated to the orders of the corresponding commissariats of the RSFSR. . . .

The remaining commissariats, those of justice, education, internal affairs, workers' and peasants' inspection, agriculture, public health, and social security would be considered independent. . . .

The agencies for combating counterrevolution in the above-named republics would be subordinated to the orders of the GPU of the RSFSR.

Signed, commission member J. Stalin.[80]

On the basis of Stalin's draft, a new Russian Federated Republic rather than a Union of Soviet Socialist Republics would have been established, with all the other national formations becoming part of the Russian Republic.

In a letter of September 27, 1922, Lenin condemned these preliminary decisions and proposed something different, creation of a new state, the Union of Soviet Socialist Republics, on the basis of equality among the RSFSR, Ukraine, Byelorussia, and the other republics. And that was the decision made by the party.

Stalin took an incorrect position in the conflict that arose between Ordzhonikidze and the leadership of the Georgian Communist Party on questions of the economic policy of the Transcaucasian regional committee and the rights of the Georgian Soviet Republic. Lenin was very disturbed by this conflict and under its impact wrote his notes "On the Question of Nationalities" at the end of 1922. In particular he said:

From what I was told by Comrade Dzerzhinsky, who was at the head of the commission sent by the Central Committee to "investigate" the Georgian incident, I could only draw the greatest apprehensions. . . . Obviously the whole business of "autonomization" was radically wrong and badly timed. . . . I think that Stalin's haste and his infatuation with pure administration, together with his spite against the notorious "national socialism," played a fatal role here. In politics spite generally plays the basest of roles. . . . I think that in the present instance, as far as the Georgian nation is concerned, we have a typical case in which a genuinely proletarian attitude makes profound caution, thoughtfulness, and a readiness to compromise a matter of necessity for us. The Georgian who is neglectful of this aspect of the question, or who carelessly flings about accusations of "nationalist-socialism" (whereas he himself is a real and true "nationalist-

80. Central Party Archive of the Institute of Marxism-Leninism, collection 558, list 2479, sheet 137.

socialist," and even a vulgar Great-Russian bully) violates, in substance, the interests of proletarian class solidarity. . . . The political responsibility for all this truly Great-Russian nationalist campaign must, of course, be laid on Stalin and Dzerzhinsky.[81]

In January 1923 Lenin returned more than once to an examination of this conflict. Moreover, as can be judged from the notes of Lenin's duty secretaries, Stalin was preventing Lenin, who was ill, from obtaining the materials he wanted.[82]

On March 5, 1923, Lenin wrote to Trotsky:

Dear Comrade Trotsky: It is my earnest request that you should undertake the defense of the Georgian case in the Party Central Committee. This case is now under "persecution" by Stalin and Dzerzhinsky, and I cannot rely on their impartiality. Quite to the contrary. I would feel at ease if you agreed to undertake its defense. If you should refuse to do so for any reason, return the whole file to me. I shall consider it a sign that you do not accept. With best comradely greetings, Lenin.[83]

Trotsky, because of illness, failed to do what Lenin asked. Kamenev did nothing either when Krupskaya complained to him about Stalin's rudeness. On December 23, 1922, she wrote:

Lev Borisovich! Because of a short letter which I had written, in words dictated to me by Vladimir Ilyich by permission of the doctors, Stalin allowed himself yesterday an unusually rude outburst directed at me. This is not my first day in the party. During all these thirty years I have never heard from any comrade one word of rudeness. The business of the party and of Ilyich are not less dear to me than to Stalin. I need at present the maximum of self-control. What one can and what one cannot discuss with Ilyich—I know better than any doctor, because I know what makes him nervous and what does not; in any case I know better than Stalin. I am turning to you and to Grigory as to much closer comrades of V. I. and I beg you to protect me from rude interference with my private life and from vile invective and threats. I have no doubt as to what will be the unanimous decision of the Control Commission, with which Stalin sees fit to threaten me; however, I have neither the strength nor the time to waste on this foolish quarrel. I too am a living person and my nerves are strained to the utmost.

N. Krupskaya.[84]

81. Lenin, PSS, 45:356–360. [Cf. CW, 36: 605–610].
82. *Voprosy istorii KPSS*, 1963, no. 2.
83. Lenin, PSS, 54:329. [Cf. CW, 45:607.]
84. Lenin, PSS, 54:674–675. [The English wording is taken from a translation of the secret speech by Nikita Khrushchev at the Twentieth Party Congress in 1956, in which Khrushchev revealed the text of Krupskaya's letter for the first time. See *Khrushchev Remembers* (Boston, 1970), p. 563. —G. S.]

It was only at the beginning of March that Lenin learned about Stalin's insulting treatment of Krupskaya, probably from Kamenev. Infuriated to the depths of his being, even though two months had passed since the incident occurred, Lenin told his secretary to dictate the following letter:

Dear Comrade Stalin: You have been so rude as to summon my wife to the telephone and use bad language. Although she had told you that she was prepared to forget this, that fact nevertheless became known through her to Zinoviev and Kamenev. I have no intention of forgetting so easily what has been done against me, and it goes without saying that what has been done against my wife I consider having been done against me as well. I ask you, therefore, to think it over whether you are prepared to withdraw what you have said and to make your apologies or whether you prefer that relations between us should be broken off. Respectfully yours, Lenin.[85]

Of course, Stalin immediately made new apologies to Krupskaya and took back his remarks. He did not dare to break with Lenin. On the morning of the next day Lenin dictated one more letter:

To Comrades Mdivani, Makharadze and others, with copies to Trotsky and Kamenev. Dear Comrades: I am following your case with all my heart. I am indignant over Ordzhonikidze's rudeness and the connivance of Stalin and Dzerzhinsky. I am preparing for you notes and a speech. Respectfully yours, Lenin. March 6, 1923.[86]

Neither this letter nor the one to Trotsky signified that Lenin fully agreed with the position of Budu Mdivani and the majority of the Georgian Central Committee. Lenin demanded patience and consideration toward the nationalism of formerly subject nations and considered greatpower chauvinism a much greater danger.

These three letters of March 5 and 6, 1923, were the last written documents of Lenin's life. On March 6 his health took a turn for the worse, and on March 10 he suffered a new stroke that deprived him of the power of speech and intensified the paralysis in his legs and right arm. There can hardly be any doubt that this condition was accelerated by his being upset. In the summer and fall of 1923 Lenin's health again improved and he began to receive visitors, take walks, and on one occasion he even traveled to Moscow and the Kremlin from Gorki (Little Hills, the village where he was staying). He spoke with a number of

85. Lenin, PSS, 54:329–330. [Cf. CW, 45:607–608.] It is curious to note that Stalin kept this note from Lenin in his archive for the rest of his life. It was found in Stalin's desk only after his death.

86. Lenin, PSS, 54: 330. [Cf. CW, 45:608.]

prominent party and government officials; but he did not once meet with Stalin.

In late 1922 and the first half of 1923 Stalin, as general secretary, was busy with many tasks, though he never forgot to strengthen his personal position in the party. He had his own plan for party building, which was set forth in rough form in a note he wrote in July 1921 but which was not published until 1947. Entitled "Political Strategy and Tactics," this memorandum consisted of a detailed plan for a pamphlet, and Stalin would use some of the thoughts presented in it in later articles. Certain other thoughts in the memorandum were not considered publishable by its author, at least not until 1947. A sentence like "the party is the commanding body and staff of the proletariat" might have aroused objections because the concept of "vanguard" and that of "command staff" (*komandny sostav*) are far from identical. But Stalin went even further:

> The Communist Party as a kind of Order of Knights of the Sword within the Soviet state, directing the institutions of that state and inspiring their activity. The significance of the Old Guard within this knightly order and the replacement of the Old Guard by new staff people who have been steeled in the struggle.[87]

This analogy between the Communist Party and the religious order of the Teutonic Knights ("the Brothers of Christ Militant" was the official name of this crusading order of sword-bearing monks) might have occurred to the mind of a former seminary student, but not to a Lenin or a Marx. Marx called the members of these orders "dog knights" and "crusading scum." There is no doubt that Stalin was impressed by the strictly hierarchical, four-level structure of the Knights of the Sword. The fact that Stalin's memorandum was published only in 1947 shows that the idea of transforming the party into something like a religious order and then creating within the party and state apparatus some sort of secret elite ranking, a special caste of "initiates," remained with Stalin for a long time. He expressed the same thought within a group of intimates again in the late thirties. The creation of a Nomenklatura (a list of high-ranking party members with exclusive rights to fill certain official positions) secretly rewarded with special payments in envelopes (which I will describe below) was undoubtedly a step in that direction.

Lenin's illness, the final outcome of which was becoming increasingly obvious, and the strengthening of Stalin's power disturbed many leaders of the party. In the fall of 1923 in a cave near Kislovodsk an unofficial

87. Stalin, *Sochineniia*, 5: 72–73.

conference of party leaders vacationing at that town was held, including Zinoviev, Bukharin, Yevdokimov, Lashevich, Voroshilov, and several others. Formally, the strengthening of collective leadership of the party was the topic of discussion. Zinoviev proposed that the Politburo be eliminated and a special triumvirate of Stalin, Trotsky, and himself be established. Zinoviev also proposed that instead of himself it might be Kamenev or Bukharin. Opinions differed and Zinoviev's plan encountered objections. They decided to ask Stalin himself. Later at the Fourteenth Party Congress, touching on this episode, Stalin said:

> In 1923 after the Twelfth Party Congress some people who gathered in a cave worked out a platform for destroying the Politburo and politicizing the Secretariat, that is, turning the Secretariat into a political and organizational leadership body consisting of Zinoviev, Trotsky, and Stalin. . . . To the question presented to me in written form from the depths of the cave at Kislovodsk I answered in the negative, stating that if the comrades insisted I would be ready to clear out without any fuss and without any discussion, open or secret.[88]

It is entirely possible that Stalin would have been obliged to "clear out" as head of the party. But a sharp debate with Trotsky and his supporters soon began, and the situation in the top levels of the party changed. The personal hostility between Zinoviev and Trotsky was still quite intense, and for that reason Zinoviev (and Kamenev, who supported him) firmly opposed Trotsky's ambitions and energetically supported Stalin, in whom they saw their main ally in the political battle that was unfolding.

■ 7

THE DEATH OF LENIN

While Stalin was taking every available opportunity to strengthen his personal position in the party, Lenin, ill and confined to his bed, was dictating his last articles and proposals (sometimes for only five or ten minutes a day). The underlying theme of these writings was the struggle against growing bureaucratism and the danger of a split in the party. Some of Lenin's notes were addressed to specific individuals and naturally were not intended for the press. He considered some of his letters and proposals strictly confidential, but he wanted the greater part of his

88. *Chetyrnadtsatyi s"ezd VKP (b). Stenograficheskii otchet* (Moscow, 1926), p. 506. In this stenographic record of the proceedings of the Fourteenth Congress, see also Voroshilov's speech, pp. 398–399.

last writings published immediately in the party press, which he read every day with the permission of the doctors. This applied in particular to the articles "How We Should Reorganize the Workers' and Peasants' Inspection" and "Better Fewer, But Better," in which Lenin sharply criticized Rabkrin, which had been headed by Stalin. Lenin for example declared:

> Let us say frankly that the People's Commissariat of Worker's and Peasant's Inspection does not at present enjoy the slightest authority. Everybody knows that no other institutions are worse organized than those of our Workers' and Peasants' Inspection, and that under present conditions nothing can be expected from this People's Commissariat.[89]

Lenin proposed that the agencies of party and government control be reorganized completely and a relatively small supervisory apparatus be established. Its members should have all the powers of Central Committee members and be elected from among workers and peasants. These Central Control Commission members, Lenin went on, would have the duty

> . . . to attend all the meetings of the Politburo . . . [and] will have to form a compact group which should not allow anybody's authority, without exception, neither that of the General Secretary nor of any other member of the Central Committee, to prevent them from asking questions, verifying documents, and, in general, from keeping themselves fully informed of all things and from exercising the strictest control over the proper conduct of affairs.[90]

Lenin attributed fundamental importance to the presence of rank and file workers on the Central Committee and Central Control Commission, seeing it as a way of reinvigorating the top party and government leadership and making it healthier. In his preparatory notes for the article on the Workers' and Peasants' Inspection (Rabkrin) Lenin wrote:

> If we delay in this matter, we will fail to carry out one of our main duties— that is, the duty to make use of our time in power in order to teach the best elements of the working masses all the details of government.[91]

Lenin's article on Rabkrin displeased not only Stalin, who saw it as an attack on himself, but also some other members of the Politburo. Bukharin, as editor of *Pravda*, in spite of his love for Lenin and in spite of Krupskaya's insistence, could not bring himself to publish the article.

89. Lenin, PSS, 45:392–393. [Cf. CW, 33: 490.]
90. Lenin, PSS, 45:387. [Cf. CW, 33: 485.]
91. Lenin, PSS, 45: 449.

Kuibyshev proposed that one copy of a special issue of *Pravda* containing the article be printed and sent to the bedridden Lenin to set his mind at rest. This proposal was not accepted. The article was published on January 25, 1923, and "Better Fewer, But Better" appeared on March 4. Nevertheless the Twelfth Congress, held April 17–25, did not take up the question of the Workers' and Peasants' Inspection; it was not on the agenda and was hardly even discussed. The congress did not set up a Central Control Commission with the kind of broad powers that Lenin proposed. To be sure, the Central Control Commission was substantially renewed and expanded, but most of its members had long been engaged in government and party work. Although they came from worker and peasant backgrounds, they were not "rank and file workers" to whom the details of administration had to be taught, nor did the Central Control Commission acquire powers on a par with those of the Central Committee.

The intensified disagreements in the Central Committee and the struggle, both open and veiled, for power within it disturbed Lenin greatly. In the fall of 1923 his health improved noticeably. He insisted that Krupskaya read the newspapers to him every day, but he no longer intervened in party affairs. As Drabkina relates in the unpublished part of her memoirs, Lenin sat alone for hours and sometimes even cried, apparently not only because of his helplessness but also from a sense of insult and frustration. According to Krupskaya, on January 19 and 20, 1924, she read Lenin the just published resolutions of the Thirteenth Party Conference, which drew a balance sheet on the debate with Trotsky and his supporters. Listening to the text of the resolutions, which were very sharply worded and often unjust, Lenin again became agitated. In order to calm him, Krupskaya said that the resolutions had been voted unanimously. That could hardly have reassured Lenin; his worst fears were beginning to be realized. On the next day, in a state of very severe emotional distress, Lenin died.

To this very day allegations occasionally appear in the foreign press that Lenin did not die a natural death but was killed by Stalin. For example, in 1976 the journal *Vremya i my* ran such an article by Lydia Shatunovskaya entitled "The Secret of One Arrest,"[92] in which she repeats a story supposedly told to her by Ivan Gronsky, a former editor of *Izvestia* and *Novy mir*, to the effect that Stalin murdered Lenin. As

92. *Vremya i my*, 1976, no. 6. From 1975–1979 *Vremya i my* was published in Israel. Since 1980 it has been published in New York.

the story goes, Stalin was visiting at Gronsky's apartment, drank so much that he lost all self-control, and had to stay overnight; during this drinking bout Stalin told his host about the murder. This is all pure fantasy, though probably Gronsky's rather than Shatunovskaya's. It is true that Gronsky was a well-known figure in the literary world in the early thirties. He was the editor in chief of *Novy mir* and took part in preparations for the First Congress of Soviet Writers, but he was not elected even as a delegate. Stalin knew Gronsky, but to say that he was "Stalin's most trusted man on literary questions" or that he "could go and see Stalin at any time without a report to give"—these assertions were made up by Gronsky. In 1937 Gronsky was arrested and sixteen years later returned from prison with a highly tarnished reputation. In order to win people's confidence again, or at least to attract their attention, he was capable of making up the most unlikely stories about his life before and after his arrest.

Trotsky, too, spread similar stories in the last years of his life. His version was so unbelievable that *Life* magazine, which had contracted with Trotsky for an article on Lenin, refused to print it. Several other American magazines rejected the article, and it did not appear until August 10, 1940, in the Hearst publication *Liberty*. Trotsky's arguments in support of his version were highly unconvincing. He recalled that at the end of February 1923 Lenin asked for some strong poison he could take if he felt another stroke coming on. Trotsky remembers that the Politburo refused to give Lenin any poison, but in Trotsky's opinion Stalin might have done so.[93]

Although Trotsky and other members of the Politburo refused to comply, it is quite possible that Lenin asked his friends, even Krupskaya, to get him some powerful poison. For a long time after each of his strokes Lenin experienced a condition of helplessness that he found extremely difficult to bear. But Stalin did not meet with Lenin at all from the end of 1922 until his death. Moreover, given the hostile relations between them at the time, Lenin could hardly have made such a request of Stalin.

It was Stalin who came up with the idea for the Lenin Mausoleum and the mummification of Lenin's body, laying the basis for the cult of Lenin, even though his widow, Krupskaya, publicly opposed the idea. The

93. See the appendix "Did Stalin Poison Lenin?" in Louis Fischer, *The Life of Lenin* (New York, 1964), pp. 677–678. [Cf. also Trotsky's discussion of this question in his *Stalin*, pp. 376–383. His article in *Liberty* was a slightly revised version of that passage.—G. S.]

majority of the Politburo went along with Stalin. One may agree with Robert C. Tucker's view that when Lenin died "Stalin probably reacted with a huge sense of relief." In making a cult of Lenin, Stalin laid the basis for his own. "A Lenin who no longer needed to be fought and feared was a Lenin who could be venerated in the old way and towards whose precepts one could swear undying fealty."[94]

■ 8
LENIN'S "TESTAMENT"

In a broad sense, all the letters, articles, notes, and memoranda that Lenin dictated in late 1922 and early 1923, when he realized the possibly fatal implications of his illness, can be considered his "Testament." However, in a more narrow sense, the term is applied to certain specific letters he wrote discussing the functioning of the Central Committee and giving his personal characterizations of its leading members. In view of the importance of these documents I take the liberty of quoting some lengthy excerpts here.*

Letter to the Congress

I would urge strongly that at this Congress a number of changes be made in our political structure.

I want to tell you of the considerations to which I attach most importance.

At the head of the list I set an increase in the number of Central Committee members to a few dozen or even a hundred. It is my opinion that without this reform our Central Committee would be in great danger if the course of events were not quite favourable for us (and that is something we cannot count on). . . .

As for the first point, i.e., increasing the number of C.C. members, I think it must be done in order to raise the prestige of the Central Committee, to do a thorough job of improving our administrative machinery and to prevent conflicts between small sections of the C.C. from acquiring excessive importance for the future of the party. . . . I think that the stability of our party would gain a thousandfold by such a measure.

December 23, 1922

94. Tucker, *Stalin as Revolutionary*, p. 285.
*[In these excerpts I have followed the official Soviet translation, though with some stylistic changes and a few changes in the choice of words, usually giving the Russian term when I have departed from the CW version. —G. S.]

Continuation of the Notes.
December 26, 1922

By stability of the Central Committee, of which I spoke above, I mean measures against a split, as far as such measures can at all be taken. . . .

Our party relies on two classes and therefore its instability would be possible and its downfall inevitable if there were no agreement between those two classes. In that event this or that measure, and generally all talk about the stability of our C.C., would be futile. No measures of any kind could prevent a split in such a case. . . .

I have in mind stability as a guarantee against a split in the immediate future, and I intend to deal here with a few ideas concerning personal qualities.

I think that from this standpoint the prime factors in the question of stability are such members of the C.C. as Stalin and Trotsky. I think relations between them make up the greater part of the danger of a split, which could be avoided, and this purpose, in my opinion, would be served, among other things, by increasing the number of C.C. members to 50 or 100.

Comrade Stalin, having become general secretary, has unlimited authority concentrated in his hands, and I am not sure whether he will always be capable of using that authority with sufficient caution. Comrade Trotsky, on the other hand, as his struggle against the C.C. on the question of the People's Commissariat for Communications has already proved, is distinguished not only by outstanding ability. He is personally perhaps the most capable man in the present C.C., but he has displayed excessive self-assurance and shown excessive preoccupation with the purely administrative side of the work.

These two qualities of the two outstanding leaders of the present C.C. can inadvertently lead to a split, and if our party does not take steps to avert this, the split may come unexpectedly.

I shall not give any further appraisals of the personal qualities of other members of the C.C. I shall just recall that the October episode with Zinoviev and Kamenev was, of course, no accident, but neither can the blame for it be laid upon them personally, any more than non-Bolshevism can upon Trotsky.

Speaking of the young C.C. members, I wish to say a few words about Bukharin and Pyatakov. They are, in my opinion, the most outstanding figures (among the youngest ones), and the following must be borne in mind about them: Bukharin is not only a most valuable and major theorist of the party; he is also rightly considered the favourite of the whole party, but his theoretical views can be classified as fully Marxist only with great reserve, for there is something scholastic about him (he has never made a study of dialectics, and, I think, never fully understood it).

December 25. As for Pyatakov, he is unquestionably a man of outstanding will and outstanding ability, but shows too much zeal for administrating and the administrative side of the work to be relied upon in a serious political matter.

Both of these remarks, of course, are made only for the present, on the assumption that both these outstanding and devoted party workers fail to find an occasion to enhance their knowledge and amend their one-sidedness.

December 25, 1922

Continuation of the Notes.
December 26, 1922

I think that a few dozen workers, being members of the C.C., can deal better than anybody else with checking, improving and remodeling our state apparatus. The Workers' and Peasants' Inspection on whom this function devolved at the beginning proved unable to cope with it and can be used only as an "appendage" or, on certain conditions, as an assistant to these members of the C.C. In my opinion, the workers admitted to the Central Committee should come preferably not from among those who have had long service in Soviet bodies (in this part of my letter the term "workers" everywhere includes peasants), because those workers have already acquired the very traditions and the very prejudices which it is desirable to combat.

The working-class members of the C.C. must be mainly workers of a lower stratum than those promoted in the last five years to work in Soviet bodies; they must be people closer to being rank-and-file workers and peasants, who, however, do not fall into the category of direct or indirect exploiters. I think that by attending all sittings of the C.C. and all sittings of the Political Bureau, and by reading all the documents of the C.C., such workers can form a staff of devoted supporters of the Soviet system, able, first, to give stability to the C.C. itself, and second, to work effectively on the renewal and improvement of the state apparatus.

Nine days later Lenin dictated a short "Addition to the Letter of December 24, 1922," as follows:

Stalin is too rude [slishkom grub] and this defect, although quite tolerable in our midst and in dealings among us Communists, becomes intolerable in a general secretary. That is why I suggest that the comrades think about a way of transferring [peremestit'] Stalin from that post and appointing another man in his stead who in all other respects differs from Comrade Stalin in having only one advantage, namely, that of being more tolerant, more loyal, more polite and more considerate to the comrades, less capricious, etc. This circumstance may appear to be a mere trifle (nichtozhnaya meloch'). But I think that from the standpoint of safeguards against a split and from the standpoint of what I wrote above about the relationship between Stalin and Trotsky it is not a trifle [meloch'], or it is a trifle which can assume decisive importance.[95]

January 4, 1923

95. Lenin, PSS, 45:343–348. [Cf. CW, 36:593–597. In these excerpts I have followed the official Soviet translation, though with some stylistic changes and a few changes in the choice of words, usually giving the Russian term when I departed from the CW version. — G. S.]

These notes and letters were addressed to the Twelfth Party Congress, which was scheduled for the spring of 1923. They were retyped in five copies at Lenin's request: one for himself, three for Krupskaya, and one for Lenin's secretariat. Lenin asked that they be placed in sealed envelopes with a notation that they were not to be opened except by Lenin himself or by Krupskaya after his death. Maria Volodicheva, Lenin's duty secretary, did not write the words "after his death" on the envelopes but told Krupskaya about the instructions verbally.

Some of these documents were brought to the knowledge of the Twelfth Party Congress. But the main part of Lenin's Testament, including his characterizations of the six Central Committee members, was not made public. The congress did not discuss the question of removing Stalin from the post of general secretary. As I have already mentioned, the Central Committee was enlarged, but among its seventeen full members and thirteen candidate members there was not a single worker or peasant. Why wasn't Lenin's letter read to the Congress? The omission was not intentional. Only Lenin, who had been paralyzed and had lost the power of speech, could break the seals on these highly confidential documents. Krupskaya could reveal them only after Lenin's death. In other words, a situation arose that was not provided for by Lenin's instructions.

As for the content of the Testament, why did Lenin limit himself to a characterization of only six Central Committee members and say nothing about such influential figures as Rykov, Kalinin, and others? I think Lenin clearly saw that in the event of his death the six people he named would constitute the core of the party leadership and that a struggle within the Central Committee contained the threat of a split in the party. A peculiarity of Lenin's document was that it indicated not only the positive qualities of the Central Committee leaders but also their fundamental shortcomings. Lenin proposed in his letter that Stalin be removed from his post as general secretary but did not question the possibility and necessity of keeping Stalin in the leadership. That is why the word transfer *(peremestit)* was used, rather than "remove" *(smestit)*. Lenin did not propose any specific person to replace Stalin as general secretary.

Trotsky, in the autobiography he wrote after being deported from the Soviet Union, asserted that he was Lenin's hoped-for successor. Trotsky even interpreted Lenin's "Testament" in this spirit:

Lenin planned to create a commission attached to the Central Committee for fighting bureaucracy. We were both to be members. This commission was essentially to be the lever for breaking up the Stalin faction as the backbone of the bureaucracy, and for creating such conditions in the party as would allow me to become Lenin's deputy, and, as he intended, his successor to the post of chairman of the Council of People's Commissars.

Only in this connection does the full meaning of the so-called [Testament] become clear. Lenin names only six people there, and sums them up briefly, weighing each word. Unquestionably, his [purpose in writing this testament] was to facilitate the work of direction for me. He naturally wanted to do it with the least possible amount of friction.[96]

In another passage of the same book Trotsky writes:

Aside from its general political aims, the campaign that Lenin opened (on the national question) had as its immediate object the creation of the best conditions for my work of direction, either side by side with him if he regained his health, or in his place if he succumbed to his illness. But the struggle, which was never carried out to its end, or even part way, had exactly an opposite result.[97]

This was all obvious fantasy on Trotsky's part, an example of the "excessive self-assurance" Lenin mentioned in his letter. It is not accidental that Lenin did not want to name his successor. Among the six party leaders he did not see one who could replace him as the de facto, one-man leader of the party and government. In an attempt to redistribute the main duties among these men (which was the meaning of the proposal to transfer Stalin), Lenin was suggesting that only if these six men worked together under the strict control of the Central Committee and the Central Control Commission could they carry the party forward under the difficult conditions then existing. That is the real meaning of Lenin's document.

Trotsky is right of course that Lenin weighed every word in his "Testament." He did not use the sharp, cutting manner he usually employed in judging people. On the other hand, despite the outwardly gentle formulations, phrased so as not to offend anyone, an acute political meaning was concealed. Lenin had something extremely flattering to say about each of his comrades-in-arms. Stalin was one of "the two outstanding leaders of the present Central Committee." Trotsky was "perhaps the most capable man in the present Central Committee." Bukharin was "a most valuable and major theorist of the party." Pyatakov was "unquestionably a man of outstanding will and outstanding ability." But at the same time Lenin gave a political characterization of each leader that is devastating in content if not in form. After all, could "one-man rule" over

96. Leon Trotsky, *My Life* (New York, 1970), pp. 479–480.
97. Ibid., p. 488.

the party be entrusted to a rude, impatient, disloyal, and capricious Stalin or to an excessively self-assured Trotsky, who tended toward excessive preoccupation with the purely administrative aspect of things and whose non-Bolshevism, like the October episode of Kamenev and Zinoviev, Lenin did not consider accidental? And, of course, leadership of the party could not be entrusted to Bukharin, whose views could be "classified as fully Marxist only with great reserve," or to Pyatakov, who in general could not be "relied on in a serious political matter."

In this instance Lenin had a superb understanding of the importance of his assessments, and if there is a central thought in the Testament, it is that none of the men listed by Lenin should be allowed to occupy the place in the party that he himself had held. In Lenin's thinking, his appraisals would act as a bridle with which the party could restrain the political ambitions and vanity of its most outstanding leaders.

Krupskaya opened the envelope with Lenin's letter after his death. The letter was addressed to the Twelfth Congress, which had already passed. She decided to wait a few months and reveal the letter to the Thirteenth Congress, scheduled for May 1924. A few days before the congress Krupskaya brought Lenin's letter to a plenum of the Central Committee. In the book "Memoirs of Stalin's Secretary" Boris Bazhanov asserts that Lenin's "Testament" was read to that plenum before the congress began.[98] That is not true. Lenin's document was not presented to the plenum. Only some members of the Politburo read the letter, which was accompanied by a note from Krupskaya stating that "Vladimir Ilyich expressed a firm desire that this writing of his should be made known to the next party congress after his death."[99]

It has long been assumed that Lenin's characterization of the top party leaders remained unknown to them until May 1924, when Krupskaya turned the document over to a commission of the Central Committee. But in February 1988 V. P. Naumov, a leading researcher at the Institute of Marxism-Leninism, published a long, thoroughly documented article which shows that Lydia Fotieva, Lenin's secretary, informed Stalin and several other Politburo members about the essential content of Lenin's notes. Naumov reports:

98. Bazhanov, *Vospominaniia sekretaria Stalina* (Paris?, 1980), pp. 106–107. For a detailed discussion of Bazhanov and his book, see section 9 of this chapter and notes 105 and 106.

99. Lenin, PSS, 45:594.

In an explanation written on December 29, 1922, to Kamenev, Fotieva justified her action on the grounds that Volodicheva had not warned her about the
very strict orders to carry out Lenin's wishes exactly as requested. But it is
enough to look at the entries in the journal of Lenin's duty secretaries to raise
doubts about Fotieva's explanation. Consequently, Politburo members and some
Central Committee members were informed of the top secret personal characterizations Lenin had made of certain leading party figures. It is hard to imagine
they did not react in any way to these assessments.[100]

Kamenev, Zinoviev, and Stalin decided that the letter would not be
read aloud to the congress, discussed by the delegates, or included
among the official documents of the congress. First it was read to a
gathering of the Council of Elders, that is, the heads of the provincial
organizations of the party. Kamenev proposed that no record be made of
that session. It was at that gathering that Trotsky and his supporters in
the Central Committee first found out about the "Testament." Then
Lenin's letter was read in closed session to separate groups of delegates,
with the warning that no one was to take notes or refer to the document
at sessions of the congress. Kamenev and Zinoviev gave explanations to
the largest delegations. Neither Lenin's letter nor the closed sessions
were entered in the record of the congress.

After the congress, when the leading bodies of the party were being
constituted, Stalin, referring to Lenin's Testament, demonstratively declined to accept the post of general secretary. But Zinoviev and Kamenev, and after them the majority of Central Committee members, persuaded him to withdraw this resignation. Apparently a special agreement
had been reached between Zinoviev and Stalin before the Thirteenth
Congress. Stalin approved Zinoviev's candidacy as the main reporter at
the congress and thereby seemed to be pushing this ambitious and
unprincipled man toward the role of leader of the party. In turn Zinoviev
and Kamenev defended Stalin's reappointment to the post of general
secretary. This move encountered no objections from the active party
membership, especially since Stalin promised to take Lenin's criticism
into account. At the same time Stalin could not yet operate independently of the other members of the Central Committee, and that ruled
out the possibility of arbitrary action on his part. There was no question
of personal dictatorship by Stalin in those days; to the contrary, Stalin
came forward as the advocate of collective leadership. He accused Trot-

100. *Pravda*, February 26, 1988.

sky of seeking to assume one-man rule and supported Zinoviev and Kamenev in their attacks on Trotsky. Under the conditions of the bitter struggle against Trotsky and his numerous supporters, the question of Stalin's rudeness and caprice, when he was actively opposing Trotsky, seemed to many members of the Central Committee to be truly a trifle. They did not see what Lenin had seen.

The further fate of Lenin's Testament is of interest. It was published in 1926 in France by Boris Souvarine and in the United States by Max Eastman. They had apparently obtained it from opposition circles. The Soviet press declared it to be apocryphal. But in 1927 the question was raised in the Central Committee. It had to be admitted that such a document really existed. In a speech at a joint plenum of the Central Committee and Central Control Commission, after reading aloud a section of Lenin's "Letter to the Congress," Stalin stated: "Yes, I am rude, comrades, toward those who are rudely and treacherously trying to destroy the party. I have not and I do not hide this." As L. S. Shaumyan has justly noted, Stalin in this case deliberately distorted the meaning of Lenin's words. Lenin was not accusing Stalin of rudeness toward enemies of the party, but toward comrades who had done the party great services.[101]

The question of Lenin's Testament was a subject of discussion at the Fifteenth Party Congress. This is how matters stood according to Yevgeny Frolov, who took part in the proceedings:

In opening the thirteenth morning session on December 9, 1927, Grigory Petrovsky, who was chairing, said: "We forgot to vote on Comrade Ordzhonikidze's motion that the request of the joint plenum of the CC and the CCC in July 1926 be respected in regard to publication in the *Lenin Miscellany (Leninsky Sbornik)* of the letters by Lenin which are often called his Testament and which the Thirteenth Party Congress decided not to publish. Allow me to present this for a vote." Rykov, who spoke next, proposed that not only the letter called Lenin's Testament be published but also the other letters on internal party questions, and that they be made an appendix to the stenographic record of the congress. The congress supported this proposal and unanimously passed a resolution to publish the Testament and Lenin's letters on internal party matters.[102]

However, Lenin's letter was not included in the stenographic record of the congress published in 1928. Nor was it published in the *Lenin Miscellany*. Nevertheless, delegates to the Fifteenth Congress (who

101. *Filosoficheskaia entsiklopedia*, vol. 3 (Moscow, 1962), p. 114.
102. From Frolov's unpublished memoirs.

numbered 1,669) were able to read these texts in the bulletin published during the congress "for members of the party only." [103]

After the Fifteenth Congress Lenin's Testament became more widely known among active party members. In the thirties, however, people stopped talking about it. When mass repression began, the document was again proclaimed to be a forgery. Anyone who possessed a copy of the Fifteenth Congress bulletin containing it usually preferred to destroy the document. According to a number of people I have interviewed, they had occasion to meet quite a few Communists in the prisons and camps who had been sentenced to long terms for "possession of a counterrevolutionary document, the so-called Testament of Lenin."

■ 9
STALIN IN 1923–1924

At the beginning of this chapter I quoted a description of the young Stalin. Of course, he changed fundamentally by the time he was forty-four and forty-five.

Stalin behaved very confidently, but also in a simple and somewhat crude way, which created a contrast between him and the rather haughty Trotsky and the very ambitious Zinoviev. Stalin's behavior was more familiar and understandable for most party functionaries, among whom the very term *intelligentnost* was more a synonym for cowardly liberalism and softness than proletarian firmness. As Maria Joffe, the widow of the formerly prominent Soviet diplomat Adolf Abramovich Joffe, wrote in her memoirs after she had emigrated to Israel in 1975:

If there was one man whom Joffe positively could not stand, it was Stalin. . . . We often saw Stalin. For example, we would run into him at Bolshoi Theater premieres, in box seats reserved by the theater management. Stalin usually showed up surrounded by his close associates, among whom were Voroshilov and Kaganovich. . . . He behaved as such a simple, ordinary, good guy. Very sociable, on friendly speaking terms with everyone, but there wasn't a truthful gesture in any of this. I remember the first time he met me he said, "Ahh, Maria Mikhailovna, I've heard so much about you." In general, Stalin was an actor of rare ability, capable of changing his mask to suit any circumstance. And one of his favorite masks was precisely this one: the simple, ordinary good fellow

103. Bulletin no. 30, supplement 1, pp. 35–37. Only congress participants were allowed to have this bulletin, and a copy has been preserved in Frolov's library. Copies of this bulletin never reached the party organizations, although the publishing information indicated a printing run of 13,500.

wearing his heart on his sleeve. Adolf Abramovich had a splendid insight into this character trait of Stalin's. He never believed him, and long before Stalin revealed his true face Joffe knew his real worth.[104]

Maria Joffe's points are rather well taken.

Trotsky wrote a great deal about Stalin's personality. He once called Stalin "the most outstanding mediocrity in our party." This formula was often repeated in opposition circles, although it explained nothing. Trotsky accounted for Stalin's victory over his rivals as being the result less of Stalin's qualities than of the conditions that arose in the Soviet Union from 1923 to 1927. In a commentary on the trials of 1936–1937 Trotsky wrote:

> In 1923 or 1924 I. N. Smirnov, who was later executed with Zinoviev and Kamenev, objected to something I said during a private conversation: "Stalin—a candidate for dictator? But he is a mediocrity, a colorless nonentity." "Mediocrity, yes; nonentity, no," I answered him. . . . I had discussions with Kamenev on the same subject. He insisted that Stalin was "just a small-town politician." There was, of course, a particle of truth in that sarcastic characterization, but only a particle. Such attributes of character as slyness, faithlessness, the ability to exploit the basest instincts of human nature are developed to an extraordinary degree in Stalin and, considering his strong character, represent mighty weapons in a struggle. Not, of course, any struggle. The struggle to liberate the masses requires other attributes. But in selecting men for privileged position, in welding them together in the spirit of the caste, in weakening and disciplining the masses, Stalin's attributes were truly invaluable. . . . Nevertheless, he remains a mediocrity. He is not capable of generalization or of foresight. His mind is not only devoid of range but is even incapable of logical thinking. Every phrase of his speech has some immediate practical aim. But his speech as a whole never rises to a logical structure. In this weakness is Stalin's strength. There are historical tasks that can be carried out only by renouncing generalization; there are periods in history when generalization and foresight exclude immediate success: these are periods of backsliding, decline, and reaction. Helvetius once said that every social epoch requires its great people, and when none are found it creates them. . . . We can apply to Stalin what Engels said about Wellington: "He is great in his own way, which is to say, only as great as one can be without ceasing to be a mediocrity. Individual "greatness" is, in the last analysis, a social function."[105]

In this characterization there is, to be sure, more than in the remarks by Smirnov and Kamenev. But it, too, is inaccurate in many respects, as in the conclusion Trotsky draws:

104. *Vremya i my,* 1977, no. 20, p. 178.
105. See note 104.

If Stalin could have foreseen at the very beginning where his fight against "Trotskyism" would lead, he undoubtedly would have stopped short, in spite of the prospect of victory over all his opponents. But he did not foresee anything.[106]

No, Stalin would not have stopped, even if he had known beforehand the cost of his own victory and of his virtually unlimited power. It is possible that he was willing to pay an even higher price.

In trying to recall all the comments about Stalin he had heard, Trotsky also quoted Bukharin to the effect that, above all, Stalin was an extremely lazy person. This opinion (if Bukharin really voiced it) is mistaken. Stalin was leisurely and unhurried in his actions but he was by no means lazy.

A certain Boris Bazhanov published an edition of his memoirs in France in 1980, entitled *Memoirs of a Secretary of Stalin's*. Bazhanov actually did work in Stalin's secretariat and for the Politburo from August 1923 to the end of 1925. In 1928 he fled from the Soviet Union to Iran and ended up living in France. In his memoirs Bazhanov sketches a portrait of Stalin from the period 1923–1924, a portrait that does have the ring of truth. He describes Stalin as vindictive, suspicious, vulgar, and devoid of any restraining moral principles. He was a crafty and skillful intriguer, extremely reticent and self-possessed. Stalin always dressed simply and lived modestly. He displayed no taste for luxury or desire to enjoy the good things of life. He lived in the Kremlin in a modestly furnished apartment formerly occupied by a palace servant. At a time when Kamenev had already appropriated a magnificent Rolls-Royce, Stalin rode around Moscow in an old "Russo-Balte." Although not particularly well-educated, Stalin knew how to conceal his lack of culture. At Politburo meetings he was brief and to the point; he sought not so much to polemicize against others as to summarize in a few words the opinion of the majority. A man of strong will, Stalin was at the same time extremely cautious and, on occasion, indecisive as well. In difficult political situations he often didn't know what to do, but he was able to conceal his indecisiveness, frequently preferring to act after the event rather than providing leadership. Stalin was not interested in women. The one all-consuming passion of his life was power. Yet he was patient; he knew

106. [The author cites as his source for these quotations an "unpublished note" by Trotsky dated January 4, 1937. (See above, note 71.) Actually this "note" was part of a series of commentaries Trotsky wrote in 1936–1937 about the Moscow trials and the Stalinist terror and published in a book *Les Crimes de Staline*. He later used passages with quite similar wording in his *Stalin*, pp. 392–393. —G. S.]

how to wait for the right moment before striking a blow at his political rivals. He was neither unintelligent nor devoid of common sense.

All the above features in Bazhanov's portrait ring true, but he then gets carried away and begins to add false embellishments. He claims, for example, that Stalin "never read anything or took any interest in anything." He was indifferent to science, literature, and music. He didn't even read the stenographic records of his own speeches and reports after they had been edited. As Bazhanov writes:

> During the first days of my job I went into Stalin's office dozens of times each day to report on documents received for the Politburo. I very quickly noticed that neither the fate of these papers nor their content interested him at all. When I asked him what to do on some matter, he would answer: "And in your opinion, what should be done?" I would answer, "Well, in my opinion, such and such"— either that a matter should be brought up for discussion in the Politburo or referred to some subcommission of the Central Committee, or that some proposal needed more work and that the department which made it should be urged first of all to coordinate its proposal with other interested departments, and so on. Stalin at this point would express his agreement, "Good, that's how we'll do it." Very soon I came to the conclusion that there was no point in my going to see him and that I should show more initiative. That is what I did. In Stalin's secretariat they explained to me that Stalin never read any documents and took no interest in any of the business.[107]

Bazhanov's assertions fail to correspond with reality. No one could come into Stalin's office dozens of times a day without a report in 1923. Stalin hardly ever signed a document without reading it over very carefully. He read a great deal; he read the party press, the most significant literary works, material from the Western press translated especially for him, and even émigré literature, not to mention various diplomatic documents, materials relating to the internal party disputes, etc. In addition, he often attended performances at the Moscow Art Theater and the Bolshoi Theater.

The generally accepted notion of Stalin as a poor orator and polemicist also requires more precise formulation. To be sure, Stalin was not a tribune of the revolution. But he was by no means an entirely unskilled polemicist. Igor Sats, a veteran party member, writes in his memoirs:

> I must add a few words to try to explain in part Stalin's effectiveness as a writer and orator, what gave him an edge over other orators and writers who were far

---

107. Bazhanov, *Vospominaniia sekretaria Stalina*, pp. 55–56. I find highly implausible the story told by Bazhanov about a Czech engineer who installed a telephone for Stalin, so that he could eavesdrop on all phone conversations in the Kremlin. Bazhanov alleges that after the engineer had done his job he was shot on Stalin's orders.

more skilled. Kamenev, Zinoviev, Bukharin, even Trotsky were much less familiar with the texts of Lenin's writings than Stalin. These men had interacted with
the living Lenin much more closely and more often than Stalin. They had
listened to him, argued with him, and read what he had just published, but they
hardly ever reread his writings. They did not have a sufficient sense of distance
between themselves and Lenin. Unlike them, Stalin studied Lenin's texts and
knew the printed Lenin intimately. He had no trouble selecting a quotation from
Lenin if he needed it. This is not the place to mention that he called his dogmatic
(catechistic) way of thinking creative and probably thought it was. We will also
leave aside the fact that he was waging a struggle (though hardly a fully conscious
or deliberate one) against the Marxist dialectical method, the method that suf-
fused all of Lenin's thinking. The important point to bear in mind is that by
shifting political discussion onto dogmatic ground, Stalin easily placed his opponents in a most disadvantageous position while he set about manipulating quotations freely and in a very convincing way.[108]

It should be added that 1924 was the year of Stalin's most creative
activity. His writings of that year occupy an entire volume of his *Works*
(Volume 6). In 1924 Stalin published his two most important theoretical
pamphlets, *Foundations of Leninism* and *The October Revolution and
the Tactics of the Russian Communists*. In these writings Stalin showed
himself to be, if not a continuator, at least a rather skillful systematizer of
Lenin's views.

108. A copy of Satz's unpublished memoirs is in my archive.

2

THE FIGHT WITH THE OPPOSITION

■ 1
DISPUTES IN THE BOLSHEVIK PARTY

The history of the rise and development of Stalinism cannot be understood without examining, at least in rough outline, the history of the
Bolshevik Party's internal disputes from 1923 to 1930. This is no easy
task because hardly any question in Soviet history has been so flagrantly
falsified as that of the opposition groups in the party in the twenties.
Even in documents published in the twenties many facts and episodes,
as well as the general trend of the ongoing struggle, were presented in
an extremely tendentious way. Each side sought to portray its opponents
in the most unattractive light; statements were distorted, mistakes or
inaccuracies exaggerated. Not only were no steps taken to stop rude and

disloyal methods; they were encouraged on all sides, making the dispute a very sharp one from the outset.

In the thirties the Soviet press described all opposition leaders as traitors and spies for foreign governments who had been recruited to work for imperialist intelligence agencies in the first years of Soviet power. Today these charges are no longer made. But even in the sixties and seventies textbooks and monographs on the history of the CPSU were not free of tendentiousness, bias, and outright falsification in their treatment of the controversies of the twenties.

As is generally known, virtually all the active participants in the various oppositions were physically destroyed by Stalin. Only a few rank and file oppositionists returned to their families after the Twentieth Party Congress. Some of them have written memoirs that read as apologias for one or another opposition leader. Such an approach is understandable, but I cannot agree with it. While Stalin, after achieving victory over all the oppositions, indeed usurped power in the party and the country, in his struggle against the oppositions he was not totally wrong, nor were his opponents totally right.

It would be just as wrong to follow certain Western historians and portray the struggle among different groups in the party after Lenin's death as merely an unprincipled battle for power, concealed under various theoretical arguments for appearance's sake. No, there were serious theoretical and practical disagreements in the twenties, and they resulted in an important struggle of ideas, especially over the question of the methods and possibilities of socialist construction in the USSR. It is true, however, that for Stalin the question of power was the main one. Maneuvering skillfully among the various platforms and tendencies, Stalin made use of the conflict among factions in the party to weaken all his rivals and increase his own power and authority.

It is not hard to see that the entire prerevolutionary history of the RSDLP is filled with disputes among various tendencies and factions. Such conflicts continued to occur after the Bolsheviks constituted themselves as a separate party. Lenin fought against a "right" tendency among the Bolsheviks in 1917, against the "Left" Communists in 1918, the Military Opposition in 1919, and the Worker's Opposition in 1920–1922. There was also the sharp debate on the trade unions in 1920–1921. Lenin considered disputes in the party quite normal and fully consistent with the principle of democratic centralism. Limits on such disputes could only be temporary, as was stated in the resolution of the Tenth Party

Congress that temporarily banned factions. At one time Stalin himself described internal party disputes not simply as normal but actually as one of the virtues of the Bolshevik Party, which did not try to gloss over its internal differences but overcame them through struggle.[1]

Although in principle Lenin tolerated dissenters, the fight that he led against them both in the RSDLP and later in the Bolshevik Party was by no means always a model of loyal and polite polemics. He was often unjustifiably harsh and rude to his opponents, often resorted to insulting formulations, and sometimes even justified such rudeness. But it was characteristic of Lenin that in these internal party disputes he had no personal motives whatsoever. It was totally unlike him to be vengeful or nurse a grudge. His main aim was to convince the party and the workers that he was right and to whatever extent possible to convince his opponents as well. When he succeeded in winning agreement with his views, all harshness disappeared and was replaced by good will, attentiveness, and friendly support. Such a change occurred, for example, in Lenin's relations with Trotsky, which were hostile in the years 1912–1913 but became quite close in 1917–1919. Similarly, it is well know that Lenin sharply attacked Zinoviev and Kamenev in October 1917, when although they were members of the Bolshevik Central Committee, they came out publicly against the armed insurrection. But immediately after the victory of the revolution, Zinoviev and Kamenev acknowledged their mistake and were given prominent posts in the Soviet government. According to Lenin in a 1920 article on disagreements among Italian Communists:

> On the eve of the October Revolution in Russia, and immediately after it, a number of very good Communists in Russia committed an error, one that our people are now loath to recall. Why are they loath to recall it? Because, unless there is a particular reason for it, it is wrong to recall mistakes that have been completely set right.[2]

And here is what Maria Ulyanova, Lenin's sister, wrote about him:

> Lenin knew how to be indulgent toward the mistakes of his comrades, if these mistakes were not caused by ill will or negligence. . . . Afterward the defeated comrade always got complete support from Ilyich and was defended against those who demanded more severe measures in relation to the guilty party. . . . In light of this you found new strength in yourself and freed yourself of errors better than if strictness and punishments had been used—better because such a method

1. Stalin, *Sochineniia,* 9:21.
2. Lenin, PSS, 41:417; CW, 31:385.

does not cause bitterness and does not result in a person's being humiliated after acknowledging his error.[3]

Many examples of such indulgence by Lenin toward former oppositionists can be cited. For example, in 1921 at the Tenth Party Congress Lenin urged not only that a resolution of the congress take note of the services of the Workers' Opposition in the struggle against bureaucratism but also that Shlyapnikov, the leader of that opposition, be placed on the Central Committee. Lenin said:

When a comrade from the Workers' Opposition is taken into the Central Committee, it is an expression of comradely confidence. . . . [and], what is more, inclusion of the representatives of this group in the Central Committee is the party's greatest expression of confidence.[4]

When Shlyapnikov announced that he was resigning from the Central Committee, Lenin proposed a resolution to the congress that would reject Shlyapnikov's action.

In October 1920 Lenin wrote the following to the Politburo:

The Control Commission should be urged, as a special task, to adopt a careful and individualized attitude, often in the form of outright therapy, toward representatives of the so-called opposition who have suffered a psychological crisis due to failures in their administrative or party careers. We should try to calm them, explain things to them in a comradely manner, find them (without using the command method) suitable jobs congenial to their psychological nature, offer them advice and the suggestions of the Orgburo, etc.[5]

Stalin took a different attitude toward his opponents. As early as the internal party disputes of 1918–1923 he distinguished himself by his harshness, rudeness, and disloyalty, as Lenin noted in his Testament. Stalin was not in the least concerned with changing his opponents' minds and drawing them into the common work. He sought to break their resistance and subject them to his will; if this failed, he unceremoniously cast them aside. At the same time he was extremely vengeful, nursing his grudges. His opponents remained personal enemies even when the issue in dispute had faded away and harmonious collaboration was imperative. And in all this, of course, Stalin was able to conceal his real feelings quite skillfully.

A good illustration of this difference between Lenin and Stalin is the

3. Maria Ulyanova, *Iz vospominanii o Lenine* (Moscow, 1928), p. 56.
4. Lenin, PSS, 43:110–111; CW: 32:260.
5. Lenin, PSS, 41:394; CW: 42:221.

contrast in their speeches to the Communist caucus at the Fourth All-Russia Congress of Trade Unions on May 18, 1921. At that congress David Ryazanov spoke in defense of trade union independence from the party. In the caucus he introduced a resolution proposing that wages be paid in kind universally. This proposal ran counter to the line of the Central Committee, but it won support because of the sharp decline in the purchasing power of Soviet currency. The majority of the Communist caucus unexpectedly voted for Ryazanov's resolution rather than for the resolution prepared by the party's Central Committee. When Stalin arrived at the caucus meeting, he tried to get the motion repealed. But the tone of his speech was harsh and irritable, and he made rude personal attacks on Ryazanov, Tomsky, the entire caucus. This caused protests, outcries, and general upset in the hall. In reply to a comment from the floor by Ryazanov, Stalin rudely flung at him: "Shut up, you clown!" Ryazanov jumped up and answered in a like manner. Tension mounted; even delegates who had voted against Ryazanov's resolution condemned Stalin's speech.

Lenin was obliged to intervene in the conflict between the Communist delegates and the Central Committee. His speech differed from Stalin's by a mere trifle: it was argued very carefully, went to the heart of the issue, and was convincing. Lenin, too, criticized Ryazanov and Tomsky quite sharply, but he refrained from any personal attacks or insults. He won by the unshakable force of his logic. The caucus which had just voted contrary to the decision of the Central Committee now voted by an overwhelming majority to rescind Ryazanov's motion and approve the Central Committee resolution.[6]

■ **2**

TROTSKY

At the center of the internal party conflicts from 1923 to 1927, and later of the struggle against Stalin as leader of the world Communist movement, was Leon Trotsky. It is appropriate, therefore, to give a portrait, if only in rough outline, of this unquestionably outstanding and contradictory figure.

There is a vast amount of literature about Trotsky; quite a few biogra-

6. As recalled by the veteran trade unionist A. M. Durmashkin, in *O V. I. Lenine. Vospominaniia* (Moscow, 1963), pp. 528–532.

phies of him have been published in the West. Of course, the best is still Isaac Deutsher's.[7] (I have been able to read it in the German edition.) Recently an abridged translation of a book on Trotsky by Joel Carmichael has been published in Russian.[8] Trotsky also wrote a great deal about himself, and much is said about him in the memoirs of Old Bolsheviks that I have had the opportunity to read, usually in unpublished manuscript form.

Trotsky was born Leib Bronstein only two months earlier than Stalin on the estate of his father, David, one of the very few Jewish landowners in Russia. He graduated from Jewish elementary school and then went to a *realnoye uchilishche* (nonclassical secondary school) founded by the German community in Odessa. The young Trotsky joined the Social Democratic movement in 1898 after his first arrest (for organizing the South Russian Workers' Union). Exiled to Siberia, he escaped and went abroad in 1902. He took part in the Second Congress of the RSDLP, at which he sided with the Mensheviks, but he soon left the Menshevik faction without becoming a Bolshevik. For a long time Trotsky was one of those who called themselves independent Social Democrats. This helped him to become an outstanding polemicist, but he never managed to become a painstaking and persistent political organizer.

When the first Russian revolution began in 1905 Trotsky returned to St. Petersburg. He took an active part in the work of the St. Petersburg Soviet and for a while was one of its three chairmen and editor of the newspaper *Russkaya gazeta*. Within a month Trotsky and Alexander Helphand (Parvus), his political friend and co-thinker at that time, transformed this newspaper from a small, liberal sheet into a mass paper with a circulation of 500,000. Quite a few of Trotsky's articles were also published in the Menshevik daily *Nachalo*.

The St. Petersburg Soviet lasted only fifty days. Trotsky headed it for only about two weeks. It was dispersed and its leaders arrested in early December 1905. Nevertheless, these few weeks made Trotsky famous in revolutionary circles. At that time Lenin treated Trotsky with belittling irony, calling him a "windbag" and "chatterbox" typical of "half-baked

7. Isaac Deutscher, *The Prophet Armed: Trotsky, 1879–1921* (London, 1954); *The Prophet Unarmed: Trotsky, 1921–1929* (London, 1959); *The Prophet Outcast: Trotsky, 1928–1940* (London, 1963).

8. Joel Carmichael, *Trotsky* (London, 1975). The Russian edition was published in Jerusalem in 1980.

seminarist rhetoricians" and "shyster lawyers." On occasion, however, Lenin spoke of him in much more flattering terms. As Lunacharsky relates:

> Trotsky came out of the 1905 revolution with the greatest gain in the way of popularity; . . . From that time on Trotsky was in the first rank. In spite of his youth he was the best prepared; least of all was there the stamp of a certain emigre narrowness which . . . at that time hampered even Lenin. . . .
>
> I recall someone saying in Lenin's presence, . . . "Now the strong man [in the Soviet] is Trotsky." For a moment Lenin's expression seemed to darken; then he said, "Well, Trotsky has earned this by his tireless and brilliant work."[9]

After the arrest of the St. Petersburg Soviet Trotsky was exiled to Siberia. He escaped along the way, managed to leave Russia again, and in 1907 took part in the Fifth London Congress of the RSDLP. Here, too, Trotsky joined neither the Bolsheviks nor the Mensheviks, but spoke essentially in his own name. He sought to instruct Bolsheviks and the Mensheviks alike in the theory that he and Parvus had worked out—that of permanent revolution. At the London Congress, Trotsky and Stalin had the opportunity to meet for the first time, but Trotsky did not notice Stalin and did not remember any such meeting. Stalin, on the other hand, remembered Trotsky very well.

As an émigré Trotsky got to know almost all of the famous leaders of the European Social Democratic movement; he succeeded with great difficulty in organizing the publication of a small newspaper called *Pravda*. It had been published since 1903 by a group of Ukrainian Mensheviks, and in 1908 it became Trotsky's personal publication. It came out roughly once every two weeks in Vienna.

At the time when the split between Bolsheviks and Mensheviks was growing and Lenin was moving toward declaring the Bolsheviks a separate party, Trotsky took a conciliationist position, organizing the so-called "August bloc," which grouped together a very small number of his supporters. It was during this period that Trotsky criticized Lenin and his policies especially sharply. His criticism became especially violent when the Bolsheviks began publishing their own daily newspaper in St.

9. [The author cites the Russian edition of Carmichael, but the quotation is from Anatoly Lunacharsky, *Revoliutsionnye siluety* (Moscow, 1923). See the complete English translation by Michael Glenny, *Revolutionary Silhouettes* (London and New York, 1967), pp. 60–61. After the 1924 edition, Lunacharsky's book, which had no "silhouette" of Stalin, was not reprinted until 1954, and then only in drastically abridged form and without the "silhouette" of Trotsky. Apparently the author did not have access to the 1923 or 1924 editions of Lunacharsky's book. —G. S.]

Petersburg also entitled *Pravda*. It seemed to Trotsky that not only the little Vienna newspaper but its name as well were his personal property.

Trotsky's attacks did not go unanswered by Lenin. It was in those very years, 1912–1913, that Lenin, in his articles and especially in his private letters, used the harsh and extremely unflattering descriptions of Trotsky that at a later time and quite different stage of the internal party disputes began to be quoted constantly in the Soviet press. Lenin accused Trotsky of outright deception of the workers and of hiding the truth about the "liquidators." Lenin called Trotsky "the basest careerist," an "adventurist," an "intriguer," and so on. That was also when Lenin used the notorious expression "Judushka Trotsky," comparing his conciliatory activity with the hypocritical attempts at reconciling his family made by Judushka Golovyov, hero of Saltykov-Shchedrin's novel *The Golovyov Family*.

The "August bloc" did not exist for very long, and soon after the beginning of World War I Trotsky broke off all remaining ties with the Mensheviks. Trotsky's position during the war came closer and closer to that of the Bolsheviks. After the February revolution, when Trotsky succeeded in returning to Russia from the United States a month after Lenin, a huge crowd of workers with red banners carried him on their shoulders from the train on which he arrived.

In Petrograd Trotsky became head of the so-called Interdistrict Committee (Mezhraionny Komitet; its members being Mezhraiontsy). Originating in 1913, the group had no more than five hundred members, but among them were such brilliant propagandists and orators as Volodarsky, Joffe, Lunacharsky, Manuilsky, and Uritsky. In the elections to urban district dumas in Petrograd in May and June 1917 the Bolsheviks ran in a bloc with the Mezhraiontsy. At a conference in July the Mezhraiontsy passed a resolution to join the Bolshevik Party. The Sixth Bolshevik Party Congress supported this proposal. Trotsky was elected a member of the Central Committee of the Bolshevik Party. After the Bolsheviks won a majority in the Petrograd Soviet, Trotsky was elected chairman as he had been in 1905.

As chairman of the Petrograd Soviet and a member of the Central committee of the Bolshevik Party Trotsky performed very great services in the decisive weeks before October. The Old Bolshevik A. P. Spunde wrote in his memoirs:

In general Trotsky displayed his best qualities in 1917. He was the idol of mass meetings in Petrograd; his political line aroused a great feeling for him. In his actions one sensed a 1917 version of Danton. Determination and boldness showed in everything he did. No one then noticed that he lacked Lenin's depth or Lenin's ability to subordinate all his personal feelings to the victory of socialism. . . . Trotsky was one of the best orators of the revolution. He spoke everywhere with amazing brilliance and had the ability to popularize even difficult ideas with great skill, though the foundation of principles was often incommensurate with the oratorical talent.[10]

Most observers and participants in the revolutionary struggle in Petrograd held the opinion, not without reason, that in those days Trotsky was not just one of the best but the best orator of the revolution. As Maria Joffe, who made stenographic records of the speeches of Lenin, Lunacharsky, and Trotsky on assignment from the Central Committee, testifies:

Trotsky had a unique talent for bringing a crowd to the highest pitch of tension. That is what happened when he spoke at the House of the People. At the high point of his speech he held up two fingers and cried: "Swear that you will support the proletarian revolution!" And the whole audience, thousands of people, responded: "We swear!" Standing in front of me was the Menshevik Khachalava, a violent opponent of the armed insurrection; yet he too held up two fingers and repeated, "I swear!" Later, when we were out on the street, I asked Khachalava how this could have happened. He answered: "In a couple of hours I'll probably come to my senses, but you understand, when you're there listening to that man it's simply impossible not to follow him."[11]

Not long before the armed insurrection Lenin took note of Trotsky's great services when he spoke about the candidates put forward by the Bolshevik Party for the Constituent Assembly:

It goes without saying that from among the Mezhraiontsy, who have hardly been tested in proletarian work in our party's spirit, no one would contest the candidature of, say, Trotsky, for, first, upon his arrival, Trotsky at once took up an internationalist stand; second, he worked among the Mezhraiontsy for [fusion with the Bolsheviks]; third, in the difficult July days he proved himself equal to the task and a loyal supporter of the party of the revolutionary proletariat.[12]

There are many myths of the most varied kind concerning Trotsky's role in the immediate practical organization of the armed insurrection of

10. Spunde was deputy people's commissar of finance in the first Soviet government and later a member of the Central Executive Committee and a deputy chairman of the State Bank. He was not arrested in 1937 but was expelled from the party and worked as a bookkeeper, cashier, and accountant in the Moscow Trading Company, writing his memoirs in 1947–1949. He died in 1962. His memoirs remain among his family's papers.

11. *Vremya i my* (1977), no. 19, p. 178.

12. Lenin, PSS, 34:345; CW: 41:447.

Petrograd. On the one hand there is a tendency to vastly exaggerate Trotsky's role. For example, according to Professor I. K. Dashkovsky in a 1965 open letter:

> In this period the names of Lenin and Trotsky were invariably found together and embodied the October Revolution not only in posters, banners, and slogans but also solidly in the consciousness of the party, the people, and the country.[13]

Joel Carmichael writes:

> One of the principal oddities throughout this strange interval of hesitation [the period from the end of August through the end of October 1917] was that since Lenin was in hiding his place as the most authoritative Bolshevik was occupied by Trotsky, at least as far as the public was concerned. In effect this turned a man who had been an implacable opponent of the Bolsheviks for fifteen years into their most authoritative spokesman. . . . It was, in fact, Trotsky who conceived and executed the coup d'etat, supported by the Party press and apparatus and his position as the elected chairman of the Petrograd Soviet.[14]

Such assertions are mistaken; they fly in the face of generally known facts. Trotsky's name certainly did appear side by side with Lenin's during the October days, but side by side does not mean equal. Even the broad public understood the different political weight of the two men. This was no secret to the enemies of the Bolshevik Party either. As for the "consciousness of the party," there the names of Lenin and Trotsky were not at all equal. The party had only one leader, Lenin, and he alone was the inspirer and organizer of the October Revolution. It was not accidental that, while praising Trotsky, Lenin noted that the Mezhraiontsy had "hardly been tested in proletarian work in the spirit of our party."

Carmichael's assertions are absolutely wrong. Even in September 1917 the entire work of practical preparation for the armed insurrection was being carried out under powerful pressure from Lenin, who almost daily wrote articles and pamphlets and sent letters and memoranda to the Central Committee and Petrograd Committee. Lenin returned to Petro-

13. Dashkovsky's open letter to the editors of *Voprosy istorii KPSS* remained unpublished. Dashkovsky joined the party in 1917 and took an active part in the revolution and civil war, later writing extensively on economic questions. He was expelled from the party in 1927 for participation in the opposition and then for approximately thirty years was subjected to various types of repression. After the Twentieth Party Congress he was cleared of all charges. From 1956 on he lived on a pension in Kharkov, writing a substantial number of articles and essays on the history of the CPSU. The date of his death is not known to me.

14. Carmichael, p. 189.

grad in early October to convene the meeting of the Central Committee at which the decision for armed insurrection was made. The fact that Lenin was still in hiding in a conspiriatorial apartment and Trotsky was speaking legally as chairman of the Petrograd Soviet can by no means serve as a justification for assertions of the kind Carmichael makes.

It would be just as wrong, however, to belittle the importance of Trotsky in the October period. In the current official history of the CPSU the section on the armed insurrection in Petrograd speaks only of "the disorienting influence of Trotsky's speeches at the Military Revolutionary Committee."[15]

In a special Soviet encyclopedia entitled "The Great October Socialist Revolution" (*Velikaia Oktiabr' skaia sotsialisticheskaia revoliutsiia*), published on the sixtieth anniversary of the revolution, there are hundreds of brief biographies of participants but none of Trotsky, although there is a long item about Stalin that calls him one of the leaders in preparing and carrying out the revolution. Trotsky's name is not even mentioned in the article on the Petrograd Soviet, of which he was chairman; his name is found only in a long list of members of the Military Revolutionary Committee. Trotsky's role in the October days is also falsified in the three-volume "History of Great October" by Academician Isaac Mints.[16]

Despite all the differences between Lenin and Trotsky concerning the conditions and legal basis for the revolution—differences that were reduced to a minimum by the course of events—Trotsky's role in the practical preparation and implementation of the October Revolution was exceptionally important, as a great many accounts by direct participants and eyewitnesses of the October insurrection attest. I will cite only one —an article entitled "The October Revolution," published in *Pravda* November 6–7, 1918, over the signature of Joseph Stalin.

The inspirer of the overturn from beginning to end was the party's Central Committee headed by Comrade Lenin. . . . The entire work of the practical organization of the uprising was carried on under the immediate direction of the chairman of the Petrograd Soviet, Trotsky. One may state without hesitation that the party was indebted first and foremost to Comrade Trotsky for the garrison's prompt going over to the Soviet and for the able organization of the work of the Military Revolutionary Committee.

15. *Istoriia KPSS* (Moscow, 1967), 3(1):321.
16. I. I. Mints, *Istoriia Velikogo Oktiabria* (Moscow, 1978), pp. 807–809, 823, 827, and passim.

This article, which even exaggerates Trotsky's role somewhat, was included in all collections of Stalin's works until the early thirties.

Trotsky himself was more modest in his conclusions. In his diary in exile he wrote:

Had I not been present in 1917 in Petersburg, the October Revolution would still have taken place—on the condition that Lenin was present and in command. If neither Lenin nor I had been present in Petersburg, there would have been no October Revolution.[17]

I will not dwell here on Trotsky's conduct and policies during the negotiations at Brest-Litovsk for a peace treaty with Germany. Trotsky's mistaken position was demonstrated within a few months when German troops began their February offensive. But it is clear to every objective historian that in those critical days there wasn't the slightest hint in Trotsky's actions and speeches of so-called premeditated treason, capitulationism, betrayal, provocation, a deal with the counterrevolution, or complicity with aggressive imperialism, and so on. All of these charges, which can be found in historical writings of the sixties and seventies, were introduced into historical science during the time of Stalin's cult.[18] Stalin put these formulations into circulation with the indirect aim of discrediting Lenin as well, for only a person who was politically blind would have given an "accomplice of imperialism" who "gave aid and comfort to the bourgois counterrevolution" the assignment to organize and lead the Red Army.

There are also quite a few myths about Trotsky's activity during the civil war. His supporters made many attempts to portray him as virtually the chief organizer of the Red Army and its main victories over the White armies. On the other hand, there were many attempts to completely deny any contribution to the war effort on Trotsky's part, although from 1918 to 1924 he was people's commissar of war and chairman of the Revolutionary Military Council of the Republic. Historians made these attempts—not only historians in the later period but also during the civil war itself. I have already mentioned Stalin's attitude toward Trotsky's orders, on some of which Stalin inscribed the instructions: "To be

17. Leon Trotsky's *Diary in Exile 1935* (Cambridge, Ma., 1958), p. 46. [The author cites the Russian edition of Carmichael, p. 186 (see the English edition, p. 293). —G. S.]

18. See, for example, *Bor'ba partii bol'shevikov protiv trotskizma v posleoktiabriskii period* (Moscow, 1969).

disregarded." Hostility toward Trotsky was widespread among many other party activists involved in military work.

For example, the Old Bolshevik V. Trifonov, who was assigned to military duties, wrote the following to his friend Aaron Solts:

> In the south, the most shocking outrages have been and are being committed, as well as crimes, about which we should shout from the rooftops and cry out in the city squares at the top of our voice. Unfortunately, for the time being I can't do that. Given the customs that have been established here, we will never end this war but will meet our own end very quickly—from exhaustion. The Southern Front is Trotsky's "favored child," and flesh of the flesh . . . of this extremely untalented organizer. . . . It was not Trotsky who built the army but we, the rank and file army workers. Wherever Trotsky has tried to work, the most tremendous confusion has immediately arisen. There is no place for a muddle-head in an organism that must operate precisely and efficiently, and the military machine is such an organism.[19]

Sergo Ordzhonikidze also wrote to Lenin from the Southern Front:

> Something unbelievable, something bordering on betrayal. . . . Where in the world is order, discipline, and Trotsky's regular army?! How in the world could he have let things fall apart so badly? It is absolutely incomprehensible.[20]

Lenin received quite a few similar signals, both from authorized representatives of the Central Committee and commanders of particular armies and fronts. Nevertheless, he always appraised the military-organizational work of Trotsky rather highly and never raised the question of replacing him as commissar of war. The Red Army was built in exceptionally difficult circumstances, and Lenin, who was unquestionably the chief organizer of the army and the main strategist of the civil war, understood very well the importance of the work Trotsky did. There is no question that Trotsky's activity played a fundamental role in transforming the Red Army from a conglomerate of guerrilla and semi-guerrilla formations into a fairly disciplined military machine. Trotsky was able to organize tens of thousands of former tsarist officers to work in the army, from noncommissioned officers up to and including generals. If it is true that the Red Army would not have been able to win the civil war without military commissars, it is also true that it could not have done so without military specialists.

Trotsky was one of the main initiators and implementers of harsh discipline in the Red Army. His measures were strict and severe and not

---

19. Yuri Trifonov, *Otblesk kostra* (Moscow 1966), pp. 151–152.
20. S. Ordzhonikidze, *Stat'i i rechi* (Articles and Speeches) (Moscow, 1956), 1:101–102.

always just, but they helped to transform the Red Army into a more or less efficiently functioning organism. As Joel Carmichael writes:

> Trotsky also gave full expression to the ferocity inherent in civil war; in the nature of things anything short of the death penalty can be thought rectifiable by the victory of one's own side.
>
> Trotsky's wholehearted identification with an Idea made him implacable— "merciless" was a favorite word of his own. He had a certain admiral (Shchastny) executed on an indictment of sabotage. This admiral had been appointed by the Bolsheviks themselves; he had saved the Baltic Sea Fleet from the Germans and with great difficulty brought it from Helsingfors to Kronstadt and the mouth of the Neva. He was very popular among the sailors; because of his strong position vis-à-vis the new regime he behaved quite independently. This was what annoyed Trotsky, who was, in fact, the only witness to appear against him, and who denounced him without itemising any charges; he simply said in court that [Shchastny] was a dangerous state criminal who ought to be mercilessly punished. . . .
>
> Trotsky also instituted a savage general measure—the keeping of hostages: he had a register made up of the families of officers fighting at the fronts.[21]

Another well-known incident was his taking of harsh reprisals against a regiment that abandoned its position without orders. Trotsky ordered not only the commander and the commissar but also every tenth Red Army man in the regiment to be shot.

Through such severity Trotsky accumulated many enemies among party and military workers. But he also acquired many supporters in the army and the party apparatus, although he did not know how to organize a faction of his own out of them—something that Stalin was doing quite successfully even then.

Lenin usually approved all of Trotsky's severe measures and the methods of leading the army that Trotsky introduced. On one occasion Lenin emphasized his confidence in Trotsky by giving him a blank piece of paper with the letterhead of the chairman of the Council of People's Commissars. On it, he had written in longhand at the bottom of the page:

> Comrades: Knowing the strict character of Comrade Trotsky's orders, I am so convinced, so absolutely convinced, of the correctness, expediency, and necessity for the success of the cause of the order given by Comrade Trotsky, that I unreservedly endorse this order. V. Ulyanov/Lenin.[22]

21. Carmichael, p. 241.

22. Leon Trotsky, *My Life* (New York, 1970), p. 469. [The author cites the Russian edition. —G. S.]

Naturally Trotsky kept this document for the rest of his life.

In his memoirs on Lenin, Maxim Gorky wrote:

> I was very surprised by his high evaluation of Trotsky's organizational abilities. Vladimir Ilyich noticed my surprise. "Yes, I know, they talk all sorts of nonsense about the relations between Trotsky and me. But what is, is, and what is not, is not—that I also know. After all, he showed that he was able to organize the military specialists.[23]

Of course, as chairman of the Revolutionary Military Council Trotsky made quite a few mistakes, although on balance only a positive assessment can be made of his work in that position. Trotsky did not become, or try to become, a military man in the exact sense; he remained a civilian. He was commissar of war, not commander of the Red Army. He himself insisted that a new position be introduced, that of Commander in Chief of the Armed Forces of the Republic, and that the person holding the post serve on the Military Council of the Republic. From September 6, 1918, to July 1919 Ioakim Vatsetis, a former colonel in the tsarist army, held this post; he was succeeded by Sergei Kamenev, another former tsarist army colonel. Both had voluntarily joined the Soviet side.

For Trotsky, words, ideas, and political concepts remained essentially his main weapons in organizing and consolidating the Red Army. His speeches, articles, proclamations, and extensive orders of the day played a greater role than painstaking practical activity. As Joel Carmichael rightly says:

> Though essentially a civilian, Trotsky was bound to get entangled in the front. . . . [On] 6 August 1918 Kazan, the major outpost on the eastern shore of the Volga, was evacuated by the Bolshevik forces. If the Whites crossed the Volga, they would have a straight run to Moscow.
>
> The very next day Trotsky went to the front in person, in the train that he was not to leave again, except for flash trips to Moscow, for two and a half years. . . .
>
> When he got to Sviyazhsk, on the Volga across from Kazan, he found a state of chaos—desertion en masse, collapse amongst both the officers and the Bolshevik

23. Maxim Gorky, *V. I. Lenin* (Moscow, 1959), p. 12. In the first edition of Gorky's pamphlet there is another sentence that goes like this: "Banging his fist on the table, Lenin said: 'Show me another man able to organize almost a model army with a single year and win the respect of military experts. We have such a man.' " (Moscow, 1924, p. 37). In the second edition Gorky shortened this passage and added the following remarks by Lenin: "Nevertheless, he's not ours! He's with us but he's not one of us. He's ambitious. There's something not right about him, that smacks of Lassalle." I don't think Gorky made this up. In 1924 he was not about to write everything that Lenin said to him about Trotsky.

commissars. Within the range of enemy artillery, his powerful voice flooded them with eloquence. He spoke at first hand to soldiers in the grip of panic, and led them back to the firing lines in person. Accompanied by Kronstadt sailors, he even made a night raid on Kazan in a broken-down torpedo boat; the little collection of ships brought down the Volga by the Kronstadters closed down the enemy artillery on the other shore. Trotsky came back unharmed; his presence had had a decisive effect.[24]

In an essay by the Soviet writer Vasily Aksyonov, published in Moscow in 1965, another example of Trotsky's activity during the civil war is described. (The essay, "Dikoi" [The Savage One], deals with the fate of Aksyonov's father, Pavel, who fought in the civil war, was arrested in Stalin's purges in 1937, and returned to his family in 1956.) The episode, quoted from Pavel Aksyonov's memoirs, dates from the fall of 1919.

In Ryazhsk there was an assembly point for deserters, and several thousand of them had been rounded up there. It was a noisy, unruly mob of morally broken men, and we in the escort were few in number. It is difficult to say why they did not slaughter us there and then. It must simply have been impossible for them to organize themselves even for such a relatively simple task. They were united only by their hatred for the commissar who had come from Moscow to inspect the situation.

We led them to a field beyond the city and somehow or other formed them into an enormous square, buzzing like a hive of furious bees. Here, a shaky platform was put together for the highly-placed commissar from Moscow. He drove up in a large black car, its brass parts gleaming in the sun. He was dressed all in leather, wore glasses, and to our great surprise, was totally unarmed. His traveling companions were unarmed as well. He got up on the precarious, unstable platform, put his hands on the rail, and turned his thin, pale face to the crowd of deserters.

Then it started! They all began shouting, and the entire field seemed to be trembling with savage anger!

"Down with him!" shouted the deserters.

"They've come to order us around, the reptiles."

"Go feed the lice in the trenches yourself."

"Get out of here while you're still in one piece!"

"Hell, no rifle. Or I'd pick off this goddam pince-nez."

"Hey guys, what are we standing here for staring at this ugly four eyes?"

We had already raised our rifles to give the first warning shot in the air, when suddenly over the field there rolled, like slow thunder, the voice of the commissar.

"What kind of people are these?" he asked, pointing at us, the guards. "I ask, what people are these with guns?" And again the voice passed over our heads,

24. Carmichael, p. 243.

like the sound that trails after modern-day jets. The deserters were astonished by
his words and stood there in open-mouthed silence.

"Those are the guards," one of his attendants said quite distinctly.

"I order the guards to be withdrawn." He took a deep breath, his glasses
flashing in the sun, and began to roar in an even heavier, even angrier voice,
whose reverberations seemed to echo in every breast.

"These are not White Guard scum in front of us, but revolutionary fighters.
Withdraw the guards!"

In the silence that followed, a deserter's hat suddenly flew into the air and a
lone voice shouted "Hurrah!"

"Comrades, revolutionary fighters!'" The commissar's voice rumbled over us
and echoed into the distance. "The scales of history are tipping in our favor.
Denikin's bands have been smashed outside Orel."

A cry of "Hurrah!" rolled across the entire field, and within five minutes the
commissar's every sentence was being greeted with enthusiastic shouts.

"Death to the bourgeoisie!"

"Give us the world revolution!"

"Everyone to the front!"

As for us, the guards, our presence already forgotten—we were shouting too,
rooted to the spot in youthful ecstasy as we gazed at the slight figure of the
commissar shaking his fist over his head against the background of a crimson sun,
setting beyond the horizon, like the blaze of Europe in flames, like the fire of the
American, Asian, Australian, and African revolutions.[25]

There were a great many simlar episodes in Trotsky's activity during
the civil war. Therefore, without disputing the accounts cited above by
V. Trifonov and Ordzhonikidze, I must agree with Dashkovsky's statement that whenever Trotsky's train arrived on some sector of the front,
it was the equivalent of the arrival of a fresh division.'

The civil war contributed in large degree to an increase in Trotsky's
fame and popularity not only among the many who fought in the war and
among foreign observers and friends of the October revolution but within
the party as well. Hardly anyone still recalled that Trotsky had joined the
party only a few months before the revolution and that he had actively
opposed the Bolsheviks before then. But the heated dispute over the
trade unions in late 1920 and early 1921, in which Lenin and Trotsky
again opposed one another, noticeably weakened Trotsky's importance
and influence in the party.

In the aftermath of the Tenth Party Congress, after the victory of the

25. Vasily Aksyonov, *Iunost. Izbrannoe, 1955–1965* (Moscow, 1965), pp. 16–18. Of
course, in this legally published essay, Aksyonov did not mention Trotsky by name. But
both father and son have confirmed that the "highly-placed Moscow commissar" was none
other than Trotsky.

Lenin majority in the trade union dispute, many of Trotsky's supporters failed to be reelected to the Central Committee and lost their positions in the Orgburo and Secretariat. Nevertheless, in 1921–1922 Trotsky was considered the second most important figure in the Bolshevik leadership. Greetings in honor of Comrades Lenin and Trotsky were announced at many rallies and meetings, and portraits of Lenin and Trotsky hung on the walls of many Soviet and party institutions. Trotsky's name occurred in songs and military marches. This period was undoubtedly the high point of Trotsky's career as a revolutionary and political leader of the Soviet state. Lenin's attitude toward Trotsky at this time was one of emphatic respect, as was Trotsky's toward Lenin. Therefore, to say as R. Palme Dutt says, that "Trotsky always had a vicious, almost pathological hatred of Lenin, for the main principles of his doctrine in general, and for the Bolsheviks in particular," is to speak obvious lies.[26]

The Old Bolshevik V. Gromov wrote in his memoirs:

Trotsky was an outstanding revolutionary. To be sure, he was not a Leninist, but he worked with Lenin in our party with full loyalty. Our party, which was built by Lenin, was a force that paralyzed Trotsky's unlimited ambition and hidden careerism. . . . No one in our party knew Trotsky better than Lenin. Everything that was good and bad in this contradictory man was described with care and precision by our leader. . . . Don't believe what Stalin wrote about Trotsky. . . . Trotsky was the only opponent who did not decline the fight imposed upon him by Stalin, because after Lenin's death Trotsky thought it possible that he would take the post of party leader. Trotsky valued his reputation highly and always guarded it. As a vain person, he was always swayed by the applause of his contemporaries, but more than anything he was concerned with being recognized by future generations. As they say, he had his sights fixed on history *(on bil na istoriyu)*. . . . Lenin himself demonstrated . . . what attitude to take toward Trotsky. . . . In his letter to the congress Lenin called Trotsky "the most capable man on the present Central Committee." These are not empty words but the final considered opinion of the founder of our party about a man with whom he worked for more than twenty years under circumstances that were extremely tense and not always clear.[27]

Trotsky's position in the party and the government at the beginning of 1923 was such that, as Lenin's illness grew worse, not only outside observers but also a significant section of the Bolshevik Party sincerely thought him the most likely successor to Lenin. However, within the

26. R. Palme Dutt, *The Internationale* (London, 1964), p. 183. [The author quotes the Russian translation *International* (Moscow, 1966), p. 188—D. J.]

27. V. Ye. Gromov (pseudonym), Stalin. Mysli i fakty (Stalin: Thoughts and Facts), unpublished manuscript, 1966–1967.

party leadership there were highly influential forces that chose at all costs to prevent matters from taking such a course.

■ 3

THE TWELFTH PARTY CONGRESS AND DISPUTES
IN THE POLITBURO, 1923

In the first few months of 1923 the political and economic situation in the young Soviet republic was still very difficult. Industry and transport had taken the first steps to extricate themselves from the grip of economic dislocation. Agriculture was slowly recovering from the effects of two wars and a drought. Material conditions were extremely hard for the workers and peasants. Especially tragic was the fate of millions of homeless children and millions of unemployed industrial and office workers.

At this very time, however, NEP was gaining strength. In both town and country private commerce was developing, and private industrial enterprises, stores, printing houses, restaurants, and so on made their appearances. Small businessmen, craftsmen, merchants, and rich peasants began to recover from the shock caused by the revolution and the policies of "war communism," such as the requisitioning of farm products. The growth of private enterprise contributed to an improvement in the general economic situation and made it easier to solve the most pressing economic problems. But it also created many political complications and difficulties for the party.

In January and February 1923 Lenin, already seriously ill, continued to dictate his last articles and letters and asked to be read literature on international relations, the cooperatives, and the scientific organization of labor. Vladimir Ilyich was in a hurry to work out in greater detail the fundamentals of the new policies of the party, its new tasks and new structure, and also to expound a deeper understanding of socialism. However, after March 10 this work was interrupted by the most serious stroke he had yet suffered. To those who belonged to the upper levels of the party, it became more and more obvious that Lenin would not be able to return to full political activity. Naturally, the question of a successor to Lenin arose.

Reading with alarm the government report on the serious worsening of Lenin's health, party functionaries and activists understood perfectly that there was not and could not be an adequate replacement for Lenin as creator and leader of the Bolshevik Party and Soviet government. However, just as an army during a military campaign needs a new commander if its previous leader has been seriously wounded, and just as a church needs a new chief priest if its previous spiritual mentor is leaving for a better world, so too a political party—especially in difficult political conditions—needs not only a collective leadership but also a new political chief and interpreter of its ideological doctrine.

Lenin foresaw that there were only three men who could aspire to the role of party chief: Stalin, Trotsky, and Zinoviev (supported by Kamenev). In fact, a triumvirate of Zinoviev, Kamenev, and Stalin had already been formed. Stalin thoroughly concealed his aspirations for the leading position. In the triumvirate he modestly remained in the shadow of Zinoviev and Kamenev. Zinoviev's claims to the top position were based on his long-standing closeness to Lenin. Trotsky's claims were based on his services in preparing and carrying out the October insurrection and leading the Red Army during the civil war and on his popularity, which seemed obvious to everyone. It was Trotsky whom foreign observers usually chose when they attempted to predict the outcome of the succession to Lenin. In fact, however, Trotsky was alone on the Politburo, and in the decisive slots of the party apparatus he had few supporters. This greatly weakened his position and made it impossible for him to automatically become the party's new top leader. A struggle for power was at hand, and signs of it could already be seen in the first months of 1923. On March 14, 1923, *Pravda* published Karl Radek's article "Leon Trotsky —Organizer of Victory." Soon after that, anonymous pamphlets against Trotsky began to circulate unofficially, primarily reminding readers of his "non-Bolshevik" past. Robert C. Tucker suggests that these pamphlets were inspired by Stalin.[28]

Lunacharsky became one of the first to try to raise Zinoviev's authority. In several publications Yaroslavsky emphasized Stalin's important role in the revolution and civil war. All of these literary exercises were outward expressions of the behind-the-scenes struggle in the party apparatus, with the triumvirate taking the initiative. Of course, there was much that Trotsky didn't know, but he saw a lot and guessed a lot more. He had many opportunities to oppose the intrigues of the triumvirate with his own decisive actions. But the first thing he did was refuse to

28. Robert C. Tucker, *Stalin as Revolutionary, 1879–1929: A study in History and Personality* (New York, 1972) p. 335.

give battle. To Trotsky the very idea that it was necessary to fight for power, to organize his own supporters, and carry out backstage maneuvers was repugnant. He apparently thought that the transfer of leadership in the party from Lenin to him would have the character of an automatic ceremonial procedure. However, even when things were going in this direction Trotsky acted capriciously, refusing to take advantage of positions and opportunities that were favorable from the standpoint of the struggle for power.

As is well-known, Lenin did not occupy any formal leadership post in the party; he was its creator and leader on the strength of his moral authority. But Lenin was the head of the Soviet government—chairman of the Council of People's Commissars (Sovnarkom). This post was then considered the most important in the power structure. In 1922 Lenin had three deputies in the Sovnarkom: Kamenev, Rykov, and Tsyurupa. In April 1922 Lenin proposed that Trotsky also become his deputy in the Sovnarkom. Trotsky refused, on the grounds that Lenin wanted to make a purely nominal figure of him. But that was not so. Trotsky's authority was so great that he would not have become a nominal figure; he undoubtedly would have become first among Lenin's deputies. After a few months Lenin took up this question again. This is how Trotsky himself relates this important episode:

Lenin proceeded to state his plan with passionate conviction. He had a limited amount of strength to give to the work of direction. He had three deputies. "You know them. Kamenev is, of course, a clever politician, but what sort of an administrator is he? Tsyurupa is ill. Rykov is perhaps an administrator, but he will have to go back to the Supreme Economic Council. You must become a deputy. The situation is such that we must have a radical realignment of personnel." Again I pointed to the "apparatus" that made even my work in the war department increasingly difficult. "Well, that will be your chance to shake up the apparatus," Lenin retorted quickly, hinting at an expression I had once used. I replied that I referred to the bureaucracy not only in the state institutions, but in the party as well; that the cause of all the trouble lay in the combination of the two apparatuses and in the mutual shielding among the influential groups that gathered round the hierarchy of party secretaries. . . . After thinking it over for a moment, Lenin put the question pointblank: "You propose then to open fire not only against the state bureaucracy, but against the Organizational Bureau of the Central Committee as well?" I couldn't help laughing, this came so unexpectedly. "That seems to be it." The Organizational Bureau meant the very heart of Stalin's apparatus.

"Oh, well," Lenin went on, obviously pleased that we had called the thing by its right name, "if that's the case, then I offer you a bloc against bureaucracy in general and against the Organizational Bureau in particular."

"With a good man, it is an honor to form a good bloc," I replied.

We agreed to meet again some time later.[29]

Trotsky immediately told his closest friends—Ivan Smirnov, Sosnovsky, Rakovsky, and a few others—about Lenin's proposal. But he did not write anything about it, although his friends advised him to. In any case, it is well know that on this occasion, too, Trotsky did not accept Lenin's proposal, and the "Lenin-Trotsky bloc" aimed against Stalin did not become a political reality.

The Twelfth Party Congress was to be held at the end of April 1923. Lenin was recovering with difficulty from the effects of his third stroke, and it was obvious that he would not be able to take part in the work of the congress. The question arose as to who would give the report in the name of the Central Committee. The most authoritative figure in the Central Committee was still Trotsky. Therefore, it was completely natural that at a meeting of the Politburo Stalin proposed that Trotsky prepare the report. Stalin was supported by Kalinin, Rykov, and even Kamenev. But Trotsky again declined, falling into confused rationalizations to the effect that "the party will be ill at ease if any one of us should attempt, as it were personally, to take the place of the sick Lenin."[30] Trotsky proposed instead that the congress proceed without a main political report. This was an absurd proposal, and was, of course, voted down. At one of the next meetings of the Politburo a decision was made—to assign Zinoviev, who had just returned from vacation, to prepare the political report. Trotsky undertook to give the report on industry, which was heard at the eighth session of the congress.

I have discussed above the extremely harsh statements and letters in which Lenin condemned Stalin's position on the national question in general and, more specifically, in regard to Georgia. Lenin wanted to raise these problems at the Twelfth Party Congress, but, fearing that he would not be able to take part in the congress, asked Trotsky in writing to take on this task. Lenin sent his request to Trotsky through Fotieva, one of his secretaries in Gorki.

Trotsky admits, and most historians agree with him, that had he fulfilled Lenin's request and spoken at the congress on the national ques-

29. Trotsky, *My Life*, p. 478.
30. Ibid., p. 489.

tion, making public all of Lenin's documents and letters, including those which Lenin had planned to give him through Fotieva, then any discussion on this question would have ended in Stalin's political defeat, and Stalin's election as general secretary would have become very difficult. Nevertheless, Trotsky refused to fulfill Lenin's request, leaving the Georgian delegation without any support. Lenin's last written document concerned solidarity with this delegation.[31]

Trotsky called Lenin's secretariat and refused to fulfill Lenin's request, pleading illness.[32] He invited Kamenev to his office and informed Kamenev that he was not going to speak at the congress on the national question and that he did not want to raise any controversial questions at it, although he was essentially in agreement with Lenin. Trotsky even added that he did not want the sanctions against Stalin, Dzerzhinsky, and Ordzhonikidze, that Lenin was demanding. Trotsky stood for the preservation of the status quo.

Remember and tell others that the last thing I want is to start a fight at the congress for any changes in organization. . . . I want . . . honest co-operation in the higher centers. . . . There must be an immediate and radical change. . . . It is necessary that Stalin . . . revise his behavior. Let him not overreach himself. There should be no more intrigues, but honest co-operation.[33]

This was a refusal to fight—in a bloc with Lenin, against Stalin's great-power ambitions. Trotsky voluntarily let pass an important and, as later became evident, the most realistic chance to weaken Stalin's position and that of the triumvirate as a whole. Of course, Kamenev, Zinoviev, and Stalin were satisfied. But some of Lenin's documents were known to other members of the Central Committee, for example, Mdivani. Therefore Trotsky went further and agreed with the decision of the Politburo to prohibit anyone from reading Lenin's documents and letters on the national question at the congress.

Trotsky later attempted to explain his behavior by certain moral considerations:

Lenin's letters on the national question and his will remained unknown. Independent action on my part would have been interpreted, or, to be more exact, represented as my personal fight for Lenin's place in the party and state. The very thought of this made me shudder. I considered that it would have brought

31. Lenin, PSS, 54:330.
32. Ibid, p. 674.
33. Trotsky, *My Life*, p. 485.

such a demoralization in our ranks that we would have had to pay too painful a price for it even in case of victory.[34]

It is difficult to agree with the arguments that Trotsky gives here. Some of Lenin's letters on the national question were known in the Politburo. And after all, Lenin did ask Trotsky to read this material to the congress, including documents that no one yet knew about, and to make known that these were Lenin's own letters. Lenin wrote directly to Trotsky saying that this question worried him very much and that he would rest easy only if Trotsky took on this task himself. Naturally Trotsky's refusal only increased Lenin's uneasiness and concern. Trotsky had the opportunity to change his decision when the most important of Lenin's letters—"The Question of Nationalities or 'Autonomization' "— was turned over to the Politburo by Fotieva on April 16—that is, a few days before the congress. By his silence Trotsky helped keep this document secret from the party. In fact it was not published until 1956.[35]

If Trotsky was so sure that he was Lenin's desired successor; if Trotsky saw that Lenin was not simply ill but paralyzed and unable to speak and write; if Trotsky also saw that Zinoviev and Stalin aspired to Lenin's place in the party and considered this dangerous to the party; then it is quite impossible to consider his conduct in March and April 1923 correct for a political person. Trotsky writes:

> I avoided entering into this fight as long as possible, since its nature was that of an unprincipled conspiracy directed against me personally, at least in the first stages. It was clear to me that such a fight, once it broke out, would inevitably take on extremely sharp features and might under the conditions of the revolutionary dictatorship lead to dangerous consequences. This is not the place to discuss whether it was correct to try to maintain some common ground for collective work at the price of very great personal concessions or whether I should have taken the offensive all along the line, despite the absence of sufficient political grounds for such action. The fact is that I chose the first way and, in spite of everything, I do not regret it. There are victories that lead into blind alleys, and there are defeats that open up new avenues.[36]

These arguments are unconvincing to a political person. The struggle for power and influence is not something shameful for a person involved

34. Ibid., p. 482.
35. *Kommunist* (1956), no. 9.
36. From "What Happened and How: Six Articles for the World Press" (written in early 1929 immediately after Trotsky's deportation from the Soviet Union). See *Writings of Leon Trotsky, 1929* (New York, 1975), p. 42. [The author quotes the Russian text published in pamphlet form by the International Left Opposition, *Chto i kak proizoshlo* (Paris, 1929).— G. S.]"

in politics; it is part of his or her life and profession. In the struggle within the Politburo in the spring of 1923 (a struggle imperceptible to the outside observer) Trotsky displayed complete passivity and in so doing condemned himself to defeat. This defeat did indeed open new avenues and perspectives—for the rise of Stalin, who turned out to be not only less scrupulous but also more cunning, intelligent, and crafty than Trotsky imagined.

■ **4**

THE TROTSKYIST OPPOSITION, 1923–1924

The Twelfth Party Congress went by without any great sensations. The delegates were acquainted with some of Lenin's documents, including his letter on nationalities and "autonomization," but only in a confidential manner. Mdivani's attempt to quote passages from the letter was stopped by Kamenev, who was chairing. Moreover, Yenukidze stated outright at the congress that Lenin "in the private question at hand . . . had been the victim of one-sided, inaccurate information."[37] This issue, which Lenin considered particularly important and a matter of basic principle, was referred to by Ordzhonokidze in his speech as "the Georgian squabble, which everyone is sick of hearing about." The Mdivani group was condemned unreservedly as "national-deviationist."

The congress gratified Trotsky's vanity. The delegates gave him the longest applause, and many greetings to the congress mentioned his name along with Lenin's. But from a political and organizational point of view the congress strengthened the positions of the triumvirate headed by Zinoviev. Stalin of course was reelected general secretary.

The report on industry presented by Trotsky was perhaps the most interesting, although it had its debatable aspects. In the first months after the congress, however, Trotsky spent most of his time on issues that were not particularly urgent. As Joel Carmichael writes:

> In the summer and autumn of 1923 he devoted his energies to the analysis of trade cycles in the nineteenth and twentieth centuries; he also wrote on the conflict between the Freudian and the Pavlovian schools of psychology. . . . In the late summer of 1923, in which no doubt his political fate, and eventually, indeed, his very life, were at stake, he devoted a series of essays to the normal behaviour of ordinary people. In addition to such subjects as family life he wrote

37. *Dvenadtsatyi s'ezd RKP(b). Stenograficheskii otchet* (Twelfth Party Congress: Stenographic Record) (Moscow, 1968), p. 590.

articles on such things as 'Civility and Politeness', 'Vodka, the Church and the Movies', 'Russian Swearing' etc. To educationalists, librarians, journalists and so on, he gave countless speeches on the terrible standards of the press, the crying need of the Russian language whose beauties were now being polluted by the flood of party bilge. His puritanism was outraged.[38]

Meanwhile the economic situation was improving very slowly. The peasants were dissatisfied with the high prices for industrial goods, and the workers were dissatisfied with the low wages, which, moreover, were not paid regularly. In July and August 1923 a wave of strikes swept through many large industrial centers, including Moscow, Kharkov, and Sormovo, causing the party leadership great concern. It was necessary to have a profound discussion on the economic situation and the party's economic policies. Insufficient internal democracy in the party, however, prevented a wide and deep discussion of these questions, as did the arbitrariness and bureaucratism within the party and government apparatuses. The question of democracy came to the fore, not in the general form of democracy for the population as a whole but in the narrower framework of the party.

One of the first to raise this question quite emphatically was Dzerzhinsky, who did so in a number of speeches. In September 1923, in connection with the disturbances among the workers and the activity of the Workers' Group—an opposition group that existed both in the party and the unions and was led by Gabriel Myasnikov[39]—a plenum of the Central Committee was called. In his speech at this plenum Dzerzhinsky referred to the stagnation evident in internal party life. He also said that the new practice of appointing party secretaries instead of electing them was becoming a political danger paralyzing the party. A commission headed by Dzerzhinsky was established to look into the internal party situation. This commission was charged with the task of drafting and proposing specific suggestions for improving the internal party regime. There is no question that Dzerzhinsky was sincere in his concern. But it should be kept in mind that in 1923 he was not only commissar of

38. Carmichael, *Trotsky*, p. 313.

39. Myasnikov's fate was unusual and tragic. He joined the Bolshevik Party at the age of seventeen in 1906. As an active participant in the revolution, he had disputes with Lenin himself on questions of democracy (see Lenin, PSS, 44:78–83). After being expelled from the party and arrested, he managed to emigrate and worked for more than twenty years as an ordinary auto worker at a factory in France. In 1945 Myasnikov, like many other émigrés, was invited to return to the Soviet Union with the promise of immunity. He returned but was arrested and died in confinement in 1946.

railways but also chairman of the GPU and people's commissar of internal affairs. We must assume that the arrest of Myasnikov, which happened even before the plenum, could not have been carried out without Dzerzhinsky's knowledge. Aleksandr Bogdanov, one of the organizers of the "Proletcult," was also briefly detained.[40]

Trotsky and his co-thinker Preobrazhensky refused to take part in Dzerzhinsky's commission, who apparently criticized Trotsky's behavior. Trotsky unexpectedly walked out of the Central Committee plenum. A group of delegates from the Central Committee was sent to Trotsky's home to ask him to return, but Trotsky refused.

In the fall of 1923 several semi-legal opposition groups formed within the party—some within its leading circles, most taking left positions. Among these groups there was an extensive exchange of opinions and work on a united platform. However, there was no authoritative leader until Trotsky assumed leadership of this incipient opposition. He finally set aside his many months of vacillations and decided to head the opposition to Stalin and the triumvirate. There is no question that pressure from many of his friends and supporters influenced Trotsky's decision, but he also felt that he was gradually being pushed out of power. Even in the commissariat of war, where Trotsky was used to regarding himself as master of the situation, his position had been weakened. By a decision of the Politburo two old opponents of Trotsky's, Voroshilov and Lashevich, had been added to the Revolutionary Military Council of the Republic and the Council of Labor and Defense.

On October 8, 1923, Trotsky sent a letter to the members of the Central Committee and the Central Control Commission sharply criticizing the party leadership. Most of Trotsky's remarks about bureaucratization of the party apparatus and the stifling of party democracy were absolutely correct. But there were quite a few exaggerations in his letter, if we bear in mind the situation in 1923. For example, according to Trotsky, "The regime which had essentially taken shape even before the Twelfth Congress and which, after it, was fully consolidated and given finished form, is much farther removed from workers' democracy than was the regime during the fiercest periods of war communism." The letter also hinted at the need for changes in the party leadership, al-

40. Bogdanov was not only the founder of "Proletcult" but also of the Institute for Blood Transfusion in Moscow. He died in 1928. Bogdanov had not been a Bolshevik for a long time, although that did not prevent him from taking an active part in public and scientific life in Soviet Russia.

though Trotsky stated that his intentions were only to change wrong policies, not to attack the existing leadership. He also stressed that he considered his letter an internal document and did not propose to present his views to the entire party. Copies of the letter became known to many of Trotsky's supporters, however, and in 1924 it was published in the émigré Menshevik newspaper *Sotsialisticheskii vestnik*.[41]

On October 15 the Central Committee received an even more harshly worded statement signed by forty-six well-known party members. There is no question that the content of this document had been made known to Trotsky in advance. This document, which is generally known as the "Letter of the Forty-Six" (or "Platform of the Forty-Six"), asserts:

> The regime established within the party is completely intolerable; it destroys the independence of the party, replacing the party by a [hand-picked] bueaucratic apparatus which acts without objection in normal times, but which inevitably fails in moments of crisis, and which threatens to become completely ineffective in the face of the serious events now impending.[42]

The authors of the letter sharply criticized the work of the Central Committee in economic matters, arguing that because of the incompetence, lack of system, and arbitrary decision of the Central Committee, instead of successes and achievements there was a serious economic crisis in the Soviet economy. The "Letter of the Forty-Six" was signed by such political co-thinkers of Trotsky as Preobrazhensky, Serebryakov, Kosior, Pyatakov, Smirnov, Beloborodov, Alsky, and Danishevsky. The letter was also signed by former members of the Democratic Centralist opposition, which had been formed in the party in 1920–1921, including Osinsky, Sapronov, Maksimovsky, Smirnov, Boguslavsky, Bubnov, and others. Some other prominent party activists such as Antonov-Ovseyenko also signed the "Letter of the Forty-Six." It was not published in the Soviet Union, but it did circulate in private copies to many party members and reached many units and organizations of the party.

41. *Sotsialisticheskii vestnik*, May 28, 1924, pp. 11–12. This newspaper was published in Berlin at first, under the editorship of Martov and, after his death, of Fyodor Dan. [A full English translation of Trotsky's October 8 letter, which is quoted in part above, can be found in Leon Trotsky, *The Challenge of the Left Opposition, 1923–25* (New York, 1975), pp. 55–56. —G. S.]

42. The "Letter of the Forty-Six" was translated from Trotsky's archives at Harvard University and published in E. H. Carr, *The Interregnum* (London, 1954). In West Berlin a multivolume collection of the writings of the Left Opposition, *Die Linke Opposition in der Sowjetunion, 1923–1929*, was published in the 1970s by Ulle and Wolter. This letter is in vol. 1 (Berlin, 1976), pp. 211–219. [A similar three-volume collection in English is Leon Trotsky, *The Challenge of the Left Opposition* (New York, 1975–1981). —G. S.]

The fact that Trotsky was at the center of the struggle for party democracy might have appeared stranger to many party activists than the concern about party democracy expressed by the head of the GPU. Trotsky never had a reputation as a democrat in party and government circles, and his methods of work in the army and the transport industry were distinguished by extreme authoritarianism. It was Trotsky who in late 1920 and early 1921 had called for the militarization of labor and for "shaking up" the trade unions and completely subordinating them to the state. This authoritarianism was combined with extreme individualism and haughtiness, which gave grounds for even people close to Trotsky to call him lordly. Maria Joffe, one of his closest associates, says this about him in her memoirs:

Trotsky bore himself as a man who knew his own worth and was sure of his place in the party. In general, unlike Stalin, who was always putting on an act and was ready to be chummy with everyone, including an enemy, for the sake of achieving his goals, one felt in the relations between Trotsky and those around him that imperceptibly he held people at a distance. Sometimes not a very great distance, but a distance nevertheless. Only with a very few people, among them Adolf Abramovich [Joffe] and myself, did he allow himself to be relaxed and familiar. Others saw in his manner pride and unapproachability, which the Stalinist apparatchiks and demagogues used skillfully to discredit Trotsky. Still, nothing could force him to betray his own values.[43]

These qualities helped Trotsky carry out particular assignments within the existing party system, especially under conditions of revolution and civil war, when authoritarian methods prevailed at all levels. But they always hampered Trotsky in purely political activity. Even Lunacharsky, in his friendly portrait of Trotsky, comments:

Trotsky was very bad at organising not only a party but even a small group. He had practically no partisans of his own at all: he was hampered by the extreme definiteness of his personality. . . . if he was impressive within the Party it was exclusively because of his personality . . . An enormous authoritativeness, and a sort of inability or unwillingness to be in the least caressing and attentive to people, an absence of that charm that always enveloped Lenin, condemned Trotsky to a certain solitude.[44]

Be that as it may, it was precisely Trotsky who took the lead of the Left Opposition in the party, and that predetermined many of the successes and failures of that opposition from then on.

43. *Vremya i my* (1977), no. 20, p. 183.
44. Lunacharsky, *Revoliutsionnye siluety*, pp. 21–25, as quoted in Carmichael, p. 296.

The party leadership could not allow Trotsky's letter to the Central Committee and the "Letter of the Forty-Six" to go unanswered. On October 25–27, 1923, in Moscow a joint plenum of the Central Committee and Central Control Commission was held together with representatives of ten party organizations. The plenum condemned these documents as a step toward a split in the party and as an example of factional activity. The plenum resolution was not published until several months later.[45] The party leadership understood that it was impossible to avoid a big new debate, but it did not want to allow Trotsky's letter or the "Letter of the Forty-Six" to become the basis for discussion.

The Politburo majority decided to take the initiative in the debate. On November 7, 1923, *Pravda* published a long article in a spirit of self-criticism by Zinoviev entitled "New Tasks of the Party." In particular Zinoviev says:

> In the internal life of the party in the recent past too much of a dead calm has been observed, and in some cases there has been outright stagnation. . . . Our main difficulty is often that all the most important questions come from the top down, decided in advance. This narrows the possibilities for creative intervention by the vast majority of party members and reduces the initiative of the base organizations of the party. . . . In order to satisfactorily carry out the tasks outlined above, in order to meet the requirements of international events that are now demanding our attention, it is necessary that internal party life become much more intensive. . . . It is necessary that workers' democracy within the party be applied in practice—free discussion within the party must be reinforced on general political, economic, and other questions, and in particular the attention of the rank and file party members must be drawn to the burning questions of economic production.

Pravda called on party members to generate a broad discussion in the press and within party organizations on the basis of Zinoviev's article. On November 13 *Pravda* began printing discussion articles and a variety of materials on problems of internal democracy. The discussion aroused tremendous interest within the party. Articles by supporters of Trotsky as well as his opponents were published. In many respects, the articles did not differ very much: both sides acknowledged the abnormality of the situation in the party and called for democracy to be advanced by all possible means. In the process quite a few sensible arguments and proposals were made, many of which are pertinent to this very day. On the whole the discussion was rather constructive, opening the way for a

45. *Trinadtsataia konferentsiia RKP(b). Biulleten'* (Moscow, 1924).

possible compromise. And a compromise was reached. On December 5, 1923, a joint session of the Politburo and the Presidium of the Central Control Commission was held. After long and difficult argument a resolution was passed *unanimously* and published in *Pravda* on December 7. It said in part:

Only a constant, vital ideological life can maintain the character of the party as it was before and during the revolution, with constant critical study of its own past, correction of its own mistakes, and collective discussion of the most important questions. Only these methods can provide real guarantees against the transformation of episodic disagreements into the formation of factional groups. . . .

In order to avert this, the leading party bodies must heed the voices of the broad party ranks and must not regard every criticism as a manifestation of factionalism, thereby impelling honest and disciplined party members to withdraw into closed circles and fall into factionalism. . . .

The network of party discussion clubs must be expanded, without unjustifiable appeals being made to "party discipline" when it is a matter of the right and duty of party members to discuss questions of interest to them and to make decisions. . . .

It is necessary to pass from words to deeds by proposing that the party cells on the base level, and party conferences on the district, region, and province levels, systematically renew the party apparatus from the bottom up at the regular party elections, by promoting to responsible positions activists who are capable of ensuring internal party democracy in practice. . . .

A particularly important task of the control commissions at the present time is to combat bureaucratic distortions in the party apparatus and in the practical work of the party and to call to account any party officials who hinder the implementation of the principles of workers' democracy. . . .[46]

Voting for this resolution, among others, were Trotsky, Stalin, Zinoviev, and Kamenev. This unanimity proved to be none too stable, however. For Stalin and Zinoviev the resolution of December 5 was something of a concession to pressure from the opposition. At any rate, they were forced to admit that substantial elements of bureaucratism were present in the party apparatus and to call on the entire party to uproot these bureaucratic deformations. This was a purely "paper" concession, however. After December 5 the Politburo did not engage in any substantial effort to expand internal party democracy or increase the number of discussion clubs. To the contrary, many apparatus officials took the resolution of December 5 as a signal to end discussion and in fact began to

46. The December 5 resolution was never subsequently reprinted in any collection of party resolutions. [A full translation in English is in Trotsky, *Challenge of the Left Opposition, 1923–1925*, New York, 1975, pp. 404–413—G. S.]

reduce the possibilities for "conscientious and disciplined party members" to engage in "continuous, critical study of their past, to correct mistakes, and collectively discuss the most important questions."

The Left Opposition was not about to retreat, however. It had not achieved any fundamental changes in the party leadership, and that, despite Trotsky's assurances, was its most important aim. Therefore it decided to use the partial victory it had gained to increase the pressure on the Politburo. It is true that Trotsky was then suffering from a prolonged undiagnosed illness. He was able to write, however, and soon several articles by him led to a renewal of the discussion between the Politburo and the opposition—this time in terms more heated than before.

On the evening of December 8, at a meeting of party activists of the Krasnaya Presnya district in Moscow, a letter by Trotsky, addressed to party meetings and entitled "The New Course," was ready. It consisted of Trotsky's personal comments on the resolution that had just been adopted by the Politburo and Central Control Commission. Trotsky declared that the December 5 resolution was a turning point in the life of the party, that it was addressed first of all to rank and file party members, who should make use of the opportunity provided them. "Some conservatively minded comrades," Trotsky writes, "who are inclined to overestimate the role of the apparatus and underrate the self-activity of the party, take a critical attitude toward the Politburo resolution. They say that the Central Committee is assuming impossible obligations, that the resolution will only engender illusions and produce negative results." The party should not go along with these conservatives, Trotsky argues. He counterposed the party to its apparatus, stating that it was not for the apparatus to decide when and how far party democracy should be encouraged. These problems should be decided by the party itself, and the ranks of the party should "subordinate the apparatus to themselves."[47]

According to Trotsky, there were many in the party apparatus who gave a hostile reception to the "new course." He therefore called for a purge of all bureaucratic elements in the apparatus and their replacement by "fresh" cadres. Above all, Trotsky argued, the leading posts in the party "must be cleared of those who, at the first words of criticism, of

47. [The author bases his account of Trotsky's letter on the text in German in *Die Linke Opposition* (see note 42). A full English translation is in *Challenge of the Left Opposition, 1923–25*, pp. 123–130. —G. S.]

objection, or of protest, brandish the thunderbolts of penalties at the critic. The 'new course' must begin by making everyone feel that from now on *nobody* will dare to terrorize the party." These hints were understood by everyone at the time.

Trotsky's letter received a hostile reception not only from the triumvirs but from the majority of the party apparatus as well. Nevertheless, it was published in *Pravda* on December 11 with a number of additions and annotations by Trotsky himself. Trotsky still enjoyed too much influence for his letter to be suppressed. In reply to reproaches by some activists Stalin stated:

> They say that the Central Committee should have banned publication of Trotsky's article. That is wrong, comrades. That would have been a very danger-ous step on the part of the Central Committee. Just try to ban an article of Trotsky's that has already been read aloud [at party meetings] in Moscow dis-tricts! The Central Committee could not take such a heedless step.[48]

Trotsky's article provided the pretext for a new flareup of controversy. General party meetings and factional meetings of Left Opposition sup-porters were held everywhere. Some party organizations passed resolu-tions supporting the line of the majority of the Central Committee; others supported the line of the opposition. Trotsky's side received the most support from student youth, office workers in Soviet institutions, and many members of party organizations in the military. In the factories the opposition most often remained in the minority. On December 11 Lev Kamenev spoke at a meeting of the active party membership of Moscow against Trotsky's arguments. On December 15 Zinoviev pre-sented a report on the internal dispute to a meeting of the active party membership in Petrograd. Also on December 15 *Pravda* published a long article by Stalin entitled "The Discussion, Rafail, the Articles by Preobrazhensky and Sapronov, and Trotsky's Letter."

Trotsky, because of his prolonged illness, could not take a direct part in the meetings and conferences being held everywhere. His absence undoubtedly weakened the ranks of the Left Opposition. As a continua-tion of his letter of December 8, Trotsky wrote two long articles, which were published in *Pravda* on December 28 and 29, 1923. All these articles were brought together—along with some other material—in a pamphlet entitled *The New Course*, which came out in early January 1924. In this pamphlet Trotsky enlarged the scope of the discussion. He

48. Stalin, *Sochineniia*, 6:33.

not only hinted at the possibility of degeneration of the party's Old Guard but also called for an orientation toward the youth, and first of all, the student youth, whom he called "the most reliable barometer of the party." This statement was greeted enthusiastically in many student organizations but did not find support even among some signers of the "Letter of the Forty-Six." Trotsky's opponents did not object to many of the Left Opposition's critical remarks concerning bureaucratization of a section of the party apparatus, but they accused Trotsky of trying to counterpose the apparatus to the party and of trying to form his own faction in the party, which, they said, could lead to a split. They also emphatically rejected the suggestions of a possible degeneration of the party's Old Guard. Constant references were made at the same time to the fact that Trotsky, who had joined the party only in the summer of 1917, could not be called an Old Bolshevik.

Replying to these hints and gibes, Trotsky rather haughtily took the position that he and his closest supporters were the real "Leninists," the genuine standardbearers of "Leninism."

I do not by any means consider the road by which I came to Leninism to be less sure and reliable than those of others. I came to Lenin fighting, but I came to him fully and all the way. And if the question is to be placed on the plane of biographical investigations, it should be done thoroughly.

It would then be necessary to reply to some thorny questions. Were all those who were faithful to the master in small matters also faithful to him in great ones? Did all those who showed such docility in the presence of the master thereby offer guarantees that they would continue his work in his absence? Does the whole of Leninism lie in docility?[49]

Trotsky not only hinted at his own services in the October revolution and civil war but also sought to demonstrate that as commissar of rail transport in 1920 he had been the first in the Soviet Union to give an example of how to draw up economic plans and practice economic planning. He also informed his readers that as early as February 1920—that is, a year before Lenin—he had come to the conclusion that the requisitioning of farm products had to be replaced by a tax in kind, but his proposals had not met with understanding from the rest of the party leadership at that time.[50]

49. [The author cites Trotsky's 1924 pamphlet *Novyi kurs* (Moscow, 1924), p. 48. A full English translation of Trotsky's *New Course* is in *Challenge of the Left Opposition, 1923–25*, pp. 63–144. —G. S.]

50. [See chs. 6 and 7 of Trotsky's *New Course*, in *Challenge . . . 1923–25*, pp. 101–123. —G. S.]

These very biographical references undermined Trotsky. Stalin and Zinoviev were not overly scrupulous in this instance. Soon after Lenin's death, which briefly interrupted the polemic with the opposition, various documents from the archives of the tsarist police were transferred to the Institute of Party History, which had just been established. Among these documents was a letter written by Trotsky in 1913 and addressed to the Menshevik leader Chkheidze. In this letter Trotsky wrote about Lenin with undisguised hostility, describing him in rude and unflattering terms. This was a common occurrence in the émigré squabbling before the revolution. Lenin's letters and articles of that time frequently contained rude references to Trotsky, Radek, and many other future Bolsheviks, not to mention his remarks on the Mensheviks. However, publication of Trotsky's letter to Chkheidze just at the time when the party was mourning the loss of Lenin dealt a heavy blow to Trotsky's presitge.

Hardly anyone compared the date when the letter was written to the date of its publication, but everyone read the insulting and unjust remarks about Lenin that Trotsky made in a letter to one of Lenin's political enemies, who had actively opposed the October revolution and who in 1921 had fled from Georgia to exile in the West. Trotsky was furious. He declared that the use made of his letter was "one of the greatest frauds in world history," exceeding by far in its cynicism the false documents produced by the French reactionaries in the Dreyfus case. However, Trotsky could not deny that he had written this letter with its abusive remarks about Lenin and had sent it to Chkheidze. Although the letter had been written long before the October revolution, Trotsky himself saw that in the minds of readers "chronology was disregarded in the face of naked quotations."[51]

The balance sheet of the first phase of the discussion was drawn at the Thirteenth Party Conference held in January 1924. The party cell meetings preceding the conference showed that the Left Opposition still had significant influence. Even at district party conferences in Moscow 36 percent of the votes went to the Trotskyist opposition. None of the subsequent oppositions gathered such a large number of votes from the party rank and file. Nevertheless, on the whole the opposition suffered a defeat. At the Thirteenth Party Conference in January 1924 it was condemned as a "petty bourgeois deviation." The decisions of the conference were approved at the Thirteenth Party Congress, held at the end of May

51. Trotsky, *My Life*, p. 516. [The author cites the Russian edition, *Moia zhizn'* (Berlin, 1930), 2:259. —G. S.]

1924. The congress voted to have the resolutions of the Thirteenth Conference added to its own official decisions.

Trotsky did not attend the Thirteenth Party Conference. He had gone for a rest cure to Sukhumi in the Caucasus. Nor did he return to Moscow after receiving word of Lenin's death. All the political and organizational decisions made by the Politburo after Lenin's demise were put through without Trotsky's participation. It was probably a matter of indifference to him at the time whether the person appointed as chairman of the Council of People's Commissars was Kamenev or Rykov. In Trotsky's absence opposition activities in Moscow were directed for the most part by three of his supporters, Preobrazhensky, Osinsky, and Sapronov.

Trotsky did take part in the work of the Thirteenth Congress. His appearance on the speaker's platform was greeted with applause almost as lengthy as it had been at the Twelfth Congress. Trotsky's speech was conciliatory rather than aggressive. He defended himself and the opposition as a whole rather weakly. It was in this speech that he uttered his famous remark that "the party is always right," a statement hardly consistent with his actual activity and with the positions he had previously taken. In particular he said:

None of us wants to be or can be right against his own party. The party in the last analysis is always right, because the party is the only historical instrument given to the proletariat to resolve its fundamental tasks. . . . I know that it is impossible to be right against the party. One can be right only with the party and through the party, for history has not created any other way of determining what is right. The English have a saying: My country, right or wrong. With much more historical justification we can say: Right or wrong on any particular, specific question at any particular moment, this is still my party.[52]

This was empty rhetoric, and Trotsky's opponents did not consider it satisfactory. Even Krupskaysa, who had sent Trotsky a warm letter when he was in Sukhumi a short time before, saying that Lenin had remembered him during the last days of his life, said in her speech at the congress that if the party is always right, Trotsky should not have started the discussion. Zinoviev remarked rather acidly that "the party has no need of bitter-sweet compliments." Stalin rejected Trotsky's rhetoric even more emphatically. He said that in the given instance Trotsky had once again made an assertion that was incorrect in principle:

52. *Trinadtsatyi s"ezd RKP(b). Stenographicheskii otchet* (Thirteenth Party Congress: Stenographic Record) (Moscow, 1924) p. 372.

The party often makes mistakes. Ilyich taught us to teach the party the art of correct leadership on the basis of its own mistakes. If the party made no mistakes, there would be nothing with which to teach the party. Our task is to catch these errors, reveal their roots, and show the party and the working class how we erred and how we are going to correct these errors in the future. Without this, progress would be impossible for the party. Without this, the forming of party leaders and cadres would be impossible, because they are formed and trained through the struggle against their own errors, by overcoming those errors. I think that a statement like Trotsky's is somewhat of a compliment with somewhat of an attempt at mockery—an attempt, of course, that failed.[53]

It was evident that the majority of the Politburo had decided to carry the fight with the Left Opposition through to the end. But the opposition was not about to lay down its arms.

During this period quite a few disputes went on over problems of the Communist movement and the international situation. In 1923 the revolutionary actions of the working class in Germany ended in some serious defeats, which were caused above all by the objective and subjective conditions in Germany. Trotsky and his supporters, however, tried to place the main responsibility for the failures of the German proletariat on the leadership of the Comintern, headed at the time by Zinoviev. A certain stabilization was taking place in the capitalist world, and the question of revolution was temporarily taken off the agenda. This put the question of the prospects for the Russian revolution on a new plane: Was it possible successfully to build socialism in one country, especially in such a backward country as Russia?

As far back as 1906 Trotsky had written:

Without direct state aid from the European proletariat the working class of Russia will not be able to retain state power and transform its momentary dominance into a prolonged socialist dictatorship. This cannot be doubted even for a minute.[54]

And in 1917 Trotsky wrote in a pamphlet entitled *Programma mira* (Peace Program):

Now, after the so very promising start of the Russian revolution, we have every reason to hope that in the course of this war a mighty revolutionary movement will develop throughout Europe. It is clear that this movement will be able to develop successfully and achieve victory only as a Europe-wide movement. If it

53. Stalin, *Sochineniia*, 6:227.
54. Trotsky, *Nasha revolutsiia* (Geneva, 1906), pp. 277–278.

remains isolated within national boundaries, it is doomed to destruction. . . . The salvation of the Russian revolution lies in its extension to all of Europe. . . . The European revolution does not have to wait for the revolution in Asia or Africa, or even in Australia and America. But a victorious revolution in Russia or England is inconceivable without a revolution in Germany, and vice versa.[55]

Trotsky's point of view did not then coincide with the opinion of Lenin, who in 1915 and 1916 argued that not only could a revolution be made and power taken in one separate capitalist country but that "socialist production could be organized" and proletarian power defended against encroachments by other countries. In the years 1918–1920 Lenin's and Trotsky's views on this question virtually coincided. First, Lenin was sure of a rapid victory for the world revolution, or at least of the European revolution. Second, the economic ruin in Russia was so severe that Lenin repeated several times that it would be impossible to build socialism in Russia without the support of a socialist Europe. However, toward the end of 1922 Lenin began to regard NEP as a longterm policy aimed at the building of socialism in Russia. Although Russia was alone and the revolutionary socialist movement had suffered defeat in Europe, Lenin confidently declared that NEP Russia would "become a socialist Russia."

Our opponents told us repeatedly that we were rash in undertaking to implant socialism in an insufficiently cultured country. But they were misled by our having started from the end opposite to that prescibed by theory (the theory of pedants of all kinds), because in our country the political and social revolution preceded the cultural revolution, that very cultural revolution which nevertheless now confronts us. This cultural revolution would now suffice to make our country a completely socialist country.[56]

In the years 1922–1924 Trotsky continued to argue that it was impossible to build socialism within the national boundaries of the Soviet Union, that "a genuine upsurge of socialist economy in Russia will become possible only after the victory of the proletariat in the most important countries of Europe."[57]

For a while Stalin too had approximately the same point of view. Later, however, under Bukharin's influence and after becoming more thoroughly acquainted with Lenin's texts, Stalin decisively changed his opinion.

55. Trotsky, *Sochineniia*, vol. 3, pt. 1 (Moscow, 1924), pp. 88–89.
56. Lenin, PSS, 45:377; CW, 33:474–475.
57. Trotsky, *Sochineniia*, 3 (1):92–93.

At the end of 1924 Stalin published a collection of his articles and speeches of that year. In the preface Stalin for the first time put forward a new formula: that it was possible to build socialism in one country even under conditions of capitalist encirclement. At the same time Stalin sharply criticized Trotsky's views on this question. Trotsky did not reply to Stalin's thrust at that time, and the main disputes over this question occurred later, at another stage of the party infighting.

Between the opposition and the majority of the party leadership serious differences arose over the economic situation and the prospects for Soviet economic development. The Left Opposition tended to exaggerate the economic difficulties and the shortcomings in existing economic policies. It did not see the real possibilities for socialist construction in the rural areas. Lenin's plan for cooperatives as a means of building socialism was regarded by the opposition as a rather utopian illusion. The opposition accused the majority of a "kulak deviation" and called for more pressure to be applied to the capitalist elements in city and country, in contradiction to the basic principles of NEP. With obviously demagogic ends in mind, the opposition greatly exaggerated the development of private capital in the USSR. N. Valentinov (Volsky), a former Menshevik and functionary of the Supreme Economic Council, who later emigrated from the Soviet Union, tells in his memoirs about the "opposition's anti-NEP way of thinking." This was expressed

with particular force in its constant outcries about the domination of private merchant capital. The opposition gave fantastic, inordinately exaggerated figures on the strength and accumulation of this type of private capital. It pointed to the fact that the overwhelming majority (70–80 percent) of all commercial operations were private but left unmentioned the fact that most of these businesses were tiny, operated by a single merchant or tradesman, who did not own a store but hawked merchandise from a table or stand or simply carried it around with him. If these peddlers had not existed, there would have been nothing. A total absence of trade would have prevailed, especially in the rural areas. The opposition kept insisting on the need to subordinate the economy to direction by a plan, "to gather all enterprises into a single system, subjecting them to a single powerful planning center." [No source given] What this meant concretely they did not explain. The peasant and peasant agriculture were outside the range of vision of the opposition. In contrast, it spoke a great deal about the "dictatorship of industry" and called for rapid and powerful industrialization, although the country did not have the wherewithal to do that. . . . All of Lenin's exhortations in his last articles, in particular his warnings against "rushing ahead too rashly and quickly," his appeals for "better fewer, but better" . . . were completely disregarded by the opposition.[58]

The Left Opposition linked its proposal for the development of industry at a forced pace with another proposal, the extraction of resources from the countryside on a more massive scale, from peasant agriculture which had not yet fully recovered from the dislocations of war and revolution. As early as 1924 one of Preobrazhensky's articles included the assertion that for the sake of socialist accumulation the proletariat must undertake the *exploitation* of presocialist economic forms.[59]

A heated discussion again erupted late in the fall of 1924 in connection with certain questions of party history. Despite the struggle against "Trotskyism" that had been proclaimed, the State Publishing House was issuing the collected works of Trotsky as well as those of Lenin. The volume of Trotsky's works being prepared for publication in the fall of 1924 contained his writings and speeches of 1917. Trotsky decided to publish these materials as a separate collection. (Stalin also published some of his writings in separate editions.) In addition, Trotsky wrote a lengthy introduction entitled "Lessons of October," which soon came out as a separate pamphlet. This publication had primarily political aims.[60]

At the end of 1924 only a small section of the party consisted of Bolsheviks who had joined before the October revolution. Most party members had a poor knowledge of the history of their own party and the biographies of its leaders. In publishing *Lessons of October* Trotsky thought to deal a crushing blow to the reputations of Zinoviev and Kamenev, who had opposed the armed insurrection in October 1917 and who after the revolution had called for the formation of a united socialist government that would include the Mensheviks and SRs. At the same time Trotsky emphasized his own outstanding role in preparing and carrying out the revolution. Moreover, in qualifying Zinoviev and Kamenev's conduct in 1917 as a "right deviation," Trotsky suggested that similar indecisiveness and lack of audacity by the leadership of the Comintern (headed by Zinoviev) had led to the defeat of the revolutionary movement in Germany in 1923.

58. N. Valentinov (Volsky), *Novaya ekonomicheskaia politika i krizis partii posle smerti Lenina* (Stanford, Ca., 1971), pp. 80–81.

59. *Vestnik Kommunisticheskoi Akademii* (1924), no. 8.

60. See the introduction in Trotsky, *Sochineniia*, vol. 3: "1917," pt. 1, (Moscow, 1924); also the pamphlet *Uroki Oktiabria*, (Moscow, 1924). [An English translation is in *Challenge of the Left Opposition, 1923–25*, pp. 199–258. —G. S.]

It cannot be said that *Lessons of October* was an outright falsification, although the work's bias was obvious. The greater the accuracy of Trotsky's facts, however, the greater the anger they aroused in Zinoviev and Kamenev. A flood of new articles and speeches poured out against Trotsky and "Trotskyism." Trotsky was now reminded of all his speeches and actions against Lenin and the Bolsheviks from 1903 to 1916. At the same time, many of Lenin's harsh comments on Trotsky, also dating from those years, were published. Trotsky's services in October 1917 were not denied by many of the authors now attacking him, but he was reminded that he had joined the Bolsheviks only in the summer of 1917, when the main preparations for the October revolution had already been made. The myth that the primary work of organizing the October insurrection was carried out by the "Party Center," to which Trotsky had not belonged, was born at this time. Stalin, in his speech dredging up the forgotten "Center," said this about Trotsky:

I am far from denying Trotsky's undoubtedly important role in the uprising. I must say, however, that Trotsky did not play any special role in the October uprising, nor could he do so; being chairman of the Petrograd Soviet, he merely carried out the will of the appropriate party bodies, which directed every step that Trotsky took. To philistines like Sukhanov all this may seem strange. . . . And yet, strictly speaking, there is nothing strange about it, for neither in the party nor in the October uprising did Trotsky play any special role, nor could he do so, for he was a relatively new man in our party in the period of October. He, like all the responsible workers, merely carried out the will of the Central Committee and of its organs. . . . It would have been enough for Trotsky to have gone against the will of the Central Committee to have been deprived of influence on the course of events. This talk about Trotsky's special role is a legend being spread by obliging "party" gossips.[61]

In this case Stalin was telling only half the truth, without bothering to make his remarks consistent with statements on the same subject he had made earlier. Trotsky was also reminded of his conduct during the Brest-Litovsk negotiations, when his position placed all of the gains of the revolution in danger.

The Central Committee voted to withdraw Trotsky's pamphlet from circulation, although publication of his *Works* continued.[62] Resolutions against Trotsky and the Left Opposition were adopted by virtually all party organizations. The Leningrad province committee, headed by Zi-

61. Stalin, *Sochineniia*, 6:327–329.

62. Seventeen volumes of Trotsky's *Sochineniia* appeared before publication was discontinued in 1927.

noviev, proposed that Trotsky be expelled from the party. Many party cells, including cells in the army and navy, urged that Trotsky be removed from his position as commissar of war. This question was to be discussed at a Central Committee plenum scheduled for January 17, 1925. At that point Trotsky again lost the will to fight. He did not reply to the attacks that appeared in the party press in November and December 1924. To be sure, he drafted a new pamphlet entitled "Our Differences," in which he attempted to refute his opponents' arguments or to clarify his own previous statements, but this work remained unfinished and was not published.[63]

Without waiting for the plenum, Trotsky sent a long statement to the Central Committee asking to be relieved of his duties as commissar of war and chairman of the Revolutionary Military Council of the Republic. He also wrote that he was prepared to "carry out any work on assignment from the Central Committee in any post or without any post and, it goes without saying, under any conditions of party supervision."[64]

The plenum was held January 17–20, 1925. It condemned the "totality of Trotsky's statements against the party" and acknowledged that "any further work by Comrade Trotsky on the Revolutionary Military Council would be impossible." At the same time the plenum decreed that the "discussion should be considered closed."[65]

Trotsky was allowed to remain on the Politburo, however. After a short time he was given new assignments as a member of the Presidium of the Supreme Economic Council, chairman of the scientific and technical division of the Supreme Economic Council, head of the electrical engineering board, and chairman of the Chief Concessions Committee.

Trotsky's defeat in the first stage of his fight against Stalin has been interpreted in various ways by Western historians. Some of them hold that Trotsky did not make use of all his advantages in this fight, especially his position as commissar of war and chairman of the Military Revolutionary Council. The idea of a military solution to the internal party conflict also occurred to some members of the Trotskyist opposition. Zinoviev, Kamenev, and Stalin had some apprehensions in this regard, which explains the changes made on the Revolutionary Military Council as early

63. [An English translation of "Our Differences" is in *Challenge of the Left Opposition, 1923–25*, pp. 259–303. —G. S.]

64. [An English translation of Trotsky's statement of resignation is in Ibid, pp. 304–308. —G. S.]

65. *VKP(v) v rezoluitsiiakh i resheniiakh s"ezdov, konferentsii i plenumov TsK* (Moscow, 1936), Pt. 1, pp. 655–656. (Hereafter cited as *VKP(b) v rezoluitsiiakh.*)

as 1924 and the removal of Vladimir Antonov-Ovseyenko as head of the
Political Directorate of the Red Army and his replacement by Andrei
Bubnov.[66]

It must be said quite emphatically, however, that at the time of the
discussion in the party there was never any real threat of a military coup,
if only because the Red Army was never just a "docile" instrument" in
Trotsky's hands. Trotsky could rely fully on the soldiers of the Red Army
when he gave the order to march on Warsaw, but he could not have
raised the Red Army against the Central Committee and Politburo.

Victor Serge, a well-known revolutionary internationalist who had taken
part in left-wing movements in many countries, was working in the
Soviet Union in the mid-twenties. He joined the Trotskyists and ultimately was arrested and sent into internal exile. However, as a result of
a campaign in France in defense of Serge, he was deported from the
Soviet Union in 1935. During World War II Serge was in North Africa,
where he wrote his memoirs. In them he claimed that Trotsky could
have easily defeated Stalin in 1924 if he had relied on the army.

[A] coup against the Politburo of Zinoviev, Kamenev, and Stalin would have
been possible, and in our Oppositional circles we had weighed this possibility.
The army and even the G.P.U. would have plumped for Trotsky if he had wished;
he was always being told this. . . . I do know that the question was discussed . . .
[and] that Trotsky deliberately refused power, out of respect for an unwritten law
that forbade recourse to military mutiny within a socialist regime; for it was all
too likely that power won in this way, even with the noblest intentions, would
eventually finish in a military and police dictatorship, which was anti-Socialist by
definition. Trotsky wrote later (in 1935):

"No doubt a military coup against the Zinoviev-Kamenev Stalin faction would
have presented no difficulty and even caused no bloodshed; but its consequences

66. Some party documents and speeches contain references to a letter from Vladimir
Antonov-Ovseyenko to the Central Committee threatening to "call to order the leaders
who have gone to far" (see, for example, Stalin, *Sochineniia*, 6:43). Anton Antonov-Ovseyenko, son of the deposed head of the Political Directorate, in his book *The Time of Stalin:
Portrait of a Tyranny* (New York, 1981) (Russian ed., *Portret tirana* [New York, 1980]),
gives more details about his father's letter, including the following alleged quotation: "This
cannot go on for long. There remains one alternative—*to appeal to the peasant masses
dressed in Red Army greatcoats* and call to order the leaders who have gone too far."
(Emphasis added.) Anton Antonov-Ovseyenko cites the unpublished memoirs of Mikhail
Polyak, apparently a member of the staff of the Political Directorate. However, some Old
Bolsheviks, such as A. V. Snegov, regard this source as inadequate and question whether
Vladimir Antonov-Ovseyenko would have used a formulation such as the one here empha-
sized.

would have been a speedier triumph for the very bureaucracy and Bonapartism against which the Left Opposition took its stand."[67]

If Trotsky in 1924 thought as he wrote in 1935, it would have been one more of his illusions. Attempts at military intervention in party affairs could not be dismissed, and just as Trotsky was sometimes capable of thinking about this, we can assume with all the more certainty that Zinoviev, Kamenev, and Stalin kept the possibility in mind as well. But a military ouster of the triumvirate and the party apparatus loyal to it would have been an extremely difficult and uncertain undertaking—an adventure with very little chance of success. If Trotsky refrained from such a step, one can assume that what held him back was not concern over Bonapartism but uncertainty of his control over the Red Army.

The German edition of Serge's memoirs contains a foreword by the prominent German revolutionary Erich Wollenberg, who went to live in the Soviet Union after the failure of the German revolution and who in the thirties fled to the West from the persecution of the NKVD and Gestapo. Wollenberg convincingly disputes the version of events presented by Serge.

What a colossal mistake in assessing the concrete situation that had arisen in the land of the Soviets within a few months after Lenin's death! I must add that at the time Lenin died I was still on military duty in Germany. As a specialist in civil war I held a prominent post in the German Communist Party. At that time I thought along more or less the same lines as Serge and as Trotsky apparently thought about all these matters for another decade or more.

But when I moved to Moscow, I saw my error. In Moscow I was forced to realize that the leading figures on the Red Army general staff, such as Tukhachevsky, with whom I became friends, admired Trotsky greatly as the organizer of the Red Army, as a man and a revolutionary, but at the same time they took a critical attitude toward his general political position.

I was at that time, from 1924 to 1926, a unit commander in the Red Army, at first in the provinces . . . and then in Moscow, in the First Red Proletarian Regiment. Later I was at the disposal of the general staff and was a member of the Presidium of the Central House of the Red Army. I had very close contact with the army in general, and through it, with the Russian village. There could

67. Victor Serge, *Memoirs of a Revolutionary* (New York, 1963), pp. 234–235. Serge died in 1947. His memoirs were first published in France in 1951. [The author cites the German edition of Serge's memoirs, *Erinnerungen Revolutionärs 1901–1941* (Wiener Neustadt, 1974)—G. S.] Victor Serge does not give the source of the remarks by Trotsky that he cites. [The source is the article "Kak Stalin pobedil Oppozitsiiu?" (How Did Stalin Defeat the Opposition?), *Biulleten' oppozitsii* no. 46, December 1935. For an English translation see *Writings of Leon Trotsky, 1935–36* (New York, 1977), pp. 171–179.—G. S.]

be no doubt that the top military command had full confidence in the party leadership. . . . And in the entire party there was an unquestionable majority in favor of the triumvirate, that is, the leading threesome formed after Lenin's death: Zinoviev, Kamenev, and Stalin. This was the order in which the importance of the three members was estimated at the time—with Stalin last.

If the Soviet constitution could have been changed for a plebiscite to be held, it is impossible to say which of Lenin's successors would have gathered the most votes. But it can be said for certain that, given the hostility of the peasants and the middle class (which was reappearing in the first half of the 1920s) in relation to Trotsky, who was considered an "enemy of NEP," the outcome would have been rather unfavorable for him.

It is necessary to state this with full clarity because to this day Trotskyists of all varieties, as well as Soviet experts in West Germany and other countries, continue to spread the tale in speech, in print, on radio and on television that after Lenin's death Trotsky supposedly missed a "sure bet." Apparently Victor Serge too believed this right up to his death.[68]

■ 5

A FEW WORDS ON ZINOVIEV AND KAMENEV

Almost immediately after the defeat of the Trotskyist Left Opposition there arose a "new," or "Leningrad," opposition headed by Zinoviev and Kamenev, about whom I shall speak briefly.

Grigory Yevseevich Zinoviev (Radomyslsky) was born in 1883 in the city of Yelisavetgrad in the province of Kherson to the family of a small Jewish entrepreneur. Having received his education at home, the young Zinoviev worked for some time as a clerk in large commercial businesses. In the late 1890s he took part in Social Democratic study groups, but in 1902 he emigrated and studied for some time at the University of Bern in Switzerland. It was there that the twenty-year-old Zinoviev became acquainted with Lenin, and when the split occurred in the RSDLP, Zinoviev took a firm stand with the Bolsheviks.

Zinoviev returned to Russia soon after the beginning of the 1905 revolution. He was active as an agitator and propagandist among the metalworkers in St. Petersburg and was elected to the St. Petersburg party committee. As a delegate from the St. Petersburg organization, Zinoviev took part in the Fifth (London) Party Congress and at this congress was chosen to be a member of the Central Committee. Having

68. Serge, *Errinerungen Revolutionärs*, pp. xi–xii. The foreword to Serge's book was the last work written by Wollenberg, who died in November 1973 at the age of 81.

returned to Russia again, Zinoviev was arrested in the spring of 1908. But he spent only about three months in jail. The tsarist Okhrana knew nearly nothing about Zinoviev and his role in the party. Therefore he was soon released under police surveillance.

Zinoviev again emigrated and remained abroad until 1917. There he took part in all of Lenin's undertakings, in particular serving on the editorial boards of the Bolshevik newspaper *Proletary* (Proletarian) and magazine *Sotsial-demokrat* (Social Democrat). Zinoviev proved himself to be a rather good propagandist and a talented polemicist, although to his acquaintances among the revolutionaries he never gave the impression of an outstanding political figure.

This is what Mikhail Yakubovich says about him in his memoirs:

The appearance of this name was news to the whole party. When the collection of articles "Against the Current" came out, on the cover stood the names of two authors—Lenin and Zinoviev. The fact that Zinoviev's name stood next to Lenin's promoted him to the front ranks. The party paid attention to him and began to listen to this party activist. The impression [that he was a figure of some importance] was strengthened when Lenin decided to organize a party school outside Paris at Longjumeau. The Longjumeau school was founded to counter the party school on Capri, begun by a group of Bolsheviks who disagreed with Lenin on a number of questions, partly political but mostly philosophical. The Capri school was headed by Aleksandr Bogdanov, an outstanding individual, whose only equal in education and talent in the party was Lenin. . . .

It was necessary to find a director for the Longjumeau school of the sort who could serve as a counterbalance to Bogdanov. Lenin's choice fell on Zinoviev. This choice surprised the Social Democrats to some degree . . . but it immediately established Zinoviev as a name in the party. Many were surprised that Lenin promoted him, and the Mensheviks treated him with great irritation because Zinoviev was a true disciple of Lenin's. Lenin was harsh in his polemics with ideological opponents; he never liked to use a conciliatory tone or to gloss over conflicts; he made a definite point of any disagreements he had with other party figures. . . . But Zinoviev, who adopted Lenin's categorical manner, carried it even farther, his polemical formulations being even harsher than Lenin's. It may be said that the Mensheviks hated Zinoviev and treated him like "Lenin's attack dog," who had been turned loose on them. That was how Zinoviev was viewed up until World War I. Everyone regarded him as Lenin's protégé, an apprentice whom Lenin had brought into the political arena. And, of course, that really was the case.[69]

69. Mikhail P. Yakubovich, "Vospominaniia o Zinovieve," unpublished manuscript. Yakubovich is also the author of interesting memoirs about Trotsky, Stalin, and Kamenev, and the events of 1917, under the general title "From the History of Ideas" ("Iz istorii idei"). Some parts of these memoirs were published in *Samizdat Register* (New York, 1977) and *Samizdat Register 2* (New York, 1981).

During this time Lenin treated Zinoviev with much warmth, as his closest disciple and aide. During the émigré years there were no disagreements between them. Zinoviev wrote a great deal in the émigré press, and also in *Pravda* after 1912. His articles were harsh and often rude, but they did not exhibit originality or theoretical independence. In this respect Zinoviev was short on both education and talent, but he made up in ambition for what he lacked in these other areas. It should also be noted that while he was abroad with Lenin, Zinoviev established many connections among Western European Social Democrats. He and Lenin took part in the Zimmerwald Conference, and both became members of the Zimmerwald Left.

After the February revolution Zinoviev returned to Russia with Lenin and immediately became a member of the newly elected Central Committee of the Bolshevik Party. After the July events Lenin and Zinoviev went underground. For a month they lived in the now famous "hunter's shack" not far from the Razliv station on the coastal railway outside Petrograd. In August Lenin moved to Finland, but Zinoviev remained underground in Petrograd. During the discussion on the question of armed insurrection, as has been noted, Zinoviev took a stand, with Kamenev, against Lenin and the majority of the Central Committee. Zinoviev published his objections in Maxim Gorky's nonparty newspaper *Novaya zhizn* (New Life) a few days before the insurrection. Lenin's rage on this occasion would be difficult to describe. He called Zinoviev and Kamenev "traitors and strikebreakers of the revolution" and demanded their expulsion from the party. Although during the weeks that followed Zinoviev and Kamenev admitted their mistake and were therefore not expelled, this "October episode" remained, as we have seen, an indelible blot on their reputations in the party.

Nevertheless, as early as the end of 1917 Zinoviev was elected chairman of the Petrograd Soviet. When the Soviet government moved to Moscow Zinoviev remained in Petrograd, where the Petrograd Commune of Labor was founded at the end of February 1918. This commune then became a part of the Union of Communes of the Northern Region, and Zinoviev remained the leader of this so-called Northern Commune.

The influence of the bourgeois elements and groups in Petrograd, the former capital of the country, was still very strong. However, in the struggle against the counterrevolution Zinoviev quite often displayed unwarranted rigor and cruelty, to which even the chairman of the Petrograd Cheka, Uritsky, felt obliged to object. After the assassination of

Uritsky and the attempt on Lenin's life by the SR Fanya Kaplan, the Red Terror raged with more fury in Petrograd than in any other city of Soviet Russia. The shooting of hostages was also a common practice there. Thus, for example, issue Number 5 of *Yezhenedelnik ChK* (The Cheka Weekly), dated October 20, 1918, contains the following brief report: "By order of the Petrograd Cheka five-hundred hostages have been shot."[70]

In his recollections Yakubovich writes further:

In the fall of 1918 Zinoviev employed mass terror and executed many people who obviously could not have taken part in terrorist measures against Soviet power, but who, because they belonged to the former ruling class, were marked for destruction. In Leningrad at that time many more people were executed than in other cities. It seems to me that Zinoviev's aggressive behavior was not dictated by calm analysis, nor by the conviction that there was no other way out. . . . Zinoviev fell into a state of panic. It is exactly this mood that explains the excessive measures of repression he employed in Petrograd, far exceeding those employed by Dzerzhinsky in Moscow. Zinoviev resorted to these measures in a state of despair; it seemed to him that the revolution was about to perish. All this was a manifestation of his pusillanimity, which we would see him display more than once if we were to trace his historical fate.[71]

Similarly, N. Verberova writes of Zinoviev in her memoirs:

It is hard now to imagine what unparalleled power was in the hands of this man who at the time of the October revolution stood in third place in the Bolshevik hierarchy after Lenin and Trotsky, leaving far behind such figures as Kamenev, Lunacharsky, Chicherin, and Dzerzhinsky. In *Petrogradskaya pravda* every morning Zinoviev would write: "I approve this," "I order that," "I forbid this," "I will punish mercilessly," "I will not tolerate—." And behind these words one felt the monstrous apparatus that supported him and the incredible power he wielded, giving neither himself nor others a moment's rest. Everything he did would of course receive approval from the Kremlin after the fact, and he knew that. He had been with Lenin in Switzerland, with Lenin he had traveled through Germany to Petrograd, and now he was the one-man dictator of the north of Russia, relying on the mighty apparatus of the Cheka built up by Uritsky. But Uritsky had been gone for a year. Because of Uritsky's assassination alone, a thousand people had been shot. But Uritsky had deputies to replace him."[72]

When the White forces of General Yudenich began to approach Petrograd, Zinoviev proved unable to organize the defense of the city. A threatening situation was developing as early as the summer of 1919.

70. *Yezhenedelnik ChK*, 1918, no. 5, p. 24. This magazine was published for a short time by a division of the Cheka.
71. Yakubovich, "Vospominaniia o Zinovieve."
72. N. Verberova, *Zheleznaia zhenshchina* (New York, 1981), pp. 124–125.

Seeing Zinoviev's inability, Lenin sent Stalin to Petrograd, and he helped turn the situation around. Yudenich's army retreated, but it was still not defeated. It began a new offensive against Petrograd in the fall of 1919, simultaneously with Denikin's attack on Moscow. Yudenich's detachments broke through to the outskirts of the city. Again Zinoviev fell into a panic and began preparing the city for evacuation. Trotsky arrived to lead the defense of Petrograd, which he later described in his memoirs:

> In Petrograd I found the leaders in a state of utmost demoralization. Everything was slipping. The troops were falling back and breaking up into separate units. The commanding officers looked to the communists, the communists to Zinoviev, and Zinoviev was the very center of utter confusion. Sverdlov said to me: "Zinoviev is panic itself." And Sverdlov knew men. In favorable periods, when, in Lenin's phrase, "there was nothing to fear," Zinoviev climbed easily to the seventh heaven. But when things took a bad turn, he usually stretched himself out on a sofa—literally, not metaphorically—and sighed. . . . This time I found him on the sofa. And yet there were brave men about him—Lashevich, for example—but even their hands hung limp. . . . [Apathy,] hopelessness, and submission to fate had infected even the lower ranks of the administrative staff.[73]

Trotsky took over the defense of Petrograd, removing Zinoviev from any important aspect of the operation. The conflict that arose between them then made them personal enemies for a long time after.

Lenin, however, did not expect military exploits from Zinoviev, seeking rather to use his abilities in a different field. After the founding of the Third, or Communist, International Zinoviev was elected, on Lenin's recommendation, chairman of the Executive Committee of the Communist International (ECCI). During this time Zinoviev remained a member of the Politburo and chairman of the Petrograd Soviet (which later became the Leningrad Soviet) and of the Executive Committee of the Soviets of Petrograd province. In 1920 he successfully spoke at the congress of the German Independent Social Democrats in Halle and led the Congress of the Peoples of the East in Baku. Zinoviev was a speaker at all of the first Comintern and party congresses. It would therefore be incorrect to deny Zinoviev some merit as a revolutionary. However, many people who knew Zinoviev well pointed out, not without some basis, not only his great energy but also his lack of endurance, unscrupulousness, inclination toward demagogy, and his exceptional ambition and vanity. He was a man who won little true sympathy from anyone.

Lev Borisovich Kamenev (Rozenfeld) was also born in 1883. At that

73. Trotsky, *My Life*, p. 427.

time his parents lived in Moscow, where Kamenev's father was a locomotive engineer on the Moscow-Kursk railway line. After graduating from the Engineering Institute in St. Petersburg, Kamenev's father began working as chief engineer at a small factory in Vilna province. Later he was given a post on the Transcaucasian railways. During the young Kamenev's last years at a Tiflis *gymnasium* he took part in the activities of some Marxist study groups. In 1901 he entered the law school at Moscow University. Kamenev was arrested for his participation in student strikes and demonstrations, expelled from the university, and sent back to his parents in Tiflis.

Soon he left for Paris, where he met Lenin, who became a lasting influence on him. After the Second Party Congress Kamenev joined the Bolsheviks. Returning to Tiflis, he became a member of the Caucasus Union Committee, to which Stalin also belonged. As a representative of the Caucasian organization, Kamenev (under the alias of "Gradov") took part in the Fifth (London) Party Congress, and after the congress, on assignment for the party, he visited many cities in Russia. During the revolution of 1905–1907 he spent much of his time in St. Petersburg working directly under Lenin. He wrote a great deal, contributing to almost all legal and illegal Social Democratic publications. After the defeat of the first Russian revolution Kamenev emigrated and for a few years was active in the group of Bolsheviks that made up Lenin's closest circle.

In 1914 Kamenev was assigned by the party to return to St. Petersburg to direct *Pravda* and the work of the Bolshevik Duma group. A few months after the beginning of World War I Kamenev was arrested and a year later appeared before the judges of the St. Petersburg judicial chamber together with the Bolshevik deputies to the Duma. Under wartime regulations the arrested Bolsheviks theoretically were faced with the death penalty. At the trial Kamenev behaved in a cowardly fashion, stating that he disagreed with Lenin's slogan favoring "the defeat of one's own imperialist government." His behavior aroused sharp criticism among the Bolsheviks. He was sentenced to exile in Siberia.

I mentioned earlier the differences between Kamenev's and Lenin's positions in March and April of 1917. It must be pointed out, however, that it was Kamenev who presided over the Bolshevik conference in April and at this conference was elected to the Central Committee on Lenin's recommendation. Defending Kamenev's candidacy, Lenin said that his debates with Kamenev enabled the party to better recognize the erroneous opinions that existed among some of the Bolsheviks and in this way to develop more convincing arguments to rally the party and the working class around correct slogans. It is true that in October 1917 Lenin demanded the expulsion of Kamenev and Zinoviev from the party. But those were the decisive days of the revolution, and it was no longer a question of theoretical differences but of the behavior of two Central Committee members who had endangered the entire cause of the Bolshevik Party. Having admitted his mistakes, Kamenev remained in the party. Moreover, it was he who was elected, on Lenin's recommendation, chairman of the Second Congress of Soviets, which approved the first decrees of the Soviet government. Kamenev was elected chairman of the Central Executive Committee for a short time and served as the first formal head of the Soviet government. Because of his disagreements with the Central Committee, however, he was recalled from that post and replaced by Sverdlov.

In 1918 Kamenev took the post of chairman of the Moscow Soviet. He went to the fronts of the civil war several times as a representative of the Council of Defense. Lenin appraised Kamenev's activity in the post-October period very favorably. In 1922, in his last public speech, Lenin called Kamenev a "superb work horse" who simultaneously pulled two carts: the work in the Moscow Soviet and that in the Sovnarkom, to which Kamenev was appointed in 1922, on Lenin's recommendation, to serve as his deputy. As Yakubovich writes in his memoirs:

Kamenev was without question a highly talented man, widely and liberally educated, devoted to the cause of socialist revolution, and able to quickly find his bearings in a complicated political situation. He also possessed an outstanding literary talent. Lenin recognized all this. . . . That is why he valued Kamenev so highly. And that is why, in particular, he repeatedly assigned Kamenev to preside at party congresses and conferences. Kamenev was a great master of formulations —no one else was able to formulate the conclusions of a discussion as clearly and precisely and record them as objectively as he.[74]

Lenin's confidence in Kamenev as a theorist is evidenced by the fact that in July 1917, when Lenin was in hiding, he asked Kamenev, "in case they do me in," to publish his notebook on the state—that is, *State and Revolution*.[75]

74. Yakubovich, "L. B. Kamenev," unpublished manuscript.
75. See Lenin, CW, 36: 454. [The author cites Kamenev's "authorized biography," which appeared in the Russian-language Granat Encyclopedia, *Entsiklopedicheskii slovar' russkogo bibliograficheskogo Instituta Granata*, 7th ed., Moscow, 1927–29. vol. 41: "Deia-

Kamenev was the chief editor of the first edition of Lenin's *Collected Works*. When Lenin became ill in 1922–1923 he entrusted his personal archives to Kamenev. From these the Lenin Institute later arose, with Kamenev as its first director. In 1923–1924 Kamenev presided at meetings of both the Sovnarkom and the Politburo. But Kamenev was not ambitious; he was pliable and gentle. He was obviously superior to Stalin and Zinoviev as a theorist, but ranked below them as a political maneuverer and as an administrator. This was what determined Zinoviev's leading role in the bloc he and Kamenev formed.

■ 6

THE "NEW OPPOSITION"

Lenin's death and the Thirteenth Party Congress not long after it brought some changes in the positions of the main figures in the Soviet leadership, which at the time seemed insignificant. The appointment of a new chairman of the Council of Peoples' Commissars (Sovnarkom) was the first order of business. There were only two candidates: Kamenev and Rykov. Kamenev had no desire for the post, although he had usually chaired Sovnarkom meetings during Lenin's illness. Rykov's candidacy was approved without any disagreements in the Politburo. At the time Kamenev's Jewish background was given as one of the reasons for not choosing him. "We must take into account the peasant character of Russia," Stalin stated during the discussion of the question. Kamenev was appointed chairman of the Council of Labor and Defense, a body established during the civil war and subordinate to the Sovnarkom. Its function was to coordinate all government departments related to defense and economic construction. Only a few of the people's commissars attended meetings of this body, along with representatives of the unions and the statistical agency.

As I have noted, Stalin remained general secretary after the Thirteenth Congress. After two years in this post his power and authority had noticeably increased. No longer was he an inconspicuous figure. He put considerable effort into building up the party apparatus, making it more and more his own. Besides this, the fight against the Trotskyist opposition not only had weakened Trotsky's political authority, but had under-

teli SSSR i Oktiabrskoi revoliutsii"), pt. 1, p. 167. An English translation of the Kamenev biography is in Georges Haupt and Jean-Jacques Marie, *Makers of the Russian Revolution: Biographies of Bolshevik Leaders* (Ithaca, N.Y., 1974), pp. 41–47. —G. S.]

mined the authority of Zinoviev and Kamenev, against whom Trotsky had dealt his main blows.

Bukharin was elected to fill the seat on the Politburo left vacant by Lenin's death. Thus, at the end of 1924 the full voting members of the Politburo were Bukharin, Kamenev, Rykov, Stalin, Tomsky, Trotsky, and Zinoviev. On all major question of domestic and foreign policy, Rykov, Tomsky, and Bukharin supported Stalin, who now had the opportunity to free himself from the tutelage of Zinoviev and Kamenev. In fact immediately after the Thirteenth Congress Stalin took steps to begin forcing Zinoviev and Kamenev out of the leading position in the triumvirate. The former friendship among the triumvirs quickly faded.

Within a few weeks after the Thirteenth Congress *Pravda* published Stalin's report, "The Results of the Thirteenth Congress," delivered at a Central Committee educational institution for secretaries of district party committees, in which he accused Kamenev of displaying his "usual carelessness regarding questions of theory, regarding exact theoretical definitions." The basis for this charge was that in Kamenev's report at the congress a quotation from Lenin had been distorted. Lenin had spoken of the transformation of "NEP Russia into a socialist Russia." Instead of *nepovskaya Rossiya* (NEP Russia) *Pravda* had printed *nepmanovskaya Rossiya* (Nepman Russia). Stalin argued that there was no such thing as "Nepman Russia" nor could there be. In fact the error was the result of carelessness by the stenographer and proofreaders, as *Pravda* explained a few days later. Stalin's report also contained an attack on Zinoviev, though without naming him:

It is often said that we have the dictatorship of the party. I recall that in one of our resolutions, even, it seems, a resolution of the Twelfth Congress, such an expression was allowed to pass, through an oversight of course. Apparently some comrades think that we have a dictatorship of the party and not of the working class. But that is nonsense, comrades.[76]

Of course Stalin knew perfectly well that Zinoviev in his political report to the Twelfth Congress had put forward the concept of the dictatorship of the party and had sought to substantiate it. It was not at all through an oversight that the phrase was included in the unanimously adopted resolution of the congress.

Zinoviev and Kamenev, reacting quite sharply to Stalin's thrusts, insisted that a conference of the core leadership of the party be convened.

76. Stalin, *Sochineniia*, 6:257, 258.

The result was a gathering of twenty-five Central Committee members, including all members of the Politburo. Stalin's arguments against the "dictatorship of the party" were rejected by a majority vote, and an article by Zinoviev reaffirming the concept was approved for publication in the August 23, 1924 issue of *Pravda* as a statement by the editors. At this point Stalin demosntratively offered to resign, but the offer was refused. A resolution was passed requiring all top leaders of the party to coordinate their actions and speeches with one another.

In the fall of 1924 Stalin did some cautious reshuffling of the party apparatus intended to weaken Zinoviev and Kamenev. Their supporter I. A. Zelensky was assigned to serve as secretary of the Central Asian Bureau of the Central Committee. For several years before that he had headed the Moscow party organization and in 1924 had been added to the Orgburo and Secretariat. His place in Moscow was taken by Nikolai Uglanov, who was by no means inclined to give unquestioning support to Kamenev and Zinoviev. Three men were chosen to be Central Committee secretaries after the Thirteenth Congress—Molotov, Kaganovich, and Andreyev; all of them followed Stalin's leadership unquestioningly.

A more serious struggle ensued in the Central Committee over the fate of Trotsky, who had already been defeated politically. Zinoviev and Kamenev demanded the expulsion of Trotsky and his closet associates from the party. On this question Stalin opposed his recent allies, and the majority of the Central Committee agreed with Stalin. Trotsky was not expelled; indeed, he remained a member of the Central Committee and the Politburo. Foreseeing a clash with Zinoviev and Kamenev, Stalin wished to neutralize Trotsky and the Trotskyists. He later said:

We did not agree with comrades Zinoviev and Kamenev because we knew that a policy of cutting off members was fraught with great dangers for the party, that the method of cutting off, the method of bloodletting—and they were asking for blood—is dangerous and contagious. Today one person is cut off, tomorrow another, the next day a third—but what will remain of the party?[77]

Most party officials were impressed by this point of view.

Zinoviev and Kamenev tried to pressure the Politburo through the leadership of the Komsomol, the majority of which consisted of their supporters. The Komsomol Central Committee passed a surprise resolution demanding the removal of Trotsky from the Politburo. The Politburo

77. Stalin, *Sochineniia*, 7:379–380.

gave a speedy reply: fifteen members of the Komsomol Central Committee were removed. All these episodes marked the collapse of the triumvirate.

For the most part these differences in the Politburo were over secondary questions, but gradually disagreements over fundamental questions emerged. In the years 1924–1925 an important shift in party policy toward the countryside was implemented. In essence this meant the elimination of the remaining vestiges of war communism and the encouragement of agricultural development within the framework of a more consistent application of the New Economic Policy. The hiring of agricultural workers was legalized, and restrictions on the renting of land were relaxed. Many administrative limitations on private capitalist (kulak) agriculture were lifted. In addition, the agricultural tax was lowered and prices for manufactured goods were reduced. The main aim of these measures was to revive the economic activity of the middle peasant, the central figure in the Soviet countryside. The well-to-do elements in the rural areas also benefited from these decisions, but so did the Soviet Union as a whole, because the production of foodstuffs and raw materials for light industry increased. The gross output of agriculture soon surpassed the 1913 level and continued to grow.[78]

As a whole the Central Committee's new decisions on agriculture and rural problems were correct, fully in keeping with the New Economic Policy. The only criticism one could make was that some decisions were premature. For example, the lowering of prices for manufactured goods, while the shortage of such goods continued, together with the reduction of the agricultural tax, resulted in an increase in the amount of money in the rural areas—that is, an increase in unsatisfied demand.

The main role in providing theoretical justification for the new agricultural policy belonged to Bukharin, who was supported in almost all respects by Rykov. They often formulated their proposals with a candor and consistency that shocked more orthodox Bolsheviks, who were accustomed to using the terms "kulak," "merchant," and "wealthy peasant" as synonyms for "enemy of the proletariat." Rykov, for example, at the Fourteenth Party Conference in the spring of 1925, called for renunciation of any administrative forms of pressure whatsoever against the kulak in general or against private capital in the urban areas. Rykov held that it

---

78. In 1926 gross agricultural output exceeded the level of 1913, a good harvest year, by 18 percent; and in 1927, by 21 percent. See *Narodnoe khoziaistvo SSSR, 1922–1972. Iubileinyi statisticheskii spravochnik* (Moscow, 1972), p. 119.

was necessary and possible to take the same attitude toward the kulak as toward the middle peasant—that is, not to squeeze him by administrative measures or put pressure on him.

This did not mean, of course, renunciation of various means of exerting economic control and pressure (for example, the tax system). The same point of view was expounded in more detail by Bukharin. At the same conference, criticizing the idea of an intensification of the class struggle in the village, Bukharin advanced the idea of peaceful development.

What elements will be in the village? The cooperatives of the poor peasants—the collective farms. The cooperatives of the middle peasants in the areas of sales, purchase, credit, etc. In some places there will also be kulak cooperatives, which will be based on credit associations. This whole ladder will merge into the system of our banks, our credit institutions, and together with them into the system of our economic institutions in general. What will we end up with in general? In general it will turn out that if the kulak grows over into the general system, that will be an element of state capitalism; if the poor peasant and middle peasant do so, that will be the very type of socialist cooperative that Vladimir Ilyich discussed. It will be a scene of many colors.[79]

A few months later Bukharin carried these ideas further in "The Road to Socialism and the Worker-Peasant Alliance":

Previously in one form or another we took from the well-to-do and from the kulaks and gave what we took to the poor peasants; that is, the well-to-do were made poorer, and in this way we achieved a certain equalization, as, for example, at the time of the Poor Peasant Committees. Now things will be different: namely, the middle peasant and poor peasant will more and more quickly work their way out of poverty with the help of their cooperative organizations, which enjoy special patronage and privileges—provided by the state power of the working class.

The more the economy as a whole moves forward, . . . the more powerful will become the support of these very sections of the peasantry, who will catch up with the well-to-do strata of the village in their standard of living but who will at the same time not be growing at the expense of the labor of others but through improved technique, through the upgrading of their farms, and through the united efforts of multiple peasant households through the cooperative organizations, which will consequently pass over into every more collective forms of management. Thus the basic network of our cooperative organizations will consist of cells not of the kulak type but of the laboring peasant type, cells growing over into our system of statewide government agencies and thereby becoming links in a single chain of socialist economy. On the other hand, the kulak nests in the

79. *Chetyrnadtsataia konferentsiia RKP(b). Stenograficheskii otchet* (Fourteenth Party Conference: Stenographic Record) (Moscow 1925), p. 187.

cooperatives will in exactly the same way (through the banks and so forth) grow over into the same system; but to a certain extent they will be an alien body in the system, similar, for example, to the concessionary enterprises. What will become of this type of kulak cooperative in the future? . . . There will be nowhere for the kulaks and kulak organizations to go in spite of everything, because the general framework of development in our country has been determined in advance by the system of proletarian dictatorship and the already considerable power of the economic organizations of this dictatorship.[80]

Although Bukharin also spoke of the need for maximum encouragement of producers' cooperatives (that is, collective farms), he did not consider speedy growth of collective farming possible because of the peasants' attachment to their own private holdings. It was first necessary to develop all the potential of small-scale peasant farming; then it would be easier to draw the peasants into cooperative production, assuming, of course, material support by the state. In the conditions of 1925, in Bukharin's opinion, the collective farm could not yet serve as the "high road to socialism."

Bukharin's slogan, "Enrich yourselves," which aroused such bitter debate, also dates from this time. Speaking at a gathering of the active party membership of Moscow on April 17, 1925, not long before the Fourteenth Party Conference, Bukharin said:

Our policy toward the countryside should develop in the direction of relaxing and in part abolishing many restrictions that put the brake on the growth of well-to-do and kulak farms. To the peasants, to all the peasants, we must say: Enrich yourselves, develop your farms, and do not fear that restrictions will be put upon you.[81]

Bukharin very soon renounced this formulation, although in doing so he stressed that it was "an incorrect formulation of an absolutely correct idea." That idea was: "We do not hinder kulak accumulation, and we do not strive to organize the poor peasants for a second expropriation of the kulak."[82]

In fact, neither Bukharin's nor Rykov's views and statements contradicted the basic postulates of scientific socialism or the views of Lenin. Socialist construction was just beginning—in the context of a backward,

80. Nikolai Bukharin, *Put' k sotsializmu v Rossii: izbrannye proizvedeniia* (The Road to Socialism in Russia: Selected Works), Sidney Heitman, ed. (New York, 1967), p. 278.

81. *Bolshevik* (1925), no. 9–10, pp. 4–5. Bukharin's speech was published earlier in a somewhat different version in *Pravda*, April 24, 1925.

82. Bukharin, *Tekushchii moment nashei politiki* (The Current Aspect of Our Policies) (Moscow, 1925), p. 35. Bukharin was obliged to make such explanations more than once.

small-peasant country. There were no ready-made prescriptions or recipes. What was needed therefore was not dogma but discussion and exploration in various directions. The tendency represented by Bukharin and Rykov was one of the most forward looking. After all, had not Lenin said in 1921–1922 as well as in 1918 that Russia suffered not so much from capitalist development as from inadequate capitalist development? Lenin had favored the development of various forms of state capitalism, which he felt could continue for many years, given the conditions in Russia, without coming into conflict with socialism. Of course, neither Bukharin nor Rykov suggested that the kulaks would become supporters of socialism, but they did not think it dangerous if kulak farming expanded along state capitalist lines. What was necessary was not only to guard the purity of certain dogmatic conceptions but also to provide food for the entire country and to "pump over" into the state budget some of the capital accumulated by the wealthy section of the peasantry.

Lenin did not have time to give finished form to his views on the possible roads to socialism. His statements often contradicted one another. It was very hard to reconcile the ideas of Bukharin and Rykov with many of the statements Lenin made at the time when the party was switching over to war communism—that is, when the system of grain requisitioning, food detachments, and poor peasants' committees was being introduced (summer 1918)—and at the time of the severe crisis of war communism (summer and fall 1920). Zinoviev and Kamenev took advantage of this to attack the Bukharin-Rykov economic policy, which enjoyed the support of the majority of the Politburo at that time. Both sides based themselves on quotations from Lenin. For example, Lenin had said that NEP was a policy of "strategic retreat by the poletarian state," and Zinoviev reminded everyone of these words, commenting on them at length. Lenin had also said that NEP was being introduced seriously and for a long time and that it was a specific form of socialist development, implying that it was not only a retreat but also an advance for socialism. Bukharin emphasized these statements, quoting and commenting on them extensively. Stalin for the most part supported Bukharin, with whom he did not entirely agree. However, he strongly opposed Zinoviev and Kamenev, who not long before had presented themselves as defenders of the peasantry.

Zinoviev and Kamenev now accused the majority of the Central Committee of a "kulak deviation." They called for an intensification of administrative pressure on the kulaks, not a relaxation. Kamenev proposed that the tax burden on the well-to-do rural elements be increased by one to two hundred million rubles per year and that there be a one-time exaction of one billion rubles from the countryside for the needs of industrialization. Zinoviev and Kamenev obviously exaggerated the relative weight and influence of the kulaks in the postrevolutionary Soviet countryside. In the mid-twenties kulak households accounted for at most 4–5 percent of the total number of peasant households, as against 20 percent in 1917. Thus the opposition's concern about the kulak danger was greatly exaggerated. The Soviet Union needed marketable grain, and therefore Kamenev's proposals, which would have partly revived "war communism," were not simply incorrect; they were actually dangerous.

To better evaluate the differences that arose in the party on the peasant question, it is instructive to compare the views of Bukharin and his opponents on the expropriation of the kulaks. On the eve of the Fourteenth Party Conference Bukharin asserted that the Soviet government would not expropriate the kulaks or the upper strata of the urban bourgeoisie even after fifteen or twenty years but would compete with them economically. Yuri Larin, speaking at the Fourteenth Party Conference, challenged Bukharin's assertions:

> We openly admit that there are exploiters in our villages, and they may continue to exist for the time being because it is more advantageous for us that they exist openly and not in disguised form. To counteract this, we organize the poor peasants, raise the level of their farming, and ease the elements of their dependency [on the kulaks]. Later, however, in fifteen or twenty years, we will confiscate and expropriate the large private farms, when the time for this comes. We will certainly confiscate them after ten, fifteen, or twenty years if they don't deliver the goods, because—what else will we be able to do?[83]

This quotation clearly shows how poorly Bukharin as well as his opponents were able to foresee the real fate of the kulaks in the Soviet Union.

In the summer and fall of 1925 Zinoviev published a long, pretentious article, "The Philosophy of the Epoch," and a book entitled *Leninism*. Both were aimed indirectly against the theories and policies of Bukharin and Stalin. A number of imprecise formulations may be found in these two works, which came out well before the Fourteenth Party Congress, probably with the hope of influencing the decisions of that congress.[84] In these works Zinoviev discussed the general conception of the New Eco-

83. *Chetyrnadtsataia konferentsiia.* The speech by Larin.
84. At the Fourteenth Congress the official name of the party was changed from Russian Communist Party (Bolshevik) to All-Union Communist Party (Bolshevik).

nomic Policy and the definition of the term "state capitalism" and went on to characterize the main Soviet industrial enterprises as state capitalist. Zinoviev's views, mistaken in Bukharin's opinion, were criticized at length in the press by Bukharin, Rykov, and their supporters.

It must be supposed that Stalin looked on with pleasure as this polemic unfolded, for it gave him greater freedom of action. He clearly distanced himself from Bukharin's call to the peasants "to enrich themselves" and said that Bukharin should acknowledge his errors. However, on Stalin's insistence the Central Committee refused to allow publication of an article by Krupskaya criticizing Bukharin's slogan. Stalin also emphatically rejected Zinoviev's arguments that there was a "kulak deviation" in the leadership of the party. Without involving himself overly much in the economic discussion, Stalin took a strong stand as defender of the possibility of building socialism in one country—that is, in the Soviet Union.

I mentioned earlier Stalin's position on this question in his polemic against Trotsky. The views Zinoviev and Kamenev expressed on this matter came close to Trotsky's, although they were phrased more cautiously, with many reservations and qualifications. At a meeting of the Politburo, Zinoviev and Kamenev criticized Stalin, accusing him of underestimating the world revolution and of being limited to a purely national perspective. The majority of the Politburo did not support Zinoviev and Kamenev. Nevertheless, they continued to argue their views, mainly in the Leningrad press. The party apparatus of Leningrad and the northern regions was almost entirely handpicked by Zinoviev from among his close supporters; not surprisingly, then, the Leningrad press spoke up strongly in support of his position. All of Stalin's efforts to penetrate the Leningrad party apparatus with his own supporters were fruitless. The result was a phenomenon quite unusual in Soviet life: an open polemic between two units of the party, the Moscow Committee and the Leningrad Committee. For example, not long before the Fourteenth Party Congress, and obviously with Stalin's inspiration, the Moscow Committee published an open letter to its Leningrad colleagues, saying in part:

Not long ago Comrades Kamenev and Zinoviev defended the point of view in the Politburo that we cannot cope with our internal difficulties because of our economic backwardness unless we are saved by the international revolution. We, along with the majority of the Central Committee, on the other hand, think that we can build socialism, are building it, and shall continue to do so regardless of our technical backwardness and in spite of it. We think that this process will go much more slowly, of course, than under the conditions of a worldwide victory. Nevertheless we are proceeding along this path and shall continue to do so. In exactly the same way we assume that the point of view of Comrades Kamenev and Zinoviev expresses lack of confidence in the internal forces of our working class and the peasant masses who follow the workers. We say that this is a departure from Leninist positions.[85]

Up to that point, a general party discussion was usually announced before a party congress. However, by decision of the Politburo, over the objections of Kamenev and Zinoviev, a union-wide discussion was not held before the Fourteenth Congress. Open criticism of some aspects of the functioning of the Central Committee and personal criticism of Bukharin were expressed only at the Leningrad Party Conference, which elected delegates to the congress.

The Fourteenth Party Congress was held at the end of December 1925. Before the congress Stalin proposed a compromise to Zinoviev but on the condition that the Leningrad party organization come under Central Committee control and cease to be under Zinoviev's personal command. Zinoviev refused. But he did try to obtain guarantees that after the congress no repressive measures would be taken against members of this so-called "New Opposition" as long as they ceased any open oppositional activity. Stalin refused to give any such guarantees. Thus he provoked the New Opposition into presenting its platform directly to the party congress, although it had no chance of success. Zinoviev was a sufficiently experienced apparatchik to understand the situation; yet he demanded the right to present a minority report at the congress. The request was granted.

In the main political report from the Central Committee to the congress Stalin said nothing about the differences with the Zinoviev-Kamenev opposition. Recalling the party's victory over the Trotskyist opposition, Stalin continued:

Now we have entered, unfortunately, into a new stage of discussion. I am confident that the party will quickly overcome this discussion as well and that nothing special will happen. . . . In order not to anticipate events or harass individuals, I will not at the present moment go into the essence of the matter. . . . I think that the members of the congress themselves will say what needs to be said, and I will sum up in my concluding remarks.[86]

85. M. Mekler, *O pobede sotsializma v odnoi strane* (On the Victory of Socialism in One Country) (Leningrad, 1926), pp. 30–31.
86. Stalin, *Sochineniia*, 7:348.

Thus Stalin placed himself in a more advantageous position. He gave Zinoviev the chance to take the first step in the new internal dispute, leaving himself free to respond in his summary.

Zinoviev's minority report was quite weak, boring, and unconvincing. An experienced orator and polemicist, in this case he was not able to win over any of the delegates at the congress; only the Leningrad delegation applauded him. The position of the New Opposition was complicated further by the fact that on many theoretical questions prominent leaders of the opposition differed fundamentally from one another, as was reflected in their speeches at the Fourteenth Party Congress.

To be sure, the speeches of the opposition delegates contained many accurate observations. Their criticism of several measures taken by the Central Committee in the agricultural sphere were not unfounded. Their references to the growing harshness of the party regime, concealed under the slogan of party unity, were also pertinent. For example, Krupskaya, who openly supported Zinoviev and Kamenev, spoke at the congress against the stifling of internal party democracy, against the practice of removing oppositionists from leading positions in the party, and against the requirement that members of the opposition not only carry out all the decisions adopted by the majority but also renounce their own views and convictions immediately and publicly. As Krupskaya put it, Lenin never made such demands of his opponents. She rightly noted that even party congresses did not always make correct decisions. "The majority should not get carried away with the fact that it is a majority, but should impassionately seek the correct decision."[87] These remarks, however, were greeted by disapproving shouts from several delegates.

Today we must acknowledge the justness of warnings by several opposition delegates in regard to the danger of the growing cult of individual leaders, above all the cult of Stalin. Kamenev spoke most emphatically on this point, saying:

We are against the theory of creating a leader; we are against building up a leader. We are against the idea that the Secretariat, which in fact unites both politics and organization, should stand above the main political organ, that is the Politburo. . . . I personally think that our general secretary is not a figure who can unite the Old Bolshevik staff around himself. . . . Precisely because I have often said this to Comrade Stalin in person and precisely because I have frequently said this to a number of Leninist comrades, I repeat this at the congress:

87. *Chetyrnadtsatyi s"ezd VKP(b). Stenograficheskii otchet* (Fourteenth Party Congress: Stenographic Record) (Moscow, 1926), pp. 165–166.

I have come to the conclusion that Comrade Stalin cannot fulfill the role of uniting the Bolshevik general staff.[88]

If these words had been uttered at the previous party congress, the thirteenth, in the context of Lenin's Testament, which had just then become known, it is very unlikely that Stalin would have been able to keep his post as general secretary. However, at the Fourteenth Congress these remarks were interrupted by indignant cries from the majority of delegates. The stenographic record of the congress describes what happened next:

> (Voices from the floor: "Untrue." "Nonsense." "So that's what they're up to." "Now they've shown their hand." "We won't surrender the command posts to you." "Stalin! Stalin!" The delegates rise and salute Comrade Stalin. Stormy applause. Cries of "Here's where the party's united" and "The Bolshevik general staff must be united." "Long live Comrade Stalin." Prolonged stormy applause. Shouts of "Hurrah." General commotion.)[89]

It was precisely after the Fourteenth Congress that Stalin began to be singled out among the members of the Politburo.

As was to be expected, the New Opposition suffered complete defeat at the congress. The resolution based on Stalin's report for the Central Committee was adopted by 559 votes to 65.[90] In 1925 the party rejected Zinoviev and Kamenev's claims to leadership of the Central Committee just as it had rejected similar attempts by Trotsky in 1924.

Stalin's definitive victory over the New Opposition came immediately after the Fourteenth Congress. Over Zinoviev's objections the congress passed a special message "To All Members of the Leningrad Organization of the Party," condemning the behavior of the Leningrad delegation. "The opposition," it said, "exposed itself completely at the congress," and added:

> The congress appeals to all members of the Leningrad organization to put an end . . . to the attempts to undermine the unity of our Leninist party. . . . The Fourteenth Congress has no doubt that the Leningrad organization, which has always marched in the vanguard of the party ranks, will know how to correct the mistakes made by the Leningrad delegation.[91]

Immediately after the congress a large group of delegates, headed by Molotov, Kalinin, Voroshilov, Andreyev, Kirov, Mikoyan, and Ordzhon-

88. Ibid., pp. 274–275.
89. Ibid.
90. Ibid., p. 524.
91. Ibid., pp. 710–711.

ikidze, went to Leningrad to explain the decisions and resolutions of the congress. Zinoviev and his supporters took up the challenge and defended their positions at the meetings that were then held. It was an uneven battle, however, and the opposition soon lost. First, at a meeting of the party organization at the Putilov Works (a Bolshevik stronghold since the 1917 revolution, which the Zinovievists had controlled) a motion supporting the decisions of the congress was adopted. Then similar motions were passed at meetings of most of the base organizations of the party, at district party conferences, and finally at a provincewide party conference. A total of 96.3 percent of the participants at these meetings voted against the opposition. Only 3.2 percent voted for the opposition, and 0.5 percent abstained.[92] A new party committee was elected for Leningrad province, and a new Northwestern Bureau of the Central Committee—both headed by Sergei Kirov; and new leaderships were voted in all the district committees of the party and the Komsomol.

Changes were also made at the highest levels of the party leadership. Zinoviev was recalled from his post as chairman of the Executive Committee of the Communist International (ECCI). In fact, that post was abolished, and in its place a Secretariat of the ECCI was established, headed by Bukharin. Zinoviev was left on the Politburo, but Kamenev was reduced from full to candidate membership. He was also relieved of his post as chairman of the Council of Labor and Defense and as a deputy to the chairman of the Council of People's Commissars. After a short time Kamenev was appointed people's commissar of domestic and foreign trade. Voroshilov, Molotov, and Kalinin became full members of the Politburo. In this way Stalin assured himself of a decisive majority not only in the Secretariat but in the Politburo itself.

■ 7
THE DEATHS OF FRUNZE AND DZERZHINSKY

Stalin's position in the leadership of the country and the party was strengthened not only by the defeat of two oppositions (Trotsky's and Zinoviev-Kamenev's) but also by the unexpected deaths of two prominent Bolsheviks who occupied key posts in the Soviet government: Mikhail Frunze and Feliks Dzerzhinsky.

In January 1925 the well-known civil war commander Frunze was appointed chairman of the Revolutionary Military Council of the Repub-

92. *Leningradskaia pravda,* January 22, 1926.

lic and people's commissar of war in place of Trotsky, but he held the post for only a few months. Strong-willed and intelligent, Frunze enjoyed great influence not only in the army, but also in the party. He was a loyal member of the Central Committee, but neither Stalin nor Trotsky could consider him a personal supporter. After Frunze's unexpected death in October 1925 at the age of forty, Voroshilov was appointed to replace him. Voroshilov had been Stalin's close comrade-in-arms since the time of the defense of Tsaritsyn.

Frunze's unexpected death gave rise to many conflicting rumors. He had suffered from a stomach ulcer, which from time to time had disabled him. Any experienced doctor of the day would have known that in the case of a stomach ulcer one should first try a conservative treatment and only extreme cases resort to surgery. Indeed, Frunze had not wanted an operation, but preferred the conservative treatment—especially since the illness was not bothering him much in the fall of 1925. A letter Frunze wrote to his wife on October 26, 1925—five days before his death—contains the following passage:

Well, at last an end is coming to my sufferings—tomorrow morning I'm going into the hospital, and two days from now (on Thursday) I'll have an operation. When you receive this letter, you'll probably have in your hands a telegram notifying you of the results. I feel absolutely healthy right now, and it is somehow ridiculous not only to go for an operation but even to think about it. Yet both medical councils ordered it. Personally I'm satisfied with these decisions. Let them have a good look once and for all at what's there and try to prescribe a real treatment. More and more often the thought occurs to me that it's nothing serious, for otherwise it's rather hard to explain the fact of my quick recovery after rest and treatment.[93]

Inevitably the question arises, Why despite the obvious success of the conservative treatment did the medical councils order an operation? This can be explained only by outside pressure. It is well known that the question of Frunze's illness was discussed in the Politburo and that Stalin and Voroshilov insisted on an operation. In his letter to his wife Frunze was to some extent hiding his real feelings. He was not really satisfied with the doctors' decision. However, it placed him, a brave military man, in a difficult position: he did not want to be accused of fearfulness or indecision. The memoirs of his close friend, I. K. Gamburg, contain the following passage:

93. S. Sirotinsky, "Posledniye dni" (The Last Days), *Krasnaya zvezda* (Red Star), October 31, 1930. This article was written for the fifth anniversary of Frunze's death.

Not long before the operation I went to see Frunze. He was upset and said that he did not want to put himself on the operating table. . . . A premonition of some kind of trouble, something irreparable, oppressed him. . . . I tried to pursuade Frunze to refuse the operation since the thought of it oppressed him. But he shook his head. "Stalin insists on the operation; he says that I need to get rid of this ulcer once and for all. I have decided to go under the knife."[94]

The operation took place on the afternoon of October 29. Chloroform was used as the anaesthetic, although ether was already known to be more effective. According to Gamburg, Frunze did not fall completely asleep; the anaesthesia did not seem to work on him properly. Professor Rozanov, the director of the operation, made the decision to increase the chloroform to twice the normal dosage, which was extremely dangerous for the patient's heart. The operation began around two in the afternoon, and it immediately became evident that it was not necessary. The surgeons discovered nothing but a scar where the ulcer had healed. However, during the operation Frunze contracted peritonitis, for which no effective treatment was then known. The double dose of highly toxic chloroform also caused dystrophy in the muscles of the heart, kidneys, and liver. As a result of all this, his heart stopped two hours after the operation.[95]

The circumstances surrounding Frunze's unexpected death and the extremely confused and conflicting explanations of the doctors who led the consultation and operation caused widespread perplexity in party circles. The Ivanovo-Voznesensk Communists (with whom Frunze's revolutionary activity was closely connected) demanded that a special commission be formed to investigate the causes of his death. In mid-November 1925 the administrative board of the Society of Old Bolsheviks held a meeting regarding Frunze's death, chaired by Nikolai Podvoisky. Semashko, the people's commissar of health, was asked to attend. At the meeting it came out that neither the attending physician nor Professor Rozanov had been in a hurry to carry out the operation and that many of the members of the medical council that recommended it were not competent in the treatment of ulcers. The entire case was handled not by the People's Commissariat of Health, but by the medical commission of the Central Committee, some leaders of which Semashko spoke of with great disapproval. It also became known that before the consultation

---

94. I. K. Gamburg, *Tak eto bylo* (Moscow, 1965), pp. 181–182.
95. These medical conclusions and explanations were published in *Pravda*, November 1, 1925, and in *Pravda* and *Izvestia*, November 3, 1925.

Rozanov had called in Stalin and Zinoviev. After discussing the question, the administrative board of the Society of Old Bolsheviks passed a resolution condemning the disgraceful attitude toward the treatment of honored members of the party; it was agreed that this resolution would be brought before the party congress.

The question of Frunze's death was not discussed at the party congress after all, but in 1926 the fifth issue of the literary monthly *Novy mir* appeared with a story—Boris Pilnyak's "Tale of the Unextinguished Moon"—that clearly implicated Stalin in Frunze's death, although the preface gave the following disclaimer:

> The plot of this story may suggest to the reader that Frunze's death inspired it and provided the material for it. Personally I hardly knew Frunze; I was barely acquainted with him, maybe met him twice. . . . I find it necessary to inform the reader of this, so that the reader will not look in this story for real persons or events.

In reality the story was about Frunze, presented under the name Commander Gavrilov. Pilnyak displayed detailed knowledge of many circumstances surrounding the operation and Frunze's death and stated bluntly that the "order" for the operation came from "Number One, the unbending man," who "headed the triumvirate" which "ran everything in the country." It was not surprising that the entire printrun of the magazine was quickly confiscated. Only a few issues survived by accident.[96] In the next issue of *Novy mir* the editors admitted that publication of Pilnyak's story had been an "obvious and flagrant mistake."

Anton Antonov-Ovseyenko has no doubt that Frunze's death was a political act of elimination organized by Stalin.[97] Adam Ulam, the American historian and Sovietologist, in his book on Stalin emphatically rejects this version. He feels that the whole problem had to do with the poor organization of medical service in the Soviet Union in 1925. As early as Lenin's time the practice of party intervention in medical affairs had been introduced; obligatory rest or treatment was prescribed for many party leaders. Thus the Politburo's decision about Frunze's operation was not a rare exception. Ulam considers Pilnyak's story unquestionable slander and comments:

96. In 1965 Flagon Press in London published the Russian text of Pilnyak's story in pamphlet form under the title *Ubiistvo komandira* (The Killing of a Commander). [See author's introduction "Perestroika and Stalinism," for information on publication of this work in the USSR in 1987.]—G. S.

97. Antonov-Ovseyenko, *The Time of Stalin*, pp. 41–42.

It is probably that Pilnyak was put up to it by somebody who wanted to strike at Stalin. The remarkable thing is that nothing happened at the time to Pilnyak or to the editor. . . . Whether out of contempt for the slander or a calculated restraint, or both, Stalin chose not to react to a libel which even in a democratic society would have provided ample grounds for criminal proceedings against its author and publisher.[98]

In July 1926 Dzerzhinsky unexpectedly passed away. He had headed the Cheka since its founding, as well as its successor organization, the GPU; he also held the important post of chairman of the Supreme Economic Council. Dzerzhinsky was an independent political figure who not only enjoyed a great deal of respect in the party but also had considerable influence. For a short time Dzerzhinsky's death united all the groups in the party. At the funeral Trotsky, Zinoviev, Kamenev, Stalin, Bukharin, and Rykov together carried Dzerzhinsky's coffin onto Red Square.

Menzhinsky was appointed to replace Dzerzhinsky as head of the GPU, but he did not have Dzerzhinsky's weight and influence in the country and in the party. Menzhinsky was inclined to give in to Stalin's pressure. Moreover, he was often sick and therefore spent little time on GPU business. Among Menzhinsky's deputies, Yagoda, a protégé of Stalin's, soon became prominent.

■ 8

THE UNITED OPPOSITION, 1926–1927

In 1925 Trotsky and his none too numerous supporters took no part in the struggle between the majority of the Central Committee and the New Opposition. Although Zinoviev and Kamenev attacked Stalin and Bukharin from basically left positions, often repeating arguments made earlier by the Trotskyists, Trotsky still considered Zinoviev and Kamenev to be on "the right wing" of the party and his personal enemies. As a member of the Politburo Trotsky remained demonstratively aloof from the sharp disputes that arose more and more often after late 1924 between Stalin with his supporters, on the one hand, and Zinoviev and Kamenev, on the other. Sometimes Trotsky brought a French novel to the Politburo meetings and became so engrossed in his reading that he was oblivious to the discussions among the other members. As a political

98. Adam B. Ulam, *Stalin* (New York, 1973), pp. 260–261.

person, however, he could not maintain this sideline observer's attitude for long.

In the party and circles close to it rumors began to circulate in early 1925 about an unofficial meeting between Stalin and Trotsky, held, it was said, on Stalin's initiative. Stalin supposedly sought certain concessions from Trotsky in exchange for an end to the propaganda campaign against "Trotskyism" and a prominent post for Trotsky in the Soviet government. I do not exclude the possibility that such a meeting took place, despite the extreme personal animosity between the two men. For example, Trotsky did not object to a decision in April 1925 to have Tsaritsyn renamed Stalingrad. However, at that very time the American writer Max Eastman published a book, *Since Lenin Died*, in which he quoted long and accurate excerpts from Lenin's Testament and described the battle that had been going on within the Central Committee before and after Lenin's death. Only someone fairly close to Trotsky could have been the source of the information given to Eastman, who obviously sympathized with Trotsky. Yet Trotsky disavowed Eastman, accusing him of slander against Lenin and the Soviet Communist Party. A major statement to this effect, in which Trotsky openly lied, was published in the party's theoretical magazine.[99]

During the second half of 1925 the campaign against "Trotskyism" was definitely on the wane, although this obviously could be explained by the rise of the New Opposition. At the Fourteenth Party Congress Trotsky intended to speak against Zinoviev and Kamenev, but his friends persuaded him not to. When things came to a vote, Trotsky's supporters among the delegates did vote against the platform of Zinoviev and Kamenev. (Trotsky himself had only a consultative vote at the congress.)

After the Fourteenth Congress Trotsky could no longer remain aloof from the struggle. His closest supporters disagreed on what course to follow. Karl Radek, one of the most capable party writers and journalists, advised him to bloc with Stalin against Zinoviev and Kamenev. The Old Bolshevik, Leonid Serebryakov, who at the time held important posts in the rail transport system, recommended a coalition with Zinoviev and Kamenev. Sergei Mrachkovsky, a veteran revolutionary who had distinguished himself in the civil war, warned Trotsky against both "blocs." Trotsky decided to follow Serebryakov's advice, which coincided with his own opinion. As he wrote later:

99. *Bolshevik* (1925), no. 16.

Such questions are finally decided not by psychological but by political considerations. Zinoviev and Kamenev openly avowed that the "Trotskyists" had been right in the struggle against them since 1923. They accepted the basic principles of our platform. In such circumstances it was impossible not to form a bloc with them, especially since thousands of revolutionary workers were behind them.[100]

Even before the formal agreement among Trotsky, Zinoviev, and Kamenev, they and their adherents began to support one another at Politburo and Central Committee meetings. Finally, not without hesitation on both sides, a secret meeting was organized among Trotsky, Zinoviev, and Kamenev. This was their first meeting except at official occasions since early 1923. Other meetings followed, either at private apartments in the Kremlin or at Radek's apartment.

The initiative in these talks consistently came from Zinoviev and Kamenev. They sought to expose Stalin, but portrayed him as a not very dangerous opponent. Full of optimism, Zinoviev and Kamenev were sure that as soon as the party learned of the agreement between themselves and Trotsky, the majority would take their side. Kamenev himself declared to Trotsky on one occasion, "It is enough for you and Zinoviev to appear on the same platform, and the party will say, 'Here is our true Central Committee.' " Trotsky went along with these arguments. He was ready to fight for power in a bloc with Zinoviev. He did not say at this point that the very thought of a struggle for power made him shudder. True, he later claimed that he had not shared Zinoviev and Kamenev's illusions. But if the history of the United Opposition is examined, there is reason to doubt this. In taking the leadership of this opposition, Trotsky too hoped for success. He merely urged his allies not to hope for quick success, not to think, as he later wrote, that "all we need do was join hands and victory would drop at our feet like a ripe fruit. 'We must aim far ahead,' I repeated dozens of times to Zinoviev and Kamenev. 'We must prepare for a long and serious struggle.' On the spur of the moment my new allies accepted this formula bravely."[101]

The first joint action by the Trotskyists and Zinovievists was at the Central Committee plenum April 6–9, 1926, where they called for the drafting of plans for more intensive industrialization. Three months later the United Opposition submitted to the Central Committee and Central Control Commission a lengthy document presenting a critique of fundamental aspects of Soviet reality and the activity of the majority of the

100. Trotsky, *My Life*, p. 521.
101. Ibid., p. 522.

party leadership. The headings of the major sections of this document cleary suggest its content: "Bureaucratism as the Source of Factionalism," "Causes of the Growth of Bureaucratism," "Wage Problems," "The Question of Industrialization," "Policy in the Countryside," "Bureaucratic Deformations in the Workers' State," "Bureaucratic Deformations in the Party Apparatus," "Bureaucratism and the Everyday Life of Rank-and-File Workers," "The Fight for Peace," "The Comintern," "On Factionalism," and "For Unity." The document was signed by Trotsky, Zinoviev, Kamenev, Krupskaya, Bakayev, Lashevich, Muralov, and Pyatakov, among others.[102]

Not surprisingly the unification of these two groups in the party was accompanied by a mutual pardoning of sins. In 1923–1924 Zinoviev and Kamenev had used extremely harsh words against Trotsky and his platform. Zinoviev had rejected Trotsky's warnings about bureaucratization and deformations in the party and government apparatus as "slander." Kamenev had called for the party "to maintain its trenches in fighting order against the petty bourgeois influence of Trotsky." Even when Zinoviev and Kamenev organized the New Opposition they accused the Central Committee majority of conciliationism toward Trotsky and called the policy of the Central Committee "semi-Trotskyist." The opposition leaders began to speak quite differently in 1926. For example, Zinoviev said:

There was a sad time when instead of our two groups of genuine proletarian revolutionaries uniting against the backsliding Stalin and his friends, we fired at each other's heads for a couple of years, because of certain unclear aspects of the state of affairs in the party, something we regret very much and hope will never happen again.[103]

Trotsky, in turn, declared:

There is no question that in *Lessons of October* I connected the opportunist shifts in [party] policy with the names of Comrades Zinoviev and Kamenev. As the experience of the struggle of ideas inside the Central Committee attests, this was a gross error. The explanation for this error lies in the fact that I did not have

102. This document was not published in the Soviet press. [The author cites a German translation in *Die Linke Opposition*. A copy of the Russian text is in the Trotsky archives at Harvard University. For an English translation see *Challenge of the Left Opposition, 1926–27*, New York, 1980, pp. 73–92—G. S.]

103. Grigory Zinoviev, "Rech' na prezidiume TsKK 26 iiunia 1926 g." (Speech before the Presidium of the Central Control Commission, June 26, 1926), p. 62. [The author provides no further bibliographical information on this text.—G. S.]

the possibility of following the course of the battle of ideas within the septemvirate, nor to ascertain in time that the opportunist shifts were inspired by the group headed by Comrade Stalin, as opposed to Comrades Zinoviev and Kamenev.[104]

The unexpected alliance of Trotsky, Zinoviev, and Kamenev promised a new spate of party infighting. Yet the alliance did not improve the opposition's prospects. Had it been formed in 1923 or even 1924, Stalin probably could not have overcome it. In 1926 the opposition's fight for power was doomed. It is true that in the spring and early summer of 1926 the opposition leaders campaigned quite energetically, using conspiratorial methods for the most part. Representatives of the bloc were sent to dozens of cities to acquaint their supporters with the platform of the opposition, while illegal meetings of opposition supporters were held in many local areas, with new members being recruited to the opposition faction. One such illegal meeting, at which Lashevich spoke, was held secretly in a woods outside Moscow.

The first open confrontation between the opposition and the majority of the Central Committee took place at a joint plenum of the Central Committee and the Central Control Commission in July 1926. Trotsky spoke for the opposition bloc. Now the party saw Trotsky, Zinoviev, and Kamenev on the same platform but hardly anyone said "Here is our true Central Committee." The overwhelming majority of the Central Committee condemned the opposition. Zinoviev was removed from the Politburo, on which Trotsky remained as the sole oppositionist.

It is not possible to analyze here all the details and episodes of the fight in the party or all aspects of the opposition platform, especially on international questions. Unquestionably many of the opposition's criticisms were justified. It was no myth that bureaucratization had gone very far in both the government and party apparatus, for example, and much of the opposition's criticism of aspects of the leadership's economic policies was well taken. Although industrial production was expanding at a rapid rate in 1925–1926 (as much as 30 to 35 percent annually), certain dangerous disproportions in the Soviet economy became evident during those very years. The shortage of manufactured goods ("goods famine"), was worsening even though industrial production was rising, because consumer demand—both urban and rural—was growing even faster.

104. *Ob"edinennyi plenum TsK i TsKK* (The Joint Plenum of the Central Committee and Central Control Commission, July 14–23, 1926), 4:103. [The author gives no further bibliographical information about this source. —G. S.]

The "goods famine" discouraged the peasants from selling their grain surpluses. Exports also fell off noticeably, grain exports in particular. Consequently imports had to be cut back as well. A decline in cotton procurements created difficulties for the textile industry. Soviet foreign trade showed a growing negative balance, resulting in increased indebtedness to foreign banks and corporations. In order to maintain confidence in the Soviet Union as a trading partner on the world market, the export of gold was increased, along with other measures.

The opposition's demand that the theory of "social fascism" be condemned was absolutely correct. This concept, used in reference to Social Democracy, served to discredit the Communists in the eyes of left-wing Social Democrats, aided the right-wing Socialist leaders, and prevented unity of action by the working class against fascist attacks. Yet the responsibility for this theory originally lay with Zinoviev as well as Stalin.

Despite the opposition's many accurate observations, however, the general thrust of its platform was mistaken. As before, the opposition held that it was impossible to build full socialism in an isolated, backward country like the Soviet Union without governmental aid from a victorious working class in one or more Western countries. As one statement by opposition theorists said:

> The technical backwardness of our country and the resulting low level of labor productivity is of course an enormous obstacle on the road of socialist construction. Because of this backwardness the transition to a truly socialist organization of production (in which the worker is transformed from mere labor power into the master of production, and commodity production is eliminated) is impossible for us without aid from the advanced countries, without a world socialist revolution.[105]

In the heat of polemics the opposition leaders greatly exaggerated the shortcomings that really existed, thus causing party cadres to protest. Something that existed as a tendency or trend was portrayed as an already completed process. The degeneration that had so far affected only part of the apparatus was presented as the degeneration of virtually the entire body. Thus, the opposition's call for a "revolution in the party regime" was seen as ultra-left by the majority of the party. The opposition depicted the party's course as an uninterrupted retreat. From the fact that the kulaks and Nepmen had grown somewhat, which was entirely natural under NEP, the opposition drew the conclusion that Stalin,

---

105. *Oppozitsionnyi neomen'shevizm* (Moscow, 1927), p. 4.

Rykov, and Bukharin were restoring capitalism. One of the opposition platforms asserted:

There are two fundamental, mutually exclusive positions in our country: one, the position of the proletariat, which is building socialism; the other, the position of the bourgeoisie, which strives to turn things back onto the capitalist track. . . . Stalin's line proceeds between these two positions—moving ever closer to the latter position and consisting of short zigzags to the left and deep ones to the right.[106]

Also untrue was the opposition's assertion that the private sector was accumulating at a faster rate than the public sector. In general, the opposition, for obviously demagogic reasons, exaggerated the extent and danger of capitalist development in the Soviet Union. As one of the programmatic documents of the opposition stated:

Capitalism in the countryside is in fact growing both relatively and absolutely, growing at great speed, and with every passing day the dependence of the Soviet state and its industry on the raw material and export resources of the well-to-do and kulak elements in the countryside becomes greater. The growth of agrarian capitalism, which gives added support to the tenacious existence of urban capitalism, has proven sufficient to arouse all the bourgeois elements in our country to an awareness of their strength. Moreover, behind their backs they sense the enormous reserves of world capitalism.[107]

It is true that the Soviet state was obtaining increased quantities of raw materials and exportable products from the rural areas, but that was beneficial not only to the well-to-do sections in the countryside but to the society as a whole.

Another untrue opposition claim was that representatives of the bourgeois and non-Communist intelligentsia, who had been drawn into the work of Soviet economic management as specialists, controlled industry and finance to a greater degree than the Bolshevik Party. Zinoviev declared for example:

The ambassadors of Ustryalov (and, yes, of Milyukov) in Moscow . . . actually direct the work of the Commisariat of Agriculture, the Commissariat of Finance, and the State Planning Commission, more than Kalinin and I do. Formally they merely "work under us," but in fact these Smenovekhovite professors make the decisions."[108]

106. *Bolshevik* (1927), no. 19–20, p. 13.
107. A. Kuznetsov, *Partiia i oppozitsiia* (Moscow-Leningrad, 1928), p. 31.
108. *Partiia i oppozitsiia po dokumentam*, vol. 1, (Moscow, 1927), p. 57. [Smenovekhovite refers to the point of view expressed in the early 1920s by a group of Russian émigrés

Similarly, Trotsky declared:

More and more the ruling circles are growing together with the upper echelons of Soviet Nepman society. Two separate strata are being formed, two ways of life, two customs and habits, two types of relationships, or, if we are to use harsh words, elements of dual power are taking shape in everyday life, and if this development continues, it could turn into political dual power, and political dual power would already be a direct threat to the dictatorship of the proletariat. . . . The proletariat must understand that at a certain historical period, given a wrong policy, the Soviet government too could become an apparatus through which power would shift away from its present proletarian base and pass over to the bourgeoisie, who would then kick away the Soviet pedestal on which power rested and transform the Soviet government into a structure of the Bonapartist type.[109]

Needless to say, no such process was under way in 1926. The upper strata of the Nepman bourgeoisie were not growing together with the top echelons of the party and government. The danger of a transfer of power to the bourgeoisie or kulaks was insignificant. The degeneration of some sections of the party was a much more complex process.

While rightly criticizing the policy of reducing wholesale and retail prices under conditions of "goods famine," some opposition leaders proposed that prices for manufactured goods be raised by 20 or 30 percent, which would also have been wrong. Although some price increases for the goods in shortest supply was necessary in that period (since private traders were making profits by reselling such goods at higher prices), an overall rise in prices for manufactured goods would not have been desirable.

The opposition's economic program was worked out mainly by Preobrazhensky. Opposing him, for the Central Committee majority, were Bukharin and a group of his followers (Aleksandr Slepkov, Dmitry Maretsky, Aleksei Stetsky, Valentin Astrov, Pyotr Petrovsky, Aleksandr Aikhenvald, D. P. Rozit, and several others).

Preobrazhensky presented his theory in fullest detail in his book *The New Economics,* which appeared in 1926. A brief exposition of his views is contained in a preface he wrote especially for this book, in the form of an answer to Bukharin's article "K voprosu o zakonomernostiakh perek-

---

who published an anthology *Smena vekh* (A Change of Landmarks). Ustryalov was their best-known spokesman. They held that with the introduction of NEP the Russian state was gradually reverting to what it had been before the revolution, and therefore the Bolsheviks should be supported. —G. S.]

109. Ibid., p. 58.

hodnogo perioda" (On the Question of the Laws of the Transition Period). Preobrazhensky was unquestionably an experienced and knowledgeable economist, and his studies of the road to industrializtion in an economically backward country contain many important and valuable points. It was probably Preobrazhensky who introduced the concept of "socialist accumulation" to Soviet economics. At the same time, Preobrazhensky advocated several terminological and theoretical positions with which it is difficult to agree. There was no question, for example, that socialist industrialization in a relatively backward country had to utilize not only capital accumulated in the socialist sector itself but also part of the surplus product from other sectors of the economy, such as peasant agriculture. Over the long term the development of socialist industry was beneficial for the peasants themselves because it promised to place agriculture on a scientific and industrial basis and to raise peasant living standards accordingly. It was important, however, to determine the correct degree to which resources should be "pumped over" this way from the countryside to the city and from the private sector to the socialist sector.

In the opinion of Bukharin and his school neither taxes on the private sector nor the prices for the products of socialist industry should be so large as to hinder the development of the private sector and individual peasant farms. The peasants' incentive to expand their farms should not be destroyed because the deterioration of private farming would also result in a reduced possibility of financing socialist accumulation from that source. In other words, not only should the socialist sector be developed; so should the private sector, even if at a slower rate, because expanded reproduction in this sector was beneficial to the whole society and provided additional resources for accelerating the expanded reproduction of the socialist economy. A certain balance between these sectors would not hinder the development of socialism and could continue to exist for a fairly long time.

The scheme that Preobrazhensky developed was different. In his view the prolonged coexistence of private commodity production was incompatible with the socialist system. Not mincing his words, Preobrazhensky wrote that one of these systems must inevitably "devour" the other. In other words, either socialist production would subordinate small private production completely to itself or the private capitalist sector would gain the upper hand over the socialist sector. Therefore Preobrazhensky did not simply advocate the "pumping over" (*perekachka*) of resources from the other sectors to the socialist sector; he argued that resources should be "pumped over" at a rate that would gradually squeeze all the nonsocialist sectors out of economic existence and eliminate them. He was not ashamed to use the terms "exploitation" and "expropriation" for this process, and even likened such "pumping over" from the countryside to the city in the Soviet Union to the capitalists' extraction of resources from the colonies to the metropolis. Preobrazhensky used the term "primitive socialist accumulation" for the utilization by the proletarian state of the surplus product from the nonsocialist sectors for the purposes of socialist development. He considered the "law of primitive socialist accumulation" the fundamental law of the Soviet economy.

Preobrazhensky writes:

The more economically backward, petty bourgeois, and peasant a country is that is making the transition to socialist organization of production, and the smaller the material legacy the proletariat of a given country iherits to put into its socialist accumulation fund at the time of socialist revolution—the greater relatively will socialist accumulation have to base itself on the alienation of part of the surplus product from the presocialist economic forms.[110]

He noted:

A country like the Soviet Union will have to go through a period of primitive accumulation, dipping very liberally into the well of presocialist economic forms.[111]

And he contended:

The task of the socialist state is not to take less from the petty bourgeois producer than capitalism took but to take even more.[112]

Stalin tried not to get drawn into economic debates with the opposition leaders, leaving that to Bukharin and his disciples. Adroitly taking advantage of the unfavorable situation in which the United Opposition found itself, Stalin accused the opposition leaders above all of unprincipled conduct. This charge was not hard to substantiate by quoting lengthy excerpts from the harsh attacks they had made on one another not long before. In addition, Stalin lumped together all of Trotsky's, Zinoviev's and Kamenev's past mistakes (from the point of view of orthodox Bolshevism). This was rather weighty ballast for any opposition group to carry. Putting the main stress on party unity, Stalin accused the United Opposition of

110. Yevgeny Preobrazhensky, *Novaia ekonomika* (Moscow, 1926), pp. 101–102.
111. Ibid., p. 63.
112. Ibid., p. 67.

whipping up factional disputes. In this he correctly voiced the sentiments not only of the party apparatus but of the party ranks, who were tired of endless debates, especially in light of the relatively difficult material conditions.

As early as autumn 1926—that is, only a few months after the United Opposition was formed—it became evident that it had not been able to win over the party ranks and had suffered a political defeat. Realizing this, the opposition leaders gave the signal for retreat. On October 16, 1926, they submitted a letter to the Central Committee admitting some of their mistakes. This letter said in part:

At the Fourteenth Party Congress and afterward we disagreed with the majority of the congress on a number of questions of principle. Our views were presented in official documents and in speeches given by us at the congress, at Central Committee plenums, and in the Politburo. We stand on the basis of these views even now. We categorically reject the theory and practice of "freedom of factions and groupings," recognizing that such theory and practice are contrary to Leninism and the decisions of the party. We consider it our duty to carry out the decisions of the party regarding the impermissibility of factional activity.

At the same time we consider it our duty to acknowledge openly before the party that we and our co-thinkers, in putting forward our views on a number of occasions after the Fourteenth Congress, have committed acts that violated party discipline, and that we have followed a factional course that goes beyond the limits laid down by the party regarding ideological struggle within the party. In recognizing these acts as wrong, we declare that we emphatically renounce factional methods of propagating our views, as these methods endanger the unity of the party, and we call on all comrades who share our views to do the same. We call for the immediate dissolution of all factional groupings that have formed around the views of the "Opposition."[113]

Having achieved victory over the opposition, Stalin hastened to consolidate his victory organizationally. At the joint plenum of the Central Committee and Central Control Commission, held October 23–26, 1926, a resolution was adopted expelling Trotsky from the Politburo and dropping Kamenev as a candidate member of that body.

Although the opposition statement of October 16 spoke of an end to all factional activity, the opposition was unable to refrain from renewed factionalism. In the spring of 1927 new and serious difficulties arose in the Soviet economic situation. International tension also increased, and the party leadership feared that war might be declared against the Soviet

113. *Pravda,* October 17, 1926.

Union. Britain broke diplomatic and trade relations with the USSR. The revolutionary movement in China, on which the Comintern had placed high hopes, suffered a defeat. Chiang Kai-shek, the head of the Kuomintang, renounced his alliance with the Chinese Communist Party and carried out a counter revolutionary coup. The opposition considered this a favorable situation for once more speaking out openly against the party leadership, accusing it of mistaken policies.

In May 1927 Trotsky, Zinoviev, and more than eighty of their supporters addressed a lengthy statement to the Central Committee calling for a confidential plenary session of that body to discuss the failures of the revolutionary Communist movement in China. The document criticized various aspects of both the foreign and domestic policies of the Stalin leadership.[114] Simultaneously, throughout the Soviet Union groups of opposition supporters were reestablished and the circulation of various letters, articles, and other material critical of Politburo policies was organized. Among these materials was a long article by Trotsky on the problems of the Chinese revolution. Trotsky also took up these problems in two speeches at the Eighth Plenum of the Executive Committee of the Comintern at the end of May 1927[115] However, the Comintern leadership rejected Trotsky's accusations.

On June 9, 1927, a gathering to bid farewell to Ivar Smilga developed into an opposition demonstration of sorts. Smilga, a prominent figure in the party and one of Trotsky's co-thinkers, had been appointed to a minor post in the Far East, an honorable form of exile imposed because he was an oppositionist. (Earlier, Kamenev had been sent as Soviet ambassador to Italy and Rakovsky as ambassador to France.) At the Yaroslavl Station in Moscow thousands of Smilga's oppositionist friends and supporters gathered to see him off. A spontaneous rally was held, with both Trotsky and Zinoviev giving speeches. Although Trotsky tried to avoid any controversial subjects and even called on all party members to be "doubly faithful" in view of the "dangers to our country," Stalin and the Politburo judged the demonstration at the Yaroslavl Station to be a factional move and a violation of the promises made in the opposition's statement of October 16, 1926.

114. [See the "Declaration of the Eighty-Four," in *Challenge of the Left Opposition, 1926–27*, pp. 224–239. The author cites *Die Linke Opposition.* —G. S.]

115. [The "long article by Trotsky" was probably "The Chinese Revolution and the Theses of Comrade Stalin," which Trotsky dated May 7, 1927. See *Leon Trotsky on China* (New York, 1976), which also contains Trotsky's two speeches at the plenum of the ECCI. The author cites *Die Linke Opposition.* —G. S.]

Actually Trotsky wanted to try another test of strength with the Politburo. It seemed to him that the mood in the party had shifted in his favor. Dozens of oppositionists who came to see him at the offices of the Chief Concessions Committee assured him that this was so. Thus Trotsky decided on a renewal of factional political activity, which was conducted on a large scale and attracted more supporters than in the fall of 1926. The opposition groups in the various Soviet cities had their own local leaderships and their own faction discipline, and dues were collected from members. Opposition materials were published secretly on government printing presses, and a small illegal printshop was set up in Moscow for the same purpose. Trotsky knew about, and fully approved of, the use of such prerevolutionary conspiratorial methods. Assessing these events several years later, Trotsky wrote:

In a very short time it was apparent that as a faction we had undoubtedly gained strength—that is to say, we had grown more united intellectually, and stronger in numbers. But the umbilical cord that connected us with power was cut by the sword of Chiang Kai-shek. His totally discredited Russian ally, Stalin, now had only to complete the crushing of the Shanghai workers by routing the opposition within the party. The backbone of the opposition was a group of old revolutionaries. But we were no longer alone. Hundreds and thousands of revolutionaries of the new generation were grouped about us. This new generation had been awakened by the October revolution. . . .

The nearer grew the time for the Fifteenth Party Congress, set for the end of 1927, the more the party felt that it had reached a cross-roads in history. Alarm was rife in the ranks. In spite of a monstrous terror, the desire to hear the opposition awoke in the party. This could be achieved only by illegal means. Secret meetings were held in various parts of Moscow and Leningrad, attended by workers and students of both sexes, who gathered in groups of from twenty to one hundred and two hundred to hear some representative of the opposition. In one day I would visit two, three, and sometimes four of such meetings. They were usually held in some worker's apartment.[116]

In this passage Trotsky obviously exaggerates the extent of opposition influence among rank-and-file party members. He overstates even more the extent to which Stalin had been discredited by the Chinese events. Moreover, most of the illegal meetings and opposition materials were no secret to Stalin and his immediate circle. He followed the activities of the opposition leaders very closely. In cases where information coming to him through party channels was insufficient Stalin unhesitatingly made use of the GPU, whose new head, Menzhinsky, usually complied with

116. Trotsky, *My Life*, pp. 530–531.

all of Stalin's wishes. Nor did Stalin find it suitable to make a truce with Trotsky. Stalin, sensing that he was master of the situation and had preponderant strength, strove to crush his political rivals completely and establish his own total control over the party. While calling on the opposition to be honest and sincere and condemning it for hypocrisy, Stalin himself acted hypocritically and deceived the party by concealing his own real aims even from those closest to himself.

One of the reasons for the opposition's defeat was the GPU's discovery of the opposition's illegal printshop. Those working at the shop were arrested, along with M. achkovsky, who was in charge of it. One of those arrested had in the past been a White Guard officer, although at the time of his arrest he was a secret agent for the GPU, as Menzhinsky himself later admitted. The case of the underground printshop and the "White Guard officer" was used to maximum advantage to discredit Trotsky and the opposition. A joint plenum of the Central Committee and Central Control Commission at the end of October 1927 passed a resolution expelling Trotsky and Zinoviev from the Central Committee while allowing them to remain as party members.

On November 2, 1927, *Pravda* published Trotsky's speech at the October plenum, his last political speech at a Central Committee meeting. The speech demonstrates rather clearly the full unreality of the platform of the Left Opposition and that of Trotsky personally. A platform of this kind—with its sharply worded criticism of the shortcomings of the party leadership, combined with elements of demagogy—could never have been successful with the leadership or even most of the membership of a *ruling* party. On the other hand, the rudeness of Trotsky's opponents leaves a very ominous impression. Among these rude opponents were Petrovsky, Skrypnik, Unshlikht, Voroshilov, Goloshchekin, Chubar, Lomov, and Kalinin. Trotsky's speech was accompanied by constant frenzied shouts from these men and others. The stenographic record contains such interruptions from the floor as "Liar," "Traitor," "Loudmouth," "Get down, scum!" "Down with the renegade!" and "Gravedigger of the revolution!"[117] The stenographer recorded the following at the end of the speech:

117. See the supplement entitled "Diskussionnyi listok" (Discussion Bulletin), no. 2, in *Pravda*, November 2, 1927. [*Pravda* printed a number of these "Discussion Bulletin" supplements devoted to the discussion preceding the Fifteenth Party Congress of December 1927. —G. S.]

[Renewed whistling. A constantly increasing commotion. Nothing can be heard. The chairman calls for order. More whistling. Shouts of "Get down from the podium." The chairman adjourns the meetings. Comrade Trotsky continues to read his speech, but not a single word can be made out. The members of the plenum leave their seats and begin to file out of the hall.]

Zinoviev too was obliged to leave the podium without finishing his speech to cries of "Get down" and "Get out."[118]

In reply to the decision to expel Trotsky, Zinoviev, and Kamenev from the Central Committee, the opposition attempted to organize its own demonstration to mark the tenth anniversary of the October revolution. This proved, however, to be not so much a demonstration of strength as of weakness. There were hardly any workers in this "parallel" demonstration; student youth and office workers from various institutions predominated. The demonstrators carried such slogans as "Let Us Carry Out Lenin's Testament," "Fire Against the Right—Against Kulak, Nepman, and Bureaucrat," "Down with Stalin," "Down with Thermidor," "Long Live Trotsky," "Against Opportunism and a Split—For the Unity of Lenin's Party," and "Long Live Trotsky and Zinoviev, Leaders of the World Revolution." Many participants in the demonstration sang a song with the words "Long live Trotsky, leader of the Red Army."

During this demonstration of the opposition leaders gave speeches from the balcony of a house on the corner of Vozdvizhenka and Mokhovaya streets, but compared with the official demonstration of Moscow workers, the opposition demonstration was a sorry spectacle. It was easily dispersed by the workers' vigilante groups and militia units quickly organized for this purpose. The first arrests were made on the streets at that time. Posters with opposition slogans and portraits of Trotsky were torn out of demonstrators' hands and ripped to pieces. Many students were beaten up. The attempt to organize an opposition demonstration in Leningrad was even less successful. Zinoviev, who obviously had overestimated his influence in that city, came close to being beaten up during the march celebrating the tenth anniversary of the revolution.

On November 14 a plenum of the Central Committee and Central Control Commission expelled Trotsky and Zinoviev from the party. Other active members of the opposition who were still on the Central Committee and Central Control Commission likewise were expelled from those bodies. Any further open discussion with the opposition before the Fif-

118. Ibid.

teenth Congress was forbidden. Hundreds of oppositionists were expelled from the party in Leningrad and other cities.

Trotsky's expulsion was one of the reasons for the suicide of Adolf Joffe, a prominent Soviet diplomat who suffered from serious illness. Joffe was a major figure in the party and had served it well, especially in negotiating the Brest-Litovsk treaty. For this reason official funeral ceremonies were organized for him. Mikhail Yakubovich, an eyewitness to the funeral, describes it in his memoirs:

> The coffin containing Joffe's body was in the building of the Commissariat of Foreign Affairs on Lubyanka Square, waiting to be taken to the Novodevichi Cemetery. A huge crowd filled all the streets around the building and blocked traffic. It was with difficulty that Trotsky made his way through this crowd, accompanied by Radek and Muralov. . . . (Among those who followed the coffin to the cemetery, incidentally, was Nadezhda Alliluyeva, Stalin's wife.) A lot of people followed the coffin—for the most part Komsomol student youth who had Trotskyist leanings. There were quite a few former military and military-political officials who had worked under Trotsky in the past. The procession sang songs of the civil war era, with Trotsky's name in them. . . . At the cemetery, after the official funeral speech delivered by Chicherin on behalf of the Central Committee, Trotsky, Zinoviev, and Kamenev spoke. Trotsky's speech was largely an appeal for the restoration of party unity. . . ; it contained no harsh thrusts, the name of Stalin was not mentioned at all. But Zinoviev spoke in a vehement, aggressive tone; he spoke of the crimes of Stalin, who had betrayed the party's interests, violated its members' rights, and misrepresented the will of the party. When the participants were leaving the gates of the Novodevichi Monastery after the funeral, a military unit stood nearby in formation, probably sent to fire the funeral salute. A young man in the group around Trotsky broke away, ran to the unit, and shouted: "Red Army comrades! Give a cheer for the leader of the Red Army, Comrade Trotsky!" A critical minute followed. No one moved in the formation. Dead silence reigned. Trotsky stood some distance away, also silent, looking at the ground. Then he turned and went to a car, followed by Zinoviev and Kamenev. It must have been obvious for those watching this scene that Trotsky's cause was hopelessly lost. The new generation of Red Army soldiers did not know him, had not taken part in the civil war, were raised in a new spirit. The name of Trotsky meant little or nothing to them. The composition of the funeral demonstration also made one stop and think, for there were no workers in it. The United Opposition had no proletarian support.[119]

In December 1927 the Fifteenth Congress confirmed the expulsion of Trotsky and Zinoviev and resolved to expel seventy-five additional members of the Opposition, including Kamenev, Pyatakov, Radek, Rakovsky,

119. M. P. Yakubovich, *L. D. Trotsky: Mysli o ego deiatelnosti i istoricheskoi roli,* manuscript.

Smilga, Lashevich, Safarov, and Ivan Smirnov. The congress also called on the party organizations to purge their ranks of "all obviously incorrigible elements of the Trotskyist opposition."

The congress completed the organizational defeat of the opposition. An atmosphere of intolerance prevailed, speeches by oppositionists were rudely interrupted, and harsh, insulting shouts were heard from all parts of the hall. Many delegates to the congress demanded that even more rigorous measures be taken against opposition supporters and that all discussion inside the party be strictly limited. Calls for an even stricter party regime were heard. K. Ryndin, a delegate from Chelyabinsk, said:

> No confidence can be placed in these deceivers of the party. . . . [We can have] no faith in their promises. . . . Enough of this mockery of the party; the party and the proletariat will not stand for it. We want to work; we have no time for squabbling or setting up commissions to deal with every criticism. We want to work. As for those who want to prevent us from working—out of the party with them!

Goloshchekin, a Central Committee member, declared:

> Comrades, it seems to me that we have to take a harder line; we have to free the party from the blathering of the opposition. . . . We must establish a strict regime in the party; and a strict regime must be established in government work. If we pussyfoot around with the opposition, comrades, we'll be cutting our own throats.

Rykov, the chairman of the Council of People's Commissars, even said:

> Despite the situation the opposition has tried to create, there are only a few in prison. I do not think I can give assurances that the prison population won't have to be increased somewhat in the near future. (Voices from the floor: "Right!")

G. Mikhailovsky, a delegate from Moscow, distorting historical facts, argued against discussion in the party in general.[120]

At the congress itself several prominent leaders of the Zinovievist opposition made statements renouncing opposition activity and asking to be reinstated in the party. The congress passed a resolution that such statements of recantation would be considered only on an individual basis and that no decisions would be made until six months after such a statement was submitted. After the congress Kamenev, Bakayev, Yevdokimov, and several other Zinovievists announced that they would abide by the decisions of the congress. Soon after, Zinoviev too capitu-

120. *Piatnadtsatyi s"ezd VKP(b). Stenograficheskii otchet*, (Moscow, 1928). See the index for the speeches by the various delegates.

lated. In mid-1928 Zinoviev, Kamenev, and many of their supporters were readmitted to the party and given posts in the government and economic appartus.

As for the Trotskyists, their intention was to continue the struggle against the "Stalin faction." The Central Committee therefore decided to widen the scope of repression against them. Nearly all Trotskyists who had not submitted written statements denouncing their own views were arrested and placed in special isolation prisons for political offenders (*politizolyatory*) or banished to remote parts of the Soviet Union. A decision was made to deport Trotsky to Central Asia. He was informed of this decision four days in advance. A large number of Trotsky's supporters appeared at the Kazan Station in Moscow to see him off, making it evident that he was still popular. According to M. A. Solntseva, some who had come to see him off lay down on the tracks.[121] Trotsky's departure was postponed to January 18. But on the 17th a group of GPU agents and Central Committee staff members came to Trotsky's apartment to take him to a train for immediate departure. When Trotsky refused to go, he was carried from his home by force and pushed into a car waiting outside. He was taken to the Yaroslavl Station and put on a train to Kazakhstan. Trotsky's son, Leon Sedov, began shouting to the railroad workers: "Look who they're shipping off—Trotsky!" But no one interfered, and the train left the station.

Trotsky and his family lived in Alma-Ata for a year. He maintained ties with his supporters, legally and illegally, carrying on a vast correspondence. He was still very optimistically inclined. In a letter he sent to the Politburo, which was circulated in manuscript copies among exiled Trotskyists, he said:

> The incurable weakness of the reaction headed by the apparatchiks, in spite of their apparent power, lies in the fact that "they know not what they do." They are executing the orders of the enemy classes. There can be no greater historical curse on a faction, which came out of the revolution and is now undermining it.
>
> The greatest historical strength of the Opposition, in spite of its apparent weakness, lies in the fact that it keeps its fingers on the pulse of the world historical process, that it sees the dynamics of the class forces clearly, foresees the coming day and consciously prepares for it.[122]

121. Solntseva was an active young party member in the 1920s who sympathized with the opposition and knew several leaders of the party and the opposition. In the 1930s she was arrested. After her rehabilitation in 1956, she did not seek readmission to the party. She died in the mid-1970s.

122. Trotsky, *My Life*, p. 560.

However, Trotsky's letters to his supporters do not corroborate the claim that he saw "the dynamics of the class forces clearly." When a "right deviation" appeared in the party, Trotsky at first favored an alliance with the "center" (Stalin) against the "rights," whom he considered more dangerous than the Stalin group. Soon thereafter he began to try to establish illegal contacts with the Bukharin group against Stalin. For a time Trotsky feared that under peasant pressure a military dictatorship would be established headed by Voroshilov and Budyonny and aimed against Stalin. In such a case he urged his supporters to back Stalin against Voroshilov.

In 1929 a decision was made to deport Trotsky. In February he and his family were secretly moved to Odessa and placed on the steamer *Ilyich,* which removed them from the USSR. By an agreement with Turkey, which then had good relations with the Soviet Union, Trotsky was allowed to take up residence on the island of Prinkipo in the Sea of Marmora. There he spent more than four years, engaging mainly in literary activity. In addition to several books and a great many articles, which were published in the West, Trotsky wrote much of the material in the *Bulletin of the Opposition,* which he founded in exile. He was still full of hope for the success of his movement. In November 1929 he wrote:

> The twelfth anniversary finds the Soviet republic in a condition in which outstanding progress is combined with the gravest difficulties; and at the same time both the progress and the difficulties continue to mount. In this is found the chief characteristic of the situation and its principal enigma. . . .
>
> The thirteenth year will be a year of deepening contradictions. The party, stifled and rendered powerless, may be caught off guard. . . . The centrist apparatus will show that it is an apparatus and nothing more. The proletarian nucleus will need leadership. And only the Communist Left, tempered in struggle, will be able to provide it. [123]

A few months later Trotsky continued to assert that the Left Opposition was growing stronger and increasing its numbers.

> In spite of all the lies of the official press, the Left Opposition is growing and fortifying itself ideologically throughout the world. Progress has been especially great during this past year. [124]

123. *Biulleten' oppozitsii* (1929), no. 7, p. 4. [Cf. *Writings of Leon Trotsky, 1929,* pp. 362, 368. —G. S.]

124. *Biulleten' oppozitsii* (1930), no. 10, p. 4. [Cf. *Writings of Leon Trotsky, 1930* (New York, 1975), p. 142—G. S.]

These were illusions, and they were very soon dispelled.

The expulsion of Trotsky from the Soviet Union, the policy of severe repression against oppositionists, the fight that began against the "right deviation," the implementation of an increasingly harsh antikulak and anti-Nepman policy, of accelerated industrialization, and the beginning of total collectivization, marking a clear turn "to the left" on Stalin's part —all this caused the Trotskyist opposition to fall apart rather quickly. The will of most of the prominent oppositionists to continue the fight against Stalin was broken. On various pretexts Radek, Preobrazhensky, and others began crossing over to Stalin's side.

According to Isaac Deutscher, Radek wrote in one of his letters, "The Stalinists have proven to be more worthy than the Opposition thought." Radek and Preobrazhensky dissociated themselves from the theory of permanent revolution, which they had previously supported. Their aim was to dissociate themselves from Trotsky as well. Preobrazhensky, in an appeal "To All Comrades of the Opposition," wrote that the opposition had been defeated precisely because its ideas had triumphed. Isaac Deutscher summarizes and quotes from Preobrazhensky's documents as follows:

> To be sure, Stalin had initiated the left course in a manner very different from the one they [the Oppositionists] had championed. The Opposition wanted industrialization and collectivization carried out in the broad daylight of proletarian democracy . . . ; whereas Stalin relied on the force of the decree and coercion from above. All the same, the Opposition had stood for what he was doing. . . . [The] Opposition's present duty was to come closer to the party and then return to it . . . in order "to hold out together against the pressure of that discontent which must be aroused in a peasant country by a policy of socialist accumulation and a struggle against agrarian capitalism." . . . "[If readmitted,] we shall have to bear responsibility for things against which we have warned and to submit to [methods] to which we cannot give assent. . . . If we are reinstated we shall, each of us, receive back the partbilet [membership card] as one accepts a heavy cross." Yet for those who wished to serve the cause of socialism effectively nothing was left but to take up the cross.[125]

In June 1929 Radek was on his way back to Moscow under guard to make his peace with Stalin. His train stopped at a station in Siberia, where by chance a group of oppositionists met and spoke with him. Radek urged them to surrender to the Central Committee. He spoke of the difficult situation in the Soviet Union, the shortage of bread, the discontent of the workers, and the threat of peasant revolts. In this

125. Deutscher, *Prophet Outcast*, pp. 69–71.

situation, Radek said, the opposition should admit that it had been wrong and rally to the party. "We ourselves have driven ourselves into prison and exile," he argued, and declared: "I have definitely broken with Lev Davidovich [Trotsky]—we are political enemies now."[126] Smilga, Serebryakov, and Ivan Smirnov soon broke with Trotsky as well.

Rakovsky continued to resist longer than others. He argued this way:

Those who made their peace with Stalin, because he was carrying out the economic part of [the Opposition] program and who hoped that he would carry out the political part as well, were behaving like old-type reformists contenting themselves with the piecemeal realization of their demands. . . . A party leadership which extracted from Oppositionists confessions of imaginary errors merely imitated the Catholic Church, which made the atheist recant on his deathbed—such a leadership "loses every title to respect; and the Oppositionist who changes his conviction overnight deserves only utter scorn."[127]

Toward the end of 1929 Rakovsky and his group (Sosnovksy, Muralov, Mdivani, etc.) wrote an "Open Letter to the Central Committee," which although it contained criticism of Stalin's policies and demanded the return of Trotsky, to the USSR, was very conciliatory in its tone. Soon the majority of this group capitulated fully and returned to Moscow, where many of them were given posts recently held by members of the Bukharinist opposition. Rakovsky was perhaps the last of Trotsky's prominent adherents, but he too capitulated after Hitler's rise to power in 1933.

In 1932 Zinoviev and Kamenev were once again expelled from the party for "contacts with the Ryutin group." They were arrested and placed in a *politizolyator*. After one more recantation, however, they were freed and readmitted to the party. At the Seventeenth Party Congress (in 1934) they gave speeches confessing their sins.

In fact, of all the leaders of the United Opposition, Trotsky alone tried to continue the struggle against Stalin—from abroad. He carried on a voluminous correspondence with supporters in various countries, trying to establish Trotskyist groups or factions and find ways of sending the *Bulletin of the Opposition* and other Trotskyist literature into the Soviet Union. However, hardly any supporters of Trotsky, even secret ones, were left there. Trotsky remained in his own mind a revolutionary and not "a counterrevolutionary heading toward fascism," as Stalin declared. However, because of his inherent dogmatism, his tendentiousness, and

126. Ibid., pp. 72–73.
127. *Biulleten' oppozitsii* (1929), no. 6, quoted in Deutscher, *Prophet Outcast*, p. 78.

his lack of information Trotsky could not understand or properly evaluate the complex processes taking place in the Soviet Union and the world Communist movement in the thirties. As a result, he was not able to formulate an alternative Marxist program. He was unable even to understand correctly the reasons for his own defeat. For example, several years after his deportation he wrote the following:

The historian of the Soviet Union cannot fail to conclude that the policy of the ruling bureaucracy upon great questions has been a series of contradictory zig-zags. . . . On the basis of . . . irrefutable facts and documents, the historian will be compelled to conclude that the so-called "Left Opposition" offered an immeasurably more correct analysis of the processes taking place in the country, and far more truly foresaw their further development.

This assertion is contradicted at first glance by the simple fact that the faction which could not see ahead was steadily victorious, while the more penetrating group suffered defeat after defeat. That kind of objection, which comes automatically to mind, is convincing, however, only for those who think rationalistically, and see in politics a logical argument or a chess match. A political struggle is in its essence a struggle of interests and forces, not of arguments. The quality of the leadership is, of course, far from a matter of indifference for the outcome of the conflict, but it is not the only factor, and in the last analysis is not decisive. Each of the struggling camps moreover demands leaders in its own image. . . .

It is sufficiently well known that every revolution up to this time has been followed by a reaction, or even a counterrevolution. This, to be sure, has never thrown the nation all the way back to its starting point, but it has always taken from the people the lion's share of their conquests. The victims of the first reactionary wave have been, as a general rule, those pioneers, initiators, and instigators who stood at the head of the masses in the period of the revolutionary offensive. In their stead people of the second rank, in league with former enemies of the revolution, have been advanced to the front. Beneath this dramatic duel of "coryphees" on the open political scene, shifts have taken place in the relations between classes, and, no less important, profound changes in the psychology of the recently revolutionary masses.

[Thus in Russia] after an unexampled tension of forces, hopes, and illusions, there came a long period of weariness, decline, and sheer disappointment in the results of the revolution. The ebb of "plebeian pride" made room for a flood of pusillanimity and careerism. The new commanding caste rose to its place upon this wave. . . .

The reaction within the proletariat caused an extraordinary flush of hope and confidence in the petty bourgeois strata of town and country, aroused as they were to new life by the NEP, and growing bolder and bolder. The young bureaucracy, which had arisen at first as an agent of the proletariat, began now to feel itself a court of arbitration between the classes. Its independence increased from month to month. . . .

To be sure, tens of thousands of revolutionary fighters gathered around the banner of the Bolshevik-Leninists. The advanced workers were indubitably sympathetic to the Opposition, but that sympathy remained passive. The masses lacked faith that the situation could be seriously changed by a new struggle. Meantime the bureaucracy asserted: "For the sake of an international revolution, the Opposition proposes to drag us into a revolutionary war. Enough of shakeups! We have earned the right to rest. We will build the socialist society at home. Rely upon us, your leaders!" This gospel of repose firmly consolidated the apparatchiki and the military and state officials and indubitably found an echo among the weary workers and still more the peasant masses. Can it be, they asked themselves, that the Opposition is actually ready to sacrifice the interests of the Soviet Union for the idea of "permanent revolution"? . . .

The Opposition was isolated. The bureaucracy struck while the iron was hot, exploiting the bewilderment and passivity of the workers, setting their more backward strata against the advanced, and relying more and more boldly upon the kulak and the petty bourgeois ally in general. In the course of a few years, the bureaucracy thus shattered the revolutionary vanguard of the proletariat.

It would be naive to imagine that Stalin, previously unknown to the masses, suddenly issued from the wings fully armed with a complete strategical plan. No indeed. Before he felt out his own course, the bureaucracy felt out Stalin himself. He brought it all the necessary guarantees: the prestige of an Old Bolshevik, a strong character, narrow vision, and close bonds with the political machine as the sole source of his influence. . . . A secondary figure before the masses and in the events of the revolution, Stalin revealed himself as the indubitable leader of the Thermidorian bureaucracy, as first in its midst.[128]

In an attempt to reinforce his argument, Trotsky quotes something Krupskaya allegedly said in 1926 in the presence of oppositionists (she continued to sympathize with the Left Opposition until early 1927): "If Ilyich were alive, he would probably already be in prison." The implication was that since Lenin himself could not have defeated Stalin and his political machine, Trotsky's defeat was certainly unavoidable.

The lengthy passage I have quoted from Trotsky contains a number of correct ideas, but it is hard to agree with it as a whole. Politics is the art of the possible. That saying embraces the essence of astute policy making. If it is true, as Trotsky asserts, that the Left Opposition made a more correct analysis of the processes under way in the Soviet Union and foresaw their future development more accurately, why did it not adapt

128. [The quotation is from the section "Why Stalin Triumphed," in Ch. 5 of Trotsky's *The Revolution Betrayed* (New York, 1945), pp. 86–93. The author cites pp. 73–78 of the Russian text, which was published by the Fourth International in Paris in the early 1970s in a photocopied facsimile edition of Trotsky's typed manuscript using Trotsky's original title *Chto takoe SSSR i kuda on idet* (What the Soviet Union Is and Where It Is Going). Although the book was published in many languages in 1937 and after, no Russian edition had previously appeared. —G. S.]

its policies to these accurate analyses and predictions? If the working class and the peasantry were extremely exhausted after many years of unexampled tension and strain, would it not have been more correct to let them work calmly in their fields and factories and help them feed and clothe their families, rather than calling on them for new sacrifices and exertions? After all, Lenin too had had time to see the tiredness, disillusion, and decline of the working class and the discontent of the peasantry. Lenin's "correct analysis" gave rise to the NEP, a policy that Trotsky's slogans contradicted.

Trotsky claims that tens of thousands of Bolshevik-Leninists rallied to the banner of the opposition. He admits, however, that the sympathy of the workers remained passive, that the workers did not support his slogans. Yet Lenin repeated many times that the Bolsheviks could retain power only if they knew what the moods and desires of the masses were and expressed them in their policies. It can be said with certainty that if Lenin were still alive in 1926–1927, he would have continued to develop and improve the policy of NEP. Lenin would surely have continued a determined struggle against bureaucratism, but in the economic sphere he surely would not have supported the slogans of Trotsky, Zinoviev, and Preobrazhensky. Nevertheless, as we shall see, Stalin soon gave energetic support to those slogans.

One Soviet historian has written:

Many veteran revolutionaries and heroes of the civil war belonged to the Left Opposition. They were sincerely convinced that they were fighting for the ideals of the revolution. Their main fire was concentrated on criticism of Stalin, accusing him of every mortal sin. Of course if we view this criticism through the prism of the crimes that Stalin later committed, it seems justified. But if a historical approach is used to assess Stalin, then it must be acknowledged that the charges against him were excessive and in many respects unjust. As an unintended side effect of these accusations, the party apparatus rallied around Stalin more closely than ever. The other party leaders could not fail to defend their general secretary, because in so doing, they were defending the policies of the party, which they had laid out and were implementing together with Stalin.[129]

N. Valentinov (Volsky) makes a similar point:

The methods used by the Politburo in the fight against the [Left] Opposition were repugnant to me as well as to many others, in particular the savage dispersal or disruption of Opposition meetings by gangs of zealots recruited especially for that purpose. But that was not the reason for the Opposition's demise. Except for

129. Yu. Golosov (pseud.), Zametki po istorii partii (Comments on the History of the Party), unpublished manuscript, pp. 266–267.

some very small groups it had no support in the country. As a matter of fact, what classes could it count on for sympathy? Certainly not the peasantry, since it called for applying pressure to the countryside. . . . it had no support from the "bureaucrats," the non-Communist intellectuals, specialists, engineers, and technicians, who considered the socio-economic program of the Opposition demagogic and harmful, sensing that behind it lurked something like a return to war communism. . . . The overwhelming majority of workers in the two main political centers, Moscow and Leningrad, took an attitude of indifference toward the Opposition. Zinoviev was cruelly mistaken in assuming that the Leningrad workers would stand up for him the moment he called. The bulk of the workers, who at that time felt satisfied, who had never eaten so well, who were living better than in tsarist times, and who enjoyed a whole series of privileges, followed the lead of the government and displayed no taste for adventures, upheavals, or new revolutions.[130]

Of course the workers never dreamed that their comfortable life would soon come to an end, that the Soviet Union would be subjected to new torments and upheavals, and that all this would result from the new "left turn" taken by Stalin and his immediate entourage.

The United Opposition suffered total organizational and ideological defeat at the Fifteenth Party Congress. At the very first Central Committee plenum after that congress, Stalin offered to resign as general secretary. But his real aim was to gain a free hand in the new stage of his struggle for power. Addressing the Central Committee, he said:

I think that until recently there were circumstances that put the party in the position of needing me in this post as a person who was fairly rough in his dealings, to constitute a certain antidote to the opposition. . . . Now the opposition has not only been smashed; it has been expelled from the party. And still we have the recommendation of Lenin, which in my opinion ought to be put into effect. Therefore I ask the plenum to relieve me of the post of general secretary. I assure you, comrades, that from this the party only stands to gain.[131]

At Stalin's insistence this proposal was put to a vote. His resignation was rejected virtually unanimously (with one abstention). Stalin immediately went on to use the special powers implied by this reaffirmation of his leading position.

■ 9
BUKHARIN

The noisy battle with the United Left Opposition had barely died down when a fight began with the so-called right deviation. In the course of

130. Valentinov (Volsky), *Novaia ekonomicheskaia politika*, p. 227.
131. From the unpublished stenographic record of the plenum.

this struggle the label "right deviationist" was pinned on many old and famous figures in the party leadership. The leading figure and main theorist in this new group of Stalin's opponents was unquestionably Bukharin.

Nikolai Ivanovich Bukharin was born in Moscow on September 27 (October 9, N.S.), 1888. Both Bukharin's father and mother were elementary school teachers and, as Bukharin himself later recalled, raised him "in the typical spirit of the intelligentsia." As a child, Bukharin loved to read and became passionately interested in natural history. He also took a keen interest in drawing, in which he displayed considerable ability. Early in his childhood Bukharin "adopted an ironical attitude toward religion."[132] In elementary school and in the *gymnasium* Bukharin was among the top students, although he put no special effort into his studies. At the beginning of the century a significant number of *gymnasium* students were revolutionary-minded; as early as the age of thirteen or fourteen, they were reading illegal literature and taking part in study groups. From the beginning of the 1905 revolution Bukharin, together with other students, took an active part in rallies and demonstrations and even helped organize strikes. He became acquainted with Marxist literature quite early and took a particular interest in Marxist economic theory. In 1906 the eighteen-year-old Bukharin officially became a member of the RSDLP and began illegal work. After only two years he was co-opted onto the Moscow City Committee of the party. After several arrests he was exiled to Onega. From there, after learning that his case would be brought to court and that he would be faced with hard labor, Bukharin escaped abroad. As he later recalled:

Emigration marked a new phase in my life, from which I benefited in three ways. Firstly, I lived with workers' families and spent whole days in libraries. If I had acquired my general knowledge and a quite detailed understanding of the agrarian question in Russia, it was undoubtedly the Western libraries that provided me with essential intellectual capital. Secondly, I met Lenin, who had an enormous influence on me. Thirdly, I learned languages and gained practical experience of the labor movement. It was abroad, too, that my literary activity began in earnest. . . . I tried to take an active part in the labor movement wherever I could.[133]

132. Haupt and Marie, *Makers of the Russian Revolution*, p. 31.

133. Ibid., p. 33. [This quotation and the preceding one (see note 132) are taken from Bukharin's brief autobiography written for the Russian-language Granat Encyclopedia, as translated in Haupt and Marie. The author cites the Russian original, *Entsiklopedicheskii slovar' russkogo bibliograficheskogo Instituta Granata*, 7th ed., vol. 41, pt. 1, pp. 54–55. —G. S.]

Bukharin spent time in almost all of the major Western European countries and the United States and not only acquired a highly diversified familiarity with post-Marxist theoretical thought but also established wide connections in the socialist movement. Besides many articles, Bukharin wrote two books while abroad: *The Economic Theory of the Leisure Class* and *Imperialism and World Economy*. He displayed an obvious bent for socialist theory and rather quickly gained a reputation as the second most important Bolshevik theorist after Lenin.

While abroad Bukharin became acquainted with both Lenin and Stalin, who had gone to Cracow for a Bolshevik conference and stayed there to work on his pamphlet *Marxism and the National Question*. Stalin knew no Western European languages, and when he went to Vienna for a short time, Bukharin, who lived there, helped him by translating some works by Otto Bauer and Rudolph Springer, which Stalin criticized in his pamphlet. While abroad, Bukharin also made Trotsky's acquaintance. Despite political differences they worked together on the New York émigré newspaper *Novy mir* and were on friendly terms. Bukharin met with Lenin in Cracow and Vienna, and they corresponded for some time. Although Lenin took a very warm and friendly attitude toward the youthful Bukharin, whose intellectual qualities were quite attractive, theoretical arguments arose between them more than once. Abroad, Bukharin, took a very skeptical attitude toward the revolutionary potential of the peasantry and petty bourgeoisie; he also opposed Lenin's call for the right of nations to self-determination.

Bukharin, who was in New York when news of the February revolution arrived, could not reach Russia until May 1917. A native Muscovite, he returned to Moscow rather than Petrograd and immediately plunged into party and revolutionary work. He not only became a member of the Moscow City Committee and Moscow regional bureau of the Bolshevik Party but also was chosen at the Sixth Party Congress to be a member of the Central Committee. An an organizer and orator, his role was tremendously important in overcoming the hesitations of the Moscow Bolshevik organization and in mobilizing the masses to carry out the armed insurrection in Moscow.[134] After the victory of Soviet power in Moscow Bukharin and Ivan Stukov were chosen to establish connections between the new Bolshevik Moscow and the Soviet government in Petrograd.

In the first months after the October Revolution Bukharin proved himself to be not only an active Bolshevik and outstanding leader but

134. Bukharin, *Na podstupakh k Oktiabriu: stat'i i rechi mai-dekabr' 1917 g.* (Moscow-Leningrad, 1926).

also an extreme radical who took ultra-left positions on many questions. Bukharin not only spoke out against the Brest-Litovsk peace treaty but actually headed the Left Communist faction, against which Lenin had to exert great efforts. This faction persisted after the signing of the peace treaty, arguing against many aspects of the Soviet government's economic policy in the spring of 1918. The core of the Left Communists consisted, in addition to Bukharin, of such prominent Bolsheviks as Bubnov, Lomov, Osinsky, Pyatakov, and Radek. Frunze, Muralov, Kuibyshev, Dzerzhinsky, Pokrovsky, Solts, Uritsky, Yaroslavsky, Krestinsky, Zemlyachka, and many others joined the Left Communists at various times. However, by the end of the summer of 1918 the disagreements between the party majority and its left-wing minority lost their acuteness. The period of civil war and "war communism" began. The Left Communist faction admitted some of its mistakes, while many of its demands (e.g., for industry to be nationalized more rapidly) became part of the policy of "war communism." The defeat of Germany in World War I and the Soviet government's repudiation of the Brest-Litovsk treaty eliminated the last basis for disagreement. Bukharin wrote in the fall of 1918:

I must admit honestly and openly that we . . . were not right; Comrade Lenin was right, for the breathing spell gave us the opportunity to concentrate our strength and organize a strong Red Army. Now every good strategist should understand that we should not disperse our strength but direct it against the strongest enemy. Germany and Austria are no longer dangerous. The danger comes from the former Allies, mainly England and America.[135]

During the summer of 1918 Bukharin was in charge of *Pravda* and remained its chief editor until the end of the twenties. In spite of former differences personal relations between Lenin and Bukharin were characterized by trust and even friendship. As Stephen Cohen correctly observes:

No leading Bolshevik challenged Lenin's views more often than Bukharin; yet he had become Lenin's favorite. Affection, even love, and mutual respect bound them together.[136]

After the Eighth Party Congress the first Politburo was formed, consisting of five full members and three candidate members. Bukharin was one of the three candidate members.

135. *Pravda*, October 11, 1918.
136. Stephen F. Cohen, *Bukharin and the Bolshevik Revolution* (New York, 1973), p. 81.

During the civil war Bukharin did not directly take part in military work. He became one of the directors of the party's publications and propaganda and also helped organize the party's international connections. At the same time he continued his theoretical work. In 1920 he finished his major contribution, *The Theory of Historical Materialism.* The book *ABC's of Communism, or A Popular Explanation of the Russian Communist Party's Program*, coauthored by Bukharin and Preobrazhensky, brought him particular fame. It ran into many editions and was translated into several foreign languages. During this period the thirty-year-old Bukharin began teaching. A group of students and followers began to form around him almost automatically, laying the basis for the subsequently famous "Bukharin school."

In May 1920 Bukharin's *Economics of the Transition Period* was published. This was a generalization of the policy of "war communism," which Bukharin at that time regarded not as a temporary policy in wartime but as a basic method for transforming a capitalist society into a socialist one. No one in the Bolshevik Party, Bukharin included, had foreseen the introduction of NEP, which turned out to be a much more reasonable policy, and under the conditions in Russia in 1920–1921, the only possible transitional policy. Thus, *The Economics of the Transition Period* soon became obsolete and was never reprinted. It is possible, of course, to take from this book many quotations that do the author no honor. But this was not his private error. It was a collective mistake, which Lenin also shared. In fact, Lenin made a careful reading of Bukharin's book, inserting many comments in the margins. Many of these comments were critical, but on the whole Lenin appraised the book as "splendid" and wrote about "the superb qualities of this outstanding book."[137]

During the so-called trade union discussion in early 1921 Bukharin supported neither Lenin nor Trotsky but tried to work out his own "buffer" position, which only complicated and dragged out the discussion. Lenin was completely exasperated by this, as is evident in his pamphlet "The Party Crisis":

Trotsky, who had been "chief" in the struggle, has now been "outstripped" and entirely "eclipsed" by Bukharin, who has thrown the struggle into an altogether new balance by talking himself into a mistake that is much more serious than all of Trotsky's together. . . . We know how soft Comrade Bukharin is; it is one of

137. V. I. Lenin, *Zamechaniia na knigu N. Bukharina "Ekonomika perekhodnogo perioda"* (Moscow-Leningrad 1931), p. 54.

the qualities that endears him to people, who cannot help liking him. We know that he has been ribbed for being as "soft as wax." It turns out that any "unprincipled" person, any "demagogue," can leave any mark he likes on this "soft wax." The sharp words in quotation marks were used by Comrade Kamenev, during the January 17 discussion, and he had a perfect right to do so. But, of course, neither Kamenev nor anyone else would dream of attributing or reducing it all to unprincipled demagogy.[138]

At the Tenth Party Congress Bukharin signed the resolution written not by Lenin but by Trotsky. Also signing this resolution were Dzerzhinsky, Pyatakov, Kalinin, Preobrazhensky, Rakovsky, and 49 others. However, during the voting this resolution received 50 votes in all, whereas Lenin's resolution received 336 out of a possible 406 votes.[139]

As far as NEP is concerned—that is, the New Economic Policy proclaimed at this same Tenth Congress—it was adopted well nigh unanimously, and Bukharin quickly became one of its main defenders and promoters. The conflict between Lenin and Bukharin faded into the past. While many Bolsheviks treated NEP as primarily a tactical or strategic maneuver, Bukharin took a different approach:

NEP . . . is not only a strategic retreat but also the solution to a major problem of social organization, or more specifically, a problem of the relationship between the spheres of production that we must rationalize and those that we cannot rationalize. We will say frankly: we attempted to take on the task of organizing everything—even organizing the peasantry and the millions of small producers . . . From the standpoint of economic rationality this was madness.[140]

When Lenin was forced to withdraw from leadership of the party because of his illness, Bukharin visited and conversed with him more often than many others. Bukharin fervently supported the "new view" of socialism and the course of its future development that Lenin expressed in his last few articles, "On Cooperation," "Better Fewer, But Better," and so on. It is true that Bukharin proved to be even more of an evolutionist than Lenin. In Bukharin's view:

We will be growing into socialism for many decades: through the expansion of our industry, through the cooperatives, through the growing influence of our banking system, through a thousand and one intermediate forms.[141]

138. Lenin, PSS, 42:242©, 32:51.

139. *Desiatyi s"ezd RKP(b). Stenograficheskii otchet* (Tenth Party Congress. Stenographic Record) (Moscow, 1963), p. 399.

140. *Chetvertyi Vsemirnyi Kongress Kominterna. Izbrannye materialy* (Fourth World Congress of the Comintern: Selected Materials) (Moscow-Petrograd, 1923), p. 75.

141. *Pravda,* June 30, 1923.

At the Twelfth Party Congress Bukharin, who knew about Lenin's notes on "autonomization," tried to take up "the defense of the Georgian question"—that is, he tried on his own initiative to do what Lenin had asked Trotsky to do. At that time Bukharin's authority was not great enough to influence the decisions of the congress. In the struggle against the Trotskyist opposition Bukharin completely supported the triumvirate, while preserving a certain independence in his opinions. In the struggle against the New Opposition, on the other hand, Bukharin was already a full member of the Politburo and played perhaps the major role in opposing Zinoviev and Kamenev. Many party leaders addressed Bukharin with generous compliments: "the best theorist of the party," "the best party worker," a person "who has the courage to express his thoughts and when they go contrary to the party, has the courage to openly state that he was mistaken," a person "whom we all love and will support." That was how Ordzhonikidze, Kalinin, Molotov, Zhdanov, Stalin, and several other speakers at the Fourteenth Party Congress referred to Bukharin.[142]

Earlier in this chapter I quoted some of Bukharin's most important statements on problems of socialist construction, in particular, his statement that the kulaks and capitalist elements could "grow over into socialism." These statements by no means indicated rejection of the principle of class struggle. Bukharin did not think, of course, that the kulaks would voluntarily contribute to the building of socialism or would continue to exist in a fully socialist society. However, he insisted on a slower and more evolutionary course for the development of socialism, and on the preservation of a voluntary alliance between the working class and peasantry. His political position was such that he could not go into detail about the future fate of the kulaks, who at the time were providing the country with a considerable part of its marketable grain. Further, Bukharin's views at that time coincided with and expressed the views of the majority of the party leadership, which did not wish for a "third" revolution. Here, for example, is what Kalinin, chairman of the Central Executive Committee, wrote about the prospects for the countryside:

Many perceive the growth of the kulak as an annoying result of an annoying process of stratification in the countryside. . . . But is it possible to talk seriously about a real growth of production in the countryside without a parallel growth in stratification? . . . Stratification of the countryside is a necessary consequence of

142. *Chetyrnadtsatyi s"ezd*, pp. 223, 471–472, and passim.

its economic growth. Soviet power uses all the means it has at its disposal to help the economic growth of the countryside, and that also means indirectly helping stratification. Those who want to seriously inhibit stratification must also want an end to economic growth in the countryside. The positive elements in the process of stratification overcome the negative aspect. After all, along with stratification the general welfare improves, including that of the poor peasants. If one is to speak the truth, rather than try to ingratiate oneself with the poor peasants, the expansion of the productive forces in the countryside is the only means of betterment for the weak peasant. It is clear that a violent struggle against stratification, inasmuch as it would inhibit the growth of production, is economically harmful and politically senseless. . . .

An increase in the percentage of strong working-peasant farms at the expense of weak ones must be welcomed, it seems to me, because it serves as an indication of the development of peasant farming and of increased productivity in the countryside. Many seem frightened by the development of initiative among the strong working-peasant elements, fearing that along with the growth of their farms a corresponding growth of bourgeois-kulak ideology will occur within this stratum of the peasantry. . . . Under the Soviet system . . . the ideological influence of our government is much stronger than that of the bourgeoisie. The stratification of the countryside creates a layer of true petty bourgeoisie in the form of farmers, tradesmen, handicraftsmen, and a very limited number of high-level market farmers. But if we allow private capital in trade and make agreements with foreign concessionaires in the hopes of using them in the interest of developing our collectivist economy, there is no doubt that the rural petty bourgeoisie will contribute to the growth of the socialized economy through the state credit, state trade, and cooperative systems.

To sum up, I maintain that the stratification of the countryside not only does not inhibit the growth of the collectivist economy but the opposite—it increases productivity and marketability in agriculture and, accordingly, prepares the elements for collectivism and, although it may seem paradoxical, clears the ground for a Soviet countryside.[143]

Of course, not everything in Bukharin's views and theories of the mid-twenties was completely thought out; he made quite a few statements that were vulnerable to orthodox Marxist criticism. Here in particular the scholasticism in Bukharin's thinking made itself felt, the scholasticism that Lenin wrote about and from which Bukharin never freed himself to the end of his life. In analyzing Bukharin's theoretical works on economics, politics, the world Communist movement, philosophy, and literature (Bukharin's enormous erudition is beyond question), we can clearly see the elements of schematic thinking and oversimplification in almost all of his theoretical constructs. It was extremely important to him to find a particular formula or schematic outline, although such formulas or sche-

143. *Izvestia*, March 22, 1925.

mas hardly ever took in all of the most essential aspects of one or another phenomenon. However, Stalin, as Raskolnikov later correctly wrote, was even more of a schematic thinker and scholastic than Bukharin.

Bukharin's major theoretical work, in which he presented his conception of NEP and the prospects for its evolution, was *The Road to Socialism and the Worker-Peasant Alliance*. First published in 1925, it was reprinted in 1926 and 1927. Answering his critics in 1929, Bukharin stated that he saw nothing erroneous in this work.

The victory over the Zinovievist opposition moved Bukharin to the position of one of the most authoritative members of the party leadership. Bukharin became the official party theorist and also headed the Comintern. Several Western researchers, not without reason, refer to the period 1926–1928 as that of the "duumvirate" of Stalin and Bukharin. As Stephen Cohen writes:

> Official Bolshevism in 1925–7 was largely Bukharinist; the party was following Bukharin's road to socialism. Nor was his influence limited to the Soviet party and internal affairs. He systematically wrote his theories into the resolutions of the Comintern. . . . From 1926 onward, he, almost alone, shaped official Bolshevik understanding of the outside world, of international capitalism and revolution.
>
> There was, generally speaking, a rough division of labor between Bukharin and Stalin, between policy formulation and theory on one side and organizational muscle on the other. . . .
>
> Bukharin also contributed more practical political assets to the duumvirate. The most important was his control of the party's central publications. To his editorship of the daily *Pravda* was added in April 1924 the Central Committee's new biweekly journal, *Bolshevik*. . . . Control of the Central Committee's two principal organs of opinion gave Bukharin an important weapon in the factional struggle. . . .
>
> [Leadership] of the Comintern [also] had its advantages. It enhanced Bukharin's personal prestige as well as the prestige and authority of the duumvirate. . . .
>
> Bukharin had "tremendous authority" among party youth, especially those chosen for advanced preparation as future Bolshevik intellectuals. . . .
>
> Those who encountered him over the years testify that the gentle, open, good-humored Bukharin, who in his traditional Russian blouse, leather jacket, and high boots conveyed the aura of Bohemia-come-to-power, was the most likable of the Bolshevik oligarchs. . . . There was about him none of Trotsky's intimidating hauteur, Zinoviev's labored pomposity, or the intrigue and mistrust surrounding Stalin. . . .
>
> In the last analysis, however, Bukharin's authority rested on his standing as Bolshevism's greatest living Marxist. . . .[144]

144. Cohen, *Bukharin*, pp. 215, 216, 219, 227.

The most consistent and authoritative of Bukharin's allies in the soon-to-follow struggle between Stalin and the "Right" were Aleksei Rykov and Mikhail Tomsky.

Rykov was also one of the most prominent and well-known party officials. His family background was proletarian, and after becoming a Bolshevik, he took part in the underground struggle against the tsarist regime. Several times he was sent into internal exile. It was during his term of exile in Narym that news of the February revolution reached him. After the October revolution Rykov became a member of the first Soviet government as people's commissar of internal affairs. During the civil war he headed the Supreme Economic Council, then became a deputy chairman of the Sovnarkom and chairman of the Council of Labor and Defense. In 1924 Rykov was appointed chairman of the Sovnarkom —that is, to the post that only Lenin had occupied before him. This was a great honor and a tremendous responsibility for the forty-three-year-old Bolshevik.

Tomsky, who came from a proletarian family, worked as a printer. He joined the Bolsheviks as early as the first Russian revolution and immediately became prominent as an organizer and leader of the trade union movement. After the defeat of the revolution he was active in underground work in Moscow and Petrograd. Arrested and sentenced to five years of hard labor, he was freed by the February revolution. He again returned to party and trade union activity and soon after the October victory became the acknowledged leader of the trade union movement and organizations in Soviet Russia. As head of the All-Union Central Trade Union Council throughout the twenties, Tomsky enjoyed enormous authority among union activists.

■ 10
STALIN'S FIGHT AGAINST THE "RIGHT DEVIATION"

In 1925–1927, in spite of the Left Opposition's attacks, a course was taken toward overall development of the productive forces in the countryside, including the development, to use Kalinin's terminology, of "strong working-peasant farms." The result of this policy was the fairly quick growth of agricultural production, which considerably surpassed the prewar level in gross output. However, the country's overall economic situation remained difficult and complicated. The recovery period had ended; yet the reactivated plants and factories were not functioning in the best way—their equipment was worn out and their output was often characterized by high cost and low quality. Significant unemployment persisted, and foreign trade was developing slowly because the government did not have sufficient goods for export. Although the party had already proclaimed a course toward industrialization, its resources were not sufficient to carry it out. This very lack of resources inhibited the modernization and re-equipment of the Red Army, although during this period the Soviet Union's international position was still unstable and gave cause for considerable apprehension. It was necessary to think about expanding the sources of "primitive socialist accumulation" at the expense of the capitalist elements in the countryside and city. Bukharin himself took the initiative in revising several basic postulates of the "general line." Thus, for example, at the Eighth Moscow Trade Union Congress, he stated:

The implementation of the line of the Fourteenth Conference and Fourteenth Congress reinforced the alliance with the middle peasant and strengthened the proletariat's position in the countryside. Now together with the middle peasant, and relying on the poor peasant and on the growing economic and political forces of our Union and party, it is possible and necessary to make a transition to an accelerated offensive against the capitalist elements, primarily the kulaks.[145]

With Bukharin's participation the Fifteenth Party Congress passed a number of resolutions aimed at restricting the capitalist elements in the city and countryside. However, contrary to the demands of the Left Opposition, it was proposed that these restrictions be carried out primarily through economic means—that is, within the framework of NEP and not by the methods of "war communism." Moreover, placing restrictions on the capitalist elements or going on the offensive against them did not at all mean that they should be squeezed out of economic life or "liquidated." Therefore the Fifteenth Congress took a firm stand against the Left's proposal for compulsory requisitioning of grain from the prosperous strata in the countryside. The congress also opposed any hasty mass collectivization, since neither the subjective nor the objective preconditions for it had been created.

The agricultural policy proclaimed by the Fifteenth Party Congress was not put into effect. Even before the congress, in the fall of 1927, serious difficulties had arisen in the process of grain procurements. Although the harvest had been good, the peasants, especially the better-off

145. *Pravda*, October 13, 1927.

ones, were in no hurry to sell grain to the government. The peasants still had surpluses left over from 1925–1926, and many of them wanted to wait for the spring in order to sell their grain at a higher price. Many peasants demanded not money but manufactured goods. These difficulties in relations with the peasants had not been overcome by the beginning of winter. The peasants had fulfilled their obligation to pay an agricultural tax, which was not too burdensome and could now be paid in money rather than in kind, but they refused to sell grain to the government at the comparatively low fall purchase price. Meanwhile, the government did not have emergency reserves of grain, since grain at that time was also an important export item. A large grain shortage developed that threatened to seriously affect food supplies for the cities and the army as well as export commitments.

Seeking to avert the consequences of the grain shortage, the Central Committee issued a number of directives authorizing the use of emergency measures against the kulaks and well-to-do peasants, including forced requisitioning of grain reserves. Although the directives termed these measures temporary, what was really involved was an abrupt change, completely unexpected by local officials, in the party's entire previous policy toward the countryside, a change that contradicted the recently adopted resolutions of the Fifteenth congress and that was more in the spirit of the proposals of the just defeated Left Opposition.

The directives were passed with the consent of the entire Politburo, including Rykov, Bukharin, and Tomsky. In order to accelerate grain procurement, thousands of party members were sent to help the rural party organizations. Many Central Committee members were dispatched to various regions of the country. Stalin himself left his office in the Kremlin and on January 15, 1928, went to Siberia, where, according to the information of the procurement agencies, especially large grain reserves had accumulated. Stalin went to Novosibirsk, Barnaul, and Omsk. There he organized meetings of party and government activists, at which he rudely and harshly condemned the local officials for their indecisiveness in the use of emergency measures against the rich peasants.

Pressure on the rich peasantry resulted in some increase in grain procurement. But in April 1928 the flow of grain to the procurement centers again decreased, and Stalin gave the order for even more widespread application of emergency measures, which had already affected the bulk of the middle peasants. Simultaneously in the Supreme Economic Council under Kuibyshev's leadership measures were devised to accelerate the process of industrialization and expand capital construction, which required significant government outlays.

It was possible to foresee that the new sharp turn in Stalin's economic policy would cause disagreements in the Politburo and the Central Committee. In the spring of 1928 debates in the Politburo became increasingly bitter. It was not only Bukharin, supported by Rykov and Tomsky, who spoke out against Stalin's policy. Two other Politburo members, Kalinin and Voroshilov, took moderate positions. Voroshilov, as people's commissar of defense, feared that troubled relations with the peasantry would affect the army's morale. "Unhealthy" moods in some sections of the army were reported to him through confidential channels. Kalinin, as chairman of the Central Executive Committee, was concerned about the alliance with the peasantry. He valued his reputation as the "all-union peasant elder," the defender of and spokesman for the interests of the working peasants. Two other Politburo members, Ordzhonikidze and Rudzutak, were wavering. Of those who had become Politburo members since the Fifteenth Party Congress, essentially only Kuibyshev and Molotov supported Stalin unconditionally. This forced Stalin to maneuver and play a waiting game. Stalin's support in the ranks of the Central Committee and in a number of important regional party organizations was not strong enough. The leadership of the Moscow party organization, headed by Politburo candidate Uglanov, came out decisively on Bukharin's side. The apparatus of the Sovnarkom and State Planning Commission were also on the side of the "moderates." Whereas Menzhinsky, the new chairman of the GPU, supported Stalin, two of Menzhensky's deputies, Trilisser and Yagoda, spoke out for the more moderate policy.

Bukharin was a theorist and ideologist; he was not afraid to get into an argument with either Lenin or Stalin. But at the same time he was too soft a man, poorly suited for the harsh conditions of political infighting. He did not strive for power in the party as did Trotsky or Zinoviev. The fresh memory of the bitter struggle with the Left Opposition prevented Bukharin from even considering the launching of a new party discussion and appealing for support from the party as a whole in his dispute with Stalin. Bukharin did not want to create a new faction and work out an opposition platform. Moreover, the alignment of forces within the Central Committee allowed Bukharin to hope that he would be able to gain the upper hand while keeping the discussion within the framework of the Central Committee and Politburo. I hardly need comment on the advantages this attitude provided for Stalin.

In May and June of 1928 Bukharin sent two letters to the Politburo that were supported by Rykov and Tomsky. In these letters Bukharin pointed out that many of the Central Committee's measures were turning into a new line that differed from the line of the Fifteenth Congress and that the party was being disoriented ideologically by all this. Bukharin maintained that the party leadership had neither a commonly held opinion nor a coherent plan. He demanded that a free and general discussion be held at the Central Committee plenary session, which was to take place on July 4. Unlike Trotsky's letters to the Politburo, Bukharin's letters were not "open" or circulated among the party organizations.

Stalin announced that Bukharin's recommendations had been accepted. However, Stalin did not want to leave the initiative to Bukharin; it was also important for him to split the ranks of Bukharin's supporters. A pretext was provided by Mikhail Frumkin, deputy people's commissar of foreign trade and finance, who sent a letter to the Politburo on June 15 protesting the policies then being carried out. Frumkin strongly objected to the new financial plan, which, in his opinion, exceeded the country's potential. Frumkin maintained that the reason for the difficult economic situation appeared to be the extraordinary measures, which were exhausting the country. He objected to the forced creation of collective farms (kolkhozes) and state farms (sovkhozes) and to excessively large capital investments. Frumkin's letter became well known to a relatively large number of people in party circles, and Stalin insisted that the Politburo answer Frumkin. However, a general answer was not agreed on; at that point Stalin wrote an answer on his own and circulated it among the Politburo members.[146]

The discussion of Stalin's letter caused an outburst of sharp disagreement at the Politburo meeting on June 27, 1928. Bukharin, Rykov, and Tomsky read a declaration that spoke of the dangers of a rupture in the alliance between the working class and peasantry. The authors of the declaration called for immediate cancellation of the extraordinary measures and reopening of the peasant markets. They proposed that no kolkhozes and sovkhozes be created until the government was able to provide them with immediate material aid. The party's attention should be focused on providing incentives for poor and middle peasant households. Molotov called Bukharin's document "anti-party," but Stalin was more careful. A commission consisting of Bauman, Bukharin, Mikoyan,

146. Stalin, *Sochineniia*, 11; 116–126.

Rykov, and Stalin was formed to resolve the disagreements that had arisen. The commission prepared compromise theses on the grain procurement policies. These were approved at the next Politburo meeting on July 2. It was decided to cancel the extraordinary measures, raise grain procurement prices, and restore the rural markets.

A few days later the Central Committee plenum opened in Moscow. Rykov, who gave the main speech at the plenary session, appraised the country's situation as very bad and even brought up the dangerous possibility of a new civil war with the peasantry. He repeated the demand for eliminating the extraordinary measures, raising procurement prices, maintaining the principles of NEP, and supporting the poor and middle peasantry.

Stalin was not about to back down. He made sure he had the support of the majority of regional party secretaries and devoted his speeches at the plenary session to justifying the policies carried out up to that time. He centered his arguments on the need for a faster pace of industrialization. But since Rykov had not accused Stalin, Stalin did not direct any accusations against Bukharin or Rykov in his speeches at the plenary session. Stalin spoke only against certain views expressed by Trotsky, Preobrazhensky, or Frumkin. At the July plenum Stalin first introduced his theory that the class struggle would intensify the closer the Soviet Union moved toward socialism. He stated:

The advancement of the working class toward socialism cannot help but lead to the opposition of the exploiting elements, . . . cannot help but lead to the inevitable intensification of the class struggle.

Stalin not only spoke in favor of "eliminating the need for any kind of extraordinary measures whatsoever" but also stated:

People who think about turning the extraordinary measures into a permanent or protracted course for our party are dangerous people, for they play with fire and create a threat to the smychka [the bond between the working class and the peasantry].

Yet in the same speech Stalin said that it was impossible to think of completely rejecting the future use of extraordinary measures in the countryside if "extraordinary circumstances" arose.[147]

The July plenum concluded with the passing of compromise resolutions that were much closer to the position of the "Rights" than to

147. Ibid., p. 172, 173–174.

Stalin's. Yet this was not a victory for Bukharin, for Stalin was able to carry the majority of the Central Committee and to win Kalinin and Voroshilov over to his side. Now he had a definite majority within the Politburo, which was more important than any resolution of the plenum. Bukharin also understood this. Just as the July plenum was taking place, about forty Left Oppositionists, including Kamenev, were readmitted to the party and returned to Moscow. On July 11 Bukharin arranged through Sokolnikov to have a meeting with Kamenev. Bukharin tried to talk Kamenev out of a bloc with Stalin against the "Right," assuring him that all of the difference between "Right" and "Left" meant nothing compared to their overall goals in the struggle with Stalin. This secret meeting accomplished nothing for Bukharin. Although Kamenev had promised to keep his talks with Bukharin a secret, he made a detailed record of them, which he showed to Zinoviev. This transcript fell into the hands of the Trotskyists, and Trotsky, who was indignant about Kamenev's and Zinoviev's "capitulation" and who did not have any sympathy for Bukharin, later made the Bukharin-Kamenev conversation public.

Rumors about disagreements in the Politburo and Central Committee circulated within the party as well as beyond its bounds, although the Politburo members, by mutual agreement, emphatically denied these rumors, maintaining the temporary equilibrium. At the end of July the Sixth Comintern Congress was to be held in Moscow. On July 30, 1928, all of the Politburo members signed the following document:

> The undersigned members of the Politburo of the Central Committee declare to the Council of Elders of the congress that they protest in the strongest possible manner the circulation of any rumors whatsoever about disagreements among the members of the Politburo.

On September 30, 1928, Bukharin published in *Pravda* his well-known article "Notes of an Economist," which criticized many of Stalin's economic policies, particularly that of industrialization at a forced pace. Bukharin simultaneously proposed an extensive program for overcoming the country's economic difficulties through developing and modernizing NEP. He spoke out against a new "revolution," advocating restrictions on the kulaks, development of cooperatives, and a more correct price policy. He defended the principle of economic planning, but opposed "hypertrophied" planning, since not everything could be foreseen in a plan. Industrial planning, he argued further, had to keep pace with agricultural development and take into account the Soviet Union's available resources. Industrialization could not be accomplished at the expense of agricultural production, he asserted, stressing that the rate of industrialization should be realistic. Bukharin's criticism was formally directed against "Trotskyism," but in fact he was arguing against Stalin's economic policies. It is not surprising that Bukharin's followers promoted this article in every way possible. At the October 8 Politburo meeting, the publication of Bukharin's article "without the Central Committee's knowledge" was condemned by a majority of votes over Rykov, Tomsky, and Bukharin's objections.[148]

However, Stalin evaded the discussion. In one of his speeches he even stated that Bukharin's "Notes of an Economist" posed a number of theoretical questions in a completely valid and acceptable way.[149]

At the same time Stalin took a number of measures to weaken Bukharin's position. The all-out struggle in the Comintern against the "right deviation" in the Communist movement was indirectly aimed against Bukharin and his followers. New elections were held at the Institute of Red Professors, resulting in the replacement of the "Bukharinist" party bureau there. Another loyal Stalinist, Kaganovich, was added to the presidium of the All-Union Central Trade Union Council. Bukharin's position in charge of the party's publications was weakened. The loyal Stalinist Yaroslavsky was given an increasingly important role on the editorial board of *Pravda*. Bukharin's supporter Pyotr Petrovsky was removed from his post as chief editor of *Leningradskaya Pravda*, and Slepkov, Astrov, Maretsky, Zaitsev, and Tsetlin were removed from the editorial boards of *Pravda* and *Bolshevik*. Although Bukharin still remained the chief editor, it was now difficult for him to set the tone and content of the party's publications.

At this point Stalin's followers in the Moscow party organization were also activated. They succeeded in having new elections held to replace pro-Bukharin party secretaries in several district committees. In mid-October 1928, while Bukharin was on vacation at Kislovodsk, a plenary session of the Moscow regional and city party committee was called. Uglanov proved to be in the minority. At the plenary session Stalin himself spoke, accusing Uglanov of right deviation. As a result of the voting Uglanov and his followers were not reelected to the leadership of the Moscow party organization. Instead, Kaganovich became its head.

This was in effect a decisive defeat for Bukharin. His group became

148. F. M. Vaganov, *Pravyi uklon v VKP(b) i ego razgrom*, Moscow, 1970, pp. 161–163.
149. Stalin, *Sochineniia*, 11; 260.

demoralized; even Rykov began making concessions in the discussions under way in the Politburo. Only now did Bukharin cut his vacation short and return to Moscow, where he found his position in the upper levels of the party had been greatly weakened. Moreover, the country's situation was again becoming strained. Grain procurement was going poorly, and the question of using extraordinary measures was again raised. Bukharin, Rykov, and Tomsky spoke against them. When the Politburo rejected their protest, they handed in a collective resignation. Stalin was not completely sure of his strength at this point, for Kalinin and Voroshilov again showed signs of wavering. Therefore Stalin proposed a compromise to which Bukharin agreed. Stalin promised, in particular, to stop harassing "Bukharinists" and to reduce capital investment in industry. Rykov was confirmed as the main speaker at the next Central Committee plenum.

The November plenum demonstrated that Stalin clearly had the advantage, and it further strengthened his position. At the plenum he gave his speech "On the Right Danger in the Party," in which he named only such party officials as Frumkin and Uglanov as "bearers of the Right danger." "As far as the Politburo is concerned," he said, "we are all of one mind." [150]

Bukharin did not attend most of the plenum meetings. Needless to say, Stalin did not abide by the compromise he and Bukharin had agreed to before the plenum. In the Comintern, under the pretext of a fight against the "Right," the leadership of many Communist parties was changed, making Bukharin only the nominal head of the Comintern. At the Eighth Trade Union Congress Tomsky and his followers proved to be in the minority among the delegates and were defeated as early as the vote on the agenda. Although Tomsky was reelected chairman of the Trade Union Council, the majority of the new Central Council consisted of Stalin's followers.

Certain of his defeat, Tomsky handed in his resignation. Although it was not accepted, Tomsky did not go back to work at the Trade Union Council. Bukharin followed his example. He stopped attending meetings of the Comintern executive committee and *Pravda*'s editorial board. It is true that at the end of January 1929 Bukharin was asked to give the speech at the memorial meeting marking the fifth anniversary of Lenin's death. In this speech, entitled "Lenin's Political Testament," Bukharin stated in detail Lenin's views on aspects of building socialism in the

150. Ibid., 11: 290.

Soviet Union, basing himself on an analysis of Lenin's articles and speeches of 1921–1923. To a careful listener or reader of Bukharin's speech it was obvious that Stalin's political and economic line was a far cry from Lenin's plan for building socialism. As things turned out, however, this indirect attack on Stalin was not particularly effective.

The struggle, which had not in fact gone beyond the framework of the Central Committee and various clashes within the apparatus, was approaching its denouement. Stalin no longer needed compromises. Bukharin took up the challenge, and a bitter conflict was fought out between them at Politburo meetings during January and February 1929. At this time Bukharin, together with Tomsky and Rykov, wrote up a detailed document—a kind of "right opposition" platform (it was called "the platform of the three"), which contained criticism of Stalin's policies and offered an alternative program for the country's economic and political development. Rykov read this platform at one of the Politburo's meetings, but it was not brought up for discussion by the party as a whole or even by the Central Committee. It was in this document that Bukharin accused Stalin of "military-feudal exploitation of the peasantry." The Politburo rejected this accusation as "slander" and reprimanded Bukharin.

The situation was heating up, and wavering was evident on the part of a number of Bukharin's closest supporters. Rykov withdrew his resignation and returned to work on the Sovnarkom. One of Bukharin's closest disciples, Stetsky, unexpectedly condemned him.

The end came in April at a joint plenum of the Central Committee and Central Control Commission, where the Bukharinists were clearly in the minority. Stalin presented a lengthy critique of "the group of Bukharin, Tomsky, and Rykov," which had supposedly just been discovered in the Politburo, as though no one had known of its existence before. Stalin's speech was sharp, rude, and full of distortions. He went over every mistake Bukharin had made from the beginning of his political career. Bukharin's writings, which had served as the basis for the party line in the years 1925–1927, were proclaimed to be incorrect. In his usual insulting manner Stalin called Tomsky a "a narrow trade unionist and political intriguer." Stalin accused Bukharin of "singing the tune of Messieurs the Milyukovs and tailing along behind the enemies of the people," adding that he was "a man of inflated pretensions" who had been "in the ranks of Trotsky's disciples until a short time ago." Bukharin's theories were "nonsense," and the declaration by the Bukharin group was "insolent and rude slander," etc., etc. The attempts by Bukharin, Tomsky, and Uglanov to soften the sharpness of Stalin's attacks by referring to their recent personal friendship were emphatically rejected by Stalin, who declared that "all these cries and lamentations are not worth a brass farthing."[151]

Bukharin, Rykov, Tomsky, and Uglanov did not recant at the plenum but instead defended their views and criticized Stalin's policies. Bukharin in particular accused Stalin of undermining NEP and establishing "monstrously one-sided" relations with the peasantry that were destroying the "bond between the working class and the peasantry" and declared that such a policy meant total capitulation to Trotskyism. Bukharin supported the plans for rapid industrialization but warned that without the simultaneous development of agriculture, industrialization was bound to fail. He accused Stalin of creating a bureaucratic state and of robbing the peasants, condemning Stalin's theory about a constant intensification of the class struggle as the USSR advanced toward socialism:

This peculiar theory takes the bare fact that an intensification of the class struggle is now taking place and elevates it into some sort of inevitable law of our development. According to this strange theory, it would seem that the further we advance toward socialism, the more difficulties will pile up and the sharper the class struggle will become, and at the very gates to socialism we apparently will either have to start a civil war or, perishing from hunger, lay down our bones to die.[152]

Bukharin's speech, like most of the record of the April plenum, was never published. Stalin had a solid majority at the plenum. But he was afraid that in the broader circles of the party and especially among rural Communists sympathy for Bukharin's program would be much greater than among the members of the Central Committee and Central Control Commission. There could be no question that among the peasantry at large and among the non-Communist intelligentsia as well as in a significant section of the working class Bukharin at that time enjoyed much greater popularity than Stalin. Even Stalin's speech at the plenum was not published in full. A major portion of it, primarily the part criticizing Bukharin and his platform, was left out. Only twenty years later was the speech published in full, in Volume 12 of Stalin's *Works*.

Stalin's fear of making his polemic with Bukharin public indicated he was unsure of the soundness of his own ideological and political platform.

151. Ibid., 12: 1–107.
152. From the unpublished stenographic record of the plenum.

Today we can see that a large proportion of the "rightist" criticisms of Stalin's policies of 1928–1929 were completely justified. The "Right" correctly opposed the transformation of the extraordinary measures into the permanent policy of the party in the countryside. They correctly protested against the policy of forced and hasty collectivization, whose only result could be a decline in agricultural production, aggravating the problem of food supplies for the cities and disrupting export plans. The "Right" also had good reason to oppose "gigantomania" in industrial construction and excessive capital expenditures, which often made no sense economically. Their proposals for a change in the prices the state paid the peasants for grain were also sensible. The grain prices in 1927 were very low, lower than the actual cost of production, which obviously gave the peasants no economic incentive to increase the amount of grain they sold to the state.

In 1928 Bukharin and his political friends proposed that the Soviet government purchase light industrial goods and even grain from abroad rather than resort again to extraordinary measures. It is possible that under existing conditions that would have been the lesser evil. The "Rights" were quite justified in pointing out that the development of light industry was being slighted. While it was correct to maintain priority for heavy industry, light industry should have been developed more rapidly because it provided a large part of the goods needed for sale both in city and country and probably would have provided the necessary financial means for all the government's projects and requirements. If the necessary proportions were not maintained, inflation and the "goods famine" were sure to continue, with administrative pressure substituting for economic incentives.

Even in 1928–1929 Bukharin was sure that NEP, as the party's basic line in economic policy, had not yet been exhausted, that there was still room in the Soviet economy for the development not only of socialist enterprises but also certain elements of capitalism. Only in the more distant future would the development of socialism result in the elimination of the bourgeois Nepman sector and the exploitative kulak farm. Bukharin felt, however (and until 1928 Stalin supported him in this view), that the urban and rural capitalist elements would be squeezed out basically by economic not by administrative pressure—that is, as a result of competition in which the socialist sector would gain the upper hand over the capitalist sector by proving itself more efficient economically. The "Leftists," who called for a new revolution and new expropriations, might dispute this point of view, but it had every right to exist and to be tested in practice. The experience of the European socialist countries since World War II (Poland, East Germany, Hungary, Yugoslavia) shows clearly that it is possible to have the most varied combinations of socialist industry in the cities and large-scale socialist enterprises in agriculture, on the one hand, and a small-scale private sector, including small capitalist businesses, on the other. This means that various approaches are possible toward the peasantry and the petty bourgeoisie while overall socialist perspectives are maintained.

Stalin, in his policies toward the peasantry, adopted Trotskyist conceptions of "primitive socialist accumulation" along with Zinoviev and Kamenev's proposals for excessive taxation of the well-to-do strata in the countryside, while substantially broadening and deepening these proposals and conceptions. It was logical for Stalin to bring in many prominent former Left Oppositionists to carry out his new policy.

Stalin also criticized Bukharin's leadership of the Comintern from an incorrect "ultra-left" sectarian point of view. There is no question that Bukharin had once shared the mistaken position of the Comintern toward the Social Democratic parties, including the formula of "social fascism," but in the mid-twenties he showed signs of revising his stand. As the danger of fascism in Europe grew, Bukharin found it possible for agreements against fascism to be made with base organizations of Social Democratic parties and Social Democratic trade unions. Stalin demanded, to the contrary, an intensified struggle against Social Democracy. Moreover, he urged that the Communists focus their attacks on the leftist tendencies in Social Democracy, although these very tendencies were potentially the most likely allies of the Communist parties.

In his speech on "The Right Deviation in the CPSU(B)," for example, Stalin said:

In Bukharin's theses it was stated that the fight against Social Democracy is one of the fundamental tasks of the sections of the Comintern. That of course is true. But it is not enough. In order that the fight against Social Democracy be carried on successfully, a special stress must be placed on fighting the so-called "Left" wing of Social Democracy, that "Left" wing which, by playing with "Left" phrases and thus adroitly deceiving the workers, is retarding their mass defection from Social Democracy. It is obvious that unless the "Left" Social Democrats are smashed, it will be impossible to overcome Social Democracy as a whole. Yet in Bukharin's theses the question of "Left" Social Democracy was entirely ignored. That of course was a great defect. The delegation of the CPSU(B) [at the Sixth

Congress of the Comintern] was therefore obliged to introduce to Bukharin's theses an amendment to this effect, and this amendment was subsequently adopted by the Congress.[153]

The erroneousness of Stalin's position is obvious. It frustrated any moves toward a united front with other left forces in the working class, and branded many in the Soviet Communist Party and quite a few Party members and activists in the West as "bearers of the right deviation."

In polemicizing against Bukharin and his group, Stalin and his supporters often made crude use of the method of vulgar sociologism, which is alien to Marxism. This method consists, in particular, in the linking of almost any cultural phenomenon or political statement with the political moods or interests of one or another class.

Since Bukharin's platform in 1928–1929 was preferable to Stalin's among not only the broad masses of working people but also the urban and rural capitalist elements, Stalin and his supporters immediately branded Bukharin as a "defender of the capitalist elements," "exponent of the ideology of the kulaks," "a transmission belt for kulak influences within the party," and so on. Some would add the qualifying term "objectively," but later it was usually left off. With such a vulgar sociological approach it would have been possible to call Lenin "a defender of kulak-capitalist elements" in 1921–1922 because of the introduction of NEP.[154]

Bukharin, Rykov, and Tomsky never established any kind of strictly defined faction within the party. Stalin himself admitted this. "Do the Right deviators have a faction?" he asked in one of his speeches. "I think not. Can it be said that they do not obey the decisions of our party? I don't think that we have any basis for accusing them of this. Is it possible to affirm that the Right deviators are necessarily organizing their own faction? I doubt this."[155] Thus the "Right" did not violate the resolution of the Tenth Party Congress on party unity. Therefore, by taking repressive measures against the "Rightists," by starting an organizational fight against them, and declaring the defense of "Rightist" views incompatible with party membership, Stalin greatly narrowed down the liberties guar-

153. Stalin, *Sochineniia*, 12: 21–22.

154. Most of these unjust assessments of Bukharin, Tomsky, and Rykov continue to appear in present-day literature on party history. For example, Sergei Trapeznikov writes, "The Bukharin-Rykov group openly took the side of the kulaks and all the reactionary forces in the country." (*Leninizm i agrarno-krest'ianskii vopros* [Moscow, 1967], 2: 187.)

155. Stalin, *Sochineniia*, Vol. 12. 287.

anteed by the party rules, under which every party member was supposed to be able to freely discuss questions of party policy.

Only after the April Central Committee plenum did an extremely
intensive campaign against the "right deviation" begin at meetings and
in the press, with criticism directed specifically against Bukharin, Rykov,
and Tomsky. All of Bukharin's works since the beginning of his political
activity were reexamined from a biased angle. While this was going on,
the leaders of the "Right" were themselves forced to be silent, although
they remained Politburo members and Rykov headed the Sovnarkom as
usual. Stalin wanted to extract from them the public capitulation he had
not been able to obtain at the April plenum. And he got what he wanted.
As early as November 1929, at the Central Committee plenum, Rykov
read a written statement from Bukharin, Tomsky, and himself, stating
that the "group of three" unconditionally stood for the general party line
and disagreed with the majority of the Central Committee only in regard
to certain methods of implementing this line. At the same time, the
"group of three" noted in their statement that "in general, very positive
results have been achieved on the rails of the accepted party method of
conducting the general line." Therefore, Bukharin, Rykov, and Tomsky
declared that "the disagreements between us and the majority of the
Central Committee have been eliminated."[156] But even this statement
was called "unsatisfactory." The November plenum therefore removed
Bukharin from the Politburo and issued a warning to Rykov, Tomsky,
and Uglanov.

Right after the November plenum Bukharin, together with Rykov and
Tomsky, submitted a new statement acknowledging their "mistakes."
The "Right" Opposition leaders' will to fight had been broken, as had
that of the Left Opposition leaders. It is said that on the night of January
1, 1930, there was an unexpected knock on the door of Stalin's apartment, where he was merrily celebrating the New Year with his friends.
On the threshold stood Bukharin, Rykov, and Tomsky with wine. They
had come to Stalin's for a friendly reconciliation. And although outwardly
there was a reconciliation, none of the leaders of the "Right" regained his
former status in the party. After the Sixteenth Party Congress Tomsky
was removed from the Politburo, and at the December 1930 plenum of
the Central Committee Rykov was likewise removed. In 1931 Rykov was
replaced by Molotov as chairman of the Sovnarkom and reassigned to the

156. *Bolshevik* (1930), no. 2, p. 8.

job of people's commissar of posts and telegraph. Bukharin was appointed leader of the scientific research planning sector of the Supreme Economic Council, and a few years later also became chief editor of *Izvestia*. The Sixteenth Party Congress again elected Bukharin, Rykov, and Tomsky to the Central Committee, but after the Seventeenth Congress all three were reduced to the rank of candidate members of the Central Committee. Although in the early thirties many dramatic events shook the Soviet Union, Bukharin, Rykov, and Tomsky never again raised their voices in protest.

Despite their submission during the first Five Year Plan the entire Soviet press continued to abuse the former proponents of the "Right." Even in 1935 the magazine *Bolshevik* continued to call Bukharin a "right capitulator," who had allegedly wanted the Soviet Union to renounce industrialization and the collectivization of agriculture and to grant unlimited freedom to the private capitalist elements. The same magazine said, of course, that the "kulak essence" of this program had been exposed by the party under the leadership of Stalin. That was Stalin's style. He denounced his opponents with increasing ferocity even after they had been defeated.

The question arises, could the "Right" opposition have defeated Stalin? A categorical "no," as in the case of the Left Opposition, would be incorrect. The Bukharin-Rykov group had many opportunities for victory. Under certain conditions their platform could have won a majority in the Politburo, the Central Committee, and wide party circles, as well as support from the majority of peasants and industrial and office workers. But the leaders of the "Right" proved unable to exploit these opportunities. They were not firm and persistent enough as political leaders; they did not have the will to fight for power in the party and the nation; they actually shied away from the struggle, just as Trotsky had in 1923–1924.

In analyzing the reasons for the defeat of the Bukharin group, Stephen Cohen gives an excellent, detailed analysis of the inner-party struggle in the late twenties:

How, then, is Stalin's lopsided victory over Bukharin to be explained? Of the several circumstances favoring the general secretary, the most important was the struggle's narrow arena and covert nature. This situation, abetted by Bukharin, Rykov, and Tomskii, confined the conflict to the party hierarchy where Stalin's strength was greatest, and nullified the Bukharin group's strength, which lay outside the high party leadership and indeed outside the party itself.

For, unlike the Bolshevik Left, which remained to the end a movement of dissident party leaders in search of a social base, the Right was an opposition with potential mass support in the country. That its rural policies were preferred by the peasant majority was clear to almost everyone, Bukharinists, Stalinists, and noncombatants alike. In addition, the purges that ravaged administrative agencies, from central commissariats to local soviets and cooperatives, echoed in the prolonged press campaign against "rightism in practice," indicated that Bukharin's moderate views were widely shared by nonparty officials, especially those involved with the countryside and outlying republics. Nor was the appeal of Bukharinism exclusively rural. Even after [Tomsky's] disgrace, rightist sentiment among rank-and-file unionists (and presumably the urban working class itself), expressed chiefly in stubborn resistance to Stalin's industrial policies, was a persistent fact. Its extent may be judged from the wholesale reconstitution of factory committees in 1929–30: in the major industrial centers of Moscow, Leningrad, the Ukraine, and the Urals, 78 to 85 per cent of their membership was replaced.

Latent Bukharinist support was also considerable inside the party itself, again as evidenced by the clamorous attack on "right opportunism" at all levels. . . . Bukharin's tragedy, and the crux of his political dilemma, lay in his unwillingness to appeal to this popular sentiment. Where the general population was concerned, his reluctance is simply explained. It derived from the Bolshevik dogma that politics outside the party was illegitimate, potentially if not actually counter-revolutionary. This was an outlook intensified by the fear, shared by majority and opposition groups alike, that factional appeals to the population might trigger a "third force" and the party's destruction. From it came the axiom that intra-party disputes ought not even to be discussed before nonparty audiences. It was, as one Trotskyist said in explaining the Left's plight, a matter of "party patriotism: it both provoked us to rebel and turned us against ourselves." So, too, with the Right, who were additionally constrained by a crisis in the country. Certain that Stalin's course was dangerously unpopular as well as economically disastrous, Bukharin, Rykov, and Tomsky remained nonetheless silent before the nation. Public opinion intruded into the struggle only obliquely, in a running debate over the significance of letters pouring into the center to protest the new rural policies. For Bukharinists they were "the voice of the masses," for Stalin unrepresentative manifestations of "panic."

But Bukharin was restrained by another consideration as well. In Marxist eyes, the social groups thought to be most receptive to his policies, notably peasants and technical specialists, were "petty bourgeois" and thus unseemly constituencies for a Bolshevik. . . .

His reluctance to carry the fight against Stalin to the party-at-large derived from similar inhibitions. For party politics outside the leadership area had also become suspect and atrophied. . . . Still, despite his complicity in imposing the proscriptive norms, Bukharin was tempted to appeal to the whole party. He agonized over his dilemma: "Sometimes at night I think, have we the right to remain silent? Is this not a lack of courage?" . . .

Finally, believing that the party hierarchy he sought to win over would "slaughter" any leader who carried the struggle beyond its councils, he conformed to "party unity and party discipline," to the narrow, intolerant politics he had helped create. He shunned overt "factionalism," and so was reduced to ineffectual "backstairs intrigues" (like his Kamenev visit) easily exploited by his enemies. His position was politically incongruous: driven by outraged contempt for Stalin and his policies, he remained throughout a restrained, reluctant oppositionist.

Apart from public appeals too Aesopian to be effective, Bukharin, Rykov, and Tomsky therefore colluded with Stalin in confining their fateful conflict to a small private arena, there to be "strangled behind the back of the party." . . .

That all this gave Stalin an enormous advantage over Bukharin, who once described himself as "the worst organizer in Russia," is unquestionable. But machine politics alone did not account for Stalin's triumph. In terms of the Central Committee, it served mainly to guarantee him the allegiance or acquiescence of low- and middle-ranking delegates who had risen through his patronage, and about whom a disillusioned Stalinist remarked: "We have defeated Bukharin not with argument but with party cards." Their Central Committee membership notwithstanding, however, these junior officials played a secondary role in 1928–29. In effect, they ratified an outcome already decided by a smaller, informal group of senior Central Committee members—an oligarchy of twenty to thirty influentials made up of high party leaders and heads of the most important Central Committee delegations (notably those representing Moscow, Leningrad, Siberia, the North Caucasus, the Urals, and the Ukraine). . . .

By April 1929, these influentials had chosen Stalin and formed his essential majority in the high leadership. They did so, it seems clear, less because of his bureaucratic power than because they preferred his leadership and policies. To some extent, their choice doubtless expressed their identification with the general secretary as a forceful "practical politician," compared to whom, perhaps, the gentle, theoretical-minded Bukharin seemed "merely a boy." [157]

I must agree with the majority of Cohen's arguments. In my opinion, he is incorrect in only one thing: within the party hierarchy the strength of Bukharin and his group was not completely lacking; in the first months of the struggle Bukharin's proposals were supported by a majority even in the Politburo. But Bukharin was not able to take advantage of this favorable situation; he really was one of the worst organizers in Russia.

It would seem that by the end of 1929 Stalin no longer had any adversaries or opponents in the Central Committee. In that Committee's greeting to Stalin on the occasion of his fiftieth birthday he was called "the best, most stable and consistent of Lenin's immediate disciples and comrades-in-arms." The greeting also said:

You, like no one else, have combined in yourself a deep theoretical knowledge of Leninism with the ability to boldly adapt it to life at various stages of the revolutionary struggle. This has helped the party to successfully deal with the

157. Cohen, *Bukharin*, pp. 322–328.

most difficult historical tasks with the minimum expenditure of time and energy, and it has helped the party maintain true Leninist unity.[158]

Hardly any of the Central Committee members who signed this greeting would live to see the end of the decade. Most of them fell as victims in the bloody purges of the thirties. For Stalin's victory over the various opposition groups was not a victory for Leninism. It was a victory for Stalinism, which established its supremacy over the country and party for a long time. The Soviet Union was about to go through the most difficult and bloody decades of its history.

177   158. *Stalin: Sbornik statei k 50-letiiu so dnia rozhdeniia* (Stalin: A Collection of Articles
178   on His Fiftieth Birthday) (Moscow-Leningrad, 1929), pp. 8–11.

3

MISTAKES AND CRIMES IN COLLECTIVIZATION AND INDUSTRIALIZATION

COOPERATIVES AND COLLECTIVIZATION IN AGRICULTURE

For several years after the introduction of NEP and in almost all of Soviet Russia's territory, a considerable revival of economic activity was observable in all sectors and within the framework of all existing economic structures. Industrial production, the foundation of the socialist sector in the economy, was being restored and expanded. Handicraft production was developing. Government and private trade was expanding. On tens of millions of small peasant farms the situation was improving and production increasing. Peasant agriculture on a larger scale, with occasional or regular employment of hired labor (referred to in that period as kulak agriculture), was growing and gaining strength. Small and medium-sized capitalist businesses were springing up everywhere, like mushrooms after a rain. Concessionary production and state-capitalist production based on foreign credit were also growing, though not to the extent that Lenin had expected. And the volume of foreign trade was increasing. There was still a considerable element of spontaneity in this economic revival, and it is not surprising that various imbalances arose here and there in the economy. The task of overcoming these was sometimes easy and sometimes very difficult.

In 1926–1927 the most striking imbalance emerged in the development of industry and agriculture. In the absence of foreign aid and sufficient credit the Soviet economy could develop only on the basis of internal accumulation. But industry still provided too little accumulation. The main hopes were placed on the development of agriculture, but this meant first of all increased rural production for the market, especially of marketable grain. In this respect, however, Soviet economic progress was unimpressive. By 1927 the value of gross agricultural output was 21 percent greater than it had been in 1913, the best year of the prerevolutionary period, but this increase was mostly in livestock and industrial crops. Indeed, grain production fell far short of the prerevolutionary level both in acreage of cultivation and in gross output. An especially sharp decline occurred in the production of grain for the market. Between 1909 and 1913 the amount of marketed grain (within the pre-1939 boundaries) averaged more than 1 billion poods a year (the pood is 36.113 pounds); between 1923 and 1927 the average was 514 million.[1]

This decline can be attributed to many factors. The prices the government paid for grain were low, giving the peasant no incentive to expand grain farming. In 1926–1927 the price index for livestock products (using 1913 as the base year) was 178 percent; for industrial crops it was 146 percent; for grain, only 89 percent.[2] This disparity was not the result of a mistake by the procurement agencies. An increase in prices paid for grain required a major rise in the production of consumer goods and agricultural machinery needed by the peasants; banknotes alone were of no use to them. But industry was not able to end the shortage of goods either in the cities or the countryside. A rapid increase in marketed grain was also hindered by the new structure of agriculture that issued from

---

1. *Narodnoe khoziaistvo SSSR v 1958. Statisticheskii ezhegodnik* (Moscow, 1959), p. 351.

2. S. P. Trapeznikov, *Leninizm i agrarno-krest'ianskii vopros*, 2d ed., 2 vols. (Moscow, 1972), 2:55.

the October revolution. The gentry's estates, which had been the basic source of marketed grain, were liquidated. Under "war communism" a severe blow had also been dealt to kulak farms, which before the war had provided a substantial quantity of grain for the market. The major producers of grain after the October revolution were the poor and middle peasants. Their farms produced 4 billion poods of grain toward the end of the 1920s, as against the 2.5 billion that they produced before the revolution. But these farms put little of their grain on the market—around 440 million poods, or 10–11 percent of the grain they produced. And that was the main reason for the enormous difficulties on the grain front.

Such difficulties could have been foreseen as early as the proclamation of the Decree on Land in 1917. In explaining the fundamentals of NEP, Lenin quite clearly outlined the way to overcome these difficulties. First of all, it was necessary to give all possible help to the poor and middle peasants, and such support was the main agrarian goal in the first stage of NEP. But it was impossible to ignore the farms of the well-to-do peasants. The development of kulak agriculture in the early years of NEP was no threat to the dictatorship of the proletariat. The alarmist declarations on the rise of the kulaks made by the Left Opposition were largely unfounded. The countryside, as Lenin repeatedly pointed out, suffered not so much from capitalism as from an insufficient development of capitalism. Therefore from the very beginning of NEP Lenin urged that all peasants who showed enterprise and initiative be encouraged in every possible way. He even proposed that prizes be given to kulaks for increased production, although it is true that he suggested rewarding them with consumer items, not machinery or equipment that could be used as means of production.[3]

Of course, such a policy, while completely correct in the first part of NEP, could not become the basic policy of the dictatorship of the proletariat in the countryside for the entire transitional period from capitalism to socialism in Russia. No one in the Bolshevik leadership proposed basing the long-term development of Soviet agriculture on kulak production. Even before coming to power, the Bolsheviks had worked out an agrarian program that foresaw the creation of large-scale model agricultural enterprises of the socialist type, based on the more efficiently managed estates of the gentry. The Bolsheviks did not succeed, however,

3. *Istoriia SSSR*, 1965, no. 2, p. 18.

in leading the countryside along this course. It proved necessary to search for more complicated and roundabout methods, making a temporary compromise with the wealthy strata in the rural areas. In considering the party's tasks in the countryside for a fairly protracted period, Lenin urged that the development of all sorts of cooperatives, including producers' cooperatives, be encouraged in every possible way. Revising his former views on cooperatives, Lenin stated that the growth of cooperatives within the context of proletarian dictatorship was identical to the development of socialism in the Russian countryside.[4]

Although the cooperative plan that Lenin proposed was no more than a rough sketch, he understood what a long and complicated process the collectivization of agriculture was—impossible without many years of intense labor, without the development of literacy and culture in the countryside, without the mechanization of agriculture and the gradual training of the peasants to manage their own economy collectively. In 1923 he wrote:

> To achieve through NEP the participation of the entire population in the cooperative movement requires an entire historical epoch. We may get through this epoch successfully in one or two decades. But in any case, this will be a special historical epoch, and without this epoch, without universal literacy, without a sufficient degree of explaining, of teaching the population how to use books, and without a material basis for all this, without a certain guarantee, if only, let us say, against crop failure, against famine, and so on—without that we shall not attain our goal.[5]

Lenin's opinions in his last writings gave the party several important guidelines, but they never constituted a "Leninist general line," the slightest deviation from which would be considered a "left" or "right" opportunistic deviation. That kind of "general line" was invented by Lenin's successors. H. G. Wells, after his interview with Lenin, put it this way:

> Lenin, . . . whose frankness must at times leave his disciples breathless, has recently stripped off the last pretense that the Russian revolution is anything more than the inauguration of an age of limitless experiment. "Those who are engaged in the formidable task of overcoming capitalism," he has recently written, "must be prepared to try method after method until they find the one which answers their purpose best."[6]

4. See, for example, Lenin, PSS, 43: 148–149.
5. Lenin, PSS, 45: 372.
6. H. G. Wells, *Russia in the Shadows* (London, 1921), p. 133.

The extreme complexity of the economic situation in the early twenties gave rise not only to continuous discussions but also to considerable difficulties, to which the party was not always able to find quick and wise solutions. Restoration of the economy, which had been ruined by two wars, began with agriculture. However, as early as 1923 the development of the countryside ran into a number of serious difficulties. The peasant farms had almost no stock of capital and almost no surplus produce to sell, while both the cost of production and the price of manufactured goods were high. Thus, despite the weakness of industry, a crisis of oversupply arose, a glut of manufactured goods that caused some industrial enterprises to shut down and others to suspend wage payments, with strikes resulting. To avert a general economic crisis, prices were lowered on many items that the village needed, while the prices of agricultural products were raised. A system of easy credit was introduced in the villages, especially for the poor and middle peasants. Finally, in 1925, following a proposal of the Fourteenth Party Conference, a law was passed enlarging the right to hire agricultural labor and to lease land from the state and from fellow peasants. This law was advantageous to the better-off peasants, but also to the government. To some degree it was even advantageous to the poor peasants, since it legalized the hiring of day laborers, which had been fairly widespread even before 1925, and established supervision over the conditions of hire.

The glut of manufactured goods was eliminated by these measures, and a certain equilibrium was achieved between the development of industry and of agriculture. Important changes along this line were introduced in the city as well as the country. An intensive campaign conducted in 1924 against "private traders" was suspended, and working conditions were improved for handicraftsmen and artisans as well as private manufacturers. A monetary reform was also completed successfully, so that the Soviet ruble acquired unprecedented stability.

The equilibrium thus achieved was very brief, however. New disproportions began to arise in 1925–1926. Industrial production developed more slowly than rural demand, which was backed up by the ability to pay. Meanwhile, the Soviet government continued to implement a number of measures to encourage capital accumulation in agriculture. Thus, for example, the agricultural tax was lowered in 1926 from 312.9 million rubles to 244.8 million rubles. The middle peasants benefited most: their tax payments were reduced by 60 million rubles.[7] Still, in view of the

7. *Istoriia SSSR*, 1963, no. 4, p. 199.

large harvests of 1926–1927 the tax cut favored all of the better-off peasants, whose agricultural surpluses increased considerably. In 1923–1924 the peasants' purchasing power was estimated to be 1.6 billion gold rubles; in 1925–1926 it reached 2.6 billion. In 1923–1924 16.8 percent of the peasants' purchasing power was withdrawn by the agricultural tax, and in 1925–1926 only 10.8 percent was withdrawn in this way.[8] But the swift rise in peasant purchasing power was not matched by a corresponding increase in the manufactured goods that the peasants needed. The problem was no longer a glut but rather a shortage of manufactured goods.

In spite of the newly emerging disproportions, both wholesale and retail prices on manufactured goods were significantly lowered. With goods in short supply the cut in retail prices did not reach the consumer but did enrich the private merchants, who controlled 40 percent of the retail trade.[9] At the same time, the reduction of wholesale prices lowered the profits of industrial enterprises. Meanwhile industry's need for the accumulation of capital was increasing sharply since 1925–1926 marked the turn from the restoration of old industrial enterprises to the construction of new ones. Because of these shortcomings in pricing policy the supply of goods grew in volume but did not grow in value.

At the end of 1927 the manufacture of goods for general consumption was only 1 to 2 percent above the previous year, while the total wage bill in state industry was up by 16 percent, and the earnings of peasants—counting only receipts for grain sold to the state, minus taxes—were up by 31 percent. All in all, the purchasing fund of the cities and the countryside had risen by more than 20 percent.[10]

In 1927 the well-to-do elements in the countryside accumulated a great deal of currency with which it was impossible to buy the goods they needed. In such circumstances it is not surprising that the principal possessors of grain surpluses, the kulaks and the well-to-do middle peasants, had no immediate interest in selling their grain surpluses to the state, especially at the low fixed prices. The relatively low agricultural tax could be paid by the receipts from the sale of secondary products and industrial crops, for which the state paid fairly high prices. And, in fact, more flax, sunflower seeds, hemp, beets, cotton, butter, eggs, hides,

---

8. *Bolshevik*, 1926, no. 19–20, p.52.

9. *KPSS v rezoliutsiiakh i resheniiakh s"ezdov, konferentsii i plenumov Tsk*, 7th ed., 3 vols. (Moscow, 1954), 2:351. (Hereafter cited as KPSS v rezoliutsiiakh.)

10. *Piatnadtsatyi s"ezd VKP(b). Stenograficheskii otchet* (Moscow, 1962), 2:857.

wool, and meat were bought by the state in the fall of 1927 than in 1926. But the purchase of grain was a completely different story.

■ 2

GRAIN PROCUREMENT DIFFICULTIES, 1927–1928

The economic miscalculations of Stalin, Rykov, and Bukharin and the reluctance of the well-to-do peasants to speed up grain sales to the state brought the USSR to the verge of a grain crisis at the end of 1927. Although there was a bumper crop, grain procurements were much lower than in previous years. The state granaries held insufficient grain reserves; nevertheless the majority of peasants tried to keep their grain until the spring, when they could sell it at higher prices. By January 1928 the government had acquired barely 300 million poods—in sharp contrast with the figure of 428 million in January 1927. The supply of bread to the cities and the army was seriously endangered.

Various proposals were made. The Left Opposition, for example, held that the time had come for a decisive assault on the kulaks. It proposed that at least 150 million poods of grain be taken by force from the kulaks and prosperous middle peasants. In a resolution dated August 9, 1927, a plenary meeting of the Central Committee rejected this proposal as "absurd and demagogic, calculated to create additional difficulties in the development of the national economy."[11]

The opposition's proposals were also unhesitatingly rejected at the Fifteenth Party Congress in December 1927, when the grain crisis was in full effect. Stalin's report to the congress carefully evaded the underlying difficulties, but he did speak plainly on the party's policy toward the kulaks:

Those comrades are wrong who think that we can and should do away with the kulaks by administrative fiat, by the GPU: write the decree, seal it, period. That's an easy method, but it won't work. The kulak must be taken by economic measures, in accordance with Soviet legality. And Soviet legality is not an empty phrase. Of course, this does not rule out the application of some administrative measures against the kulaks. But administrative measures must not replace economic ones.[12]

Many of Stalin's supporters spoke in much stronger terms. For example, in a special speech on the party's agrarian policy, Molotov de-

11. *KPSS v rezoliutsiiakh*, 2:160–161.
12. *Piatnadtsatyi s"ezd VKP(b)*, 2: 1222.

clared that those who proposed a "forced loan" from the peasantry were
enemies of the alliance between the workers and peasants; they were
proposing "the destruction of the Soviet Union." At that point Stalin
called out, "Correct!" [13]

Mikoyan discussed the problem of grain procurement in greater detail.
He argued that the imbalance between prices for manufactured goods
and those for agricultural products was the main reason for peasant
reluctance to sell grain. He urged a determined effort to deliver large
supplies of low-priced manufactured goods to the villages, at the expense
of temporary shortages in the cities. Only in this way could the peasants
be persuaded to part with their grain. [14] Virtually admitting that the
shortages in grain procurement were due to the oversights and mistakes
of the government, Mikoyan proposed economic measures as the least
painful way out of the mess, and the Fifteenth Congress incorporated his
proposals in its resolutions.

The delegates, however, had barely returned to their home districts
when completely different instructions came flying after them from Moscow. A few days after the end of the congress, which had expelled the
leaders of the Left Opposition from the party, Stalin made a sudden
sharp turn "to the left" in agricultural policy. He began to put into effect
the forced requisition of grain that the entire party had just rejected as
"adventurist." In late December Stalin sent out instructions for the
application of extraordinary measures against the kulaks. Local party
officials, who had just heard and read the speeches of the Fifteenth
Congress, must have been thunderstruck. They did not hasten to carry
out the new instructions. Then, on January 6, 1928, Stalin issued a new
directive, extremely harsh in both tone and content, which ended with
threats against local party leaders if they failed to achieve a decisive
breakthrough in grain procurements within the shortest possible time.
There followed a wave of confiscations and violence toward wealthy
peasants throughout the entire country.

The result was a significant increase in grain procurements, but only
briefly. In the spring of 1928 the sale of grain to the state dropped off
sharply once again, and Stalin explained the reason:

If we were able to collect almost 300 million poods of grain from January to
March, it was because we were dealing with the peasants' reserves that had been

13. Ibid., pp. 1094–95.
14. Ibid.

saved for bargaining. From April to May we could not collect even 100 million poods because we had to touch the peasants' insurance reserves, in conditions when the outlook for the harvest was still unclear. Well, the grain still had to be collected. So we fell once again into extraordinary measures, administrative willfulness, the violation of revolutionary legality, going around to farms, making illegal searches, and so on, which have caused the political situation in the country to deteriorate.[15]

Today it is clear that the decision to apply "extraordinary measures" in the winter and spring of 1927–1928 was extremely hasty and mistaken. Although the economic errors of 1925–1927 left little room for political and economic maneuvering, there were still some possibilities for the use of economic rather than administrative measures—for the methods of NEP rather than those of "war communism." But high politics—the management of the state and party—has its own laws, its own logic. If the state gets off one road, it often cannot get back on it. That was the case with the use of extraordinary measures against the kulaks.

When Stalin issued his directives in December 1927 and January 1928 he evidently did not plan to make them the basis of agrarian policy for many years to come. He knew that the Kulaks would inevitably react to extraordinary measures by curtailing their production and, since there were very few state and collective farms at the time, the result would be famine. Stalin, it seems, only wanted to frighten the kulaks into submission, to make them more compliant about selling their grain to the state, as the new directives that went out to the rural areas in the spring and summer of 1928 indicate: use no more extraordinary measures, raise grain prices by 15 to 20 percent, increase the supply of manufactured goods in the countryside. In July 1928 Stalin, speaking to the Leningrad Party organization, stressed the necessity of avoiding further searches and seizures of grain, of reestablishing strict legality in dealing with the peasants, and of relying on economic incentives to obtain grain.[16]

But Stalin was unable to carry out this new reversal. For in effect the extraordinary measures in the winter of 1927–1928 had been a declaration of war against the kulaks, the end of NEP in the countryside. And although several months later Stalin ordered the termination of military operations against the kulaks and even moved toward substantial concessions to the affluent strata of the countryside, it was impossible to return to the former methods of procuring grain. Hundreds of thousands of the

15. Stalin, *Sochineniia*, 11:206.
16. Ibid., p. 211.

better-off peasants had already countered the use of extraordinary measures by sowing less grain. Many kulaks "liquidated themselves"; they sold their basic means of production and hid their money and valuables. Middle peasants had no incentive to increase production, since they might then be labeled "kulaks." Thus, in the fall of 1928 the grain procurement plan was once again in danger, despite the good harvest and the economic concessions of the summer.

Deliveries of some industrial crops to the state also declined, disrupting the textile industry; raw material reserves were depleted, reducing export possibilities and thereby the receipt of hard currency from abroad. Forgetting about his promises of July, Stalin sent out orders at the end of 1928 for even harsher administrative measures to be taken against the wealthy peasants.

The renewal of the extraordinary measures increased grain procurements for a few months. But in February and March of 1929 there were again great difficulties, and by April 1929 less grain was collected than in the same period of the previous year. The sale of bread was often interrupted even in Moscow, and the gap widened between market and government prices of grain. Various kinds of black market operations began. The new pressure on the kulaks also caused a new decrease in the amount of land sown and a new wave of "self-liquidation." Efforts were made to increase the amount of land sown by poor and middle peasants, but this could not produce a noticeable increase in the quantity of marketable grain. In 1929, despite a relatively good harvest, rationing of grain and many other agricultural products had to be introduced in the cities.

A dangerous situation thus developed in the middle of 1929. The undeclared war with the better-off section of the peasantry threatened the Soviet Union with disorganization of its entire national economy, even with famine. Something had to be done, but Stalin's incorrect policies left even less room for political or economic maneuvering than in 1927–1928. Three possible solutions remained. One was to admit that mistakes had been made and to undertake major concessions to the kulaks and well-to-do middle peasants. But that was an extremely difficult course to follow. The more prosperous peasants had lost faith in NEP. For the situation to be stabilized, substantial concessions had to be made to those strata, but that course of action was unacceptable to Stalin as well as to the majority of the Central Committee. Another possibility was to make substantial purchases of grain from abroad, which would have meant reducing the scope of planned industrialization and revising the targets of the first five-year plan. This course of action was also rejected. The final possibility was to speed up the collective-farm movement in order to limit and ultimately destroy the kulaks' monopoly on marketable grain. As we know, the party chose the latter course, which was also very difficult. Unfortunately, Stalin was unable to carry out this new reversal of the party's agrarian policy—the fourth in two years— without making more serious mistakes and committing new excesses.

■ 3

DISTORTIONS AND MISTAKES IN COLLECTIVIZATION

Despite Lenin's advice and instructions, the cooperative movement grew very slowly in the twenties. The main emphasis fell on the development of purchasing and marketing cooperatives. Even in mid–1928 less than 2 percent of all peasant households belonged to collective farms; they accounted for no more than 2.5 percent of the total cultivated area in the Soviet Union and only 2.1 percent of the area sown with grain.[17] Many of these communes and collective farms (kolkhozy) had been founded as early as 1918–1920. The Fifteenth Party Congress resolved to speed up collectivization, saying that "the unification and transformation of small individual peasant households into large collectives should be made the primary task of the party in the countryside."[18]

All the delegates who spoke on work in the countryside, however, pointed to the need for caution and for proceeding gradually in regard to collectivization. For example, Molotov said:

The transition from individual to socialized (collective) farming requires quite a few years. . . . We must understand that the seven-year experience of NEP has been enough to teach us that Lenin was right when he said as early as 1919: no rashness, no haste on the part of the party and Soviet power in relation to agriculture. What we studied so much to learn during the first seven years of NEP will prove very useful to us in carrying out our new tasks in the countryside —namely, that in building socialism in the countryside, the important skills are circumspection, caution, patience, a gradual approach, etc.[19]

Many delegates to the congress spoke of the government's lack of sufficient material resources to support collective farms, the shortage of

17. *Itogi Noiabr'skogo plenuma Tsk* (Moscow, 1929), p. 75.
18. *VKP(b) v rezoliutsiiakh*, 2:230.
19. *Piatnadtsatyi s"ezd VKP(b)*, vol 2.

agricultural equipment, and the weakness of the party's rural organizations. Taking all these conditions into account, the congress indicated that the development of collective farms should go hand in hand with all possible aid to individual poor and middle peasant farms because "the privately owned farm will continue to be the basis of all [Soviet] agriculture for a significant time to come."[20]

At one of the Central Committee plenums in 1928 Stalin stated:

There are people who think that individual peasant farming is finished, that it is not worth supporting. This is not true, comrades. Such people have nothing in common with our party line. . . . We need neither belittlers nor boosters of the individual farm. We need sober politicians who know how to get the maximum of what can be gotten from the individual peasant farm, and know at the same time how to switch the individual farm onto the rails of collectivism.[21]

According to the optimal variant of the first five-year plan, adopted at the Sixteenth Party Conference, in April 1929, 23 percent of the peasant farms were to be collectivized in the next five years, thereby putting into the socialized sector 17.5 percent of the total cultivated area and 43 percent of grain production for the market. At the same time plans for the first year of the five-year plan (July 1928–July 1929) were very modest: the level of collectivization was to be raised merely from 1.7 to 2.2 percent.

However, the seriousness of the situation and the problems arising in the countryside in early 1929 required the revision of these plans. Progress in collectivization began to be visible in the middle of 1929: by July 1, more than 1 million peasant households had joined collective farms instead of the projected 564,200. This was still a modest increase; only 4 percent of all households had joined collective farms. In 1929 less than 10 percent of the cultivated area was worked by tractors, while harvester combines were still counted in the hundreds. The collective farms had almost no cattle sheds or silos.

Stalin, however, was not able to appraise the situation in the countryside correctly. At the first signs of progress, he embarked on a characteristically adventuristic course. Apparently he wanted to compensate for years of failure and miscalculation in agricultural policy and to astonish the world with a picture of great success in the socialist transformation of agriculture. So at the end of 1929 he sharply turned the bulky ship of agriculture, without checking for reefs and shoals. Disregarding the ob-

20. *VKP(b) v rezoliutsiiakh*, 2:253.
21. Stalin, *Sochineniia*, 11:208.

jective conditions, Stalin, with the support of Molotov, Kaganovich, and several other Politburo members, pushed for excessively high rates of collectivization, driving the local organizations in every possible way.

At the beginning of November 1929 there were approximately 70,000 collective farms, but most of these were small cooperatives that had amalgamated 1,919,400 peasant households, or 7.6 percent of the total. The overwhelming majority of collective farmers were poor peasants; only in a few villages and districts had sizable numbers of middle peasants joined the collective farms. But Stalin hastily generalized these scattered facts, interpreting them as the beginning of a crucial breakthrough. His article on the year's results was entitled "Year of the Great Breakthrough" (*God velikgo pereloma*). Moreover, in the fall of 1929 Stalin called for total collectivization, which in the real conditions of that time was clearly premature. Most of the middle peasants were still wavering, while the kulaks were not yet neutralized or isolated from the middle peasants, especially the more prosperous ones. In such a situation the call for total collectivization unavoidably led to perversions in the collective-farm movement, to administrative pressure on all peasants, and to the use of force against the middle peasant—all of which happened at the end of 1929 and beginning of 1930.

In the period after the October 1964 Central Committee plenum (at which Khrushchev was ousted) many historians began a new debate over whether Stalin and his entourage had really made mistakes in the first stage of collectivization. For example, according to F. Vaganov

The second half of 1929 was marked by a rapid upsurge in the collective-farm movement. . . . The major feature of this period was the influx of middle peasants into the collective farms, which made that section of the peasantry active participants in socialist construction. Collective farms in the country numbered 67.4 thousand. They held 3.6 percent of the cultivated land and produced 4.9 percent of the agricultural marketings. All this shows that the necessary material, technical, and political preconditions had been created for total collectivization.[22]

Vaganov deliberately withholds the data on the percentage of collectivized households. Even a simple juxtaposition of the figures—7.6 percent of the peasant households but only 3.6 percent of the cultivated land—shows clearly that the middle peasant had not yet joined the collective farms. It is also obvious that 3.6 percent of the cultivated area and 4.9 percent of marketings simply cannot be construed to prove that the

22. F. Vaganov, "Preobrazovanie sel 'skogo khoziaistva," *Kommunist*, 1966, no. 3, p. 95.

material, technical, and political preconditions for immediate total collectivization had been created.

At the end of 1929 a special commission of the Central Committee was established to draft a decree on the organization of collective farms. Many members of the Central Committee, though agreeing that collectivization must be speeded up, protested against an excessive and unnecessary speed-up, for which neither the subjective nor the objective preconditions existed. The commission took these views into consideration. But Stalin severely criticized the commission's draft decree. At his insistence the draft was stripped of rules indicating what portion of livestock and farm implements should be collectivized and what procedures should be followed in the creation of indivisible funds and circulating capital. In the final version the period of collectivization in the North Caucasus and the Middle Volga was reduced to one or two years, and rules were omitted concerning socialization of instruments of production. In other words, the peasants' right to keep small livestock, implements, and poultry was omitted. Also deleted were guidelines for liquidating the kulaks, including a proposal that the kulaks be used in the kolkhozy if they would subordinate themselves and voluntarily carry out all the duties of collective-farm members. In the final version collectivization was to be completed in the major grain-producing regions by the fall of 1930, or in any case by the spring of 1931. In other areas it had to be completed by the fall of 1931 or the spring of 1932.[23]

The Central Committee's decree "On the tempo of collectivization and measures to help the organization of collective farms" was adopted by the Central Committee on January 5, 1930. Right after its publication many party organizations in the provinces and union republics decided to overfulfill the plan and finish collectivization not by the fall but by the spring of 1930. In January and February 1930 the newspapers were full of reports to this effect. But neither the local party and Soviet organizations nor the peasants themselves were prepared for such an accelerated campaign. In order to carry out the orders that came from above, not only in written but often in oral form, almost all party and Soviet bodies were forced to put administrative pressure on the peasants and also on lower-level officials. In short, an emergency situation was created in the countryside and with it an increase in the role of the GPU.

Marx spoke of the voluntary and gradual transition from private to

23. See N. I. Nemakov, *Kommunisticheskaia partiia—organizator massovogo kolkhoznogo dvizheniia* (Moscow, 1966), pp. 98–102.

collective ownership of the land. Lenin often expressed the same ideas, and they were endorsed by a special resolution of the Eighth Party Congress in 1919. Stalin's own speeches contained many valid comments on this subject. However, in 1929 Stalin issued a call for *implanting* collective and state farms. In December 1929 he said:

> It is necessary . . . to *implant* in the village large socialist farms, collective and state farms, as bases of socialism, which, with the socialist city in the vanguard, can drag along the masses of peasants. . . . The socialist city can drag along the small peasant village in no other way than by *implanting* in the village collective and state farms and by reshaping the village on new socialist lines.[24]

And in fact, at the end of 1929 and the beginning of 1930, Lenin's principle of voluntary collectivization was violated almost everywhere, under pressure from Stalin and his closest aides. Organizational and explanatory work among the peasants was replaced by crude administrative fiat and force directed against the middle peasants and even some of the poor peasants. They were forced to join collective farms under threat of "dekulakization." In many areas the rule was quite simple: "Whoever does not join collective farms is an enemy of the Soviet regime." Along with force many local organs tried all kinds of fantastic promises. They promised the peasants tractors and considerable credit. "Everything will be supplied—join the collective farms." In many districts an attempt was made to create not collective farms but communes, which meant that the peasants were forced to put all their livestock, poultry, and household gardens into the collective pool. Instead of offering financial and material aid, the authorities in some provinces began squeezing all the resources they could out of the individual peasants, forcing them, before they joined the kolkhoz, to contribute to its credit fund and seed supply and to pay membership dues.

Such perversions aroused great dissatisfaction among the peasants, especially the middle peasants, except for an enthusiastic few. Before joining the collective farms, many peasants, slaughtered their livestock: cows, sheep, pigs, even poultry. In February and March of 1930 alone, approximately 14 million head of cattle, one-third of all pigs, and one-fourth of all sheep and goats were destroyed. Although the percentage of collective farms rose rapidly, tension also increased. In some areas anti-kolkhoz outbursts occurred among the peasantry.

The situation began to ease up only in March 1930, following the

24. Stalin, *Sochineniia*, 12:149.

publication of Stalin's article "Dizzy with Success," which he wrote at the demand of the Central Committee. In his article Stalin rightly criticized many of the "excesses" in collectivization, although he shifted the responsibility for these mistakes onto local officials. This threw them into complete confusion because for the most part they had acted on orders from the "center" and the local leadership. Special reports had been sent regularly, every seven to ten days, from the localities to all members of the Politburo. It was Stalin who, at the end of 1929 and the beginning of 1930, had endorsed the proposal made by some of his colleagues for the collectivization of farm implements, small livestock, milch cows, and so on.[25] Moreover, the newspapers were filled with pledges to speed up total collectivization. "Comrade Stalin," wrote Comrade Belik, a worker from Dnepropetrovsk:

I, a rank-and-file worker and a reader of *Pravda,* have all this time been following the newspapers closely. Is the person to blame who could not help hearing the uproar about collectivization, about who should lead collective farms? All of us, the lower ranks and the press, messed up that crucial question of collective-farm leadership, while Comrade Stalin, it seems, at that time was sleeping like a god, hearing nothing, his eyes closed to our mistakes. Therefore you too should be reprimanded. But now Comrade Stalin throws all the blame on the local authorities, and defends himself and the top people.[26]

A similar protest against Stalin's insincerity was made by Krupskaya in the summer of 1930 in a speech to a party conference of the Bauman district of Moscow. According to delegates S. I. Berdichevskaya and M. Tsimkhles, Krupskaya said that collectivization was not being carried out in a Leninist manner and that the methods being used had nothing in common with Lenin's plan for developing cooperatives. In pushing collectivization, the leaders of the Central Committee had sought advice from no one, neither the party nor the lower ranks nor the people. And it made no sense, said Krupskaya, to accuse local officials of the mistakes made by the Central Committee itself. Kaganovich and Bubnov harshly and rudely spoke out against Krupskaya, the latter even saying, "Krupskaya is not the beacon that guides our party toward what is best for it."

In the spring of 1930 there was mass repression of local officials in many provinces, and in many districts there were trials of "left deviationists." Many of the defendants did deserve punishment for violating revo-

25. *Voprosy istorii,* 1965, no. 3, p. 12.
26. *Istoricheskii arkhiv,* 1962, no. 2, p. 194.

lutionary legality in the countryside. Bewilderment and resentment were aroused, however, by the fact that most of the bigger officials, whose instructions had been carried out by the local leaderships, were not brought to justice.

Soon after the publication of Stalin's "Dizzy with Success," the Central Committee adopted a resolution "On the struggle against distortions of the party line in the collective-farm movement," which proposed to stop the use of force and to allow peasants to leave the collective farms if they so wished. This resolution led to a mass exodus of peasants from the collective farms. More than ten million peasant households had joined the kolkhozy, but by July 1, 1930, less than six million remained in them, that is, less than one-fourth of all poor and middle peasants. In several provinces nearly all the collective farms were dissolved. But in the fall pressure on the peasantry was renewed. Those who left the collective farms were simply not allowed to take their livestock and land back with them. It is not surprising that the figures for collectivization soon began to rise again.

The collectivization of agriculture in its Stalinist variant did great harm to agricultural production. Collectivization was supposedly designed to achieve a rapid increase in total agricultural output. Thus the first five-year plan forecast an increase in gross agricultural output from 16.6 billion rubles in 1927–1928 to 25.8 billion rubles in 1932–1933, an increase of 52 percent. But gross agricultural output declined throughout the first five-year plan. If 1928 agricultural output by all categories of farms is taken as 100 percent, in 1929 it was 98 percent, in 1930 94.4 percent, in 1931 92 percent, in 1932 86 percent, and in 1933 81.5 percent. There was an especially sharp drop in livestock production, which in 1933 stood at 65 percent of the 1913 level. The total number of cattle dropped from 60.1 million head to 33.5 million. The number of goats, sheep, and pigs decreased to less than half its prewar level. The number of draft animals, especially horses, declined by more than half. As a result, supplies of organic fertilizer declined sharply.

In short, by 1933 gross agricultural output had fallen to 13.1 billion rubles.[27] The consequences of this fall continued to be felt even during the second and third five-year plans. For example, the average annual production of grain in the second half of the thirties was less than in 1913

27. The data are taken from the yearbooks of the Central Statistical Administration, 1956–1960.

(for the area within Soviet borders before September 17, 1939), and although the population of the country had increased, meat production did not even reach the 1913 level.

■ 4

COLLECTIVIZATION AND RENEWED PERSECUTION OF THE ORTHODOX CHURCH

One form of government and party pressure on the peasantry was the intensification of pressure on the Orthodox Church. Antireligious propaganda began to gain strength in the Soviet Union at the beginning of 1928, and by the fall of that year it had developed into outright terror against the church. All religious organizations and church groups suffered, but the focus of this struggle against so-called "religious superstition" was the Orthodox Church. Many prominent and authoritative church officials were arrested and exiled. For example, in 1928 a major Russian religious thinker, Pavel Florensky, was banished and later arrested. He died in one of the northern prison camps during the Patriotic War. In 1928 and 1929 all the monasteries were closed, though many of them were operating as model agricultural cooperatives; thousands of monks and nuns were exiled to Siberia. In mid-1929 the Central Committee held a conference on antireligious work, followed shortly by the Second All-Union Congress of Militant Atheists. After this congress antireligious terror increased universally, with the focus shifting from the city to the countryside. Apparently the Stalinist top brass regarded the church as one of the main obstacles to collectivization. Therefore, in village after village the decision to collectivize was accompanied by the closing of the local church. Often the cross was knocked from the church's cupola, and icons and many other objects of worship were burned. Many village priests were arrested, as were some peasants who tried to resist the destruction of the churches. Thousands of people suffered in this way not because of their social status but because of their religious beliefs.

By the beginning of 1930 the campaign of terror against the church had taken on especially broad dimensions. A frightened Academy of Sciences passed a special resolution withdrawing protected status from most historical monuments associated with "religious cults"; as a result, local authorities began to tear down many churches and monasteries that were extremely valuable architectural monuments. This occurred in such old Russian towns as Tver, Nizhny Novgorod, Pskov, Novgorod, Samara,

Vyatka, Ryazan, and Tula. But it was Moscow that suffered the most: churches were destroyed even inside the Kremlin walls, to which not only Lunacharsky objected but Yenukidze as well. Lunacharsky's former secretary, I. A. Sats, tells in his unpublished memoirs about taking part in a hasty review of Lunacharsky's papers after the latter's death, under the watchful supervision of the chairman of the Central Party Archives. Among these papers Sats found an excerpt from a Politburo resolution signed by Stalin: "Comrade Lunacharsky's letter was read. Resolved: To declare Lunacharsky's letter incorrect in content and nonparty in form." The subject of the letter was the destruction of the churches in the Kremlin. The official attitude at that time was reflected in a song sung by Komsomol members:

We'll fan a fire the world around
To level the churches and jails to the ground.

As Mikhail Agursky writes in one of his articles:

Antireligious terror reached such proportions that in January 1930 Pope Pius XI appealed to all Christians for a world-wide day of prayer on March 16, 1930, on behalf of the persecuted faithful of Russia. This appeal was joined not only by most Christian churches but by Jewish religious circles, alarmed by the news of terror against Judaism, especially the report that twenty-five members of the Jewish clergy had been arrested in Minsk. The protest campaign outside the USSR reached the point where it began to threaten Soviet political and economic interests. Demands for breaking diplomatic relations with the Soviet Union were heard on all sides.[28]

Undoubtedly this massive protest campaign prompted Stalin not only to suspend antireligious terror for a time but even to disavow it, attributing it to "local excesses." In his article "Dizzy with Success," published in *Pravda* on March 2, 1930, Stalin wrote:

And what about those "revolutionaries," if one may call them that, who begin the job of organizing collective farms by taking the bells from the churches. To take a bell—just think—how r-r-revolutionary![29]

On March 15, 1930—one day before the world-wide day of prayer declared by Pope Pius—Soviet newspapers published the decree on "distortions" of the party line in the cooperative movement. This decree

28. Mikhail Agursky, "Novye izmereniia stalinizma," p. 10. [The author quotes from a manuscript copy of Agursky's article, written in Moscow in 1973. In 1974 Agursky emigrated to Israel. —G. S.]
29. Stalin, *Sochineniia*, 12:198.

referred to the administrative closing of churches as an error committed
by local officials and threatened severe punishment for anyone offending
the feelings of believers. All this was undoubtedly a concession to world
public opinion. However, the temporary cessation of antireligious terror
was accompanied neither by the restoration of ruined churches and the
reopening of those that had been closed nor by the return of most of the
people who had been exiled to Siberia and the north for religious reasons. By the end of 1930 roughly 80 percent of the village churches had
been closed and among the "dispossessed kulaks" were a substantial
number of clergymen.

■ 5
"LIQUIDATION OF THE KULAKS AS A CLASS"

Before the October revolution the kulaks had been a major force in the
Russian countryside. They even improved their position immediately
after the revolution as a result of the expropriation of the noble landowners' estates. At that time as many as 20 percent of the peasants were
kulaks, and they owned more than 40 percent of the land.[30]

The first clash between the Soviet government and the kulaks occurred
in the spring and summer of 1918, when the Bolsheviks began forcibly
confiscating surplus agricultural products and turned the power in the
villages over to committees of poor peasants *(kombedy)*. In that period
Lenin insisted on a determined struggle against the kulaks. In August
1918 he wrote:

> There can be no doubt at all that the kulaks are rabid enemies of the Soviet
> regime. Either the kulaks will cut down an infinite number of workers, or the
> workers will mercilessly cut down the risings of the robbing kulak minority
> against the regime of the toilers. There can be no middle way.[31]

In this case Lenin was not completely correct, for an acceptable "middle
way" was found by the Bolsheviks three years later, when NEP was
introduced, requisitioning was replaced by a tax in kind, and power was
again transferred from the poor peasant and revolutionary committees to

---

30. In Russian Marxist sociology "kulak" was the term for a wealthy peasant who not
only worked his farm himself but regularly hired farm laborers and poor peasants. Kulaks
also used other forms of exploitation, such as lending money or grain at high interest rates
and charging for the use of their machinery, mills, etc.

31. Lenin, PSS, 37:41.

the village soviets. It is important to note, however, that although Lenin called for the ruthless suppression of kulak risings, he never demanded the complete expropriation of the entire kulak population, much less the physical annihiliation or banishment of the kulaks and their families. He insisted repeatedly that the kulaks were not to be stripped of their property like the landlords and capitalists. Part of what they had was the fruit of their own labor on the land. If they rebelled they should be put down, but they should not be expropriated.[32]

When planning NEP as an entire historical period of economic competition between socialism and private capital, Lenin thought of squeezing out the kulaks by economic measures. "If you can give the peasants machines," he wrote, "you will raise them up, and when you give them machines or electrification, tens or hundreds of thousands of petty kulaks will be crushed."[33]

During the mid-twenties the kulaks strengthened and widened their economic positions and influence. But the question of their liquidation was raised only by the most extreme Left Oppositionists. This question was still being discussed in the party press in 1928–1929, but not one writer posed the question of forced expropriation and eviction of the kulaks. The discussion concerned only under what conditions the kulaks could be allowed into the collective farms and whether or not this was possible at all. Opinions differed, and the problem was being solved differently in different locations. In Siberia and the Northern Caucasus it was decided not to admit kulaks into the collective farms. The territorial committee of the party in the Middle Volga region spoke, with some reservations, in favor of allowing the kulaks into the collective farms. The more moderate position on this question was held by Politburo members such as Voroshilov and Kalinin, who were by no means supporters of the "right deviation."

In December 1929 a special commission of the Politburo on collectivization as well as a subcommission specifically on the kulaks were formed. Stalin did not wait for recommendations from this subcommission. In a speech at a conference of Marxist students of the agrarian question at the end of December 1929, Stalin called for "liquidation of the kulaks as a class" and stated that "dekulakization" (dispossession of the kulaks) should be an essential aspect of the formation of the collective farms in carrying

32. Ibid., 38:19, 145.
33. Ibid., 43:69–70.

out complete collectivization. Even the official ideologist and neo-Stalinist Sergei Trapeznikov notes that a decision of such importance should at least have been discussed at a Central Committee plenum.[34]

After Stalin's speech a campaign to dispossess the kulaks got under way almost everywhere. All of the subsequent resolutions and telegrams of the Politburo were an attempt to introduce some order into the brutal operation that had already been set into motion.

In its first recommendations the commission on collectivization had proposed that kulak farms be divided into three categories:

(1) Kulaks who actively opposed the organization of collective farms and carried on counterrevolutionary subversive activities. These should be arrested or exiled to remote regions.

(2) Kulaks who less actively opposed the measures designed to bring about total collectivization. These were to be banished from their own *oblast* or *krai*.

(3) Kulaks who were prepared to submit to steps toward collectivization and to behave loyally toward the Soviet regime. The commission thought it possible to accept such kulaks as members of collective farms, but without the right to vote for three to five years.

Stalin, however, strongly objected to these recommendations and especially to accepting kulaks from any group into the collective farms. Under pressure from Stalin the kulaks were categorized in a different way in the instructions issued by the Central Executive Committee and the Council of People's Commissars on February 4, 1930.

The first category consisted of active counterrevolutionary kulaks who organized revolts and acts of terrorism. They were to be isolated at once, by incarceration in prisons and corrective labor camps; and if necessary, they were to be shot. All members of their families were to be banished to distant regions. It was proposed that approximately 60,000 households could be assigned to this category.[35]

The second category included the rest of the wealthy and politically active kulaks. The commission proposed that they and their families be banished to remote regions of the country or to remote localities in their

34. S. P. Trapeznikov, *Istoricheskii opyt KPSS v osushchestvlenii kooperativnogo plana* (Moscow, 1965).

35. In 1928 on the entire territory of the RSFSR 1123 terrorist acts by kulaks were recorded (see *Istoriia SSSR*, 1966, no. 1, p. 96). We can assume, therefore, that the Central Committee commission, in issuing what could be called "control figures" for reprisals against kulaks, exaggerated rather than underestimated the number of "active counter-revolutionary kulaks."

own regions. It was indicated that there would be about 150,000 of these households.

In the third category were less powerful kulak households. It was proposed that they be left in their own districts but that they be resettled outside the collectivized villages with new allotments of land apart from the collective-farm fields. These kulaks, according to the instructions, were to be assigned production goals and duties. It was proposed that the majority of kulak households be assigned to this category—about 800,000.

Nothing was said in these instructions and decrees about "kulak supporters" (also called "subkulaks"—*podkulachniki*) or about prosperous middle peasants.

Even these severe recommendations were exceeded in most areas. By the end of 1930 the number of kulaks who had been banished to remote, usually northern regions, sent to corrective labor camps, or shot was much greater than the number planned for at the beginning of the year. In 1931 the same kind of repression was carried out on an even broader scale. It is difficult to determine the full dimensions of these cruel operations. According to data presented to the January plenum of the Central Committee in 1933, from the beginning of 1930 to the end of 1932, 240,757 kulak families (about 1 to 1.5 million people) were banished to remote regions. There is good reason to believe that these figures are greatly understated. Later studies, published in the seventies, give different figures. They report that the liquidation of the kulaks was carried out in two stages. In the first stage—up to October 1930—115,231 families were banished to northern regions. In February 1931 a resolution was passed to implement a second stage. During that year 265,795 more kulak families were banished.[36] Thus, the total number of deported families was 381,000. These were official figures, which were not reported to the Central Committee plenum in 1933 but were based on reports by the GPU units that carried out the deportation operations as well as on materials from a verification carried out in the fall of 1931 by members of the Central Control Commission's presidium.[37]

Still, even these figures cannot be considered exhaustive or exact. They do not include the kulak households that were resettled within the regions of complete collectivization. Nor do they include the hundreds of

36. *Istoriia KPSS*, vol. 4, pt. 2, (Moscow, 1971), p. 56; *Leninskii kooperativnii plan* (Moscow, 1970), p. 121.

37. *Voprosy istorii KPSS*, 1975, No. 5, p. 140.

thousands of poor and middle peasants who were exiled as "kulak supporters." Moreover, it is well-known that massive deportation of peasant
and Cossack families to the north was still under way in 1932—that is,
after the verification in 1931. It would hardly be sinning against the truth
to put the total number of "dispossessed kulaks" at close to one million
families, of which not fewer than half were exiled to the northern and
eastern regions of the country.

Soviet historical literature usually explains the massive exile of kulak
families by the intensification of the class struggle, the responsibility for
which it places on the kulaks alone. But this is neither accurate nor fair.
The class struggle in the countryside did begin to intensify in 1928, but
this was related to the use of the extraordinary measures and the massive
breach of Soviet legality by the authorities. The intensification of the
class struggle was also a result of the excesses and perversions in setting
up collective farms in 1929–1930. These excesses caused dissatisfaction
among the middle peasants as well as the kulaks. Thus the kulaks were
not isolated and neutralized, a situation that facilitated and encouraged
their resistance. In itself the eviction of the kulaks was an act of civil war
that, naturally, provoked attempts at active resistance from some of the
wealthy peasants. Terror descended not only on the "counterrevolutionary kulak activists" but also on substantial numbers of well-to-do middle
peasants, who only occasionally used hired labor or did not use it at all.
In addition, a procedure was established under which the personal property of wealthy peasant families—property not used for agricultural production—was distributed among the poor peasants. This procedure encouraged the placing of many well-to-do middle peasants on lists of those
subject to "dekulakization."

In many areas the authorities' blows fell on lower-middle peasants,
poor peasants, and even farm laborers, who for various reasons refused
to join the collective farms and who for the convenience of repression
were given the senseless label of "kulak supporter."

Much information can be gleaned from Soviet literature on "dekulakization" in 1930–1932. The dramatic scenes of the deportation of well-to-
do peasant families in Mikhail Sholokhov's *Virgin Soil Up-turned* are
quite true to life. Dreadful episodes from these terroristic operations are
also described by Fyodor Panfyorov in his novel *Bruski*. Sergei Zalygin's
short novel *Na Irtyshe*, published in 1964, gives a similarly truthful
picture of collectivization in the Siberian countryside, where many honest and hard working middle peasants fell victim to "dekulakization."

And Viktor Astafyev, in his novel *Tsar-ryba,* also writes about the brutal excesses that accompanied collectivization in Siberia. Incidentally, it was in Siberia that the victims of "dekulakization" were particularly numerous because the relatively well-off Siberian peasantry was in no hurry to join collective farms. In one western Siberian region alone, in just one year — 1932 — 43,000 families were exiled to the north. According to the documents, all of them went as "kulaks" or "kulak supporters."[38]

In 1930–1931 the party press published much about abuses during dekulakization. For example, in many *raiony* dekulakization preceded collectivization, when there were no grounds for such action and neither the poor nor middle peasants were ready for it. Dekulakization was therefore carried out suddenly, by the administrative apparatus, and produced negative results. In 1930 *Bolshevik,* the organ of the Central Committee, reported that levying a special tax on peasants who would not join a collective farm was widely regarded as a preliminary to deprivation of the franchise, which in turn was a preliminary to dekulakization. *Bolshevik* reported cases of middle peasants being subjected to dekulakization because they had once sold a dozen scythes, some grain, a cow, shoe soles, or hay. In some places groups of poor peasants explicitly decreed the expropriation of middle peasants, ordering the confiscation of such luxuries as sewing machines, mirrors, and beds. In one *raion* investigation revealed that only three of thirty-four households subjected to dekulakization were actually kulak.[39]

There were thousands and thousands of such cases. The following scene of dekulakization is taken from an unpublished short novel by M. N. Averbakh, who took part in the collectivization campaign. In 1930, when he was still quite young, Averbakh was one of the industrial workers sent to the countryside in special brigades to help "liquidate the kulaks as a class."

The door opened. The brigade burst into the house. The GPU officer in charge of the operation was in front, brandishing a revolver.

"Hands up!"

Morgunov was barely able, in the gloom, to make out the frail figure of the class enemy. He was wearing white drawers and a dark undershirt, and was barefoot. A tangled beard stuck out on a face that was long unshaven. The eyes, wide with terror, glanced from place to place. The deeply lined face winced; the coarse brown hands were trembling. Hanging by a worn, old cord, on his bare chest was a little cross grown dark with age.

38. Ibid.
39. See A. Angarov in *Bolshevik* (1930), no. 6, p. 20.

"Oh Lord Jesus! Save us, have mercy on us . . ."

Freezing air swirled into the well-heated peasant hut. The members of the dekulakization brigade were already standing at each window; their expressions were stern; they all expected something terrible to happen, were ready to rush into battle for their cause, for Soviet power, for socialism. But the kulak's accomplice Terentyev never dreamed of resisting. He kept blinking and crossing himself, shifting from one foot to the other, as though he were standing on live coals, and suddenly he began to sob. Convulsive gasps doubled up his whole body. He bent over in an unnatural position as his body shook and small gleaming tears followed one another down the calloused, weatherbeaten face. His wife, not a young woman, jumped down from the high sleeping bench and began to wail at the top of her voice. The children began crying. A calf lying beside the stove, apparently not in very good health, began to bawl.

Morgunov looked around, aghast. He saw that the hut contained nothing but the one room and the big Russian stove. In the front corner, beneath the icons, were two simple wooden benches and a crude table made of planks. No chest of drawers, no beds, no chairs. On the shelves were some simple wooden bowls, worn by long use, and some wooden ladles of equal vintage. By the stove were some oven forks and buckets of water, and to the left, by the wall, was a large old-fashioned trunk.

The class enemy!

The representatives of authority had already announced to Terentyev that he was under arrest. He was being dekulakized and deported right away. All his property was being confiscated. His family would follow him shortly, but where they were going was not known. He could take with him only the clothes he could wear and a change of underwear.

Terentyev trembled and wept: "What kind of kulaks are we? What for? What did I do?"

No one answered him. Rudely breaking the locks, they threw open the trunk and the food cupboard. They dragged out some footgear, sack cloth, and food-stuffs.

"What for? What did I do? . . ."

"Nothing! You're a kulak, a podkulachnik! You're against the kolkhoz! You don't want to join and you're disrupting the work! That's all there is to it!"

They set about making a list of his goods and possessions.[40]

The brutal directive ordering the deportation of the entire famly of the expropriated kulak was the result first and foremost of the fact that in 1930–1931 the Soviet government did not have the necessary financial resources to assist the collective farms that were being organized. Therefore it was decided to give the collective farms practically all the possessions of the kulak households. In May 1930, in half of the collective farms kulak property constituted 34 percent of the indivisible fund of the

40. M. N. Averbakh, "K viashchei slave gospodne," unpublished manuscript, p. 71.

collective farm.[41] Thus, the forced pace of collectivization encouraged the use of the most brutal methods in dekulakization. In unheated railway cars hundreds of thousands of peasants with their wives and children went east, to the Urals, Kazakhstan, Siberia. Many thousands died en route from hunger and cold and disease. E. M. Landau, a veteran party member, met a group of these transportees in Siberia in 1930. In winter, during a severe frost, a large group of kulaks with their families were being taken in wagons three hundred kilometers into the *oblast*. One of the muzhiks, unable to endure the crying of a baby sucking its mother's empty breast, grabbed the child from his wife's arms and dashed its head against a tree.

In many cases the kulak alone was arrested and sent to a labor camp or jailed or shot, while his family was not touched at first. Agents only made an inventory of the property, leaving it in the family's care, as it were. The deportation of the family would occur a few months later.

Many former kulaks and members of their families died in the first few years of life in the underpopulated and untamed regions of the Urals, Siberia, Kazakhstan, and the northeastern section of European Russia. Thousands of kulak special settlements were established in these remote regions. The inhabitants of these exile colonies were denied freedom of movement. The exiles' situation changed in 1942, when young men from the special settlements began to be drafted into the Red Army because of the Soviet army's severe losses in the war. At the end of the war the commandants' offices for supervising these colonies were closed, and the residents of the former special settlements obtained relative freedom of movement.

From 1951 to 1954 I worked as a teacher in the Visim *raion* of Sverdlovsk *oblast*. The school had been built in a prosperous industrial workers' settlement, whose residents were miners of platinum, gold, and diamonds. But children from the former special settlements for kulak and podkulachnik deportees from central Russia also attended our school. The natives of this region in the Urals and the mine workers lived in spacious houses with sheltered courtyards. They were even allowed to keep horses—a rare occurrence in those days. The former special settlement residents lived in small, rickety prefabricated structures, with only half a house assigned to each family. There was no collective farm; potatoes and vegetables were grown on personal plots. Since it was

41. *Sovetskoe krest'ianstvo* (Moscow, 1970), p. 257.

difficult for the residents of this settlement to get work in the mines, mostly elderly people and children lived there, while the rest worked in plants and factories in other towns in the Urals.

It is a highly instructive fact that after World War II, although many of the new socialist countries (or "people's democracies") took up the task of "liquidating the kulaks as a class," they did so by restricting and squeezing out the wealthy peasants, not expropriating them totally. In fact, former kulaks and their families were allowed to join collective farms under certain conditions. In a number of countries, such as Poland and Yugoslavia, there are many farms that still employ hired labor, and they are not threatened with expropriation.

■ 6

ADMINISTRATIVE REPRESSION IN THE COUNTRYSIDE, 1932–1933

The decline in agricultural production during the first five-year plan had a negative effect on food supplies for the quickly growing urban population. It is not surprising that Stalin, with his predilection for rule by fiat and abuse of power, saw only one way out of this situation: to resort once again to the forced extraction of agricultural surpluses—and not only surpluses. Despite the reduction in gross agricultural output government procurement of agricultural products constantly increased, reaching the level of 40 percent of all harvested grain by 1934. At the same time procurement prices were very low, several times lower than their cost of production—a situation that caused legitimate dissatisfaction among the collective farmers. The government's procurement policies essentially amounted to forced requisitioning.

In the collective farms these policies caused a collapse of labor discipline and mass theft of grain. Although most of the kulaks had been exiled, anti-kolkhoz and anti-Soviet agitation increased in many areas. "Grain strikes" of a kind broke out in some regions that were relatively rich in grain—that is, not only individual peasants but collective farmers too cut back their acreage, refused to surrender grain to the state, and buried it in the ground. This happened particularly in the rich Black Earth region of the southern Ukraine, the Northern Caucasus, and the Don. Stalin, instead of correcting his errors or raising procurement prices, responded by intensifying the use of force. Draconian measures were taken against the theft of grain in the collective farms. Many peasants, convicted of stealing products they themselves had raised, were sentenced to long terms of imprisonment or were even shot. In certain regions a policy of mass terror was introduced. Goods were not delivered to *raiony* that did not meet their grain procurement quotas; state and cooperative stores were closed down.

In some cases whole villages were resettled to the far northern regions. For example, in the fall of 1932 a commission headed by Kaganovich, which was granted virtually unlimited powers, was sent to the Northern Caucasus to investigate the difficulties in grain procurement. In November 1932 the bureau of the Northern Caucasus party organization, with Kaganovich taking part, resolved to "smash all the saboteurs and counterrevolutionaries" responsible for the failure of the grain collection and the fall sowing.[42] As a result sixteen villages of the Northern Caucasus, including Poltavskaya, Medvedovskaya, Urupskaya, and Bagaevskaya, were moved to the far north. The entire populations of these villages, including poor and middle peasants and both individual and collective farmers, were deported. Peasants from the non-Black Earth regions were resettled in these "vacated" areas. Under the leadership of Molotov and Kaganovich mass repression was also carried out in the Ukraine and Belorussia (the resettlement of the so-called *chernodosochnye raiony*).

There is a revealing letter from Mikhail Sholokhov to Stalin on the outrageous actions of the grain procurers in Veshenskaya and other *raiony* of the Don. On April 16, 1933, Sholokhov wrote that "disgusting methods" were being used to collect grain, including cursing, beating, and torture, and he asserted:

These examples can be multiplied endlessly. They are not isolated cases of deviation; they are the "method" of procuring grain that has been decreed for the whole raion. I have heard these facts either from Communists or from the collective farmers themselves, who experienced all of these "methods" and afterwards came asking me to write about it in the newspaper. Do you remember, Joseph Vissarionovich, Korolenko's essay "In a Pacified Village?" Here the "disappearing act" has been performed, not on three peasants suspected of stealing from the kulak, but on tens of thousands of collective farmers. And, as you can see, it's been done with a richer application of technical methods and more sophistication.

Sholokhov asked Stalin to look into what was happening in the Don region and to investigate not only the people who used intolerable methods against collective farmers but also the higher-ups who directed them.[43]

42. See the newspaper *Molot*, November 5, 1932.
43. Khrushchev quoted Sholokhov's letter in a speech published in *Pravda*, March 10, 1963. For Korolenko's "In a Pacified Village," a 1911 account of brutal mistreatment of

But Stalin remained deaf to such appeals. He even tried to give this terror against the peasantry his own kind of "theoretical foundation." At a Politburo meeting in November 1932 he said:

What is the collective farm peasantry? The collective farm peasantry is the ally of the working classes. The vast majority of these peasants support the Soviet regime in the countryside. But this does not mean that, among the collective farmers, there cannot be individual groups who are against the Soviet regime and support the sabotage of grain procurements. It would be stupid if Communists, merely because collective farms are a socialist form of enterprise, did not counter the blows of these individual collective farmers and farms with crushing blows of their own. [44]

The newly formed state farms also experienced repression. A typical example was a decree "On the work of livestock state farms," published in the spring of 1932 and signed by Stalin, Molotov, and Yakov Yakovlev, people's commissar of agriculture. The decree named thirty-four directors of state farms who had tried "to gloss over shortcomings resulting from their own poor leadership by referring to the fact that livestock state farms are in the early stages of construction." The decree "proposed" that these thirty-four be fired and brought to trial; it also listed ninety-two other directors, who were only to be fired.

■ 7

FAMINE IN THE COUNTRYSIDE, 1932–1933

For the Soviet countryside the first five-year plan ended not only with mass collectivization but also with a terrible famine that took millions of lives. An increasingly severe food shortage was already being experienced in the rural districts in 1930–1931 as gross agricultural production shrank and government requisitioning expanded. In the late fall of 1932 vast regions of the country were affected by a fierce famine. Its ravages were especially harsh in the Southern Ukraine, the Middle Volga, the Northern Caucasus, and Kazakhstan. The dimensions of this famine considerably surpassed the famine in the Volga region in 1921, which had actually extended beyond the Volga region. In 1921, however, all of the newspapers reported on the famine. Funds were collected around the world, international aid for the starving was begun, and special aid

---

peasants under the last tsar, see V. G. Korolenko, *Sobranie sochinenii*, vol. 5 (Moscow, 1955), pp. 392–402.

44. *Bolshevik*, 1933, no. 1–2, p. 19.

organizations were established. There was none of this in 1932–1933. A ban was placed on all information about the famine. Neither in the Soviet Union nor abroad were there any campaigns to aid the victims of starvation. On the contrary, the very fact of a massive famine was officially denied.

Hundreds of thousands and even millions of starving people fled to the cities and more prosperous regions, but few managed to reach their goals since military barricades and checkpoints were set up on highways and at railway stations to halt and turn back peasants from the famine-stricken regions. Even those who reached the cities did not receive help. The peasants did not have ration cards, and stores would not sell them bread. In Kiev and in many other cities in the south the gathering of the corpses of dead peasants began early in the morning; they were loaded onto wagons and brought outside the city to be buried in large anonymous graves.

Nothing was said about the famine at the first All-Union Congress of Collective Farm Shock Workers, held in Moscow in February 1933 — that is, at the very height of the famine in the south. At this very congress Stalin issued the call to "make all the collective farmers prosperous." Even at Politburo meetings Stalin refused to discuss the famine. For example, in 1932 R. Terekhov, a secretary of the Ukrainian Communist Party's Central Committee, reported to Stalin on the terrible situation developing in the villages of Kharkov *oblast* as a result of the crop failures and asked Stalin to send some grain there. Stalin's reaction was strange. Sharply interrupting the speaker, he said:

We've been told that you, Comrade Terekhov, are a good speaker; it seems that you are a good storyteller—you have made up quite a fable about famine, thinking to frighten us, but it won't work! Wouldn't it be better for you to leave the post of *obkom* secretary and the Ukrainian Central Committee and join the Writer's Union? Then you can write your fables, and fools will read them.[45]

In the thirties, however, it was impossible to read any "fables" about the famine of 1932–1933. Any reference to it was prohibited in the Soviet presss until 1956; in fact, during the thirties many people were arrested as "counterrevolutionary agitators" for uttering the words "famine in the south." Only after the Twenty-Second Party Congress did several writers begin to touch on this previously forbidden topic. In *Bread Is a Noun*, Mikhail Alekseev described the harsh winter of 1932–1933:

45. *Pravda*, May 26, 1964.

After the kulak the middle peasant left the village, but voluntarily. In accordance with one order or another, all the grain and all the fodder were taken away. Horses began to die en masse, and in 1933 there was a terrible famine. Whole families died, houses fell apart, village streets grew empty, more and more windows became blind—those who went to the city boarded them up. . . .

Akimushka's face became blacker than a furnace. His eyes shone like white incandescence, and his fellow villagers often looked into them as if to ask: "What is this? How can this be, Akimushka? After all, we followed you? You're a party man!" He answered as he was able. He said that there at the top they were going to investigate. Stalin would send his own man to Vyselki, where he would look things over and punish the guilty—all would be well. No one came to Vyselki, but people like Akimushka fortunately did not lose heart and let everything go, so that the collective farm slowly began once again to climb uphill.[46]

Similarly, Vladimir Tendryakov wrote in his novel *Death:*

In Petrakovskaya cattle died for lack of fodder, people ate bread made from nettles, biscuits made from one weed, porridge made from another. And not only in Peatrakovskaya. A year of hunger moved through the country, nineteen hundred and thirty-three. In Vokhrovo, the *raion* capital, in the little park by the station, dekulakized peasants expelled from the Ukraine lay down and died. You got used to seeing corpses there in the morning; a wagon would pull up and the hospital stable hand, Abram, would pile in the bodies. Not all died; many wandered through the dusty mean little streets, dragging bloodless blue legs, swollen from dropsy, feeling out each passer-by with doglike begging eyes. In Vokhrovo they got nothing; the residents themselves, to get bread on their ration cards, queued up the night before the store opened. Thirty-three.[47]

In his unpublished memoirs Kamil Ikramov wrote that in 1933 hundreds of thousands of hungry people from all regions of Central Asia rushed to Tashkent. All of the stations were filled with people, and despite the roadblocks, many of them made their way into the city. Emaciated in the extreme, they quietly wandered the streets hoping for charity. Many died right in the streets.

Vasily Grossman, one of the major Soviet writers, also described the harrowing scenes of famine in the southern Ukraine in his novel *Forever Flowing*, which was published abroad after his death.[48]

Aleksei Kosterin, another Soviet writer, who died in 1969, described the famine this way in his memoirs:

46. *Zvezda*, 1964, no. 1, p. 37.
47. *Moskva*, 1968, no. 3, p. 37.
48. Vasily Grossman, *Forever Flowing* (New York, 1972). [The description of the famine appears in chapter 14, pp. 139–170.—G. S.]

It was frightening to walk through villages in 1933–1934. And I had occasion to pass through dozens of villages in Stavropol, on the Don, Kuban, and Terek, and in Saratov, Orenburg, and Kalinin oblasti. . . . Houses with boarded up windows, empty barnyards, abandoned equipment in the fields. And terrifying mortality, especially among children. The fields and household gardens grew wild. In the Kuban the Cossacks grimly joked: the wolves have gathered in the weeds outside the village.

And the people wandered about as though they weren't all there.[49]

In 1934 the daughter of the prerevolutionary Russian writer Vladimir Korolenko wrote a letter to her former teacher, Nadezhda Krupskaya. In a very calm but clear manner Sofia Korolenko described the situation in the Poltava region of the Ukraine. Krupskaya did not answer her student, whom she had prepared for admission to a *gymnasium* as early as 1898. It was not only Stalin who brushed aside reports of famine in the south.

As for Stalin, he continued to export grain to the European countries in spite of the famine. Of the 1928 harvest less than 1 million centners (1 centner = 100 kilograms) of grain were exported, but in 1929, 13 million centners were exported; in 1930, 48.3 million; in 1931, 51.8 million; and in 1932, 18.1 million. Even in the worst year of the famine, 1933, close to 10 million centners of grain were shipped to Western Europe.[50] Because of the depression in Western Europe, Soviet grain sold at a very low price. Yet only half of the grain that was exported in 1932–1933 would have been sufficient to save all the southern regions from famine.

In Western Europe people ate Soviet bread, which had been taken from hungry and dying peasants, and ate it quite calmly. All rumors of famine in Russia were emphatically denied as anti-Soviet propaganda, even by official figures. George Bernard Shaw, who traveled to the Soviet Union in 1931, wrote on returning to the West that the rumors about famine in Russia appeared to be made up; he was certain that Russia had never before been so well supplied with goods as at the time that he was in that country. Pasternak saw a completely different picture in the Soviet countryside. He later wrote:

In the early 1930s it became fashionable among writers to travel to the collective farms and gather material about the new Soviet village. I wanted to be like everyone else, and so I set out on such a trip with the idea of writing a book. What I saw there cannot be conveyed in words, any words. There was such inhuman, unimaginable misery, it was such a terrible disaster, that it began to

49. Aleksei Kosterin, *Vospominaniia* (unpublished manuscript), p. 6.
50. *Narodnoe khoziaistvo SSSR* (Moscow, 1935), p. 222.

seem almost abstract, beyond the bounds that the conscious mind could admit. I fell ill. For an entire year I could not write.[51]

To this day no one knows how many peasants died of starvation in 1932–1933. Many observers give the figure 5 million; others say 8 million, and the latter is probably closer to the truth. The number of dead was larger than in 1921 or than in China during the terrible famine of 1877–1878. Indirect data attest to this. The book *Narodonaselenie SSSR* gives figures on the number of Ukrainians in the Soviet Union: according to the 1926 census, there were 31.2 million; according to the 1939 census, the number was 28.1 million. The total decrease over thirteen years was 3.1 million people. However, during those thirteen years the number of Belorussians increased by 1.3 million—that is, by almost 30 percent. During the years from 1926 to 1939 the number of Kazakhs decreased by 860,000, and several other minority nationalities suffered similar losses.[52]

As one specialist on the demography and statistics of the Soviet Union explains:

The famine of 1933–1934 was accompanied by the mass death of children, especially newborns. While the figure for persons born in the years 1929–1931 is given in the 1970 census as 12.4 million, the figure for births in 1932–34 is only 8.4 million. This decrease cannot be viewed as the result of conscious birth control on the part of the population. Although the most intense years of collectivization were in 1929–1931, the decline in the birth rate during those years was relatively small in comparison with the years 1926–1928. The famine in 1933 was too unexpected an occurrence, and furthermore, there was no knowledge of birth control in the countryside at that time. Probably no less than 3 million children born in 1932–1934 died of starvation.[53]

For the six years 1933–1938 the yearbooks of the Central Statistical Agency repeat the same figure for the population of the Soviet Union that was recorded as of January 1, 1933: 165.7 million people. Speaking in December 1935 at a meeting of advanced combine operators, Stalin said:

Among us everyone now says that the material conditions of working people have significantly improved, that living has gotten better and happier. This, of

51. From the unpublished memoirs of Boris Pasternak.
52. A Gozulov and M. Grigoriants, *Narodonaselenie SSSR* (Moscow, 1969).
53. M. Maksudov, Poteri naseleniya SSSR v 1918–1958 gg. [Maksudov's essay circulated in typescript in the Soviet Union long before being published abroad in several languages. An English version is "Population Losses in the USSR, 1918–1958," in *Samizdat Register II*, New York, 1981, pp. 220–276.—G. S.]

course, is true. But this has resulted in the situation that the population has begun to multiply much more quickly than in the old days. The mortality rate has decreased, the birth rate has increased, and the net population increase has become much greater. This is good, of course, and we welcome it. Now every year the net growth of the population is around 3 million. This means that every year we have a population growth equal to all of Finland.[54]

But Stalin was premature with his conclusions about an increase in the growth rate and about life becoming "happier." The 1939 census gave the figure of 170.4 million people. Thus the growth rate had remained less than 1 million per year. As for the "happier" life in the Soviet Union, I will discuss that in the next section.

■ **8**
INTERNAL PASSPORTS

The imposition of a passport system on part of the Soviet population in the early thirties constituted a kind of repressive campaign in its own right.

In tsarist Russia the passport system primarily served the purpose of police surveillance and restriction of movement within the country. The passport system complicated the lives of ordinary people so much that one of the main demands of the revolutionary-democratic movement in the late nineteenth and early twentieth centuries was for abolition of internal passports and guaranteed freedom of movement. It was natural for the passport system to be abolished after the October revolution; this measure was considered one of the most important democratic reforms of the new proletarian government. In the first edition of the *Small Soviet Encyclopedia*, published from 1928 to 1931, the following passage appears:

> The passport system is an important instrument of police control and tax policy in what is called a "police state." Tsarist Russia had such a system. Especially burdensome for the mass of working people, a passport system is also restrictive to the civil and commercial circulation desired by the bourgeois state, which therefore abolishes or greatly relaxes such a system. Under Soviet law there is no passport system.[55]

In the Soviet Union during the twenties citizens were issued passports only for travel abroad. Vladimir Mayakovsky's ode extolling his "red-

54. *Pravda*, December 4, 1935.
55. *Malaia sovetskaia entsiklopediia*, 6:342–343.

skinned" Soviet passport is included in all native anthologies for Soviet literature.

The situation began to change, however, with the beginning of collectivization and even more with the famine. In contrast to the civil war period, when millions of city dwellers escaped hunger by moving to the countryside, in the early thirties rural inhabitants sought to escape the famine by moving to the cities, where despite everything the supply of food was better. Knowing no other way to control this spontaneous migration of millions of people, Stalin's government made the decision to reintroduce the passport system. Under this system only industrial and office workers had the right to carry passports; peasants could not. Their freedom of movement was thus severely restricted, and control over the movements of all citizens was increased.

In early 1930 the journal *Bolshevik* published some remarks by Christian Rakovsky as an example of "Trotskyist slander against the party." Rakovsky wrote in part:

Behind the fiction of collective farmers who are all equal owners and behind the fiction of elected management, relations are taking shape that will leave far behind what we see now on the state farms. The fact is that the collective farmers will not be working for themselves. The only thing that will grow, develop, and flourish on the collective farms will be a new collective farm bureaucracy. It will be of all sorts and types. The brainchild of bureaucratic fantasy, . . . the collective farms, uniting under one roof all the strata of the peasantry except for obvious kulaks, will be hemmed in on all sides by the steel hoops of the bureaucratic apparatus. The collective farms will suffer from want in all respects, but this poverty will be compensated for by a surfeit of officials and guardians both open and secret. This confirms once again that bureaucratic socialism in turn produces bureaucrats and that the socialist society that we have come right to the verge of, as we are assured by all the official scribblers, will be nothing but the kingdom of bureaucrats. . . .

Finding themselves in a difficult situation, the poor peasants and farm laborers will begin to flock to the cities en masse, leaving the countryside without working hands. Might it then happen that our proletarian government would pass a law under which the poor and middle peasant would be bound to the collective farm and under which our Red militia would be obliged to detain escapees on the streets and hustle them back to their authorized places of residence?![56]

Many of Rakovsky's bitter prophecies, which in early 1930 were interpreted by the readers of *Bolshevik* as inconceivable for the proletarian government, became reality at the end of 1932 and beginning of 1933.

56. *Bolshevik*, 1930, no. 7, pp. 18–19.

Through the passport system the Soviet government actually did bind the poor and middle peasants to their collective farms and did require the "Red militia" to catch and return starving peasants from railroad stations and cities.

The passport system served not only to attach the peasant to his collective farm but also to restrict many residents of Moscow, Leningrad, Kiev, and other large cities. They, too, could be denied passports. The militia would not issue passports to thousands of former capitalists, noblemen, and other "disenfranchised" persons (those who had been denied voting rights). These people were forced to leave the capitals and large cities for small provincial towns where they usually held minor office jobs in local institutions.

In 1920 the economist and writer A. V. Chayanov, a prominent figure in the cooperative movement, published under the pseudonym Ivan Kremnev a small book in Moscow entitled *My Brother Aleksei's Journey to the Land of Peasant Utopia*, with an introduction by the prominent Bolshevik writer V. V. Vorovsky. The year the book was published was one of sharply intensified conflict between the city and countryside in Russia, when a wave of peasant uprisings was sweeping the country, which the Red Army was taking stern measures to suppress. Describing the possible future development of this conflict, the author predicted that over the course of years the countryside would gradually overcome the cities. At first the peasantry would gain equal voting rights with the workers and would win a majority in all the highest institutions of the Soviet government. By 1932 political power in Russia would be firmly in the hands of the peasant leaders, who would gradually reorganize the entire economy on the basis of individual peasant farming and cooperative associations. The cities would eventually be destroyed. A revolt by city dwellers against the peasant power would be suppressed in 1937, and the cities would be dissolved in the surrounding rural regions in a way that would not interfere with scientific and technical progress or the maintenance of the military strength of the new peasant state, which would be able to cope quite easily with military aggression on the part of urban industrial Germany. By 1984 Russia would consist of nothing but villages and land.[57] Needless to say, events in the Soviet Union took a

57. This book by A. V. Chayanov (Ivan Kremnev), *Puteshestvie moego brata Alekseia v stranu krest'ianskoi utopii*, was published in French in Geneva and in English in the *Journal of Peasant Studies* (October 1976), vol. 4. no. 1. It was reprinted in Russian (New York, 1981) by Serebryany Vek publishing house.

course completely different from the one predicted in Chayanov's "utopia."

SHORTCOMINGS AND MISTAKES IN INDUSTRIALIZATION

The mistakes and abuses of power that occurred during collectivization
have often been criticized in Soviet and foreign literature alike. Much
less has been said about Stalin's shortcomings and abuses in the course of
industrialization.

I am not about to deny the major successes achieved by the Soviet
Union during the first five-year plan. In the period from 1928 to 1933
alone, 1,500 big enterprises were built and the foundations were laid for
branches of industry that had not existed in tsarist Russia: machine-tool
production automobile and tractor manufacturing, chemical works, airplane factories, the production of powerful turbines and generators, of
high-grade steel, of ferrous alloys, of synthetic rubber, artificial fibers,
nitrogen, and so on. Construction was begun on thousands of kilometers
of new railroads and canals. Major centers of heavy industry were created
in the territories of the non-Russian minorities, the former borderlands
of tsarist Russia—in Belorussia, the Ukraine, Transcaucasia, Central
Asia, Kazakhstan, Tataria, the Northern Caucasus, and Buryat Mongolia.
The eastern part of the country became a second major center for metallurgy and the oil industry. A modern defense industry was established.
And hundreds of new cities and workers' settlements were founded.
Stalin put considerable effort into the huge task of building a modern
industry in the Soviet Union. But in this area as in others he often acted
not as a wise statesman but as a voluntarist and promoter of unrealizable
schemes *(prozhektor)*. Thus, Stalin's leadership frequently created unnecessary difficulties for the party and the country.

It is well-known, for example, that the first five-year plan of 1928/29–
1932/33 was drawn up in two variants: a basic *(otpravnoi)* variant and an
optimum one, the first setting goals about 20 percent lower than the
second. The plan was drawn up in two variants because of both a lack of
experience in central planning and the impossibility of foreseeing such
factors of importance to the five-year plan as the condition of agriculture
and the possibilities for receiving Western credit and goods through foreign trade. The first year of the plan showed not only that it was sensible
to have two variants but also that the basic variant should have become

the main guideline for the planning period. However, in the discussion of the draft plan most of the targets set by the basic variant were dismissed as "concessions to the right deviation." Stalin oriented all of the party organizations toward the optimum variant, which was in fact ratified at the Sixteenth Party Congress.

In the first two years of the five-year plan it became obvious that some of the major conditions for fulfilling the optimum variant had not materialized. There was no great increase in credit from the capitalist countries, nor did the Soviet Union's capacity to export show dramatic growth. On the contrary, the industrial and agricultural crisis that hit the major capitalist countries in 1929–1930 created unforeseen difficulties for the USSR. World prices of raw materials dropped sharply, and for each machine imported it was necessary to export more than twice the amount the plan had provided for. Nor was there a steep rise in the qualitative indices of economic development (lower cost of production, higher productivity of labor, and so on).

In addition of course there was the decline in Soviet agricultural production. Earlier it had been assumed that agricultural production would increase and that the capital accumulated in that sector could be used extensively for industrialization; these calculations had to be revised. On the average, 33.4 percent of the surplus product derived from agriculture was used for industrial development during the first five-year plan. At the beginning of the planning period the figure was close to 50 percent, but in 1932 it fell to 18.1 percent.[58] At the end of the first five-year plan the starving villages were hardly able to help industrialization.

Thus it is not surprising that despite great exertions the first five-year plan did not get off to a successful start. For example, the production of pig iron and steel increased by only 600,000 to 800,000 tons in 1929, barely surpassing the 1913–1914 level. Only 3,300 tractors were produced in 1929. The output of food processing and light industry also rose slowly. And in the crucial area of transportation the railways worked especially poorly.

Under these conditions it was necessary to reduce many of the targets and control figures of the five-year plan and to revert to the basic variant. Instead at the Sixteenth Party Congress in June 1930 Stalin announced sharp increases even in the optimum planning targets—for pig iron, from 10 million to 17 million tons by the last year of the plan; for tractors,

58. A. A. Barsov, *Balans stoimostnykh obmenov mezhdu gorodom i derevnei* (Moscow, 1969), p. 134.

from 55,000 to 170,000; for other agricultural machinery and trucks, an increase of more than 100 percent; and so on. He dismissed as "hopelessly bureaucratic" the argument that such arbitrary increases undermined the whole principle of planning.[59]

Stalin's proposals were seriously questioned not only by many of the nonparty specialists but also by eminent Bolshevik executives. Stalin, however, did not wish to consider their arguments. When A. S. Shakmuradov, the chief director of the Central Board of Nonferrous Metals, gave a convincing critique of the fantastic new targets in nonferrous metallurgy, he was demoted and later fell victim to repression.

Of course repression and threats of repression did not speed up the development of industry. For example, in 1930 Stalin predicted an increase in industrial output of 31 to 32 percent.[60] The actual increase, according to the yearbooks of the Central Statistical Administration, was 22 percent. For 1931 a new target was adopted: an increase of 45 percent. The actual increase in 1931 waas 20 percent. In 1932 it dropped to 15 percent, and in 1933 to 5 percent. In 1932 the slogan "17 million tons of pig iron" was dropped, along with many other unrealistic goals in metallurgy and machine production.

In January 1933 Stalin reported that the first five-year plan had been fulfilled in four years and three months, that industrial output in 1932 had reached the goals set for 1933. He told the Central Committee plenum which met that month that the plan as a whole had been fulfilled at the end of 1932 by 93.7 percent, and in Group A (heavy industry) by 103.4 percent. A noisy propaganda campaign was launched on the occasion. Stalin wanted to use this campaign to cover up the difficult situation that existed in the Soviet Union because of the serious food shortage and the famine in the major agricultural regions.

Of course industry did make great strides during the first five-year plan. But this "leap forward" was not nearly as great as Stalin reported to the January plenum in 1933. Stalin's figures were based on deliberate falsification.

The Supreme Council of the National Economy had planned that gross industrial output would increase 2.8 times from 1927–1928 to 1932–1933, with heavy industry increasing 3.3 times. In fact, over the five-

59. Stalin, *Sochineniia*, 12:345–347.
60. The targets of the five-year plan are indicated in Stalin, *Sochineniia*, 13:29–30. The facts on the actual increase in production are taken from the yearbooks published by the Central Statistical Administration since 1956.

year period gross industrial output approximately doubled and heavy industry increased by 2.7 times, considerably short of the planned targets. The output of consumer goods was supposed to rise by 240 percent, but the actual increase was only 56 percent.[61]

In a number of cases even the increase that was registered was purely statistical. This was because the value of a half-finished product was now counted twice: first in evaluating the performance of the enterprise turning out the half-finished product, then in evaluating the work of the enterprise making a finished product out of the half-finished one.

If fulfillment of the first five-year plan is analyzed not only on the basis of gross output but also on the basis of physical indices of goods produced, the results prove to be much more modest than the propaganda claimed. Toward the end of the plan almost none of the optimum goals, as expressed in physical units, was reached. Even further from fulfillment were the unrealistic goals that Stalin spoke of at the Sixteenth Party Congress.

Ten million tons of pig iron were planned for the last year of the five-year plan, and in 1930 Stalin declared this goal raised to 17 million tons. In 1932, 6.16 million tons were poured. On the eve of the war, in 1940, 15 million tons of pig iron were poured. Only in 1950 did the figure pass 17 million.[62] Instead of the 10.4 million tons of steel planned for 1932 under the optimum variant, around 6 million tons were poured, and the output of the rolling mills was 4.43 million tons in 1932 instead of the planned 8 million.

The Sixteenth Party Congress endorsed a control figure of 22 million kilowatt hours to be generated in the last year of the plan; in fact, 13.4 million kilowatt hours were generated in 1932. The production of coal and peat that year fell short of the target by 10 to 15 percent. Petroleum output was somewhat better: already in 1931, 22.4 million tons were extracted, more than planned for 1932–1933. In the next two years, however, petroleum production dropped: in 1932 to 21.4 million tons and in 1933 to 21.5.

61. See *Promyshlennost' SSSR*, pp. 12–13, and *Kratkii kurs istorii SSSR*, vol. 2 (Moscow, 1964), p. 234.

62. The targets of the five-year plan in this case are taken from the three-volume text of the plan published by the State Planning Commission in 1928–1929, *Piatiletnii plan narodno-khoziaistvennogo stroitel'stva SSSR*, and from the stenographic record of the Sixteenth Party Congress, *Shestnadtsatyi s"ezd VKP(b). Stenograficheskii otchet*. The facts on plan fulfillment are taken from the yearbooks published by the Central Statistical Administration since 1956. See also *Istoriia sotsialisticheskoi ekonomii SSSR* (Moscow, 1977), 8:113.

The optimal goals in the production of building materials were not met. Instead of the 9.3 billion bricks planned, 4.9 billion were produced in 1932. It was even worse with mineral fertilizers. The plan called for 8 to 8.5 million tons in 1932, but only 920,000 were produced in 1932 and 1,030,000 in 1933 (the plan called for 3.4 million tons of superphosphates in 1932, but only 182,000 tons were produced). Approximately 30 percent of the target for production of sulphuric acid was actually reached.

Many of the more important goals in the machine industry were not reached, including the production of agricultural machinery. According to the plan, 100,000 automobiles and trucks were to be produced in the last year of the plan, and in 1930 Stalin declared this goal doubled. In fact, 23,900 were manufactured in 1932 and 49,700 in 1933. Not until 1936 did automobile manufacture pass the 100,000 mark. In 1932, 49,000 tractors were produced, as against the 55,000 planned. As for Stalin's declared figure of 170,000 tractors, it was reached neither before the war nor during the first postwar decade. Nor was Stalin's unrealistic goal of 40,000 harvester combines attained by 1932.

In light industry and food processing many important branches showed no growth at all during the first five-year plan. In cotton cloth, for example, 2.678 billion meters were manufactured in 1928 and 2.694 billion in 1932, whereas the plan called for 4.588 billion. Woolen cloth: 86.8 million meters were manufactured in 1928 and 88.7 million meters in 1932, when the plan called for 270–300 million meters. Linen cloth: 174.4 million meters in 1928 and 133.6 million meters in 1932, in comparison with the planned 500 million meters. The production of sugar was to have increased twofold; in reality it stood 30 percent lower in 1932 than in 1928. A similar decline occurred in the production of meat and milk. And there were many other important sectors of the economy where the optimum targets were not reached: paper, footwear, railway tonnage, and so on.

Despite the nonfulfillment of the plan's physical indices, the working class population grew much faster than planned. From 1928 to 1933 the number of workers increased not by just a third, as the plan had forecast; it nearly doubled.[63] This was due to a number of unforeseen circumstances: extended delays in completing many big industrial projects, the mass exodus of peasants to the cities because of the bad situation in the countryside, and failure to achieve the planned increase in the productiv-

63. *Voprosy istorii KPSS*, 1967, no. 2, p. 58.

ity of labor. The immoderate growth of the urban population created a multitude of disproportions.

The transfer to the cities of millions of peasants, most of them poor, was accompanied by an improvement in their standard of living. And of course the material position of the former unemployed was improved; now they all had work. But the standard of living of the regular workers grew worse. The Fifteenth Party Congress adopted a resolution saying that "any further increase in wages must be in real wages, not just in monetary units," but this was not carried out.[64] At the very beginning of the first five-year plan the purchasing power of the ruble fell and prices on the open market rose severalfold. "Commercial"—that is, unrationed—stores appeared, where scarce goods could be bought at high prices. The historian O. I. Shkaratan's data show that in 1930 the real wages of Leningrad factory workers in all sectors were lower than their 1928 level. This tendency remained in 1931–1932, and real wages did not reach their 1928 level until 1940.

It goes without saying that the difficulties in fulfilling the first five-year plan can be explained in part by the fact that it was the *first* five-year plan in history. But much can be blamed on the mistakes of Stalin.

Stalin introduced the "willful" *(volevoi)* method of planning into Soviet economic life, and there are many cases that prove how wrong it was. It will suffice to recall the development of synthetic rubber.[65] The first batch of experimental synthetic rubber was produced in January 1931, and immediately, the construction of one or two large factories was proposed. All the leading engineers, including academician S. V. Lebedev, whose process had been used to produce the synthetic rubber, doubted the practicality of such a program. Nonetheless, striving for a rapid development of the Soviet chemical industry, the participants in the discussion endorsed a plan to build one or two factories. The specialists were astonished to learn that the government had decided, on Stalin's proposal, to build ten big synthetic rubber factories during the first five-year plan. Lebedev himself categorically opposed such a grandiose project in an area of production that still had many unsolved problems. Opposition was also expressed by Jan Rudzutak, chairman of the Committee on Chemical Production. But Stalin brushed aside these well-founded objections. The search for construction sites and building materials began. Such resources as were available were spread out over ten

64. *Piatnadtsatyi s"ezd VKP(b)* (Moscow, 1962), 2:1450.
65. See *Istoriia SSSR*, 1964, no. 3, pp. 34–38.

units. Finally, in 1932–1933 starts were made on only three factories; the rest were not built either in the first or in the second five-year plan. As a result vast resources were frozen for a very long time.

There are many similar examples of Stalin's incompetence and adventurism, which greatly complicated the already complex job of industrialization.

Several Old Bolsheviks, in their memoirs, point out the difference between the style and atmosphere of meetings on economic problems chaired by Lenin and by Stalin. For example, Yu. Flakserman, a prominent Soviet economic manager, writes:

Lenin never overpowered anyone with his authority. An atmosphere of camaraderie prevailed at the Sovnarkom meetings; everyone felt comfortable. During discussions opinions were often expressed that didn't coincide with Lenin's, but he always listened attentively and, if he perceived a sensible idea, would correct his own proposals accordingly.

I will never forget, in contrast, a meeting of one of the Central Committee commissions headed by Stalin. It was in 1931. The topic of discussion was the structure and location of a large new industrial complex in which power engineering played a large role, which is why I was invited. At the time I was a power engineer and had become chairman of the Center for Power Engineering (Energotsentr). The commission worked in the afternoon in the auditorium where Sovnarkom meetings were held. I installed myself off to the side, by the windows, where I used to sit in 1918 under Lenin. The members of the commission, various people's commissars, Ordzhonikidze [head of the Supreme Economic Council] and other members of the Presidium of that Council—all sat at the long conference table in the center of the room. Stalin walked around, smoking his pipe. For the most part, the officials of the Supreme Economic Council spoke. Then Stalin took the floor. He sat off to the side, at the chairman's table, with his face toward the conference table. He spoke so softly that no one could hear what he said. At first we all began involuntarily to cup our hands behind our ears, but that did not help. Then everyone practically lay on the table, straining to hear the speaker. Everyone remained in this position until he had finished his speech. When he finished speaking the meeting was closed: there was no more discussion, the truth had been spoken in its final form. How dissimilar this was to the way it had been under Lenin.[66]

It is possible to say with certainty that industrialization during the first five-year plan proceeded at a slower pace and higher price not least of all because Stalin was the head of the party and the government. A more competent leadership would have been able to attain far different results.

66. *Voprosy istorii*, 1964, no. 8, pp. 38–39.

4

NEW CRIMES BY STALIN IN THE EARLY THIRTIES

■ 1

SOVIET POWER AND THE "BOURGEOIS" INTELLIGENTSIA

The serious miscalculations in economic and social policy from 1928 to 1932 lowered the standard of living for the majority of the Soviet population and resulted in the introduction of strict rationing in food supply and retail trade. This in turn caused discontent among substantial numbers of working people. It was hard to ascribe all these shortcomings to "the kulaks," most of whom were deported to remote parts of the country. Nor was any self-criticism on the part of Stalin and his entourage to be expected. Instead, Stalin once again looked for a scapegoat and found it in the form of the specialists from among the prerevolutionary Russian (and Ukrainian) intelligentsia.

It is well known that some of the intelligentsia actively opposed the Bolsheviks during the civil war and that quite a few were exiled from Soviet Russia in the early years of NEP. In Lenin's view, however, it was possible and desirable to use the experience and knowledge of the old "bourgeois" intelligentsia to build the Soviet economy and develop Soviet science in the same way that many thousands of former tsarist officers had been used to build the Red Army. The specialists were willing in their professional capacities to collaborate loyally with the Soviet government, even though they hoped that in the end that government would gradually degenerate, reverting to the features of the prerevolutionary Russian state. Lenin stressed the need to make use of the "human material" available to the Soviet government.

Marxism is distinguished from the old utopian socialism precisely by the fact that the latter wanted to build a new society not out of the masses of human material created by bloody, dirty, moneygrubbing, rapacious capitalism, but out of especially virtuous people raised in special greenhouses and hothouses.[1]

Further, in his view:

Unless our leading bodies, i.e., the Communist Party, the Soviet government and the trade unions, guard as the apple of their eye every specialist who does his work conscientiously and knows and loves it—even though the ideas of communism are totally alien to him—it will be useless to expect any serious progress in socialist construction.[2]

The policy outlined by Lenin was subsequently implemented fairly consistently during the first years of NEP. It is not surprising therefore that during the first five-year plan many of these so-called bourgeois specialists, who derived from the old intelligentsia and from the classes overthrown by the October revolution, were working in the Soviet economic apparatus, industrial enterprises, scientific and educational institutions, agricultural agencies, the State Plannning Commission (Gosplan), and the statistical offices. Many former Mensheviks and SRs who had abandoned oppositional political activity also worked in these areas.

The aggravation of all internal contradictions in the Soviet Union, especially between the government and the peasantry, and incompetent

1. Lenin, PSS, 37:409.
2. Lenin, PSS, 44: 350–351. [Cf. CW, 33:194.]

government intervention in the economy, causing many losses and difficulties, could not help but affect the attitudes of the intelligentsia. It was natural that a large number of them sympathized mainly with that section of the party leadership termed the "right deviation." Some specialists, however, actually became involved in anti-Soviet activity, including conspiratorial work. In the early thirties several counterrevolutionary organizations and groups sprang up inside the Soviet Union as well as abroad. (The GPU itself founded some of these groups for purposes of provocation, as in the case of the organization called The Trust, which later gained much notoriety.) Such people were an insignificant minority among the old intelligentsia. The overwhelming majority continued to work honestly, trying to help the party leaders in charge of the various economic organizations. Many of the specialists were genuinely inspired by the tremendous scope of the first five-year plans.

It is not surprising that the GPU quickly suppressed the few isolated and feeble operations organized by émigré groups or groups inside the Soviet Union with the aim of overthrowing Soviet power. At the same time it was necessary to make a strict differentiation in the application of repressive measures so that the loyalty many of the old intelligentsia and specialists felt toward the Soviet regime would be maintained. Their know-how and experience were essential to the job of socialist construction.

Stalin's speeches, articles, and statements of that time contain quite a few assertions about the need to care for the old bourgeois intelligentsia in every possible way. His actions, however, were quite different.

First of all, he increasingly demanded of these people not simply loyalty to the Soviet government but also acceptance of Communist ideology. Repression was often used against them because of their non-Communist or non-Marxist views or their activities before the revolution. Secondly, in campaigning to place the responsibility for the mistakes in industrialization and planning on the "bourgeois specialists," Stalin and some of his closest associates began to carry out a policy aimed at discrediting and crushing a significant section of the nonparty specialists.

The political trials staged in the late twenties and early thirties occupied a special place in this campaign. They require the closest scrutiny by historians.

■ 2

THE POLITICAL TRIALS OF 1928–1930

The first major political trial to have the effect of seriously aggravating the internal political situation in the Soviet Union was the so-called Shakhty case. The defendants were engineers and technicians in the coal industry of the Donetsk basin (Donbass). They were accused of "wrecking," deliberately causing explosions in the mines, and maintaining criminal ties with the former mineowners, as well as less serious crimes, such as buying unnecessary imported equipment, violating safety procedures and labor laws, incorrectly laying out new mines, and so on.

The indictment was drawn up by Nikolai Krylenko, senior assistant to the public prosecutor of the Russian Socialist Federated Soviet Republic (RSFSR), and P. A. Krasikov, prosecutor of the USSR Supreme Court. The case was heard by the Supreme Court in Moscow in the summer of 1928. Presiding at the hearings was Andrei Vyshinsky, a former Menshevik and a lawyer by profession, who worked for the Commissariat of Enlightenment and was the head of Moscow State University. The choice of Vyshinsky was intended by the organizers of the trial to ensure the appearance of objectivity. The trial, however, was obviously staged for political purposes.

Besides the specialists and several workers from the Donbass, various directors of Ukrainian industry were on trial, alleged to be the leaders of a "Kharkov center" that directed the wrecking activity. Representatives of a "Moscow center" were also present, accused of connections not only with various organizations of Russian émigré businessmen but also with representatives of Belgian, French, and Polish capital. According to the indictment, Western capitalists had financed the Donbass wreckers' organizations and activities.

At the trial some of the defendants confessed their guilt, but many denied it or confessed to only some of the charges. The court acquitted four of the fifty-three defendants, gave suspended sentences to four, and prison terms of one to three years to ten. Most of the defendants were given four to ten years. Eleven were condemned to be shot, and five of them were executed in July 1928. The other six were granted clemency by the All-Union Central Executive Committee.

The "Shakhty affair" was discussed at two plenary sessions of the Central Committee and provided the occasion for a prolonged propaganda campaign. The term "Shakhtyite" become virtually a synonym for "wrecker." However, anyone who closely examines the trial materials, which were discussed extensively in the press, is bound to ask: How well founded were the indictments and verdicts in the Shakhty case?

In one of Stalin's prison camps the Old Bolshevik A. M. Durmashkin met an NKVD executive, sentenced in 1937 to fifteen years, who told him that many of the charges in the Shakhty trial were false. In prison the writer Varlam Shalamov met two specialists, N. N. Boyaryshnikov and Miller, who had been through the Shakhty affair. (At first Boyaryshnikov was condemned to be shot but the sentence was reduced to ten years' imprisonment.) They told Shalamov that in 1928 investigators used such methods as the "conveyer" (uninterrupted interrogation, allowing the accused no sleep) as well as solitary confinement and cells with hot or cold floors—torture that forced many of the accused to give false testimony during investigation and at the trial.

V. Brodsky, a former Menshevik who was in prison for almost thirty years (from the late twenties until 1956), wrote the following to me:

> I saw a countless number of people who had been accused of wrecking and many who were still facing such charges, and *all* of them denied that even isolated instances of deliberate wrecking by specialists had occurred. There had been cases of damage to equipment, they said (such as sand in bearings), but this had been done directly by production workers (especially new arrivals from the villages). However, even these instances could have been the result of ignorance and unskilled operation of machinery. All of the specialists I met explained the accidents (particularly in the Donbass) as the result of haste in trying to fulfill or overfulfill the plan, incompetence on the part of administrators who were not specialists, and the low level of skills among the workers, most of whom had come from the countryside.

On the other hand, according to Suren Gazaryan, a veteran Chekist who was head of the economic section of the NKVD in Transcaucasia (and was arrested in 1937), there was such a thing as wrecking. Still, this form of anti-Soviet activity was comparatively insignificant. Wrecking as a conscious policy, pursued by the entire stratum of bourgeois specialists, never existed. Gazaryan said that there really was criminal mismanagement in the Donbass in 1928, which was the cause of many serious accidents (flooded mines, explosions, and so on). Both central and local management were still understaffed; there was a lot of casual help and many negligent persons; in a number of Soviet and economic organizations, bribery, thieving, and disregard for the interests of the workers flourished. These crimes should obviously have been punished with the full severity of Soviet law. There may also have been individual cases of wrecking in the Donbass in 1928. (One of the engineers had actually received a letter from a former manager who had left the country.) But none of this justified a major political trial. Yet all sorts of accusations of wrecking and of connections with foreign counterrevolutionary organizations were added to various criminal accusations—thieving, bribery, mismanagement—in the course of the investigation. This was intended "to mobilize the masses," "to arouse their wrath against the imperialists," "to intensify vigilance," and so forth. In reality the aim of these false charges was to divert the dissatisfaction of the masses from the party leadership, which was encouraging haste in pursuit of a maximum rate of industrialization.

Nikolai Ustryalov, one of the most prominent ideologists of the bourgeois intelligentsia and "Nepman" bourgeoisie, wrote the following in his book *Na novom etape,* published in 1930 in Harbin, Manchuria:

Wrecking is a senseless, disgraceful, and most pernicious crime, a betrayal, a direct transition to anti-Soviet and anti-Russian positions; today even Milyukov, in exile, would not defend it. . . . As for so-called passive neutrality, from our point of view it merits unconditional condemnation in principle. The job of the technical intelligentsia is not to stand aside or refuse its active participation and contribution . . . in the great task of rebuilding our country.

Ustryalov was giving his followers, the specialists—the Smenovekhites who were working for the Soviet government—a clear-cut directive. "What are the old specialists to do? There can be only one answer: maintain an irreproachable loyalty to the state, and do all that is in your power to assist it."

Stalin, however, did not wish to look into the subtleties of the situation in regard to the old intelligentsia. He found it advantageous to support the notion of deliberate "wrecking" by the bourgeois intelligentsia. Eager to generalize the "lessons" of the Shakhty case, he called on party members to seek out "Shakhtyites" on every level of the government and party appartus. In April 1929 Stalin told the Central Committee:

The so-called Shakhty affair must not be considered an accident. "Shakhtyites" are now ensconced in every branch of our industry. Many of them have been caught, but by no means all have been caught. Wrecking by the bourgeois intelligentsia is one of the most dangerous forms of opposition to developing socialism. Wrecking is all the more dangerous in that it is connected with international capital. Bourgeois wrecking is a sure sign that the capitalist elements have by no means laid down their arms, that they are massing their forces for new attacks on the Soviet government.[3]

After such instructions it is not surprising that the terror against so-called bourgeois specialists sharply increased. In the Ukraine in 1929 there was an open political trial concerning the Union for the Liberation of the Ukraine (SVU). S. A. Yefremov, the vice-president of the Ukrainian Academy of Sciences, was declared to be the leader of this organization. Forty other people were also on trial. There were scientists, teachers, clergyman, activists in the cooperative movement, and medical workers. Almost all of them were accused of "bourgeois nationalism," wrecking, carrying out the orders of foreign Ukrainian nationalist organizations, and working as agents for the intelligence and counterintelligence services of several foreign governments. The SVU was also charged with forming a secret alliance with Poland in order to separate the Ukraine from Russia.

According to the Old Bolshevik A. V. Snegov, who held a responsible position in the party in the Ukraine at the time, the trial of the SVU was primarily organized by the GPU of the Ukraine, headed by Vsevolod Balitsky, who was carrying out the direct orders of Stalin. Also involved in organizing the trial were the leaders of the Ukrainian Communist Party: Stanislav Kosior, Mykola Skrypnik, and Vlas Chubar. The chief government prosecutors were L. Akhmatov and Mikhailik, and the prosecutors representing the public were P. P. Lyubchenko, Academician A. N. Sokolovsky, and the writer A. A. Slisarenko. In Snegov's opinion, although nationalist feelings were quite strong within a certain section of the Ukrainian intelligentsia, most of the accusations were false and the SVU as an organization did not really exist. This is confirmed by two of the defendants who were still alive after twenty-five years of imprisonment and in the seventies were still living in the Ukraine: V. Gantsov, a professor of philology, and B. F. Matushevsky, an engineer. Anyone reading the records of the trial today would reach the same conclusion, for it is impossible to find in this material any real evidence or convincing proof of the guilt of the accused.[4]

Also in 1930 the discovery of a new counterrevolutionary organization was announced: the so-called Toiling Peasant Party (TKP). Among the supposed leaders were Professor N. D. Kondratiev, an economist who

3. Stalin, *Sochineniia*, 12:14.
4. See the materials in *Ukrainskaia kontrrevoliutsiia na kul 'turnom i literaturnom fronte* (Kiev-Kharkov, 1930).

had been an assistant to the minister of food in the Provisional Government, the economist L. N. Yurovsky, the economist and writer A. V. Chayanov, whom I have discussed above, and the prominent agronomist A. G. Doyarenko. All these men were loyally working in Soviet governmental and economic institutions at the time. The TKP was accused of having nine major underground groups in Moscow: in the system of agricultural cooperatives and agricultural credit, in the commissariats of agriculture and finance, in the newspaper *Bednota* (The Poor Peasantry), in research institutes of agricultural economics, and in the Timiryazev Agricultural Academy. According to the GPU, the TKP also headed a considerable number of underground groups in the provinces, especially in agricultural agencies and among former kulaks and Social Revolutionaries. Membership in this underground party was estimated at 100,000 to 200,000.

The GPU began to organize a great open trial. The necessary testimony was prepared, and a large number of people were to be included in the trial, mostly agronomists and organizers of cooperatives. The trial was almost completely rehearsed, but for some reason Stalin changed his mind about having an open political trial. Apparently something went wrong in the preparations. The arrested "members and leaders of the TKP" were condemned in a closed court. The press concentrated not so much on the concrete deeds of TKP members as on the theoretical pronouncements and writings of the Moscow professors who supposedly had headed the party. Today Chayanov, Kondratiev, and Doyarenko have been rehabilitated.[5] Nevertheless, a number of publications, including the latest edition of the *Great Soviet Encyclopedia*, still refer to them as the leaders of the counterrevolutionary Toiling Peasant Party.[6]

In the fall of 1930 it was announced that the GPU had uncovered a sabotage and espionage organization in the food-supply system, especially in the meat, fish, and vegetable agencies. According to the GPU, this organization was headed by the former landowner and professor

5. See, for example, the article on Chayanov in *Literaturnaia entsiklopediia*, vol. 8 (Moscow, 1975) and the articles on Chayanov, Kondratiev, and Doyarenko in *Ekonomicheskaia entsiklopediia* (Moscow, 1979–1980).

6. See, for example, the article "Prompartiia" (The Industrial Party) in *Bol'shaia sovetskaia entsiklopediia*, vol. 21 (Moscow, 1975). (This encyclopedia and the literary encyclopedia cited in note 5 were produced by the same official Soviet publishing house, and the two volumes with conflicting attitudes toward the alleged TKP leaders appeared in the same year, 1975). Slanderous accusations about the TKP were also printed in *Istoricheskaia entsiklopediia*, vol. 11 (Moscow, 1968), p. 609.

A. V. Ryazantsev, the former landowner and general Ye. S. Karatygin, and other former noblemen, industrialists, Cadets, and Mensheviks, who had wormed their way into responsible positions in the Supreme Economic Council, the Commissariat of Trade, the meat, fish, and vegetable and fruit agencies (Soyuzmyaso, Soyuzryba, Soyuzplodoovoshch), and other such institutions. The press reported that these men had succeeded in disorganizing the supply of food products to many cities and workers' settlements and causing famine in several parts of the country. They were also responsible for the increase in prices on meat and for the distribution of poor-quality canned goods. All forty-six who were brought to closed trial were sentenced to be shot. These verdicts were far more severe than in other similar trials. Of course, today such accusations and sentences cause legitimate doubts.

■ 3
THE "INDUSTRIAL PARTY" AND "UNION BUREAU" TRIALS

From November 25 to December 7, 1930, a new political trial was held in Moscow, this time an open one. A group of prominent technical specialists were accused of wrecking and counterrevolutionary activities as members of an alleged Industrial Party (Prompartiya). Again the presiding judge was Vyshinsky and the main prosecutor was Krylenko; the defense attorneys were I. D. Braude and M. A. Otsep. Eight men were accused of wrecking and espionage activities: Leonid K. Ramzin, director of the Institute of Heat Engineering and a foremost specialist in heat engineering and boiler construction, V. A. Larichev, another prominent specialist in technology and planning, and I. A. Kalinikov, N. F. Charnovsky, A. A. Fedotov, S. V. Kupriyanov, V. I. Ochkin, and K. V. Sitnin.

The eight defendants were accused of being the executive committee of the underground "Industrial Party," which was supposedly founded in the late twenties. Their alleged aims were to organize wrecking, diversionary actions, sabotage, and espionage and to prepare for the intervention of the Western powers and the overthrow of the Soviet government. The founding of the Industrial Party was linked with Pyotr Palchinsky, a prominent engineer and former industrialist. (He had been arrested at the time of the Shakhty affair and executed without public trial in either 1928 or early 1929.) The organizers of the new trial apparently wanted to connect the Shakhty affair and the trial of the "Prompartiya." Approximately two thousand people were alleged to be members of the Industrial Party, most of them highly qualified technical specialists.

At the trial the defendants confessed their guilt and willingly gave the most improbable detailed testimony about their wrecking and spying, their connections with foreign embassies in Moscow, even with Raymond Poincaré, the president of France. A wave of meetings swept the country, with the speakers demanding that the leaders of the Industrial Party be shot. The court obligingly sentenced most of them to death, but a decree of the Central Executive Committee granted clemency, reducing the sentences to various terms of imprisonment.

In the West there was also a wave of protests and appeals against the trial in Moscow. Poincaré himself published a special declaration:

I do not know whether Professor Ramzin and the other members of the Industrial Party organized a conspiracy against the government of their country. I am not their confessor. . . . But in any case—and I affirm this once again—if there really was such a conspiracy, no one in France was involved in it. There must be rather gullible people in Moscow, if some actually believe or believed these fairy tales. . . . If by chance there are still judges in Moscow, they would do well to unmask the accusers and the accused, who are acting against their own interests in this strange affair and are participating in the dissemination of falsehood. In any case, I must repeat that neither Briand nor I nor the French general staff ever had any knowledge of the real or imaginary plans of an Industrial Party, whether in 1928 or before or after, and therefore we did not approve and did not encourage such plans. If I had known of such adventures, I would have condemned them as dangerous folly. I would like to be informed in what room the Russian conspirators conversed with my double, and by what authorization he gave them an audience. Above all, I would like them to send me the supposed plans of the French general staff and to inform me where, when, and under what conditions the supposed attack was to take place.[7]

It is significant that the complete text of Poincaré's declaration was published in *Pravda* and entered in the court record. Evidently this was done to show the court's objectivity. Since public confidence in Soviet courts was only slightly shaken in 1930, the bulk of Soviet citizens regarded Poincaré's declaration as proof of a real plot.

In March 1931, a few months after the trial of the Industrial Party, another open political trial was held in Moscow, that of an alleged Union Bureau of the Central Committee of the Menshevik Party. Among the fourteen defendants were: V. G. Groman, a member of the Presidium of Gosplan; V. V. Sher, a member of the board of the State Bank; Nikolai

7. *Pravda*, December 3, 1930.

Sukhanov, a writer; A. M. Ginzburg, an economist who headed the commission that drew up Vesenkha's first draft five-year plan in 1927; Mikhail Yakubovich, deputy director of the division of supply of the Commissariat of Trade; V. K. Ikov, a writer; and I. I. Rubin, a professor of economics. This time the presiding judge was Nikolai Shvernik, a member of the Central Committee of the Soviet Communist Party; Krylenko was again the main prosecutor; and the attorneys for the defense were I. D. Braude and N. V. Kommodov. Most of the accused had left the Menshevik Party between 1920 and 1922 and held responsible posts in economic and planning agencies. They were accused of secretly rejoining the Mensheviks at the end of the twenties and of organizing a center for that party within the Soviet Union.

The "Union Bureau" was accused of wrecking, especially in the drafting of plans for economic development. If the indictment is to be believed, the accused systematically lowered all the draft plans, trying thereby to slow down the development of Soviet industry and agriculture. The Mensheviks were also supposed to have formed a secret bloc with the Industrial Party and the Toiling Peasant Party to prepare for armed intervention from without and insurrection from within. Each contracting party was assigned a certain function: the Industrial Party was to conduct preliminary negotiations with representatives of the countries that were supposed to inspire or take part in armed intervention, to organize flying brigades of engineers for diversionary and terrorist actions, and to arrange for military conspiracies with certain individuals in the high command of the Red Army; the Toiling Peasant Party was to organize peasant revolts, supply the rebels with weapons and munitions, and create disturbances in Red Army units; and the Union Bureau was to prepare a citizens' guard in the cities, which could seize government institutions and provide the initial support for a new counterrevolutionary government.

The indictment contained clear hints of connections between the Mensheviks and the former opposition groups within the Bolshevik Party, primarily the Trotskyists and rightists. Some of the testimony was openly directed against David Ryazanov, who was then the director of the Marx-Engels-Lenin Institute. A major theorist and historian of Marxism, Ryazanov was known for his negative and even scornful attitude toward Stalin.

At the trial all the defendants confessed, giving highly detailed accounts of their wrecking activities. As prosecutor, Krylenko tried at one session to demonstrate the objectivity of the court by reading a special declaration from the émigré leaders of the Menshevik Party. They categorically denied any connection between the Menshevik Party and the defendants, who had quit the party in the early twenties or had never belonged to it at all. The émigré center declared that it had sent genuine Mensheviks into the Soviet Union to try and keep the organization alive, despite the ban that the Bolsheviks had placed on all parties but their own. But the Menshevik emissaries never tried to organize wrecking or prepare for armed intervention. In any case, none of the accused had ever been in touch with the emissaries of the Menshevik Party. After this declaration had been read, the accused, at the suggestion of the presiding judge, refuted it and reaffirmed their guilt. A few days later the court sentenced all fourteen defendants to terms of imprisonment ranging from five to ten years.

■ 4
THE FRAUDULENCE OF THE 1928–1931 POLITICAL TRIALS

Even after the Twentieth and Twenty-Second Party congresses many historians continued to treat the political trials of 1928–1931 in the same way as the press had four decades earlier. The latest edition of the *Great Soviet Encyclopedia* and the *Historical Encyclopedia (Istoricheskaia entsiklopediia)* contain special articles on the Shakhty affair and the Prompartiya trial. S. A. Fedyukin's book *The Soviet Regime and the Bourgeois Specialists* contains a substantial and interesting analysis of Bolshevik policies toward the bourgeois specialists, but Fedyukin's viewpoint in the first part of the book is strangely contradicted in the second part, where a large number of the specialists are suddenly converted to counterrevolution and wrecking at the end of the twenties.[8] Today it is possible to write in such a way only with an extremely uncritical attitude toward the materials and documents, which were openly published in the USSR in 1928–1931 and to which it is not difficult to obtain access.[9]

It should be said that a careful reading of the proceedings of the trials,

8. S. A. Fedyukin, *Sovetskaia vlast' i burzhuaznye spetsialisty* (Moscow, 1965).

9. See the following books and collections: *Protsess Prompartii* (Moscow, 1931); *Protsess kontrrevoliutsionnoi organizatsii men'shevikov* (Moscow, 1931); *Sotsial-interventy pered sudom proletarskoi diktatury* (Moscow, 1931); *Vrediteli piatiletki* (Moscow, 1931); *Vrediteli rabochego snabzheniia* (Moscow, 1930); A. A. Sadovskii, *Zavershim razgrom kondrat'evshchiny* (Moscow-Leningrad, 1931); *Ekonomicheskaia kontrrevoliutsiia v Donbasse* (Moscow, 1928).

indictments, and statements of the prosecutors and defendants leads me to the firm conviction that most of the charges were intentionally falsified.

In the case of the Industrial Party, the discrepancies begin with the indictment, especially with the explanation of the defendants' motives for establishing counterrevolutionary organizations. Before the revolution almost all the ringleaders were alleged to have been big industrialists and capitalists or to have held the highest paying managerial posts under them. But it became clear during the trial that not one of the eight defendants had ever been a capitalist or even the son of a capitalist. They came from families of artisans, peasants, civil servants, or middling landlords. Only three had worked in private industry before the war, one of them for only three years.

One of the prime reasons for the creation of the "counterrevolutionary organization," the indictment also said, "is the political convictions of the old engineers, which usually vacillated between Cadet and right-wing monarchist." This assertion was not proved at the trial. Of the eight defendants, only Fedotov had clearly expressed Cadet views. The rest had little interest in politics, and some had been Russian Social Democrats. Even prosecutor Krylenko was obliged to characterize some of the accused as people without a political ideology, for whom "political questions do not play any role."

The indictment also stated that the political feelings of the accused were "reinforced by the difference in the professional and material position of engineers before and after the revolution, and by the Soviet regime's natural mistrust of engineers." However, the trial materials make it clear that all the defendants held major posts before their arrest, so that it is difficult to see any mistrust in the government's treatment of them. Their material position was for the most part better at the time of their arrest than before the revolution. In general, the motives behind the "wrecking activity" of the Industrial Party were left unclear at the end of the trial.

Krylenko wiped out everything he had said earlier when he declared in his summation:

They had and have no ideas or even inner convictions, nor could they have any, for you have seen the price for which everything was done. . . . Lacking any ideological support, they leaped into the camp of outright counterrevolution and began to work for money, like mercenaries, renouncing any pretensions of ideological and political commitment. . . . Ramzin is not one of those people who work selflessly for an idea. It is nonsense to say he did not receive any money for this.

Even Ramzin, who had supported almost every accusation, felt obliged to retort to Krylenko in his final speech:

Was it possible that I risked my neck, became a traitor and a saboteur, out of purely financial considerations, for the sake of a 10–20–30 per cent addition to my salary? I doubt whether anyone will believe that. . . . What could I hope to gain from a change of the regime? Nothing better, in any case, than what I had, because rarely could a foreign scientist even dream of having what I have had in the Soviet Union, in terms of standard of living and favorable conditions for research.

A great many absurdities and inconsistencies can be found in the defendants' testimony about their counterrevolutionary activity. Ramzin, for example, the supposed leader of the Industrial Party, gave extremely dubious testimony. During his trip to Paris, he allegedly asked the White Guard organizations to prove the existence of serious plans for French intervention, whereupon a meeting was arranged with some eminent officials of the French general staff. Besides informing Ramzin about the French government's decision for intervention in the near future, they handed over to him the detailed operational plans of the French high command, including the direction of the main attacks by the French expeditionary force and by its allies, the debarkation points, and the time schedules. Ramzin made a clean breast of this at the trial. But it is obvious that no general staff would let a man such as Ramzin into their plans, even if such plans had existed.

The very possibility of organizing, on Soviet territory, entire underground parties with thousands of members, central committees sending instructions to the provinces and maintaining close contacts with foreign centers, embassies, and so on is to be doubted. The investigative agencies frankly informed the court that they could not produce any material evidence or documents proving the existence of underground parties. There was much talk about instructions and directives, appeals to members, circular letters, resolutions, and records of plenary meetings, but not one of these documents was presented to the court and the press. The defendants were said to have destroyed all such documents before their arrest. Krylenko said in his summation:

Let us analyze this problem further. What evidence can there be? Are there, let us say, any documents? I inquired about that. It seems that where documents existed, they were destroyed. . . . But, I asked, perhaps one of them has accidentally survived? It would be futile to hope for that.[10]

Krylenko tried to prove that "sincere" confessions made any material evidence unnecessary. But then he could not explain what motivated the accused to make "sincere" confessions in the complete absence of any material evidence. After all, these were supposed to be class enemies, spies, diversionists, murderers. Krylenko himself declared in his opening speech: "I cannot take Citizen Ramzin and the others at their word; I cannot believe them, despite their declarations of sincere repentance."

The mix-up concerning the Ryabushinskys—a well-known family of big capitalists—was typical. According to the indictment, P. P. Ryabushinsky was slated to be Minister of Trade and Industry in the future Russian government. Further on the indictment said that "in October 1928, two members of the Central Committee of the Industrial Party, Ramzin and Larichev, got in touch with P. P. Ryabushinsky." Palchinsky and Fedotov, two other members of this supposed committee, were also said to have had close connections with Ryabushinsky. But as soon as the indictment was published in the newspapers, almost all the foreign papers reported that the head of the Ryabushinsky family had died before 1928 and only his sons were living abroad. Ramzin, who had said earlier that he had met P. P. Ryabushinsky in Paris, now declared:

> I am not completely sure about the first name of the Ryabushinsky with whom I spoke in Paris. It may have been Peter or Vladimir. . . . I can describe his appearance, if that would be of interest.
> *Krylenko:* It is important to establish that it was evidently Vladimir.
> *Ramzin:* That is most likely.

A similar mix-up occurred concerning a well-known Soviet historian, Academician E. V. Tarle. The indictment said that he was to have been minister of foreign affairs in the White Guard government. Naturally he was immediately arrested and expelled from the Academy of Sciences. But soon afterward Tarle was quietly freed and reinstated in the Academy. It turned out that Stalin had another use for him.

There was a multitude of inconsistencies in the testimony on other matters, too: on the composition of the Central Committee of the Industrial Party and the distribution of assignments; on the composition of the future government, on the amount of money received from abroad and what had happened to it, and so on. Confusion marked the testimony on

10. *Proletarskii prigovor nad vrediteliami-interventami* (Moscow, 1930), p. 32.

concrete acts of wrecking. Sometimes the president of the court had to prompt the accused openly. There was, for example, this curious dialogue between Vyshinsky and Fedotov:

Vyshinsky: Was there a directive to build new factories while existing factories were insufficiently used?
Fedotov: No, there was no such directive.
Vyshinsky: There wasn't?
Fedotov: Excuse me, there was a directive to build factories although factories already existed.
Vyshinsky: No, there is no wrecking in that. Factories must be built.

And Vyshinsky went on, leading Fedotov to say that "the directive was to build factories while existing factories were not working at full capacity." Fedotov was brought to agree that "if it had not been for wrecking, fewer factories would have been built. Not, it is true, much fewer, maybe one or two, but still some foreign currency would have been saved."

Insufficient contact between scientific research institutions and industry was also declared to be wrecking, along with many other shortcomings that are often discussed in the press to the present day. Even draining swamps in border areas was declared to be wrecking, since it allegedly facilitated imperialist intervention in the USSR.

Just as many absurdities and inconsistencies can be found in the trial of the Menshevik "Union Bureau" in 1931. The most vulnerable point of the indictment was the connection of the Union Bureau with the Industrial Party, a connection that was discussed in considerable detail. An utterly improbable secret agreement was introduced, supposedly concluded between the Industrial Party and the Menshevik Party. In fact the Union Bureau had not been mentioned at the trial of the Industrial Party; no reference had been made to any connections or individuals, even though at the time of the Industrial Party trial (December 1930) all the leading figures of the Union Bureau had already been arrested. To explain this discrepancy, it was said that "frank confessions" had been obtained from the members of the Union Bureau only toward the end of December 1930. But the truth was that Stalin and his aides had the idea of organizing the Union Bureau trial only after the "success" of the Industrial Party trial and then began to prepare the appropriate legends.

Several annoying discrepancies arose. For example, the indictment said that collusion between the Union Bureau and the Industrial Party was discussed at the third plenum of the "Bureau," which allegedly met in April 1930. But according to the testimony of the preceding trial, the

Industrial Party had been broken up by April 1930, and the Mensheviks could have had no connections with it. Therefore Sher, in his testimony, introduced a correction: the bloc with the Industrial Party was discussed not at the third but at the second plenum of the Union Bureau, in 1929. The indictment quoted Sukhanov's deposition which said that he had met with Ramzin three times and had received 30,000 rubles from him. But at the trial Ramzin declared that he had never negotiated personally with Sukhanov and that in general he didn't know Sukhanov, had never met him. Sukhanov was obliged to confirm this. Further questioning "cleared up" the matter: it was not Sukhanov but Groman who had received the money from the Industrial Party, and it was not Ramzin but Larichev who had handed it over.

The membership of the so-called Union Bureau also remained unclear at the trial. During the questioning it became apparent that most of the accused had not had any connections with the Menshevik Party for a long time, while some had never been Mensheviks until, as they put it, they entered that party in 1927–1928. How then did they so quickly become its leaders in the Soviet Union?

A. Yu. Finn-Yenotayevsky's testimony on this score was incoherent, including his answers to the defense lawyer. Great confusion also marked the defendants' testimony on the program committee of the Union Bureau, on the subjects of discussion at various meetings of the Union Bureau, and about meetings with Rafail Abramovich, one of the leaders of the émigré Mensheviks, who was alleged to have come illegally to the Soviet Union to give instructions.

The examples of wrecking activity were completely unbelievable. This is how A. L. Sokolovsky described one of his acts of "wrecking":

> In the control figures for 1929–30, the Presidium of the Supreme Economic Council set the task of lowering costs of production by 10 percent. I put down only 9.5 percent and began to insist on this figure, arguing with genuine facts. During that entire period, with the exception of 1927–28, the actual decline of production costs was lower than the planned figure, and in 1925–26 costs did not drop, as you may recall, but rose. I even think that the figure of 9.5 percent was also not achieved.

While the members of the Industrial Party had confessed that they had inflated many goals of the plan for the purposes of wrecking, the members of the Union Bureau were accused of deflating goals. Various speeches were quoted in which the accused had objected at Gosplan meetings to excessively high control figures in the five-year plan. Since Stalin and

Molotov had demanded a considerable increase in the control figures in 1930, it is not surprising that almost all the earlier targets set by Gosplan were declared to be wrecking. Now that we know that most of the goals in physical units were not actually achieved, it is difficult to agree with such accusations. Many of the speeches made by the defendants at Gosplan meetings, which were quoted at the trial, were rational warnings by specialists against the adventurism and unrealistic schemes of some party leaders.

A person attending the trials of 1930–1931 might have thought that the first five-year plan had not been discussed in detail at the Sixteenth Party Conference in April 1929 and had not been ratified at all levels of the party and state. Similarly, anyone hearing the defendants' testimony about their deliberate disruption of the food supply, about their organization of famine in some rural areas, about the deliberate spoiling of millions of tons of vegetables, meat, fish, and grain, about the slowing down of coal and peat production, about the organization of a crisis in the supply of electricity might have thought that wreckers were in complete control of the commissariats dealing with the economy. Yet the crucial decisions on food supply and other economic matters were made by the Politburo, not the commissariats.

Testimony on the activities of the Second International was also obviously staged. Such testimony was intended to support the mistaken doctrine of "social fascism" (which will be discussed in section 11) but it did not correspond to reality.

The variegated fate of the accused was also strange. All forty-six "wreckers of the food supply" were shot, although their organization was pictured in the indictment as merely an affiliate of the Industrial Party. Yet Leonid Ramzin, the leader of this party, a "candidate for dictator," "spy," and "organizer of diversions and murders," was for some reason pardoned. And not only pardoned; in prison he was allowed to do research on boiler construction. Barely five years after his trial he was freed and given the Order of Lenin. He died, according to the *Great Soviet Encyclopedia*, in 1948, holding the same post, director of the Moscow Institute of Heat Engineering, that he had held before the trial of the Industrial Party.

■ 5

BEHIND THE SCENES OF THE TRIALS

I have already said that Stalin tried to cover up his own mistakes and miscalculations during the first years of collectivization and industrializa-

tion by blaming them on the "wrecking" activities of bourgeois specialists. On top of that, Stalin desired to win credit for thwarting foreign
intervention and breaking up nonexistent underground counterrevolutionary organizations. He wanted to accumulate political capital—fictive
to be sure, but crucial for him in that period. He was deliberately forcing
tension in the country to silence his critics and once again cast the
shadow of suspicion on the leaders of all the former opposition groups.

A question arises, however: how did Stalin succeed in forcing the
accused to publicly denounce themselves and many others and to make
up nonexistent organizations and crimes that had never been committed?
This was accomplished through the use of torture and many other illegal
means of influencing arrested persons. Stalin did not succeed in destroying all the witnesses to his crimes, however. Despite the hardship of
twenty-four years in prisons and camps and a long stay in a home for
invalids in Karaganda, Mikhail Yakubovich, one of the main defendants
in the trial of the "Union Bureau," survived until 1980, dying at the age
of ninety. After being freed, he continued to live in the invalid home in
Karaganda but visited Moscow every year. He met with me several
times, providing detailed accounts of the methods by which the trials of
the early thirties were set up. Having decided to reveal the truth about
those trials, Yakubovich also talked with Solzhenitsyn in 1966–1967 and
gave him details similar to those he had given me. Solzhenitsyn asked
Yakubovich about his entire life, about the 1917 revolution, and about
the leading figures in the various left-wing parties whom Yakubovich had
known well.

Some of this information was published in the first volume of Solzhenitsyn's *Gulag Archipelago*. Unfortunately, in this work Solzhenitsyn
distorted many details of Yakubovich's testimony. For example, Solzhenitsyn explained the false testimony Yakubovich gave in the Union Bureau trial as the result of a voluntary agreement on his part, the expression of his sincere desire to help the Communist Party in its fight against
Menshevism. Solzhenitsyn asserted that there was a voluntary agreement between Yakubovich and the prosecutor Krylenko, but he omitted
the fact that Yakubovich ended up in Krylenko's office only *after* many
weeks of terrible torture, an attempt at suicide, and a warning that unless
he confessed he would be tortured indefinitely. Yakubovich was a man
who, according to people in the camps with him, displayed the finest
human qualities during his imprisonment. But Solzhenitsyn describes
him as virtually a conscious provocateur, a real "find for the prosecutor."
All because Yakubovich, who in 1917 had been a Menshevik, later collab-

orated with the Bolsheviks and remained a socialist even after surviving the camps.

Fortunately, Yakubovich did not limit himself to oral accounts. In May 1967 he sent a special deposition on the trials of the early thirties to the Procuracy of the Soviet Union, giving copies to several of his friends. The following is the text of his deposition, with a few minor omissions indicated by ellipses.

Yakubovich's Deposition

To the General Procurator of the USSR:

In connection with your office's reexamination of the case in which I was convicted in 1931, I present the following explanation:

No "Union Bureau of Mensheviks" ever existed in reality. Not all the defendants knew each other, nor had they all belonged to the Menshevik Party in the past. Thus, A. Yu. Finn-Yenotayevsky . . . had been a Bolshevik since the Second Party Congress in 1903, and although he left the party during the imperialist war of 1914–1917, he never had any connection with the Mensheviks. A. L. Sokolovsky had belonged in the past to the Zionist socialists but was never a Menshevik. Most of the defendants, however, had been connected to some degree with the Menshevik Party, some very accidentally and slightly, others belonging to the main leadership cadres. . . . But both the former and the latter had long since broken with the Mensheviks under various circumstances and for various reasons. The only participant in the trial who really had maintained a connection with a Menshevik center, as I learned from him later on in the Verkhneuralsk *politizolyator* [a prison for politicals only], who had even been the chairman or secretary of a Menshevik Bureau, was V. K. Ikov. But he never breathed a word about these activities during the investigation or the trial, and the very existence of the "Moscow Bureau" remained undiscovered during the investigation and the trial.

. . . The OGPU investigators did not make the least effort to discover the real political connections and views of Ikov or of any other defendant. They had a ready-made scheme of a "wrecker" organization that could have been constructed only with the participation of big, influential officials; real underground Mensheviks, who did not hold such offices, were unsuitable for such a scheme. Evidently this scheme was suggested to OGPU officials by the leading figures in trials of the "Industrial Party" and the "Toiling Peasant Party," Ramzin and Kondratiev, who subsequently testified for the prosecution at the trial of the "Union Bureau." For the sake of balance, to round out the political picture, they had to add a third politico-wrecking organization—a Social Democratic one. This was the explanation given to me by Professor L. N. Yurovsky, who confessed to being the minister of finance in Kondratiev's "shadow cabinet." He was planted in my cell for several days, evidently to explain the nature of the investigation to me.

Kondratiev's idea was taken over wholeheartedly by his personal friend V. G.

Groman, who was found in Kondratiev's apartment when the OGPU came to arrest Kondratiev, and on this ground was himself subjected to investigation. He was promised restoration of his job and complete pardon if he cooperated in the trial of the Menshevik wreckers. Subsequently, when the people convicted in the trial of the "Union Bureau" were brought to the Verkhneural'sk *politizoliator*, Groman, who was in the prison "station," shouted out loud, in despair and indignation, "They tricked me!" Groman's willingness to cooperate was reinforced by his alcoholism. The interrogators would make him drunk and get all the evidence they wanted. Once, during the trial, while I was being sent back to the inner OGPU prison, I found myself in the same car as Groman, where I heard a conversation between him and the investigators. "Well, Vladimir Gustavovich," they said to him, "should we fortify ourselves with a little cognac?" "Hee hee," laughed Groman, "of course, as always." His active helper, in making up the story of the wrecking Menshevik organization, was the defendant Petun, an unintelligent man who had joined the Menshevik Party after the February Revolution and left it after the October victory of the Bolsheviks. According to his account, told afterwards in Verkhneuralsk, he "calculated" that he would gain the most, given his arrest, by actively cooperating in setting up the wrecking trial. For this he would receive a reward from OGPU — that is, the restoration of freedom and a job. If he didn't cooperate, he could get a long term in prison or even die. It was Petun who got the idea of creating the "Union Bureau" on the principle of departmental representation: two people from the Supreme Economic Council, two from the Commissariat of Trade, two from the State Bank, one from the Central Trade Union Council, and one from Gosplan. The "departmental representatives" he named were leading officials in appropriate departments, of whom he had heard it said that they were former Mensheviks. Not knowing precisely, however, the political past of the people he named, he made such mistakes as including in his list the Zionist Sokolovsky as a "representative" of the Supreme Economic Council. Such an "inaccuracy" did not bother the investigators; they had to get "confessions" out of the victims and did not care whether they were really Mensheviks.

Then came the extraction of "confessions." Some, like Groman and Petun, yielded to the promise of future benefits. Others, who tried to resist, were "made to see reason" by physical methods. They were beaten — on the face and head, on the sexual organs; they were thrown to the floor and kicked, choked until no blood flowed to the face, and so on. They were kept on the *konveier* without sleep, put in the *kartser* (half dressed and barefoot in a cold cell, or in an unbearably hot and stuffy cell without windows), and so on. For some, the mere threat of such methods, with an appropriate demonstration, was enough. For others, application of the methods was necessary to some degree, on a strictly individual basis, depending on the man's resistance. The most stubborn were A. M. Ginzburg and myself. We knew nothing of each other and sat in different prisons, I in the northern tower of Butyrskaya, Ginzburg in the Inner Prison of the OGPU. But we came to the same conclusion: we could not endure the methods used; we would be better off dead. We opened our veins. But we did not succeed in dying.

After my attempt at suicide, they no longer beat me, but for a long time they did not let me sleep. My nerves reached such a state of exhaustion that nothing on earth seemed to matter—any shame, any slander of myself and others, if only I could sleep. In such a psychological condition, I agreed to any testimony. I was still restrained by the thought that I alone had fallen into such cowardice, and I was ashamed of my weakness. But I was confronted with my old comrade V. V. Sher, a man who had joined the workers' movement long before the victory of the revolution, though he came from a rich bourgeois family—that is, a man unconditionally committed to ideas. When I heard from Sher's own lips that he had confessed to being a participant in the Menshevik wrecking organization, the Union Bureau, and had named me as one of its members, I surrendered right there at the confrontation. I no longer resisted and wrote any testimony I was told to write by the investigators: D. Z. Apresyan, A. A. Nasedkin, D. M. Dmitriev. During the investigation some of the accused, myself included, were taken to Suzdal for more intensive methods of physical coercion. There we were kept in an old monastery prison used in tsarist times for the incarceration of so-called heretics. Once, when told to write some improbable confession, I said to investigator Nasedkin: "But you understand that never happened and could not have happened." Nasedkin, a very nervous man, who never took part in torture, replied: "I know it didn't happen, but Moscow demands it."

Was there any wrecking in the Commissariat of Trade, in the planning for the utilization of industrial goods? That is what L. B. Zalkind and I were charged with. Not only was there none; none was possible. The plans for the "supply of industrial goods" throughout the economic *raiony* were drawn up by me and the Board of Industrial Goods, which I directed. These plans were reported by me to meetings of the Collegium of the Commissariat of Trade, with a detailed explanation and justification of each point. The meetings of the Collegium were attended by responsible and experienced party officials and experts from various departments—from the Supreme Economic Council, the Commissariat of Finance, and from big economic aggregates such as the textile syndicate. A. I. Mikoyan presided over the Collegium, and he critically, even hypercritically, examined each figure before agreeing to endorse it. What kind of wrecking could have occurred under such conditions? Was everyone blind except me? Such an absurd supposition cannot be made. Yes, I enjoyed the confidence of the Collegium, of the Commissariat, and of all responsible officials who knew me. But this confidence was earned by the substantial and persuasive quality of my reports, by many years of work in the Soviet state apparatus, beginning with its very first organization, and finally by the "Soviet political line" that I followed, first in the ranks of the Menshevik Party and afterward, when I had broken with it because I became convinced that I could not turn it onto the "Soviet path." In the record of the investigation there is a deposition written in my hand, in which wrecking documents are listed with their file numbers in the Commissariat of Trade. But I did not see a single document in prison, and no one ever showed me any. Those numbers were taken out of thin air, in the expectation that no one would ever check them.

    . . . When the "Union Bureau" had been "formed" on an "international basis," additional members joined, as the investigators directed. Among these, to the surprise of the main "participants," was V. K. Ikov. How this addition was made can be seen from the example of M. I. Teitelbaum. The composition of the Union Bureau had already been determined and agreed upon by the investigators and the accused when investigator Apresyan summoned me from my cell. In his office I found Teitelbaum, whom none of the accused had named in their depositions. I had known Teitelbaum for years as a party official, a Social Democrat. Originally a Bolshevik, he had gone over to the Mensheviks during the First World War; in 1917 he was the secretary of the Moscow Committee of Mensheviks, but after the October revolution he broke with the Mensheviks and worked abroad for the Commissariat of Foreign Trade. When I entered, Apresyan got up and went out, leaving us two alone. Teitelbaum said to me: "I've been in prison for a long time. They beat me, demanding a confession that I took bribes abroad from capitalist trading firms. I couldn't stand the torture and 'confessed.' It's terrible, terrible to live and die with such shame. Investigator Apresyan suddenly said to me, 'Perhaps you want to change your testimony, to confess participation in the counterrevolutionary Menshevik Union Bureau? Then you would not be a common criminal but a political.' 'Yes, I want that,' I replied; 'how do I do it?' Apresyan said, 'I will call Yakubovich in now. Do you know him?' 'Yes.' So he called you. Comrade Yakubovich, I beg you—take me into the Union Bureau. I would rather die as a counterrevolutionary than a rotten crook." At this point Apresyan came into the room. "Well, have you reached an agreement?" he asked me with a mocking grin. I was silent. Teitelbaum begged me silently with despairing eyes. "I agree," I said. "I confirm the participation of Teitelbaum in the Union Bureau." "Well, good enough," said Apresyan. "Write a deposition, and the others will sign it after you. And you, Teitelbaum, rewrite all your depositions, and I will destroy the old ones." That is how the "Union Bureau" was formed.

Several days before the beginning of the trial, the first "organizational meeting" of the "Union Bureau" was held in the office of the senior investigator, D. M. Dmitriev, who presided. In addition to the fourteen accused, the investigators Apresyan, Nasedkin, and Radishchev took part in this "meeting." The accused got acquainted with each other, agreed upon their behavior at the trial, and rehearsed it. This work was not finished at the first "meeting," so it was repeated.

I was beside myself. How should I behave at the trial? Deny the depositions I had made during the investigation? Try to disrupt the trial? Create a worldwide scandal? Whom would that help? Wouldn't it be a stab in the back for the Soviet regime and the Communist Party? I had not joined the Communist Party when I quit the Mensheviks in 1920, but politically and morally I was with it and remain with it. Whatever crimes were committed by the OGPU *apparat*, I felt I ought not betray the party and the state. I won't hide the fact that I had something else in mind. If I repudiated my earlier depositions at the trial, what would the investigators, the torturers, do to me? It was terrible just to think about it. If it were only death. I wanted death. I sought it, I tried to die. But they wouldn't let me die; they would slowly torture me, torture for an infinitely long time. They wouldn't let me sleep until death came. And if it came from lack of sleep?

Probably madness would come first. How could I bring myself to that? In the name of what? If I had been an enemy of the Communist Party and the Soviet state, I would perhaps have found moral support for my courage in hatred. But I wasn't an enemy. What could have roused me to such desperate behavior at the trial?

With such thoughts and in such a state of mind I was summoned from my cell and taken to the office of N. V. Krylenko, who had been named state prosecutor for our trial. I had known him for a long time, from prerevolutionary days. I knew him intimately. In 1920, when I was commissar of supplies for Smolensk province, he came to Smolensk as a plenipotentiary of the party Central Committee and the Soviet Central Executive Committee to observe and direct the collection of grain. He lived in my apartment for some time; we slept in the same room. That year Smolensk province was the first in the RSFSR to fulfill its quota of forced grain requisitions, earning approval and praise from Lenin himself. In short, Krylenko and I knew each other quite well.

Offering me a seat, Krylenko said: "I have no doubt that you personally are not guilty of anything. We are both performing our duty to the party—I have considered and consider you a Communist. I will be the prosecutor at the trial; you will confirm the testimony given during the investigation. This is our duty to the party, yours and mine. Unforeseen complications may arise at the trial. I will count on you. If the need should arise, I will ask the presiding judge to call on you. And you will find the right words." I was silent. "Have we agreed?" Krylenko asked. I mumbled something indistinctly, but to the effect that I promised to do my duty. I think there were tears in my eyes. Krylenko made a gesture of approval. I left.

At the trial a complication did in fact arise, as Krylenko had foreseen. The so-called "Foreign Delegation" of the Menshevik Party sent the court a lengthy telegram that disproved the depositions before the court. Krylenko read the telegram to the court, and, when he had finished, asked N. M. Shvernik, the presiding judge, to call on defendant Yakubovich for a reply. My position would have been very difficult if the telegram of the "Foreign Delegation," which honestly refuted the fabrications about wrecking done on its orders, had also expressed sympathy for the accused, obliged by force to give false testimony. What could I have replied to such a statement? But the "Foreign Delegation" itself made my job easy. Though refuting the prosecutor's case, it also declared that the defendants did not have and had never had any relations with the Social Democratic Menshevik Party, that they were nothing but provocateurs hired by the Soviet government. On this point I could speak truthfully and honestly, accusing the "Foreign Delegation" of lies and hypocrisy, recalling the role and service of a number of the defendants in the history of the Menshevik Party, and charging the Menshevik leaders with betraying the revolution, the interests of socialism, and the working class. I spoke emotionally, with the strength of conviction. That was one of my best political speeches. It made a great impression on the audience in the packed Hall of Columns. (I could sense this from my experience as a speaker.) It was, if I may say so, the culminating point of the trial and assured its political success. My promise to Krylenko had been kept.

The next day A. Yu. Finn-Yenotaevsky began his testimony by saying that he was in complete agreement with everything I had said about the "Foreign Delegation" and added that in this matter I spoke for all the defendants.

The trial ran smoothly and from the outside had the look of truth, despite the crude errors made by the investigators in its staging. The story of an illegal visit to the Soviet Union by the Menshevik leader R. A. Rein-Abramovich was especially clumsy. You had to know Abramovich, as I knew him, to understand the utter absurdity of this story. In the whole "Foreign Delegation" there was no one less capable of such a risk than he. Both during the investigation and during the interrogation in court, I managed to avoid corroborating my meeting with him. But Groman and some other defendants vied with each other in telling about their meetings with him. I later heard that Abramovich published in the West irrefutable proof of his alibi.

In his concluding speech, Krylenko demanded the supreme measure of social defense against five defendants, including myself. He did not humiliate me in his speech; he said that he did not doubt my personal integrity and disinterestedness, called me an "old revolutionary," but characterized me as a fanatic for my ideas and called my ideas counterrevolutionary. That is why he demanded that I be shot. I was grateful to him for his characterization of me, for not degrading me before my death; he didn't drag me in the mud. In my "defense" speech I said that the crimes I had confessed deserved the supreme penalty, that the state prosecutor had not demanded excessive punishment, that I was not asking the Supreme Court to spare my life. I wanted to die. After giving false testimony in the investigation and the trial, I wanted nothing but death. I did not want to live in shame. When I returned to my place on the defendants' bench after my speech, Groman, sitting next to me, grabbed my hand and whispered, in anger and despair, "You're out of your mind! You'll destroy us all! You had no right, with respect to your comrades, to speak that way!"

But we were not condemned to death.

After the sentencing, when they were taking us out of the hall, I bumped into Finn-Yenotaevsky at the door. He was older than all the other defendants, twenty years older than I. He said to me, "I will not live to see the day when the truth about our trial can be told. You are the youngest; you will have more chance than all the others to see that day. My bequest to you is to tell the truth."

In fulfillment of this bequest of my older comrade, I am writing this statement, and have also given oral depositions in the office of the Procurator of the USSR.

MIKHAIL YAKUBOVICH
May 5, 1967

Yakubovich's statement is not the only document revealing the mechanics of the political trials in 1930–1931. Another came into my hands, "B. I. Rubina's Memoir," concerning her brother I. I. Rubin, who was also a participant in the trial of the "Union Bureau." Rubin, a professor of economics, had taken part in the revolutionary movement since 1905.

He first belonged to one of the Bund[11] organizations and later joined the Mensheviks. In 1924 he abandoned political activity and worked at Marxist economics.[12] In 1926 he became a research associate in the Marx-Engels Institute, where he enjoyed the confidence of the Institute's director, D. B. Ryazanov. It is obvious that Rubin was included in the "Union Bureau" primarily to compromise Ryazanov, whom Stalin hated. Immediately after Rubin's "depositions" had been obtained and even before the trial of the "Union Bureau" had begun Ryazanov was removed from his job at the institute he had founded and was expelled from the party, "for treason to the party and direct aid to the Menshevik interventionists."

After the trial Rubin spent three years in solitary confinement; then his sentence was commuted, and he was exiled to the town of Aktyubinsk. His wife joined him there, and later his sister, to whom he described the circumstances that compelled him to give false testimony about himself and Ryazanov.

B. I. Rubina's Memoir

This is what I learned from my brother. When he was arrested on December 23, 1930, he was charged with being a member of the "Union Bureau of Mensheviks." This accusation seemed so ridiculous that he immediately submitted a written exposition of his views, which he thought would prove the impossibility of such an accusation. When the investigator read this statement, he tore it up right there. A confrontation was arranged between my brother and Yakubovich, who had been arrested earlier and had confessed to being a member of the "Union Bureau." My brother did not even know Yakubovich. At the confrontation, when Yakubovich said to my brother, "Isaac Ilyich, we were together at a session of the Union Bureau," my brother immediately asked, "And where was this meeting held?" This question caused such a disruption in the examination that the investigator interrupted the examination right there, saying, "What are you, a lawyer, Isaac Ilyich?"

My brother in fact was a lawyer, had worked in that field for many years. After that confrontation the charge that Rubin was a member of the "Union Bureau" was dropped. Soon after, my brother was transferred to Suzdal. The circumstances of that transfer were so unusual that they were bound to inspire alarm

11. [The Bund—The Jewish Socialist Party of prerevolutionary Russia.—D. J.]

12. An article about Rubin describing him as a major economist whose position was close to that of "Austro-Marxism" appeared in *Ekonomicheskaia entsiklopediia*, vol. 3 (Moscow, 1979), p. 510. The encyclopedia made no charges of a political nature against Rubin, thus indicating that he had been "rehabilitated." According to the encyclopedia, the date and place of his death are unknown.

and fear. On the station platform there was not a single person; in an empty railroad car he was met by an important GPU official, Gai. To all of Gai's attempts at persuasion my brother replied with what was really true: that he had no connections with the Mensheviks. Then Gai declared that he would give him forty-eight hours to think it over. Rubin replied that he didn't need forty-eight minutes.

. . . The examination at Suzdal also failed to give the investigators the results they wanted. Then they put Rubin for days in the *kartser*, the punishment cell. My brother at forty-five was a man with a diseased heart and diseased joints. The *kartser* was a stone hole the size of a man; you couldn't move in it, you could only stand or sit on the stone floor. But my brother endured this torture, too, and left the *kartser* with a feeling of inner confidence in himself, in his moral strength. . . . Then he was put in the *kartser* for a second time, which also produced no results. At that time Rubin was sharing a cell with Yakubovich and Sher. When he came back from the *kartser*, his cellmates received him with great concern and attention; right there they made tea for him, gave him sugar and other things, and tried in every way to show their sympathy. Telling about this, Rubin said that he was so amazed: these same people told lies about him and at the same time treated him so warmly.

Soon Rubin was put into solitary confinement; in those circumstances he was subjected to every kind of tormenting humiliation. He was deprived of all the personal things he had brought with him, even handkerchiefs. At that time he had the flu and walked about with a swollen nose, with ulcers, filthy. The prison authorities often inspected his cell, and as soon as they found any violation of the rule for maintaining the cell they sent him to clean the latrines. Everything was done to break his will. . . . They told him his wife was very sick, to which he replied: "I can't help her in any way, I can't even help myself." At times the investigators would turn friendly and say: "Isaac Ilyich, this is necessary for the party." At the same time they gave him nighttime interrogations, at which a man is not allowed to fall asleep for a minute. They would wake him up, wear him out with all sorts of interrogations, jeer at his spiritual strength, call him the "Menshevik Jesus."

This went on until January 28, 1931. On the night of January 28–29, they took him down to a cellar, where there were various prison officials and a prisoner, someone named Vasilyevskii, . . . to whom they said, in the presence of my brother; "We are going to shoot you now, if Rubin does not confess." Vasilyevskii on his knees begged my brother: "Isaac Ilyich, what does it cost you to confess?" But my brother remained firm and calm, even when they shot Vasilyevskii right there. His feeling of inner rightness was so strong that it helped him to endure that frightful ordeal. The next night, January 29, they took my brother to the cellar again. This time a young man who looked like a student was there. My brother didn't know him. When they turned to the student with the words, "You will be shot because Rubin will not confess," the student tore open his shirt at the breast and said, "Fascists, gendarmes, shoot!" They shot him right there; the name of this student was Dorodnov.

The shooting of Dorodnov made a shattering impression on my brother. Re-

turning to his cell, he began to think. What's to be done? My brother decided to
start negotiations with the investigator; these negotiations lasted from February
2 to 21, 1931. The charge that Rubin belonged to the Union Bureau had already
been dropped in Moscow, after the confrontation with Yakubovich. Now they
agreed that my brother would consent to confess himself a member of a program
commission connected with the Union Bureau, and that he, Rubin, had kept
documents of the Menshevik Center in his office at the Institute, and when he
was fired from the Institute, he had handed them over in a sealed envelope to
[D. B.] Ryazanov, as materials on the history of the Social Democratic movement. Rubin had supposedly asked Ryazanov to keep these documents for a
short time. In these negotiations every word, every formulation was fought
over. Repeatedly the "confession" written by Rubin was crossed out and corrected by the investigator. When Rubin went to trial on March 1, 1931, in the
side pocket of his jacket was his "confession," corrected with the investigator's
red ink.

Rubin's position was tragic. He had to confess to what had never existed, and
nothing had: neither his former views; nor his connections with the other
defendants, most of whom he didn't even know, while others he knew only by
chance; nor any documents that had supposedly been entrusted to his safekeep-
ing; nor that sealed package of documents which he was supposed to have handed
over to Ryazanov.

In the course of the interrogation and negotiations with the investigator it
became clear to Rubin that the name of Ryazanov would figure in the whole
affair, if not in Rubin's testimony, then in the testimony of someone else. And
Rubin agreed to tell the whole story about the mythical package. My brother told
me that speaking against Ryazanov was just like speaking against his own father.
That was the hardest part for him, and he decided to make it look as if he had
fooled Ryazanov, who had trusted him implicitly. My brother stubbornly kept to
this position in all his despositions: Ryazanov had trusted him personally, and he,
Rubin, had fooled trustful Ryazanov. No one and nothing could shake him from
this position. His deposition of February 21 concerning this matter was printed
in the indictment and signed by Krylenko on February 23, 1931. The deposition
said that Rubin handed Ryazanov the documents in a *sealed* envelope and asked
him to keep them for a while at the Institute. My brother stressed this position
in all his statements before and during the trial. At the trial he gave a number of
examples which were supposed to explain why Ryazanov trusted him so much. . . .

Putting the problem in such a way ruined the prosecutor's plan. He asked
Rubin point-blank: "Didn't you establish any organizational connection?" Rubin
replied, "No, there was no organizational connection, there was only his great
personal trust in me." Then Krylenko asked for a recess. When he and the other
defendants got to another room, Krylenko said to Rubin: "You did not say what
you should have said. After the recess I will call you back to the stand, and you
will correct your reply." Rubin answered sharply: "Do not call me any more. I
will again repeat what I said." The result of this conflict was that, instead of the
agreed three years in prison, Rubin was given five, and in his concluding speech
Krylenko gave a devastating characterization of Rubin like that of no one else.

Everyone interested in the case could not understand why there was so much spite and venom in this characterization.

Rubin set himself the goal of doing everything in his power to "shield" Ryazanov. . . . At the trial the possiblity of defining in this way his position with respect to Ryazanov gave Rubin a certain moral satisfaction. But these legal subtleties made little sense to anyone else. Politically, Ryazanov was compromised, and Rubin was stricken from the list of people who have the right to a life worthy of man. Rubin himself, in his own consciousness, struck himself from the list of such people as soon as he began to give his "testimony." It is interesting what my brother felt when they took him back to Moscow from Suzdal. When, sick and tortured, he was put into the sleigh, he remembered, in his words, how self-assured and internally strong he had been when he came to Suzdal and how he was leaving morally broken, destroyed, degraded to a state of complete hopelessness. Rubin understood perfectly well that by his "confession" he had put an end to his life as an honorable, uncorrupted worker and achiever in his chosen field of scholarship.

But that was not the main thing; the main thing was that he was destroyed as a man. Rubin understood perfectly well what repercussions his confession would have. Why had Rubin borne false witness against himself? Why had he also named Ryazanov? Why had he violated the most elementary, most primitive concepts of human behavior? Everyone knew with what mutual respect these two men were connected, Rubin and Ryazanov. Ryazanov, who was considerably older than Rubin, saw in him a talented Marxist scholar who had devoted his life to the study and popularization of Marxism. Ryazanov had trusted him unreservedly; he himself was bewildered by what had happened. Here I want to recount an episode, a very painful one, the confrontation between Rubin and Ryazanov. The confrontation took place in the presence of an investigator. Rubin, pale and tormented, turned to Ryazanov, saying, "David Borisovich, you remember I handed you a package." Whether Ryazanov said anything and precisely what, I don't remember for sure. My brother right then was taken to his cell; in his cell he began to beat his head against the wall. Anyone who knew how calm and self-controlled Rubin was can understand what a state he had been brought to. According to rumors, Ryazanov used to say that he could not understand what had happened to Isaac Ilyich.

The defendants in the case of the "Union Bureau" were sentenced to various terms of imprisonment, and all fourteen men were transferred to the political prison in the town of Verkhneuralsk. Rubin, sentenced to five years, was subjected to solitary confinement. The others, who received terms of ten, eight, and five years, were placed several men to a cell. Rubin remained in solitary confinement throughout his imprisonment. During his confinement he continued his scholarly work. Rubin became sick in prison, and lip cancer was suspected. In connection with this sickness, in January, 1933, he was taken to Moscow, to the hospital in Butyrskaya Prison. While in the hospital Rubin was visited twice by GPU officials who offered to make his situation easier, to free him, to enable him to do research. But both times Rubin refused, understanding the price that is paid for such favors. After spending six to eight weeks in the prison hospital, he was taken back to the political prison in Verkhneuralsk. . . . A year later, in 1934, Rubin was released on a commuted sentence and exiled to the town of Turgai, then an almost unpopulated settlement in the desert. Aside from Rubin there were no other exiles there.

After several months at Turgai Rubin was permitted to settle in the town of Aktyubinsk. . . . He got work in a consumer cooperative, as a plan economist. In addition he continued to do his own scholarly work. In the summer of 1935 his wife became seriously sick. My brother sent a telegram asking me to come. I went right away to Aktyubinsk; my brother's wife lay in the hospital, and he himself was in a very bad condition. A month later, when his wife had recovered, I went home to Moscow. . . . My brother told me that he did not want to return to Moscow, he did not want to meet his former circle of acquaintances. That showed how deeply he was spiritually shaken by all that he had been through. Only his great optimism that was characteristic of him and his deep scholarly interests gave him the strength to live.

In the fall of 1937, during the mass arrests of that time, my brother was again arrested. The prison in Aktyubinsk was overcrowded, the living conditions of the prisoners were terrifying. After a short stay in the prison, he was transferred somewhere outside of Aktyubinsk. We could find out nothing more about him.

The tragic fate of N. N. Sukhanov, the author of *Notes on the Revolution*, also deserves recording. Broken by the preliminary investigation, Sukhanov did not let down his investigators at the trial. But later on he found strength to protest, and after several hunger strikes he was released. Then in 1937 he was arrested again and shot. As for V. Ikov, Yakubovich's testimony has been contradicted by D. Vitkovsky, who asserted, in a conversation with me, that the Moscow Menshevik underground was completely destroyed by 1925–1927 and that Ikov was virtually the only Menshevik who remained at liberty until 1930. Thus he could not give any information about an underground Menshevik organization in Moscow, since such an organization did not exist. Vitkovsky obtained his information from the Mensheviks he met in camps in the years of Stalin's arbitrary rule.

■ 6

MASS REPRESSION AGAINST THE INTELLIGENTSIA
AND SPECIALISTS

The political trials of the late twenties and early thirties produced a chain reaction of repression against the old technical intelligentsia, whose representatives worked in various commissariats, educational institutions, museums, the Academy of Sciences, the cooperatives, and even the army. Although there were hardly any Marxists among them, there were quite a few former Cadets, moderate monarchists, and participants in various nationalist movements, as well as former Mensheviks, SRs, and People's Socialists. Only a very small number had joined the Bolsheviks during the twenties. The majority preferred not be be involved in politics. Some prominent figures from the old intelligentsia, however, taking advantage of the relative freedom of the NEP era, were active in certain religious and ethical circles and groups as well as literary and nationalist associations.[13]

Between those of the old intelligentsia who emigrated during the years 1918–1923 and those who remained in the USSR certain contacts existed, but these connections were hardly ever criminal in nature, even from the point of view of Soviet law. Undoubtedly many of the old intelligentsia took an ironic or frankly contemptuous attitude toward the Bolshevik leaders, Stalin among them. For these people Lenin was no idol. They expressed such attitudes only among themselves, however, not in public. The fact was that on the whole the specialists were quite loyal to the Soviet government and served the nation well with their knowledge and experience.

From 1929 to 1932 the main blow of the punitive agencies fell on the technical intelligentsia. The Soviet press asserted that wrecking by "bourgeois specialists" had penetrated everywhere and that the public trials had exposed only the leaders of the wrecking organizations, not the broad membership.[14] The word went out that "90 to 95 percent of the old engineers absolutely must be considered as counterrevolutionary in their mood."[15]

Recalling this difficult period, the chemical engineer D. Vitkovsky wrote the following in his autobiographical short novel *Polzhizni:*

In January 1931 the wave of arrests swept me into prison. The jails were filled to overflowing. I was put in a cell that evidently had been converted in haste for prison use from a small cellar storeroom with a tiny air vent opening onto the street then called the Little Lubyanka. . . .

Explanations began quickly and energetically, as in a detective story. It turned out I was an activist in a widely ramified anti-Soviet conspiracy. . . . I had

13. One such circle, led by the philosopher A. A. Meier, is described in the essay "The Voskresenie (Resurrection) Circle." See N. P. Antsiferov, "Tri glavy iz vospominanii," *Pamiat'*, no. 4 (Paris, 1981), pp. 57–72.

14. See, for example, *Vyvody i uroki iz protsessa "Prompartii"* (Moscow, 1931), p. 3.

15. See the pamphlet *Klassovaia bor'ba putem vreditel'stva* (Moscow-Leningrad, 1930), p. 9.

concocted poisons to kill members of the government. . . . Soviet military men had been part of the conspiracy. . . . Invisible police agents were hot on their heels. . . . Everything was known and all that was lacking was our confession.

Alas, I could not help the investigators in any way. All I could do was reiterate that I did not know of any conspiracy and had had no dealings with conspirators. . . . The interrogation sessions were conducted only at night. Many of them all night long. To the point of exhaustion. . . .

After being worked over for a month, I was transferred to the Butyrskaya prison. Many of the prisoners slept directly on the cement floor, some without any bedding under them. In my cell there were between sixty and eighty men— among them several professors, mostly from technical fields, and no less than fifty engineers, as well as a few writers, artists, and military men. No wonder the wits in those days called the prisons "engineer-technician vacation homes." . . .

Almost all the prisoners at that time gave in to the investigators and endorsed the fantastic charges against themselves. In fact there was no real investigation. There was only a system for forcing false confessions out of people by threatening to have them shot, to have members of their families arrested, or by promising an easing of their lot. . . .

And was there any sense in resisting? Everyone had learned the lessons of the Shakhty and Ramzin trials very well: you could save your skin only by denouncing yourself and others. Anyone who tried to maintain his human dignity would perish. No one had any illusions about the real aim of these confessions. Some suffered tragically over their own downfall; the majority dismissed the ethical side of the question with a wave of the hand: you can't buck the tide. . . . I didn't want to take this well-worn trail, and for that I was punished. I was sentenced to be shot, but the sentence was reduced to ten years in prison.[16]

The aviation engineer S. M. Dansker recalled similar experiences in his unpublished memoirs:

After my graduation from an institute in early 1930 I was sent to an aircraft factory. . . . On the grounds of plant No. 39 there was a one-storey wooden hangar, refurbished for dwelling purposes. In it lived twenty prisoners, under guard, most of them middle-aged engineers, who had the right to go out only onto the factory grounds. The employees of the plant referred to these engineers who had been deprived of their freedom as "the engineer wreckers." My memory has retained the names of thirteen of them: D. P. Grigorovich and N. N. Polikarpov, airplane designers; A. V. Nadashkevich, a designer of weapons for

16. Vitkovsky was cleared of the charges against him only after the Twentieth Party Congress. The last years of his life were spent in Moscow. He submitted his short novel *Polzhizni* (Half My Life) to *Novy mir*, but the magazine was unable to publish it despite chief editor Aleksandr Tvardovsky's stong desire to do so. Tvardovsky passed the manuscript along to me. After Vitkovsky's death I published *Polzhizni* in Russian in *Dvadtsatyi vek* (Twentieth Century; a collection of uncensored samizdat writings) (London, 1976), pp. 138–236.

aircraft, P. M. Kreison, a test engineer; B. F. Goncharov, a specialist in aerodynamics; I. M. Kostkin, an organizer of production processes; Tissov and Voznesensky, planners; Shcherbakov, a designer of electric furnaces; Dneprov, a specialist in motors; Nerkasov, a professor; and A. N. Sidelnikov, a designer. I began to keep a close eye on the wreckers who lived in hangar No. 7. Over the course of two years I had the opportunity to observe with special care those with whom I had workaday contact on the production line. From this I came to the conclusion that they were not criminals but highly decent, even noble people. If something was needed in production, even in the middle of the night, after being awakened by me through one of the Red Army men who guarded their hangar, they would leave their beds, come to the design office, make the necessary calculations, and write out technical solutions to the problems, so that production of the experimental aircraft we were making would not be held up even for the night. After two years of observation, this is what I thought of them: "These are cultured and intelligent specialists, highly organized, with a profound technical education, conscientious engineers, and decent and honest workers, from whom young people, engineers like myself, have a very great deal to learn. These are not 'wreckers' at all."[17]

Among the "bourgeois specialists" arrested in the years 1929–1931 were such outstanding scientists and engineers as N. I. Ladyzhensky, chief engineer of the Izhevsk military works; A. F. Velichko, a highly prominent specialist in rail construction and shipping and a former general in the tsarist army who had gone over to the side of the Soviet government; A. G. Lorkh, one of the most important specialists in the breeding of potato varieties; and Academician P. P. Lazarev, a very important physicist.

Repression struck not only at the technical intelligentsia but also many "adjacent" areas. Many military specialists were arrested in 1930 on a trumped up charge of creating a monarchist counterrevolutionary organization. Most of them were loyal commanders, such as the prominent military specialist Nikolai Kakurin and the former head of the General Staff Academy, Andrei Snesarev, to whom the Central Executive Committee had just given the Hero of Labor award.[18]

17. In 1932 at plant no. 156 of the People's Commissariat of the Aircraft Industry a special Central Design Office-29 (TsKB-29) of the NKVD, was organized, consisting entirely of prisoner personnel. Most of the aircraft industry specialists listed by Dansker were transferred to this design office. Their subsequent fate is related in a document that circulated anonymously in samizdat for many years but that later was published in Germany: see A. Sharagin (pseud. of Professor G. Ozerov), *Tupolevskaia sharaga* (The Tupolev Prison Research Institute), (Frankfurt, 1971).

18. Both Kakurin and Snesarev have been completely rehabilitated. See *Voenno-istoricheskii zhurnal* (1965), no. 11.

Arrests were widespread as well among scholars in the humanities—historians, linguists, geographers, philosophers. A number of academicians (members of the Soviet Academy of Sciences) were arrested, including S. F. Platonov, Yevgeny Tarle, N. P. Likhachev, S. V. Bakhrushin, and S. I. Tkhorzhevsky.

This was also the time when the case of the Slavicists was fabricated: some prominent linguists, including Academician V. V. Vinogradov, were accused of active struggle against the Soviet regime and arrested. Among agronomists and biologists there were similar mass arrests. The great plant breeder V. V. Talanov, one of the founders of the varietal testing system in the Soviet Union, was imprisoned from 1931 to 1935. In Leningrad Professor B. E. Raikov, a major specialist in the teaching and history of science, was arrested, along with some of his students. Among the dozens of other well-known scientists and scholars arrested or sent into exile in this period were the philosopher A. A. Meier, the historians V. V. Bakhtin and I. M. Grevs, and the literary scholar M. M. Bakhtin.[19]

The subsequent fate of these people worked out in different ways. Many of them were freed after a few years and went on to brilliant scholarly careers; such was the case for Tarle, Lorkh, Vinogradov, and Talanov. In the forties and fifties they headed the most important scientific institutions in the Soviet Union, enjoyed great respect, and were awarded the highest honors. Some of the most important specialists, however, died in confinement. They were exonerated only posthumously. This was true not only of Kakurin and Snesarev but also of Lazarev and Platonov. Some writings by these men have been reprinted and brief articles about them can be found in present-day Soviet encyclopedias. Many of the specialists arrested from 1929 to 1931, however, have not been rehabilitated to this day. They have simply been forgotten.

There would have been many more arrests among the intelligentsia had it not been for the protests of important party leaders, whose opinions still had to be taken into consideration by Stalin and the GPU. The intercession of Army Commander Iona Yakir and the prominent Chekist Yefim Yevdokimov won the release of many loyal military specialists. Yakir persuaded the Politburo to discuss the "case of the military specialists" and to review the sentences given by the GPU. Lunacharsky frequently protested against excessive purges in the institutions of higher education and managed to save many scholars from prison or internal

19. See *Pamiat'*, no. 4 (Paris, 1981).

exile. As minister of heavy industry, Ordzhonikidze protested emphatically against the arrest of valuable technical specialists. He had no illusions concerning the kind of "wreckers" who were in prisons and camps in the early thirties. "I've heard that you need specialists," he said in 1934 to A. V. Snegov, who was the party organizer for Military Kombinat No. 9. "I'll give you three outstanding specialists—'wreckers.' They'll do good work for you, if you treat them well and don't bring up the past." And in fact, three specialists were soon brought under guard to the Kombinat, where they helped to get production going.

■ 7
THE END OF NEP

I have already mentioned that the exceptional measures against the kulaks in 1928 meant the de facto end of NEP in the countryside. The "liquidation of the kulaks as a class" and the campaign for total collectivization put a formal end to the New Economic Policy Lenin had initiated for the rural areas in 1921. This premature and coercive "revolution from above," as Stalin himself defined it, also affected the position of the Nepmen in the cities. The overall worsening of the economic situation, the introduction of rationing, the disruption of financial equilibrium in the economy, and the falling value of the ruble—all this made it extremely difficult to continue NEP in the industrial centers, although economically and politically NEP's possibilities were far from exhausted.

But by this time Stalin had no intention of continuing NEP. From the beginning of the first five-year plan the Soviet government suffered from a severe shortage of the capital necessary to complete many major industrial projects. Increased taxation on urban private enterprise served as an important, if limited, source of financial means for industrialization. Even earlier, such taxation had been very stringent, taking as much as 50 or 60 percent of the private entrepreneurs' profits (and in some cases 90 percent). For that reason the party had rejected the proposal of the Left Opposition (in 1926–1927) that private businessmen be taxed an additional 200 million rubles. The party had argued with good reason that such tax pressures would amount to the expropriation of private capital and signify the abandonment of NEP. In the early thirties, however, Stalin himself began a policy of increased taxation of private businessmen, forcing them in fact to close down their businesses. It is true that Stalin did not call for the arrest and deportation of former Nepmen and their families. Instead, an unannounced decision was made to confiscate a goodly part of their wealth.

Especially memorable in this connection was the "gold campaign" conducted throughout the Soviet Union. In closing out their businesses, most of the Nepmen, who had no confidence in the paper currency of the Soviet government, sought to convert their wealth into gold, jewelry, and similar valuables. The civil code of the RSFSR permitted such operations. Article 54 of that code, on "The Right of Property," stated:

> The following are allowed as items of private property: nonmunicipal structures, commercial enterprises, industrial enterprises hiring no more workers than the number provided for under special laws; equipment and means of production, money, securities, and other valuables, including gold and silver coins, foreign currency, household items, items of personal consumption, goods whose sale is not forbidden by law, and any other property not excluded from private trade.[20]

All such statutes were eliminated. Without troubling themselves to abide by the law too closely, the financial agencies required former private businessmen to turn in all their gold to the state. Those who were slow in complying with this demand were arrested by the GPU and held as hostages until their relatives produced the gold. Much of the gold extracted in this way had only recently been sold to the Nepmen on the free market by disguised agents of the GPU. The idea was to strengthen the declining value of the ruble and to decrease the quantity of paper money in circulation. Needless to say, this campaign represented a gross abuse of power.

In general, Stalin was not fussy about methods for bringing more gold and foreign currency into the treasury. He decided, for example, to sell some national treasures, and sent abroad paintings by Titian, Raphael, Velazquez, Rembrandt, Rubens, and Watteau, taken from the Hermitage and other museums. They were sold mostly to wealthy collectors in the United States but also to an American millionaire, S. Gulbenkian. Some furniture and other objects of value from the tsars' palaces were also sold.

Some historians place the end of NEP in 1934 or even in 1937, on the grounds that a significant part of the peasantry had not been collectivized in the first half of the thirties and that private production by artisans and

20. *Grazhdanskii kodeks RSFSR* (Moscow, 1928), p. 19.

craftsmen persisted. I think this dating is wrong. NEP provided not only for small private farming and craft production but also for capitalist elements in agriculture, domestic trade, and small-scale or even medium-scale industry, of course under government restriction and regulation. Yet capitalist elements were completely eliminated in both town and country by 1931–1932. The entire first five-year plan—not to mention the second—was already beyond the limits of NEP.

Stalin terminated NEP without proper economic justification. The possibilities of NEP had not been fully utilized, with the result that economic development was not speeded up but slowed down. In correctly opposing the demands of the Left Opposition, the party's Central Committee had often pointed out that NEP had been introduced "seriously and for a long time," that until state industry, state trade, and the cooperatives were able to satisfy the needs of the Soviet economy 100 percent, there would be room not only for the individual farmer and artisan or craftsman but also for the private capitalist, who would be allowed to function under definite conditions and under vigilant government supervision. It is hardly necessary to demonstrate that in the period 1932–1937 neither state industry, state trade, nor the cooperatives were able to meet the needs of the economy 100 percent. If we keep in mind the fact that these needs have grown constantly—and at a rate faster than the possibility of satisfying them—it cannot be said categorically even today that there is no room in the Soviet Union for the small private entrepreneur, whether in industry, commerce, or services. In any case the question of the premature ending of NEP and the real potential for a NEP-style policy in socialist society stands in need of additional and profound investigation.

The Old Bolshevik Yevgeny Gnedin, a journalist and diplomat, wrote memoirs not long before he died. In this summing up of his life and work he had the following comment about NEP.

I will take the liberty of saying, without going into any proofs, that the liquidation of NEP—that is, the destruction of the preconditions for the favorable development of our country on the basis of a mixed economy, with government planning and gradual progress in peasant agriculture—was an historic crime of the party bureaucracy under the supremacy of Stalin.[21]

For my part, I can only endorse Gnedin's conclusion.

21. Gnedin, *Vykhod iz labirinta* (New York, 1982), p. 54.

■ 8

REPRESSION INSIDE THE PARTY

The increasingly brutal methods of rule in the country as a whole, the mass repression directed against the better-off peasants, the Nepmen, and the "bourgeois" intelligentsia, were accompanied by increasingly harsh rule within the party itself. For example, soon after the trial of the "Union Bureau," David Ryazanov, the founder of the Marx-Engels Institute, who had done much to discover and publish the manuscripts of valuable Marxist classics, was expelled from the party and then arrested. Even before the revolution Ryazanov had begun publication of the collected works of Marx and Engels at the behest of the German Social Democratic Party; he subsequently continued this project in Moscow. In the 1920s there was no one in the Soviet Communist Party more knowledgeable than he on the history of Marxism. Although Ryazanov had often differed with Lenin, he treated Lenin with great respect. Toward Stalin, however, Ryazanov did not hide his ironic, even sarcastic attitude. Little wonder that his name came up in the fabricated depositions at the trial of the "Union Bureau."

Many Trotskyists were arrested in the early thirties. Trotsky had been expelled from the Soviet Union in 1929, and most of his supporters were broken, both in an ideological and an organizational sense. They bowed down before Stalin and severed their connections with Trotsky. But some maintained or sought such connections, and this was used as a pretext for repression. Thus in 1932–1933, hundreds of Trotskyists were arrested, some for a real but many for an imaginary connection with Trotsky. Among them was Ivan Smirnov, who had earlier been an eminent party official, one of the leaders of the armed uprising in Moscow in 1905, chairman of the Siberian Revolutionary Committee in 1919, and people's commissar of posts and telegraph in the twenties.

The fate of the former Left SR Yakov Blumkin also requires clarification. In 1918, on his party's orders, Blumkin assassinated the German Ambassador Mirbach, then turned himself in to the Cheka. Although the assassination occurred on July 6, Blumkin was not brought to trial until the end of November 1918. He was sentenced to three years forced labor, but was granted amnesty the following year by a special decree of the Presidium of the CEC.[22] Blumkin joined the Bolshevik Party and

---

22. *Krasnaia kniga VChK*, vol. 1 (Moscow, 1920), p. 235.

took part in the civil war, working for a time in Trotsky's military secretariat and on Trotsky's armored train. Later Blumkin worked for the
GPU. In 1929 he was sent to Turkey on a secret assignment. When he
returned to the Soviet Union, he was arrested and shot. According to
one account (heard from I. I. Sandler, a Latvian Old Bolshevik and
former underground activist, later imprisoned in Vorkuta), Blumkin's
main assignment was to kill Trotsky, who had always considered Blumkin
his devoted supporter. Although Blumkin was able to meet Trotsky and
win his confidence, he could not bring himself to kill him, and was shot
for this on his return to Moscow. According to other reports, Blumkin
was sympathetic to Trotsky and even agreed to carry out a number of
assignments for him, in particular to help establish contact between
Trotsky and his earlier supporters in the USSR. One of them was Radek,
who without even unsealing the letter from Trotsky that Blumkin brought
him, turned it over to Stalin.[23] When Trotsky heard about Blumkin's
arrest and execution he made a public issue of it. Without going into
detail about the mission he had entrusted to Blumkin, Trotsky acknowledged that they had met in Turkey. Trotsky called on his supporters
throughout the world to organize protests over the shooting of Blumkin
as an impermissible act of violence against a revolutionary of long standing. But the campaign over Blumkin and in support of Trotsky met with
no success.

At the beginning of the thirties a fair-sized campaign was also launched
against "nationalist deviations." It would be incorrect to deny the existence of nationalist currents in the union republics, including among
Bolsheviks. Lenin had urged that a very cautious approach be taken in
dealing with such sentiments, that they be overcome by political means,
not repression. In the first decade after the formation of the USSR the
union republics still enjoyed considerable autonomy in resolving their
internal problems. Stalin did not like this, and under the guise of a
struggle against nationalism he began a systematic restriction of the rights
of the union republics, a violation of the nationalities policy that had
been worked out under Lenin. This caused many party members to
protest, whereupon these internationalists were arbitrarily reviled as
"national deviationists." Moreover, Stalin frequently exaggerated the
mistakes of party leaders in the union republics whom he found inconvenient. Unjustified criticism of this sort was heaped on Mykola Skrypnik,

23. [Cf. the account in a letter to Trotsky from Moscow, "Ubiistvo Bliumkina" (The
Murder of Blumkin), *Biulleten' oppozitsii* no. 9, February–March 1930. —G. S.]

one of the leaders of the Ukrainian Bolsheviks and a member of the Executive Committee of the Communist International.

Friction between Stalin and Skrypnik began at the Sixth Party Congress in August 1917, when Skrypnik criticized Stalin for taking an unclear and indecisive stand on the question whether Lenin should appear before a court of the Provisional Government. And in 1918—as we have seen—Skrypnik sharply criticized the way that Stalin, as commissar for nationality affairs, was treating the Ukraine. At the Tenth Party Congress in March 1921 Skrypnik criticized Stalin's speech on the nationality question as abstract and inane. "The nationality problem," said Skrypnik, "is important, critical. Not the slightest solution was proposed in Comrade Stalin's speech this morning."[24] Stalin did not forget these affronts.

To be sure, Skrypnik's own pronouncements were not always correct. The process of "Ukrainization," which he directed, sometimes aroused justifiable criticism from Bolsheviks working in the Ukraine. But instead of criticizing Skrypnik's mistakes in a comradely manner, instead of an open discussion of the difficult problems of nationality policy in the Ukraine, Stalin and his henchman Pavel Postyshev (whom Stalin made a secretary of the Central Committee in 1930) launched a political campaign against Skrypnik, accusing him of "objectively" giving support to "class enemies" on the cultural front and other mortal sins.

The fraudulent trial of the "Union for the Liberation of the Ukraine" was used for this purpose. This trial, said Postyshev in one of his speeches, "has shown . . . that the strongest nuclei of the nationalist counterrevolution [have existed] in higher education and in vocational schools, in the [Ukrainian] Academy of Sciences, in publishing houses, in writer's organizations." And he asked rhetorically, "Did the Ukrainian Communist Party draw the necessary conclusions from this trial? No, it did not." In 1933 Postyshev further declared that as a result of this

weakening, and even, in some cases, this loss of Bolshevik vigilance, the sector which Comrade Skrypnik has directed until recently—I have in mind the Commissariat of Education and the entire educational system of the Ukraine—has been completely infested with wrecking, counterrevolutionary, nationalist elements. It is in these very institutions that wrecking elements were given completely free rein, placing their people in the most responsible, the leading, sectors of the ideological front.[25]

24. *Desiatyi s"ezd RKP(b). Stenograficheskii otchet* (Moscow, 1963), p. 210.
25. P. Postyshev, *Ot XVI do XVII s"ezda. Stat'i i rechi* (Moscow, 1934), pp. 59, 203.

Many valuable cadres of the Ukrainian national intelligentsia were discredited and removed from their posts, and quite a few were arrested. Skrypnik, as a result of the slanderous campaign against him, committed suicide in July 1933. Postyshev, who was made a candidate member of the Politburo, returned to Kiev to become head of the party organization in the Ukraine together with Vlas Chubar.

In Armenia in the early thirties the well-known Armenian Bolshevik N. Stepanyan was dismissed from his post as commissar of education on a charge of "nationalism." The outstanding Armenian poet Ye. Charents and the writer Aksel Bakunts were also subjected to persecution.[26] Many officials of the party and government apparatus in Uzbekistan were also arrested for "nationalism" in the early thirties.

Severe repression came down on members of small opposition groups that arose inside the party in these years. By the early thirties, as we have seen, all the former opposition leaders (except the exiled Trotsky) had been broken psychologically and no longer opposed Stalin's policies, although they saw what a distressing economic situation those policies had produced. Dissatisfaction with the extremely painful material conditions of the masses and related social conflicts penetrated the ranks of the party. One person who expressed this discontent was V. V. Lominadze, who in early 1930 was first secretary of the party's Transcaucasian Committee (kraikom). Lominadze spoke out against the neglect of the workers' and peasants' needs, against fakery, and against what he called the "feudal and seignorial degeneration" of some party officials in Transcaucasia. On the last issue Lominadze prevailed upon the kraikom to adopt a special resolution.

Dissatisfaction with Stalin's policies was also expressed by the talented official Sergei Syrtsov, a candidate member of the Politburo and chairman of the Council of People's Commissars for the RSFSR. He and his sympathizers protested against excessive expansion of capital construction and called attention to the serious situation in the countryside, especially in stockbreeding. Syrtsov declared that it was too early to speak of the victory of socialism in the countryside or the imminent completion of the foundations for a socialist society in the Soviet Union.

In 1930 Lominadze visited Moscow, and Syrtsov invited him to his home. For several hours they talked over party and state affairs. Later Syrtsov incautiously spoke of this meeting among his close acquaintances.

26. Ts. Agayan, *N. Stepanyan* (Yerevan, 1967), pp. 44–47.

Even in those days Stalin made wide use of informers and tried to place some in the entourage of every important government official. When Stalin learned about the Syrtsov-Lominadze meeting he was intensely angered, for both men had been his protégés and owed their promotions to him. A joint session of the Politburo and the Presidum of the CEC was immediately convened, and there Stalin accused Syrtsov and Lominadze of forming a "rightist-leftist" bloc. The press began a campaign against this nonexistent bloc and its alleged members, including N. Chaplin and L. Shatskin, both prominent young party leaders at the time. Syrtsov and Lominadze were removed from the Central Committee. Syrtsov was demoted from chairman of the RSFSR Council of People's Commissars to director of a factory producing phonograph records. Lominadze was transferred from the Transcaucasian *kraikom* to work in the Commissariat of Trade and then was sent to Magnitogorsk as secretary of the city's party committee.

Another anti-Stalin group that arose inside the party in the early thirties was the Ryutin group. M. N. Ryutin worked in the Central Committee apparatus and for several years headed the party committee of Moscow's Krasnaya Presnya district. Disturbed by failures in collectivization and industrialization and by Stalin's increasingly harsh rule within the party, Ryutin and his friend P. A. Galkin organized an opposition group in Moscow, although its membership was fifteen at the most. This group drafted a lengthy document, known to history as the "Ryutin Platform." Robert Conquest asserts that the members of the Ryutin group circulated "this document . . . widely in the leading circles of the party."[27] Actually, only a very small circle was acquainted with the Ryutin Platform; conditions were such in those days that documents of that kind could not have been circulated widely. Some of Bukharin's friends and students—Nikolai Uglanov, Pyotr Petrovsky, Aleksandr Slepkov, Dmitry Maretsky—knew about the document, as did the philosopher Yan Sten. Some fragments of the platform were also made known to Zinoviev and Kamenev. Ryutin and his group called for a decisive change in the party's economic policy and an easing of the pressure on the countryside as well as for an end to repression inside the party and democratization of the party. The main prerequisite for such changes, however, was the removal of Stalin from the party leadership.

27. Robert Conquest, *The Great Terror: Stalin's Purge of the Thirties*, rev. ed. (New York, 1968), p. 52. (The text of the Ryutin Platform has not come down to us. It was never published and only relatively short summaries of it are known.)

Nearly one-fourth of the platform was taken up with the condemnation of Stalin. Ryutin had joined the party in 1914 and knew its leaders well. According to his friends, Ryutin had always held a very low opinion of Stalin and had criticized the Politburo for its recommendation that Stalin be elected general secretary. The unpublished memoirs of R. G. Alikhanova, who knew Ryutin well, mention that he asserted more than once, among his closest co-thinkers, that the assassination of Stalin was not only possible but actually the only way to get rid of him. The Ryutin group, however, did not make any preparations or attempts to carry out such an assassination.[28]

When Stalin found out about the group through the GPU or his own private informers, he struck swiftly. Demagogically accusing Ryutin and his co-thinkers of a counterrevolutionary plot, of creating a "kulak organization," and attempting to restore capitalism, Stalin insisted on the arrest of the group's members and demanded that its leaders be shot. The majority of the Politburo, however, did not agree with Stalin. An unwritten law still existed at the time—that excessively severe measures should not be taken against party activists. The decision was made to expel the "Ryutinites" from the party, and to exile most of them to remote areas.

Ryutin himself was expelled and arrested first. On October 11, 1932, *Pravda* published a decree of the Central Control Commission on the expulsion of twenty persons from the party "as degenerate elements who have become enemies of communism and of Soviet power, as traitors to the party and the working class, who tried to form an underground bourgeois-kulak organization under a fake 'Marxist Leninist' banner for the purpose of restoring capitalism in general and kulakdom in particular in the USSR."

Besides Galkin, Slepkov, and Maretsky the list of expelled party members included M. S. Ivanov, P. M. Zamyatin, P. P. Fedorov, V. I. Demidov, V. N. Kayurov, M. I. Mebel, and S. V. Tokarev. They were all banished from Moscow. Sten, Petrovsky, Uglanov, and M. E. Ravich-Cherkassky were expelled from the party for one year. They were given the right "after a year, depending on their conduct, to raise the question of a review of the present decree."

Many of these people soon "recanted," were reinstated in the party,

28. R. G. Alikhanova is the wife of G. Alikhanov, who was a prominent figure in the Comintern and one of the founders of the Communist Party of Armenia. She is also the mother of Yelena Bonner, the wife of Aleksandr Sakharov.

and returned to Moscow. With the beginning of mass repression in 1936–1938, however, they were all arrested and physically destroyed.

■ 9

THE SUICIDE OF NADEZHDA ALLILUYEVA

On November 9, 1932, Stalin's wife, Nadezhda Alliluyeva, committed suicide. According to some biographers, her death had a profound effect on his personality, for in his way he had loved her very much. In my opinion, however, the effect of this tragic episode should not be exaggerated. Stalin's personality was fully formed by the end of 1932.

As I said in chapter 1, Alliluyeva was Stalin's second wife; his first—Yekaterina Svanidze—died in 1907, when their son Yakov was only one year old. A photograph still exists showing Stalin wearing a beard, standing with the relatives of his first wife next to her coffin. The photo was given by Svanidze's mother to a daughter of Prokofy Dzhaparidze. (Dzhaparidze was one of the twenty-six Baku commissars executed by the counterrevolution in 1918; he was also known by the party name Alyosha).

Stalin first met Sergei Alliluyev, the father of his second wife, in 1903, when Alliluyev came to Tiflis to make arrangements for the Baku underground printing press.[29] A few years later fate brought them together again in Baku, and Stalin may at that time have made the acquaintance of Alliluyev's six-year-old daughter, Nadya. The Alliluyev family soon moved to St. Petersburg, where their apartment served as a secret meetingplace for the Bolsheviks. After the July events in 1917 Lenin hid at this apartment for several days. Stalin was also a frequent visitor at the Alliluyevs' apartment, as we have seen; his relationship with Nadezhda Alliluyeva dated from that time. In 1918 she joined the party and went with Stalin to the Tsaritsyn front. After returning to Moscow, she served in Lenin's secretariat and after Lenin's death worked for the magazine *Revolyutsia i kultura* (Revolution and Culture). In the late twenties she began studying at the newly formed Industrial Academy in order to learn the technology of synthetic fiber production. In the early thirties she transferred to work for the party's Moscow Committee, without having completed her studies.

I cite these facts because quite a few rumors and myths have arisen about Alliluyeva and her relations with Stalin. (Earlier I mentioned

29. Sergei Alliluyev, *Proidennyi put* (Moscow, 1956), p. 60.

Essad-Bey's tale that Stalin kept her confined like an Oriental patriarch). In fact, Nadezhda Alliluyeva was an extremely sociable person, who was close with many prominent party figures, particularly the family of Abel Yenukidze, the relatives of Alyosha Dzhaparidze, and the entire Svanidze family. Molotov's wife, Polina Zhemchuzhina, was a very close friend of hers; and she had good relations with Nikita Khrushchev, whose acquaintance she made at the Industrial Academy. Her relations with Yakov Dzhugashvili, only five years younger than herself, were most affectionate. The frequent quarrels between Stalin and Yakov distressed her, and she was stunned by Yakov's unsuccessful attempt to shoot himself. Svetlana Alliluyeva indicates that Yakov was a perfectly loyal son but refused to make an idol of his father. "Father always speaks in ready-made formulas," Yakov once said to Svetlana.[30] Stalin treated Yakov coldly, even with hostility. This in fact was the reason for Yakov's suicide attempt. "Luckily he was only wounded," writes Svetlana. "My father used to make fun of him and sneer, 'Ha! He couldn't even shoot straight!' My mother was horrified."[31]

Nadezhda Alliluyeva's life with Stalin became increasingly difficult. There were frequent quarrels. On one occasion she took the children and left him, but after a few months under gentle pressure from her father and other relatives she returned to him. In almost every case when the quarrels between Stalin and Nadezhda were carried outside the household her relatives sided with Stalin. The disagreements were not only personal but political as well. Finding no sympathy or understanding among her closest friends and relatives, Alliluyeva began to think about suicide. When her brother Pavel, who served as an army engineer in the civil war and was later commissar of the tank and armored-car administration of the Red Army, went abroad on business, she asked him to get her a revolver. Pavel complied with this request, presenting her with a small ladies' pistol he had obtained in Berlin.

There were several versions of Nadezhda Alliluyeva's suicide, which differ in minor ways only. In *Twenty Letters to a Friend* Svetlana tells what she heard from her nurse and from her mother's close friend Polina Zhemchuzhina, the wife of Molotov. Neither of these women could bring herself to inform Stalin's daughter of the details of her mother's death until 1955, when they had returned from internal exile and finally freed

30. Svetlana Alliluyeva, *Twenty Letters to a Friend*, (New York, 1967 paper ed.), p. 170.
31. Ibid., p. 113.

themselves from the fear of Stalin that had gripped them for so many years.

Svetlana's nurse and the housekeeper Carolina Till were the first to find Nadezhda Alliluyeva lying in a pool of blood next to her bed with a small pistol in her hand. They called Yenukidze, who lived nearby, Polina Zhemchuzhina, and K. V. Pauker, the chief of the Kremlin guard. Voroshilov and Molotov also came to Stalin's apartment. They informed Stalin of Nadezhda's death when he awoke and came into the dining room. Zhemchuzhina also told Svetlana about the dispute that occurred between Stalin and his wife the evening of her death at a banquet in the Kremlin to celebrate the anniversary of the October revolution.[32]

I consider this account the most reliable. It coincides with what I happened to hear from a relative of Pavel Alliluyev. At one time I also recorded an account given by a person who had known the family of Abel Yenukidze well. His account went as follows. On November 8 a group of families of Bolshevik leaders gathered to celebrate the fifteenth anniversary of the revolution. Nadezhda was there but Stalin was late. When he arrived Nadezhda made a sarcastic remark. In a burst of temper Stalin said something rude in reply. He happened to be smoking a cigarette rather than a pipe, as he sometimes did. Taking his anger out on his wife, he suddenly threw the lit cigarette in her face. The cigarette fell down the cleavage of her dress but she managed to get it out and jumped up from the table. Stalin meanwhile had turned on his heel and left the room. Nadezhda also left almost immediately. Stalin had gone to his dacha outside Moscow, and Nadezhda went back to their apartment in the Kremlin. The celebration of the revolution had been ruined but within a few hours something even worse happened. There was a call from the Stalin apartment for Yenukidze and Ordzhonikidze to come immediately. Nadezhda had shot herself. Next to her lay a small ladies' pistol and a letter to Stalin, which no one of course could bring him- or herself to open. Stalin was called at his dacha, and he soon arrived. He was stunned by what had happened but said nothing.

The press of course did not mention suicide. A notice about the sudden illness and death of Stalin's wife appeared in the newspapers, along with a falsified medical report. All the servants of the Stalin household were soon replaced. To be sure, rumors that Stalin's wife had killed herself began to circulate rather widely and reached the foreign press. The

32. Ibid., pp. 119–122.

rumor was accepted as fact, for example, by Boris Souvarine, a well-known French socialist writer, who had helped to organize the Comintern and the French Communist Party but later broke with Communism. His book on Stalin, published in 1935, is quite interesting and of value to historians. Souvarine's book was reissued in 1977, but not revised. In a lengthy introduction to the reissued version Souvarine explained:

> The author did not feel he had the right to change or correct the text published in 1935. . . . His advanced age has prevented him from reviewing the vast amount of additional material that has appeared and continuing this account of Stalin's life to its end.

Nevertheless in the introduction and in the even longer afterword to the 1977 edition Souvarine did attempt a survey of the many new books and publications on Stalin and Stalinism and in the light of these to make some corrections in his original text. Among these corrections was a note on the death of Nadezhda Alliluyeva. Commenting on the appearance of the two books by Nadezhda's daughter Svetlana, Souvarine wrote:

> She believes in her mother's suicide, but she is repeating what was said in the Kremlin, where everyone lies. Today the suicide story, which seemed plausible at one time (and which I accepted in this book), has unofficially been rejected in Kremlin circles and is refuted by weighty evidence.[33]

Souvarine does not give the sources for his information on the views he attributes to "Kremlin circles" nor does he cite the "weighty evidence" that supposedly disproves the assumption that Alliluyeva killed herself.

Lydia Shatunovskaya also advances the notion that Stalin killed his wife. Among her arguments—or more exactly, speculations on the motives for this alleged murder—Shatunovskaya cites the "sexual incompatibility" between the passionate Nadezhda and Stalin, who was quite "cold."[34] All this is made up out of whole cloth.

Now that people know about Stalin's monstrous crimes, the murder of hundreds of thousands of people on his orders, including many of his own relatives and former friends, it is understandable that he should be thought capable of killing his own wife if she became an obstacle in some way. Of course Stalin's perfidy and his capacity for secret murder to supplement his open reign of terror cannot be doubted. But we must also bear in mind that in the fall of 1932 conditions in the Kremlin were still fundamentally different from those that existed in the fall of 1937. In

33. Boris Souvarine, *Stalin* (Paris, 1977), p. 605.
34. Lydia Shatunovskaya, *Zhizn' v Kremle* (New York, 1981).

1932 it was possible to conceal Alliluyeva's suicide from the broad masses by an official announcement about a sudden fatal illness. But in the narrower circles of those who lived in the Kremlin or "government house" ("the house on the embankment") her suicide could not be kept secret. If Stalin had killed his wife, he could not have hidden the fact from Kremlin circles nor from the large Alliluyev family. Significantly, the members of the Alliluyev family did not condemn Stalin for Nadezhda's death; their first impulse was to try to help him overcome the tragedy. Nadezhda's brother Pavel immediately returned from Berlin and took up residence at Stalin's dacha for several years together with his whole family. Stalin talked with them a number of times about Nadezhda. From time to time he felt guilty and tried to justify himself to Pavel. "I did everything she wanted. She could go anywhere, buy whatever she wished. What could she have lacked? Look!" Stalin opened a small locked drawer of his desk. It was crammed full of ten, twenty, and thirty-ruble notes.[35]

Robert Conquest, among others, asserts that after Nadezhda's death Stalin lost confidence in her brother, Pavel.

Nadezhda's brother, the Old Bolshevik Paul Alliluyev, was political commissar of the Armoured Forces. He was put under special surveillance. Later he told an old acquaintance that he had been kept away from Stalin since his sister's death and had had his Kremlim pass taken from him. It was clear to him that Yagoda and Pauker had suggested that he might be personally dangerous to Stalin in avenging his sister.[36]

This, too, is pure conjecture. Pavel Alliluyev's relatives and two sons still live in Moscow. They remember well the fact that their whole family lived with Stalin at his dacha until 1935, and they remember particular meetings with Stalin. Of course Pavel also had an apartment in Moscow, but he like the others lived for a long time at Stalin's place "in the bosom of nature." In 1935 his family was moved to Mikoyan's dacha, but Pavel was still able to enter the Kremlin freely and sometimes visited Stalin at his Kremlin apartment. As Svetlana writes:

Both the Svanidzes, Uncle Pavel, and the Redenses still used to come to our apartment in the Kremlin. But with my mother gone nothing was the same.

35. Svetlana Alliluyeva reports that even after the war Stalin did not spend the huge sums he was paid for the various posts he held. The envelopes of money he received were stashed in a drawer of his desk without being opened.

36. Conquest, *Great Terror*, p. 68.

Everything had collapsed—the sense of a home, relationships, the feeling of friendly concern each one had for all the others.[37]

Many stories have been made up as well about Nadezhda Alliluyeva's funeral. To this day some of Stalin's ardent followers say that Stalin followed his wife's coffin on foot from the Kremlin to Novodevichy cemetery. Stories are also told that late at night once a week Stalin would go to his wife's grave and sit there for several hours under the streetlights. The truth was otherwise. Alliluyeva's coffin with her remains was on display in the building that is now the GUM department store (in the thirties several Kremlin offices were located there). Stalin came to view the coffin before the memorial service. After approaching the coffin, he suddenly made a gesture as though to push the coffin away and said distinctly, "She left me as an enemy!" Then he turned away and departed. He did not attend his wife's memorial service or burial, nor did he visit her grave even once in his life. Not only does his daughter attest to this; so do all of Nadezhda Alliluyeva's relatives and the party and government figures who had a hand in the funeral arrangements in 1932.

After the death of Nadezhda Alliluyeva, Stalin remained a widower to the end of his life. He had a few brief affairs with women. Some children resulted from these liaisons, but they all bear their mothers' names. None of these women had any influence on him, and he never saw any of these children. In fact to the end of his days, he would see only three of his eight legitimate granchildren (children of Yakov, Vasily, and Svetlana). Family life ended for him in 1932.

■ 10
REPRESSION IN THE SOCIAL SCIENCES AND LITERATURE

An abnormal situation was also created in the social sciences at the beginning of the thirties. The first wave of repression among Marxist historians was precipitated by Stalin's famous letter to the editor of *Proletarian Revolution,* laying down extremely fallible views on the history of Bolshevism in an extremely nasty manner. Many historians were fired, and some were even expelled from the party without cause. At the end of 1931 the Institute of History reported to the Presidium of the Communist Academy that it had carried out Stalin's instructions by firing

---

37. Alliluyeva, *Twenty Letters,* p. 147.

people who did not write the history of Bolshevism in the prescribed way. In particular, I. M. Alter and A. G. Slutsky were fired from the Institute, and Slutsky's candidate membership in the party was subsequently canceled. N. Elvov and G. Vaks, contributors to the multivolume *History of the CPSU,* were expelled from the party, while the editor, Yemelyan Yaroslavsky, was severely criticized.[38]

Repression also hit many other disciplines. The Leningrad Branch of the Communist Academy reported in 1933 that it had rooted out "Trotskyism, Luxemburgism, and Menshevism, not only on the historical but also on the economic, agrarian, literary, and other fronts."[39]

On April 10, 1932, Academician Mikhail Pokrovsky, a member of the Central Committee of the Soviet Communist Party, died at the age of sixty-four. He had become a Marxist and joined the Bolshevik Party at the turn of the century, when he was already an established Russian historian. After the October revolution he was the recognized leader of Soviet historical science, serving as deputy people's commissar of enlightenment for the RSFSR and as head of the Communist Academy and its Institute of History and of the Institute of Red Professors as well. Pokrovsky was also chairman of the Society of Marxist Historians, director of the Central Archive, and chief editor of the journals *Istorik-marksist* (Marxist Historian) and *Borba klassov* (Class Struggle). According to the official obituary:

Pokrovsky was a world famous Communist scholar, one of the most prominent organizers and leaders on our theoretical front, and an untiring promoter of Marxist-Leninist ideas.[40]

Pokrovsky's authority was an obstacle to Stalin, who aspired to the leading position in the sphere of Marxist theory. Under Kaganovich's leadership and with Stalin's support, a savage campaign was launched against Pokrovsky, whose mistakes as a historian were enormously exaggerated. A de facto ban was imposed on the reprinting of his books and articles.

There were also intolerable excesses "on the philosophical front." I cannot here review all the issues involved in the formation and evolution of Soviet Marxist philosophy. Some of these issues are taken up in a

38. See the article by V. A. Dunaevsky in *Evropa v novoe i noveishee vremia* (Moscow, 1966), pp. 508–510.
39. Ibid., p. 509.
40. *Pravda,* April 12, 1932.

recently published book by I. Yakhot, a well-known Soviet philosopher who emigrated from the Soviet Union.[41] I will note only that in the twenties a debate on fundamental questions was carried on in the Soviet philosophical journals between the so-called "mechanists," represented primarily by Skvortsov-Stepanov, Timiryazev, and Varyash, and the "dialecticians," led by A. M. Deborin, Yan Sten, and N. Karev. Both these tendencies of course considered themselves Marxists and proponents of both materialism and dialectics. Gradually a group of younger philosophers was drawn into the debate; they were mainly students at the Communist Academy and the Institute of Philosophy. This younger group, which constituted the majority of the party bureau at the Institute of Philosophy, was headed by Mark Mitin, Pavel Yudin, and V. Raltsevich, and they were joined later by Fyodor Konstantinov, M. Iovchuk, and others.

Deborin was the most authoritative Soviet philosopher at that time, and his supporters had clearly gained the upper hand in the ongoing debate. Suddenly the situation on the philosophical front changed radically. The younger group, headed by Mitin and Yudin, began to attack both the "mechanists" and Deborin's "dialecticians," calling for the "Bolshevization" of philosophy and defending the "Leninist stage" in the development of Marxist philosophy. On December 9, 1930, Stalin had met in person with the party bureau at the Institute of Philosophy, which was part of the Institute of Red Professors. There is no detailed record or even brief summary of the meeting. It was at this meeting, however, that Stalin characterized the views of Deborin and his group with the absurd term "Menshevizing idealism," which implied "enemy of Marxism-Leninism," thus opening the door for any charge at all to be brought against Deborin without his having a chance to defend himself. Yet Deborin had never been an idealist. For several years he had been a Menshevik, but that fact did not alter his world view. (After all, the great Marxist philosopher Georgy Plekhanov had also been a Menshevik in his later years.) At the meeting with the party bureau Stalin also condemned the "mechanists," calling on the "young" philosophers to give battle on both fronts. This they proceeded to do with great zeal, stifling everything fresh, vital, and creative in Soviet philosophy. From then on for more than two decades Soviet philosophical literature was dominated by a stereotypical,

41. I. Yakhot, *Podavlenie filosofii v SSSR (20–30 gody)* (New York, 1981).

superficial mechanism draped with mere phrases about dialectics and the "Leninist" (or "Leninist-Stalinist") stage in the development of philosophy.

Many pseudoscientific struggles erupted at the beginning of the thirties. There were fights against "Menshevizing counterrevolutionary Rubinism" in economics, against "the Bogdanovian mechanistic theories of Bukharin" in social theory, against "Raikovism" in the methods of teaching biology, against "Voronskyism" and "Pereverzevism" in literary criticism, against the theory of "the withering away of the school" in pedagogy, and so on. In almost every case insignificant differences in phraseology were elevated "to principled heights." In the tiniest phraseological inaccuracies someone would try to find enemy influences; in the guise of "revolutionary vigilance" narrow-minded sectarians cultivated intolerance and viciousness. Here, for example, is the reasonable advice given to journalists in one article:

Fellow newspapermen, the reader begs you not to admonish him, not to teach, not to exhort, not to goad, but to give him clear and understandable exposition, to analyze, to explain what, where, and how. Lessons and exhortations will emerge from such writing by themselves.

And here is what was said about that reasonable advice in a special resolution adopted by the Communist Institute of Journalism:

These are very harmful [*vredneishie*, which is close to wrecking, *vreditel'skie*] bourgeois theories; they reject the organizing role of the Bolshevik press and should be destroyed once and for all.

Such talk is scarcely distinguishable from the wall posters of the Red Guards in China.

In the years 1930–1933 Trofim Lysenko and others less famous adventurists began their meteoric careers in science. An intolerable situation also developed in literature, the theatre, and the arts in general. Stalin himself denounced Mikhail Bulgakov's play *Beg* (The Flight) as anti-Soviet and an "attempt to justify or partially justify the White Guard cause."[42] In the sixties and seventies Soviet audiences by the millions have enjoyed many different productions of this play as well as a film based on it. The Kamerny Theatre in Moscow, founded by the outstanding Soviet director Aleksandr Tairov, was condemned by Stalin as "truly bourgeois."[43] And he engaged in rude vilification of the poet Demyan

42. Stalin, *Sochineniia*, 11:327.
43. Ibid., p. 329.

Bedny, a man closely linked with the party and the entire history of the October Revolution. To be sure, Bedny's poetry can be criticized from various standpoints, but in the conditions of 1930–1931 for Stalin to refer to Bedny (who was considered with good reason to have been the founder of "proletarian poetry" and who had joined the Bolshevik Party in 1912) as a "frightened intellectual" who "does not know the Bolsheviks"[44] was enough to close the doors of most Soviet editors and publishers to him.

As a result of such condemnations, the Soviet intelligentsia was divided into factions. Quarreling, slander, informing, and defamation became a way of life in most research institutes, in institutions of higher education, and in writers' and artists' organizations. And this abnormal way of life was justified by reference to the intensification of the class struggle in the Soviet Union.

Not long ago the writer Veniamin Kaverin described his astonishment on leafing through a notorious journal of the late twenties, *On Literary Guard.* He found literature sharply divided into two camps, enemy and friendly. Although the dividing line shifted constantly and weirdly, at any given moment enemies and friends were clearly set apart, the one as an object of hatred and poorly concealed envy, the other being patted on the back. And behind it all was a lust for a share in power, a lust so obvious that at times it seemed rather ludicrous to Kaverin.[45] Kaverin was writing about the period 1928–1930, but the situation continued to heat up in 1931 and 1932, right up until the surprising decision of the party's Central Committee to dissolve the Russian Association of Proletarian Writers (RAPP) and establish a single Soviet Writers' Union. The outburst of liberalism and hope, which accompanied the First Congress of Soviet Writers in 1934, did not last long and was succeeded by times that were even worse, as we shall see below.

■ 11

STALIN'S POLICIES IN THE INTERNATIONAL WORKING CLASS MOVEMENT

Increasingly harsh rule in the Soviet Union as a whole and inside the Soviet Communist Party inevitably led to the same thing in the Comintern; an intensification of factional disputes in the individual Communist parties. A bitter struggle against "right" and "left" deviations was waged

44. Ibid., 13:26–27.
45. *Novy mir*, 1966, no. 11, pp. 141–142.

in these parties, often borrowing the methods and slogans of the Soviet party with little relevance to the internal situation in the foreign party or the country in which it was located. Every one of the Communist parties had to approve automatically whatever happened in the Soviet Union and its ruling party. Under the rigid structure of the Comintern these parties were stripped of political independence and turned into semi-autonomous sections of a worldwide Communist organization. This situation often resulted in the expulsion of valuable and far-sighted political leaders and prevented the Communist parties from becoming truly mass-based political organizations. In 1928 the total membership of all the Communist parties outside the USSR was only 400,000. The same year the members of Social Democratic parties numbered approximately 6.5 million.[46]

The first arrests of Western Communists working in the Soviet Union occurred in the early thirties—for example, of the well-known French revolutionary Victor Serge, who had actively supported the Left Opposition. Serge spent several years in prison and internal exile but was freed as a result of a protest campaign in the West. His memoirs, published while Stalin was still alive, are a valuable aid to understanding events in the Soviet Union and Western Europe in the twenties and thirties.

Severe blows were dealt to the small Communist parties of the Western Ukraine and Western Byelorussia. In the early thirties the leadership of the Communist Party of the Western Ukraine was unjustly accused of nationalism and betrayal. Many of its leaders, including M. T. Zayachkovsky and G. V. Ivanenko, were arrested.[47] In 1933 the same treatment was given to the Communist Party of Western Byelorussia. P. P. Voloshin, F. I. Volynets, and I. E. Gavrilik—former deputies in the Polish Sejm—and other Communists who, after long prison terms in bourgeois Poland, had been released in a prisoner exchange with the Soviet government and given political asylum in the Soviet Union, were falsely accused of anti-Soviet and counterrevolutionary activity and arrested. Along with them some other leaders of the Western Byelorussian party went to jail, among them Ya. Bobrovich, A. G. Kaputsky, P. A. Klintsevich, and L. I. Rodzevich.[48]

I must speak briefly about the effect of Stalin's policies on the international working-class movement in the early thirties. The depression of

46. *Kommunist*, 1968, no. 2, p. 90; and 1980, no. 5, p. 34.
47. See the newspaper *Pravda Ukrainy*, October 11 and November 18, 1963.
48. *Kommunist*, 1963, no. 10, pp. 37–47.

1929–1933, which profoundly shook the Western capitalist system, brought about far-reaching political and social changes. These differed in the United States and Western Europe. In the United States the depression brought in Franklin D. Roosevelt and his New Deal, producing drastic changes in the functioning of the capitalist system while maintaining the basic institutions of bourgeois democracy. Although Roosevelt's main concern was to strengthen the capitalism system through reforms, some of those reforms—expanded government regulation of industry and agriculture, social security and unemployment benefits, increased rights and opportunities for trade unions, laws on fair hiring practices, and so on—allow one to suppose that the social legislation introduced earlier in the Soviet Union might have had some influence on New Deal policies.

The economic crisis had different results in Western Europe. The drastic deterioration in conditions for the working class and the petty bourgeoisie brought increased support for the revolutionary left. However, the right-wing nationalist mass movements that, in Soviet political theory, were grouped under the general term "fascism" began to grow even more rapidly. The most reactionary and extremist of mass movements, fascism used social demagogy and exploited nationalist prejudices in an effort to win over all discontented elements, create a mass base, then isolate and smash the most organized and conscious section of the working class. Fascism aimed its blows in equal measure at the Communists and at the Social Democrats, trade unions, and other progressive workers' organizations. It opposed all forms of bourgeois democracy, seeking to establish a one-party totalitarian system. Fascism had been victorious in Italy in the early twenties. In the early thirties the deadly danger of victory for an even more aggressive fascist dictatorship arose in Germany, the largest and economically most advanced country of Western Europe.

Among the factors that aided the victory of fascism in Germany were some related to the existence of the Soviet Union and its policies. Soviet historians usually emphasize the Western bourgeoisie's fear of socialism in general and Bolshevism in particular. It can be shown that the Nazis made skillful use of these fears to secure the support of certain influential circles in Britain and France. They also made effective use of another factor: the disillusionment of many workers and most petty bourgeois in socialist Russia, which instead of becoming a paradise for workers and peasants was experiencing convulsions of mass repression one after another. It is quite evident that the wave of violence in the Soviet countryside in the late twenties and early thirties, the abolition of NEP and the Nepmen, the mass confiscation of small businesses, the "gold campaign," the terror against technical specialists and specialists in the humanities were all played on by Western propagandists to weaken the revolutionary movements in those countries. Why else did the unparalleled crisis of capitalism from 1929 to 1933 strengthen the Communist movement only to a very small extent, without giving rise to any revolutionary situations? Why did substantial numbers of peasants, petty bourgeois, and even workers move to the right rather than to the left during the years of crisis, providing a mass base for the fascist movement? There can hardly be any doubt that the news coming from the Soviet Union contributed in no small degree.

Stalin's policy of splitting the international working-class movement, however, was his main "gift" to fascism. The formation of the Comintern, as is generally known, involved a bitter struggle between the young Communist parties and various tendencies and groups in Western Social Democracy that were rebuilding their organizations and reestablishing ties after the terrible upheavals of World War I. I cannot analyze the history and causes of this deplorable division in the ranks of the workers' movement. Each side has presented (and continues to present) quite weighty arguments in defense of its own policies and positions.[49]

The political and ideological battle between the two Internationals went on throughout the twenties, when not only Stalin but also Trotsky, Zinoviev, Kamenev, and Bukharin vied with one another in denouncing the Social Democrats. Virtually the most insulting accusation to be leveled against a Bolshevik in those days was to be charged with Social Democratic or Menshevik views.

There can be no question that it was wrong to call the Social Democrats "social fascists," the "moderate wing of fascism," or "the main social support for fascism," although such characterizations were included in the program adopted in 1928 at the Sixth Congress of the Comintern. This political extremism on the part of the Bolshevik leadership became particularly dangerous in the period 1929–1933. The fascist offensive in the West made a change in Communist policy absolutely essential. The main political task was not to fight the Social Democrats but to establish a united front of the working class and a general people's front against fascism. In other words, a policy of rapprochement and unity of action

49. I have given a brief historical analysis of this problem in my *Leninism and Western Socialism* (London, 1981), ch. 6.

with the Social Democratic parties, the dominant force in the Western labor movement, was called for.

There can be no doubt that Lenin would have known how to carry out the necessary change of policy. It is well known that during the civil war in Russia the Bolsheviks not only arrested but shot SRs, Mensheviks, and Anarchists. Quite a few Bolsheviks also fell from bullets fired by SRs and Anarchists, especially on territory controlled by SR-Menshevik and Anarchist detachments, armies, or "governments." Nevertheless, when the White armies of General Denikin were threatening Moscow in 1919, Lenin ordered the release of SRs and Mensheviks from the jails, and they immediately went voluntarily to the battlefront, sometimes as military commissars, to fight for Soviet power. An alliance was also made with the rebel army of the Anarchist Nestor Makhno, which was officially made a unit of the Red Army and went on to smash the best regiments of Denikin's army in the southern Ukraine.

It is undoubtedly true that after World War I the right-wing Social Democrats helped maintain the capitalist system in Western Europe. Finding themselves in power in several Western countries, they gave not a moment's thought to the problem of carrying out a transition to socialism. In many cases, however, the bourgeoisie did not wish to agree to the partial reforms that the Social Democratic parties were trying to introduce. Thus, the bourgeoisie, once its system had been stabilized, began to rely more and more on its own political parties. In countries like Italy, Germany, and Japan a major part of the capitalist class placed its bets on the fascist movement. The Social Democratic parties were forced to go into opposition. Many Social Democratic groups and leaders began to take a more clear-cut stand against fascism. But Stalin seemed not to notice these changes; he continued to insist on fighting Social Democracy. Under his influence in 1931, for example, the Eleventh Plenum of the Executive Committee of the Comintern passed the following resolution:

A successful struggle against fascism requires of the Communist parties . . . immediate and decisive correction of mistakes that are essentially reducible to the fact that they counterpose fascism to bourgeois democracy in a liberal way; they counterpose the parliamentary forms of bourgeois dictatorship to its openly fascist forms. This is a reflection of Social Democratic influences in Communist ranks.[50]

50. *Kompartii i krizis kapitalizma. XI Plenum IKKI. Stenograficheskii otchet* (Moscow, 1932), p. 626.

Stalin's attacks were particularly zealous against the left Social Democrats, who enjoyed considerable influence in the working class. He called
them the most dangerous tendency in the Social Democratic movement
because in his opinion they concealed their opportunities beneath a
phony revolutionism and thus lured the working people away from the
Communists. Stalin too quickly forgot that the left tendencies in Social
Democracy had served as the basis for the founding of the Communist
parties. Lenin, for example, had called Rosa Luxemburg an "eagle," a
"great Communist woman," and "a representative of the revolutionary
proletariat and of unfalsified Marxism," while Stalin, for his part, unleashed a campaign against "Luxemburgism" in the early thirties.

This sectarian policy was especially harmful in Germany, where the
fascist threat was the greatest. In the Reichstag elections of 1930 the
Nazis won 6.4 million votes, an eightfold gain in comparison with 1928.
But more than 8.5 million voted for the Social Democrats, and 4.5
million for the Communists. In 1932 13.75 million voted for Hitler's
party, 5.3 million for the Communists, and roughly 8 million for the
Social Democrats. If there had been a united front of the two workers'
parties, it could have stopped Hitler's drive to power in 1930 or even in
1932. But there was no united front. On the contrary, the leaderships of
the two parties fought each other as bitterly as ever. For example, a
leaflet distributed by the Communist Party of Germany (KPD) at this
time asserted: "Another variety of fascist, which is very hard to distinguish but is particularly treacherous, is the social fascist."

Even in July 1932, only a few months before Hitler came to power, a
document of the KPD stated:

The SPD (Social Democratic Party of Germany) is the main social support of the
bourgeoisie. . . . The working class will be incapable of a united struggle against
fascism and the bourgeoisie as long as the Social Democratic leaders have any
influence on the masses.[51]

Also in 1932 the KPD Central Committee sent a special circular to
local organizations, declaring:

The left Social Democrats belong to the vanguard of the counterrevolutionary
bourgeoisie; they are among the most vicious enemies and traitors of the proletariat.[52]

51. See the article by L. I. Gintsberg in *Evropa v novoe i noveishee vremia* (Moscow,
1966), pp. 675–676.
52. L. I. Gintsberg, *Na puti v imperskuiu kantseliariiu* (Moscow, 1972), p. 269.

Within the KPD the group led by Heinz Neumann and Hermann Remmele was particularly ardent in promoting Stalin's theories. In 1931 Remmele even declared in the Reichstag: "Fascist rule, a fascist government, does not frighten us. It will collapse sooner than any other."[53]

The veteran Soviet commentator Ernst Henri (S. N. Rostovsky) described the situtation vividly in his 1966 open letter to Ilya Ehrenburg:

Stalin's words were just as much an order for the Comintern as his instructions were for the Red Army or the NKVD. They divided workers from each other as though by a barricade. . . . Old Social Democratic workers everywhere were not only insulted to the depths of their souls; they were infuriated. They could not forgive the Communists for this. And the Communists, gritting their teeth, carried out the order for a "battle to the death" [against the Social Democrats rather than the fascists]. An order is an order, party discipline is party discipline. Everywhere, as if they had gone out of their minds, the Communists and Social Democrats raved at each other before the eyes of the fascists. I remember it well. I was living in Germany in those years and will never forget how old comrades clenched their fists seeing how everything was going to ruin, how the Social Democratic leaders were rejoicing, how the theory of social fascism month by month, week by week, was paving the way for Hitler. They clenched their fists as they submitted to the "mind" and "will" of Stalin and marched toward the doom that was already waiting for them in the SS torture chambers.[54]

Even after the fascist victory in Germany the sectarian attitudes were so strong within the Comintern that when Maurice Thorez addressed a proposal to the French Radical Party for the establishment of a Popular Front, the Comintern leadership considered it an opportunist act and requested Thorez to withdraw his proposal. The French Communist Party, however, rejected the Comintern request. That was one reason why fascism was unable to gain a victory in France.[55]

■ 12

BEGINNING OF THE STALIN CULT

The early thirties was also the time of a constantly growing cult of Stalin, whose personality was being identified more and more with everything done by the party and government. This cult did not spring up overnight. Even in the early twenties an uncritical attitude toward such institutions

---

53. *Evropa v novoe i noveishee vremia*, p. 676. [Both Heinz Neumann and Hermann Remmele were subsequently arrested by the NKVD.—D. J.]

54. "Otkrytoe pis'mo Il'e Erenburgu," unpublished manuscript.

55. *Problemy mira i sotsializma*, 1965, no. 12, p. 20.

as the party and the government was encouraged among Soviet citizens in general and party members in particular. For the sake of the party and the government, whose decisions were always correct, Communists had to be ready to do anything required of them. After Lenin's death a cult of Lenin was begun, one aspect of which was the establishment of the Lenin Mausoleum, although it was opposed by Krupskaya and others, as we have seen.

Gradually the cult of the party and of Lenin was transferred to Lenin's "disciples," above all, the members of the Politburo. Their names were affixed to streets, factories, collective farms (the Rykov plant, the Bukharin streetcar depot, etc.), and to cities as well. In 1924–1925, with the approval of the Politburo, not only Leningrad and Stalingrad but cities such as Trotsk and Zinovievsk appeared on the map. But as the composition of the Politburo changed, tributes to Stalin became more and more immoderate.

Some authors date the rise of Stalin's cult from 1926–1927. Many speeches by leaders of the Left Opposition in those years contain protests against the incipient cult of Stalin. But this was only the beginning phase in his rise to preeminence. Outwardly, he tried to behave in an exaggeratedly democratic manner, as though to contrast himself to the "aristocrat" Trotsky. Stalin was relatively accessible, simple, and rough-hewn (*grubovat*). He walked freely about the Central Committee building and the Kremlin and took strolls outside the Kremlin with hardly any bodyguards. Sometimes he would drop in at the Institute of Red Professors to have a chat with students there who were party activists.

In the early twenties portraits of Lenin and Trotsky were hung in most official institutions (although after 1924 Trotsky's portrait was removed from nearly all), but there were no portraits of Stalin anywhere. Only in 1930 did portraits of Stalin begin to appear almost everywhere, after his fiftieth birthday had been celebrated, in December 1929, with a pomposity that was unusual at that time. The greetings to Stalin in some cases included such words as "remarkable," "outstanding," "great," and even "genius." The State Publishing House issued a special anthology, entitled *Stalin*, with contributions by Kalinin, Kuibyshev, Kaganovich, Voroshilov, Ordzhonikidze, and other leaders. Exaggerations and distortions abounded, especially one that was insistently repeated:

During Lenin's lifetime, Comrade Stalin, though he was one of Lenin's pupils, was nevertheless his single most reliable aide, who differed from the others by never faltering, by always moving hand in hand with Vladimir Ilyich at all the crucial stages of the revolution, at all the sharp turns through which Lenin took the party.[56]

Some contributors also tried to make the case that although Stalin was best known in the party as a practical leader, he actually was a major theorist of Marxism-Leninism. Voroshilov's "Stalin and the Red Army" contained an unusually large number of distortions, especially on the defeat of Denikin in the civil war. Voroshilov assigned to Stalin the main role in planning his defeat, although his role was actually modest. Also in 1929 the book *Lvov-Warsaw* appeared, not without Stalin's knowledge, altering the facts to blame the mistakes in the Polish campaign of 1920 on S. S. Kamenev and Tukhachevsky and denying any mistakes whatsoever on Stalin's part.

By 1931 V. V. Adoratsky was writing, in the preface to a six-volume collection of Lenin's works, that Stalin's works were the indispensable guide to Lenin's. At the same time, Bubnov, Yaroslavsky, and other historians were bringing out cultist revisions of their books on party history.

After the Central Committee plenum in January 1933, there was an extraordinary intensification of Stalin worship. There was some sincerity in this flood of praise for Stalin, but most of it was carefully encouraged fawning. The simple fact that members of the Politburo (especially Molotov and Kaganovich) were the first to extol Stalin immediately bestowed on such praise the character of official policy, and as such it had to be endorsed even by those who had not previously considered Stalin an infallible genius.

Former oppositionists joined the general chorus of praise: indeed their voices often sounded louder than the rest. One after the other Zinoviev, Kamenev, Bukharin, and other opposition leaders published articles confessing again that they had erred while the "great chief of the toilers throughout the whole world," Comrade Stalin, had always been right. The first issue of *Pravda* for 1934 carried a huge two-page article by Radek, heaping orgiastic praise on Stalin. This former Trotskyist, who had led active opposition to Stalin for many years, now called him "Lenin's best pupil, the model of the Leninist party, bone of its bone, blood of its blood." Stalin, according to the article, was distinguished by "the greatest vigilance against opportunism" combined with "adamantine composure"; he personified "the entire historical experience of the party";

56. *Stalin* (Moscow, 1929).

"more than any other pupil of Lenin, he has fused with the party, with its basic cadres." He was "as farsighted as Lenin," and so on. This seems to have been the first large article in the press specifically devoted to adulation of Stalin, and it was quickly reissued as a pamphlet in 225,000 copies, an enormous figure for the time. To his former associates in the opposition Radek offered the following explanation of the praise he had lavished on Stalin: "We should be grateful to Stalin. If we [the opposition] had lived at the time of the French Revolution, we would long ago have been shorter by a head." Events soon showed how little Radek knew Stalin.

After Radek's article tributes to Stalin became grotesquely hypertrophied. Genius and more than genius, great and the greatest, wisest of the wise, all-knowing and all-seeing—these are but a few of the phrases that accompanied almost every reference to Stalin.[57]

The cult of Stalin not only catered to his vanity but also served the aims of his immoderate lust for power. It placed him in a special position, raising him to unattainable heights, far above the party, and protecting him completely from any criticism. With Stalin beyond the control of the Central Committee, a certain vital balance within the party leadership was lost. This can be seen in the contrast between the Sixteenth and Seventeenth party congresses. The businesslike speeches of the delegates to the Sixteenth Party Congress in 1930 had not included praise of Stalin. Indeed, most of the delegates, when speaking about the party's achievements, did not even mention Stalin's name. The Seventeenth Party Congress in 1934 was quite different. Nearly every speaker dwelt on Stalin's greatness and genius. At times it seemed that the congress was convened to celebrate Stalin, that the nation owed all its achievements to Stalin alone. For the first time in the party's history a congress did not adopt a detailed resolution in accordance with the report of the Central Committee but instead directed all party organizations simply "to be guided in their work by the theses and objectives set forth in Comrade Stalin's speech."[58]

There was another consideration in the creation of the Stalin cult. As we have seen, the early thirties were a very difficult time for the Soviet

57. Soon after Radek's pamphlet, a special album was published, *I. V. Stalin: Zhivopis'. Plakat. Grafika. Skulptura* (J. V. Stalin in Painting, Posters, Graphics, and Sculpture) (Moscow, 1934). Almost all the artistic representations of Stalin that had been made in the previous several years were collected in this volume.

58. *KPSS v rezoliutsiiakh* (Moscow, 1953), 2:744.

Union. There was famine in many areas, agricultural output decreased, food was rationed. Serious difficulties were also apparent in industry. An objective analysis would have led to the conclusion that Stalin's leadership in the building of socialist industry and socialist agriculture was unsatisfactory. For that reason Stalin and his sympathizers cast aside any objectivity, replacing it with boundless glorification of Stalin, eradicating any criticism before it could start. Thus, extravagant tributes to Stalin originated not so much from successes as from the need to cover up the miscalculations, the mistakes, and the crimes that Stalin had committed, was committing, and was preparing to commit.

Through the Comintern Stalin's cult began to be implanted in all other Communist parties. The example of the CPSU encouraged many parties to create cults of their own leaders and to pervert democratic principles of party life.

There was no precedent for this in the history of the Marxist movement. Marx and Engels were hostile to adulation. Marx wrote to Wilhelm Blos:

Out of hatred for any cult of personality, I never allowed publication of the laudatory messages with which I was pestered from various countries during the life of the International. I never even sent answers, except for a few rebukes.[59]

Lenin felt the same way. He reacted with disapproval to the tribute that was spontaneously paid to him at the closing session of the Ninth Party Congress in 1920. He walked out of the meeting to protest against this modest attempt on the part of the delegates to show their affection and respect. Lunacharsky recalls that in 1918, soon after he was seriously wounded, Lenin called in V. D. Bonch-Bruevich and some other people and said:

I've noticed with great displeasure that my personality is beginning to be extolled. This is annoying and harmful. We all know that our cause is not in a personality. I myself would find it awkward to forbid any such phenomenon. That would be somewhat ridiculous and pretentious. But we must gradually put the brakes on this whole business.[60]

Lenin was also quite upset by Gorky's tributes—the article "V. I. Lenin" and the open letter to H. G. Wells—which were permeated with the spirit of the cult of personality. As soon as Lenin read them, he wrote the following draft for a Politburo resolution:

59. Marx and Engels, *Sochineniia*, 2nd ed., 34:241.
60. *Leninskie stranitsy* (Moscow, 1960), p. 100.

The Politburo considers the publication of Gorky's articles in *Kommunistichesky Internatsional*, no. 12 (1920), to be extremely inappropriate, especially as the feature piece, for there is nothing Communist in these articles but much that is anti-Communist. Henceforth in no case shall such articles be published in *Kommunistichesky Internatsional*.[61]

But how did Stalin react to the growing cult of his personality? The facts show not only that he accepted it calmly and as his due, which was improper enough for a Marxist-Leninist, but also that he directed and encouraged this praise himself. The facts show that he reacted hostilely not to praise but to insufficient praise, to belittling of his "great services." Far from checking his servile flatterers, he supported and promoted them.

In a 1937 interview with Lion Feuchtwanger, Stalin made a show of mild disapproval of the praise being showered on him. Feuchtwanger raised the subject of tasteless and immoderate tributes, whereupon

Stalin shrugged his shoulders. He apologized for his workers and peasants, who are too busy with other things to cultivate good taste. He joked a little about hundreds of thousands of portraits of a man with a mustache, blown up to monstrous size, which flit before his eyes at demonstrations. I pointed out that even people who obviously had taste put up busts and portraits of him—and what busts and portraits!—in utterly inappropriate places, for example at a Rembrandt exhibition. At this point he became serious. He suggested that these are people who have accepted the existing regime rather late and now are trying to prove their loyalty with doubled zeal. Yes, he considers it possible that this could be a plot of wreckers to discredit him. "A timeserving fool," said Stalin angrily, "does more harm than a hundred enemies." He tolerates all this ballyhoo, he declared, only because he knows what naive joy the festive hubbub gives to its organizers, and he knows that all this relates to him not as an individual person, but as the representative of the trend which believes that the building of a socialist economy in the USSR was more important than permanent revolution.[62]

In encouraging the cult of his own personality, Stalin was actually putting into effect some ideas of some very early opponents of Lenin, the "god-builders," who sought to make a god of "the collective power of humanity," who preached a new "socialist" religion "without a god." This school of religious philosophy, which emerged from the ideological disarray that followed the defeat of the 1905 revolution, urged that scientific

61. Lenin, PSS, 54: 429.

62. Lion Feuchtwanger, *Moskva 1937* (Moscow, 1937), pp. 51–52. [There are versions in other languages, including English, *Moscow, 1937: My Visit Described for My Friends* (New York, 1937)—D. J.]

socialism be declared the most religious of all religions. Adapting themselves to the most backward part of the popular masses, they presented socialism in a religious form. Lenin severely castigated this fideism, calling belief in any god necrophilia. Stalin ignored Lenin's fight against god-building. He put its basic ideas into effect and went much further, seeking to create a "socialist religion" with a god. And the all-powerful, all-knowing, all-holy god of the new religion was himself, Stalin.

■ 13
BUKHARIN IN THE EARLY THIRTIES

Bukharin was not chosen as a delegate to the Sixteenth Party Congress. Of course he could have attended the congress as a member of the Central Committee, but he preferred not to take part in the congress, especially since he was ill at the time. Stalin demanded new confessions from the former leaders of the right opposition, and Rykov, Tomsky, and Uglanov were expected to give speeches of recantation at the congress. Bukharin refused to follow this procedure, declining even to send a letter to the congress—an action that brought sharp criticism from many of the delegates. All the same, the congress elected not only Rykov and Tomsky but also Bukharin members of the Central Committee. Bukharin still enjoyed popularity with a substantial section of the party.

Bukharin gradually expanded his work at the Supreme Economic Council and the Academy of Sciences. Although he did not meet with former members of his "school," he met and conversed with many prominent scholars and scientists and spoke at meetings of the Academy. He helped to edit Lenin's collected works, wrote articles to mark the fortieth anniversary of Gorky's debut in literature and public affairs, and wrote articles and pamphlets with critical analyses of world capitalism. Bukharin was very interested in literature and poetry; he was good friends with Gorky and also with Osip Mandelstam. Bukharin encountered Stalin a few times at Gorky's house; they hardly ever met to discuss things, but after a while Bukharin began to write letters to Stalin rather frequently. Stalin never answered these letters; he only acknowledged that he had received them. He continued to demand a full, public recantation from Bukharin.

Bukharin did not make a condemnation of his "right-deviationist" theoretical platform until the January Central Committee plenum in 1933. At that time he declared:

Now the question stands point-blank—for the party or against the party—and no middle position is possible. Former struggles and problems have been set aside by the passage of time, for we are now a new country in our technological capacities; we are a new country in our economic structure; . . . we are a new country in our alignment of class forces.[63]

Bukharin's self-criticism was considered inadequate, and that was indicated in the plenum's resolution.

In January 1934 the Seventeenth Party Congress was held in Moscow. There Bukharin finally capitulated completely to Stalin. His lengthy speech included the following statements:

It is clear that the "Rights," of whom I was one, had a different political line, a line opposed to the all-out socialist offensive, opposed to the attack by storm on the capitalist elements that our party was beginning. It is clear that this line proposed a different pace of development, that it was in fact opposed to accelerated industrialization, that it was opposed to . . . the liquidation of the kulaks as a class, that it was opposed to the reorganization of small peasant agriculture, . . . that it was opposed to the entire new stage of a broad socialist offensive, completely failing to understand the historical necessity of that offensive and drawing political conclusions that could not have been interpreted in any way other than as anti-Leninist. . . . It is clear, further, that the victory of this deviation inevitably would have unleashed a third force and that it would have weakened the position of the working class in the extreme. . . . It would have led to intervention before we were ready . . . and, consequently, to the restoration of capitalism as the combined result of the aggravated domestic and international situation, with the forces of the proletariat weakened and the unleashing of antiproletarian, counterrevolutionary forces. . . . It is clear, further, that Comrade Stalin was completely right when he brilliantly applied Marxist-Leninist dialectics to thoroughly smash a whole series of theoretical postulates advanced by the right deviation and formulated mostly by myself.[64]

It is difficult to imagine that Bukharin said all of this sincerely. He made a compromise with his conscience. The excuse for him personally, as can be judged from the text of his speech, was the strengthening of the fascist threat in the West and East. In the face of this danger, as Bukharin suggested, it was necessary to put aside disputes and rally around the existing leadership—that is, Stalin.

This capitulation did not go unnoticed. Although Bukharin was chosen at the congress only as a candidate member of the Central Committee,

63. *Pravda*, January 14, 1933.

64. *Semnadtatyi s"ezd VKP(b). Stenograficheskii otchet* (Seventeenth Party Congress: Stenographic Record) (Moscow, 1934), pp. 124–125.

this demotion was accompanied by a return to active political and journalistic activity. In February 1934 Bukharin was appointed editor-in-
chief of *Izvestia*, the second most important Soviet newspaper. Bukharin
managed to make this newspaper interesting—by Soviet standards, of
course. The main theme of his frequent articles in *Izvestia* was the fascist
threat, but like all other Soviet newspapers *Izvestia* contributed to the
cult of Stalin, who was, in Bukharin's words "the best of the best revolutionaries, a glorious field marshal of the proletarian forces."

■ **14**
TROTSKY IN THE EARLY THIRTIES

After being deported to Turkey in February 1929, Trotsky lived for a
short time in Istanbul, then took up residence on the small island of
Prinkipo in the Sea of Marmara, an hour and a half from the Turkish
capital. There he plunged into exceptionally intensive literary-political
activity. The Western press published many articles and several books
by him. He kept up constant correspondence with his not very numerous
supporters among Western leftists, and with the help of Leon Sedov, his
son, managed to arrange publication of a Russian-language magazine, the
Bulletin of the Opposition, in which nearly half the material was written
by Trotsky himself.

Trotsky's critical comments on Stalin's policies were in most cases
completely justified. Trotsky proposed suspending "complete" collectivization, replacing it with the cautious organization of cooperatives on a
strictly voluntary basis and in accordance with the Soviet Union's actual
resources. He called for an end to the administrative dispossession of the
kulaks and a return to the policy of government restrictions on kulak
agriculture. He also urged that Stalin's unrealistic superindustrialization
plans be reduced. But at the same time Trotsky took at face value the
trials against "wreckers" from the bourgeois intelligentsia. He even criticized the sentences against leaders of the "Industrial Party" as too lenient.

In the *Bulletin of the Opposition* Trotsky published an article accusing
Stalin and his supporters of having promoted "hired agents of foreign
capital and of the Russian émigré comprador bourgeoisie" to leading
positions in the Soviet economy. The article says in part:

Isn't it clear that the indictment of the Industrial Party by Krylenko is at the same time an indictment of the Stalinist upper crust, which, in its struggle against the Bolshevik-Leninists, was really the political instrument of world capitalism?[65]

Trotsky also believed in the existence of the mythical "Working Peasants' Party." When in 1931 the show trial of the "Union Bureau" was staged in Moscow Trotsky would not credit the convincing arguments of the émigré Menshevik leadership but instead accepted the unsubstantiated arguments of the prosecutor Krylenko. Although there was no evidence except confessions by the defendants, Trotsky wrote that the guilt of the defendants had been "irrefutably established."[66]

Not until five years later, in a note to an article in the *Bulletin of the Opposition*, did Trotsky write:

The editors of the *Bulletin* must acknowledge that at the time of the Menshevik trial they greatly underestimated the degree of shamelessness of Stalinist "justice" and in light of this took too seriously the confessions of the former Mensheviks.[67]

Trotsky energetically protested against the execution of Blumkin. But when he commented on the Ryutin affair [of September–October 1932], he seemed to gloat over the defeat of the "Ryutin group," recalling that it was Ryutin who, with Uglanov, had led the struggle against the Trotskyists in the Moscow party organization.

Nor did Trotsky abandon his general theoretical constructs. In 1930, for example, he still argued as follows:

It is true that the fundamental difficulties of socialist construction are beyond the power of the leadership; they lie in the impossibility of establishing a socialist society in a single country, moreover a particularly backward country.[68]

Even when Trotsky acknowledged the considerable success of socialist industry in the Soviet Union and the stability of the system established there, he did not forget to add that the long-term success of socialist construction was possible only on the basis of worldwide proletarian revolution and an international planned economy.

65. *Biulleten' oppozitsii* (November–December 1930), no. 17–18, p. 21. [Cf. *Writings of Leon Trotsky, 1930–1931* (New York, 1973), p. 67.—G. S.]

66. *Biulleten' oppozitsii* (April 1931), no. 20, p. 9. [Cf. *Writings of Leon Trotsky, 1930–1931*, p. 219.—G. S.]

67. *Biulleten' oppozitsii* (July–August 1936), no. 51, p. 15. [The editors' note was appended to an article by Victor Serge exposing the Stalinist frame-up methods in the "Union Bureau" case.—G. S.]

68. *Biulleten' oppozitsii* (April 1930), no. 10, p. 2. [Cf. *Writings of Leon Trotsky, 1930* (New York, 1975), p. 136.—G. S.]

I have mentioned above that in 1934 in some sections of the Comintern a movement began toward a united front with the Social Democrats, with the goal of preventing any further fascist gains and reducing the threat of world war. But at this time Trotsky was exerting great efforts to establish the Fourth International, and in his treatment of the Social Democrats he continued to defend a position that even Stalin found it necessary to gradually abandon. In May 1934 a document entitled "The Fourth International and War" was published. It included the following assertions:

A modern war between the great powers does not signify a conflict between democracy and fascism but a struggle of two imperialisms for the redivision of the world. Moreover, the war must inevitably assume an international character and in both camps will be found fascist (semifascist, Bonapartist, etc.) as well as "democratic" states. . . .

The incompatibility of Social Democratic policy with the historic interests of the proletariat is incomparably deeper and sharper now than on the eve of the imperialist war. The struggle with the patriotic prejudices of the masses means, above all, an irreconcilable struggle against the Second International as an organization, as a party, as a program, as a banner.[69]

It can be assumed, of course, that if in 1924–1925 the Trotsky group and not the Stalin group had come to power, the "Great Terror" of the middle and late thirties would not have occurred. But Trotsky cannot be idolized; the Left Opposition was not able to establish an acceptable alternative to the Stalin leadership. In the early thirties Trotsky made the following observations about the capitulations of his recent followers:

Revolution is a harsh school. It is unsparing of spines, whether physical or moral. An entire generation has spent itself, becoming drained physically and spiritually. Only a few have survived. The overwhelming majority of the Stalinist tops consists of men drained to the core. The appurtenances of the apparatus invest them with an imposing appearance, serving them as a parade uniform serves a senile general. Historical events will continue to expose and to confirm the hollowness of the Stalinist "[Old] Guard" at each new trial. The capitulations on the question of Trotskyism have served thousands and tens of thousands as training in the art of capitulation as such. The succession of political generations presents a major and a very complex problem which is posed in its own peculiar manner before each class and each party. But all must face it. Lenin often castigated the so-called "Old Bolsheviks," even remarking on occasion that revolutionists on reaching the age of [fifty] should be consigned to the hereafter. This grim jest contains a serious political thought. Each revolutionary generation becomes, after attaining certain limits, an obstacle to the further development of

69. *Chetvertyi Internatsional i voina. Tezisy* (Geneva, 1934), pp. 13, 16. [Cf. *Writings of Leon Trotsky, 1933–1934* (New York, 1975), pp. 307, 310. —G. S.]

those ideas which it had served. Generally speaking, men are quickly drained by politics and all the more so by revolution. Exceptions are rare. But there are exceptions. Otherwise there would be no such thing as ideological continuity. . . . Today the theoretical education of the younger generation is our supreme task. This is the meaning of the struggle we are waging against the epigones who despite their seeming strength have already been drained ideologically.[70]

Trotsky was not an "Old Bolshevik," and here he is most likely distorting the meaning and form of what Lenin might have said. Besides, for Trotsky, who was in exile when he wrote this, it was just words. He no longer possessed the power to consign people to the hereafter. But Stalin, who read Trotsky's articles and books in those years, sometimes listened closely to what he had to say. If we compare Trotsky's words given above with what Stalin accomplished in 1936–1939, consigning to the hereafter the major part of the Leninist Old Guard, that is, the entire generation of "Old Bolsheviks" who were close to fifty years of age, we might even think that Stalin had followed Trotsky's advice. But this is not so. Stalin was completely independent in his decision, and he destroyed an entire generation of Bolsheviks not because it was "drained" and "spiritually spent." These people were not "an obstacle to the further development which they had served" but to the development and deepening of Stalin's autocratic power. That is what led Stalin to the idea of consigning all of the "Old Bolsheviks," for whom he felt as much hostility as Trotsky, to the hereafter and relying on the younger generation of party activists, who had not gone through the school of revolution sufficiently but who had quite thoroughly passed through the Stalin school of falsification.

70. Leon Trotsky, *Stalinskaia shkola falsifikatsii* (Berlin, 1932), pp. 110–111. [Cf. Trotsky, *The Stalin School of Falsification* (New York, 1971), pp. 98–99, —G. S.]

STALIN'S USURPATION OF POWER, AND THE GREAT TERROR

5

THE KIROV ASSASSINATION AND THE PURGE TRIALS

■ 1

THE BEGINNINGS OF NEW OPPOSITION, 1934

Despite the very severe situation in the Soviet Union in the years 1930–1933 there was no serious opposition to Stalin. No one disputed his role as party leader because first of all, his personal power was very great in the early thirties. He had virtually unchallenged control not only over the rapidly growing and highly centralized party apparatus but also, through Voroshilov, over the Red Army and, through Yagoda and Ya. D. Agranov, over the security organs. Under these conditions opposition to Stalin was extremely dangerous; many who in the past had been quite critical of him now felt frozen by fear. Secondly, many of the miscalculations and crimes that Stalin committed before 1934 were not fully revealed until later, some only after his death. Only a very few people, for example, were privy to the secret rigging of the 1930–1931 trials. Moreover, some of Stalin's crimes and blunders were extolled by the propaganda machine as great achievements.

It is important to bear in mind that the exceptional situation that arose in the Soviet Union in the early thirties actually contributed to the strengthening of Stalin's power. Faced with unprecedented difficulties, many party leaders—even those dissatisfied with Stalin—thought it impossible to begin a new struggle within the party, lest the situation in the country become even worse. They did not see anyone in higher party circles worthy of replacing Stalin and were afraid that if a different course were taken or an attempt made to stop or retreat on the course being followed, everything might be lost. Even a Trotskyist made the comment: "If it were not for that so-and-so [Stalin] . . . everything would have fallen to pieces by now. It is he who keeps everything together."[1] In addition, by 1933–1934 many party leaders had greatly changed. Stalin succeeded in subjecting—and corrupting—a significant portion of the party cadres. Many of the party leaders actively participated in the mistakes and crimes of the late twenties and early thirties, and these people could hardly have become energetic critics of Stalin. (This aspect of the question will be discussed further below.)

Nevertheless, simultaneously with the growing cult of Stalin, a certain estrangement did emerge in the early thirties between Stalin and a significant portion of veteran cadre elements in the party. These were Old Bolsheviks, not former opposition leaders; in fact, they belonged to the basic nucleus of party leadership that took shape in the struggle against the oppositions. Stalin sensed this estrangement and, beginning in the early thirties, relied more and more on young party officials, handpicked by himself, slighting many veterans of the revolution, who, as he saw it, had played out their roles. At this time, on Stalin's suggestion, the Society of Old Bolsheviks was disbanded.

For their part some Old Bolsheviks became increasingly dissillusioned with Stalin, disturbed by the growth of his arbitrary rule. Stalin's unchanging nastiness and increasing unwillingness to consider any opinion but his own brought some party leaders to protest, although Stalin cut such objections short. Even I. P. Tovstukha, who had once been Stalin's personal secretary, began to express dissatisfaction. Once, for example,

1. Robert Conquest, *The Great Terror: Stalin's Purge of the Thirties*, rev. ed. (New York, 1968), p. 60.

when Tovstukha was away, Stalin reorganized the section of the Central Committee Tovstukha headed, firing some people and transferring others. When Tovstukha learned of this, he sent in a strong protest against such arbitrary action. Stalin disposed of the protest with this notation: "Ha, ha, ha. Here's a real bantam." After this conflict with Stalin, Tovstukha was reassigned to the Marx-Engels Institute. An early death saved him from a more painful end.

In this connection it is worth examining the case of the Eismont-Tolmachev-Smirnov group, which was taken up at a joint session of the Central Committee and Central Control Commission in January 1933. The three men involved were well-known party leaders: A. P. Smirnov had headed several different people's commissariats in the twenties and had served as a Central Committee secretary and member of the Collegium of the Supreme Economic Council; N. B. Eismont was people's commisar of food supply in the early thirties; and V. N. Tolmachev was people's commissar of internal affairs for the RSFSR and a member of the Central Executive Committee. The January 1933 plenum passed a resolution condemning their formation of an underground factional group, allegedly dedicated to the disruption of industrialization and collectivization and the restoration of capitalism, the kulaks in particular. It was therefore resolved to expel Eismont and Tolmachev from the party, while Smirnov was removed from the Central Committee with a warning that expulsion from the party would follow if his future work did not merit trust.[2]

Today we know that the chief sin of Smirnov, Eismont, and Tolmachev was a little discussion among a few people about replacing Stalin as general secretary. "Only enemies," Stalin told the Central Committee meeting, "can say that you can remove Stalin and nothing will happen."[3]

The Eismont-Tolmachev-Smirnov group did not represent a real danger to Stalin. It is another matter altogether, however, when we consider the disagreements in the Politburo, which did not always end in victory for Stalin. I have noted above that in the fall of 1932 Stalin insisted that Ryutin and the leaders of his group be shot, whereas the Politburo passed a resolution merely sending them into internal exile. Gradually there took shape a group of more moderate members of the Politburo, consisting of Kirov, Kalinin, Ordzhonikidze, Kuibyshev, and Stanislav Kosior.

During the famine of 1933 in the Ukraine and Northern Caucasus

2. *KPSS v rezoliutsiiakh*, 2nd ed. (Moscow, 1953), 2:742. A few years later Smirnov was shot on Stalin's orders, as was Tolmachev. Eismont died earlier as the result of an accident.

3. *Vsesoiuznoe soveshchanie istorikov* (Moscow, 1964), p. 291.

Stalin insisted on intensified repression against peasants fleeing their villages, while Kirov called for restraint. In one of his speeches at the Politburo Kirov called for "restoration of Soviet power in the country-side," where a state of emergency had been in effect since collectivization began and where the political sections of the MTSs wielded the real power, rather than the official institutions of power—the village soviets. Soon after Kirov's speech, by a decision of the party's Central Commit-tee, the special political departments of the MTSs were abolished. In most rural areas the powers of the village soviets were restored. Within the MTSs a new official post was established: deputy director for political work.

During 1933 Kirov spoke in the Politburo several times in favor of more flexible policies and a certain "liberalization." These speeches met with a positive response from leading party officials. It was not without Kirov's influence that Zinoviev and Kamenev were restored to party membership during 1933. In Leningrad Kirov opposed repression against former oppositionists. Those who accepted the "general line" were read-mitted to the party. Kirov also spoke in favor of improving the party's relations with writers and with other groups among the creative intelli-gentsia, and he had a part in the decision to abolish the Russian Associa-tion of Proletarian Writers (RAPP) and begin preparations for the First Congress of Soviet Writers. (For more about RAPP, see below, ch. 6, section 11.)

Dissatisfaction, disillusionment, and protest over the situation in the Soviet Union and Stalin's policies were noticeable not only among some Old Bolsheviks but also among some young people in the party and Komsomol. Often in the mid-twenties Komsomol activists had enthusi-astically taken up the slogans of the Left Opposition. On the other hand, Bukharin had enjoyed great personal popularity among Komsomol mem-bers in the twenties. In the early thirties younger party members suf-fered disillusionment not only with the behavior of their former idols but also with the policies of Stalin. This resulted in the formation of many small discussion circles *(kruzhki)*. In most cases matters were limited to meetings and discussions among small groups of friends at one another's homes or at parties. At times, however, things went as far as public demonstrations or the scattering of leaflets, actions that were immedi-ately judged to be "counterrevolutionary." In the summer of 1933 the NKVD arrested several groups of young people. Stalin insisted on ex-tremely rigorous punishment, but the Politburo decided to apply "the supreme measure" only in exceptional cases. In fact, the sentences given to those taking part in oppositional demonstrations were relatively mild.

In light of all this tension, certain events connected with the Seventeenth Party Congress in January–February 1934 acquire special significance. To a superficial observer this congress was a demonstration of love and devotion to Stalin. What went on in the corridors at that congress is a different matter. If some scanty reports from Old Bolsheviks are put together, it can be concluded that a considerable number of leading party members formed an illegal bloc at this congress, consisting basically of secretaries of *oblast* committees and secretaries of the non-Russian central committees, people who had felt the results of Stalin's policy errors more than anyone else. The reports say that one of the active members of this bloc was I. M. Vareikis, who then held the post of secretary of the party's province committee in the Central Black Earth region. Conversations were held at the Moscow apartments of several highly placed officials, with Ordzhonikidze, Mikoyan, Mamia Orakhelashvili, and Grigory Petrovsky taking part. Suggestions were made that Stalin be transferred to the post of chairman of the Council of People's Commissars or chairman of the Central Executive Committee and that Kirov be elected general secretary. A group of delegates to the congress had a talk with Kirov on these matters, but he emphatically opposed such a plan, and without his consent it could not be carried out. In *History of the CPSU*, a textbook published in 1962 under the editorship of Boris Ponamarev, a secretary of the Central Committee, there is a very sparing reference to these corridor discussions at the Seventeenth Congress.

The abnormal situation developing in the party alarmed some Communists, especially the old Leninist cadres. Many delegates at the congress, especially those who were familiar with Lenin's Testament, thought that the time had come to transfer Stalin from the post of general secretary to some other job.[4]

Dissatisfaction with Stalin was also expressed in the election of the Central Committee by the Seventeenth Congress. The voting took place at the evening session of the congress on February 9, 1934. The chairman of the elections commission was V. P. Zatonsky, who had replaced Skrypnik as commissar of education in the Ukraine. His deputy was the Old Bolshevik V. M. Verkhovykh. When the elections commission opened the ballot boxes late that night it turned out that Stalin had received

4. *Istoriia KPSS* (Moscow, 1962), p. 486. Later editions of this textbook omitted the sentence I have quoted, along with many other sentences and paragraphs critical of Stalin.

fewer votes than any other candidate. Only three votes had been cast against Kirov, while 270 delegates voted against Stalin, who was elected only because there were exactly as many candidates as there were members to be elected.[5]

The elections commission could not bring itself to announce these results even to the congress delegates. According to Verkhovykh, who by some miracle survived all the horrors of Stalin's purges, prisons, and camps, Zatonsky immediately reported the voting results to Lazar Kaganovich, who was running the organizational side of the congress. Kaganovich ordered the removal of almost all the ballots on which Stalin's name was crossed out. On February 10 the congress was told that only three votes had been cast against Stalin, the same as against Kirov. Neither in the newspapers nor in the stenographic record of the congress was any reference made to the number of votes cast for one or another candidate. But Stalin knew the actual results, and he also found out about some of the discussions among congress delegates concerning his transfer to a lesser post.

Rumors about the unfavorable vote for Stalin in February 1934 circulated in Moscow and reached beyond Soviet borders. It was even said that Stalin had not won enough votes to be elected to the Central Committee. *The Socialist Courier*, published in Paris by the Mensheviks, reported that Stalin had received fewer votes than two other candidates and that the largest number of votes had been for Kalinin.[6]

In his book about Stalin the American historian Adam Ulam disputes the evidence cited above in regard to vote tampering at the Seventeenth Congress. Without presenting any proof, Ulam states, "There is every reason to believe that the election of the Central Committee was unanimous." Ulam considers Verkhovykh's account suspect, since his recollections "show unfamiliarity with the voting procedures for the Central Committee. The voting was secret, and ever since 1923 the announced results had not included the number of votes received by successful candidates."[7] In this instance, it is Ulam who is mistaken. In a memorandum submitted to the Central Committee even before the Twentieth Party Congress, Verkhovykh described in detail how the votes were

5. Anton Antonov-Ovseyenko, in *The Time of Stalin: Portrait of a Tyranny* (New York, 1981), pp. 80–83, gives the figure of 292 votes against Stalin. The difference between his information and mine is not very great.

6. *Sotsialisticheskii vestnik*, February 25, 1934.

7. Adam B. Ulam, *Stalin: The Man and His Era* (New York, 1973), p. 374.

counted in the Central Committee election at the Seventeenth Congress. It is true that the voting was always by secret ballot and that after 1923 the results were no longer published in the press or in the stenographic records of congresses, but they were still announced to the congress delegates. In any case, it would have been difficult to keep the results secret, since the elections commission had many members—more than forty at the Seventeenth Congress.

In 1957 a special commission of the Central Committee was established to check into Verkhovykh's report. It examined the documents and materials in the party archives relating to the Seventeenth Congress, and broke open the sealed packages containing the ballots cast in the 1934 vote for the Central Committee. The commission was headed by Olga Shatunovskaya, a veteran Communist and member of the Party Control Commission. According to her, 267 ballots were missing from the packages, which were opened in the presence of responsible officials of the party archives and Pyotr Pospelov, the then director of the Institute of Marxism-Leninism. In other words, in 1934 the elections commission had announced a figure different from the actual number of ballots preserved in the sealed packages. In Verkhovykh's opinion the ballots had simply been destroyed. It may be assumed, however, that they were taken away for thoroughgoing analysis by the GPU.

The composition of the Central Committee was altered significantly at the Seventeenth Congress. A number of former members undesirable to Stalin were not reelected, among them Filipp Goloshchekin, E. I. Kviring, N. N. Kolotilov, V. V. Lominadze, G. I. Lomov, Mamia Orakhelashvili, Lavrenty Kartvelishvili, and K. A. Rumyantsev. Among those reduced to candidate membership were Bukharin, Rykov, Tomsky, and S. Shvarts. Such prominent officials of the security police as Vsevolod Balitsky and Yefim Yevdokimov were for the first time elected to the Central Committee. (Previously they had not been even candidate members.) Lavrenty Beria and Nikolai Yezhov likewise became full members without having been candidate members, as did Nikita Khrushchev. They were all favorites of Stalin at the time. Lev Mekhlis and Aleksandr Poskrebyshev, who were not even delegates to the congress but served in Stalin's personal secretariat, became candidate members of the Central Committee. Genrikh Yagoda and Dzhafar Bagirov of the security police also became full and candidate members, respectively.

After the Seventeenth Congress Yezhov and Mekhlis were given key posts in the Central Committee apparatus. The GPU was reorganized as the NKVD (People's Commissariat of Internal Affairs), although this was taken by some at the time as a sign of liberalization. Kirov was elected a secretary of the Central Committee, and Stalin insisted that he move to Moscow from Leningrad, but Kirov was reluctant to do so. In support of Kirov's position a delegation of Leningrad Bolsheviks went to see Stalin, who gave them a very cold reception. This is reported by A. M. Durmashkin, who knew Kirov well. Stalin agreed that Kirov could remain temporarily as head of the Leningrad party organization, but during 1934 Stalin gave Kirov several assignments far exceeding the duties of Leningrad party secretary (such as to help with the harvest in Kazakhstan).

According to Durmashkin, an obvious estrangement between Stalin and Kirov could be felt in 1934, although previously they had been considered close friends. Stalin had been in the habit of calling Kirov in Leningrad quite frequently, but these calls stopped almost completely. Nevertheless, Kirov continued to work energetically and rather independently. For example, he allowed Ryazanov, an "unreconstructed" opponent of Stalin's policies, who had been expelled from the party, to move to Leningrad. When disagreements arose in the Comintern on the question of relations with the Social Democrats, Kirov invariably spoke in support of those who called for a turn toward a united front policy.

From everything I have said above the conclusion may be drawn that despite the expressions of praise and support, the events at the Seventeenth Congress showed a growing lack of confidence in Stalin among wide circles of party activists. Stalin was always extremely sensitive to such signals. He felt that his position and power were in danger, and this danger was personified for him by Sergei Mironovich Kirov.

■ 2

THE KIROV ASSASSINATION

On December 1, 1934, in Smolny, a shot in the back killed Sergei Mironovich Kirov, member of the Politburo, secretary of the Central Committee, and first secretary of the Leningrad oblast committee. Several details of this crime can be learned from biographies of Kirov published in the sixties.[8] However, in many respects the real motives and circumstances of the assassination, which became the first link in a long

---

8. For example, S. Sinel'nikov, *S. M. Kirov—zhizn' i deiatel 'nost'* (Moscow, 1964); and S. Krasnikov, *Kirov* (Moscow, 1964).

chain of tragic events lasting for many years, have remained unclarified to this day.

The reports of the assassination said that the shot was fired by a young party member, Leonid Nikolaev, who had been caught while trying to escape. It would seem that this would have made possible a careful investigation. In fact the investigation in December 1934 was carried out in complete violation of the law, of common sense, of the desire to find and punish the real culprits. Nor was the truth established by further NKVD investigations in 1936 and in 1937–1938.

At the Twentieth Party Congress Khrushchev noted several suspicious aspects of the 1934 investigation of the Kirov murder. A special commission of the Central Committee was established in 1956 to make a new investigation. Although the events had occurred more than twenty years earlier, the new investigation lasted several years, obtaining a very large amount of material. Testimony was taken from more than three thousand persons. Naturally much of this evidence was imprecise, contradictory, and dubious, but there was some extremely important testimony that did not raise any doubts and that allowed the commission to draw some conclusions in a final document summarizing its work. The document was not published, however. According to Olga Shatunovskaya, a member of the commission, who was awarded the Order of Lenin for the work accomplished and then retired on a pension, Khrushchev himself, when he read the commission's conclusions, locked the document in his safe and said: "As long as imperialism exists in the world, we will not be able to publish this document."

No honest historian could consider Khrushchev's decision justified or his reasoning persuasive. Without claiming to have a full account or explanation of the murder, I will present some evidence and hypotheses relating to the Kirov assassination. First, let me cite some personal recollections. In 1934 my family lived in Leningrad, and I remember well the strong emotions felt by my parents and everyone around us at the news of Kirov's death. In the thirties children began to take an interest in politics very early, and after the Kirov assassination I began to read the newspapers regularly, not only the Leningrad youth paper *Smena*[9] but many others as well, including *Pravda* and *Izvestia*.

Some Western studies report that certain sections of the Soviet popu-

9. The first published item signed "Roy Medvedev" appeared in *Smena* on December 1, 1935. It was entitled "On the Death of Kirov."

lation were pleased by the Kirov assassination. Adam Ulam, for example, says:

Anyone familiar with the history of the Russian revolutionary movement must know how intoxicating the news of a successful political assassination can be to victims of political repression. "A sixteen-year-old student was said to have declared, 'They killed Kirov; now let them kill Stalin,' " states one of the many similar reports found in the archives of the Smolensk party organization.[10]

Of course there can be no question that there was room in Soviet society for the most varied responses to the Kirov assassination. However, among victims of political repression the predominant mood was not one of "intoxication," as Ulam suggests, but fear, which proved to be well founded. Among the majority of Soviet young people the assassination aroused profound grief and anger, feelings that also prevailed among the working class of Leningrad, where Kirov was quite popular. At any rate, I remember well the workers' silent torchlight procession, full of grief, along the embankment of Vasilyevsky Island, culminating in an immense memorial rally at the Winter Palace on the night that Kirov was killed.

On the morning of the next day, December 2, the rumor spread through Leningrad that Stalin had arrived. He came by a special train with Molotov, Voroshilov, Yezhov, Yagoda, Zhdanov, Yakov Agranov, and Leonid Zakovsky. The leaders of the Leningrad party organization, headed by Mikhail Chudov, second secretary of the oblast committee, and the Leningrad NKVD, headed by Filipp Medved, went to welcome Stalin at the station. It was said that when Stalin stepped onto the platform he refused to shake hands with the welcoming party and that without removing his gloves, he struck Medved in the face. Right after his arrival, Stalin took complete charge of the investigation.

Kirov's assassination was obviously not the work of Nikolaev alone. Pyotr Chagin, a prominent party official and close comrade of Kirov, has told me that several attempts had been made on Kirov's life in 1934, including an attempt during his trip to Kazakhstan in the summer of 1934. It was a real manhunt, directed by a strong hand.

As for Nikolaev, all sources agree that he was a psychologically unbal-

10. Ulam, p. 385. Ulam quotes from Merle Fainsod, *Smolensk Under Soviet Rule* (Cambridge, Mass., 1958), p. 422. The Smolensk archives were captured by the Germans during the invasion of the Soviet Union in 1941. Later the archives fell into British and American hands. [For more on the Smolensk archives, see below, Chapter Seven, note 14. —G. S.]

anced individual who acted at first on his own initiative. A vain and embittered failure, he imagined himself a new Zhelyabov[11] and planned the murder of Kirov as an important political act. Kirov liked to walk around Leningrad, and Nikolaev carefully studied the route of these walks. Of course Kirov was carefully guarded; his guards, headed by the NKVD official Borisov, walked before and after him in civilian clothes.

One day the guards' suspicions were aroused by a passerby who tried to get too close. He was detained. This was Nikolaev. His briefcase had a slit in the back, through which a revolver could be drawn without opening the briefcase. And a revolver was there, loaded, along with a map of Kirov's route. Nikolaev was immediately arrested and sent to Leningrad NKVD headquarters, where he was questioned by Ivan Zaporozhets, the deputy director of the Leningrad NKVD, who was a close confidant of Yagoda's and who had just been appointed to the Leningrad post. (It was subsequently explained that Zaporozhets and other officials of the Leningrad NKVD were active participants in the plot. But the director, Filipp Medved, apparently did not take part in the planning of the assassination.) After questioning Nikolaev, Zaporozhets did not report to his superior, Medved, who was a close acquaintance of Kirov's, but instead phoned Moscow and reported everything to Yagoda, then commissar of internal affairs and one of the people Stalin most trusted. A few hours later, Yagoda instructed Zaporozhets to let Nikolaev go. With whom had Yagoda consulted in the meantime? During the trial of the so-called "Right-Trotskyite bloc" in 1938, the defendant Yagoda confirmed these facts, but claimed that he got his instructions in 1934 from Yenukidze and Rykov. Nowadays this story is not believed by anyone: Yagoda had far more influential patrons.

When Nikolaev was released, he acted in a very clumsy way, and a few days later, on a bridge, he was again arrested by Kirov's guards. For a second time the same loaded revolver was taken from him. The strange liberalism of the Leningrad NKVD officials, who again let Nikolaev go, aroused serious suspicions among Kirov's guards. Some tried to protest, but they were told at the NKVD that it wasn't their business. Individual guards had their party cards temporarily taken away and were then threatened with expulsion. Nevertheless, Borisov told Kirov about these suspicious incidents.

As we know, Nikolaev was released again, and soon succeeded in

11. [Zhelyabov was the main leader of the People's Will group that assassinated Tsar Alexander II in 1881. —G. S.]

killing Kirov. Stalin, after arriving in Leningrad, decided to question Nikolaev personally. What happened at this interrogation can be pieced together from several reports, including those of Zhdanov's assistant I. M. Kulagin, who was present, the above-mentioned Pyotr Chagin, and V. Sh——, a friend of Mikhail Chudov.

Behind a table in a large room sat Stalin, Molotov, Voroshilov, Zhdanov, and several others. In back of them stood a group of Leningrad party officials, headed by Chudov, and, standing apart from them, a group of Chekists. (On the day of Kirov's murder Zaporozhets was vacationing in the south and could hardly have returned to Leningrad by the following day.) Nikolaev was brought in, held under the arms on both sides. Stalin asked him why he shot Kirov. Falling on his knees and pointing at the group of Chekists standing behind Stalin, Nikolaev shouted, "They made me do it!" Then several Chekists ran over and began to beat Nikolaev with their pistol butts. Covered with blood and unconscious, he was carried out of the room. Some of those present, including Chudov, believed that Nikolaev had been killed, and that another person was substituted for Nikolaev in the trial at the end of December. Chudov later told this to Sh——.[12] Actually, this was not the case. Nikolaev had been taken to the prison hospital after the interrogation and was revived with difficulty by alternating hot and cold baths. Neither Chudov nor Kulagin could understand why Stalin had not stopped the Chekists from beating Nikolaev or how they could have so grossly exceeded their authority in his presence.

Borisov was to be interrogated after Nikolaev. He had been arrested immediately after the assassination. Although all others arrested in the case were brought to the interrogation in automobiles, for some reason Borisov was brought in a closed truck guarded by several Chekists armed with crowbars. One sat behind the driver. On Voinov Street, as the truck was passing the blind wall of a warehouse, the Chekist suddenly jerked the wheel. The driver nonetheless managed to avoid hitting the wall head-on; the truck struck it a glancing blow and then managed to reach the place of the interrogation. But Borisov was dead, killed by the crowbars. The autopsy report drew the false conclusion that he had died

---

12. In most cases persons I interviewed gave me permission to refer to them by name in publishing their testimony. However, there were exceptions, Sh—— being one of them. Stalin's interrogation of Nikolaev is also described by Antonov-Ovseyenko in *The Time of Stalin*, p. 93, but with certain details that seem doubtful to me. In particular, Stalin would hardly have kicked Nikolaev with his boot.

in the truck accident. Some of the doctors who signed this report were alive after the Twentieth Party Congress in 1956, and they gave written testimony to the commission that they had been forced to write the autopsy report and that Borisov had died from the blows of heavy metal objects on his head.

The strange story of Borisov's death, following his repeated efforts to prevent the assassination of Kirov, was reported to the Twenty-Second Party Congress in 1961 by Khrushchev. He added that the men who killed Borisov were themselves shot, and he promised a careful investigation.[13] Following this revelation and others at both the Twentieth and Twenty-Second congresses, hundreds of people wrote to the Central Committee expressing their doubts about the official account of Kirov's assassination and providing much testimony that shed new light on the crime. Copies of some of their letters are in my archive. For example, I. P. Aleksakhin, a veteran party member, told what he had heard at the Linkovy mine from a fellow prisoner by the name of Duboshin, who had earlier been head of the Petropavlovsk NKVD. Duboshin told Aleksakhin that when he was living in the Hotel Selent in Moscow in 1934, an NKVD executive closely connected with the central leadership dropped in on him and said: "A terrible assassination is being planned in Leningrad." At the time Duboshin did not attach any importance to these words, but after Kirov's assassination he said to the same executive: "It appears that some of you knew about the plans for the attempt on Kirov's life." But the other man could give no convincing explanation.

Yevgeny Frolov, a party member since 1919, who in 1934 was head of the Machine Building Sector of the Central Committee's Industrial Section, submitted this report: On the morning of December 1, 1934, Yezhov, who was then head of the Industrial Section and was also charged by Stalin with checking up on NKVD activity, went to Stalin's office and spent a good part of the day there. That was unusual; there had not previously been an occasion for Yezhov to spend so many hours with Stalin. Yezhov did not return to the Industrial Section until 7 P.M., when he called one of his assistants, V. Tsesarky, and ordered him to get ready for an immediate trip to Leningrad.

It is well known that Kirov was soon replaced as the first secretary of the party's Leningrad oblast committee by Andrei Zhdanov. I. M. Kulagin, Zhdanov's assistant, submitted this report: Several months after

---

13. *Dvadtsat' vtoroi s"ezd KPSS. Stenograficheskii otchet* (Moscow, 1962), 2:582–584.

Kirov's assassination, Borisov's wife came to the party headquarters in Smolny. She said that she had been put by force into an insane asylum but had managed to escape, and she asked to be taken into protective custody since "they" wanted to poison her. She also told Kulagin that the NKVD had interrogated her, trying to find out whether her husband had told her anything before Kirov's assassination. She was willing to be transferred into an ordinary hospital. At that time Kulagin could not do this without notifying the Leningrad NKVD. He phoned the deputy director and got permission for the woman to be admitted to the city hospital. Some time later Kulagin learned that the woman died in the hospital; there were indications of poisoning.

M. Smorodina, the daughter of Pyotr Smorodin, one of Kirov's chief aides, reported that when Medved, the head of the Leningrad NKVD, heard of Kirov's murder, he rushed to Smolny without hat and coat in the middle of the winter. But he was stopped at the entrance by unknown Chekists from the Moscow NKVD, who had somehow appeared at the entrance before him. Kirov was killed right outside the office of Mikhail Chudov, Kirov's deputy (second secretary of the party's Leningrad obkom). When Chudov heard shots, he ran out of his office. Kirov was already dead. Chudov ordered that nothing be touched so as not to interfere with the investigation, then he immediately phoned Stalin in Moscow. Stalin ordered that the meeting of the active party membership of Leningrad, scheduled for that day, be canceled and that Smolny be surrounded by NKVD troops. Medved was not at his office in NKVD headquarters at the time, and the orders were carried out without his knowledge. Apparently Medved and the NKVD units called out by Chudov did not "recognize" one another.

According to S. N. Osmolovskaya, the wife of Kirov's close friend Pyotr Petrovsky, an attempt had been made on Petrovsky's life a few days before Kirov's assassination. Two strangers came up to him on the boulevard and began to beat him with iron objects, but he managed to cover his head and escape. When he learned of Kirov's assassination, he immediately declared that it was Stalin's work. Quite a few such stories could be cited.

Soon after Kirov's assassination, Medved, Zaporozhets, and several other leading figures in the Leningrad NKVD were removed from their positions on charges of criminal negligence. But they were given light punishment at first; they were sent to work for the NKVD in the Far East. Only in 1937 were they shot. "It is possible," Khrushchev stated in his "secret speech" to the Twentieth Party Congress, "that they were later shot to cover up all traces of the organizers of Kirov's assassination."

The following sequence of events is also noteworthy. On the evening of December 1, 1934, by an order from Stalin over the telephone and without the approval of the Politburo—which was formally obtained by a referendum only two days later—the secretary of the Presidium of the Central Executive Committee, Yenukidze, signed a decree that would later serve as the basis for a great deal of repression: (1) Investigating authorities were to speed up their work on cases of those accused of preparing or carrying out terrorist acts. (2) Judicial authorities were not to postpone the execution of sentences of capital punishment because of appeals for clemency by criminals of this category, since the Presidium of the Central Executive Committee did not consider it possible to consider such appeals. (3) The agencies of the NKVD were to execute sentences of capital punishment on criminals of the above-mentioned category immediately after such sentences had been issued.[14]

This decree, unprecedented in peacetime, specified that the entire investigation of such cases be concluded in not more than ten days and that the indictment be handed over to the accused only one day before the trial. Moreover, the trial was to be conducted without contesting parties—that is, without defense lawyers. Thus any decision of the court was immediately regarded as correct and was not subject to any kind of review. The decree gave the widest scope to lawlessness, since any "political case" could be represented as preparation for a terrorist act. Also, the ten-day limit encouraged superficial examination and outright fabrication. It obstructed the determination of the guilt or innocence of suspects as well as the discovery of all those really involved in a crime.

On the basis of this decree, dozens of cases of counterrevolutionary crimes, which were in no way connected with Kirov's murder but happened to be at various stages of investigation on December 1, were quickly transferred to the Military Collegium of the Supreme Court and just as quickly decided there. On December 5, in closed session, the Military Collegium sentenced almost all the accused to be shot. They were shot at once. This was reported the following day, which was the day of Kirov's funeral. In Leningrad thirty-nine people were shot this way, in Moscow twenty-nine. During the next few days twelve people were reported arrested in Minsk, nine of whom were shot, and thirty-

14. The text of the decree is in *Sbornik materialov po istorii sotsialisticheskogo ugolov-nogo zakonodatel'stva* (Moscow, 1938), p. 314.

seven in Kiev, twenty-eight of whom were shot. It was also reported that the Military Collegium remanded some cases for further investigation, which demonstrates the juridical absurdity of the order to speed up investigations.[15]

The investigation of Kirov's assassination was also carried out with unusual haste. On December 22 a report said that Nikolaev belonged to an underground terrorist organization set up by members of the former Zinovievist opposition, who killed Kirov on the order of the "Leningrad Opposition Center" in revenge for Kirov's struggle against the opposition. The same report named the members of the "Leningrad Opposition Center" who were arrested by the NKVD. Most of them had been members of the Zinovievist opposition. On December 27 the indictment of the "Leningrad Center" was published, signed by Vyshinsky, procurator of the Soviet Union, and by Lev Sheinin, investigator for especially important cases. The indictment asserted that Kirov's murder was part of a long-range plan for the murder of Stalin and other party leaders. Two conspiratorial terrorist groups had allegedly been discovered: one led by Shatsky, the other by I. I. Kotolnyov, who ordered Nikolaev to kill Kirov. (In the twenties Kotolynov had been a member of the Central Committee of the Komsomol and secretary of the Komsomol organization in Leningrad's Vyborg district.) The murderer was said to have received five thousand rubles from a foreign consul, who connected the conspirators to Trotsky. (At the end of 1934 the consul general of Latvia, George Bissenieks, was expelled from the Soviet Union, though the Latvian government categorically denied his participation in the assassination of Kirov.)

It is obvious from this indictment that only Nikolaev and two of his friends, who had not been Zinovievists, had confessed to Kirov's murder. The rest of the accused confessed only to participation in a Zinovievist group. Not one of them named Nikolaev as a member of the "Leningrad Center." The only proof that the Zinovievists were involved in Kirov's assassination and that Nikolaev was a member of their group was the deposition of Nikolaev himself, which contradicted the other defendants' testimony and all the other evidence as well. The material evidence— addresses, various notes, Nikolaev's diary—did not confirm the existence of the "Leningrad Center." But this fact was brushed aside; the

---

15. Two of those arrested were later rehabilitated, after the Twentieth Congress: the Ukrainian writers A. V. Krushelenitsky and V. A. Masyk. The fates of the others are unknown to us.

indictment declared that all the papers and notes found on Nikolaev were fabrications designed for "camouflage."

This indictment, riddled with contradictions, was the only document published in the case. Neither the text of the verdict nor the depositions of the accused nor their final speeches were ever published. There were no speeches for the prosecution or for the defense because the case was tried without prosecuting and defense attorneys and also without the right to appeal or the right to petition for clemency. According to the military jurist A. B———r, who attended the trial, Nikolaev behaved quite differently during the trial than during his interrogation by Stalin. He confessed to the premeditated murder of Kirov on instructions from the "Leningrad Center," and named the other members of the "Center." But most of the other defendants did not confess, and many claimed that they had never seen Nikolaev before. All received the death sentence and were shot immediately. The papers reported the execution on December 30.

There is also the important testimony of Katsafa, a former NKVD agent, who was one of the constant guards in Nikolaev's cell (to keep him from committing suicide). Nikolaev told Katsafa that the assassination had been arranged by the security police and that he had been promised his life if he implicated the Leningrad Zinovievites. He asked Katsafa whether he would be deceived. When his sentence was read out loud, he began to shout and struggled with the guards. It was natural that in 1934 Katsafa did not believe a word that Nikolaev said, but in 1956 he submitted his testimony in written form to the Central Committee.

At the very beginning of the investigation Stalin asked the Leningrad NKVD for a thorough report on the former Zinovievists. There was in fact a small group of them in the city, who gathered occasionally on a semi-legal basis. The NKVD knew the members and had even asked Kirov to authorize their arrest. But Kirov had refused, since he believed that former oppositionists should not be repressed but won over ideologically. The list of the Leningrad Zinovievists, together with Kirov's decision, had been put in NKVD files. Now the list was brought to Stalin. From it, and from a list of Moscow Zinovievists, Stalin himself put together the "Moscow Center" and the "Leningrad Center." The roll, written in Stalin's own hand, is still preserved in his papers. (According to Olga Shatunovskaya, a member of the Commission of Party Control, it was there in the years immediately following the Twentieth Party Congress, when a photocopy was made and submitted to handwriting experts.) Stalin shuffled some of the names from the "Moscow Center" to the "Leningrad Center," and vice versa. Everyone on his list was arrested.

In 1934 Stalin's story that Zinoviev and his supporters were the organizers of Kirov's murder seemed plausible. Everyone knew that in 1926 Kirov had succeeded the Zinovievist Grigory Yevdokimov as leader of the Leningrad party organization. It is therefore not surprising that right after the murder the thoughts of many people turned toward the former Leningrad opposition. But it is just this obvious plausibility that obliges us to have doubts about Stalin's story. The Zinovievist opposition would have gained no political benefit from the murder of the man who was at that time the most popular party leader after Stalin. On the contrary, the character of the investigation directed by Stalin and the chain of subsequent events makes it plausible to assume that Kirov was killed with Stalin's knowledge. Kirov had been Stalin's friend a long time, but personal friendship meant little to Stalin when his political goals were involved.

The section of the decree in which the Central Executive Committee ordered a speed-up of investigations was a dead letter following the Kirov case; in most subsequent "political cases" the investigation dragged on for months. But in the Kirov case it was important for Stalin to achieve the swiftest judicial vengeance in order to hide all the inconvenient evidence. The other points in the "Law of December 1," however, were actively used by the authorities. The charge of terrorist activity was a favorite in 1937–1938 since it permitted all legal restrictions to be disregarded in the investigation and trial.

The portrait of Kirov should not be gilded. He had many characteristics of Stalin's entourage, and many reprehensible events of the late twenties could not have occurred without his participation. Still, as an individual Kirov was in many ways different from Stalin. His simplicity and accessibility, his closeness to the masses, his tremendous energy, his oratorical talent, and his excellent theoretical training—all made him a party favorite. His influence grew steadily, and in 1934 his authority in the party was without doubt second only to Stalin's. It is known that in the summer of 1934, when Stalin was seriously ill for the first time, the question of a possible successor to him as general secretary arose, and the Politburo unanimously expressed itself in favor of Kirov.

Nasty, suspicious, cruel, and power-hungry, Stalin could not abide brilliant and independent people around him. Kirov's growing popularity and influence could not have failed to arouse Stalin's envy and suspicion. Kirov's great authority among Communists and his reluctance to go along with Stalin unquestioningly served to impede the realization of Stalin's ambitious plans. It can therefore be said with assurance that Stalin had no regrets at Kirov's death. Moreover, his assassination gave Stalin a desired pretext for reprisals against everyone obstructing his road to power. The Kirov assassination was an important link in the chain of events leading to Stalin's usurpation of all power in the country. That is why Stalin's guilt in the assassination, which would have seemed improbable in 1934–1935, nowadays appears plausible and, logically and politically, almost proven. On the other hand, Zinoviev's and Kamenev's guilt, which seemed reasonable in 1934–1935, today appears quite unlikely.

It is curious to note that one of the first articles in the first issue of Trotsky's *Bulletin of the Opposition* said the following:

> There remains only one thing for Stalin: to try to draw a line of blood between the official party and the Opposition. He absolutely must connect the Opposition with assassination attempts, preparations for arms insurrection, etc. . . .
>
> The impotent policy of maneuvering and evading problems, the growing economic difficulties, the growing distrust within the party toward the leadership have made it necessary for Stalin to stun the party by putting on a large-scale show. He needs a blow, a shock, a catastrophe.[16]

The point was also made that "this is the kind of thing—and the only kind—that Stalin thinks through to the end."

On the basis of this quotation one could credit Trotsky with great perspicacity, noting only that he was wrong about the timing. It is all the more peculiar, then, that five years later Trotsky completely misinterpreted the Kirov assassination. In his article on the event he said in part:

> Nikolaev is depicted by the Soviet press as a participant in a terrorist organization made up of members of the party. If the dispatch is true—and we see no reason to consider it an invention, because it was not easy for the bureaucracy to admit such a thing—we have before us a fact that must be considered of great symptomatic significance. There is always the possibility of a chance shot fired by a man for personal reasons. But a terrorist act prepared beforehand and committed by order of a definite organization is, as the whole history of revolutions and counterrevolutions teaches us, inconceivable unless there exists a political atmosphere favorable to it. The hostility toward the leaders in power must have been widespread and must have assumed the sharpest forms for a terrorist group to crystallize out within the ranks of the party youth or, more properly speaking,

---

16. *Biulleten' oppozitsii* (July 1929) no. 1–2, p. 2. [Cf. *Writings of Leon Trotsky, 1929* (New York, 1975), pp. 61–62.—G. S.]

within its upper stratum, which is intimately connected with the lower and middle circles of the bureaucracy.[17]

Trotsky obviously did not understand the events of late 1934 and early 1935 in the Soviet Union. Nevertheless in his appeals to the working class he called on the "vanguard of the proletariat" to carry out a "ruthless purge of the bureaucratic apparatus, starting at the top."[18] Such advice suited Stalin perfectly well at that moment for he was preparing exactly that kind of a purge.

■ 3
REPRESSION IN EARLY 1935

Immediately after the assassination meetings were held in every enterprise and office throughout the country. In Moscow, Zinoviev, then a member of the administration of the Central Trade Union Council, spoke at the Council meeting that denounced the vicious murder. On the evening of December 1, Grigory Yevdokimov, head of the Central Milk Board, spoke at the meeting of his organization. But a few days later, Zinoviev, Yevdokimov, Kamenev, and many other leaders of the former Zinovievist opposition were arrested. One of them was Pyotr Zalutsky, who in the past had been a prominent Bolshevik, one of the organizers of the Central Committee's Russian Bureau and the party's Petrograd Committee, an active participant in the civil war, and a secretary and member of the presidium of the Central Executive Committee of the Soviets. In the twenties Zalutsky joined the Left Opposition, for which he was expelled from the party for a year, but his part in those internal disputes could not discredit his irreproachable revolutionary record. The same could be said about most of those who were arrested.[19]

In January 1935, following a brief investigation, the first political trial of former opposition leaders was held. On the bench of the accused sat Zinoviev, Kamenev, Yevdokimov, Ivan Bakaev, A. M. Gertik, A. S.

17. *Biulleten' oppozitsii* (January 1935) no. 41, p. 6. [Cf. *Writings of Leon Trotsky, 1934–35* (New York, 1971), pp. 121–122. —G. S.]

18. *Biulleten' oppozitsii* (February 1935) no. 42, p. 4. [Cf. *Writings of Leon Trotsky, 1934–35*, p. 163. —G. S.]

19. After the Twentieth and Twenty-Second congresses Zalutsky was rehabilitated, as can be seen from articles about him in two reference works: *Grazhdanskaia voina i inostrannaia interventsiia v SSSR* (Moscow, 1982); and *Velikaia Oktiabr'skaia sotsialisticheskaia revolutsiia v SSSR* (Moscow, 1977), p. 185. Most of the other prominent party figures arrested in 1935 have not been rehabilitated.

Kuklin, Ya. V. Sharov, B. L. Bravo, S. M. Gessen, and ten others—
nineteen people in all. During the unusually brief trial meetings were
held throughout the country demanding that all the accused be shot. But
the investigators in this case apparently had not used "unlawful methods"
—the Stalinist euphemism for torture—and thus were not able to "prove"
the direct responsibility of the "Moscow Center" in the assassination of
Kirov. To quote the verdict of the court: "The investigation did not
establish facts that would provide a basis for describing the crimes of the
Zinovievites as instigation of the assassination of S. M. Kirov." Therefore
Zinoviev's sentence was "only" ten years in prison, and Kamenev's five.
The other defendants received similar punishment.

At the same time a special board (*osoboe soveshchanie*) of the NKVD,
without any legal judicial proceedings, sentenced a large group of once
prominent party members to two to five years for belonging to the
Leningrad and Moscow "Centers." These included Pyotr Zalutsky, I. K.
Naumov, I. V. Vardin-Mgeladze, A. P. Kostin, V. S. Bulakh, A. I.
Aleksandrov, and I. I. Zelikson. On January 18, 1935, a confidential
letter from the Central Committee was sent to all party organizations,
demanding the mobilization of all forces to destroy enemy elements and
to root out counterrevolutionary nests of enemies of the party and the
people. Every oblast, Leningrad especially, was swept by the first wave
of mass arrests, which later in the camps was called the "Kirov flood."
Simultaneously former noblemen and their families were deported en
masse from Leningrad, although the vast majority of them had not carried on any underground anti-Soviet activity.

Anatoly Krasnov-Levitin, one of the witnesses to this tragic operation,
described it later in his reminiscences:

In March a mass relocation (*vyselenie*) of "alien elements" from Leningrad
began. The newspapers published a brief notice to the effect that a "certain
number of citizens of the tsarist aristocracy and the former exploiting classes" had
been relocated. The editor of *Leningradskaya pravda* wrote that "only genuine
proletarians, only honest working people" had the right to live in the city of
Lenin.

I went to the Shpalernaya to have a look at the deportees. I will never forget
that day. Before I reached the Shpalernaya I saw an old lady, over seventy, from
very high society, who could barely move on her gout-stricken feet. She was
carrying some sort of green paper in her hand and complained loudly to acquaintances she met that she was being asked to move to Bashkiria on twenty-four
hours' notice. All the streets adjoining the Shpalernaya were full of such elderly
people. People with fine manners, loaded down with things. The Liteiny Pros-

pekt area was one of aristocratic mansions, and many surviving former owners of those mansions still found shelter in the servants' quarters or basements of those houses. Now they all had to go. Where? Why? No one knew. When I reached the Shpalernaya it was very hard to get through to the main drawing room. . . . But Lord, what I found when I got there! The large room was jammed full of people. I had never seen such despair, such horror. The procedure was as follows. A person was arrested and then after two days was released with instructions to come back with his or her passport; the passport was taken away, and in its place a document was issued, ordering the person to leave for a particular locality within twenty-four hours. (The same green paper I had seen in the hands of the old lady.) In the large reception hall there were a great many former officers. This was evident from their posture and the remnants of old uniforms on some of them. They behaved with forced good cheer, even joking with one another, but in their faces I saw fear and despair. . . .[20]

The relocation process was carried out on the basis of the following principle: an old directory or social register entitled *Ves' Peterburg (All of St. Petersburg)* was examined, and any surviving persons listed in it were deported. Some were also deported as a result of denunciations by informers. All "former people" were removed: former aristocrats and members of the nobility, former officers, and former businessmen or merchants.

■ **4**

CONTINUED REPRESSION, 1935–1936

During the whole of 1935 and the first half of 1936 the economic situation began to improve noticeably. For example, rationing was ended in the cities. However, political tension increased steadily after the trial of the former Zinovievists. In every party organization there was a campaign for "confessions" and "recantation." Eugenia Ginzburg described it in her memoirs:

Large and crowded lecture halls were turned into public confessionals. Although absolution was not at all easy to come by—expressions of contrition were more often than not rejected an "inadequate"—the torrent of confessions grew from day to day. Every meeting had its chosen theme. People repented for misunderstanding the theory of permanent revolution and for abstaining from the vote on the program of the opposition in 1923; for failing to purge themselves of great-power chauvinism; for underrating the importance of the second Five-Year

20. Anatoly Krasnov-Levitin, *Likhie gody, 1925–1941* (Paris, 1977), pp. 266–269.

Plan; for having known personally some "sinner" or for liking Meyerhold's theater.[21]

Soviet laws gradually grew harsher. On March 30, 1935, a decree of the Central Executive Committee introduced punishment of "members of families of traitors to the homeland." All close relatives of "traitors" were to be banished to remote regions, even though they might have had nothing to do with the crime committed. Thus the hostage concept became part of Soviet law. Although the decree spoke of "traitors that have fled the country," in subsequent years no distinction was made between "traitors" and "enemies of the people." On April 7, 1935, the Central Executive Committee enacted a decree making children aged twelve and older criminally accountable. The effect of this law was to extend to children all penalties existing in the criminal code of that time, up to and including the death penalty.

"Selective" repression never let up throughout 1935 and the first half of 1936. In every oblast and republic, dozens and dozens of people were arrested—not only former oppositionists but Communists who had never belonged to any opposition. At the same time, hundreds were expelled from the party "for a connection with hostile elements" or "for lack of vigilance." The party purge which had begun in 1933 continued, not to the end of 1934, as had been proposed, but to the end of 1935. In fact, the admission of new members to the party was closed until the middle of 1936. Nevertheless, until the fall of 1936 most of the former oppositionists remained free and even held responsible positions in the commissariats, in publishing, and in educational institutions. Bukharin, for example, was editor of *Izvestia* and was allowed to travel abroad to negotiate purchases from the archives of the German Social Democratic Party for the Marx-Engels-Lenin Institute. Pyatakov was exerting himself intensely as first deputy people's commissar for heavy industry, and articles by Radek appeared almost daily in the central papers and magazines.

The higher circles were as yet scarcely touched by repression. But some middle-level party officials were arrested, such as Pavel Shabalkin, a member of the bureau of the Far Eastern kraikom, and V. V. Dyakov, a leader of the Volga-Don Administration.

In 1935, Vladimir Nevsky was arrested. A prominent historian of the party, who had once been a leader of the Central Committee's Military Organization, he was the director of the Lenin Library at the time of his

21. Eugenia Ginzburg, *Journey Into the Whirlwind* (New York, 1967), p. 11.

arrest. M. A. Solntseva reports that he refused to discard a significant part of the library's holdings in political literature, despite a written order from Stalin. "I am not running a baggage room," Nevsky declared. "The party directed me to preserve all this."

Only one member of the Central Committee seems to have suffered: Abel Yenukidze, the secretary of the CEC. He was expelled from the party but was not arrested at the time. Not without reason, Yenukidze was considered one of Stalin's few close friends. Their friendship went back to the turn of the century, the years when they worked together in Transcaucasia. In spite of this, Yenukidze was accused of loss of vigilance and of moral corruption (these charges have now been rescinded). The pretext was that several former Mensheviks, SRs, and members of the nobility were found on the CEC staff. For example, the CEC's legal counsel was the former Menshevik E. E. Pontovich. However, all these persons had previously been active in the Russian revolutionary movement and were doing good, hard work on the staff of the Central Executive Committee, loyally carrying out directives from the Communist Party's Central Committee. In those days the staffs of the State Planning Commission, the Procuracy, and the NKVD itself contained former Mensheviks, SRs and members of the nobility. None of this was any secret to Stalin. The real reason for Yenukidze's disgrace and removal was his indignation over Beria's work of falsification *From the History of the Bolshevik Organizations in Transcaucasia*, in which Stalin was given credit for things he never did, things that had actually been done by Yenukidze. At the Central Committee meeting that examined Yenukidze's case, Stalin remained silent, as though the whole affair was being decided without him. Yenukidze was also silent. Although several people spoke against him, Yenukidze neither repented nor argued back. Only when detailed and obviously false testimony from arrested Central Executive Committee staff members began to be read aloud to the meeting did Yenikidze exclaim from his seat: "If Yagoda's power was in my hands, I could have even more absurd testimony read aloud here!" After the Central Committee meeting the "working over" of Yenukidze in all units of the party continued for several weeks.

Maxim Gorky's situation also grew more complicated during 1935. Shortly after the Kirov assassination a decree was passed to strengthen the guards in attendance on all "leaders" *(vozhdi)* and members of the

Soviet government.[22] This decree incidentally increased the NKVD's ability to monitor the activities of all such persons. Gorky was included in the list of "leaders." To his great surprise on the morning of December 3, 1934, two days after the Kirov assassination, he found that virtually an entire squad of NKVD men had been assigned to guard him. This deprived him of all freedom of action, since from then on he had to obtain agreement for any trips not only from his physicians but also from the head of his bodyguard. The memoirs of I. S. Shkapa, a longtime collaborator of Gorky's, contain the following account of a visit to Gorky in September 1935:

On Friday, September 20, again I was in Gorky's office. He was listening to a report I was giving . . . [when] a telephone rang in the next room. Kryuchkov [Gorky's chief secretary] went out for a few minutes. Gorky and I were left alone. Suddenly, leaning over to me, Gorky said: "What's going on, my friend? Isn't it possible to root out bungling (*golovotyapstvo*)?" . . . Getting no answer he continued:

"I'm terribly tired. . . . How many times I've wanted to visit the countryside, even to live there, as in the old days. Can't do it. It's as though they've surrounded me like a fence; can't get through!"

His words about the countryside were in response to my frequent advice that he spend two or three days among collective farmers but I held my tongue, because I knew that Gorky was restricted from going anywhere except Moscow, the Crimea, and Lenin's former residence at Gorki.

Then I heard him saying: "They have surrounded me . . . hemmed me in. . . . I can't go forward or backward. And I can't adjust to it!"[23]

Even in the early thirties it was very difficult to get to see Gorky, but in 1935–1936 the famous writer's guards and secretaries stopped allowing "undesirable persons" to see him at all. On one occasion an attempt was made to prevent Mikhail Prishvin, the elderly and renowned Russian writer (who, incidentally, avoided political topics in his writings), from seeing Gorky. Kryuchkov, Gorky's chief secretary, tried to stop Prishvin, but Prishvin simply pushed him aside and went into Gorky's office. When Gorky heard about his secretary's behavior he remarked with embarrassment: "Didn't you really know that I'm under house arrest?"

22. In early 1936 the party Central Committee abolished the right of party members to carry arms, a right they had enjoyed since the time of the civil war. In preparing for mass terror against the party, Stalin had a fear of retaliatory action against himself.

23. I. S. Shkapa, *Sem' let s Gor'kim* (Moscow, 1966), pp. 383–4.

On another occasion Bukharin, who often dropped in on Gorky, was stopped outside the house by the guards. Bukharin did not have his papers with him to prove he was a Central Committee member; and he had not bothered to call Gorky in advance to have a pass issued. Something of a prankster, Bukharin went around to the back of the house and simply climbed over the high fence. Here too he was detained by two guards. Kryuchkov came out to see what the fuss was and, recognizing Bukharin, authorized his admission. But after the incident Bukharin and Gorky were hardly inclined to joke about it.

By no means everyone noticed the increased political tension; many party leaders, members of the Central Committee, obkom secretaries, people's commissars, and top military men sensed no danger. Stalin knew how to conceal his intentions.

The second five-year plan brought unprecedentedly high rates of industrial growth. In 1934 gross industrial output rose by 19 percent, in 1935 by 23 percent, and in 1936 by 29 percent. The majority of people's commissars and obkom secretaries in 1935–1936 were awarded the Order of Lenin, which at that time was a rare and very high honor. In 1936 no more than two or three hundred persons bore this honor. At the same time the title of marshal was introduced in the Soviet Army, being awarded not only to Stalin's cronies Voroshilov and Budyonny but also to Tukhachevsky, Yegorov, and Blyukher.

After several years of stagnation, agricultural production also began to increase: in 1935 gross agricultural output was 20 percent higher than in 1933. Soon after rationing was ended, collective farms were permitted to sell grain on the open market, which stimulated farmers' interest in increasing grain production. (The system of grain procurements did not create such a stimulus because of low procurement prices.) Consumer goods prices began to drop. The acute food crisis of the early thirties was apparently over. The standard of living, both urban and rural, rose appreciably. It was at this time that Stalin uttered his famous phrase: "Life has become better, comrades; life has become more joyful." [24]

Life really did become a bit "more joyful," and this atmosphere engendered a certain enthusiasm. But the Soviet propaganda machine attributed all the economic successes to Stalin's "wise leadership," and the cult of his personality grew unceasingly. This cult was not of course the

24. [The slogan is from Stalin's speech at the First All-Union Conference of Stakhanovites, November 17, 1935. See Stalin, *Problems of Leninism* (Moscow, 1953), p. 670. —Tr.]

result of the spontaneous enthusiasm of the masses. Stalin himself permitted and encouraged this unrestrained adulation of his person, as did the political leaders closest to him, such as Molotov, Kaganovich, and Voroshilov.

A good indication of the situation in the Soviet Union is provided by many of the strained circumstances of Andre Gide's visit to the Soviet Union in the summer of 1936. In the early 1930s this prominent French writer, who was then in his sixties, proclaimed himself an enemy of capitalism and began to express open sympathy for the Soviet Union and for Stalin personally. He was invited to the USSR, where an edition of his works soon came out in Russian translation. Gide was received with great pomp, with Mikhail Koltsov serving as the organizer of the grand welcome. Great feasts and banquets were arranged wherever Gide went; tables groaned under the weight of good food and drink. Gide protested but to no avail. To his friends he said: "I am frightened by these feasts. I dislike them very much. They are not only absurd; they are immoral." Gide was supposed to follow a prearranged itinerary on his trip. He made frequent speeches but they were all strictly censored. The following "seditious" passage, for example, was deleted from a speech he was to give in Leningrad. The speech was never delivered.

When the revolution is triumphant, installed and established, art runs a terrible danger, a danger almost as great as under the worst fascist oppression—the danger of orthodoxy. . . . What the triumphant revolution can and should offer the artist is, above all else, liberty. Without liberty, art loses its meaning and its value. . . . And as, quite naturally, the assent of the greatest number, with its accompanying applause, success and favors, goes to the qualities the public is best able to recognize, that is to say to conformity, I wonder with some anxiety whether perhaps in this great Soviet Union there may not be vegetating obscurely, unknown to the crowd, some Baudelaire, some Keats, or some Rimbaud, who by [the] very reason of his worth cannot make himself heard.[25]

While Gide was in Moscow, Gorky died there. During the funeral Gide stood on the reviewing platform of the Lenin mausoleum beside

25. [The author cites "materials in the archives of Ilya Ehrenburg" as his source for the account of Gide's visit and the quotations from Gide's book. These include items that seem to be abridged translations into Russian of passages from Gide's book *Retour de l'U.R.S.S.* (Paris, 1936). Where the author quoted these, I have used the wording from the English version, *Back from the USSR* (New York, 1937). The censored passage from the speech that was not delivered is on pp. 81–82 of that edition. The incident of the telegram to Stalin is described on pp. 66–68 (the materials in Ehrenburg's archives mistakenly report that Gide refused to send the telegram). The other quotations are, respectively, on pp. 45, 63, and 66. —G. S.]

Stalin, Molotov, and Mikoyan. But he was not allowed to meet with Bukharin, although Bukharin was still editor in chief of *Izvestia*. During his tour of Georgia, Gide decided to send Stalin a telegram of greetings from Stalin's birthplace of Gori. In the appropriate space on the telegram form Gide began to write: "Passing through Gori, in the course of our wonderful journey, I feel the need to send you. . . ." Here the interpreter accompanying Gide interrupted to tell him that he could not write simply "you" when referring to Stalin, but needed to add something like "you, the great leader of the workers." The interpreter refused to send the telegram unless it was changed, and Gide finally submitted.

There was an unspoken agreement that Gide would write a book about the USSR. It appeared in 1936, with much praise of the country and its leaders but also with some justified criticism. Here are some sample excerpts:

In the USSR everybody knows beforehand, once and for all, that on any and every subject there can be only one opinion. . . . I doubt whether in any other country in the world, even Hitler's Germany, thought be less free, more bowed down, more fearful (terrorized), more vassalized. . . . Stalin's effigy is met with everywhere; his name is on every tongue; his praises are invariably sung in every speech. . . . Is [this the result of] adoration, love, or fear?[26]

Of course Gide's book was insultingly attacked in the Soviet press. It was called a "vicious anti-Soviet caricature" although most of its criticism was valid and even understated. Harsh personal attacks on Gide were also published in the Soviet press. Although his works had been published in Russian in 1935–1936, a strict ban on them was imposed. I would hardly be in error to assert that to this day not one new book has been published in Russian translation by this celebrated French author, who was awarded the Nobel Prize for literature in the postwar era. Gide was further criticized by such colleagues as Romain Rolland, Lion Feuchtwanger, and Ilya Ehrenburg. The year after Gide's visit, Feuchtwanger "corrected" Gide's errors. He similarly toured the USSR and wrote the book *Moscow: 1937*, which I will discuss further below.

■ 5

THE FIRST MOSCOW TRIAL, 1936

On August 19, 1936, in the October Hall of the House of Soviets in Moscow, the first monstrous show trial of former opposition leaders

26. See note 25.

began. The main defendants had been leaders of the "New Opposition," but others were former Trotskyist leaders, and some were not major figures at all. Many were going on trial for the second time in two years. The group of sixteen defendants was charged in the indictment with constituting a "Trotskyite-Zinovievite Terrorist Center." During the court hearings, which lasted until August 24, the defendants no longer refused to admit their guilt.

Zinoviev, for example, declared:

My waning Bolshevism was transformed into anti-Bolshevism, and because of Trotskyism I went all the way to fascism. . . . We took the place of the Mensheviks, SRs, and White Guards, who could not come out openly in our country.

Kamenev in turn stated:

Is it any accident that next to Zinoviev and myself there are sitting emissaries of foreign secret agencies, people with false passports, dubious biographies, and undeniable ties with Hitler and the Gestapo? No, it is no accident.[27]

The defendants willingly and smoothly told about their roles in the assassination of Kirov and about their plans to kill Stalin, Molotov, Kaganovich, Chubar, Postyshev, Kosior, and Eikhe. (As things turned out, the last four were murdered without any help from former oppositionists; they were shot later—on Stalin's orders.) Zinoviev said that Stalin was to have been killed during the Seventh Congress of the Comintern in order to move Communists throughout the world to support Trotsky and to shake up the Central Committee of the CPSU so badly that it would have to start negotiations with Trotsky, Zinoviev, and Kamenev and invite them to take over the leadership. Only one of the defendants, Ivan Smirnov, the alleged leader of all the Trotskyists in the Soviet Union, tried to refute the charges. He was, however, "exposed" by the testimony of other defendants—Mrachkovsky, Ter-Vaganyan, Yevdokimov, Kamenev.

The trial of the "United Center" was ostensibly public, but only a few hand-picked representatives of "public opinion" were present in the room. The rest of the spectators were actually NKVD employees. Elementary rules of judicial procedure were violated. No material evidence or documentary proof of the guilt of the accused was presented to the court by the prosecutor, Vyshinsky, nor did the Military Collegium of the Soviet Supreme Court, headed by Vasily Ulrikh, ask for any. The

27. *Delo trotskistsko-zinov'evskogo terroristicheskogo tsentra* (Moscow, 1936), p. 170.

entire case rested on the contradictory "depositions" and "confessions" of the accused. Moreover, they were deprived of the right to defense counsel; a number of foreign lawyers offered to defend them, but the offers were rejected.

The trial was brief, the testimony of the accused uniform. Basically it consisted in the enumeration of various monstrous crimes or, more often, the plans for such crimes, prepared both by the "Center" and by groups "affiliated" with it.

Today the falsity of such "depositions" is not hard to prove (and I will return to that subject below [section 10]), but in 1936 the party and the majority of the people still trusted Stalin, the NKVD, and the Soviet courts. There were a few who had doubts, but hardly any dared to express them, even to their closest friends.

The trial and the shooting of the accused engendered a new wave of repression throughout the country. First to be arrested were former members of the Left Opposition. The papers were filled with exposes of "hidden Trotskyites," although many of them had never dreamed of hiding themselves or their past. Hundreds of articles appeared with such headlines as: "A Secret Trotskyite," "Protectors of Trotskyites," "Trotskyites on the Ideological Front," "Trotskyite Subversion in Scholarship," "The Trotskyite Salon of the Writer Serebryakova," "Clues to Trotskyites in the Uzbekistan Commissariat of Agriculture."

Some of the defendants in the trial of the "Trotskyite-Zinovievite Center," unexpectedly adding to their pretrial depositions, began to talk about their "criminal" connections with Bukharin, Rykov, and Tomsky, and also with Radek, Pyatakov, Sokolnikov, Serebryakov, Uglanov, Shlyapnikov, and other ex-oppositionists who had not yet been arrested. On August 21, 1936, the newspapers carried an order from Vyshinsky starting a new investigation into the counterrevolutionary conspiracy of the people mentioned. In offices and factories throughout the country meetings demanded a full investigation of "the connections of Bukharin, Rykov, Tomsky, and others with the despicable terrorists." The same issue of *Izvestia* that included this demand in its lead article listed Bukharin as its editor in chief on the last page.

Tomsky did not wait for investigation; he committed suicide. According to his son Yuri (the only surviving member of the Tomsky family), Stalin showed up at the Tomskys' apartment in the Kremlin with a bottle of wine in hand and locked himself up with Tomsky in the latter's study. After a while, loud shouting could be heard from the study: Tomsky was denouncing Stalin in unprintable language. Then the door was flung open and Tomsky ordered Stalin out. Stalin left, shaking with anger; a few minutes later a shot rang out in the study. During those same days Rykov tried to shoot himself, but members of his family literally tore the revolver from his hands, something they greatly regretted later on.

As for Bukharin, during the second half of August he was in the Pamir Mountains on vacation and knew nothing about the show trial. Only after he came down out of the mountains and reached the city of Frunze, did he learn about the events in Moscow. He was stunned. This was a political "turn" he had not expected from Stalin. Despite Bukharin's relative political naïveté, he understood that the mention of his name and those of Tomsky and Rykov at the Moscow trial was not accidental. Bukharin was especially shocked by the news of Tomsky's suicide.

Bukharin thought he would be arrested in Frunze, but he was not. Leaving all his baggage in Frunze, he bought a ticket on the first plane to Moscow after sending Stalin a telegram asking that the death sentences not be carried out until he could confront the convicted defendants who had accused him. Waiting to meet Bukharin in Moscow were not NKVD men but his private automobile with a driver and his worried young wife, Anna Larina. Once he was home in his Kremlin apartment, Bukharin immediately telephoned Stalin. But Stalin was not in Moscow. Immediately after hearing with pleasure that Zinoviev, Kamenev, and the others had been shot (the Chekists who carried out the sentence reported directly to Stalin), he had left for Sochi to "have a rest." For several days Bukharin stayed at home and was seen by no one.

On September 10 Vyshinsky published a report: "The investigation has not established a juridical basis for legal proceedings against N. I. Bukharin and A. I. Rykov, as a result of which the present case is discontinued." Thus Bukharin, Rykov, and the majority of the former "right" oppositionists remained free. But Vyshinsky's report did not mention Radek, Serebryakov, or the other former Left Oppositionists. On September 11 Radek, in a cold sweat, came to see Bukharin. "Please ask Stalin to let my case be handled by him personally, and not by Yagoda," Radek begged, imagining that Bukharin could help him somehow. "Remind Stalin [what I did for him] about Blumkin." Radek, who had published an article against Zinoviev and Kamenev on the first day of their trial, was soon arrested, along with Serebryakov, Sokolnikov, and many others. When Bukharin learned of this he wrote Stalin a letter but received no reply.

■ 6

THE FALL OF YAGODA AND PROMOTION OF YEZHOV

On September 25, 1936, Stalin and Zhdanov sent a telegram from Sochi to Kaganovich, Molotov, and other Politburo members:

We consider it absolutely necessary and urgent that Comrade Yezhov be appointed to head the People's Commissariat of Internal Affairs [NKVD]. Yagoda has obviously proved unequal to the task of exposing the Troskyite-Zinovievite bloc. *The OGPU was four years late in this matter.* All party officials and most of the NKVD agents in the oblasti are talking about this.[28]

The next day Yagoda was removed from the NKVD and appointed people's commissar of railways and roads. The central newspapers appeared that day with large photos of the two commissars, Yezhov and Yagoda. However, Yagoda was soon removed from his new post as well, and in early 1937 he was arrested. I will return to his fate below, but first a few words about Yezhov.

Nikolai Yezhov, the new commissar of internal affairs, had not gained this post by accident. This man, who was fated to play one of the briefest but most terrible roles in the history of the country, had risen relatively quickly as a favorite of Stalin.[29]

Robert Conquest has referred to Yezhov as "a tested and ruthless operator."[30] Taking exception to this characterization, I. A. Sats, a veteran party member, man of letters, former secretary to Anatoly Lunacharsky, and one who knew well the backstage aspect of many events of the thirties, said the following in his memoirs:

Even before his appointments [to top-level posts] Yezhov was in charge of the Central Committee department concerned with party cadres. According to the comments of people who knew him well, he was not at all a "ruthless operator" at that time, when he worked in the middle levels of the party hierarchy, or even earlier on lower levels. When he worked in the provinces, he gave people the impression of a nervous but well-meaning and attentive person, free of arrogance and bureaucratic manners. Perhaps this was a mask. But it is more likely that he was turned into a butcher by the Stalinist system and the personal influence of

28. The test of the telegram was quoted by Khrushchev in his secret speech to the Twentieth Congress. [Cf. *Khrushchev Remembers*, (Boston, 1970), p. 575. —G. S.]

29. As Adam Ulam writes (in his *Stalin*, pp. 392–393), "Yezhov's career . . . was short-lived. But how momentous! As long as there is history, *Yezhovshchina,* 'the Yezhov time,' will figure in it."

30. Conquest, The *Great Terror: Stalin's Purge of the Thirties*, p. 127.

Stalin himself. In any case Yezhov's later role, behavior, and fate were a surprise to many who knew him before the NKVD.[31]

Nadezhda Mandelstam got to know Yezhov at a government dacha in Sukhumi to which she and her husband were invited in 1930 by Nestor Lakoba, the influential Caucasian Bolshevik who was chairman of the Central Executive Committee of Abkhazia. She writes:

The Sukhumi Yezhov was a modest and rather agreeable person. He was not yet used to being driven about in an automobile and did not therefore regard it as an exclusive privilege to which no ordinary mortal could lay claim. We sometimes asked him to give us a lift into town and he never refused. . . .

On the day of Mayakovsky's death we were walking in the garden with a proud and elegant Georgian, a specialist in radio. The guests had all gathered in the dining room for their evening's entertainment. . . . Our companion said: "Georgian People's Commissars would not dance on the day on which a Georgian national poet had died." M. nodded to me and said: "Go and tell that to Yezhov." I went into the dining room and passed on the Georgian's words to Yezhov, who was in very high spirits already. The dancing ceased, but I don't think anybody apart from Yezhov knew the reason.[32]

Indeed Yezhov was by no means a demonic figure. He came from a poor working-class family, was orphaned early in his life, and was raised by the Shlyapnikovs from the age of twelve. He joined the Bolshevik Party in 1917. As a young man he was not distinguished by negative traits such as treachery and viciousness, unlike the young Beria, who was notorious for those features. People who knew Yezhov in Komsomol work, in party work, in an oblast of Kazakhstan, or during his short term as people's commissar of agriculture have told me that Yezhov was a very ordinary person at that time, not cruel in any way—not a bad sort at all. But from the time of his first meeting with Stalin, which apparently occurred during Stalin's trip to Siberia in 1928, Stalin's influence on Yezhov became total, unlimited, almost hypnotic. Stalin noticed this and quickly began to push Yezhov up the ladder of the party and government hierarchy.

At the end of the twenties Yezhov was still a little-known obkom secretary in Kazakhstan. In 1929 he was made deputy commissar of agriculture for the entire USSR. Still, at the Sixteenth Party Congress in 1930 he was only a delegate with a consulting vote. That same year he was transferred to work in the party apparatus and became chief of two

31. I. A. Sats, "Iz vospominanii," unpublished manuscript.
32. Nadezhda Mandelstam, *Hope Against Hope* (New York, 1970), pp. 322, 325.

Central Committee departments, for assignments (Raspredotdel) and for cadres (Otdel kadrov). Although not even a member of the Central Committee, he acquired enormous influence in party circles because of his power to make important assignments and transfers.

After the Seventeenth Party Congress in 1934, at which Yezhov was elected to the Central Committee for the first time, he moved rapidly to the top. He became a member of the Organizational Bureau, deputy chairman of the Commission of Party Control, and head of the Central Committee's department for industry. For unknown services to the international Communist movement he was elected to the Executive Committee of the Comintern. In 1935 Yezhov became one of the secretaries of the party Central Committee and chairman of the Commission of Party Control. Stalin put Yezhov in charge of monitoring the activity of the NKVD for the Central Committee, which greatly displeased Yagoda. Yezhov not only carried out this overall supervisory function but also took an active role in preparing the 1936 trial of Zinoviev, Kamenev, and the rest. He was present at interrogation sessions and gave orders to highly placed NKVD officials. As Alexander Orlov writes:

> Yagoda was jealous of Yezhov's interferences in the affairs of the NKVD and was watching his every move, hoping to take advantage of Yezhov's first blunder in order to discredit him before Stalin and thus get rid of Yezhov's control. . . .
>
> For Yagoda . . . his whole career was at stake. Yagoda knew that the members of the Politburo feared and hated him and that it was under their influence that Stalin had sent to the OGPU, in 1931, a member of the Central Committee, Akulov, to be his superior. At that time, soon after Akulov had been appointed, Yagoda managed to discredit him and to persuade Stalin to dismiss him from the OGPU. But Yezhov was Stalin's favorite and as such he was a much more dangerous rival to Yagoda than Akulov had ever been.[33]

Together with Yagoda, many leading officials of the NKVD were fired and later arrested. No fewer than ten or fifteen prominent NKVD men committed suicide. Yezhov brought several hundred new people with him to work in the NKVD, mostly middle-level party functionaries. But many of Yagoda's protégés continued to serve under Yezhov, who still had a poor grasp of the mechanics of the punitive organs. He was helped

33. Alexander Orlov, *The Secret History of Stalin's Crimes* (New York, 1953), pp. 119, 124–125. Orlov was a prominent NKVD official who, while serving in Spain in 1937, refused to return to the Soviet Union. His book was not published until after Stalin's death. Not everything in the book is reliable, since Orlov often uses rumors or chance conversations as sources. Yet on the whole the book is an important document. [The author cites a Russian translation: *Tainaia istoriia stalinskikh prestuplenii* (New York, 1983), pp. 126, 131–132. —G. S.]

to master them by such men as Leonid Zakovsky, Stanislav Redens, Mikhail Frinovsky, and Genrikh Lyushkov.

With the appointment of Yezhov the NKVD apparatus was substantially enlarged, but the wave of repression that began in the summer of 1936 abated somewhat in the autumn. The main reason for this was the mass turnover of personnel in the security organs and the reorganization of their functioning. The orgy of terror was apparently checked also by the nationwide discussion on the new constitution that guaranteed—in words—the inviolability of the individual and many other democratic rights. It is not surprising that Yagoda's replacement by Yezhov was not perceived as a sign of intensified terror to come. In fact, many who feared arrest began to breathe easier, and some who had survived the terror of 1934–1935 began to hope for an improvement in their lot. These hopes were of course soon dashed. In 1937, terror and repression descended on the party and all citizens of the Soviet Union on a scale previously unheard of. To this day the word "1937" has less meaning as a date in time than as a synonym for monstrous mass terror.

■ 7

THE TRIAL OF THE "PARALLEL CENTER"

The year 1937 began with a major new show trial. The Military Collegium of the Supreme Court now put seventeen people on trial: Yuri Pyatakov, Karl Radek, Grigory Sokolnikov, Leonid Serebryakov, Nikolai Muralov, Mikhail Boguslavsky, Yakov Drobnis, Ya. A. Livshits, and nine others. Most had been prominent activists from prerevolutionary days. From 1923 to 1928 almost all had supported the Left Opposition or the United Opposition, but afterward they had publicly broken with Trotsky and were readmitted to the party. Now they were accused of belonging to a "Parallel Center," of plotting terrorists acts (including once again the murder of Kirov), of espionage, and of trying to provoke a war with fascist Germany and Japan and bring about a Soviet defeat in this war. This time some rules of judicial procedure were observed, although the state-appointed defense lawyers did not really try to defend the accused. Convinced of the efficiency of his "investigative machinery," Stalin invited many foreign correspondents and diplomats to the trial—although no documents or material evidence were produced. As soon as the procurator declared that certain documents of "the G——n intelligence service" were to be presented, the session was closed. In plain fact, the only evidence offered at the trial were the confessions of the accused.

What then made the prisoners confess? The indictment says that they had long ago lost all shame and conscience, had become hired assassins and diversionists and could hope for no mercy. Almost all of them declared that they had not been tortured or coerced. Prosecutor Vyshinsky turned to these "murderers, wreckers, traitors, and spies" and prodded them to explain what motivated their sincere confessions. He asked Muralov why, after repeatedly denying his guilt, he had finally decided to confess. Muralov gave his reasons: his hot temper, his attachment to Trotsky, and, "you know, in every cause there are extremists," but suddenly realized to his horror that he would become the symbol of counterrevolution, the opposite of everything he had fought for. "For me that was decisive, and I said: O.K., I'll go and tell the whole truth."[34] Explicit accusations were made against Bukharin and Rykov. Radek, for example said that friendship had long prevented him from implicating Bukharin. He had very much wanted to give his friend the chance to disarm himself by volunteering honest testimony. But now, Radek said, he had decided that he could not enter the court hiding another terrorist organization.[35] He and others offered detailed stories about their counterrevolutionary "connections" with the Bukharin-Rykov group. Radek and other members of the "Parallel Center" thus decided the fate of the former right deviation. On January 17, 1937, *Izvestia* appeared without the signature of its editor in chief, Bukharin. Rykov, too, was removed from his post. But Stalin still put off arresting these now universally proclaimed "enemies of the people."

Back in the fall of 1936, as I have said, Bukharin expected to be arrested; he continually wrote letters to Stalin, who did not reply. Stalin played a far more complicated game with Bukharin and Rykov than he had with Zinoviev and Kamenev. According to Anna Larina, on November 7, 1936, Bukharin decided to celebrate the holiday at Red Square—not, as usual, from the top of Lenin's tomb, but in the stands with his wife. But Stalin saw him there and had him invited up.

After the holiday, however, the most painful phase of Bukharin's life began. He was not summoned to the Lubyanka, but personal confrontations between him and arrested "leftists" and members of the "Bukharin school"—that is, his closest disciples—were arranged in the Kremlin itself. After a face-to-face encounter with Radek he had another with Sokolnikov and one with Serebryakov, then one with Yefim Tseitlin, one

34. *Pravda*, January 27, 1937.
35. *Izvestia*, January 30, 1937.

of his closest followers. They all told of their alleged criminal ties with Bukharin, of the existence of another counterrevolutionary terrorist center headed by Bukharin and Yagoda. For example, in Bukharin's presence Tseitlin alleged that Bukharin had given him a revolver and placed him on the corner of a street down which Stalin was supposed to travel that day but that Stalin's car had taken a different route so that the assassination attempt failed.

In addition to personal confrontations every day there were brought to Bukharin's and Rykov's apartments copies of "testimony" from party figures who had been arrested and from whom the NKVD investigators were extracting ever new legends about their "terrorist" and "wrecking" activities. Bukharin and Rykov's names figured in these transcripts quite frequently. Similar packets of material were being circulated to other full and candidate members of the party's Central Committee.

One day after returning home from the latest face-to-face encounter, Bukharin was unable to endure the psychological pressure any longer. He took his revolver from his desk. Attached to its handle was a gold plate engraved with these words: "To a leader of the proletarian revolution from Klim Voroshilov." Bukharin said goodbye to his wife and after locking himself in his study sat there holding the revolver in his hand for a long time, but he could not shoot himself. Such incidents occurred several times, but most often they ended in hysterics or in one more letter to Stalin, which invariably began, "Dear Koba." In early December 1936 a group of Chekists came to Bukharin's apartment in the Kremlin and served him notice of his eviction from the apartment. Bukharin panicked. He was especially concerned over the fate of his huge library and archive. Where could they be moved to? Suddenly the internal Kremlin phone rang. It was Stalin.

"How are things with you, Nikolai?" he asked as though everything were perfectly normal. Bukharin lost his presence of mind; still, he did manage to say that he was being served an eviction notice. Without asking anything further, Stalin roared, "Chase them the hell out of there!" The uninvited guests left immediately.

In December 1936 Bukharin hardly went out of his apartment, as though under voluntary house arrest. He accepted calmly the decision for his removal as editor in chief of *Izvestia* since he was no longer doing any work for the paper. Nevertheless, during the trial of the "Parallel Center" he was in a constant state of nervous tension and slept hardly at all.

The trial ended on January 30, 1937. Thirteen people were condemned to be shot. Radek, Sokolnikov, and V. Arnold were sentenced to ten years in prison and M. S. Stroilov to eight. The NKVD agents and representatives of "public opinion" present in the courtroom greeted the verdict with shouts of approval, as did a crowd of Muscovites gathered outside the House of Trade Unions. On the next day the party's Moscow city committee, headed by Nikita Khrushchev, called a huge mass rally on Red Square, where hundreds of thousands of industrial and office workers approved the "severe but just" verdict.

■ 8

THE FEBRUARY–MARCH PLENUM OF 1937

Soon after the end of the Radek-Pyatakov trial a Central Committee plenum was scheduled. The agenda, which was sent to Central Committee members in advance, consisted of two points: (1) Bukharin and Rykov; and (2) preparing the party organizations for elections to the Supreme Soviet of the USSR.

When Bukharin received this notification, he realized that it meant his and Rykov's expulsion from the Central Committee and the party, which many Central Committee members had demanded at the previous plenum. Seeing no other way to fight back, he went on a hunger strike, informing Stalin and several other Central Committee members of the fact. Stalin again called Bukharin on the internal Kremlin line. "Who are you on hunger strike against? Against the party?" "What else can I do?" Bukharin replied. "Since you're getting ready to expel me from the party." "No one's getting ready to expel you," Stalin answered and hung up.

The plenum began on February 25, 1937. Yezhov presented information on Bukharin and Rykov's "criminal activities" and the "espionage and wrecking activity" of a new counterrevolutionary center. Then the Central Committee members began to make their speeches, in extremely harsh and insulting tones. There is a legend that some of them defended Bukharin and Rykov and spoke out against the mass repression that had begun. That did not happen. No one opposed the overall policy of Stalin and the NKVD; the condemnation and denunciation of Bukharin and Rykov was unanimous. Everyone demanded that they be called to account.

At the plenum numerous examples were presented of poor functioning in factories and offices, the alleged result of "wrecking" by former oppositionists. Of course, not all the speeches at the plenum were equally base. For example, I. Ye. Lyubimov, the commissar of light industry, tried to minimize the extent of "wrecking" in his sector, which brought a sharp attack on him by I. Vareikis. G. M. Kaminsky, the commissar of health, not only expressed doubts about the correctness of some acts of repression in Transcaucasia but also expressed distrust of Beria, who in fact was Stalin's proxy in Georgia and Transcaucasia. Pavel Postyshev expressed doubt about the arrest of one of his closest assistants, who had never engaged in oppositional activity, but Postyshev himself was under a cloud at that time and felt that his own career was in danger. He had just been relieved of his duties as first secretary of the party's Kiev oblast committee in January 1937, although he remained for the time second secretary of the Ukrainian party's Central Committee. The Kiev oblast committee was accused of bureaucratism, crude political mistakes, and "ties with Trotskyites."

The atmosphere at the plenum was already quite heated when Bukharin was given the floor. After refuting the charges made against him, he declared, "I am not Zinoviev or Kamenev, and I will not tell lies against myself." To this Molotov replied from the floor: "If you don't confess, that will prove you're a fascist hireling. Their press is saying that our trials are provocations. We'll arrest you and you'll confess!" Bukharin read a joint statement in which he and Rykov declared all the depositions against themselves, both at the Pyatakov-Radek trial and by other arrested persons, to be slanderous. Such depositions, they argued, proved once again that something was wrong in the NKVD and that a commission should be appointed to investigate its activities. "Well, we'll send you there, and you can take a look for yourself!" Stalin called out.

The plenum set up a commission, consisting of approximately thirty members, with Mikoyan as chairman, to decide the fate of Bukharin and Rykov. For two days, while this commission met, the plenum was in recess. Bukharin spent these days at home. Having lost all hope, he composed a letter, "To a Future Generation of Party Leaders," and asked his wife, Anna Larina, to memorize it. "You're still young," he said, "and you'll live to see the time when the party is headed by new people." Several times he tested her to be sure she had memorized it word for word. Then he burned the letter.

Larina managed to survive the long and difficult years of prison camps and internal exile. Countless times she repeated her husband's letter to herself, and after her release she wrote it down. After the Twentieth

Party Congress she submitted the text of the letter to the party's Central Committee:

I am leaving life. I am lowering my head not before the proletarian ax, which must be merciless but also virginal. I feel my helplessness before a hellish machine, which, probably by the use of medieval methods, has acquired gigantic power, fabricates organized slander, acts boldly and confidently.

Dzerzhinsky is gone; the remarkable traditions of the Cheka have gradually faded into the past, when the revolutionary idea guided all its actions, justified cruelty to enemies, guarded the state against any kind of counterrevolution. That is how the Cheka earned special confidence, special respect, authority and esteem. At present, most of the so-called organs of the NKVD are a degenerate organization of bureaucrats, without ideas, rotten, well-paid, who use the Cheka's bygone authority to cater to Stalin's morbid suspiciousness (I fear to say more) in a scramble for rank and fame, concocting their slimy cases, not realizing that they are at the same time destroying themselves—history does not put up with witnesses of foul deeds.

Any member of the Central Committee, any member of the party can be rubbed out, turned into a traitor, terrorist, diversionist, spy, by these "wonder-working organs." If Stalin should ever get any doubts about himself, confirmation would instantly follow.

Storm clouds have risen over the party. My one head, guilty of nothing, will drag down thousands of guiltless heads. For an organization must be created, a Bukharinite organization, which is in reality not only nonexistent now, the seventh year that I have had not a shadow of disagreement with the party, but was also nonexistent then, in the years of the right opposition. About the secret organizations of Ryutin and Uglanov, I knew nothing. I expounded my views, together with Rykov and Tomsky, openly.

I have been in the party since I was eighteen, and the purpose of my life has always been to fight for the interests of the working class, for the victory of socialism. These days the paper with the sacred name *Truth (Pravda)* prints the filthiest lie, that I, Nikolai Bukharin, have wished to destroy the triumphs of October, to restore capitalism. That is unexampled insolence, that is a lie that could be equaled in insolence, in irresponsibility to the people, only by such a lie as this: it has been discovered that Nikolai Romanov devoted his whole life to the struggle against capitalism and monarchy, to the struggle for the achievement of a proletarian revolution. If, more than once, I was mistaken about the methods of building socialism, let posterity judge me no more harshly than Vladimir Ilyich did. We were moving toward a single goal for the first time, on a still unblazed trail. Other times, other customs. *Pravda* used to carry a discussion page; everyone argued, searched for ways and means, quarreled, made up, and moved on together.

I appeal to you, a future generation of party leaders, whose historical mission will include the obligation to take apart the monstrous cloud of crimes that is growing ever huger in these frightful times, taking fire like a flame suffocating the party.

I appeal to all party members! In these days, perhaps the last of my life, I am confident that sooner or later the filter of history will inevitably sweep the filth from my head. I was never a traitor; without hesitation I would have given my life for Lenin's, I loved Kirov, started nothing against Stalin. I ask a new young and honest generation of party leaders to read my letter at a party plenum, to exonerate me, and reinstate me in the party.

Know, comrades, that on that banner, which you will be carrying in the victorious march to communism, is also my drop of blood.

N. Bukharin.

This letter reveals not only Bukharin's personal tragedy but also his failure, to the very end, to comprehend the frightful meaning of events. Bukharin defends only himself in his letter; he writes nothing about Zinoviev, Kamenev, Pyatakov, and the other party leaders who had already been destroyed by Stalin. He writes that he knew nothing about the existence of Ryutin's and Uglanov's secret organizations, but he does not question their existence. Above all, he stresses that for seven years he had had no differences with the party and that he had "started nothing against Stalin."

To be sure Bukharin's letter was not conceived as a political document of great profundity, the testament of a statesman sharing the wisdom of experience; it was a cry of despair. Boris Souvarine is partly right in his comment that Bukharin's letter is an astonishing document not least of all because of its naïveté, its contradictions and inconsistency, its rhetorical manner and pathetic tone.[36]

Nevertheless it is a very important human document, which was left unanswered by several "future generations of party leaders" (until the time of "perestroika" under Gorbachev). It should not be forgotten, as well, that Bukharin wrote the letter not only for future leaders but also for his young wife, who might have been frightened by a letter with contents of a different kind.

The commission established to decide Bukharin and Rykov's fate met under the chairmanship of Mikoyan. It included almost all the top party leaders, many of whom would fall victim to harsh repression during the next two years. To reach a decision, a voice vote was taken by alphabetical order [following the Cyrillic alphabet of course—G. S.]. One after another the Central Committee members rose—Andreev, Bubnov, Voroshilov, Kaganovich, Molotov—and uttered three words: "Arrest, try, shoot." When Stalin's turn came he said: "Let the NKVD handle the

36. *Est et Ouest* (Paris, April 1–15, 1973), no. 507.

case," and several other people then repeated this formula, which in 1937 meant about the same as the first one. It is worth noting that Mikoyan, who called the roll, did not express his own opinion, and it is not recorded in the minutes.

After the two-day interlude the plenum resumed its work. Bukharin and Rykov were summoned to the meeting to hear the decision. They had no doubts about the outcome. In leaving home, Bukharin kissed his nine-month-old son, then fell on his knees in tears before his wife, begging her forgiveness. Regaining his self-possession, he stood up and said: "Remember Anya, I'm not guilty of anything. History has all sorts of twists and turns. Raise our son to be a firm Bolshevik."

The plenum was being held in the Kremlin, so that Bukharin had only to cross the yard and enter the building where it was in session. The coatroom was deserted, except for Rykov, who entered at the same time as Bukharin. As they were handing their coats to the attendant, eight men emerged from the shadows along the walls and approached Bukharin and Rykov, four converging on each. This was the arrest. From the Central Committee building they were sent straight to the Lubyanka, while two other groups of agents appeared at their apartments to carry out searches. The members of the two men's families were not arrested immediately, not even evicted from the Kremlin. They were needed by the investigators for purposes of blackmail and pressure on the new prisoners.

While the plenum was listening to the report from the commission on Bukharin and Rykov, while those attending the plenum were voting to expel them from the Central Committee and the party, the two were already undergoing their first interrogation at NKVD headquarters. Speaking at one of the last sessions of the plenum, Stalin, who only a few days before had told Bukharin that he would not be expelled from the party, gave a speech calling for an intensified struggle against "enemies of the people" whatever flag they might fly, Trotskyist or Bukharinist.

■ 9

THE TRIAL OF THE
"ANTI-SOVIET RIGHT-TROTSKYITE BLOC"

The investigation of the "rightists" dragged on for more than a year. The trial, the last open and big political trial of "enemies of the people," did not begin until March 2, 1938. Presiding over the Military Collegium of the Supreme Court was the same Vasily Ulrikh, with Andrei Vyshinsky again as prosecutor. In many respects this was the most important of the three major purge trials, serving allegedly to "unmask" the most secretive and numerous of all the "anti-Soviet centers."

The twenty-two defendants were a mixed lot. Besides Bukharin, the chief defendant, and Rykov, who for many years had been premier of the Soviet Union (chairman of the Council of People's Commissars), there were men who had never taken part in any opposition and were arbitrarily put into the "rightists" group by Stalin himself following their arrests. Besides Yagoda, who had been people's commissar of internal affairs, four other defendants had been people's commissars: A. P. Rosenholz (Rozengol'ts), M. A. Chernov, G. F. Grinko, and V. I. Ivanov. There were also former Left Oppositionists, so that Stalin could call this the trial of "the Right-Trotskyite Center." Among them were Nikolai Krestinsky, one of the top Soviet diplomats, and Christian Rakovsky, a major figure for years in the Russian and international working-class movements. Also among the defendants were Akmal Ikramov and Faizul Khodzhaev, former leaders of the Uzbek SSR; P. P. Kryuchkov, the former secretary of Maxim Gorky; and two prominent Kremlin doctors, D. D. Pletnev and I. N. Kazakov.

In addition to the charges made at the 1936 and 1937 trials, which were now repeated (Kirov's murder, preparations for Stalin's murder, and so on), Bukharin, Rykov, and the others were accused of murdering Gorky, Kuibyshev, and Menzhinsky, of attempting to kill Lenin in 1918, and of trying to give away not only the Ukraine, Byelorussia, and the Far East but also Central Asia and Transcaucasia.

At the first session of the court Ulrikh read the indictment and asked each of the accused, "Do you admit your guilt?" Bukharin, Rykov, and Yagoda replied, "Yes, I admit it." But when it was Krestinsky's turn, he unexpectedly answered:

I do not admit my guilt. I am not a Trotskyite. I never took part in the "Right-Trotskyite Bloc" and wasn't aware of its existence. I never committed a single one of the crimes imputed to me, and in particular I do not confess myself guilty of contacts with German intelligence.

Shaken, Ulrikh repeated the question but received the same firm answer. Then he questioned the other prisoners, who confessed their guilt. After that a twenty-minute recess was called. What happened during that recess? The schedule of questioning was certainly changed.

The first to be questioned when the trial resumed was Sergei Bessonov, who played a special role in the preparations for the trial and in the script followed at the performance itself. It was Bessonov who established the alleged connection between the Trotskyists and Zinovievists, and the "rights" (Bukharin, Rykov, and Tomsky). While working for the Soviet trade mission in Berlin, Bessonov had allegedly organized meetings between oppositionists and Trotsky, as well as Leon Sedov, and passed on Trotsky's orders to the "Right-Trotskyite Bloc." Unlike Krestinsky, Bessonov immediately affirmed his willingness to carry on with the part assigned to him.

After Bessonov told of his efforts to establish connections between the former left and right oppositionists, Vyshinsky asked Bukharin to confirm Bessonov's testimony. Bukharin replied that the "rightists" had negotiated with Pyatakov and other "Trotskyists" even before meeting with Bessonov. "You were negotiating about united actions against Soviet power?" Vyshinsky asked. "Yes," Bukharin tersely replied.

But when Vyshinsky asked Krestinsky to confirm some of Bessonov's assertions, Krestinsky repudiated all of them. For the first twenty years of Soviet rule Krestinsky had been one of the major figures in the party and government. Before his arrest he was deputy commissar of foreign affairs. Although he had sympathized with some of the actions of the Left Opposition, he had not been a Trotskyist and did not take part in the internal disputes of the twenties, if for no other reason than because until 1930 he was Soviet ambassador to Germany. During the investigation he had quickly signed everything he was asked. Apparently he understood that a major new trial was in preparation and therefore decided to save his strength for the trial itself, where he would tell the truth. When Vyshinsky questioned him a second time, Krestinsky declared loudly and clearly that he had never spoken with Bessonov about links with the Trotskyists and that Bessonov was lying. When Vyshinsky asked him about the testimony he had given during the pretrial investigation Krestinsky replied that that testimony had been false. "Why did you not tell the truth in the preliminary investigation?" Vyshinsky asked. Krestinsky was slow to respond, and Vyshinsky hastily interjected: "Hearing no reply, I have no further questions." A short time later, however, when the prosecutor addressed Krestinsky again, Krestinsky stated that he could not and did not wish to state the truth during the pretrial investigation because he was convinced that his protestation of innocence would not reach "the leaders of the party and the government" unless he saved it for the trial, "if there should be such a trial." Vyshinsky returned to questioning Bessonov, and then declared a two-hour recess.[37]

Krestinsky's testimony certainly did reach "the leaders of the party and government." The defendants spoke into a microphone whose wires led not only to the amplifiers in the courtroom but also to the Kremlin. On various parts of the stage and in the courtroom there were additional hidden microphones for monitoring the entire performance. In addition the trial was filmed from start to finish.

During the two-hour recess the entire "headquarters staff" in charge of the trial gathered in premises especially reserved for them. Because the trial was such a major spectacle, it required an experienced stage director and a large group of assistants. Comfortable rooms not far from the October Hall had been equipped for this staff; the entrances were carefully concealed, well guarded, and known only to the initiated.[38] The staff was headed by the veteran security police official Leonid Zakovsky, who had held prominent posts in the Cheka-GPU-NKVD under all its previous leaders and continued to do so under Yezhov.

We do not know what discussion went on at "trial headquarters" in regard to Krestinsky. At the evening session of March 2 Vyshinsky questioned Rosenholz and Grinko. When they testified about their connections with the fascists, supposedly established through Krestinsky, Vyshinsky again turned to Krestinsky, who again denied any connections with the fascists.

At the morning session of March 3 Vyshinsky questioned Ivanov, Bukharin, Zubarev, and Vasilyev. No questions were directed to Krestinsky. But at the evening session, during the interrogation of Rakovsky, Vyshinsky again turned to Krestinsky, who at that point caved in. He agreed with Rakovsky's accusations against himself and reaffirmed his own pretrial depositions.

"Why, then," asked Vyshinsky, "did you engage in that Trotskyite

37. See the complete court record: *Sudebnyi otchet po delu antisovetskogo pravo-trotskistskogo bloka. Polnyi tekst stenograficheskogo otcheta* (Moscow, 1938), pp. 49–146. It is significant that the abridged record and the newspapers omitted a good part of the questioning of Krestinsky. The complete court record was published only in a small edition.

38. I cite all these details on the basis of the account given by Yevgeny Gnedin, who was responsible, through his position in the Foreign Affairs Commissariat, for the diplomatic corps and all foreign correspondents. He was the chief censor of foreign correspondents covering the Moscow trials and knew almost all the details of the organization of the trials. Gnedin died in 1983. During the last years of his life he published memoirs that told in part about his own participation in the Moscow trials.

provocation at yesterday's session?" Krestinsky answered that he had been ashamed to tell the truth, and had denied his guilt "mechanically" (*mashinal'no*).

VYSHINSKY: Mechanically?

KRESTINSKY: I didn't have the strength to tell world public opinion the truth, that I have all this time been carrying out Trotskyite work against the Soviet regime. I ask the court to record my declaration that I wholly and completely confess myself guilty of all the serious accusations made against me, and I confess myself completely responsible for the betrayal and treason done by me.

VYSHINSKY: At present I have no more questions for the defendant Krestinsky.

Today it is difficult, of course, to answer the question of what happened the night of March 2 to make Krestinsky change his testimony so sharply. S. I. Berdichevskaya, a party member since 1919, relates the testimony of a woman doctor from Lefortovo prison. Berdichevskaya had known her during the civil war and met her again at a transit prison during her years of confinement. On the second day of the 1938 trial this doctor had seen Krestinsky in Lefortovo prison savagely beaten and covered with blood. Berdichevskaya therefore suggests that Krestinsky himself appeared in court for the first session, but that in subsequent sessions a double took his place. Yevgeny Gnedin, who worked for the Commissariat of Foreign Affairs at the same trial, considers such conjecture quite possible. Kamil Ikramov, son of the defendant Akmal Ikramov, tells of a man he met in camp who knew Krestinsky quite well before 1937 and then saw him at the trial. He told Ikramov: "You know, Kamil, they must have done something awful to Krestinsky, because I simply didn't recognize him on the second day. Even his voice was different."

Alexander Orlov, basing his view on rumors rather than hard facts, had the following to say about this matter:

In foreign countries, among people who had been following through newspaper reports the progress of the trial, a significant question was asked: "What did they do to Krestinsky on the night from the 2nd to the 3rd of March?" That question evoked in the minds of men horrible thoughts of torture.

In reality, however, the inquisitors didn't have to coerce Krestinsky anew, because the whole scene of his repudiation of the testimony, which he had previously signed at the NKVD, was only a sham theatrical act staged on Stalin's instructions. Stalin was aware of the suspicion which had been aroused abroad by the fact that at the first two Moscow trials all the defendants, with one voice, admitted their guilt and, instead of pleading extenuating circumstances, each tried to ascribe to himself the lion's share in the crime.

Stalin realized that the foreign critics hit upon a very weak spot in his first two trials and that the defendants had overacted their parts. He therefore decided to show at the third Moscow trial that in his courts not all the defendants confessed like automatons. For that purpose the scene with Krestinsky was enacted. The choice fell on Krestinsky because he was one of the most pliable defendants and because, as a former lawyer, he oriented himself better in the setting of the trial and was able to catch better than the other defendants the meaning of the tricky moves of the prosecutor and adjust his part to them.[39]

I do not find Orlov's account of the Krestinsky incident particularly convincing.

Bukharin's testimony was also rather out of the ordinary: at any rate, it provided food for thought. It seems to have followed two separate plans. For the Soviet man in the street this testimony portrayed an enemy of Stalin and of Soviet power, but for anyone who wanted to look into the matter more thoughtfully a great many hints were thrown out calling into question the official version. For example, Bukharin confessed that he had belonged to the counterrevolutionary "Right-Trotskyite Bloc," but asserted that this organization was not fully aware of its own aims, had not "dotted all the i's." Admitting his own leadership of the "bloc," Bukharin noted that as leader he could not have known all the specific actions committed by its individual members. While stating that the "bloc" had aimed at the restoration of capitalism in the Soviet Union and that "we were all transformed into embittered counterrevolutionaries, traitors, spies, and terrorists," Bukharin emphatically denied every particular criminal act he was accused of, such as the murders of Kirov, Menzhinsky, Gorky, and Kuibyshev. He was just as categorical in denying that he had planned to murder Lenin in 1918, when he headed the "Left Communist" oppositional faction inside the Bolshevik Party.

While admitting at first that they had all become "spies," Bukharin later denied any knowledge of espionage activity by the "bloc." Throughout the trial he continued to assert that he had not engaged in espionage and knew nothing of any such acts. While describing in detail his "contacts" with Trotsky and preparations for a "coup d'état," he allowed a great many contradictions to appear in this testimony and consistently denied any connection with White Guard or fascist organizations or with British intelligence.

39. Orlov, *Secret History*, p. 290.

In his final words Bukharin gave a juridical appraisal of the trial. "Confessions of the accused," he said, "are not essential. Confessions of the accused are a medieval juridical principle." And this was said at a trial based entirely on confessions of the accused. It is not surprising that the "judges" were annoyed with Bukharin. At one point Ulrikh said to him: "So far you've been beating around the bush, saying nothing about the crimes." Vyshinsky also took note of Bukharin's tactics:

> You are obviously using certain tactics and do not want to tell the truth. You are hiding in a stream of words, in pettifoggery, side-tracking into politics, philosophy, theory, and so on. You should forget about these things once and for all. You are accused of espionage and are obviously, according to all the data of the investigation, a spy for a foreign intelligence agency. So stop the pettifoggery.

The newspapers also referred to Bukharin's special tactics: "He has a system, a tactic," wrote *Izvestia;* "his aim is to deflect all concrete charges from himself by wholesale declarations of his responsibility for everything."[40]

At the morning session on March 11, 1938, Vyshinsky gave his final speech as prosecutor, declaiming melodramatically:

> Time will pass. The graves of the despised traitors will be overgrown with weeds and thistles and covered with the eternal scorn of all honest people, the entire Soviet population. . . . And our people will march forward, as before, along the road swept clean of the last foul and dirty remnant of the past, headed by our beloved leader and teacher, the great Stalin.[41]

Late on the evening of March 12 the court recessed for six hours, reconvening at 4 A.M. on March 13. Moscow was deserted; there was no one around the trade union building, the scene of the trial. For about thirty minutes Ulrikh read the verdict, which all present heard standing up. The majority of the defendants were condemned to be shot. Pletnev was given twenty-five years in prison, Rakovsky twenty, and Bessonov fifteen.

On the night of March 15 Bukharin, Rykov, and their comrades in misfortune were shot. It is known that after the executions of those whom Stalin knew personally or for whom he had a special hatred, he almost always waited to hear with sadistic satisfaction a first-hand report from the executioners. I will not describe the way many once prominent

40. *Izvestia*, March 9, 1938. See also the editorial in the magazine *Oktyabr* (1938), no. 3, pp. 5–6.
41. *Izvestia*, March 12, 1938.

Bolsheviks behaved when facing execution. Not all of them were able to maintain self-possession. Bukharin did remain calm, though. He asked for a pencil and sheet of paper in order to write a last letter to Stalin, and his request was granted. The brief letter began with the words: "Koba, why did you need my death?" For the rest of his life Stalin kept this letter in one of the drawers of his desk, together with Lenin's sharp note about Stalin's rude treatment of Krupskaya and some other, similar documents.

■ 10
THE FRAUDULENCE OF THE MOSCOW SHOW TRIALS

In 1936–1938 the overwhelming majority of Soviet citizens, not only industrial and office workers but intellectuals as well, had no doubt that real enemies of the people were seated on the defendants' bench in the House of Trade Unions. Twelve- or thirteen-year-old schoolchildren, such as I was, believed this too, as did people like Yevgeny Gnedin who took part in the organization of these trials. In his memoirs Gnedin writes:

The October Hall in the House of Trade Unions invariably arouses painful memories for me. It is as though the room still held the fluids and nervous currents produced by the suffering and horror that in those days seized both the victims and the observers of those monstrous judicial crimes. As I sit in the room the phantoms of the executed servants of the Soviet state rise before me. Rykov, the former chairman of the Council of People's Commissars, as he assents to the absurd fabrications, holds tight to the back of a chair as though to a life preserver, or perhaps simply not to fall over from weakness. Next to him a manly face has turned into a death mask. It is Pyatakov, once the strong-willed organizer of Soviet industry. From the back of the stage of mournful-looking Akmal Ikramov, former secretary of the Central Committee of Uzbekistan, comes forward, while at stage front there sits the elegantly dressed former chairman of the Uzbekistan Council of People's Commissars Khodzhaev. A palefaced Bukharin, answering the prosecutor's questions, gazes searchingly out into the courtroom—or more exactly, into the future—with the hope that the real meaning of his evasive answers and philosophical argumentation will be understood.

In a loud, clear voice Krestinsky declares his innocence; then later (is this the real Krestinsky?) in uncharacteristically bureaucratic language he confirms his own guilt; Radek, after the reading of the verdict, turns his face to the onlookers and gazes out into the courtroom with a miserable farewell smile; Rosenholz, the former commissar of foreign trade, in concluding his final remarks, tries to sing the patriotic song "Fair is my native land," but breaks down after the first line. And Yagoda, the former commissar of internal affairs, who always had the fierce look of a wolf, now looks like a wolf at bay and pleads in his final remarks: "Comrades of the Cheka, Comrade Stalin, if you can, forgive me!" (as though he had done them some wrong, and not they him). The prosecutor Vyshinsky, giving his bloodthirsty closing speech, makes the deliberate gestures of an orator, as though he were speaking, not in front of a courtroom with restricted attendance, but before a vast audience. Meanwhile, the first five rows are occupied by a crew of peculiar and unpleasant types, some with massive square features, others sharp-nosed and vicious. These are the investigators, watching closely to see how their victims conduct themselves. Above the courtroom are several small windows covered with thin dark fabric. From behind these curtains it is possible to see down into the room, while from the courtroom floor it is possible to see that behind those curtains smoke is curling from a pipe. The chief stage director and chief villain of the piece is curious . . . to see how, at his command, this monstrous act of evil is proceeding.

I participated in the trials of the thirties as a representative of the Commissariat of Foreign Affairs. . . .

Surely Dostoevsky was right when he said, "It is a great misfortune that it is possible not to think of oneself as loathsome, and in fact not to be loathsome, while doing an obviously loathsome thing."

A great misfortune? Or a terrible wrong? In spite of everything, I think it is a misfortune. We became victims of the butchers long before we fell directly into their hands. Even when people are not behind bars, they can be fettered by unseen chains. One of many possible illustrations of this thought is the attitude people had toward the frame-up trials. Not only out of primitive fear did the loyal citizen dismiss any doubts that such a huge number of wreckers, spies, and enemies of the people were at large in the Soviet Union. The web in which we were caught was more complex than handcuffs and irons. We were bound by prejudices and illusions. We subjected ourselves to dogmas, not wishing to lose hope. In our minds there lurked a hidden fear of quite a special kind: If the trials of enemies of the people were analyzed consistently, the chain of logical conclusions could become a noose around our own necks. . . . I can explain things this way today as I write my memoirs. But I was incapable of such reasoning at the time of which I write. Among people of my acquaintance—and I am referring to unquestionably honest people—I did not know a single one who would have taken upon himself the burden of the final logical conclusions from an analysis of the political events of that time, in particular, the trials.[42]

The British Communist R. Palme Dutt, in a book published after the Twenty-Second Congress of the CPSU, wrote that "the final verdict on the trials, whose validity is disputed by many living, will rest with future historians."[43] There is no need to wait for future historians. The truth is that the trials were completely fraudulent. They were monstrous theatri-

42. Yevgeny Gnedin, *Katastrofa i novoe rozhdenie* (Amsterdam, 1977), pp. 281–284.
43. R. Palme Dutt, *The Internatsionale* (London, 1964), p. 246. [The author quotes the Soviet translation: *International* (Moscow, 1955), p. 251—D. J.]

cal productions that had to be rehearsed many times before they could be shown to spectators.

Only a small part of the testimony of the accused corresponded to the truth. It is obvious that Yagoda, the former commissar for internal affairs, did have a definite connection with the assassination of Kirov, which was not, however, committed on the instructions of "the Right-Trotskyite Bloc." There is also some truth in the testimony of Krestinsky and Bessonov about their contacts with the German army. But these contacts did not involve any espionage or treason. Both men had in fact met with representatives of the German army in 1921–1922—with Lenin's knowledge—in connection with the secret part of the Rapallo agreement between the Soviet and German governments. As a Politburo member, Stalin also knew about these meetings. In the early twenties the Soviet government was anxious to end its diplomatic and economic isolation. Thus, certain agreements with defeated Germany, even on military matters, were advantageous to the Soviet Union. It was absurd, seventeen years later, to represent these international agreements as the work of Krestinsky, Bessonov, and Trotsky.

Most of the testimony consisted of outright lies, deliberately fabricated in the torture chambers of the NKVD and put into the mouths of the accused by sadistic investigators. Today no one charges the former opposition leaders with the murders of Kirov, Gorky, Kuibyshev, and Menzhinsky. The complete and unconditional rehabilitation of Tukhachevsky, Yakir, Gamarnik, Uborevich, and other Soviet military leaders reveals the falsity of most of the charges made at the trial of the "Right-Trotskyite Bloc." A basic theme of the testimony at this trial was the defendants' "criminal connection" with the military leaders. Some of the accused "sincerely and frankly" confessed that Yakir in collusion with the "rightists" ordered one of the terrorists to murder Yezhov, while Gamarnik ordered another to slay Stalin.[44] The "rightists" also testified that in 1934 Tukhachevsky and Gamarnik had worked out plans to seize the Kremlin, kill the members of the Central Committee, and arrest the delegates to the Seventeenth Party Congress.

V. F. Sharangovich, one of the obscure defendants, "sincerely" confessed that Goloded and Chervyakov, the leaders of the Byelorussian Communist Party, were ready to turn Byelorussia over to Poland. Both Goloded and Chervyakov have been completely rehabilitated, as have

44. Somehow none of the dozens of carefully prepared assassination attempts was successful—except in the case of Kirov.

the Uzbek leaders Ikramov and Khodzhaev, who allegedly tried to hand over Central Asia to the British.[45] At the same trial the "rightists" repeatedly named the Old Bolshevik Yan Rudzutak as their accomplice; he has been posthumously rehabilitated. So has Yenukidze, who, Rykov testified, attended the underground meeting where the decision was made to kill Kirov.

A 1934 attempt on Molotov's life in the town of Prokopyevsk loomed large in the trial of the "Parallel Center." Many of the accused spoke at length about the organization of this attempt and told who had insisted on killing Molotov. We know now, from Nikolai Shvernik's speech to the Twenty-Second Party Congress, that no such attempt ever took place; Molotov made up the whole story for the sake of provocation. A plot to kill Yezhov was a major theme in the trial of the "Right-Trotskyite Center." In his speech of March 11, 1938, Vyshinsky accused the conspirators of planning to poison the air in Yezhov's office by a mixture of mercury and acid. After Yezhov was killed as an enemy of the people, this fantastic story vanished from all publications, which continued to describe the crimes of the "Right-Trotskyite Bloc." Vyshinsky's allegation of this crime was simply removed from subsequent printings of his speeches.

Krestinsky, too, has been fully rehabilitated. In 1963, in an article entitled "A Diplomat of the Leninist School" Academician Ivan Maisky presented a true portrait of Krestinsky and his contributions to Soviet foreign policy.[46] In February 1964 *Pravda* included G. F. Grinko, one-time commissar of finance, and I. A. Zelensky, onetime chairman of the Central Trade Union Council, among the Bolsheviks who directed the great work of economic construction and cultural advancement during the first five-year plan. In the 1938 trial they were accused of spying, wrecking, and serving as agents of the tsarist secret police before the revolution.[47] Another such "agent"—from the time he was in the eighth grade—was V. I. Ivanov, former commissar of forestry; he too has been fully rehabilitated. So have Gorky's personal secretary, P. P. Kryuchkov, Dr. Pletnev, and others. The list of such examples, proving the fraudulence of the political trials of the thirties, could be greatly extended.

45. For example, *Pravda*, on April 9, 1964, referred to Ikramov as a "loyal fighter in the Leninist Old Guard," and *Izvestia* of May 24, 1966, called him "a fighter for the great cause."
46. *Izvestia*, September 23, 1963.
47. *Pravda*, February [?], 1964.

At the present time almost all the defendants in the Moscow political trials have been rehabilitated as citizens, and about twenty have been posthumously restored to party membership. But until 1988 there was no formal, public annulment of the verdicts. Most of the chief defendants —Bukharin, Rykov, Zinoviev, Kamenev, Pyatakov, Radek, and the rest —had not been reinstated as party members, although they held prominent posts in the party and government at the time of their arrests.

Not one of the books on party history or the history of the Soviet Union that appeared after the Twentieth Party Congress mentioned the trials of the thirties. A 1962 textbook on party history had two lines on the subject: "The repression of the thirties was begun against former ideological opponents, who were represented as agents of imperialism and foreign intelligence services." All subsequent editions of this textbook, edited by the top party leader and Academician Boris Ponamarev, dropped those two lines. In 1964 a preliminary version of the ninth volume of a *History of the USSR*, printed in one thousand copies and circulated among historians for discussion, contained a one-page criticism of the Moscow trials as undeniably fraudulent. This page was deleted from the final text.[48]

Suggestions or demands for a formal annulment of the verdicts in the purge trials were made many times in the sixties and seventies. After the Twenty-Second Party Congress four old party activists[49] sent the following letter to the Politburo:

Dear Comrades, Members of the Presidium of the Central Committee [i.e., the Politburo]:

We appeal to you on an important matter. The path of the Bolshevik revolutionary N. I. Bukharin, stretching over thirty years, was complex. On that path he committed serious mistakes of a theoretical and political order, for which he caught it from Lenin more than once. But Lenin's criticism of Bukharin's mistakes never questioned his devotion to the party and the revolution; that was criticism and arguments with *a man who shared his views on the basic problems of Bolshevism*.

N. Bukharin was noted for his ability to admit his mistakes and correct them without false pride. For that very reason in Lenin's time he was not put out of the party for his mistakes; he was a member of the Politburo and for twelve years the editor of the central organ, *Pravda*.

48. [A translation of that page appears in the first edition of *Let History Judge*, p. 182.— G. S.]

49. The authors were: Yelena Stasova, party member since 1898; Vyacheslav Karpinsky, member since 1898; P. Katanyan, member since 1903; and A. Rudenko, member since 1905.

Lenin, in his Testament, giving as it were final characterizations of some party officials, a stocktaking of the entire past, called Bukharin the biggest and the most valuable theorist in the party.

Bukharin was expelled from the party and removed from the Central Committee only in 1937, on the basis of testimony given during the "investigation" of his alleged espionage and terrorist activity, the absurdity of which is now clear to everyone. P. Pospelov, a member of the Central Committee, at the All-Union Conference of Historians in December 1962, declared unequivocally (and this was published in the press) that Bukharin was no terrorist or spy. How then, after such a definite declaration at a gathering of two thousand people and in the press, can one preserve the verdict of the court and the expulsion from the party in the absence of a *corpus delicti?*

This discredits the court. . . . Annulment of the illegal verdict and reinstatement of Bukharin in the party will not only be acts to restore justice personally in relation to one of our party's outstanding leaders of the Leninist period; they will also play a big role in the further elaboration of the party's history during the relevant periods, which is extremely hampered just now by the forbidden position of Bukharin's name: only bad things can be written about him now, which leads to distortion of these sections of history in general.

We think that restoration of the truth and annulment of decisions based on false documents will raise still higher the party's authority and our country's prestige.

We, who knew Bukharin personally at many stages of our glorious history, with his shortcomings and his merits as a Bolshevik revolutionary, fully understand and share such warm words of Lenin, spoken by him in the last few minutes of his life, as a sort of farewell to the party, such words about Nikolai Bukharin as the Testament does not have concerning any one else: the rightful favorite of the party.

Those words are a great obligation on all of us, and that forces us to turn to you, members of the party's Presidium, with the request not to let the name of the man who was so appreciated by Lenin remain in the camp of traitors and to rehabilitate Bukharin from the charges made in 1937 by annulling the verdict and reinstating him in the party.

A man whom Lenin called the rightful favorite of the party cannot remain in the list of traitors and outcasts from the party.[50]

All four of the Old Bolsheviks who signed this letter have died. Their appeal remained unanswered until 1988.

From 1978 to 1980 an intensive campaign was waged in various European countries for the rehabilitation of Bukharin, mostly by Communist and other left organizations. Appeals for his rehabilitation, signed by prominent figures from the workers' and Communist movements, were published. In Italy, France, Yugoslavia, and even China collections of

---

50. A copy of this appeal is in my archive.

Bukharin's most important writings appeared, and major Communist newspapers carried articles about him. At that time the Central Committee of the CPSU did not respond in any way, preferring the absurd and laughable pose of silence, which only discredited the Soviet Union.

It was ridiculous for Soviet historical scholarship to maintain this silence, to pretend that there were no political trials in the mid-thirties; that Trotsky, Bukharin, Rykov, Tomsky, Pyatakov, Kamenev, and Zinoviev were not outstanding leaders; that they never worked under Lenin; that they did not, despite their mistakes, do great and useful work in our party. It was ridiculous that their names were not to be found even in encyclopedias and handbooks, or, if they were included in the index to Lenin's works or the record of a party congress, their names were followed by a careful list of only sins, blunders, and mistakes.

Another crucial question arises: What methods did Yezhov and Yagoda use to obtain "confessions" from the prisoners, many of whom had formerly been tough revolutionaries? It has been said that Bukharin, Kamenev, Rakovsky, and the others did not really appear in court; skillfully made-up and specially trained NKVD agents supposedly took their place. But some who attended the trials and who knew many of the defendants well, including Yevgeny Gnedin, Ilya Ehrenburg, and others whom I personally interviewed in the sixties denied this supposition.[51]

Ehrenburg expressed his confidence to me in a conversation that it really was Bukharin, Rykov, Krestinsky, Rosenholz, and Rakovsky who sat on the defendants' bench. Ehrenburg did notice, however, their general inertia and sluggishness. They gave their testimony in a kind of mechanical language, without the intonation and temperament peculiar to each of them. Although each one used some of his stylistic peculiarities, for the most part they all used the language of an average office clerk, with turns of speech that they had never employed previously. At the same time they did not give the impression of people who had been recently subjected to prolonged torture. Ehrenburg said that he thought many of the prisoners had been given some kind of drug that takes away one's will *(obezvoliaiushchii preparat)*. The suggestion merits consideration. There are medicines that can temporarily transform an energetic and resolute man into an obedient puppet. The use of such methods as

51. Ehrenburg was a childhood friend of Bukharin's. Stalin himself saw to it that Ehrenburg was issued a pass to attend the trial. "Arrange for a pass for Ehrenburg," Stalin told the new editor of *Izvestia.* "Let him have a look at his old buddy."

hypnosis and subliminal suggestion are also possible. It is worth noting that a well-known hypnotist, Arnoldo, disappeared in the mid-thirties.

Some foreign authors have suggested that certain ideological and psychological techniques were effectively used on the defendants before the trials. For example, the historian François Fejto argues that the accused in such trials cooperate in their own destruction because of their abiding faith in Stalinism as a form of Marxist Leninism. They agree that the cause must be subject to strict discipline—in other words, to the will of the leaders. Thus, in a time of savage class struggle, the very fact that the leaders accuse them proves "objectively" (or subconsciously, as people say in the West) they have indeed become allies of enemy forces. The only service they can still do for the cause is to strengthen the party's unity by condemning themselves.[52] Arthur Koestler gives a similar interpretation in his 1947 novel *Darkness at Noon*.

Such methods were undoubtedly used on some of the defendants. There are many indications that this was the way the investigators succeeded in making Radek talk and getting him to help write the basic scenario for the trials. But it is unlikely that such primitive arguments could have convinced Bukharin. More likely, he was blackmailed by threats of reprisal against his young wife, his elderly and sick father, and his newborn son. There is much evidence that such blackmail occurred. During the first months of the investigation the Bukharin family was allowed to continue living in their old apartment in the Kremlin, and notes from Bukharin's wife were delivered to him, together with books that he requested from his library and photographs of his son. All of this ended once Bukharin was broken and began to "testify." His wife was arrested even before the trial began.

Despite some of the methods mentioned above, it may be concluded from the available evidence that the main instrument of the investigators was the most refined torture, which broke the prisoners' will and made them sign any story of their "crimes" prepared beforehand by the investigators. N. K. Ilyukhov reports that in 1938 he shared a cell in Butyrskaya prison with Bessonov, who had received a long prison term in the trial of the "Right-Trotskyite Bloc." Bessonov told Ilyukhov, who had been his colleague at the Institute of Red Professors, that he was subjected to long and painful torture before his trial. To begin with he was kept on the "conveyor" for seventeen days without food or sleep. He

52. [The author cites François Fejto, *La tragedie hongroise* (Paris, 1956), p. 90, from the Soviet translation: *Vengerskaia tragediia* (Moscow, 1957), p. 55.—D. J.]

would fall down and pass out, but they would bring him to and force him again and again to stand up. Then he was methodically beaten, especially on the kidneys, until this once healthy and strong man became emaciated. The defendants were warned that such tortures would be continued even after the trial if they did not give the necessary testimony.

Some defendants were promised their lives and assignment to party or Soviet work in Siberia or the Far East. They were persuaded that their testimony was needed at the time in connection with the complex international situation, that their sentences would be mere formalities, and that they would be reinstated in the party later, although they might have to work under assumed names for several years. Drobnis' wife states that such a promise was made to her husband during the preparations for the trial of the "Parallel Center." He managed to send word of this promise to his family, asking them "not to worry."

■ 11
MASS REPRESSION AMONG FORMER OPPOSITIONISTS

On March 5, 1937, Stalin told the Central Committee that only active Trotskyists still loyal to their exiled leader had to be repressed. "Among our comrades," he said, "are a certain number of former Trotskyites who abandoned Trotskyism a long time ago and are fighting against it. It would be stupid to defame these comrades."[53] Following the publication of this speech, some local NKVD agencies began to scale down the repression. Soon, however, they received appropriate explanations of Stalin's speech, and the terror revived with new intensity. In fact, by the end of 1937 almost all the ex-oppositionists had been arrested, regardless of the views they held at the time.

The fate of Vladimir Antonov-Ovseyenko is indicative. As a member of the Military Revolutionary Committee and leader in storming the Winter Palace, he had arrested the Provisional Government. Later, this legendary hero of the October revolution commanded armies and entire fronts of the civil war. In 1923–1927 he was aligned with Trotsky, but broke with him in 1928 and was appointed Soviet ambassador to Czechoslova-

53. Stalin, *Sochineniia*, 14:228–229. At the time of Stalin's death only thirteen volumes of his works had been published. After his death no further work was done on the Soviet edition. However, the Hoover Institution in Stanford, California, completed the task, publishing volumes 14–16 in 1967, in Russian, using the same format and typescript as the Soviet edition.

kia. When the Spanish Civil War broke out in 1936, he was sent as Soviet consul to Barcelona, where he served as one of the chief Soviet advisers to the Republican government of Catalonia. In late August 1937 he was recalled to Moscow, without any explanation. His son describes what happened:

> In the lobby of Building No. 2 of the Council of People's Commissars [Antonov-Ovseyenko] met the frightened gaze of the elevator operator. The door of nearly every office in the seven-story building was sealed with the large wax seal of the NKVD. . . . A week passed, then another. Each morning he got up with nothing to do and spent the day aimlessly, and the long night, waiting—for what?
>
> Stalin called Antonov to the Kremlin in the thirtieth day after his return to Moscow. [Stalin] began with some reproaches. It seemed that Antonov had functioned too independently in Spain, hadn't coordinated the steps he took with the Soviet Commissariat of Foreign Affairs. Many complaints against him had come in.
>
> [Antonov] explained: "It was sometimes necessary to take risks and make bold decisions on the spur of the moment, as required by combat conditions." Apparently his interlocutor was convinced, for his appointment as commissar of justice [of the RSFSR] came a day later. However, in the gray building on Bolshaya Dmitrovka, in an office on the fifth floor, Public Prosecutor Vyshinsky had already prepared the warrant for the arrest of the new people's commissar.[54]

Antonov-Ovseyenko was arrested on October 11, 1937. He had held the post of commissar of justice for less than two weeks. After a short time he was shot.[55]

A similar fate befell the revolutionary Ye. Eshba, who had actively participated in the revolution and civil war in the Caucasus, leading the uprising in Abkhazia in 1921. In 1926 he belonged to the Trotskyist opposition, but soon left it and, having admitted his mistakes, was reinstated in the party. Later, at responsible posts in the Commissariats of Foreign Trade and of Heavy Industry, he did much for the construction of socialism. But in 1937 Eshba was arrested on the charge of Trotskyist activity and perished.[56] Both Antonov-Ovseyenko and Eshba have been

54. Anton Antonov-Ovseyenko, *Portret tirana* (New York, Press, 1980), p. 193. The son of Vladimir Antonov-Ovseyenko himself spent many years in prison. His book contains many inaccuracies, is not written in a professional manner, and received many bad reviews in the Russian émigré press. Yet I consider it an important document. The conditions necessary for professional work on current historical topics do not exist for Soviet historians today.

55. For an account of the courage displayed by this hero of October in the last days of his life, see the essay by Yuri Tomsky in *Novy mir*, 1964, no. 11.

56. See *Zaria vostoka*, March 20, 1968.

rehabilitated, as has the popular literary critic Aleksandr Voronsky. One of the old-time Leninists, Voronsky belonged to the Trotskyist opposition from 1925 to 1928 but then broke with it.

The man who held party card number one of the Petrograd Committee of the RSDLP, Grigory Fyodorov, suffered the same fate. A self-taught worker who was elected to the Central Committee at the April Conference of 1917 and took an active part in the October insurrection, he had become in the mid-thirties director of the All-Union Cartographic Trust. In 1967 *Izvestia* devoted a long article to Fyodorov, which failed to note that he had been shot in 1937.[57]

The NKVD also struck at former members of earlier and smaller oppositions—at the short-lived Democratic Centralist group of 1920–1921, for example. N. Osinsky, director of the Central Statistical Agency, I. Stukov, and I. K. Dashkovsky were among its former adherents who were arrested in 1937. Most members of the Workers' Opposition of 1920–1922 also perished, including Aleksandr Shlyapnikov, who was shot in 1937. He was one of the major leaders of the Petrograd Bolshevik organization during the February revolution, and during the difficult year 1916 he had headed the Russian Bureau of the Bolshevik Central Committee. Shlyapnikov became people's commissar of labor in the first Soviet government and later served on the Revolutionary Military Committee of the Southern Front and of the Caucasian Front. Before his arrest in 1937 he was chairman of the Soviet executive committee of an oblast and a member of the All-Union Central Executive Committee of the Soviets.

Ye. N. Ignatov, a prominent leader of the Moscow Bolsheviks during the October revolution, also perished. Within the Workers' Opposition he headed his own subgroup. Later in the twenties he withdrew from all oppositional activity, and in the mid-thirties he was director of advanced courses in Soviet structure for the All-Union Central Executive Committee. The NKVD also eliminated A. S. Kiselev, who had been a party member since 1898 and a member of the Central Committee of the RSDLP before the revolution; from 1924 to 1938 he was secretary of the Soviet government's Central Executive Committee. This long period could not atone for his brief adherence to the Workers' Opposition in the early twenties; he was arrested and shot. The same fatal flaw was in the record of N. A. Kubyak, who in the twenties and thirties had served as a

57. L. Shinkarev, "Mandat Revoliutsii," *Izvestia*, April 6, 1967.

secretary of the party's Central Committee, commissar of agriculture, and chairman of the Central Executive Committee's council on city management.

Most of the Syrtsov-Lominadze group also perished; the same was true for the Ryutin group. In the union republics there was mass repression of party members who had at some time been accused of "national deviationism." Of course Stalin did not miss the chance to settle scores with his personal enemy, Budu Mdivani, who in the thirties served as deputy chairman of the Council of People's Commissars of the Georgian Soviet Republic. In 1936 he was expelled from the party and soon annihilated. Lenin, of course, had sided with Mdivani and his supporters in the 1922 conflict with Stalin, Ordzhonikidze, and Dzerzhinsky. The conflict with Mdivani had nearly ruined Stalin's career, and he did not forget it. Nor did Mdivani, who at important party gatherings often gave witty speeches with implied criticism of Stalin, as I. A. Sats relates in his memoirs:

Budu Mdivani was a big favorite of Stalin's as an actor and witty raconteur, whose talent was deeply marked by the Georgian national character. Stalin's later attempts at political reconciliation with Mdivani—after their first clash in 1922 —led to nothing, however. In the late 1920s Budu told others that he had replied to all attempts at persuasion with these words: "Koba can ask me anything he wants and I'll do it. But not that." His speeches at party congresses critically and satirically describing Stalin's methods were widely known. Here, for example, is one of his pronouncements from the rostrum: "The Central Committee does not give orders. The Central Committee (here Mdivani would roll up his sleeve and make a fist) only makes—r-r-recommendations!" And another: "We must not deviate to the Left. (A gesture with the left hand.) We must not deviate to the Right. (A gesture with the right.) We must go straight down the middle with the general line. (A convoluted gesture, as of a snake crawling.)" [58]

Such things were more than Stalin could forgive.

Thus, many thousands of party members who had long ago ceased opposition activity were suddenly arrested and destroyed. (In emphasizing their cessation of political opposition, I do not mean to imply, of course, that oppositional activity, past or present, should be regarded as a criminal offense.) These arrests and killings were major crimes committed by Stalin and the NKVD.

At the same time that the NKVD was arresting and destroying former members of opposition groups within the Bolshevik Party, it was doing

58. I. A. Sats, "Iz vospominanii," unpublished manuscript, p. 21.

no less to the party's defunct rivals. Socialist Revolutionaries, Mensheviks, Bundists, Anarchists, Cadets, Mussawatists, Dashnaks, and so on who had chosen to quit their parties and stay in the Soviet Union were now punished for their choice. Many of them had already been in Soviet prisons in the twenties, and in the mid-thirties they had the status of internal exiles, working in small towns or cities away from the main centers. Although they kept in touch or corresponded with one another as friends, they did not engage in any political, let alone anti-Soviet, activity. (I am not referring, of course, to such former Mensheviks as Vyshinsky, who were serving Stalin out of both fear and devotion.) Those arrested included, for example, among former leaders of the Left SRs, Maria Spiridonovna, Boris Kamkov, I. A. Mayorov, A. A. Izmailovich, and Irina Kakhovskaya, and among Right SRs, Abram Gotz and K. Gogua.

Nor did Stalin spare members of the old generation of the People's Will. Almost immediately after the Kirov assassination the Society of Former Hard Labor Prisoners and Internal Exiles was dissolved and its magazine *Katorga i ssylka* (Hard Labor and Internal Exile) was suppressed. The NKVD rounded up first of all people who had been involved in terrorist activity before the revolution. Two such persons, A. V. Pribyl and N. M. Salova, were among those arrested in 1935. People's Will supporters who had not engaged in terrorism before the revolution were also arrested. Ye. N. Kovalskaya, who had been active in the Southern Russia Workers' Union and was a permanent member of the editorial board of *Katorga i ssylka*, was imprisoned in 1935, and a number of others, such V. I. Sukhomlin and A. I. Pribylova-Korba, were arrested later.

Almost all these people died. In the flood of rehabilitated persons in 1956–1957 I succeeded in finding only one former Menshevik, whose name I have forgotten, one former Anarchist (Z. B. Gandlevskaya), and one Left SR (Irina Kakhovskaya). The latter, shortly before her death, gave her friends some brief reminiscences about the terrible years in Stalin's prisons and camps.[59]

N. V. Ustryalov, the ideologist of the Change of Landmarks trend, was also arrested and shot at this time. Formerly one of the leaders of the Cadet Party, he lived in Harbin in the twenties. After his reconciliation

---

59. For a somewhat abridged English translation of Kakhovskaya's memoirs, see *An End to Silence: Uncensored Opinion in the Soviet Union* (New York: 1982), pp. 81–90. The Russian original is in *Politicheskii dnevnik* (Amsterdam, 1974), pp. 707–742.

with the Soviet regime, he began to work for the Soviet-owned Chinese Eastern Railway as the director of a library. When Japan seized Manchuria many employees of the railway returned to the Soviet Union, among them Ustryalov.

Quite a few former members of other parties had broken with their pasts and joined the Soviet Communist Party, fighting on the Bolshevik side in the civil war and later holding responsible positions in the government, the party, and the Comintern—among them, V. F. Malkin, G. Zaks, A. P. Kolegaev, F. Yu. Svetlov, Ye. Yarchuk, G. B. Sandomirsky, and V. Shatov. These people were destroyed without open political trials; indeed, their arrests were hardly mentioned in the press. Apparently their criminality was considered too obvious to need publicity, since former members of defunct intraparty oppositions had become "enemies of the people."

A question naturally arises; what impelled Stalin to physically destroy all former oppositionists and members of other parties, when they represented no serious threat to Soviet rule? This is part of a larger problem that will be treated later on. Only a few comments are in order now.

First of all, Stalin carried out a planned, premeditated, political act. In January 1933, speaking before a Central Committee plenum, Stalin declared that desperate resistance by the defeated classes—*byvshie liudi*, he called them at one point, the Russian equivalent of *les ci-devants*— would increase as the Soviet state approached the final victory of socialism.

Defeated groups of the old counterrevolutionary parties, the SRs, the Mensheviks, the bourgeois nationalists of the center and the borderlands, may revive and stir; fragments of the counterrevolutionary elements of the Trotskyists and right deviationists may revive and stir. This, of course, is not frightening. But all this must be kept in mind, if we want to get rid of these elements quickly and without special sacrifices.[60]

Stalin thus left no doubt about his desire to "get rid of these elements," although they had not yet stirred and perhaps might never do so.

The physical destruction of former opponents was not dictated by any real fear on Stalin's part that a new and more dangerous opposition would be formed. Such considerations hardly troubled him. In part, this operation was simply a matter of political revenge against his former opponents, who had sometimes made unrestrained comments about him. In

60. Stalin, *Sochineniia*, 13:212.

the twenties Stalin was not powerful enough to take physical vengeance on them. He patiently waited for his chance. When most of the opposition leaders capitulated, Stalin gave only formal acknowledgment to their actions. He hypocritically said one thing and planned another, and as soon as he felt strong enough he destroyed the activists of the former oppositions. Their destruction helped him, in turn, to strengthen his own power and influence. Stalin's resentment and vindictiveness, however, were not the main reason for the course of action he took.

By organizing political trials of former oppositionists, people who were already discredited, defenseless, powerless, Stalin sought to terrorize the party and the people, to create an emergency situation, and thereby to allow himself, the "warrior" and "savior" of the state, to concentrate more power in his own hands. Another important motive was undoubtedly his desire to blame the "enemies of the people" for the political and economic difficulties that still existed in the country. Every despot building the cult of his own person needs a scapegoat. In 1928–1932 it was the "kulaks" and the "wreckers" among the bourgeois intelligentsia; in the mid-thirties it was the former members of various oppositions.

But Stalin could not and would not limit himself to the destruction of former oppositionists. The logic of the struggle for power and the logic of crime led Stalin further, until he finally decimated the main cadres of party and state personnel and anyone not to his liking in the fields of science and culture, regardless of whether they had belonged to an opposition. Thus, the trials and repression I have discussed were only a prologue to an even more frightful campaign of mass terror, one unprecedented in world history.

■ 12

TROTSKY IN THE MIDDLE AND LATE THIRTIES

At the first major show trial in August 1936 Trotsky was condemned to death in absentia. At that time he was in Norway, where he was formally prohibited from political activity. When he heard the first details of the Moscow trial, however, he immediately violated this prohibition. He began to issue press releases and sent telegrams to the League of Nations and statements to various public meetings. The Norwegian government reacted immediately; it proposed that Trotsky leave the country. But since no other Western country wanted him on its territory, he had to remain for the time being in Norway, where he was kept under strict house arrest and not allowed to make public statements. Of course, this placed him at a great disadvantage. His eldest son, Leon Sedov, took up his father's defense, but Sedov's every step was known to the NKVD through informers whom Sedov thought were his loyal collaborators. In late December 1937 Mexico agreed to give Trotsky political asylum. Under guard and in deepest secrecy Trotsky and his wife were put on a tanker hired by the Norwegian government, which sailed for the Americas. On January 9 it arrived in Mexico. Two weeks later the trial of the "Parallel Center" began in Moscow ,with former Trotskyists predominating among the defendants.

In Mexico Trotsky threw himself into activity with great energy, but this was not reflected in the world press, for Trotsky was not popular in either liberal or conservative bourgeois circles; nor was he popular among Social Democrats or Communists. Moreover, Trotsky did not have a good understanding of what was going on in Moscow; in his public statements he often mistook wish for reality, as in the following example:

> While temporarily saving Stalin's rule, the bloody purge has definitively shaken asunder the social and political props of Bonapartism. Stalin is drawing close to the termination of his tragic mission. The more it seems to him that he no longer needs anyone, the closer draws the hour when he himself will prove needed by nobody. Should the bureaucracy succeed in changing the forms of property and extruding from itself a new property-owning class, this new class will find itself other leaders who will not have ties with the revolutionary past and who will be —more literate. It is hardly likely that Stalin will thereupon receive a single word of gratitude for the work he has done. The open counterrevolution will make short shrift of him, most probably on the charge of—Trotskyism. . . .
>
> This path, however, is not at all predestined. . . . It is quite probable that revolutionary upheavals in Europe and Asia will forestall the overthrow of the Stalin clique by capitalist counterrevolution and prepare the way for its downfall under the blows of the working masses. In that event Stalin will have even less cause to count on gratitude.[61]

Immediately after the trial of the "Parallel Center" Trotsky decided to organize a countertrial to expose the judicial farce put on in the Soviet Union. Most prominent and prestigious Western intellectuals, however, refused the invitation to participate in the countertrial. Some of them believed much of what was said in Moscow. Others did not believe it but had a negative attitude toward Trotsky. With great difficulty and thanks especially to the assistance of his American followers Trotsky succeeded

---

61. *Biulleten' oppozitsii* (September–October 1937) no. 58–59, p. 4. [Cf. *Writings of Leon Trotsky, 1936–1937* (New York, 1978), pp. 331–332. —G. S.]

in having a special commission formed to inquire into the charges against him; it was headed by the eighty-year-old American philosopher and educator John Dewey, a man whose reputation as an objective scholar was beyond question. The commission held hearings in Trotsky's house in Mexico under heavy police protection. Dewey visited the Soviet Embassy in Mexico City and the headquarters of the Mexican Communist Party, asking that they send representatives to the commission hearings. Of course his request was refused. The hearings began on April 10, 1937, and lasted for a week, but the Western press paid little attention to them. Several months after the hearings (during which time the commission members studied the documents and testimony presented by Trotsky) the commission's verdict was published. It said in part:

The Commission finds:
(1) That the conduct of the Moscow trials was such as to convince any unprejudiced person that no effort was made to ascertain the truth.
(2) While confessions are necessarily entitled to the most serious consideration, the confessions themselves contain such inherent improbabilities as to convince the Commission that they do not represent the truth, irrespective of any means used to obtain them.

After rejecting all the specific charges against Trotsky and his son as unproved and finding that "the Prosecutor fantastically falsified Trotsky's role before, during and after the October Revolution," the Commission concluded:

(22) We therefore find the Moscow trials to be frame-ups.
(23) We therefore find Trotsky and Sedov not guilty.[62]

The public meeting where the commission's verdict was announced was attended by 2,500 people. Isaac Deutscher, Trotsky's biographer, writes:

Trotsky received this verdict with joy. Yet its effect was small, if not negligible. Dewey's voice commanded some attention in the United States; but it was ignored in Europe, where opinion was preoccupied with the critical events of the year, the last year before Munich, and with the vicissitudes of the French Popular Front and the Spanish Civil War.[63]

62. [*Not Guilty: Report of the Commission of Inquiry into the Charges Made Against Leon Trotsky in the Moscow Trials*, 2d ed. (New York, 1972), pp. xiii–xv. A Russian translation of the commission's verdict is in *Biulleten' oppozitsii* (February 1938) no. 62–63, pp. 1–2. —G. S.]
63. Isaac Deutscher, *The Prophet Outcast: Trotsky, 1929–1940* (London, 1963), p. 393.

The commission's verdict could not of course save Trotsky from Stalin's vengeance. After the last show trial in Moscow Stalin ordered the NKVD to give top priority to the task of killing Trotsky. A special department was established within the NKVD to carry out this task and to deal with several former Soviet diplomats and intelligence agents who had refused to return to the Soviet Union in the period 1936–1938. In early 1938 Leon Sedov died under suspicious circumstances in a French hospital after a successful operation for appendicitis. Inside the Soviet Union Trotsky's second son, Sergei, who had been nonpolitical and had refused to go abroad with his parents, was arrested and soon died. At the same time mass shootings of Trotskyists were carried out in the camps. Former Trotskyists who had capitulated were shot as well as those who had remained loyal to Trotsky and been imprisoned since the late twenties. Hardly any survived.[64]

The trial of the "Right-Trotskyite Bloc" took place, as I have indicated, after the Dewey commission's verdict. Trotsky continued to defend himself against slander, demonstrating the absurdity of the charges against Rykov, Bukharin, Yagoda, and others. But his voice was not very audible. Moreover, the enormous scale of the terror eluded Trotsky, who no longer had direct contacts in the USSR. Nor did Western reporters and observers have any detailed or exact information about the events under way. As Isaac Deutscher notes:

While the trials in Moscow were engaging the world's awestruck attention, the great massacre in the concentration camps passed almost unnoticed. It was carried out in such deep secrecy that it took years for the truth to leak out. Trotsky knew better than anyone that only a small part of the terror revealed itself through the trials; he surmised what was happening in the background. Yet even he could not guess or visualize the whole truth. . . . He still assumed that the anti-Stalinist forces would presently come to the fore, articulate and politically effective; and in particular that they would be able to overthrow Stalin in the course of the war and to conduct the war towards a victorious and revolutionary conclusion. He still reckoned on the regeneration of the old Bolshevism to whose wide and deep influence Stalin's ceaseless crusades seemed to be unwitting tributes. He was unaware of the fact that all anti-Stalinist forces had been wiped out; that Trotskyism, Zinovievism, and Bukharinism, all drowned in blood,

64. After the rehabilitations of 1956–1957 several tens of thousands of survivors of the terrible years of the Gulag returned to Moscow. Among them were several thousand Communist Party members of various generations, including Old Bolsheviks. Among them I managed to meet only two former Trotskyists, two people who had only voted on some occasion for Trotsky's platform, and one Zinovievist.

had, like some Atlantis, vanished from all political horizons; and that he himself was now the sole survivor of Atlantis.[65]

In 1938 Trotsky was preoccupied with the organization of the Fourth International. In September of that year his supporters managed to convene a founding congress of the new organization, but in fact it was a narrow gathering consisting exclusively of Trotskyists, with only twenty-one delegates present from eleven countries. Trotsky himself could not attend the congress, which was held in great secrecy near Paris and lasted only one day, from morning till night.

Trotsky placed great hopes in the Fourth International. He was certain that the new organization would play virtually the decisive role in the class battles of the decade ahead and that a new war would work in favor of the Trotskyists. He wrote that "in the course of the coming ten years the program of the Fourth International will gain the adherence of millions, and these revolutionary millions will be able to storm heaven and earth."[66] History took a different and more complicated course, however. The ultra-left organizations that called themselves (and still call themselves) "Trotskyist" were not able to win significant influence in the working class either during the war or in the postwar decades.

As for Trotsky himself, his fate was tragic. Stalin's agents continued the "hunt" against him, with several prominent Mexican Communists taking part. Trotsky's house in Coyoacan was turned into a veritable fortress, constantly under guard. One night in May 1940 the house was attacked by an armed group led by the Mexican artist and Communist Party leader David Siquieros. The attack, which included the machine-gunning of the villa, failed, although the attackers succeeded in disarming the police guard and occupying the entire Trotsky house for twenty minutes. Not far from the place where Trotsky and his wife lay huddled under a bed in a dark room, nearly a hundred machine-gun shells were later found. The villa was guarded more closely after that, and new fortifications were put up around it. By then, however, the provocateur Ramon Mercader, a young Spanish Communist pretending to be an American businessman, had insinuated himself into Trotsky's closest circles. On August 20, 1940, Mercader assassinated Trotsky by driving a mountain climber's ice ax into his skull; he had smuggled it into Trotsky's office under his coat. The murderer was caught and after a long trial was

65. Deutscher, *Prophet Outcast*, p. 419.
66. Ibid., p. 426.

sentenced to twenty years in prison. L. Eitingen, the NKVD colonel who directed the operation, and the assassin's mother, Caridad Mercader, who also participated in the preparations for this terrorist act, were able to avoid detection although they were close enough to hear the shouts and commotion in the Trotsky house.

Stalin had triumphed. Mercader was awarded the title Hero of the Soviet Union; his mother was awarded the Order of Lenin and was received personally by Beria. Stalin told Eitingen that as long as he, Stalin, was alive not a hair on Eitingen's head would be touched. Eitengen was promoted to the rank of NKVD general. Until then it had been Stalin's rule to eliminate anyone who knew too much. In this case he suspended his own rule.[67]

67. Ramon Mercader was released from prison in 1960 and took up residence in the Soviet Union, on Lenin Prospect in Moscow. When it became known where he was living several Western Trotskyists, visiting the Soviet Union as tourists, tried to see him. Fearing such encounters, Mercader moved to Czechoslovakia, where he died in the 1970s. His mother left the Communist movement and died in Paris. [In the Western press it was reported that Mercader died of cancer in a hospital in Havana, Cuba, on October 18, 1978, and that his remains were sent to Moscow for burial. —G. S.] Eitingen was arrested in 1953 along with Beria's closest accomplices and spent eight years in prison. After that he worked for a long time in the modest post of editor and translator for Progress Publishers in Moscow.

6

THE ASSAULT ON PARTY AND STATE CADRES, 1937–1938

The illegal repression of former oppositionists was a painful blow to the party and government, but it was only the beginning. Within the first few months of 1937 most of the former "Lefts" and "Rights," who probably numbered no more than fifty or sixty thousand altogether, had been jailed and many had been shot. Nevertheless, throughout 1937 and 1938 the flood of repression rose, assuming more and more massive and sinister proportions.

The NKVD, guided and directed by Stalin, virtually ceased to make a distinction between former members of opposition groups and former loyalists, between those who had opposed Stalin's policies and those who had actively supported him, helped him rise to the top, and took part themselves in many earlier acts of political terror. Stalin and the NKVD undertook the organized and systematic destruction of the basic cadres of the Bolshevik Party and Soviet state. This pitiless extermination of millions was the most frightful act in the tragedy of the thirties.

■ 1

THE ASSAULT ON CADRES OF THE CENTRAL PARTY, GOVERNMENT, AND ECONOMIC INSTITUTIONS

First of all, the Central Committee was attacked. By the beginning of 1939, 110 of the 139 members and candidate members elected at the Seventeenth Party Congress in 1934 had been arrested. They were all destroyed soon after their arrests. Dozens of outstanding leaders perished, including:

Vlas Chubar, Politburo member and deputy chairman of the Council of Commissars, posted to Solikamsk, then arrested and shot. Stanislav Kosior, first secretary of the Ukrainian Central Committee; in January 1938, accused of insufficient vigilance, transferred to high posts in Moscow, but arrested anyhow and, on February 26, 1939, at age 50, shot. Pavel Postyshev, demoted from the Politburo and the Ukrainian Central Committee to a provincial post, then arrested and shot. Robert Eikhe, first secretary of the West Siberian Party Committee and candidate member of the Politburo, appointed commissar of agriculture in 1937, then arrested and shot. Yan Rudzutak, a deputy chairman of the Council of Commissars and candidate member of the Politburo, arrested and shot in May 1937.

Many top officials of the Central Committee apparatus were shot, including:

Karl Bauman, head of the Science Section of the Central Committee and formerly a member of the Orgburo; Yakov Yakovlev, head of the Agricultural Section of the Central Committee and formerly commissar of agriculture; B. M. Tal, head of the Press and Publications Sections of the Central Committee; Aleksei Stetsky, head of the Agitation and Propaganda Section of the Central Committee; and A. M. Nazaretyan, a well-known Old Bolshevik who in the thirties worked on the Central Committee's Bureau of Complaints and on the Commission of Soviet Control; in 1922 he had been appointed Stalin's assistant on Lenin's advice.

The Commission of Party Control was also devastated; most of the people elected to it at the Seventeenth Party Congress were arrested and none of them survived.[1]

1. They included I. M. Bekker, N. S. Berezin, V. S. Bogushevsky, S. K. Brikke, Ye. B. Genkin. M. L. Granovsky, V. Ya. Grossman, F. I. Zaitsev, N. N. Zimin, M. I. Kokhiani, A. A. Levin, I. A. Lychev, Zh. I. Meyerzon, K. F. Pshenitsyn, N. N. Rubenov, A. A. Frenkel, and S. K. Shadunts.

Not only leaders but also most of the subordinate personnel of the central party apparatus, such as "instructors" and technical personnel, were arrested.

Government and economic institutions were also hard hit by repression. Most members of the Presidium of the Central Executive Committee (CEC) were arrested. I have already mentioned the fate of Yenukidze, secretary of the CEC and long a close friend of Stalin's; expelled from the party's Central Committee and assigned to a minor post in the health resorts administration, he was arrested in 1937 and after a brief, closed trial was shot. As a rule the arrests of CEC members had to be sanctioned by Kalinin, the "all-union peasant elder" who was chairman of the CEC and later chairman of the Presidium of the USSR Supreme Soviet. During one session of the CEC in 1937 Kalinin's secretary called four members of the CEC from the meeting room to Kalinin's office, one after the other. There Kalinin, sobbing, signed the authorization for their arrests, which were immediately carried out by an NKVD group waiting in the next room.[2]

The apparatus of the State Planning Commission (Gosplan) was devastated. V. I. Mezhlauk, an experienced party leader and economic manager who had headed Gosplan for years, was among those who perished. His successor, G. I. Smirnov, only thirty-four years old, was also arrested in 1937. E. I. Kviring, a deputy chairman of Gosplan, and G. I. Lomov-Oppokov, a veteran party activist who had worked for Gosplan a very long time, were also shot.

The Council of People's Commissars had its share of victims. For example:

V. Schmidt and N. K. Antipov, deputy chairmen of the USSR Council; D. Ye. Sulimov, chairman of the RSFSR Council, and his deputies D. Z. Lebed, S. B. Zoznochenko, and T. Ryskulov; M. L. Rukhimovich, commissar of defense industry; I. Ye. Lyubimov, commissar of light industry; S. S. Lobov, commissar of the forest industry; I. Ya. Veitser, commissar of domestic trade; Grigory Kaminsky, commissar of health; I. A. Khalepsky, commissar of communications; M. I. Kalmanovich and N. N. Demchenko, commissars of state farms producing grain

2. This was reported by Pavel Aksyonov, chairman of the party's city committee in Kazan and a member of the CEC, who was also arrested in Kalinin's office. Father of the writer Vasily Aksyonov and husband of Eugenia Ginzburg, Pavel Aksyonov survived seventeen years in confinement. After being rehabilitated, he lived in Kazan. Vasily Aksyonov told about his father's fate in "Dikoi," in *Iunost': Izbrannoe, 1955–1965* (Moscow, 1965), as did Eugenia Ginzburg in her memoirs, *Journey into the Whirlwind*, published in many languages and countries, but not in the Soviet Union.

and livestock; N. I. Pakhomov, commissar of water transport; A. Bruskin, commissar of machine building; S. L. Lukashin, chairman of the Committee on Construction under the Council of Commissars; L. Ye. Maryasin, chairman of the board of the State Bank; N. Popov, commissar of agricultural procurements, one of the youngest members of the Soviet government, not yet thirty-five; B. Z. Shumyatsky, head of the State Committee on Cinematography; and Nikolai Krylenko, commissar of justice.

Most of the people's commissars of the RSFSR also perished, among them K. V. Ukhanov, commissar of local industry, and Andrei Bubnov, who from 1929 to 1937 was RSFSR commissar of education. Under the tsars Bubnov was arrested and exiled thirteen times but always managed to escape. In 1937 he was arrested for the fourteenth time and shot.

Most of these government and economic leaders were also members or candidate members of the party's Central Committee. Of course, commissars were not arrested by themselves in 1937–1938; the commissariats they headed were decimated. For example, the NKVD cooked up a story about a "gang of spies and wreckers" in the Commissariat of Heavy Industry, headed by Ordzhonikidze's deputy Pyatakov. The leading officials in this commissariat were arrested even before Ordzhonikidze's death; afterwards all the major departments were ravaged. The victims included:

A. P. Serebrovsky, A. I. Gurevich, and O. P. Osipov-Shmidt, deputy commissars. K. A. Neiman, A. F. Tolokontsev, I. V. Kosior, A. I. Zykov, Yu. P. Figatner, S. S. Dybets, and Ye. L. Brodov, directors of various departments and sections and members of the Commissariat collegium.

The same fate befell all the other commissariats of the USSR and the RSFSR. Among the many thousands of talented executives who perished were:

Sh. Z. Eliava, N. P. Bryukhanov, A. M. Lezhava, A. B. Khalatov, Paul Oras, Vladimir Milyutin, K. P. Soms, V. I. Polonsky, V. Naneishvili, M. V. Barinov, I. I. Todorsky, V. A. Kangelari, S. S. Odintsov, V. A. Trifonov, I. I. Radchenko, M. M. Maiorov, G. I. Blagonravov, A. I. Muralov, Ya. L. Bobis, K. Danishevsky, and G. Dzhabiev.

The Commissariat of Foreign Affairs was savagely purged in 1937–1939. Among the victims:

Levon Karakhan and Boris Stomonyakov, deputy commissars; the following ambassadors or attaches: K. Yurenev, ambassador to Japan; M. A. Karsky, ambassador to Turkey; Ye. V. Girshfeld; V. Kh. Tairov, ambassador to Mongolia; Bogomolov, ambassador to China; Ostrovsky, ambassador to Rumania; G. S. Astakhov;

I. S. Yakubovich, ambassador to Norway; and the following heads of departments: A. V. Sabinin, A. F. Neiman, M. A. Plotkin, A. V. Fikhner, Yevgeny Gnedin.

M. Rozenberg, a diplomat who had contributed greatly to the Soviet-French rapprochement, was jailed, and two other prominent diplomats, V. V. Yegoryev and B. Mironov-Kornev, perished in the purges. Fyodor Raskolnikov, ambassador to Bulgaria, and Alexander Barmine, ambassador to Greece, who refused to return to certain death in Moscow, were declared outside the law. Many foreign correspondents for Soviet newspapers and for TASS were also victims of repression.

■ 2

THE DEATH OF SERGO ORDZHONIKIDZE

The terror of 1937–1938 was marked not only by mass arrests but also by many suicides. For example, N. N. Rabichev, a deputy director of the Central Committee's department of agitation and propaganda, sensing that he was doomed, ended his own life.

The death in February 1937 of Sergo Ordzhonikidze, one of the party's most popular leaders, was later said to have been a suicide. Famous from the time of the October revolution and the civil war, he was in 1937 a member of the Politburo and commissar of heavy industry.

On February 19, 1937, a special government bulletin reported that on the previous day he had died in his own apartment of a heart attack. The papers carried a detailed medical report, signed by Grigory Kaminsky, the commissar of health, and by three doctors. Only nineteen years later, at the Twentieth Party Congress, was it officially announced that Ordzhonikidze had died by his own hand. Those mainly to blame for this tragedy were Stalin, Yezhov, and Beria.

Stalin had decided to avoid direct charges against Ordzhonikidze, preferring to compromise and demoralize him instead. An older brother, Populia, was arrested and shot after terrible tortures, and a falsified record of the interrogation was sent to Ordzhonikidze. Nearly every day Ordzhonikidze learned of the execution of a close friend or associate. Mass arrests of executives in heavy industry, appointed by Ordzhonikidze, also occurred. The NKVD made these arrests without sanction by the commissar of heavy industry, since Ordzhonikidze refused to give it. Stalin or Molotov authorized the arrests instead. Then Stalin sent Ordzhonikidze the false depositions extracted from the prisoners by torture, with the comment, "Comrade Sergo, look what they're writing about you."

Ordzhonikidze was not impressed by the depositions and hotly protested the arrests. In some cases he ordered officials of his commissariat to check the grounds that the NKVD gave for the arrests. Stalin and Yezhov ignored Ordzhonikidze's protests, and the Politburo, on a motion by Stalin, directed Ordzhonikidze to give the report on "wrecking" in industry at the Central Committee plenum scheduled to begin in late February 1937. Stalin even ordered a search of Ordzhonikidze's Kremlin apartment. Ordzhonikidze, humiliated and enraged by this provocation, tried all night to phone Stalin.

Toward morning he got through to Stalin and received the reply: "The NKVD can even search my apartment. There's nothing strange about that. . . ." There was a conversation with Stalin the morning of the 17th. Eyeball to eyeball for several hours. A second conversation after Sergo returned home was uncontrollably angry, full of mutual insults and Russian and Georgian swearing. No more love or trust. Everything destroyed. . . . Sergo could not begin to share responsibility for what he had no power to prevent. He would not become a corrupt timeserver; that would mean wiping out his whole past life. . . . All he could do was leave.[3]

Today some Old Bolsheviks say that Ordzhonikidze was murdered, pointing out that the day before he died he had worked at his commissariat and even issued a number of orders and made some appointments for the following day. Yevgeny Frolov writes in his memoirs that the circumstances surrounding Ordzhonikidze's death were not investigated in 1937; even the bullet hole was not examined. All the doctors who signed the medical report were soon arrested. Right after Ordzhonikidze's death, his chief bodyguard, V. N. Yefremov, and his personal secretary, Semushkin, were arrested. A. Cherkassky, who at that time was a driver in the Kremlin motor pool, says that Ordzhonikidze's entire bodyguard was arrested, along with almost everyone who worked for him, even the watchman at his country home. His former deputy Vannikov has reported that a few days after the death he was summoned to Yezhov's office and told to write a report on the "wrecking" directives issued by Ordzhonikidze. Frolov reports that many of Ordzhonikidze's papers were removed and later transmitted—for "study"—to Beria, who was a personal enemy of Ordzhonikidze, and that later Ordzhonikidze's brothers Konstantin and Vano (Ivan) were arrested, along with almost all his

3. I. Dubinsky-Mukhadze, *Ordzhonikidze* (Moscow, 1963), pp. 6–7.

relatives.[4] The entire chain of events raises many questions; still, there are not sufficient grounds to dispute the version of suicide. Alexander Orlov insists that Ordzhonikidze was murdered, but admits that he bases his belief on rumors and stories he heard from NKVD agents arriving in Spain.[5]

According to Zinaida Gavrilovna Ordzhonikidze, the wife of Sergo, he did work at the commissariat on February 17, but on the morning of February 18, the day before the Central Committee plenum was scheduled to meet (this meeting was subsequently put off for ten days), he did not get out of bed, did not begin to dress, and refused breakfast. He asked not to be disturbed and spent the morning writing something. His friend G. Gvakharia came to visit the afternoon, but Ordzhonikidze would not see him, only ordered that he be fed in the dining room. Ordzhonikidze himself refused the afternoon meal. His wife was extremely worried and phoned her sister, Vera Gavrilovna, asking her to come over. February days are short, and as it began to grow dark, just after five, Zinaida Gavrilovna decided to go into her husband's room, but while she was on her way, turning on the light in the living room, a shot exploded in his bedroom. Running in, she saw her husband lying on the bed, dead, the bedclothes stained with blood.

According to Zinaida Gavrilovna, the apartment had a side entrance, which everyone used, and a main entrance that was always closed, with bookshelves against it. Moreover, the main entrance led into the living room, where Zinaida Gavrilovna was at the moment the shot was fired; so it could not have been used by an assassin.

Ordzhonikidze's wife immediately phoned Stalin. Although his apartment was just opposite Ordzhonikidze's building, Stalin did not come at once to see his former friend. First he sent for all the Politburo members. Ordzhonikidze's sister-in-law Vera ran in before Stalin. Entering the bedroom, she saw some sheets of paper on the desk, covered with Ordzhonikidze's tiny handwriting. She automatically picked them up and clutched them in her hand, but she did not feel up to reading them. When Stalin and the other Politburo members finally arrived, Stalin caught sight of the papers immediately and tore them from her hand. Sobbing, Ordzhonikidze's wife shouted at Stalin, "You didn't protect Sergo for me or for the party." "Shut up, you idiot," Stalin replied.

4. A copy of Frolov's memoirs is in my archives.
5. Alexander Orlov, *The Secret History of Stalin's Crimes* (New York, 1953), p. 187–189.

Sergo Ordzhonikidze's younger brother Konstantin survived sixteen years of confinement to set down his reminiscences of that tragic day.

I will tell a few details connected with the death of my dear brother Sergo, who committed suicide on February 18, 1937, at 5:30 P.M.

That evening, after skating in Sokolniki Park, I went as usual to see my brother in the Kremlin. At the entrance Sergo's chauffeur, N. I. Volkov, said to me, "Hurry up!"

I did not understand anything. When my wife and I reached the second floor, we went to the dining room, but were stopped at the door by an NKVD agent. Then we were let into Sergo's office, where I saw G. Gvakharia. "Our Sergo is no more," he said.

I ran to the bedroom but my way was barred, and I was not allowed to see the body. I returned to the office, stunned, not understanding what had happened.

Then Stalin, Molotov, and Zhdanov arrived. First they went to the dining room. Zhdanov had a black bandage on his forehead. Suddenly Gvakharia was led out of Sergo's office (for some reason through the bathroom). After that Stalin, Molotov, and Zhdanov went from the dining room to the bedroom, where they stood a while beside the body, then returned to the dining room. The words of Zinaida Gavrilovna reached me from the dining room. "This must be reported in the press." Stalin answered. "We will say that he died from a heart attack." "No one will believe that," retorted Zinaida Gavrilovna, and added: "Sergo loved the truth; the truth must be printed." "Why won't they believe it? Everyone knew that he had a bad heart, and everyone will believe it." Thus Stalin put an end to the dialogue.

The doors to the bedroom were shut. Opening them slightly, I saw Yezhov and Kaganovich sitting on chairs at the feet of the deceased. They were discussing something. I closed the door immediately to avoid unnecessary reproach.

Sometime later the Politburo members and a number of other high-placed persons gathered in the dining room. Beria also appeared. In the presence of Stalin, Molotov, Zhdanov and the rest, Zinaida Gavrilovna called Beria a rat (*negodyai*). She went toward him and tried to slap him. Beria disappeared right after that and did not come to Sergo's apartment again.

The body was taken from the bedroom to the office, where Molotov's brother photographed the deceased together with Stalin, Molotov, Zhdanov, other members of the government, and Zinaida Gavrilovna. All this time I stood by the wall and didn't think that maybe I had to go somewhere else. Then the well-known sculptor S. D. Merkulov came and made a mask of Sergo's face.

Zinaida Gavrilovna asked Yezhov and Pauker to notify Sergo's relatives in Georgia so that they could come to the funeral. She also wanted our older brother Populia to attend. Yezhov replied to that: "Populia Ordzhonikidze is in confinement, and we consider him an enemy of the people. Let him serve out his punishment; you may help him by sending warm clothing and food. We will inform the rest of the family; just give us their addresses." I gave them the addresses of brother Ivan and sister Julia, and also Populia's wife, Nina.

Late that evening Yemelyan Yaroslavsky arrived. When he saw the deceased, he fainted. With difficulty we laid him on the couch. When Yaroslavsky came to, he was driven home. Then Semushkin arrived. It was his day off, and he had been resting in his cottage at Tarasovka. When Semushkin saw the awful scene, he began to rave and had to be sent home almost tied down.

Sergo's secretary, Makhover, overwhelmed by what he saw, uttered words that stick in my memory: "They killed him, the rats *(merzavtsy)!*"

. . . On the night before February 20, 1937, the body was cremated. The funeral was held on the twentieth. Brother Ivan and his wife and sister Julia and her husband were late in getting to Moscow.

After some time, intensified arrests began. M. D. Orakhelashvili and his wife were arrested. Semushkin and his wife were arrested, and so were many officials in the Commissariat of Heavy Industry who were close to Sergo.

Two Ordzhonikidzes were arrested: the wife of our older brother Populia, and another relative, G. A. Ordzhonikidze.

And finally, on May 6, 1941, they arrested me too.[6]

■ 3
THE FATE OF NADEZHDA KRUPSKAYA

Lenin's widow, Nadezhda Krupskaya, also met tragedy in the late thirties. I have already described how she was "worked over" in the midtwenties and at the height of collectivization. When her *Reminiscences of Lenin* were published in 1934, Stalin himself phoned to congratulate her on a good and useful work. But only a few days later a harsh and unfair review appeared in *Pravda*. The reviewer, a young historian named Pyotr Pospelov, charged that there were mistakes in her portrayal of Lenin and her treatment of certain problems of party history. Obviously this was not done without Stalin's knowledge.[7]

When mass arrests began in 1936, Krupskaya repeatedly tried to protect many party leaders whom she knew well. For example, at a Central Committee plenum in 1937 she spoke against the arrest of Iosif Pyatnitsky, who had been labeled a provocateur for the tsarist secret police. Krupskaya said that he had been a responsible official in the Bolshevik underground; he had been in charge of communications between Russia and the émigré leaders, and he had never once deviated from the party line. But almost all these protests were ignored. Only in a few cases did she win the release of some loyal party members. For example, I. D.

---

6. From my archives.
7. See *Sovetskaia istoricheskaia entsiklopediia* (Moscow, 1966), 8:192.

Chugurin, who had issued a party card to Lenin on April 3, 1917, was released as a result of Krupskaya's intervention.[8]

Soon Stalin and the NKVD began to ignore her protests completely. At a meeting honoring Lenin in January 1937, when Krupskaya asked Yezhov about the fate of some comrades, Yezhov simply turned and walked away. Krupskaya died at the very beginning of 1939, shortly after her birthday, which she celebrated with a small number of her closest friends. While the small group was gathered at her apartment, a huge cake was brought in—"from Stalin." Later, this became the basis for rumors that she had been poisoned. However, Stalin had sent her the same kind of gift on every birthday, and none of her guests who shared the cake were affected. Krupskaya was buried with all the honors, and Stalin was among the leaders who carried her ashes at the funeral. But the very next day her apartment was searched and many of her papers were seized. And very soon the publishing house of the Commissariat of Education received an order: "Don't print one word about Krupskaya."[9] Her name was consigned to oblivion. Under various pretexts her books were taken off library shelves, and even an exhibition devoted to the newspaper *Iskra* contained not one word about her work for it.

When news of Krupskaya's death reached Trotsky he wrote an obituary that included the following passage:

> Nothing could be further from our minds than to blame Nadezhda Konstantinovna for not having been resolute enough to break openly with the bureaucracy. Political minds far more independent than hers vacillated, tried to play hide and seek with history—and perished. Krupskaya was to the highest degree endowed with the feeling of responsibility. Personally she was courageous enough. What she lacked was mental courage. With profound sorrow we bid farewell to the loyal companion of Lenin, to an irreproachable revolutionist and one of the most tragic figures in revolutionary history.[10]

Trotsky's position in this case can be understood. In trying to provide evidence of his closeness to Lenin (citing Lenin's words, for example, "there has been no better Bolshevik" [than Trotsky]), he often referred to certain personal letters Krupskaya wrote him after Lenin's death. If he had expressed a poor opinion of Krupskaya, he might have discredited this evidence.

8. See *Pravda*, December 22, 1962.
9. *Vsesoiuznoe soveshchanie istorikov* (Moscow, 1964), p. 260.
10. *Biulleten' oppozitsii* (March–April 1939) no. 75–76, p. 32. [Cf. *Writings of Leon Trotsky, 1938–39*, 2nd ed. (New York, 1974), p. 198. —G. S.]

A historian cannot completely agree with Trotsky's assessments, however. There can be no question about the tragic position of Krupskaya, who witnessed the destruction of many of Lenin's and her best friends and comrades. But she very quickly stopped even her timid attempts to interfere with the NKVD's actions. She did not object when lengthy passages praising Stalin were inserted in her speeches and articles. Many Communist Party members in prison asked themselves how Krupskaya's behavior could be explained. Certainly Stalin and Beria could secretly kill her, but they would not dare to arrest her. Essentially there was one simple explanation: Krupskaya was broken long before 1937.

In *The Great Terror* Robert Conquest quotes a story told by Alexander Orlov, a former NKVD official, who heard it from other NKVD agents. Stalin reportedly remarked on one occasion that unless Krupskaya stopped criticizing him, the party would proclaim that the Old Bolshevik Yelena Stasova was really Lenin's widow, not Krupskaya. "Yes," he said, "the party can do anything!"[11]

Rumors like that, unfortunately, are an important source of information in the Soviet Union. Only someone who lives in the country and studies its political life carefully and at first hand can separate rumors that correspond to real events from accidental and unreliable ones, rumors deliberately put into circulation for purposes of "disinformation." The veteran party member I. A. Sats made the following comment on the rumor reported by Conquest:

> In this case we are dealing not with *evidence*, true or false; it is clear from the construction of the quotation that we are dealing with an *anecdote*. Many anecdotes circulated in those days; most of them attributed to Karl Radek. I think it quite possible that in the wake of the Fourteenth Party Congress [at which Krupskaya criticized the majority led by Stalin] the cynical and clever Radek (or someone else) could have started a rumor like this and that it could have reached the ears of GPU agents. Nevertheless, even if such an anecdote to some extent symbolizes the social atmosphere of the time, to take it as a fact or as historical evidence is to say the least naive.[12]

According to Sats, Krupskaya was broken by the early thirties. She agreed to lengthy cuts in her reminiscenses of Lenin. She was in fact kept from having any contact with ordinary workers and peasants, even from any vital interchange with educationists, and she herself began to

---

11. Robert Conquest, *The Great Terror: Stalin's Purge of the Thirties*, rev. ed. (New York, 1968), p. 126. Conquest cites Orlov, *Secret History of Stalin's Crimes*, p. 216.

12. I. A. Sats, Iz vospominanii, manuscript.

refuse such meetings and to abandon participation in the life of the Communist Party in general. She concentrated on her work at the Commissariat of Education, but she began to be disregarded even in the field of education, where she had done so much—especially after Lunacharsky retired as "commissar of enlightenment" and was replaced by Bubnov. Since Krupskaya did not agree with many of the changes that began to be introduced in public education, she submitted her resignation, but the Politburo ordered her to continue her duties as a deputy commissar of education of the RSFSR. She submitted, refusing to make an issue of it even when Bubnov insulted her directly at meetings of the governing board of the commissariat. She retreated into private life and virtually ceased to visit her office at the commissariat. The explanation for all this, however, was not a lack of "mental courage" but an understandable lack of strength in a woman who was elderly, tired, and unwell.

■ **4**

THE FATE OF OTHERS CLOSE TO LENIN

Many of the oldest party members who had worked with Lenin for many years escaped arrest in 1936–1939, including:

Gleb Krzhizhanovsky, Felix Kon, Pyotr Krasikov, Vladimir Bonch-Bruevich, Nikolai Podvoisky, Aleksei Badaev, Dmitry Manuilsky, Matvei Muranov, Fyodor Samoilov, Nikolai Semashko, Isaak Shvartz, Aleksandra Kollontai, Yelena Stasova, and Lydia Fotieva.

But all these people were pushed out of the leadership, terrorized, and deprived of any influence. Stalin treated them with undisguised contempt, calling them *intelligenty* (members of the intelligentsia), incapable of leading the proletariat under the new conditions.

Grigory Petrovsky, who had been a close comrade of Lenin, a Bolshevik deputy in the Duma before the revolution, and chairman of the Ukrainian Central Executive Committee in the Soviet period, was deeply shaken by the arrest of such close friends and colleagues as Vlas Chubar, Stanislav Kosior, and K. V. Sukhomlin. His older son, Pyotr, a hero of the civil war and subsequently an editor of *Leningradskaya pravda*, was arrested. His younger son, Leonid, also a civil war hero and one of the first Komsomol organizers, was expelled from the party and fired from his job as commander of the Moscow Proletarian Division. Petrovsky's son-in-law, S. A. Zeger, chairman of the Chernigov Soviet executive committee, was arrested and shot. At the end of 1938 Petrovsky himself was suddenly called to Moscow. After a short but painful meeting with Stalin this Old Bolshevik, whose sixtieth birthday had recently been given nationwide observance, was dismissed from all his posts in the Ukraine and accused of connections with "enemies of the people." At the Eighteenth Party Congress in 1939 he was not reelected to the Central Committee, and for a long time he had no work at all. Just before the war he was made deputy director of the Museum of the Revolution, in charge of the economic section.

Demyan Bedny, Bolshevik poet and close comrade of Lenin, also suffered, as he had in the early thirties. In 1935 Stalin made some moves to resume relations with Bedny, twice inviting him to his country house. But a new break came very quickly and further publication of the poet's work was stopped. In 1938, when Bedny wrote a pamphlet about fascism under the title "Hell," Stalin not only prohibited publication but wrote on the manuscript, "Tell this latter-day Dante that he can stop writing." In August 1938 Bedny was expelled from the party and then from the Writers' Union. Until the war began, newspapers and journals were closed to him.[13]

Many of Lenin's most trusted associates were arrested. As early as 1935 this happened to Nikolai Yemelyanov, the Petrograd worker who had hidden Lenin in the hut at Razliv, helping to save him from arrest in the summer of 1917. In 1921 Lenin wrote in a letter:

Please show the *most complete confidence,* and give all possible assistance, to Comrade N. A. Yemelyanov, whom I've known from before the October revolution, an old party activist and one of the leaders of the working-class vanguard of St. Petersburg.[14]

At the time of Yemelyanov's arrest, he was already retired on a pension. According to A. V. Snegov, Krupskaya tearfully begged Stalin to spare Yemelyanov's life. He remained in confinement until Stalin's death, and his whole family was also arrested: his wife, and his sons Kondraty, Nikolai, and Aleksandr, who as little boys had helped to hide Lenin at Razliv.

Another Old Bolshevik victim was Aleksandr Shotman, the leader of the famous Obukhov defense in 1903. In the summer of 1917, when Lenin went underground, Shotman was the sole liaison between Lenin

13. *Vospominaniia o Dem'iane Bednom* (Moscow, 1965), pp. 220–222.
14. Lenin, PSS, 54: 24.

and the party's Central Committee. Shotman was also given the job of guarding Lenin's life and of arranging his journey from Razliv to Finland. In 1918 Lenin wrote: "Shotman is an old party comrade, whom I know quite well. He deserves absolute trust." But Shotman was arrested and perished in 1939.[15]

The terror also killed Fritz Platten, a well-known Swiss left Socialist, later a Communist and a leader of the Third International. In 1917 he arranged the passage of Lenin and his comrades through Germany to Russia. In fact Platten went with them and took an active part in the Russian revolution. On January 1, 1918, he saved Lenin's life from a counterrevolutionary attempt to assassinate him; Platten suffered an arm wound. Subsequently he brought his family to live in the Soviet Union, only to be arrested along with his wife, who was working for the Comintern. Platten had been in the prisons of tsarist Russia and landlord Romania, in the torture chambers of Petlyura in the Ukraine and the Kovno jail, in the Moabit of Berlin and the prisons of Switzerland. But he died in Kargopollag, a camp for invalids, making shingles and weaving baskets.[16]

In September 1937 another of Lenin's comrades was shot: Jakob Hanecki, a leader of the Polish workers' movement whom Lenin had personally recommended for membership in the Russian Party. In August 1914 Hanecki obtained the release of Lenin, who had been arrested by the Austrian authorities as a Russian spy. In 1917 he helped arrange Lenin's return to Russia, meeting him in Sweden and securing his journey to revolutionary Petrograd. After the October revolution Hanecki held important diplomatic and economic posts in the Soviet Union, eventually becoming director of the Museum of the Revolution in Moscow.

S. I. Kanatchikov, who had belonged to the Union of Struggle for the Emancipation of the Working Class, the organization Lenin founded in St. Petersburg in 1895, was also arrested and killed.

Stalin did not spare Old Bolsheviks who had long since retired because of age or illness. N. F. Dobrokhotov, who held many important posts until a serious disease forced him to retire in 1929, was arrested and perished. Stalin did not even spare the dead: some Old Bolsheviks were posthumously declared enemies of the people, others consigned to oblivion. Pyotr Stuchka, for example, commissar of justice in Lenin's first

15. See T. Bondarevskaia, *A. Shotman* (Moscow, 1963).

16. *Leningradskaia pravda*, October 1, 1964.

government and at the end of 1918 head of the short-lived Latvian Soviet Republic, died in 1932 and was buried in Red Square. But in 1937–1938 he was declared a propagator of harmful ideology and virtually a deliberate wrecker in the field of jurisprudence. Similarly, Sergei Gusev, a colleague of Lenin and an outstanding leader of the revolution and the civil war, was buried with military honors in Red Square in 1933 but was subsequently expunged from the history of the party and of the civil war. Many of his friends and relatives were arrested. The name of the legendary underground Bolshevik Kamo (S. A. Ter-Petrosyan) was also suppressed. The small monument on his grave in Tbilisi was destroyed, and his sister was arrested. Yakov Sverdlov's brother, Veniamin M. Sverdlov, a member of the collegium of the commissariat of education, was killed. And many famous Bolsheviks, such as Krasin, Nogin, Chicherin, Lunacharsky and others, were erased from the pages of history.

■ 5

THE ASSAULT ON CADRES IN THE PROVINCES AND UNION REPUBLICS

The wave of repression that hit the central party organs also swept through every oblast and republic. In the RSFSR around 90 percent of all obkomy (oblast party committees) and the majority of city, okrug, and raion committees were ravaged. In some oblasti several successive party committees were arrested. In the RSFSR the following obkom secretaries were arrested and perished:

L. I. Kartvelishvili, I. M. Vareikis, I. P. Nosov, N. N. Kolotilov, A. I. Krinitsky, A. I. Ugarov, F. G. Leonov, V. V. Ptukha, I. D. Kabakov, K. V. Ryndin, D. A. Bulatov, P. I. Smorodin, V. P. Shubrikov, B. P. Sheboldaev, E. K. Pramnek, M. I. Razumnov, I. V. Slinkin, I. P. Rumyantsev, M. S. Chudov, M. Ye. Mikhailov, N. M. Osmov, P. A. Irklis, A. S. Kalygina, Ya. G. Soifer, G. Baituni, I. I. Ivanov, N. D. Akilinushkin, B. P. Bekker, Ye. I. Ryabinin, G. P. Rakov, P. M. Tonigin, S. P. Korshunov, V. Ya. Simochkin, A. Ya. Stolyar, S. M. Sobolev, S. M. Savinov, V. Ya. Simyakin, and many others.

Chairmen of krai and oblast executive committees who were destroyed included:

G. M. Krutov, N. I. Pakhomov, P. I. Struppe, Yan Poluyan, F. I. Andrianov, S. B. Ageev, M. L. Volkov, N. I. Zhuravlev, V. V. Ivanov, I. F. Novikov, A. N. Burov, D. A. Orlov, I. N. Pivovarov, G. D. Rakitov, I. I. Reshchikov, A. A.

Shpilman, I. F. Gusikhin, I. Ya. Smirnov, I. F. Kodatsky, chairman of the
Leningrad Soviet, and many others.

The arrest of the obkom secretary and the chairman of the oblast
executive committee usually meant that all the leading cadres in that
oblast would be ravaged. For example, in Moscow oblast the following
party secretaries were arrested, and most of them shot:

A. N. Bogomolov, T. A. Bratanovsky, Ye. S. Kogan, N. V. Margolin, N. I.
Dedikov, V. S. Yegorov, M. M. Kulkov, S. Z. Korytny, N. A. Filatov, chairman
of the Moscow oblast executive committee, his deputy S. Ye. Guberman, I. I.
Sidorov, chairman of the Moscow Soviet, and many others.

By the middle of 1939 only 7 out of 136 raikom secretaries in Moscow
and the Moscow oblast were still at their posts.[17] Almost all the rest had
been arrested and most of them shot, including:

V. P. Tarkhanov, N. Ye. Volovik, I. Levinshtein, B. Ye. Treivas, S. Ye. Gorbul-
sky, Ye. Pershman, and dozens of others.

Many heads of departments in the Moscow oblast and city committees
were destroyed, including:

M. D. Krymsky, T. R. Voroshilov, Kurenkov, Verklov, and Barleben.

Some prominent Moscow Bolsheviks, V. Furer, for example, committed
suicide. The majority of party instructors were also arrested.

In Gorky during 1937–1938, a special block of the city prison held the
entire city party committee, headed by its secretary, L. I. Pugachevsky,
and the entire city soviet, headed by its chairman A. P. Grachev. Here,
too, were the secretaries of nine of the city's raikoms (district committees) together with many other city and oblast officials. In 1938 the head
of the local NKVD, Lavrushin, told the Sixth Party Conference of Gorky
oblast that "entire hordes of counterrevolutionaries have been smashed."[18]
Almost all the party leadership was exterminated in Leningrad and in
many other major cities of the RSFSR.

Virtually none of the autonomous republics of the RSFSR escaped. In
Karelia Gustav Rovio, first secretary of the obkom, the "Red policeman"
of Helsingfors who had helped to hide Lenin in 1917, was destroyed. So
were the chairman of the Council of Commissars, E. Giulling, and the
chairman of the republic's Central Executive Committee, N. V. Arkhi-

---

17. In 1936–1937 Moscow oblast included areas of what are now Ryazan, Kaluga,
Kalinin, and Tula oblasti.

18. *Ocherki istorii Gor'kovskoi organizatsii KPSS* Pt. 2 (Gorky, 1966), p. 392.

pov. Nearly all the leadership of the Buryat-Mongol autonomous republic was destroyed, including M. N. Yerbanov, one of the founders of the Soviet regime in Buryat-Mongolia.

In the Tatar autonomous republic A. K. Lepa, obkom secretary, G. G. Baichurin, chairman of the republic's Central Executive Committee, K. A. Abramov and A. M. Novoselov, chairmen of its Council of Commissars, and dozens of lesser officials were arrested and executed. S. Said-Galiev also perished, the first chairman of Tataria's Council of People's Commissars. He had once criticized Stalin, the commissar of nation aliities, for lack of principle in relation to petty-bourgeois Tatar nationalities.[19]

Betal Kalmykov, first secretary of the Kabardino-Balkar obkom, died in confinement, as did G. N. Sukharev and M. P. Khavkin, secretaries of the party committee in the Jewish Autonomous Region, M. Ibragimov and A. Sameidov, chairmen of the Council of People's Commissars of the Crimean Autonomous Republic, Z. P. Bulashev, head of the government in Bashkiria, Ch. I. Vrublevsky, secretary of the party committee in the Mari Autonomous Republic, Ye. E. Frener and D. G. Rozenberg, leaders of the Volga German autonomous republic, and many thousands of other officials in these areas.

In Dagestan and Ossetia, in Checheno-Ingushetia and Chuvashia, in Mordovia and Udmurtia, in Yakutia and Karachai-Cherkessia, the party suffered enormous losses. In Northern Ossetia, for example, nine out of eleven members of the obkom bureau were arrested. In two years four obkom secretaries were removed, including S. A. Takoev and K. S. Butaev. A large part of the Ossetian intelligentsia was also wiped out.[20] Even in such a small, out-of-the-way place as the Komi autonomous republic, a fourth of all Communists, starting with obkom secretaries A. A. Semichev and F. I. Bulashev, were arrested.[21]

I have already mentioned the destruction of Chubar, Postyshev, and Kosior, former party leaders in the Ukraine. Along with them almost all leading officials of the republic were arrested, including:

V. P. Zatonsky, I. Ye. Klimenko, K. V. Sukhomlin, M. M. Khataevich, V. I. Chernyavsky, Ye. I. Veger, F. I. Golub, S. A. Zeger, S. A. Kudryavtsev, A. S. Yegorov, O. V. Pilatskaya, V. D. Yeremenko, A. V. Osipov, A. K. Serbichenko, N. I. Golub, G. I. Stary, and M. I. Kondakov.

19. *Ocherki po istorii partiinoi organizatsii Tatarii* (Kazan, 1962).
20. *Istoriia Severo-Osetinskoi ASSR* (Ordzhonikidze, 1966), p. 247.
21. *Istoriia Kommunisticheskoi partiinoi organizatsii Komi ASSR*, (Syktyvkar, 1964).

Of all these leaders only Osipov and Pilatskaya were allowed to live. A. P. Lyubchenko, chairman of the Ukrainian Council of Commissars, fearing that his family would be arrested after his death, shot his wife and son and then himself. Almost all of the famous revolutionary Zaporozhets family were arrested: Viktor and Anton, Mariya Kuzminichna, and her husband, Taranenko. Iury Kotsiubinsky, Bolshevik son of the famous Ukrainian revolutionary democrat, perished. When Nikita Khrushchev was appointed first secretary of the Central Committee of the Communist Party of the Ukraine and was preparing a party congress to reestablish a party leadership it was discovered that the repression had reduced the membership of the Ukrainian party from 433,500 in 1934 to 285,800 in 1938.[22]

In Belorussia, where mass repression began much earlier than in the other republics, party membership dropped by more than a half. By 1937 there was actually no one to work in the Central Committee. Party officials were rapidly transferred from the oblasti to Minsk, but there in the capital they, too, fell into the gigantic meat grinder. Almost all the leading Bolsheviks perished, including:

N. M. Goloded, A. G. Chervyakov, who, the newspapers reported, killed himself "for family reasons," M. O. Skakun, S. D. Kamenshtein, A. M. Levitsky, D. I. Volkovich, A. F. Kovelev, N. F. Gikalo, a famous hero of the civil war, Ya. I. Zavodnik, A. I. Khatskevich, and hundreds of others.

Perusal of the current official Encyclopedia of Belorussia (*Belorusskaia entsiklopediia*) shows that of all the deservedly famous people in Belorussia in the thirties only a few survived, among them the writers Yakub Kolas and Yanka Kupala. All the others were arrested and most of them perished.

In Transcaucasia repression in Azerbaijan was directed by Stalin's protege Bagirov. Among the victims were:

G. M. Musabekov, former chairman of the Council of Commissars of Transcaucasia, a chairman of the USSR Central Executive Committee, and a member of the Comintern Executive Committee; Gusein Rakhmanov, secretary of the Central Committee and chairman of the Council of People's Commissars of Azerbaijan; S. M. Efendiev, chairman of the Central Executive Committee of Azerbaijan; and such prominent party and government figures as M. D. Guseinov, A. P. Akopov, R. Ali-Ogly Akhundov, D. Buniatzade, M. Tserafibekov, A. G. Karaev, M. Kuliev, M. A. Narimanov, G. Sultanov, and A. Sultanova.[23]

22. *Ocherki po istorii Kommunisticheskoi partii Ukrainy* (Kiev, 1964).
23. *Ocherki po istorii Kommunisticheskoi organizatsii Azerbaidzhana* (Baku, 1964).

The Georgian Party organization also suffered heavy losses in 1937–1938:

Mikha Kakhiani, Levan Gogoberidze, Jason Mamulia, Soso Buachidze, Peter and Levan Agniashvili, and Ivan Bolkvadze were killed or died in confinement. Mamiya Orakhelashvili, one of the founders of the Bolshevik organizations in Transcaucasia and long first secretary in that krai, perished. So did his wife, Maria, a party member since 1906 and a leader of the women's movement. G. Mshaloblishvili and L. Sukhishvili, successive chairmen of the Georgian Council of Commissars, were arrested, along with most of the people's commissars of Georgia, the heads of many factories and government agencies, and faculty members in higher educational institutions. The Abkhazian leader Nestor Lakoba, a close friend of Ordzhonikidze, Kirov, and Kalinin, was shot, and so was A. S. Agrba, first secretary of the obkom. M. A. Lakoba, a member of the obkom bureau, also perished.

The scale of repression in Georgia is revealed by this figure: of the 644 delegates to the Tenth Georgian Party Congress, which met in May 1937, 425, or 66 percent, were soon after arrested, exiled, or shot.[24]

In Armenia mass repression began very early. The Armenian leadership was displeased when Beria became first secretary of Transcaucasia, and Beria knew it. Moreover, Beria's wretched little book on the history of Bolshevism in Transcaucasia was condemned for its falsehoods by local party leaders, such as the Armenian commissar of education, Nersik Stepanyan. Beria responded with a shrill article, "Destroy the Enemies of Socialism," slandering Stepanyan and demanding his physical annihilation. The terror against the Armenian party actually began in 1935, when the NKVD fabricated cases against some leading officials and writers. The goal was to compromise the first secretary, A. Khandzhyan. On July 9, 1936, the bureau of the party's Transcaucasian territorial committee (Zavkraikom) heard an NKVD report "On the Discovery of a Counterrevolutionary Terrorist Group in Georgia, Azerbaijan, and Armenia." Khandzhyan was accused of lack of vigilance. That very evening he was dead. Some say he killed himself.[25] Other, more believable accounts (by Aleksandr Shelepin, Suren Gazaryan, Olga Shatunovskaya, and A. Ivanova) say that he was shot by Beria personally. After his death G. Amatuni and S. Akopov, Beria's creatures, became the new leaders of Armenia, and started to terrorize honest party and state cadres on the pretext of fighting nationalism and Dashnak counterrevolution. The victims included:

24. *Ocheriki po istorii Kommunisticheskoi partii Gruzii* (Tbilisi, 1963).
25. Ts. Agayan, *N. Stepanyan* (Yerevan, 1967).

four secretaries of the Armenian Central Committee—S. Srapionyan (Lukashin), A. Ioannisyan, G. Ovsepyan, and A. Kostanyan; S. Ter-Gabrielyan, former chairman of the Council of People's Commissars of Armenia; S. Martikyan, chairman of the Central Executive Committee of Armenia's soviets; P. M. Kuznetsov (Dabrinyan), chairman of the Armenian party's Commission of Party Control; five people's commissars—Nersik Stepanyan, A. Yerzinkyan, V. Yeremyan, A. Yesayan, and A. Yegizaryan; and the veteran Communists D. Shaverdyan, A. Melikyan, and A. Shaksuvaryan.[26]

In September 1937 Anastas Mikoyan and Georgy Malenkov arrived in Armenia. They took part in an intensification of the terror, which also swept away the newly appointed leaders Amatuni and Akopov.[27]

In Central Asia Kazakhstan experienced extreme repression. In 1937 every single member of the Central Committee bureau elected at the republic's first party congress was arrested and shot. Among the victims were:

L. I. Mirzoyan and S. Nurpeisov, secretaries of the Kazakhstan Central Committee; U. Kulumbetov, chairman of the republic's CEC; U. D. Isaev, chairman of the republic's Council of Commissars; and I. Yu. Kabulov, a member of the bureau of the Kazakhstan Central Committee and a prominent scholar.

At the same time most Central Committee members and party secretaries at all levels were arrested, including such founders of the Soviet regime in Kazakhstan as:

U. K. Dzhandosov, S. Segibaev, Yu. Babaev, A. Rozybakiev, and A. M. Asylbekov.

Today these Communists have been completely rehabilitated.[28]

Tadzhikistan lost:

A. Rakhimbaev, the president of its Council of Commissars, who had been elected to the All-Union Central Committee on Lenin's recommendation; Sh. Shotemor, secretary of the Tadzhik Central Committee; and such other party leaders as Kh. Bakiev, S. Anvarov, B. Dodobaev, K. Tashev, and A. T. Rcdin.[29]

In Kirgizia the victims of terror included:

M. K. Ammosov, first secretary of the Kirgiz party's Central Committee, its second secretary, M. L. Belotsky, D. S. Sadaev, chairman of the Kirgiz Control Commission, and many others.[30]

26. *Ocherki po istorii Kommunisticheskoi partii Armenii* (Yerevan, 1964).
27. See the newspaper *Kommunist* (Yerevan), September 22–30, 1937.
28. *Ocherki po istorii Kommunisticheskoi partii Kazakhstana,* (Alma-Ata, 1963).
29. *Ocherki po istorii Kommunisticheskoi partii Tadzhikistana,* (Dushanbe, 1965).
30. *Ocherki po istorii Kompartii Kirgizii,* (Frunze, 1966).

Turkmenia lost:

A. Mukhamedov and Ya A. Popok, secretaries of the Turkmen party's Central Committee; K. Atabaev, chairman of the republic's Council of People's Commissars; N. Aitakov, chairman of the Central Executive Committee of the Turkmen soviets; and such prominent party leaders and public figures as Ch. Vellekov, Kh. Sakhatmuradov, K. Kuliev, O. Tashiazarov, D. Mamedov, B. Ataev, and Kurban Sakhatov.

For several months there was not even a Central Committee Bureau in Turkmenia.[31]

The Communist Party of Uzbekistan also suffered heavy losses. I have already discussed the fate of Akmal Ikramov, its first secretary, and Faizul Khodzhaev, chairman of the Uzbek Council of Commissars. Hundreds of other leaders in that republic were arrested and died, including

D. Tyurabekov, D. Rizacv, D. I. Manzhara, N. Israilov, and R. Islamov.[32]

What I have presented thus far is sufficient to demonstrate that the cutting edge of the terror of the late thirties was mainly aimed at the party. This was obvious to nonpolitical Soviet citizens, who slept more soundly in those years than party members. In *The Gulag Archipelago* and in many articles published since his expulsion from the Soviet Union, Aleksandr Solzhenitsyn has frequently stated that he cannot regard the Communists arrested in 1936–1939 as *victims* of Stalin's terror because they themselves had taken part in the Red Terror from 1918 to 1922 and had directly or indirectly assisted in the violent campaigns against the peasantry and the intelligentsia in the years 1928–1933. He asks:

If until the last moment a person has helped the executioner, turning others in to be slaughtered and holding the axe himself, to what extent is he a victim rather than just another executioner?[33]

The opposite point of view may be encountered as well, one that idealizes the generation of party leaders that perished in 1936–1939. The Old Bolshevik Kirill Rublev, the hero of a novel by Victor Serge, writes the following in his diary shortly before being shot on Stalin's orders:

We are all dying without knowing why we have killed so many men in whom lay our highest strength. . . . We were an exceptional human accomplishment,

31. *Ocherki po istorii Kompartii Turkmenii* (Ashkhabad, 1965).
32. *Ocherki istorii Kommunisticheskoi partii Uzbekistana*, (Tashkent, 1964).
33. *Russkaya mysl* (Paris), January 16, 1975.

and that is why we are going under. A half century unique in history was required to form our generation. . . . We grew up amid struggle, escaping two profound captivities, that of the old "Holy Russia" and that of the bourgeois West, at the same time that we borrowed from those two worlds their most vital elements: the spirit of inquiry, the transforming audacity, the faith in progress of the nineteenth-century West; and a peasant people's direct feeling for truth and for action, its spirit of revolt, formed by centuries of despotism. . . .

We acquired a degree of lucidity and disinterestedness which made both the old and the new interests uneasy. It was impossible for us to adapt ourselves to a phase of reaction; and as we were in power, surrounded by a legend that was true, born of our deeds, we were so dangerous that we had to be destroyed beyond physical destruction, our corpses had to be surrounded by a legend of treachery. . . .

The weight of the world is upon us, we are crushed by it. All those who want neither drive nor uncertainty in the successful revolution overwhelm us; . . . to those who were comfortably established inside our own revolution, we represented venturesomeness and risk. . . . We demanded the courage to continue our exploit, and people wanted nothing but more security, rest, to forget the effort and the blood. . . .[34]

The truth lies somewhere in between these extremely negative and extremely positive interpretations. In spite of everything Solzhenitsyn is right to some extent. Neither Yagoda, Yezhov, Zakovsky, nor many other butchers can simply be called "victims" of the terror, nor can their direct accomplices who knew what they were doing—even though when their turn came the charges against them were fabricated. Nevertheless, in rejecting Solzhenitsyn's opinion regarding other Communist Party members, I am not by any means justifying the cruel terror against the peasants during collectivization or against alleged "wreckers" or "class enemies" from the former educated classes, the *byvshie lyudi*. I will discuss further below the fact that many of the party and government leaders who were later exterminated went to considerable lengths to destroy their own party comrades.

Among the Communists who died in the purges of the thirties were people who differed considerably in their careers, the motives for their actions, their personal qualities, and the degree of responsibility they bore for the crimes committed during or after the revolution. There were many honest, self-sacrificing people among them who sincerely wished to create a just society and firmly believed they were helping build one, fighting only against the enemies of such a society. Quite a few were

---

34. Victor Serge, *The Case of Comrade Tulayev*, (New York, 1963), pp. 358–360. [The author cites a Russian edition: *Delo Tulaeva* (Belgium, 1972), pp. 469–472. —G. S.]

deceived or sincerely mistaken or fell victim to a cult of a different kind, the cult of party discipline. There were people who understood a great deal, but not until it was too late. There were people who never understood, right up to the end. There were thinking people who were painfully aware of what was going on but who in many respects still believed the party leadership and the official propaganda. They appealed to Stalin and other leaders but usually fell victim to the monstrous meat grinder soon afterward. Others no longer believed in Stalin or the party propaganda but had no idea how to alter the situation. And of course there were those who were simply afraid. It is terribly wrong to lump all these people together as criminals who "got what they deserved." One may speak in general about the historical and political responsibility of the party membership for the tragedies of the twenties and thirties. This applies to the Chekists as well, although their responsibility for the events of the thirties is very great. I cannot, however, take the same attitude toward Yagoda or Zakovsky as I do toward a well-known Chekist, Artuzov, who before he was shot wrote in his own blood on the wall of his prison cell: "It is the duty of an honest man to kill Stalin."

■ **6**

REPRESSION IN THE TRADE UNIONS AND THE KOMSOMOL

Long before 1937, immediately after Tomsky withdrew from leadership of the All-Union Council of Trade Unions, almost all the old leaders were removed. Under the pretext of the "anti-rightist" campaign these people were transferred to minor posts in government agencies or economic institutions. In 1937–1938 almost all of them were falsely accused and arrested, including:

G. N. Melnichansky, A. I. Dogadov, Ya. Yaglom, V. Mikhailov, B. Kozelev, F. Ugarov, and V. Shmidt.

In 1937 a large part of the newly elected secretariat of the All-Union Council of Trade Unions, headed by Nikolai Shvernik, was not touched by repression. But many well-known trade union officials, such as Ye. N. Yegorova, secretary of the Trade Union Council, were arrested. In 1917 she had been the secretary of the Vyborg raikom in Petrograd who filled out a party card for Lenin. In July 1917 she helped to hide Lenin. This old friend of Krupskaya was accused of anti-Soviet activity and killed.[35]

35. *Sovetskaia Latvia*, March 22, 1964.

Many others who were then in the trade union leadership, including A. A. Korostelev, perished.

The Komsomol leaders had a more tragic fate, including many who had moved on to other jobs but preserved a connection with the youth organization. Among these were:

Oskar Ryvkin, who had been elected chairman of the Komsomol at its first congress in 1918; he was the party secretary in Krasnodar in 1937 when he was arrested. Lazar Shatskin, who had been first secretary of the Komsomol in 1920–1921, was working in the Comintern when he was taken away. Pyotr Smorodin, first secretary of the Komsomol from 1921 to 1924, who spoke for the organization at Lenin's funeral, had become a secretary of the Leningrad party committee and a candidate member of the Central Committee in 1937, when he was arrested and shot. Nikolai Chaplin, general secretary of the Komsomol from 1924 to 1928, was head of the Southeastern Railway when he perished. Aleksandr Milchakov, who was general secretary from 1918 to 1929, was also arrested.

In short, Stalin and the NKVD would have us believe that every chief of the Komsomol from 1928 to 1929 was an "enemy of the people."

Some Komsomol leaders of the new generation were also arrested, but not as many as Stalin wished. Aleksandr Milchakov, Valentina Pikina, and A. Dimentman report that in June 1937 Aleksandr Kosarev and the other secretaries of the Komsomol CC were summoned to Stalin's office. Yezhov was there. Stalin began to reprimand Kosarev for the failure of the Komsomol Central Committee to help the NKVD in discovering "enemies of the people." None of Kosarev's explanations helped. For an hour and a half Stalin continued to reproach him. Analogous charges against Kosarev were included in the resolutions of the Fourth Plenum of the Komsomol CC, which met in closed session in 1937 to hear a report by Kosarev "On the Work of Enemies of the People Within the Komsomol." Malenkov and Kaganovich were also present at the plenum. A resolution adopted by the plenum stated that the bureau of the Komsomol's Central Committee and Kosarev personally were to blame for lateness and lack of initiative in unmasking enemies of the people and for spreading the idea among the membership that there were no such enemies within the Komsomol.[36]

Repression of Komsomol officials increased considerably following the plenum. Among those arrested were:

36. This information is from the stenographic record of a meeting in honor of Kosarev's sixtieth birthday, held at the Museum of the Revolution in Moscow, November 1963. The text is in the archive of the Kosarev family.

P. S. Gorshenin and Fainberg, secretaries of the Komsomol CC; Vasily Chemodanov, member of the executive committee of the Communist Youth International; D. Lukyanov, G. Lebedev, and A. Kurylev, members of the Komsomol CC; V. M. Bubekin, editor of *Komsomolskaya pravda;* and four secretaries of Komsomol organizations on the union-republic or oblast level: S. Andreev, secretary of the Ukrainian Komsomol CC, K. Taishitov, secretary of the Kazakhstan Komsomol CC; I. Artykov secretary of the Uzbekistan CC; and V. A. Aleksandrov, secretary of the Komsomol's Moscow oblast committee.

At the end of 1938 it was Kosarev's turn. On November 19–22 there was a plenum of the Komsomol CC chaired by A. A. Andreev, with Stalin, Molotov, and Malenkov in attendance. With slander supplied by Olga Mishakova, a Komsomol apparatchik, Stalin turned the plenum into an attack on the Komsomol leadership. Kosarev and most of the other leaders were removed from their posts and soon after arrested. *Komsomolskaya pravda* attacked Kosarev for obstructing the war on enemies by arguing that the Komsomol was less infested by them than other groups. This despicable effort to demobilize the vigilantes was defeated, the paper said, by the direct intervention of the Central Committee and by Stalin personally. The war on enemies could now proceed. "There is no doubt that the enemies and politically corrupt people who have led the Komsomol have managed to implant their 'cadres' in many sectors. This political scum is still far from destroyed."[37] And this was published only a few weeks after the twentieth anniversary of the Komsomol had been celebrated with stories of its glorious past and great triumphs.

Many of Kosarev's friends and colleagues were arrested, including Pikina, Bogachev, and Vershkov. Milchakov, one of the few who survived many years of confinement, recalls the following names among those arrested:

Oskar Tarkhanov, Rimma Yurovskaya, Vladimir Feigin, Andrei Shokhin, Dmitry Matveev, Georgy Ivanov, Gusein Rakhmanov, Ignaty Sharavyev, and Sergei Saltanov.[38]

Only a few of these people had reached thirty-five. The life of most resembled that of Nikolai Ostrovsky and his autobiographical hero, Pavel Korchagin. Indeed, many of the Komsomol leaders who perished were personal friends of Ostrovsky, who did not live to see what happened to them.[39] And these energetic young people, who had already done so

37. *Komsomolskaya pravda*, November 24, 1938.
38. Alesksandr Milchakov, *Pervoe desiatiletie* (Moscow, 1965).
39. See Nikolai Ostrovsky, *Kak zakalialas' stal'* (Moscow, 1935). [In this semi-autobio-

much for their country but still had more to do, were declared enemies of the people. Most of them died in the camps or were shot on Stalin's orders.

■ 7

DESTRUCTION OF THE CADRES OF THE RED ARMY

In the late thirties the Soviet Union, sparing neither effort nor resources, was preparing for what seemed to be an inevitable war with the fascist states, which had already begun their aggression in Spain, Abyssinia, China, and central Europe (Czechoslovakia). Precisely in that perilous time Stalin and the NKVD struck at the best cadres of the Red Army; in the course of two years they destroyed tens of thousands of loyal commanders and commissars.

The first arrests were made in late 1936 and early 1937, snatching such heroes as:

I. I. Garkavy, I. Turovsky, G. D. Gai, Yu. V. Sablin, D. M. Shmidt, B. Kuzmichev, and Ya. Okhotnikov.

They were accused of ties with Trotskyists and Zinovievists.

On June 11, 1937, the papers announced the arrest, trial, and hasty execution of the most important generals:

Mikhail Tukhachevsky, Iona Yakir, I. P. Uborevich, B. M. Feldman, A. I. Kork, R. P. Eideman, V. M. Primakov, and V. K. Putna.

The death of Tukhachevsky, who had been deputy commissar of defense until shortly before his arrest, was an especially painful blow to the Soviet army. He was the Soviet Union's greatest military strategist after Frunze, a brilliant organizer with a special interest in the technical modernization of the armed forces.[40] Yakir, hero of the civil war, member of the Central Committee, recognized internationally for his military talent, was commander of the Kiev special military district before his arrest. Uborevich, at the age of twenty-two, had led the Soviet Four-

---

graphical work, *How the Steel Was Tempered*—also translated as *The Making of a Hero*—the young author-hero, dying of an incurable disease, reviews with pride his service to the Communist cause. —D. J.] The book is very popular in the Soviet Union. Tens of millions of copies have been published, and to this day it is required reading for all secondary school students and members of the Komsomol.

40. *Voenno-istoricheskii zhurnal* (1963) no. 4, p. 65.

teenth Army to victory over Denikin's elite divisions in 1919 outside Orel. In 1922 he commanded the army of the Soviet Far Eastern Republic in the liberation of Vladivostok. At the time of his arrest he was commander of the Belorussian military district. Primakov was famous as a commander of "Red Cossacks" in the civil war. Eideman, hero of the battle of Kakhovka in the civil war, was head of the Soviet civil defense organization Osoaviakhim at the time of his arrest; he was also a well-known poet and one of the founders of Soviet Latvian literature.

At the same time the papers announced the suicide of another "enemy of the people," Yan Gamarnik, a member of the party's Central Committee, head of the army's Political Administration, and a deputy commissar of defense.

However serious the loss of Tukhachevsky, Yakir, and their comrades, it was only the beginning. Speaking in August 1937 to a meeting of the army's political officials, Stalin called for the extirpation of "enemies of the people" who were hiding in the army. The next day Commissar of Defense Voroshilov and Commissar of Internal Affairs Yezhov issued an order to the armed forces stating that a far-reaching network of spies existed in the army. Everyone who knew or suspected anything about spying activity was ordered to report it.

The NKVD then proceeded, in the second half of 1937 and in 1938, to assault the core of the military command: the central apparatus of the Commissariat of Defense, the Political Administration of the Army, the Revolutionary-Military Council of the USSR, the military districts (okrugi), the navy, and most of the corps, regiments, and divisions. Almost all the most outstanding Red Army commanders who had risen to prominence during the civil war perished. Marshal A. I. Yegorov, chief of the General Staff, who had routed Denikin in 1919, was arrested and killed. Marshal Vasily Blyukher, commander of the Special Far Eastern Army, a legendary hero of the civil war, was shot. He was tremendously popular in the army and in the country as a whole. For that reason Stalin did not announce his death. Rumors circulated that he was fighting in China under a different name. I. F. Fedko, a hero of the civil war and bearer of four Orders of the Red Banner, also perished.

Other victims included:

V. M. Orlov and Ya. I. Alksnis, deputy commissars of defense for the navy and air force, respectively; A. I. Sedyakin, E. F. Appog, G. Bokis, N. N. Petin, Ya. M. Fishman, R. V. Longva, and A. I. Gekker, heads of departments in the

Commissariat of Defense; I. Ye. Slavin, commissar; G. A. Osepyan and A. S. Bulin, deputy chiefs of the army's Political Administration; and G. D. Bazilevich, secretary of the Committee of Defense under the USSR Council of Commissars.

Almost all the commanders of the country's military districts and fleets were arrested and shot, including such heroes of the civil war as:

Pavel Dybenko, who had commanded several military districts, including that of Leningrad; N. V. Kuibyshev, brother of V. V. Kuibyshev, commander of the Transcaucasian military district; S. Ye. Gribov and N. D. Kashirin, commanders of the Northern Caucasus military district; M. D. Velikanov, commander of the Transbaikal military district; I. P. Belov, commander of the Belorussian military district; I. K. Gryaznov, commander of a district; Ya. P. Gailit, commander of the Siberian military district; I. I. Dubovoi, commander of the Kharkov military district; A. N. Borisenko, commander of the mechanized corps; M. K. Levandovsky, commander of the Primorskaya group of the Far Eastern Army; V. V. Khripin, commander of the Special Aviation Army; and A. Ya. Lapin, commander of air forces in the Far East, who had led the Amur Army during the civil war.

Today all these heroes have been completely rehabilitated.

More victims:

Ye. I. Kovtyukh, the hero of the Taman campaign described by Serafimovich in his novel *The Iron Flood;* I. I. Vatsetis, former commander of the Lettish Rifle Division, and commander in chief of the RSFSR armed forces; I. S. Kutyakov, who at the age of twenty-two had replaced V. I. Chapaev as commander of the famous 25th Division and who helped to produce the film *Chapaev;* D. F. Serdich, I. Ya. Strod, B. S. Gorbachev, and V. M. Mulin, civil war heroes; and G. Kh. Eikhe, former commander of the Fifth Army of the Eastern Front, which defeated Kolchak in Irkutsk, one of the few army commanders to survive many years of imprisonment.

Many naval officers were arrested and shot, including:

M. V. Viktorov, commander of the Pacific Fleet; I. K. Kozhanov, commander of the Black Sea Fleet; K. I. Dushenov, commander of the Northern Fleet; A. K. Vekman, head of the naval forces in the Baltic Sea; Admirals and Vice Admirals A. S. Grishin, D. G. Duplitsky, G. P. Kireev, I. M. Ludri, R. A. Muklevich, G. S. Okunev, V. M. Smirnov, E. S. Pantserzhansky, and S. P. Stavitsky.

Almost all the military academies were devastated. Among the victims were:

S. A. Pugachev, head of the Military Transport Academy; B. M. Ippo, head of the Military Political Academy; M. Ya. Germanovich, head of the Military Academy of Motorization and Mechanization; D. A. Kuchinsky, head of the General Staff Academy; A. Ya. Sazontov; and A. I. Todorsky, a talented journalist and military leader, head of the Air Force Academy and of the administration of higher schools within the Commissariat of Defense, was arrested but managed to survive.[41]

Hundreds of teachers and students in these academies also perished, including such outstanding military scientists as

P. I. Vakulich, A. I. Verkhovsky, A. V. Pavlov, and A. A. Svechin.

The Lenin Military-Political Academy was especially hard hit in 1937–1938. To justify senseless arrests of the army's political officials, Stalin brought up the "Belorussian-Tolmachev opposition." In 1928 some political officials of the Belorussian military district and the Academy, which was then named after N. G. Tolmachev, had criticized the introduction of one-man control [edinonachalie].[42] By 1937 this "opposition" had been forgotten—except by those who started arresting and shooting members of the military councils and directors of the political departments in almost every military district. Most of the victims—such men as M. P. Amelin, L. N. Aronshtamm, G. I. Veklichev, G. D. Khakhanyants, A. M. Bitte, and A. I. Mezis—had never had any connection with this "opposition." What is more, in 1937 Stalin himself revived the institution of political commissars in the army, thereby limiting "one-man control." In 1940 one-man control was reestablished, but in 1941 political commissars were reintroduced, only to be abolished in 1942, this time for good. The crucial fact was Stalin's repression of the army's best commanders and commissars; he encouraged distrust of command and of political cadres and thereby undermined discipline in the army.

Many former military leaders who had moved to civilian posts were also arrested, including:

I. S. Unshlikht, director of the main administration of the Air Force, candidate member of the Central Committee, from 1935 secretary of the USSR Central Executive Committee; R. I. Berzin, commander of armies on the Eastern and Southern Fronts during the civil war, who later worked in the war industry and the Commissariat of Agriculture; and Dmitry Zhloba, a civil war hero who subsequently did economic work in the Kuban.

41. Todorsky's tragic fate and courageous behavior were described in Boris Dyakov's story *Iz perezhitogo* (Moscow, 1963).

42. [*Edinonachalie* is the principle that a single individual has ultimate authority and responsibility within an organization, whether a military unit, a factory, or a governmental agency. In conflict with the revolutionary goal of popular participation and with the notion of collective leadership, *edinonachalie* occasioned disputes in many areas of Soviet life during the twenties. —D. J.]

Nor did Stalin spare retired officers. V. I. Shorin, to take a notable example, was shot at the age of sixty-eight. A commander of armies and fronts during the civil war, he had retired for reasons of health in 1925. The Revolutionary Military Council of the USSR had issued an order granting him lifetime membership in the Red Army in recognition of his colossal labors in its creation, his talented leadership throughout the civil war, and his personal heroism. This was the first time in the army's history that a man was so honored, but Stalin struck his name from the army rolls and had him shot.

Stalin vented his enmity even on dead military leaders, consigning to oblivion such well-known soldiers as:

V. Triandofilov, K. Kalinovsky, Ya. Fabritsius, S. S. Kamenev, and S. Vostretsov.

The army suffered not only from the arrest but also from the demotion and discharge of thousands of talented commanders and commissars, who were expelled from the party "for loss of vigilance." Even if this type of casualty is ignored, the total losses of the army and navy were enormous: three of the five marshalls, fifteen of the sixteen army commanders, all of the corps commanders and almost all division commanders and brigade commanders, and one-third of the regimental commissars.[43] The navy suffered equally heavy losses. There were also huge losses among the field-grade and junior officers. The shocking truth can be stated quite simply: never did the officer staff of any army suffer such great losses in any war as the Soviet army suffered in this time of peace.

Years of training cadres came to nothing. The party stratum in the army was drastically reduced. In 1940 the autumn report of the Inspector General of Infantry showed that, of 225 regimental commanders on active duty that summer, not one had been educated in a military academy, 25 had finished a military school, and the remaining 200 had only completed the courses for junior lieutenants. At the beginning of 1940 more than 70 percent of the division commanders, about 70 percent of the regimental commanders, and 60 percent of the military commissars and heads of political divisions had occupied these positions for a year only.[44] And all this happened just before the worst war in history.

The destruction of the best officers of the Red Army caused great rejoicing among the Germans. It was a major consideration in Hitler's

43. *Kratkaia istoriia Velikoi Otechestvennoi voiny* (Moscow, 1965), pp. 39–40. A. I. Todorsky arrived at similar estimates.

44. V. A. Anfilov, *Nachalo Velikoi Otechestvennoi voiny* (Moscow, 1962), p. 28.

plans for an attack on the Soviet Union. At the Nuremberg trial Marshal Keitel testified that many German generals had warned Hitler against attacking the Soviet Union, arguing that the Red Army was a strong opponent. But Hitler rejected their misgivings. "The first-class high-ranking officers," he told Keitel," were wiped out by Stalin in 1937, and the new generation cannot yet provide the brains they need." On January 9, 1941, Hitler told a meeting of Nazi generals planning the attack: "They do not have good commanders."[45]

■ 8

REPRESSION IN THE NKVD, THE COURTS, AND THE PROCURACY

Stalin relied on the punitive organs of the state to carry out his mass repression. But an important part, a precondition, was the physical destruction of thousands of officials in the punitive organs themselves.

This ruthless purge began as early as the fall of 1936. The officials in these organs could hardly be described as good Chekists. Most officials in the NKVD, the courts, and the procuracy had taken part in the eviction of millions of kulaks and middle peasants in 1930–1933, the repression of "bourgeois specialists," the "gold campaign" of 1930–1931, and the illegal repression of former oppositionists in 1935–1936. But the process of degeneration and political corruption going on among these officials was not rapid enough to suit Stalin. NKVD officials who had readily consented to provocation and fraud against people of alien classes or against ex-oppositionists were not so ready to turn the same weapons against the basic cadres of the party and the Soviet state. So Stalin decided to change the composition of these organs radically. Not the least factor in this decision was that these people "knew too much." Tyrants have little liking for witnesses of and participants in their crimes.

Earlier I mentioned the arrest and shooting of Yagoda. His deputies and closest assistants Vsevolod Balitsky, Yakov Agranov, G. A. Molchanov, L. G. Mironov, M. I. Gai, A. M. Shanin, and Z. B. Katsnelson were destroyed along with him. A. A. Slutsky, the head of the foreign section of the NKVD, was poisoned. Stalin also authorized the execution of K. V. Pauker, the head of the NKVD's operations section, the commandant of the Kremlin and head of the Kremlin guard—a man who many had thought was one of Stalin's most trusted henchmen.

45. A. I. Poltorak, *Niurnbergskii epilog* (Moscow, 1965), pp. 324–326.

Yefim Yevdokimov, the first Chekist to receive four Orders of the Red Banner, was also arrested. He had helped to organize the trial of the "Industrial Party," and, transferring to party work in 1936, had exerted himself to purge Rostov oblast of ex-oppositionists. In 1937 Yevdokimov himself was arrested and shot. That same year Terenty Deribas was arrested and shot. He had managed the NKVD in the Far East, and some party officials from that region, notably Pavel Shabalkin, say that Deribas opposed the repression of party and government cadres.

In 1936–1937 many well-known Chekists were arrested and shot, including

Martyn Latsis, S. Messing, N. Bystrykh, S. Styrne, Artur Artuzov, G. Blagnonravov, S. Arshakuni, A. Pillyar, V. R. Dombrovsky, M. V. Slonimsky, N. G. Krapivyansky, G. Ye. Prokofyev, L. B. Zalin, T. Lordkipanidze, B. A. Zak.

According to the former Chekists and veteran party members Suren Gazaryan, M. V. Ostragradsky, and M. M. Ishov, most of these people were well-meaning Communists who did not want to take part in the destruction of party and state cadres. Artuzov, for example, made the following statement in an NKVD meeting in 1937:

Given the sergeant-major style of leadership that has been established since the death of Menzhinsky certain individual Chekists and even entire sectors of our organization have taken the dangerous road of degeneration into simple technicians of an apparatus for internal control, with all its attendant defects, putting us on a par with the despicable political police of the capitalists.[46]

After this speech Artuzov was arrested and soon shot.

Other victims included:

V. N. Mantsev, a personal friend of Dzerzhinsky—shot. I. M. Leplevsky, Belorussian Commissar of Internal Affairs, who refused to apply the "new methods" —shot. F. T. Fomin, one of Dzerzhinsky's cohorts—arrested but survived.[47] M. S. Pogrebinsky, organizer of many communes for delinquent and abandoned children, the inspiration of the excellent film *Putevka v zhizn* (The Road to Life); appointed director of the NKVD in Gorky oblast, Pogrebinsky killed himself to avoid participation in lawlessness, as his suicide letter reveals.

The head of one of the Ukranian NKVD agencies, Kozelsky, also committed suicide. Indeed, a wave of suicides swept through the NKVD in 1937, taking away not only honorable officials but also some who had already traveled pretty far on the road to crime. Kursky, for example,

46. T. Gladkov and M. Smirnov, *Menzhinsky* (Moscow, 1969), p. 327.
47. See Fomin's *Zapiski starogo chekista*, (Moscow, 1964).

who not long before had received the Order of Lenin for his "successful" preparation of the trial of the "Parallel Center," shot himself.

The former NKVD official Alexander Orlov writes that Yezhov was cautious at first in destroying the top NKVD aides who had worked with Yagoda, but then began to act more boldly.

He started mass arrests of the interrogators who had taken part in the preparation of the [first two] Moscow trials, and of all other officers who knew or might know the secrets of Stalin's falsifications. They were arrested one by one during the daytime in their offices and at night in their homes. Many of the officers did not await their turn and committed suicide. When in the early hours of the morning a patrol came to the apartment of Chertok, the interrogator who had distinguished himself by his cruel treatment of Kamenev, Chertok shouted, "You won't get *me!*" and plunged to his death from the balcony of his twelfth floor apartment.

Felix Gursky, an officer of the Foreign Department who several weeks before had been decorated for "devotion to duty" with the Order of the Red Star, threw himself from the window of his office on the ninth floor. Two interrogators of the Secret Political Department did the same thing. . . . The inquisitors of the NKVD, who not long before had driven fear into the hearts of Stalin's captives, were now themselves shaking with indescribable horror. . . .

There was even no pretense of investigating the cases of the arrested officers. They had been summarily accused of Trotskyism and espionage and shot without trial.[48]

Other victims included:

E. P. Berzin, head of Dalstroi, organizer of the first camps in the Kolyma region, former secretary of Dzerzhinsky and former commander of the Lettish Rifle Division, arrested in 1937 and shot in 1938; I. D. Kashirin, second of the Kashirin brothers to perish, member of the NKVD collegium; Gleb Boky, member of the NKVD collegium, party member since 1900, survivor of eleven terms in the Peter-Paul Fortress; and Yakov Peters, a close associate of Dzerzhinsky's.

In his unpublished book Eto ne dolzhno povtorit'sia (It Must Not Happen Again), Suren Gazaryan, an old Chekist of the Dzerzhinsky school, gives a good description of the terror that arose within the NKVD itself. He headed the Economic Section of the NKVD in Georgia and Transcaucasia in 1937, when he was arrested He survived all sorts of torture and prolonged confinement to tell how dozens of honorable NKVD officials in Georgia were seized and placed in hastily built prisons by their former friends and subordinates. Many Chekists, faced with the choice between criminal actions and arrest, committed suicide. On the

48. Orlov, *The Secret History of Stalin's Crimes*, pp. 215–216.

other hand, it was in just those years that Beria's creatures won swift promotion, first in the Georgian, then in the USSR NKVD—men like Kobulov and Khazan, Krimyan and Savitsky, Dekanozov and Merkulov, Goglidze and Milshtein.

Soviet intelligence was also decimated, both the NKVD branch and the branch within the Commissariat of Defense. Soon after Slutsky was done away with, his successor, Shpigelglas, was arrested and shot. Many foreign agents were recalled to Moscow, sent to sanatoria, and then, after a "rest," arrested and shot. Among the victims were Nikolai Smirnov (Glinsky), NKVD resident in France, and Lvovich of the military intelligence. However, quite a few refused to return to certain death. To get even with these people, with diplomats who would not return, and with other people who were inconvenient to Stalin, Yezhov set up a special task force to work abroad. After long manhunts, many people were killed, including:

Ignace Reiss, tracked down and killed in Switzerland; Walter Krivitsky, NKVD resident in Holland, who was tracked down and killed in the United States; Agabekov, former NKVD resident in Turkey, who had quit Soviet intelligence in 1929 and was tracked down and killed in Belgium in 1938.

The founder and director of Soviet military intelligence, Ya. K. Berzin, who in 1937 was named chief advisor to the Spanish Republican government, was recalled and shot. Twice Berzin had been sentenced to death by tsarist courts for revolutionary activity in the Baltic region. But it was the sentence of a Soviet court that secured the death of this outstanding leader, who trained hundreds of fighters on the secret front, including Richard Sorge, Hero of the Soviet Union. Sorge's comrade Karl Ramm was recalled from Shanghai and shot. Aino Kuusinen, wife of Otto Kuusinen, was recalled from Japan and arrested. She had been working with Sorge, carrying out a number of assignments for him. Sorge's wife, Yekaterina Maksimova, who was in Moscow, was arrested and perished. Sorge himself was called to Moscow for the same treatment but refused to return on the grounds that there was no one to replace him and that the connections he had were of unique importance. The numerous books about Sorge published today indicate that his information helped the Soviet forces defeat the Germans in the fighting outside Moscow in the fall and winter of 1941. These books do not say, however, that after arresting Sorge in October 1941, the Japanese authorities offered to exchange him for several important Japanese agents arrested in the

Soviet Union. Stalin refused to authorize the exchange, and in 1944 Sorge was hanged by the Japanese.

S. P. Uritsky, who replaced Berzin as head of military intelligence, was shot. His uncle, M. S. Uritsky, had been killed in 1918, when he was head of the Petrograd Cheka—by White Guardists.

These events were unheard of in the history of intelligence. A vast and superbly organized intelligence network was destroyed by its own leadership, quite consciously and deliberately.

The judicial and procuratorial organs were also savagely purged in 1936–1938. In addition to Nikolai Krylenko, the commissar of justice whose fate has already been described, Ivan Akulov, procurator general of the USSR, was dismissed and then arrested. One of the oldest Bolshevik activists, he had organized the famous demonstration of 60,000 Petrograd workers in 1912. In the thirties Akulov tried to fight Yagoda's abuse of power, but Yagoda together with Vyshinsky—and, of course, with Stalin's support—got rid of Akulov. Many other leading judicial officials were arrested and done to death, including:

A. V. Medvedev, a member of the Supreme Court; V. A. Degot, procurator of the RSFSR; N. M. Nemtsev, member of the Supreme Court and chairman of the Moscow city court; R. P. Katanyan and M. V. Ostrogorsky, high officials in the procuracy; and such officials of the military procuracy and military tribunals as N. N. Gomerov, Yu. A. Dzervit, Ye. L. Perfilyev, and L. Ya. Plavnik.

In 1938, without any explanation, Pyotr Krasikov, who had been one of Lenin's oldest comrades and vice-president of the Second Party Congress in 1903, was dismissed from his seat on the Supreme Court. As early as 1936 Krastin, the deputy procurator general of the USSR, shot himself. According to R. G. Alikhanova, Krastin left a suicide note saying that the upcoming trials of opposition leaders were fabrications in which he could not participate.

Yuri Trifonov has told the tragic story of Aron Solts, famous in his time as the "conscience of the party." Working in the procurator's office, he was one of the few to demand evidence of "enemy" charges. He did so when Valentin Trifonov, the author's father, was caught up in such a case. Vyshinsky told him:

"If the NKVD has arrested him, it means he is an enemy." Solts grew red and shouted: "You're lying! I've known Trifonov for thirty-four years as a true Bolshevik, but I know you as a Menshevik." He threw down his briefcase and left. . . . Solts began to be taken off cases. He did not give in. In October 1937, at the height of the repression, Solts suddenly began to criticize Vyshinsky at a party conference in Sverdlovsk. He demanded the creation of a special commission to investigate Vyshinsky's activity as procurator general. He still believed that the methods introduced when Lenin was still alive had some force. . . . Some of the audience froze with terror, but most began to shout, "Down with him! Get off the platform! A wolf in sheep's clothing!" Solts kept on speaking. Some enraged vigilantes ran up to the old man and dragged him off the stand. It's hard to say why Stalin did not get even with Solts the simple way, by arresting him. . . . In February 1938 Solts was finally dismissed from the procuracy. He tried to get an appointment with Stalin. He had worked with Stalin in the Petersburg underground in 1912–13, even sharing a bunk with him, but Stalin would not see him. Solts still did not give in; he announced a hunger strike. Then they stuck him in a psychiatric hospital. Two hefty orderlies came to his house on Serafimovich Street, grabbed the little man with the big head of grey hair, bound him, and carried him down to the ambulance. Later he was released, but he was broken.[49]

Ostrogorsky says that Solts announced his hunger strike after Vyshinsky tried blackmail, showing him some depositions that denounced Solts. In his letters to Stalin Solts continued to use *ty*, the familiar form of "you," and to call Stalin "Koba." When every meeting began the ridiculous practice of electing an "honorary presidium" of Politburo members, who were not even present, Solts, according to A. V. Snegov, refused to stand and applaud during this religious rite. But that was the protest of one man. Solts's death, during the war, was briefly noted only in the wall newspaper of the procurator's office.

Hundreds of Soviet legal officials shared Solts' fate. They were pushed aside in favor of unprincipled, cruel people, such as Vyshinsky, Ulrikh, I. O. Matulevich, G. P. Lipov, S. Ya. Ulyanova, and A. A. Batner.

■ 9
REPRESSION AGAINST ACTIVISTS OF THE COMINTERN AND FOREIGN COMMUNIST PARTIES

In the mid-thirties most non-Soviet parties were underground. To preserve the leading core of these parties, many of their Central Committee members lived in Moscow, which was the center of the Comintern, the Communist Youth International, the Peasant International, the Trade Union International, and so on. It is not surprising therefore that these organizations were seriously hurt by the campaign of terror in the USSR.

First of all, many Soviet officials of these international organizations were arrested and perished, among them:

49. Yuri Trifonov, *Otblesk kostra* (Moscow, 1966), pp. 26–27.

Iosif Pyatnitsky, secretary of the Comintern's Executive Committee, who had been a leader of the Moscow insurrection and was greatly esteemed by Lenin; Rafael Khitarov, for many years the head of the Communist Youth International; Pavel Mif, rector of Sun Yat-sen University, leading figure in the Comintern and expert on China; G. Alikhanov (Alikhanyan), head of the Comintern's department of cadres and one of the founders of the Communist Party of Armenia; K. I. Smolyansky, G. Safarov, B. A. Vasilyev, P. L. Lapinski, Mirov-Abramov, and Kraevsky, leading officials in the Comintern apparatus.

M. A. Trilisser, who had been a deputy chairman of the GPU, became director of a special section of the Comintern in the mid-thirties. According to V. S——, one of the jobs assigned to Trilisser was to purge the Comintern of "enemies of the people." Soon Trilisser himself fell victim to that savage purge.

Along with Soviet officials, many foreign Communists were killed. Bela Kun, the leader of the short-lived Hungarian Soviet Republic in 1919, was arrested and shot. Other leaders of the Hungarian Communist Party perished, including F. Karikas, D. Bokanyi, Farkas Gabor, and L. Magyar. Twelve former commissars of the Hungarian Soviet Republic died in the torture chambers of the NKVD. (Most of them were also members of the Soviet Communist Party, since simultaneous membership in two or even several Communist parties was common at the time.)

The Polish Communist Party was especially hard hit. Virtually all its leaders and rank-and-file members in the Soviet Union were arrested. Victims included:

Juljan Leszczynski-Lenski, general secretary of the party's CC; A. Warski, one of the founders of the Social Democratic and then of the Communist Party of Poland, arrested and shot at the age of seventy; Wera Kostrzewa (Maria Koszucka), who had given more than forty years of her life to the Polish workers' movement; G. Henrykowski and Jerzy Ryng, members of the party's Politburo, who were lured from Poland "for consultation," then arrested and shot.

Dozens of other leading Polish Communists were also arrested, including CC members Edward Pruchniak and Bronkowski. Most of them perished, together with leaders of the Western Ukrainian and Western Belorussian Communist parties, including: R. D. Volf, I. K. Loginovich, M. S. Maisky, and N. P. Maslovsky.

In the summer of 1938 the Executive Committee of the Comintern announced the dissolution of these two parties along with the Polish Communist Party, the Polish Young Communist League, and all other Communist organizations in Poland—just at a time when the formation of an antifascist front and a united effort to combat the threat of German invasion was progressing. This blow to the Polish revolutionary movement and the possibility of repelling German aggression was justified by the alleged penetration of Polish secret police agents into the leadership of the Polish Communist Party.

This action and the arrest of all the party leaders in Moscow had a depressing and demoralizing effect on Communists in Poland, many of whom were in Polish prisons when the news reached them. Marian Naszkowski recalls the impact in his memoirs:

A little item buried in the columns of the *Kurjer codzienny* [Daily Express] reported the dissolution of the Polish Communist Party. We were stunned.

At first we thought this report was a base provocation. . . . But the next day's papers had more detailed reports, and however we tried to suppress our anxiety, they continued to reveal the sorry truth. Finally, someone who had just been arrested brought official confirmation.

An oppressive silence fell over the prison.

How could anyone believe such terrible accusations? How could we reconcile the monstrous crimes imputed to these people with the splendid image that we had formed of them?

Lenski, Warski, Wera Kostrzewa, Henrykowski, Pruchniak, Rwal, Bronkowski —such heroic individuals, such coryphaei of our movement. . . . People tried to figure out the causes by digging up the old history of factional struggle between "majority" and "minority." . . . But none of the pieces fitted; the whole thing seemed very implausible.

After all, the "liquidated agents," as the Comintern report called them, included people from the "majority" as well as the "minority." . . .

However, even if in the final analysis we accepted the news that the entire leadership of our party was consumed by provocation, then we had to face the most important question:

What would happen to the movement?

Who were we now?

Could it be that our glorious militant party, which we took such pride in, which had raised us, for which each of us would give his life, could it be an agency of the Pilsudskyites?

And we all answered, No, a thousand times no.

A party that had done so much to awaken the revolutionary spirit of the masses, a party that had led mighty working-class brigades to war with capitalism, with fascism, could not be a fraud.

. . . Shaken to the depths of our souls, accepting, with pain, with bitterness, the "truth" about our leaders' treachery, not for a moment did we doubt our idea or the rightness of our movement, our party. That gave thousands of Communists the strength to live through the difficult times that had arrived. That was the basis for the resurrection of the party later on.[50]

50. M. Naszkowski, *Nespokoinye dni. Vospominaniia o tridtsatykh godakh*, trans. from Polish (Moscow, 1962), pp. 209–210.

The slanderous accusations made against the Communist parties of Poland, the Western Ukraine, and Western Belorussia were retracted only after the Twentieth Party Congress in 1956. The Communist parties of the Soviet Union, Finland, Bulgaria, and Italy joined the Polish United Workers' Party in issuing a special declaration on this subject. The Polish Communist leaders who had perished in the years of Stalin's cult were completely rehabilitated.

Serious losses were also suffered by the Communist parties of Latvia, Lithuania, and Estonia, many of whose leaders lived in the Soviet Union. The innocent victims included:

Hans Pogelman and Jan Anvelt, Estonian Communists and Comintern officials; Berzin-Ziemelis, Ia. Lentsmanis, Jan Krumins-Pilat, and E. Apine, Latvian Communists; and Rudolf Endrup, E. Tautkaite, N. Janson, F. Delgav, R. Mirring, O. Riastas, I. Kiaspart, R. Vakman, E. Zandreiter, F. Pauzer, and O. Dzenis.

As a result of this repression the Central Committees of these parties either ceased to function or struggled on in isolation from the Comintern.[51] Thousands of political émigrés from the Baltic countries were arrested, with the result that the Latvian division of the Herzen Pedagogical Institute in Leningrad was closed, as were the Latvian house of culture and the Estonian club, along with Latvian and Estonian newspapers that had been published in the Soviet Union.

Numerous arrests were made among Communists from Bessarabia, Romania, Iran, and Turkey. The Iranian Communist leader A. Sultan-Zade, who had emigrated to the Soviet Union in 1932, perished. The Mexican Communist leader Gomez was arrested but managed to survive.

The leadership of the Yugoslav Party was decimated. Among the victims were:

Filip Filipovic (Valija Boskovics), one of the party's founders; Milan Gorkic (Josip Cizinski), the general secretary of its CC, who had been working in Moscow since 1932 and was also a member of the Soviet party's CC; Vlada Copic, a secretary of the Yugoslav party's CC, who had returned from Spain, where he had commanded the Eighteenth International Lincoln Brigade; S. Cvijic, D. Cvijic, Horvatin, Ciliga, Popovic, and Novakovic.

Tito disclosed that the dissolution of the Yugoslav Party was not even discussed, since all its leaders living in the Soviet Union had been arrested. "I was alone," Tito writes. The Comintern gave Tito permission to form a new CC, and he quickly moved the party's leadership to

51. See *Ocherki po istorii kompartii Estonii*, vol. 2 (Tallin, 1963); and *Ocherki istorii kommunisticheskoi partii Latvii*, vol. 2 (Riga, 1966).

Yugoslavia, where in the underground he felt safer than he had in the Hotel Luxe in Moscow. All told, more than a hundred activists of the Yugoslav party died in NKVD torture chambers.[52]

The Bulgarian party suffered heavy losses. Its representatives in the Comintern, Iskrov and Stomonyakov, were arrested. So were Popov and Tanev, who together with Georgi Dimitrov at the famous Leipzig trial in 1934 had obliged a fascist court to acquit them. They had been given Soviet citizenship, but three years later Popov and Tanev were arrested, and this time a Soviet court condemned them on false charges. (Only Popov lived to see the Twentieth Congress.) Other prominent figures in the Bulgarian party who were arrested included:

Ml. Stoyanov, I. Vasilyev, I. Pavlov, and G. Lambrov.

Hundreds of other Bulgarian Communists perished. Most had emigrated to the Soviet Union to live and work in the Odessa region, quite close to their homeland. Dimitrov managed to save a few of his fellow countrymen, but in most cases he had to look on in silence or even to sanction arrests in the Comintern on the basis of falsified dossiers brought to him by the NKVD and filled with allegations he had no way of checking. In fact, the NKVD put together a special file against Dimitrov himself.

Many Chinese Communists were arrested, including Go Shao-tan, their party's representative in the Comintern. The entire Korean section of the Comintern in the Soviet Union was liquidated. Mukherjee, Chattopadhyaya, Luhani, and other leaders of the Indian Party were destroyed.

The arrests of German Communists require special mention. Theirs was the largest colony of foreign Communists and antifascists, since they had fled to the Soviet Union—or, on party orders, had moved—to save themselves from Hitlerite terror. But an even crueler terror was waiting for many of them in the USSR. The NKVD tried to give an "ideological basis" to the mass arrests of German antifascists. For example, the *Journal de Moscou* declared: "It is no exaggeration to say that every Japanese living abroad is a spy, or that every German citizen living abroad is an agent of the Gestapo."[53] Toward the end of April 1938, the arrest of 842 German antifascists had been recorded by the German representative on

52. See the Yugoslav newspaper *Borba*, April 20, 1949.
53. *Journal de Moscou* (April 12, 1938) no. 19.

the Executive Committee of the Comintern. The actual number was considerably greater. Many Germans were arrested right in the House of Political Emigres, in Moscow. Among the arrested were:

Three members of the Politburo of the Communist Party of Germany—Hermann Remmele, Fritz Schultke, and Hermann Schubert; and such members of that party's Central Committee as Hans Kappenberger, the leader of the illegal military apparatus of the German CC; Leo Flieg, a secretary of the German CC; Heinz Neumann; Heinrich Susskind, the chief editor of *Rote Fahne;* Werner Hirsch, secretary and friend of Ernst Thälmann; Hugo Eberlein, a participant in the first Comintern Congress, secretary of the German CC and its representative on the Comintern's Executive Committee.

Willi Münzenberg, one of the best Comintern officials, was expelled from the party for refusing to leave Paris for Moscow and certain death. He was killed in France in 1940 under suspicious circumstances.

Several hundred members of the Schutzbund, the workers' militia that had carried out an armed uprising against the fascist seizure of power in Vienna in 1934, fled to the Soviet Union after their defeat. At first they were greeted as heroes, but in 1937–38 nearly all of them ended up in Soviet prisons.

Suren Gazaryan tells about a large group of German Communists confined in Solovetskaya prison. When they were being transferred to a camp, they organized obstructive actions to protest the inhuman conditions of transportation. N. P. Smirnova reports that a large group of German women, members of the Communist youth organization, were in the prisons of Vladivostok. When Eugenia Ginzburg was in Butyrskaya prison, she talked to a German Communist woman whose body showed terrible scars of torture, first by the Gestapo and then by the NKVD. According to S. I. Berdichevskaya, Willi Burdich, one of the leaders of the Bavarian Soviet Republic, was arrested in 1937 and later died. Like others, he was tortured terribly during interrogation. Showing his cellmates, Soviet Communists, his fingers flattened by torture, he declared: "For this the German working class will never forgive you."

After the friendship pact with Germany was signed, in September 1939, Stalin committed yet another crime unprecedented in history: a large group of German antifascists and Jews, who had fled from the Gestapo to the USSR, were handed over to Nazi Germany. The Gestapo in turn delivered to the NKVD a small number of persons, whose names and fates remain unknown to us. Actually, most of the Germans turned over to the Gestapo were "lucky"; almost all of them lived to see the end of the war, whereas most of the German antifascists in Soviet prisons perished. Also in the fall of 1939, the Soviet borders were closed to refugees from enslaved Europe.

Many Italian Communists perished in the purges, including Edmondo Peluso, who had done many responsible assignments for the Comintern. P. Robotti, a relative of the Italian Communist leader Palmiro Togliatti, was arrested and tortured, but survived. After Stalin's death the Italian party published a list of its members who had died in the Stalinist terror. The list contained more than 120 names.

Among those arrested in 1937–38 were Belgian (M. Villems), Turkish (Salikh), British (Charlie Johnson), Romanian (M. Pauker, A. Dobrogeanu), Mongolian, Czechoslovakian, French, American, Finnish, Spanish, and Brazilian Communists.

It was not only Communists who suffered, but also all foreign nationals living in the USSR. Some specialists, who under various agreements during the first five-year plan had come to the Soviet Union with their families, stayed on. In 1937–1938 many of them were arrested, as were members of their families. From Leningrad a group of French women was sent into internal exile—all of them quite elderly teachers of the French language. In earlier years many families in the capital had hired them as tutors or governesses. The French embassy paid a small pension to such citizens who had lost their jobs and grown old in Russia.

All of the collective farms and agricultural communes that had been founded by foreigners were dissolved by the end of the 1930s. Not many people today know that in the early 1920s, long before forced collectivization, groups of agricultural enthusiasts had come to the Soviet Union from various countries and established such farms with the help of the local and central Soviet authorities. Most of them had been model operations, well supplied with machinery. According to V. I. Volgin, the Seyatel (Sower) commune, a highly productive farm near Rostov on the Don, which had been organized mainly by people from the United States, was shut down. Most of the Americans in the commune were arrested and sent into internal exile, although for many years their farm had delivered quality produce to Rostov at low prices and had served as a model for collective and state farms in the area.

■ 10

REPRESSION AMONG THE SCIENTIFIC AND TECHNICAL INTELLIGENTSIA

Soviet science could not escape the terror and universal suspicion that developed in the mid-thirties. Thousands of scientists, engineers, and business managers died, both as a result of Stalin's direct interference and because various kinds of careerists and adventurers took advantage of the spy- and wrecker-phobia. Many disputes that began at conferences or in the pages of scientific journals ended in the torture chambers of the NKVD.

In history, for example, tendentious criticism of Mikhail Pokrovsky's mistakes turned into a political pogrom. Many of his students and followers were labeled Trotskyists, wreckers, and terrorists, and then were arrested. "It is not accidental," runs a directive of the time,

that the so-called school of Pokrovsky became a base for wrecking, as the NKVD has discovered; a base for enemies of the people, for Trotskyite-Bukharinite hirelings of fascism, for wreckers, spies, and terrorists, who cleverly disguised themselves with the harmful anti-Leninist concepts of M. N. Pokrovsky. Only unforgivable, idiotic carelessness and loss of vigilance by people on the historical front can explain the fact that this shameless gang of enemies of Leninism long and safely carried on their wrecking work in the field of history.[54]

Victims of Stalinist terror included:

Yu. M. Steklov, a leading historian and revolutionary, one of the first editors of *Izvestia;* V. G. Sorin, one of the first biographers of Lenin, editor of the first collections of Lenin's works, deputy director of the Marx-Engels-Lenin Institute; V. G. Knorin, director of the Institute of Party History at the Institute of Red Professors, member of the party's Central Committee; N. M. Lukin, director of the Institute of History under the Academy of Sciences; Academician M. A. Savelyev, a revolutionary activist, editor of the journal *Proletarian Revolution,* and chairman of the Presidium of the Communist Academy; N. N. Popov, a secretary of the Ukrainian Communist Party's CC; N. Keldysh, brother of the future president of the USSR Academy of Sciences; N. N. Vanag, S. A. Piontkovsky, S. Bantke, G. S. Fridland, E. Veis, V. M. Dalin, Yu. T. Tevosyan, and S. P. Korshunov—all of whom perished; and S. Lotte, S. M. Dubrovsky, and P. F. Preobrazhensky, who lived to see their rehabilitation.

Monstrous forms of struggle appeared on the philosophical "front" too. Fundamental arguments between different groups had ended in 1930–

54. *Protiv istoricheskoi kontseptsii M. N. Pokrovskogo* (Moscow, 1939), 1: 5.

1932, with "victory" going to a group of relatively young but extremely active Stalinists, who pushed other tendencies into the background, branding them "Menshevizing idealists" and "vulgar mechanists."[55] Despite the unwarranted harshness of the debates of the early thirties, they had not led to repression. In 1936–1937, however, the victorious group, which held the dominant positions in institutions and the press concerned with philosophy, took advantage of the situation to settle old scores. In the pages of *Pod znamenem marksizma*[56] accusations of philosophical mistakes turned into charges of wrecking and even terrorist activity. As a result of this pogrom, organized by such people as Mark Mitin, Pavel Yudin, Fyodor Konstantinov, and B. A. Chagin, dozens of Soviet philosophers were arrested—not only former "mechanists" or "Menshevizing idealists," but fully orthodox dialecticians and materialists. The victims included:

A. I. Varjas, I. K. Luppol, B. Milyutin, I. Razumovsky, N. Karev, V. Rudas, S. Pichugin, G. S. Tymyansky, A. R. Medvedev,[57] M. Furshchik, and G. F. Dmitriev. Most of them died in confinement.

The outstanding philosopher and party official Jan Sten is remembered by his friend Yevgeny Frolov:

Hardly anyone knew Stalin better than Sten. Stalin, as we know, received no systematic education. Without success Stalin struggled to understand philosophical questions. And then, in 1925, he called in Jan Sten, one of the leading Marxist philosophers of that time, to direct his study of Hegelian dialectics. Sten drew up a program of study for Stalin and conscientiously, twice a week, dinned Hegelian wisdom into his illustrious pupil. (In those years dialectics was studied by a system that Pokrovsky had worked out at the Institute of Red Professors, a parallel study of Marx's *Capital* and Hegel's *Phenomenology of Mind*.) Often Sten told me in confidence about these lessons, about the difficulties he, as the teacher, was having because of his student's inability to master Hegelian dialectics. Jan often dropped in to see me after a lesson with Stalin, in a depressed and gloomy state, and despite his naturally cheerful disposition, he found it difficult to regain his equilibrium. Sten was not only a leading philosopher but also a political activist, an outstanding member of the Leninist cohort of old Bolsheviks. The meetings with Stalin, the conversations with him on philosophical matters, during which Jan would always bring up contemporary political problems, opened his eyes more and more to Stalin's true nature, his striving for one-man rule, his

55. See I. Yakhot, *Podavlenie filosofii v SSSR (20–30 gody)* (New York, 1981).
56. [Under the Banner of Marxism, the chief journal of Soviet philosophy from 1922 to 1944.—D. J.]
57. Aleksandr Romanovich Medvedev was my and my brother Zhores' father.

crafty schemes and methods for putting them into effect. . . . As early as 1928, in a small circle of his personal friends, Sten said: "Koba will do things that will put the trials of Dreyfus and of Beilis in the shade." This was his answer to his comrades' request for a prognosis of Stalin's leadership over ten years' time. Thus, Sten was not wrong either in his characterization of Stalin's rule or in the time schedule for the realization of his bloody schemes.

Sten's lessons with Stalin ended in 1928. Several years later he was expelled from the party for a year and exiled to Akmolinsk. In 1937 he was seized on the direct order of Stalin, who declared him one of the chiefs of the Menshevizing idealists. At the time the printer had just finished a volume of the *Great Soviet Encyclopedia* that contained a major article by Sten, "Dialectical Materialism." The ordinary solution—and such problems were ordinary in those years—was to destroy the entire printing. But in this case the editors of the encyclopedia found a cheaper solution. Only one page of the whole printing was changed, the one with the signature of Jan Sten. "Dialectical Materialism" appeared over the name of M. B. Mitin, the future academician and editor in chief of *Problems of Philosophy (Voprosy filosofii)*, thus adding to his list the one publication that is really interesting. On June 19, 1937, Sten was put to death in Lefortovo prison.[58]

A similar pogrom was organized in jurisprudence by Vyshinsky, acting as Stalin's mouthpiece. Many prominent jurists died, most notably Ye. B. Pashukanis.

Education was also engulfed in tragedy. After the arrest of Bubnov, people's commissar of education, many of his assistants and members of the collegium of his commissariat perished, including M. S. Epshtein and M. A. Aleksinsky. Also lost in the purges were such outstanding educational administrators and theorists as:

A. P. Pinkevich, S. M. Kamenev, A. P. Shokhin, M. M. Pistrak, S. A. Gaisinovich, and M. V. Krupenina.

In almost every autonomous and union republic the commissariat of education was decimated. Not only administrators but tens of thousands of ordinary teachers perished. One of the most gifted victims was Aleksei Gastev, who had been a professional revolutionary, organizing workers' brigades under the name Lavrenty. He was also a poet, author of the book *Poetry of the Workers' Attack*. After the revolution he applied all his energy to the study of vocational training and to a new branch of science, time and motion study. After he and many of his assistants were arrested, the Central Institute of Labor, which he directed, was closed, and all serious research in the field of time and motion study and industrial psychology was stopped.

58. From the archive of Yevgeny Frolov.

Soviet linguistics also suffered considerable losses. N. M. Siyak, director of the Linguistics Institute in Kiev, died. In 1919 his application for party membership had been endorsed by Lenin. Arrest and death were also the lot of the outstanding linguist Ye. D. Polivanov and of N. A. Nevsky, the brilliant Orientalist who deciphered Tangut hieroglyphics.[59] His great scholarly work, *Tangut Philology*, preserved in the archives of the Academy of Sciences, was posthumously published in 1960 and awarded a Lenin Prize in 1962.

Among many other talented scholars lost to science were:

N. P. Gorbunov, secretary of the Academy of Sciences, former secretary of Lenin, and adminstrative chief of the Council of People's Commissars; I. Z. Surta, president of the Belorussian Academy of Sciences; N. F. Bogdanov, secretary of the All-Union Geographical Society; G. I. Krumin, economist, a director of the *Great Soviet Encyclopedia;* I. N. Barkhanov, economist; I. F. Yushkevich, chemist; I. A. Teodorovich, a leading agrarian economist and Old Bolshevik, head of the Society of Political Prisoners and Deportees, which had been dissolved; R. L. Samoilovich, organizer of the All-Union Arctic Institute; A. V. Odintsov, economist and public administrator; A. Ya. Kantorovich, economist and expert on international affairs; O. A. Yermansky, a specialist in time and motion study (the "scientific organization of labor"); and A. Gaister and other directors of the Agrarian Institute, which was closed.

"Intensified class battles," to quote the journal *Soviet Science*, raged in all the natural sciences. Almost all the best physicists of the country—for example, Igor Tamm and V. A. Fok—were attacked by the press as "idealists" and "smugglers of enemy ideas." Many were arrested, including:

Four future academicians—A. I. Berg, Lev Landau, P. I. Lukirsky, and Yu. B. Rumer, jailed for "only" two or three years; M. P. Bronshtein, a brilliant theoretical physicist, shot in 1938 at the age of thirty-two; Academician A. I. Nekrasov, a specialist in mechanics; V. K. Frederiks, a well-known theoretical physicist; Yu. A. Krutkov, a specialist in mechanics and mathematical physics; S. P. Shubin, a young theorist, one of Tamm's best students; A. A. Vitt, a founder of the Soviet school of nonlinear oscillations; and I. N. Shpilrein, who, like the previous four, never returned to his family or his job.

Even mathematics experienced "heightened class struggle." In the summer of 1936 *Pravda* attacked the great mathematician N. N. Luzin, one of the founders of the Moscow mathematical school, calling him a

---

59. [Tangut was a Tibetan kingdom in the eleventh, twelfth, and thirteenth centuries.—D. J.]

"Black Hundredist," a "counterrevolutionary," and a "wrecker on the mathematical front." Fortunately, he was not arrested. The entire Moscow mathematical school, including such outstanding mathematicians as A. N. Kolmogorov. M. V. Keldysh, and S. L. Sobolev, was declared reactionary and bourgeois.

Some scientists, fearing repression, refused to return from trips abroad. Among these "nonreturners" (nevozvrashchentsy) were A. Y. Chichibabin and N. N. Ipatyev, outstanding chemists, and N. V. Timofeev-Resovsky, geneticist. It is hardly surprising that in the second half of the thirties Stalin cut down foreign trips to the barest minimum.

The years of terror brought special tragedy to biology and the agricultural sciences. As early as 1936 some leading biologists were arrested on false charges of Trotskyism, espionage, and wrecking activity; they included:

Academician I. I. Agol, geneticist, secretary of the Ukrainian Academy of Sciences; S. G. Levit, director of the Institute of Medical Genetics, the leading Soviet specialist on the subject (the institute was closed); Ya. M. Uranovsky, distinguished Darwinist and historian of science.

The young agronomist Trofim Lysenko took advantage of these early arrests to mount a noisy campaign of slander against many leaders of biology and the agricultural sciences. Lacking any serious knowledge of world science, he and his aide, I. I. Prezent, made up for their ignorance by unrestrained demagogy, including unfounded political accusations against their scientific opponents. As a result arrests were especially extensive among biologists and agricultural specialists. Institutes of cotton, stockbreeding, agrochemistry, and plant protection saw their leaders decimated. I have space for only a small list:

A. I. Muralov, president of the Lenin Academy of Agricultural Sciences, arrested and shot; G. K. Meister, a major plant breeder, awarded the Order of Lenin shortly before he perished; N. K. Koltsov, another of the country's leading biologists, was defamed and fired and soon died.

The arrest and death of these scientists did not stop the discussion in biology. It continued in the same intolerable manner, still accompanied by arrests. N. I. Vavilov, a great plant breeder, geneticist, geographer, administrator of science, founder and first president of the Lenin Academy of Agricultural Sciences, was arrested in 1940 and died in prison in 1943. At the same time, his pupils were arrested—G. K. Karpechenko,

G. A. Levitsky, L. I. Govorov, and N. V. Kovalev—and most of them died.

In that period Lysenko and Prezent worked mainly in the biological sciences, closely cooperating, however, with V. R. Williams[60] and a group of his supporters, who mounted an assault on agronomy. Research agronomists who disagreed with Williams' grassland *(travopolnaya)* system of crop rotation were falsely accused of wrecking and arrested. Many crop specialists in the Commissariat of Agriculture, in Gosplan, and in the All-Union Institute of Fertilizers shared their fate.

Academician N. M. Tulaikov, a Communist scientist, was sent to die in a concentration camp; Sh. R. Tsintsadze, one of the best products of Pryanishnikov's school of agricultural chemistry, also perished.

Not only the fields mentioned but all branches of biological science suffered great losses. For example:

Academician P. F. Zdradovsky, V. A. Barykin, O. O. Gartokh, I. L. Krichevsky, M. I. Shuster, L. A. Zilber, A. D. Sheboldaeva, and G. I. Safronova—microbiologists, nearly all of whom died in confinement; Academician G. A. Nadson, brother of the poet, microbiologist, age seventy-three when arrested, died in an Arctic camp; K. A. Mekhonoshin, who fought in the civil war, director in the thirties of the Institute of Oceanography and the Fishing Industry; A. A. Mikheev, botanist, beaten to death by a guard in the Kolyma region; I. N. Filipyev, botanist; and A. V. Znamensky and N. N. Troitsky, entomologists.

Neither did medical science escape. V. S. Kholtsman, director of the Central Tuberculosis Institute and world-renowned specialist, perished. K. Kh. Kokh, a distinguished surgeon, was shot in the Kolyma region for failing to fulfill his quota in the gold mines. Not all the arrested doctors worked in the gold mines; some hospitals in the Gulag system rivaled the best in Moscow in their number of eminent physicians.

Repression struck at thousands of the technical intelligentsia, including leading inventors, designers, directors, engineers, even shop superintendents. In contrast to the early thirties the main blow fell on prominent representatives of the new "Soviet" intelligentsia, most of them party members whose careers had begun after the revolution.

The Soviet aviation industry was hard hit:

N. M. Kharlamov, one of the directors of the Central Aviation Institute, arrested along with a large group of his colleagues; the major airplane designers—A. N.

60. [Williams was the Russian son of an American engineer who helped build the first major railroad in Russia. —D. J.]

Tupolev, V. M. Petlyakov, V. M. Myasishchev, D. L. Tomashevich, R. Bartini, K. Stsillard, and I. G. Neman.

In order to maintain production of new airplanes after these arrests, a special prison institute (TsKB-29, or Central Design Office No. 29) was established under NKVD control. Many well-known engineers and designers in addition to those mentioned above were assigned to it, including:

V. L. Aleksandrov, B. O. Vakhmistrov, A. A. Yenglbaryan, A. M. Izakson, M. M. Kachkaryan, D. S. Markov, S. M. Markov, S. M. Meerson, A. V. Nadashkevich, A. I. Putilov, V. A. Chizhevsky, and A. M. Cheremukhin.

Specialists from related fields were also sent there, including:

A. S. Fainshtein, N. N. Bazenkov, B. A. Saukke, N. G. Nurov, A. R. Bonin, Yu. V. Kornev, Yu. V. Kalganov, and G. A. Ozerov.[61]

Some of these scientists and engineers were freed in the period 1940–1942, and others were freed after the war, but quite a few prominent figures in aviation engineering were rehabilitated only posthumously in 1956.

Several prominent construction engineers were arrested, including

A. Dzhordzhavadze, a specialist in bridge construction, and I. Ter-Astvatsatryan and V. Chichinadze, specialists in the construction of hydroelectric power plants.

Many rocket experts died in confinement, including the leaders of a small group of enthusiasts in the field of rocketry, designers and builders of the first rocket engines, in particular, I. T. Kleimenov, director of the Jet Power Research Institute, and his deputy G. E. Langemak, the actual inventor of the famous Katyusha rocket. S. P. Korolev, one of the great rocket experts of the century, who became the chief designer in the Soviet missile program, was also arrested. His investigator told him, "All your fireworks and pyrotechnics are unnecessary, even dangerous for our country." Korolev ended up at hard labor in Kolyma, and was transferred to TsKB-29 only later. He was not freed until after the war when his "pyrotechnics" became very necessary.

61. Ozerov later described many aspects of life at TsKB-29 in his book *Tupolevskaia sharaga*, a manuscript copy of which I have in my archive. It circulated in samizdat for a long time before it was published in the West. *Sharaga*, or *sharashka*, was a term used for this type of prison institute or design office. Solzhenitsyn's *First Circle* describes another such institution.

Many other designers in the armaments industry were destroyed, including:

V. I. Bekauri, creator of many new types of weapons; V. I. Zaslavsky, tank designer; and L. Kurchevsky, inventor of the best recoilless cannon.

Repression in the Agency for Anti-Aircraft Defense had serious consequences. It is a known fact that theoretical and practical work in the field of radiolocation was begun in the Soviet Union earlier than in the United States or Britain. But in August 1937 P. K. Oshchepkov, the leading radar engineer within the Agency for Anti-Aircraft Defense, was arrested. So was N. Smirnov, director of the radar program, along with many other people in the agency. As a result, the Soviet army entered World War II without radar. The first radar stations used against German aircraft were bought from England and the United States at the end of 1941.[62]

Another important figure in defense-related science was arrested: M. Leitenzen, founder of the Society for Interplanetary Travel at the Air Force Engineering Academy.

Thousands of executives, chief engineers, plant managers, and the like were arrested and perished, including such prominent figures as:

S. M. Frankfurt, head of Kuznetsstroi; V. M. Mikhailov, chief of construction at Dneproges; I. P. Bondarenko, director of the Kharkov Tractor Factory; Chingiz Ildrym, chief of construction at the Magnitogorsk Metallurgical Complex; V. Ye. Tsifrinovich, director of the Solikamsk Potash Trust; M. Lurye, director of the Zaporozhye Metallurgical Complex; G. V. Gvakharia, director of the Makeevka Metallurgical Plant; S. S. Dyakonov, director of the Gorky Auto Factory; V. I. Mikhailov-Ivanov, director of the Stalingrad Tractor Factory; K. M. Ots, director of the Kirov (former Putilov) Factory; Glebov-Avilov, director of the Rostov Agricultural Machinery Plant; G. P. Butenko, director of the Kuznetsk Metallurgical Complex; Ya. S. Gugel, director of Azov Steel; I. P. Khrenov, director of the Kramatorsk Metallurgical Plant; M. A. Surkov and M. M. Tsarevsky, directors of the Sormovo Auto Plant; P. I. Svistun, director of the Kharkov Tractor Factory; P. G. Arutunyants and L. T. Strezh, directors of large chemical enterprises; G. K. Kavtaradze, head of the Ryazan-Ural Railway; Z. Ya. Prokofyev, head of the Tashkent Railway; L. R. Milkh, head of the Odessa Railway.

The management of the Amur Railway and of almost all other railways was entirely destroyed. When Vladimirsky, head of the Belorussian Railway, heard of the arrest of his friend Ya. Livshits, a deputy commissar of

62. P. K. Oshchepkov, *Zhizn' i mechta* (Moscow, 1965).

rail communications, he shot his wife, his son, and then himself. Only his younger son escaped.

The extent of repression in industry can be judged by the case of metallurgy, where practically all the executives in the Central Administration and even the majority of plant directors and shop superintendents were arrested. Experienced officials were generally replaced by inexperienced people, many of whom then provided the NKVD with new victims. In 1940, of 151 directors of large enterprises in the Commissariat of Ferrous Metallurgy, 62 had worked less than a year, 55 from one to two years; of 140 chief engineers, 56 had worked for less than a year. In contrast, before the mass repression—that is, in 1935—only five directors in the entire system under the Commissariat of Heavy Industry were replaced, and only one chief engineer in ferrous metallurgy.[63] At the end of 1935 the journal *Bolshevik* boasted that the 200 biggest machine-building plants were directed almost entirely by party members, 73 percent of whom had joined the party before 1920, most of them manual workers by origin.[64] By 1939 almost all these directors had been arrested, despite their proletarian background, and many were no longer alive. Repression on the same mass scale struck the electrical and chemical industries and many other branches of the economy in 1937–1938.

■ 11
REPRESSION IN LITERATURE AND THE ARTS

In the fierce struggle among literary groups in the twenties and early thirties, the Russian Association of Proletarian Writers (RAPP) was especially vicious, sectarian, and dogmatic. Many writers hoped that the liquidation of RAPP and the formation of an all-inclusive Union of Soviet Writers would put an end to sectarian and dogmatic restrictions in literature. These great expectations were expressed by nearly all the speakers at the First All-Union Congress of Soviet Writers in 1934, but they were doomed to disappointment. The rise of Stalin's cult and the increase in bureaucratic centralism turned the Union of Soviet Writers into an agency for bureaucratic control. The same thing happened with the artists' union and other organizations in culture and the creative arts. Far from abating, factional fights for control over Soviet cultural life were intensified. Ilya Ehrenburg recalls the situation in 1935 this way:

63. *Voprosy istorii KPSS* (1964), no. 11, pp. 72–73.
64. *Bolshevik* (1935), no. 18.

At meetings of theater people . . . Tairov and Meyerhold were vilified. . . . Film people went after Dovzhenko and Eisenstein. The literary critics first attacked Pasternak, Zabolotsky, Aseev, Kirsanov and Olesha, but, as the French say, the appetite grew with the eating, and soon Kataev, Fedin, Leonov, Vsevolod Ivanov, Lidin, and Ehrenburg were found guilty of "formalist stumbling." Finally they got to Tikhonov, Babel, the Kukryniksy.[65]

In 1936 arrests began. The well-known writer Boris Pilnyak—Stalin had old scores to settle with him—and the young writer Galina Serebryakova were declared "enemies of the people." "In our midst," V. Stavsky, secretary of the Writers' Union, told a meeting of Moscow writers,

we have had Serebryakova, a sworn enemy. We accepted her as a comrade and did not recognize the enemy in her. The loss of vigilance among certain comrades reached the point where many evenings were devoted to discussion of Serebryakova's works. We served the enemy with our own hands. . . . Now we have expelled people such as Serebryakova. But who can guarantee that there are no more sworn enemies of the working class in our midst?[66]

No one could guarantee it; writers continued to be arrested on an ever-widening scale. It would be hard to list all the writers arrested and destroyed in 1936–1939. Some calculations put the number in excess of six hundred, nearly one-third of the Union's total membership, including:

Isaac Babel, died in confinement in 1941. Bruno Jasienski, also died in confinement. Osip Mandelstam, the outstanding poet, arrested a second time in 1938 and shortly after died of hunger in Magadan. Pavel Vasilyev, talented poet, shot at twenty-six. A. Ya. Arosev a participant in the Moscow insurrection of 1917. Mikhail Koltsov, arrested in December, 1938, after his return from Spain, and shot. Prose writers, dramatists, poets, critics—including Artem Vesely, V. I. Norbut, S. M. Tretyakov, A. Zorich, Ivan Kataev, I. M. Bespalov, B. P. Kornilov, G. K. Nikiforov, Nikolai Klyuev, Viktor Kin, A. I. Tarasov-Rodionov, M. P. Loskutov, Wolf Erlich, G. O. Kuklin, M. P. Gerasimov, N. K. Guber, V. T. Kirillov, N. N. Zarudin, G. Ye. Gorbachev, R. Vasilyeva, V. M. Kirshon, and L. L. Averbach—all perished. Among those who survived many long and difficult years in confinement were A. K. Lebedenko, Aleksei Kosterin, A. S. Gorelov, S. D. Spassky, Nikolai Zabolotsky, I. M. Gronsky, Varlam Shalamov, and Yelizaveta Drabkina. Olga Berggolts, the famous poet, spent two years in prison. Aleksandr Voronsky, an outstanding figure in Soviet literature, perished. The prominent literary scholar Yu. G. Oksman, was arrested but survived.

The writers' organizations in the non-Russian republics suffered great losses.

65. *Novy mir*, (1962), no. 4, p. 60.
66. *Literaturnaia gazeta*, August 27, 1936.

In the Ukraine I. K. Mikitenko, a major writer, G. D. Epik, secretary of the Ukrainian Union of Writers, the dramatist M. Kulish, and the writer V. P. Bobinsky perished. In Belorussia the poets and writers Yu. Taubin, Platon Golovach, G. Gortny, and V. I. Golubok were arrested. In Armenia the great revolutionary poet Yegishe Charents and the Communist writer Aksel Bakunts perished; Gergen Maari, Vaan Totovents, Bagram Alazan, Mkrtych Armen, and V. Norents were arrested but survived. In Georgia the great writer Titsian Tabidze perished. After several summonses to the NKVD, the poet Paolo Yashvili shot himself. Among the writers and critics who died were M. Dzhavakhishvili, N. Mitsishvili, P. Kikodze, and Benito Buachidze. In Azerbaijan T. Shakhbazy, V. Khuluflu, R. Akhundov, Husein Dzhavid, and Seid Husein were among the arrested. In Kazakhstan Saken Seifulin, one of the founders of Soviet Kazakh literature, I. Dzhansugurov, and V. Mailin were among those who perished. In Tataria the outstanding writer and leading figure in Soviet Tatar culture Galimjan Ibrahimov and his colleagues K. Tinchurin, K. Nadzhmi, and others were killed.

Dmitry Korepanov-Kedra and Mikhail Konovalov, the founders of Udmurt literature, Mahomet Dyshekov, the first Cherkess prose writer, and B. Khodzhera, the first Nanai writer, all perished. Ipai Olyk and I. T. Chaivan, important figures in Mari literature, died in the purges, as did Ts. Don and I. Dambinov, the first Buryat writers, Said Baduyev, the first Chechen writer, the Bashkir writers A. G. Amantai, S. Galimov, G. Davletshin, and I. Nasri, and the Khakass writer V. Kobyakov. Platon Oyunsky, the founder of Yakut literature and the chairman of the CEC of the Yakut autonomous republic, died in confinement. And this list of victims of Stalinist terror in literature could be extended.

Antal Hidas, a leading Hungarian writer, was arrested in the Soviet Union but survived seventeen years of confinement.

The tragedy that struck Soviet literature was expressed with great force in a poem that Bruno Jasienski wrote in prison and managed to pass on to his friends before he died:

> Over the world rages the desert wind of war,
> Alarming my country with its nasal howl,
> But I, locked in a stone shroud,
> Am not among her sons at this moment.
> · · · · · · · ·
> But I do not reproach you, motherland.
> I know that only by losing faith in your sons
> Could you put faith in such heresy,
> And break my song like a sword.
> · · · · · · · ·
> March on, my song, in the banner formation.
> Don't cry that we shared life for such a short time.
> Our lot is dishonorable, but sooner or later
> The fatherland will see its mistake.[67]

67. Bruno Jasienski, *Slovo o Yakube Shele. Poemy i stikhi*, (Moscow, 1962).

The fatherland did see its mistake but much too late. Not until eighteen years after Jasienski wrote that poem were the writers I have named rehabilitated, nearly all of them posthumously. Their books have been reprinted, but no one can ever print the books they had in mind—and most of them were under forty when they were arrested. Even much of what they had written can never be published, for their manuscripts were usually confiscated and destroyed by the NKVD. The same happened with the manuscripts of arrested scientists and scholars.

Every kind of creative person and organization was struck by repression: painters, actors, musicians, architects, and film people. In Moscow, for example, Yelena Sokolovskaya was arrested. The legendary head of the Odessa underground during the civil war, she had become the artistic director of Mosfilm in the thirties. In the Leningrad film company, A. I. Piotrovsky, head of the script department, was arrested and died. A. F. Dorn, who had made a photo chronicle of the October revolution, was arrested.

The death of the great director Vsevolod Meyerhold was an enormous loss. A party member since 1918, he had devoted his life to creating a theater "in tune with the epoch." The persecution of Meyerhold began early: A pejorative term was coined for the purpose: "Meyerholdism" (*meierkholdovshchina*). By 1936 the campaign was in full swing, but Meyerhold would not repent. At a 1936 meeting where artistic formalism was condemned and Meyerhold excoriated he spoke out strongly against a narrow understanding of realism. He opposed the establishment of any rigid model for theatrical art, such as the Moscow Art Theater. He opposed "prophylactic control," saying: "The theater is a living creative thing, where passions boil. We must be given freedom—yes, freedom." [68] He was not given freedom, however. In January 1938 his theater was closed, and soon after that this remarkable man was arrested and killed after especially severe and refined torture.

In 1956, after Meyerhold's rehabilitation, at a meeting of the All-Russia Theatrical Society, Ilya Ehrenburg read the text of Meyerhold's final statement before the closed NKVD court that condemned him. He bore himself bravely and renounced all the testimony he had given during the investigation, since it had been forced out of him by torture. In conclusion he asked that when the times changed the text of his last words be shown to his children. The court sentenced Meyerhold to be shot on two

68. *Literaturnaia gazeta*, March 15, 1936.

absurd charges—spying for Japan and formerly working for the tsarist Okhrana.

Among other victims from the theatrical world were:

Les Kurbas, the "Ukrainian Meyerhold." The directors and actors Sandro Akhmetelli, Igor Terentyev, K. Eggert, I. Pravov, L. Verpakhovsky, Mikhail Rafalsky, Natalya Sats, Olga Sherbinskaya, Z. Smirnova, and Yevgeny Mikeladze.

At the end of the thirties the actor Aleksei Dikoi was arrested, but he was released in 1941 and later played the part of Stalin without the Georgian accent that Stalin was notorious for. Earlier G. Gelovani had played Stalin with an accent. Stalin liked Dikoi's accent-free version better.

The painter V. I. Shukhaev, a former émigré who had returned to the Soviet Union, was arrested. The Leningrad painter Sharapov was also arrested, after he had been called to Moscow to paint the "chief's" portrait. Two sittings sealed his fate. Stalin probably disliked the sketches, which showed his deformed arm. (Stalin assiduously hid this defect throughout his life.)

The editors of most of the central newspapers, as well as those on the republic and oblast level, also perished in 1937–1938; they included:

G. Ye. Tyspin (editor of Vechernyaya Moskva), D. V. Antoshkin (Rabochaya Moskva), Bolotnikov (Literaturnaya gazeta), S. M. Zaks (Leningradskaya pravda), D. Braginsky (Zarya Vostoka), N. I. Smirnov (Bednota), Ye. S. Kusilman (Proletarskaya pravda), S. Modonov (Krasnyi Krym), and A. V. Shver (Tikhookeanskaya pravda). Hundreds of journalist were arrested along with them.

■ **12**

REPRESSION AMONG THE POPULACE AT LARGE

About seven hundred victims have been named here, chiefly the best known officials, military commanders, writers, artists, and scholars. But repression was not limited to the upper strata. It struck a vast number of officials at the middle and lower levels; it touched all strata of the population.

An analysis of the party statistics shows that between 1936 and 1939 more than 1 million members were expelled from the party. Under the conditions of the time such expulsion almost always meant arrest. To this number should be added the 1.1 million expelled in the purges of 1933–

1934, most of whom were also arrested. To be sure, nonparty people were also arrested, but most often they were relatives, friends, or co-workers of arrested Communists. The oldest members were special victims, as the composition of the congresses shows. At the Sixteen and Seventeenth Congresses, 80 percent of the delegates had joined the party before 1920; the figure was only 19 percent at the Eighteenth Congress. The losses among the party's younger intellectual stratum were also enormous.

Losses among rank-and-file industrial workers were also very great. For example, according to L. M. Portnov, more than a thousand people were victims of repression at the Electric Factory in Moscow, including not only the executives but also many rank-and-file office workers and shock-brigade workers. The Kirov Factory in Leningrad was short every week of shop superintendents, engineers, Stakhanovites, and office workers.[69] Dozens of executives and hundreds of workers, both manual and white-collar, in the construction of the Moscow subway were arrested. There was the same senseless destruction of people in thousands of other enterprises. In the process the NKVD arrested above all those workers, engineers, and white-collar personnel who had gone to American and German factories for practical training.

The farms also suffered great losses. A. I. Todorsky met in confinement one of the lesser officials of the grain-procurement system of the Northern Caucasus. He told Todorsky that two hundred party activists in his *raion* were arrested the same night as he and kept temporarily in the *raion* political prison. Many ordinary peasants were also arrested. Eugenia Ginzburg tells about an old woman from kolkhoz who was accused of being a Trotskyist *(trotskistka).* The old woman thought they were talking about a tractor driver *Traktoristka)* and argued that in her village old people were not put on tractors. The Belorussian party official Ya. I Drobinsky tells in his unpublished memoirs about an old man from a kolkhoz who sat in the corner of his cell:

He had grown terribly thin. At every meal he put aside a piece for his son, who was a witness for the prosecution. A healthy young peasant who could not bear the beating and abuse or for some other reason, he had testified that his father had talked him into killing the chairman of the kolkhoz. The old man denied it; his conscience would not let him lie. No beatings or tortures could shake him. He went to the confrontation with his son with the firm intention to stick to the truth. But when he saw his tortured son, with marks of beatings on him, some-

69. *Istoriia Kirovskogo zavoda* (Moscow, 1966), pp. 535–542.

thing snapped in the old man's spirit, and turning to the interrogator and his son, he said: "It's true; I confirm it. Don't worry, Iliushka, I confirm everything you said." And right then he signed the record of the confrontation.

. . . Preparing to meet his son in court, the old man put aside a part of his food every day, and when he was taken out, he broke away from his guard for a second and handed it to Ilyushka. Then Ilyushka could not stand it; he fell on his knees in front of the old man and tearing his shirt, howling and groaning, he shouted: "Forgive me, Pa, forgive me, I lied about you, forgive me!" The old man babbled something, carressed him on the head, on the back. . . . The guard was embarrassed, upset. Even the judges of the tribunal were shaken when they saw the sight. They refused to try the old man and his son. But the case was not closed. The old man remained in prison. Specialists in our cell thought that the case had gone to the Special Assembly. The old man was almost always silent, and continued to put away part of his starvation rations for his next "meeting with Ilyushka."[70]

Such tragedies occurred by the tens and hundreds of thousands.

Something should also be said about the wave of lesser "open" trials that swept over the country in 1937–1938. This term usually refers to the major show trials of former opposition leaders, held in Moscow and attended by dozens of foreign correspondents. Similar trials were held in other parts of the Soviet Union in those years. In fact, almost every republic, oblast, even raion had its own "open" trial. These trails of local importance were not as a rule reported in the central newspapers, but the regional press gave them full coverage. There were also various types of "closed" trials in the provinces. Some were not reported in the press, but others were given fairly detailed local coverage—which is to say that the indictments and verdicts were published. Most of the arrests and verdicts were carried out without any respect for legal procedure.

In the second half of 1937, in hundreds of raiony, the accused were kolkhoz members and officials of the raion party organization and economic agencies, usually accused of "wrecking," "anti-Soviet," and "right-Trotskyite" activity. As a rule, the trial was conducted by a special collegium of the oblast court, with the oblast procurator in attendance. Usually the same ranks of officials were put on trial everywhere, indicating a uniform scheme worked out at the center—for example, the raikom

70. From the archive of Aleksandr Tvardovsky. For five years after the 1962 publication of Solzhenitsyn's "One Day in the Life of Ivan Denisovich" in *Novy mir*, which Tvardovsky edited, that magazine received a large number of stories and memoirs on the subject of Stalin's prisons and camps. Many of these works were of the highest artistic quality, but *Novy mir* could no longer publish them. [Before Tvardovsky died in 1973 he turned over his archive with this material to Roy Medvedev. —G. S.]

party secretary, the chairman of the raion executive committee, the head of the raion grain procurement section *(raizo)*, the director of the Machine Tractor Station, two or three kolkhoz chairmen, a senior agronomist, and sometimes the raion livestock specialist and a veterinarian. As a rule the "open" trials were held in raiony where kolkhoz output was lower than the oblast average. All the faults of the collective and state farms—late harvesting, poor cultivation of the land, loss of cattle, lack of fodder—were treated as "wrecking" or "counterrevolutionary activity" by the group on trial, whose aim had been to arouse dissatisfaction with the Soviet regime among workers and peasants.

A typical trial occurred at the end of 1937 in the Red Guard raion of Leningrad oblast. A special collegium of the oblast court, with the participation of the oblast procurator, B. P. Pozern, tried raikom party secretary I. V. Vasilyev, chairman of the raion executive committee A. I. Dmitrichenko, senior land supervisor A. I. Portnov, and some other officials. The charges were that for purposes of wrecking they had brought the kolkhozy to a state of ruin, placed the local kolkhozy in debt to the government, and paid the collective farmers at extremely low rates. The purpose of all this, as stated in the indictment, was "to restore capitalism in the USSR."

Raikom party secretary Vasilyev admitted that the kolkhozy were in a bad way but categorically denied any deliberate wrecking or participation in any anti-Soviet organization. The other defendants, however, made full "confessions" of their "counterrevolutionary activities." After the procurator's speech, completely reaffirming the charges, the defendants were all sentenced to be shot.

Sometimes the show trial was put on in the capital of a union republic or autonomous republic. Thus in Minsk, the capital of the Belorussian republic, "wreckers" of Zagotzerno were tried at the food workers' club in 1937. In Ordzhonikidze, capital of the North Ossetian Autonomous Republic, from October 23 to 28, 1937, leaders and collective farmers of the village of Dargavs were tried by a special collegium of the Supreme Court of the Ossetian Republic on charges of "wrecking" and of participation in an imaginary "counterrevolutionary kulak insurrectionary organization." Six of the thirteen defendants were sentenced to be shot.[71] Similar trials were held in Kuibyshev, Voronezh, Yaroslavl, and other cities.

71. *Istoriia Severo-Osetinskoi ASSR* (Ordzhonikidze, 1966). The state's punitive organs went much further than the state's interest required.

In many oblasti and republics there were show trials of "wrecking" officials in the field of trade. They were charged with premeditated organization of stoppages in the supply of staple goods, with the aim of fomenting discontent among the workers. Similar trials were held for officials in other branches of the economy, especially in the railways. For example, on May 9, 1937, the case of the "Trotskyite espionage terrorist group" on the Amur Railway was taken up by the Military Collegium of the USSR Supreme Court on circuit in the town of Svobodny. Forty-six persons were sentenced to be shot. On June 4, 1937, a second trial was held in the same town, and 28 people were shot. On July 4 there was a third trial, with 60 people sentenced to death, and on October 9, a fourth trial, with 24 executed. Thus, in Svobodny alone, counting only the sentences reported in the local press, 158 officials of the Amur railway were shot in six months. Similarly, on circuit in Khabarovsk and Vladivostok the Military Collegium tried officials of the Far Eastern Railway, and more than a hundred people were sentenced to be shot.

In some oblasti NKVD officials accused children of counterrevolutionary activity. In Leninsk-Kuznetsk, sixty children between the ages of ten and twelve were arrested on a charge of forming a "terrorist counterrevolutionary group." The NKVD chief in the city, A. T. Lunkov, the divisional chief, A. M. Savkin, the operational plenipotentiary, A. I. Belousov, and the acting city procurator, R. M. Klipp, were in charge of this case. The children were kept in the city prison for eight months, while the investigators put more than a hundred other children through interrogation. The workers of the city were so outraged that *oblast* organizations interfered. The children were released and "rehabilitated" and the NKVD officials themselves brought to trial.[72]

The clergy of various faiths were also severely repressed. I have already discussed persecution of the churches in the late twenties and early thirties. In 1937–1938 persecution was resumed with new intensity. Hundreds of churches and temples were closed or torn down. In Petrograd in the early twenties there were ninety-six places of worship, belonging to various branches of the Russian Orthodox Church. By the end of the thirties only seven remained. The situation was the same in all parts of the country. When war began in 1941 no more than 150 churches were still in operation in the older part of the Soviet Union. In the new territories of Western Ukraine, Western Belorussia, Bessarabia,

72. *Sovetskaia Sibir'* (1939), nos. 39–45.

and the Baltic republics there were several hundred churches. The information I have indicates that even before the Yezhovshchina about a hundred higher church officials and no less than a thousand regular priests were still imprisoned. In 1936–1938 approximately eight hundred higher officials of the Orthodox and the "New Church" and many thousands of ordinary clergy were arrested. Thousands of churchgoers were also arrested, primarily among diverse sects such as the Baptists and Seventh-Day Adventists, which were legal bodies under Soviet law. The Catholicos of Armenia, Khoren I. Muradbekyan, a popular leader, was killed in 1937 in his residence.

The great number of prisons built under the tsars proved to be too small for the millions of people arrested—even though several prisoners were put into cells built for one, while up to a hundred were packed into cells built for twenty. Dozens of new prisons were hastily built, and former monasteries, churches, hotels, and even bathhouses and stables were converted into prisons. Some of the most famous tsarist prisons, including Lefortovo, had been converted into museums, with wax figures in the cells. But when the mass repression began, the wax figures were thrown out, and the jail, filled once again with living people, was modernized and expanded. A small prison for especially important prisoners was even built in the Kremlin at the end of the thirties. New concentration camps were put up all over the country, especially in the Far East, Siberia, Kazakhstan, and the northern part of European Russia.

Between 1936 and 1938 Stalin broke all records for political terror. Tens of thousands of Romans perished during the reigns of the tyrannical emperors from Sulla to Nero. The Spanish Inquisition killed about 350,000 people, of whom more than 30,000 were burned alive. During the hundred-year persecution of the Huguenots in France about 200,000 were killed, several thousand in the infamous St. Bartholomew's massacre. The *oprichnina* of Ivan the Terrible killed some tens of thousands; at its height ten to twenty people were killed daily in Moscow. In the Jacobin terror, historians estimate, 17,000 people were sent to the guillotine by revolutionary tribunals, and no less than 70,000 were imprisoned. In nineteenth-century Russia several dozens were executed for political reasons and several hundred, or at most several thousand, "politicals" died in prison and exile. After the suppression of the 1905 revolution in Russia tens of thousands were shot by special courts martial.

The scale of the Stalinist terror was immeasurably greater. I know, from sources deserving the fullest confidence, that the NKVD records show that in 1936 the number of death sentences was 1,116. In 1937 the number rose to 353,680. I do not know the figures for 1938, but an estimate of 200,000 to 300,000 could hardly be wrong. During those three years a total of no less than 5 million persons were arrested for political reasons. In 1937–1938 there were days when up to a thousand people were shot in Moscow alone. If we take only the Lubyanka, the central prison of the NKVD, over 200 executions were recorded per day. These were not streams, these were rivers of blood, the blood of Soviet citizens. The simple truth must be stated: not one of the tyrants and despots of the past persecuted and destroyed so many of his compatriots.

REHABILITATION AND REPRESSION, 1938–1941

The vast scale of the repression of 1937–1938 began more and more to affect the political atmosphere in the Soviet Union and even the economic situation. All the prisons and camps were filled to overflowing, and the available NKVD personnel could not cope with the interrogation and guarding of so many prisoners. The aims Stalin had set when he unleashed the terror had been realized. Now some changes were needed to consolidate what had been gained—and as a master technician of the political lightning rod, Stalin knew this.

On his suggestion the Central Committee unexpectedly appointed a special commission to investigate NKVD activity; it included, among others, Beria and Malenkov. During the discussion of this matter in the Politburo, Kaganovich suggested that Beria be appointed deputy people's commissar of internal affairs in order to "facilitate his access to all the materials of the NKVD." This proposal was accepted.

Hardly anyone paid attention to this appointment either within the Soviet Union or outside its borders. But for Yezhov and his circle it was an alarming signal. Beria transferred several of his closest friends from Georgia to Moscow, and in the higher apparatus of the NKVD some changes were made. One evening at the end of September, Ilyitsky, one of Yezhov's closest assistants, got into a boat, rowed out to the middle of the Moscow River, and, leaning over the side, shot himself in the head.

On November 17, 1938, the Central Committee and the Council of People's Commissars endorsed two secret decrees: one, "On arrests, procuratorial supervision, and the conduct of investigation"; the other, "On recruitment of honest people for work in the security agencies." These decrees posed the task of "normalizing" the work of the punitive organs.

In April 1938 Yezhov, while remaining head of the NKVD, was appointed to a second post as commissar of water transport. At the time this appointment did not raise any eyebrows. People recalled that at one time Dzerzhinsky, too, held two posts, head of the Cheka-GPU and commissar of rail transport.

On December 8, in the back pages of the central newspapers in the section "News Items," a short notice appeared: N. E. Yezhov had at his own request been released from his duties as commissar of internal affairs; he would be serving solely as commissar of water transport. Replacing Yezhov as commissar of internal affairs was Beria.

As soon as Yezhov was replaced by Beria, the NKVD was hit by the usual wave of dismissals and arrests. Almost all of Yezhov's close associates and dozens of leading NKVD officials were arrested and shot. Among those arrested were Frinovsky and Zakovsky, men left over from Yagoda's days; Maltsev, "chief executioner" of Novosibirsk oblast; Berman, the sadistic head of the Belorussian NKVD; Lavrushin, head of the Gorky NKVD, and his deputies Kaminsky and Listengurt. Among others who were arrested and soon shot was Stanislav Redens, husband of Nadezhda Alliluyeva's sister. In 1937 he had directed the mass repression in Moscow and then, as NKVD chief in Kazakhstan, had decimated the party and government apparatus of that republic. The head of the Ukrainian NKVD, Uspensky, was also eliminated. Most prison wardens got a taste of their own prison discipline, including Popov of Butyrskaya, Vainshtok of Yaroslavl, and the warden of Solovetskaya. They were all quickly shot, as were most of the heads of the major prison camps and administrative units of the Gulag. As a rule, these people had occupied their posts in the NKVD for only a short time, from the removal of Yagoda to the removal of Yezhov. The former prisoners with whom I spoke could not even recall the names of these officials.

The panic that shook the NKVD following Yezhov's arrest is revealed in the case of Genrikh Lyushkov. In the early thirties he had been in charge of a special NKVD group for fighting Trotskyists, which made extensive use of provocation. It was Lyushkov who headed the investigation of Zinoviev and Yevdokimov in 1935. In 1937 he became NKVD chief in Rostov oblast, where he decimated party and government cadres, and then became chief in the Far East, where he repeated his performance. When he learned of Yezhov's arrest, Lyushkov fled to Manchuria, taking foreign currency, documents, and seals from the NKVD. He revealed to the leaders of Japan's Kwantung Army the distribution of Soviet troops in the Far East and "exposed" Stalin's crimes, in which he himself had taken an active part.

Meanwhile, Yezhov remained at liberty for another few months. He appeared alongside Stalin at the Bolshoi Theater on January 21, 1939, for the fifteenth anniversary of Lenin's death. As a member of the Central Committee he appeared at the Eighteenth Party Congress and sat on the presidium of the congress during the first few sessions. However, his name did not appear on the list of members of the new Central Committee. There is no mention of Yezhov in the stenographic record of the congress, which was published shortly after it.

In late 1938 and the first part of 1939 E. G. Feldman acted as first secretary of the party's Odessa oblast committee. He was a delegate at the Eighteenth Party Congress, and as the leader of an oblast organization he joined the Council of Elders of the congress, which traditionally discussed and decided the membership of the new Central Committee. Feldman left his friends the following memorandum about this gathering:

When the congress was ending, the Council of Elders gathered in one of the halls of the Kremlin. In front of the elders at a long table, as if on a stage, sat Andreev, Molotov, and Malenkov. Behind them, far to the rear, in a corner to the left sat Stalin, puffing away at his pipe. Andreev stated that since the congress was finishing its work, it was necessary to nominate candidates for the Central Committee that was to be newly elected. The first to be named were members of the previous Central Committee, except of course for those who had fallen. They came to Yezhov. Andreev asked, "What do you think?" After a short silence someone said that Yezhov was one of Stalin's people's commissars, everyone knew him, he should be kept. "Any objections?" Everyone was silent. Then Stalin took the floor. He got up, walked to the front table, and, still smoking his pipe, called out:

"Yezhov! Where are you? Come up here!"

From one of the back rows Yezhov came up to the table.

"Well! What do you think of yourself? Are you capable of being a member of the Central Committee?"

Yezhov turned pale and in a broken voice answered that his whole life had been devoted to the party and to Stalin, that he loved Stalin more than his own life and didn't know anything he had done wrong that could provoke such a question.

"Is that so?" Stalin asked ironically. "And who was Frinovsky? Did you know him?"

"Yes, of course I knew him," answered Yezhov. "Frinovsky was my deputy. He—"

Stalin cut Yezhov short, asking who Shapiro was, what Ryzhova had been (Yezhov's secretary), who Fyodorov was, and who others were. (By this time all these people had been arrested.)

"Joseph Vissarionovich! You know it was I—I myself!—who disclosed their conspiracy! I came to you and reported it . . ."

Stalin didn't let him continue. 'Yes, yes, yes! When you felt you were about to be caught, then you came in a hurry. But what about before that? Were you organizing a conspiracy? Did you want to kill Stalin? Top officials of the NKVD are plotting, but you, supposedly, aren't involved. You think I don't see anything?! Do you remember who you sent on a certain date for duty with Stalin? Who? With revolvers? Why revolvers near Stalin? Why? To kill Stalin? And if I hadn't noticed? What then?!"

Stalin went on to accuse Yezhov of working too feverishly, arresting many people who were innocent and covering up for others.

"Well? Go on, get out of here! I don't know, comrades, is it possible to keep him as a member of the Central Committee? I doubt it. Of course, think about it. . . . As you wish. . . . But I doubt it!"

Yezhov, of course, was unanimously struck from the list; after a recess he did not return to the hall and was not seen again at the congress.[1]

Yezhov was not arrested right away, however. He continued to appear at the offices of the Commissariat of Water Transport. His behavior showed evidence of severe depression and even psychological disorder. While attending meetings of the collegium of the Commissariat, Yezhov remained silent and did not intervene in any way. Sometimes he made doves and airplanes out of paper, sailed them, and went after them, at

1. E. G. Feldman, notes. From my archives.

times even crawling under the tables and chairs. All this in silence. A few days after the congress, when a group of NKVD operatives entered the conference room of the collegium, Yezhov rose and said, with his face almost aglow, "How long I have waited for this!" He put his gun on the table and they led him away.[2]

Yezhov's arrest was not reported in the press. The man whom *Pravda* had called "the nation's favorite," who possessed "the greatest vigilance, a will of iron, a fine proletarian sensitivity, enormous organizational talent, and exceptional intelligence" was not mentioned again in any newspaper.

Yezhov was not shot right after his arrest. A long investigation was conducted in connection with his case. He was not tortured, since he readily confessed to all charges, changing or correcting them when necessary and, in general, calmly acceding to all the demands of the investigators. The Old Bolshevik Pavel Shabalkin, who died in 1965, gave me the following account of Yezhov's subsequent fate:

When they took me from the Solovetskie Islands back to Butyrskaya prison for reinterrogation, I found myself in a cell with D. Bulatov, a well-known party official. Bulatov was refusing to testify and demanding interrogation by Yezhov himself. (A few years earlier Bulatov and Yezhov, when they were in charge of CC departments, had lived next to each other and often visited each other.) In the fall of 1938 Bulatov was taken to interrogation for the fifth time. Suddenly a door in the wall opened and Yezhov entered the interrogator's office. "Well," he said, "is Bulatov testifying?" "Not at all, Comrade General Commissar," replied the investigator. "Then lay it on him good," said Yezhov, and left by the same door. . . . After that Bulatov was beaten several times, but then they seemed to forget about him. A few months later, in 1939, Bulatov was again taken to interrogation and for more than a day did not return to the cell. When he came back, he fell on his bunk and began to sob. Two days later Bulatov told Shabalkin that they had taken him to some other prison and into an investigator's office, where he saw Yezhov, now arrested and held in confinement. This was a confrontation. In a monotonous and indifferent voice Yezhov began to tell how he had been preparing to get rid of Stalin and seize power and how Bulatov had been one of the members of his organization, whom, for "better protection," they had decided to keep in Butyrskaya prison. Bulatov naturally denied this slander, but Yezhov kept to his story. After several hours of interrogation they took Yezhov away and put Bulatov in a car, took him to Lefortovo Prison, forced him to strip naked, and took him down to the basement. There he saw another naked man, whom he recognized as the head of one of the departments of the Moscow NKVD. "What are they getting ready to do with us?" Bulatov asked him. "Probably shoot us," replied Yezhov's former colleague, who was very familiar

2. Testimony of M——, a former member of the Commissariat of Water Transport.

with such matters. But a few hours later they took Bulatov upstairs, gave him his clothes, and took him back to Butyrskaya prison. Bulatov was killed later on, but Yezhov was shot earlier.[3]

According to A. V. Snegov, Yezhov was shot in the summer of 1940.[4] The last few weeks of his life he spent in the NKVD's special Sukhanovo prison outside of Moscow, where "especially dangerous enemies of the people" were kept. In the spring of 1940 the microbiologist P. F. Zdrodovsky, among others, was being kept there. The investigator in charge of his case pointed out to him, through the window, a small chapel in which, according to the investigator, Yezhov "himself" was being held. Rumors circulated among the population that Yezhov had gone mad and was in a lunatic asylum. It is likely that these rumors were spread deliberately, to give an apparent explanation of the mass repression and thus to serve as a political lightning rod.

■ 2
BERIA'S POLITICAL CAREER

Lavrenty Beria, the new commissar of internal affairs, was a worthy heir and continuer of the "Yezhov tradition." Beria had never been a Marxist or a revolutionary. He began his dreadful career as an inconspicuous inspector of housing for the Baku city soviet. During the civil war the adventurer Bagirov gave Beria a job in the Cheka. (Quite a few adventurers and chance elements ended up in the Cheka, as Dzerzhinsky himself admitted on more than on occasion. M. A. Bagirov, who became the head of the Azerbaijan Cheka, was one of this type. He later became head of the party organization in Azerbaijan, in a position he retained until Stalin's death.) During the civil war the Soviet regime was not firmly established in the Caucasus, and it is not surprising that the young Beria tried to ensure himself against all eventualities. His trial in 1953 established that as early as 1919 he had connections with the intelligence service of the Azerbaijani nationalists (the Mussawat Party, which was in power then) and in 1920 with the security division of the Menshevik government of Georgia. Beria did not deny the fact that he made these contracts, but claimed that he had done so on instructions from the Cheka. The question of Beria's suspicious or questionable practices had

---

3. Shabalkin's account is in my archives.
4. Sources in which I have full confidence have made known to me that Yezhov was shot on July 10, 1940.

been raised even earlier. In 1921 Mikhail Kedrov, one of Dzerzhinsky's closest assistants and head of a special division of the GPU checking up on the work of the Azerbaijan Cheka, whose chairman then was Bagirov, with Beria as vice-chairman, established that Beria had released enemies of the Soviet regime and condemned innocent people. Suspecting treason, Kedrov reported this to Dzerzhinsky in Moscow and suggested that Beria be removed from his post as untrustworthy. For reasons unknown, Kedrov's letter produced no results at that time.[5]

In the twenties Beria's career in the Cheka-GPU went quite well. By intrigues and crimes and with Bagirov's support Beria rose to the position of chairman of the GPU of Georgia and then of the entire Transcaucasian Federation.

Stalin did not know Beria personally before 1931, although he must have heard of him. He must also have known that Beria was an enemy of the party's first secretary in Transcaucasia, Lavrenty Kartvelishvili, and that Bagirov was Beria's protector. Kartvelishvili asked several times that Beria be removed from Tiflis, but his request went unanswered. Kirov and Ordzhonikidze also expressed negative opinions of Beria. Many prominent Bolsheviks from the Caucasus would not greet Beria when they met him (Ordzhonikidze, Alikhanov, Khandzhyan, and others).

According to A. V. Snegov, who in 1930–1931 held a responsible position in the apparatus of the Transcaucasian Party Committee, Stalin and Beria met under the following circumstances.

In the summer of 1931 the Transcaucasian party committee received a special decree from the Politburo about a rest cure for Stalin. The Transcaucasian committee was to make all the arrangements. Tskhaltubo was chosen as the place, with Beria as chief of security. In an impressive flurry, he sent a multitude of GPU agents to Tskhaltubo and took personal command of Stalin's bodyguard for a month and a half. During these weeks, repeatedly talking with Beria, Stalin could see that he was a "useful" man.

In late September or early October Stalin returned to Moscow, but he did not forget Beria. Soon the Tbilisi officials received an order to prepare a report for the Politburo on the three Transcaucasian republics. No more specific topic was specified. All members of the party's Transcaucasian Bureau and of the three republics' Central Committees went to Moscow. Kaganovich presided at the Politburo meeting. Of course, Stalin was also there, clearly in a bad mood. First Lavrenty Kartvelishvili spoke, then G. Davdariani for the Georgian Central Committee, V. Polonsky for the Azerbaijan CC, and A. Khandzhyan for the

5. See the book on Kedrov by I. Viktorov, *Podpol'shchik. Voin. Chekist*, (Moscow, 1963), pp. 81–83.

Armenian CC. For some reason Ordzhonikidze was absent. Snegov asked his neighbor why, and received the reply: "Why should Sergo attend the coronation of Beria? He's known that crook for a long time."

After the officials from Transcaucasia had finished, Stalin delivered a long speech. He spoke of nationality policy in Transcaucasia, of the production of cotton, of oil. Turning to organizational matters at the end of his speech, he suddenly proposed the promotion of Beria to be second secretary of the Transcaucasian Party Committee, that is, Kartvelishvili's deputy. Many people were stunned and Kartvelishvili said loudly, "I will not work with that charlatan." Not everyone, to be sure, supported Kartvelishvili; Vladimer Polonsky in particular was beginning to play some game with Beria. Still, the majority of the Transcaucasian Bureau objected to Stalin's proposal because of Beria's bad reputation in the Georgian party organization. Stalin, red with fury, said, "Well, so what, we'll settle this question the routine way." The meeting ended.

Many members of the Transcaucasian Bureau went straight from the meeting to Ordzhonikidze's apartment. They found him extremely depressed. Everyone began to ask him why he agreed to Beria's promotion. How could they return to Tbilisi? Sergo tried to change the subject but then, unable to contain himself, said: "For a long time I've been telling Stalin that Beria is a crook, but Stalin won't listen to me, and no one can make him change his mind."

The very next day, in "the routine way," the composition of the Transcaucasian leadership was settled. Kartvelishvili was sent to West Siberia as kraikom second secretary; A. I. Yakovlev, the second secretary of the Transcaucasian party committee, was appointed director of the Eastern Gold Trust; G. Davdariani was sent to study at the Institute of Red Professors; A. V. Snegov was sent to a party job in Irkutsk.[6]

Mamiya Orakhelashvili became first secretary of the Transcaucasian party committee; Beria, the second secretary. Within two or three months Beria became first secretary of the Georgian CC and soon of the entire Transcaucasian Federation. Orakhelashvili was called to Moscow as deputy director of the Marx-Engels-Lenin Institute. In Georgia a mass turnover of party cadres began. Thirty-two directors of raion NKVD agencies became first secretaries of raion party committees.

The conflict in the Transcaucasian party organization gave rise to rumors about Beria's former connections with the Mussawatists. Ye. D. Gogoberidze says that Levan Gogoberidze and Nestor Lakoba discussed this subject as early as 1933. There were various versions about the first political ventures in Beria's life. According to one of them, during the occupation of Baku by the Turks Beria worked for the Mussawatist police (not their intelligence service) but offered his services to the underground Bolshevik committee, making his admission to the Bolshevik

6. This account by A. V. Snegov, taperecorded in the late 1960s, is in my archives.

Party a condition for such collaboration. The question was taken to Mikoyan, who agreed, and Beria was accepted into the party. One thing is indisputable: Beria was rude, ignorant, indulgent in the pleasures of the flesh, but also crafty and skillful. Among the Transcaucasian party intelligentsia Beria's ignorance was legendary; they said he had not read a single book "since the time of Gutenberg." Nevertheless, he was greatly feared.

Letters and reports about Beria's crimes and moral corruption reached Stalin from many party members in Transcaucasia. But he ignored these materials. The logic followed by so many despots was at work. The more dubious was Beria's past, the more devoted he would be to Stalin personally in the present. There is no doubt that it was on Stalin's advice, and under Beria's direction, that in Georgia several researchers began an urgent hunt through the archives to find material about the early period of Stalin's revolutionary activity in Transcaucasia. At the same time a pseudo-scientific falsification of the entire history of the Social Democratic and Bolshevik organizations in Transcaucasia was carried out. In the process the role of many important Marxists and Bolsheviks was minimized and Stalin's role was undeservedly exaggerated. On the basis of this "research," which at first was kept secret even from the Tbilisi branch of the Marx-Engels-Lenin Institute, an extensive report was written, which Stalin himself undoubtedly read. On June 21–22, 1935, Beria read this report at a meeting of the most active members of the party, and it was then published in *Pravda* and in the Transcaucasian papers. Soon it came out in book form. The first edition of Beria's book *On the Question of the History of the Bolshevik Organizations in Transcausasia* provoked many protests among historians and famous Bolsheviks such as Yenukidze, Filipp Makharadze, Orakhelashvili, and others. They still remembered well the events Beria wrote about. After the wave of terror had eliminated the majority of prominent activists in the Transcaucasian revolutionary movement, Beria published a second edition of his book, in which Stalin appeared as not only the most important but virtually the only actor on the stage.[7]

Even the open speech by Grigory Kaminsky at the 1937 Central Committee plenum, in which he made a number of serious accusations against Beria, did not impede Beria's rise. Among other things, Kamin-

7. L. Beria, *K voprosu ob istorii bol'shevistskikh organizatsii v Zakavkaz'e* (Moscow, 1937).

sky spoke of the young Beria's extremely suspicious ties with the Mussa-watists. At that time Kaminsky was much better known in the party than Beria. He held the post of people's commissar of health. Moreover, after the October revolution Kaminsky had headed various party organizations in the RSFSR, and in 1920, right after the establishment of Soviet power in Azerbaijan, he had worked for two years as a secretary of the Azerbai-jan Central Committee and served as chairman of the Baku Soviet. Even then a bitter conflict arose between Kaminsky, on the one hand, and the leaders of the Azerbaijani Cheka, Bagirov and Beria, on the other. Thus the Cheka organs often acted without sanction or approval from the party organs not only in the outlying regions but also in Baku. Eventually this conflict ended, but not in Kaminsky's favor. Although his policy was considered correct and although not only Ordzhonikidze, the head of the Caucasus Bureau, but also Lenin had supported Kaminsky, the decision was made to return him to work in the RSFSR. Kirov was chosen as the leader of the Azerbaijan party organization, and Bagirov and Beria had to submit to his authority.[8]

Kaminsky's speech against Beria in 1937 had (or probably simply speeded up) tragic consequences for Kaminsky, who was arrested and immedi-ately shot. Beria remembered who had opposed him in the twenties and early thirties and in 1937–1938 he sought revenge. Some former Cauca-sian leaders (Kartvelishvili, Orakhelashvili, and Asribekov) were brought to Georgia not only from Moscow but even from the Far East and were subjected to especially refined tortures under Beria's direct supervision.[9]

Thus Stalin placed the punitive organs of the entire country under none other than this vile and suspect individual—Lavrenty Beria.

It should be noted, however, that in 1938–1939 not many people knew Beria for what he really was, so that the replacement of Yezhov by Beria was received as a hopeful sign. And in fact, right after Yezhov's replace-ment mass repression was discontinued for a while. Hundreds of thou-sands of cases then being prepared by the NKVD were temporarily put aside. The special commission appointed to investigate NKVD activity continued its work, with A. A. Andreev as its new chairman. Andreev himself had been very active during 1937–1938 in the assault on "ene-mies of the people," and this was Stalin's chief consideration in selecting him to head the commission.

8. A. Lozhechko, *Grigorii Kaminskii* (Moscow, 1966).
9. Suren Gazaryan, Eto ne dolzhno povtorit'sia, unpublished manuscript.

■ **3**

PARTIAL REHABILITATIONS, 1939–1941

The hopes for rehabilitation felt by millions of innocent prisoners and their close relatives were doomed to disappointment. There was much talk at the Eighteenth Party Congress in 1939 about rehabilitating the unjustly condemned—Zhdanov's speech especially aroused hope—but the actual rehabilitation was quite limited. No more than two out of every hundred were released. Indeed there could not have been a mass rehabilitation in Stalin's lifetime, for hundreds of thousands of people had already been shot, and their rehabilitation would have meant that Stalin was admitting his monstrous crimes.

First, some prisons in Moscow and in the provinces were "unloaded" (emptied of their prisoners). Prisoners whose preliminary investigations had not been completed were released. In Moscow, for example, the party worker A. M. Portnov, whose testimony has already been cited, was rehabilitated. The Austrian physicist Alexander Weissberg, whose arrest had aroused concern among Western scientists, was also released. After the war his account of the Stalinist terror was published while Stalin was still alive.[10]

In late 1939 and early 1940 several thousand Red Army commanders were rehabilitated because of the extreme shortage of officers and the incompetence demonstrated during the Soviet-Finnish war. Generally officers up to the level of divisional commanders were rehabilitated. The rehabilitated included many future heroes of the Great Patriotic War, such as:

Konstantin Rokossovsky, future marshall; Kirill Meretskov, future marshall; Aleksander Gorbatov, future army general; S. I. Bogdanov, future commander of the Second Tank Army; G. N. Kholostyakov, future vice-admiral; S. V. Rudnev, future commissar of partisan units in the Ukraine—all of whom were later named Heroes of the Soviet Union. Also, N. Yu. Ozeryansky, hero of the defense of Leningrad, awarded two Orders of Lenin and three Orders of the Red Banner; and Leonid Petrovsky, the younger son of Grigory Petrovsky, appointed commander of the 63rd Rifle Corps, who died a hero's death on the Dnieper in August 1941.

But many equally talented officers and commissars remained in labor camps and prisons throughout the war, although most of them begged to be sent to the front. Grigory Petrovsky, after the death of his younger

10. Alexander Weissberg, *The Accused* (New York, 1951).

son, Leonid, wrote to Stalin asking that his older son, Pyotr, and his son-in-law, S. A. Zager, be released and sent to the front. "At the beginning of the war with the fascists," he wrote, "I sent the CC a letter, addressed to you, asking that my son Pyotr be freed from prison, so that he, like Leonid, would fearlessly fight in the war against the fascists. I received no reply. . . . In the fight against the fascists every patriotic individual will relieve the nation's strain. 'Everything depends on people.'[11] I have lost everything that was near and dear to me, but it is better to lose it in the war against the fascists than the devil knows where. Once again I appeal to the CC to release Pyotr Petrovsky and Zager from prison, to give them a chance at the front or in the rear to work for the Red Army."[12] Stalin did not answer this letter either. Pyotr Petrovsky, civil war hero, leader of the defense of Uralsk, was shot in 1942.

Some scientists and technologists were rehabilitated. The physicists A. I. Berg and Lev Landau were released even before the war, and at the beginning of the war a number of engineers and airplane designers, including Tupolev, Petlyakov, V. Myasishchev, and N. Polikarpov, were given their freedom. Frightened by the threat of epidemics, Stalin released the microbiologist Pavel Zdrodovsky, one of the country's leading epidemiologists. Also freed was the microbiologist B. A. Zilber.

According to Aleksandr Gorbatov, during rehabilitation each recent "zek" (political prisoner) was required to sign a special pledge saying that he would not under any circumstances divulge what he had seen in the prisons and camps. The majority of rehabilitated prisoners fulfilled this demand. Of course, there were exceptions. Some of the rehabilitated persons wrote letters to Stalin and to the Central Committee, risking imprisonment once again. I was told about an incident in which a rehabilitated commander of the Red Army in Kiev, encountering on the street an investigator who had subjected him to severe torture during the investigation, shot him right then and there. An extraordinary incident took place in Moscow in August 1939. Albrecht, a former high official in the People's Commissariat of Forestry and a German by nationality, was arrested in 1937 and released in 1939. While Ribbentrop was in Moscow, Albrecht went to the German embassy and asked Ribbentrop for political asylum. As a sign of "friendship," Stalin allowed Ribbentrop to take Albrecht back to Germany. There Albrecht wrote two books: *Butyrskaya Prison: Cell Number 99* and *The Revolution They Betrayed.*

11. A famous quotation from Stalin.
12. From the papers of the Petrovsky family.

According to Lev Kopelev, who served in a unit that engaged in countering enemy propaganda during the war, the German propagandists made wide use of Albrecht's books—in the Wehrmacht every unit had copies.

A 1963 *Encyclopedia Britannica* article on Karl Radek alleges that he was freed in 1941 "to work as a propagandist."[13] This is obviously a mistake. Radek was shot—according to one source, in 1939, according to another, in 1942.

Some contemporary historians try to present the removal of Yezhov and the partial rehabilitations of 1938–1941 as a political "defeat" for Stalin. In the French publication *Liberté* the historian G. T. Rittersporn published a long article in which, referring to the "Smolensk archives,"[14] he argued that during the "great purges" of 1936–1938 Stalin "was not always free to direct the course of events" and even suffered a "political defeat" during this period. Rittersporn claims that Stalin wanted to "sanitize" the party apparatus but ran into the opposition of the cadres who did not wish to find themselves dead after the purge. This "muted" struggle continued until 1939 and, in Rittersporn's opinion, ended at the Eighteenth Party Congress, at which Stalin was forced to accept the positions of his opponents. Although Stalin suffered a defeat in the political sense, he still remained the head of the party.[15]

Rittersporn's argument is not borne out by the actual course of events during the Great Terror. Stalin had his way and asserted his dominant position in the party in every respect. It is not possible to speak of any "defeat" for Stalin in 1937–1938 or at the Eighteenth Party Congress. Weak attempts to oppose Stalin's dictatorship were made not at the Eighteenth but at the Seventeenth Party Congress. Even then it was relatively easy for Stalin to crush the resistance, and he always managed to carry the majority of the party with him.

The partial rehabilitations that began in 1939 were not a sign of any setback for Stalin. For Stalin and for the NKVD they were only a diver-

13. *Encyclopedia Britannica*, vol. 18 (1963), p. 873.

14. During the Great Patriotic War, despite the rapidity of the German troops' advance nearly all the regional archives, including those of Belorussia, the Ukraine, and Moldavia, were either removed or destroyed. The archives of Smolensk oblast, however, fell into German hands. Later they came into the possession of the U.S. and British authorities, and the major documents were published in the United States. It must be kept in mind that the documents in Soviet archives, especially those of the NKVD, often did not reflect, but rather falsified reality.

15. *Liberté* (1978), no. 4; and (1979), no. 6. See also *Le Matin*, September 27, 1979.

sionary maneuver. At this point Stalin hoped to calm public opinion somewhat and also to give an explanation for Yezhov's disappearance. In addition, from Stalin's point of view a few rehabilitations were useful as a way of emphasizing that for the most part the repression was correct and justified.

■ 4
NEW REPRESSION, 1939–1941

Arrests of NKVD officials and partial rehabilitations were not, of course, the only activity of the new NKVD leadership. Soon Beria and his men resumed the repression. Admittedly, the mass scale of 1937–1938 was not approached, but Stalin had begun to use terror, and he could not stop; arrests and executions accompanied him to the last days of his life.

When Yezhov was replaced there was a temporary halt in the implementation of death sentences previously imposed. A spark of hope arose in the overcrowded cells on death row. But executions soon resumed in the cellars of the NKVD. Reconsideration was not granted even to those accused of plots against Yezhov and other people who had been declared "enemies of the people." Ukrainian party officials who had been arrested on the basis of testimony by S. Kudryavtsev, former second secretary of the Ukrainian CC, were not freed even though Zhdanov, in his speech at the Eighteenth Congress, had cited Kudryavtsev's testimony as an example of slander.

It was in 1939–1940 that a number of people mentioned in the previous chapter were arrested, including Kosarev, Vavilov, Meyerhold, and Isaac Babel. In 1941 the poet and dramatist Daniil Kharms (Yuvachev) was arrested and soon died of starvation in a Leningrad prison.

Another who died in this period was the Old Bolshevik Mikhail Kedrov, a prominent activist in the civil war and in the Cheka and GPU. (As I have mentioned, he had recommended the removal of Beria from the security police as early as 1921.) In 1939 Kedrov was already retired. One of his sons, Igor, an investigator in the central NKVD from the time of Yagoda and Yezhov, was in fact notorious for his cruelty. What Mikhail Kedrov felt about the activities of his son, of Yagoda, and of Yezhov is not known. But when he learned of Beria's appointment as commissar of internal affairs, he and his son sent Stalin a number of letters exposing Beria. That was in February and March of 1939. The first reply to these letters was the arrest and shooting of Igor Kedrov. In April 1939 the elder Kedrov was arrested too.

He then sent a well-known letter—it was read to the Twentieth Congress in 1956—to CC secretary Andreev, a man who played no small role in Stalin's machinery of mass terror.

From a gloomy cell in Lefortovo prison, I appeal to you for help. Hear my cry of horror, don't pass on by; intercede, help to destroy a nightmare of interrogations, to discover the mistake. . . . I am an innocent victim. Believe me. Time will show. I am not an agent-provocateur of the tsarist secret police, not a spy, not a member of an anti-Soviet organization, as I am accused on the basis of slanderous declarations. And I have committed no other crimes against the party or the homeland. I am a stainless Old Bolshevik; for almost forty years I have fought honorably in the party ranks for the good and happiness of the people. . . . Now the investigators are threatening me, an old man of sixty-two, with measures of physical coercion even more severe, cruel, and humiliating. They are in no condition to recognize their mistakes and admit the illegal and intolerable nature of their behavior in relation to me. They seek to justify it by picturing me as a vile enemy who refuses to disarm, and by intensifying repression. But let the party know that I am innocent and that no measures will succeed in turning a true son of the party, devoted to it to the grave, into an enemy. . . . To everything, however, there is a limit. I am utterly worn out. My health has been undermined, my strength and energy have dried up, the end approaches. To die in a Soviet prison branded as a contemptible traitor and betrayer of my native land—what can be more terrible for an honorable man? What a horror! Boundless pain and sorrow press and convulse my heart. No, no! This will not happen, this must not happen, I shout. Neither the party nor the Soviet government will allow such a cruel and irremediable injustice to be committed. I am convinced that calm, dispassionate investigation, without disgusting abuse, without spite, without terrible degradation, will easily establish the groundlessness of the charges. I deeply believe that truth and justice will triumph. I believe, I believe.

Kedrov's innocence was so obvious that even the Military Collegium of the Supreme Court completely exonerated him. In spite of this decision Beria did not permit his release, and in October 1941 Kedrov was shot. A new, back-dated verdict was drawn up after the shooting.

Also arrested and shot was Filipp Goloshchekin, elected to the CC at the Prague Conference of 1912 and in the late thirties chief of arbitration for the Council of People's Commissars. The fate of such dissimilar types as Kedrov and Goloshchekin, who nevertheless both belonged to the first generation of Bolsheviks and occupied prominent posts in the organs of proletarian power during the civil war and during the twenties, prompts me to return to the theme of moral appraisal of the Stalinist terror of the late thirties.

In the seventies Lydia Shatunovskaya emigrated from the Soviet Union. She had at different times been the wife of two highly placed officials and during the terror had lived in the so-called "house on the embankment," where many members of the Soviet elite lived. With her husband she would occasionally visit the homes of even higher officials whose apartments were at the time located in the Kremlin. She has now published in the West a book called *Life in the Kremlin*[16] and several articles, in which real facts are oddly intertwined with all sorts of rumors and sometimes pure invention.

In one of her articles, expressing a fairly widespread point of view among émigrés, Shatunovskaya wrote:

> Do I feel badly about the fate of the Old Bolsheviks who were so ruthlessly exterminated by Stalin? Do I sympathize with them? Simply out of humaneness I feel sorry for many of those whom I knew personally and who in their private lives were not bad people. But when I think of the Old Bolsheviks as a social group, I cannot find any pity or sympathy in my heart for them. Of course they did not commit and did not intend to commit any of the crimes against the party and the state which they were accused of. But they are guilty of something else, something far worse—they not only established this government but also unconditionally supported its monstrous apparatus of arbitrary and lawless oppression, violence, and terror as long as the apparatus was not directed against themselves. I am not religious in the usual sense of the word, but in my heart there is an undying belief in some kind of Higher Justice in which "it shall be given unto each according to his deserving." . . . And if it is possible to apply the word "justice" to the activities of the Soviet security organs, then perhaps the extermination of the Old Bolsheviks was in some sense the most just of all their completely unjust acts. The Old Bolsheviks created this monstrosity, and because of it they were killed.[17]

In the first chapters of this book I did not conceal the brutal acts for which the Bolshevik Party undoubtedly carries a moral and political responsibility. But following Shatunovskaya's logic, any cruelty can be justified and the blame can be placed on anyone, not just the Bolsheviks. Did not the tens of thousands of "specialists" who were eliminated in 1929–1932 help the Bolsheviks build their economy and even the Red Army? And did not the Mensheviks and SRs, who were virtually wiped out during the civil war and early twenties, help set the stage for the victory of the October revolution? By the same logic Solzhenitsyn reproaches the officer corps of the Russian army, which had a million

16. L. Shatunovskaya, *Zhizn' v Kremle* (New York, 1981).
17. *Kontinent* (1981), no. 27, pp. 340–341.

members and in 1917 did not support the overthrown monarch, the same monarch who preferred to renounce the desperate struggle for the throne to which his empress called him. However, Solzhenitsyn goes further into the past and even blames Peter the Great, who not only "opened a window onto Europe" but also opened the door to "destructive" Western influences and placed the church under secular power. Logic like that of Shatunovskaya and Solzhenitsyn is nothing other than Stalin's notorious "class logic," but in reverse. Bolshevik propagandists wrote in the same categorical manner that they pitied the individual landlords and capitalists as human beings, but that both classes had supported an immoral social order in Russia and an autocratic government opposed to the people and that they should therefore be exterminated "in the name of a higher justice." And was not the universal destruction of all wealthy peasants explained by such a "higher justice"?

I do not belong to that group of people who see a "higher justice" in the extermination of the Old Bolsheviks. They were revolutionaries who were sincerely striving to destroy the injustices and defects of society in Russia and the world of their time. The result was not what they had been striving for; the theory and practice of socialism began to diverge immediately after the victory of the revolution. Everyone knows that good intentions do not automatically produce good results. This has been the problem of many revolutions and many revolutionaries in different countries and provides no basis for rejoicing over the fate of the Old Bolsheviks or of revolutionaries and socialists in general.

After the dismissal of Maxim Litvinov as commissar of foreign affairs, there were new arrests of Soviet diplomats. Preparations began for a special trial of "enemies of the people in the Commissariat of Foreign Affairs," but this project was later dropped. Reverses in the Soviet-Finnish war resulted in new arrests of army officers. N. Ye. Varfolomeev, chief of staff of the Leningrad military district, disappeared without a trace.

Mass arrests of officers who had taken part in the Spanish Civil War began in 1937–1938, as has been noted. In 1938 the Soviet military attaché, V. Ye. Gorev, the real organizer of the defense of Madrid—the Spanish general Jose Miaja played almost no role—was recalled to Moscow and shot. He was given the Order of Lenin by Kalinin two days before his arrest. G. M. Shtern, a Central Committee member, returned from Spain to replace Blyukher as commander of the Far Eastern Theater, where he directed military operations at Khalkin-Gol[18] and pressed for the enlargement of the Far Eastern Army. (In December 1941 the large, well-equipped regular army in the East would play a significant role in the relief of Moscow, sending divisions west when needed.) In 1940 Shtern was suddenly called to Moscow and given a post in the Commissariat of Defense. Shortly thereafter, he shared Blyukher's fate —arrested and shot.

Just before the war against Germany another large group of Spanish Civil War veterans were arrested, including twenty-two Heroes of the Soviet Union, some of whom had twice earned the decoration. Among them were:

Ya. V. Smushkevich, who had commanded the air force in Spain in 1937–1938 and on his return had been put in command of the Soviet Air Force; P. Rychagov, Ye. S. Ptukhin, I. I. Proskurov, E. Shakht, P. I. Pumpur, and Arzhanukhin.

In all probability Stalin shot many more Soviet participants in the Spanish civil war than the number killed by fascist bullets in Spain.

Not long before the war against Hitler, A. D. Laktionov, candidate member of the CC and commander of the Baltic military district, was arrested and killed. For several months in this prewar period, it is true, there was only one arrest—that of the commissar of armaments, CC member B. L. Vannikov, who was released after the war began. But this case shows that Stalin had no scruples about taking reprisals even against CC members newly elected at the Eighteenth Party Congress of 1939.

A large number of illegal arrests in 1939–1941 occurred in Bessarabia, the Western Ukraine, Western Belorussia, and the Baltic territories.[19] Besides a few real enemies of the proletariat—agents of the tsarist secret police, reactionary politicians, members of fascist and semifascist organizations—thousands of completely innocent people were repressed. In some of these areas Stalin and the NKVD carried out a criminal deportation: tens of thousands of local people were arbitrarily sent east. This action caused widespread dissatisfaction among the local inhabitants, which led in turn to worse repression. Just before the war, all the prisons of Lvov, Kishinev, Tallin, and Riga were filled to overflowing. In the turmoil of the first days of the war the NKVD in some cities (Lvov and

18. [The Khalka River was the scene of a border clash between Soviet and Japanese forces in 1939. —D. J.]

19. [These areas were newly acquired by the Soviet Union in the period indicated. —D. J.]

Tartu, for example), unable to move prisoners, simply ordered them to be shot. The bodies were not even removed, and in Lvov, before the appearance of the Germans, the population came to the prison to identify the dead. This crime caused an outburst of indignation in the western areas and was very useful to fascist and local nationalist propagandists. The criminal actions of the NKVD were largely to blame for the slow development of the resistance movement against the fascist occupation in the western regions. It was in these areas that various nationalist groups collaborated with the Germans, finding support and recruiting members from the population.

In conclusion, I cannot overlook certain acts of repression of the prewar years that were not political in any formal sense. For example, at the end of June 1940 a law was passed making absenteeism and consistent tardiness criminal offenses. Both white- and blue-collar workers could be taken to court for being late three times, even if by only a few minutes, and also for being absent from work without a valid reason. The exact statistics relating to this law are not available to me, but it is common knowledge that an enormous number of people were convicted. At the end of 1940 all of the transport prisons and regular prisons were filled with people convicted under this law. Many of these prisoners were not released until the end of the war even though their relatively short sentences had expired long before.

■ 5

INTERNATIONAL RESPONSE TO THE REPRESSION OF 1936–1938

Varied and contradictory, the international response to the repression did not cause Stalin and the NKVD any great problem. By contrast, in the Brezhnev era the repression, though much smaller in scale, aroused much greater concern in the rest of the world.

Of course, news of political terror in the Soviet Union was widely used by the bourgeois press, including in the fascist countries, for purposes of anti-Communist propaganda. No one, it is true, knew the real scale of Stalinist terror, and the attention of the Western press was focused mainly on the show trials in Moscow. Although many details and the inner mechanism of these trials were unknown, Western observers (not to mention the intelligence services whose agents the defendants supposedly were) could easily see that most of the testimony was fraudulent.

For example, at the first "open" trial Holtzman stated that in 1932 in Berlin he had arranged with Sedov, Trotsky's son, to meet Trotsky at the Bristol Hotel in Copenhagen and did meet him there. But six days after the trial ended, the Danish Social Democratic paper reported that the Bristol Hotel had been torn down in 1917. This report made news around the world. Stalin was infuriated, but such mistakes were repeated. At the second trial Pyatakov testified that on the night of December 25, 1935, he flew to Oslo for a meeting with Trotsky. Two days after this testimony a Norwegian paper published a statement by the airport director that not a single foreign plane had landed there in December 1935.

In reporting on the terror in the Soviet Union, most Western newspapers voiced no sympathy for the victims. The Russian émigré papers expressed their satisfaction that some Communists were killing others. On the other hand, many Western liberals, left intellectuals, Social Democrats, and Communists were dismayed. They could not understand what was going on in Moscow. Some continued to believe in Stalin. Others had doubts but said nothing. Still others made protests.

An instructive case in point was that of Lion Feuchtwanger, who traveled to the Soviet Union in early 1937 and was immediately received and given special treatment by Stalin. He was given a pass to the trial of the "Parallel Center" and completely accepted all the charges against the accused. In this book *Moscow, 1937* Feuchtwanger described how he was converted from skepticism to faith in Stalin's justice. During the trial of Zinoviev and Kamenev he had been in the West and found the confessions impossible to believe. He sympathized with friends whose vision of a new world died along with Zinoviev and Kamenev. But when, during the next big trial, he sat in the Moscow courtroom and heard the confessions of Radek and Pyatakov with his own ears, his doubts vanished and he accepted the whole fantastic story.

Many Western commentators wondered why, instead of denying the charges, the accused tried to outdo each other in their confessions. Why did they depict themselves as filthy criminals? Why did they not defend themselves, as people on trial usually do? If they believed in Trotsky's theories, why did they not openly support their leader? Speaking for the last time before the masses, why did they not state their beliefs?

Feuchtwanger tried to answer these questions with a primitive, obviously inconsistent version of the argument that the accused cooperated with their accusers because all were loyal to the party and wanted to make it function as effectively as possible. He may fairly be charged with dishonesty. Conceding that he could not understand many aspects of the trials, Feuchtwanger reaffirmed his faith by quoting Socrates on the dark passages in Heraclitus: "What I understand is superb. Hence I conclude that the rest, which I do not understand, is also superb."

Feuchtwanger described Stalin, whom he interviewed, as a "simple, good-natured man," who "appreciated humor and was not offended by criticism of himself." Feuchtwanger's explanation of why Stalin staged the political trials is quite unconvincing. He rejects the suggestion that Stalin was a despot who took pleasure in terror because he was possessed by feelings of inadequacy, lust for power, and a boundless thirst for revenge. Feuchtwanger links the trials to—of all things—the *democratization* of Soviet society. The government, in his words, did not want the Trotskyists to take advantage of this democratization.

Stalin was quick to use Feuchtwanger's book. A Soviet translation was soon published, with a huge printing. The author received a large fee not only for this book but for his novels, which had been published earlier in the Soviet Union. At that time hardly any Western author whose works were published in Soviet translations received payment.

Romain Rolland, a true friend of the Soviet Union, experienced great inner torment over the repression of 1936–1938. However, he expressed his thoughts only in his personal diary.

It is a system of absolutely uncontrolled arbitrary rule, without the slightest guarantee provided for elementary freedoms, the sacred rights of justice and humanity. I feel pain and indignation arising within me, but I suppress the need to write and speak about it. All I would have to do would be to make public the slightest criticism of this system, and its mercenary enemies . . . would seize upon my words as a weapon, poisoning them with the most criminal ill will.[20]

When Rolland finally did speak, he defended the Soviet Union as a bulwark against the danger of fascism in Western Europe and explained to his friends, in regard to Stalin and his associates, that "the cause is bigger than they are."[21]

The truth about Stalin's crimes was so frightful that some idealists among progressive Western intellectuals refused to believe it. George Bernard Shaw, for example, continued to the end of his life to praise Stalin, identifying his deeds with the ideas of socialism. But then Shaw could not bring himself to believe in the German death camps either; he

20. Gabriel Perrieux, *Romain Rolland et Maxim Gorky* (Paris, 1968).
21. *Novy mir* (1966), no. 1, pp. 233–235.

could not accept the fact that the Nazis killed almost all the Jews in occupied Europe.[22]

It was not only friends of the Soviet Union who failed to understand the Moscow trials but even such a figure as Roosevelt's special ambassador to Moscow, Joseph E. Davies. In his secret dispatches to Secretary of State Cordell Hull, in letters to his daughter, and in his diary this diplomat, who personally attended the second and third Moscow trials, invariably asserted that the defendants were certainly guilty of treason and espionage and that the trials were in no way staged. Davies claimed that most of the diplomats accredited to Moscow shared this view. As he wrote in *Mission to Moscow*, published several years later:

In re-examining the record of these cases [the trials of 1937 and 1938, which I had attended and listened to], . . . I found that practically every device of German Fifth Column activity, as we now know it, was disclosed and laid bare by the confessions and the testimony elicited at these trials of self-confessed "Quislings" in Russia. . . .

All of these trials, purges, and liquidations, which seemed so violent at the time and shocked the world, are now quite clearly a part of a vigorous and determined effort of the Stalin government to protect itself from not only revolution from within but from attack from without. They went to work thoroughly to clean up and clean out all treasonable elements within the country. All doubts were resolved in favor of the government.

There were no Fifth Columnists in Russia in 1941—they had shot them. The purge had cleansed the country and rid it of treason.[23]

Davies' writings were of great help to the pro-Communist journalists Michael Sayers and Albert E. Kahn, whose book *The Great Conspiracy*, published just after World War II, had the same aim as Feuchtwanger's: to whitewash and justify everything done by Stalin and the NKVD, citing "objective" Western sources.[24]

As well-informed a man as Winston Churchill believed the false information spread in the West by the NKVD. In his account, President Benes of Czechoslovakia

. . . became aware that communications were passing through the Soviet Embassy in Prague between important personages in Russia and the German Gov-

22. Emrys Hughes, *Bernard Shaw* (Moscow, 1966), p. 272. [There is no English edition of Hughes' book, which was written for a Soviet publisher—D. J.]

23. Joseph E. Davies, *Mission to Moscow* (New York, 1941), pp. 274–280.

24. Michael Sayers and Albert E. Kahn, *The Great Conspiracy* (New York, 1946). [The author cites the Russian edition: *Tainaia voina protiv Sovetskoi Rossii* (Moscow, 1947).— G. S.]

ernment. This was a part of the so-called military and Old-Guard Communist conspiracy to overthrow Stalin and introduce a new regime based on a pro-German policy. President Benes lost no time in communicating all he could find out to Stalin. Thereafter there followed the merciless, but perhaps not needless, military and political purge in Soviet Russia, and the series of trials in January, 1937, *[sic]* in which Vyshinsky, the Public Prosecutor, played so masterful a part.

To this passage Churchill appended a footnote:

There is, however, some evidence that Benes' information had previously been imparted to the Czech police by the [GPU], who wished it to reach Stalin from a friendly foreign source. This did not detract from Benes' service to Stalin, and is therefore irrelevant.

Churchill continued:

Although it is highly improbable that the Old-Guard Communists had made common cause with the military leaders, or vice versa, they were certainly filled with jealousy of Stalin, who had ousted them. It may, therefore, have been convenient to get rid of them at the same time, according to the standards maintained in a totalitarian state. Zinoviev, Bukharin, Radek, and others of the original leaders of the Revolution, Marshal Tukhachevsky . . . and many other high officers of the Army, were shot. In all not less than five thousand officers and officials above the rank of captain were "liquidated." The Russian Army was purged of its pro-German elements at the heavy cost to its military efficiency.[25]

Significantly, Churchill does not question the content of "Benes' information," although in fact that was the most "relevant" aspect of this Stalinist provocation. It is evident that Churchill was more ready to be understanding toward Stalin than to sympathize with the ousted party leaders, such as Zinoviev, Bukharin, and Radek, or the mythical "pro-German elements" in the Soviet army.

Certainly many Western public figures did speak out against the terror in the Soviet Union. Robert Conquest discusses the position taken by some:

There was, indeed, much resistance among the tougher-minded Left. Edmund Wilson, reading the charges against Zinoviev and Kamenev while still in Russia, saw at once that they were faked. In the United States, the Commission headed by the eighty-year-old Professor Dewey had as its lawyer John F. Finerty, who had appeared for the defence in the Mooney and Sacco-Vanzetti trials. The Liberal Manchester Guardian was the strongest and most effective of British exposures of the trials. The orthodox Labour Party press did the same: that party

25. Winston Churchill, *The Gathering Storm* (Boston, 1948), pp. 288–289.

also put out Frederick Adler's forthright and accurate pamphlet on the subject. And on the extreme Left some of the most effective exposure was done by Emrys Hughes in the Scottish *Forward*. In fact some Leftists (and not only Trotskyists and so on who had a direct partisan interest) were perfectly clear-headed about the matter, while some people opposed to the principles of Communism accepted the official version.

But on the whole, in the atmosphere of the late thirties, Fascism was the enemy, and a partial logic repressed or rejected any criticism of its supposed main enemy, the USSR.[26]

Such prominent and influential writers as André Gide and H. G. Wells were thrown into confusion. They did not want to support Stalin, but neither did they want to side with Trotsky. For a long time Bertolt Brecht, too, did not credit the reports about lawlessness in the Soviet Union. He was cheered by Feuchtwanger's explanation of the trials and wrote to Feuchtwanger that his book was the best thing on the subject.[27] But when Brecht made a brief visit to the Soviet Union in the spring of 1941, he learned of the arrest of many German antifascists, the closing of the Thälmann Club and the Liebknecht School, the disappearance of his intimate friend Karole Neger, [?], and the shooting of his friend and teacher in Marxism, the Soviet writer Tretyakov. Then Brecht wrote the following poem:

Is the People Infallible?

1

My teacher,
Big, friendly,
Has been shot, condemned by a people's court.
As a spy. His name is damned.
His books are destroyed. Talk about him
Is suspect and hushed.
Suppose he is innocent?

2

Sons of the people have found him guilty.
The kolkhozes and the factories of the workers,
The most heroic institutions in the world,
Have seen an enemy in him.
No voice has been raised for him.
Suppose he is innocent?

26. Robert Conquest, *The Great Terror; Stalin's Purge of the Thirties,* rev. ed. (New York, 1968), pp. 669–670.
27. Lev Kopelev, *Brecht* (Moscow, 1966), p. 255.

. . . .

5

To speak of enemies who may be sitting in the people's courts
Is dangerous, for the courts need their authority.
To demand papers on which guilt is proved black on white
Is foolish, for there must be no such papers.
Criminals hold proofs of their innocence in hand.
The innocent often have no proofs.
Suppose he is innocent?

6

What five thousand have built, one can destroy.
Among fifty who are condemned,
One can be innocent.
Suppose he is innocent?
Suppose he is innocent
How could he go to his death?[28]

Telegrams and letters sent to Stalin, Vyshinsky, and Kalinin by leaders of Western science and culture show how disturbed many Western friends of the Soviet Union were. Here is one such letter, written in June 1938, by three Nobel laureates, Irene and Frederic Joliot-Curie and Jean Perrin, following the arrest of two outstanding German antifascist physicists:

The undersigned, friends of the Soviet Union, believe it to be their duty to bring the following facts to your attention:

The imprisonment of two well-known foreign physicists, Dr. Friedrich Houtermanns, who was arrested on December 1, 1937, in Moscow, and Alexander Weissberg, who was arrested on March 1 of the same year in Kharkov, has shocked scientific circles in Europe and the United States. The names of Houtermanns and Weissberg are so well known in these circles that it is to be feared that their imprisonment may provoke a new political campaign of the sort which has recently done such damage to the prestige of the country of socialism and to the collaboration of the U.S.S.R. with the great Western democracies. The situation has been made more serious by the fact that these scientific men, friends of the U.S.S.R. who have always defended it against the attacks of its enemies, have not been able to obtain any news from Soviet authorities on the cases of Houtermanns and Weissberg in spite of the time which has gone by since

28. B. Brecht, *Gesammelte Werke*, vol. 9 (Frankfurt, 1967), pp. 741–743. Medvedev quotes a Russian verse translation by N. Gorskaya. This English translation from the German is by D. Joravsky. —D. J.]

their arrest, and thus find themselves unable to explain the step that has been taken.[29]

On May 16, 1938, the greatest physicist of the twentieth century, Albert Einstein, sent a special letter to Stalin, protesting the arrest of many famous scientists. Stalin did not answer this letter; he turned a deaf ear to most such appeals.

The Western Socialist parties sharply condemned the terror. In 1937 many believed in the "plot" of Tukhachevsky and his comrades. The Gestapo did its best to have "reliable" reports about this "plot" reach Czechoslovak and French intelligence. From there the reports passed to activists of the Socialist parties. But on the whole, European Socialists had no doubts at all about the perversions of socialist democracy in the Soviet Union. They differed among themselves only in their explanations of the causes of this tragedy. Some thought the Soviet Union, rapidly degenerating into a state of the fascist type, was destroying old revolutionaries who were still true to their ideals. Others argued that a savage struggle for power was going on within the Soviet system, with Stalin relying on the new Soviet generation, who were eager for practical action and indifferent to such things as the theoretical quarrels between Trotskyists and Bukharinists. In this view the industrial and agrarian revolution from above was inevitably accompanied by reprisals against dissidents. A third group attributed the slaughter of Old Bolsheviks simply to Stalin's megalomania and persecution mania.

Foreign Communist parties were in an especially difficult position, since their leaders in that period unreservedly endorsed everything that happened in the USSR. Their press usually repeated everything that appeared in *Izvestia* or *Pravda.* Their main argument was simply that a Soviet court was a proletarian court and therefore had to be just. As for the rumors of torture, the Communist papers rejected them as vicious slander. They did not even raise questions about the arrest and shooting of foreign Communist leaders in Moscow. And at the time most activists really believed that dangerous traitors and conspirators were being destroyed in the Soviet Union. The American Communist Hershel Meyer recalls that it was impossible to believe that Stalin was destroying inno-

29. The Russian text of this letter is in my archives. Weissberg was released in 1941, as I have said above. Houtermanns' fate is unknown to me. [This translation of the letter, from French to English, is printed in Weissberg, *The Accused,* pp. xviii–xix. The complete text declares that Einstein, P. M. S. Blackett, and Niels Bohr also had an active interest in the case. —D. J.]

cent people; such stories were simply dismissed as anti-Soviet propaganda.[30] But this trustfulness of the leaders and activists was by no means always shared by rank-and-file workers, including those who were Communists. Ivan Maisky, then Soviet ambassador to Britain, recalls the situation vividly:

Socialists and reformists of all kinds quickly seized on the news of arrests and repression in the USSR, and popularized it in the factories, saying: "Look what Communism leads to." I well remember how English Communists whom I used to see in those years would ask me with bitterness, almost with despair, the same question as Wells: "What is happening in your country? We cannot believe that so many old and honored party members, tested in battle, have suddenly become traitors." And they told how the events in the USSR were alienating the workers from the Soviet land and undermining Communist influence among the proletariat. The same thing happened in France, Scandinavia, Belgium, Holland, and many other countries.[31]

Some Soviet diplomats and intelligence agents who refused to go back to the Soviet Union addressed appeals to Western public opinion, which had some effect. In December 1937 European papers (including Pavel Milyukov's *Poslednie novosti*) carried the "open letter" of General Walter Krivitsky, which he addressed to the French Socialist Party, the Communist Party of France, and the Fourth International. Krivitsky wrote that he had served the Communist cause for a long time, since he joined the party in 1919. For his services to the Red Army he had received two decorations and constant evidence of trust. But the arrest and shooting of many innocent people had finally obliged him to give up his position and devote himself to the rehabilitation of those who were unjustly accused and destroyed. The letter concluded:

I know—and have proof—that a reward has been offered for my head. I know the GPU will stop at nothing to silence me by murder. Dozens of people, ready for anything, are at Yezhov's disposal and have already been after me. I consider it my duty as a revolutionary fighter to report all this to international working-class opinion.

Krivitsky (Walter)
December 5, 1937[32]

30. Hershel D. Meyer, *Doklad Khrushcheva i krizis levogo dvizheniia v SShA* (Moscow, 1957), p. 10. [For the original, see Hershel D. Meyer, *The Khrushchev Report and the Crisis of the American Left* (New York, 1956). —D. J.]

31. Ivan Maisky, *Bernard Shaw i drugie* (Moscow, 1967), p. 83.

32. Krivitsky's words about being followed were no exaggeration. Stalin had ordered him killed. An experienced operative, Krivitsky skillfully hid himself for several years and managed to publish a book defending those Stalin had destroyed. But in February 1941 he was found shot to death in a hotel room in Washington, D.C.

A few days later many European papers published a similar letter from Alexander Barmine, the former Soviet ambassador to Greece, which he sent to the League for the Rights of Man and Citizen. He had been a Communist for nineteen years, he wrote, and now could see preparations for the mass destruction of all those who had made the revolution and the working class state. Thus he was faced with a tragic dilemma;

to return to my native land and meet certain death there, or, refusing to see my fatherland, to risk being shot abroad by GPU agents, who have recently been following my footsteps. To remain in the service of the Soviet government would mean losing all moral right and sharing the responsibility for crimes committed every day against the people of my country. It would mean betraying the cause of socialism to which I have devoted my entire life.[33]

Of special interest is a statement by Fyodor Raskolnikov, a hero of the October revolution and civil war and an outstanding political writer.[34] From 1930 to 1939 he was a Soviet diplomat, first in Estonia and Denmark, later in Bulgaria. Raskolnikov was increasingly alarmed by the cult of personality and the destruction of the best party cadres. He noticed that he was always followed by NKVD agents. Slow to respond to an order from the Foreign Affairs Commisariat that he return to Moscow, he was removed from his post as Soviet ambassador to Bulgaria in the summer of 1939, when he was in France. Learning that he had been declared an enemy of the people and an outlaw, he replied with a public statement, "How They Made Me an Enemy of the People," vigorously defending himself and other innocent victims. Some weeks later he wrote "An Open Letter to Stalin":

Stalin, you have begun a new stage, which will go down in the history of our revolution as the "epoch of terror." No one feels safe in the Soviet Union. No one, as he goes to bed, knows whether he will escape arrest in the night. . . . You began with bloody vengeance on former Trotskyists, Zinovievists, and Bukharinists, went on to destroy the Old Bolsheviks, then slaughtered party and state cadres who rose in the civil war and carried through the first five-year plans; you even massacred the Komsomol. You hide under the slogan of a fight against "Trotskyite-Bukharinite spies," but you did not get power only yesterday. No one

33. Barmine managed to publish a book, *One Who Survived* (New York, 1945). His subsequent fate is unknown to me. Russian translations of Barmine and Krivitsky's letters circulated in manuscript form in Moscow in the 1960s. Certain passages published in Western works indicate the accuracy of these translations, which as a rule were done by anonymous contributors to samizdat.

34. Raskolnikov had been chairman of the Bolshevik Party's Kronstadt committee in 1917, then served as deputy commissar for naval affairs and as a fleet commander, first on the Volga and Caspian and later on the Baltic.

could be appointed to an important post without your permission. Who placed the so-called "enemies of the people" in the most responsible government, army, party, and diplomatic positions? . . . Joseph Stalin! Who put the so-called "wreckers" in every pore of the Soviet and party apparatus? . . . Joseph Stalin!

With the help of dirty forgeries you have staged trials which, in the absurdity of the accusations, surpass the medieval witch trials you know about from seminary textbooks. . . . You have defamed and shot long-time colleagues of Lenin, knowing very well that they were innocent. You have forced them before dying to confess crimes they never committed, to smear themselves in filth from head to toe.

. . . You have forced those who go along with you to walk with anguish and disgust through pools of their comrades' and friends' blood. In the lying history of the party, written under your direction, you have plundered those whom you murdered and defamed, appropriating their feats and accomplishments to yourself.

On the eve of war, you are destroying the Red Army. . . . At a moment of the greatest military danger, you continue to massacre army leaders, middle-rank officers, and junior commanders.

. . . Under pressure from the Soviet people, you are hypocritically reviving the cult of the heroes of Russian history: Alexander Nevsky, Dmitry Donskoi, Mikhail Kutuzov, hoping they will help you more in the coming war than our executed marshals and generals.

This open letter, as Admiral V. Grishanov rightly said in *Izvestia* in 1964, is a credit to its author. It appeared in a White-émigré paper, *Novaya Rossiya*, on October 1, 1939, when World War II was beginning, and passed almost unnoticed. Raskolnikov probably had sent it to a French news agency, which served many newspapers, including some émigré ones. He had no other way to reach public opinion. In 1964 his widow, a resident of France, brought the original of the letter to Moscow, where a commission on Raskolnikov's literary heritage had been set up in the Writers' Union. Raskolnikov himself died in September 1939. According to the French newspapers, he committed suicide by jumping —or being thrown?—from a window. The circumstances of his death were never properly investigated, and it may be assumed that he was tracked down and killed by NKVD agents.[35]

35. Raskolnikov was not rehabilitated until 1963. Several articles about him appeared in the Soviet press, and in 1964 his war memoirs were published. In the late 1960s, however, at the insistence of conservative figures in Brezhnev's entourage (Sergei Trapeznikov in particular), no further mention of Raskolnikov was permitted. There are no articles about him in the Great Soviet Encyclopedia and the Historical Encyclopedia, nor in encyclopedias about the civil war and October revolution. The commission on his literary heritage was dissolved. [In 1987 material about Raskolnikov again began to appear in the Soviet press, including the text of his "Open Letter to Stalin."—G. S.]

8

ILLEGAL METHODS OF INVESTIGATION AND CONFINEMENT

■ 1
TORTURE

Mass arrests of innocent Soviet citizens were only the first in a sequence of crimes performed by Stalin's machine of terror. The purpose of this machine was not merely to isolate or destroy objectionable people but to crush their wills, humilitate them, force them to call themselves "enemies of the people" and to confess to various crimes and conspiracies. But it was obvious to Stalin and his accomplices that even partial adherence to legal methods of investigation would make it impossible to achieve this goal. So, in 1937 Stalin prescribed massive application of "physical methods of influence."

Some former NKVD officials have tried to deny that torture was extensively used, despite the reports of thousands of rehabilitated people. One of the memoirs I have is by a former high official in the NKVD, who wrote:

> We declare, with full responsibility, that only individual, morally unstable, and unprincipled Checkists went so far as to apply physical torture and torment, for which they were shot in 1939, following the November [1938] letter to the Politburo on excesses in investigation.

A "responsible" declaration of this sort is a deliberate distortion of the truth. Physical torture was used by the NKVD not on its own initiative but with the approval and even at the insistence of Stalin's Politburo. Of course, this policy did not spring up in a single day but developed gradually over several years. Back at the beginning of the first five-year plan, in the campaign to extract gold from alleged Nepmen, the GPU beat arrested people, deprived them of sleep and food, and kept them in prison until they or their relatives handed over gold "for the needs of industrialization."

Beatings, the "conveyor," deprivation of sleep, and the heat, cold, hunger and thirst treatments—all these methods of "investigation" were used extensively against "wreckers" in 1929–1931. Arrested Communists, however, were treated more "humanely" at the beginning of the thirties. Until the spring of 1937 torture was used only against certain prisoners and only by certain specially selected investigators—for example, in the preparation of the trials of the "Trotskyite-Zinovievite" and "Parallel" centers. Other investigators were permitted to use only such methods as the "conveyor." But after the February–March plenum of the Central Committee in 1937, most investigators were permitted to apply even the most refined tortures to "stubborn enemies of the people," which meant that almost all prisoners who offered any resistance were tortured. And this was not stopped in 1939, when Yezhov was removed. V. I. Volgin, who was interrogated in one of the prisons of Rostov-on-Don, tells what changes came with the appointment of Beria:

> Previously the investigators would say to us: "Come on, you gangster, write; or we'll make mincemeat of you." Now they spoke differently: "Come on, Vasily Ivanovich, write, write," using the polite second person now; "sign it, buddy; you'll get twenty years anyway."[1]

The use of torture was one of the worst crimes of Stalin and his terror machine. Torture was, of course, extensively employed during the "in-

---

1. From my archives.

quests" in Russia in the sixteenth and seventeenth centuries. Even then the deficiencies of torture as a method of investigation were recognized. Hence a rule arose: "The informer gets the first knout." That is, the informer should be tortured before the accused, to verify his information. Torture provoked such strong protests that Catherine II decreed its end: "No bodily punishments of any kind shall be used on anyone, in any government office, in any cases, for the discovery of the truth." But this ban was by no means always obeyed, especially after the Pugachev rebellion. So in 1801 Alexander I ordered the Senate

to reaffirm most strictly everywhere and throughout the empire, that nowhere, under no form, neither in higher or in lower offices or courts, no one shall dare to use or to allow or to undertake, any torture, under pain of unavoidable and severe punishment. . . . The very word "torture," which is a disgrace and reproach to humanity, must be eradicated forever from the nations' memory.[2]

Of course these decrees were not strictly observed by the investigating organs of tsarist Russia, although under Alexander II the use of torture and corporal punishment was greatly reduced after the abolition of serfdom. In periods of intense revolutionary conflict tsarist officials and members of the Black Hundreds used the most refined tortures on many revolutionaries, including women. Many embittered counterrevolutionaries revived torture on a mass scale during the civil war. The Bolsheviks, for their part, often shot captives but rarely resorted to other forms of violence.

There were officials of the Cheka who publicly called for the use of torture on "enemies of the revolution." The following incident is typical of the young Soviet state. In the summer of 1918 the Cheka uncovered a conspiracy against the Soviet regime headed by the British diplomat Bruce Lockhart. The conspirators were arrested, and Lockhart was expelled from the Soviet Union. The newspapers reported that "the exposed English diplomat representative left the Cheka greatly embarrassed."[3] About the same time a small journal, the *Cheka Weekly*, was started in Moscow. An early issue published a letter—"Why the Kid Gloves?"—from the chairman of the party committee and of the Cheka in Nolinsk:

We will say it plainly. . . . The Cheka has not broken with petty-bourgeois ideology, the cursed legacy of the prerevolutionary past. Tell us why you did not

2. Vladimir Korolenko, "Russkaia pytka v starinu," in his *Sochineniia* vol. 9 (1914), p. 215.

3. *Izvestia*, September 3, 1918.

subject him, this Lockhart, to the most refined tortures, to get information and addresses, which such a bird must have a lot of. With those measures you could have easily discovered a whole series of counterrevolutionary organizations, perhaps even have eliminated the possibility of future financing, which is certainly equivalent to wiping them out. Tell us why, instead of subjecting him to such tortures, the mere description of which would make counterrevolutionaries' blood run cold, tell us why you let him "leave" the Cheka greatly embarrassed. Or do you think that subjecting a man to horrible tortures is more inhumane then blowing up bridges and warehouses of food with the purpose of finding an ally, in the torments of starvation, for the overthrow of the Soviet regime? . . . Let every British worker know that if an official representative of his country is doing such things, he must be subjected to torture. And it is safe to say that the workers will not approve the system of explosions and bribes carried out by such a rat, directed by rats of higher rank. No more kid gloves. Stop this contemptible game of "diplomacy and representation."[4]

The appeal of the Nolinsk officials was not supported by the Cheka. According to a writer who was Sverdlov's secretary in 1918, "Why the Kid Gloves?" caused widespread indignation in party circles. Readers sent the newspapers letters of protest, some of which were published. Sverdlov heard of this polemic. When he read the relevant materials, his indignation was boundless. The question was raised in the highest governmental body, which adopted the following resolution:

The Presidium of the All-Russia Central Executive Committee, having discussed the article "Why the Kid Gloves?" which appeared in the third issue of the *Cheka Weekly*, has taken note that the thoughts expressed in it on the struggle with the counterrevolution are in gross contradiction with the policy and the tasks of the Soviet regime. Although the Soviet regime resorts of necessity to the most drastic measures of conflict with the counterrevolutionary movement, and remembers that the conflict with the counterrevolution has taken the form of open armed conflict, in which the proletariat and poor peasants cannot renounce the use of terror, the Soviet regime fundamentally rejects the measures adovcated in the indicated article, as despicable, dangerous and contrary to the interests of the strugggle for Communism. The Presidium of the Central Executive Committee most severely censures both the authors of the article and the editors of the *Cheka Weekly* who printed the article and provided it with commentary.

It was also decided to close down the *Cheka Weekly* for publishing the article, to dismiss the authors from their jobs, and to forbid their holding office in the Soviet government.[5]

Such a resolution was not an accident. It was consistent with the best

4. *Ezhenedel'nik VChK* (1918), no. 3, pp. 7–8.
5. Yelizaveta Drabkina, "Memuary," unpublished manuscript. Part of Drabkina's memoirs were published under the title *Zimnii pereval*, (Moscow, 19568).

traditions of the Russian revolutionary movement. Russian revolutionaries of all persuasions had always been intolerant of any form of physical torture. This was even true of those who engaged in terrorism. When S. L. Zlatopolsky, for example, a member of the Executive Committee of the People's Will (Narodnaya Volya),[6] was in the Trubetskoi ravelin of Peter-Paul Fortress, in the solitary cells for "especially dangerous state criminals," he managed to send the People's Will a long letter, which was then circulated as a sort of proclamation throughout the country. After describing the cruel regimen established in the Peter-Paul Fortress for political prisoners, Zlatopolsky closed with a dying man's appeal:

Friends and brothers! From the depths of our dungeon, speaking to you for probably the last time in our life, we send to you our bequest: On the day of revolutionary victory, the triumph of progress, may the revolution not pollute its sacred name by acts of violence and cruelty against the defeated enemy. Oh, if we could serve as a redeeming sacrifice not only for the creation of freedom in Russia but for an increase in humanitarianism in all the rest of the world! Mankind must renounce solitary confinement, force, and torture in any form, as it has renounced the wheel, the rack, the stake, etc. Regards to you, regards to my relatives, regards to everything alive.[7]

Beatings or whipping in prisons of the early twentieth century provoked stormy protests from all the revolutionary parties outside, and many collective hunger strikes, riots, and, in exceptional cases, even mass suicides inside. Even tsarist prison officials were forced to pay attention to these protests. It is not surprising, then, that after the October revolution the conscience of a true revolutionary could not accept the physical torture even against enemies of the revolution. Thus, when Stalin permitted and even forced the use of torture, he was committing an outrage to the memory of the Russian revolutionaries.

Torture not only conflicts with the principles of a proletarian state, it is the least effective method of investigation. In most cases it yields not truth but a distortion of the truth, since the accused will agree to say anything to stop the unbearable torment. Thus torture is aimed not so much at finding the guilty person as at making the innocent one guilty, forcing him to calumniate himself and others. Medieval inquisitors were well aware of this when they forced their victims to testify about their contacts with the devil. The intelligence agencies of most countries are also aware of it. The British intelligence agent Oreste Pinto writes:

6. The organization that carried out the assassination of Alexander II in 1881.
7. From the archives of Yuri Trifonov.

There is no doubt that physical torture will ultimately break any man, however strong in body or determined in mind. I knew one incredibly brave man who fell into the hands of the Gestapo and who had all his fingernails and toenails forcibly extracted and one leg broken without uttering a word of useful information. But he himself admitted that he was at the end of his resistance. It so happened that his torturers were baffled and gave up at that stage. Had they gone on, even with some minor discomfort compared to the exquisite agony he had so far suffered, he would have broken and confessed all.

. . . Physical torture has one overwhelming disadvantage. Under its spur an innocent man will often confess to some crime he has never committed, merely to gain a respite. . . . He will even invent a crime involving the death penalty, preferring a quick death to a continuation of his agony. Physical torture will make any man talk but it cannot ensure that he will tell the truth.[8]

Stalin and the NKVD officials understood this very well when they forced devoted Communists to testify about their connections with genuine enemies of our nation.

Even the Inquisition tried to put some limit on the willfullness of the inquisitors. "Heretics" could be whipped, stretched on the rack, or tortured by water, hunger, and thirst. But the rules of the Inquisition forbade the spilling of blood. The "heretic" could be tortured only once in the course of an interrogation, and the torture was supposed to last no more than an hour—so as to let the clerk, the torturer, and the inquisitors rest. The NKVD investigators tortured prisoners for many hours at a stretch, and repeatedly. Brutalized interrogators disfigured prisoners. They not only beat them and kept them from sleep, food, and water; they gouged out eyes and perforated eardrums, pulled out fingernails and toenails, broke arms and legs, burned their victims with redhot irons, and mutilated sex organs.

R. G. Alikhanova tells about I. Khansuvarov, a well-known party member, who was made to stand in water for ten days straight. Stanislav Kosior's wife told Alikhanova that her husband's captors, unable to break him with torture, brought his sixteen-year-old daughter into the room where the investigation was taking place and raped her before her father's eyes. Afterwards Kosior signed the entire "confession," and his daughter, having been released from prison, committed suicide by throwing herself under a train. In Butyrskaya prison there were cases when a husband was tortured in front of his wife or a wife in front of her husband.

Besides Lefortovo, one of the worst prisons was Sukhanovo. The mi-

8. Oreste Pinto, *Spy-catcher* (New York, 1952), pp. 24–25. The author quotes the Soviet translation, *Okhota za shpionami* (Moscow, 1964).

crobiologist Pavel Zdrodovsky, a prisoner there, was told, "Keep in mind that in this prison we're allowed to do everything." Almost all the inmates of this prison had been members of the "elite" of society, but the first interrogation often began with a brutal beating of the prisoner. By this method interrogators wanted to humiliate the prisoner and break his will. Zdrodovsky told me, "I was lucky; they punched me in the face but didn't flog me." The fate of Populia Ordzhonikidze's wife was different. At Sukhanovo they lashed her to death.

Some survivors' stories make the blood run cold. When sadistic investigators in Butyrskaya prison did not obtain the testimony they needed from one Communist, they tortured him in front of his wife and then tortured her in front of him. A. V. Snegov tells about torture chambers of the Lenigrad NKVD where prisoners would be put on a concrete floor and covered by a box with nails driven in from four sides. On top was a grating through which a doctor looked at the victim once every twenty-four hours. In 1938, both Snegov, a small man, and Pavel Dybenko, who was big, were put into such a box—one cubic meter in size. (This method was borrowed from the Finnish secret police. Other methods were taken directly from the Gestapo.) One NKVD colonel, on getting a prisoner for interrogation, would urinate in a glass and force the prisoner to drink the urine. If he refused, he was liable to be killed without being interrogated.

Suren Gazaryan tells what was done to Soso Buachidze, commander of a Georgian division and son of a hero of the revolution. When he would not give the required testimony, his stomach was ripped open, and he was thrown, dying, into a cell. In the same cell was David Bagration, one of Buachidze's friends, who had just been arrested. Gazaryan, who had been an executive in the Transcausian NKVD until June 1937, was also subjected to inhuman torture. Similar ghastly scenes are recorded in works by Solzhenitsyn, Shalamov, Eugenia Ginzburg, Lev Kopelev, M. Maksimovich, L. Bershadskaya, and many others.

I will cite just one excerpt from the memoirs of Ya. I. Drobinsky, the Belorussian party official, illustrating the methods of "investigation" used in the Minsk Central Prison in 1938:

At ten they took him again through that corridor to that room, but what a difference! . . . During the day this was a quiet corridor, with respectable offices in which neat, well-groomed people shuffled papers. In the evening Andrei felt he was running a gauntlet—the screams of the tortured, the filthiest gutter curses of the torturers, coming from every room. Sometimes a glimpse of a body on the floor. Andrei saw a familiar face, turning purple. . . . It was Lyubovich, an Old Bolshevik, deputy chairman of the republic's council of commissars and chairman of its State Planning Commission. He had been in the first government created by Lenin in 1917. He had entered it as the deputy commissar of communications under Podbelsky. He had been a member of the Little Council of Commissars and had worked with Lenin. Now he lay on the floor, they were whipping him with rubber hoses, and he, a sixty-year old man, was screaming "Mama!" . . . An instant, but it was etched in Andrei's memory forever.

. . . A torture room of the sixteenth century. He was taken into an office. As in the daytime, there were two: Dovgalenko and the sportsman. "Well," asked the captain, businesslike, "have you thought it over?" Andrei shook his head. . . .

"Take off your jacket." . . . Andrei didn't move. With a sharp movement the young man tore it off; the jacket split, fell down. "Ah, just once I'll give it to him." Andrei jerked his right fist toward the young man's chin and hit the air. The same instant, he received two karate chops on his arms. A sharp pain pierced them, and his arms hung like vines. And right away the young man hit him hard, once, twice, three times in the chest. . . . Andrei leaned against the wall. Those creatures went to a large closet, took out two thick sticks, and got down to work. From both sides they beat rhythmically, the back of his head, his ribs, his back. Clenching his teeth, Andrei groaned—the main thing was not to scream, not to give those creatures the satisfaction. . . . The pain was unbearable, then it grew dull. Then they poured something on him, iodine or salt water or simply water, and then the pain became horrible, insufferable. His body was being torn by the teeth of some wild beasts, hundreds, thousands of dogs were biting this poor tormented body.

"Well, are you going to write?"

He didn't answer. To answer he had to open his mouth, and then he would begin to scream. He must not scream. They were screaming from the other rooms. "Murderers, fascists!" screamed the voice of a young woman, "don't you dare, don't you dare. How can you?" "My God," thought Andrei, "what are they doing to her?"[9]

A few words should be said about the behavior of people who were tortured by the NKVD. Most of them could not withstand the torture and signed the false statements prepared for them by the investigators. The Old Bolshevik Sergei Pisarev relates the following:

In just two prisons, in the Inner Prison of Lubyanka and in Lefortovo, I was subjected to forty-three sessions of monstrous insult, with spitting in the face and foul language—sessions inappropriately termed "interrogations." Of these, twenty-three instances involved physical torture of many varieties, simply because I

9. From the archives of Aleksandr Tvardovsky. The character "Andrei" was actually Dubinsky, former secretary of the party's Mogilev city committee. During the October revolution Lyubovich commanded the detachment that occupied the Central Telegraph Office in Petrograd. Later he headed the postal and telegraph workers' union and the signal corps of the Red Army.

refused to slander myself. During that awful time there were few prisoners who were "favored" with tortures that were so long and tiring for the prison guards. . . . All told, during those years in the different cells of the four major Moscow prisons I had approximately four hundred cellmates, prisoners just like myself. Except for two men, all were Communists. Almost all of them had substantial records of service to the party. The highest ranking in terms of service to the party was the Latvian Bolshevik Landau, who had been a member of the party since 1905 and who had headed the Aniline Trust (a group of enterprises in the chemical industry) in Moscow for many years. There were professors, regimental officers of the Red Army, many military men and political workers from the Spanish front, literary men, even a public prosecutor named Subotsky. And out of all these worthy Communists, only *four* [Pisarev's emphasis] were able to withstand the torture and slandered neither themselves nor anyone else. I was one of those four. Everyone expected either execution or a sentence in prison camp. Most dreamed of a sentence in prison camp, as of deliverance from torture and escape from execution. [10]

Most of the victims could not endure the torture and signed fraudulent interrogation records. They should not be judged too harshly. Demoralized and confused, they did not understand what was happening in the country so that their will to fight was unavoidably weakened. Much of their behavior can be explained, if not completely justified. Therefore, I cannot agree with General Aleksandr Gorbatov, whose memoirs reveal anger not so much against the torturers as against the people who succumbed to the torture. [11]

Of course, different prisoners behaved in different ways. Some immediately complied with the desires of the investigators; without any sort of resistance they gave false testimony not only about themselves but about dozens and hundreds of their comrades. M. V. Ostrogorsky tells how the former editor of *Krestyanskaya gazeta* (The Peasant Newspaper), Semyon Uritsky, when grabbed by the NKVD, at once began to give false testimony about dozens of his colleagues. Some of these weak-willed people went even further than the investigators demanded; they gained cruel satisfaction out of voluntarily denouncing co-workers and friends, demanding their arrest, though they had no doubt about their innocence. Frequently, such people continued to collaborate with the NKVD be-

10. Pisarev had held various posts in the party, from the district-committee level all the way up to the Central Committee. In the thirties and forties he was arrested four times. After being rehabilitated, he joined the human rights movement in the 1960s and was expelled from the party. Before he died in the late 1970s he entrusted to me many of his letters and memoranda to the Central Committee.

11. *Novy mir* (1964) nos. 3–5. [For an English version see Gorbatov, *Years Off My Life* (New York, 1965). —G. S.]

yond the investigation; they became stool pigeons *(seksoty, stukachi)*, who informed on their mates in the prison cell or the camp barracks.

After the first interrogations, many prisoners committed suicide by breaking their heads on the washbasin or the prison wall, throwing themselves on the guards during walks, jumping from a window or down a stairwell, or opening their veins. Others resisted stubbornly but finally broke down under torture and put their signatures to fraudulent depositions. Suren Gazaryan says that the Georgian Communist David Bagration was tortured for fifteen nights in a row, until he lost control of his actions and signed. I. P. Aleksakhin says that Pavlunovsky, an official in the Commissariat of Heavy Industry, held out for several months. But when they threw him in a solitary cell, full of water and swarming with rats, he caved in, banged on the door, shouting: "Barbarians, write what you want!" And then he signed.[12] M. V. Ostrogorsky tells us that Krylenko, the former commissar of justice, gave in only after cruel tortures. He asked for some paper in his cell, and there, in the presence of his comrades in misfortune, he began to create his counterrevolutionary organization. He would mumble: "Ivanov? No, he's a good official and a man, I won't put him down. But Petrov, he's a louse; let's sign him up."

When M. R. Maek, an executive of the Leningrad *obkom*, was arrested, he was shown the testimony of B. P. Pozern, who "confessed" that he had recruited Maek into his counterrevolutionary organization. Maek knew Pozern to be an honest and intelligent man, one of the founders of the Red Guard in 1917. Unable to believe that Pozern would sign such a deposition, Maek demanded a confrontation, which took place the next day. Many years later, after he had been rehabilitated, Maek recalled how an utterly emaciated old man entered the investigator's office, whom he hardly recognized as Pozern. Maek asked him: "How, Boris Pavlovich, how could you write such ridiculous stuff, that you recruited me into an anti-Soviet organization?" But Pozern, looking down, began suddenly to say: "It doesn't matter, it doesn't matter, my friend; I recruited you, I recruited you." Everything was immediately clear to Maek.

Some people would sign any deposition against themselves but absolutely refused to compromise their comrades. Mikhail Baitalsky writes in his memoirs:

12. Pavlunovsky had been a party member since 1905 and a member of the Military Revolutionary Committee in Petrograd in 1917. Until 1930 he worked in the Cheka and GPU and after that in the Commissariat of Heavy Industry.

I don't want to pretend that I behaved like a hero during the interrogations and didn't sign any records. I would sign if the matter concerned me alone, or if it was well-known stuff. But when the investigator would tie people to me who were still alive, there I refused. They pinned my first sergeant (*starshina*) to me —I would not give in. They were even more energetic in tying in Boris Gorbatov. I defended him—that is, I disowned him as much as I could. And, it seems, not without success. He died in his bed and not in a camp, although the investigators told me: "Prizewinners aren't worth beans to us, and your military decorations have the same value. Be good a thousand times, but if you fall once, that's all. Understand?" [13]

Many prisoners did not sign anything, despite severe torture. Suren Gazaryan signed nothing. Neither did Pisarev, as we have seen. N. S. Kuznetsov, North Kazakhstan obkom secretary, withstood the most refined tortures. Once he stood before his tormentors without sleep or food for eight days in a row. On the ninth day he lost consciousness and fell, but did not sign the prepared statement. [14]

Nestor Lakoba, poisoned by Beria and posthumously declared an "enemy of the people," left a wife who would not sign any false statements about him. A young and beautiful woman, rumored to be a Georgian princess, she was arrested and put in the Tbilisi prison soon after her husband's death. Nutsa Gogoberidze, the wife of Levan Gogoberidze, who shared a cell with Lakoba's wife, tells how this silent and calm woman was taken away every evening and in the morning was dragged back to the cell, bloody and unconscious. The women cried, asked for a doctor, and did what they could to revive her. When she came to, she told how they demanded that she sign an essay on the subject "How

13. Baitalsky, *Tetradi dlia vnukov*, unpublished manuscript. Baitalsky gave me a manuscript copy of his memoirs for my archives in 1967, with permission for mc to quote them using the pseudonym "D. Mikhailov." Later he wrote under the pseudonyms Aronovich, Ilsky, Domalsky, and others. His articles, essays, verse, and reminiscences circulated widely in samizdat and appeared in the samizdat magazines *Politicheskii dnevnik* and *Yevrei v SSSR*. His extremely interesting study of alcoholism in the Soviet Union, entitled *Commodity Number One* and signed with the pseudonym Krasikov, appeared in Russian in *Dvadtsatyi vek*, No. 2 (London, 1977), and in English in *Samizdat Register* and *Samizdat Register II* (New York, 1977 and 1981). Shortly before his death in 1978 he asked that all his pseudonyms be made known. In the quotation cited above the reference is to interrogations that took place in the postwar period.

14. N. S. Kuznetsov, to whose memoirs I shall refer below, was one of only two obkom secretaries known to me who was rehabilitated while still alive rather than posthumously. After being rehabilitated, he took work as a forest ranger in the Northern Caucasus. Konstantin Simonov acquainted me with Kuznetsov's memoirs and kept them in his archives until his death. Kuznetsov personally gave them to Simonov, a writer and an editor of the magazine *Znamya*.

Lakoba sold Abkhazia to Turkey." Her reply was brief: "I will not defame the memory of my husband." She stood fast even when faced with the ultimate torture: her fourteen-year-old son was shoved crying toward his mother, and she was told he would be killed if she did not sign. (And this threat was carried out.) Even then Lakoba's wife would not defame her husband. Finally, after a night of torture, she died in her cell.

Kosarev and most of the other leaders of the Komsomol Central Committee were also unyielding. These young and strong people could not be broken by the worst tortures. According to Valentina Pikina, the unyielding behavior of Kosarev and his colleagues kept the NKVD from organizing an open trial of youth. General Gorbatov also did not bear false witness against himself or his comrades.

I cannot help condemning willing false witnesses. Nor can I overlook the strength of such people as Gazaryan, Kuznetsov, Lakoba's wife, Kosarev, and Gorbatov, who displayed fortitude in conditions far worse than on the battlefield. But I do not have the right to condemn such people as Bagration or Pavlunovsky, whose strength gave out in the unequal struggle. Gorbatov was wrong when he wrote that these unfortunate people "misled the investigation" when they put their signatures to false statements. What took place in the NKVD torture chambers was not investigation; it was deliberate crime.

Sharing a cell with a friend who had given false testimony against him, N. Kuznetsov did not turn his back; he embraced his comrade. And Gazaryan did the same. Gorbatov behaved differently with his companions in misfortune. "By your false testimony," he declared, "you have committed a serious crime, for which they are keeping you in prison."[15] This behavior contrasts poorly with the words of Eugenia Ginzburg, who refuses "to put on the tragic buskins of the hero or the martyr" and does not condemn those who surrendered to unbearable torment. She writes that she was simply lucky—her investigation ended before the massive use of "special methods" began.[16]

The diary of Pavel Shabalkin, who died in 1965, contains some interesting reflections on the behavior of prisoners. This veteran party official, who was also a philosopher, was twice subjected to investigation and trial and spent about twenty years in prisons and camps. During his second investigation he could not hold out against the torture and signed false

15. *Novy mir* (1964), no. 4, p. 119.
16. Eugenia Ginzburg, *Journey into the Whirlwind* (New York, 1967).

statements. In prison camp for more than ten years he was manager of a mess hall, which suggests a certain degree of collaboration with the camp administration. He eased his conscience by not allowing the criminals any privileges and secretly giving extra food to some of the political prisoners. Before his death Shabalkin showed me his diary, which included the following entry:

Why did so many people who were devoted to the revolution, ready to die for it, who had endured tsarist prisons and exile and had more than once looked death in the eye—why did so many of these people give in during interrogation and sign false statements, "confessing" to every sort of crime they never committed? The cause of these "confessions" and "self-defamation" consists in the following:

(1) Right after the arrest the prisoner starts to be worked over. First it is done verbally, with the preservation of a certain amount of politeness; then come shouting and cursing, humiliations and insults, spitting in the face, light blows, and mockery. "You bastard," "You rat," "You traitor, spy, garbage," and so on and so forth. They humiliate a man without limit, convince him that he is nothing.

This goes on day after day, night after night. The so-called conveyor is set up: the interrogators change but the prisoner stands or sits. For days. They kept me, for example, on the conveyor for eight days. They don't let you sleep. They force tea into you. The conveyor is a terrible torture. And all the while they kick you, insult you; if you resist, they beat you. The job of the conveyor is to break a man morally, turn him into a rag.

But if you withstand the conveyor and don't crack, physical torture follows. They get the tortured man to the point where he becomes indifferent to everything, and he is inclined to accept everything they suggest.

"You're a rat." "Yes a rat."

"You're a traitor." "Yes a traitor."

"You were a provocateur." "Yes, I was a provocateur."

"You wanted to kill Stalin." "Yes, I wanted to kill Stalin." And so on.

At this time they take stories made up by the investigators and push them on the prisoner, who accepts them without murmur. The investigators hurry to exploit their success. They compile the first record of interrogation, a "hand-written deposition."

(2) Next is the stage of consolidating the "achievements." They begin to feed the prisoner decently. They give him cigarettes, parcels from his family, even let him read books and newspapers. But work on the unfortunate does not stop. They convince him that now he cannot turn back, that he can save himself only by "sincere repentance," that he himself must now think what he can still tell the investigators. They supply him with paper and pen to write "depositions" in his cell, suggest the theme, and check his work.

Frequently, the victims of this ordeal started to vacillate. But the NKVD thought up thousands of ways to suppress these vacillations. They would arrange confrontations with other people just as unfortunate. "Interaction" would take place. Additional methods of physical influence would be used. They would take prisoners to see the "procurator," who would be an investigator in disguise. Provocational "court" sessions would be arranged, and so on.

(3) If the prisoner had to be brought before a court—an absolute majority of prisoners were condemned in absentia by various *troiki*, special assemblies *(oso-bye soveshchaniia)*, etc.—then there would be additional work on him, a peculiar rehearsal for the trial. Here every method was used: threats, suggestion, "serious conversations"—"Bear in mind that we will not simply shoot you; we will torture you, tear you to pieces"—and so on. They convinced many people that they would not be shot; that was only for the press, while everybody really remained alive and unharmed. As proof, they would show "shot" people who were still alive. (Afterwards they shot these people anyway, but for the time being they used them to trick the living.) During the trial the torturers were kept right before the prisoners's nose. They were a living reminder of what would happen if he changed his mind. . . .

(4) The investigators developed a complex system of "the individual approach" to the investigated. First they studied him through stool pigeons in his cell, or, if he was in solitary, by brief summons to the investigator. They would work him over in the cell, or in the office. One they would take by fear, another by persuasion, a third by promises, and a fourth by a combination of methods. But the main thing was that they immediately deprived the prisoner of any chance of defending himself.

(5) Yet the main reason why strong-willed people who had more than once looked death in the eye frequently broke down in the investigation, and agreed to monstrous self-accusations, was not the terrible cruelty of the investigation. The crucial thing was that these people were suddenly cut off from the soil on which they grew up. Here a man was like a plant torn from the ground and thrown to the mercy of the winds and weather, deprived of food, moisture, and sun. His ideals were shattered. Facing you were not class enemies. The people, the Soviet people, were against you. You were an "enemy of the people." There was nothing to lean on. A man was plunging into the abyss and didn't understand the reason. Why? What for? . . .

Of course there were many who gave in without a fight. The atmosphere of terror in the prison created feelings of hopelessness. Many "fresh" prisoners immediately signed everything that was put in front of them, feeling that resistance was useless and defense impossible. In this way a new phenomenon developed in the investigatory process: the parties would reach a peaceful agreement on the "crime" and the "punishment." Very many military men amazed me by such "softness." They said: "No, I will not let them beat me. If they don't need me, let them shoot me. I'll sign everything they want." And they did this without any struggle or resistance. . . . And this too was a sort of protest against arbitrary rule.

■ 2

THE FARCE OF A TRIAL: JAILS AND PRISONER TRANSPORTS

Although most political prisoners were convicted in absentia by various special assemblies and *troiki,* in many cases a closed trial was held, without spectators, procurators, or defense lawyers. Even in complicated cases these trials did not last more than five or ten minutes. Kosarev's trial took fifteen minutes, but that was a rare exception. Gorbatov, whose trial lasted five, tells how delighted he was when he came to court, convinced that he was going to be acquitted. He denied that he had committed any crime, and when he was asked why ten condemned people had testified against him he told the judges how sixteenth-century witchcraft trials had extracted confessions. Immediately the judges pronounced him guilty and sentenced him to fifteen years, which came as such a shock that he fainted on the spot.[17]

Although Eugenia Ginzburg's trial was supposed to be public, only the Military Collegium of the Supreme Court—three officers and a secretary —faced her and two guards in an empty room. The bored judges were startled by her demand to be told which official she had plotted to kill. They mentioned Kirov's murder. She replied that she had never been in Leningrad, which they dismissed as casuistry. "People with her views" had killed Kirov, and that made her "morally and criminally responsible." About to faint as the sentence was read —she expected death—she was revived by the concluding words: ten years. The whole procedure took seven minutes.

For many prisoners, including most of the high officials, the day of the trial was the last day of life. By the law of December 1, 1934, the death sentence was to be executed immediately. Some of those sentenced to be shot were kept in the death chamber for a few days or months, but the majority were killed right after the trial. They were shot in various ways: some in the back of the head on the stairs to the basement; others in the basement of the Lubyanka or Lefortovo prison, where some prisoners said a tractor engine drowned out the shots. From other Moscow prisons the condemned were taken to the outskirts of the city to be shot. Yevgeny Frolov wrote down the story of one of the soldiers who escorted people condemned to death. He told Frolov that he would take such people to a place of execution in the Krasnaya Presnya district of

17. *Novy mir* (1964), no. 4, p. 122.

Moscow. There in a deserted area bordering a cemetery was a lot surrounded by a wall, against which the condemned were shot. This job was done by special people, two of them, who lived in a dugout. When the escort brought condemned people, a hollow-faced man would come out of the dugout, take over the prisoners and their documents, and shoot them on the spot. In the dugout, the soldier said, stood two bottles—one with water, the other with vodka.

Not only men were shot but women, not only young people but old ones, not only healthy but sick. The Old Bolshevik A. P. Spunde tells how a well-known Latvian Communist, Yu. P. Gaven, died. He had joined the RSDLP in 1902, taken part in the 1905 revolution, done years of hard labor in tsarist prisons, where he contracted tuberculosis. After the revolution he was chairman of the Central Executive Committee of the Crimean Autonomous Republic and worked in the diplomatic service. In the twenties he had expressed distrust of Stalin. In the thirties he was carried on a stretcher to be shot.[18] Also carried on a stretcher to be shot was Lieutenant General Ya. V. Smushkevich, head of the Soviet air force, twice honored as Hero of the Soviet Union, who was recovering from severe injuries after a plane crash. (This was reported by his daughter.)

For those who were not killed, there were long years in prison and then in camps.

No scientific history of the Stalinist prisons, camps, and exile system, similar to M. N. Gernet's multivolume study of the history of the tsarist prisons,[19] has yet been produced, and no one knows when the conditions for such work will appear. Many contributions to this history have been made, however, through creative literature and memoirs. My bibliography contains nearly two hundred books under the heading "Prison Camp Literature." Nearly half of these have been published, but almost exclusively by foreign publishers. The most significant of these are unquestionably the works of Aleksandr Solzhenitsyn, Eugenia Ginzburg, and Varlam Shalamov, but the first books about Soviet prisons and camps began to appear in the twenties and thirties, and quite a few came out later. Yu. Margolin's book *Journey to the Land of Ze-Ka* deserves mention here. A Polish citizen, Margolin was released at the end of his term

18. V. Baranchenko, *Gaven* (Moscow, 1967). (A volume in the series "Lives of Remarkable People.")

19. M. N. Gernet, *Istoriia tsarskoi tiur'my*, 3rd ed., 5 vols., (Moscow, 1960).

in 1945 and managed to emigrate. He wrote his book in Tel Aviv in 1946–1947.[20]

In the present work I shall limit myself to a brief commentary on the prisons and camps, with references for the most part to little-known or unpublished memoirs and studies.

Concentration camps and temporary prisons for political prisoners or hostages were established in Soviet Russia during the civil war that followed the revolution. But it was not until the early twenties that a more or less regular penitentiary system began to be introduced and laws elaborated to apply to it. The regimen for political prisoners in the twenties was relatively lenient. They received extra food, were exempt from forced labor, and were not subjected to humiliating inspections. In political jails *(politizolyatory)* self-government was allowed; the politicals elected "elders," who dealt with the prison administration. They kept their clothes, books, writing materials, pocket knives; they could subscribe to newspapers and magazines. Their imprisonment was regarded as temporary isolation during a national emergency.

For example, on December 30, 1920, when the civil war had barely ended, the Cheka issued a special order:

Information received by the Cheka establishes that members of various anti-Soviet parties arrested in political cases are being kept in very bad conditions. . . . The Cheka points out that the above-listed categories of people must not be regarded as undergoing punishment, but as temporarily isolated from society in the interests of the revolution. The conditions of their detention must not have a punitive character.[21]

One incident highlights the prison customs of the time. When Peter Kropotkin, the Anarchist patriarch, died in his home near Moscow,[22] hundreds of Anarchists who had been put in Butyrskaia prison for anti-Soviet activity demanded permission to attend the funeral of their teacher. Dzerzhinsky ordered that the Anarchists be let out on their honor. After the military funeral they all returned, to a man. Subsequently they published, from jail, an anthology, *On the Death of Kropotkin.*

20. Iu. B. Margolin, *Puteshestvie v stranu ze-ka,* 1st ed. (New York, 1952), 2nd ed. (Tel Aviv, 1976).

21. M. Ya. Latsis, *Chrezvychainye komissii po bor'be s kontrrevoliutsiei* (Moscow, 1921).

22. Lenin had personally helped with Kropotkin's living arrangements after the seventy-five-year-old anarchist returned to Russia from abroad; and Lenin met several times with the celebrated old revolutionary.

In those days only SRs, Mensheviks, Anarchists, and other members of socialist and left-wing parties that had fought against the tsarist regime were admitted to the category of "politicals." Members of procapitalist or monarchist parties or participants in the White Guard movement were called counterrevolutionaries and imprisoned together with criminals. Harsh punitive conditions were established for them in glaring violation of the principles proclaimed shortly after the October revolution.

Of course, in the early twenties there were quite a few instances that could be classified as insulting treatment of prisoners by the GPU. Still, this was the exception, not the rule. The Corrective Labor Code of 1924, which regulated conditions for all prisoners, including criminals and "counterrevolutionaries," stated (p. 49):

The regimen should be devoid of any trace of cruel or abusive treatment (*muchitelstvo*), the following by no means being permitted: handcuffs, punishment cells, solitary confinement, denial of food, keeping prisoners behind bars during conversations with visitors.

In most cases this code was observed at the time.

In the early twenties Commissar of Health Semashko pointed with pride to the establishment of a humane prison regime, which could not exist in capitalist countries. To be sure, some deterioration can be noted even in the twenties. At the end of 1923, for example, the exercise period was cut down, which provoked a much publicized clash between Social Revolutionaries and guards at Solovketskaia prison. There were other "excesses," but at the time they were exceptions rather than the rule.

In the early thirties the deterioration continued. The "wreckers" imprisoned then could not dream of having the kind of prison conditions that had existed in the early twenties. But it was the mass repression later in the decade that reduced prisons to the most savage regime imaginable. As we have seen, the cells became brutally overcrowded. Prisoners were forbidden to go to the window, to lie on the bunks in the daytime, sometimes even to talk. On the slightest pretext they were thrown into the punishment hole (*kartser*), deprived of exercise, correspondence, or books. In many cells it was nearly impossible to breathe.

There are many firsthand accounts of the inhuman prison regime during Stalin's time. Here, for example, is an excerpt from the memoirs of M. M. Ishov, onetime military procurator of the West Siberian district, who was put into the Novosibirsk transfer prison in 1938.

I was taken to the second floor and ordered to halt in front of the door to one of the cells. The guard turned the lock with a key, opened the door, and literally squeezed me in. I say squeezed because so many people were there that you could push through only with great difficulty. If you recall the ancient tales about heaven and hell and try to visualize them, then that cell was real hell. Alas, it was no tale but grim reality. About 270 men were kept in a cell 40 square meters in area. They were supposed to find places in the two-tiered system of bunks. People squirmed under the bunks, even on the cover of the big *parasha* [prison slang for chamber pot] standing in the corner. Prisoners piled up at the doors, in the passageway. There was nowhere to sit down and nowhere to move to. Many, standing on their feet, fainted from exhaustion. They wanted just to sit and rest a little. But there was nowhere to sit or lie down. The prisoners, lying on the floor, standing in the passageway, cursed each other. Everyone was extremely irritated and mean. A more ill-assorted crowd can hardly be imagined. There were big bandits, thieves, crooks, murderers, profiteers, various victims of circumstance, and we, accused of crimes listed in Article 58 of the Criminal Code. In the cell we were called the "Counters" [short for counterrevolutionaries]. How depressing it was to hear this! We had many former military men, from various branches of the service. There were officials of big and medium industry, manual workers, office workers, peasants, students. . . . There were juveniles—petty thieves. There were strong people but there were weak and sick people too. At times it became unbearable to be in the cell. A little window, 30-by-40 centimeters [12 by 16 inches], was open all the time, but the flow of air was negligible. The cell was stifling. There was a heavy noisome stench. It became hard to breathe. Not only the new arrivals but the earlier inmates felt very sick and breathed with great difficulty. It is even hard to imagine how so many people were put into such a small cell.[23]

Some months later, Ishov found himself in Lefortovo prison in Moscow, where it was not so crowded: only two people were put into a cell built for one. But the regime was stricter than in the overcrowded provincial prisons.

The regime was just as savage in almost all the prisons. V. I. Volgin, a Rostov agronomist, recalls

. . . cell Number 47 in the inner prison, around 35 square meters in area. There were always fifty to sixty men in the cell. It was the beginning of June 1939. It got hot in the courtyard and burning in the cell. We used to press to the cracks in the floor to suck some fresh air and took turns crowding near the door to feel the cross draft through its cracks. The old men could not bear it, and soon were carried away to eternal rest.[24]

23. M. M. Ishov, "Gody potriasenii i tiazhelykh ispytanii" (unpublished manuscript, Leningrad, 1966), pp. 94–95. A copy of this manuscript is in my archives.

24. V. I. Volgin "Rasskazy iz kammennogo meshka" (unpublished manuscript, Rostov-on-Don, 1965), p. 16. A copy of this, too, is in my archives.

Eugenia Ginzburg tells how the guards in Yaroslavl prison threw an Italian Communist into a cold solitary cell and drenched her with ice water from a hose. In Kuibyshev many prisoners were put into the prison basement, where the central heating pipes passed through. In the summer they counted thirty-three species of insects, including, of course, lice, fleas, and bedbugs. In the winter, heat killed off the insects; the people endured, their bodies covered with painful sores.

In Sukhanovo prison outside of Moscow the prisoners suffered from hunger. After two months of prison food a person was reduced to skin and bone. The prison was located in the basement and lower floors of the building, the top floors of which were a recreation area for employees of the NKVD.

According to the Old Bolshevik I. P. Gavrilov, in the Barnaul municipal prison the terrible conditions caused a mass demonstration by the inmates who managed to break out of the overcrowded cells and reached the prison yard. Following this incident several people were shot, although the regimen changed a little for the better. Stories of this sort could be told endlessly.

After investigation, trial, and imprisonment, inhuman cruelty pursued the prisoners who were being transported. Frequently twenty to thirty prisoners were shoved with rifle butts into each compartment of the "Stolypin" prison cars,[25] intended for only six people. On some trains people stood for days on end, pressed against each other, fed on salted fish and receiving only one cup of water a day, though the train was not crossing a desert. These trains moved east for weeks, and almost every stop was marked by the graves of prisoners.

Mikhail Baitalsky, in the following excerpts from his memoirs, gives a description of conditions on these trains:

Without waiting for a sympathetic glance from the passers-by, I clambered up the steps of the railroad car. They crammed us in, locked the door, and in the passageway in front of the bars appeared the head of the escort guards, a young sergeant with excellent posture.

"Attention, imprisoned enemies of the people! Announcement! You will be allowed water twice a day. One bucket per car. You will be brought to the toilet once a day. Understood?"

The sergeant used the word "toilet" to be polite. The enemies of the people grumbled. But the sergeant was not afraid of these down-and-outers.

25. ["Stolypin cars" were named after Pyotr Stolypin, the tsarist prime minister who presided over suppression of the 1905 revolution. —G. S.]

"Announcement! You're talking a lot. Those who make noise will not be allowed to use the toilet. Understood?"

. . . His accent was that of a person from Vologda. In the camps we often heard the saying "Vologda escort guards don't fool around." Sergeants like this one would repeat this saying with pride. What a thing to be proud of.

Two, three, four days passed. We sat hunched up, pressing our folded arms against our stomachs. We tried not to drink, in order to ease the pain. But it is more difficult not to drink than not to eat. On the trip they gave us dry rations: bread and herring. Every day of the trip we were hunched up more and more; it was as if we had cobblestones in our intestines. The train stood for a long time at the stations.

"Attention, imprisoned enemies of the people!" announced the sergeant. "The train is stopping for an indefinite period of time. You can go to the toilet when the train begins moving again."

For eight days he did not make a single exception for anyone. He maintained politeness, relentless politeness, which he had been persistently taught. . . . He believed that we were fascists. We were abused that way quite often—by escort guards, supervisors, and criminals. I don't blame the sergeant. He was simply putting into practice what the exponents of the supreme ideology had couched in theoretical terms.

We didn't know where we were going, couldn't read the names of the stations. After eight days they finally let us out. Vorkuta![26]

Ye. G. Veller-Gurevich describes a similar journey in her memoirs:

We came to a freight car standing on a siding; they ordered us to line up and climb into the car by a steep ladder. The car was lighted by one dull lamp in the corner. Inside there were three tiers of bunks in each half of the car. In the middle was a hole in the floor, serving as a "toilet," and an iron stove. A hundred women were put in this car, which was intended for the transport of eight horses. We pressed against each other to warm up a little. My brain could not take in everything that was going on. . . . The journey by stages from Moscow to Tomsk lasted nineteen days. They were infinitely long days: unbelievable crowding, hunger, cold, thirst, parasites, filth, stink, sickness, the impossibility of moving, the struggle between despair and hope.[27]

The Leningrad Communist Yelena Vladimirova, who like millions of others made the frightful journey east, described it in her poem Kolyma, the following passage from which is given here in a prose version:

The prison train was a new stage in his discoveries. When, calling sheep dogs to help, they got the people ready for the road, dumb with anger and shame, he saw the guards, undressing people until they were naked, twirl their sickly bodies

26. Baitalsky, "Tetradi dlia vnukov."

27. Ye. G. Veller-Gurevich, "Iz vospominanii o 37-m," unpublished manuscript. A copy is in my archives.

in coarse insulting paws; he saw how they kept the people in trains for two days without drink, feeding them salted fish; saw cripples on crutches and women, locked in cars, with nursing babies in their arms.[28]

Conditions were even worse on the ships taking prisoners from Vladivostok to the Kolyma region. In their crowded holds people often lay on top of each other, and bread was thrown to them through the hatches as if they were beasts. Those who died during the voyage—and they were many—were simply thrown in the sea. A riot or an organized protest was met with icy water, poured into the hold from the Sea of Okhotsk. Thousands of prisoners died after such a bath or were delivered frostbitten to the prisons of Magadan.

Many prisons kept politicals and criminals separate. Thus for many politicals the first encounter with the criminal gangs was during transport to the camps. Such encounters frequently had tragic results. "The criminals," according to V. I. Volgin,

robbed the politicals almost openly, because they had the guards' protection. They would let the current victim glimpse a knife in their clothes, and shift his things into their own hands. In most cases resistance was unthinkable, because it could only be bloody and unsuccessful. We would have been slashed, to the guards' joy and with their encouragement. On the road we learned about this frightful experience, and no one wanted to lose his liver over a rag. Then we learned too that the transports were the most frightful experience for politicals, and that this new torture was maintained by camp administrations as a means of extermination. The rule of separate transit stockades for politicals and criminals had never been repealed; it was even strictly observed in the old days. But in our time it was deliberately not observed, so that politicals might be torn up by criminals.[29]

Solzhenitsyn, Shalamov, and Eugenia Ginzburg have dealt at length with this subject of terror imposed on the politicals by the criminals. Therefore, I will limit myself to the above-cited quotations and comments. I will also limit myself to a brief discussion of the camp system.

■ 3

THE "CORRECTIVE-LABOR CAMPS"

The fundamental place of detention was not the jails but the thousands of camps that like a thick net covered the country in Stalin's time, especially

28. Vladimorova's long narrative poem "Kolyma" and her shorter verse have not been published.
29. Volgin, "Rasskazy iz kamennogo meshka."

in the northern part of European Russia and in Siberia, Kazakhstan, and the Far East.

So-called corrective-labor camps were organized in some outlying regions in the early thirties. In Karelia camps were set up to dig the White Sea-Baltic Canal, in Siberia to build the Baikal-Amur Railroad, while the inmates of Siblag, Dmitrovlag, and others worked on other projects. Labor camps also began to go up in the Kolyma region (Dalstroi, the Far Eastern Construction Complex), the Komi Autonomous Republic, and other areas. The composition of the inmate population was quite varied even then, but the majority were peasants, religious believers, petty offenders, and hardened criminals.

A very detailed, though not always objective, history of the first prison camps can be found in the second volume of Solzhenitsyn's *Gulag Archipelago*. Solzhenitsyn writes that "a stubborn legend persists in the Archipelago that 'the camps were thought up by Frenkel.' " Further, Solzhenitsyn actually adheres to this legend, telling the reader in detail the history of the "Turkish Jew Naftaly Aronovich Frenkel." He also writes of other important founders of the first camps such as Rappoport, Berman, Kogan, and others whose Jewish descent is emphasized by the photographs in Solzhenitsyn's book.[30] Curiously, Solzhenitsyn did not include photographs of Yezhov, Beria, Berzin, and many other leading participants in the Gulag with Russian, Georgian, Latvian, and Ukrainian names.

Of course, Frenkel did not invent the camps, although he did put a lot of effort into the organization of this forced-labor system. The basic idea of corrective-labor camps, to a much higher degree than the "political isolators" or prisons, was consistent with the nature of socialist society, which should strive not only toward the punishment but the rehabilitation of offenders. However, the actual labor camp system was as far from its original idea as Stalinism was from socialism. And it was Stalin who really founded the camps that Solzhenitsyn writes about. Stalin's chief accomplices in this work were Yagoda, Yezhov, and Beria; people like Frenkel merely added some refinements to the system.

In the first "corrective-labor camps" of the thirties it was possible to find many examples of extreme cruelty. The shores of the Moscow-Volga Canal and the White Sea-Baltic Canal are strewn with the unmarked graves of prisoners. But there were quite a few sincere attempts to help

---

30. Aleksandr Solzhenitsyn, *The Gulag Archipelago Two* (New York, 1975).

the criminals. These camps were not considered secret, and they were often closed down on completion of a project or even ahead of schedule. The books written about these camps by such contributors as Gorky, Kataev, Zoshchenko, Inber, Yasensky, Averbakh, and others are full of omissions and distortions, but there are elements of truth in them which should not be forgotten.[31]

Harsh as nature was in the Kolyma region, few people died in the Dalstroi camps in the years 1932–1937. There existed a system of examinations which allowed ten-year sentences to be reduced to two or three years, excellent food and clothing, a workday of four to six hours in winter and ten in summer, and good pay, which enabled prisoners to help their families and to return home with funds. These facts may be found not only in the book by Vyaktin, a former head of one of the Kolyma camps, but also in Shalamov's *Tales of the Kolyma Camps.*[32]

In 1937 all these liberal systems were abolished by Yezhov and Stalin. Such liberalism was declared to have been wrecking by "enemy of the people" Berzin and his aides, who were accused of wanting to win favor with the prisoners and to separate the Kolyma region from the Soviet Union. The other camps were also changed. New orders from Moscow and a new generation of camp bosses quickly turned the corrective-labor camps into hard-labor camps, calculated not so much to correct as to destroy the prisoners.

Unbelievably difficult and dull labor, rarely ten hours but more often twelve, fourteen, and even sixteen hours a day, a savage struggle for existence, hunger, ragged clothing, poor medical care—all this was not the exception but the norm of life in the Stalinist camps after 1937. Especially harsh conditions existed in all kinds of penal and "special" camps, in the Kolyma gold mines and the logging camps, which literally became death camps for the prisoners. In the Kolyma gold mines it took only a month to turn a healthy man into a wreck. At the end of the gold-mining season brigades did not have a single man left of those who had started, except the brigadier himself, his orderly, and some of his personal friends. The rest of the brigade had moved into the hospitals, the so-called convalescent crews, invalid settlements, or had died.

31. See Maxim Gorky, I. L. Averbakh, and S. G. Firin, eds., *Belomoro-baltiiskii kanal imeni Stalina* (Moscow, 1934); and I. L. Averbakh, *Ot prestupleniia k trudu* (Moscow, 1936).
32. See V. Vyaktin, *Chelovek rozhdaetsia dvazhdy* (Magadan, 1964); and Varlam Shalamov, *Kolymskie rasskazy* (London, 1978).

The regimen in most Kolyma and northern camps was deliberately calculated to destroy people. Stalin and his circle did not want their victims to return; better that they should disappear forever. Most inmates of the camps soon realized they had been brought there to die. V. I. Volgin writes in his memoirs:

In the first place, they handed out a ration that clearly meant starvation—given the ten-hour workday. The ration was intentionally harmful to health. . . . Prisoners were taken out to work during the worst frosts. The barracks were not given enough heat, clothing would not dry out. In the fall they kept people, soaked to the skin, out in the rain and the cold to fulfill norms that such hopeless wrecks could never fulfill. . . . Prisoners were not dressed for the climate in the Kolyma region, for example. They were given third-hand clothing, mere rags, and often had only cloth wrapping on their feet. Their torn jackets did not protect them from the bitter frost, and people froze in droves.

In such conditions there was a mass of sick people. Their treatment was often directed, as the staff put it, toward *padezh* [murrain, the death of a herd of cattle]. The sick looked for salvation only where the doctors were themselves prisoners. . . . In the Kolyma region there were so called *slabosilki* [infirmaries], where they kept convalescents after discharge from the hospital. Here they were confined for three weeks. The ration was indeed better: 700 grams of bread [about 1½ pounds]. But three weeks for a wreck were the same as a bone for a hungry dog. I regarded those infirmaries as a way of covering up the *padezh* of the arrested cattle. As if to say, "We took suitable measures, but they did not want to work and live."[33]

And over the gates of all the camps in the Kolyma region was the inscription required by the camp statute: "Labor is a matter of honor, valor, and heroism." (Can one fail to recall here that the gates of Auschwitz carried the inscription "Arbeit macht frei"?)

The destruction of political prisoners was not achieved only through exhausting work. By putting both types of prisoners in the same camp, the administration was in fact "sicking" the criminals like attack dogs on the politicals. According to a former criminal, G. Minaev:

On every suitable occasion they tried to let us know that we thieves were still not lost to the homeland; prodigal, so to speak, but nevertheless sons. But for "fascists" and "counters" [i.e., politicals] there was no place on this mortal earth and never would be in all ages to come. . . . And if we were thieves, then our place was beside the stove, while the "suckers" (*frayery*) and all that sort had their place by the doors and in the corners.[34]

33. Volgin, "Rasskazy iz kamennogo meshka."
34. *Literaturnaya gazeta*, November 29, 1962.

Criminals traditionally have some sort of organization dating back for decades, in some countries for centuries. Prisons and camps do not destroy this organization but often strengthen it. The idea of the Stalinist punitive agencies to thrust criminals and politicals into the same camps was no better or worse than the idea of creating gas ovens in Auschwitz, Treblinka, and the other Nazi death camps.

It wasn't until 1949, when the MVD (formerly, the NKVD) was divided into two independent ministries—the MVD and MGB—that political and criminal prisoners were separated in the prisons. However, even after 1949 there were still a few criminals in the "political" camps, such as those who had received additional sentences for attempting to escape, for "sabotage," for anti-Soviet tattooing, etc. The strength of the criminals and their organizations was significantly weakened, and conditions in the camps improved. Each "corrective" or "special" camp had its own production plan which it was required to fulfill. After 1948–1949, however, the influx of "labor power" into the camps declined. The general exhaustion of the prisoners in the early postwar years was so great that in many instances, out of two or three thousand men on the rolls only about one hundred would turn out for work in the mines. These "economic" causes alone induced the camp administration to look after its "labor power." Of the people arrested and placed in the camps in 1937–1938, no more than 10 to 15 percent survived and made it to freedom.

Many of the camp bosses taunted the political prisoners and delighted in dreaming up humiliations. On receiving a group of prisoners exhausted by a long journey, a boss in a large northern camp lined them up in front of the gates and ordered: "Those with higher education, one step forward." Some took the step, hoping apparently that their knowledge would be used somehow in the camp. "OK, you scholars," he said to those who had stepped out, "forward, march! Clean the outhouses!"

In 1938 a wave of undisguised terror on a massive scale struck down thousands of innocent people without trial or investigation, following charges of sabotage or attempted rebellion or simply on the basis of lists sent from Moscow. According to A. I. Todorsky, in 1938 commissions were sent to the northern camps, where they finished off political prisoners who had received five- and ten-year sentences. Most of them were former members of opposition groups and had been imprisoned since the early thirties. One such commission, consisting of a special NKVD official, Kashketin, the head of the special section of Camp Administration,

Grigorishin, and the head of the third operations section of the NKVD, Chuchelov, sentenced many prisoners in the Ukhta camp in the Komi Autonomous Republic to be shot. This same Kashketin commission also terrorized Vorkuta. The commission had its own special execution squad. Kashketin's men, covering themselves with declarations about some kind of counterrevolutionary organization preparing a prison rebellion, shot several thousand political prisoners.

According to A. Pergament, who belonged to the Trotskyist opposition in the twenties and who by some miracle survived the Vorkuta camp, most of the executions at Vorkuta occurred near the Vorkuta brick factory, where prisoners at first were kept in hastily erected tents; later they were told they were being transferred to a different part of the camp, only to be machine-gunned as they marched along, never suspecting what was in store for them.[35]

After Kashketin and his commission had fulfilled their terrible mission, they were themselves arrested and killed. As Baitalsky writes in his memoirs:

In the spring of 1938, special groups of prisoners selected on the basis of certain lists were brought to Vorkuta from the various camp locations along the river—Kochemas, Sivaya Maska, etc. They marched on foot, driven by the guards. But the guards did not succeed in getting some of them across the swollen streams, and it took the prisoners a long time to find out what the hurry was for. The guards were in a hurry to kill them. Those whom they managed to get to Vorkuta on time, they shot. During that year the Vorkuta camps were at the mercy of a ferocious man, a man whose name was uttered only after looking over one's shoulder. Later, from a window at the Kotlas prison could be heard the cry, "Tell the people that I am Kashketin! I am the one who shot all the enemies of the people! Tell the people!"

These cries were heard that very year, but no one told about it until many years later. The platoon of guards who had carried out the massacres also disappeared.

Of course, Kashketin had precisely fulfilled the orders of his superiors, and they in turn had specific orders from god himself [i.e., Stalin]. The Kashketins were dispatched everywhere: to the northern camps of Siberia, to the camps of Pechora, the Far East, and elsewhere, the "isolators" and the prisons. The Kashketins carried out a secret purge of the party wielding machine-guns. . . . The death sentences were handed down on the basis of a list that would be sent to Moscow for confirmation. The executioners awaited the official stamp from Moscow saying "Approved." By whom it did not say.[36]

35. In the early 1920s Pergament was one of Trotsky's assistants. Trotsky of course was then a member of the Politburo. I interviewed Pergament several times in the 1960s.
36. Baitalsky, "Tetradi dlia vnukov."

Local camp authorities did not lag behind these central commissions. They had the right to kill prisoners even without lists approved by Moscow. In 1938, on charges of sabotage and other fabricated charges, at least 40,000 prisoners were shot in the Kolyma region by the head of Dalstroi, Pavlov, his assistant, Colonel Garanin, and their apprentices. Garanin went especially wild. Arriving at a camp, he would order all "shirkers" to be lined up. This usually meant sick people and physical wrecks. Some could not stand on their feet. Garanin would walk down the line in a fury, shooting many at close range. Two soldiers followed him, taking turns reloading his revolver. The guards often stacked the corpses at the gates like a dam of timbers, and the work brigades passing by would be told, "The same thing will happen to you for shirking."

In 1939 Garanin, like Kashketin, was shot on charges of "espionage" and "wrecking." Many prison camp directors were removed and even shot. This was a result of Yezhov's ouster from the leadership of the NKVD. But to the prisoners this brought only a brief respite. When the Great Patriotic War began, their situation again became unbearable; almost everywhere the workday was lengthened, and the starvation rations were "temporarily" reduced. According to P. I. Negretov, in 1942 in the logging division of the camps in the Komi ASSR the entire complement of prisoners often died out in the course of a hundred to a hundred and fifty days. The average number of prisoners in the Soviet Union in 1941–1942 was approximately equal to the number of soldiers on active duty in the army. At that time the loss of people in the East and West was also approximately equal.

■ 4
NKVD PERSONNEL: THEIR CONDUCT AND RESPONSIBILITY

The question of the *pridurki,* the "trusties," the inmates who found fairly warm and easy positions in the camps, the question whether there was a certain degree of collaboration between such prisoners and the camp administration—this question, which has greatly exercised all authors of camp memoirs, goes beyond the framework of this book. I will note only that nearly all who managed to survive the difficulties of life in the camps and went on to describe that life spent most of their terms employed elsewhere than at ordinary manual labor ("general work," as it was called in the camps). This goes for Solzhenitsyn as well as Boris Dyakov, for

Eugenia Ginzburg, and Lev Kopelev, Varlam Shalamov and I. P. Gavrilov, Pavel Shabalkin and Yelizeveta Drabkina, A. I. Todorsky and Suren Gazaryan. For that reason alone it would be wrong to judge too harshly those who found relatively soft spots for themselves in Stalin's death camps. The most important question is whether these people tried to ease the sufferings of others, to help others survive, or whether they themselves became part of the monstrous machinery for destroying prisoners.

On the other hand, I will speak at some length about the people who worked the system of terror that Stalin organized, who ran the machine of suppression, only parts of which have been sketched here. There were, of course, different types in the NKVD even during the height of the Stalinist terror. Many soldiers and junior officers among the NKVD troops, those who hardly ever came in contact with the prisoners, who served as guards outside the camps, did not know that they were guarding innocent Soviet citizens, rather than criminals.

Others knew the truth but did not fully understand the causes of the frightful tragedy. Such officials often tried somehow to help prisoners. There is considerable evidence of this in the writings of Dyakov, Ginzburg, Shalamov, and Gazaryan and in other published and unpublished materials.

Yelizaveta Drabkina has given me a curious example. There was an industrial enterprise in the north, where the workers were mostly politicals, while all but the highest offices were held by thieves. For a long time it had not fulfilled its production plan. At the beginning of the war a new director, V. A. Kundush, was sent out from Leningrad, as a punishment for his "liberalism." He asked the factory controller, a former party member, for a list of former Communists in the work brigades. From this list he picked replacements for all the thieves in important jobs. The enterprise immediately became a pacemaker, and throughout the war held the Red Banner for Management. After the war Kundush obtained the early release of many prisoners "for good work" but soon found himself a prisoner.

The majority of Yezhov's and Beria's subordinates were men of a different type. They understood very well that their bosses were criminals, their victims innocent, but the realization only intensified their sadistic ardor in fabricating cases and extracting confessions. The writer Boris Dyakov tells how investigator Melnikov sneered at him: "Prove to us you are 100 percent crystal pure and you'll get ten years, otherwise a piece of lead."[37]

Gazaryan tells of an old teacher in Barnaul, Siberia, A. A. Afanasyev, who was originally accused of creating, during the civil war, a terrorist group to kill Lenin *if he should come to Barnaul*. But the chief would not endorse the case because the accusation was so fanciful. So the investigator made a new accusation: Afanasyev was a Japanese spy. "Well, so what?" said the sick old man. "I can become a Japanese spy." But once again the case was not endorsed by the central office because there was no indication of how Afanasyev sent his reports to Japan. So new searches began in Barnaul for the spy's accomplices. This time they found the "resident" of Japanese intelligence in the city—a railroad worker. And all these people were shot.

Fritz Platten, the Swiss Communist, was accused of having been a German spy since 1917, when he arranged Lenin's return to Russia. In spite of savage torture, he refused to sign the deposition because it would have cast a shadow on Lenin. Finally he and the investigator compromised: he would confess to spying for some country other than Germany —the United States or Argentina, my source does not recall exactly which.[38]

In Rostov-on-Don, according to V. I. Volgin, a captain of the river fleet was asked to sign a statement that when he was a commander of the tanker *Smely* he had sunk the torpedo boat *Burny* with an explosive shell. The captain laughed and asked the investigator if he knew what a tanker was. "Tanker, tank," the interrogator muttered, "it's an armed boat." "No, not at all," explained the captain. "It's a boat that carries oil and cannot destroy a torpedo boat." "Well, to hell with you," said the investigator calmly. "Write it the other way round, the way it has to be, and you can go to a camp with fresh air. But here you'll rot." Twenty-seven people in the same cell were forced to sign a statement that they had burned down the Rostov mill for diversionary purposes, while thirteen men "confessed" to having blown up a railway drawbridge over the Don. But both the mill and the bridge are still standing in Rostov, in good condition except for the damage done during the war.

According to Ya. I. Drobinsky, one of the commanders of the Belorussian military district, Povarov, admitted that he had formed a counter-

37. *Oktyabr* (1964), no. 7, p. 82.
38. M. F. Pozigun, a party member since 1920, heard this from Platten in a prison hospital.

revolutionary military organization and named more than forty people whom he had allegedly recruited—made-up names of nonexistent commanders. On the basis of this "evidence," Povarov was tried and condemned. The investigators did not know that the people named were nonexistent, but they knew very well that anyone named in an investigation would not run away. The local NKVD had already fulfilled its plan with the required number of arrests, so that these names could be put "in reserve," to fulfill future arrest plans.

Plans and "control figures" for arrests actually did exist. Local areas received their arrest plans from Moscow. Telegrams in code reported that "in your oblast, according to the information of the central investigating agencies, there were so many terrorists or ASAs [anti-Soviet agitators]. Find them and try them." The NKVD agencies had to fulfill these quotas and wait for a new quota the next month or quarter.

One day in 1937 the chief editor of a Ukrainian newspaper, A. I. Babinets, was summoned to the NKVD. He was told to edit the introductory part of an indictment of "a kulak terrorist center." Working at night in the NKVD director's office, Babinets heard the director calling the regional offices of the NKVD, demanding increases in the "index figures" of the fight against "enemies of the people." "How many did you take today?" he would shout. "Twelve! Not enough, far from enough." "And you?" he would say to another raion. "Sixty? Good, great work. Only watch you don't drop off at the end of the month." To a third: "What! You arrested only five people? Have you already built complete communism in your raion, or what?" And then, turning to Babinets, he said, "I have to put the pressure on. Soon they'll phone from Moscow, and then what could I tell them, what sort of report could I make?"[39]

It is astonishing—and instructive—to see how careless most NKVD searches were. In making the arrests, the agents usually seized papers and letters but did not bother to open floors, sofas, mattresses, and the like. (They also took articles of value, such as gold, but those items never appeared in the record of the search.) They knew from experience that they would not find "compromising" documents and did not waste time. It was much easier and faster to think up some story and get its confirmation by torture. Neither did they waste much time analyzing papers seized during arrests; after a brief examination such material would as a rule be destroyed. It is hard to imagine how much valuable material was

39. As told to me by Babinets.

lost this way. A vast number of precious manuscripts and papers were taken from Academician Vavilov and other scientists, from hundreds of writers and poets, from prominent government and party leaders. All vanished without a trace. Almost none of the investigators regarded confiscated papers as evidence they could use to expose the criminal. According to the playwright A. K. Gladkov, one arrested scholar had three original letters of Immanuel Kant. One would think that these letters, written in German, would attract the investigators' special attention. Not at all. The letters were burned without even being translated. In the record, which was shown to the prisoner after rehabilitation, they are listed as letters "by an unknown author in a foreign language."[40]

In a number of cases arrests, even of important officials, were made with no searches at all. The Moscow apartment of Livshits, deputy commissar of communications and one of the main defendants in the trial of the "Parallel Center," was not searched. Livshits was arrested in Khabarovsk, brought to Moscow, and after several months of investigation and trial was shot. During all this time, according to his widow, their Moscow apartment was never searched. No one showed any interest in the contents of his desks, his papers, letters, or notes. After he had been tried and shot, she phoned the appropriate agency to come and take her husband's gun.

Most of the judges and procurators must have known what they were doing when they sanctioned the arrest of innocent people and then sentenced them to be shot or imprisoned. These officers of the law knew that they were creating lawlessness, but they chose to be its creators rather than its victims. "Without a shudder constricting my heart," writes M. M. Ishov, a military procurator who refused to serve the terror machine,

it is impossible for me to recall the name of Sonya Ulyanova. She worked in the second section of the Chief Military Procuracy. All the cases fabricated in the NKVD against good Soviet citizens passed through the bloodstained hands of this woman, who was ready to climb over mountains of corpses of loyal Communists to save her own worthless life.[41]

Likewise, virtually all camp directors and officers understood what kind of prisoners they were dealing with but went ahead with their savage job anyhow.

40. This account is based on letters to me from Gladkov.
41. Ishov, *Gody potriasenii i tiazhelykh ispytanii.*

What turned many NKVD officials into sadists? What forced them to break all the laws of humanity? Many of them were once good Communists or Komsomol members, who joined the NKVD on orders, not at all by inclination. Many influences were at work on them. In the first place, there was the fear of becoming prisoners themselves, which overrode all other feelings. One of the well-informed people with whom I spoke told me, "Out of fear of being shot or tortured, many of those who had been arrested confessed, almost without resistance to anything at all during investigation, thus becoming NKVD collaborators. But the majority of NKVD personnel were shackled by this very same fear." Secondly, a terrible process of selection went on within the NKVD, sifting out some officials, leaving the worst. Especially addressing this question of the "wolf-tribe of butchers," Solzhenitsyn points out that many NKVD personnel were corrupted by the unlimited power over the prisoners that Stalin gave to the NKVD. Recalling how he himself changed after being given power over people along with his rank as an officer in the Soviet army, how he personally carried out many minor but base actions because he had power, how at the institute they were trying to recruit him to join not only the military academy but also the department of the NKVD, Solzhenitsyn exclaims:

I credited myself with unselfish dedication. But meanwhile I had been thoroughly prepared to be an executioner. And if I had gotten into an NKVD school under Yezhov, maybe I would have matured just in time for Beria.[42]

Solzhenitsyn cites Tolstoy's words about the corrupting influence of material power. Dostoevsky also wrote in his *Notes from the House of the Dead:*

Whoever has experienced the power, the complete ability, to humiliate another human being . . . with the most extreme humiliation, willy-nilly loses power over his own sensations. Tyranny is a habit, it has a capacity for development, it develops finally into a disease. I insist that the habit can dull and coarsen the very best man to the level of a beast. Blood and power are intoxicating. . . . The man and the citizen die within the tyrant forever; return to human dignity, to repentance, to regeneration, becomes almost impossible.[43]

NKVD personnel were especially trained to be capable of carrying out any order, even the most criminal. The special brigades of torturers, for

42. See the chapter "The Bluecaps" in Solzhenitsyn, *The Gulag Archipelago*, (New York, 1974), p. 168.
43. Fyodor Dostoevsky, *Sobranie sochinenii* Vol. 3, (Moscow, 1956), pp. 596–597.

example, usually included students from the NKVD schools, young people eighteen to twenty years old. They were taken to torture chambers, as medical students are taken to dissection laboratories, and thus were turned into sadists. Many of Yezhov's and Beria's torturers were destroyed in the Stalin era, and others were punished in 1953–1955 and in the period following the Twentieth Congress. But quite a few got off with only a mild scare: they were dismissed from their jobs and retired or given other work. Most of them attributed—and continue to attribute— their crimes and inhuman cruelty to orders from above, to the decrees of Stalin, Yezhov, Beria and other "bosses." But the International Military Tribunal at Nuremberg decided—and the Soviet Union endorsed the decision—that orders which contradict basic rules of morality, which flout the ethical imperatives on which human society is founded and destroy the very foundations of human community, cannot serve as a moral or legal justification for those who carry out such orders.

In the last pages of Vladimir Maksimov's novel *Quarantine* there is a description of a prophetic dream that comes to the hero Boris:

A silent procession stretched past them from one horizon to the other, and the end of this purposeful movement was not visible. In overcoats and padded jackets, in bandages and on crutches, covered with decorations and number cards, in the armor of dinner jackets and uniforms, in front of Boris passed his "neighbors of this century," his contemporaries, countrymen, and workmates— ministers, ordinary laborers, thieves, marshals who had been shot, guards, judges, executioners, saints and sinners, righteous men and good-for-nothings, poets and tradesmen.
  "Will they make it?"
  "They will."
  "Do they have something to repent?"
  "They do."
  "Which of them is guilty?"
  "All and none."
  "Does that mean they are cleansed?"
  "Now they are, yes."
  The measure of pain which befell them is greater than their sins. They washed their path on earth with such blood and tears that they cannot arouse any feeling but pity and compassion. There is no punishment for them and no one to judge them. Who would dare throw stones at them?
  Who can say that, in the night of fear and hatred through which they had to pass, he himself would have remained bright and stainless? Did they really know what they were doing when they persecuted and tortured each other? It was equally horrible for the persecutors and the persecuted. The truth made its way

through the sufferings they experienced in common. His love is with them, all of them.[44]

I don't know how this philosophy of absolution, making equal the butchers and their victims, scoundrels and righteous men, agrees with the principles of Christianity. I only know that the degree of pain, blood, and tears that befell my "neighbors of this century" was very unequal, and many of the butchers were completely aware that they were doing evil, not good. I am sure that an unequal fate awaits the butchers and their victims before the judgment of history (and, some of my friends think, before the judgment of God).

STALINISM:
ITS NATURE AND CAUSES

9

THE PROBLEM OF STALIN'S RESPONSIBILITY

STALIN'S LEADING ROLE IN THE REPRESSION OF 1937–1938

To many people in the Soviet Union the mass repression of 1937–1938 was a terrifying and incomprehensible calamity around which numerous legends and stories arose almost immediately. Explanations abounded, some of them representing a search for the truth; most often, however, they were attempts to escape the cruel truth, to find some formula that would preserve faith in the party and Stalin. Some of these legends and stories are worth examining, especially since many people still believe them. One of the most widespread stories was that Stalin did not know about the terror, that all those crimes were committed behind his back.

Of course it was ridiculous to suppose that Stalin, master of everyone and everything, did not know about the arrest and shooting of members of the Politburo and Central Committee, people's commissars, secretaries of oblast party committees, the military high command, top economic officials, Comintern leaders, leading writers and scholars, and his own relatives and friends. It was naive and ridiculous to picture Stalin as a man completely cut off from reality, ignorant of what was happening on this earth, and still to worship him. But this is a peculiarity common to the religious type of mentality, which blindly believes in some sort of higher being. This kind of thinking has its own logic: it identifies everything good as coming from the deity and everything bad as the work of Satan. It is this peculiarity of the religious mentality that explains the stories about Stalin's ignorance of what was going on.

"We thought," writes Ilya Ehrenburg, "(probably because we wanted to think so) that Stalin did not know about the senseless ravaging of Communists, of the Soviet intelligentsia." Ehrenburg tells about an encounter with Pasternak, who "waving his hands among the snowdrifts, kept repeating: 'If only someone would report all this to Stalin!' Meyerhold, too, kept repeating: 'They're hiding it from Stalin.' "[1]

Many people thought that wreckers, headed by Yezhov, had wormed their way into the NKVD and were destroying the party's best cadres without Stalin's knowledge. This kind of thinking is typified by the conversation that occurred between F. A. Stebnev, commissar of the 29th Rifle Division, and A. Ya. Vedenin, commander of the Vyazma Military District and future commander of the Kremlin.

"What's going on, Andrei Yakovlevich?" Stebnev asked me. "What's going on?" He walked nervously about the room. "I don't believe there are so many enemies in the party. I don't believe it. Can it be that in some high party office, in the security organs, there are alien people? It's as if they are deliberately destroying the party's cadres. I would bet my head that Joseph Vissarionovich doesn't know about this. Warnings, complaints, protests are being intercepted and don't reach him. Stalin must be informed. Otherwise, disaster. Tomorrow they'll take you, and after you me. We can't keep quiet."[2]

That was the opinion of hundreds and thousands of officials, rank-and-file party members, even many prisoners and their relatives. D. A. Lazurkina, an official in the Leningrad obkom, survived to tell the Twenty-Second Congress:

1. *Novy mir* (1962), no. 5, p. 152.
2. A. Ya. Vedenin, *Gody i liudi* (Moscow, 1964), p. 55.

When they arrested me . . . I felt such a horror, not for myself but for the party. I couldn't understand why they were arresting Old Bolsheviks. For what? . . . I told myself something horrible was happening in the party, probably wrecking. And this gave me no rest. Not for one minute, though I spent two and a half years in prison, then was sent to a camp, then into exile, . . . did I ever accuse Stalin. I always stood up for Stalin when other prisoners cursed him. I would say: "No, it cannot be that Stalin has permitted all that has happened in the party. It cannot be."[3]

The philosopher Arnosht Kolman was arrested several years after World War II. He found himself in the same cell as G. A. Vorozheikin, a marshal of the air force, who had fought in both world wars and in the civil war. Vorozheikin, because of his high position, had frequently encountered Stalin and formed an opinion about him, blaming him specifically for the mass repression. Kolman writes:

I tried to convince Vorozheikin that he was profoundly mistaken. He was blinded [I said] by a fully understandable feeling of personal offense, which he felt especially strongly because his own merits were especially great. He was looking at these ghastly events subjectively and not from the only correct point of view, as part of a historical process brought about by the class struggle. It wasn't a matter of Stalin personally. Stalin was a theoretician of genius and a revolutionary leader, who was carrying forward Lenin's cause, just as Lenin had carried forward that of Marx and Engels. But Stalin was as much a victim of the Fifth Column as we were. The imperialists, seeing the failure of their attempts to finish off the Soviet Union from the outside, through war and intervention, were trying to destroy it from within through such agents as Yagoda, Yezhov, and Beria.[4]

This naive conviction of Stalin's ignorance was reflected in the word "Yezhovshchina," "the Yezhov thing," the popular name for the tragedy of the thirties. The sudden disappearance of Yezhov seemed to confirm this story, which was only a new version of the common people's faith in a good tsar surrounded by lying and wicked ministers.

But it must also be acknowledged that this story had some basis in Stalin's behavior. Secretive and self-contained, Stalin avoided the public eye. Although his name was on everyone's lips, he acted through unseen channels. He tried to direct events from behind the scenes, making basic decisions by himself or with a few aides. He rarely addressed meetings in 1936–1938 and never advertised his part in the mass repression,

3. *Dvadtsat' vtoroi s"ezd KPSS. Stenograficheskii otchet*, (Moscow, 1962), 3:119.
4. Arnosht [Ernest] Kolman, *My ne dolzhny byli tak zhit'* (New York, 1982), pp. 290–291. Kolman emigrated from the Soviet Union in 1976 and went to Sweden. He died there in 1979.

preferring to put the spotlight on other perpetrators of these crimes, thereby retaining his own freedom of movement. Moreover, many of his speeches gave the impression that he was not well informed about the repression. For example, at the February–March Plenum of the Central Committee in 1937 he demanded that there be no arrests of Trotskyists and Zinovievists who had broken all ties with Trotsky and ended oppositional activity. At that very time thousands of such people were being arrested. Stalin also rebuked those who considered it a trifle to expel tens of thousands from the party. At that very time not tens but hundreds of thousands were being expelled and arrested.

Shortly before the arrest of the civil war hero D. F. Serdich, Stalin toasted him at a reception, suggesting that they drink to "Bruderschaft."[5] Just a few days before Blyukher's destruction, Stalin spoke of him warmly at a meeting. When an Armenian delegation came to him, Stalin asked about the poet Charents and said that he should not be touched,[6] but a few months later Charents was arrested and killed. The wife of A. Serebrovsky, a deputy people's commissar of Ordzhonikidze's, tells of an unexpected phone call from Stalin one evening in 1937. "I hear you are going about on foot," Stalin said. "That's no good. People might think what they shouldn't. I'll send you a car if yours is being repaired." And the next morning a car from the Kremlin arrived for Mrs. Serebrovsky's use. But two days later her husband was arrested, taken right from the hospital.

R. G. Alikhanova tells about the case of G. I. Broido, one of Stalin's former aides in the Commissariat of Nationalities. When NKVD men came to his door late at night, rather than let them in he rushed to the internal Kremlin telephone and called Stalin. "Koba, they've come for me," said Broido. "Foolishness," Stalin replied. "Who could bring charges against you? Go calmly to the NKVD and help them establish the truth." Still, Broido was lucky. After only two years in prison he was freed in 1940. It was a different story with Nikolai Krylenko, commissar of justice of the USSR. After being removed from his post, he spent several days turning things over to the new commissar, N. M. Rychkov. Then Krylenko went to his dacha outside Moscow, where his family had gathered. Suddenly a phone call came from Moscow. It was Stalin. "Don't get upset," he said. "We trust you. Keep doing the work you were assigned to on the new legal code." Stalin's phone call calmed Krylenko and his

5. I. D. Ochak, *D. Serdich* (Moscow, 1964).
6. The artist M. Saryan told Ehrenburg of this incident.

family, but that very night a special operations group of the NKVD surrounded Krylenko's dacha. After bursting into his home, they arrested him and almost all the members of his family.[7]

A. V. Snegov reports that L. Ye. Maryasin, director of the USSR State Bank, took the occasion of a meeting with Stalin to tell him that he feared for his own fate. Stalin embraced Maryasin with these words: "But you're not an oppositionist. You're our own Red banker. What have you got to be afraid of?" Within a week Maryasin was arrested.

The famous historian and publicist Yu. Steklov, disturbed by all the arrests, phoned Stalin and asked for an appointment. "Of course, come on over," Stalin said, and reassured him when they met: "What's the matter with you? The party knows and trusts you; you have nothing to worry about." Steklov returned to his friends and family, and that very evening the NKVD came for him. Naturally the first thought of his friends and family was to appeal to Stalin, who seemed unaware of what was going on.[8] It was much easier to believe in Stalin's ignorance than in such subtle perfidy. In 1938 I. A. Akulov, onetime procurator of the Soviet Union and later secretary of the Central Executive Committee, fell while skating and suffered an almost fatal concussion. On Stalin's personal orders outstanding surgeons were brought from abroad to save his life. After a difficult recovery lasting many months, Akulov returned to work, whereupon he was arrested, and in 1939 he was shot.[9]

In 1937 Aleksandr Milchakov, who was working in the administration of the gold mining industry, was suddenly removed from his job and expelled from the party. But a few days later the party organizer of the administration searched him out and said anxiously, "Let's go to the Kremlin; Stalin's asking for you." In the Kremlin office were Stalin and Kaganovich. "What have things come to," said Stalin, "if they're expelling people like Milchakov?" Then he said to Milchakov: "We're appointing you deputy chief of Glavzoloto (the Chief Administration for Gold Mining). Go and carry out your duties." Two or three weeks later Milchakov became the head of Glavzoloto, after the arrest of Serebrovsky. After another two months, however, Milchakov was arrested and did not see Moscow again for sixteen years. Quite a few such cases could be cited.

It was Stalin who called a special plenum of the Central Committee in

7. *Partiia shagaet v revoliutsiiu* (Moscow, 1964), p. 236.
8. This episode is reported by I. P. Aleksakhin.
9. Reported by M. V. Ostrogorsky.

January 1938, when more than half the members of the Central Committee had already been arrested, to pass the resolution "On the mistakes of party organizations in expelling Communists, on the bureaucratic handling of the appeals of those expelled, and on measures to eliminate these shortcomings." Presenting scattered figures on expulsions that had been rescinded by the Control Commission and on "enemy" accusations that had been proved groundless by the NKVD, the resolution attacked the expellers and accusers:

All these facts show that many of our party organizations . . . have not exposed the cleverly masked enemy who hides . . . behind shouts for vigilance, . . . and tries to slaughter our Bolshevik cadres and sow distrust and excessive suspiciousness in our ranks.[10]

Whereupon the Central Committee ordered all party organizations to cease "mass, wholesale expulsions," to decide each case on an individual basis, to get rid of party officials who did not take the individual approach, and to review the appeals of expelled members within a three-month period.

Much of this resolution, edited and in parts actually written by Stalin himself, was ambiguous, but it roused great hopes for an end to mass repression and a review of arrests already made. Those hopes were strengthened by press reports in January and February 1938 that some expelled Communists had been reinstated in the party and some false accusers had been punished. But the January plenum was nothing more than a political diversion. Repression resumed in the spring of 1938 on a scale even greater than in 1937. Mass expulsions from the party (based on lists) also continued. It was in 1938 that conditions in the camps worsened drastically, with mass executions being carried out, and in the prisons permission was granted for the use of torture on all categories of political prisoners under investigation.

Stalin's decisive role in the activities of the punitive organs was discussed in many oblast and republic party meetings in 1937–1938. When Kaganovich, Andreev, Malenkov, Mikoyan, Shkiryatov, and others arrived in the provinces to direct the repression, they invariably made the point that they were acting on Stalin's orders. Their speeches, however, were not published. Only on the eve of the Eighteenth Party Congress, after Yezhov's dismissal, did the press begin to emphasize Stalin's leading role in the assault on "enemies of the people." The theme was continued

10. *Pravda*, January 19, 1938.

by many speakers at the congress itself in March 1939. Shkiryatov, for example, declared:

Comrade Stalin has directed the work of purging enemies who have wormed their way into the party. Comrade Stalin taught us how to fight wreckers in a new way; he taught us how to get rid of these hostile elements quickly and decisively.[11]

Some delegates gave enthusiastic details. Mishakova, for example, told how Stalin helped her purge the Komsomol. She began on her own in Chuvashia, but the Komsomol Central Committee tried to curb her.

Kosarev's gang . . . were entrenched in the CC. . . . I sent a letter to Comrade Stalin telling him of the irregularities in the Komsomol Central Committee. Although he was very busy, Comrade Stalin found time to read my letter. The result was an investigation . . . and the Stalinist resolution adopted at the Komsomol CC's seventh plenum.[12]

Many years later, further details were made public. At first Shkiryatov was given the job of checking Mishakova's accusations. He supported her, but only to the extent of suggesting that Kosarev be reprimanded for "persecuting" Mishakova. Shkiryatov sent this proposal to Stalin, with a covering note: "Dear Joseph Vissarionovich: As always, I am sending this memo to you. If something is not right, you will correct me." And Stalin did "correct" Shkiryatov. In his speech to the seventh plenum of the Komsomol CC, Shkiryatov shouted: "You, Kosarev, wanted to kill everything Stalinist and Bolshevik in Mishakova, but you didn't succeed, because Stalin intervened in this matter."[13]

Even then Stalin continued to cover up the traces of his crimes. He told a group of delegates to the Eighteenth Congress that Yezhov had arrested many more people than he was "allowed." He repeated this story more than once in the period before the war when the acute shortage of qualified people became apparent. The airplane designer A. S. Yakovlev recalls the following in his memoirs:

In the summer of 1940 Stalin said these precise words in a conversation with me:

11. *Vosemnadtsatyi s"ezd VKP(b). Stenograficheskii otchet* (Moscow, 1939), p. 175.
12. Ibid., p. 561.
13. From a speech by Valentina Pikina at a meeting in the Museum of the Revolution on November 21, 1963, in honor of Kosarev's sixtieth birthday.

"Yezhov is a rat; in 1938 he killed many innocent people. We shot him for that."

I wrote these words down immediately after returning from the Kremlin.[14]

Today many details and documents have become known showing beyond any doubt that Stalin knew about all the main acts of repression; they were, in fact, done on his direct instructions. Here is one such document, read to the Twenty-Second Congress by Z. T. Serdyuk:

Comrade Stalin:
I am sending for confirmation four lists of people whose cases are before the Military Collegium:
    (1) List No. 1 (general)
    (2) List No. 2 (former military personnel)
    (3) List No. 3 (former NKVD personnel)
    (4) List No. 4 (wives of enemies of the people).
I request approval for first-degree condemnation of all these people.

                                                   Yezhov

Condemnation in the first degree *(pervaia kategoria)* meant shooting.

While personally directing repression at the center, Stalin spurred on his aides and accomplices. Armenia provides a typical example. After Ter-Gabrielyan was fired—he had been chairman of the Armenian Council of Commissars—and after Khandzhyan was murdered—he had been first secretary of the Armenian Central Committee—state and party cadres were subjected to mass terror. The new party chiefs, G. Amatuni, S. Akopov, and K. Mugdusi, striving to win the favor of Stalin and Beria, killed many leading officials, including Ter-Gabrielyan. But Stalin was still dissatisfied with their work. Mikoyan was sent to Armenia, accompanied by Malenkov. At a plenary session of the Armenian Central Committee they read a letter from Stalin dated September 8, 1937, criticizing the republic's economic and cultural development, its disorderly agriculture and industrial stagnation, its toleration of Trotskyist and anti-party elements. In this context Stalin rebuked the Armenian party leaders for "protecting" enemies of the people, asserting that "enemy of the people" Ter-Gabrielyan had been killed prematurely to prevent the exposure of other enemies. "It is intolerable," the letter said, "that enemies of the Armenian people should be playing around freely in Armenia." Consequently Amatuni, Akopov, and Mugdusi were expelled from the party and arrested. G. A. Arutyunyan was made first secretary, and repression became especially massive and bloody.[15]

---

14. A. S. Yakovlev, *Tsel' zhizni: zapiski konstruktora* (Moscow, 1966), p. 179.
15. *Ocherki po istorii KP(b) Armenii* (Yerevan, 1964), p. 355.

Stalin took an equally active part in the destruction of cadres in Uzbekistan. It was on Stalin's personal orders that Khodzhaev, the chairman of the Uzbekistan Council of People's Commissars, was arrested. Earlier, in the revolutionary period, Khodzhaev had been one of the founders of the Young Bokhara movement (the Jadids). After the occupation of Bokhara by the Red Army he headed the government of the Bokhara Democratic Republic but did not join the Bolshevik Party until 1922. For some Bolsheviks Khodzhaev's nationalist past might have seemed suspicious. However, the man who replaced Khodzhaev as chairman of the Uzbekistan Council of People's Commissars—A. Karimov—was also arrested after a few months. At that point the Uzbek party leader Akmal Ikramov telephoned Stalin to say that he did not understand the NKVD's actions, that Karimov was a man who had been tested thoroughly and was irreproachable, that he could not be involved in any counterrevolutionary activities. It is not known what Stalin said in reply. Although Ikramov remained first secretary of the Uzbekistan Central Committee, no more phone calls from him were allowed to go through to Stalin.[16] Soon a secret letter signed by Stalin and Molotov arrived in Tashkent and was read to a special plenum of the Uzbekistan party's Central Committee. The letter accused Ikramov of political blindness toward bourgeois nationalists, allegedly headed by Khodzhaev, and of ties with Bukharin, A. V. Smirnov, I. Zelensky, and other ex-oppositionists who had already been arrested in Moscow. After the letter was read, a special committee was set up at the plenum, which hastily "established" the justice of the charges against Ikramov. The plenum then expelled Ikramov from the party and handed the matter over to the NKVD.[17] Ikramov was immediately arrested.

Stalin not only ordered arrests, but also closely followed many investigations. Sometimes, he interrogated prisoners himself, in his office. On occasion Stalin even gave orders about what kind of torture was to be used on one or another party official. And if the investigator still could not obtain the desired testimony, Stalin reprimanded the NKVD agents for "defects in their work." When the depositions of tortured prisoners included the names of their "accomplices," Stalin, without seeking further proof, wrote on the record "Arrest," or "Arrest everyone." When Yezhov, in one of his reports, told about the arrest of a group of officials —with the list attached—and declared that information on other persons

16. From the memoirs of the writer Kamil Ikramov, son of Akmal Ikramov.
17. *Ocherki istorii KP Uzbekistana* (Tashkent, 1964), pp. 295–296.

was being checked, Stalin underlined Yezhov's final words and wrote: "No need to check, arrest them."[18]

From speeches at the Twenty-Second Party Congress by Serdyuk, deputy chairman of the Commission of Party Control, and Aleksandr Shelepin, head of the KGB, it is evident that Stalin personally signed approximately four hundred lists of proscribed persons. These lists bore the names of 44,000 people, mostly party and government leaders, military personnel, and cultural figures. It is significant that in looking over these lists, Stalin sometimes deleted one name or another, with no concern whatsoever about the charges filed against the persons in question. For example, from a list of literary figures slated for arrest Stalin deleted the name of Lily Brik. "We won't touch the wife of Mayakovsky," he told Yezhov. Later Stalin "bestowed his mercy" on Mikhail Sholokhov, who had secretly fled to Moscow from his home in Veshenskaya, when a group of Chekists arrived to arrest him.

Many officials in local areas protested to Stalin, as Ikramov did, against the actions of the NKVD. A typical conversation occurred in September 1937, between Stalin and Vareikis, the secretary of the Far East kraikom.

"What did he tell you?" Vareikis' wife asked him. "It's terrible even to say," Vareikis replied. "At first I thought it wasn't Stalin but someone else on the phone. But it was him. . . . Yes, him. Stalin shouted: 'It's none of your business! Don't mix in where you don't belong. The NKVD knows what it's doing.' Then he said that only an enemy of the Soviet regime could defend Tukhachevsky and the others, and he slammed down the receiver."[19]

A few days later Vareikis was urgently summoned to Moscow and arrested. Four days later his wife was also arrested in Khabarovsk.

As for torture, Stalin not only knew about it; he initiated that method of "investigation." After the removal of Yezhov many local party leaders began to criticize NKVD agents for using torture, whereupon Stalin sent a coded telegram to obkom and kraikom secretaries and to officials of the NKVD, saying:

The Central Committee explains that from 1937 on the NKVD was given permission by the Central Committee to use physical influence. All bourgeois intelligence agencies use physical influence against representatives of the socialist proletariat. . . . Why should the socialist intelligence agency be more humane in relation to dedicated agents of the bourgeoisie, sworn enemies of the working

18. N. R. Mironov, *Programma KPSS i voprosy dal'neishego ukrepleniia zakonnosti i pravoporiadka* (Moscow, 1962), pp. 7–8.

19. *Pravda*, September 18, 1964.

class and the collective farmers? The Central Committee believes that the method of physical influence must necessarily be used in the future too, as an exception, against obvious and stubborn enemies of the people, as a completely correct and expedient method.[20]

Stalin knew perfectly well about the inhuman conditions in the "corrective-labor" camps. Early in 1938 a group of officials in the Kolyma region sent Stalin a telegram complaining about the arbitrary actions being committed by Pavlov, the new head of Dalstroi, and his aide Garanin. Stalin replied:

> To Nagaevo. The newspaper *Sovetskaia Kolyma*. To Osmakov, Romashev, Yagnenkov. Copy to Pavlov of Dalstroi. . . . Received long telegram of Osmakov, Romashev, and Yagnenkov with complaint about the regime in Dalstroi and the shortcomings in the work of Pavlov. The telegram does not take into consideration the difficulties in the work at Dalstroi and the specific conditions of Pavlov's work. I consider your telegram demagogical and unfounded. The newspaper should help Pavlov, not throw a wrench in the works. Stalin[21]

This telegram provoked an even greater orgy of terror in the Kolyma region, against Chekists as well as prisoners.

Of course Stalin did not and could not know about every instance of lawlessness. But the most important arrests and directives originated with him. While serving a term in a labor camp, the old Communist Pavel Shabalkin met a Chekist who had been in Stalin's personal bodyguard in 1937–1938. He told Shabalkin that Yezhov came to Stalin almost daily with a thick file of papers and that they would consult together for three or four hours. It is not hard to guess what those consultations were about. There is no reason to place the main responsibility on Yezhov or any other official supposedly acting without Stalin's knowledge. The main responsibility for what was truly "the Great Terror" lies unconditionally with Stalin—which does not relieve his aides of responsibility.

What drove Stalin to such unprecedented crimes, to the mass destruction of the basic cadres of the Soviet state and the Communist Party?

■ 2

WAS STALIN "DECEIVED"?

The contrast between the people's image of Stalin and the terrible truth revealed after the Twentieth Party Congress was so great that it was only

---

20. Khrushchev quoted this telegram in his secret speech to the Twentieth Congress.
21. *Sovetskaia Kolyma*, January 17, 1938.

natural for many Communists and friends of the Soviet Union abroad to try to soften that contrast, to ease the kind of shock a person would experience on suddenly learning that one's father, best friend, or beloved teacher was a criminal. This reaction, often combined with a desire to dampen criticism aimed at oneself or at the Communist movement as a whole, gave rise to a new story, which many people still believe: the tragedy of the "deceived" Stalin.

Conceding that Stalin killed tens of thousands of innocent people, that he was personally responsible for the mass repression of the thirties, these people argue that he intended no evil, that he was led astray by careerists, adventurers, and foreign intelligence agents, who wormed their way into the NKVD, in order to wipe out the best cadres and demoralize the people. Anna Louise Strong, for example, finds

the key [to the terror], most probably, in actual, extensive penetration of the GPU by a Nazi fifth column, in many actual plots and in the impact of these on a highly suspicious man who saw his own assassination plotted and believed he was saving the revolution by drastic purge. . . . Stalin engineered [the country's modernization] ruthlessly, for he was born in a ruthless land and endured ruthlessness from childhood. He engineered suspiciously, for he had been five times exiled and must have been often betrayed. [As if other Bolsheviks had not gone through the same hard experiences. — R.M.] He condoned, and even authorized, outrageous acts of the political police against innocent people, but so far no evidence is produced that he consciously framed them.[22]

Even after the Twenty-Second Party Congress this legend was repeated. I. Verkhovtsev, for example, pictured "Stalin's nasty and sick suspicious nature playing into the hands of foreign intelligence agencies, and also careerists, adventurers, and hostile elements, who wormed their way into the security organs and fabricated cases against leading party and state officials."[23] V. Tarianov follows the same line to conclude that Yezhov, Merkulov, Beria, and Abakumov were responsible, not Stalin.[24] Stalin's daughter, Svetlana, puts up the same defense of her father. Listing the many relatives and friends who were arrested and shot with his knowledge and consent, she cries:

How could father have done that? I know only one thing: he could not have thought it up by himself. . . . I believe that Beria was craftier, sneakier, more treacherous, more brazen, clearer in his goal, firmer, and consequently stronger

22. A. L. Strong, *The Stalin Era* (New York, 1956), pp. 68, 125.
23. I. Verkhovtsev, *Leninskie normy partiinoi zhizni* (Moscow, 1962), p. 29.
24. V. Tarianov, *Nevidimye boi* (Moscow, 1964), pp. 74–75.

than my father. My father had his weak points—he could feel doubts, he was more gullible, coarser, and rougher; he was simpler and could be taken in by a trickster like Beria.[25]

Some Western Communists have indulged in even wilder fancies, picturing Yezhov and Beria as the leaders of deep conspiratorial organizations, which systematically deceived Stalin on the direct orders of bourgeois intelligence agencies. They even claim that those agencies inspired the show trials of the thirties. This primitive tale has already been refuted by the facts I have cited.

The myth of the "deceived" Stalin is still supported by most of the writers and cultural figures who, in the Brezhnev era, zealously continued the effort to clean up and restore the image of Stalin as "the great father of the peoples." For example, A. Serdyuk, who suggested in an earlier novel, *Voina* (War), that Tukhachevsky and Yakir really were guilty, has recently written about Rokossovsky as follows:

It sometimes happened that disaster would break into the accustomed course of a busy life and shake up everything with its unexpectedness and essentiality. That's how things had happened in 1937—the groundless arrest, the absurd charges of spying for foreign intelligence, concocted by enemies of the October revolution who had hidden themselves deeply, who dreamed of restoring the old order and reacquiring their lost riches, and who for that purpose had done everything possible to weaken the command staff of the Red Army and bring discord into the ranks of the party and its leadership. They had brought many misfortunes upon the Soviet people. . . . But they had not broken Konstantin Rokossovsky; they had not planted bitterness and anger in his heart.[26]

Of course, Stalin was not clairvoyant. He was a very limited and suspicious man. Thus it is not surprising that at Stalin's "court," as at the court of every despot and tyrant, all kinds of intrigues and fierce struggles for power and influence were constantly in progress among his retinue. Cut off from the people by a wall of armor, Stalin was ill informed about the state of affairs in the the country and the party. This made it easy to lead him astray and to deceive him. Thus it is probable that some of his aides used slander and provocation to rouse his suspicions of individuals whom he had trusted in order to obtain his sanction for their arrest and execution. Beria was a master of such provocations. The 1955 trial of Beria's creatures in Georgia established, for example, that an attempt on

25. S. Alliluyeva, *Dvadtsat' pisem k drugu* (New York, 1968), pp. 74, 130. [Cf. the English edition, *Twenty Letters to a Friend*, pp. 88, 148.—G. S.]
26. See Serdyuk's novel "Moscow, 1941" in *Ogonyok*, 1985, No. 27, p. 23.

Beria's and Stalin's lives during a boat ride on the Black Sea was organized by Beria himself and that Stalin's life was not actually threatened. Some hoodlums hired by Beria shot in the air from the mountains, deliberately missing the target—and when they came to collect their reward, they were killed. This gave Beria the pretext he wanted to take revenge on Lakoba, chairman of the Central Executive Committee of Abkhazia, who was considered a personal friend of Stalin's. I would not be surprised to learn that Stalin himself was let in on the secret of this provocation. Rumors of such an attempt on his life were more important to Stalin than to Beria.

We know today that some foreign intelligence agencies did try some provocations aimed at deceiving Stalin. According to Fyodor Raskolnikov, for example, Bulgarian counterintelligence palmed off forged documents on Yezhov's agents and succeeded in provoking the arrest of almost all the members of the Soviet embassy in Bulgaria, from the chauffeur, M. I. Kazakov, to the military attache, V. T. Sukhorukov. But it would be a major mistake to see such intrigues and provocations as the main cause of the mass repression. To the contrary, it was the terror unleashed by Stalin that created favorable conditions for such intrigues by foreign intelligence.

The tragic fate of Tukhachevsky is illuminating in this respect. As early as the twenties the Western press tried to compromise him, attributing overweening ambition to him as a "Red Napoleon." The German generals knew Tukhachevsky and other Soviet military leaders from the period of Soviet-German military cooperation in the twenties and early thirties, when they met at maneuvers and when many "Red generals" studied at German military academies. The German military men appreciated the formidable talents of their prospective adversaries. As the purges began the Nazi leaders surmised that the vain and pretentious Stalin would probably come into conflict with his own talented generals. This prompted the Gestapo to organize a provocation to compromise Tukhachevsky and his colleagues.

In early 1937 the Gestapo forged a letter allegedly sent by Tukhachevsky to his "friends" in Germany, telling of the intentions of himself and his "sympathizers" to overcome civilian control by a coup d'etat. Not only Tukhachevsky's handwriting but also his characteristic style was imitated. On the forged letter were genuine Abwehr stamps: "top secret" and "confidential." Hitler himself wrote a note on it—an order to shadow the German generals who supposedly were in contact with Tukhachevsky. Today even the name of the engraver who forged Tukhachevsky's signature is known, as is the name of the Gestapo official in charge of the operation—Alfred Naujochs.[27]

To reach Stalin with this letter and other materials, there was a fake theft of Tukhachevsky's "dossier" by Czechoslovak intelligence agents during a fire in the Abwehr building. Eduard Benes tells in his memoirs how he received unofficial information in January 1937 that Hitler was negotiating with Tukhachevsky, Rykov, and others to overthrow Stalin and set up a pro-German government. Benes immediately passed all this information on to Moscow via the Soviet embassy in Prague.[28]

Thus one might think that with respect to Tukhachevsky Stalin really was tricked by German intelligence. But the true story of Tukhachevsky's destruction is more complicated, and much remains unclear. Reinhard Heydrich, second in command of the Gestapo, did not think up the idea of the Tukhachevsky "plot" himself; it was suggested to him by a Russian émigré general, Nikolai Skoblin, who had connections with the NKVD as well as the Gestapo. It was Skoblin who organized the kidnapping of General A. P. Kutepov, who headed the main émigré White Guard military organization, the Russian All-Military Alliance (ROVS), after the death of General Wrangel.[29]

Stalin had "reliable information" about Tukhachevsky's "treason" at the very beginning of 1937, but he let him continue as deputy commissar of defense. Moreover, the forged letters did not figure either in his trial or in the pretrial session of the Military Council that met June 1–4, 1937, to examine the case. The members of the Military Council were given fraudulent "depositions" by officers who had already been arrested, accusing Tukhachevsky and the others of planning a coup d'état. The forgeries made by the Gestapo were tacked onto the Tukhachevsky case only after Tukhachevsky and his comrades had been shot.

Stalin was an extremely secretive person; he never told anyone his true intentions. In this sense—and only in this sense—he had no partners in crime to whom he entrusted his plans. This opens the door to all sorts of

---

27. Gunther Reis, *Naujochs, l'homme qui declencha la guerre* (Paris, 1961), p. 88, cited in M. Heller and A. Nekrich, *Utopia u vlasti* (London, 1982), 1:325.

28. E. Benes, *Memoirs* (London, 1954), pp. 19–20, 47.

29. See Aleksandr Nekrich, *1941, 22 iiunia* (Moscow, 1965), pp. 86–87. See also Wilhelm Hoettl (pseudonym: Walter Hagen), *The Secret Front* (London, 1954), pp. 77–85; Victor Alexandrov, *The Tukhachevsky Affair* (Englewood Cliffs, N.J., 1964); and the memoirs of Walter Schellenberg, former head of the Gestapo, *The Labyrinth* (New York, 1956). [There is an English translation of Nekrich, which appeared under the name of V. Petrov, *June 22, 1942* (Columbia, S.C., 1968).—G. S.]

speculation about his motives. To the end of his days he insisted both in conversation and in his writings that all those he had destroyed were enemies of the people. In this case he deceived others but not himself. Actually, Stalin was totally preoccupied with the preservation of his unlimited power and contemptuous of almost everyone around him and of human life in general. The elimination of hundreds of thousands of people posed no moral problem to him. He undoubtedly knew that the thousands of party leaders arrested on his orders were neither spies nor traitors. All his behavior shows that his accusations against these people were deliberate slander.

If one were to go by the materials from the NKVD files of the thirties, one would have to conclude that far-flung networks of "right-Trotskyite, spy-terrorist, diversionist-wrecking organizations and centers" existed in almost every krai, oblast, and republic, for some reason always headed by the local first secretaries of the party organizations. It was not hard to see that the great bulk of these false accusations did not come to the NKVD from without; they were fabricated by its own investigators. A real factory of lies was in operation, turning out hundreds of thousands of false stories about all kinds of "plots," "terrorist acts," "espionage," and "diversions."

It would be a mistake to think that these false accusations were the main cause of the destruction of so many leading party figures. More often Stalin himself set the line to be followed by the investigators. The NKVD men had no authority to question or try to verify the accusations that came from Stalin. Their job was to "fill in the details" and obtain a confession from the accused by any means necessary. Khrushchev, in his secret speech to the Twentieth Congress, described a typical situation. Such top party leaders as Kosior, Chubar, and Kosarev were investigated by a man named Rodos—

an insignificant man with the mental horizon of a chicken, and the morality, literally, of a degenerate. . . . Could such a man on his own possibly have carried out an investigation to prove the guilt of men such as Kosior? No, he could not have done much without appropriate instructions. He said to the Presidium [i.e., the Politburo]: "They told me Kosior and Chubar were enemies of the people; therefore I, as the investigator, had to extract from them the confession that they were enemies."

There were, of course, some NKVD officials with well-developed intellects, such as Vyshinsky and Lev Sheinin, the investigator for specially important cases who went on to become a well-known author. But morally they were probably even more degenerate than Rodos.

Any serious investigation would have exposed the Nazi forgery against Tukhachevsky, but Stalin did not order an expert investigation. It would have been even easier to establish the falseness of many other materials produced by the NKVD, but neither Stalin nor his closest aides checked or wanted to check the authenticity of these materials.

When sanctioning the arrest and execution of his former colleagues and friends, Stalin never expressed a desire to meet and interrogate these people himself. He closely followed the reports of many investigations, so he knew that some prisoners would not admit their guilt despite the cruelest tortures. Nonetheless, he sanctioned their executions. He was also given last letters and declarations by many of his former colleagues, in which they reaffirmed their innocence, their devotion to the party and to Stalin, and asked Stalin to see them and to listen to them. But he invariably ignored these declarations and requests, although he put some of them in his safe and kept them for the rest of his life.

Eikhe's appeal, which was read to the Twentieth Party Congress, was especially moving. Writing on October 29, 1939, he confessed to one genuinely criminal act: signing a false confession. He described the torture that had extracted this confession from him: he had an imperfectly mended spine, which was used by the NKVD investigator to cause him unbearable pain. He pointed out the absurd disregard for facts that the investigator displayed and pleaded with Stalin to save the party from its real enemies, the people who were destroying innocent cadres. Stalin paid no more attention to this than to any other appeal. It was simply passed to Beria, and Eikhe was shot on February 4, 1940.

Another candidate member of the Politburo, Rudzutak, completely repudiated his confession at his trial before the Military Collegium of the Supreme Court. His hard-hitting accusation of his accusers and affirmation of his utter loyalty also went unanswered.[30] Stalin refused to talk with him, and Rudzutak was shot.

Lion Feuchtwanger reports in *Moscow 1937* that Stalin told him about a long letter from Radek, protesting his innocence. But Stalin had no desire to meet with Radek. One can imagine what Stalin's reaction to that letter was, for on the very next day he told Feuchtwanger that Radek had now "confessed" to all his crimes.

If we assume that Stalin was deeply convinced of the guilt of people repressed on his orders, it is impossible to explain why he took such pains to keep the investigations secret, making sure that no outside

---

30. Rudzutak's statement was also read by Khrushchev in his secret speech to the Twentieth Congress.

person, not even the procurator, could gain admittance to the torture chambers of the NKVD. Why did he take pains to revoke all due process with respect to political prisoners? Why did he take away their right to defense, to prove their innocence? Why did the usual political trial take place in prison and last only a few minutes? Why was such a trial an empty formality, with the sentence typed in advance? Why were many political prisoners given long prison terms in absentia, without any trial at all, by the decision of a so-called troika? Why were individuals labeled enemies of the people and expelled from the party as soon as they were arrested, long before investigations were finished? Why did Stalin establish the illegal system whereby the NKVD all by itself carried out the arrests, the investigations, the trials, the sentencing, and the executions? Such questions can never be answered if we start with the notion that Stalin was "deceived."

In some oblasti the NKVD, unable to handle its huge quota of repression, drastically simplified the investigation. M. M. Ishov, the former military procurator, tells how NKVD agents in Novosibirsk not only made up stories themselves; they even signed for the prisoners. Then the sentence was pronounced in absentia, often a death sentence. And people were shot, without being tortured, without even being interrogated.

In Moscow, however, as in many large cities, and also in most big cases the NKVD tried to preserve an appearance of legality. Forcing prisoners to tell lies against themselves and to invent all sorts of conspiracies, the NKVD demanded that they sign depositions in their own hand. In case of resistance the signature would be secured by days, even months, of torture, a procedure that seems strange to some commentators. The idea was not only to break the prisoner's will, to degrade him, but also to cover up the crime, to give murder some semblance of legality. That is why torture was introduced in the NKVD on Stalin's insistence.

Only the same motives can explain the terrible conditions that were created on Stalin's orders in the camps. When the Nazis sent millions of people to Auschwitz and the other death camps, they would write on accompanying documents: "Return undesirable." Stalin and his aides behaved more hypocritically. On many files is the inscription "Use only for hard physical labor." But the meaning was the same, since "hard physical work" under existing conditions meant death 99 percent of the time. All this shows that Stalin deliberately tried to erase all traces of his crimes.

In 1955–1958 some open trials of former NKVD executives were held in various cities. The trials revealed that in the years of the cult the NKVD leadership became a rallying point for all sorts of adventurers and careerists, some with dark political and criminal pasts. Stalin needed precisely such people in his "secret police" organization. They had one priceless virtue: they were completely dependent on the man who gave them almost unlimited power, and they were ready to do anything he ordered without thinking, without pangs of conscience. There was nothing new in this situation. Many other tyrants and despots have functioned in exactly the same way. Stalin kept firm control of the punitive organs, removing some officials and promoting others. None of these facts can be explained away by the primitive tale that Stalin was "deceived."

It is not hard to imagine a man with weak nerves, mistrustful and fearful, finding himself at the head of the only socialist state in the world. Such a man would begin to see enemies and conspiracies everywhere. He would thrash about, not knowing what to do, wind up killing his best and most devoted friends, surrendering the country to a small group of incompetent but ambitious adventurers who knew how to win his confidence. But Stalin bore no resemblance to such a leader. He was unquestionably a man of strong nerves, inflexible will, and iron self-control. He had a forceful personality, which was, to a great extent, the secret influence over those around him. His fundamental actions and orders were not the product of fear or deception; they were the well calculated moves of a man determined to stop at nothing to reach his goals. "It's not so easy to fool Comrade Stalin," he once said about himself.[31]

■ 3
WAS STALIN MENTALLY ILL?

Historians have often been obliged to turn to psychiatry, for history offers many cases of rulers with abnormal minds. It is therefore not surprising that Stalin's behavior is also attributed to acute mental illness. For example, at a meeting of Old Bolsheviks with delegates to the Twenty-Second Party Congress in 1961 and in a number of other speeches, N. A. Alekseev, a party member since 1897 and a physician by profession, argued that Stalin was mentally sick and incompetent (nevmenyaemy). Another old party member, I. P. Aleksakhin, who returned to Moscow after seventeen years in confinement, propounded the same story to the

31. Stalin, Sochineniia, 12:113.

active party membership of Moscow's Krasnaya Presnya district in 1961. According to Dmitri Shostakovich, for example, a friend of his family, the well-known surgeon I. Grekov, told them that a detailed diagnosis of Stalin's mental condition was somehow done as early as 1927 by V. Bekhterev, one of the most prominent of Russian psychiatrists, who concluded that Stalin was mentally ill. Bekhterev was seventy at the time, and died soon after seeing Stalin. Grekov assured those to whom he told this story that Bekhterev had been poisoned.[32] Grekov himself died in the late thirties, but the story of Bekhterev's psychiatric examination of Stalin (some add that it was done secretly, at the instigation of the opposition) still survives. Many foreign Communists argued the same way after the Twentieth Party Congress obliged them to face the facts of Stalin's terror. For example, the American Communist Hershel Meyer, denying that the development of socialism necessitated terror, tried to show that an accident was to blame: Stalin's paranoid psyche. In this interpretation Stalin was convinced that he was destroying real enemies and saving the revolution from those who sought to restore capitalism.[33]

According to medical textbooks, paranoia is a psychological disorder characterized by wildly distorted, frenzied ideas, which, however, affect only a limited area of perception and develop with little or no hallucinations and without a marked change in personality.[34] Paranoia develops primarily among people in their early forties, of strong but uneven temper. The sickness is accompanied as a rule both by megalomania and by a persecution mania. Other typical symptoms are egocentrism, grudge-bearing, unsociability, obstinacy, and a striving for dominance. Paranoiacs get special satisfaction from unmasking their "enemies." They hate people who once helped them and to whom they are somehow obligated. "A paranoiac," writes psychiatrist P. I. Kovalevsky, "has no friends. . . . Suspiciousness, mistrust, secretiveness, and cruelty show through all his actions. . . . Often the cruelty is joined with a thirst for blood . . . and

32. [See *Testimony: The Memoirs of Dmitri Shostakovich*, as related to and edited by Solomon Volkov (New York, 1979). The author cites the German edition (Hamburg, 1979), p. 212. Cf. a somewhat different version of Bekhterev's encounter with Stalin in Antonov-Ovseyenko, *The Time of Stalin*, p. 254. —G. S.]

33. See Hershel D. Meyer, *Doklad Khrushcheva i krizis levogo dvizheniia v SShA* (Moscow, 1957), pp. 15–20. [The original is Hershel D. Meyer, *The Khrushchev Report and the Crisis in the American Left*, (New York, 1956). —D. J.]

34. *Bol'shaia meditsinskaia entsiklopediia* (Moscow, 1961), 23:224. The story that Stalin had schizophrenia must be rejected out of hand, for the symptoms—splitting of the psyche, atrophy in the emotional and volitional sphere, disintegration of the logical thought processes, aural and other hallucinations—were clearly absent.

with great cunning." At the same time, the paranoiac retains his memory and intellect and frequently manages to carry on his professional functions. Many historians and psychiatrists call Ivan the Terrible a typical paranoiac.[35]

From this description it is clear that the story about Stalin's mental sickness is not entirely unfounded. It is not difficult to detect pathological elements in his behavior. Morbid suspiciousness, noticeable throughout his life and especially intense in his last years, intolerance of criticsm, grudge-bearing, an overestimation of himself bordering on megalomania, cruelty approaching sadism—all these traits, it would seem, demonstrate that Stalin was a typical paranoiac. Nevertheless this view is inadequate.

Medicine makes a serious distinction between a real mental illness, in which a person is acknowledged incompetent and must be placed in a psychiatric hospital, and various abnormal states of personality, in which a person knows what he is doing and bears full responsibility for his behavior. This distinction between the person with psychopathic traits and the person who is genuinely sick must be applied to Stalin. Despite all the pathological changes in his personality during the last twenty years of his life, which took on the characteristic features of paranoid psychopathology, despite the fact that his behavior clearly shows not only acute moral degeneration but also serious psychic derangement—I am profoundly convinced that *Stalin was beyond doubt mentally competent (vmenyaemy) and fully aware of what he was doing.* No court, including the court of history, can excuse and explain Stalin's actions by reference to incompetence.

For all his suspiciousness and mistrust, Stalin acted with great self-control. After he chose a victim, he almost never struck without preparations. His were not the actions of an abnormal man, driven only by a persecution mania. Before taking vengeance, he organized vilification of his victim, entangling him in a web of slander.

There were basically two different methods of assault on the cadres. One could be called "from the top down." First, in a chosen oblast, republic, or institution, the entire complement of leaders would be thrown out by an unexpected swift move, using depositions fabricated in Moscow. The leaders, labeled "Trotskyites," "enemies of the people,"

35. P. I. Kovalevsky, *Psikhiatricheskie eskizy iz istorii,* vol. 3, [Kharkov? 1893?], pp. 65–75. And see, for example, Kovalevsky's article "Ioann Groznyi ego dushevnye sosto-ianiia," in his *Psikhiatricheskie eskizy iz istorii;* also A. Lichko, "Glazami psikhiatra," *Nauka i religiia* (1965), nos. 10 and 11.

and "spies," would be arrested. Then came the turn of lesser officials—members of editorial boards, directors of institutions and enterprises, heads of raion party committees and raion executive committees, and, in the central institutions in Moscow, department and section heads or many rank-and-file staff members. It was considered self-evident that "enemies of the people" who had headed an oblast or an institution for years had planted their agents everywhere.

The second method could be called "from the bottom up." Without consulting the leaders of the chosen oblast, republic, or commissariat, the NKVD would arrest several rank-and-file officials and label them "wreckers," "enemies of the people," "spies." The central newspapers, and frequently the local ones, too, would raise a great hullabaloo: what had the local leaders been doing? The arrests would spread, reaching individual officials in the oblast or republic apparatus, or section heads in the commissariat. At the same time some close associates of the leaders would be taken: a personal chauffeur, a researcher, an editor, a secretary, a relative. The natural desire of the leaders to save people they knew to be honest and loyal would be interpreted as protection of enemies of the people. The newspapers' tone would become more wild and menacing, openly charging that some leaders were helping enemies of the people, alluding to "Trotskyite" or other compromising connections of these leaders. All this stimulated the flow of denunciations. In some cases the central press even appealed over the heads of the oblast or commissariat leaders, inviting rank-and-file Communists to come out against their chiefs. A typical article in *Pravda* was headlined "Time for the Bolsheviks of Omsk to Speak Up," and continued: "If the leaders of the Omsk obkom do nothing and protect Trotskyite-Bukharinite spies, then it is time the Omsk Bolsheviks began to make their voices heard."[36] The leaders would thus be isolated from the rank and file, demoralized, paralyzed. All sorts of careerists and time-servers would be mobilized and united. The business would end with the destruction of the victim selected by Stalin.

These actions bear little resemblance to those of a paranoiac.

It is also instructive to observe how Stalin frequently limited himself, at first, to shifting a major figure without arresting him, although the NKVD already had fabricated testimony against him. The man would be transferred to a less important or sometimes a more important post; he would be sent from Moscow to a province, or he would be called from a

36. *Pravda*, September 28, 1937.

province to Moscow. One way or another, Stalin would remove his "opponent" from his familiar milieu, from the collective that knew and trusted him. There were cases in 1937–1938 when a leading Communist would be transferred three or four times. Dybenko, for example, was relieved of his command in the Volga military district in 1937 and appointed commander of the Leningrad military district. But a few months later he was removed from this post for "insufficient vigilance," appointed deputy commissar of the forest industry, and sent to the Urals. There, in April 1938 he was finally arrested.[37] Before their arrests Postyshev was sent to be the obkom secretary in Kuibyshev, Chubar to be gorkom secretary in Solikamsk. Tukhachevsky, a few weeks before he was shot, was sent from Moscow to Kuibyshev to be commander of the Volga military district. Kosior, dismissed as first secretary of the Ukrainian Central Committee, was moved from Kiev to Moscow to be deputy chairman of the All-Union Council of Commissars. Yagoda, after he ceased to be commissar of internal affairs, became commissar of communications. On September 27, 1936, his picture appeared in all the newspapers beside that of Yezhov. Kosarev was not arrested right after the Seventh Plenum of the Komsomol Central Committee, which practically declared him an enemy of the people. His wife says that he was watched from behind every tree at his dacha but for some time was not touched. These maneuvers also have little resemblance to those of an incompetent man.

It is further significant that many people who had been close to Lenin were not arrested, though they were out of Stalin's favor and had been close friends with those already condemned as enemies. These individuals were merely demoted. Stalin did not arrest Podvoisky, Kon, Petrovsky, Stasova, Tskhakaya, Makharadze, or many other once prominent leaders whose names were mentioned in slanderous denunciations and confessions.

Why did Stalin order the destruction of some Old Bolsheviks but spare others? Why did he sometimes cross out names on the lists of people to be arrested? Why, looking over interrogation records that named dozens of "accomplices" and "accessories," did Stalin refrain from noting that this, that, or the other individual should be arrested? Did Stalin, like many tyrants, enjoy his unlimited power not only to break and kill people but also to leave some alive, to show that he was free to "execute and

37. *Voenno-istoricheskii zhurnal* (1965), no. 10.

pardon"? This does not seem to be the chief factor. Stalin's main considerations were political. He had identified himself as Lenin's closest friend
and colleague. It was therefore necessary and desirable that some genuine friends and colleagues of Lenin remain alive in order to demonstrate
the continuity between Lenin's time and the Stalin era. These people
were continually forced to praise Stalin; on his birthday they signed
collective congratulations to Stalin, "the true Leninist." All this shows
that Stalin was not guided by the frenzy of an abnormal person but by
clear-cut political calculation.

An illuminating case in point is the fate of Maxim Litvinov, commissar
of foreign affairs and a close comrade of Lenin. Litvinov, unlike nearly
everyone else in his commissariat, was not arrested. The story goes that
in 1907 during the Fifth Party Congress in London, Stalin got in a fight
with some dock workers and Litvinov helped him out. In 1937–1938
Litvinov expected to be arrested any night and even had a suitcase with
underwear ready. But arrest did not come. Later on Litvinov asked the
reason for this "indulgence." "I haven't forgotten that time in London,"
answered Stalin. Even if this story is authentic, Stalin was not sincere.
Gratitude was never one of his characteristics, but he realized that he
needed Litvinov as a diplomat in the event of a new shift in the international situation (which occurred in 1941). Litvinov could not be replaced
as easily as other commissars or obkom secretaries. According to
A. Yevstafyev, the writer and journalist Mikhail Koltsov, after being
broken during investigation, gave testimony implicating the well-known
Soviet diplomat Constantine Oumansky. But Oumansky was not arrested. He went on to hold many important posts and after his tragic
accidental death in Mexico was buried with honors next to the Kremlin
wall.

The same was true of many cultural leaders. In the fabricated depositions of arrested artists, writers, and film workers there were allegations
against hundreds who were not arrested. For example, Boris Pasternak
and Yuri Olesha were named as accomplices of Babel and Meyerhold in
the so-called diversionary organization of literary people. But Stalin did
not order the arrest of Pasternak and Olesha. Another remarkable writer
who was spared arrest was Mikhail Bulgakov, although many denunciations of his "anti-Soviet attitudes" reached the NKVD. Stalin angrily
walked out of a performance of Shostakovich's *Lady Macbeth of the
Mtsensk District*, and the talented young composer found himself out of
favor for a long time. His friendship with Meyerhold and connections

with Tukhachevsky were also well known. Every night Shostakovich waited to be arrested; he had a "prison suitcase" packed and ready and could hardly ever sleep. But Stalin did not authorize his arrest, or that of Zoshchenko or Akhmatova. Just as inexplicably Boris Pasternak and Andrei Platonov were allowed to remain free. Nor did Stalin permit the arrest of many leading film directors, although the NKVD prepared more than one case against them. Stalin liked to watch films when he was relaxing; he saw some favorites fifty or a hundred times—and forced his retine to watch them too.[38] His weakness for the cinema obviously saved many Soviet directors.

Careful calculation in Stalin's crimes, rather than mental illness, is also evident in cases where he arrested the wife or some other close relative of a leader but kept the leader in his important job and continued to meet him both officially and socially. I have already mentioned the arrest of Kalinin's wife in 1937 and of Molotov's after the war. Similarly arrested were two of Mikoyan's sons, Ordzhonikidze's brother, the wife and the son of Otto Kuusinen,[39] the wife of A. K. Khrulev, the wife of Poskrebyshev, two of Mikoyan's sons, Khrushchev's daughter-in-law, and others. Mikhail Kaganovich, an older brother of Lazar Kaganovich, committed suicide after being accused of belonging to a "fascist center."

Sometimes Stalin made a show of mercy by releasing one of his aide's relatives. Kalinin's wife, for example, was released in a few weeks. Yuri Karyakin says that one day Stalin, while talking with Otto Kuusinen, asked him why he didn't try to get his son freed. "Evidently there were serious reasons for his arrest," he answered. Stalin grinned and ordered the release of Kuusinen's son. The case of Poskrebyshev, Stalin's personal secretary, is instructive. His wife was the sister of Sedov's wife, and Sedov was Trotsky's son. But that did not prevent Poskrebyshev from being one of the people closest to Stalin. Stalin did finally order the arrest of Poskrebyshev's wife but kept him as his secretary. Poskrebyshev was fired only a few months before Stalin's death and still was not arrested.

38. Among Stalin's favorites, according to film director Mikhail Romm, were *The Great Waltz, Lights of the Big City, Lenin in October, Volga, Volga,* and *Kuban Cossacks.*

39. Aina Kuusinen, like her husband, Otto, had been a Comintern official. She was arrested for "connections with a foreigner." M. A. Solntseva, who shared bunks with Aina in 1938–1941, tells us that Aina used to receive parcels from her husband regularly, signed by a domestic servant. Once on New Year's Eve, Solntseva relates, a screechy radio loudspeaker was installed in their barracks, and Aina, dressed in rags, got to listen to a New Year's speech given by Otto from the Kremlin.

These accounts reveal Stalin's great contempt for his aides, not any fear of them. And they simply cannot be reconciled with the notion of Stalin's incompetence.

It was very hard to guess how Stalin would decide the fate of certain people who had been close to him. Consider, for example, Stalin's strange behavior toward his old comrade Sergei Ivanovich Kavtaradze, who had done Stalin many favors during the underground years. Kavtaradze had risked his own safety on one occasion to help Stalin hide from detectives in St. Petersburg. In the twenties Kavtaradze joined the Trotskyist opposition and left it only when the opposition leadership called on its supporters to stop oppositional activity. After Kirov's murder Kavtaradze, exiled to Kazan as an ex-Trotskyist, wrote a letter to Stalin saying that he was not working against the party. Stalin immediately brought Kavtaradze back from exile. Soon many central newspapers carried an article by Kavtaradze recounting an incident of his underground work with Stalin. Stalin liked the article, but Kavtaradze did not write any more on this subject. He did not even rejoin the party and lived by doing very modest editorial work. At the end of 1936 he and his wife were suddenly arrested and after torture were sentenced to be shot. He was accused of planning, with Budu Mdivani, to murder Stalin. Soon after sentencing, Mdivani was shot. Kavtaradze, however, was kept in the death cell for a long time. Then he was suddenly taken to Beria's office, where he met his wife, who had aged beyond recognition. Both were released. First he lived in a hotel; then he got two rooms in a communal apartment and started doing editorial work again. Stalin began to show him various signs of favor, inviting him to dinner and once even paying him a surprise visit along with Beria. (This visit caused great excitement in the communal apartment. One of Kavtaradze's neighbor's fainted when, in her words, "the portrait of Comrade Stalin" appeared on the threshold.) When he had Kavtaradze to dinner, Stalin himself would pour the soup, tell jokes, and reminisce. But during one of these dinners Stalin suddenly went up to his guest and said, "And still you wanted to kill me."[40]

40. Based on the oral account of Ye. D. Gogoberidze, a translator who knew Kavtaradze well. In 1941 Kavtaradze was even appointed a deputy minister of foreign affairs. He took part in the Yalta and Potsdam conferences and was ambassador to Romania. He approved the revelations about Stalin made at the Twentieth Congress and was a delegate to the Twenty-Second. According to Gogoberidze, Kavtaradze wrote some detailed memoirs during the last years of his life, but the fate of those memoirs remains unknown to me. Kavtaradze died in 1971 at the age of eighty-six.

Some historians may see this comment as proof of Stalin's paranoia. But Stalin knew very well that Kavtaradze never tried to kill him. He could not, however, admit this openly, for then he would have had to reconsider the execution of Budu Mdivani and many other Communists involved in the case. It was much simpler to "forgive" Kavtaradze alone. Similarly, he sent word to Alyosha Svanidze that he would be "forgiven" if he asked Stalin's pardon. Svanidze, considering himself innocent, refused to ask for pardon and was shot. All these actions reveal a misanthropic tyrant, not a mentally ill person who did not know what he was doing.

Stalin usually turned down appeals to free people. Still, in a number of cases, he felt obliged to give in. The physicist Lev D. Landau tells how he

was arrested because of a ridiculous denunciation. I was accused of being a German spy. . . . I spent a year in prison and it was clear I wouldn't last another six months. I was simply dying. Kapitsa went to the Kremlin and declared that he was demanding my release. If it was not granted, he would be forced to leave the Institute [of Physical Problems]. I was freed.[41]

It stands to reason that Kapitsa's fame as a scientist did not influence Stalin as much as his need for Kapitsa as head of the institute.

By comparison with Landau's case, the case of P. K. Oshchepkov, an engineer and inventor who built the first Soviet radar devices, was rather long and drawn out. During the war the Soviet government passed a resolution calling for the most rapid possible development of radar devices made in the USSR. Academician A. F. Ioffe at that point sent a special memorandum to the government, calling attention to Oshchepkov's great services and asking for his release. Ioffe wrote to Oshchepkov, who was in prison in Saratov:

I am sure that our government will appreciate your great services at their true worth and find those who are to blame. I am sending you whatever groceries I can find at home—it's impossible to buy anything. If you have scurvy, drink rose hip tea. . . . I will be in Moscow soon and will again raise the question of you.[42]

41. *Komsomolskaya pravda*, July 8, 1964. [The Institute of Physical Problems, specially created for Kapitsa on his return from a long stay in England (1923–1935), was mainly devoted to the study of low-temperature physics and superconductivity. In 1946 Kapitsa ceased to be director, reportedly because he refused to work on the development of nuclear arms. After Stalin's death he was made director again.—D. J.]

42. P. K. Oshchepkov, *Zhizn' i mechta* (Moscow, 1965), p. 118.

After the Soviet-Finnish war and in the first months after the German invasion of the Soviet Union Stalin allowed the release of several thousand Red Army officers, many of whom were promoted to high posts during the war. Among those released was B. Vannikov, former people's commissar of armaments, who went directly from prison to a Politburo meeting. Stalin said that Vannikov should take over since the defense industry was in bad shape. Vannikov refused. Stalin turned to the other members of the Politburo and said, "His feelings are hurt, and he's taking it out on us." By decision of the Politburo Vannikov was appointed deputy people's commissar of armaments and a short time later people's commissar of munitions. He accepted these assignments, not wishing to return to prison.

At almost the same time, in October of 1941 and the summer of 1942, Stalin ordered a large group of leading Red Army officers serving sentences in the camps to be shot; he considered them a threat to himself in the event of unfavorable developments on the Soviet-German front.[43] Such behavior is not characteristic of a mentally incompetent person suffering from a persecution mania.

The fact that Stalin surrounded himself with men of such murky political background as Beria and Abakumov does not accord with the idea that Stalin was mentally ill. He chose his accomplices carefully and craftily, knowing their true nature. He knew, for example, that under Kerensky the Menshevik Vyshinsky had been head of the militia in Moscow's Arbat district and in the summer of 1917 had signed orders for the arrest of Bolsheviks. Why did Stalin entrust the procuracy of the Soviet Union to this man and later the post of minister of foreign affairs? Why did he prefer Vyshinsky and Beria to members of the Leninist old guard? His motive was clearly political.

Stalin received much compromising material on many of his aides, whom he nevertheless kept in high places. Voroshilov's name was included in the fabricated depositions of some military officers.[44] An old party member, F. Zastenker, says that in Sverdlovsk oblast alone several poods of depositions against Kaganovich and Molotov were "prepared." Many against Molotov were stored in Kuibyshev oblast. Investigators tortured President Kalinin's wife until she signed statements compromising her husband. Stalin was aware of all this; he suggested some of these depositions himself. But for the time being he ignored them.

43. Recounted by Konstantin Simonov.
44. Varlam Shalamov informed me of this.

Stalin was not only rude, ill-tempered, self-centered, and cruel; he was a morbidly suspicious man. "If one's heart is so constructed," Krylov wrote long ago, "that it feels neither friendship nor love, . . . one sees everyone as an enemy." Many criminals, afraid of exposure, begin to fear those around them, and the result may be more and more crimes. Something of this sort must have happened to Stalin. Having wiped out most of the Leninist old guard and almost all his erstwhile friends and comrades, having cast aside all laws of the party and state, of friendship, of simple humanity, Stalin had good reason to be afraid of people. And this fear steadily increased throughout his life. "Evil rulers," says an Eastern proverb, "are always haunted by fear of their subjects." Stalin's fear of exposure and retribution drove him to commit more and more crimes. But we should not attribute the tidal wave of repression in the thirties to maniacal suspiciousness. Every despot is suspicious, but suspicion does not explain despotism.

■ 4

THE MYTH OF STALIN'S "PERMANENT REVOLUTION"

Not long after the Twentieth Congress I first heard, from a highly placed official, a strange explanation of the blood purges of the thirties. Yes, he said, Stalin knew very well that his victims were not spies and wreckers. All those charges were deliberately fabricated. Judged by the usual moral and legal standards, Stalin's actions were of course lawless. Still they were necessary for the further development of the revolution. The people Stalin got rid of were very powerful and popular. They, as much as Stalin, had taken part in the revolution. They could not have been simply fired from their jobs or expelled from the party. They had to be accused of monstrous crimes, of plotting against the Soviet regime and attempting to restore capitalism, of espionage and conspiring with the imperialists. Then with the masses deceived, those people could be destroyed.

"But why," I asked, "was it necessary for the revolution to get rid of its active participants?"

That is the logic of all revolutions, he answered. Many of the people Stalin destroyed had stopped being revolutionaries by the mid-thirties. They had degenerated into officeholders and bureaucrats. They were pushing the party and state machine not toward socialism but toward state capitalism. Stalin had to get rid of those who were interfering with the further development of the socialist revolution; he had to push up[45] young officials who were capable of leading the revolution forward.

I have discovered that this story has wide currency among retired party officials who were "pushed up" in the thirties and forties. Of course it is not expounded publicly but retailed "confidentially," especially in conversation with young officials. It may even have its source in some comments of Stalin himself. Some foreign writers have expressed the same point of view. Isaac Deutscher, for example, discussing the causes of Stalin's purges in *The Prophet Outcast*, argues that Stalin feared the bureaucracy's metamorphosis into a new capitalist class and therefore decimated it "on the pretext of fighting Trotskyism and Bukharinism." Deutscher contends that one of the effects of the purges was to prevent the

managerial groups from consolidating as a social stratum. This was one of the most obscure, least discussed and yet important consequences of the permanent terror. While on the one hand the terror annihilated old Bolshevik cadres . . . , it kept, on the other, the whole of the bureaucracy in a state of flux, renewing permanently its composition, and not allowing it to grow out of a protoplasmic or amoeboid condition, to form a compact and articulate body with a socio-political identity of its own. . . . Just as he had "liquidated" the kulaks, so Stalin was constantly "liquidating" the embryo of the new bourgeoisie; and in this he once again acted, in his own barbaric autocratic manner.[46]

What can be said of this legend, which is essentially the same as the official explanation for the Chinese "cultural revolution" of 1965–1969, with its appeal to the Maoist Red Guards to "open fire on headquarters" and to overthrow "those in authority taking the capitalist road"? The degeneration of many officials did occur in the postrevolutionary period (and I will discuss the nature and extent of this degeneration in Chapter 11). To some extent it was inevitable in a huge and relatively backward country where, in 1917 alone, the party increased more than a hundred-fold as it was transformed from an underground political organization into the ruling party. And from 1918 on it did not share its power with any other party; it ruled by dictatorial methods, uncontrolled for all practical purposes.

Who were affected by bureaucatic degeneration? First of all, petty-

45. [The verb *vydvinut'*, to push up or advance, and the noun *vydvizhenets*, the person pushed up or advanced, were endlessly used in the thirties to describe the official policy of placing lower-class people in top jobs. —D. J.]

46. Deutscher, *Prophet Outcast*, pp. 306–307.

bourgeois revolutionaries who had joined the proletarian cause but were unable to overcome the temptations of the transitional period. Also some proletarian revolutionaries, who were firm in the struggle against tsarism and the bourgeoisie but could not cope with the exercise of governmental power. There were tens of thousands of old officeholders whom the Soviet regime were forced to bring into the state apparatus. They did not need to degenerate; they knew no other methods of governing than bureaucratic.

It was not inevitable that degeneration would affect the entire regime and the party as a whole. In its first decades the Soviet government waged a struggle against bureaucratism, careerism, and petty-bourgeois degeneration, raising a whole stratum of young and talented officials in this spirit. Was Stalin so dissatisfied with this struggle that he wanted a swift, massive purge of bureaucratic officials, even if he had to use barbaric methods, in order to accelerate the socialist revolution? Such a suggestion does not withstand the slightest criticism.

In the first place, in 1936–1939, not only were bureaucratized leaders repressed, but also an enormous number of devoted officials, as well as army officers, business managers, scientists, and artists, were arrested. And not only highly placed leaders but also masses of middle-rank officials perished; not only members of alien classes but also the most educated section of the party intelligentsia, who had been carefully trained by the Soviet regime. In the second place, most of these people were replaced by less experienced, less reliable, less educated cadres. I will not even mention the triumph of people like Molotov, Beria, Kaganovich, Mekhlis, Bagirov, Malenkov, Voroshilov, Shkiryatov, and Vyshinsky. They—and Stalin—represented the worst elements in the party and could truly be called degenerates, incapable of carrying the revolution further or tapping the revolutionary potential of the Soviet system.

An explanation diametrically opposite to Deutscher's is given in *Nomenklatura* by Michael Voslensky,[47] formerly a highly placed Soviet official. Unlike Deutscher, who claimed that Stalin used terror to destroy the embryo of a new class, Voslensky argues that in destroying the Bolshevik old guard, Stalin was laying the foundations for a new class, which Voslensky calls the Nomenklatura. By the mid-thirties, Voslensky

---

47. Voslensky, *Nomenklatura: The Soviet Ruling Class* (New York, 1984), pp. 53–55. [The author quotes apparently from a Russian edition, *Nomenklatura* (Paris, 1980), pp. 82–86.—G. S.]

claims, there had arisen within the framework of the Soviet ruling stratum a large group of ambitious and extremely aggressive young leaders, closely linked together, men who had been "pushed" by Stalin—for example, Zhdanov, Shcherbakov, Pospelov, Mitin, Yudin. They were precisely the embryo of a new class, says Voslensky, both supporting Stalin and pressuring him directly to carry through his campaign of savage terror. They were not only pushed by Stalin; they also pushed him forward as their leader and influenced his decisions.

Voslensky writes:

In 1937, twenty years after the revolution, the Bolshevik old guard was no longer young, but it could still look forward to, say, another fifteen years of life. The newcomers of the nomenklatura [the *vydvizhentsy*] were unwilling to grant them this, for they coveted the leading positions occupied by these old revolutionaries. The nomenklatura, the "new aristocracy" . . . had arrived; it had passed through a hard school and had learned how to rule; the only remaining hurdle was the liquidation of the old guard. . . . The Leninist old guard owed their appointments to their former membership in the organization of professional revolutionaries. Individual Leninists could be dismissed, but there was no ordinary procedure by which they could all be eliminated at a stroke.

The only way of wiping out the old guard was to destroy its moral authority and turn its long years of service to the revolution into a crime.

Stalin was well aware of the envious glances the nomenklaturists cast at the Leninists. Those old men who still preserved some loyalty to the revolution in spite of their good jobs, their prestige, and the good life they led were alien and antipathetic to the newcomers. The latter needed only a signal to fling themselves like a pack of wolves on the enfeebled old fogies who were keeping them out of good positions.

The signal was given by the murder of Kirov. . . .

It is wrong to regard the *yezhovshchina* as the work of Stalin alone, and it is still more wrong to regard Yezhov as the only guilty man.

In giving the green light for the extermination of the Leninist old guard, Stalin fulfilled the wishes of his creatures. It was not a heroic campaign. One may have an unfavorable opinion of its victims, the Leninist professional revolutionaries, but the settling of accounts with them was appalling.

The enormous scale of the repression resulted in a grave shortage of cadres. Hundreds of thousands of officials had to be pushed up from below. Tens of thousands of Stakhanovite workers became factory directors. Ordinary soldiers became platoon and company commanders, company commanders were placed in charge of battalions and regiments, battalion and regiment commanders rose to command divisions and entire armies. Many rank-and-file scientists took over laboratories and big institutes. In short, this was a time when hundreds of thousands of people made lightning careers, ending up in positions they could not have dreamed of before. They cannot be put in political categories such as Stalinist or Leninist, nor were they specially selected protégés of Stalin's top-ranking Nomenklatura men. Most of these *vydvizhentsy* were subjectively honest, having great respect for both Lenin and Stalin, but they could not make out clearly the essence of the changes going on. They wanted to work for the good of the Soviet regime and often did so with great vigor. Still, there is no reason to applaud such a forcible "renewal" of cadres. For the situation in the Soviet Union after the Great Terror was quite different than it had been before. Many *vydvizhentsy*— including those who had been ordinary industrial or office workers or peasants—were corrupted by power much more quickly than had been observable during the twenty years before that (as will be shown in detail in Chapter 11).

■ 5
THE MYTH OF STALIN'S "NATIONAL REVOLUTION"

In examining the various explanations for Stalin's purges of 1936–1939, I cannot avoid considering the legend of Stalin's "national revolution," one that stubbornly persists among certain circles of the intelligentsia. One of the first to state this hypothesis, as early as 1943, was the Russian religious philosopher and historian Georgy Fedotov, who emigrated from the Soviet Union in 1925. In his article "The Riddle of Russia" Fedotov seeks to explain the reasons for the prewar terror as follows:

Every great revolution, no matter what universal ideas it is born with, culminates in nationalism. People who have wrested their homeland from the grip of their class enemies begin to feel that it is truly theirs. It is impossible—even for a foreigner—to rule a country for twenty years without becoming knitted together with it, without at least acquiring the sense of ownership, proprietorship. In the eighteenth century a German woman on the Russian throne conducted a Russian policy. And a Corsican who rose to the head of the French revolution, for all his universal plans, was first of all emperor of the French. Of all Lenin's disciples, Stalin was most suited for the "nationalization" of the Russian revolution. He never took part in the international socialist movement, never was interested in the theoretical problems of Marxism. A practical organizer, he put all his efforts into the Russian revolution, leaving to his more cultured and independent comrades the work with the International. Today he has liquidated almost all of Lenin's comrades in arms. Together with them thousands of true Leninists have been shot or expelled from the party, and their places taken by new people who have no connection with the international movement. Are all these purges of the late 1930s accidental—the Moscow trials? the replacement of virtually the entire diplomatic staff? They can hardly be explained as nothing more than personality clashes between Stalin and the Leninist old guard. If ideological disagreements lie behind these clashes, it is most natural to look for them in the changing of landmarks: the triumph of the new nationalism.[48]

This point of view was put forward in more detail in a series of articles by Mikhail Agursky, a Moscow scholar and writer on current affairs who emigrated in the mid-seventies. In Agursky's opinion the 1917 revolution was a national as well as social revolution, for it brought about the victory of the "colonies," the outlying national regions, over Great Russia, the "metropolis." As a result, non-Russian elements tended to predominate in the leadership of the new government. But in the mid-thirties a new trend began. Agursky describes it as follows:

> The causes of the purges were much deeper. Under the purges' mantle there took place a profound social and (no less important) national transformation, as a result of which there came to power a new stratum of people, mostly of peasant origin, among whom there were virtually no aliens any more (Jews, Latvians, Lithuanians, Poles, etc.). This was the reaction of a vast Slavonic country to the internationalist, cosmopolitan experiments of the 1920s and 1930s, which ignored the national factor. Stalin merely summoned the new stratum to power: he did not create it. Without exaggeration, the purges of 1936–38 can be regarded as one of the final stages of the civil war in Russia.
>
> To replace the old elite—which need not be idealized—there came a new stratum which had no continuity with its predecessors, for the purges took place in different phases, and in the end liquidated the entire body of activists who had taken any direct part in the revolution and civil war, or had participated in party life and knew the party's structure before 1937. Evidently an indispensable condition for the formation of the new elite was also the fact that until 1937 its members had been on only the lowest level of public life.[49]

Some who espouse this viewpoint go even further. For example, A. Ivanov, an active contributor to the Moscow samizdat journals *Veche* and *Moskovskii sbornik*, openly calls himself a modern Russian nationalist and apparently quite deliberately chose the pseudonym Skuratov for his articles.[50] Ivanov-Skuratov links the purges of the thirties with the victory of the Soviet Union in the Great Patriotic War. In his article "The

48. Georgy Fedotov, *Rossiia i svoboda (Sbornik statei)* (New York, 1981), pp. 143–144.
49. M. Agursky, "The Birth of Byelorussia," *Times Literary Supplement*, June 30, 1972.
50. Malyuta Skuratov was Ivan the Terrible's favorite *oprichnik* and the cruelest of that cruel band.

Question of the Role of Aliens (Inorodtsy) in the Victory of Soviet Power" he writes:

Alien domination in the first decade after the revolution was an indisputable fact. With the fall of Trotsky, Zinoviev, and Kamenev it was weakened somewhat but in 1929–1930 was reintensified. In the early thirties the number two man in the party after Stalin was Kaganovich, and his fellow tribesmen [i.e., Jews] gathered the most important commissariats into their hands—Litvinov the Foreign Affairs Commissariat, Yagoda the NKVD, Yakovlev (Epstein) the Commissariat of Agriculture; Gamarnik, and after him Mekhlis, the Political Directorate of the Red Army. But in the mid-thirties a decisive change occurred. The spontaneous, unconscious dissatisfaction of the party's Russian rank and file had a chance to express itself, though at times in a deformed and cruel way. Yet no other reaction was possible to the anti-Russian cruelty that had gone before. On the other hand, the lasting values of Russian culture and history were rehabilitated, the principle of Russian statehood, and this was a positive result of the decade, achieved at terrible cost but helping [Russia] to stand its ground in the war, which would have been lost at the count of two if the leadership had maintained its anti-Russian positions of the twenties and early thirties.[51]

Theories of Stalin's "national revolution" single out only one, and certainly not the most essential, aspect of the events of 1917–1920 and of 1936–1939. It is common knowledge of course that not only the Bolshevik Party but all the Russian revolutionary parties—including the Socialist Revolutionaries, Mensheviks, Anarchists, and Anarcho-Communists—had a disproportionately large number of Jews, Latvians, Lithuanians, Georgians, Armenians, Finns, Poles, and other "aliens" (*inorodtsy*, i.e., non-Russians) in their membership. For a long time the Russian empire had not been a purely Russian national state. In 1917 out of a population of 170 million only 43 percent were "Great Russians."[52] Nearly 100 million of that population consisted of Ukrainians, Poles, Finns, Belorussians, Germans, Jews, Moldavians, Greeks, Georgians, Armenians, Azerbaijanis, Tatars, Kazakhs, Chechens, Ingush, Kurds, Ossetians, Bashkirs, Latvians, Lithuanians, Estonians, and many others. More than 150 nations and national groups, large and small and at various stages of economic and social development, inhabited the territory of old Russia. Today there is no need to document the fact that in addition to various forms of social oppression the non-Russian nationalities experi-

51. From my archive.

52. Official statistics before the revolution artifically counted Ukrainians and Belorussians as part of the "Russian" population, even though that did not correspond to the real state of affairs or to the national consciousness of most of the population in the Ukraine and Belorussia.

enced national oppression, which most people find particularly painful and insulting. It was quite natural therefore that revolutionary propaganda elicited such a favorable response among the non-Russian national groups and that the Russian revolutionary parties obtained a substantial proportion of their cadres from this source. The national question was one of the most important problems the Russian revolution had to resolve, and the slogans of internationalism and elimination of national oppression were a very important part of Bolshevik ideology.

However, it was not the national conflicts in the vast Russian empire that were the main cause of the revolution. Of prime importance was the profound discontent of the peasants in the main provinces of central Russia. The peasants—who constituted the bulk of the population—continued to suffer from land hunger, persisting elements of serfdom, and lack of rights relative to the large landowners, who still held the greater part of the cultivable land. World War I, which placed no less than ten million peasants under arms, only intensified the agrarian contradictions, while the Provisional Government, formed after the downfall of the monarchy, postponed implementation of the long overdue land reform. In fact, by September 1917 the mass peasant movement began to develop into a genuine peasant war that no punitive expeditions could stop.

The second most important cause of the revolution was the extreme war-weariness not so much of the population as a whole as of the twelve million member army. The war had been going on for four years, and its aims were incomprehensible to the mass of soldiers, suffering from inadequate food supplies and a shortage of arms and munitions. The soldiers did not trust the officers and generals and refused to spend another year or two in the trenches. Yet the Provisional Government insisted on continuing the war "to a victorious conclusion" when the soldiers could see no end to the war and had no faith in victory.

Lastly, the third most important cause of the revolution was the constantly worsening living conditions of the urban population, above all the working class in the main industrial centers and particularly in Petrograd, the capital. The February revolution actually began as a result of food riots in the capital. Still, the Provisional Government was unable to improve conditions for the workers in the cities.

The main forces of the political army of revolution—that is, the most active elements among the masses, without whose participation and support no political party could have been victorious—were shaped by the three causal factors listed above. The main forces behind the Bolsheviks were the working class in the chief industrial centers, the sailors of the Baltic fleet, and a substantial number of soldiers in the garrisons of the capital and the other large cities (peasants in uniform). Moreover, while most of the army was politically neutralized, the determined actions of the peasants and soldiers contributed to the Bolsheviks' victory. The outlying national regions of the Russian empire were drawn into the revolution belatedly, and in those areas separatist moods and organizations clearly predominated at first. In fact, some of the outlying regions became strongholds of the counterrevolution.

The active role of non-Russians in the revolutionary parties naturally resulted in their having a significant presence in the government bodies that began to take shape after the October revolution. In evaluating the importance of this fact, however, all the contributing factors should be taken into account, rather than drawing up arbitrary lists or devising tables of arbitrary facts based on preconceived notions.

For example, those who wish to demonstrate the "alien" character of the first agencies of Soviet power point to the fact that the chairman of the Central Executive Committee of the Soviets was Sverdlov, a Jew, that the head of the Cheka was Dzerzhinsky, a Pole, and that the head of the Red Army was Trotsky, also a Jew. In the summer of 1918 the most battleworthy unit of the Red Army was the Latvian Division, while many combat units of the Cheka were made up of Hungarians, Czechs, Chinese, Latvians, and Finns. In focusing on these facts, however, many other more important ones are ignored.

The Sixth Congress of the Bolshevik Party was its last before the October revolution. This was the congress that approved the policy of armed insurrection and the delegates to this congress became the main driving force in the leadership of the October revolution in the capital and local areas. What did this congress represent from the national point of view? Of the delegates at the congress 55 percent were Russians, 3 percent Georgians and Armenians, 17.5 percent Jews, 10 percent Latvians, 4 percent Poles, and 3.5 percent Lithuanians and Estonians. The congress elected a Central Committee consisting of twenty-eight full and candidate members. Sixteen of them were Russians or Russified Ukrainians, six were Jews, two were Georgians, two Latvians, one was an Armenian, and one a Pole.[53] These figures reveal the significant political activism of

53. *Protokoly VI s"ezda RSDRP(b)* (Moscow-Petrograd, 1919), p. 239.

Jews and Latvians in 1917, but they certainly do not confirm the thesis that the role of Jewish and Latvian revolutionaries was decisive.

The main government body after the October revolution was the Sovnarkom, or Council of People's Commissars, elected by the Second Congress of Soviets. The first Sovnarkom consisted of twelve Russians, one Pole, one Georgian, and one Jew. Although Trotsky was the head of the Red Army, Russians made up the bulk of the command staff, including more than ten thousand former officers of the tsarist army. It is true that many "internationalist" units fought on the side of Soviet power—Hungarians, Czechs, Germans, Latvians, Chinese—but altogether they constituted an insignificant part of the Red Army, which totaled three million and was predominantly Russian.

At the height of the civil war, in March 1919, the Eighth Party Congress was held in Moscow. As can be seen from the questionnaires that were filled out, 63 percent of the delegates were Russians, 16 pecent Jews, 7 percent Latvians, 4 percent Ukrainians, and 3 percent Poles.[54] At the Ninth Party Congress out of the 530 delegates who filled out questionnaires 70 percent were Russians, 14.5 percent Jews, 6 percent Latvians, 3 percent Ukrainians, 2 percent Belorussians. All other national groups at the congress added up to about 4 percent.[55] As we can see, there was an obvious tendency for the number of Russians to increase and the number of Jews and Latvians to decline.

The myth of the non-Russian, or more narrowly, the Jewish, character of the October revoloution and Soviet government first arose during the civil war. The White Guard press and later the Russian émigré press were full of references to the "Kike-Bolshevik commissars" and the "Kike-Bolshevik Red Army." Even the London *Times* wrote on March 5, 1919, that Jews held 75 percent of the leading positions in the RSFSR. The proceedings of the 439th and 469th sessions of the U.S. Senate contain the assertion that "in 1918 the government in Petrograd consisted of 16 Russians and 371 Jews, with 265 of those Jews having come from New York."[56] This story is still being told in many Russian émigré publications, though not in such fantastic form.[57]

---

54. *Vos'moi s"ezd RKP(B). Protokoly* (Moscow, 1959), p. 451.

55. *Protokoly IX-go s"ezda RKP(b)* (Moscow, 1934), p. 551.

56. See *Novy zhurnal* 1977, no. 127, p. 280.

57. See, for example, *Kontinent*, 1977, no. 11, pp. 190–191; and *Informatsionnyi biulleten' rossiiskogo Natsional'nogo ob"edineniia* (Belgium), March–April, 1976). [This is a publication by semi-underground Russian emigres, who are deliberately vague about where their "Bulletin" is published.]

The figures I have quoted above provide in my opinion a sufficiently convincing refutation of this tale. The national composition of the Politburo of the Bolshevik Party provides additional refutation. In 1922 there were four Russians, three Jews, and one Georgian on the Politburo. By 1927, however—ten years before Stalin's alleged "national revolution" —the Politburo consisted of thirteen Russians, two Ukrainians, one Georgian, one Armenian, and one Jew. In summarizing my argument on the national character of the October revolution, let me quote two important statements from what would seem to be two opposing ideological camps. First, a comment from Trotsky:

[Reactionary] enemies of the Executive Committee [of the Petrograd Soviet in the first half of 1917] . . . made a great point of the "preponderance" in it of non-Russians: Jews, Georgians, Latvians, Poles, and so forth. Although by comparison with the whole membership of the Executive Committee the non-Russian elements were not very numerous, it is nevertheless true that they occupied a very prominent place in the presidium, in the various committees, among the orators, etc. Since the intelligentsia of the oppressed nationalities—concentrated as they were for the most part in cities—had flowed copiously into the revolutionary ranks, it is not surprising that among the old generation of revolutionaries the number of non-Russians was especially large. Their experience, although not always of a high quality, made them irreplaceable when it came to inaugurating new social forms. The attempt, however, to explain the policy of the soviets and the course of the whole revolution by an alleged "predominance" of non-Russians is pure nonsense. Nationalism in this case again reveals its scorn for the real nation—that is, the people—representing them in the period of their great national awakening as a mere block of wood in alien and accidental hands. But why and how did the non-Russians acquire such miracle-working power over the native millions? As a matter of fact, at a moment of deep historic change, the bulk of a nation always presses into its service those elements which were yesterday most oppressed, and therefore are most ready to give expression to the new tasks. It is not that aliens led the revolution, but that the revolution made use of the aliens. It has been so even in great reforms introduced from above. The policy of Peter I did not cease to be national when, swinging out of the old tracks, it impressed into its service non-Russians and foreigners.[58]

Nicholas Berdyaev, the prominent twentieth-century philosopher, wrote essentially the same thing, though in a different form and to make a different point.

A long historical path leads to revolutions, and in them national peculiarities are revealed even when they deal a heavy blow to national might and national dignity. Every people has its own revolutionary style, just as it has its own

58. Leon Trotsky, *History of the Russian Revolution* 1:225–226.

conservative style. The English revolution was national, just as much as the French. The past of England and of France can be recognized in each of them. Every people makes a revolution with the spiritual baggage that it has accumulated in its past; it brings to the revolution its own sins and defects but also its own capacity for sacrifice and enthusiasm. The Russian revolution was antinational in its character. . . . But even in this antinational character the national peculiarities of the Russian people were reflected, and the style of our unfortunate and destructive revolution is the Russian style. Our old national illnesses and sins brought about the revolution and determined its character. The spirits of the Russian revolution are Russian spirits.[59]

Let me return to the question of the "national character" of Stalin's terror of 1936–1939. It is quite obvious that it was not a Russian "national revolution" or "national transformation." Russians active in the party and government suffered no less than those of other nationalities. For example, while it is true that in 1936–1937 almost all NKVD leaders with Jewish names, Yagoda first of all, were shot, it also true that in 1939 almost all the new NKVD leaders, with purely Russian names, were likewise shot. The leading role in the NKVD leadership, which rose above the Central Committee itself in importance, was played by Georgians, Armenians, and Azerbaijanis (e.g., Beria, Bagirov, Merkulov, Dekanozov, Rukhadze, Kobulov).

Agursky is wrong to say that there was no continuity between the old and new leaderships. The upper echelons of the "new elite" actually did come from a section of the old elite. The Politburo elected after the Eighteenth Party Congress in 1939 included seven members of the Politburo elected in 1934 (Stalin, Molotov, Kaganovich, Voroshilov, Kalinin, Andreev, Mikoyan). Among the new full and candidate members were Zhdanov, Khrushchev, Shvernik, and Beria, men who cannot in any way be described as coming from "the lowest level of public life." There were quite a few such men at the middle levels of government. The repressive measures of 1936–1939 noticeably reduced the number of Latvians, Estonians, Finns, Poles, and Hungarians within the Soviet elite, but this can be explained by the fact that Latvia, Estonia, Finland, Hungary, and the Baltic countries were not part of the Soviet Union and could not serve as a source of new cadres. The number of Germans and Jews in the elite was also reduced, although many Jews continued to hold leadership posts in the party and government. Mikhail Baitalsky, author of a major study of the Jews in Russia, had the following comment on this question.

59. *Iz glubiny. Sbornik statei o russkoi revoliutsii* (Paris, 1967), pp. 71–72. This is a reprint of an anthology compiled and published semi-legally in 1918.

The repression of the thirties hit the Soviet intelligentsia and members of the government and party apparatus much harder than it hit ordinary workers. Within the intelligentsia and the official staffs, in turn, the Communists were hit much harder than non-Communists. Finally, among the Communists themselves repression struck at old members with much greater force than at those who had recently joined. But it was precisely among the Jews that there were more white-collar workers and intellectuals than industrial workers; the percentage of Jewish Communists was two, three, sometimes four times greater than among other nationalities; and if we look at national composition within the party, there was a disproportionately large number of Jews among older party members. The result of this combination of factors was that, although the repression was not specifically aimed at the Jews, it struck them harder, in a kind of ricochet effect, than it did other nationalities, sweeping away in the process the most progressive section of the Jewish nation, those most devoted to the revolution.[60]

This point of view is much closer to the truth than are the arguments of Agursky, Fedotov, and Ivanov-Skuratov. After 1939 a large number of posts that had previously been held by Jews, Poles, Latvians, or Hungarians were taken by people from the Caucasus, Central Asia, and Kazakhstan.

In the early thirties the Nazi ideologue Alfred Rosenberg wrote the following in his book *The Future Path of German Foreign Policy:*

The essence of the Russian revolution, if it is viewed from the racial-historical standpoint, is that unconscious Mongoloid forces were victorious in the Russian national organism over the Nordic ones and set about the task of eradicating the latter, which they considered an alien and hostile essence.[61]

In July 1941 the same Rosenberg assured Hitler that "Bolshevism had destroyed the old ruling stratum in Russia and replaced it by a new one, of Caucasian-Asiatic origin."

This was not the dominant point of view among the Nazi theorists, however. Even after Stalin's purges a common theme of Nazi propaganda was that on the basis of the main elements in its leadership the Soviet Union remained—a Jewish country. The Nazi newspaper *Angriff* said the following, for example, even after the attack on the USSR:

In the Soviet Union the Jews have carried out what they are preparing for all mankind. . . . Therefore Jewry and its world must be destroyed, as is now

60. Baitalsky, "Russkii evrei vchera i segodnia," unpublished manuscript.
61. Quoted by Bukharin in his speech to the Seventeenth Party Congress. See *Semnadt-satyi s"ezd VKP(b). Stenograficheskii otchet* (Moscow, 1934), p. 138.

happening on the territory of the Bolshevik "Soviet paradise," so that a free road can be opened for the success and development of true socialism.[62]

It is true that Stalin promoted Russian great-power nationalism and that it was reflected in his personnel policy. But that happened during and after the war, especially in 1948–1949 and is a subject for separate discussion.

■ 6
THE MYTH OF STALIN'S "ANTI-COMMUNIST REVOLUTION"

The repression of the thirties completed Stalin's long-planned usurpation of power, which he had carried out by stages. At the end of the twenties Stalin was already being called a dictator, and with good reason, but the totally unlimited personal dictatorship that he established in the late thirties had no precedent in history. For the last fifteen years of his life Stalin wielded such power as no Russian tsar or any other dictator of the past thousand years has possessed. In his hands were not only the full plenitude of political and military power but also the uncontrolled power to dispose of all the material resources of the Soviet Union, unilaterally to decide all fundamental questions of foreign policy, and personally to direct Soviet literature, art, and science.

In the period of revolution and civil war the Soviet government did not concern itself overly much with questions of law and legality in regard to those individuals, groups, parties, or entire social strata that were considered class enemies of the proletariat; the same was true in the NEP era and in the late twenties and early thirties. Such arbitrariness was usually justified by referring to the "dictatorship of the proletariat," which—it was said—could not tie its own hands with legal niceties but had to rely directly on force and violence when necessary. In reality, what existed was not so much a dictatorship of the proletariat as a dictatorship of the Communist Party, which gradually turned into the dictatorship of the strongest faction of the party, and in the first half of the thirties became the dictatorship of the top echelons of the party, a special kind of "dictatorship of the leaders."[63]

62. *Angriff*, August 12, 1941. (Quoted from archival materials by the Soviet Information Bureau during the war.)

63. For a more detailed discussion of the process of degeneration of the dictatorship of the proletariat in the Soviet Union, see Roy Medvedev, *Leninism and Western Socialism* (London, 1981), pp. 29–93.

The upper echelons of the party, while they did not observe any laws in relation to "class enemies" and gave little consideration to the rank-and-file membership, not to mention oppositionists of various kinds, still demanded observance of certain party norms and principles of collective leadership. This outlook conflicted with Stalin's plans. In carrying through the final and decisive phase in his usurpation of power, Stalin gradually violated all the earlier established party norms and traditions, one after the other, until he had thrown them out entirely.

For example, Stalin totally disregarded all rules and prerogatives of the Central Committee, as well as such governing bodies of the CC as the Politburo and the Secretariat, although these institutions were not formally abolished. Originally the Central Committee had been designed as a democratic body based on collective leadership. The party rules provided for plenums of the Central Commitee and congresses of the party to be held regularly. To prevent arbitrary action against members of the Central Committee, the rules stipulated that no member of the CC could be removed from its ranks without a decision to do so by a party congress or in exceptional cases the decision of an enlarged plenum of the Central Committee.

Nevertheless after the arrest of Bukharin and Rykov in January 1937 Stalin stopped holding Central Committee plenums to consider action against CC members. In deciding to have Bukharin and Rykov arrested and shot, Stalin acted on his own, discussing only certain technical details of the forthcoming "operation" with Yezhov and Beria.

For the majority of CC members arrest was a complete surprise, unaccompanied by even the minimum formalities. Iona Yakir, a CC member, after being summoned to Moscow, was arrested right in his compartment on a train when it stopped at Bryansk. In the middle of the night NKVD agents entered the compartment where he was sleeping. One of them took the army commander's pistol from under his pillow then awakened Yakir and told him he was under arrest. "But where's the CC resolution?" Yakir asked. "When you arrive in Moscow they'll show you all the resolutions and authorizations," the NKVD man replied.[64] Rudzutak, a candidate member of the Politburo, was arrested at his dacha in the midst of a lively conversation with the artists V. N. Meshkov, A. M. Gerasimov, and P. M. Shukhmin.[65] According to D. Yu. Zorina, who formerly held a position as "instructor" for the Central

64. *Komandarm Yakir. Sbornik vospominanii* (Moscow, 1963).
65. G. A. Trukan, *Yan Rudzutak* (Moscow, 1963).

Committee, the arrest of Ya. A. Yakovlev, head of the CC's agricultural department, occurred in his office at work. "Have we had a counterrevolutionary coup or what?" he asked the NKVD agents. "I am a member of the CC and the government. What right have you to arrest me without Central Committee authorization?" His protest remained unanswered. Andrei Bubnov, a prominent party leader, member of the CC, and people's commissar of education, was refused admission by the Kremlin guard to a CC plenum in October 1937. Several other CC members found themselves in the same position. Extremely upset, Bubnov went to his office at the Commissariat of Education and remained there until evening. From the evening news on the radio he learned that he had been removed from his post as commissar of education. A few days later he was arrested.[66] Stalin's actions against other members of the CC and the Soviet government were equally brazen and illegal.

It is not surprising that Stalin also disregarded the deadlines specified by the party rules for holding congresses and CC plenums. In the first ten years after Lenin's death four party congresses, five party conferences, and forty-three CC plenums were held. In the next twenty years (1934–1953) only three party congresses, one party conference, and twenty-three CC plenums took place. There was a thirteen-year interval between the Eighteenth and Nineteenth party congresses, and from 1941 to 1951 only two CC plenums were held.[67]

The view that no substantial changes took place in the Soviet system in the second half of the thirties is upheld frequently and quite persistently by Western Sovietologists and Russian émigrés. Stalin's terror, in the opinion of many authors, was a direct continuation of the Red Terror of civil war times, the terrorist methods of collectivization, and the terror against "bourgeois specialists" and "hostile class elements" in the early thirties. They argue that although the dictatorship of the Communist Party became harsher in the late thirties, its fundamental character did not change. For them no specific phenomenon called "Stalinism" ever existed—only the normal and natural development of the basic principles of "Leninism" carried to their logical conclusion. "Stalinism" and "Leninism," in their eyes, were different stages in the process by which the system of "totalitarian socialism" worked out by Marx and Engels, or socialism in general, was put into practice.

The question of the relation between Stalinism and Leninism, and

66. *Andrei Bubnov* (Moscow, 1964).
67. *Istoricheskaia entsiklopediia*, vol. 8, (Moscow, 1965), p. 275.

between the Marxist and Leninist doctrines of socialism, on the one hand, and the Soviet reality of the thirties and forties, on the other, requires special examination and I will take it up in later chapters.

For now I will note only that the views described above coincide almost completely with those of official Soviet historians, who see no difference in principle between Leninism and Stalinism and who in general deny the validity of the term "Stalinism." Official Soviet history regards the events of the thirties as the natural and logical continuation of socialist construction in the Soviet Union along the lines laid down by Lenin and by Marxist-Leninist theory. Of course for many Western authors and émigrés from the Soviet Union any socialist system is hateful and inimical, regardless of whether it is called Leninist, Stalinist, democratic, or totalitarian, while official Soviet writers spare no eulogies in describing the socialism of the thirties as well as the "existing socialism" of today. The authors of one textbook on party history write, for example:

> The cult of personality . . . could not alter the nature of the socialist system, could not shake the party's Leninist foundations. The party and its local units continued to live their own active, autonomous life. In constant conflict with the unhealthy tendencies engendered by the cult of personality, the genuinely Leninist principles lodged in the very foundations of the party invariably won out.[68]

Another example of this point of view is *Essays in the History of the CPSU (Ocherki po istorii KPSS)*, a textbook for schools teaching Marxism-Leninism, which was reprinted many times from 1966 to 1975. It was prepared under the direction of Sergei Trapeznikov, with the assistance of G. N. Golikov, A. I. Titov, G. A. Deborin, and others. It takes up the events of 1936–1939 in a section entitled "The Victory and Consolidation of Socialism." Here we read about the adoption of a new, and "more democratic" Soviet constitution and a new, "more democratic" electoral system and about the growth of democracy within the party. Nothing is said about the mass repression or the extermination of the greater part of the cadres of the party, army, and government. Without mentioning a single victim of Stalin's arbitrary rule, the authors of this textbook make only a cryptic reference to abuses of power and to Stalin's mistaken notion that the class struggle would intensify in proportion to the successes of socialism in the USSR.

A similar tendency can be detected in the multivolume *History of the*

68. *Gody ratnykh trudov i podvigov* (Moscow, 1966), p. 9. This book was one of the series "On the History of the CPSU for Young People."

CPSU (*Istoriia KPSS*), whose publication has been going on for twenty years and is still not complete.[69] This major official history treats the events of 1937 in a chapter entitled "The Victory of Socialism in the USSR" (volume 4, chapter 24), and the events of 1938–1939 in a chapter called "The Entry of the USSR into the Period of the Completion of Socialist Construction" (volume 5, chapter 1). In these chapters we find quite a few discussions of progress in the development of Soviet democracy, the strengthening of the party units, the ideological training of party members, and the sociopolitical unity of the Soviet people, but there is not one chapter, section, or paragraph on the savage terror and mass repression of the prewar years.

In contrast to this viewpoint, quite a few Western and émigré authors regard Stalin's usurpation of power as a complete break from socialism and the Leninist revolution, as a counterrevolutionary, monarchist, or even fascist coup.

As early as the civil war some theorists of the White movement discussed the idea that the October revolution, like many previous revolutions in other countries, would eventually culminate in the establishment of a new monarchy. Vasily Shulgin, a prominent Russian nationalist and monarchist, in his book *1920* presented a conversation he had in late 1920 with an official of the Soviet embassy in Constantinople. Shulgin argued that as a result of objective conditions the Bolsheviks would inevitably reestablish Russia's military might, return the borders of the Russian state "to their natural limits," and also prepare the way for "the advent of an autocrat of all the Russias." Neither Lenin nor Trotsky could become such an autocrat, Shulgin wrote, because they could not abandon socialism:

With the help of socialism they overthrew the old order and seized power. They must carry this sack on their back to the end, even though it will crush them. . . . Then there will come "Someone" who will take from them their *dekretnost* (habit of issuing decrees) . . . , their decisiveness in making incredible decisions on their own authority. Their cruelty—in carrying out what has once been decided on. But he will not take from them their heavy sack. He will be truly Red in his will power and truly White in the goals he will pursue. He will be a Bolshevik in his energy and a nationalist in his convictions. It is a difficult

69. The chief editors of Volume 1 (1964) were Pyotr Pospelov, Ye. I. Bugaev, Lev Ilyichev, Vyacheslav Karpinsky, D. M. Kukin, Isaak Mints, I. D. Nazarenko, Boris Ponomarev, and P. A. Satyukov. Chief editors of Volume 5, Part 2 (1980) were P. N. Fedoseev, Ye. I. Bugaev, A. G. Yegorov, A. A. Yepishev, A. S. Kapto, Isaak Mints, A. D. Pedosov, Boris Ponomarev, and Sergei Trapeznikov.

combination, I know. . . . But everything that is going on now, the entire horror that is hanging over Russia, is only the terribly difficult, dreadfully painful birth pangs. The birth of an autocrat. . . . And do you think it is easy to give birth to a true autocrat, especially one of all the Russias?[70]

It is not surprising that some right-wing and Cadet émigrés evaluated Stalin's usurpation of power as a kind of monarchist overturn. A letter from Pavel Milyukov, the onetime leader of the Cadet Party, was found in Prague in 1945 in the archives of Yelena Kuskova, a prominent public figure and writer who was expelled from Soviet Russia in 1922. The letter, dated September 18, 1936, said in part:

In your opinion, these executions are because the [correct political] line has been lost. But the line continues; consequently, there is nothing to be lost. Let them continue to believe in the correctness of the line right up until they mount the scaffold. While I characterize the means (the outward form) as barbarous, I believe the end for which these means are used to be entirely correct. . . . All the more I wish Stalin good health, so that there will be no backward zigzags.[71]

Georgy Fedotov was even more definite in an article entitled "Stalinokratia" (The Stalinocracy) published in 1937 in *Sovremennye zapiski.*

The ice has broken. The enormous blocks that have pressed Russia down with their weight for seventeen years are melting from below and breaking up one after the other. This is a true counterrevolution carried out from above. . . . The liquidation of Communism under way in Russia is wrapped in a defensive veil of lies. The Marxist symbolism of the revolution has not yet been eliminated, and this prevents people from seeing the facts. . . . Stalin is a "Red monarch," such as Lenin never was. Stalin's regime fully deserves the title of monarchy, even though this monarchy is not hereditary and has not yet found an appropriate name for itself.[72]

Mikhail Kuzenits, then a young Communist, was told by one of his cellmates, an old monarchist officer, imprisoned since 1920:

Now I am happy. At last the dreams of our beloved Nicholas [II], which he could not carry out because of his gentleness, are being fulfilled. After all, the jails are full of Jews and Bolsheviks. Don't you understand that a new dynasty is being established in Russia?[73]

70. V. Shulgin, *1920 god* (Leningrad, 1927), pp. 269–273. Arrested in Yugoslavia in 1944, Shulgin was held in a Soviet prison until 1956. He died in the Soviet Union in 1976.
71. Reported by S. Petrikovsky, a member of the CPSU.
72. Georgy Fedotov, *Rossiia i svoboda. Sbornik statei* (New York, 1981), pp. 63–76.
73. Reported by Mikhail Borisovich Kuzenits.

In the late thirties the notion that a "Red fascist" regime had been established in the Soviet Union was brought up among a small number of surviving members of the SR Party who managed to keep in touch with one another in Stalin's prisons and camps. Benito Mussolini expressed the same opinion quite independently of the SRs. Among his close friends Mussolini openly praised Stalin. In 1937 the Italian fascist journals wrote that Bolshevism was moving toward the formation of a state of the fascist type. In Spain the fascist dictator Franco also expressed admiration for Stalin's methods.[74]

The notion that Stalin was a conscious opponent of the Soviet Communist Party in particular and of the world Communist movement in general is still expressed sometimes. For example, Valery Chalidze, a former Soviet dissident who now lives in the United States, wrote a small book on this subject entitled "Conqueror of Communism" (*Pobeditel' kommunizma*), which says in part:

He fooled all of us and the entire world. To this day nearly everyone believes that Stalin established a socialist state and that his goal was to build communism. Yet a closer analysis demonstrates that Stalin gained a victory over the socialist revolution, destroyed the Communist Party, and restored the Russian empire in a much more despotic form than that which existed before 1917. In doing all this he was forced to use Marxist phraseology and conceal his true intentions. . . .

The [events of] 1937–1938 did not resolve the problem. This was merely the first blow against the Communists. Preparations were being made for the next steps—to maintain the structure of the party formally, while removing the Communists from it, not only the Old Bolsheviks, but all believers in communism, even young ones, who had taken the pestiferous doctrine seriously, not realizing that all that was in the past, that the goals were completely different now, that now it was a party of Stalinists building a mighty empire with solid state power.[75]

Unfortunately it is precisely a convincing analysis that is lacking in Chalidze's booklet; analogies, as everyone knows, do not constitute proof.

While Chalidze, Fedotov, and others contend that Stalin restored the monarchy or established a new dynasty, or a fascist regime, or a modern variant of "the Asiatic mode of production," an Asiatic despotism, their arguments have been subjected to thorough criticism by other émigrés. While opposing socialism of any kind and Leninist socialism in particular, these émigré authors seek to demonstrate, not without reason, that many

74. Reported by Victor Serge in *Erinnerungen revolutionärs*. See also, Victor Alba, *Oppozitsiia vyzhivshikh* (Barcelona, 1978), p. 226.
75. Valery Chalidze, *Pobeditel' kommunizma* (New York, 1981), pp. 3, 39.

elements of the Leninist heritage were not destroyed by Stalin.[76] They point out that Stalin did not establish a monarchy and did not kill all the Communists and socialists. On the contrary, he used the mechanism of the Communist Party and its dictatorship to usurp power and establish his personal dictatorship, physically eliminating all real or potential rivals or opponents. Unfortunately, the advocates of this view look only for the elements of similarity between Lenin's time and the Stalin era and fail to see the vast differences between them, the fact that in many respects they were polar opposites.

Stalin's usurpation of power was a change not only in the outward form of Soviet rule. In essence it was a *partial* counterrevolution, as I will discuss further below. Nevertheless, Stalin did not intend to carry this counterrevolution through to the end, nor could he even if he had wanted to. He had no intention of establishing a new dynasty in the Soviet Union, of returning the large landowners and capitalists who had been driven out of the country, or of creating a new "Soviet aristocracy," a new ruling class. Stalin sought to combine in some form the new social system with his antidemocratic regime of absolute personal power. One can speak therefore of different varieties of Stalinist barracks socialism, but not of a new absolutist monarchy.

Since the label "Bonapartism" is frequently attached to the Stalinist regime, it should be enlightening to compare Stalin's actions with those of Napoleon. After coming to power, Napoleon did not try to return the land seized by the French peasantry to its former owners. He retained all the basic advances made by the bourgeoisie, including its leading role among the classes in French society of that time. Having the solid support of the bourgeoisie and the peasantry, Napoleon was able to act openly. He was not afraid to proclaim himself dictator for life or to have the emperor's crown placed on his head. In contrast, Stalin's terror and usurpation of power were not in keeping with the interests of the proletariat and peasantry, the classes on which the October revolution and Soviet power rested. Therefore, where Napoleon acted openly, Stalin resorted to deception. Where Napoleon went all the way, Stalin stopped at the halfway point. Stalin did not wish to assume the title of emperor, nor could he have done so, considering the sentiments existing in Soviet society. In words he presented himself as Lenin's most loyal disciple, carrying on the work of the October revolution. Together with the terror,

76. See, for example, Dora Shturman, *Zemlia za kholmom* (Ann Arbor, Mi., 1983), pp. 143–156.

this claim contributed to the stability of his regime. Until the end of the thirties Stalin did not assume any government post other than member of the Presidium of the Central Executive Committee of the Soviets (later the Presidium of the USSR Supreme Soviet). Only on the eve of the war did Stalin become chairman of the Council of People's Commissars (the equivalent of premier). During the war he assumed the title of marshal, then generalissimo. Yet without monarchical titles, Stalin concentrated such power in his hands as Napoleon never had or could have had. The British historian E. H. Carr had the following comment on this historical paradox.

The Bolsheviks knew that the French revolution had ended in a Napoleon, and feared that their own revolution might end in the same way. They therefore did not trust Trotsky, who among their leaders looked most like a Napoleon, and trusted Stalin, who looked least like a Napoleon.[77]

■ 7
WAS STALIN A POLICE AGENT?

The tsarist secret police, the Okhrana, in its struggle against the Russian revolutionary parties, made wide use of secret agents, both provocateurs who were sent into those parties and agents recruited from among unstable party members who would agree to work for the police. Many local and even central organizations of the Bolshevik Party were penetrated by such agents. After the revolution many facts about the history of Bolshevism, based on documents from the Moscow Okhrana, were published. One book included a list naming twelve secret agents who had worked in the RSDLP:

M. I. Brandinsky, Ya. A. Zhitomirsky, M. G. Krivov, A. I. Lobov, R. V. Malinovsky, A. K. Marakushev, A. A. Polyakov, A. S. Romanov, I. P. Sesitsky, M. Ye. Chernomazov, V. Ye. Shurkhanov, and a "Vasily" whose identity had not been discovered.

According to these police files, agents had even participated in the Prague Party Conference of 1912, sending in reports of its resolutions and practical decisions.[78]

Most of the police spies were exposed right after the February revolution of 1917. But some were not exposed until much later. One reason

77. E. H. Carr, *What Is History?* (New York, 1962), p. 90.
78. *Bol'sheviki (Dokumenty po istorii bol'shevizma s 1905 do 1916 gg. byvshego Moskovskogo Okhrannogo Otdeleniia)* (Moscow, 1918).

for the delay was that many of the documents of the Petrograd Okhrana were burned by the insurgent workers in the palace of the Department of Police in the first days of the February revolution. This was obviously a gross error by the revolutionaries, probably provoked by someone with an interest in having these documents destroyed. A second reason was that some of the more important police provocateurs were known only to one or two top directors of the Okhrana. For example, it was not until the twenties that an agent named Serebryakova, who had betrayed many Bolsheviks to the tsarist secret police, was found out.

In the mass repression of the thirties Stalin and the NKVD made use of the popular hatred for police spies. False charges of this kind were directed against such respected party members as Zelensky, Pyatnitsky, Razumov, and many other officials who have now been completely cleared. Even Meyerhold was accused in 1938 of having worked for the tsarist secret police under the name Semenych. Few realize that similar accusations have repeatedly been made against Stalin himself.

As early as the twenties émigré papers carried reports that Stalin had been an agent of the tsarist secret police. One of the first to make this charge was the leading Georgian Menshevik Noi Zhordania, who recounted what Stepan Shaumyan had told him about his, Shaumyan's, arrest in Tiflis in 1909. He was apprehended on the first day of an illegal visit to that city, when only one person knew the date of his arrival and the address where he was supposed to stay. That person, if we can believe Zhordania's report of what Shaumyan said, was Stalin. Zhordania's allegations were published in Boston in a Dashnak journal entitled *Airinik* and later reprinted in a Russian émigré newspaper.[79] References to Stalin's alleged ties with the Okhrana are also found in an unpublished manuscript at the Hoover Institution by another Georgian Menshevik, Grigory Uratadze. The reports by Zhordania and Uratadze can be interpreted in various ways, but we know that Shaumyan was quickly released after his 1909 arrest and that he maintained friendly relations with Stalin after that incident.

More reports of this kind came out in the West after the Twentieth Party Congress of 1956. I have already cited Alexander Orlov's book *The Secret History of Stalin's Crimes*, which was first published in English in 1953, not long after Stalin's death, and which was recently reissued in Russian. In May 1956 Orlov published a long article in *Life* magazine entitled "Stalin's Sensational Secret," containing material that had not

79. See "Stalin po vospominaniiam N. N. Zhordania," in *Poslednie novosti* (Paris, December 15, 1936).

appeared in his 1953 book.[80] In particular Orlov claimed that for many years before the revolution Stalin had collaborated with the Okhrana.

According to Orlov, in February 1937, when he was in a French clinic with a bad back, he was visited by his cousin Zinovy Borisovich Katsnelson, an NKVD plenipotentiary in the Ukraine and a member of the Central Committee. Katsnelson was a great friend of Stanislav Kosior and other prominent figures in the party. He said to Orlov that Stalin told Yagoda, when they were preparing the first Moscow trial, that it would be useful to connect some of the intended victims with the tsarist police. Yagoda decided to try to find a former officer of the secret police, which at that time was not an easy matter. The largest collection of police archives was kept in the Lubyanka office of Yagoda's predecessor, Menzhinsky. An NKVD official named Shtein was told to search these archives. He discovered a file in which a police official named Vissarionov had kept his papers. "There," wrote Orlov, in his 1956 article,

were reports and letters in longhand, addressed to Vissarionov, in the handwriting of the dictator that was so familiar to Shtein. The file, as Shtein discovered, concerned Stalin all right—not Stalin the revolutionary but Stalin the agent provocateur who had worked assiduously for the tsarist secret police.

Shtein then went to the Ukraine, to his former chief and friend, Vsevolod Balitsky, head of the Ukrainian NKVD. Balitsky submitted the papers to expert analysis and established their authenticity. Then Balitsky informed Katsnelson, Yakir, Kosior, and other highly placed officials. Many photocopies of the documents were made, and Yakir flew to Moscow and told Tukhachevsky, Gamarnik, Kork, and others. The military commanders drew up a plan to destroy Stalin. They proposed to pick two Red Army units loyal to them to accomplish an overturn in the Kremlin, without any disturbances in the country. All this Katsnelson is supposed to have told Orlov in February 1937, four months before the arrest of Tukhachevsky and his friends. Orlov wrote that he went to Spain soon after receiving this report, and there he heard the news of Tukhachevsky's arrest over the French radio. Subsequently everyone who could possibly have been involved in the affair was arrested and shot. In short, according to Orlov, a large part of the 1937 mass repression was due to Shtein's accidental discovery.

Orlov's 1953 book is based on real events—or on genuine rumors which, even if they did not correspond to the facts, are interesting and

80. See *Life* (May 14, 1956), no. 10.

symptomatic of the times. There are hardly any elements of fabrication in the book. It remains a noteworthy publication. But Orlov's article in *Life* is a deliberate fabrication inspired by sensationalism and the big fees paid by the magazine.

Orlov's allegations do not withstand even superficial criticism. Katsnelson, to begin with, was neither a member nor a candidate member of the Central Committee in 1937. The "conspirators" Orlov names were not arrested all at once but over a long period of time, and none of them tried to hide on learning that their "plot" had failed. Kosior was arrested and shot almost a year after Tukhachevsky's arrest. As for the many photocopies that were allegedly made of the "Vissarionov file," not one is extant, although many of the "conspirators" could easily have sent them to friends abroad. We know the details of the arrest of the military leaders and these facts are utterly incompatible with the existence of a widespread conspiracy to kill Stalin. It is also improbable that no one had searched the archives of the tsarist secret police before 1937. Similarly, many officials who were close to Kosior and Yakir—Grigory Petrovsky, for example—were not arrested. Orlov is even wrong in his account of Khrushchev's speech to the Twentieth Party Congress. Khrushchev said nothing in that speech about the case of Marshal Tukhachevsky and the other generals, who were rehabilitated only in 1957. There are many more such distortions and errors in Orlov's article. His explanations of why he was silent for so long and why, even in his 1953 book on Stalin's crimes, he did not mention Katsnelson's story, sound unconvincing. It is obvious, in short, that Orlov's 1956 article is a clumsy fabrication. It is understandable, therefore, that Orlov and his publishers have never included that article in later editions of *The Secret History of Stalin's Crimes*.

The same issue of *Life* carried an article by Isaac Don Levine, who had written one of the first Western biographies of Stalin. The article included a document that had supposedly come into Levine's hands proving that Stalin had been an Okhrana agent. Levine soon published a book on this subject, *Stalin's Great Secret*, including this document in it. It was a letter dated July 12, 1913, from a certain Yeremin to the chief of the Yenisei department of the secret police, A. F. Zheleznyakov:

Joseph Vissarionovich Stalin, who had been administratively exiled to the Turukhansk region, gave the head of the Tiflis Agency of S[tate] G[endarmes] valuable undercover information when he was arrested in 1906.

In 1908, the Head of the Baku Secret Police got a number of reports from

Stalin, and later, when Stalin arrived in St. Petersburg, Stalin became an agent of the Petersbug Division of the Secret Police.

Stalin's work was distinguished by precision, but it was sporadic.

After Stalin's election to the party's Central Committee in Prague, Stalin, upon his return to Petersburg, became completely opposed to the government and entirely broke off his connection with the Secret Police.[81]

This letter contradicts Orlov's claim that Stalin worked for the police after the Prague Conference of 1912. Levine's attempt to explain the discrepancy, without disavowing Orlov's material, is unconvincing. His account of the document's history fails to explain how it could have passed through several owners over a thirty-year period without being published.

The reference to Stalin's arrest in 1906 is entirely unsubstantiated. Levine argues that Stalin could have been arrested when the Avlabar secret printing press was destroyed in April 1906. But Stalin had no real involvement with the work of that printshop. We know today that the Avlabar press was organized by Mikho Bochoridze.[82] If Stalin had been arrested in the Avlabar case, it would not have gone unnoticed, for twenty-four people were known to have been arrested then. Levine's argument that Stalin could have been arrested for just a few hours, then released as a reward for the valuable information he provided as an agent and allowed to go to Stockholm to participate in the Fourth United Congress of the RSDLP stretches credibility.

Levine discusses the type of paper and ink used in the letter and details of its text, all of which supposedly prove the authenticity of the document. But the expert analysis was carried out by an American chosen by Levine; for objectivity's sake a commission of international experts having no stake in the matter should have been established. Levine determined that Zheleznyakov and Yeremin actually did work for the Okhrana in 1913. Yeremin's signature was verified by General Spiridovich, formerly of the tsarist gendarmerie, who in 1956 was living outside Paris. But, first, of all, it is hard to rely on the memory of a man past eighty. Second, the authors of fake political documents usually use the signatures of real persons and forge them quite skillfully. The fact

81. [See frontispiece of Levine, *Stalin's Great Secret* (New York, 1956), for a photocopy of this document. —D. J.]

82. *Bol'shaia sovetskaia entsiklopedia*, 3rd ed., vol. 1 (Moscow, 1970), pp. 189–190. (In the first edition of *Let History Judge* I mistakenly named Yenukidze as the organizer of the Avlabar press. In fact, he organized the no less famous Nino press in Baku.)

that American Sovietologists no longer cite Levine's "document" demonstrates once again that it is an unconvincing counterfeit item.

Another publication on the same subject is by Edward Ellis Smith, who worked at the U.S. embassy in Moscow for many years and who presents himself in his preface as something of an authority on the history of the Okhrana.[83] To him the allegations of Uratadze and Zhordania are quite important, but he rejects Orlov's testimony and Levine's document. To Smith it seems strange that when there were mass arrests in Tiflis on March 21–22, 1901, Stalin was not arrested. Stalin's later escape from Siberian exile (January 1904) strikes Smith as a police ruse. Smith does not agree that Stalin might have been arrested for a few hours in the Avlabar press case, but the very fact that he was not arrested seems suspicious to Smith. Similarly in Smith's eyes, the fact that Stalin was able to pass through all police checkpoints to attend the Stockholm congress and return to Russia could be confirmation of his ties with the Okhrana. Yet many other delegates reached Stockholm and returned in spite of the police. In 1908, after being arrested and escaping again, Stalin ended up in Bailov prison in Baku. For some reason Stalin's appearance in this prison strikes Smith as suspicious. He believes that Stalin ultimately broke with the Okhrana in 1913, when he had to choose between the police and the party. Then on July 2, 1913, he was arrested and sent into exile in the Turukhansk region. All this indirect evidence is unconvincing. It does not prove anything.

Following the Twentieth Party Congress, stories on this subject began to circulate among some of the old Bolsheviks. Here are a few that I heard and recorded in the sixties.

(1) As we have already seen, a 1918 collection of police documents indicated that an unidentified Vasily was an agent within the party; some Old Bolsheviks recall that in 1912, after escaping from Siberian exile and while sharing a room with Aron Solts at T. A. Slovatinskaya's in Petersburg, Stalin had the pseudonym Vasily.[84]

(2) In the early thirties the historian Professor Sepp, author of *The October Revolution in Documents*, happened upon the file of a police agent, Joseph Dzhugashvili. The file contained Dzhugashvili's request to be released from arrest. A note was written on this request: "Free him,

83. E. E. Smith, *The Young Stalin: The Early Years of an Elusive Revolutionary* (New York, 1967).
84. Yury Trifonov, *Otblesk kostra* (Moscow, 1966), p. 52.

if he agrees to give the Gendarme Department information about the activity of the Social Democratic Party." Sepp at that time was working in the Agitprop section of the Central Committee of Georgia. He went to Beria and showed him the file. Beria took it and flew to Moscow to see Stalin. Stalin looked through the file, destroyed the documents, and told Beria that it was all nonsense but that Sepp had to be taken care of. Following Beria's return to Tiflis, Sepp was arrested and shot.[85]

(3) In the mid-thirties Beria had Transcaucasian NKVD officials gathering materials from police archives on the activity of the Social Democratic Party. (Beria needed this material for his book on the history of Marxist organizations in Transcaucasia.) In the Kutais archives, a denunciation of a group of Social Democrats was found, signed by Joseph Dzughashvili. The denunciation was brought to Kobulov, Beria's closest aide, who gave it to Beria himself.[86]

(4) The old Bolshevik V—— has told how he once dropped in on Stalin in a conspiratorial apartment in Tiflis and found a high-ranking gendarme with him. After the gendarme left, V—— asked Stalin: "What do you have in common with the gendarmes? Why was that gendarme here?"

"Uh—he's helping us—in the gendarmerie," Stalin answered.[87]

(5) At the end of 1916, because of the deteriorating situation at the front, the army decided to draft a group of Social Democrats exiled in Siberia, including Stalin. After the exiles had arrived at Krasnoyarsk under guard, Stalin asked for a day's leave in the city. He did not return and did not go to the front. Although he lived in Krasnoyarsk practically without hiding, the police showed no evidence of interest in his activity.[88]

(6) Following the Prague Conference of 1912, Ordzhonikidze was assigned a number of important jobs by the Central Committee and set out on a trip to many Russian cities. As soon as he crossed the border, detectives "latched onto" him and shadowed him during his whole long journey. At one station Stalin came on the train and sat down with Ordzhonikidze, who told him about the decisions of the conference. They went to sleep in the railway car. But in the morning Stalin was gone. Five years later, after the February revolution, Ordzhonikidze asked Stalin where he had gone. "I noticed someone following me and didn't

---

85. From the personal papers of Yevgeny Frolov, party member since 1918.
86. The story was told to Suren Gazaryan by a member of Kobulov's family.
87. From the papers of Yevgeny Frolov.
88. From the memoirs of the Old Bolshevik Boris Ivanov.

want to get you in trouble," Stalin answered. Later, the report of the agents who had followed Ordzhonikidze was found in the police files. It described his entire journey, without one word about his meeting with Stalin.[89]

(7) During the 1905 revolution Stalin organized a number of "expropriations"—that is, armed robberies. (The Bolsheviks considered expropriations permissible in the context of a revolutionary situation.) In some cases guards were killed. The legal penalty was very severe, up to and including death. Stalin's participation would have been difficult to hide from the police. But all the sentences he received were relatively light. Some historians feel that such leniency was not accidental.

For most procurators in the Stalin era these stories would have justified an order for the arrest of Joseph Dzhugashvili—had he not stood at the head of the party, the government, and the NKVD itself. But it is not hard to see that all these "proofs" of Stalin's connections with the tsarist secret police are based on questionable second- or even third-hand reports. They have as little credibility as the accounts in the foreign press. Why, for example, did Stalin not have Beria and Kobulov shot, since they knew about this sinister secret from his past? Who can vouch for the truthfulness of the story of the Old Bolshevik who supposedly saw a high-ranking gendarme in Stalin's apartment? Such a visit by a gendarme in a uniform to the conspiratorial apartment of a Bolshevik is highly improbable.

The coincidence between Stalin's pseudonym in 1912 and that of some unidentified police spy also tells us nothing. Stalin had a great variety of cover names; and many other Bolsheviks could have had the cover name Vasily. According to police reports, Stalin customarily used the pseudonyms Koba and Kavkazets.

As for the story of Professor Sepp, was there actually a historian by that name? I have not been able to find his name in present-day historiography of the October revolution. It is an Estonian name. A Communist revolutionary by the name of A. Sepp took part in an uprising in Estonia in 1919 after the collapse of Soviet power in that country, but the revolt was suppressed and most of its leaders were killed. If Sepp did exist, who can say what were the real reaons for his arrest and execution?

T. Firsova's story about Stalin and Ordzhonikidze's trip is inaccurate. In fact, the police did have reports about their meeting, which noted that

89. Recounted by G. L. Mekhanik, who heard it from T. Firsova, who heard it from Zinaida Ordzhonikidze.

Stalin met Ordzhonikidze in Moscow and went with him to St. Petersburg on April 9, 1912. A Colonel Zavarzin sent a telegram to this effect to the head of the Petersburg secret police. Three experienced detectives were sent along to tail Stalin and Ordzhonikidze. The train arrived in St. Petersburg April 10. Ordzhonikidze was arrested on April 14, Stalin on April 22. It is possible that this happened precisely because he slipped away from the train. Of course, he should have alerted Ordzhonikidze to the fact that they were being followed, but his failure to do so does not prove that he had ties with the police. After being sentenced to three years of exile in the Narym territory, Stalin escaped from that remote region and lived in St. Petersburg until his last arrest, in 1913. As for the "expropriations," the tsarist police may not have known of Stalin's part in them.

There was undoubtedly a special file on each Bolshevik leader in the central offices of the gendarmerie. But during the February revolution, as I have mentioned, a crowd of workers and soldiers broke into the Petrograd police archives, threw a lot of papers from cabinets and safes into the courtyard, and burned them. Many documents were thereby irretrievably lost, but the insurgents did not find all the police safes and hidden materials. Part of the archives of the Central Gendarme Administration dealing with RSDLP activists was stolen by N. A. Maklakov, the former Russian ambassador to France, and taken abroad. This material was sold to the Hoover Institution in the United States. As far as I know, this material has been opened but nothing sensational has been found in it. (Similarly, there was nothing sensational when the closed section of Trotsky's archives were opened in 1980. Trotsky sold his papers to Harvard University in 1940 with the stipulation that part of them would remain sealed for forty years.)

Another Russian émigré, a Colonel Gerasimov, who was the head of the St. Petersburg Okhrana, personally dealt with a number of agent-provocateurs without making these dealings known to his colleagues. Boris Nicolaevsky, an émigré Menshevik and one of the most conscientious historians of the Russian revolutionary movement, wrote the following, based on statements by Gerasimov:

In regard to the secret agents of central importance who worked under Gerasimov's direction, not all their identities were later revealed. The role of a whole series of them remains absolutely unknown to this day. The reason for this is that Gerasimov made no reports about them to the Department of Police (and it was on the basis of such reports that the names of most St. Petersburg agents became known . . .). Only Gerasimov himself had any dealings with these agents; no one else knew them, and after Gerasimov left his post as head of the Okhrana, these agents also abandoned police work. According to Gerasimov, up to now none of them has been uncovered.[90]

There is no reason to think that Stalin-Dzhugashvili might be one of the agents whose identity Gerasimov claimed had never been discovered. Of course the Okhrana had quite a few documents on Stalin, especially since he frequently was arrested, interrogated, sent into exile, and escaped from exile. None of the documents known to me confirm the story that he collaborated with the police. I will present only a few of them here. The first dates from 1904.

Circular of the Ministry of Internal Affairs, Department of Police, Special Section, May 1, 1904. No. 5500

To all governors of provinces, mayors, chiefs of police, heads of provincial gendarmerie and of railroad police administrations, and to all border posts.

The Department of Police has the honor of sending you herewith, for appropriate disposition, the following: (1) a list of persons being sought in connection with political cases; (2) a list of persons for whom search may be terminated; and (3) a list of persons named in previous circulars, still being sought. . . .

List 1—Persons being sought in connection with political cases (Entries No. 1–185).

. . .

Entry No. 52 (p. 20)

Dzhugashvili, Joseph Vissarionovich; peasant from the village of Didi-Lilo, Tiflis district, Tiflis province; born 1881; of Orthodox faith, attended Gori church school and Tiflis theological seminary; not married. Father, Vissarion, whereabouts unknown. Mother, Yekaterina, resident of the town of Gori, Tiflis province. On the basis of an order of His Majesty, issued on the 9th day of May, 1903, the subject was banished for three years, under open police surveillance, to Eastern Siberia for crimes against the state and was placed in residence in Balagan district, Irkutsk province, from whence he disappeared on January 5, 1904.

Description: height, 2 arshins, 4 1/2 vershki [about 5 feet, 4 inches]; average build; gives the appearance of an ordinary person; hair of the head, dark brown; mustache and beard, reddish-brown; straight hair, not curly or wavy; eyes, dark brown, of average size; shape of head, ordinary; forehead flat, not high; nose,

---

90. Boris Nicolaevsky, *Istoriia odnogo predatelia* (New York, 1980). (This book was first printed in the early 1930s.) It should be noted that Colonel Gerasimov not only gave interviews to Nikolaevsky in the late twenties and early thirties but in 1934 himself published a long book in German about the Okhrana and the agents and informers who worked for it, Azef being the main one. The book was also published in French and recently appeared in a Russian edition: A. V. Gerasimov, *Na lezvii s terroristami* (Paris, 1985).

straight, long; face, long swarthy, covered with smallpox marks; right lower jaw, front molar missing; a person of moderate size, with a sharp chin, soft voice, ears of average size; normal gait; birthmark on left ear; second and third toes of left foot joined together.

Detain and telegraph Department of Police for further instructions.[91]

It is doubtful that a document of this kind would be sent to all police units and border posts in order to capture an agent of the tsarist police.

The other two documents date from 1911. They are letters between police officials in Moscow and Vologda.

Absolutely Secret
Personal

MVD, Chief of the Division
for the Preservation of Social
Safety and Order in Moscow
August 17, 1911
To: The Chief of the Vologda Gubernia Gendarme Administration

According to repeated and trustworthy information give to my Department by secret agents, at the present time an active and very serious member of the Russian Social Democratic Labor Party, bearing the pseudonym "Koba," is living in Vologda, where he is serving, or has already served, a term of administrative exile.

The above-named "Koba" has been in direct touch within the party center abroad and has now been told to go abroad for the necessary instructions to fulfill the obligations of a traveling agent for the Central Committee.

The following address is used for communication with the above-named "Koba": Peter Alekseevich Chizhikov, Ishmematov's Store, Vologda; money for Koba's traveling expenses will be sent to this address.

Absolutely Secret

Chief of the Vologda Gubernia Gendarme Administration
To: The Chief of the Moscow Branch of the Secret Police
August 21, 1911

The nickname "Koba" indicated in your communication of August 17, No. 260990, belongs to the former political exile Joseph Vissarionov Dzhugashvili, who is temporarily living in Vologda. A copy of the report on him addressed to the Director of the Department of Police on March 14 of this year, No. 53, was at the same time forwarded to you by the Chief of the Tiflis Gubernia Gendarme Administration.

From the files of the Administration entrusted to me it appears that on Febru-

91. Central State Archives of the October Revolution, collection DO — Department of Police, Special Section, file 167, 1905, records in the case of Shimon Abramovich Zilban, person of the townsman caste (meshchanin), sheets 4–36.

ary 27, 1909, Dzhugashvili arrived under guard in the place of exile designated for him, Solvychegodsk, whence, on July 24 of the same year, he disappeared. Arrested in Baku on March 24, 1910, he was taken back to Solvychegodsk, whence on July 27, 1911, upon finishing his term of exile, he was released, and with a transit document arrived in Vologda, where in accordance with his petition, he was permitted to stay temporarily, for two months until September 19 of this year.

According to our agents' information, Dzhugashvili together with other exiles (Ivan Petrov Petrov, Ivan Mikhailov Golubev, Nikolai Matveev Ilyin, Aleksandr Yankelev Shur, Irodion Isaakov Khasimov, Fedor Ignatyev Syaponovsky, Mikhail Alekseev Kalandatze, Georgy Alekseev Korostylev, and Grigory Ivanov Zhavoronkov) tried to organize a Social Democratic faction in Solvychegodsk, and held meetings at which papers were read and political questions were discussed. The goal of these meetings was to produce propagandists. This information of our agents was forwarded by my predecessor to the raion on May 17 of this year, No. 216. On his arrival in Vologda on July 19, Dzhugashvili moved into the house of Bobrova on Malo-Kozlenskaya Street, and from July 24 came under observation under the nickname "Kavkazets."

. . . Since Dzhugashvili will probably soon be going to St. Petersburg or Moscow to see representatives of organizations there, he will be accompanied by an observer on his departure from Vologda.

Taking into consideration the fact that Dzhugashvili is very careful and could therefore be lost by an observer, it would be better to make a search and arrest him now in Vologda. To this end, please inform me whether you have at your disposal information necessary to make a case against Dzhugashvili, and whether there are any objections on your part to a search of this person now.

We might add to the foregoing that it is impossible to count on favorable results from a search of him in Vologda, in view of the extremely conspiratorial nature of his actions.

Simultaneously with the search of Dzhugashvili all the people with whom he is in contact here will also be searched.

> Certified signature:
> Colonel Konissky[92]

It is hard to suppose that such letters would be exchanged concerning a provocateur. Thus there is no proof that Stalin had connections with the tsarist secret police or that fear of exposure of such connections was what drove him to mass repression. Nevertheless, Stalin was a typical provocateur, though in another sense of the word. In his struggle for power provocation was his favorite weapon, and he used it with great skill. As early as the intraparty struggle of the twenties he inflated disagreements, set leaders against each other, encouraged enmity among them. Whatever is believed about Kirov's murder, it cannot be denied

---

92. Central State Historical Archives, collection 102, item 267/1911 g., DO, 1911.

that Stalin used the murder for provocative ends, cleverly directing popular anger against the former opposition. As for the political show trials of the thirties, they were among the basest provocations of the twentieth century, with the most painful consequences.

In 1937 at a meeting of the Military Council Stalin said that he had received a denunciation of Blyukher signed by one of his deputies. Stalin added that he did not believe the denunciation. In fact he had not received it; he merely wanted Blyukher to quarrel with one of his colleagues, who was soon arrested with Blyukher's tacit consent.[93] Stalin often gave his agents and subordinates criminal orders—verbally, of course—and then had them arrested for carrying out those orders.

Under Stalin's influence NKVD investigators used provocation as well as torture.[94] A highly complex provocation was organized against the prominent Bolshevik Betal Kalmykov. He was married to a woman whose first husband had been a White officer and then became an émigré, although her son by her first husband was going to school in Moscow. On some pretext the youngster was persuaded to go to Belorussia, where he was arrested on charges of trying to leave the Soviet Union illegally to go live with his father. After the son's arrest a case was concocted against Kalmykov. In a similar case an NKVD general was told to go at once to a certain border point to check on the functioning of the border guards there. When the general arrived, he was arrested and accused of trying to flee abroad. The postwar "Leningrad case" and the "doctor's case" were typical provocative actions organized by Stalin and some NKVD executives.[95]

Actions of this kind have caused Stalin to be compared not only to Ivan the Terrible and other tyrants but also to famous provocateurs. Grigory Pomerants, for example, compares Stalin to Yevno Azef, head of the Combat Organization of the Socialist Revolutionary Party, who was at the same time an agent of the secret police.[96] Mikhail Yakubovich makes the same comparison in his interesting notes on Stalin:

93. Recounted by Pyotr Yakir.

94. Eugenia Ginzburg tells of one such provocation in her *Journey into the Whirlwind* (New York, 1967). See the chapter "Pugachev Tower," pp. 180–188.

95. For these cases, see below.

96. G. Pomerants, "Nravstvennyi oblik istoricheskoi lichnosti," unpublished manuscript. Pomerants's essay circulated widely in manuscript form in the Soviet Union in the sixties. A copy is in my archive.

Why did Azef play with human lives, destroying people on both sides—his revolutionary comrades and his superiors in the police? I believe that such activity was above all his way to satisfy his love of power—or rather, his lust for power—in the manner available to him in those times. The power of life and death is the greatest power, of all its possible variations; to kill people is the sharpest and fullest satisfaction of this lust for power. Of course, if a power-hungry man is characterized by blood-thirsty cruelty as well, by a capacity for ruthlessness, by contempt for people and lack of faith in any ideas, then he has the capacity to play with ideas and juggle them at will, just as pragmatism requires.

All these qualities were possessed in full by Yevno Azef and likewise by Joseph Stalin. In the same cold blood, without any regret or pangs of conscience, Stalin sent his party comrades to be shot, just as Azef sent them to the tsarist gallows. And the motives of both were the same—an unchecked, boundless thirst for power, which was satisfied most fully by the murders they committed. The only difference between them was that they lived in dissimilar historical contexts: Stalin realized his power through the apparatus of the state security agencies subordinated to him, while Azef did so through the apparatus of the tsarist courts and the tsarist police, or by the hands of the SR Combat Organization. If Azef had found himself at the helm of government, he probably would have ruled by the same methods as Stalin. . . . The psychological similarity between them is remarkably great. They are soul brothers.[97]

■ 8

STALIN'S PERSONALITY AND THE MOTIVES FOR HIS CRIMES

I have examined critically the various accounts of why Stalin unleashed the terror of 1936–39. There is no need to overly complicate the explanation. His main motive (and here I agree completely with Yakubovich) was lust for power, boundless ambition. This all-consuming lust appeared in Stalin much earlier than 1936. Even though he had great power, it was not enough—he wanted absolute power and unlimited submission to his will. He understood at the same time that the generation of party and government leaders formed in the years of underground work, revolution, and civil war would never become totally submissive. They too

97. Mikhail Yakubovich, "Stalin. Razmyshleniia o ego lichnosti i istoricheskoi roli," unpublished manuscript, a copy of which is in my archive. [Medvedev's four-paged quotation from this manuscript has been greatly abridged here, for much of it tells the familiar story of Azef. —D. J.]

had taken part in the creation of the party and the state and demanded their share of the leadership. But Stalin did not want to share power.

As early as 1926, when Kirov was elected first secretary of the Leningrad party committee, Stalin revealed himself at a dinner celebrating the event. The conversation turned to a favorite question of that period: how to govern the party without Lenin? Everyone, of course, agreed that the party should be governed by a collective. Stalin at first did not take part in the discussion, but then he got up and, walking around the table, said, "Don't forget we are living in Russia, the land of the tsars. The Russian people like to have one man standing at the head of the state." Then he added, "Of course, this man should carry out the will of the collective." No one took exception to Stalin's remark, but no one present thought Stalin had himself in mind as this great chief of Russia.[98]

Stalin may have been serious in his argument that class struggle would intensify as the country moved toward socialism. Inclined to schematic thinking, to a simplified, mechanistic understanding of reality, Stalin was often deeply convinced that the schemes he created were uniquely correct. But he was certainly not sincere when he extended this argument beyond members of former exploiting classes to veterans of the revolution and the basic cadres of the party and the state. Stalin spoke respectfully of some of his victims even after he had destroyed them. According to A. I. Todorsky, at a Politburo meeting in 1938 Stalin unexpectedly began to praise Tukhachevsky, who had already been shot. Stalin noted Tukhachevsky's unquestioned military talent, his great sense of responsibility when given a job, and his striving to keep abreast of the fast-changing theory, technology, and practice of military affairs. And after Uborevich had been shot, Stalin said to Kirill Meretskov: "Train our troops the same way you trained them under Uborevich."[99]

Generally, though, Stalin referred to his victims with bitterness and hatred. He feared conspiracies and he feared many of his colleagues. Politburo members who met each other for tea or visited each other's homes could fall under suspicion. They and other highly placed officials were under constant surveillance by the NKVD. Each of Stalin's dachas outside Moscow had several bedrooms, and on each bed was a change of linen. Usually Stalin himself would put the sheets on the bed. Often

98. Recounted by Pyotr Chagin, one of the leaders of the Leningrad party organization, who was a close friend of Kirov and who was present at the dinner along with Kirov, several other Leningrad leaders, Tomsky, and Stalin.

99. *Komandarm Uborevich* (Moscow, 1964).

before going to sleep, he would look under the bed. For his convenience in doing this the lamp in the bedroom usually had no shade and could easily be lowered to the floor. Each dacha had two exits and was carefully guarded all seasons of the year, whether Stalin was living there or not.

In the late twenties Stalin often went for walks outside the Kremlin. He would have bodyguards with him but they were not obvious. Inside the Kremlin and in the Central Committee building Stalin walked around without any visible guard. Some Old Bolsheviks recall riding in the elevator with Stalin at the Central Committee building or meeting him in the corridor. Almost all prominent Bolsheviks carried weapons, a practice surviving from the civil war. After Kirov's assassination rank and file party members were forbidden to carry guns but leaders such as Voroshilov and Budyonny, Beria and Kaganovich, Ordzhonikidze and Lyubchenko walked around with pistols in their holsters. Tomsky and Gamarnik shot themselves with their own pistols; Bukharin and Rykov tried to. Nestor Lakoba, chairman of the CEC of Abkhazia, where Stalin went on vacation almost every summer, liked to do target practice with his Browning. All these "freedoms" were gradually curtailed, then abolished before the war. At the Kremlin and at Stalin's dachas only NKVD personnel who were on guard outside the buildings and would therefore not come into contact with Stalin were allowed to have weapons. People received by Stalin, if they carried weapons, were supposed to surrender them before entering his office or room. Some highly placed visitors were even searched. This was the fear of a tyrant and usurper worried about his power and his life; it was not the vigilance of a leader responsible for the first socialist state in the world.

Stalin's destruction of the party's old guard was a deliberate policy, not the result of some persecution mania. The facts show that Stalin had a plan to destroy the cadres of the party, state, and military cadres, and this plan, to use Todorsky's expression, was not inferior to the mobilization plan of a great army. It was carefully thought out, richly supplied, and masterfully executed. It was a crime whose equal is hard to find in world history.

We know from history that a ruler's excessive ambition does not automatically lead to mass repression and the murder of his opponents and rivals, even when there are no serious obstacles to such reprisals. Thus, in considering the personal aspect of the repression in the thirties, we must take into account not only Stalin's ambition and vanity but also his cruelty and viciousness. We must also note the contradiction between

Stalin's limitless ambition and his limited abilities. It was this very contradiction that drove Stalin into conflict not only with those he saw as his present or future opponents but also with many Old Bolsheviks who were personally devoted to him, never said anything against him, and carried out all his orders. From his early years Stalin had an inferiority complex. Combined with the ambition and vanity that developed in him quite early, his inner sense of inferiority intensified such characteristics as spitefulness and envy, which originally arose out of the conditions of life in his family home, the church school, and the seminary.

Nero, fancying himself a great actor and poet, sometimes killed not only those who gave him too little applause, but also those who excelled him in versifying or declaiming. When he took part in competitions of singers or actors, he was always the victor, but that was not enough; he ordered that the statues of past winners be dragged into privies. Many of Stalin's actions amounted to the same thing. People who had done as much or more than he for the revolution merited destruction by that very fact. And everywhere he put up monuments to himself—thousands upon thousands of factories and firms named for Stalin, and many cities: Stalinsk, Stalino, Stalinir, Stalingrad, Stalinbad, Stalinkan, Stalin, Stalinovarosh—more than can be counted. This again recalls Nero, who wanted to name Rome Neropolis.

Before the revolution Stalin did not belong to the nucleus of leaders grouped around Lenin. Not until 1912 was he placed on the Central Committee, and his exile to the Turukhansk region deprived him of the chance to play much of a leading role. His earlier work in the Transcaucasian Bolshevik organizations was much more modest than later legends asserted. Lenin was only slightly acquainted with Stalin before the revolution, despite the story that dates their "friendship" from the Tammerfors Conference in 1905.

When Stalin was encouraging the cult of his personality, he wanted praise not just for his current activity but for his entire party career. He and his cohorts shamelessly falsified party history, twisting and suppressing many facts and producing a flood of books, articles, and pamphlets filled with distortions. People who knew party history at first hand got in Stalin's way. So Stalin arranged deliberate provocations to remove these people, from life and—so he thought—from history as well. They knew, for example, that the newspaper *Brdzola*, which Stalin edited and which Beria praised so much in his falsified history of Bolshevik organizations in Transcaucasia, had been a sheet slightly larger than a leaflet and had appeared only four times; thus it was absurd to put it on the same level as Lenin's *Iskra*.[100] They also knew that when Beria credited Stalin with founding the famous underground press in Baku, it was a lie. Their knowledge of the real history was sufficient reason for Stalin and Beria to destroy many Old Bolsheviks, whose past services were then attributed to Stalin. In the same way other myths were created—that of the "two chiefs" of the October revolution, Lenin and Stalin, and that of Stalin's "decisive role" in the victories of the Red Army during the civil war.

Stalin's "modesty" is often stressed in the various memoirs about him published during the Brezhnev era with the aim of partly rehabilitating Stalin. These publications tell us that Stalin disliked luxury, that he preferred simply food and modest quarters. When the Potsdam Conference, attended by Stalin, Churchill, and Truman, was being arranged for July 1945 an order was sent to the appropriate unit of the Soviet occupation army to prepare a villa for Stalin "no worse than for Roosevelt and Churchill." When General Vlasik, the head of Stalin's bodyguard, arrived from Moscow, he ordered everything rearranged, because "Stalin does not like luxury." The fine beds and rugs were quickly removed. A simple oak table was put in the office and a sofa in the bedroom, while carpet runners replaced the rugs.[101] It is true that Stalin did not appropriate former royal palaces and residences for his own use, as Tito did. He simply appropriated the services to the revolution made by those he had killed.

Stalin did not wish to live in palaces, but he apparently nourished the dream of a godlike chief from his earliest years. His first meeting with Lenin was therefore disappointing, as he confessed in 1924:

Lenin had been drawn in my imagination as a giant, stately and imposing. How disenchanted I was to see a most ordinary man, below average height, in no way, literally in no way, different from ordinary mortals. . . .

Usually a "great man" is expected to arrive late at a meeting, so that the members of the meeting should wait for his appearance with baited breath, should warn each other . . . "Shhh . . . quiet . . . he's coming." Such ceremony seemed to me not superfluous, because it was impressive and inspired respect. How disenchanted I was when I learned that Lenin had arrived at the meeting before the delegates and, hiding in some corner, was simply having a conversa-

100. [*Iskra* was the Russian newspaper, published abroad in 1900–1903, that served as the chief means of organizing the Russian Social Democratic Labor Party (RSDLP). *Brdzola* ("The Struggle") was an underground Georgian newspaper whose four issues appeared in 1901–1902.—D. J.]

101. N. A. Antipenko, "Den' Pobedy," *Novy mir* (1981), no. 8, p. 227.

tion, a very ordinary conversation with very ordinary delegates. I won't conceal the fact that this seemed to me at the time a kind of violation of necessary rules.[102]

People who knew Stalin often mention not only his ambition, vanity, and cruelty, but also his coarseness, his lack of culture, of intellectuality. K. K. Ordzhonikidze, an older brother of Sergo Ordzhonikidze, tells the following incident:

It is common knowledge that Stalin and Sergo were good friends. Since I was often at my brother Sergo's place, I got to know not only Stalin but also many eminent leaders of the Communist Party and our country, in the first place Dzerzhinsky, Voroshilov, and Mikoyan. I especially remember Stalin's arrival in Tiflis in June 1926. He came on the first of June and stayed in Tiflis more than a week. Mikoyan arrived with him in Tiflis. Sergo then lived on Ganovskaya Street (now it is called Tabidze Street). Stalin and Mikoyan stayed in Sergo's apartment. Then I got to know them well.

In connection with Stalin's arrival, leading Georgian and Caucasian officials gathered at Sergo's apartment. The table was set. We drank a lot of wine and sang drinking songs. Stalin poured me a tumbler of Georgian wine, which I tossed off at one draft. Then he poured me another tumblerful, which I also drank, and continued to sing along with everybody.

There was a moment of silence, and Stalin, taking advantage of it, began to sing in the Georgian language. It was an indecent song. He went on singing even though there were women sitting at the table. Maria Platonovna Orakhelashvili did not need a translation, but Zinaida Gavrilovna [Sergo's wife], who did not know Georgian, asked Sergo to translate the words of the song into Russian. At first Sergo refused, but she kept insisting, seeing the embarrassment of many and the unusual reaction of those present. When Sergo whispered a few words of this obscene song to Zinaida Gavrilovna, she blushed with shame and embarrassment.

That Stalin was foul-mouthed is well known, but that incident graphically convinced me that he was so used to foul words that he even sang songs abounding in them, and what was most astonishing was that he was not at all inhibited by the presence of such highly moral women as Maria Platonovna Orakhelashvili and Zinaida Gavrilovna Ordzhonikidze.

On the day of Stalin's departure from Tiflis, there were guests at Sergo's again. There was abundant refreshment. Then the guests went from Sergo's to Mamiya Orakhelashvili's place. Orakhelashvili lived at that time not far from Sergo, on Paskevich Street (now it is called Filipp Makharadze Street). Stalin did not want to go to Orakhelashvili's but Sergo talked him into it. Stalin was visibly convinced by words of Sergo that I still remember: "How can you do that! He's the head of our government—it will be awkward if you avoid him." At that time Mamiya Orakhelashvili was chairman of the Council of Commissars of the Transcaucasian Republic.

102. Stalin, *Sochineniia*, 6: 54.

Subsequent years would show that Stalin hated Orakhelashvili. Evidently he had come to dislike him long before and thus showed such reluctance to go to his house.[103]

In other cases Stalin could be the most charming host, even tender, paying compliments to his guests and serving them special Caucasian dishes with his own hands. Lydia Nord's book on Tukhachevsky contains a great deal of mistaken or inaccurate information. The author apparently was unable to distinguish between solid fact and empty rumor. The following description of Stalin in that book, however, is fairly accurate.

Today I often hear that Stalin could be charming when he wanted to. That is as true as the fact that his face was pockmarked. The qualities that make a person charming were as few as the traces of the pox on his face. He was not a bad psychologist, it's true. He knew when to be polite with those he needed. Until he became dictator, he was often ingratiating toward people. He was not begrudging with flattery, and sometimes he flattered a person so flagrantly and crudely that the object of flattery was thrown off and in the end attributed it all to the ingenuousness of Stalin's southern nature, taking it all for good coin. . . . But Stalin could also be terribly boorish, especially when he was drunk. He was aware of this himself and so as not to overdo it, he would drink only wine, and never very much. If he had offended someone, he would constantly excuse himself, if he thought that necessary, but subsequently everyone of whom Stalin had at one time asked forgiveness was executed or killed on his orders.[104]

Stalin was extremely unforgiving. If he felt humiliated or criticized, he never let it pass, even if his opponent went on to extol him for many years. Yet he found it easy to forgive an insult aimed at one of his entourage; sometimes he was quite amused by such a thing. In the first half of the thirties Stalin often visited Maxim Gorky's home. There, members of the government would encounter well-known members of the intelligentsia in an informal setting. In one such encounter Yagoda, the all-powerful commissar of internal affairs, came up to the well-known author and playwright Vsevolod Ivanov with the intention of clinking glasses and having a talk. "I don't drink with butchers," Ivanov said loudly. Everyone present fell silent, not knowing how to react. But Stalin burst out laughing and clapped Yagoda on the back. "I guess he told you off," Stalin said just as loudly as Ivanov had. Ivanov, after he sobered up, suffered nothing worse than humiliation and fright. On the other hand,

103. From K. K. Ordzhonikidze's unpublished memoirs, a copy of which is in my archives.
104. Lydia Nord, *Marshal M. N. Tukhachevsky* (Paris, 1978).

within a year Yagoda was removed from his post and within two years was shot.

Stalin's great willpower has frequently been noted in memoirs by those who knew him. In 1939 Fyodor Raskolnikov wrote in his diary:

The fundamental psychological trait of Stalin, which gave him a decisive advantage, as the lion's strength makes him king of the jungle, is his unusual, superhuman strength of will. He always knows what he wants and, with unwavering implacable methodicalness, gradually reaches his goal. "Inasmuch as power is in my hands," he once said to me, "I am a gradualist." In the silence of his office, in deep solitude, he carefully figures out a plan of action and with fine calculation strikes sudden and true. Stalin's strength of will suffocates, destroys the individuality of people who come under his influence. He easily succeeded in "crushing" not only the soft and weak-willed Kalinin but even such willful people as Kaganovich. Stalin does not need advisers, he only needs executors. Therefore he demands from his closest aides complete submission, obedience, subjection—unprotesting, slavish discipline. He does not like people who have their own opinion, and with his usual nastiness drives them away.

He is poorly educated. . . . He lacks the realism that Lenin possessed and, to a lesser degree, Rykov. He is not farsighted. When he undertakes some step, he is unable to weigh its consequences. He is after-the-fact. He does not foresee events and does not guide the spontaneous flow, as Lenin did, but drags at the tail of events, swims with the current. Like all semi-intellectuals who have picked up scraps of knowledge, Stalin hates the genuine cultured intelligentsia, party and nonparty in equal measure. Stalin lacks the flexibility of a man of state. He has the psychology of Zelim Khan, the Caucasian robber, who greedily seized one-man rule.[105] Scorning people, he considers himself complete master over their life and death. A narrow sectarian, he proceeds from a preconceived scheme. He is the same kind of schematist as Bukharin, with this difference, that Bukharin was a theoretically educated man. Stalin tries to force life into a ready-made framework. The more life resists being forced into the narrow Procrustean bed, the more forcefully he mangles and breaks it, chopping limbs off it. He knows the laws of formal logic, and his conclusions logically follow from his premises. But against the background of more outstanding contemporaries, he has never shone intellectually. Instead he is unusually tricky. . . . No one can compete with Stalin in the art of trickery. At the same time he is sneaky, treacherous, and vengeful. "Friendship" is an empty word for him. He flung aside and sent to execution such a close friend as Yenukidze. In his home life Stalin is a man with the requirements of an exile. He lives very simply and modestly, because with

105. Raskolnikov's widow turned his diaries over to the commission on his literary heritage in 1964 during her visit to the USSR. In this passage Raskolnikov was mistaken about Zelim Khan, who was not a Caucasian robber, but an *abrek*, a rebel fighter whose actions were an expression of protest against the tsarist authorities' policy of national oppression and terror in the Caucasus. See his biography written by a modern Chechen writer: M. Mamanaev, *Zelim-khan* (Grozny, 1971).

the fanaticism of an ascetic he scorns the good things in life: life's comforts, such as good food, simply do not interest him. He does not even need friends.

Raskolnikov knew Stalin well, and he drew a basically accurate portrait of the man's psyche. But the portrait is not exhaustive. Of course, Stalin was a strong-willed man, unwavering in attaining his goals. His quiet firmness and taciturnity impressed many Bolsheviks, won him the reputation of an unflinching fighter, even gave him a certain attraction in the eyes of many party members. But his strong will is not a sufficient explanation of his ascendancy. The fact that he destroyed some leaders of the party and subordinated others to himself does not mean that he was firmer or more strong-willed than, say, Kirov, Ordzhonikidze, Chubar, Yakir, or Dybenko. An assassin who shoots from ambush hardly needs a stronger will than his victim. An honorable man abstains from crimes not because he lacks a strong character; his character is simply directed toward other goals. Too often we call a man strong who violates all the accepted norms of human relations and all the rules of honorable struggle; the more he flouts these rules, the stronger and more resolute he seems to some people. In fact, most crimes evince not strength of will, but weakness of moral principles.

Stalin did have a strong personality. But he did not have the superhuman strength of will that some of his contemporaries attributed to him. He simply lacked firm moral principles; he never loved or respected people, never tried to serve them. And he never recognized any rules of honorable political struggle. Taking advantage of his superior position in the party, striking from ambush, he was able to destroy many strong people. But we do not know how he would have behaved if he himself had been tortured in the cellars of the NKVD.

Raskolnikov is also inadequate on Stalin's cunning. Stalin was not simply crafty; he was a man of unusual hypocrisy. He achieved a great deal by his ability to put on any mask. I have already discussed his extraordinary cruelty. Zinaida Ordzhonikidze used to tell her friends that she always found it unpleasant to visit Stalin, who liked to make fun of his "friends." His personal secretary Poskrebyshev was a frequent butt. One New Year's Eve Stalin rolled pieces of paper into little tubes and put them on Poskrebyshev's fingers. Then he lit them in place of New Year's candles. Poskrebyshev writhed in pain but did not dare take them off. Cruel practical jokes were also played on highly placed officials invited to visit Stalin. The newcomer might be pushed into the pond at Stalin's dacha "just for fun," or he might be asked to give a toast, and

while he was doing so, a cake or ripe tomato would be placed on the seat
behind him.

Yet as I have said, Stalin could be the most affable host, even bringing
his guests roses from his garden. (I may note, only as a chance coincidence, that Hitler also liked to make gifts of flowers and to smell roses.)
Stalin played the role especially with foreign guests, which misled many
of them. I have already cited Lion Feuchtwanger's enraptured comments
on Stalin. H. G. Wells also failed to understand Stalin, who received him
in 1934.

I confess that I approached Stalin with a certain amount of suspicion and preju-
dice. A picture had been built up in my mind of a very reserved and self-centered
fanatic, a despot without vices, a jealous monopolizer of power. I had been
inclined to take the part of Trotsky against him. . . . All such shadowy undertow,
all suspicion of hidden emotional tensions, ceased forever, after I had talked to
him for a few minutes. . . . I have never met a man more candid, fair and honest,
and to these qualities it is, and to nothing occult and sinister, that he owes his
tremendous undisputed ascendancy in Russia. I had thought before I saw him
that he might be where he was because men were afraid of him, but I realize that
he owes his position to the fact that no one is afraid of him and everybody trusts
him. The Russians are a people at once childish and subtle, and they have a
justifiable fear of subtlety in themselves and others. Stalin is an exceptionally
unsubtle Georgian. His unaffected orthodoxy is an assurance to his associates that
whatever he does would be done without fundamental complications and in the
best possible spirit. They had been fascinated by Lenin, and they feared new
departures from his talismanic directions.[106]

This is obviously a portrait of Wells rather than Stalin.

Many prominent figures in Soviet life succumbed to Stalin's favors.
Marshal Konstantin Rokossovsky, for example, while resting at his own
dacha in 1947, was invited by phone to dinner with the "boss." The
dinner was quite relaxed, with Stalin often rising and walking about the
room. At one point he went up to the marshal and asked: "I heard
recently that you were in confinement?" "Yes, Comrade Stalin," was the
reply. "I was in confinement. But, as you see, they figured out my case
and let me go. But how many good and remarkable people perished
there," Rokossovsky unexpectedly concluded.

"Yes," said Stalin slowly. "We have a lot of good, remarkable people."
He turned quickly and went out into the garden. Everyone at the table
fell into a frightened silence. "What did you say to Stalin?" Malenkov
whispered indignantly, "and why?" A few minutes later Stalin came back,

106. H. G. Wells, *Experiment in Autobiography*, (New York, 1934), pp. 684–689.

carrying roses. He gave one bouquet to Rokossovsky, another to his wife. The marshal, who had been preparing himself for the worst, was overcome, and never again reminded Stalin of his fallen comrades.

For people he wanted to impress, Stalin sometimes put on elaborate acts. After the war, for example, when he was receiving an admiral in his office, he suddenly called Poskrebyshev, who put on his desk a pile of books on linguistics and, running down a list, which included prerevolutionary works, said that he had not yet been able to get some of them. "What doesn't Stalin study!" thought the admiral. Academician Eugene Varga told his friends that every time he visited Stalin, Marx's *Capital* was lying on Stalin's desk.

During the war a story gained wide popularity about a pilot who had been awarded the title Hero of the Soviet Union. Returning home after the award ceremony through the streets of Moscow, darkened against air raids, the pilot shot a man who was harassing a young woman. A police patrol detained the pilot, and the case was reported to Stalin. He asked what could be done for the pilot *under Soviet law*. He was told that he could vouch for the pilot so that he would be released on his own recognizance until the trial. Stalin personally sent a statement to the Presidium of the Supreme Soviet. The pilot was temporarily returned to his unit but soon died in aerial combat.[107]

A typical example of Stalin's hypocrisy was recalled by the widow of Aleksandr Kosarev at the meeting dedicated to his memory.

When Papanin's group[108] returned to Moscow in the summer of 1938, there was a reception and a big banquet in the Kremlin. Molotov proposed a toast to those present, including Kosarev. Everyone who was toasted went up to Stalin to clink glasses. Sasha also went up. Stalin not only clinked his glass but embraced and kissed him. Returning to his seat, Sasha, pale and agitated, said to me: "Let's go home." When we had left, I asked why he was so upset. He replied: "When Stalin kissed me, he said in my ear, 'If you're a traitor, I'll kill you.' " Some months later Sasha was in fact killed, although he had not acted against Stalin.[109]

While it is a mistake to consider Stalin a superman of invincible will, it is also wrong to regard him simply as an ambitious, sadistic hypocrite

107. Air Marshal A. Ye. Golovanov recounted this forgotten story in his memoirs as an example of "Stalin's respect for Soviet law" (*Oktyabr*, 1970, no. 5, p. 195). Yet Golovanov surely knew how cruelly Stalin dealt with the leadership of the air force both before and after the war and how many pilots died, not in aerial combat, but in prisons and camps.

108. [I. D. Papanin directed an Arctic expedition, which determined ocean currents by drifting on a floe for an extended period. — D. J.]

109. From the unpublished stenographic record of the meeting at the Museum of the Revolution on the sixtieth anniversary of Kosarev's birth, November 21, 1963, p. 49.

who gained control of the party by intrigues and crimes. Both as a person and as a leader, Stalin was a much more complex and contradictory figure. Certainly he cannot be called a genuine Marxist or Leninist as some Western Sovietologists and Russian émigrés of a certain persuasion do, along with many official Chinese and Soviet publications. Some do this in order to glorify Stalin; others to belittle Lenin. In his published works Stalin used Marxist terminology but not the Marxist method. If Lenin could write that it was highly doubtful whether Bukharin's theoretical views were entirely Marxist, Stalin's works deserve such an appraisal even more. Of course, Stalin often wrote and spoke like a Marxist, for he could not ignore the party's ideology or avoid the use of Marxist terminology, but he was never a Marxist in essence.

Socialist doctrine, of which Marxism-Leninism represents certain forms and stages, is not only a system of concepts; it is also a system of convictions and moral principles, which Lenin did not always set forth accurately. As for Stalin, he was totally lacking in such qualities. In fact, Stalin was not so much a participant in the socialist revolution as one of its *fellow-travelers*.

What motivates people to join a revolutionary movement? Support for revolution usually comes from those who are dissatisfied with the existing order, who suffer acutely from the prevailing political and economic system. A violent revolution is usually preceded by an abrupt deterioration in the already difficult conditions of the masses or by some provocative action by the ruling classes. Such a revolution is an explosion of anger and desperation on the part of the oppressed who have lost hope for any improvement in their situation under the old dispensation and who are ready to suffer and die to establish a new order. The political army of the revolution comes first of all from the lower strata of society. Some members of the intelligentsia and the intermediate strata join the movement as well, and tend to predominate in the leaderships of the revolutionary parties. Some of them enter the camp of revolution with noble motives, seeking to realize the ideal of a just society. Others join the revolution for personal reasons, sometimes with rather ulterior motives, hoping to occupy a better position in the new society than they had in the old one.

There are many historical examples of unstable and dishonorable people who join a revolutionary movement and later degenerate into tyrants or the servants of tyrants. Joseph Fouché, for example, the all-powerful minister of police in Napoleon's government and in the Bourbon restoration, one of the richest men in France, began as one of the most radical Jacobins. When he was proconsul of a province he threatened moderates, confiscated the property of the rich, and attacked the church. In Lyons he had hundreds of people shot on charges of being enemies of the people. In 1794 he was elected president of the Jacobin Club. But ten years later the same Fouché hunted down Jacobins, and ten years after that he pursued Bonapartists. After reading Stefan Zweig's book *Joseph Fouché*, which was translated in the Soviet Union in the thirties, Stalin commented: "There was a man for you. He outwitted everyone, made them all look like fools." Stalin said approximately the same thing about Talleyrand after reading a book about him by the Soviet historian Yevgeny Tarle. Mussolini is another case in point. He began as a member of the most radical wing of the Italian Socialist Party and wound up as a fascist dictator.

In his novel *The Devils* (also known as *The Possessed*), Dostoevsky gives a distorted picture of the Russian revolutionary movement in the second half of the nineteenth century, but some of the types he portrays deserve scrutiny. The Russian revolutionary movement included not only the heroic types pictured in Chernyshevsky's novel *What Is To Be Done?* but also people like Dostoevsky's Liputin, a petty provincial official, an envious, coarse despot, a miser and a usurer; and like his Verkhovensky, a cheat, scoundrel, and murderer, who wanted to unite his few followers not by common ideals but by joint responsibility for the crimes committed. That such "socialists" did exist is proved by the activity of Sergei Nechaev in the late 1860s. He sincerely believed that he was a socialist, which he understood as follows:

> To become a good socialist, one must reject all tender, soft feelings of kinship, friendship, love, gratitude, and even honor itself. . . . He is not a revolutionary who pities anything in this world. . . . A revolutionary knows only one science— the science of destruction and extermination. He lives in the world with this sole aim. To leave not one stone on another, as many ruins as possible, the extinction of most of the revolutionaries—that is the perspective. Poison, the knife, the noose—the revolution consecrates everything.

Blind obedience to the chief, a system of mutual spying and involuted deception of all the members of the organization—such were Nechaev's methods for the triumph of socialism. He murdered Ivanov, a student in the Agricultural Academy, accusing him of betrayal, although Ivanov had only opposed Nechaev's arbitrary ways. In an interesting article on Dostoevsky, Yuri Karyakin has drawn an anology between Stalin and Ne-

chaev that has some validity.[110] Karyakin has also informed me of a
suggestive fact: Nechaev's archive, thought to be lost, was returned to its
place after 1953, from Stalin's office.

Crimes committed during and after a revolution may be viewed as
grounds for condemning all revolutions and revolutionaries. But as Yevgeny Gnedin has written:

> I am inclined to defend the revolutionary personality. This is not an easy task,
> and it is one that I inwardly resist when I think about the unbridled extremists in
> the West who call themselves "revolutionaries" but commit crimes against hu-
> manity.
> The personality that I interpret in a positive sense is not filled with hatred and
> must be free of narrow fanaticism and dogmatic limitations. I remind the reader
> that the productive and innovative revolutionary spirit, which is at the same time
> the spirit of tragedy, is inseparable from the history of mankind and from the
> destinies of individuals. World history and literature are rich with vivid confir-
> mations of this truth. In Soviet society the revolutionary personality, the idealist,
> the revolutionary romantic, is for many reasons both praised to the skies and
> ridiculed, regarded as a great contributor and a source of destruction, one that
> reaches for the stars or flounders in the mire. Today in Soviet society the
> passionate youth who reject our stagnant system of government regard the
> revolutionary type with anger and condemnation, and view the self-satisfied
> defenders of the system with vicious irony. Both the noble opponents of violence
> and the self-seeking bureaucrats who base themselves on the violence of the state
> reject revolution. Yet for a number of years rebellious moods were a mass phe-
> nomenon in our country, when hopes rose high that Russia, having taken the
> road of revolution, would perform a world-historical mission. These "cosmopoli-
> tan" aspirations aside, revolutionary character took shape in various strata of
> society in those years, especially in the working class, but among the peasants as
> well, when it seemed that the ancient hopes for a just redivision of the land
> would be realized. The longing for justice was an integral part of the revolution-
> ary character.[111]

Maxim Gorky expressed similar ideas, though in a more pointed and
precise way, in one of his articles written in 1918. He distinguished two
types of revolutionary: the revolutionary for all time and the revolutionary for this day. The first type is eternally Promethean, dissatisfied in any
social system, because he believes humanity can go on creating the
better out of the good forever. The second type has a keen feeling for the
wrongs of contemporary society and accepts current revolutionary ideas,
but

110. *Problemy mira i sotsializma*, 1963, no. 5. An English translation is in *World Marxist
Review*, 1963, no. 5.
111. Yevgeny Gnedin, *Vykhod iz labirinta*, (New York, 1982), pp. 76–77.

. . . in the whole structure of his feelings he remains a conservative. He presents the sorry, often tragicomic spectacle of a being who seems to have been put on earth only to take the cultural, humanitarian, all-human content of revolutionary ideas and to distort and degrade them, to make them ridiculous, repulsive and stupid.

He feels offended above all for himself, for the fact that he is not talented, not strong, that he has been insulted, even for the fact that he has been in jail. . . . He thinks that he is completely emancipated, but inside he is chained by the heavy conservatism of zoological instincts, fathered by a thick mesh of petty grudges, which he has no power to rise above. The habits of his thought drive him to seek in life and in man above all the negative phenomena; in the depths of his soul he is full of contempt for man, on whose behalf he suffered once or a hundred times, but who has himself suffered too much to notice or appreciate the torment of another. . . . He has toward people the attitude that an untalented scientist has toward the dogs and frogs picked for cruel scientific experiments, with the difference that the untalented scientist, though usefully tormenting the animals, does it in the interest of man, while the revolutionary for this day is not constantly sincere in his experiments on people.

People for him are material: the more suitable the less exalted it is. . . . He is a cold fanatic, an ascetic; he emasculates the creative force of the revolutionary idea.[112]

Gorky's definition of a revolutionary for this day is completely applicable to Stalin. It is strange that within ten years Gorky himself was expressing quite different thoughts, and in the mid-thirties was quite close to Stalin. Gorky did not speak up on behalf of the "bourgeois specialists" arrested in the period 1929–1931, and he did not want to hear about the harsh methods used during collectivization, or about the famine of 1932–1933. To the contrary, it was in that very era that he produced his ill-famed remark, "If the enemy does not surrender, he will be destroyed," a phrase NKVD investigators loved to repeat during the terror. Not long before his death Gorky called for a stern judgment against Zinoviev and Kamenev, who were falsely being blamed for Kirov's death.[113]

I am profoundly convinced that Stalin never sought to restore capitalism. Nevertheless, his criminal actions did great harm to the cause of

112. Gorky's article, which first appeared in *Novaya zhizn (Petrograd)*, no. 109, June 6 (May 24), 1918, was reprinted in *Nesvoevremennye mysli* (Paris, 1971), pp. 256–260. [For the complete essay in English, see Gorky, *Untimely Thoughts* (New York, 1968), pp. 229–233. The translation given here is by David Joravsky and Colleen Taylor. —D. J.]

113. We do not share the view expressed by Isaac Don Levine in his book *The Life of Maxim Gorky* that in 1936 Stalin ordered Gorky killed because of the latter's alleged attempts to save people from police repression and his "firm determination" to oppose Stalin's terror.

socialism, effectively abolishing the already quite limited degree of socialist democracy existing in the Soviet Union. Stalin also undermined the leading role of the party in Soviet society and caused serious damage to the alliance of workers and peasants.

Although Stalin was extremely destructive, he was often obliged to adapt himself to the irreversible changes that had taken place in Soviet society after the revolution and to the moods and demands of the mass of working people. He was not only required to take correct Marxist positions in words; on occasion he had to act like a Marxist. Although he devastated the intelligentsia, the state could not do without trained specialists, and therefore measures continued to be taken during the thirties to expand the educational system and create a new Soviet intelligentsia. Although his repression in the Red Army and the Comintern was a great service to fascism, he opposed fascism after Germany's attack on the Soviet Union and thereby helped the worldwide fight against it.

Stalin was concerned about preserving both his power and his popularity. He was indifferent to neither the opinion of his contemporaries nor to that of future generations. He wanted his influence to last for decades, even centuries, a desire reflected in his actions. It was not out of love for suffering humanity that Stalin came to socialism and the revolution. He joined the Bolsheviks because of his ambition and lust for power.

When he joined the most radical wing of the revolutionary movement, he already believed in his own special mission. In exile in Turukhansk he not only read but studied Machiavelli's *Prince* with great attention. The son of a famous Bolshevik tells this revealing episode. In 1912, when he was only nine, a Caucasian came to his parents' apartment in Moscow. After a little talk his father went out, leaving the Caucasian, who was pleased by the boy's conversation. Four hours later the doorbell rang. The boy jumped up but the man stopped him. "Wait, wait," he said, taking him by the shoulder and hitting him on the cheek as hard as he could. "Don't cry," the Caucasian said, "don't cry, little boy. Remember, today Stalin talked to you." When the boy told his parents about their guest's strange behavior, they were outraged and baffled, until, later on, they heard of a custom in many mountain villages of Georgia: if a prince came to a peasant's hut, the peasant would call in his son and hit him hard on the cheek, saying, "Remember that today Prince So-and-so visited our house."[114]

114. Recounted by the film director Mikhail Romm, a friend of the one who got slapped.

For Stalin the party was always just an instrument, a means of reaching his own goals. To be sure, the propagandists of his cult pictured him as a man who constantly thought of the people's needs, as a simple, accessible, sensitive man. In reality, Stalin was inaccessible to rank-and-file workers; he met no ordinary people and did not visit the factories and farms where socialism was being built. He was indifferent to the fate of individuals; for him they were merely cogs in the enormous, soulless state mechanism. Thus the ideas of socialism lost the meaning given them by Marx, Engels, and Lenin; they were only arid dogma for Stalin. His socialism took on many features of Nechaev's. "What a splendid model of barrack communism!" Marx exclaimed about Nechaev's *Bases of the Future Social Structure*, where people must "produce as much as possible and use as little as possible," and where all personal relations are strictly regimented.[115]

Believing in his uniqueness and infallibility, Stalin lost his sense of reality. He evidently assumed that his crimes would seem insignificant in comparison with the magnificence of his historical deeds, the unavoidable price for progress. In fact no enemies of the Communist Party and the October revolution could have done more harm to the cause of socialism.

115. Marx and Engels, *Sochineniia*, 2d ed., 18:414–15.

OTHER CAUSES OF MASS REPRESSION

■ 1
THE CHAIN REACTION OF ARRESTS

Besides destroying most prominent leaders of the party and government, who were well known to Stalin, the repression of 1936–1938 struck millions of people who were unknown to him and were no serious threat to his power. Only the intertwining of many causes and processes can explain this mass repression.

The most widely used formula for justifying the mass repression was the old Russian saying "When you cut down the forest, woodchips fly." This implied that the arrested party leaders really were enemies of the people who had created a far-reaching counterrevolutionary organization based on the former oppositions. The further implication was that some excesses and distortions were unavoidable in the decisive assault on this counterrevolutionary organization.

Yezhov, for example, in a speech to NKVD executives, declared that the Soviet Union was going through a dangerous period, that a war with fascism was imminent, and that therefore the NKVD had to destroy all the nests of fascists in the country. "Of course," Yezhov said,

there will be some innocent victims in this fight against fascist agents. We are launching a major attack on the enemy; let there be no resentment if we bump someone with an elbow. Better that ten innocent people should suffer than one spy get away. When you cut down the forest, woodchips fly.[1]

Today we know what kind of forest was cut down, what trees were felled, and what chips were flying. Still there is a certain weird sense in this argument. As we have seen, the destruction of every party leader was accompanied by the arrest of hundreds, even thousands, of people directly or indirectly connected with him. Stalin spread the story of a vast fascist underground, a fifth column permeating every pore of Soviet society. By means of terrible tortures, arrested people were obliged not only to confess their own guilt but also to reveal their "accomplices" and "confederates." In some NKVD agencies there were even quotas: if the second secretary of an oblast committee had to name at least twenty "confederates," then the first secretary had to implicate at least forty. The arrest of a people's commissar brought repression against hundreds of officials in his commissariat. The arrest of a CC secretary, Politburo member, or former opposition leader resulted in repression of thousands.

Some of those arrested conceived a peculiar theory. If, they argued, we confess to any and every imaginary crime and name hundreds of innocent people as our "confederates," more and more innocent people will be arrested, until the party wakes up to the monstrous stupidity of the whole process and restrains the NKVD. Eugenia Ginzburg tells about one of Bukharin's followers, the biologist Slepkov, who named 150 people as his "confederates" in Kazan alone. "You must disarm yourselves before the party!" he would shout at the confrontation with the people who had been arrested because of him, although none of them had ever "armed themselves" in the first place. General Gorbatov tells of a fellow prisoner who denounced more than three hundred innocent people. In a cell of the Inner Prison at Luubyanka, Yevgeny Gnedin met a mechanic

---

1. Recounted by Yevgeny Frolov, a veteran party member and longtime official in the Central Committee apparatus.

who said he had "written down the names of the entire steamship" where he worked. And Suren Gazaryan writes of a prisoner who on his own initiative denounced all the party officials and even all the ordinary Communists he knew in his raion. He too believed that the more people arrested, the sooner the absurdity of his depositions would come to light. But his expectations were disappointed. A court accepted his depositions and sentenced him to be shot. The people he denounced were also severely punished.

"In the Minsk central prison at the end of 1937, . . . there were two conflicting points of view," writes Ya. I. Drobinsky in his memoirs.

The first was: "Write more, fulfill and overfulfill the investigators demands. The repressions are a provocation, a festering boil; the faster it grows, the sooner it will burst. To make it grow, drag in more people. Every action has an equal and opposite reaction." . . . The other point of view was to fight, to make no compromises. Do not bear false witness against yourself or others. Endure all tortures, torment, hunger; if you have not endured, if you have slipped, rise again, tear into them, even if they rip your skin off; to your last ounce of strength, fight, fight, fight.[2]

The same arguments went on in other prisons. The Old Bolshevik N. K. Ilyukhov tells about his encounter with Grigory Sokolnikov, who urged him not only to sign the interrogation records but to think up denunciations against all those who were helping Stalin—against Postyshev, against the party appartchiki, against NKVD officials. "Drag down with you as many bad people as you can, protect good ones." Obviously such a position was not correct or moral; it suited Stalin's plans completely. It enabled him to destroy the basic party cadres as well as former oppositionists. The huge scale of the repression did not frighten Stalin. Moreover, voluntary cooperation with the NKVD demoralized the prisoners, deprived them of unity in the face of lawlessness. But even without such voluntary "testimony," the NKVD often arrested many colleagues, friends, even chance acquaintances of the "enemies of the people," for "prophylactic" purposes. Thus, almost every arrest started a series of new arrests, and the chain reaction was hard to stop.

Another reason the repression of 1936–1938 became so massive was the practice of arresting relatives of "enemies," especially wives, grown children, and often brothers, sisters, and parents. The family of Tukhachevsky, for example, was cruelly ravaged: his wife, mother, and two brothers died in prison, and his daughter and four sisters were arrested.

2. From the copy of Drobinsky's unpublished memoirs in my archives.

Even many women rumored to be close to Tukhachevsky were arrested. Eight members of Yenukidze's family perished, and the same fate struck hundreds of thousands of completely innocent people.

"In May of 1938, seven months after my husband, they took me," recalls Kaledina-Shver.

They took little Sasha away from me. . . . He died in the NKVD's holding center for children of arrested parents *[detpriemnik]*. . . . In our prison cell there were forty or fifty "ChSIR"—"members of families of traitors to the motherland." Gritting our teeth, we endured mockery and humiliation. We believed in a happy ending, we were waiting for it. But three months went by, and we were taken away. Where, why—no one knew. . . . For two weeks we were transported in cattle cars. . . . A long, long train, filled only with women. . . . Once, the train stopped in a field. An officer climbed into the car, opened a briefcase, and started to take out one folder after another, reading off names and terms. . . . "For what?"—this question burned in my head, in my soul. . . . "Eight years! . . . Five! . . . Eight! . . . Eight! . . . Five!" I heard my name: "Kaledina-Shver—eight years!"

Someone asked: "Why do some get eight, others five? We all have the same fault: we're the wives of our Communist husbands. And many of us are Communists ourselves."

The officer was slow in answering, then smiled and said: "Wives who are loved get eight years; the unloved ones get five!" He made some other jokes, too, that defender of despotic caprice! They took us to Akmolinsk. And from there to Point 26, thirty kilometers away, where behind barbed wire stood barracks for three to four hundred people. Up to eight thousand women were jammed into the camp. We called it ALZHIR [i.e., Algiers, and also an acronym for] Akmolinsk Camp for Wives of Traitors to the Motherland.[3]

There were many such camps in all the remote regions of our country —in Kolyma and Vorkuta, for example—where tens of thousands of women were sent to do logging, construction, and agricultural labor.

Vasily Grossman described the situation as follows:

Wives, wives—from Moscow, Leningrad, Kiev, Kharkov, some hard and practical, some otherworldly, some sad, some sinful, some meek and mild, some ill-tempered, some quick to laugh, all in convicts' jackets. The wives of doctors, engineers, artists, agronomists, the wives of marshals and chemists, the wives of prosecutors and dekulakized villagers, of Russian, Belorussian, and Ukrainian sowers of seed. They all followed their husbands into the Scythian gloom of barrowlike barracks. The more illustrious the fallen "enemy of the people," the wider the circle of women who took the road to the camps in his trail: his current

3. Boris Dyakov, *Povest' o perezhitom* (Moscow, 1966), pp. 180–181.

wife, his previous wife, his very first wife, his sisters, his secretaries, his daughters from his present and earlier marriages, and his wives' women friends.[4]

In certain cases the minor children of prominent officials were arrested. Such children, aged fourteen to sixteen, included Yakir's son, the daughter of Antonov-Ovseyenko (his son was arrested at the age of twenty), and the children of Postyshev, Kosior, Kamenev, Medved, Garkavy, Bauman, Kodatsky, Tomsky, Sosnovsky, Popov, and many others. In Georgia, Gazaryan informs us, the son of Nestor Lakoba, aged fourteen, and three of his schoolmates were killed on Beria's orders. They were all between fourteen and sixteen years of age. The indictment in this case said:

> The investigation has established that Rauf Nestorovich Lakoba, after the exposure of his father, Nestor Lakoba, as an enemy of the people and head of a counterrevolutionary, spying, and terrorist group of rightists in Abkhazia, grouped around himself the sons of other enemies of the people, against whom repressive measures had been taken, and together with them carried on disruptive work at school, engaging in systematic agitation aimed at discrediting measures taken by the party and government. . . . Taking their counterrevolutionary views from their parents, enemies of the people, all the accused in this case, being fervent opponents of the existing system, formed themselves into a counterrevolutionary group in 1937 and began their subversive work. . . . In view of the fact that all the accused were minor children at the time of their crimes, the present case is to be turned over for consideration to a Special Board of the NKVD.[5]

This shocking lawlessness is not excused by the law, adopted a few years before the mass repression, providing that all members of traitors' families be exiled to remote regions. Both in letter and in spirit that law applied to the families of people who were beyond the reach of the courts because they had fled abroad. Even in such cases it was unjust to punish not the traitor himself but his relatives, most of whom were quite innocent. But in 1937–1939 and frequently in later years, too, this savage law was unjustly extended to "enemies of the people" who had made no attempt to flee.

Many children of "enemies of the people" were arrested and exiled later, when they had grown older. In 1944, for example, the children of Bubnov and Lominadze were arrested, and in 1949 there was a big

4. Vasily Grossman, *Vse techet*. Quoted from the Russian manuscript, a copy of which is in my archives. At the time of writing, the novel had not been published in the Soviet Union but was published abroad (Frankfurt, 1970). [See the English translation, *Forever Flowing* (New York, 1972). —G. S.]

5. A copy of this document is in my archives.

campaign for such arrests in Leningrad and Moscow. The victims included young students from the families of the writer Artem Vesyoly, of Army Commander Bazilevich, of Shlyapnikov, former leader of the Workers' Opposition, of Pyotr Smorodin, of Nikolai Bukharin, and of many others.

■ 2

THE CONCEPT "POLITICAL CRIME"

Even in the twenties a very broad interpretation of the concept "political crime" was typical of the Soviet court system. In the thirties this concept was expanded beyond all limits. At one time Karl Marx had written that no one should be put in prison or deprived of property or other legal rights on the basis of political or religious beliefs.

This elementary proposition of any democratic system was discarded. Not actions, not even intentions, but opinions became the basis for criminal prosecution and physical annihilation. For a long time people whose opinions were nonsocialist had been victimized by the punitive agencies even if they were completely loyal to the Soviet regime. But as the Stalinist system developed, all Soviet citizens, including party members, who objected to specific measures taken by the Soviet government or to particular decisions made by the Central Committee, or who only disagreed with certain aspects of the party line—all such persons fell into the category of "enemies of the people" and became victims of repression. And since a great many incorrect decisions were made in the thirties, the number of "enemies" became quite large.

For example, after the first elections to the Supreme Soviet in late 1937 a worker expressed some criticism to his close friends concerning the new electoral system, under which only one candidate appeared on the ballot. Another worker at a trade union meeting asked why semolina was sold to managers and officials at closed distribution stores but had long been unavailable in stores for ordinary workers. Both workers were quickly arrested and sentenced to ten years imprisonment for "anti-Soviet agitation."

The NKVD was especially zealous about protecting Stalin's prestige. In fact, after 1934–1935 the label "state and political criminal" was applied to any person, however devoted to the ideas of socialism, who spoke against Stalin personally, expressed disapproval of his actions, or spoke or acted in a way that could be interpreted even indirectly as belittling Stalin. It was enough to tell an anecdote about Stalin, to damage a picture of him accidentally, or to express doubt about one of his pronouncements on theory for a person to become an "enemy of the people." In Germany the Academy of Law declared love for the führer to be a legal concept and therefore dislike of the führer to be a crime. In the Soviet Union, love of Stalin became obligatory for all, and dislike of him or even the slightest criticism of his activities was a crime.

In the first years of the Soviet regime some leaders expounded the false thesis that the "subjective" and "objective" aspects of a person's behavior were identical. But the real triumph of this thesis occurred in the Stalin era. It was declared unimportant whether a person was subjectively devoted to the working class and the Soviet regime. If, in the opinion of the leadership, that person hurt the proletarian dictatorship and helped the country's enemies by some theoretical or practical mistake, then he or she had to be considered an enemy of the Soviet people, regardless of subjective motives. "Conciliators," people who themselves committed no mistakes but called for leniency toward those who were being criticized and repressed, were also cruelly persecuted and sometimes arrested.

Another cause of the mass repression in the thirties was the fact that almost all of Stalin's laws and secret orders went into effect retroactively. For example, the NKVD punished people on the basis of denunciations it received concerning disrespectful comments about Stalin made many years earlier, during the stormy party debates of the twenties. Those debates had been accompanied by a fair amount of repression, with many thousands of party members ending up in regular prisons, "political isolators," labor camps, or places of internal exile. By 1934 most of them were free and behaving "prudently," but in 1936–1937 nearly all of them were arrested again. No new charges were brought against them; yet hardly any political prisoners of this category survived until rehabilitation in 1956.

■ 3

MASS PARTICIPATION IN THE REPRESSION

One of the most terrible features of the repression in the thirties was that the masses, trusting the party and Stalin, were drawn into it. Hundreds of thousands of simple and essentially honorable folk, guided by the best motives, were led astray by the campaign against "enemies of the people." Millions were poisoned by suspicion. They believed Stalin's story about a ubiquitous underground and were caught up in the spy mania. The campaign against "enemies" and "wreckers" acquired a mass character, like the Stakhanovite movement. The central newspapers were especially zealous in inflaming this mass psychosis. Almost every issue of *Pravda* and *Izvestia* called on the workers to seek out and expose enemies of the people. "Enemies and Their Protectors," "Wrecking in the Selection of Cadres," "Wreckers in Radio Stations," "Who's in Charge of Pryazhinsky Raion?," "Uproot Enemy Nests in the Commissariat of Trade," "Enemy Outburst in Sverdlovsk"—hundreds of such articles roused the masses to struggle.

"Enemies of the people" were to be sought everywhere. *Pravda* declared that

... not one disorder, not one accident, should go unnoticed. We know that assembly lines do not stop by themselves, machines, do not break by themselves, boilers do not burst by themselves. Someone's hand is behind every such act. Is it the hand of the enemy? That is the first question we should ask in such cases.

Pravda went on to denounce officials who believed in the inevitability of accidents and who hesitated to expose enemies.[6]

Robert Eikhe, while first secretary of the West Siberian *oblast* committee, told a Novosibirsk party meeting: "We are now so well equipped and have so many devoted people that there can be no breakdowns. When accidents and failures begin to take place in a factory the first thing to do is look for an enemy."[7] And in May 1937 the Moscow Party Conference adopted this resolution: "For every drop of blood they spill, the enemies of the USSR will pay with gallons of the blood of spies and diversionaries." All the oblast papers published this resolution calling for mass executions as an example to be imitated.

Such appeals had mass results. The smallest error of a manager, miscalculation of an engineer, misprint overlooked by an editor or proofreader, or publication of a bad book was taken to be deliberate wrecking and cause for arrest. People looked everywhere for secret signs or fascist symbols and found them in drawings in books, in notebooks, in scout badges.[8] Even such difficulties as the low pay of teachers, shortages of

6. *Pravda*, February 2, 1937.
7. *Sovetskii Sibir'*, January 1937.
8. I remember that in 1937 or 1938, when I was a member of the Young Pioneers, we were ordered to turn in all previous clips used for holding our Pioneer ties. In the designs on these clips someone had detected the seditious initials "L" and "T" (for "Leon Trotsky").

funds, high dropout rates from high school, and the wearing out of equipment were demagogically attributed to sabotage.

There were even such absurdities as a report that bayonets were bending as a result of wrecking. A special commission sent from Moscow established that a certain ordnance technician had started the fuss. One day he decided to fasten the end of a bayonet in a big vise, and, putting the weight of his whole body against the rifle stock, to try and bend the bayonet. He succeeded. After a careful investigation the commission declared that the bayonets were eminently suitable for battle.[9]

An anonymous denunciation of A. Ya. Vedenin, military commander of the Kirgiz Republic, said that he deliberately chose spotted horses for the army in order to spoil the camouflage of the cavalry in any future encounter with the enemy.[10] One Communist, the head of a fire department, was asked during a political lesson who had commanded the Red Guard in Moscow in 1917. Upon answering, quite correctly, that Muralov had, he was immediately arrested as a counterrevolutionary. The writer A. Pismenny tells about a mining engineer named Baudouin whom he met in the postwar period and who had been arrested in 1937 because of his foreign name, although he was a cousin of a well-known Russian linguist, Baudouin de Courtenay. As torture, he was subjected to constantly cold conditions for half a year until he finally confessed to being a spy.

People were put in prisons or camps for "disseminating the verses of Pasternak or Yesenin" and "for connections with Ilya Ehrenburg," although none of those writers had been arrested. "Plotting to resurrect Austria-Hungary" was another charge, and even "suspicion of intending to betray the motherland." In one of the Ufa prisons R. G. Zakharova met a teacher who was accused of a connection with Finland: after the overthrow of the Soviet regime she was to be proclaimed "queen of the Mari," a Finnic-speaking nationality in the Volga-Ural region. In a Minsk clothing factory, according to Ya. Drobinsky, an old cutter and Communist, Solnyshkov, was accused of fomenting discontent among the people by designing too narrow pockets in the pants of work clothes. A number of Old Bolsheviks were charged with joining the party in its early years for the sole purpose of "disrupting it from within." In Novosibirsk a group of construction workers born in 1913–1914 were accused of sup-

9. N. N. Voronov, *Na sluzhbe voennoi* (Moscow, 1963), pp. 118–119.
10. A. Ya. Vedenin, *Gody i liudi* (Moscow, 1964), p. 58.

porting Kolchak's armies in the civil war of 1918–1921. One of the directors of a lying-in hospital in Gomel was accused of instructing the chief doctor to infect all the babies with syphilis. The artist V. I. Shukhaev and his wife were accused of belonging to the Borotbist Party. The naive artist, poorly prepared for the new way of life, kept asking his cellmates who these Borotbisty were.[11]

In Moscow a large group of stamp collectors were arrested for exchanging stamps with foreign collectors. They were accused of sending secret information abroad. Varlam Shalamov tells about the arrest of all members of an Esperanto society in Moscow; the name of this artificial language apparently frightened the security organs. Dozens of athletes, especially those who had participated in international competitions, were arrested on absurd charges. A denunciation to the NKVD was an easy way to get rid of athletic rivals. The world champion swimmer Semyon Boichenko was removed from competition that way, as were the Starostin brothers, soccer players on the Spartak team.

It was enough for a Vladivostok cinema to show a newsreel that included a shot of a Moscow official arrested two months earlier to cause *Pravda* to print "Enemy Outburst," an article calling for an investigation to see if there were enemies of the people among the officials in this cinema, in the film organization of Vladivostok, and in the Main Repertory Commission in Moscow. Even such an innocuous book as *An Index of Literature for Viola and Viola d'Amore* was declared by *Pravda* to be subversive and fascistic because the works of some contemporary German composers were included in it.

Pravda and *Izvestia* also kept a careful eye on other newspapers, whipping up laggards. "If you study the Kiev paper *Proletarskaya pravda*," wrote *Pravda*, "you are struck by a strange fact. Not one enemy of the people has been unmasked by the paper. As a rule, the paper exposes enemies who have already been exposed."[12]

Even Komsomol members and schoolchildren were dragged into the feverish search for "enemies of the people." On July 10, 1937, *Pravda* reported elections in 1,525 primary Komsomol organizations, complaining that "you can count on the fingers of one hand the electoral meetings

---

11. [The Borotbist Party was a Ukrainian revolutionary group whose political position was analogous to that of the Left SRs in Russia. They fused with the Bolshevik Party in 1920.—G. S.]

12. *Pravda*, October 11, 1937.

at which . . . the offspring of fascist agents who had wormed their way into the Komsomol were unmasked."[13] Whereupon arrests of Komsomol members and leaders increased significantly.

Thousands of plenipotentiaries traveled around the country during those years, feverishly checking on reports from the provinces. Some of these officials may have had good intentions; others acted out of stupidity or careerist considerations; still others were simply mad with fear. But almost all of them ordered or sanctioned the arrest of innocent people. The work of one of these officials, Zemtsov, is typical. With nothing but unverified newspaper articles about "enemy" activity in a rural raion, Zemtsov called a raion party meeting without making any kind of check and declared that the raion leaders were enemies. Then he ordered the arrest of the raikom secretary, and it was done. Zemtsov put together a list of Communists to be expelled and told the raikom to do it. By evening of that day seventeen Communists were expelled from the party. Then Zemtsov took away the keys and seal from the members of the raikom, handed them over to the raion division of the NKVD, and, sealing up the raikom building, left. In one day he had liquidated the raikom.[14] In Kiev special commissions were attached to the raikomy to gather compromising materials on party members and candidate members. Thousands of libelous statements were collected. In Kiev's Petrovsky raion, 111 people in a single party organization in the Academy of Sciences were denounced, although there were only 130 Communists in the entire Academy.[15]

Under these conditions all sorts of careerists and scoundrels tried to use slander to destroy their enemies, to get a good job, an apartment or a neighbor's room, or simply to get revenge for an insult. Some pathological types crawled out of their holes to write hundreds of denunciations. In short, the abolition of law and justice aroused the basest instincts. Lenin at one time had warned the Cheka against false accusations and urged the severest punishment for them, including the death penalty. But under Stalin most slanderers went unpunished, and a flood poured into the NKVD offices, where big receptacles "for statements" were placed in reception rooms. The usual NKVD response to a denunciaton was to arrest the victim and only later to bother about "checking" the charges made against him.

13. *Pravda*, July 10, 1937.
14. *Vosemnadtsatyi s"ezd VKP(b). Stenograficheskii otchet* (Moscow, 1939), p. 569.
15. Ibid.

If many ordinary citizens took advantage of the terror to pursue their own despicable aims, what could be expected from the leaders on all the various levels, including Stalin's closest aides? In drawing these people into his crimes, Stalin had to give them carte blanche to deal with their own opponents and personal enemies, as well as with people they simply found inconvenient. Many took full advantage of these possibilities. In Georgia, for example, thousands of people Beria and his gang found objectionable were destroyed. In Azerbaijan more than ten thousand people were shot on the sole charge of attempting to assassinate Stalin's henchman Bagirov.

It was impossible for the system of personal dictatorship to be limited to the top levels of power. The newly appointed people's commissars, directors of major enterprises and institutions, obkom and raikom secretaries, and state security officials were given the right to decide the fate of Soviet citizens. Each of them was virtually the master of his domain, and many of them abused this power, forming cliques of hangers-on and unprincipled careerists around themselves. Thus a basis was created for ceaseless mass repression.

CONDITIONS FACILITATING STALIN'S USURPATION OF POWER

POSING THE PROBLEM

I have described the general character of the repression of the thirties and discussed the reasons for it, but there are other questions of no less importance. How did Stalin manage to deal such a terrible blow to the party? Why didn't his actions encounter decisive opposition from the people, the party and the leadership?

Marx and Engels often referred to the possibility, or even the inevitability, that a revolution would degenerate if it occurred in objective historical conditions that did not correspond to its aims. Plekhanov also wrote about this several times in his arguments with the populists. If the people, Plekhanov declared, approach power when social conditions are not ripe, then the "revolution may result in a political monstrosity, such as the ancient Chinese or Peruvian empires, i.e., in a tsarist despotism renovated with a Communist lining."[1] Some persons I have spoken with see prophetic truth in these words. They argue that in the Soviet Union of the twenties it was inevitable for the likes of Stalin to come to power. "If Lenin had lived another ten or twenty years," one opponent, V. K—— declared, "he would certainly have been pushed out of the leadership by the 'new' people, whose embodiment was Stalin." "The system created after the October Revolution," said another opponent, the economist I. P——,

was based on outright dictatorship, on force, to an excessive degree. Disregard of certain elementary rules of democracy and lawful order inevitably had to degenerate into Stalinist dictatorship. It was Stalin who fitted this system ideally, and he only developed its latent possibilities to the maximum degree. The whole trouble was that a socialist revolution in a country like Russia was premature. In a country that has not gone through a period of bourgeois democracy, where the people in its majority is illiterate and uncultivated, in such a country genuine socialism cannot be built without the support of other more developed socialist countries. By prematurely destroying all the old forms of social life, the Bolsheviks raised up and turned loose such forces as must inevitably have led to some form of Stalinism. Approximately the same thing is happening today in China and Albania.

I cannot agree with this point of view. Various possibilities exist in almost every political system or situation. The triumph of one of these possibilities depends on both objective and subjective factors, some of which are obviously accidental. Even the tsarist regime in early twentieth-century Russia could have developed in various ways, and the fragile system of bourgeois democracy that existed in Russia from February to October 1917 was not inevitably doomed. Of course, a question always arises about the *degree of probability* that events will take one turn rather than another, but even the smallest possibility should not be dismissed.

As the historian A. Ya. Gurevich has written:

The path of history is not a course or route that has been laid out beforehand once and for all. History is not programmed or predetermined by anyone. Historical development is an open system with the widest possibilities and a limitless set of probabilities and variants. . . . That which has transpired seems

1. Georgy Plekhanov, *Izbrannye filosofskie proizvedeniia*, vol. 1, (Moscow, 1956), p. 323.

to us inevitable, but only insofar as other possibilities were not realized. Naturally, the historian seeks a basis for events that have occurred and proposes an explanation of them, for nothing in history happens without a reason. When certain potentialities have been realized and all others by the same token have been excluded, there arises the concept that the path events have taken was the only one possible, and this thought grows into a firm conviction in proportion as we expose the inner logic in the chain of historical events. The realized variant of historical development receives its explanation and is declared to be a regular, law-governed process. However, the historian who portrays the historical process as something irreversible and proceeds from the conviction that what has happened was the only possible result of all that preceded, wrongly excludes other unrealized possibilities and fails to study the various, perhaps even diametrically opposed tendencies that are always present in society.[2]

From this point of view Stalinism was not at all inevitable. I do not think by any means that the political conception the Bolsheviks brought to the October revolution was free of defects. The system of Soviet rule in the early years of the revolution also had quite a few defects, but it had many merits as well. For the young Soviet state the road of development was not determined in such a way that it necessarily had to grow into the Stalinist system. Various possibilities existed, and Stalinism was not the only one or even the main one. I will discuss this question further in subsequent chapters.

Many foreign thinkers, including Communists, have studied this problem. After the Twentieth Congress, in March 1956, Palmiro Togliatti published his famous objection to a simple inversion of the cult of personality: blaming all evil on the superman who had formerly been praised for all good. Togliatti suggested that the system called "Stalinist" was to be explained by reference to the development of bureaucracy, deriving from prerevolutionary conditions and from the desperate need for centralized power during the civil war. This context favored the rise of Stalin, a typical apparatchik.[3]

Truly we are confronted with this question: How, in spite of the monstrosity of his crimes, did Stalin manage to retain not only his power but also the respect and trust of the majority of Soviet people? It is an unavoidable fact that Stalin never relied on force alone. Throughout the

2. See Gurevich's article in the collection *Filosofskie problemy istoricheskoi nauki* (Moscow, 1969), pp. 74–75.

3. See P. Togliatti, *Problemi del movimento operaio internazionale (1956–61)* (Rome, 1962), pp. 99–106. [An English translation may be found in *The Anti-Stalin Campaign and International Communism: A Selection of Documents* (New York: 1956), pp. 97–139. — D. J.]

period of his one-man rule he was popular. Aleksandr Zinoviev, in his recent book *The Flight of Our Youth* correctly notes that it is wrong to describe the Stalinist system as one based solely on force and deception "when at bottom it was the voluntary creation of the many-millioned masses who could be organized into a single stream only by means of force and deception."[4] The longer Stalin ruled the Soviet Union, cold-bloodedly destroying millions of people, the greater seems to have been the dedication to him, even the love, of the majority of the people. When he died in March 1953 the grief of hundreds of millions, both in the Soviet Union and around the world, was quite sincere.

How can this unprecedented historical paradox be explained? We must look more closely at the conditions that facilitated Stalin's usurpation of power.

■ 2

AGAIN ON THE STALIN CULT

One condition that made it easy for Stalin to bend the party to his will was the hugely inflated cult of his personality. Ilya Ehrenburg writes in his memoirs:

For 1938 it is more correct simply to use the word "cult" in its original religious meaning. In the minds of millions Stalin was transformed into a mythical demi-god; all trembled as they said his name, believed that he alone could save the Soviet Union from invasion and collapse.[5]

The deification of Stalin left the party unable to control his actions and justified in advance everything connected with his name. The embodiment of all the achievements of socialism in his person tended to paralyze the political activism of the other leaders and of the party membership as a whole, preventing them from finding their own way in the welter of ongoing events, leading them to place blind faith in Stalin. The cult of Stalin, following the logic of any cult, tended to transform the Communist Party into an ecclesiastical organization, producing a sharp distinction between ordinary people and leader-priests headed by their infallible pope. The gulf between the people and Stalin was not only deepened but idealized. The business of state in the Kremlin became as remote and

4. A. Zinoviev, *Nashei iunosti polet* (Lausanne, 1983), p. 10.
5. *Novy mir* (1962), no. 5, p. 152.

incomprehensible for the unconsecrated as the affairs of the gods on Olympus.

In the thirties and forties the social consciousness of the people took on elements of religious psychology: illusions, autosuggestion, the inability to think critically, intolerance towards dissidents, and fanaticism. As Yuri Karyakin put it, a secular variant of religious consciousness arose in the Soviet Union.[6] Perceptions of reality were distorted. It was difficult, for example, to believe the terrible crimes charged against the Old Bolsheviks, but it was even more difficult to think that Stalin was engaged in a monstrous provocation to destroy his former friends and comrades.

The religious cult of Stalin's personality was accompanied by the belittling of everyone else, especially ordinary working people. Conformism, uniformity of behavior and thought, was implanted in the Soviet people. Serving socialism was transformed into serving Stalin; it was not he who served the people but they who served him. His praise, his encouragement, his smile were considered the highest reward.

For the sake of future beatitude, religious believers are expected to endure without complaint any misfortune their in earthly lives.[7] Just as believers attribute everything good to God and everything bad to the devil, so everything good was attributed to Stalin and everything bad to evil forces that Stalin himself was fighting. "Long live Stalin!" some officials shouted as they were taken to be shot.

Of course the cult of Stalin varied in its effect on people of different age groups and social status. Its most powerful effect was on young people, as was true of the Mao cult thirty years later in China. Schools and institutes became the main breeding grounds for the cult. The daughter of Maxim Litvinov, Tatyana Litvinova, who emigrated to the United States in the seventies, when asked what attitude she had taken toward Stalin, answered quite sincerely that she had experienced a feeling of intense ecstasy:

I saw him only once. Around 1936. Papa gave me a guest ticket to a Congress of Soviets. I heard him and saw him. . . . His Georgian accent was so strong that for the first fifteen minutes it was hard for me to understand h   , which I hadn't expected, because I had only read his speeches in newspapers. It was also surprising how he held his audience in the palm of his hand. He spoke slowly,

6. Yuri Karyakin, "Epizod iz sovremennoi bor'by idei," *Problemy mira i sotsializma* (1964), no. 9.
7. Yuri Levada, *Sotsial'naia priroda religii* (Moscow, 1965).

with pauses, as a very calm person. . . . I have never heard a public speaker so unhurried, so confident not only that every word of his was being listened to but also that he could make whatever pauses he liked and they would not seem empty. Everything was in his hands. And that produced a kind of blissful ecstasy on top of the excitement I already felt. You know, he was like a stage director, pausing at places where there should be laughter, and we would laugh. . . . I clapped; everyone clapped. I was ecstatic, in a state of exaltation. And then there was the thrill of being in the presence of the tremendous power that could be felt all around. It was a feeling like the one Tolstoy describes when one of his characters—Nikolai Rostov, I think, or Petya—saw Tsar Alexander riding across the parade ground.[8]

Of course there were some young people who did not feel any ecstasy or enthusiasm toward Stalin, but they were usually older, in their twenties. Most often they stayed away from politics or protest, however. In the thirties children were drawn into politics from the earliest years and became preoccupied with it. As I have said, at the age of ten I myself wrote a poem about Kirov, which was published in the Leningrad newspaper *Smena*. On May 1, 1936, I also published verse about Stalin in our school newspaper. Certainly the arrest of our father affected me terribly, but I perceived it then as only an isolated case of injustice. Not until after the war did I begin to take a more critical attitude toward reality, and even then that attitude grew and developed slowly.

It was not only young people between twelve and seventeen who were enraptured by Stalin and believed in him. The Soviet writer Boris Gorbatov is an example of sincere delusion in this regard, as Mikhail Baitalsky's description indicates:

Of all my friends Boris Gorbatov was probably the greatest enthusiast. He was a man of pure conscience. For me and my other Odessa friends, for all of us who had been in the Left Opposition, faith, once it had been cracked and glued back together again, no longer gave off such a clear crystal tone. But Boris in the early thirties rang out just as clear as ten years earlier when he first joined the Komsomol. . . . The characteristic features of the times had been etched into him. Times change, but a person's traits of character remain, and in the new circumstances those traits can be of assistance to hypocrites hiding behind the backs of honest people to deceive the youth, who are used to trusting honest people. Several generations in a row trusted Gorbatov, believing in his sincerity and open-heartedness, not knowing that he himself had been deceived and was unwittingly promoting deception. . . . He is a believer. Can a believer imagine that the devil has taken up residence in the holy sepulcher? Seeing the horns sticking out behind the golden halo, the believer does not trust his own eyes and

8. Tatyana Litvinova, *Otvetstvennost' pololeniia* (New York, 1981), pp. 30–31.

thinks he is imagining something. He crosses himself three times and utters the Lord's name. And soon he has convinced himself that this was a mirage and the devil's gold-tinted horns swim before his eyes, taking on the features of a nimbus around the head of a saint. And he prays to the devil and makes his children pray too. But that is no saint they are praying to.[9]

This kind of religious outlook crippled the will even of those people who had stopped believing in Stalin and had begun to see where Stalin was taking the party. Why did Ordzhonikidze shoot himself rather than Stalin? Why was there not one real attempt to remove Stalin during the twenty years of bloody crimes? Those who were capable of such an act were stopped not so much by fear for their lives as by fear of the social consequences, which could not be predicted in the conditions of the cult. The hero of a novel of the mid-sixties puts the case clearly:

It's terrible that we ourselves helped to strengthen blind faith in him, and now are powerless before that faith. Sacred truth looks like a terrible lie if it does not correspond to people's actual beliefs. You can imagine what would happen if someone got on the radio, say, and told the entire country what was going on, told the truth about Stalin. From that instant even a person who had his doubts would believe that we are surrounded by enemies; he would believe anything. And any cruelty would be justified.[10]

As in the time of Ivan the Terrible, people created an earthly god and then could not raise a finger against the idol they had created. A nineteenth-century radical historian described with horror how "Prince Repnin, impaled on a stake and dying slowing, . . . praised the tsar, his lord and executioner." The historian ascribed such behavior to "the inculcation of distorted views, for self-abasement and submission to the tsar were unalterably sacred ideals for these people from the time of their early youth, with the result that their strength of spirit acted only to stifle the indignation within them and the natural impulse to rebel."[11]

The deification of secular or religious leaders has occurred quite frequently in human society in different parts of the world from the earliest stages of social development. In ancient and medieval times such forms of religious consciousness were particularly widespread. Personality cults of various kinds have not been uncommon in the modern era for that matter. Hitler, for example, wrote that "the personality cult is the best form of government."

9. M. D. Baitalsky, *"Tetradi dlia vnukov."*
10. Grigory Baklanov, "Iiul' 41 goda," *Znamya*, 1965, no. 2, p. 16.
11. See S. M. Stepniak-Kravchinskii, *Rossia pod Vlast'iu tsarei* (Mosow, 1965), pp. 59-60. [This is a reprint of a famous work by a nineteenth-century populist *(narodnik)*. — D. J.]

Unfortunately the concept of the godlike hero leading the "crowd" has frequently penetrated modern revolutionary movements. It would have seemed that the Bolsheviks were best protected against the rise of any kind of religious psychology or personality cult within their midst or in the government they established. Why then did the cult of personality arise and exist for so long in the Soviet Union?

As we have seen, the boundless praise of Stalin did not arise spontaneously; it was organized by Stalin and his creatures. And this well-organized campaign did its job. From their earliest years schoolchildren were taught that everything good came from Stalin. But it would be naive to attribute the success of Stalin's cult only to clever propaganda. That is what simpleminded opponents of Christianity do when they attribute its spread to deception and stupidity, instead of studying the historical conditions that explain its success.

Some historians think that the success of Stalin's cult was considerably facilitated by the petty-bourgeois character of tsarist Russia, which carried over into the postrevolutionary era. They also point to the low educational and cultural level of the masses and the absence of strong democratic traditions in a country so recently emancipated from despotism. For centuries the cult of the tsar, the ideology of absolutism, had been ingrained in Russia. While taking this notion into consideration, it would be a mistake to regard the ignorance of the masses or the religious illusions of peasants and petty artisans as the only preconditions for Stalin's cult. There were others, inherent in the revolution itself. It brought such sweeping change in such a short time that the leaders seemed to be miracle makers. Indeed, the tendency of the masses to glorify their leaders appears spontaneously in every mass revolution. It is an expression of the masses' great enthusiasm, pride in their revolution, their gratitude to the leaders who did so much for their liberation. Of course this idealization of the leaders need not inevitably lead to a cult of the leaders, or become idol worship. Much depends on concrete historical circumstances and on the character and world view of the leaders themselves.

Paradoxical as it may seem, another important factor explaining the triumph of Stalin's cult was the vast scale of the crimes committed in the thirties. For Stalin did not commit them by himself. Taking advantage of the people's revolutionary enthusiasm and trustfulness, the enormous power of party and state discipline, and the low educational level of the proletariat and the peasantry, Stalin involved millions of people in his crimes. Not only the punitive organs but also the entire party and government apparatus participated actively in the repressive campaigns of the thirties. Thousands of party officials were members of the *troiki*, the three-member "special boards" that condemned innocent people. Tens of thousands of officials sanctioned the arrest of their subordinates, as required by a Politburo resolution in 1937. People's commissars had to sanction the arrest of their deputies, obkom secretaries the arrest of party officials in the oblasti, while the chairman of the Union of Writers sanctioned the arrest of many writers. Hundreds of thousands of Communists voted for the expulsion of "enemies of the people." Millions of ordinary people took part in meetings and demonstrations demanding severe reprisals against "enemies"—frequently against their former friends.

The majority of Soviet people believed in Stalin and the NKVD in those years and were sincere in their indignation against "enemies of the people." But many citizens, even members of the NKVD, had their doubts, if not about the general trend, then at least about particular acts of repression. These people reacted to the voice of conscience in different ways. Some took a stand against the particular acts they questioned. Others resigned themselves and kept quiet. Either way, people who felt some doubts could not admit to themselves that they were in some measure accomplices in crimes. So they forced themselves to believe in Stalin, who knew everything and could not make mistakes. They found mitigation for themselves in the cult of his personality.

The writer A. Pismenny, who wrote many novels justifying the repression of the thirties—for example, *The Verdict (Prigovor)*—and who in his later years deeply regretted having done that, gave the following explanation:

Of course I could not believe that Ivan Kataev, Nikolai Zarudin, Boris Guber, Mikhail Loskutov, Sergei Urnis, or many other friends of mine were spies, bomb-throwing Anarchists planning to kill Stalin, loathsome poisoners of reservoirs, or enemy agents. . . . However I might try today to ridicule my tossing and turning and—why hide it, when everything is being said?—my search for spiritual peace; the fact is that then above all I wanted to understand. Yes, yes, I repeat once again, I wanted not only to believe but to understand what was happening. . . . But in those years it was impossible to understand what was happening. You could become an informer, go mad, commit suicide, but if you wanted to live, the most convenient way for an unhappy, distraught, but honorable person clinging with his last ounce of strength to his place in society—I repeat and will go on repeating a thousand times—was to believe. To believe without reasoning, without second thoughts, without proofs, as people believe in omens, in god, in the devil, in life beyond the grave. The thought that all social actions could be prompted by the criminal designs of a single man who had appropriated the full plenitude of power, and that this man was Stalin, was blasphemous, was unbelievable.[12]

In fact this complex mixture of contradictory feelings was one of the main sources of strength for Stalin's cult, especially among officials, many of whom feel this way even now.

Thus there was a two-way cause-and-effect relationship between the terror and the cult of Stalin's personality. Stalin's cult facilitated his usurpation of power and the destruction of inconvenient people, while his crimes, supported by the apparatus and also by the deluded masses, extended and reinforced the cult of personality.

The cult of personality does not automatically lead to mass repression; much depends on the personality. Not every deified emperor or pharaoh was a cruel and bloodthirsty despot. But the most dangerous feature of the cult of personality is that the leader's conduct depends not on laws or other rules but on his own arbitrary will. For the Soviet Union it is an intolerable situation if the personal qualities of the leader of the party and government are the only guarantee of citizens' rights, indeed of their very lives.

■ 3
THE ABSENCE OF OPEN DISCLOSURE AND FREEDOM OF CRITICISM

The main Bolshevik newspaper was called *Pravda* (Truth) for good reason. In 1917 all parties enjoyed freedom of speech. By publicizing their slogans and demands, the Bolsheviks managed to rally the majority of the working class behind them, along with a significant portion of the soldiers and peasants. In their struggle against the tsarist regime and the bourgeois Provisional Government, the Bolsheviks advocated maximum public disclosure (glasnost) and freedom of criticism. Stalin, on the other hand, in his struggle against his political opponents, in his intrigues, provocations, and demagogy had no interest in criticism or public disclosure. The entire functioning of the NKVD in the thirties was surrounded by secrecy, and any attempt to penetrate the veil was itself regarded as a crime.

A wall of silence, for example, surrounded the fate of Postyshev,

12. From an unpublished manuscript by Pismenny in my archive.

Kosior, Chubar, Eikhe, and Rudzutak. The arrest of hundreds of other leaders was not reported in any newspaper and could only be deduced from certain hints or from brief oral reports given at some party meetings. The newspapers were full of appeals for struggle against the "enemies of the people," but this was not true public disclosure. The charges against most of Stalin's victims were not made public. As a rule, even well-informed people knew of arrests only in their own oblast, in their own line of work, in their own circle of acquaintances. The vast scale of the terror escaped them. This ignorance was heightened by the orgy of transferring officials from one oblast to another, from one post to another, that characterized the time of troubles. Often people did not know whether an official had been arrested or transferred. In many cases even the relatives did not know. The NKVD usually did not inform relatives of execution or death by other causes. Playing on hopes and illusions, the NKVD invented a formula about the exile of "enemies of the people" (even those who had been shot) to distant camps "without the right of correspondence."

Stalin and the NKVD often preferred methods of disguised terror to straightforward arrest. Sometimes, the NKVD staged "robberies," during which the intended victim would be killed. That is how the actress Zinaida Raikh, Meyerhold's wife, died, while she was struggling for her husband's release. The robbers who raided her apartment stabbed her seventeen times, took all her papers, and left many valuables untouched.[13] Some officials were murdered in their homes, in hotels, on hunting parties, in their offices, thrown out of windows, poisoned—and then were reported dead of heart attacks, accidents, or suicides. The body of Nestor Lakoba, who was poisoned but who was said to have died of a heart attack, was sent from Tbilisi to Sukhumi with great ceremony. (Later, when Lakoba was posthumously declared an "enemy of the people," the coffin with his remains was dug up, removed from its resting place in the center of Sukhumi, and reinterred in an unmarked grave somewhere else.)

The fate of Khandzhyan, first secretary of the Armenian Central Committee, is typical. He was murdered on July 9, 1936, in Beria's office in Tbilisi by Beria himself.[14] A. Ivanova, who was then an official in the party Control Commission, happened to be in the office next to Beria's on the day of the murder, where she heard the shot. Khandzhyan's body

13. Recounted by Ilya Ehrenburg.
14. Reported by Shelepin at the Twenty-Second Party Congress.

was taken to the hotel where Armenian officials usually stayed, and Beria's accomplices put the body on a bed and fired a shot in the air. According to Suren Gazaryan, two forged letters were placed in the corpse's pockets: a farewell to his wife, Rosa, and a confession to Beria, saying he had made a mess of his affairs and had decided to put an end to himself. Beria and his clique then insulted the memory of the dead man, accusing him of shameful cowardice. Meetings were held throughout Transcaucasia in July of 1936 to condemn Khandzhyan's "cowardly act." The lead article in the Armenian Party paper declared suicide

an especially shameful act of treacherous cowardice when committed by a party leader. . . . For the past three or four years . . . the steadfast leader of the Transcaucasian Bolsheviks, Lavrenty Beria, has extended enormous help to the Communist Party of Armenia . . . and its former leader Khandzhian . . . , [who] shot himself at a time when he had been raised to lofty heights as leader of the entire party organization. That shot we cannot help calling a traitor's shot.[15]

There were hints that Khandzhyan had connections with suspicious people, and a few months later he was retroactively named an enemy of the people. On this basis almost the entire leadership of the Armenian Party was cut down.

Stalinist officials committed ordinary as well as political crimes. They built themselves luxurious private houses and villas, illegally spending millions of rubles and state funds. Some, like G. F. Aleksandrov, a leading ideologist and administrator, created dens of debauchery near Moscow. Beria used to drive around Moscow in his car, looking for young women who were then delivered to his dacha. And all this was made possible by the lack of a free press. To get proper leaders, Lenin said, there must be full public disclosure of all the activities and qualities of the candidates. The masses should have the right to check up on every step of their leaders' activities.[16]

Freedom of speech and of the press have been demanded by every truly democratic revolution. As the French "Declaration of the Rights of Man and Citizen" pointed out, the necessity of making the demand is itself evidence of despotism.[17]

15. *Kommunist* (Yerevan), July 15, 1936.
16. Lenin, PSS, 8:96.
17. See Filippo Buonarotti, *Zagovar vo imia raventstva* (Moscow, 1948), p. 89. [A translation of Buonarotti's *Conspiration pour l'égalité dite de Babeuf* (Brussels, 1828). — D. J.]

For Marx, freedom of the press was never even a debatable question. At the very beginning of his revolutionary activity he wrote: "The absence of freedom of the press makes all other freedoms illusory. One form of freedom governs another, just as one limb of the body does another."[18]

In September 1917 Lenin wrote a special article on freedom of the press, outlining the method by which the Soviet government would guarantee the freedom to all groups of citizens.[19] A few days after the October Revolution he signed the "Decree on the Press," which allowed restrictions on the press in times of crisis, but promised full freedom "within the limits of responsibility, as judged by a court, in accordance with the broadest and most progressive law" once normal conditions had set in.[20] The civil war forced the Bolshevik government to keep this temporary decree in effect for several years and to intensify administrative measures against the publications of other parties. In 1918, for example, the newspapers and publishing houses of the Mensheviks and SRs were shut down. A few months after the civil war ended, Lenin projected a number of measures to extend freedom of speech and the press, although his letter to Myasnikov in August 1921 shows that he then opposed freedom of the press in general, "from the monarchists to the anarchists":

The bourgeoisie (all over the world) is still very much stronger than we are. To place in its hands yet another weapon like . . . freedom of the press . . . means facilitating the enemy's task. . . .

We clearly see this fact: "freedom of the press" means in practice that the international bourgeoisie will immediately buy up hundreds and thousands of Cadet, Socialist Revolutionary, and Menshevik writers and will organize their propaganda, their fight against us. That is a fact. "They" are richer than we are and will buy a "force" ten times larger than we have, to fight us. But no, we will not do it; we will not help the international bourgeoisie.[21]

Thus, censorship of the press was maintained with the full agreement of Lenin and the leadership of the Soviet Communist Party, although it was relaxed significantly during the first years of NEP. In a keynote article, "Freedom of the Press and the State," which set out government policy at the beginning of 1921, Lunacharsky, the commissar of educa-

18. Marx and Engels, *Sochineniia*, 2d ed., 1: 63. [Cf. Marx, "Debates on Freedom of the Press," in Marx and Engels, *Collected Works*, 1: 180. —G. S.]
19. Lenin, PSS, 34: 212–213.
20. *Dekrety Sovetskoi vlasti*, vol. 1 (Moscow, 1957), p. 24.
21. Lenin, PSS, 44: 79; CW, 32: 505–506.

tion, wrote that censorship was necessary to prevent the dissemination of counterrevolutionary ideas.

But the person who says "Down with all these prejudices about free speech; state control of literature suits our Communist system; censorship is not a horrible feature of the transitional period but something inherent in a well-ordered socialized life"—the person who infers from this that criticism should be transformed into some sort of denunciation, or into cutting down a work of art to fit primitive revolutionary patterns, such a person shows only that under the Communist, if you scratch him a little, you will find a Derzhimorda.[22] Whatever power he gets, he sees nothing in it but the pleasure of throwing his weight around, the pleasure of bullying, and especially of grab-'em-and-don't-let-'em-go. . . . We do show such symptoms; we cannot help it; we are a people with too low a level of culture. The danger of a strong proletarian regime, vested in junior agents and accidental spokesmen, being transformed into a police regime . . . is real and present, and must be avoided by every means.[23]

Stalin was precisely the kind of "junior agent" Lunacharsky warned against. Under his direct influence, from the mid-twenties on, there was a steady restriction in the publicity attending party and state affairs. Not only "monarchists" or "anarchists" were denied the freedom to express their views; so were some of the most prominent figures in the Communist Party itself. When Stalin achieved one-man rule in the thirties he extended his personal control of all sources of information to an unheard-of degree. Party members and citizens in general were given no other information than Stalin and his aides thought necessary. No motion picture could be shown to the public unless Stalin personally had seen and approved it. The idea of a proletarian monopoly on the press, which Lenin meant as a purely temporary measure, was perverted by Stalin. The press was closed not only to enemy criticism and mudslinging, which was quite proper, but also to criticism from party positions, to criticism of the political, economic, and cultural perversions that abounded in the years of the cult.

Engels wrote long ago that in a country where all sources of knowledge are under government control, where nothing can be spoken or printed without prior permission from the government, it is very difficult to arrive at correct ideas. Stalin had no desire for Soviet citizens to develop a correct understanding of things. He knew that the absence of public

22. [Derzhimorda: a character in Gogol's *Inspector General*, whose name—its literal meaning is "Hold the snout"—has become an eponym for officials who rule by browbeating and force. —D. J.]

23. *Pechat' i revoliutsiia* (1921), no. 1, p. 7.

disclosure enabled him to deceive the party and the people more effectively. When even the most important officials were denied information that Stalin knew about, it allowed him to be the master of the situation. It seemed to all that Stalin knew much more than they, which deprived them of confidence in their own powers and initiative. In her open letter to *Izvestia* on the fifteenth anniversary of Stalin's death, Lydia Chukovskaya described the situation:

What got us into this unprecedented trouble? Into this utter defenselessness of people in front of a machine rolling over them? Into this historically unexampled merger, fusion, union, of the state security organs (which were breaking the law every minute of the day and night) with the procuratorial organs that exist to uphold the law (yet became obsequiously blind for years on end), and finally with the newspapers, which are supposed to defend justice but instead excreted planned, mechanized slander on the persecuted—millions of millions of lying words—on "hardened," "vicious" enemies of the people, who had "sold themselves to foreign intelligence services," and are now rehabilitated? When and how was this accomplished, this combination, undoubtedly the most dangerous of all the chemical combinations known to scientists? How was it possible? . . . The murder of the truthful word—it too derives from the cursed time of Stalin. And it was one of the blackest crimes in all history. The loss of the right to independent thought closed the door in Stalin's time to doubt, questioning, cries of alarm, and opened it to the self-confident, shameless, multi-copied, and multi-persistent lie. The hourly repeated lie kept people from finding out what was being done in their native country to their fellow citizens; some did not know because of their simplicity, their naiveté, others because they did not want to know. Whoever knew or guessed was condemned to shut up, keep quiet, for fear of perishing the next day; not fear of trouble at work, unemployment or poverty, but plain physical destruction. What a great honor was shown to words in that time: for them people were killed.[24]

Thus Stalin used the party's temporary monopoly of the printed word to the detriment of the party itself and the Soviet people.

■ 4

THE DOMESTIC AND INTERNATIONAL SITUATION

Because of the absence of open discussion and public disclosure the Soviet people knew little about Stalin's despotic and criminal side. Official propaganda emphasized other, essentially positive aspects of reality, which were invariably linked with Stalin's name. The heroic and the tragic were closely intertwined in the Soviet Union in the thirties. As the

24. Lydia Chukovskaya, *Otkrytoe slovo* (New York, 1976) pp. 42–43.

prominent Soviet writer Sergei Smirnov pointed out, "the meaning of those years is too complex and contradictory to permit, only two or three decades later, a completely dispassionate and conclusive judgment."[25] It was an epoch not only of political reaction but also of revolutionary progress, which influenced Stalin as well as everyone else.

Stalin's activity did not consist of crimes alone. Besides issuing orders for arrests and executions, as leader of the first socialist state in the world he had to decide many questions of economic and cultural development, of foreign policy and the international workers' movement. As I will discuss below, he made many mistakes that dearly cost the Soviet people. But he had to consider the ideology and aspirations of the party, the principles of Marxism and Leninism, the principles of socialism. The cult of Stalin's personality slowed down or reversed the progress of Soviet society in some areas but could not stop relatively rapid development in others. That is one reason why to this day it is difficult to expose the crimes of Stalin, for official propaganda attributed all the achievements of the Soviet people to him.

It was known that party and state leaders were being arrested as "enemies of the people," but at the same time new schools, factories, and palaces of culture were rising everywhere. Military leaders were being arrested as spies, but the party was building a strong, modern army. Scientists were being arrested as wreckers, but Soviet science developed rapidly with the party's support. Writers were being arrested as "Trotskyites and counterrevolutionaries," but some literary works appeared that were real masterpieces. Leaders in the union republics were being arrested as nationalists, but the formerly oppressed nationalities were improving their lot, and friendship among the peoples of the Soviet Union was growing. And this obvious progress filled Soviet hearts with pride, engendering confidence in the party that was organizing it and in the man who stood at the head of the party.

Stalin even profited from the accidental fact that 1937, the most frightful year of repression, happened to be blessed with the most bountiful harvest of the prewar period. Claude Roy has compared Stalin to the savage warriors who move into battle driving the wives and children of their opponents before them. Stalin sheltered himself behind a people advancing out of ignorance and backwardness. His opponents could not strike at him without striking their loved ones.[26] Although the metaphor

25. "Smert' komsomolki," *Komsomolskaia pravda*, November 16, 1966.
26. *Libération* (Paris), June 25, 1963.

does not give a completely accurate picture of the period, there is a great deal of truth in it.

Some writers and memoirists try to explain the behavior of people in the thirties primarily by fear. Nikolai Aseev, for example, describes people's feelings on the death of Stalin in his poem "Faithful to Lenin":

> Why the crowd at the grave?
> People run from all sides
> To check, to see for sure.
> What he will leave after death.
> . . . .
> And then, by the mortal remains,
> We didn't know how to behave,
> To remain petrified with fear
> Or begin to talk loudly?

Such an interpretation of the recent past is misleading and insincere. Of course many people were afraid of Stalin, especially those close to him; Stalin knew how to inspire dread. Many people feared the NKVD, feared repression. In a 1961 poem "Fears" Yevtushenko described the situation very graphically:

> I remember their power and force
> In the court of the conquering lie.
> Fears slid everywhere like shadows,
> Penetrated every storey.
> Quietly they trained people,
> And left their mark on everything,
> Taught shouting where silence should be
> And silence where one ought to shout.

Pismenny writes about the same thing in his memoirs:

There was something animal-like—this must be admitted—probably some affinity with the zoological instinct of self-preservation, in the complex, I would even say diseased, process of learning to believe, of submitting to the implacable and at the same time dubious logic of social life in the thirties. Perhaps this was the most unbearable part. Behind all the lofty reasoning, the vast calculations, the ideological and political conjectures, hiding and dancing in my noble mind was a little demon of ordinary fear. It was not preaching lofty principles and was not given to the speechifying cant that had become so customary. The little demon of the instinct of self-preservation, with its ugly lewd face, was naive and shrewd. It did not get involved with political analysis. In its common sense there was more wisdom of everyday life than in dozens of learned books. Its skeptical ideas about the surrounding world had to be kept hidden from other people because, though these ideas were perhaps closest of all to the truth of everyday life, they might have been considered philistine and even reactionary.[27]

For many people, however, fear of repression was not simply blind animal fear for their lives but fear of being disgraced. These people trusted Stalin and the party, believed that they were sincerely serving the people, saw the growth of socialism around them, and feared being outside this mainstream. Boris Yefimov, people's artist of the RSFSR, wrote the following in his memoirs:

It would take a really talented writer . . . to reproduce the thoughts and feelings that possessed thousands and thousands of people in that period. There was agonizing bewilderment and a passionate desire to understand something; there was unspeakable fear and faith in common sense; there was hope flooding the heart and despair laying waste the soul. How can one describe the condition of people who sensed with all their being the approach of a terrible disaster and did not know how to escape it, how to save themselves, and remained bound and helpless as in a nightmare? . . . How can one describe the mood of people who had no possibility of explaining anything because questions were lacking, who had no possibility of vindicating themselves because there were no charges against them, who understood the full horror of their position, the ominous danger hanging over them and those close to them, and at the same time had to act as if there was no cause for concern, as if everything was all right, had to preserve their cheerfulness and capacity to work?[28]

To understand why it was easy for Stalin to convince people of the existence of an extensive fascist underground, we must also recall the grim atmosphere of the thirties. As early as 1907 Aleksandr Bogdanov, who was still a Bolshevik at the time, foresaw the possibility that the first socialist states might be islands in a sea of capitalist states, which would try to destroy them by repeated attacks.

It is difficult to predict the outcome of those clashes. But even where socialism would hold out and emerge the victor, its character would be profoundly and lastingly distorted by the many years of its besieged condition, of unavoidable terror and a military regime. . . . That would not be our socialism by a long shot.[29]

Much of this prediction came painfully close to reality. Throughout the twenties and thirties the Soviet Union was the only socialist country in

27. From a copy of Pismenny's unpublished memoirs in my archives.

28. Boris Yefimov, *Mihail Kol'tsov, kakim on byl* (Moscow, 1965), p. 69.

29. A. Bogdanov, *Krasnaia zvezda* (St. Petersburg, 1907). "Our" refers to the ideal socialism of the Martian who says these words in this utopian science-fiction novel by Bogdanov.

the world, while the imperialist powers were very much the masters of the world situation. Soviet citizens were sure that a life-and-death struggle with imperialism and fascism was not only inevitable but actually imminent. The result was an atmosphere of alarm as well as exaltation.

The intense and cruel class struggle of the preceding decade was fresh in everyone's memory. Some of those who had been defeated formed counterrevolutionary organizations, though as a rule they were small and uncoordinated. The espionage and subversive activities of imperialist intelligence agencies, especially those of the fascist states, were stepped up in those years. But even the alarming international situation of the thirties did not justify the spy mania, the artificial incitement of passions, or the mass repression. Ordinary people and even most leading officials lacked sufficient information to appraise political opponents, and this myth of a widespread counterrevolutionary underground seemed reality to many people. Konstantin Simonov, in commentary accompanying his war diaries of 1941, testifies to the overwhelming influence of the conviction that war was near at hand:

In the spring of 1937, when I heard about the trial of Tukhachevsky, Yakir, and the other military commanders—as a boy in the twenties I had seen Tukhachevsky several times—I trembled, but I believed that what I read was true, that a military conspiracy really did exist, and the participants were connected with Germany and wanted to carry out a fascist coup in our country. At the time I had no other explanation for what was happening.[30]

The widespread belief in the existence of a fascist fifth column facilitated Stalin's realization of his criminal plans. His cruelty and mistrust even seemed desirable qualities to many people. Thus in the years of the terror Stalin continued to rely on the masses, keeping them deceived and exploiting their urge for a better future and love for their homeland. His apostasy regarding the ideals of the socialist revolution was always masked by ultrarevolutionary phrases, which prevented working people and the youth from discerning the real motives behind his actions. Thus he secured the support of the people, without which even such a despot as Stalin could not have maintained himself. At the same time he could not stray too far outside the framework of the socialist system; he could not destroy all the gains of the revolution. By deceiving the people, Stalin was able to direct his fire at the veterans of the revolution, portray-

---

30. Simonov's war diaries were published in *Novy mir*, 1966, no. 10. However, the entire run of that issue was destroyed. Only a few copies were saved, one of which was given to me by *Novy mir* editor Aleksandr Tvardovsky.

ing them as enemies, but he could not come out openly against the revolution itself, against Lenin and socialism. Stalin greatly slowed the wheel of history but he could not turn it back.

The "before-the-storm" atmosphere of tension and vigilance in the thirties also helps to explain why officials who understood that innocent people were perishing refrained from opposing Stalin and the NKVD. "Stalin had already managed to get a death grip on power," writes Grigory Pomerants,

and to strike at Stalin meant to strike at the Soviet system. But the Soviet system was one of the strongest obstacles to fascism. Not by reason of Stalin's dislike for Hitler—he may have liked him—but by the logic of the system itself, which was stronger than Stalin's will. And it was impossible to perform surgical operations, to strike at the Soviet system even to cure it, with Hitler standing there.[31]

Pomerants runs together the war and the prewar years, so his reasoning is only partly correct. The dilemma—Stalin or Hitler?—arose in the war, not before. When it did, even White émigrés were faced with the choice. Some took Hitler's side, some took neutral positions, but many, including Milyukov, supported the Red Army.[32] If even émigrés supported Stalin during the war, Soviet people were all the more obliged to do so. This choice was not so categorical in the years before the war. Stalin's crimes were so great that, had they been known, it would have been impossible to support him even by reference to the threat of fascism. But that, once again, was the problem: no one at the time knew the scale of those crimes or realized how dangerous they were.

"Of course there was a lot we did not know, and did not even suspect about Stalin's monstrous plans," one Old Bolshevik has said to me. (He helped build Magnitogorsk and then spent many years in jails and camps.)

However, we did see all around us many faults, mistakes, even crimes. Why did we not immediately rise up against them? In the thirties we felt as if we were at war, at war with the entire old world, and we believed that in war you should act like there's a war on. In other words, we should swear at the blunders of the high command not during the conflict but after the battle. While the conflict was on,

31. G. Pomerants, "Nravstvennyi oblik istoricheskoi lichnosti," unpublished manuscript.
32. In 1942, in a Russian emigre paper published in Vichy France, Pavel Milyukov endorsed the formula, "If you're not for Stalin, that means you're for Hitler." The fact that Milyukov chose the Soviet side is to his credit. But the reasons he gave for the choice are curious. He saw in Stalin's "new form of one-man dictatorship . . . a new step forward in the evolution of the Russian state organization." The full text of Milyukov's article circulated in the USSR in copies made on a duplicator. Some passages from it are quoted in A. Lyubimov, *Na chuzhbine* (Moscow, 1963).

a conflict to the death, it was necessary to maintain iron discipline no matter what. We considered it natural to ignore the successes of the enemy and to exaggerate our own still very modest successes in every way possible. That's always how it is in a war.[33]

Yelena Vladimirova speaks about these reflections somewhat differently in one of her prison poems:

Afraid to break the structure of customary thought,
Fearing to see the truth naked,
We seek grounds to preserve our calm
And avoid spiritual schism.
Hiding our cowardly heads under our wings,
Submissively accepting any evil,
We say, "Let it be hard on us,
We will forgive our homeland anything."
Forgive . . . whom? and what?
If only the country needed our pain, then we would accept
Pain and any sentence without a word about forgiveness.
In the dread hour that has come upon our land,
Under storm clouds of war that threaten every hour,
We should not forgive, but answer,
Where is the truth and where the lie, where the
Path and where the danger?
We must give an answer: Who needed
The monstrous destruction of the generation
That the country, severe and tender,
Raised for twenty years in work and battle?

Such misgivings, such insights into Stalinism, can be found to a much greater extent among former prisoners than among those who remained free. Only when people landed in prison did they come to see the frightful inside truth of the Stalinist dictatorship and the extraordinary dimensions of the terror. As the Polish writer Jerzy Lec puts it: "Certain thoughts come into your head only when you're being marched along under guard."

■ 5
CENTRALIZATION AND LENGTH OF TERM IN OFFICE

Long before the October revolution, the Bolshevik Party was based on strict centralization. Indeed, this was one of its distinguishing features;

---

33. Even Trotsky in the early thirties wrote an article entitled " 'Down with Stalin' Is Not Our Slogan," although after 1935 his views apparently changed.

many arguments between Bolsheviks and Mensheviks focused on the relationship between democracy and centralism. The Mensheviks protested against strict organization, the increasing authority of party centers, and the transformation of party members into "cogs in the party machine." Plekhanov's article "Centralism or Bonapartism" was characteristic.[34] Lenin always decisively rejected the Mensheviks' arguments and protests as symptoms of petty-bourgeois individualism and the lack of discipline typical of intellectuals. Fears of excessive centralism in the party had unquestionably more basis to them than merely "the slackness of the intelligentsia." Lenin's polemical sallies on this point were not always sufficiently well founded. Still, he did perceive the many dangers in excessive centralism. At the same time, he invariably pointed out that in a country like Russia socialists needed strict discipline and centralization no less than correct policies to win out in the revolutionary struggle. It was necessary to choose what seemed at the time to be the lesser of two evils.

In the first years after the October revolution centralism was intensified. In fact, one may speak not so much of the centralization as the militarization of the party and Komsomol in that period. The Soviet government was also organized on the basis of strict centralization. Without it, and without military discipline, the Bolsheviks could hardly have mobilized all the resources of the exhausted and devastated country for the struggle against its numerous enemies. From a purely theoretical standpoint many of the reproaches made by Rosa Luxemburg and even by Karl Kautsky against the dictatorial practices of the Bolsheviks were justified. However, in the summer of 1918, at the beginning of the civil war, when Lenin and the Bolsheviks found themselves in a critical situation after suffering a series of major defeats and having lost control of the greater part of Russian territory, it was difficult for them to follow any logic other than that of intense military combat, and in that period greater centralization of power and limitation of democracy were not only natural but indispensable. Lunacharsky wrote in 1921:

The idea of revolution is firmly connected in most people's minds with the idea of freedom. . . . In fact, no revolution creates a regime of freedom or can create it. Revolution is civil war, invariably accompanied by external war. . . . That is why even a socialist revolution, which announces an end to all wars and the abolition of all state power as its ultimate ideals, is forced in its first stage to intensify the spirit of its own kind of militarism, to intensify the dicta-

34. Plekhanov, *Sobranie sochinenii*, 13:81–93.

torial quality of state power and even, so to speak, its quality as a police state.[35]

The Comintern, too, was committed to the strictest centralization. Each of its member parties was regarded only as a section of the central organization, and "an iron discipline bordering on military discipline" was required of these sections.[36]

For some young Communist parties working underground or faced with anti-Communist terror, such centralization was necessary—but only as a temporary measure. It was a mistake to make extreme centralization a necessary condition for all Communist parties simply because centralization was necessary for the Bolsheviks in the midst of revolution and civil war, especially when such extreme centralization had not existed in the Bolshevik Party in the prerevolutionary period. Many Communist parties that were founded after the October revolution worked in economic, political, and historical conditions quite different from those in Russia. The military system introduced into those parties could therefore only hinder their political growth and expansion. Lenin himself soon came to understand this, learning from the example of the Bolshevik Party itself. Immediately after the end of the civil war the Bolshevik Central Committee adopted a number of measures to decrease centralization and develop democracy. The Ninth Party Conference, of September 22–25, 1920, resolved:

It is necessary in the internal life of the party to achieve broader criticism, both of local and of central party institutions. The Central Committee is instructed to indicate ways to broaden intraparty criticism at general meetings. Publications should be created that would be capable of achieving a more systematic and broader criticism of the party's mistakes (discussion bulletins, etc.) . . . Any repression of comrades for being dissidents on certain issues that the party has already decided is intolerable.[37]

The banning of factions at the Tenth Party Congress in 1921 represented a significant restriction on democracy inside the party. On the other hand, that very same congress took note of many negative aspects of excessive centralization: bureaucracy, isolation from the masses, rule by force, decline in party morale. The resolutions of the Congress called for a revival of intraparty democracy to correct these abuses.[38]

35. *Pechat' i revoliutsiia* (1921), no. 1, pp. 3–4.
36. See Term 13 of "The Terms of Admission to the Communist International," in Lenin, PSS, 41: 208–209; CW 31:210.
37. *KPSS v rezoliutsiiakh* . . . (Moscow, 1954), 1:509.
38. Ibid., pp. 517–519.

Of course, elimination of centralization was out of the question. Communists never conceived of socialist society as an agglomeration of self-governing communes, not subject to any central authority. Centralization was necessary to combat counterrevolution and defend the country against foreign intervention. Without a strong and authoritative central government an economically weak and dislocated country like Russia could not build a modern industry quickly, especially certain branches of the machine industry. Only a strong central authority could redistribute accumulated wealth, transferring it from certain existing sectors of the economy to create new branches of industry, while enforcing an appropriate tax policy and a monopoly of foreign trade. Another objective basis for centralization lay in the constantly growing economic system of modern socialist society, which could not function without a coordinated, effective, firm leadership.

There was, of course, a need for moderation and balance in all this. The Soviet Union needed not blind, thoughtless, unlimited centralism but a wise combination of centralization with local initiative and individual creativity, of state discipline with personal freedom. Stalin did not find—he did not even seek—such a combination. Thus the work of democratizing the party and public life, begun in the first half of the twenties, was not continued. Instead, Stalin constantly pressed for greater one-sided centralization. Covering himself with the thesis that the class struggle was intensifying, he gradually accumulated more and more power. The repression of the thirties completed the process. Centralization was transformed into absolutism. But this repression became possible only when Stalin's power had already exceeded all reasonable bounds. Such excessive power could corrupt even the best people; in the hands of a limited, ambitious, and spiteful careerist it inevitably led to the criminal abuse of power.

Another factor helping Stalin was the length of time he was allowed to remain in power. It is not unusual in many countries for a political figure to become the leader of his party for life, especially in the case of a truly outstanding politician. In democratic societies with multiparty systems, however, leaders and parties must periodically renew their mandates, and that is by no means a purely formal procedure. Moreover, in a democracy there is usually a limit on the length of time one may occupy a top government post. This tradition dates back to the Roman republic, in which consuls were elected for no more than one year at a time and could not serve two successive terms. Yet in the Soviet Union to this day there exists no system for regularly changing the leadership of the party and government.

Of course Lenin was chief of the Bolshevik Party continuously for a quarter of a century, but he was also the founder of the party and of the Soviet government; he was a political genius of a type that appears perhaps once in a century. Some Sovietologists also rate Stalin's political abilities quite highly. For example, an article by Steven Blank in a Russian émigré journal states:

> [Stalin] must be recognized as a political genius. Regardless of the criminal methods he resorted to, he also knew how to maneuver politically when that was required to satisfy his inordinate ambition. This can be seen quite well in his actions on the international arena. He was denied the option of having Churchill or Roosevelt shot. Still, he brilliantly outmaneuvered them. Thus we find in Stalin, in addition to his criminal willfullness, incredible cruelty, and contempt for morality, both political astuteness and political talent. To doubt this would be to underestimate Stalin.[39]

Steven Blank exaggerates Stalin's accomplishments in foreign policy, but there is an element of truth in what he says. It was precisely because of inordinately ambitious "political geniuses" of Stalin's type that a different system for the succession of political leadership and different limits for the length of time in office should have been established for Lenin's successors. Yet after Lenin's death, as before, the party had no system of limits on the length of time an individual might remain at the head of the party and the state. This allowed a man like Stalin the time to carefully lay the basis for the total usurpation of power by gradually eliminating all opponents one after the other.

■ **6**

THE BOLSHEVIK PARTY'S POLITICAL MONOPOLY

It is hardly necessary to demonstrate that the one-party dictatorship that arose in the Soviet Union in the early twenties was a very important condition for Stalin's usurpation of power, providing extremely favorable soil for all the crimes and abuses of power connected with his name. It may be said that this system was a product of history. But in saying this, I do not mean to justify the system or suggest that it is the best one for building a socialist society. Some explanations are in order.

39. *Tribuna* (Paris, 1983), no. 2, p. 3.

After the fall of the autocracy in Russia power passed to the main bourgeois parties in the State Duma. They at first formed a Provisional Committee, then a Provisional Government. Initially, the dominant influence in this government was the Cadet Party, headed by Pavel Milyukov.

At the same time the workers and soldiers of the capital city and of the other main cities were the chief driving force behind the February revolution. They did not regard the Duma as a body expressing their interests. There immediately arose a need to establish representative institutions reflecting the interests and political will of the workers and soldiers not only to "represent" the masses but also to direct their actions. In this way the Soviets of Workers' and Soldiers' Deputies came into existence, created by the people themselves. The result was "dual power" in Russia, for the Soviets appeared as an addition to the already existing Duma, as a unique kind of "lower chamber" of an imaginary parliament. The "upper chamber" (the Duma and the Provisional Government) represented the ruling classes of society; the Soviets represented the working people. A compromise between these two bodies was possible only by establishing a new representative institution that would reflect the will of the entire nation. The demand for the formation of such an institution arose immediately after the revolution with the call for a Constituent Assembly. But the Provisional Government constantly put off convoking such an assembly, fearing that the bourgeois parties would be a minority in it.

The slogan "All Power to the Soviets," raised by Lenin and the Bolsheviks in 1917, was not a call for a one-party system. All the left and socialist parties belonged to the Soviets at that time—the SRs, Mensheviks, Bolsheviks, Anarchists, and many other, less influential political groups. In June and July 1917 the Bolsheviks were still a minority in the Soviets. Not until September did they gain a majority in the Petrograd and Moscow Soviets, as well as in the other working-class centers. Nevertheless, at the time of the October revolution, when the Second Congress of Soviets convened in Petrograd, it was still not certain that the Bolsheviks would receive the support of the majority of delegates.

The Bolshevik Party was the only one represented in the first Soviet government, the first Council of People's Commissars. Lenin strongly opposed the creation of a "united socialist government," which would have included right Socialist Revolutionaries and Mensheviks, although within the Bolshevik leadership quite a few favored that alternative. In fact, under other circumstances that would have been a wise move, widening the political base of the new government and reducing the danger of civil war. The Bolsheviks were not the only advocates of socialism in Russia; a government based on a coalition of socialist parties could have been an important step in the peaceful development of the socialist revolution. I do not say this to condemn Lenin's point of view. The problem in October 1917 was not how to build socialism but whether to continue the world war, which had been going on for nearly four years. On that question it turned out that no compromise was possible. That was what prevented the formation of a "united socialist government."

Even then Lenin did not advocate a total political monopoly by the Bolsheviks. Within weeks after the October revolution, when the SRs split into two parties, the Left SRs were invited to enter the Council of People's Commissars and were given seven of the eighteen seats, including the Commissariats of Agriculture, Justice, and City and Local Self-Government. Nor was the political activity of other parties banned right after the October revolution, with the exception of the Cadets and monarchists. Lenin was sure that the Bolshevik Party could establish its hegemony in Russia mainly by carrying out urgently needed social and economic reforms, not by the use of force against its opponents. Indeed in November and December 1917 the political influence of the Bolsheviks grew quickly and that of the Mensheviks and Right SRs fell just as quickly. That fact enabled the Bolsheviks to disperse the Constituent Assembly and prevented the Right SRs and Mensheviks from keeping that assembly alive. In January 1918 at the Third Congress of Soviets, the Bolsheviks had 66 percent of the delegates. Of the 360 members of the Central Executive Committee elected by that congress, 160 were Bolsheviks, 125 Left SR's, 7 SR-Maximalists, 7 Right SRs, 3 Anarchist-Communists, 2 Menshevik-Internationalists, and 2 Menshevik-Defensists.[40]

Events did not continue as the Bolsheviks would have wished. The question of the Brest-Litovsk treaty caused a split not only between the Left SRs and the Bolsheviks but within the Bolshevik Party itself. An overly rapid nationalization of industry and the dictatorial methods of the Commissariat of Food Supply, with its grain-requisitioning detachments, caused a still sharper conflict between the Bolshevisk and the Left SRs,

---

40. *Velikaia Oktiabr'skaia sotsialisticheskaia revoliutsiia. Entsiklopediia* (Moscow, 1977), p. 606.

whose influence among the peasants began to grow swiftly. Under these conditions the Bolsheviks chose to restrict the rights of the other socialist parties. They hoped that this measure would help them bring the country through the difficult transitional period more easily. On June 14, 1918, citing Right SR and Menshevik participation in the fight against the Soviet regime, the Central Executive Committee decreed the expulsion of the Right SRs and Mensheviks from all Soviets. Earlier, in April 1918, all Anarchist groups had been expelled from the Soviets. In July 1918, after the rising of the Left SRs, the same decree was issued for them. But even after their expulsion from the Soviets, the SR and Menshevik parties continued to exist as legal, active political organizations. Moreover, when the Menshevik Central Committee at the end of 1918 opposed foreign intervention and collaboration with the bourgeoisie and rejected the proposal for a Constituent Assembly, the Central Executive Committee rescinded the decree of June 14 with respect to the Mensheviks. In February 1919 the same was done with respect to those Right SR groups that took a position against foreign intervention. Some anarcho-syndicalist groups also existed legally.

In the summer and fall of 1918 the main forces opposing the Bolsheviks in the incipient civil war were the left "petty bourgeois" parties—the SRs, Mensheviks, Anarchists, various nationalist groups—in alliance with the Czech Legion. By the end of 1918 the monarchist generals supported by armed units from England, France, Japan, the United States, and several other countries had become the main anti-Bolshevik force. This changed the political situation inside the Soviet Republic. In 1919, for example, the so-called Irkutsk Political Center, led by SRs and Mensheviks, came out against the leader of the Whites in Siberia, Admiral Kolchak. The Maximalist SRs and Bundists also opposed Kolchak in 1919, and the Bolsheviks did not decline temporary agreements with those groups. During 1919 the SRs and Mensheviks held legal congresses and other meetings in the Soviet Republic. Imprisoned SRs and Mensheviks were freed by an amnesty, and in many cases they left immediately for the front lines of the civil war. Some SRs and Mensheviks even became political commissars in units of the Red Army. During Denikin's offensive in 1919 the Bolsheviks concluded a very important military-political alliance with Makhno, an anarchist whose army was a major force in the southern Ukraine at that time. The successful raids in Denikin's rear carried out by Makhno's units, which were formally made part of the Red

Army, helped to weaken the Whites' offensive against Moscow and later to smash the armies of Denikin and Wrangel.

An analysis of Lenin's speeches and articles during 1917–1920 shows that he did not assume the existence of a one-party system in Soviet Russia nor a complete ban on other left and socialist parties. On the contrary, he said that after basic revolutionary changes had been carried out, free elections should be held. He did not doubt that the Bolsheviks would win, but it was taken for granted that the other socialist parties would have a chance to present their programs in these elections. Lenin considered it possible that in other countries or under other conditions supporters of bourgeois parties would also continue to have electoral rights.

Of course the civil war, devastation, and famine made the holding of free elections impossible. In large areas of the country elections to the Soviets were eliminated and the elected Soviets were replaced by "revolutionary committees" appointed from above. Because of these conditions the holding of relatively democratic elections was delayed but not entirely ruled out.

The end of the civil war brought with it an exceptionally complicated political situation. The evolution of the various political parties in the RSFSR and the other Soviet republics took a new turn. In 1920 the Left SRs, the Maximalists, and the Populist Communists decided to end their existence as parties. In March 1920 the Borotbists (the Left SRs of the Ukraine) were taken into the Ukrainian Communist Party. In 1921 the left wing of the Bund also decided to join the Communist Party, as did certain leftwing members of the Menshevik and Right SR parties (some for careerist reasons, but most on the basis of political principles). The Right SRs, the Mensheviks, and the Anarchists went through a serious crisis at the beginning of the decade and could not work out any definite program or enduring organization. The Communist Party was also going through a serious crisis; it was shaken by internal debates. Several factions formed within it, including the Workers' Opposition and the Democratic Centralist group.

A significant section of the working class was dissatisfied with the deteriorating standard of living, the poor functioning of industry, and food shortages. Still greater dissatisfaction with the policies of "war communism" and grain requisitioning was expressed by the peasantry in dozens of rebellions, large and small, breaking out all over the country. The largest of these was the Kronstadt revolt of March 1921, in which sailors of the Baltic fleet took part along with workers and residents of the Kronstadt fortress. A peasant revolt in Tambov province led by an SR member, A. S. Antonov, lasted for several months. At the height of the Antonov insurgency the rebels had about fifty thousand fighters, organized into twenty-one regiments. In the spring and summer of 1921 fierce fighting with the mobile units of Makhno's army spread through most of the Ukraine. Dozens of other armed units fought the Communist authorities in the Don region, the Northern Caucasus, the Volga region, the Urals, and Siberia. This was in fact a continuation of the civil war, with the counterrevolution no longer led by monarchist generals but by significant "petty bourgeois" groups, headed primarily by SRs and Anarchists but sometimes by people who had been Communists until shortly before then. Winning this battle was more difficult for the Bolsheviks than defeating the campaigns of the Entente. It was not so much the suppression of the Kronstadt revolt or the Antonov uprising as the abandonment of "war communism" and the introduction of the New Economic Policy that enabled the Communist Party to retain power.

Although the Communists remained in power, their social and political base had shrunk substantially; the sympathies of the majority were no longer on their side. The working class that had been the main social support of the Bolsheviks in 1917 simply no longer existed. This is how Lenin described the situation in 1921:

Our proletariat has been largely declassed; the terrible crisis and the closing down of the factories have compelled people to flee from starvation. The workers have simply abandoned their factories; they have had to settle down in the country and have ceased to be workers. Are we not aware of the fact that the unprecedented crises, the civil war, the disruption of proper relations between town and country, and the cessation of grain deliveries have given rise to a trade in small articles made at the big factories—such as cigarette lighters—which are exchanged for cereals, because the workers are starving, and no grain is being delivered? . . . That is the economic source of the proletariat's declassing and the inevitable rise of petty bourgeois, anarchist trends.[41]

The peasantry was also different than it had been in 1917, when it obtained legal right to the landowners' estates from the Bolshevik government. Since then it had gone through the experiences of "war communism," grain requisitioning, food detachments, dekulakization, and the Poor Peasants' Committees.

For the Bolsheviks to hold free elections, if only in the Soviets, giving

41. Lenin, PSS, 43: 42; CW, 32:199.

free rein to the "petty bourgeois" socialist parties would almost certainly have meant loss of the political power they had fought a long and stubborn armed struggle to retain. That they could not allow. Political freedom was again postponed to the indefinite future. In the present it was necessary to speak openly about the renunciation of "pure" democracy. Soviet elections were held quite differently from those of 1917. A complex system of indirect, multiphase elections was established. Instead of direct voting with a secret ballot and equal suffrage, one worker's vote was the equivalent of five or six votes (sometimes even more) by peasants or "petty bourgeois." In addition, quite a large number of persons who had by no means belonged to the exploiting classes previously were denied the right to vote.

Gradually the Bolsheviks banned all other political parties, establishing the dictatorship of their party. Lenin did not equate the "dictatorship of the proletariat" with that of the party, but he did not reject the formula "dictatorship of the party," despite Stalin's later assertions to the contrary.

One of many examples was the following statement made by Lenin at the Second Comintern Congress in 1920:

[We are told that] by the dictatorship of the proletariat we actually mean the dictatorship of the organized and class-conscious minority of the proletariat. True enough, in the era of capitalism . . . the most characteristic feature of working-class political parties is that they can involve only a minority of their class. A political party can comprise only a minority of a class, in the same way as the really class-conscious workers in any capitalist society constitute only a minority of all workers.[42]

In 1920–1921 the demand for free Soviet elections was raised by the Mensheviks and SRs. In 1921 the Menshevik Central Committee urged its members to take "an active part in electing Soviets of Workers' Deputies and in the work of the Soviets themselves."[43] As the Menshevik leader Fyodor Dan acknowledged, "free Soviet elections as the first step in replacing the dictatorship by the rule of democracy—that was our political slogan."[44] The Right SRs pursued approximately the same policy. Where it was impossible to present their own slate in

42. Lenin, PSS, 41: 236. CW, 31: 235.
43. *Sotsialistichesky vestnik* (1922), no. 1, p. 17.
44. F. Dan, *Dva goda skitanii* (Berlin, 1922), pp. 113–114.

electing a Soviet, they put their candidates forward as "nonparty people."[45]

At first the Bolsheviks responded to these tactics by placing numerous practical restrictions on the Menshevik and Right SR parties, later imposing a formal, legal ban on their activities. The penal code of the RSFSR, drafted and approved in 1922, equated Menshevik or SR activity directly with counterrevolution. The liberal economic policies of NEP were accompanied by political terror against the Bolsheviks' recent allies in the struggle against the tsarist autocracy. Many of the techniques used by the Bolsheviks in this campaign against the Mensheviks and SRs were by no means above reproach.

The open trial of the leaders of the Right SRs is a case in point. The trial lasted from June 8 to August 7, 1922. We do not know what part Lenin played in its preparation, for he was seriously ill from the end of May through the summer of 1922. Certainly the trial could not have been organized without the participation of the general secretary, Stalin. (The chairman of the Supreme Tribunal of the Central Executive Committee was Pyatakov, and the chief prosecutor was Krylenko.)

Of course the Right SRs had a long record of crimes against the Soviet government. Suffice it to recall Fanny Kaplan's attempt to kill Lenin in 1918, the assassinations of Uritsky and Volodarsky, and the crimes of SR authorities in the Volga region during the summer of 1918 and in Arkhangelsk. Nonetheless, in 1919 the Soviet government had declared an amnesty and legalized the Right SR Party, which began to publish its newspaper, *Delo naroda*, in Moscow. In 1920–1921 the SRs were outlawed again, for they took part in many of the peasant revolts in those years, although Lenin himself admitted that the peasants had valid reasons for discontent with Soviet policies. From the Bolsheviks' point of view NEP was a policy turn of enormous importance. Still, many of the measures introduced under NEP had been proposed long before by the SRs and Mensheviks.

Although there was sufficient basis for a criminal investigation of the Right SRs, the Soviet court should have proceeded carefully and objectively. Deliberate crimes had to be distinguished from political mistakes, and the personal responsibility of each leader had to be established, for the SR Party was never a tightly centralized organization. The court

45. K. V. Gusev, *Partiia eserov* (Moscow, 1975), p. 346.

should have taken into account also that in early 1922 the Central Executive Committee had declared an amnesty for participants in the peasant revolts of the preceding years. In painful fact, the trial took a very different course. The organizers of the trial resorted to outright falsification in pursuit of unsavory political aims. In addition to the real leaders of the Right SRs, who strove to defend themselves and justify their party's activities, there were defendants who had not been leaders and, in a number of cases, had not even been members. These people zealously agreed with the indictment and repented for crimes they had taken no part in.

One such defendant was Rufina Stavitskaya (or Faina Stavskaya). She was well known to a number of eminent Bolsheviks as an activist of the Anarcho-Communists. In 1922 she had applied for admission to the Bolshevik Party. According to the unpublished memoirs of her husband, the Old Bolshevik V. Ye. Baranchenko, a peculiar test was set for her: to expose the Right SRs at the trial. She agreed, and her husband tries in his memoirs to justify her action, which is a disgrace for any true revolutionary.

1922 was an extremely hard year for Rufina Stavitskaya. In her youth she had taken the revolutionary path and ceaselessly sought to give her life to the cause of world social revolution. Now she was faced with the prospect of giving not her life but something that is dearer for every revolutionary. In the interests of the dictatorship of the proletariat and its socialist revolution, she was asked to give her revolutionary honor, as the old revolutionaries and political prisoners understood that honor. She was obliged by the will of the leading force of the proletarian revolution to take part in a big trial that exposed and destroyed the enemies of the proletarian regime who were at that time ideologically and politically the most wicked, the most dangerous. . . . Soon afterward she was admitted to the Communist Party, which she had served as well as she could until then.[46]

There is reason to doubt the confessions and conduct of several other defendants at this trial. Three of them, Semyonov, Usov, and Konopleva, were undoubtedly acting as provocateurs. The Supreme Tribunal sentenced Stavitskaya to two years of solitary confinement. But the same decision also stated:

46. V. Ye Baranchenko, "Vozvrashchenie chesti. Zhizn' i gibel' Fainy Stavskoi," unpublished manuscript. (Baranchenko and Stavskaya were arrested in 1937. Stavskaya died in confinement and was posthumously rehabilitated. Her husband wrote a number of articles and books about revolutionaries of the Crimea, one of which, on Yu. P. Gaven, I have cited above. Baranchenko's book about Stavskaya was submitted to Soviet publishing houses but they refused to print it.)

With respect to Semyonov, Konopleva, Yefimov, Usov, Zubkov, Fyodorov-Kozlov, Pelevin, Stavitskaya, Dashevsky, the Supreme Tribunal finds: these defendants were honestly mistaken when they committed their serious crimes, for they believed that they were fighting in the interests of the revolution. . . . The above-named defendants have completely recognized the full gravity of the crime they committed, and the Tribunal, in complete confidence that they will courageously and selflessly fight for the Soviet regime in the ranks of the working class, . . . petitions the Presidium of the Central Executive Committee to release them from all punishment.[47]

All the above-named "defendants" were freed after the trial and given jobs. Their subsequent fates are not known to us, with the exception of Stavitskaya, who was sent to work in the Crimea and accepted as a member of the Communist Party. Later she became director of a historical library in Moscow, but in 1937 she was arrested and shot.

Fifteen defendants, including such members of the SR Central Committee as Gotz, Donskoi, Gendelman, Gershtein, Likhach, Ivanov, and Timofeev, were sentenced to be shot. The Central Executive Committee confirmed the verdict but gave a stay of execution on the condition that the SR Party cease its "conspiratorial, terrorist, and espionage activities." "If this party does not abandon armed struggle against Soviet power," said the CEC ruling, "the sentence against its counterrevolutionary leaders will be put into effect."[48]

The Right SR leaders were thus to be kept on death row as hostages. They were held in the Inner Prison of the GPU on Lubyanka Square (now Dzerzhinsky Square). One of them, S. D. Morozov, could not bear the stress and committed suicide on December 20, 1923. Western socialists responded with a flood of protests, and in early 1924 the death penalty for the Right SR leaders was reduced to five years imprisonment.[49]

After this trial both the Right SR and the Menshevik parties were banned. Legal political activity was now possible only for the Communist Party. Under the harsh and all-embracing one-party dictatorship, the repeated attempts of the SRs and Mensheviks to resume illegal activity were unsuccessful. Lacking a uniform program or tactics, they broke into many small groups. Only among émigrés were central organizations

47. *Prigovor Verkhovnogo revoliutsionnogo tribunala po delu partii eserov* (Moscow, 1922), pp. 28–29.

48. Ibid., pp. 33–34.

49. They were released after five years, but were sent into internal exile and assigned to economic work of various kinds. In 1937–1938 those who were still alive were rearrested and died in confinement.

established representing the non-Bolshevik socialist parties and some nationalist parties. Their leaflets and other publications, including newspapers—the *Sotsialistichesky vestnik* of the Mensheviks and *Revolyutsionnaya Rossiya* of the SRs—were printed abroad. Only a few of these publications, however, managed to reach the USSR. They did contain some just criticism of the Bolsheviks. For example, the SRs, while fully supporting socialist agrarian cooperatives—that was one of the main points in their own program—criticized Stalin's methods of establishing cooperatives. SR and Menshevik publications attacked the bureaucratization of the state apparatus, the repression of technical specialists, and the trials of the "Industrial Party" and the "Union Bureau." At the same time a significant number of SRs opposed terror, declaring themselves in favor of "ethical socialism." The movement toward the goal, they reasoned, should be advanced not by any means whatever but by means that would educate militants for communism. They also spoke out against all arbitrary rule and even against the state itself, for they continued to draw their ideas from Lavrov and Chernyshevsky.

Despite hard times and widespread dissatisfaction in the Soviet Union during the late twenties and early thirties, the SRs and Mensheviks had no success with their propaganda. Their publications were printed in insignificant numbers, their agitators were easily caught by the GPU, and their illegal organizations were invariably liquidated a few months after formation. At the same time a massive propaganda campaign constantly portrayed any opposition as counterrevolutionary.

It is not my intention here to take up the defense of the SRs and Mensheviks; each of these parties committed quite a few political errors and even some crimes. But I do not defend the one-party dictatorship either. A political monopoly by one party results in an end to open public discussion, to freedom of opinion and criticism, and contributes to the prolongation and deepening of mistakes by the ruling groups and concealment of their crimes. The assertion that in view of the social homogeneity of Soviet society there is no basis for more than one party is profoundly wrong. Marxism has by no means solved all problems in social, political, and economic science, and not everything that is considered solved has been solved correctly. Nor is Leninism by any means the last word in the political and social sciences. Lenin himself changed his proposals on the ways and means of building socialism in Russia. Various approaches to this question are possible, and this provides philosophical and ideological justification for the existence of different political parties and groups in a socialist society. That would prevent a degeneration into despotism, for socialist society has a vital need not only for a ruling party but also for a legal opposition.

■ 7
PERVERSION OF LENIN'S CONCEPTION OF PARTY UNITY

Close study of Stalin's record, I am convinced, demonstrated that he perverted Lenin's concepts of unity and discipline in the party. Lenin never gave independent significance to the question of party discipline, apart from the convictions of the members, the principles of communism, and the rightness or wrongness of the policies of the party's central bodies. Lenin never construed party unity to mean absolute suppression of groups and tendencies in the party, independent of concrete historical conditions and the actual policies of the party leaders at a given time. Unity obviously gives any party great strength. But sometimes unity, in the absence of debates among different tendencies, is a manifestation of weakness, especially when an entire party is moving as one man in the wrong direction. That is why Lenin emphatically rejected a dogmatic interpretation of party unity. As early as 1904, in the very first stages of party building, Lenin wrote:

There will always be controversy and struggle in a party; all that is necessary is to bring them within party bounds—and that only a congress can do. . . .

[The] entire experience of the postcongress struggle [shows], . . . that it is necessary to include, in the party rules, guarantees of minority rights, so that the disagreements, dissatisfactions, and irritations that will constantly and unavoidably arise may be diverted from the old, philistine, circle channel of rows and squabbling into the still unaccustomed channels of a constitutional and dignified struggle for one's convictions. As one of these essential guarantees, we propose that the minority be allowed one or more literary groups, with the right to be represented at congresses and with complete "freedom of speech." In general, the widest guarantees should be given as regards publication of party literature criticizing the activities of the central party institutions.[50]

In 1911, Lenin wrote the following in reply to Trotsky, who ostensibly opposed the formation of factions in the party.

How empty—under the present circumstances—are the shouts against "factionalism," especially coming from those who have just formed their own faction.

50. Lenin, PSS, 9: 8–10. [Cf. CW, 7: 450–452.]

Surely it is time for them to understand that shouts against factionalism divert attention from the really important question, that of the pro-party or anti-party content of the activity of the various factions.[51]

When a proposal to condemn the struggle among groups in the party was made by V. Kosovsky-Shvartzman at the Prague Conference of the RSDLP in 1912, Lenin opposed it, declaring that internal struggles in the party could not be condemned in general. To condemn the struggles of groups in general, he said, would be to condemn the struggle of the Bolsheviks against the Liquidators.[52]

Among the Bolsheviks in Lenin's time there were always various groups and factions, which was considered natural and normal. Only in 1921, at a time of acute crisis for the Bolshevik government (as described above), did Lenin call for a temporary halt to factional struggle within the party and for the dissolution of all groups and factions then in existence. The resolution Lenin proposed on party unity did not, however, take away the members' right to criticize party policy. It not only eliminated the possibility of debate and discussion within the party, but also spoke openly of the desirability of such discussion.[53]

In speaking at the Tenth Congress against two factions—the Workers' Opposition and the Democratic Centralist group—Lenin did not demand that their members immediately change their views and convictions; he proposed only that they cease the propagation of their views at large among party members. Indeed he stressed the necessity of publishing divergent views in "special collections."[54]

Moreover, in proposing the resolution for party unity, Lenin emphasized that it applied to the current period and to the disagreements under discussion at the Tenth Congress. He strongly opposed a broad interpretation of the resolution. When Ryazanov proposed an amendment forbidding not only factional activity but also election campaigns to future congresses on the basis of platforms, Lenin disapproved:

I think that Comrade Ryazanov's wish is, however unfortunate that may be, unrealizable. We cannot deprive the party and the members of the Central Committee of the right to appeal to the party, if a basic question provokes disagreement. I can't imagine how we could do this. The present congress cannot in some way control elections to future congress. Suppose some question like the

51. Lenin, PSS, 20: 300–304. [Cf. CW, 36: 180–184.] (This article was not published until 1956, in the journal *Kommunist*, No. 5.)

52. *Voprosy istorii KPSS*, 1965, no. 2, p. 34.

53. *Desiatyi sahezd RKP(b). Stenograficheskii otchet* (Moscow, 1963), pp. 572–573.

54. Ibid., p. 523.

Treaty of Brest-Litovsk comes up.[55] . . . If circumstances give rise to fundamental disagreements, can we prohibit their presentation to the judgment of the entire party? We cannot![56]

The resolution on party unity to some extent played a positive role in the early twenties, but it could not prevent the emergence of serious differences in the party or the rise of new opposition. The opposition tendencies existed openly and an open struggle was waged against them. Of course from the very start there were attempts to interpret the Tenth Congress resolution dogmatically. Among the first to do so were Zinoviev and Kamenev in 1923–24. Speaking against the Trotskyist opposition at a meeting of Moscow's active party membership, for example, Zinoviev said:

> If you think the time has come to legalize factions and groups, then say so openly. We believe the time has not come and will not come during the period of the dictatorship of the proletariat. [Stormy applause] It cannot come because this issue is connected with the issue of freedom of the press, and in general with the issue of political rights for the nonproletarian strata of the population.[57]

Later, Zinoviev's distortion of the rule on factions was turned against his own opposition group.

In the mid-twenties most party activists had the concept that when there are serious differences on important questions, party members have the right to criticize the upper echelons. In short, they had the right of opposition. The right was implicitly recognized in a typical resolution of the Central Committee, such as that adopted on July 23, 1926:

> The party hoped that the opposition would in the process of day-to-day work realize and correct its mistakes. Thus the opposition was given full opportunity to defend its views in the normal party way when disagreements arose on various questions. Although the opposition persisted in its mistakes, which were pointed out by the Fourteenth Party Congress, and introduced elements of flagrant factional irreconcilability into the work of the Politburo and the Central Committee, the opposition's defense of its views within the Central Committee in the normal party way did not arouse serious concern about the preservation of unity either in the Central Committee or the Central Control Commission.[58]

55. [Lenin was originally outvoted in the Central Committee on the question of the Brest-Litovsk treaty. He threatened to resign and take his case to the party at large.— D. J.]

56. Ibid., p. 523.

57. Grigory Zinoviev, *Sud'by nashei partii* (Moscow, 1924), pp. 95–96.

58. *KPSS v rezoliutsiiakh* . . . , vol. 2 (Moscow, 1953), p. 161.

The resolution went on to accuse the opposition of overstepping the limits of permissible discussion, a charge that will not be assessed here. The point is that the resolution acknowledged the opposition's right to uphold its views.

As Stalin became master of the party, he decisively changed the interpretation of the principle of party unity. He began to denounce not only the views of particular opposition groups but opposition in general. Conscious discipline was replaced by blind obedience to the will of the Leader. Party members were instilled with the conviction that Stalin and his leadership could make no mistakes and that any opposition was the work of petty-bourgeois and bourgeois-imperialist circles. This distorted interpretation of the Tenth Congress resolution played a sorry role in the history of the party. Opportunism, taking the form of Stalinism, won out in the upper ranks of the party. The slogan of unity, dogmatically interpreted, served Stalin as an important tool in consolidating his personal dictatorship and crushing the Leninist core of the party. He exploited the admirable concept of the unity of the working class and of all Communists to actually split the party and exterminate any party member he found unsuitable.

■ 8

STALIN'S PERSONAL CONTROL OVER THE AGENCIES OF REPRESSION

The system of personal dictatorship that Stalin created was complex and strong. The deceived masses, the strictly censored mass media, the central and local party and government apparatuses, and the armed forces obedient to Stalin's will—all these were components of the system. But the chief role was played by the special punitive organs, which were under Stalin's personal control.

Before the revolution Lenin hypothesized that the proletariat would be able to break the resistance of the bourgeoisie fairly easily and that relatively limited punitive measures would suffice to put down counterrevolution. Reality proved to be more complex. The Soviet government was obliged to establish special repressive agencies shortly after the revolution. The first session of the Cheka, or Extraordinary Commission to Combat Counterrevolution and Sabotage, was held in December 1917. During the civil war, 1918–20, it reached a peak of activity, especially in areas near the front lines. In that period its units were thought of not as juridical or investigative agencies, but as military-administrative punitive agencies. Just as a soldier at the front kills his opponent simply because he sees him with a weapon in his hand, so the Cheka's mission was to seek out and destroy counterrevolutionaries and saboteurs, the internal enemy.

In 1921, Martyn Latsis (real name: Jan Sudrabs), head of a secret section of the Cheka and one of Dzerzhinsky's close collaborators, explained the tasks and functions of the Cheka as follows.

> The Extraordinary Commission is not an investigating commission or a court. Or a tribunal. It is a combat arm operating on the internal front of the civil war, and in the course of its struggle it uses the methods of investigative bodies and courts, military tribunals and outright military forces. It does not try the enemy; it strikes him down. It does not pardon or forgive but pulverizes anyone with a weapon on the other side of the barricades who cannot in any way be used to serve us. . . . But it is not a guillotine, severing heads after a decree by a revolutionary tribunal. No, it either destroys the enemy without a trial after catching him at the scene of the crime or it isolates him from society by confining him in a concentration camp or it turns him over to a tribunal when a thorough investigation and wide publicity are needed. It simply determines the harmfulness or harmlessness of a given individual or the degree of his harmfulness to Soviet power and accordingly either destroys him or isolates him from society, thereby rendering him harmless and preventing a repetition of hostile acts against Soviet power. For us, as for the Israelites, it is necessary to build the world of the future under constant fear of enemy attack, under constant enemy fire. The Extraordinary Commission secures the possibility of peaceful labor for all supporters of Soviet power by standing on guard within the country and protecting it from open and secret counterrevolutionaries.[59]

The Soviet government and Red Army could hardly have defeated their opponents without the help of the Cheka, without its acts of mass repression, without the Red Terror. But it was precisely the "extraordinary" functions of the Cheka, not always strictly defined, that often resulted in mistakes and abuses. Latsis himself was inclined to make too broad an interpretation of the concept "counterrevolutionary."

> The three-year struggle of Soviet power has shown with obvious clarity that there are no longer just counterrevolutionary individuals but that entire classes are counterrevolutionary. Under the dictatorship of the proletariat, first of all, the entire big bourgeoisie is counterrevolutionary. But counterrevolution also lurks among the petty bourgeoisie. The active fighting forces of the counterrevolution are recruited mainly from this milieu. Military cadets and officers of the

---

59. Latsis, *Chrezvychainye komissii po bor'be s kontrrevoliutsiei*, Moscow, 1921.

old regime, teachers, university students, and all youth in school are in their overwhelming majority a petty-bourgeois element, and it is they who have constituted the fighting forces of our opponent, from which White Guard regiments have been formed.[60]

These arguments were profoundly mistaken and harmful for the development of the revolution. Undoubtedly some part of the petty bourgeoisie constituted a reserve that the counterrevolution could draw on, but if the revolutionary party pursued a correct policy, the bulk of the petty bourgeoisie could be a source of support for the revolution. Otherwise, in a country like Russia, the revolution had no chance of winning. Among the Bolshevik leaders themselves there were more who had come from the intelligentsia, the lesser gentry, the universities and schools, and the ranks of teachers and junior officers, than directly from the proletariat. I leave aside the tens of thousands of military and technical specialists who during the civil war helped the Bolsheviks, not their enemies.

The moods and attitudes reflected in Latsis's pamphlet were especially harmful and dangerous because, as Latsis himself noted, the Cheka attracted to its ranks psychotics and also "swindlers and simply the criminal element, who use the title 'agent of the Cheka' for blackmail, extortion, and lining their pockets."[61]

Latsis's pamphlet was written in 1921, but as early as 1918 the same Latsis, calling for intensified struggle against the counter-revolution, gave the agents of the Cheka the following instructions:

Don't search the records for whether someone's revolt against the Soviet was an armed or only a verbal one.[62]

Social origin alone was sufficient basis, said Latsis, for declaring someone to be an enemy of Soviet power. Such instructions evoked protests within the Communist Party itself, and the matter came to Lenin's attention. He called Latsis's arguments "a complete absurdity," which "not even one of the best and most experienced Communists should go so far as to utter," and added:

Political distrust of the members of a bourgeois apparatus is legitimate and essential. But to refuse to use them in administration and construction would be the height of folly, fraught with untold harm to communism. . . . [Petty-bourgeois] democracy is not a chance political formation, not an exception, but a

60. Ibid., p. 13.
61. Ibid., p. 11.
62. *Krasnyi terror* (Kazan), 1918, no. 1, p. 2.

necessary product of capitalism. . . . After all, even backward Russia produced
. . . capitalists who knew how to make use of the services of educated intellectuals, be they Menshevik, Socialist-Revolutionary, or nonparty. Are we to be
more stupid than those capitalists and fail to use such "building material" in
erecting a communist Russia?[63]

In his 1921 pamphlet Latsis claimed that throughout Russia from 1918
through 1920 the Cheka shot only 12,733 persons. Undoubtedly this
figure was grossly understated, for in September 1918 alone, after the
Red Terror was proclaimed, several thousand hostages and "socially alien
elements" were shot. The exact number of people destroyed by the
Cheka during the civil war will probably never be known, but there can
be no doubt that the Whites killed many more Communists, Komsomol
members, captured Red Army men, and ordinary workers and peasants.
The White armies rarely took prisoners or established concentration
camps. The very first campaigns of the Volunteer Army, led by Generals
Kornilov and Denikin and resulting in the occupation of most of the
Northern Caucasus in 1918, were accompanied by the execution of thousands and thousands of Red Army men, not to mention civilians active in
support of the Soviets.

The Cheka's punitive actions were not limited to shooting. Many
people were put in concentration camps, but this confinement was regarded as temporary—only for the duration of the civil war. As soon as
the war ended, the Cheka leadership began a campaign to empty the
prisons and camps and to change its working methods. A Cheka decree
of January 8, 1921, acknowledged that

the prisons are filled to overflowing, not with bourgeois but for the most part
with workers and peasants [involved in theft or speculation]. This legacy [of the
civil war] must be done away with; the prisons must be emptied and we must
carefully see to it that only those who are really dangerous to the Soviet regime
should be put there.

The decree went on to stress the self-defeating nature of mass repression,
which increases the number of discontented people. A great program of
patient re-education was now the proper way to deal with ordinary
people; to catch genuine enemies, very careful investigation must replace
"the crude distinction between ours and not-ours simply according to
class character."[64]

Change in the Cheka's methods was not enough. With the end of the

63. Lenin, PSS, 37: 407–411.
64. Latsis, pp. 19–21.

civil war the necessity for a swift-striking punitive agency gradually disappeared. A special investigative apparatus was still needed to catch spies, subversives, and counterrevolutionaries, but this apparatus had to be deprived of the right to punish without a trial, that is, as an act of administration. The functions of judgment and punishment had to be transferred to juridical agencies. That is why in 1921, under peacetime conditions, when the main problem was to guarantee greater legality and the rights of the individual, Lenin raised the question of limiting the functions of the Cheka. On his initiative, the Ninth Congress of Soviets adopted a resolution that led to a major reorganization of the Cheka.[65] On February 6, 1922, it was transformed into the GPU (Glavnoe politicheskoe upravlenie—Main Political Administration). The GPU was given the job of combating only especially dangerous state crimes: political and economic counterrevolution, espionage, and banditry. Moreover the GPU did not have the right to apply repressive measures against criminals. In all cases, including those which were investigated by the GPU, the power of judgment belonged exclusively to the courts.

Lenin wrote that "previously the combat agencies of Soviet power were mainly the Commissariat of War and the Cheka, but now an especially big role falls to the Commissariat of Justice."[66]

The reconstruction of the Cheka-GPU went on for some years in the first half of the twenties. But it slowed down after the deaths of Lenin and Dzerzhinsky; indeed things started moving in an entirely different direction. The GPU gradually began to resume the functions that were appropriate only for a period of civil war. Under pressure from Stalin, a punitive organization reappeared, with the right to put people in jail and camps, to exile them to remote places, and later even to shoot them without any juridical procedure, simply as an administrative act.

Vyacheslav Menzhinsky, the head of the GPU after Dzerzhinsky's death, was an old party official, but he lacked the influence and authority of his predecessor. He was sick for long periods and rarely interfered in the day-to-day activity of the GPU. The real boss by the late twenties was his deputy, Yagoda, who was strongly influenced by Stalin. Stalin and Yagoda introduced a new style of work, for example, in the seizure of valuables from Nepmen by massive use of violence and arbitrary force. The GPU was also assigned the job of transporting hundreds of thousands of kulak families to the northern and eastern districts of the country.

65. *Izvestia*, December 30, 1921.
66. Lenin, PSS, 44: 306.

Stalin relied on the GPU to carry out the lawless repression of the intelligentsia in the late twenties and early thirties. At that time some GPU employees, with tacit support from above, were already creating false evidence, forcing prisoners to sign false interrogation records, inventing all kinds of plots and organizations, and beating and torturing prisoners. When one victim, Mikhail Yakubovich, told his interrogator at the end of 1930 that such methods would have been impossible under Dzerzhinsky, the interrogator laughed: "You've found someone to remember! Dzerzhinsky—that's a bygone stage in our revolution."

The GPU gradually increased in size and in 1934 it was reorganized as the NKVD (People's Commissariat of Internal Affairs), which included the "militia" (the regular police) and the border guards. After Menzhinsky's death in 1934 Yagoda was officially made head of the NKVD. Beginning in 1935 Yagoda monitored the work of the NKVD for the party's Central Committee, but long before that Stalin had in fact established his complete and undivided control over the GPU-NKVD.

In 1934 the powers of the NKVD were substantially enlarged. A Special Assembly (Osoboe Soveshchanie) was established within the NKVD by a decree of the Sovnarkom and Central Executive Committee with the right to confine people in prisons or camps or to send them into internal exile for as much as a five-year term without any court proceedings. The Special Assembly consisted of the commissar of internal affairs, his deputies, the head of the militia, and the chief prosecutor of the USSR or his deputy. A decision of the Special Assembly could be reversed, in the event of a protest by the procuracy, only by the Presidium of the Central Executive Committee.[67]

After the murder of Kirov and especially after the first two Moscow trials, Stalin and Yezhov carried out a "general purge" of the NKVD, as described above in chapter 6. It is important to note that in 1937 the pay of NKVD employees was approximately quadrupled. Previously a relatively low pay scale had hindered recruitment; after 1937 the NKVD scale was higher than that of any other government agency. NKVD employees were also given the best apartments, rest homes, and hospitals. They were awarded medals and orders for success in their activities. And, in the latter half of the thirties, their numbers were so swollen as to become a whole army, with divisions and regiments, with hundreds of thousands of security workers and tens of thousands of officers. NKVD

---

67. *Sbornik materialov po istorii sotsialisticheskogo ugolovnogo zakonodatel'stva* (Moscow, 1938), p. 311.

agencies were set up not only in every oblast center but in each city, even in each raion center. Special sections were organized in every large enterprise, in many middle-size ones, in railroad stations, in major organizations and educational institutions. Parks, theaters, libraries—almost all gathering places (even smoking rooms) came under constant observation by special NKVD operatives. An enormous network of informers and stool pigeons was created in almost every institution, including prisons and camps.

Dossiers were kept on tens of millions of people. In addition to the sections that kept tabs on Cadets and monarchists, SRs and Mensheviks, and other counterrevolutionary parties, in the Fourth Administration *(upravlenie)* of the NKVD a section was created for the Communist Party. It maintained surveillance over all party organizations, including the Central Committee. All raikom, gorkom, and obkom secretaries were confirmed in their posts only after the approval of the appropriate NKVD agencies. Special sections were also created to watch the Chekists themselves, and a special section to watch the special sections. The Chekists were trained to believe that Chekist discipline was higher than party discipline. "First of all," they were told, "you are a Chekist, and only then a Communist." Their training included learning the history of the trade, beginning with a very serious study of the Inquisition.[68]

Stalin paid special attention to surveillance of his closest aides, the members of the Politburo. "The secret service of the sovereign," says an ancient Indian book, "must keep its eyes on all the high officials, directors of affairs, friends and relatives of the ruler, and likewise his rivals."[69] Stalin watched every step of his closest aides, using the notorious law "On the protection of chiefs," enacted after Kirov's murder. While Stalin personally selected and completely controlled his own bodyguard (headed by General Vlasik), the protection of other leaders was entrusted to the NKVD. They could not go anywhere without the knowledge of their guard, could not receive any visitor without a check by the guard, and so on.

Although the powers of the NKVD were unusually great in the early

68. Chekists also received practical training in torture and many other things that were condemned in theory. Posted prominently in NKVD offices, even on the local level, was a saying by Lenin, "The slightest illegality is a hole through which counterrevolution can creep in." This hypocrisy was fully in the spirit of Stalin.

69. *Tirukaral. Kniga o dobrodeteli, o politike i o liubvi*, Moscow, 1963, p. 79. [This is a translation of the Tamil classic *Tirukkural*. See C. and H. Jesudasan, *A History of Tamil Literature* (Calcutta, 1961), pp. 41–51.—D. J.]

thirties, in the summer of 1936 the Central Committee passed a resolution, on Stalin's proposal, to grant the NKVD extraordinary powers for one year—to destroy completely the "enemies of the people." At the June Plenum of the Central Committee in 1937 these powers were extended for an indefinite period. At the same time the NKVD's juridical functions were significantly expanded. Within a day after the June plenum eighteen Central Committee members were arrested.

In addition to the Special Assembly, an extensive system of troiki, or three-man boards, was created, subordinated to this Special Assembly. These illegal bodies, whose very existence violated the Constitution of the USSR, independently examined political cases and passed sentences, completely ignoring the norms of jurisprudence. In this way the punitive organs were exempt from any control by the party and the soviets, the courts, and the procurator. Even when the NKVD investigators passed cases to the procurator's office or the courts, the latter obediently handed down verdicts prepared beforehand by the agency. In many oblasti procurators issued back-dated sanctions several months after an arrest, or even signed blank forms on which the NKVD subsequently entered any names they wanted. In reality, only one man had the right to control the activity of the punitive organs—Stalin himself.

This kind of repressive system obviously had its own kind of inertia, since a large percentage of the privileged NKVD officers would naturally desire to continue in their positions and therefore had an interest in finding and imprisoning more and more "enemies of the people" to justify their own existence. Thus the ever-expanding punitive agencies, besides being a firm foundation of the Stalinist regime, became a source of never-ending repression.

Mention must also be made of the demand for labor by the great network of labor camps, established for the most part in outlying regions of the country. In the mid-thirties prison camp labor was used mainly to build canals, at first the Baltic-White Sea canal and then the Moscow-Volga canal. By the late thirties the situation had changed; the headlong expansion of the prison camp system coincided with the expansion of industrial construction. State plans assigned an increasingly important role to the Main Camp Administration (GULAG). By the end of the thirties GULAG was responsible for much of the country's lumbering and extraction of copper, gold, and coal. GULAG built not only canals but also strategic roads and many industrial enterprises in remote regions.

This widespread use of forced labor had dangerous consequences. In the first place, the harsh regime established in 1937 used up labor quickly, with a consequent need for rapid replacement. Secondly, because Stalin did not find a rational solution for the problem of building in remote regions, he constantly increased the number of projects assigned to GULAG. Thirdly, the apparent "cheapness" and "mobility" of GU-LAG labor prompted many construction organizations and other economic units to employ such labor even in the central regions of the USSR. By the early fifties GULAG was working several mines in the Donbass and some sewing factories, ran virtually the entire lumber industry in Arkhangelsk oblast, and had built the Moscow University skyscraper as well as several other buildings in Moscow. Sanatoria in the Crimea and Sochi and residences for NKVD personnel in Orel were built by prisoner labor. The planning agencies frequently put pressure on GULAG through the apparatus around Stalin to speed up certain projects. Planning was done not only for projects assigned to GULAG but also for the growth of its labor force. Planning even encompassed the mortality rate in the camps—and in this respect achievement far exceeded plan goals. Before some large construction projects were begun, many oblast NKVD agencies would receive an order to provide the necessary labor force. Thus another vicious circle: the system of forced labor became a cause as well as an effect of mass repression.

■ 9
ENDS AND MEANS IN THE SOCIALIST REVOLUTION

The socialist revolution sets itself great and humane goals: the elimination of all exploitation, the end of wars and violence, and the harmonious, all-round development of the human personality. But to reach these goals the proletariat must go through a long struggle, both with its enemies and with its own deficiencies. Thus revolutionaries become involved in the problem of choosing ways of fighting, in the relationship between ends and means.

It is well known that neither Marxism nor Leninism denies the need for violence in the revolutionary struggle. (In this they differ from Gandhism, for example.) Marx often remarked that violence is the midwife in the birth of a new society, and Lenin frequently said that revolutions are not made with white gloves on. When the enemies of Soviet power tried to overthrow it, the Bolsheviks accepted the challenge. It was their firmness in struggle, their relatively skillful combination of force and persuasion, and in a number of cases the use of terror that secured their victory in the revolution and civil war. But true Marxism must not and cannot take the position that the revolutionary goal justifies in advance any means used to attain it.

The proposition "the end justifies the means" was devised, not by revolutionaries, but by their opponents. Its most consistent expression was found in the actions of the medieval church when it felt its existence threatened. In establishing the Inquisition and the Jesuit order, it freed them in advance from any moral obligations. Everything was justified for the sake of maintaining the unity of the church, including treachery, murder, and lies. It is well known what atrocities have accompanied the numerous religious wars, crusades, and campaigns of religious persecution that have occurred in so many countries.

The Jesuits' name was applied to the idea that the end justifies the means. Another version of this viewpoint was endorsed by the fascists in modern times. "When we win," asked Goebbels, "who will question us about our methods?"[70]

This point of view has frequently passed from the enemies of revolution to its advocates, among whom there have been not only unprincipled careerists but also fanatics and dogmatists ready to move toward the chosen goal without regard to means. This indiscriminate attitude was typical of many participants in bourgeois-democratic revolutions. One of the proclamations that appeared in France in 1792 said:

Everything is permitted to those who act in the spirit of the revolution. For a Republican there is no danger except that of lagging behind the laws of the republic. Often the one who goes beyond them, who might seem to have outstripped the goal, is still far from the point of completion.[71]

The Jacobin dictatorship and the Reign of Terror helped the French revolution drive back its domestic and foreign foes and to carry through a number of very important socioeconomic changes. But later the terror sapped the strength of the revolution, leading to the downfall of the Jacobins and the discrediting of the revolutionaries. Directed at first against royalists and counterrevolutionaries, the terror soon began to strike at revolutionaries too, if they stood a little to the right or left of the Jacobins themselves. Terror became the main, if not the only, means of

70. Quoted in Ye. Rzhevskaia, *Berlin, mai 1945* (Moscow, 1965), p. 73.
71. Quoted in Stefan Zweig, *Izbrannoe*, vol. 2 (Moscow, 1957), p. 172.

political combat. The simplified legal procedures accompanying the terror opened the way for abuses of power, and these possibilities were utilized not only by fellow travelers of the revolution but also by the Jacobin leaders themselves, Robespierre and Couthon. With Robespierre's knowledge and at his insistence slanderous charges were brought against political opponents and fraudulent trials were staged, with many loyal supporters of the republic being executed as a result. The Jacobins also replied with terror to the demands of the urban poor for an improvement in living conditions.

In the nineteenth century there were many revolutionaries who recognized no restrictions in their choice of means. Nechaev has already been discussed. Bakunin also saw revolution as universal destruction, as revenge, whose weapons could be "poison, the knife, the noose." Only a little while before his death did Bakunin realize that jesuitry and revolution were incompatible, that "you will build nothing vital or strong by jesuitical trickery, that, for the sake of success itself, revolutionary activity must seek support not in low, base passions; without the highest human ideal, no revolution triumphs."[72]

In 1871 the shooting of hostages by the Paris Commune was censured by many progressive democrats, although it was done in reply to the execution of captured Communards by the Versailles forces.

In the Soviet revolution and civil war examples of unjustified cruelty, suspicion, and misuse of violent methods were unfortunately not rare. In the first months after the October insurrection, lynching *(samosud)* of "suspects" was fairly frequent. Two former ministers of the Provisional Government, A. I. Shingarev and F. Kokoshkin, came to an end that way, and John Reed barely escaped. The civil war was accompanied not only by historically justified forms of revolutionary violence but also by superfluous cruelty. B. M. Dumenko, who organized the first cavalry units of the Red Army, was shot, and so was the commander of the Second Cavalry Army, F. Mironov. (They were not rehabilitated until 1964–65.) In the novel *Tikhii Don* Sholokhov has given a vivid description of the mass shooting of Cossacks on the Upper Don, which was a major cause of the Veshenskaya Cossack rising against the Soviet regime.

During the civil war it was not only Stalin who frequently misused violence but also such figures as Trotsky, Gusev, M. S. Kedrov, and many other commanders, commissars, and plenipotentiaries. The wide-

72. Quoted in *Voprosy istorii*, 1964, no. 10, p. 85.

spread taking of hostages, which began in the first months of the civil war, was also a mistake. Sometimes justification could be found for temporarily isolating certain individuals who were potentially dangerous to Soviet rule, but the method used by the Bolsheviks entailed not only temporary isolation but also the physical annihilation of some for the crimes of others. This was stated plainly in an order sent by telegraph to all Soviets in September 1918 by Grigory Petrovsky, the commissar of internal affairs.

The assassination of Volodarsky and Uritsky, the attempted assassination and the wounding of the chairman of the Council of People's Commissars, Vladimir Ilyich Lenin, the mass execution, by the tens of thousands, of our comrades in Finland, the Ukraine, and finally, in the Don region and the area controlled by the Czechs, the plots constantly being uncovered in the rear of our army, the open admission by the Right SR's and other counterrevolutionary scum of participation in these plots, and at the same time the extremely minor extent to which severe repression or mass execution has been used by the Soviets against the White Guards and the bourgeoisie—all this shows that despite the constant talk about mass terror against the SRs, the White Guards, and the bourgeoisie, this terror does not in fact exist. This situation must be overcome decisively. We must immediately put an end to slackness and pussyfooting (*mindal'nichan'e*). All Right SRs known to the local soviets must be immediately arrested. A substantial number of hostages must be taken among the bourgeoisie and former tsarist officers. If there is any attempt at resistance or the slightest movement in the White Guard milieu, the method of mass execution must be applied unconditionally. The provincial soviet executive committees must display special initiative in this regard.[73]

Petrovsky's order actually did result in the seizure and execution of hostages on a mass scale. Issue No. 5 of the Cheka weekly reported the execution of five hundred hostages in Petrograd alone. It is impossible to agree with such harsh measures, even considering the difficult situation in 1918. Such executions did not uproot the counterrevolution but merely embittered the conflict, causing more casualties on both sides.

Many of the executions carried out by the Cheka were unnecessary, especially some shootings of hostages. In 1920 the Soviet government proclaimed an amnesty for all former White Guardists hiding in the Crimean mountains, but the local authorities shot some of those who gave themselves up, including some who had been forcibly drafted into the White Army. Doubts are also raised by Frunze's order to surround

73. See the weekly bulletin of the Cheka *Ezhenedel'nik Chrezvychainykh Komissii* (Moscow), 1918, no. 1, p. 11.

and eliminate a three-thousand-member brigade of Makhno's army, which had taken part in the storming of Wrangel's defenses on the Crimea. In 1919–1920 Makhno's army was an important ally of the Red Army. It is not ruled out that the problems of Makhno's movement, which had a mass base among the peasants and which marched under anarchist banners, might have been resolved by political means, thus avoiding a long and bloody conflict lasting until mid-1921.

Many leaders of the Communist Party and Soviet government spoke out against various kinds of extreme and unjustified cruelty, only a few examples of which we have given above. Dzerzhinsky wrote, for example, in a memorandum to Unshlikht: "Better to err a thousand times in the direction of liberalism than send one innocent man into internal exile, from which he will return an active opponent and his sentencing will be used against us." Did the Cheka follow this wise counsel often enough? As early as the end of 1918, on a motion by Lenin, the Council of Defense granted the people's commissariats, and the party's local committees the right to participate, through delegated representatives, in investigations of citizens arrested by the Cheka. The Cheka was to release anyone vouched for in writing by two members of the collegium of a commissariat or by two members of a party committee. Did the commissariats and party committees avail themselves of this right very often? Did the Cheka itself give much consideration to this decree by the Council of Defense?

The conclusion of the civil war required that the Soviet government strengthen observance of legality. Many forms of violence that had previously been justified became impermissible and dangerous at that point. The transition was difficult, however, because many leaders considered the introduction of legality as equivalent to "disarming the revolution."[74]

In 1920 after a visit to Soviet Russia Bertrand Russell wrote:

> The evils of war, especially of civil war, are certain and very great. . . . In the course of a desperate struggle, the heritage of civilization is likely to be lost, while hatred, suspicion, and cruelty become normal in the relations of human beings. . . . Experience of power is inevitably altering Communist theories, and men who control a vast governmental machine can hardly have quite the same outlook on life as they had when they were hunted fugitives. If the Bolsheviks remain in power, it is much to be feared that their Communism will fade.[75]

74. See V. M. Kuritsyn, "NEP i revoliutsionnaia zakonnost'," *Voprosy istorii*, 1967, no. 9.

75. Bertrand Russell, *The Practice and Theory of Bolshevism* (New York, 1964), pp. 30–31.

As Kalinin noted:

The civil war has created huge cadres of people for whom the only law is expedience, ordering, power. To govern, as far as they are concerned, means to issue orders in complete independence, without submitting to the regulating articles of the law.[76]

The historian Pokrovsky wrote in 1924 about Communists returning from the civil war full of assurance that the methods which "produced such brilliant results in regard to Kolchak and Denikin would help in dealing with all remnants of the past in any other field." Victory in the civil war gave them the hope "that things would go just as quickly in economic construction; the only thing needed was to put military methods to work."[77]

Marx and Engels held the view that the proletariat would need a period of ten or fifteen years of civil war to free itself from its own defects. Perhaps war does free people from some defects, but it instills many others that are very hard to get rid of afterward. Besides, war and terror create not only habits but also institutions, which are even harder to eliminate.

The transition to new methods was difficult even for Lenin. In the spring of 1922, when the Commissariat of Justice was preparing the first Criminal Code of the RSFSR, Lenin sent a letter to Commissar of Justice Dmitry Kursky concerning the definition of counterrevolutionary activity. He urged that the definition should be

a politically truthful (and not only a juridically narrow) proposition, giving the grounds for and justification of terror, its necessity, its limits.

The courts should not eliminate terror—to promise that would be self-deception or deception—but should give it a legitimate basis, principled, clear, without hypocrisy or adornment. The formulation must be as broad as possible, for only a revolutionary sense of the law (*pravosoznanie*) and revolutionary conscience will provide the conditions for a wider or narrower application in each case.[78]

Lenin then sketched three possible drafts, two of which were indeed "as broad as possible," for they held a person guilty of counterrevolutionary crime and subject to execution if he engaged in propaganda or agitation that "objectively aided" or might be "capable of aiding" the

76. Mikhail Kalinin, *O sotsialisticheskoi zakonnosti* (Moscow, 1959), p. 166.

77. Mikhail Pokrovsky, *Oktiabr'skaia revoliutsiia. Sbornik statei* (Moscow, 1929), p. 375.

78. Lenin, PSS, 45: 189–191. [Cf. CW, 33: 358–359.]

international bourgeois enemy.[79] These formulations, which would have encouraged a multitude of abuses, did not appear in Article 57 of the Criminal Code of the RSFSR, published June 15, 1922. That article defined a counterrevolutionary action as one "*directed* toward the overthrow" of the Soviet regime or toward aid to its foreign enemies.[80] Nevertheless, Lenin's letter, which was published in 1924, hardly contributed to the development of the fledgling judiciary.

Marx's comment that revolutions are the locomotives of history is well known.[81] Lenin's statement, made long before the October revolution, is also frequently cited: "Revolutions are festivals of the oppressed and the exploited."[82] Recalled much less frequently are Engels's words that "in every revolution a great many stupidities are committed."[83] Certainly revolutions can vary in their results and character, but after the experience of the twentieth century it is hard to compose hymns in honor of violent revolution. Revolutions are necessary when obsolete and reactionary institutions and social strata refuse to make any concessions, so that a violent political explosion is the only way out. Yet it is difficult to regulate armed conflict between classes and even more difficult to foresee its outcome, for the desires and goals of the revolutionaries are achieved only after a bitter struggle, whose end results turn out to have little similarity to the original conception.

Dmitry Pisarev, the nineteenth-century Russian radical writer, made the following sound observations more than a hundred years ago.

In the lives of nations, revolutions occupy the same place as when an individual is forced to kill someone. If you have to defend your life, your honor, or the life or honor of your mother, wife, or sister, it may happen that you will kill the scoundrel attacking you. . . . The same can be said about violent revolutions, which can also be likened to defensive wars. Every revolution and every war in and of itself does both material and moral harm to a nation. But if the war or revolution is the result of imperious necessity, the harm done is negligible compared to the harm from which one is being saved.[84]

One may agree with Pisarev, with the qualification that while the harm done may be unavoidable, it is by no means negligible.

79. Ibid.
80. [Italics added. In other words, the burden of proving treasonable *intent* was placed on the prosecution, whereas Lenin's formulation removed that burden. —D. J.]
81. Marx and Engels, *Sochineniia*, 2d ed., 7:86.
82. Lenin, PSS, 11: 103. [Cf. CW, 9: 113.]
83. Marx and Engels, *Sochineniia*, 2d ed., 18:516.
84. From Pisarev's 1867 article "Heinrich Heine."

Raissa Lert, a journalist and veteran party member who actively participated in events in our country from the twenties through the seventies
told the author of this book:

A revolution was necessary, Russia being the country it was, and this revolution could not have done without violence. We could not have won the civil war
without mass terror, without violence against the officers and the kulaks. . . .
Truly what broke out was a war to the death, and if the Communists had not
won, the Whites would have slaughtered them all. But we, as a revolutionary
party, made a mistake when we portrayed revolutionary violence as a heroic
exploit rather than an unfortunate necessity. Mass violence and terror, even the
Red Terror, remained an evil all the same. Granted that this evil was temporarily
necessary, still it was an evil; yet it soon began to be portrayed as a virtue. We
began to think and say that everything useful and necessary for the revolution
was good and moral. But that is not true. The revolution contained not only good
but evil as well. To avoid violence in the revolution was impossible, but it should
have been understood that we were talking about a temporary admission of evil
into our life and into our practical actions. In romanticizing violence, we gave it
added life, we preserved it even when it became absolutely surperfluous, when
it became an absolute evil. . . . Nonresistance to evil, the refusal to resist evil by
force, is not our philosophy; in many cases that can only help evil triumph.
However, in using very harsh (*krutye*) methods, we should not have changed our
moral evaluation of such acts of violence.[85]

If the misuse of violence was already fairly common during Lenin's
lifetime, it became standard practice once Stalin became leader of the
party. Long before the repression of 1936–1938 he pressed upon official
cadres the belief that there could be no restrictions on the methods used
to fight those he proclaimed to be enemies of the revolution. Mass terror
against peasants who were prosperous or simply lacked class consciousness, lawless repression of the bourgeois intelligentsia, arbitrary treatment of the oppositions and all dissidents—all these were practical
applications of "the end justifies the means." And torture made its appearance during collectivization: kulaks and "subkulaks" were beaten,
and drenched in cold water during winter. In Sholokhov's *Virgin Soil
Upturned* Nagulnov summed up the Stalinist attitude: "Place in front of
him dozens of old men, children and old women," and if he is told that it
is necessary for the revolution, he will "finish them off with a machine
gun."[86]

85. In the late 1970s Raissa Lert, after fifty years in the CPSU, announced her resignation
from the party. She had taken an active part in the human rights movement of the 1970s.
86. [See Sholokhov, *Podniataia tselina* (Moscow, 1931). Translated as *Seeds of Tomorrow*
(New York, 1935). —D. J.]

Stalin was not the only proponent of such methods; many other leaders and also rank-and-file participants in the revolution agreed. The constant inculcation of the idea that any means could be used in the practical work of government agencies, especially the punitive agencies, so long as it was "in the interests of the revolution" made it easier for Stalin to achieve his aims. All he had to do was to say "enemies of the people" and those unfortunates were outside the law; any cruelty, torture, or violence against them was immediately justified.

By no means all officials willingly took part in the Stalinist methods of collectivization from 1929 to 1933. Many activists sent to the countryside during collectivization returned home sick over what they had experienced. In 1936–1938 numerous officials found it hard to sanction mass arrests of their party comrades. Many NKVD employees obeyed the instructions to use torture with grave misgivings. But the customary logic —it is necessary for the revolution—eased their consciences and clouded their brains, preventing a realistic appraisal of events, transforming honorable revolutionaries into blind instruments of Stalin's arbitrary rule— and often into his victims as well, later on.

Nikolai Krylenko is a typical case. A decade after the civil war, when its terroristic methods were revived against technical specialists, many of whom were arrested and severely punished simply by fiat without any trial, the first to protest should have been the Commissar of Justice Krylenko. Instead he was an especially zealous defender of extralegal repression:

> To bourgeois Europe and to broad circles of the liberalish intelligentsia, it may seem monstrous that the Soviet regime does not always deal with wreckers by putting them on trial. But every class-conscious worker and peasant will agree that the Soviet regime is behaving correctly.[87]

Nor did Krylenko protest the unconstitutional edict of December 1, 1934, or the lawless acts of the NKVD in 1935–1937. He probably realized his mistake in 1938, when he himself was condemned and shot without any legal procedure.

Another typical case is that of B. P. Sheboldaev, first secretary of the Northern Caucasus kraikom. In the early thirties he joined with Kaganovich in deporting from the Kuban not only groups of people belonging to hostile classes but whole villages. On November 12, 1932, in Rostov, Sheboldaev said:

87. Krylenko, *Klassovaia bor'ba putem vreditel'stva* (Moscow, 1930).

We openly proclaimed that we would send off to northern regions malicious saboteurs and kulak agents who do not want to sow. Didn't we in previous years deport kulak counterrevolutionary elements from this same Kuban? We did, in sufficient numbers. And today when these remnants of the kulak class try to organize sabotage, oppose the demands of the Soviet regime, it is even more correct to give away the fertile Kuban land to collective farmers who live in other krais on poor land, and not enough even of that poor land. . . . And those who do not want to work, who defile our land, we'll send them to other places.

That's fair. We may be told: "What? Earlier you deported kulaks, and now you're talking about a whole village, where there are both collective farms and conscientious individual peasants? How can that be?" Yes, we must raise the question of a whole village, because the collective farms, because the really conscientious individual peasants in the present situation must answer for the condition of their neighbors. What kind of support for the Soviet regime is a collective farm, if right next to it another collective farm or a whole group of individual farms oppose the measures of the Soviet regime?"[88]

Five years later Stalin found that the entire Northern Caucasus kraikom, with Sheboldaev at its head, was not a reliable support for the Soviet regime. Sheboldaev was arrested and shot.

In 1936 the Old Bolshevik M. O. Stakun, secretary of the Gomel obkom, in a speech to his activists criticized even the NKVD for "liberalism" and demanded the arrest of an old woman who had cursed the Soviet regime for the bread shortage. A year later the NKVD was sufficiently illiberal to arrest Stakun himself.

Also in 1936 Vladimir Antonov-Ovseyenko, a hero of the October insurrection who in the twenties had joined the Trotskyists, was sent as a Soviet emissary to Spain. His task, for which he was given special powers, was to organize the liquidation of the anarchist groups in Catalonia, the extreme left organization POUM, which was then called "Trotskyist" or "semi-Trotskyist," and all other "Trotskyist" elements. And indeed, Antonov-Ovseyenko participated in the swift liquidation of the left groups and anarchists in Catalonia, even though they were active in the fight against Franco's fascists. A year later Antonov-Ovseyenko was recalled to Moscow and shot as an alleged "Trotskyist."

For many years Leopold Averbakh, as general secretary of RAPP (the Russian Association of Proletarian Writers), harassed all "nonproletarian writers." As early as 1929 he viciously criticized the outstanding Soviet writer Andrei Platonov. In the magazine *On Literary Guard* Averbakh wrote: "They come to us propagating humanism, as though there were

88. A. Radin and L. Shaumian, *Za chto zhiteli stanitsy Poltavskoi vyseliaiutsia s Kubani v severnye kraia*, (Rostov on Don, 1933), p. 14.

something more humane in the world than the class hatred of the proletariat." In 1938 Averbakh himself was shot as an "enemy of the people," an object of the class hatred he promoted.

In 1936–1937 V. F. Sharangovich, as first secretary of the Belorussian Central Committee, decimated Belorussian cadres. When A. G. Chervyakov committed suicide after Sharangovich publicly demanded his removal, Sharangovich declared at a party congress in Minsk: "A dog's death for a dog!" A year later Sharangovich was one of the defendants in the Bukharin-Rykov trial, where the prosecutor Vyshinksy had this to say: "The traitors and spies who were selling our country to the enemy must be shot like dirty dogs!"

Some old Bolsheviks in their memoirs assert that everything bad began in 1937. For example, in "The Return of Honor" V. Baranchenko writes of the twenties and thirties in the most enthusiastic tones; everything was fine until that cursed 1937 arrived. Ya. I. Drobinsky takes a different view. The hero of his memoirs, Andrei Fomin, brought before the Military Collegium, delivers a silent soliloquy:

People! Communists! How did you come to this? . . . You have suddenly changed! . . . But that's the rub, Andrei, it wasn't sudden. It was prepared for imperceptibly—no, not even imperceptibly, but before our eyes. Gradually, slowly, but in systematic small doses, this poison of infamy was administered, and cadres were prepared for this operation. The poison accumulated in the organism, and when the defensive forces had weakened, it took over the entire organism. It was being prepared back then when muzhiks' families were broken up, when the muzhik's ancient nests were broken up, when he was driven to the end of the earth, into camps, when he was labeled a subkulak for daring to say that it was wrong to dekulakize his friend, a middle peasant, a laboring man! This poison was accumulating back then when they forced a peasant to turn in flax though they knew very well that it had not grown, when directives were issued to crack down on sabotage, to bring saboteurs to trial, though they knew once again that there was no sabotage and no saboteurs, because there was no flax, it had not grown. When they brought such "saboteurs" to trial, and seized the last little cow, the procurator knew that there was no sabotage at all, but still he sanctioned the arrest. The judges also knew that the muzhik was honest, but they tried him. And now the same procurator has sanctioned your arrest and the same judges are trying you. The principle hasn't changed. It is simply being given wider application. Back then you didn't understand this. But that was when the cadres were being prepared for these cases, cadres of people for whom it's not important whether you are guilty of anything; but it is important that there is a directive to consider you guilty. Remember how you said to Gikalo back then: "Nikolai Fedorovich, that flax did not grow." "I know that myself," answered

Gikalo, "but the country needs flax and Moscow believes neither tears nor objective reasons."[89]

The vile methods of the Bolsheviks are a favorite theme of Western anti-Soviet literature. In Arthur Koestler's novel *Darkness at Noon,* for example, the investigator Ivanov tries to convince himself and others that the repression of 1937 is justified. Dostoevsky's Raskolnikov, he argues, would have been in the right if he had killed the old woman on party orders, to get money, for a strike fund. There are only two possibilities in ethics: the Christian, humanist rule that the individual is sacred and rational calculation is therefore excluded from morality, or the socialist rule that the individual must be sacrificed to the rationally calculated good of the collective.[90]

In the Soviet press Koestler's novel has been called "defamatory" and the investigator Ivanov's views are said to have nothing in common with Marxist-Leninist ethics. Yet in a recent Soviet novel a positive hero, the party official Naletov, reasons as follows.

How will future generations be able to judge our deeds correctly? And how accurate will their judgments be? Will they understand that it could not have been otherwise? Who could weigh and calculate carefully when everything around us was ablaze? And who would have thought to take measurements to see whether sometimes we paid too much, whether there were unnecessary sacrifices? No, he, Nikita Petrovich Naletov, had a different philosophy. And so far it had enabled him to stand his ground firmly, without wavering at difficult moments. Do you see the goal before you? Do you believe in it? Storm the ramparts. Win at any cost. Do you have to sacrifice? Then do it. But don't measure it out, making an exact count. Do it with plenty to spare. If you pinch pennies, it'll cost you more in the end. The goals are so grand that any sacrifices (including of course your own life) are nothing by comparison.[91]

It is undoubtedly true that the philosophy of Ivanov and Naletov has nothing in common with socialist ethics; nevertheless, Stalinists of every kind are quite comfortable with such an outlook.

The Soviet political writer and sociologist Yuri Karyakin has rightly commented:

89. From Drobinsky's unpublished memoirs, a copy of which is in my archives.

90. See Koestler, *Darkness at Noon* (New York, 1961), p. 141. In the 1960s, "homemade" translations of Koestler's novel circulated in the Soviet Union in manuscript copies. A professional Russian translation is *Slepiashchaia t'ma* (New York, 1978).

91. See Aleksandr Putko, "Svoya nosha," in tbe magazine *Oktyabr,* 1969, no. 6, p. 58.

Marxists recognize [the need for] class violence, but only under one condition: so long as there are aggressors *(nasil'niki)*, it must be applied to them and them alone. This is humane because it signifies the emancipation of the overwhelming majority from oppression by the insignificant minority. Without the fight for such emancipation there is no freedom of the individual, no individual self-improvement, but only the downfall of the individual. The inevitable sacrifices on the road of class struggle are not a matter of "enriching the soil" for future generations but of sowing for the future. It is not a case of slaughtering rams upon the altar of an unknown deity but of the upsurge and enthusiasm of the masses, conscious of their enslaved condition under capitalism, conscious of their strength and their ideals. It is even more the free choice of the human individual becoming more truly human. . . . The humanism of the ends that Communists pursue determines the humaneness of the means they choose, while any kind of jesuitry is . . . a perversion of both the ends and the means. The truest ideas, when upheld by jesuitical methods, are inevitably transformed into their opposite.[92]

Of course, a revolution has a vast arsenal of means to choose from, and much depends on the concrete circumstances. In the Soviet revolution there have been situations when extremely cruel methods had to be used, such as the shooting of the tsar's family in Yekaterinburg,[93] the sinking of the Black Sea fleet, and the Red Terror of 1918. Still, not all such methods are permissible. The revolutionary party must carefully study each concrete situation and decide what means will reach the goal at the least cost and by the best route (not necessarily the quickest). Which methods should not be used in a given situation, and which should not be used in any situation, should also be determined. A Soviet philosopher, arguing that the great moral goal of communism requires the use of moral methods to reach it, discerns a certain autonomy in morality. Some objective criteria of morality are above the practice of a given moment and set limits to the choice of methods. Rigorous observance of these limits will help Communists achieve their long-run goal

92. *Problemy mira i sotsializma*, 1963, no. 5, p. 36.
93. The Russian tsar and tsarina deserved the death penalty no more than did Louis XIV, Marie Antoinette, or Charles I of England. It is possible that the interests of the revolution required the execution of all adult members of the tsar's family, guilty of many crimes. But even in the critical situation in which the executions took place, a revolutionary tribunal should have been set up; they should not have been shot without a trial. As for the killing of the innocent son and daughters of the tsar, and the tsar's physician and servants, no alleged interests of the revolution could justify that action. It is worth noting that A. G. Beloborodov, the 27-year-old chairman of the Soviet of the Urals region, who directed the execution of the tsarist family, was later one of the creators of the early Stalinist prison system. In 1937 he was shot as a "Trotskyite," also in the "interests of the revolution."

by helping them to win and hold the confidence of the masses.[94]

The revolutionary who does not recognize these tenets can have only temporary success. A revolutionary party that uses vile methods inevitably loses the trust and support of the people, and this in turn limits its possibilities of choosing methods that depend on mass action and popular initiative. Thus, vile methods are evidence of a party's weakness, not its strength. In any country a movement advocating communism must train honest, upright, and humane leaders, not sadists and cynics.

Stalin gave no thought to the relation between ends and means. To him, in the pursuit of his personal aims, all means were suitable, including the most inhumane. As a result the cause of socialism was dealt a horrendous blow.

■ **10**

INCOMPREHENSION AND LACK OF SOLIDARITY

The fact that most of the Soviet people trusted Stalin, the party leadership, and the punitive agencies placed the victims of repression in a tragic position. They were not guilty, but most people did not believe them, and turned their backs. Only a few friends and relatives believed in their innocence. An incident in the interrogation of Vladimir Antonov-Ovseyenko reveals the terrible situation. The radio happened to be on when the investigator called the old revolutionary an enemy of the people, and was answered back, "You're the enemy of the people, you're a real fascist." At that moment some sort of meeting was being broadcast on the radio. "Do you hear," said the investigator, "how the people hail us? They trust us completely, and you will be destroyed. I've already received a medal for you."[95]

Incomprehension was even more serious than the lack of solidarity, the feeling of isolation, in depriving many people of the strength to resist. Even such a well-informed and intelligent man as Mikhail Kolstov could not comprehend what was going on.

"What is happening?" Kolstov used to repeat, walking up and down in his office. . . . "I feel I'm going crazy. I am a member of the editorial board of

94. See M. G. Makarov, *Filosofiia marksizma-leninizma o kategorii "tsel'"* (Leningrad, 1960), p. 12.

95. See the note by Yuri Tomsky (who heard this account from Antonov-Ovseyenko in Butyrskaya prison) in *Novy Mir*, 1964, no. 11, p. 212.

Pravda, a well-known journalist, a deputy (to the Supreme Soviet): it would seem that I should be able to explain to others the meaning of what is happening, the reasons for so many exposés and arrests. But in fact I, like any terrified philistine, know nothing, understand nothing. I am bewildered, in the dark."[96]

Many of those arrested thought that there had been some accidental mistake, that soon everything would be cleared up and things would return to normal. "I'll be home tomorrow," Yan Gamarnik's deputy G. Osepyan told his wife when the NKVD came to his apartment one night. A similar "constitutional illusion" was revealed by Valery Mezhlauk, the former chairman of Gosplan. In prison he continued to think about the problems that occupied him when he was free. Just before he was shot, he wrote "On Planning and Ways to Improve It."[97] Similarly, when Andrei Bubnov was expelled from the Central Committee and fired as commissar of education, he simply turned things over to the new commissar and went to the construction site of the State Public Library, which he had been supervising. He was convinced that the injustice being done to him would be corrected.[98]

Sergei Pisarev, a longtime party professional, described his reaction this way:

When I found myself in prison I was not at all frightened or angry, but rather surprised. It seemed to me that to make such a mistake and arrest me, an irreproachable party member, who had always been active, who had been tested a thousand times and was virtually at home in the Central Committee apparatus, being well known to everyone, from Stalin, Kalinin, Poskrebyshev, Vyshinsky, and Yaroslavsky on down—that this was the crudest kind of error, an absurdity that inevitably would be swiftly corrected. I considered everyone who had been arrested by the NKVD by then to be arch conspirators and fascists. . . . So what was I there for?! I had always been an outgoing and energetic party member, always visible to the Central Committee, to my district committee, and to hundreds of authoritative Communists at all stages of my work in the party ranks and in the leading bodies of the party apparatus. . . . No, I was not frightened in the least; at the time of my arrest after a nighttime search, at 5 A.M., I calmly sat down to eat breakfast, as was my custom—an action that alarmed the search party. I was naive like a little child. Even after my arrest, as I sat for an entire week in a tiny solitary cell on the fourth floor of the Taganka prison, into which twelve of us recent arrestees had been squeezed and on whose floor only half of us at a time could lie, pressed against one another,—we took turns sleeping; the rest stood or sat on their haunches—at that time, too, I still considered all my cellmates genuine enemies of the people and did not exchange a single word

96. *Mikhail Koltsov, kakim on byl* (Moscow, 1965), p. 71.
97. *Izvestia,* February 19, 1963.
98. *Andrei Bubnov* (Moscow, 1964).

with any of them for the entire week. The others behaved the same way. . . . My eyes were opened only after my transfer to the Lubyanka, to the Inner Prison, for "active investigation."[99]

Calm, self-control, and nonresistance were also the parting advice to his friends from Iosif Pyatnitsky, a close colleague of Lenin's. On the day before his arrest Pyatnitsky met Tsivtsivadze, who had been expelled from the party, though his loyalty could not be doubted. "For the party," said Pyatnitsky, "we must endure everything, just so that it remains alive."[100] Within a few months both Tsivtsivadze and Pyatnitsky were shot.

Even after torture many arrested people continued to believe that legality would prevail, if not during the investigation then at the trial. Another reaction reveals the same underlying lack of comprehension: When the entire membership of the party committee in a Siberian city were grabbed one night and put into a single cell, they decided that a counterrevolutionary coup had taken place in their city, and, expecting to be shot at once, they began to sing the "International."

Isolation and incomprehension engendered confusion, passivity, even resignation. "The impunity and relative ease with which Stalin took vengeance on millions of people," Varlam Shalamov wrote in one of his stories, "were due precisely to the fact that these people were not guilty of anything."[101] Most people, even when they were expecting arrest, did not try to hide and escape destruction. Many even turned themselves in. For example, after Yakir was shot, M. P. Amelin, head of the political administration of the Kiev Military District, was called to Moscow. He knew quite well what was in store for him. "I don't know whether I'll come back," he told his friends and family, "but believe me, I have never been an enemy of my country or government."[102]

I. P. Belov, commander of the Belorussian Military District, also had forebodings when he was suddenly summoned to Moscow. Through the entire journey he kept walking up and down the empty corridor of the official railway car or stood at the dark window for long periods. Several times he turned to his traveling companion, L. M. Sandalov, with questions, from which it was easy to see that he was thinking of his predecessor, I. P. Uborevich, who had also been suddenly called to Moscow and

99. Sergei Pisarev, "Iz vospominanii," unpublished manuscript.
100. Recounted in the diary of Pyatnitsky's wife, which is in the possession of S. Petrikovsky, a member of the CPSU.
101. V. Shalamov, *Kolymskie rasskazy.*
102. *Voenno-istoricheskii zhurnal,* 1964, no. 7, p. 119.

had not returned. Belov's anxiety was not groundless. As soon as he arrived in Moscow he was arrested and soon perished.[103]

Pavel Shabalkin was unusual in his refusal to submit to arrest when NKVD agents came to his office. A member of the bureau of the Far Eastern *kraikom,* he demanded that his case be discussed in the *obkom* bureau. But the *obkom* secretary, who also did not understand what was going on, urged Shabalkin to submit. And Shabalkin did so, surrendering his gun to the NKVD agents.[104] Even diplomats recalled from broad, who usually knew what would happen to them, almost always obeyed the order to return.

Sometimes, after long and painful expectation of arrest, people felt a certain relief to be finally in jail. "Well, comrades," the old Bolshevik Dvoretsky told his cellmates when he was brought into Minsk prison, "Tonight I will probably get a good night's sleep. The first in three months. . . . For three months I've been in torment, waiting for them to come for me. Every day they took people but didn't come for me. They took all the commissars, but me they just would not take. I was simply worn out. Why don't they call me? Why don't they take me? And then, glory be! . . . Today a phone call from the NKVD. And I've been in bed for almost a year, my legs don't function. Some director calls up. 'Can't you come over for an hour? We need to consult with you,' he says. 'Of course I can,' I say. 'Send over a car.' "[105]

In one prison Shabalkin met a group of party officials who argued that if the Soviet government was obliged to take such harsh measures, that meant they were necessary. After suffering the most refined tortures, they still sang the song with the words: "I know no other country where people breathe so freely."

In 1937 at the Food Industry Club in Minsk (Club Pishchevik) a frame-up trial was held of a group of "wreckers" from the grain procurement agency Zagotzerno. Chudnovsky, one of the defendants, who had headed the Belorussian office of Zagotzerno and was an Old Bolshevik and a former organizer of the Soviets' First Donetsk Army, was accused of contaminating grain with insects. Before the trial his cellmates begged him to tell the truth and show how he had been tortured. A hoarse voice was heard in reply, "How can I do that, boys? The investigator said the

103. *Voenno-istoricheskii zhurnal,* 1963, no. 6, p. 76.
104. Recounted to the author by Shabalkin.
105. From the unpublished memoirs of Ya. I. Drobinsky.

Polish consul will be there. How can I disgrace our country in front of him?"[106]

If in some places primary party organizations defended their members, they did so only before the NKVD stepped in. After a person was arrested, the same party organization would nearly always expel him or her unanimously without any discussion of the charges.

A veteran party member wrote the following to me.

What could Communists have said at meetings? Give new material to informers? The whole problem was that no one dared to tell anybody anything bad about Stalin; everyone was obliged—even if he knew something, even if he knew or guessed the truth—to shout hallelujah. Try not to shout hallelujah, if you're, say, a district agitator. Try not to "give a rebuff to the enemy outburst"! The result was that everyone had to work out his world view in solitude, disregarding everything he heard from people around him. And anyone who worked out his own view, but could not play the hypocrite for ten years and somehow gave himself away, ended up in a camp.

It is impossible to condone such logic, although it was fairly widespread during the years of the cult. There is a frightful paradox here. Thousands upon thousands of people, arrested in 1937–1938 on charges of plotting against Stalin and his aides, could be reproached today for insufficient resistance to evil and for excessive faith in their leaders.

This complex mixture of contradictory feelings—incomprehension and panic, faith in Stalin and fear of the terror—fragmented the party and made it fairly easy for Stalin to usurp total power. Of course he did more than take advantage of the confusion; he encouraged dissension in every way, pitting people against each other, one part of the Central Committee against another, thus enabling him to destroy people in groups. The ban on factions did not end quarrels among separate groups of leaders on various issues, both principled and unprincipled. Denied an open forum, these quarrels became distorted and vicious. Stalin, a master of treacherous intrigue, encouraged such quarrels for his own ends. He took advantage of differences of opinion, personality clashes, and the excessive ambition of some officials and played on the very worst qualities of the people around him—envy, malice, vanity, stupdity. It was probably Stalin who kept alive the antagonisms among the other members of the Politburo, and he encouraged conflicts between Litvinov and Krestinsky in the Foreign Affairs Commisariat, between Voroshilov and Tukhachev-

106. Ibid.

sky in the Commissariat of Defense, between Ordzhonikidze and Pyatakov in the Commissariat of Heavy Industry, and so forth.

The lack of solidarity was felt at every level. Military leaders like Belov, Blyukher, Dybenko, and Alksnis, who were arrested and shot in 1938, had been members the year before of the Military Collegium that imposed death sentences on Tukhachevsky, Yakir, Uborevich, Primakov, and the other generals. It had not been easy for them to sign the sentences. Ilya Ehrenburg writes in his memoirs:

> I remember a terrible day at Meyerhold's. We were sitting and peacefully examining a monograph on Renoir when one of Meyerhold's friends, Army Commander I. P. Belov, came in. He was very excited. Ignoring the fact that, besides Meyerhold, Lyuba and I were in the room, he began to tell how they had tried Tukhachevsky and other military men. Belov was a member of the Supreme Court's Military Collegium. "They sat just like this, opposite us. Uborevich looked me in the eye . . ." I still remember Belov's remark: "And tomorrow I'll be put in their place." [107]

Examples of this kind can be adduced endlessly. V. Smirnov, appointed commissar of the navy in 1938, made a special tour of the fleets to purge "enemies of the people." He was highly successful, but at the end of the year he himself was arrested and shot. And Eikhe, as first secretary of the West Siberian kraikom, sanctioned many arrests of "Trotskyites and Bukharinites," who were then forced to bear false witness against Eikhe, with the result that he was later shot as the leader of the "Trotskyite-Bukharinite" underground in West Siberia. Similarly, K. A. Bauman and Ya. A. Yakovlev, as heads of the Central Committee Divisions of Science and of Agriculture, supported the persecution of many outstanding scientists in 1936–1937 — until their own turn came.

Pavel Postyshev is an especially egregious case in point. As secretary of the Ukrainian CC he worked hard to decimate the national cadres of the republic. In 1932–1933, together with Stalin, he organized the persecution of Skrypnik, driving him to suicide. In 1937 Postyshev sent Vsevolod Balitsky, the NKVD plenipotentiary in the Ukraine, dozens of lists containing the names of hundreds of innocent people. To be sure, Postyshev became alarmed when some people close to him were repressed on orders from Moscow. Speaking at the February–March Plenum of the Central Committee in 1937, he expressed doubts about the justice of some arrests. But these misgivings did not stop Postyshev from contin-

107. *Novy Mir*, 1962, no. 3, pp. 152–153.

uing to sanction thousands of arrests in the Ukraine. He did not stop even when, in 1937, his wife was arrested. He was nevertheless demoted "for insufficient vigilance" to the post of first secretary of the Kuibyshev kraikom—although he remained a candidate member of the Politburo. He did not change his mind then either. In 1938 the Kuibyshev krai, which then included Mordvinia, was purged of "enemies" with a savagery unexampled even in other oblasti. Postyshev sanctioned the decimation of almost all organizations on the krai level and also 110 raion committees. He organized the open trail of the krai agricultural administration, as a result of which hundreds of agricultural officials were shot. He changed many of the sentences sent to him for his signature, requiring death where the procurator and investigator thought eight or ten years in confinement were sufficient. And then, when the krai had been purged, Postyshev was removed from his job on the charge of "exterminating cadres"—Stalin must have grinned when he mouthed this formula—and arrested and shot.

Divisions were created even in families that had been solidly united a short time before. The veteran party member Baitalsky wrote about this in his memoirs:

In Odessa in 1937 men and women party members were summoned one after another to the bureau of the Voroshilov district committee. The bureau remained in session sometimes through the night: they were in a hurry to expel those who had been arrested. Their Communist wives were interrogated: why didn't you report on your husband? After all, he's an enemy!

Many wives would answer, "Well, actually I did notice something strange about him. But I didn't realize what it was all about. Yes, I am to blame."

I had known these women for a long time—they had been our fighting girls, strapped in leather [during the revolution and civil war]. Now they were expelled from the party (or if they managed to come up with "material" against friends of their husbands, action was limited to a reprimand). They were subject to condemnation not for informing, but for failure to inform.

But what can you do? It was natural for people to behave that way in those days. But there was one who didn't—Oksana Lazareva. Her husband, Isaev, had already been arrested. She was asked the same question: Why didn't you report on him?

"I don't believe," she said, "that my husband could be an enemy of the people. I know that the truth will be uncovered, and as a token of my certainty I am leaving my party card with you. The day will come when you will call me in and give it back to me." None of those present approved her action. Everyone was indignant: How dare she behave that way? The standard of behavior was already quite different than it had been. . . .

Eighteen years later Oksana was rehabilitated, reinstated in the party. But those who expelled her could not call her in. They had been shot soon after approving the arrest and execution of her husband.[108]

Of course incomprehension and confusion were not universal. There were people who had a good idea what was going on. A seventy-five-year-old Bolshevik explained the situation to two former officials who could not understand why they were in Sol-Iletskaya Prison:

Your logic is childish. You have understood nothing. Don't you see that Lenin predicted present events twenty years ago? To be sure, these words of Lenin have been kept under lock and key. The broad party masses cannot know what Lenin said could happen if a nonobjective man concentrated unlimited power in his hands. Lenin's words of genius have come true. All those who could at some time have stopped this man from realizing his unlimited power, from carrying out his policy without consulting anyone, all those people have been physically destroyed.[109]

Even some young people mistrusted the adulation of Stalin, though it had been drilled into their heads since infancy. Mikhail Molochko, a Komsomol member and student from Minsk, wrote in his diary on February 3, 1935:

It is interesting to read the newspapers, especially *Komsomolets*. Interesting materials of the seventh Congress [of Soviets]. I read the inspired, colorful speech of the writer A——, devoted to Comrade Stalin. To tell the truth, I don't like the constant adulation of this "great strategist," "wise chief," and so on. This is systematic, unceasing ruination of the man. Well, speak, write, give some reward; but they are giving only epithets as rewards. All the speeches at the Congress are permeated with a single spirit, the spirit of tacking Stalin's name on every place and district. I don't see and I can't see why everyone praises and loves Stalin so much. I personally do not feel this love or even great respect.[110]

A question inevitably arises about those who understood the real situation: What should they have done? After the Twenty-Second Party Congress in 1962 a well-known Soviet poet, Pavel Antokolsky, wrote:

108. From Baitalsky's unpublished memoirs, "Tetradi dlia vnukov."
109. From the unpublished memoirs of Suren Gazaryan, "Eto ne dolzhno povtorit'sia." The Old Bolshevik was I. I. Radchenko, former head of Glavtorf [the Central Peat Agency]. His audience was M. Belotsky, former secretary of the Kirgiz Central Committee, and Gazaryan, a former NKVD official. [Part of the quotation, predicting the triumph of the party over Stalin, is omitted. —D. J.]
110. *Neman* (Minsk), 1962, no. 4, p. 141. Molochko joined the Red Army as a volunteer during the war with Finland and died in 1940. The writer "A——" was A. O. Avdeyenko. It was not Molochko but the magazine *Neman* that withheld the full name.

We are all his regimental mates,
Who were silent when
From our silence grew
A national disaster.
Hiding from each other,
Spending sleepless nights,
While out of our circle
He was making executioners.
Let our great-grandsons score us
With their contempt
All alike, equally,
We do not hide our shame.

Antokolsky won a Stalin Prize in the years of the cult. He was not silent during that period, although he saw and knew more than many others; he heaped praise on Stalin and lived quite well. After the Twentieth and Twenty-Second congresses, feeling awkward and ashamed, he tired to hide behind all of Stalin's contemporaries, suggesting that they should all be condemned—and not by their sons or grandsons but by "great-grandsons." But not all should be condemned. People behaved in various ways and have varying degrees of responsibility. Much depended on their distance from the epicenter of the catastrophe, on the choices they faced. The responsibility of a people's commissar or even a writer cannot be equated with that of a rank-and-file party member, worker, or collective farmer. The responsibility of the head of a concentration camp or prison cannot be equated with that of a simple guard. Much also depended on the degree of comprehension. And finally, a great deal depended on qualities of character, on courage and sense of honor.

Many people actively helped Stalin in his crimes and made for lawlessness themselves, slandering citizens on their own initiative. Such aides to the executioner should not only be "scored with contempt" but punished by a court. There were many who freely chose to denounce others to the NKVD or who, when called in by the NKVD, out of fear signed any deposition put before them. Many groveled and shouted Stalin's praise of their own free will, with genuine zeal.

But there were also individuals who in one way or other resisted. I know of instances of passive resistance, when officials, sensing imminent arrest, fled their home towns, sometimes even became illegal and changed their names. There were also many petitioners and protesters. The Central Committee, the procurator's office, and Stalin personally received letters not only from relatives and friends of prisoners but also from leading cultural, scientific, government, and party figures. Kapitsa's demand for Landau's release, which was granted, has been mentioned. Academician D. N. Pryanishnikov was not so fortunate in his stubborn efforts on behalf of N. I. Vavilov. After having been rejected by Molotov and Beria, he decided on a desperate step: he recommended the imprisoned Vavilov for a Stalin Prize. Marietta Shaginyan, in her brief note "Pages from the Past," tells how the arrested poet David Vygodsky was defended by fellow writers. At considerable risk to themselves Yury Tynyanov, Boris Lavrenyov, Konstantin Fedin, M. Slonimsky, Mikhail Zoshchenko, and Viktor Shklovsky wrote declarations and guarantees, pleading for the release of their comrade.[111] Vygodsky, like Vavilov, was not released; both died in prison. When the Old Bolshevik N. N. Kulyabko, who had recommended Tukhachevsky for party membership, learned of his friend's arrest, he sent a letter of protest to Stalin—and was immediately arrested.[112] In 1937, when the physicist M. P. Bronshtein was arrested, a letter in his defense was signed by academicians S. I. Vavilov and V. A. Fok and by the writers Samuil Marshak and Kornei Chukovsky.[113] The fact that these protests were disregarded, as were hundreds of thousands of others, does not mean that they were entirely pointless.

There were also people in the party apparatus with access to investigatory materials who tried to oppose lawlessness. N. S. Kuznetsov, an obkom secretary in Kazakhstan, sanctioned the arrest of many communists in the first months of the mass repression. Then, he began to have doubts. He went to the oblast prison to interrogate some friends, became convinced of their innocence, sent obkom party officials into the NKVD apparatus, and took control of NKVD operations in his oblast. He obtained the release of many Communists and forbade the use of torture. Gathering an enormous amount of material on the lawlessness of the NKVD and its penetration by all sorts of suspicious people, including former White Guard officers, Kuznetsov went to Moscow and obtained a meeting with Stalin. Stalin listened only a few minutes and broke off the conference, advising Kuznetsov to report the whole thing to Malenkov. Malenkov also brushed him off, telling him to go back to Kazakhstan and send in a written report by government courier. Returning, Kuznetsov

111. From the unpublished memoirs of Shaginyan, "Stranitsy proshlogo," a copy of which is in my archives.

112. *Marshal Tukhachevskii: sbornik vospominanii* (Moscow, 1965), p. 30.

113. V. Ia. Frenkel, *Ia.I. Frenkel'* (Moscow, 1966), p. 13.

learned that he had been transferred to another obkom. A few months later he was called to a meeting in Alma Ata and arrested in his hotel. The two oblast committees he had headed were decimated, and the Communists who had been released on Kuznetsov's demand were rearrested.[114]

In 1937 the party's Central Committee in Kirgizia also tried to interfere in the actions of the security organs. The Bureau of the Central Committee, hearing of the torture of the prisoners, set up a special commission to investigate—with tragic results: the entire commission was repressed by the NKVD.[115]

The Belorussian NKVD also had a heroic though futile defender of justice: Bikson, a Bolshevik since 1905 and a comrade of Dzerzhinsky's. In 1937, as chairman of the Special Collegium of the Supreme Court of Belorussia, he refused to consider many baseless cases. Hearing of the use of torture, he went to the Belorussian Central Committee, only to be asked by its secretary, Volkov: "What intelligence agency are you serving? The Polish or the English?" Bikson replied: "I have been a Bolshevik since 1905." "We know these Old Bolsheviks," Volkov shouted, and phoned the head of the Belorussian NKVD, Berman. "There is an old counterrevolutionary here, an agent of Polish intelligence, your employee Bikson. He's going to a lot of trouble for enemies of the people." Bikson was arrested in the Central Committee office and soon died in prison. A few months later Volkov was removed from his post and given a less important position in Tambov, where he committed suicide in a hotel.[116]

M. M. Ishov, a military procurator in the West Siberian Military District, also tried to oppose the terror. On an inspection tour in Tomsk he discovered that the local NKVD investigators humiliated the prisoners, deprived them of food and water, and beat them during interrogations. Many prisoners were not questioned at all; the investigators made up interrogation records and signed them themselves. Cases were sent to a *troika,* which handed out death sentences in absentia. Ishov arrested some of these investigators, and sent them under guard to Novosibirsk. He then gathered material on the activities of four NKVD

114. From Kuznetsov's unpublished memoirs, preserved in the archives of the writer Konstantin Simonov. Kuznetsov survived arrest and imprisonment and was rehabilitated in 1955, after which he took a job as a forester—the farther away from people, the better.
115. *Ocherki istorii Kommunisticheskoi partii Kirgizii* (Frunze, 1966), p. 289.
116. From the unpublished memoirs of Ya. I. Drobinsky.

agencies in the West Siberian Military District, and began sending reports on their lawlessness to the Chief Military Procurator of the USSR, Rozovsky, to the General Procurator of the USSR, Vyshinsky, and to Stalin, Molotov, and Kaganovich. He achieved a discussion of the problem by the *obkom* party bureau, and he managed to save a few Red Army officers and civilian officials from being shot. But otherwise he was unsuccessful. His appeals to Moscow usually went unanswered. The obkom Buro, after listening to his speech, instructed the head of the Novosibirsk NKVD agency to "correct the situation." The result was the arrest of Ishov's sister and brother and an NKVD report to Moscow:

Military Procurator Ishov is opposing the NKVD, impeding the investigation of the cases of enemies of the people, refusing to sanction their arrest. He has taken the law in his own hands, arresting NKVD agents. By his actions he is undermining the authority of the agencies. We ask that he be removed from his post and that his arrest be sanctioned.

In March 1938 Ishov went to Moscow, and submitted additional material on NKVD terror to the Chief Military Procurator's Office. In July he went to Moscow again, and was seen by Vyshinsky. Ishov recounts in his memoirs:

When we entered his office, Vyshinsky pointed to a chair alongside his desk, asked me to sit down, and asked for what reason and precisely with what business I had come to him. Taking documents out of my briefcase and putting them on the desk, I asked him to hear me out. . . . I asked him to pay special attention to the techniques and methods used to extract false testimony: beating, humiliation, the medieval methods of the Inquisition. When he had heard me out, Vyshinsky responded with words that stuck deep in my memory, for my whole life. He said: "Comrade Ishov, since when have the Bolsheviks decided to treat enemies of the people in a liberal fashion? You, Comrade Ishov, have lost your sense of party and class. We don't intend to pat enemies of the people on the head. There's nothing wrong with beating enemies of the people on their snouts. And don't forget what the great proletarian writer Maxim Gorky said, that if the enemy doesn't surrender, he must be destroyed. We will have no mercy on enemies of the people.[117]

Ishov tried to show Vyshinsky that it was not enemies but innocent people whom the NKVD had forced to lie. But Vyshinsky reacted coldly, and only for appearance's sake told Rozovsky, who attended the conversation, to check on Ishov's materials. No check, of course, was ever

117. From the unpublished memoirs of M. M. Ishov, a copy of which is in my archives.

made. Returning to Novosibirsk a few days later, Ishov was arrested. Authorization for the arrest was signed personally by Vyshinsky.

All these attempts at resistance failed. For one thing, they were uncoordinated and isolated. Also, it was too late to do much. Stalin could have been stopped at the end of the twenties, and there were still some chances of removing him by regular party procedure at the beginning of the thirties. But after 1934 Stalin could have been removed only by force, and no one was prepared to take that step for fear of the possible consequences and the difficulties of such an undertaking. Not everyone understood that Stalin was engaged in a premeditated usurpation of power; so people turned to the usual forms of protest. They wrote to the proper office and hoped for help "from above." They did not understand that entirely different forms of struggle were required than complaints and petitions to the very people who were ruling illegally. The usual ways of fighting the enemy were unsuitable, and so were the usual methods of correcting the mistakes of individual party members. No one could think of ways to combat lawlessness that came from the party's own leaders. It is difficult to blame the Soviet people. In their overwhelming majority they were honorable workers and fighters, who overcame countless difficulties during the first two five-year plans and fought courageously against Nazi Germany, despite enormous losses. Soviet citizens had no historical experience to guide themselves by in trying to build a new society; they did not realize that it was necessary and possible to oppose the arbitrary methods of rule practiced by their own leaders. The party, the people, and the government were caught unaware, for the blow came from an unexpected direction. World War II showed that Soviet society and the Soviet form of government had the capacity to stand up to any danger from without. But they were helpless when stabbed in the back by their own leaders.

■ 11

BUREAUCRATIZATION AND DEGENERATION

The development of the cult of Stalin and the Stalinist system was facilitated to a large degree by the social processes taking place in the Soviet Union after the revolution—processes that cannot be reduced solely to the struggle between the proletariat and the bourgeoisie. Of no less importance was the struggle between petty bourgeois tendencies and aspirations, on the one hand, and proletarian socialist ones, on the other, both inside the Communist Party and Soviet government and outside of them.

As Lenin once wrote:

> Whoever expects a "pure" social revolution will never live to see it. . . .
> The socialist revolution . . . cannot be anything other than an outburst of mass struggle on the part of all and sundry oppressed and discontented elements. Inevitably, sections of the petty bourgeoisie and of the backward workers will participate in it—without such participation mass struggle is impossible; without it no revolution is possible—and just as inevitably will they bring into the movement their prejudices, their reactionary fantasies, their weaknesses and errors.[118]

Marxist sociology includes in the petty bourgeoisie not only peasants, artisans, small merchants, and the lower sections of office workers and professionals but also declassed elements at the bottom of society, a large group in Russia and many other backward capitalist countries. They are people who have lost or have never had even petty property; they have not grown accustomed to labor in capitalist industry and live by occasional earnings. The significant stratum of agricultural workers, or hired hands (batraki), in old Russia also had little experience of collective labor, although they were called the "rural proletariat." Despite great diversity, all these petty bourgeois strata have certain features in common, including political instability and vacillation, a degree of anarchism, and small-proprietor individualism. Because of their political instability they may provide the reserves for revolution or for reaction, depending on circumstances. Unsettled and disoriented after World War I, for example, they supported fascist dictatorship in some European countries.

Under the autocratic regime in Russia, which was waging an unpopular and burdensome war, the Bolshevik Party was able to win over not only the greater part of the industrial proletariat but also a substantial section of the semiproletarian and petty bourgeois masses. It would be naive to think, however, that the tens of millions of semiproletarian and petty bourgeois elements would be completely transformed by several years of revolutionary struggle, freeing themselves from the shortcomings and limitations of their class backgrounds. It would also be a mistake to idealize the proletariat, picturing it as purely virtuous. Not only in Russia

118. Lenin, PSS, 30:54–55. [CW, 21: 356.]

but also in many industrially developed countries a good part of the proletariat was infected with ideas, convictions, and attitudes quite far removed from the socialist ideal.

Thus, it was not possible for the Bolshevik Party to somehow isolate itself from the surrounding petty bourgeois element. That environment inevitably exerted great pressure on the party through the most varied channels and had a significant effect on the revolutionary cadres, the party and government apparatus of the young Soviet republic.

As is generally known, most of the professional revolutionaries, who formed the backbone of the party, came not from the working class but from the intelligentsia, the lesser gentry, the civil service, the lower strata of the merchant class, artisans and craftsmen, and the clergy. These origins did not prevent most of these people from merging heart and soul with the proletariat and thus becoming proletarian revolutionaries in the full sense of the word. But by no means all the party activists experienced a complete transformation. Besides, the revolution and the civil war produced many new leaders who had not gone through the rigorous school of underground struggle before the revolution. That many individuals who were not true proletarian revolutionaries became leaders of the party both under Lenin and after his death was therefore not an accident or the result of insufficient wisdom. It was the natural result of a proletarian revolution in a petty bourgeois country like Russia. Lenin's remarks about the need to build socialism out of the human material left by capitalism applied to the Bolshevik Party as well.

Lenin was well aware that one of the most difficult problems of the proletarian revolution in Russia was to safeguard the party cadres from bureaucratic degeneration, to overcome the increasing pressure from the petty bourgeois element on the proletariat and the Bolshevik Party. He saw that the transformation of the party from an underground organization to a ruling party would greatly increase petty bourgeois and careerist tendencies among old party members and also bring into the party a host of petty bourgeois and careerest elements that had previously been outside. As early as the Eighth Party Congress, in 1919, Lenin said:

We must avoid everything that in practice may tend to encourage individual abuses. In some places careerists and adventurers have attached themselves to us like leeches, people who call themselves Communists and are deceiving us, and who have wormed their way into our ranks because the Communists are now in power, and because the more honest government employees refused to come and work with us on account of their retrograde ideas, while careerists have no ideas, and no honesty. These people, whose only aim is to make a career, resort to coercion in local areas and imagine they are doing a good thing.[119]

A resolution adopted in 1921 on Lenin's initiative, which dealt with "cleansing" the party of alien elements, said the following:

A situation is gradually taking shape in which one can "rise in the world," make a career for oneself, get a bit of power, only by entering the service of the Soviet regime.[120]

Lenin argued that petty-bourgeois intellectuals would always:

worm their way into the Soviets, the courts, and the administration, since communism cannot be built otherwise than with the aid of the human material created by capitalism, and the bourgeois intellectuals cannot be expelled and destroyed, but must be won over, remolded, assimilated, and reeducated, just as we must—in a protracted struggle waged on the basis of the dictatorship of the proletariat—reeducate the proletarians themselves, who do not abandon their petty bourgeois prejudices at one stroke, by a miracle, at the behest of the Virgin Mary, at the behest of a slogan, resolution, or decree, but only in the course of a long and difficult mass struggle against mass petty bourgeois influences.[121]

In his last writings Lenin concentrated on this very problem: the interrelation of petty bourgeois and proletarian elements in Soviet society and government and the bureacratization and degeneration of the party and government apparatuses. As late as 1922, after five years of the revolution, Lenin's opinion of the party's composition was not particularly high.

There is no doubt that our party, to judge from the bulk of its present membership, is not sufficiently proletarian. . . .
If we do not shut our eyes to reality, we must admit that at the present time the proletarian policy of the party is not determined by the character of its membership, but by the enormous, undivided prestige of that very thin stratum which may be called the party's Old Guard. A small conflict within this stratum would be enough, it not to destroy this prestige, in any event to weaken it to such a degree as to rob this stratum of its power to determine policy.[122]

In his "Letter to the Congress" (part of what is called "Lenin's Testament") he wrote:

119. Lenin, PSS, 38: 199. [CW, 29: 209–210.]
120. *Pravda*, July 27, 1921.
121. Lenin, PSS, 41: 100. [CW, 31: 115.]
122. Lenin, PSS, 45: 20. [Cf. CW, 33: 256–257.]

The apparatus we call ours is, in fact, still quite alien to us; it is a bourgeois and tsarist hodgepodge, and there has been no possibility of getting rid of it in the course of the past five years without the help of other countries. . . . There is no doubt that the infinitesimal percentage of Soviet and Sovietized workers will drown in that tide of chauvinistic Great Russian riffraff like a fly in milk.[123]

Similarly, Lenin's opinion was not particularly high in regard to the Soviet working class itself, at least in the form it took in the wake of the upheavals and catastrophes of world war and civil war.

There is no doubt that we constantly regard as workers people who have not had the slightest real experience of large-scale industry. There has been case after case of petty bourgeois, who have become workers by chance and only for a very short time, being classed as workers. All shrewd White Guardists are very definitely banking on the fact that the alleged proletarian character of our party does not in the least safeguard it against the small-proprietor elements gaining predominance in it, and very rapidly too.[124]

Lenin's concern for the preservation of the socialist character of the Soviet government and the proletarian policy of the Bolshevik Party was fully justified. He was, however, speaking only of the *danger* of bureaucratic and petty bourgeois degeneration, not its fatal inevitability. For in addition to the impact of petty bourgeois ideology on the proletariat and its party, an opposite process was under way—a decisive reshaping of the psychology, ideology, and morals of the petty bourgeois masses and the backward strata of the proletariat itself. The party protected itself against degeneration not only by regular purges of its ranks but also by organizing the education and reeducation of the masses on an unparalleled scale. The civil war weakened the proletariat, but it left the power in Bolshevik hands. Through the Soviets, the trade unions, the press, the school system, through groups organized to eradicate illiteracy, through "reading-room huts" (*izby-chitalni*) set up in countless villages, through the Red Army, and by all other available means the Bolshevik Party sought to lodge socialist ideology firmly in the consciousness of the masses. Considerable progress was made in this area even during Lenin's lifetime. After his death the effort began to flag, because Stalin took the leadership of the party. Stalin's views and personality combined the outward features and terminology of a proletarian revolutionary with the character traits of a petty bourgeois revolutionary and careerist inclined toward degeneration. With his petty bourgeois background and his train-

123. Lenin, PSS, 45: 357. [Cf. CW, 36: 606.]
124. Lenin, PSS, 45: 18. [CW, 33: 254.]

ing in church schools Stalin lacked the qualities of a genuine proletarian revolutionary.

But the problem did not lie in Stalin alone. Moral decay and bureaucratic degeneration to one degree or another affected a section of the party's Old Guard, on which Lenin placed such high hopes and of which he spoke with such pride. First of all, within this Old Guard throughout the twenties, as we saw in part I, there was a fierce ideological battle, which at the same time was a struggle for leadership of the party. Secondly, great progress in socialist construction and considerable power turned the heads of many members of the Old Guard. Further contributing to this process was the steadily increasing centralization of power in both party and government, not matched by any increase in control from below. Symptoms of arrogance, conceit, intolerance of criticism, and susceptibility to flattery began to appear among some who previously had seemed to be modest and reliable revolutionaries. In their way of life, behavior, and material comforts these men moved farther and farther away from the ordinary people, and they did nothing to hinder the immoderate praise that in the late twenties began to be heaped upon them.

It is only fair to note that degeneration of a part of the revolutionary cadres is the rule in every revolution, which attracts many people who are motivated by a desire for power or wealth. The French Revolution brought to the fore not only leaders like Marat but also careerists like Fouché, Talleyrand, Barras, and Tallien. The October revolution did not escape the same fate. "Every revolution has its scum," Lenin said once. "Why should we be any exception?"

Mikhail Razumov provides a typical example. A party member since 1912, secretary of the Tatar and then of the Irkutsk obkom, he turned into a magnate before the startled eyes of Eugenia Ginzburg, who records the process in her memoirs. As late as 1930 he occupied one room in a communal apartment. A year later he was building a "Tatar Livadia" (reminiscent of the former tsar's palace at Livadia in the Crimea). In 1933, when Tatary was awarded the Order of Lenin for success in the kolkhoz movement, portraits of the "First Brigadier of Tatary" were carried through the city with singing. At an agricultural exhibition his portraits were done in mosaics of various crops, ranging from oats to lentils.

Similarly, on May Day in 1936 N. Demchenko, secretary of the Kharkov oblast committee of the party, ordered (indirectly, through others) that portraits of himself be hung from balconies and on the facades of buildings. Such portraits had been printed in advance in large numbers, in spite of a paper shortage; Demchenko had given permission for paper reserved for school textbooks to be used to print the portraits.[125]

Betal Kalmykov, leader of the Kabardin-Balkar Bolsheviks, also developed into a petty dictator, and a cruel one. He went to great lengths in destroying "enemies of the people" in the Karbardin-Balkar republic, until he himself ended up on the list of "enemies."

By 1937 a genuine personality cult also existed around E. P. Berzin, the head of the Kolyma labor-camp complex called Dalstroi, who had likewise been blinded by power. This morally degenerate man was removed by Yezhov not really because he was "excessively humane" toward prisoners, as the charge went, but because Yezhov naturally wanted his own man as head of Dalstroi.

Jakob Hanecki, a veteran revolutionary and close associate of Lenin, turned into a full-fledged bureaucrat, according to reports by people who worked under him. In the thirties he held a variety of prominent positions, at first in economic work and foreign trade and later in the State Association for Music, the Stage, and the Circus. In 1935 he was appointed director of the Museum of the Revolution.

A. P. Serebrovsky became notorious in the thirties for his rough and rude treatment of subordinates. He had been a revolutionary well known to Lenin. Later he was a leading figure in economic work, a deputy people's commissar for heavy industry and head of Glavzoloto. We could cite equally unflattering reports about many other veteran party members, figures who with full justification could be counted as members of Lenin's "Old Guard."

There were various reasons for this lamentable turn of events. People's paths away from the ideals and moral standards of the revolution were as varied as the ways by which they had come to the revolution in the first place. It is easy to understand the degeneration of Vyshinsky, the Menshevik turncoat: he had apparently always been an unprincipled, cowardly person, hungry for power and fame. (Thus, it is not surprising that he persecuted first his former Menshevik comrades and later his new comrades, the Bolsheviks.) It is harder to understand why men like Yaroslavsky or Kalinin who had once been staunch Bolsheviks broke and became totally submissive to Stalin's will. Personalities aside, the general

125. Reported by Mikhail Baitalsky.

rule is apparent. It was not the struggle with the autocracy, not jail or exile, that was the real test for revolutionaries. Much harder was the test of power, having the vast and powerful resources of the state at one's disposal.

Of course the degree to which Bolshevik leaders degenerated also varied. Bureaucratic degeneration reached great extremes in the cases of men like Postyshev, Krylenko, Sheboldaev, and Betal Kalmykov, not to mention such intimates of Stalin as Molotov, Kaganovich, and Voroshilov. The moral collapse of many other members of the Old Guard was not so profound. But they did acquire the habit of commanding, of administration by fiat, ignoring the opinion of the masses. Cut off from the people, they lost the ability to criticize Stalin's behavior and the cult of his personality; on the contrary, they became increasingly dependent on him. Their change in life-style aroused dissatisfaction among workers and rank-and-file party members. One result was the relative ease with which Stalin subsequently destroyed such people, for he could picture their fall as the result not only of a struggle against "spies" and "wreckers" but also of the proletariat's struggle against corrupt and degenerate bureaucrats, a struggle to purge the party of petty bourgeois elements.

Of course after Stalin's purges the composition of the higher echelons of party and government grew even worse. Most of the new officeholders were not young and honest revolutionaries but unprincipled careerists who were willing to carry out any order Stalin gave, with no concern for the interests of the people and socialism. Nevertheless, even after rising to the party leadership, such people could not operate with a free hand. The concrete conditions of the Soviet system were such that they had to declare, at least in words, their devotion to the proletariat and the Communist movement. Thus a whole stratum of "Soviet" philistines and "party" bourgeois took shape, differing from traditional bourgeois philistines only by their greater sanctimoniousness and hypocrisy. The influence of such petty bourgeois elements was especially strong in the union republics where the proletarian nucleus was not as great and the revolution not as profound as in the basic regions of Russia.

Thus, we see that the Stalin cult was not just a religious or ideological phenomenon; it also had a well-defined class content. It was based on the petty bourgeois, bureaucratic degeneration of some cadres and the extensive penetration of petty bourgeois and careerist elements into the ruling elite of Soviet society. Stalin was not simply a dictator; he stood at the peak of a whole system of smaller dictators; he was the head bureaucrat over hundreds of thousands of smaller bureaucrats.

Some sociologists have voiced the hypothesis that in the Stalin era the proletarian socialist core of the party and government were completely destroyed and that with the advent to power of purely petty bourgeois bureaucratic elements a society of the state capitalist type was created. This is a mistaken conception and a distortion of reality, although it contains an element of truth.

The extremely complex social processes in the Soviet Union in the twenties, thirties, and forties are still waiting for genuine scientific analysis. But certain trends are apparent. On the one hand, the working class, growing with exceptional speed, absorbed the declassed urban bourgeoisie and petty bourgeoisie and the millions of peasant migrants to the cities. In 1929–1935 new workers of these types were several times more numerous than the working class of the past. This rapid change in the composition of the working class was bound to affect its psychology and behavior and also the composition of the party, thereby facilitating the degeneration of some parts of the apparatus.

As the veteran party member B—— wrote in his unpublished memoirs:

> Virtually the most important of the changes that took place was the change in the composition of the working class. Beginning with the first five-year plan, enormous masses of peasants began flooding rapidly into industry (the construction industry first of all), including many dekulakized peasants. Is this a fact of small importance? From time immemorial the Russian proletariat had consisted of former peasants. But it had grown at a measured pace and had always managed to digest its new replenishments from the peasantry. Now, however, because of the stormy pace of industrialization, dictated by the revolution and vitally necessary for the revolution, another process began to occur in parallel. The elemental petty bourgeois peasant mass began to encroach on the inner essence of the proletariat, on the proletarian psychology and social outlook, its attitude toward the individual, toward property, toward its work and the cause of socialism. The petty bourgeois element was on the offensive from within, wearing worker's overalls and carrying worker's tools. . . . When the factory didn't have the strength to proletarianize the peasants (and it couldn't have happened any other way, because of the rapid peasant influx and its enormous numerical growth), there immediately began the "peasantization" of the workers. With this change in composition something also changed in the worker's soul. And these changes could not help but affect the party.

At the same time, alongside these negative processes in the thirties and forties, an opposite process was taking place: the transformation of the ideology and consciousness of enormous masses through the propagation of socialist ideology and morality, even though the forms and formulations were significantly distorted. In the deep recesses of Soviet society processes were under way that ultimately strengthened rather than weakened the role and influence of socialist elements. Through the press, the army, and especially the school system socialist ideology was spread to vast numbers, including the nonproletarian population. A new generation of young people grew up and a new intelligentsia. The work of educating and reeducating the populace was done on a vast scale, and although many gave only lip service, a great many more, especially among the youth, adopted socialist ideology and morality as the basis of their conduct and inner convictions. And this process proved to be the most important.

It would be unjust to say that in the thirties the Soviet state apparatus represented nothing but bourgeois and tsarist philistinism. Its composition was changing. But this process of socialist transformation proceeded in various ways on various levels and among various strata of the party, government, and society. The spread of proletarian ideology and Communist morality was most intensive in the twenties and thirties among the new generations and on the lower levels of society. The greatest changes in this respect were observable in the lower echelons of the party, government, and economic apparatus, where the losses from the mass repression were fewer than in the upper echelons. In the leadership of base-level organizations of the party and Komsomol, of individual factories, shops, and farms, among teachers, doctors, sports organizations, and so on the majority were not bureaucrats and careerists but honest and devoted cadres.

Of course they too were affected by the distortions connected with the cult. Many wrong and even criminal directives were carried out by primary party organizations. But there was far more sincere error and honest self-deception on these lower levels than there was higher up. Most of the directives sent down to them breathed the spirit of revolution, speaking about struggle with the enemies of socialism, concern for individuals, the need to advance the cause of the revolution. The lower organizations, failing to see the gap between the words and deeds of Stalin and his associates, tried to adhere to political and moral norms that many people at the top did not consider binding on themselves. Rank-and-file Communists and Komsomol members and apparatus cadres on the lower level sincerely tried as much as they were able to put into practice the socialist slogans, which for many careerists and bureaucrats at the top were just empty words.

Even at the top, however, there was some variety. One group, the

Stalinist guard, consisted of cruel, unprincipled men, ready to destroy anything that blocked their way to power. But since these people were incapable of managing a big, complex governmental organism, Stalin had to bring into the leadership people of another type, comparatively young leaders who supported Stalin in almost everything but were not informed of many of his crimes. Although they shared certain characteristic faults of Stalin's entourage, they also wanted to serve the people, the party, and socialism. They lacked sufficient political experience to analyze and rectify the tragic events of the Stalinist period, and some of them perished toward the end of it. But others survived, and after Stalin's death gave varying degrees of support to the struggle against the cult and the effort to establish more normal conditions for Soviet society.

■ 12

CONSERVATISM AND DOGMATISM AMONG SOME REVOLUTIONARY CADRES

The petty bourgeois degeneration of a section of the party and government cadres took such forms as self-seeking, careerism, bureaucratism, lack of principle, conceit, vainglory, and time serving. It was this degeneration that facilitated the rise of the Stalin cult, and it was from this milieu that Stalinism drew its main cadres.

Within the proletariat and the proletarian core of the party, however, there were also conservative and dogmatic tendencies that contributed to the extended hegemony of Stalinism.

According to Marxist doctrine, the proletariat is the most advanced class of bourgeois society, but neither Marx nor Lenin idealized it. Lenin made the following point in his *"Left-Wing" Communism—An Infantile Disorder:*

Within every class, even in the conditions prevailing in the most enlightened countries, even within the most advanced class, and even when the circumstances of the moment have aroused all the spiritual forces of this class to an exceptional degree, there always are—and inevitably will be as long as classes exist, as long as a classless society has not fully consolidated itself, and has not developed on its own foundations—representatives of the class who do not think and are incapable of thinking. Capitalism would not be the oppressor of the masses that it actually is, if things were otherwise.[126]

126. Lenin, PSS, 41: 52–53. [Cf. CW, 31: 68–69, footnote.]

A creative approach to both reality and theory is considered the chief claim of Marxism and scientific socialism to superiority over other systems, but it would be wrong to place one's trust solely in the creative aspect of socialist ideology and underestimate the strength of dogmatism. It would be naive to think that dogmatism always repels people, while a creative approach is always attractive. Unfortunately, the opposite has more often occurred.

For a large number of people who lack the necessary education and training, dogmatism proves to be more attractive because it frees them from the need to think, to take initiative, to continually raise the level of their own understanding. Instead of studying ever-changing reality, they use a few fixed rules. Human history in general and the history of religions and ideologies in particular have shown us the immense force of dogmatic thinking. Things are always harder for creative thinkers and innovators than for dogmatists. Although a revolution represents the victory of new ideas over old dogmas, in time any revolutionary movement becomes overgrown with its own dogmas. In tsarist Russia such a tendency was more likely than usual, for a great many revolutionaries lacked education. In such a situation Stalin's ability to make extreme simplifications of complex ideas was not the least factor in his rise. Many party cadres knew Marxism and Leninism only in its schematic Stalinist form, unaware that Stalin had impoverished and vulgarized Marxism, transforming it from a developing, creative doctrine into a kind of religion.

Thus it would be wrong to attribute every mistake of former revolutionaries to petty bourgeois degeneration. Many of their errors were due not to a change in their earlier views but to an incapacity for change—in other words, to dogmatism.

Many dedicated revolutionaries, indifferent to personal advantage, were nevertheless incapable of carrying the revolution forward when a new stage required new methods. More and more their thought revealed the doctrinaire rigidity, the sectarian ossification, that Thomas Mann had in mind when he spoke of "revolutionary conservatism." Many leaders who excelled in the period of civil war were not effective at building a new society. Accustomed to resolving most conflicts by force of arms, they were incapable of complex educational work, which had to be the chief method in the new period. Instead of learning, some Communists even began to boast of their lack of education. "We never finished *gimnazii* [secondary schools], but we are governing *gubernii* [provinces]," a well-known Bolshevik declared in the late twenties, and his audience applauded. When such people ran into difficulties, they often turned into simple executors of orders from above, valuing blind discipline most of all. The closed mind, the refusal to think independently, was the epistemological basis of the cult of personality. It was not only degenerates and careerists who supported the cult; there were also sincere believers, genuinely convinced that everything they did was necessary for the revolution. They believed in the political trials of 1936–1938; they believed that the class struggle was intensifying; they believed in the necessity for mass repression. They became willing or unwilling accomplices in Stalin's crimes, although subsequently many of them also became his victims.

Mikhail Baitalsky, in his memoirs, gave a very accurate description of one such dogmatist and follower of orders from above—his first wife, Yeva.

Yeva could have served as a model worker among the masses. She was not particularly educated. What of it? She knew everything necessary for her work in fixed and final form; it was incontrovertible. She read the newspapers and even more systematically—the directives. . . .

During all the years of her work in the central uniform shops . . . Yeva was secretary of the local Komsomol cell. . . . When she got beyond Komsomol age, she became an activist in the Women's Department (in the 1920s a special department of the party existed for mass work among women). Later she transferred to party work, again as a secretary. And so it went almost until the day of her death. . . .

Yet never in her life was Yeva an apparatchik fossilized in leadership work. On the contrary, she always remained an enthusiast. It's simply amazing how little she changed! Just as she began with faith in the revolution, so she believed faithfully to the end. . . .

She could not think of herself outside of the revolution. For her the revolution merged totally with the party, and so she could not think of herself outside the party, which in her heart was always spelled with a capital letter. . . . Since the Party had sanctioned the shooting of its previous leaders as "self-confessed spies and murderers," that meant they actually were spies and murderers. No other proof was required for Yeva, so long as there was a Decision by the Party. . . .

Was Yeva good? Did she love people? Those are questions I find difficult to answer with a simple "Yes." Cruelty sickened her; to cause people pain in order to take pleasure at the sight of it was not within her nature. . . . But her goodness gave way before another feeling, which had grown within her to incredible dimensions—the sense of duty she had acquired over the years. The notion of good or evil in Yeva's consciousness was built on the firm foundation of the political knowledge obtained, first, in Komsomol study circles, then at the provincial party school, then from party resolutions.

Believers must be ready to scorn not only their own suffering but also that of others when their duty to the faith requires it. . . .

Yeva, with her faith, did not demand clarity in her own thoughts; she undoubtedly felt that such clarity was dangerous for her bright, serene faith. Yeva needed only clarity in the instructions sent from above: Do this, don't do that. The dogmas of the faith must be indisputable. Therefore, there is no more convincing theoretical argument than a resolution, a decision, a decree.[127]

Rigidity of this type was manifested by many leaders in the period under review and is well portrayed by a novelist in a character named Onisimov. He is an Old Bolshevik who has become an important manager, a commissar, devoted to socialism, scrupulously honest, simple in his way of life, never using his high post for personal advantage, but also a conservative, a worshipper of blind discipline. He is a zealous servant, who thinks only of how to carry out his orders "from above," from "the boss." Nothing else interests him. Although he hates Beria personally, like Beria he is a pillar of the Stalinist regime.

When he was reporting to Stalin on the problem of East Siberian metallurgy, he had no idea of the paradoxes, the contradictions of the era. Questions that might have disturbed his reason and conscience as a Communist were set aside, avoided in the simplest way: It's not my business; it doesn't concern me; it's not for me to judge. His favorite brother died in prison; in his soul he mourned for Vanya, but even then remained firm in his "don't argue!" For him the expression "soldier of the party" was no empty phrase. Later, when "soldier of Stalin" came into use, he considered himself such a soldier, with pride and undoubtedly with reason.[128]

> Neither torture nor words can burn out of me
> Loyalty to my country and the people.

These words appear in a poem, "The Vow," written in prison in 1939 by Yevgeny Gnedin, a former official of the Foreign Affairs Commissariat. He sent the poem to his family, even though he had been tortured and beaten for many days, including in Beria's office and with Beria's participation. Gnedin survived seventeen years in prisons, camps, and internal exile. In the late sixties and early seventies he wrote lengthy

127. From Baitalsky's unpublished memoirs, "Tetradi dlia vnukov."

128. From the novel by Aleksandr Bek, *Naznachenie* (The Appointment) [which has now been published in the Soviet Union. —G .S.] In the 1960s the novel was prepared for publication by the magazine *Novy mir*, whose editor, Aleksandr Tvardovsky, several times submitted it to the censors only to have it rejected. In 1971, not long before Bek's death, the text of the novel found its way out of the Soviet Union. It was published in West Germany by the Russian emigre publishers Posev. The quotation is from p. 53 of that edition.

memoirs. Analyzing his views and attitudes during the first phase of his imprisonment, Gnedin had this to say:

In the first version of this poem, which I recited to myself and thought of reciting to the investigator, I said "Neither violence nor words." I didn't say "torture." I also said "loyalty to the leader and the people," not "to my country and the people." Thus, even in an unwritten poem that I recited to myself, I couldn't bring myself to use that ominous word "torture," and although I had been tortured, I swore allegiance to the sinister man who was our "leader." . . .

It is natural and unobjectionable that an innocent person of principle, a patriot thrown into prison, should avow his loyalty to his homeland and people. But such was the pernicious influence of the Stalinist system that a thinking person who himself had fallen victim to arbitrariness and who knew that thousands of other innocents had been destroyed by Stalin's accomplices still gave assurances in his thoughts of political loyalty to the Stalinist regime, which was so unjust and destructive for the Soviet people. In trying to be completely accurate and self-critical, I must state that my firmness in defense of my innocence and my emphatic refusal to give false testimony against anyone else—this courageous behavior while under the third degree—still did not rule out the possibility that if I had suddenly found myself free again, I might willingly and without any coercion have remained an obedient servant of the regime.

I gradually freed myself from the psychology of a devoted bureaucrat and dogmatist as my thoughts became freer through the deep reflection and rigorous thinking that constituted my inner spiritual life in the prisons and camps.[129]

How narrow and dogmatic people could be is revealed in a song composed by wives of "enemies of the people" at a transit prison.

In accord with severe Soviet laws
Answering for our husbands,
We have lost our honor and freedom,
We have lost our beloved children.
We don't cry, though we feel bad.
With our faith firm we will go anywhere,
And to any part of our measureless country
We will take our ardent labor.
This labor will give us the right to freedom.
Our country, like a mother, will accept us again.
And under the banner of Lenin and Stalin,
We will give our labor to the country.[130]

Similarly, V. I. Volgin has written the following:

129. Yevgeny Gnedin, *Katastrofa i vtoroe rozhdenie: memuarnye zapiski* (Amsterdam, 1977), pp. 164–166.

130. Quoted in Ye. G. Veller-Gurevich, "Iz vospominanii o 37-m," unpublished manuscript.

Forgetting all insults, we submitted statements asking to be sent to fight on the battlefront. Our requests were denied with suspicion and contempt. We consoled ourselves with the thought that the mining of gold and tin was also a battlefront, as was the provision of firewood for the power plants that served the work of gold mining, and that perhaps this front was no less important in economic terms than the actual battlefront stretching across the continent. I was the work-brigade leader and demanded that the norms be overfulfilled. Seryozha Postyshev often sat while others worked, and once I cursed him out roundly for that. "Your father," I said hotly, "set out to teach the entire people, but he raised his only son to be a sponger." There was no point in my berating him so. This young man had just graduated from the Yeiskaya school of aviation when his father was arrested and Seryozha himself, as a member of the family of an "enemy of the people," was given fifteen years in the camps by a special three-man board. Embittered and depressed over his father's fate and his own, he would sit motionless for hours, lost in thought. But at the time I took this to be "sabotage."[131]

Here Volgin touched on a question that was often the topic of sharp dispute among political prisoners in the camps. One of the extreme points of view was that labor in the Stalin camps was slave labor and that the best way to curb the repression and stop forced labor was to work as poorly as possible, to sabotage production goals, to try to damage equipment without being noticed, even to damage the seedlings in the hothouses where vegetables were grown for the feeding of prisoners. This point of view was unquestionably wrong because it only resulted in an intensification of the terror in the camps, in a harsher regimen and poorer provisioning. The majority of prisoners did not accept this extreme view; they did not organize strikes and demonstrations or damage equipment, but they also did not show any enthusiasm for the work, avoiding it whenever doing so was not too dangerous. Their main aim was to survive.

Among the inmates of the camps, however, there were those who tried to convince themselves and others that work in the camps contributed to the building of socialism and therefore should be performed as conscientiously as possible. It is not surprising that this was the view that especially stirred the sympathies of the magazine *Oktyabr*, when after the Twenty-Second Congress it found itself obliged to write at least something about the camps and the mass repression. It printed a long narrative poem entitled "From Dewdrop to Star" by Vladimir Firsov, a

131. From Volgin's unpublished memoirs, a copy of which is in my archives.

neo-Stalinist poet of the "rural school," which includes the following lines:

> We were victorious!
> But then how did those live
> Who were innocently slandered,
> When they were sent off from the people
> And lies hurled after them?
> • • • • • • • •
> What of courage? It could not come
> All by itself to Soviet people.
> It grew in labor, from battle to battle.
> In the taiga, too, it grew as before!
> The courage that gave them strength at times
> When metal cracked from the icy cold,
> The strength to work for Soviet Russia
> And not for those who'd slandered them.
> O, how many deaths they were to see!
> Yet their labor worked toward Victory.
> In the name of the life of Lenin's ideas!
> Granted they did not fight at the front.
> Cities still rose beneath their hands
> And factories high above the taiga,
> In the distant dark, in the name of life.
> They have no need for medals and honors.
> Why would they want belated flowers?
> The sole reward they'd want is Their Land,
> From sunlit dewdrop to star above.[132]

Of course the labor of political prisoners in Stalin's camps was not performed "in the name of socialism" or "in the name of the life of Lenin's ideas." It was slave labor in the name of eternalizing the Stalinist tyranny.

It is important to note that dogmatism, stereotyped thinking, and an oversimplified approach to reality were evident not only in the behavior of various leaders. Through propaganda and the educational system many primitive dogmas and clichés were drilled into the masses as well, becoming for them a guide to action.

Reminiscing about his youth as a Komsomol member, for example, the poet Naum Korzhavin wrote that he "used to open the journal *Prozhektor* (Searchlight) with the greatest interest":

132. Vladimir Firsov, "Ot rosinki do zvezdy," *Oktyabr*, 1964, no. 10, pp. 8–9.

Lying down on the floor I would draw a kulak with a sawed-off gun. I recall how, before a holiday, I would spare neither India ink nor whiting; I would divide the whole world unconditionally into Whites and Reds. Eager, skinny, short, I marched gaily, and suspected a bourgeois in every fat man.[133]

This kind of dogmatic and sectarian thinking on a mass scale only served the victory of Stalin and Stalinism.

■ 13

THE SOCIALIST STATE IN THEORY AND PRACTICE

The question of the state occupied an important place in nineteenth-century socialist literature. Should the victorious proletariat make use of the old machinery of state or destroy it? If destruction was the answer, a question still remained: should a new proletarian state be created on the ruins of the old, or could the proletariat do without a state altogether? If there were to be a proletarian state, should it exist for a long time? With the passage of time might it not turn into a clique of privileged function-aries standing above the people?

Revolutionaries expressed many different views on these questions. The anarchists, for example, drew a sharp line between society and the state. In any society, they held, the state was the main conservative force, the most serious obstacle to the development of equality and freedom. Therefore the revolution meant the immediate destruction of any state; socialism and the state were incompatible. For the anarchists there was no problem of a transitional period to put down the upper classes and reeducate the lower in the spirit of socialism. They believed that any proletarian state would inevitably degenerate into the rule of the minority over the majority and would represent a new form of the oppression of the masses. The abolition of the state, in their view, should occur on the very first day after the revolution.

Mikhail Bakunin, the anarchist theoretician, argued as follows:

Since any form of state power, any government, by its very nature and position is placed apart from and above the people and must invariably strive to subject the people to aims and usages alien to the people, we therefore proclaim our-selves the enemies of any form of governmental or state power, enemies of governmental organization in general. We think the people can only be happy and free when they have organized themselves from the bottom up through

133. Korzhavin's poem is from a typed anthology circulated in the 1960s, a copy of which is in my archives.

independent and totally free associations apart from any official supervision, though not apart from the influence of various individuals and parties that are equally free. The people itself will create its own life. These are the convictions of social revolutionaries, and because of them we are called anarchists. We do not protest this name because we truly are enemies of all authority, for we know that state power has just as corrupting an effect on those vested with it as on those obliged to submit to it. Under its pernicious influence some become greedy, power-hungry despots and exploiters of society . . . while others become slaves.[134]

Naturally the anarchists were opposed to a proletarian state. "What does it mean to say that the proletariat will be elevated to be the ruling class?" asked Bakunin in a polemic with Marx.

Can the entire proletariat stand at the head of the government? . . . Then there would be no government, there would be no state. . . . This dilemma is easily resolved in the theory of the Marxists. By popular government they mean government of the people by a small number of representatives elected by the people. . . . And so, whatever way you look at this problem, you reach the same sorry conclusion: the government of the enormous majority of the popular masses by a privileged minority. But this minority, say the Marxists, will consist of workers. Yes, of former workers, who, as soon as they become rulers or representatives of the people, will cease to be workers and will begin to look upon the whole world of common laborers from the heights of the state system. They will represent not the people but themselves and their claims to govern the people.[135]

Marx and Engels objected strongly to this gloomy picture. Socialist society, they argued, cannot arise in a single day; it can be created only by many years of struggle to reconstruct the social organism on new principles and to suppress the opposition of the overthrown exploiting classes. In other words, a more or less prolonged transitional period would be needed between capitalist and communist societies, and during that period the proletariat could not do without governmental power. After destroying the old state machine, the proletariat would have to create its own, the dictatorship of the proletariat, giving this state a "revolutionary and transitional form."[136] In a famous critique of antiauthoritarian revolutionaries, Engels wondered whether they had ever seen a revolution.

Revolution is without doubt the most authoritarian thing possible. Revolution is an act in which part of the population forces its will on another part by means

134. Bakunin, *Polnoe sobranie sochinenii* (St. Petersburg, 1907), 2: 166.
135. Ibid., p. 217
136. Marx and Engels, *Sochineniia*, 2d ed., 18: 297.

of guns, bayonets, cannon—that is, by extremely authoritarian instruments. And the victorious party is necessarily obliged to maintain its rule by means of the same fear that its weapons inspire in the reactionaries.[137]

Of course the Marxists also faced the problem of how to keep the proletarian state from degenerating, from becoming transformed from society's servant to its master. But this problem was never satisfactorily solved in nineteenth-century Marxist writings—for good reasons. In the first place, it was hard to work out rules for a proletarian state without any concrete experience of building such a state. Marx and Engels made some recommendations on this matter only after the Paris Commune: every official should be subject to recall at any moment, and the salary of any official should be no higher than a workman's pay. But the experiment of the Paris Commune lasted only seventy-two days, which was too short to test the efficacy of these measures or to discover what else might be necessary to prevent degeneration.

In the second place, Marx and Engels assumed that the socialist revolution would triumph in all the major capitalist countries at the same time. Therefore the revolutionary state would be necessary only for a short period. They regarded the state as a necessary evil, to be endured only "until the generation that grows up in the new free social situation will be in a condition to cast aside this whole rubbish of state systems."[138]

In the most famous comment of all, Engels summed up the issue:

The first act in which the state really comes forward as the representative of society as a whole—the taking possession of the means of production in the name of society—is at the same time its last independent act as a state. The interference of the state power in social relations becomes superfluous in one sphere after another, and then ceases of itself. The government of persons is replaced by the administration of things and the direction of the processes of production. The state is not "abolished"; it withers away.[139]

Lenin took the same point of view in *State and Revolution* (1917), though of course he was primarily concerned with the establishment of proletarian hegemony over the bourgeoisie. Lenin did not believe in the simultaneous victory of the socialist revolution in the major capitalist countries. He considered it more likely that socialism would triumph

137. Ibid., 18: 304–305.
138. Ibid., 22: 201.
139. Ibid., 20: 291–292. [This English translation is by Emile Burns. See Engels, *Herr Eugen Dühring's Revolution in Science (Anti-Dühring)* (New York, 1939), pp. 306–307.—D. J.]

first in one country, which would lead to an inevitably savage struggle between the proletariat and the overthrown exploiting classes, lending new urgency to the maintenance of a strong proletarian state. "We are not utopians," Lenin wrote.

We do not "dream" of suddenly doing without all government, all subordination. Those are anarchist dreams, essentially foreign to Marxism, based on a failure to understand the tasks of the dictatorship of the proletariat. In fact, they only serve to put off the socialist revolution until people are different.[140]

Lenin did not reject the idea of a gradual withering away of the proletarian state. He wrote in *State and Revolution* that the only government the proletariat needed was one that would immediately start to wither away and that could not help but wither away. He stressed that only Soviet power could lay the basis for the total withering away of all state structures by drawing the organized masses of working people into regular, unrestricted participation in administering the government.

In 1917, since the possible degeneration of the proletarian state did not seem to be an urgent problem, Lenin merely repeated some of Marx's and Engels' ideas without elaboration.

The workers, after winning political power, will smash the old bureaucratic apparatus, shatter it to its very foundtions, and raze it to the ground; they will replace it by a new one, consisting of the very same workers and other employees against whose transformation into bureaucrats the measures will at once be taken which were specified in detail by Marx and Engels: (1) not only election but also recall at any time; (2) pay not to exceed that of a workman; (3) immediate introduction of universal control and supervision, so that all may become "bureaucrats" for a time and therefore nobody may become a "bureaucrat."[141]

The reality of postrevolutionary Russia very quickly showed the impracticality and utopian character of the measures "specified in detail by Marx and Engels." The old bureaucratic apparatus actually was smashed and shattered to its foundations, but the creation of a new apparatus "of the very same workers and other employees" proved impossible. In order to create a new state apparatus, fragments of the old one had to be used. Lenin himself was forced to admit that truly Sovietized workers would drown among this tsarist and bourgeois riffraff "like a fly in milk."[142] The state apparatus in Soviet Russia stood over and above not only the

140. Lenin, PSS, 33:49.
141. Ibid., p. 201.
142. [The phrase is from Lenin's December 1922 notes on "The Question of Nationalities or 'Autonomization.'" See CW, 36:605–611. —G. S.]

classes of capitalists and landowners who had been overthrown by the revolution and whose resistance it actually was necessary to suppress. The bulk of the population consisted of various strata of the petty bourgeoisie, with their unstable ideology, their vacillations, and their reluctance to reorganize society on socialist foundations. Therefore election and recall of government bodies "at any moment" could have had the quick result of removing the Bolshevik Party from power. Thus the de facto principle of appointment from above took precedence over the principle of election from the bottom up, which was formally retained. Moreover, as early as the spring of 1918 the Bolsheviks were obliged to introduce pay rates for "bourgeois specialists" that were many times higher than the average pay of an industrial worker. Limits on rates of pay were maintained in the twenties, but only for party members (the so-called "party maximum"), but here too there were many levels and the highest pay rates exceeded that of an average industrial worker by a factor of three or four, sometime even five. Not only people of bourgeois and petty bourgeois social origin but also party members and people with working-class backgrounds succumbed to the corrupting effects of power and turned into bureaucrats.

The chief agency of supervision and control, above all other governmental institutions, was the Bolshevik Party itself. The party's best people were placed in key government posts, and all state institutions were obliged to account for themselves to party organizations and to carry out directives issued by the party. But such control by the party could not prevent the process of bureaucratic degeneration in important sectors of the state apparatus. Besides, many components of the party itself were affected by bureaucratization.

Under the system of one-party rule, the Bolshevik Party, especially in the case of its leading bodies, ceased to be just an association of like-minded people. The party apparatus became the most important part of the governmental system. Certain party bodies, in particular the Central Committee and the party congresses, in fact became the legislative organs of the Soviet system. Lenin viewed this fusion of the upper echelons of party and state and the party's key role in the power structure as fundamentally positive, because to him the party, forged in the fire of two revolutions, was the principal bearer of socialist ideas. It tied together all the parts of the new social organism.

But in fact there were also negative results. Top party leaders had more power than directors of government agencies, and this prompted some party leaders to abuse their power. They began to use their power and influence for purposes that were by no means in the interest of the workers. Elements of corruption began to penetrate certain sections of the top party apparatus. Special privileges were established for some party leaders—privileges that in some cases became an end in themselves, taking on independent value. On the other hand, the heightening of the party's influence weakened that of the soviets as representative bodies. Soviet congresses did not so much discuss and draft legislation as give formal approval to directives made by party congresses and the party Central Committee.

Lenin, who watched these processes closely, planned to write a second part of *State and Revolution,* which would have analyzed and generalized the experience of the young Soviet state. But he never managed to carry out this plan. Unfortunately, that kind of analysis and generalization, one of the most important tasks of scientific socialism, was not carried out after Lenin's death either. On the contrary, Stalin skillfully used the incompleteness, both in theory and practice, of the proletarian state to promote his own ends. The absence of effective mechanisms of popular control over the government to check the abuse of power, especially by the highest leaders, enabled Stalin to strengthen his own position and gradually to usurp all power. The question of control over the government deserves more detailed analysis. In the next section I shall look at this question more closely.

■ 14
LACK OF EFFECTIVE POPULAR CONTROL

In modern times it is impossible to administer a country without a large number of government officials, as well as party, economic, and military officials. In the view of Marxists capitalist society cannot do without bureaucracy, government by privileged people elevated above the masses. But the capitalist class maintains control of these officials by many informal as well as formal means. Indeed, the upper strata of the bureaucracy belong to the exploiting class and cannot become an independent social force. To this I must add that in Western multiparty systems the periodic election of new governments and presidents is not just an empty formality.

Strange as it may seem at first glance, it was in socialist society that bureaucratic officialdom proved to be a greater potential danger from the point of view of this stratum becoming an independent social force not controlled by society.

After destroying the old state machine, the working class needs to create its own state, whose proletarian character is determined first of all by the class composition of the personnel staffing the highest bodies of the state and of the ruling proletarian party. However, in the context of a one-party dictatorship there exists the danger that many of those called upon to exercise power in the name of the people will start to abuse their power and use it against the people's interests. This can happen, as in the Stalin era, in the case of officials endowed with the plenitude of state power. The result is a difficult position for the popular masses. Protected against their former rulers and external enemies, they are practically helpless against the arbitrary rule of their own leaders. Thus one of the most important tasks of the proletarian revolution should be the establishment of effective control by the workers and peasants over their representatives in the state and party apparatus.

This sort of problem was recognized long before the Russian revolution. Robespierre, for example, noting that the people's sovereign power is unlimited, asked who would control the individuals to whom such power is delegated.[143] He had an incorrect answer to that sensible question: the benefactor of the people would exercise control. The Babeuvists saw the danger more clearly[144] and proposed a more sensible solution: bodies of popular supervisors checking up on officials. Marx and Engels' sensitivity to the problem has already been noted. Perhaps the most forceful formulation came from Engels:

> When the working class comes to power, . . . it must, in order not to lose its newly won supremacy, on the one hand, get rid of the old machine of oppression which had been used against it and, on the other hand, *protect itself against its own deputies and functionaries.*[145]

Lenin was much concerned with questions of popular control. This problem was one of the most important facing the Bolsheviks after the October revolution. Within days after the revolution, a special collegium was selected by the Central Executive Committee to begin state control. In May 1918 this Central Executive Collegium was transformed into the People's Commissariat of State Control. At the same time many workers'

143. M. Robespierre, *Revoliutsionnaia zakonnost' i pravosudie* (Moscow, 1959), p. 209.
144. See F. Buonarotti, *Zagovor vo imia ravenstva*, pp. 316–317.
145. Marx and Engels, *Sochineniia,* 2nd ed., 32: 199.

and peasants' inspection organizations came into being. In 1920 they were fused with the Commissariat of State Control to form the Commissariat of Workers' and Peasants' Inspection, or Rabkrin, with Stalin appointed to head this commissariat. Lenin was quite optimistic about the new institution:

> The worker and peasant masses who have to build up our entire state must start by establishing state control. It is from among the worker and peasant masses that you will obtain this apparatus.[146]

But soon Lenin's optimism vanished. He declared:

> This agency was organized about a year ago, but thus far has shown little promise as a school for training the masses to administer the state.[147]

In February 1922 Lenin wrote that it was "ridiculous to expect more from Rabkrin than the carrying out of simple instructions."[148] At the end of 1922 he expressed himself even more sharply about the functioning of Rabkrin:

> Let us speak frankly. At present Rabkrin does not have an ounce of authority. Everyone knows that there are no institutions more poorly organized than the institutions of Rabkrin and that in its present state nothing can be expected of the Commissariat.[149]

Control organs were also set up in the party. In September 1920, on Lenin's motion, the Ninth Party Conference created the Central Control Commission (TsKK) and local control commissions, whose tasks were to

> . . . fight encroaching bureaucratism, careerism, the abuse of party and Soviet positions by party members, the violation of comradely relations within the party, the spread of unfounded and unverified rumors and insinuations, which discredit the party or its individual members, and other such reports that damage the party's unity and authority.[150]

In 1922 Lenin tried to introduce a new system of popular control. He proposed the creation of joint party and state control agencies that would rely above all on rank-and-file workers and peasants. The particulars were: (1) the expansion of the Central Control Commission by adding seventy-five to one hundred workers and peasants, who were to be

146. Lenin, PSS, 40: 200–201; CW, 30: 415.
147. Ibid., 42: 49; CW, 31: 435.
148. Ibid., 44: 369.
149. Ibid., 45: 392–393.
150. *KPSS v rezoliutsiiakh* . . . , pt. 1 (Moscow, 1953), p. 533.

carefully screened from the party point of view, since they would enjoy all the rights of Central Committee members; and (2) the assignment of some members of the Central Control Commission to Rabkrin, where they would be members of its directing apparatus and thus maintain a vital link between the two agencies of control. At the same time the apparatus of Rabkrin was to be reduced to three or four hundred people. One of the most important tasks of the new control organs was to prevent a split in the Central Committee and also to limit the "boundless power" of the party's general secretary. Lenin wrote:

Our Central Committee has become a strictly centralized and highly authoritative group, but the work of this group is not set up in conditions appropriate to its authority. The reform I am proposing should improve things: the members of the Central Control Commission, a certain number of whom would be obligatory attendants at every meeting of the Politburo, should form a solid group, which should see to it, "without respect to persons," that no authority—neither that of the general secretary nor that of any other Central Committee member—stops them from making an inquiry, from checking documents, and in general from achieving unconditional information and the strictest accuracy. [151]

Of course no system of control could be effective without active support by the Central Committee, the Politburo, and the Secretariat, which were the highest bodies of the party between congresses. Moreover, Lenin obviously exaggerated the ability of rank-and-file workers and peasants, even when invested with great authority, to supervise and control the activity of well-known and prestigious politicians. Stalin, who proved to be the key figure in the Central Committee after Lenin's death, did not continue Lenin's effort to create genuine agencies of popular control. Quite to the contrary, he limited the existing agencies to checking up on lower organizations and controlling opposition groups, while the higher administrative bodies became increasingly immune to effective control. As Stalin's power grew, the importance of the control agencies declined. In the late twenties he appreciably limited the powers of Rabkrin and the Central Control Commission. Their main function became to fight the opposition and check up on the activities of lower ranking organizations but not to interfere in the work of the Politburo and Secretariat.

Just before the Seventeenth Party Congress, in 1934, the press carried

151. Lenin, PSS 45: 387. From the memorandum "How We Should Reorganize Rabkrin," published in *Pravda*, January 25, 1923, while Lenin was still alive. However, in that and all subsequent versions until after Stalin's death, the words "neither that of the general secretary nor that of any other Central Committee member" were deleted.

a proposal by Kaganovich to replace the Central Control Commission and Rabkrin by two agencies: a Commission of Party Control (KPK) and a Commission of Soviet Control (KSK). Stalin told the congress that there was no need for the two existing agencies. Now, he said, an organization was required that "would not have the universal goal of inspecting everyone and everything, but could concentrate all its attention on the work of control, on the work of verifying the execution of the decisions of the Soviet regime's central institutions."[152] Thus, the functions of control were restricted. Such problems as fighting bureaucratic abuse or improving the functioning of the state apparatus were not even mentioned.

The functions of the Commission of Soviet Control, which later became the Commissariat of State Control, were essentially limited to inspection, auditing, and reporting on violations discovered this way. As for the Commission of Party Control it had almost no control functions at all; its main job was the reveiw of personnel problems and appeals of Communists. Rank-and-file party members and the popular masses were entirely excluded from the control function. The whole system of Rabkrin —groups and cells, sections, complaint bureaus, the "light cavalry," and so on—was dismantled. All this opened the way for an increase in bureaucratic methods of administration and weakened the struggle against lawlessness and abuse of power.

There is no question that under a centralized one-party system the creation of effective popular control is a very complex problem, somewhat analogous to trying to square the circle. The best system of control is to permit the free functioning of opposition parties and publications independent of the government. Nevertheless, even under the conditions existing in the Soviet Union far more effective systems of popular control could have been organized than the ones that existed. Yet Stalin eliminated even those "lesser grade" systems that had been organized in Lenin's time. This facilitated his usurpation of power in the party and over the entire country.

■ 15

INSUFFICIENT EDUCATION, CULTURE, AND DEMOCRATIC TRADITION

In the final analysis, the attitude of the masses is decisive. Sooner or later they overthrow all sorts of tyrants and despots, but at other times the same masses are the strongest support of despotism. "Every people,"

152. Stalin, *Sochineniia*, 13: 373–374.

said Marx, "has the rulers it deserves." An Arab thinker and social
activist of the nineteenth century expressed the idea at greater length:

> The common people are the despot's sustenance and his power; he rules over
> them and with their help oppresses others. He holds them captive and they extol
> his might; he robs them and they bless him for sparing their lives. He degrades
> them and they praise his grandeur; he turns them against each other and they
> take pride in his craftiness. And if the despot squanders their wealth, they say he
> is generous; if he kills without torturing, they consider him merciful; if he drives
> them into mortal danger, they submit, fearing punishment; and if some of them
> are reproachful, rejecting despotism, the people will fight the rejectors as if they
> were tyrants. In short, the common people cut their own throats through fear,
> which derives from ignorance. If ignorance is destroyed, fear will disappear, the
> situation will change.[153]

I have already argued that Stalin was supported by the majority of the
Soviet people both because he was clever enough to deceive them and
because they were backward enough to be deceived. Not only Stalin's
craftiness as a demagogue contributed to this but also the people's inadequate historical experience, their low level of culture and education,
and the weakness of democratic traditions. Russia's previous development prepared it for revolution but also for the possibility that the
revolution would evolve into a totalitarian system of despotic barracks-
style socialism—that is, Stalinism.

This question of the relationship and continuity between nineteenth-
century Russia and the twentiety-century Soviet Union—between the
Russia of Nicholas I and II and the Soviet state under Lenin and Stalin,
between the autocracy of the Russian tsars and Stalin's autocracy—has
been a subject of bitter dispute among various schools of Western Sovi-
etology and Russian émigré opinion as well as between offical Soviet
historians and nationalism currents in present-day Soviet literature and
journalism. Without going into all the shades of opinion on this question,
let me cite some of the extreme positions. Not so long ago the editor of
Russkaya mysl, the émigré newspaper published in Paris, wrote the
following:

> Our point of view, if it is to be condensed to its very essence, is to reject totally
> any equating of the Russian and Soviet state systems. We reject and refute this
> equation not in the hereditary and traditional way but by proceeding from a
> clear-cut understanding that on no level and in no sphere is the Communist

153. Abd al Rahman al-Kawakibi, *Priroda despotizma i gibel 'nost' poraboshcheniia*
(Moscow, 1964), pp. 25–26. [Translated from an Arabic edition (Aleppo, 1922).—D. J.]

machine that arose after the revolution connected with Russia's historical past; it cannot be placed in the stream of Russia's cultural and spiritual traditions. This machine is not a continuation of Russia even in its worst imperial and serf-owning manifestations, no matter how skillfully and successfully it made use of the basest human characteristics produced in part by those phenomena. Their very nature, the quality of the evil, is different. . . . Russian history was broken off by the Bolshevik coup just when it was clearly moving toward liberalization and democratization, toward European balance and steadiness *(uravnoveshennost')* and more-than-European humaneness. It is from there too that it must be restored.[154]

In contrast, the U.S. Sovietologist Richard Pipes attempts to demonstrate that in nineteenth-century and twentieth-century Russia not only are there fully analogous systems but also there is total continuity.

It is my central thesis that . . . Russia belongs *par excellence* to that category of states which in the political and sociological literature it has become customary to refer to as 'patrimonial.' In such states political authority is conceived and exercised as an extension of the rights of ownership, the rules (or rulers) being both sovereigns of the realm and its proprietors. The difficulty of maintaining this type of regime in the face of steadily increased contact and rivalry with a differently governed west had brought about in Russia a condition of permanent internal tension that has not been resolved to this day.

Pipes does not deny that after the abolition of serfdom a slow movement in the direction of liberalization began, but he contends that after the assassination of Alexander II by the Narodniks such movement stopped almost completely.

In its eagerness to meet the threat posed by terrorism, the imperial government greatly over-reacted. It began to set in motion, sometimes overtly, sometimes secretly, all kinds of countermeasures, which in their totality strikingly anticipated the modern police state and even contained some seeds of totalitarianism. Between 1878 and 1881 in Russia the legal and institutional bases were laid for a bureaucratic-police regime with totalitarian overtones that have not been dismantled since. The roots of modern totalitarianism, one may well argue, are sought more properly here than in the ideas of a Rousseau or Hegel or Marx. For while ideas can always beget other ideas, they produce insititutional changes only if they fall on a soil well conditioned to receive them.[155]

I am convinced that the truth lies somewhere in between these two extreme viewpoints. The course of history cannot be broken off by even the most radical revolution, and although the very nature of the social

154. Irina Ilovaiskaya, *Russkaya mysl*, September 17, 1981.
155. Richard Pipes, *Russia Under the Old Regime* (New York, 1974), pp. xxii, 298. [The author cites a Russian-language edition: *(Rossiia pri starom rezhime* (Cambridge, MA, 1980), pp. xiv, 400.—G. S.]

revolution signified a decisive break with the establishment and customary ways of the ancien regime, the character of the revolution itself and the way it turned out are related to the character and particular features of the old society. In a revolution there exists both negation of the past and maintenance of continuity; therefore it is wrong to call attention to one aspect and ignore the other in the interrelation of past and present. Besides, just as Russia passed through a number of different periods during the seven decades before the revolution, so too the Soviet Union has passed through several stages since the revolution, one of them being the era of Stalin and Stalinism.

In reply to *Russkaya mysl* I say: It was not the course of Russian history that was broken off, but *tsarist* Russian history, and the break occurred not while Russia was on its way to achieving "European balance and steadiness" but as the outcome of a murderous world war centered in Europe, which was being waged not over some humanist ideals but over colonial possessions and the redivision of the world. The Bolsheviks themselves did not want any identification between the Russian and Soviet state systems. That was why Lenin commented with such pained impatience on the numerous instances in which features of the old tsarist system became visible behind the facade of the Soviet machinery of state. Such matters were far less upsetting to Stalin. In fact, he consciously reintroduced into Soviet reality many of the customs, manners, and usages that had been typical of the Russian autocratic and bureaucratic system. But even Stalin could not restore that system "in its totality," as Pipes suggests was done.

The Bolsheviks frequently took note not only of the revolutionary character of the Russian working class but also of the extreme backwardness of the Russian masses in general. That was why, as Lenin often warned, it was comparatively easy to begin a socialist revolution in Russia, but it would be much harder to carry it through to the end, in the minds of the people as well as in the economy.

In a more advanced capitalist country the culture that the people would inherit after a socialist revolution would be mainly bourgeois and not socialist. Some revolutionaries therefore considered the illiteracy of the Russian people an advantage, not a drawback, since the people would be more receptive to revolutionary propaganda and socialist ideas, not knowing any others. But that was a dubious argument. It is true that in the tens of thousands of circles for the eradication of illiteracy created after the revolution the peasants and workers studied not only the Russian and Ukrainian alphabets, for example, but also "the ABC's of Communism." They accepted the ideology of Marxist socialism, but in an extremely oversimplified form. Later on, this situation made it possible for completely distorted concepts of socialism and Marxism to be instilled among the masses.

The Stalinist dictatorship was undoubtedly parasitic on the shortcomings of the masses in revolutionary Russia. Stalin cleverly used not only their revolutionary passion, their hatred for enemies of the revolution, but also their low level of culture. The oversimplified slogans he issued in the thirties—the intensification of the class struggle under socialism, the need to destroy "enemies of the people"—captured the mass mood, becoming thus a powerful material force in support of Stalin's dictatorship. As Mikhail Baitalsky has rightly noted:

> Lack of education is a threat to the very existence of a true commitment to ideas and principles (ideionost'). The danger is that it will turn such commitment into fanaticism. Fanaticism is devotion to the letter rather than the spirit of a doctrine. It transforms scientific theory, in the case of fanaticism in science, into an ossified dogma like religion. The fanatic is blind. The raising of his theoretical level is no help. At best fanaticism is merely enriched with more quotations. [In our country] there existed a gigantic school aimed at reeducating principled Communists to be fanatics, a school of half-education, of Talmudic literalism (nachetnichestvo), of religious sanctimoniousness, a school of dogmatism and the worship of quotations, a school that turned Marxism into something like preaching from the Koran, the transformed commitment to ideas into orthodoxy. The founder and first teacher of this gigantic Madrassa [Islamic religious school] was Stalin. By his services in this area he can rightly be awarded the title "great Koran-izer of Marxism." [156]

The problem of the relationship between Stalin's cult and the masses cannot be reduced simply to the masses' lack of education. Some historians and political commentators have tried to connect the cult of Stalin with the peculiarities of the Russian peasantry, its tsarist illusions and religiosity. Grigory Pomerants, for example, upheld this viewpoint in a pamphlet:

> Centuries of Tatar rule and serfdom left a considerable tradition of servility and shamelessness (kholuistvo i khamstvo). The revolution shook it, but, on the other hand the revolution wrenched masses of peasants away from their old nesting places, transformed whole strata of a patriarchal people into masses who had lost their old mainstays but had not assimilated much of the new ideology. These masses wanted nothing like an extension and strengthening of freedom;

156. Baitalsky, "Tetradi dlia vnukov."

they hardly understood what freedom of the individual is. They wanted a boss and order. That was Stalin's mandate No. 2. Mandate No. 3 was a decapitated religion. The muzhik believed in God; in pictures of the Savior and the Kazan Mother of God he found something to love, to worship unselfishly. . . . They explained to the muzhik that there is no god, but that did not destroy his religious feeling. And Stalin gave the toilers a god, an earthly god, of whom it was impossible to say that he did not exist. He did exist, he existed in the Kremlin, and now and then he would appear on a platform and wave his hand. He was endlessly concerned that not a hair should fall from a toiler's head.[157]

Such explanations are oversimplified. The new cult of the living god did not replace the muzhik's old god. The old religion, though weakened, retained great rural strength in the thirties and especially in the forties. Religion was not "decapitated," and therefore faith in Stalin could hardly be considered the result of the peasants' unsatisfied religious feelings. Secondly, Stalin's cult proceeded not from the village to the city but from the city to the village. It originated in the early thirties, when conditions were very bad in the newly collectivized villages. Millions of peasant families had been deported to the north and to Siberia. In many areas there was famine. The peasant masses were dissatisfied with the policy of forced state procurements at arbitrary prices. In some areas grain strikes broke out. Thus conditions in the countryside were obviously unfavorable to the rise and consolidation of Stalin's cult, which probably had its fewest devotees there.

The cult also had little appeal to the petty-bourgeois urban masses. They too were dissatisfied in the early thirties, but they were also tired and politically apathetic as a result of the long years of war, first imperialist and then civil. Such apolitical petty bourgeois were unlikely to grow ecstatic over Stalin.

In my view Stalin's cult was strongest in the party stratum of the working class, among the new young intelligentsia, and most especially in the party and state apparatus, particularly the apparatus that took shape after the repression of 1936–1938. In short, appraisal of the cult's influence requires a differential approach; the people cannot be regarded as an undifferentiated mass. Furthermore, all these problems require concrete sociological analysis.

The same rule applies to the low educational and cultural level of the workers and peasants. Obviously ignorance, lack of education, defects in moral values, and an abundance of potentially authoritarian personality

157. See Pomerants, "Nravstvennyi oblik istoricheskoi lichnosti," in his *Neopublikovannoe* (n.p., n.d.), p. 218.

types played a very important role in the establishment of the Stalinist dictatorship. "Ignorance," wrote the young Marx, "is a demonic force, and we fear that it will serve as the cause of still more tragedies."[158] But in this connection I must speak first of all not about the ignorance and rudeness of the masses but about the ignorance and rudeness of the leaders, those who found themselves at the helm of state during the years of Stalin's cult.

The theory that genuine socialism is impossible without a certain cultural and moral level in society is not new. In the nineteenth century Herbert Spencer argued this case at great length, against liberal reformers as well as socialists. He noted that voluntary associations of these people invariably acquired an authoritarian structure and asked what could be expected if they achieved state power. Drawing analogies with such disparate states as those of medieval European, Japan, and contemporary Germany, where Bismarck showed "leanings towards State socialism," Spencer envisioned a centralized bureaucratic despotism if socialists came to power. If the socialist state became involved in foreign war or internal dissension, he predicted "a grinding tyranny like that of ancient Peru," with a revival of forced labor and universal surveillance. Analogies and prophecies aside, the heart of Spencer's analysis was his insistence that

the machinery of communism, like existing social machinery, has to be framed out of existing human nature; and the defects of existing human nature will generate in the one the same evils as in the other. . . . The belief, not only of the socialists but also of those so-called liberals who are diligently preparing the way for them, is that by due skill an ill-working humanity may be framed into well-working institutions. It is a delusion. . . . There is no political alchemy by which you can get golden conduct out of leaden instincts.[159]

Dostoevsky expounded views similar to Spencer's. In 1877, for example, he wrote:

It is clear and intelligible to the point of obviousness that evil in mankind is concealed deeper than the physician-socialists suppose; that in no organization of society can evil be eliminated; that the human soul will remain identical; that abnormality and sin emanate from the soul itself; and finally, that the laws of the human spirit are so unknown to science, so obscure, so indeterminate and mysterious that, as yet, there can be neither physicians nor *final* judges, but that

158. Marx and Engels, *Sochineniia*, 2d ed., 1:112.
159. Spencer, *The Man Versus the State* (London, 1881). [The Author cites the Russian translation, *Lichnost i gosudarstvo*, St. Petersburg, 1908, pp. 31–33.—D. J.]

there is only He who saith: "Vengeance belongeth unto me; I will recompense."[160]

There is some particle of truth in these arguments, but on the whole Marxism rejects any attempt to derive the forms of social organization directly from biological and social instincts supposedly inherent in humanity. If it is true that the morality and "social instincts" of the population influence the social organization, it is also true that the social organization can very strongly influence morality and "instincts."

Nevertheless the problem that Spencer raised was not satisfactorily dealt with in Marxist writings of the nineteenth century. Both Marx and Engels expected that the socialist revolution would simultaneously triumph in the most culturally advanced countries of Europe. In the early twentieth century, as the center of the revolutionary movement shifted to Russia, the interrelation of socialism and culture was debated among Social Democrats. Not only Western socialists but also the Russian Mensheviks and even some Bolsheviks felt that a socialist revolution could not triumph in Russia because of its backwardness. The majority of Bolsheviks decisively rejected such hesitations, although they did not deny Russia's backwardness. Lenin, for example, wrote:

> If a certain cultural level is required for the creation of socialism (though no one can say just what this "cultural level" is, for it is different in each West European country), then why can we not begin from the beginning by winning the preconditions for this certain level through revolution, and then, on the basis of the workers' and peasants' power and the Soviet system, move to catch up with other nations? . . . For the creation of socialism, you will say, people must be civilized. Very good. But why could we not begin by creating such preconditions for the civilization of people as getting rid of noble landlords and . . . capitalists?[161]

This was a correct position in principle, but one that was extremely difficult to carry out. Proceeding from this premise, the Bolsheviks undertook a cultural as well as a social revolution. Nevertheless, as Lenin himself noted more than once, it was extremely difficult to raise the level of culture and civilization not only among the masses but also in the apparatus of the workers' and peasants' government, and in the Bolshevik Party apparatus itself. In discussing the creation of a truly civilized and

160. [See Dostoevsky, *Diary of a Writer* (New York, 1954), p. 787. —G. S.]
161. Lenin, PSS, 45:380–381.

socialist state apparatus in Soviet Russia, Lenin indicated the following difficulties.

What elements do we have for building this apparatus? Only two. First, the workers who are absorbed in the struggle for socialism. These elements are insufficiently enlightened. They would like to give us a better apparatus, but they do not know how. They cannot build one. They have not yet developed within themselves the level of culture and advancement that is necessary for this. And it is precisely culture that is necessary for this. . . . Secondly, we have elements of knowledge, education, and training, but they are ridiculously inadequate compared with all other countries.[162]

There is no question that with Stalin's rise to power, the general level of leadership dropped even more, from the point of view of methods as well as culture, morality, and degree of civilization. At a time when the number of specialists and educated people was increasing at the lower and middle levels of the state and economic administration, many of those in Stalin's retinue were distinguished by shocking ignorance and rudeness. Stalin himself remained to the end of his life an uneducated man, although he pretended to be a "scholar of genius" and "a coryphaeus of science." The NKVD apparatus was recruited from ignorant people who despised the intelligentsia. A glaring lack of culture was also the hallmark of many in the new intelligentsia who took prominent places in literature, art, and science in the thirties and forties.

The lack of general culture and morality was accompanied by a poor understanding of Marxism and scientific socialism, a failure to comprehend the contradictions in the new social system and the ways to overcome them. Under such a leadership the political and cultural development of the masses inevitably became extremely one-sided. The core of the working class and party kept their revolutionary spirit, their desire to build socialism and to fight fascism and imperialism, but this spirit was not supplemented by properly organized political education and moral training. Therefore, it could not serve as a substantial obstacle to the establishment of Stalin's autocracy.

The subject of Russia's backwardness and lack of culture has sometimes been handled in a very strange way by certain Western Sovietologists—to try to absolve Stalin of all sins. Theodore Von Laue, for example, is convinced that Russia in general and the October and February revolu-

162. Ibid., pp. 390–391. [From the article "Better Fewer, But Better." Cf. CW, 33: 488.—G. S.]

tions in particular cannot be judged by "Western standards." In his opinion it was the dark and reactionary masses who came to the fore in 1917 and totally destroyed the Europeanized state structure that had been erected by the tsars and the aristocracy. In the "bloody nightmare" that began in 1917 the creation of a normal state system was impossible. The illiterate, apolitical, and savage Russian masses, Von Laue claims, could be subdued only by a cruel dictator, and they even desired such a dictator. Stalin understood the needs of the country, which had been destroyed by the revolution, and therefore he was the country's best way out under the existing circumstances. Pushed forward by the reactionary and savage masses, Stalin combined revolutionary idealism with a willingness to commit crimes and in that way was able to harness the masses and mobilize them for the modernization of Russia. According to Von Laue, it was Stalin who knew how to overcome the chaos, restore order, and put the country back on its feet; he prepared the Soviet Union for war and won the war when it came; and no other methods could have achieved those results in such a savage country. [163]

Lenin's comment that it is sometimes necessary to fight against barbarism by barbarous means is fairly well known. But Von Laue carries this idea to the point of absurdity, disregarding the massive evidence that Stalin's methods of terror and violence were faulty and destructive and were by no means the only ones possible or necessary.

163. See the magazine *Union sovietique*, 1984, no. 11, pt. 1, pp. 76–79. Von Laue, an American Sovietologist, is also the author of *Why Lenin? Why Stalin? A Reappraisal of the Russian Revolution, 1900–1930* (New York, 1964). He still regards the people of the USSR as fairly ignorant, as they were in the Stalin era, and argues that for this kind of population, especially in the presence of external danger, repression continues to be necessary. In the same issue of *Union sovietique* (pp. 90–92) he disagrees with the hopes of "Medvedev and his friends" for a gradual liberalization. The KGB and the Politburo, he writes, have a better understanding of their country.

SOME CONSEQUENCES OF STALIN'S PERSONAL DICTATORSHIP

IV

12

ERRORS IN DIPLOMACY AND WAR

■ 1

STALIN'S FOREIGN POLICY IN 1939–1940

The main theme of this book, which has been determined both by my own intention and by the sources available to me, is the description and analysis of the events in Soviet society from the twenties through the forties which resulted in the establishment of Stalin's bloody one-man dictatorship. In other words, I am talking about the genesis, nature, and consequences of the phenomenon or system of Stalinism. An examination of the foreign policy of the Soviet Union under Stalin was not one of the aims I set myself, and therefore in the first part of this book I made only some brief comments on Stalin's policy in the international working-class movement in the late twenties and early thirties.

Because of a lack of sources it is not possible to analyze here Stalin's extremely ambiguous policy toward the Spanish Republic from 1936 to 1939, during the period of democratic revolution and civil war in Spain. Stalin's obvious indifference, even his veiled opposition, to the policy of a united antifascist front, proclaimed at the Seventh Comintern Congress, substantially affected the fate of Republican Spain. It is common knowledge that soon after the fascist rebellion and the beginning of the civil war in Spain the Soviet Union began to aid and support the Spanish Republic. The Communist parties of many countries also gave considerable aid to Republican Spain through the Comintern. The International Brigades, which consisted mainly of Communists from various countries, were an important part of the Spanish Republican army. However, Soviet sources do not usually indicate that at the very time when arms began to reach Spain from the Soviet Union the Spanish Republic sent to the USSR the greater part of its gold reserves, which had previously been kept in the vaults of the Bank of Spain. Although this was not meant as payment for the Soviet military deliveries, it is nevertheless highly unlikely that the Soviet Union ever returned the gold to Spain.

Soviet military aid to the Spanish Republic was many times smaller than the aid to General Franco from Fascist Italy and Hitler's Germany. By the end of 1936 the Soviet Union had supplied Spain with 106 tanks, 60 armored cars, 136 airplanes, more than 60,000 rifles, 174 field guns, 3,727 machine guns, and an unspecified amount of ammunition.[1] This was not very much aid considering the scale of the fighting in Spain. The antifascist sentiments of Soviet citizens were very strong, with tens of thousands expressing their desire to help fight fascism in Spain. But the total number of Soviet volunteers and military specialists allowed to go to Spain by Stalin was no more than 2,000, possibly as little as 1,500.

Besides, the Soviet specialists not only helped organize the army of the young republic. Quite a few of the "specialists" who arrived in Spain helped to establish a powerful repressive police apparatus that engaged in mass terror against the extreme Left—anarchist groups, anarcho-syndicalist organizations, and the more radical left-socialist groups, which were slanderously accused of "Trotskyism," ties with "fascism," and so forth. In fact these groups and organizations were in many areas the main driving force of the revolution in its early stages. In Catalonia collectivized industrial enterprises were dissolved, as were the free anarchist

1. *Istoriia KPSS*, vol. 4, bk. 2 (Moscow 1971), pp. 348–349.

communes in Aragon. Such policies, of course, completely contradicted the idea of a united front against fascism.

In 1937 the Soviet Union's military aid to the Spanish Republic began to decrease markedly, and in 1938, a year before the collapse of the republic, it dwindled to nearly nothing. Stalin's patent indifference to the needs and fate of the Spanish revolution was related first of all to internal events in the USSR. In 1937–1938 Stalin was too busy organizing the mass repression in his own country. It was at this very time that the NKVD apparatus was significantly expanded, and millions of people found themselves in camps and prisons.

It may also be assumed that Stalin wanted to take his distance from the events in Spain, that he did not want a victory over facism there that would have been seen as the result of maximum support by the Soviet Union. Such a victory would have complicated any subsequent agreement with fascist Germany—something that was on Stalin's mind long before 1939.

Certain facts are now known about the secret contacts between Soviet and Nazi diplomats from 1933 to 1938.[2] Certainly diplomacy and actual policy do not always coincide, nor can all contacts and discussions be appraised in an oversimplified, one-dimensional way. Many of the secret contacts between Soviet representatives and German diplomatic or business figures were a kind of diplomatic "reconnaissance." This "reconnaissance" showed, however, that Germany was not ready to discuss improved relations with the Soviet Union, let alone a nonaggression pact, and that the main obstacle to such moves at that time was Hitler himself. Still, the Soviet Union was able to obtain quite a large loan of credit from Germany and the signing of a Soviet-German economic accord.

At the same time, however, it was obvious that a rapprochement between the Soviet Union and France, marked by the signing of a mutual assistance treaty, was proceeding at an even more intense pace. The Soviet Union had also joined the League of Nations and was conducting intensive diplomatic and political activities aimed at curbing the aggressive aims and actions of the ruling circles in Germany, Italy, and Japan.

The policy of the Soviet Union found very little support among the ruling parties of England and France. They, like Hitler, were pursuing a double game at that time, playing now an anti-Soviet card, now an antifascist one. Under the circumstances, Soviet diplomats also had to

2. Yevgeny Gnedin, *Iz istorii otnoshenii mezhdu SSSR i fashistskoi Germaniei* (New York, 1977).

play a double game. In 1938 and early 1939 this went on to Hitler's obvious advantage. With a minimum military force he was able to annex Austria and the Sudentenland and then occupy all of Czechoslovakia.

In April 1939 diplomatic negotiations among the Soviet Union, England, and France were reactivated with the aim of establishing a system of collective security in Europe. But the most important Soviet proposals were rejected, while many of the English and French proposals were clearly unacceptable to the USSR. Moreover, the government of Neville Chamberlain secretly continued to seek an agreement with the Germans to guarantee England's security. The French and English ruling circles had obviously not abandoned their primary hope of turning German aggression eastward, against the Soviet state. Under these conditions Soviet diplomats again began to seek contacts with Germany. Stepped-up contacts of this kind required a change in the Soviet diplomatic leadership. On May 3, 1939, a decree of the Presidium of the USSR Supreme Soviet announced that Maxim Litvinov, "at his own request," was being relieved of his duties as people's commissar of foreign affairs. His replacement was Molotov, who retained his post as chairman of the Council of People's Commissars (the equivalent of premier).

Litvinov's removal caused a sensation in the world of diplomacy in Western Europe. Only the day before he had received the British ambassador in Moscow and was among the honored guests at the May Day parade and celebration. It soon became apparent that the dismissal of Litvinov, known as an active opponent of closer ties with Germany and a Jew by nationality, was an important step for Stalin on the road to a treaty with Germany. Soon after Molotov's appointment the number of contacts with Germany increased (talks between Soviet chargé d'affaires Georgy Astakhov and Julius Schnurre, an expert in the German Foreign Ministry; between Molotov and the German ambassador, Schulenburg; and others). By taking these diplomatic steps, the Soviet government sought to upset a possible agreement between Germany and the more conservative ruling circles of France and Britain. It also wanted to insure itself in the event of failure in the negotiations then being held for a mutual assistance treaty among the Soviet Union, Britain, and France. Unfortunately, these negotiations were being conducted by Britain and France in a way that made failure far more likely than success.

In July and early August of 1939 diplomatic contacts between Germany and the Soviet Union multiplied. Germany now clearly sought to conclude a nonaggression pact with the Soviet Union. For Germany the question of war with Poland had already been decided, but England and France were sure to be drawn into such a war. Hitler feared a war on two fronts and urged his diplomats to hurry in reaching an accord with Stalin. While not abandoning plans for further eastward expansion, Hitler first wanted to smash Poland and his opponents in the West.

The nonaggression pact between Germany and the Soviet Union was not the best solution for either the Soviet Union or the forces favoring peace in the world. A collective-security treaty among all the antifascist powers would have been far preferable, but the United States was keeping its distance from European affairs, while England and France were playing an insecure and dangerous political game. They dragged out the negotiations with the Soviet Union while holding secret talks with Germany, still hoping that Germany would direct its aggression eastward.[3]

England and France were assuring Poland of their support, but it was entirely possible that in the event of war between Poland and Germany, England and France would continue their policy of nonintervention. It was both advantageous and important for them that, after a decisive victory over Poland, Germany should gain wide access to the Soviet border. Meanwhile in the summer of 1939 bloody clashes were taking place in the east between Japanese units and the allied forces of the Soviet Union and the People's Republic of Mongolia. Thus the Soviet leadership was also faced with the specter of a two-front war—against Germany and Japan. Stalin, who only a short time before had wiped out his country's best military leaders, knew that the Soviet Union was unprepared for such a war. He needed to stall for time. The Soviet Union was forced to choose the lesser of two evils. In the conditions that prevailed there was no way out other than to agree to Germany's proposal for a nonaggression pact.

On August 19 Stalin made his decision. On August 20–21 there was an exchange of telegrams between Hitler and Stalin, and it was decided that a German delegation headed by Ribbentrop would go to Moscow as quickly as possible. Hitler did not conceal from Stalin that Germany had decided to invade Poland. "The tension between Germany and Poland," Hitler wrote in a telegram, "has become intolerable. A crisis could erupt any day. Germany must look after the interests of the Reich by every means at its disposal." On August 23 the German delegation arrived in Moscow, and the nonaggression pact was signed the very same day.

3. For details on these negotiations see P. A. Zhilin, *Kak fashistskaya Germaniia gotovila napadenie na Sovietskii Soiuz* (Moscow, 1966).

Most Western authors recount these events in a very tendentious manner—as though the Soviet Union were responsible for supporting Hitler in his attack on Poland and thus contributing to the outbreak of World War II. But this opinion is mistaken.

I do not intend to justify Stalin's entire policy. I have already shown how he obstructed a united front in Germany, decimated the Comintern, dissolved the Polish Communist Party, killed the best Red Army commanders. All this greatly facilitated Hitler's drive to war. But the nonaggression pact should not be added to this list of Stalin's errors and crimes.

The Soviet government was compelled to sign the pact because Britain and France, with their policy of toleration and nonintervention, had been encouraging German fascism and had helped Germany recreate a strong military machine in the hope that it would be used against Bolshevism. Some of the big corporations in the United States had also helped, with the same aim in mind. The Munich accord of 1938, agreed to by Germany, Italy, England, and France, was what truly unleashed Hitler. After the occupation of Austria and Czechoslovakia the next step for Germany was almost certainly to try to destroy Poland. It was also clear to Hitler that England and France would "give up" Poland if they could be certain that German aggression would be directed eastward. "The enemy cherishes the hope," Hitler declared at a military conference in Berlin on August 22, 1939, "that Russia will become our enemy after the conquest of Poland." Hitler considered France and Britain the weaker opponents, however, and at first planned to make war only on his Western front. To this day every document published in the West has confirmed that the Western governments of that time were responsible for the breakdown of negotiations for collective security in Europe. Under these circumstances the Soviet Union had to look after its own interests and security. In 1939 the nonaggression pact with Germany served that purpose.

Stalin's blunder was not the pact itself but the attendant psychological and political atmosphere that he created. He put too much trust in his pact with Hitler and failed to perceive Germany's real plans for an invasion. As Konstantin Simonov has written:

> It still seems to me that the pact of 1939 was founded on raison d'état, in the almost hopeless situation we were in back then, the summer of 1939, when the danger of the Western states pushing fascist Germany against us became immediate and real. And yet, when you look back, you feel that for all the logic of

raison d'état in this pact, much that accompanied its conclusion took away from us, simply as people, for almost two years, some part of that exceptionally important sense of ourselves, which was and is our precious peculiarity, connected with such a concept as "the first socialist state in the world." . . . That is, something happened which was in a moral sense very bad.[4]

Special attention must be paid to the secret protocols signed at the same time as the nonaggression pact. They provided for the division of Poland into German and Soviet spheres of influence "in the event of territorial and political changes on the territory belonging to the Polish state." Some historians regard these agreements as totally wrong and speak of the "fourth partition of Poland." In their view the Soviet Union could simply have liberated the Polish-occupied parts of Byelorussia and the Ukraine without any preliminary agreement with Germany. England and France had already declared war on Germany, they argue, and Germany would have had to resign itself to the actions of the Red Army. The fact is, however, that at the end of August 1939 no one could have said for certain how England and France would act after Germany's invasion of Poland. They might still have refrained from declaring war. Both the prospect of German troops emerging on the Soviet border after occupying all of Poland and that of Soviet troops entering Polish territory without prior agreement with Germany entailed great dangers. I must agree that the secret protocols attached to the nonaggression pact were a natural extension of that pact. The Soviet Union was unable to prevent Germany's invasion of Poland, but it could see to the strengthening of its own defensive positions in case of possible complications—especially since the territory involved was not strictly Polish but one where the local Byelorussian and Ukrainian populations had long been struggling for national liberation.

Although I view the nonaggression pact with Germany as one forced upon the Soviet Union by necessity, since in political dealings it is often necessary to choose the lesser evil, the signing of the so-called German-Soviet Friendship and Border Treaty on September 29, 1939, can be seen only as a great mistake. There was no necessity for it. Only one month earlier Stalin had reasoned far more realistically. During the August negotiations, when Ribbentrop had proposed that a preamble on the friendly nature of German-Soviet relations be added to the nonaggression pact, Stalin had categorically refused, stating:

4. Konstantin Simonov, "Uroki istorii i sovest' pisatelia," unpublished manuscript; a copy of which is in my archives.

The Soviet government could not honestly assure the Soviet people that friendly relations exist with Germany when for six years the Nazi government has been pouring buckets of slop on the Soviet government.[5]

"Friendly" relations between the Soviet Union and Germany required important changes not only in Soviet foreign policy but in ideological activity and Comintern policy as well. Beginning in the fall of 1939 there was a complete halt to antifascist propaganda. Soviet leaders began almost to justify Hitler's actions, as though Germany were being attacked by England and France. Speaking before the fifth special session of the Supreme Soviet on October 31, 1939, Molotov declared:

During the last few months such concepts as "aggression" and "aggressor" have acquired a new concrete content, have taken on another meaning. . . . Now . . . it is Germany that is striving for a quick end to the war, for peace, while England and France, who only yesterday were campaigning against aggression, are for continuation of the war and against concluding a peace. Roles, as you see, change. . . . The ideology of Hitlerism, like any other ideological system, can be accepted or rejected—that is a matter of one's political views. But everyone can see that an ideology cannot be destroyed by force. . . . Thus it is not only senseless, it is criminal to wage such a war as a war for "the destruction of Hitlerism," under the false flag of a struggle for democracy.[6]

After this speech Beria gave a secret order to the GULAG administration forbidding camp guards to call political prisoners "fascists." The order was rescinded only on June 22, 1941.

In plain violation of the resolutions of the Seventh Comintern Congress, Stalin sent a directive to all Communist parties demanding curtailment of the struggle against German fascism, naming Anglo-French imperialism as the basic aggressive force, which was to become the main target of Communist propaganda. This sudden about-face caught the Western Communist parties by surprise. The Communist parties in the Balkans, which had been making great progress, were thrown into complete disarray. Great confusion also prevailed in the Communist parties of France and England. At that time all Communist parties were considered sections of the Comintern, obliged to submit to discipline. Thus the Comintern's declaration that France and Great Britain were the aggressors, while Germany wanted peace, put the French and British Communists in an especially difficult position. The logic of the directive

5. P. A. Zhilin, *Kak fashistskaia Germaniia . . .* , p. 61.
6. *Stenograficheskii otchet vneocherednoi piatoi sessii Verkhovnogo Soveta SSSR* (Moscow, 1939), pp. 8–10.

required Communists in those countries to oppose the military efforts of their bourgeois governments.

This policy did not have much significance in Britain, where the Communist Party was relatively small. But in France, where the party was strong, this antiwar position markedly weakened national resistance to German aggression and facilitated a government ban on the Communist Party. The resulting political tension worked to Hitler's advantage in those months. At the turn of the year some illegal French Communist publications were demanding that the French government end the imperialist war with Germany. To be sure, the French CP changed its line in the spring of 1940, when German armies invaded France. The underground Central Committee informed the government that it would consider the surrender of Paris treason, and called on it to arm the people and turn Paris into an impregnable fortress. After the fall of France in June the Communists called for resistance to the occupiers, but even then some French activists believed that the German-Soviet nonaggression pact meant a nonaggression pact between Nazism and Communism. Late in 1940 some of them had serious hopes of legal activity in occupied territory and even prepared to publish *L'Humanité* legally in Paris. Only at the beginning of 1941, when Communists were arrested and shot en masse, did such illusions dissolve, and the Central Committee began to take a more clear-cut antifascist stand. However, armed struggle against the Nazis began in earnest only after the German attack on the Soviet Union.

The left Socialists, who after the Seventh Comintern Congress had worked with the Communists in the antifascist struggle in France, Spain, Italy and elsewhere, were indignant over the "friendship" between the Soviet Union and Germany in 1939–1940. Their press declared outright that the Soviet Union had deserted the front, that Moscow had destroyed solidarity with the proletariat fighting Nazism.

It is certain that the Soviet-German nonaggression pact delayed the Soviet Union's entry into the war by two years. But is is equally certain that the delay was used more effectively by Germany than by the Soviet Union. Germany increased its military potential in those years much faster. Seizing one country after another with minimal losses, Germany continually improved its strategic position while providing its army with considerable combat experience.

For example, in the spring of 1940 without any provocation Germany attacked and occupied Denmark and Norway. In the summer of 1940, in violation of the neutrality of Belgium and Holland and of existing agreements between them and Germany, Hitler's armies invaded those countries, crushed all resistance, and occupied them. German divisions went on to invade France, advancing swiftly. After several weeks France capitulated, while the British Expeditionary Corps, abandoning its heavy arms, was barely able to evacuate Dunkerque and return to Britain. France's quick defeat was unexpected even by many German generals. For Stalin, it was an extremely unpleasant surprise. He had counted on a long war in the West.

It was difficult not to condemn Germany's aggression in Western Europe, but the "friendship" treaty obliged the Soviet Union to refrain from any such statements. After the total defeat of France the Soviet press even emphasized the importance of the Soviet-German "friendship" treaty in creating "a peaceful front for Germany to its east." *Pravda* quoted complacent statements from Nazi newspapers stating that precisely because of the Soviet-German accords the German "offensive in the West developed successfully."[7]

It must be stressed that Stalin did not stop at "friendship" with Hitler. In the second half of 1940 he entered into negotiations with Germany concerning worldwide spheres of influence after the presumed defeat of Great Britain. These negotiations were begun on Hitler's initiative, since he wanted to divert Stalin's attention from German preparations for war against the Soviet Union. And to a certain extent, Stalin took the bait. He even agreed to negotiations concerning the adherence of the Soviet Union to the Tripartite (Anti-Comintern) Pact. These negotiations for an *alliance* with Germany were eventually broken off, though not by Stalin; Hitler simply stopped answering Stalin's letters on the subject.

■ 2
WAR WITH FINLAND

It is not possible for me to examine here the complex political, legal, and national problems connected with the "peaceful" incorporation into the Soviet Union of such countries as Estonia, Latvia, and Lithuania. In 1939–1940 hardly anyone was concerned about abiding by international legal standards. The Soviet Union hastened to take advantage of the

7. *Pravda*, August 26, 1940.

situation in Western Europe to establish more favorable borders and better strategic positions before its inevitable entry, sooner or later, into the world war. Stalin was also not indifferent to the question of expanding Soviet territory. He was already beginning to think in terms of the former Russian empire, hoping to "regain" a large part of the territory that once had been part of it.

The incorporation of Estonia, Latvia, Lithuania, Bessarabia, and Northern Bukovina took place without war. With Finland it was different. The Soviet Union proposed to exchange Finnish territory bordering on Leningrad for a section of land in central Karelia—a trade that could not be considered fair by any stretch of the imagination. The Karelian isthmus had great economic significance for Finland, while the territory offered in return was mainly undeveloped. The Karelian isthmus was also vital to Finland's security. Over the course of many years several lines of strong defensive fortifications had been built there (the Mannerheim Line). Deprived of those, Finland would have been left with an unprotected border, its future dependent on Stalin's good will. Not surprisingly, Finland rejected the Soviet proposal.

In and of itself, Finland posed no threat to the Soviet Union. There were no British, French, or German troops on Finnish soil at that time, and though Finland was largely under the influence of France and Britain, it had taken a neutral stand when they declared war on Germany. Thus the threat to the Soviet Union's northern border was not great enough to justify, even in part, a preventive war against Finland. Stalin, however, thought that such a war could be easily won. He sought to take advantage of the world situation not only to strengthen the Soviet Union's western border but also if possible to establish a "Soviet" Finland.

The writer Aleksandr Chakovsky, in his documentary novel *The Blockade*, which is based on historical materials made available to him, relates that the Chief Military Council met in Moscow in mid-autumn 1940. The topic of discussion was a plan for military action against Finland. Stalin rejected the plan, drawn up by the General Staff under Marshal B. M. Shaposhnikov, and harshly criticized the Marshal for supposedly underestimating the strength of the Red Army and overestimating that of the Finns. When the command of the Leningrad Military District was told to draw up a new one, based on the Chief Military Council's discussion, the result was a strategy for fighting with "little loss of blood," counting on a rapid victory, using limited forces, without a concentration of reserves. It was this plan that doomed Soviet troops to long weeks of failures and heavy losses.[8]

Stalin and Voroshilov were convinced the war would last only a few days. So sure were they of a quick victory that Shaposhnikov was not even given advance notice; he was on leave when he heard that war had begun. It did not produce a quick victory. The Red Army did not have enough experience or experienced officers (after the recent purges) to break through the Mannerheim Line in a sudden rush. Suffering heavy losses, it was stopped at the first line of defense. The Soviet Union was obliged to wage a bloody and exhausting winter campaign, concentrating between thirty and forty divisions against Finland. The number of killed, wounded, and frostbitten on the Soviet side was in the tens of thousands.

The overall plan for the war, approved by Stalin, envisaged the occupation of all of Finland and the change of its government. Soon after the outbreak of war the formation of a new "people's democratic" government of Finland, headed by Otto Kuusinen, was announced, and the program of the new government was published in the Soviet press. Little Finland's long and stubborn resistance aroused great sympathy throughout the world. It was probably the reaction of world public opinion that prompted Stalin eventually to abandon his plans for a "Soviet" Finland and dissolve the Kuusinen "government."

In the peace talks, which the Finns asked for after the Mannerheim Line was finally broken in the spring of 1940, Stalin accepted the existing government and limited himself to his original demands. He did not insist on guarantees against the possible later use of Finnish territory for an attack on the Soviet Union. In reaction to the war there was a predictable upsurge of revanchist tendencies in Finland. Incomprehensibly, Stalin stood by quietly as the Finnish army was rebuilt and Finland turned away from a British and French orientation to acceptance of German protection and the accumulation of German troops on Finnish soil. (By June 1941 the Germans had five divisions in Finland.)

Clearly it was the defeat of 1939–1940 that pushed Finland into Hitler's arms. In other words, it was Stalin's irrational foreign policy that moved Finland into the German camp, when it might have joined the antifascist coalition or in any case have remained neutral. This is not to justify the Finnish militarists for their participation in the German attack on the Soviet Union. But it was Stalin who helped the militarists dominate public opinion in Finland for some time.[9]

8. See Chakovsky's "Blokada," *Znamya* (1968), no. 10.

9. For the sake of objectivity I must note that in the spring of 1941 the internal political

■ 3

STALIN'S MILITARY-STRATEGIC BLUNDER OF 1941

The most serious of Stalin's mistakes in foreign policy was his misreading of the military situation in the spring and summer of 1941. Of course he and his entourage always kept in mind the possibility of war with the capitalist countries, and in the late thirties this meant specifically Germany and Japan. Preparations for such a war were made by creating a modern defense industry, military aviation, an up-to-date navy, civil-defense training for the whole population, and so on. In 1939–1941 the army increased by 2.5 times, many troops and supplies were transferred to the western districts, war production increased, and the number of military schools grew. Especially after the war with Finland, a great deal of work was done toward retraining the army. The development of new weapons was speeded up. More than a hundred thousand men were put to work on the fortification of the new western borders. Airfields were modernized, ordnance depots and ammunition dumps set up, and military exercises for troops and commanders carried out. Yet one cannot help drawing the conclusion from the overall picture that all this effort and preparation was scheduled for completion no earlier than the end of 1942. This supposition is confirmed by no less authoritative a figure than Marshal Georgy Zhukov, chief of the General Staff in the months just before the war, who wrote:

> The war caught the country in the stage of reorganizing, reequipping, and retraining the armed forces, in the stage of building up the necessary mobilization stores and state reserves. The Soviet people were not planning war, were striving to avoid it, putting all their efforts and resources into implementing their peaceful economic plans.[10]

---

situation in Finland was highly complex, and sentiments favoring neutrality were still quite strong. For that reason, neither on June 22 nor 23 nor 24 did the Finnish government order its troops to attack the USSR. During those first three days the Finns were not involved in any of the fighting in the northwest sector. Soviet forces had only some minor border clashes with relatively small German units, and some German planes tried to attack Leningrad from Finnish airbases. In the confusion and disorganization of the first days of war these facts were not analyzed as they should have been. Large-scale military action began on the Soviet-Finnish border only after June 25, when Soviet aircraft made a massive preventive strike on Finnish airbases and Soviet artillery opened fire on military targets in Finnish territory. In fact, until June 25 nowhere was there any official statement indicating that war had begun between the USSR and Finland. See S. Kabanov, *Na Dal'nykh podstupakh* (Moscow, 1970).

10. Georgy Zhukov, *Vospominaniia i razmyshleniia* (Moscow, 1969), pp. 246–247. [The

Zhukov also wrote:

The period between 1939 and the middle of 1941 was marked on the whole by transformations that *within two or three years* would have given the Soviet people a brilliant army.[11]

Yet overwhelming evidence in the spring of 1941 showed that war could not be postponed for long. The time bought by the nonaggression pact was clearly coming to an end; Stalin's calculation that war could be postponed until late 1942 or even 1943 was obviously unrealistic. Hitler and the German General Staff were closely following the steps being taken to reorganize and reequip the Red Army. They were not about to wait until that work was completed.

The intensive transfer of German troops and equipment to the Soviet border began in 1940. Early in 1941 it was sharply increased, becoming an uninterrupted flood in March and April. After May 25 as many as one hundred echelons were moved up each day.[12] By the middle of June the deployment of the German army for invasion was complete. Massed on the Soviet borders were 190 fully staffed and equipped divisions, both German and satellite, 3,500 tanks, around 4,000 planes, and 50,000 guns and mortars.

Efforts were made to keep these movements secret and to mislead Soviet intelligence, but so huge an operation could not be concealed. Numerous reports steadily poured in through various channels: the Soviet intelligence service, border units, and diplomatic corps, foreign friends of the Soviet Union, officials of the British and U.S. governments, deserters, and so on.

For example, the command of the Soviet border troops sent regular reports on the situation at the border to the party's Central Committee, to the Sovnarkom, and to the foreign affairs and defense commissariats. As early as 1940 there was systematic provocation by the Germans along the border. Border markers were deliberately destroyed, Soviet territory was fired upon, attempts were made to capture Soviet border units, anti-Soviet rallies and demonstrations were held in border towns, with the local population being forced to participate. Also, large numbers of fascist

---

English wording is taken from the translation by Progress Publishers: G. Zhukov, *Reminiscences and Reflections* (Moscow, 1985), 1:271. — G. S.]

11. Ibid. [Emphasis added. Curiously, the phrase "within two or three years" does not appear in the 1985 English translation by Progress Publishers, which is based on a later edition of Zhukov's book than the one cited by the author. — G. S.]

12. *Voenno-istoricheskii zhurnal* (1965), no. 10, pp. 33–39.

agents were sent into Soviet territory. From October 1939 to December 1940 alone more than five thousand German agents were neutralized. In the first quarter of 1941 the number of spies either arrested or eliminated was fifteen to twenty times greater than in the first quarter of 1940. In April and May the figure increased again by a factor of two or three. As a rule, professional intelligence agents were involved. Beginning in April 1941 large military reconnaissance groups headed by experienced officers of the Abwehr (German military intelligence) were infiltrated across the border. These groups carried equipment to be used for espionage and diversion, with instructions on actions to take under wartime conditions. Sometimes such groups were dressed in Red Army uniforms.[13]

The number of violations of Soviet airspace along the border increased constantly. Whereas in late 1939 training and sport planes may have crossed no more than two to four kilometers into Soviet airspace, by the end of 1940 German military aircraft were making incursions of between forty and two hundred kilometers inside Soviet territory. From January to June 1941 Soviet airspace was violated more than two hundred times.

Commanders of the border districts continually reported the deployment along the Soviet border of large military units, most of which had had combat experience in Western Europe. Troop movements were made mostly by night. All the main roads were guarded by active units, and in Poland the railroads were placed under military jurisdiction. Schools and other public buildings were commandeered for the quartering of troops, and large numbers of German medical personnel arrived in the border areas. It was obvious that fascist Germany was preparing to attack the Soviet Union, and the dispatches from the Soviet border districts spoke of this many times. For example, a report from the Ukrainian border district dated April 20, 1941, stated the following:

Information from the units of the NKVD forces in the period from April 10 to 20 confirm with full clarity the accelerated preparation of a theater of war being carried out by the German authorities and their high command both in the border area adjacent to the USSR and on Hungarian territory.[14]

In early June the deployment of land forces in preparation for military action was essentially complete. All Wehrmacht personnel on vacation

13. *Pogranichnye voiska SSSR (1939–iiun' 1941)* (Moscow, 1970). All the facts cited above are taken from the introductory article in this collection about Soviet border forces from 1939 to June 1941.

14. "Document No. 360," in *Pogranichnye voiska SSSR*.

had been recalled to their units, and the German forces began to occupy their jumping-off positions.

Reports from the border districts were confirmed by information from diplomatic personnel. The Soviet military and naval attachés in Berlin, for example, reported at the end of May 1941 that the frontier zones were almost saturated with men and equipment. The Soviet embassy in Berlin reported constant rumors of the impending attack. The rumored dates were quite varied, evidently to sow confusion: April 6, April 20, May 18, finally June 22—all Sundays. The embassy sent these rumors to Moscow regularly, and toward the end of May submitted a thorough report, which concluded that Germany's preparations for war against the Soviet Union were virtually complete, that the concentration of forces was too great to be intended for political pressure. But Stalin did not react to this report in any way.[15]

Very important information came from President Roosevelt, who had received from his agents in Germany precise information about the date and direction of the main German strikes and almost all the basic elements of the Barbarossa plan. He gave this information to Soviet Ambassador Constantine Oumansky.[16] On June 11 state security reported to Stalin that the German embassy in Moscow had been ordered by Berlin to prepare for evacuation in seven days and that diplomats were burning documents in the basement of the embassy.[17]

From the Soviet intelligence agent Richard Sorge in Japan came information of enormous importance. In May of 1941 and again in June, he reported not only the precise timing of the German attack but also the size of the army, the operational plans, and the directions of the main strikes. These reports were immediately given to Stalin, who wrote on them "For the archives," and "To be filed."

Marshal Zhukov, in his *Reminiscences and Reflections,* confirms the fact that the General Staff and military intelligence were informed of Hitler's plans. According to Zhukov, General F. I. Golikov, chief of the Soviet army's Intelligence Division (Razvedupr), presented Stalin with a report on March 20, 1941, containing information of exceptional significance. Zhukov quotes in part from the report:

Of the most probable military operations planned against the USSR, the following merits special attention:

15. V. Berezhkov, *S diplomaticheskoi missiei v Berlin* (Moscow, 1966), pp. 90–91.
16. A. M. Nekrich, *1941, 22 iiunia* (Moscow, 1965), p. 121.
17. *Voprosy istorii* (1965), no. 5, pp. 27–28.

Variant No. 3, according to information . . . relating to February 1941: "For the attack on the USSR," the message reads, "three army groups are being set up: the 1st group under the command of General Field Marshal von Bock will strike in the direction of Petrograd; the 2nd group under the command of General Field Marshal von Rundstedt, in the direction of Moscow; and the 3rd group under the command of General Field Marshal von Leeb, in the direction of Kiev. The tentative date for beginning the attack on the USSR is May 20." However, military action could be postponed to the beginning or middle of June.

1. On the basis of all the aforesaid statements and possible variants of operations this spring I consider that the most probable time operations will begin against the USSR is after the victory over England or the conclusion with her of an honorable peace treaty.

2. Rumors and documents to the effect that war against the USSR is inevitable this spring should be regarded as misinformation coming from the English or perhaps even the German intelligence service.[18]

Zhukov reports that Admiral N. G. Kuznetsov, people's commissar of the Soviet navy, attached a similar comment to his report.[19]

Zhukov gives the impression that Golikov and Kuznetsov were trying to deceive Stalin and that Stalin was taken in by their deception. Yet Zhukov himself indicates that while the top military leadership had no doubts that war was imminent, it could not convince Stalin. Golikov and Kuznetsov knew Stalin's mood and outlook very well, and they knew how intolerant he was. He did not want to hear anything contradicting his own mistaken thinking, and with the malice of a tyrant was ready to destroy anyone who dared to challenge his views. The actual contents of Golikov and Kuznestov's reports show that they attributed great importance to the intelligence they had received and were calling it to Stalin's attention. The comments they attached were a kind of insurance against Stalin's wrath.[20]

There is good evidence that even the German ambassador to the USSR, Schulenburg, a secret enemy of Hitler's, decided to warn the Soviet government a few weeks before the attack. The Soviet ambassador to Germany, V. G. Dekanozov, a friend of Beria and confidant of Stalin's, happened to be in Moscow. Schulenberg invited him to dinner, and in

18. Zhukov, *Vospominaniia i razmyshleniia*, p. 248. [The English wording is from Zhukov, *Reminiscences and Reflections*, 1:273. —G. S.]

19. See *Reminiscences and Reflections*, 1:273–274.

20. [Zhukov himself wrote that when Stalin was angry "he stopped being objective, changed abruptly before one's eyes, grew paler still, and his gaze became heavy and hard. Not many were the brave men who stood up to Stalin's anger and parried his attacks." (*Reminiscences and Reflections*, 1:366.)—G. S.]

the presence of his own diplomatic counselor, Gustav Schilger, and Pavlov, a man who served as interpreter for both Molotov and Stalin, Schulenberg asked Dekanozov to tell Stalin that Hitler might strike at the Soviet Union in the near future. But Stalin did not believe Schulenburg any more than he had Sorge, Roosevelt, and the others. He decided that the report of the German ambassador was only a blackmailing trick of Hitler's, to get new concessions from the Soviet Union.

Stalin blindly believed that Hitler would not break his pact with the Soviet Union. Any facts that did not fit the abstract scheme in Stalin's head were rejected. Indeed, he made a public show of his confidence in peace. When Yosuke Matsuoka, the Japanese Minister of Foreign Affairs, left Moscow in April 1941 Stalin and Molotov surprised everybody by seeing him off. The German ambassador, who was at the railroad station, reported that Stalin came over, hugged him, and remarked for all the crowd to hear: "We must remain friends no matter what, and you must now do everything to that end."

The disgraceful behavior of the Soviet government during the German attack on Yugoslavia is also revealing. At the end of 1940 and the beginning of 1941 German troops entered Hungary, Bulgaria, and Romania with the consent of their reactionary governments. The pressure on Yugoslavia increased until, in March 1941, Yugoslav Premier Dragisa Cvetkovic signed an agreement to join the Tripartite Pact. The result was a national uprising; a group of patriotic officers overthrew the pro-German government. The Soviet Union recognized the new government and on April 5, 1941, signed a treaty of friendship and nonaggression with it. Less than twenty-four hours later, German troops invaded Yugoslavia and subjected Belgrade to savage bombardment. Stalin did not condemn this aggression against a fraternal Slavic country. The report of German war against Yugoslavia appeared on the last page of *Pravda*, on April 7. Nothing was said about the bombardment of Belgrade. Moreover, the Soviet government closed the embassies of Yugoslavia, Greece, and Belgium, which signified recognition and encouragement of German aggression.

Of course the massing of four million German troops on the border could not be kept secret from the Soviet command. They even knew the numbers of most of the German divisions poised along the border. They sought permission to move Soviet troops to defensive positions and put them on military alert. Stalin refused. The work of the defense commissariat, the military construction organizations, and the industrial commissariats was not oriented toward the possibility of an early start to the war. Indeed, the army and industry were unprepared for the attack both psychologically and materially. Most divisions were short of their full wartime staffs. Many tank units did not have their full complement of men and equipment. There was a general shortage of spare parts, and repairs were slow. Also, a major reorganization of mechanized brigades and corps had not been completed. It is generally known that the USSR pioneered in the formation of large-scale mechanized units. On the basis of incorrect assessment of the experience in Spain, however, the mechanized units in the Soviet army were disbanded. Germany's success with powerful armor formations prompted the Soviet General Staff to revive its own mechanized corps. But according to Zhukov, things moved rather slowly in this area.

Stalin . . . seemed not to have made up his mind on the matter yet. . . . Time went on, and only in March 1941 was the decision made to activate the twenty mechanized corps that we had asked for.[21]

Consequently, in the first days of the war many tank troops did not have their tanks, and many tanks were without crews.

In June 1941 the Soviet army had very few tanks of the new type. The factories were still producing obsolete models. The same was true of airplanes. Approximately 70 or 80 percent of Soviet aircraft were inferior to comparable German planes in engineering and flight capabilities. The production of new models began to be arranged only in 1940. According to Zhukov, Soviet airfields were equally unprepared for the war. Only in February 1941 was a plan approved for the construction of 190 new airfields in the western regions. Meanwhile, reconstruction of the old fields began; they had to be enlarged for the new types of planes. Construction units of the NKVD went to work on most military airfields all at once, putting them out of use until the late fall. As a result, most military planes were transferred to civilian airports, which were located near the border and poorly defended against bombing attacks.

In artillery, production and development was behind schedule, and the High Command's artillery reserve was still inadequate. Antitank artillery brigades were not up to strength. Marshal G. I. Kulik, Stalin's

21. Zhukov, *Vospominaniia i razmyshleniia*, p. 213. [Cf. *Reminiscences and Reflections*, 1:236. —G. S.]

chief adviser on artillery questions, failed to appreciate the importance of such a powerful weapon as the "Katyusha" multiple rocket launcher. Its mass production began only in June 1941.

In addition, the main supplies of Soviet military equipment were stored not in the rear but in the threatened districts. And further, the network of roads in border areas was inadequate.

Some comment is required on the question of the fortified areas in the border regions. In the thirties a continuous chain of strong defensive structures had been erected along the entire western border of the Soviet Union, at considerable cost in labor and resources. The General Staff under Shaposhnikov held that even after the incorporation of the new territories the main line of defense in the west should remain along the old border, which had been thoroughly studied and was well fortified. That was where the main forces of the western military districts should have been kept, in their opinion, while the forces to be moved forward into the new territories of Bessarabia, the Western Ukraine, Western Belorussia, and the Baltic countries should consist only of sufficient units to provide a cover for the deployment of the main forces in the event of an attack on the USSR.[22]

Stalin acted otherwise. Although the new western regions were not adequately prepared for defense, the first echelons of the forces of the western military districts were transferred to them and joined by other units still in the formative stages. Stalin ordered a strong fortified line to be built along the new border, just as there was along the old one. The pace of construction was hectic, but it was not finished before the outbreak of war. Out of 2,500 reinforced concrete emplacements only 1,000 had artillery; the rest had only machine guns. Kulik, Shaposhnikov, and Andrei Zhdanov all suggested the transfer of artillery from the old line of fortifications, but Zhukov and Timoshenko did not agree, arguing that the artillery in the old fortified areas could still be very useful. Stalin supported the first point of view, allowing the earlier line of fortifications to be disarmed as of "secondary" importance. Thus the old fortified areas were weakened while construction on the new ones had not been completed. As a result, neither the old line nor the new served as a substantial obstacle to the Germans.

Many pages could be taken up with evidence of a similar kind. For example, no command posts had been prepared for effective troop con-

22. *Voprosy istorii* (1972), no. 9, p. 210.

trol under wartime conditions either by the General Staff, the Commissariat of Defense, or the commanders in the field. During the first weeks of war military leadership was exercised from civilian offices.

Incredible as it may seem, military leaders testify that the armies dislocated westward did not have definite plans of operation in the event of a German attack. Former Commissar of the Navy Kuznetsov describes the situation:

> Stalin kept military matters under his personal control. No system existed that would unfailingly go into operation in the event of war, no matter which individual might be put out of action at the critical moment. In this respect the war caught us unprepared. . . . Stalin had ideas on how to wage war, but, with his usual pathological mistrust, he kept them secret from the future executors of his ideas. Mistaken about the probable date of the conflict, he thought there was still enough time. And when the course of history speeded up, the ideas, the thoughts about a future war, could not be transformed into clear strategic conceptions and concrete plans. Yet such plans—worked out with exactitude, down to the last detail—were absolutely essential in 1939–41.[23]

Undoubtedly informed of the Soviet Union's unpreparedness, the fascist command became brazenly open in May 1941. Artillery units brought up to the border were hardly even camouflaged. In May and June combat patrols reconnoitered more and more openly, encroaching on Soviet territory and firing on Soviet border guards.

Air Marshal A. Novikov, who in 1941 commanded the planes of the Leningrad Military District, wrote the following in his memoirs:

> German planes increasingly broke into Soviet airspace, but we weren't allowed to stop them. Not long before the war began General Tikhomirov, chief of the operations department of our district, told me that it was forbidden to move troops to the border or to open fire on German planes, even when they were deep in Soviet territory. Hitler's planes flying unopposed had an oppressive effect. Several times my hand reached for the telephone to call the commander of our fighter planes and order him to speedily knock down the intruders and thereby teach a lesson to others, but discipline quickly squelched this impulse. After the war I came across an interesting document. From it I learned that Hitler's men had photographed and compiled special files on many of our airfields and important industrial and transportation sites in the western regions, including military objectives in Kiev, the ports of Odessa and Sevastopol, factories in Dnepropetrovsk, Kharkov, Mariopol, and other cities, the giant Dneproges power plant, and the main bridges across the Dnieper, Dniester, and Don.[24]

23. *Oktyabr* (1965), no. 11, pp. 147–148, 162.
24. *Novy mir*, (1970), no. 2.

On June 14, 1941, when Hitler was holding his final military conference before the attack, TASS published a government statement that had a serious effect on the preparedness of Soviet forces. It said:

According to the information of the USSR, Germany is observing the terms of the Soviet-German nonaggression pact as strictly as the USSR. Therefore, in the opinion of Soviet circles, rumors about Germany's plan to break the pact and to undertake an attack on the USSR are quite unfounded. The recent transfer of German troops, released from operations in the Balkans, to the eastern and northeastern areas of Germany is connected, it must be supposed, with other motives, which have no bearing on Soviet-German relations.

The effect of this declaration is described by L. M. Sandalov:

The anxious mood, which had become especially acute by the middle of the month, was somewhat relieved. Such a statement coming from an authoritative state agency dulled the vigilance of the troops. Among the command staff it generated confidence that there were some unknown circumstances which enabled our government to remain calm and confident about the security of the Soviet borders. Officers stopped sleeping in the barracks. Soldiers began to undress at night.[25]

The blindness of Stalin and his advisers in those days of June is unparalleled. While the German embassy in Moscow was systematically reducing the number of German citizens in the USSR, almost every day new Soviet officials were arriving in Germany with their families. Deliveries of Soviet goods to Germany continued without pause, though Germany had sharply reduced the flow of its goods as specified in the trade commitments of 1939. Shortly before the attack, all German ships left Soviet ports without even finishing unloading. In Riga, for example, more than two dozen German ships, some of which had only begun to unload, weighed anchor on June 21. The Riga harbor master, sensing something wrong, at his own risk detained the German ships and quickly got in touch with the commissariat of Foreign Trade in Moscow. Stalin was told at once, but he ordered that the German ships be allowed to leave. At the same time Soviet ships, given no instructions, continued to unload in German harbors. On June 22 they were seized as spoils of war.[26]

The Commissariat of Defense warned Stalin once again about the possibility of a German attack a few days before it happened. "You are creating panic over nothing," he replied. According to Marshal Bagra-

25. L. M. Sandalov, *Perezhitoe* (Moscow, 1961), p. 78.
26. Berezhkov, *S diplomaticheskoi missiei v Berlin*, pp. 91, 116.

myan, only on the afternoon of June 19 was the command of the Kiev
Military District warned by the Commissariat of Defense that Hitler
might attack within a few days without a declaration of war. But even
then Stalin did not put the troops in border areas on military alert, not
even the air force. Marshal Rodion Ya. Malinovsky writes that troops in
the border areas

continued their peacetime training: the artillery belonging to infantry divisions
was in artillery camps and on firing ranges, antiaircraft guns were on antiaircraft
firing ranges, engineer units were in engineer camps, and "stripped" infantry
divisions were in their separate camps. Given the threat of imminent war, this
very crude blunder bordered on the criminal. Could it have been avoided? It
could and should have been.[27]

On the evening of June 21 Molotov summoned Ambassador Schulenburg to ascertain the causes of Germany's "dissatisfaction." But Schulenburg, uninformed about Hitler's immediate plans, could not answer
Molotov's worried questions. Returning to the embassy, he found instructions from Ribbentrop waiting for him: he was to visit Molotov and
read a document containing Hitler's usual obscene denunciation of a
nation about to be invaded. It was virtually a declaration of war. In
Schulenburg's words Molotov heard him out in silence and then said
bitterly: "This is war. Do you believe that we deserve that?"[28]

Molotov had good reason to ask such a question. Not until that night,
Marshal Malinovsky tells us, was a coded telegram sent to the military
districts, warning of a German attack on June 22 or 23. Troops were
ordered to move quietly into firing positions in the fortified areas, to
disperse aircraft, to put all units on alert, and to take no other actions
without special orders. To the question whether the troops could open
fire if the enemy invaded Soviet territory, the reply was that they should
not give in to provocation and should not open fire. But this directive
never reached the troops, for within a few hours the war had begun.[29]

The incongruity between reality and Stalin's actions is so striking that
many people are still asking why. N. G. Kuznetsov suggests the following
explanation:

Under the pressure of inexorable facts, Stalin began to realize, early in 1941,
that an attack by Hitler was really possible. But once he was convinced that his

27. *Voenno-istoricheskii zhurnal* (1961), no. 6.
28. Alexander Werth, *Russia at War, 1941–1945* (New York, 1964), p. 127.
29. *Voenno-istoricheskii zhurnal* (1961), no. 6.

expectation of a later war had been proved wrong, that our armed forces and the country as a whole were inadequately prepared for war in the next few months, he tried to take advantage of everything that he thought might postpone the conflict, to carry on in such a way as to give Hitler no pretext for attack, to provoke no war.

But such an explanation is not entirely convincing; a few lines earlier Kuznetsov himself notes that Stalin,

as a man of great experience, a major politician, was obviously aware that the aggressor could be sobered up only by our readiness to give him the proper response—a blow for a blow! If the aggressor raises his fist, that means he must be shown a fist in return.[30]

Some historians cite the German campaign of disinformation as an explanation for Stalin's inaction. Directed by Goebbels, the Germans spread the word that they were concentrating troops on the Soviet border in order to lull England into a false sense of security. Still, it was not hard to see through these tricks, especially since they were far outweighed by other information. Zhukov maintains that the military were convinced war was imminent. He seems ready to accept some blame that he and his colleagues did not "do more to convince Stalin that war with Germany was inevitable in the very near future and that the urgent measures provided for in the operational and mobilization plans should be implemented in all haste."[31] Zhukov fails to mention, however, the reason for the military leaders' timidity and inaction: the atmosphere of terror that had been created in the army. As Konstantin Simonov has justly written:

Stalin is responsible not only for the fact that he refused, with incomprehensible stubborness, to consider very important intelligence reports; his worst sin is that he created a disastrous atmosphere in which dozens of competent people who had irrefutable documented information did not have a chance to show the chief of state the extent of the danger, and did not have the right to take sufficient measures to avert it.[32]

To these words of Simonov's I must add that the main cause of Stalin's mistakes in 1941 was the system of one-man rule combined with that one man's limitations. Unlimited power was in the hands of a man who lacked the profound intelligence of a true statesman. He was unable to foresee

30. *Oktyabr* (1965), no. 11, p. 163.
31. [Zhukov, *Reminiscenses and Reflections.*—G. S.],"
32. Simonov, "Uroki istorii i sovest' pisatelia," unpublished manuscript.

events, to allow for varying possibilities, and thus proved to be a poor strategist. Stalin, like any despot, based his foreign policy planning not on reality but on his own imaginings.

Of course the same reproach can be made against Hitler. The invasion of the Soviet Union was a risky adventure for Germany, especially since Hitler gambled on victory within a few weeks—in any case before winter. The German war plan did not provide for adequate reserves of manpower or industrial production. German industry was not prepared for a lengthy war of such colossal dimensions. The Nazi Army could beat the Red Army in some battles, but Germany could not enslave the whole Soviet people in addition to all the nations of Europe. Considering that the German Army suffered defeat in spite of its unbelievably favorable situation in 1941, it is useful to imagine what would have happened to it if the Soviet government had been properly prepared. Hitler was also a dictator; he too based his actions on imaginary rather that real factors. Intoxicated by the German victories in the West, he overestimated the strength of the German Army and underestimated the strength of the Soviet people and the cohesion of Soviet society. He thought of the USSR as a giant with feet of clay that would collapse after its first defeats. Hitler was an adventurist and a reckless maniac, but Stalin perceived him as a rational statesman. Stalin's tendency to mistake illusions for reality prevented him from seeing the same fault in Hitler. That is one of the main reasons why both Hitler and Stalin miscalculated in 1941.

■ 4

STALIN AS MILITARY LEADER

It is acknowledged by historians of all persuasions, both Soviet and Western, that Stalin was responsible for the Germans' great advantage of surprise and for the Soviet troops' unpreparedness. It is generally acknowledged that the Soviet Union entered the worst war in history with its best military leaders destroyed by Stalin.

I. A. Sats, who was active in the war, wrote in his memoirs:

The first months of the war with Hitler Germany revealed that the losses [from the repression] had not been made up for. Far from it. The command staffs had been affected—going all the way from the principal leaders to company and platoon commanders (who were of no less importance, even though they are not [usually] considered). So were the teaching staffs—going all the way from the main academies to the training schools and special courses. No single war could have destroyed so many commanders as did the years of unwarranted repression.

Were it not for the repression, the Germans might never have reached the Dnieper, let alone the Volga. I don't know the exact figures on the relative material strength of the two sides, but I don't think it was that much in Germany's favor. The Germans were better supplied with mortars, but it was easy to catch up with them in this area; besides, the USSR already had jet-propelled projectiles, which the Germans did not. In artillery, during the course of the war, the Germans were simply no match for our army. In aircraft, we lagged behind at the beginning, again because repression in the aviation industry impeded the production of the necessary number of new aircraft. The German heavy tank, the T-4, was inferior to our medium tank, the T-34, in maneuverability, and was no better in firing power. In the western regions of the USSR the number of Soviet and German divisions was roughly the same. The first weeks of the war inflicted such losses on our equipment and material reserves that the enemy's advantage was greatly increased. But that setback also stemmed from the main source of our temporary military weakness—the blow dealt to the army's cadres in the prewar years. The Germans' main advantage was in effective troop control and communications, the smooth working of all the components of their military machine, and the elementary topographical literacy of their middle and lower command personnel. The Soviet people paid for [the lack of these things on our side] with human losses in the millions, both at the front and among civilians, and losses of huge amounts of territory.[33]

While hardly anyone disputes the fact that Stalin committed major crimes and blunders before the war, there have been persistent, if crude, attempts to justify Stalin's conduct during the war. He is portrayed as a skillful and experienced military leader whose decisive actions helped overcome the consequences of his own mistakes and miscalculations and win the historic victory over fascist Germany. Such attempts to salvage Stalin's reputation if only as a military leader were made especially in the period 1966–1970 and afterwards in memoirs by many marshals and generals who had commented quite differently in earlier articles and memoirs in 1961–1965.

In 1969 the authoritative journal *Kommunist* carried a review article that made the following general argument on the basis of these "edited" memoirs: "For all the complexity and contradictions of his character, Stalin emerges from the generals' memoirs as an outstanding military leader."[34] The historian who wrote this review article was obviously polemicizing with Khrushchev, in particular with the section of his "secret speech" to the Twentieth Party Congress that harshly yet fairly demolished the myth of Stalin's military genius. The facts cited by

33. I. A. Sats, "Vospominaniia," unpublished manuscript.
34. Ye. Boltin, writing in *Kommunist* (1969), no. 2, p. 127.

Khrushchev in 1956 have not been disproved; in the decade following his speech they were supplemented by hundreds of authoritative accounts, most of them published in the Soviet press. The case against Stalin's military record was so overwhelming that over the past decade and a half prevarication and sophistry have been the only recourse of his apologists.

These apologists have also exploited a widespread feeling derived from the cult of personality. Stalin's name became a sort of symbol in the popular mentality existing independently of its actual bearer. During the war years, as the Soviet people were battered by unbelievable miseries, the name of Stalin and faith in him to some degree pulled the Soviet people together, giving them hope of victory. The logic of any cult was at work, attributing all defeats to other commanders or to treason, all victories to Stalin. To this day many of the soldiers and officers who went into battle with Stalin's name on their lips find it hard to reconsider their attitude toward him and the wartime events connected with his image. The historian may sympathize with this primitive psychology, but inexorable facts oblige him to oppose it.

Of course as supreme commander in chief Stalin did make correct decisions, give his subordinates correct orders, and accept from them—often after arguments and resistance—much good advice. But his personal qualities—his nastiness and narrow-mindedness, his contempt for people and boundless love of power, his suspiciousness and his bureaucratic style of leadership—were bound to affect his behavior as a commander. The result was something much worse than the mistakes that cannot be avoided in any war. Most of Stalin's wrong decisions were so extravagantly and senselessly costly that they cannot be condoned.

First of all, something must be said about the general plan of operations for the war, drawn up in advance by the Soviet General Staff. For a long time Soviet historians had no idea what this plan consisted of. It was only from Zhukov's memoirs that they found out about its main elements. Zhukov's account is as follows:

In the autumn of 1940 the previous operations plan was thoroughly revised and brought in line with the objectives that would face us in the event of attack. True, there were strategic mistakes in the plan, stemming from an erroneous conception.

As we saw it, the most dangerous strategic direction was the Southwestern (the Ukraine) and not the Western (Byelorussia) where Hitler's High Command actually concentrated and engaged its most powerful ground and air formations in June 1941. Yet the western direction was the shortest route to Moscow.

As a consequence, the 19th Army and a number of units and formations of the 16th Army, which had been concentrated in the Ukraine . . . , were rushed to the west and sent into action "on the march" under the command of the Western Front. This undoubtedly affected the defensive operations in the western direction.

When revising the operations plan in the spring of 1941 (February–April), we failed to eliminate all the effects of this mistake and did not lay down a large enough force in the western sector.

Stalin was convinced that in the war against the Soviet Union the Nazis would first try to seize the Ukraine and the Donets Coal Basin in order to deprive our country of its most important economic regions and lay hands on Ukrainian grain, Donets coal, and later, the oil of the Caucasus. During the discussion of the operational plan in the spring of 1941, Stalin said: "Nazi Germany will not be able to wage a major lengthy war without those vital resources."

Stalin was the greatest authority for all of us, and it never occurred to anybody to question his opinion and assessment of the situation. Yet his conjecture as to the main strike of the Nazi invader, although of course it did have some basis, did not take into account the enemy's plans for a Blitzkrieg against the USSR.[35]

Further on, Zhukov discusses other defects in the plan of operations:

In revising the operational plans in spring 1941, little attention was given to the new methods of warfare at the initial stage of hostilities [i.e., Blitzkrieg tactics]. The People's Commissariat of Defense and the General Staff believed that war between countries as big as Germany and the Soviet Union would follow the old scheme: the main forces would engage in battle after several days of frontier fighting. As regards concentration and deployment deadlines, it was assumed that conditions for the two countries would be the same. In fact, the forces and conditions proved to be far from equal.[36]

In evaluating Stalin's role as military leader, the historian cannot overlook, for example, the great damage done by two basic dogmas that he constantly expounded: "We will not surrender an inch of our land to the enemy," and "We will carry the war to the enemy's territory." Because of these dogmas he rejected proposals for a defense in depth. His strategic plan excluded the possibility that the enemy might break through the first line of defense. Thus neither factories nor people in the western areas were prepared for possible evacuation. Worse yet, the first line of defense was simply drawn along the national border, with all its convolutions. That made encirclement difficult to avoid and natural defense

35. Zhukov, *Vospominaniia i razmyshleniia*, pp. 227–228. [Cf. the English version by Progress Publishers, *Reminiscences and Reflections*, 1:250. —G. S.]

36. Zhukov, *Vospominaniia i razmyshleniia*, pp. 232. [Cf. *Reminiscences and Reflections*, 1:255. —G. S.]

lines—such as the Neman River and the Augustow Canal—difficult to take advantage of. Twelve armies were distributed along the borders in such a pattern as to be easily outnumbered and outflanked by the German attack.[37]

Goebbels made an entry in his diary in June 1941: "The Russians were concentrated right on the border. We couldn't hope for anything better. If they had been distributed in depth, they would have been a great danger."[38] In his history of World War II the German military historian Tippelskirch makes essentially the same point, but with a large number of factual details.[39]

Earlier, at the beginning of the thirties, the Revolutionary Military Council of the USSR foresaw the possibility of a temporary retreat at the beginning of a war and began to organize partisan units in frontier districts. These preparations were directed by Yakir, Uborevich, Blyukher, and Ya. K. Berzin, and the plans died with them in 1937–1938. Their organization of secret partisan bases was alleged to reveal "lack of confidence in the power of the Soviet state" and even "preparation for hostile actions in the rear of the Soviet armies." Many commanders of the projected guerrilla units, who were in civilian work in peacetime, were arrested as "enemies of the people" and "diversionists."[40]

Stalin displayed total confusion in the first hours and days of the war, which began so unexpectedly for him. Zhukov gives a fairly detailed description of the first hours of the war. On the night of June 21 no one at the Commissariat of Defense slept, although Stalin left the Kremlin earlier than usual and went to his country place. He retired at 1 A.M., and most of his guards were soon sleeping soundly. At 3:17 A.M., reports of German air raids began pouring in to Moscow from all the fronts and fleets, but not until 4 A.M. could Timoshenko, the commissar of defense, and Zhukov bring themselves to disturb "the Leader." According to Zhukov's account Timoshenko

ordered me to phone Stalin. I started calling. No one answered. I kept calling. Finally, I heard the sleep-laden voice of the general on duty at the security section. I asked him to call Stalin to the phone.

37. *Voenno-istoricheskii zhurnal* (1965), no. 10, pp. 33–39.

38. Goebbels' diary is quoted in Ye. Rzhevskaia, *Berlin, mai 1945* (Moscow, 1965), p. 71.

39. See Tippelskirch, *Istoriia vtoroi mirovoi voiny* (Moscow, 1956), p. 177 (a translation of his *Geschichte des zweiten Weltkriegs* [Bonn, 1951]).

40. See I. G. Starinov, *Miny zhdut svoego chasa* (Moscow, 1964).

"What? Now? Comrade Stalin is asleep."

"Wake him at once. The Germans are bombing our cities."

About three minutes later Stalin picked up the receiver.

I reported the situation and requested permission to begin retaliatory action. Stalin was silent. I heard only the sound of his breathing.

"Did you understand me?" I said.

Silence again.

At last Stalin asked: "Where is the commissar of defense?"

"Talking with the Kiev District."

"You and him come to the Kremlin. Tell Poskrebyshev to summon all the members of the Politburo." . . .

At 4:30 A.M. Timoshenko and I arrived at the Kremlin. All the Politburo members were assembled. The commissar of defense and I were called in. Stalin, his face white, was sitting at the table cradling a tobacco-filled pipe in his hand. He said:

"We must immediately phone the German embassy."

The embassy replied that Ambassador Schulenburg requested to be received in order to deliver an urgent message.

Molotov was authorized to receive him.

Meanwhile, Vatutin, the first deputy chief of the General Staff, sent word that after a powerful artillery barrage German land forces had mounted an assault at several points on the Northwestern and Western sectors.

A while later Molotov hurried into the office and said, "The German government has declared war on us."

Stalin lowered himself to his chair and fell into deep thought. A long and heavy pause ensued.

I took the risk of breaking the prolonged silence and proposed that we come down with all the strength of our forces in the border districts upon the enemy units that had broken through in order to detain any further enemy advance.

"Not detain, but destroy," Timoshenko corrected me.

"Issue a directive," said Stalin.

At 7:15 on June 22 the defense commissar's directive No. 2 was communicated to the border districts, but in view of the actual balance of forces and the obtaining situation it proved quite unrealistic and was therefore never carried out.[41]

Directive No 1, ordering that the troops in the border districts be readied for combat, had been issued at 12:30 A.M. on June 22, but never reached the troops, as we have seen. Directive No. 2 did not reach the troops until 10 or 11 A.M., when the battle was already in full swing, with a significant portion of the Soviet air force destroyed on the ground at poorly protected airfields and the advantage clearly on the German side

41. Zhukov, *Vospominaniia i razmyshleniia*, pp. 254–255. [Cf. *Reminiscences and Reflections*, 1:281–282. —G. S.]

at many points along the front. Yet Directive No. 2 called on Soviet aircraft to "destroy the enemy's aircraft on his airfields and bomb the main concentrations of his ground forces." For some reason the restriction was added that Soviet planes were not to fly more than 100–150 kilometers [60–90 miles] into enemy territory. Soviet troops were retreating, but the directive contained this warning: "Until receipt of special orders, no ground forces are to cross the border [into enemy territory]."

On the afternoon of June 22 Stalin had Directive No. 3 sent to the troops ordering them to mount a counteroffensive with the aim of smashing the enemy and advancing into his territory. "But we still don't know exactly where the enemy is striking and in what strength," Zhukov objected to General Vatutin, the deputy chief of the General Staff, who had received Stalin's order. Zhukov went on: "Wouldn't it be better to find out what is actually going on at the front by tomorrow morning and then adopt the requisite decision?"

"I share your view," Vatutin replied, "but it's already been decided."[42]

While the first two directives had surprised commanders at the front, the third aroused anger that was fully justified. As Zhukov reports:

When the Supreme Command ordered the counteroffensive it did not know the situation that had shaped up toward the close of day on June 22. Neither did the front commanders know the true state of affairs. The Supreme Command based its decision not on an analysis of the obtaining situation and not on verified estimates, but on intuition and a desire to act. It failed to take the capability of the troops into account, and that is totally impermissible at crucial moments in an armed struggle. . . . Most of the counterattacks that were in fact attempted were poorly organized, and lacking due cooperation and support, failed to achieve their objectives.[43]

Khrushchev told the Twentieth Party Congress that when Stalin heard of the Red Army's first major defeats, he believed the end had come, that everything created by Lenin had been irretrievably lost. Thereupon Stalin withdrew from direction of the war effort, until some Politburo members came to him and said that immediate measures had to be taken to correct the situation at the front. All the marshals of the Soviet Union were at the Twentieth Congress; so were Molotov, Malenkov, Kaganovich, Voroshilov, and Bulganin, and none of them found it necessary to correct Khrushchev.

42. [See Zhukov, *Reminiscences and Reflections*, p. 287. —G.S.]
43. Zhukov, *Vospominaniia i razmyshleniia*, p. 273. [Cf. *Reminiscences and Reflections*, 1:301–302—G. S.]

Was his sensational report disproved later? The central archives of the Soviet Army contain many directives issued during the opening days of the war but not a single document signed by Stalin in the period from June 24 to July 2, 1941. Nor does any order from the commissar of defense or any other military leader refer to any directive from Stalin. What did he do, where was he in those crucial days? An answer has recently been given in a documented tale that was passed by special military censorship.

Late in the evening Stalin, accompanied by some members of the Politburo, unexpectedly appeared at the Commissariat of Defense on Frunze Street. As he entered the commissar's office, Stalin was calm and self-assured. However, it was there at the directing center of the country's military effort that he first sensed concretely the magnitude of the growing danger. Enemy tank groups were forming a pincers on Minsk and it seemed that nothing could stop them. Contact with our retreating armies had been lost. . . . Stalin, usually so outwardly calm and deliberate in his speech and motions, this time could not restrain himself. He burst out with angry, insulting scolding. Then without looking at anyone, head down and stooped over, he left the building, got into his car, and went home. . . .

No one knew what was going on in Stalin's mind during the next few days. No one saw him. He did not appear in the Kremlin. No one heard his voice on the telephone. He summoned no one. And none of those who hour by hour waited for his summons dared go to him unsummoned. . . . The members of the Politburo, the people's commissars, the leaders of the Commissariat of Defense, of the General Staff, and of the army's Political Administration were overwhelmed with thousands of matters, great and small, connected with the implementation of military measures throughout the country and at the fronts. But as they worked on these problems from morning to late at night, they asked themselves time and again: Where is Stalin? Why is he silent? What was he doing, what was he thinking about, this apparently omnipotent and omniscient man, in those long terrible hours?[44]

The author tries to give the impression that the management of the war effort was proceeding normally even without Stalin. But because of the strict centralization Stalin had established, neither Zhukov nor Timoshenko nor Molotov nor Beria had the authority to give certain necessary orders. Stalin's absence from his post as head of the state and the party from June 23 to the beginning of July was an important reason why the Nazis penetrated so swiftly and deeply into the Soviet Union.

In the attempts to refurbish Stalin's reputation in the years after Khrushchev's removal some authors disputed the very fact of Stalin's

44. Chakovsky, "Blokada," *Znamya* (1968), no. 11, p. 49.

shameful desertion during the first days of the war. For example, Kuznetsov's memoirs assert that on June 23 Stalin "was working energetically" and that on June 24 Kuznetsov saw Stalin holding an important conference in his office at the Kremlin.[45] Zhukov's memoirs refer to meetings with Stalin on June 26 and 29. In some other memoirs the authors claim, if not to have met with Stalin, at least to have talked with him on the phone between June 23 and June 30. All such "testimony" is merely an example of the kind of falsification so common in Soviet historical literature and memoirs. The archives of the writer Konstantin Simonov contain extensive tape recordings with many marshals and generals, including Zhukov. In the mid-sixties the first version of Zhukov's memoirs was compiled on the basis of Simonov's interviews. The result was a typescript of approximately four hundred pages. Simonov very kindly acquainted me with all this material, which demonstrates irrefutably that Stalin was absent from Moscow and the Kremlin from approximately June 23 to June 30.[46] Marshal Grechko has also written about this: "There is nothing to indicate that during that period Stalin took any part in the decisions of General Headquarters (the Stavka)."[47]

It is hardly an accident that in the Central Archives of the Soviet Army, in those very sections with material pertaining to directives issued during the first days of the war, there are no documents whatsoever signed by Stalin from June 23 to June 30.

As a result of the Red Army's unpreparedness and the absence of the required leadership during those first days of war, the Nazi forces won major victories. The German historian Tippelskirch describes them this way:

The offensive of the army groups began quite promisingly. The enemy was caught unawares and was completely stunned. On the southern flank all the bridges crossing the river Bug fell into German hands intact. Both tank groups, after successfully breaking through the border defenses, advanced steadily eastward. On June 24 the 2d Tank Group reached the region of Slonim and the 3d Tank Group, the Vilnius area. After them came the 4th and 9th Armies. The enemy's troops in the Belostok region tried to retreat eastward to break out of the "pocket" that was gradually being formed. The attacking tank groups with the support of substantial air power managed to delay the retreating enemy until a

45. *Oktyabr* (1968), no. 8, p. 138.
46. Simonov allowed me to read most of the memoirs in his unique archives, but only on the condition that I not quote from them without permission of the authors, with whom I have unfortunately been unable to make contact.
47. *Voenno-istoricheskii zhurnal* (1966), no. 6, p. 12.

link-up was made between the 4th and 9th armies on June 29 to the east of Belostok. For two days the Russians made desperate attempts to break out to the east and southeast and escape the tightening ring of encirclement. Then their strength gave out. The encirclement was completed and the fighting in that region ended. Meanwhile the two tank groups advanced further eastward in order to encircle once again those Russian forces that had retreated. . . .

On June 27 the 2d Tank Group reached the southern outskirts of Minsk, where it met up with Tank Group 3. . . .

Now the tank groups trapped the Russian troops remaining west of Minsk in a new "pocket" and gradually tightened the ring. . . .

The army groups coming from the west then definitively completed the encirclement of this second Russian grouping. On July 9 the pocket was mopped up. A communiqué of the German High Command reported on July 11 that as a result of the first major double battle for Belostok and Minsk, 328,898 prisoners of war had been taken, including several ranking generals, and that 3,332 tanks and 1,809 field guns had been captured along with large amounts of other equipment.[48]

That was the course of events on the central sector of the German offensive. Nor do Soviet historians or military leaders dispute these facts. According to Marshal Zakharov, during the first hours of the war German planes made massive raids on Soviet airfields in the border regions, dealing heavy blows to Soviet air power particularly in the Western Military District. As of noon on June 22 1200 planes were lost, more than 800 having been destroyed on the ground. Marshal Grechko states that "the enemy managed in three weeks to put 28 of our divisions out of action, while more than 70 divisions lost 50 percent or more of their men and equipment."[49] "No organized defense," writes I. V. Tyulenev,

could be created or maintained in the first days of the war. Battles had an uncoordinated character. Instead of a solid front of defense, which could not be created because of the disorganized movement into battle of cover units, there were isolated centers of fighting.[50]

Although overall direction improved somewhat with Stalin's return to his post, the situation remained critical. Even in July and August of 1941 Stalin still could not overcome his confusion. N. N. Voronov, who was deputy commissar of defense and representative of the General Staff on many fronts, recalls:

48. Tippelskirch, *Istoriia vtoroi mirovoi voiny*, pp. 177–178. [This passage is translated from the wording in Roy Medvedev's Russian manuscript, not the German original.—G. S.]
49. *Voenno-istoricheskii zhurnal* (1966), no. 6, pp. 7–8.
50. I. V. Tyulenev, *Cherez tri voiny* (Moscow, 1962), pp. 147–148.

I rarely saw Stalin in the first days of the war. He was depressed, nervous, and off balance. When he gave assignments, he demanded that they be completed in an unbelievably short time, without considering real possibilities. In the first weeks of the war, in my opinion, he misconceived the scale of the war, and the forces and equipment that could actually stop the advancing enemy on a front stretching from sea to sea. . . . He was constantly expressing the assumption that the enemy would be defeated in a very short time.[51]

Based on his erroneous notions of the balance of forces on the fighting fronts, Stalin forbade retreat even when it was absolutely necessary. As Zhukov reports, the General Staff came to the conclusion in early August that the weakest link in the chain of Soviet defenses was the Central Front. The Germans could take advantage of this weakness to strike at the flank and rear of the Southwestern Front. The General Staff accordingly proposed that between twelve and fifteen divisions be transferred from the Far East to the Central Front and that the troops of the Southwestern Front be withdrawn behind the Dnieper. This meant abandoning Kiev. The Germans were already going around that city to the north and south and it was impossible to hold it for long, whereas an organized evacuation could save the lives of both soldiers and civilians. When Stalin heard these proposals he exploded, rejecting them as "foolish nonsense." Zhukov was removed from his post as chief of the General Staff and made commander of the Reserve Front. Nevertheless, Stalin did take into account some of the General Staff's concerns, establishing the Bryansk Front to cover the flank of the Southwestern sector. Unfortunately, the Bryansk Front was too weak to perform the tasks assigned to it.[52]

When the Germans resumed the offensive they were able fairly easily to overcome the resistance of the Bryansk Front, so that the main forces of the Southwestern Front soon found themselves under threat of encirclement. The commander of the front, General M. P. Kirponos, favored withdrawal to a new line of defense along the Sula River and the southern branch of the Dnieper.

Kirponos and his chief of staff, General Tupikov, sent Stalin a detailed report of their desperate situation, concluding with a request for permission to withdraw. An hour and a half later they got a reply: "Kiev was, is, and will be Soviet. I do not permit you to retreat to the Sula River. I order you to hold Kiev and the Dnieper. Stalin."[53]

51. N. N. Voronov, *Na sluzhbe voennoi* (Moscow, 1963), p. 179.

52. Zhukov, *Vospominaniia i razmyshleniia*, p. 320.

53. Reported by S. M. Yakimenko, who was an intelligence officer on the staff of the Southwestern Front.

When Stalin ordered that Kiev be held at all costs Marshal Budenny, the commander in chief of the southwestern armies, tried to change his mind. In a report to headquarters Budenny stressed that "delay in the withdrawal of the Southwestern Front may lead to the loss of troops and an enormous amount of material." But Stalin ignored him.

Marshal Bagramyan also recalls this catastrophe. When the encirclement was already clearly formed, General Tupikov wrote another report plainly stating that headquarters must allow a retreat or be responsible for the destruction of hundreds of thousands of people. The commander of the front would not sign the report, so Tupikov sent it on his own. In reply he was accused of panicmongering—and the very next day the enemy cut through the last lines connecting the front with the rest of the country.[54] Kirponos' troops were crushed on the left bank of the Dnieper; Kirponos, Tupikov, and most of their staff were killed in battle; and a huge breach was opened through which the German armies poured into new areas to the east and south.

Only in the fall of 1941, when the Germans had occupied almost the entire Ukraine, all of Belorussia and the Baltic republics, and had reached Leningrad and the outskirts of Moscow, did Stalin finally give up the thought of quickly destroying the enemy "in the districts where he has violated the Soviet border." He finally issued a directive that is aptly summed up in the witty remark of one officer: "It is necessary to stop the offensive and start the defense."

Another cause of chaos in these first months was the lack of a well-organized chain of command. "Only when the war had begun was organized leadership hurriedly formed," writes former Commissar of the Navy Kuznetsov.[55] On June 23 the Headquarters (Stavka) of the Chief Command of the Armed Forces was set up under Commissar of Defense Timoshenko. Stalin was listed only as a member of this headquarters. On July 10 a new body, the Headquarters of the Supreme Command, was created. On July 19, almost a month after the beginning of the war, Stalin was named commissar of defense, and only on August 8 was the Headquarters of the Supreme Command reorganized into the Headquarters of the Supreme Commander in Chief—Stalin.

From June to September, despite stubborn resistance on individual

54. *Literaturnaya gazeta*, April 17, 1964.
55. *Voenno-istoricheskii zhurnal* (1965), no. 9, p. 66.

sectors of the fronts, the Soviet armies were forced to retreat hundreds of kilometers. More than three million soldiers were killed or taken prisoner. (German losses up to September 30, 1941, numbered 555,000 men.)[56] Since it was the basic cadres of the regular army that suffered the losses, those losses were especially serious. Losses of equipment were also enormous.

At the same time it must be said that the German command was unquestionably disappointed in the results of the fighting from June to September. Hitler's original plans were that by October 1 his armies were to have crushed the Soviet Union, reached the Volga, and taken both Leningrad and Moscow. The stubborn Soviet resistance at Smolensk, Kiev, Odessa, and Leningrad disrupted all the timetables for the German advance. The Soviet leadership exerted enormous efforts to make up for its losses. From the end of June to September alone more than three hundred divisions were mobilized and sent to the front, although when planning the war the German general staff assumed that the USSR would be unable to mobilize more than sixty divisions in half a year. Also, during the Red Army's retreat more than 1,500 factories were evacuated to the east.

These facts can be interpreted in various ways, however. If the Red Army had not suffered such great losses in the summer of 1941, there would have been no need to mobilize hundreds of new divisions in such hasty fashion. More often than not those divisions were not provided with a sufficient quantity of heavy equipment or even rifles, and the military training of both new recruits and older men recalled to duty was incomplete. All reserves were thrown into battle, with no thought for the fact that the war might last several more years. The poor training of the newly formed divisions also resulted in heavy casualties, and the situation was even worse with the virtually untrained citizen's regiments, or "people's militia" *(narodnoe opolchenie)*. Stalin called for the formation of such emergency regiments in his first wartime speech to the nation of July 3, 1941.

On September 30, 1941, the Germans began a general offensive aimed at taking Moscow. They were in a hurry to end the war before the onset of winter. In the opening days of the offensive they made major gains. At

56. *Kommunist* (1966), no. 17, p. 49. According to other figures, Soviet losses in killed, wounded, and—mainly—captured from June to September 1941 were five million, while enemy losses reached one million.

several places they broke through the defenses not only of the Western Front but also of the Reserve Front—between 80 and 120 kilometers to the rear. Very large Red Army groupings were surrounded—major components of the 19th, 20th, 24th, and 32d armies in the Vyazma region, and the 3d and 13th Soviet armies near Bryansk. Enemy tank columns took Orel, Bryansk, Kaluga, Maloyaroslavets, and many other cities and towns. They were left with a clear road to Moscow, with no solid line of defenses along the way. There were not even any troops to close the gaps that had been torn in the Soviet lines. The surrounded armies continued to fight, holding up dozens of enemy divisions, but it was impossible for them to sustain resistance for long. According to Marshal A. M. Vasilevsky, the painful defeats of the Red Army in early October were partly caused by the Supreme Command's failure to determine correctly the direction of the enemy attack; as a result, the Red Army defenses were too weak along the main lines of the Germans' advance.[57]

Marshals Zhukov and Konev have also written about Stalin's serious mistakes in directing the defense of Moscow in October 1941. They point out that in the fall offensive the Nazis no longer enjoyed the advantage of surprise. It was known that from early September the German command had been concentrating its strike forces on the approaches to Moscow and preparing for an offensive. On September 15, Konev, commander of the Western Front, was summoned to Moscow. Stalin discussed several problems about building up the army and establishing two new honorary awards, the Order of Suvorov and the Order of Kutuzov. As Konev was to write later:

> At this session the Stavka did not discuss the problems of the Western Front with me; nothing was said about reinforcing the front with troops and equipment; the possibility of an offensive by the Nazi forces was not touched on. Nor did the General Staff provide any orientation.[58]

On October 4, after the German breakthrough, when there was clearly a danger that major enemy tank units would emerge in the rear of the Western Front, Konev reported the situation to Stalin over the high-frequency telephone, emphasizing that several Soviet armies were under threat of encirclement. Stalin heard him out but made no decision. Konev got on the line to Shaposhnikov, chief of the General Staff, and repeated his report. Shaposhnikov promised to notify the Stavka, but on

57. *Kommunist* (1966), no. 17, p. 52.
58. Ivan S. Konev, *Bitva za Moskvu* (Moscow, 1966), p. 33.

that fateful day the Western Front received no authorization to withdraw to the Gzhatsk defense line. The Stavka's slowness resulted in the encirclement of four Soviet divisions. When the crushing of the surrounded Soviet troops had been completed in mid-October there was still no solid line of defense to bar the Germans' way to Moscow. On October 10 the remaining troops of the Western and Reserve fronts were merged into a single Western Front, and Zhukov was appointed commander. On the right flank, covering Moscow, the Kalinin Front was formed, under Konev. Meanwhile the German troops continued their advance, with more than a twofold superiority in men and equipment.

At this point the capital was in real danger. After October 5 most government offices were relocated to Kuibyshev. On October 15 A. S. Shcherbakov, head of the Moscow party organization, called a hasty gathering of the party secretaries of the city's districts. His instructions testified to the emergency situation. Only those with special duties were to remain in Moscow: explosives experts, those who would fight on as guerrillas, etc. All others were to leave. Ironically, the main evacuation route chosen at that time was called the Highway of Enthusiasts (Shosse Entuziastov). The Gorky region was to be the nearest evacuation center. So great was the danger that Moscow would fall that the experience of 1812 was recalled as an example to be utilized; that is, if the city could not be held, it would have to be abandoned, as it had been to Napoleon. Preparations were made to blow up power plants, parts of the subway system, and factories that were too difficult to evacuate. These moves could hardly be kept secret from the population, and on the next day, October 16, a wave of alarm spread through the city. Hundreds of thousands began to leave Moscow on their own initiative. This unorganized flight created great confusion and in several instances genuine panic. A special train was made ready for the departure of the Stavka and of Stalin personally. According to many accounts, on the night of October 16 Stalin actually did leave the city, but he did not show up either in Gorky or in Kuibyshev. Konstantin Simonov says that Stalin did leave Moscow on the special train but within less than twenty-four hours, after receiving more encouraging reports from the commanders of the fronts, he decided to return to the Kremlin.

This insignificant episode, which has nothing in common with Stalin's desertion of duty at the beginning of the war, has greatly troubled many of Stalin's idolators, who prefer to deny that Stalin left Moscow even for a short time. The writer P. L. Proskurin, in his novel *Thy Name*, discusses the events of October 1941 and Stalin's behavior. To demonstrate how piously such people view Stalin I cite the following excerpt from Proskurin's novel.

He [Stalin] was thinking of the decision taken in the fall of 1941, that he had to leave Moscow immediately for Kuibyshev, and he clearly recalled that morning of OCTOBER NINETEENTH: the Rogozhsko-Simonovsky siding, the special train, the deserted platform, the comrades who had come to see him off, patiently waiting. . . . . It was one of those crucial moments of his life when the next step had to be absolutely right with no room for error; at his back, grown numb as stone, he felt the infinite watchfulness of the great city, now at the very center of desperate, unprecedented global shocks in a colossal tangle of world forces.

He could still feel it almost physically in his skin, how heavily the time had passed, and himself, in absolute isolation from the rest of the world, separate from those who were seeing him off, immune to the wind, hunched, pacing back and forth along the platform; he was after all only a man, but whether he liked it or not, concentrated in his name was the hope and despair of millions of people, dying in attacks, shedding blood in scores and hundreds of battles, and not in their own country alone. In these last hard months, he had only been a dead tired man, but just for that reason, just at that moment on the empty platform of the railway siding, pacing back and forth for a frightening two hours while not one of those present dared to approach him, he sensed not so much with his mind as with his heart the incredible burden of responsibility, and he could never shift even the smallest fraction of that burden to the shoulders of another; he felt again the almost living, anguished cry of the immortal city. No one saw his face. Coming up to the front of the platform at his characteristic unhurried pace, without saying a word to anyone, he suddenly turned, stooping more than usual, walked to his car, got in, and went back.[59]

Everything in this passage has a false ring to me—not only the pompous thoughts ascribed to Stalin but also the date of October 19, when actually the situation outside Moscow was temporarily stabilized and the question of Stalin's departure would not have arisen. Still, it is obvious that Proskurin knows the real facts about those painful days and deliberately passes over them in silence.

The memoirs of A. I. Shakhurin, former minister of the aircraft industry, include a detailed account of October 16 in Moscow. In the morning he was at one of the aircraft factories that was being evacuated when he received an urgent message to come see Stalin in the Kremlin.

The Kremlin looked deserted. After entering Stalin's apartment, I took off my coat and proceeded down the hallway. Meetings were usually held in the dining

59. *Moskva* (1977), nos. 2–5.

room. As I entered that room Stalin appeared from the bedroom. As always, he was smoking and pacing back and forth. Directly in front of the entrance to the dining room was a table, and to the left a buffet. To the right, along the wall, were bookcases, but now there were no books in them. Stalin was dressed as usual, in a tunic with his trousers tucked in his boots. (It was only later that he began wearing a military uniform.) The Politburo members came in. Stalin greeting each of them, continuing to puff on his pipe and pace up and down. We all stood. Then he stopped and, addressing no one in particular, asked: "How are things in Moscow?" Everyone kept silent, glancing at one another. I decided to speak up:

"I was at the factories this morning. At one plant they were amazed to see me. One of the women workers said, 'But we thought everyone had left.' At another, the workers were angry that not everyone had been paid; someone told them that the director of the State Bank had shipped out the paper money and there wasn't enough left at the bank."

Stalin asked Molotov, "Where's Zverev [the commissar of finance]?"

"In Gorky," Molotov answered

"Have the money sent back by plane right away."

I went on: the streetcars weren't running; the subways weren't working; the bakeries and other stores were closed.

Stalin turned to Shcherbakov and asked why things were in such a state, but without waiting for an answer he turned and again began to pace. Then he said "Well, it isn't so bad really. I thought it would be worse." And he added, addressing Shcherbakov, "Get the streetcars and subways running right away. Open the bakeries, stores, and restaurants—and medical facilities, with whatever doctors are still in the city. You and Pronin go on the radio today and call for calm and quiet. Announce that the normal operation of transport, eating places, and other public services is assured." The meeting was brief. After several minutes Stalin said, "All right, that's it." And we went our separate ways, each on his own assignment.[60]

The meeting described by Shakhurin undoubtedly took place, but the whole tone of it, as well as Stalin's remarks and his rather unusual manner, suggest that it occurred not on October 16 but two days later, when Stalin had returned to the Kremlin after his sudden departure. Otherwise, how is one to explain his ignorance of conditions in the city or his remark "I thought it would be worse"? As if someone could stop the subways and streetcars, close the bakeries and other stores, and authorize Zverev, the commissar of finance, to move to Gorky without first clearing it with Stalin. In my opinion this meeting took place on October 17, when the panic in Moscow had begun to subside. At any rate, it was on October 17 that Shcherbakov announced over the radio,

60. *Voprosy istorii* (1975), no. 3, pp. 142–143.

on behalf of the Central Committee, that the army, the citizens' regiments, and all of Moscow would fight to the last drop of blood to frustrate the Nazis' criminal designs.[61]

By the end of October, through the efforts of the defenders of Moscow, the Germans were stopped on the Western, Kalinin, and Bryansk fronts. To continue their offensive, the Germans needed to rest and regroup. For that they needed more than two weeks, a respite that the Soviet command was able to use to its own advantage. In early November Zhukov reported to Stalin that the Germans were completing their preparation of new strike forces and would apparently resume the offensive before long. Stalin ordered that preventive blows be struck to disrupt the enemy's preparations. Zhukov tried to demonstrate the inexpediency of such action, citing the absence of reserves and the overly extended Soviet lines. Stalin cut him off sharply: "Consider the question of counterattacks settled. Report your plans this evening."[62]

As was to be expected, the counterattacks did not produce the results Stalin hoped for. On the contrary, according to Zhukhov, they stripped the Western Front of its needed reserves and made it more difficult to repel the Nazi offensive, which was resumed on November 15. Nevertheless, in November the Germans were unable to break through the Soviet defenses. Moscow's defenders were reinforced at last by new divisions transferred from the Far East, and the initiative began to pass to the Red Army. Although Hitler's forces were only twenty or thirty kilometers from the capital, they could not carry their offensive further without a new regroupment, which they were not given a chance to carry out. The Western, Kalinin, and Southwestern fronts, although with fewer men and less equipment than the Germans, used the fresh, newly arrived units to go on the offensive and from December 5 to 15 inflicted major defeats on the German armies. By January 7, 1941, the first winter counteroffensive of the Red Army had been completed. The enemy was thrown back between 100 and 250 kilometers from Moscow.

The victory at Moscow had great strategic, political, and moral significance. Still, in summing up the results of the fighting in December 1941 and January 1942, a sober assessment should have been made of the capabilities of the army and the economy. The Red Army still had fewer

61. *Velikaia otechestvennaia voina Sovetskogo Soiuza. Kratkaia istoriia* (Moscow, 1970), p. 120.
62. Konev, *Bitva za Moskvu*, pp. 98–99.

men and less equipment than the Germans. The factories evacuated to the east had not yet managed to resume full production. The last months of 1941 saw the sharpest drop in output for the war effort. Current production met only half the needs of the front and the new reserve units. In planning the main objectives of the winter campaign under these conditions, the Soviet leadership should have focused mainly on increasing military production and reinforcing the army, resting and replenishing the divisions weakened by the fighting in the summer and fall. An orientation toward a defensive strategy would have corresponded to the required tasks. Offensives could have been planned for certain sectors of the front only. The General Staff understood this, but Stalin did not. Overestimating the first successes of the Red Army and underestimating the strength of the German army, Stalin gave orders for a general offensive all along the line.

Zhukov recalls the evening of January 2, 1942, when he was called to Moscow to discuss strategy. After Stalin had laid out the plan for a general offensive, Zhukov argued the case for restricting the attack to the Moscow front. Voznesensky supported him, pointing out the lack of necessary forces and equipment. Stalin, supported by Malenkov and Beria, brushed aside these objections. As they were leaving, Shaposhnikov told Zhukov that it had been pointless to argue; directives had already been sent to the fronts; the attack would begin the next day.[63]

The result was a predictable failure. Not one of the main German army groups was fully broken up. A recent history points out that this effort to achieve the impossible spoiled the attack on the Central Front, where a German army group could have been surrounded if Soviet reserves had been concentrated on the task.[64] Worse yet, when the winter offensive had spent itself and there was an urgent need to go on the defensive, Stalin insisted that the attack be continued. For example, on March 20 he ordered the enemy's major grouping in the Rzhev-Olenin-Vyazma area to be smashed. The troops of the Western Front tried to carry out this order, but to no avail. Again in April Stalin ordered an offensive, although the spring thaw had turned the roads to mud, hampering the movement of troops and supplies. As a result, Soviet troops were exhausted when the German spring and summer campaign of 1942 began. That was undoubtedly one of the reasons for the Soviet defeats that summer.

63. *Voenno-istoricheskii zhurnal* (1966), no. 10, pp. 79–80.
64. *Kratkaia istoriia Velikoi Otechestvennoi voiny* (Moscow, 1965), p. 138.

Another of Stalin's mistakes was the concentration of forces in the center, on the erroneous assumption that the Germans would focus their efforts once again on the drive toward Moscow. Intelligence reports in mid-March indicating a German concentration in the south were simply ignored.[65]

Moreover, Stalin would not completely give up the thought of ending the war in 1942. Though he accepted the General Staff plan for a defensive strategy that summer, he ordered some offensives, around Kharkov, for example, and in the Crimea. These were places where the Germans were also preparing for an offensive, and they had the superiority to justify it. Within a single month about 200,000 men concentrated on the Crimean Front, were lost, along with all their heavy artillery, which was subsequently used against the defenders of Sevastopol.

Konstantin Simonov considers the fighting on the Kerch Peninsula in the spring of 1942 a typical example of

the contrast between the right way to run a war and the false, slogan-ridden ideas of how a war should be run, which were based not only on military illiteracy but also on the mistrust of people engendered by 1937. . . . Seven years ago one of our front-line correspondents wrote me: "I was on the Kerch Peninsula in 1942. The reason for the shameful defeat is quite clear to me: the complete mistrust of the army and front commanders that emanated from Mekhlis, the stupid tyranny and wildly arbitrary ways of this military illiterate. . . . He forbade the digging of trenches so that the offensive spirit of the soldiers would not be undermined. He moved up heavy artillery and army staffs to the very front lines, and so on. Three armies were placed on a 16-kilometer front, a division occupied 600–700 meters of the front—never, nowhere, have I seen such a saturation of troops. And they all were mashed into a bloody porridge, they were thrown into the sea, they perished only because the front was commanded by a madman instead of a commander."

I was at the same place as the author of this letter, and although I don't fully agree with his choice of words, I subscribe to the substance of what he says. I have brought this up not in order to run down Mekhlis one more time; incidentally, he was a man of irreproachable personal courage and did nothing for his own glory. He was deeply convinced that he was doing right; and precisely for that reason, from a historical viewpoint, his actions on the Kerch Peninsula are of major interest.

Here was a man of that period; regardless of circumstance, he considered everyone a coward who preferred a suitable position one hundred meters from the enemy to an unsuitable position thirty meters away.

He considered everyone a panicmonger who wanted to take elementary security measures against possible failures, considered everyone unsure of our own

65. Ibid, pp. 153–154.

forces who made a realistic appraisal of the enemy's. For all his personal readiness to give his life for the homeland, Mekhlis was an obvious product of the atmosphere of 1937–38.

The commander of the front, Kozlov, to whom Mekhlis came as Stalin's representative, an educated and experienced military man, was also a product of the atmosphere of '37–38, only in a different sense: he was afraid to take on full responsibility, afraid to put a reasonable argument against a stupid onslaught— "everyone and everything forward"—afraid of the risk to himself in taking his argument with Mekhlis to headquarters.[66]

The attack near Kharkov also ended in disaster. Soviet troops managed to advance several dozen kilometers, but they were unable to consolidate their gains. On May 17, 1942, the Nazis took the offensive and threatened to encircle the Soviet armies. Vasilevsky, chief of the General Staff, proposed an immediate halt in the Soviet offensive. But Stalin, after talks with Timoshenko, rejected this proposal and ordered a continuation of the offensive. On the evening of May 18 Khrushchev asked Stalin to call off the offensive, but Stalin refused once again. Only when it was too late did he issue the order to stop. The situation was then hopeless; at least two armies were surrounded. Most of the men were killed or taken prisoner. The Southern and Southwestern fronts, which had insufficient troops to begin with, were extremely weakened by the Kharkov and Crimean disasters. The Germans were soon moving forward along the entire southern front.

The heroism of the Red Army finally stopped the enemy very deep in Russia, at Stalingrad and in the Causasus. Having exhausted the enemy in savage battles, the Soviet army resumed the offensive in November 1942, surrounding and destroying hundreds of thousands of enemy soldiers at Stalingrad. Yet again Stalin revealed his inability to assess the relative strength of the Soviet armies and the enemy's. In the second winter offensive, as in the first, he did not know when to stop the attack and go on the defensive. It took one more major defeat of Soviet troops, in the spring of 1943, to make Stalin see the real balance of forces. The enemy withdrew into the Donets Basin, to regroup and prepare a counterattack.

Stalin imagined that the Nazis were moving further west, beyond the Dnieper. So, although Soviet troops had outrun their supply bases and air support, Stalin demanded not a halt but an intensification of the offensive, to prevent the enemy from getting behind the Dnieper. The

66. Simonov, "Uroki voiny i sovest' pisatelia."

result was a powerful German attack that caught Soviet forces completely by surprise. After heavy fighting they were forced to retreat behind the Northern Donets and to abandon Kharkov and Belgorod once again. Reserves had to be sent to the southern sector of the front, and the move westward was accordingly slowed down.

My aim in this book is not to try to examine the whole war and all of Stalin's actions as supreme commander in chief. War is a complex process, whose result depends on a host of contributory elements. Despite the terrible defeats of the Red Army the war produced an immense wave of patriotism among the people. Millions of Soviet citizens rose to the defense of their country. During the war the influence of the party organizations recovered from the decline suffered during the repression. It was not the NKVD but the party that organized the people for the fight against fascism. Many officials acquired considerable autonomy in deciding important problems, and thousands of new leaders came to the fore, genuinely talented and devoted to the people. The course of events forced Stalin to rely on such individuals.

The patriotism of the people and the increasing experience of the Red Army, the colossal effort on the home front to produce all types of weapons, and the aid provided by the Soviet Union's allies—all these were primary factors that ensured a Soviet victory, despite Stalin's poor leadership.

Of course Stalin also learned something in the course of the war. Marshal Vasilevsky discusses this clearly enough, though quite cautiously:

The General Staff was turned into the working body of General Headquarters (the Stavka), which had no other special apparatus for that purpose. The General Staff supplied the necessary information, processed it, and drew up proposals that the Stavka subsequently used as a basis in issuing its orders. From the start Stalin expressed great dissatisfaction with the work of the General Staff. I cannot hide the fact, however, that Stalin did not always make the best decisions, nor did he always show an understanding of our difficulties. . . . At that time Stalin's performance suffered from miscalculations, sometimes quite serious ones. He was unjustifiably self-confident, headstrong, unwilling to listen to others; he overestimated his own knowledge and ability to guide the conduct of a war directly. He relied very little on the General Staff and made no adequate use of the skills and experience of its personnel. Often for no reason at all he would make hasty changes in the top military leadership. Under such conditions the General Staff could not develop to full capacity and was less effective than it should have been as the working body of the Stavka. . . . Stalin quite rightly insisted that the military abandon outdated strategic concepts, but he did not do so himself as quickly as we would have liked. He was to some degree more inclined toward head-on confrontations. Here, of course, aside from anything else, he was influenced by the situation at the front, the proximity of the enemy to Moscow, and his penetration deep into the heart of our country. . . . [The] battle of Stalingrad was an important milestone. But it can be argued that Stalin did not fully master the new forms and methods of armed combat until the battle of Kursk.[67]

I need hardly comment, after Vasilevsky, that the battle of Kursk took place after more than two years of war.

It can be said with certainty that had there been a more competent supreme command, a different kind of preparation for the war, a more intelligent assessment of the danger of war in June 1941—above all, if the military commanders and cadres killed in the purges of 1937–1938 had been preserved—the victory over Nazi Germany would have come much sooner and at much less cost.

It is true that by 1943–1945 Stalin's orders to the troops were more judicious than in the first two years. Still, his progress was much less noticeable than that of most of his subordinates. Although he bore the title Supreme Commander in Chief, he never commanded directly in the sense of personally leading troops in battle.

Whether the armies were retreating or advancing, Stalin stayed in his office. He had a poor picture of front-line conditions; he did not visit the army, to say nothing of the army in action. During the entire four years of war Stalin made only one trip to the front lines. This was at the beginning of August 1943, when preparations were under way for the Smolensk offensive by the forces of the Kalinin and Western fronts. On August 3 he visited the headquarters of the Western Front and on August 5 the headquarters of the Kalinin Front in the village of Khoroshevo near Rzhev. For the rest of the time Stalin conducted the war from Moscow, even when the action moved far to the west in 1944. This made work extremely difficult for the front-line commanders, who often had to leave their fronts and fly to Moscow in order to coordinate operations and have their plans approved. Zhukov testifies that Stalin had very little understanding of tactical problems; the action of military units smaller than armies was obscure to him. As for his "organizational talent," it rested

67. A. M. Vasilevsky, *Delo vsei zhizni* (Moscow, 1974), pp. 126–127.

largely on fear of repression, which did not stop during the war, as we shall see below.

Marshal Biryuzov is quite explicit on Stalin's involvement—or lack thereof—in the fighting:

He stood at a distance from the army. He was the supreme commander in chief, but the troops never saw him at the front, and not once did his eyes behold a soldier in combat. Moreover, during the very difficult initial period of the war the army in action did not even receive operational orders signed by Stalin himself. Almost all such documents were signed by Shaposhnikov, "on the instructions of the supreme commander in chief." Only when Soviet troops began to win one victory after another did orders appear over Stalin's signature.[68]

This isolation became a serious liability when Stalin tried to force his ideas on front-line commanders in contravention of the views of the front-line staff. Some commanders made independent decisions that were later attributed to Stalin's military genius. He was also given credit for decisions that were worked out by many minds at meetings of the General Staff.

In short, Stalin was in several respects a poor commander, with a weakness for abstract schematizing, for underestimating the enemy and overestimating his own forces. He was shortsighted and cruel, careless of losses, little interested in the fate of soldiers or the common people. He had much more to do with the reverses at the beginning of the war than with the victories at the end.

It is generally known that the Soviet victory cost 20 million lives (or more probably, between 25 and 30 million). No less than 10 million came back from the war as invalids. In 1940 the population of the Soviet Union was 194.1 million. In 1950, despite a record-high birth rate from 1945 to 1949, the population amounted to only 178.5 million.[69] During the war the Soviet Union also lost approximately 30 percent of its national wealth, which had been accumulated for centuries.[70] The Soviet Union did not win "with little loss of blood," nor was most of the fighting on enemy soil. By contrast, Germany's losses on all fronts and among its civilian population came to only 7 million. These figures cannot be overlooked when speaking of Stalin's role as a "military leader" in World War II.

68. S. S. Biryuzov, *Sovetskii soldat na Balkanakh* (Moscow, 1963), p. 242.
69. *Kommunist*, 1972, no. 8, p. 41.
70. *Kommunist*, 1972, no. 17, p. 18.

■ 5

REPRESSION DURING THE WAR

Finally, something must be said about the repression and other acts of illegality that continued during the war. The first big wave of repression occurred in the very first days of the war. Soviet citizens whose passports had the word "German" next to the heading "Nationality" were arrested. For centuries craftsmen and farmers had migrated from Germany to settle in Russia. In Moscow and several other major towns there had been special districts with German populations. Peter the Great had invited many scientists and skilled craftsmen to Russia from Germany. In tsarist times a significant number of families of the nobility had names of German origin. In the eighteenth century the Russian tsars and tsarinas had encouraged German immigrants to establish their settlements in the Ukraine, the Crimea, the Northern Caucasus, and Transcaucasia. Catherine the Great turned over a large area beyond the Volga in the former provinces of Saratov and Samara for German colonization. Over the course of a century, from 1764 to 1864, some 190 German settlements were established there. Germans living in Russia became subjects of the Russian state. In 1874 they began to be called up for military duty. During World War I quite a few soldiers, officers, and even generals of German nationality served in the Russian army. After the October revolution a large number of Russian Germans supported Soviet power. During the civil war three separate German regiments were formed in the Red Army, including the First German Cavalry Regiment in the First Red Cavalry Army. In late 1918 Lenin signed a decree establishing the Volga German Autonomous Region, which in 1924 became an autonomous republic. In 1941 approximately 400,000 Germans were living there. There was no question about their loyalty to the Soviet government. Almost all of them were active antifascists and expressed their desire to fight in the war against the Nazis. But Stalin took a different approach. Arrests of industrial and office workers of German nationality began in the first days of the war, and all Soviet Germans were dismissed from military service. In August 1941 the Volga German republic was abolished, and during a two-month period hundreds of thousands of Volga Germans were exiled to remote areas of Siberia and Kazakhstan. At the same time all German settlements and colonies in the Ukraine, Crimea, Kuban, and Transcaucasia were eliminated. The deportees were confined to "special settlements" in the eastern parts of the country, just as "kulaks" and "kulak supporters" had been in the early thirties. The number of Soviet Germans affected by these lawless measures exceeded 1.5 million.

Tens of thousands of Soviet citizens of Finnish nationality were similarly deported from Karelia or arrested. Approximately 300,000 Koreans were likewise moved from areas in the Soviet Far East and resettled in Central Asia and Siberia, while from Transcaucasia Stalin's government deported Kurds, Greeks, Georgian Muslims (Meskhi), and Armenian Muslims (Khemshchiny).

In 1943–1944 by order of the State Defense Committee a new wave of deportations began, this time of several nationalities in the Northern Caucasus and Volga regions. The Kalmyk, Chechen, Ingush, Karachai, and Balkar peoples were deported to Siberia and Kazakhstan. Their national autonomous districts were abolished and their property confiscated.

A friend of mine, M. N. Averbakh, was vacationing at the Armkhi Sanatorium in the Chechen-Ingush region in August 1949 (it had been made part of Georgia at that time). He came across a totally uninhabited *aul*, or mountain village, half in ruins, on the slope of Mount Stolovaya. A few days later he made the acquaintance of a militia colonel from Sverdlovsk, who gave my friend the following candid account of what had happened:

We were brought together in Beria's office in late July 1943. With the absolute secrecy of the meeting being stressed, we were told about the forthcoming operation and assigned specific tasks. Each of us was to put on the uniform of a military commander and take up a position with a military unit near the particular village assigned to him. We were to get on a friendly footing with the inhabitants of the village, winning them over with gifts and flattery, to develop close ties with influential people in the village, demonstrating profound respect for their customs and way of life, in short, to become their "blood brothers" and let them grow used to having Red Army soldiers stationed next to their village. The Chechens for the most part understood Russian well; nevertheless we were taught the rudiments of their language and instructed in their customs, habits, way of life, etc. They were all Muslims, still practiced polygamy, and consequently their women were an inert and passive lot. During the half year that we officers were supposed to live among them, we were to study them very closely and, without their knowing, draw up exact lists of the members of all families, find out where absent members were, and make preparations for a grand celebration of the next Red Army Day, to which all the men of the village in question were to be invited. We told them that the great services of the Chechen people in the struggle against the German aggressors would be celebrated on that day, that prizes and certificates from the Supreme Command would be awarded, and so on. We carried out these orders, living by the villages for half a year—I at the very one we can see from here—and we made preparations for celebrating Red Army Day, February 23, starting at 8 A.M.

On that day everyone gathered for the ceremony. A presiding committee was elected, consisting of the chairmen of the local soviets, who suspected nothing, the heads of the district NKVD units, and all the local notables. An honorary presiding committee consisting of the entire Politburo headed by Comrade Stalin was also elected. As representative of the army, I chaired the meeting. We began with speeches, awards, and comments from those who had fought in the war. There were only men at the meeting of course, since this was happening in the Muslim land of the Chechens.

At exactly 10 A.M. I stood up, pulled a printed envelope from the side pocket of my tunic, broke the wax seals, and announced that I was going to read a decree of the Presidium of the USSR Supreme Soviet. Then I read it to the stunned assemblage. The decree stated that the Chechens and Ingush had betrayed the Motherland during the war, had aided the Nazis, etc., and therefore were subject to deportation.

"Resistance or attempts to escape are useless," I added. "The clubhouse is surrounded." And turning to the NKVD officer and his deputy seated next to me, I ordered: "In the name of the party! Put your weapons on the table!"

Unimaginable confusion broke out in the hall. People flung themselves at the doors and windows but came up against the barrels of automatics and machine guns. During the ceremonies the military unit had surrounded the clubhouse with a solid cordon several rows deep. And think of it! There was no active resistance, even though everyone was dressed in ceremonial costume, wearing his dagger. We disarmed them very easily and led them in small groups under redoubled guard to the nearest railway station at Dzau-dzhikau (formerly Ordzhonikidze, and before that, Vladikavkaz), where trains of freight cars modified for the transport of prisoners were waiting.

While we were dealing with the men, others arrested the women and children, who had been left leaderless, and took them away. They too were loaded into freight cars, but not at the same station as their men, and sent off, trainload after trainload, to Kazakhstan. Some of the women offered resistance. They would not allow anyone to touch them. One threw a dagger and killed a soldier; in two other cases soldiers were wounded. After the people had been taken away, their livestock and other possessions, which had been inventoried in advance, were gathered up and carried off.

The cruel operation in Checheno-Ingushetia was directed by NKVD General Ivan Serov; overall leadership for the Caucasus as a whole was provided by Beria himself. But none of this could have happened without the approval, indeed the inspiration, of Stalin.

In May 1944, after the Crimea was liberated from the Germans, a similar punitive operation was carried out there on an even grander scale. During a three-day period, May 17–19, the entire Crimean Tatar population was deported. Families were allowed only half an hour to collect their things, and they were allowed to take with them only what they could carry. The Crimean Tatars were shipped off to Central Asia, Kazakhstan, and the Urals region.

For weeks they traveled in overcrowded freight cars—women, children, and the elderly. Tens of thousands perished along the way from hunger, thirst, and disease. Once in Tbilisi I myself happened to see a trainload of Kurdish nomads being deported from Georgia. The filthy freight cars were crammed full of women and children, from whom a constant weeping and lamentation could be heard.

This is how a Crimean Tatar woman, Tenzila Ibragimova, described the deportation:

> We were deported from the village of Adzhiatman in the Freidorf district. The operation was carried out with great brutality. At 3 A.M., while our children were fast asleep, soldiers burst in and ordered us to get ourselves together and leave our homes in five minutes. We weren't allowed to take any food or possessions with us. We were treated so rudely we thought they were taking us out to be shot. After being moved out of our village, we were detained [out in the open] for twenty-four hours without food; although we were famished, we weren't allowed to go back to our homes for something to eat. The crying of the hungry children became continuous. My husband was fighting at the front, and our three children were with me. Finally, we were loaded into trucks and driven to Eupatoria, where we were crowded like cattle into freight cars filled to overflowing. The train carried us for twenty-four days until we reached the station of Zerabulak in Samarkand province, from which we were shipped to the Pravda collective farm in the Khatyrchinsk district.

So inhuman were the conditions of transport that tens of thousands of the deported peoples died. Hundreds of thousands more perished from famine and disease when they found themselves in sparsely inhabited, inhospitable regions of Kazakhstan, Central Asia, Siberia, and the Urals. The Crimean Tatars, for example, contend that nearly half their population was lost, especially children and old people. Tenzila Ibragimova's account continued as follows:

> Thirty families were deported from our village, and of these only five families, themselves stricken with losses, survived. In the surviving families only one or two remained; the rest had perished from hunger and disease.
> My cousin . . . and her eight children were deported with us, although her husband had served in the Soviet army from the very first days of the war and

been killed in action. But the family of this fallen soldier died of starvation in penal exile in Uzbekistan. Only one daughter, named Pera, survived, but she was crippled by the horrors and hunger she experienced. . . .

Our men were at the front and there was no one to bury the dead. Sometimes for several days the corpses would lie there among the living.[71]

It is hard to estimate the total number of victims among the "punished peoples." We can assume that between four and five million were deported on the basis of their nationality, and that no less than one third died in transit or in exile. Members of the deported nationalities serving in the active army were discharged, despite their service records or the military honors they had won. At first, many of these soldiers and officers were put to work in construction battalions; later, they were sent off to their families in the east or south.[72]

In his detailed account of the tragedy of the Crimean Tatars and other deported peoples Aleksandr Nekrich discusses the question of whether those particular nationalities had been any more "disloyal" than others during the war.

[There were also] Cossack formations [that] were made a part of the Wehrmacht. In the summer of 1942, the general staff of the German land forces established a special department to handle the formation of military, auxiliary, and police forces from the ranks of former Soviet citizens. By early 1943 there were 176 battalions and 38 companies in this category, with a total of between 130,000 and 150,000. The overwhelming majority of them made up the so-called Russian Liberation Army, under the command of former Lieutenant General of the Soviet Army A. A. Vlasov. By the end of the war Vlasov had 300,000 men.

[Besides these treasonous Russians, there were] non-Russian military formations in the Wehrmacht at the end of the war numbering 700,000. Thus the total number of former Soviet citizens who took up arms on the enemy side was approximately one million. But it remains to be determined how many of them actually fought on the German side. Many of these units took no part whatsoever in military operations. . . .

Military units made up of "Oriental peoples" included the Turkestan legions and battalions (i.e., people of Central Asian origin), as well as Georgian, Armenian, Turkish, Volga Tatar, Crimean Tatar, Mountaineer (i.e., mountain peoples of the Northern Caucasus), Kalmyk, and some other legions and battalions.

But can these "legionnaires" be equated with the populations of the republics from which they came? Of course not. Those who took up arms against their homeland, who stood in the same ranks with the Nazis, placed themselves

71. From a collection of documents in my archives entitled "Appeals of the Crimean Tatar People to the Twenty-Third Party Congress."

72. See Aleksandr Nekrich, *Nakazannye narody* (New York, 1978). [Cf. the English edition, *The Punished Peoples* (New York, 1978). —G. S.]

outside the community. They were renegades and traitors to their own nationalities.[73]

To the list of military formations of former Soviet subjects who fought on the enemy side may be added the Ukrainian SS Galichina Division, Latvian, Lithuanian, and Estonian nationalist units, and some others. I cite this list, which is not particularly flattering to the Stalinist regime, simply to show that there is no basis for singling out only a few Soviet nationalities for the charge of collaboration with the enemy. There was no basis for any discrimination against them, let alone harsh repression.

In Western publications it is commonly stated that during the war Stalin pursued a relatively "mild" and conciliatory policy, seeking to unite all forces around the party and army. Reference is made to many purely nationalist slogans calling for the defense of Russia against age-old German expansionism, and also to Stalin's reconciliation with the Russian Orthodox Church. There is an element of truth in these assertions. Certainly in 1943 much of the previous persecution of the church was ended, many bishops and other clergy were released from confinement, hundreds of previously closed churches were opened, seminaries and an Orthodox Academy were allowed to open, and a Patriarchate was established.

Similarly, it was not only children of arrested Communists that were allowed to serve in the army; so were young people from former kulak families deported in the early thirties and denied freedom of movement before the war. Through some of the special service units of the NKVD abroad, contacts were made with Russian émigrés who opposed Hitler. There is evidence that even the Cadet leader Milyukov and General Denikin provided information useful to the Soviet Union during the war. Any such contacts would, of course, have required Stalin's approval or would have been made on his initiative.

Stalin had other "services" to his credit, however. Not only were "disloyal" nationalities deported but the camps of the Gulag Archipelago continued to be crowded with prisoners during the war just as before. Many political prisoners who asked to be sent to the front were instead left to suffer or die in Kolyma, Kazakhstan, Siberia, and the Urals. Thousands of knowledgeable commanders and commissars were among them, as well as capable economic administrators. All were guarded by NKVD military units that might better have been fighting the invader.

73. Ibid., pp. 10–11.

During the war local NKVD agencies were maintained in every small town or district, although there were quite enough regular police to maintain order. Thus, at the same time that Stalin was waging war on Nazi Germany he continued his own war against a sizable portion of the Soviet population.

Mention must also be made of the repression against military leaders. In the first days of the war quite a few highly placed military personnel were arrested on Stalin's orders; for example:

General D. C. Pavlov, commander of the Western Front, was arrested and shot; General V. Ye. Klimovsky, a leading participant in the Spanish civil war and chief of staff at the front, was arrested and shot; General N. A. Klich was arrested and shot; Major General S. I. Oborin, commander of the 14th Mechanized Corps, arrested on the charge that it was not ready for action; Korobkov, commander of the 4th Army, was arrested.

All these officers have since been rehabilitated. By blaming them for lack of preparedness for the war and losing the first battles, Stalin sought to make them scapegoats for his own blunders.[74]

Many generals who died in battle in the first months of the war were also made scapegoats. They were proclaimed traitors, and their families were exiled from Moscow. One example was Lieutenant General V. Ya. Kachalov.[75]

At the beginning of the war Stalin sometimes issued confused orders for arrests, then abruptly ordered the release of the victims. I have already mentioned the brief imprisonment of Vannikov, people's commissar of the defense industry. V. P. Balandin, a deputy commissar of the aviation industry, had a similar experience. He was in prison while his colleagues were anxiously consulting with Stalin about the air defense of Moscow.

Stalin repeated several times: "There are no people you can count on. . . . There aren't enough people." When Stalin began to talk about people, Dementyev whispered to me: "Let's ask about Balandin." I nodded, and we took advantage of a pause in the conversation: "Comrade Stalin, it's been over a month since they arrested our deputy commissar in charge of engines, Balandin. We don't know why he's doing time, but we can't imagine that he is an enemy. The Commissariat needs him, the supervision of engine building has become very poor. We beg you to review this case, we have no doubts about him."

"Yes," Stalin replied, "he's been doing time for forty days and hasn't signed

74. See *Kratkaia istoriia Velikoi Otechestvennoi voiny*, p. 68.
75. See *Ogonyok* (1964), no. 47.

any depositions. Maybe there's nothing on him. . . . It's very possible. . . . That does happen. . . ." The following day Vasily Petrovich Balandin, with sunken cheeks and shaved head, was back in his office at the Commissariat, continuing his work.[76]

Soldiers who broke out of encirclement were often rewarded with arrest. The agents of SMERSH[77] were actively engaged in repression both at the front and in the immediate rear. Of course German intelligence and the Gestapo did send many spies into rear lines, and tried to recruit traitors. But the reports of SMERSH, which tell of uncovering huge numbers of foreign agents, anti-Soviet elements, plots and betrayals, leave the impression that many such discoveries were deliberately contrived.

The sentences handed down by military tribunals at various levels were also unjustifiably harsh. Many soldiers and commanders were sentenced to death for the most insignificant reasons. After the disaster on the southern front in the summer of 1942, on Stalin's orders, special "barrier units" *(zagraditelnye otryady)* were set up behind the lines to prevent retreat. At a conference of officials from the military tribunals, SMERSH, and related agencies Kaganovich declared that the soldiers and commanders of the Soviet army should know that if they moved forward, what awaited them was either death or awards and honors, but if they moved backward, what awaited them was only death. Yet the ordinary soldiers and commanders were the least to blame for the retreats and defeats of 1941–1942.

Another ugly practice of the war years was the execution of inmates of prisons in cities being abandoned. Even in the spring of 1942 during the retreat from Voroshilovgrad, by order of I. O. Matulevich, a member of the Military Collegium of the Soviet Supreme Court, almost all the inmates of that town's prisons were shot.

Repression also continued away from the battlefront. For example, a group of philosophers—F. Gorokhov, I. M. Kulagin, and others—were arrested on the charge of defeatist tendencies. Near the end of the war several commissariats were subjected to savage purges, especially the Commissariat of Means of Communication, which was ravaged on March 16, 1944, with the knowledge of Stalin and Kaganovich. All the victims were rehabilitated in the late fifties, most of them posthumously.

76. A. S. Yakovlev, *Tsel' zhizni* (Moscow, 1966), p. 265.
77. [SMERSH—an acronym from the Russian words *smert' shpionam,* meaning "death to spies"—was a special agency for dealing with spies behind the lines. —G. S.]

Stalin's attitude toward prisoners of war is one of the grimmest pages in his record. No precise figures on the number of such prisoners have appeared in Soviet publications, but it is safe to say that in 1941 the Germans took no less than 3 to 4 million Soviet prisoners, plus another million or so in the spring and summer of 1942. The conditions under which they were held were extremely brutal. A great many died from starvation and the killing pace of slave labor for the Nazis. Huge numbers were simply shot. Western sources state that up to May 1944, 1,981,000 Soviet prisoners of war had died in Hitler's camps, while another 1,241,000 had been executed.[78] For the most part these Red Army soldiers had surrendered only after finding themselves in a hopeless situation, after being encircled and trying to hold out without adequate arms or supplies, without food, often badly wounded. Yet Stalin himself was to blame, as we have seen, for the disastrous experience of their units. Of course the primary blame for the cruel treatment of prisoners of war belongs to Hitler and the Gestapo. Nevertheless Stalin also took an unjustifiably harsh attitude toward them. He refused to sign the Hague Convention, with the result that Soviet prisoners received no help through the International Red Cross. Many of the Soviet prisoners who joined Vlasov's "Russian Liberation Army" were only trying to save themselves from starvation, hoping at a suitable moment to cross over to the Soviet Army or the partisans.

In late 1941 Stalin's son Yakov Dzhugashvili was one of those taken prisoner when Soviet armies were encircled near Vyazma. After the Nazi defeat at Stalingrad Hitler's government offered, through intermediaries, to exchange Yakov for Field Marshal von Paulus. Stalin refused, and his son died in captivity during the last weeks of the war. When told of the German exchange offer, Stalin's response had been: "I don't have a captured son in Germany." In "Liberation" (*Osvobozhdenie*), a Soviet film serial on the war, Stalin is portrayed as saying, "I don't exchange soldiers for field marshals," but this remark is a product of the screenwriter's imagination.

When the war ended, special officers visited the prisoner-of-war camps in the Anglo-American zone and read to the inmates an official letter, which declared that prisoners of war would not be prosecuted in their native land. This promise was not kept. Returning prisoners of war were treated like traitors. Into the concentration camps went not only real

78. Alexander Dallin, *German Rule in Russia, 1941–1945: A Study of Occupation Policies* (New York, 1957), p. 427.

traitors but also many war heroes, defenders of Sevastopol, Odessa, and Brest, partisans, people who had been tortured in the Nazi death camps of Maidanek, Auschwitz, and Dachau. The fate of Major N. S. Tkachuk is typical. A tank officer, seriously wounded near Dorogobuzh during a desperate attack on an enemy breakthrough, Tkachuk was hidden and nursed by collective farmers. When he was barely recovered, Tkachuk tried to pick his way eastward but was captured by the Nazis and put in a prisoner-of-war camp. In February 1942 he escaped but was recaptured. After a third flight, Tkachuk made contact with French partisans, and for two years actively fought the Nazis. In January 1945 he was again taken prisoner but was freed by British forces. He joined a British unit —asking to have a Soviet uniform made for him—and fought the Nazis once again. Yet when Tkchuk returned to his native land, he was put in a "filtration" camp for a year, and then was arrested and condemned on the basis of ridiculous charges.[79]

Among others arrested on their return from captivity were Major P. M. Gavrilov, one of the leaders in the defense of the Brest fortress. Stalin's security police took him away, along with virtually all other surviving participants of that heroic battle. Thousands of similar examples could be cited. Even the outstanding Tatar poet Musa Dzhalil, who was killed in Nazi captivity, was proclaimed an "enemy of the people" under Stalin.

79. Tkachuk's story is told by the prominent Soviet writer S. S. Smirnov in *Pravda*, April 5, 1964. A similar fate befell A. Karapetyan, P. Chkuaseli, and V. Moskalets, imprisoned pilots who seized three German planes in the summer of 1944 and escaped to a partisan base in the Naluboks forest in Belorussia. After the liberation of Belorussia they were arrested and sentenced to ten years in prison. See *Izvestia*, July 9, 1964.

13

CRIMES AND MISTAKES IN THE POSTWAR PERIOD

■ 1
REPRESSION AFTER THE WAR

The victory of the Soviet people in the Great Patriotic War, though won at the price of enormous sacrifices, engendered great exaltation. People tried to heal the wounds of war as quickly as possible; they lived on the hope of a better and happier future. The land was so bloodsoaked that any thought of new deaths seemed unbearable. So strong was this senti-ment that immediately after the war the Presidium of the Supreme Soviet decreed an end to the death penalty, even for the most serious crimes. The spy mania and universal suspicion that prevailed before the war tended to disappear, especially in view of the drastic change in the international situation. The Soviet Union was no longer isolated. It had become a superpower, and both its friends and its enemies abroad closely followed events inside the USSR. All this set limits on the arbitrary measures Stalin and his circle could indulge in.

Still, repression continued in the postwar period, though on a somewhat smaller scale than in the prewar years. In 1947, for example, many prominent figures in the Soviet air force and aviation industry, who had been heroes in the war, were arrested on trumped-up charges. Among them were A. I. Shakhurin, minister of the aviation industry, and three air marshals—S. A. Khudyakov-Khanferyants, A. A. Novikov, and G. A. Vorozheikin. A large number of officials in the aviation industry and military aviators were also arrested on charges of producing airplanes of "poor quality," of stopping military production too soon and switching aircraft factories over to consumer production too quickly. Stalin's own son Vasily took a hand in this affair. He was a coarse, semiliterate alcoholic, who began the war as a captain and rose to lieutenant general by the end of the war, being placed in charge of the air force of the Moscow Military District, a position totally incommensurate with his abilities.

A number of other prominent military men were arrested on false charges, including major figures in the Soviet navy. Among them were:

Admiral M. A. Galler, deputy commissar of the navy; V. A. Alfuzov, naval chief of staff; and G. A. Stepanov, Alfuzov's deputy.

These three veteran admirals were accused of giving away the secret of the parachute torpedo—when sketches of it were being sold at bookstalls. Another victim was Colonel-General V. N. Gordov, one of the heroes of the battle of Stalingrad. Galler and Gordov died in prison, but in 1953 the others were rehabilitated and restored to their positions in the army, navy, and air force.

Even Marshal Zhukov, who after the war remained minister of defense and deputy to the supreme commander in chief, as well as being the chief in command of the Soviet forces in Germany, fell into disfavor. One day Stalin called Zhukov into his office and said to him:

Beria has just written me a report on your suspicious contacts with the Americans and British. He thinks you've become a spy for them. I don't believe that nonsense. But still it would be better for you to go somewhere away from Moscow for a while. I've proposed that you be appointed commander of the Odessa Military District.[1]

1. N. K. Kuznetsov, *Nakanune* (Moscow, 1966), p. 212.

Until after Stalin's death Zhukov was obliged to stay far from Moscow, at first in Odessa, later in the Urals Military District. The press stopped writing about him; people stopped talking about him. Some thought he had been arrested. On the other hand, rumors circulated (as they once had about Blyukher) that he was leading the People's Liberation Army in China. The names of many other famous wartime commanders also vanished from the press: Rokossovsky, Meretskov, Tolbukhin, Voronov, Bagramyan, Konev, Malinovsky, Vatutin, Chernyakhovsky. Stalin was determined not to share his military glory with them.

In 1949–1951 some oblast party organizations were decimated. The "Leningrad Affair" was the most serious of such cases. On Stalin's order, and with the active participation of Beria and Malenkov, P. S. Popkov, first secretary of the Leningrad obkom, was arrested, and with him a number of other leading officials, including P. A. Tyurkin, a former commissar of education and director of the "Ice Line."[2] Indeed, nearly the entire staff of the Leningrad obkom was arrested, and mass repression fell on officials of the local Komsomol, the Soviet executive committee, on raikom leaders, factory managers, scientific personnel, and people in higher education. Thousands of innocent people were arrested, and many of them died in confinement. Among the victims of the Leningrad Affair were:

Nikolai Alekseevich Voznesensky, member of the Politburo, deputy chairman of the Council of Ministers, and chairman of Gosplan; A. A. Kuznetsov, a secretary of the Central Committee and a leader of the defense of Leningrad; M. I. Rodionov, chairman of the Council of Ministers of the RSFSR; and A. A. Voznesensky, minister of education of the RSFSR.

Many of the officials who were cut down in 1949–1952, such as Voznesensky and Kuznetsov, belonged to the new generation of leaders who rose to prominence after 1936–1937 and distinguished themselves during the war. They were significantly different from the preceding generation. As a rule, they completely accepted the cult of Stalin's personality. As their careers progressed, some of them acquired the characteristic features of Stalinists: rudeness and unjustified abruptness in their treatment of subordinates, dictatorial manners, vanity. But many of these younger officials knew little about the crimes Stalin had committed. They took a creative attitude toward their work, displaying great energy and organi-

2. [Ledovoi Magistral—the road across the ice of Lake Lagoda, by which supplies were brought to Leningrad during the nine-hundred-day siege by the Germans.—G. S.]

zational talent. They were basically honorable people who tried to do their jobs as well as possible, and with increasing frequency they came into conflict with such figures in Stalin's inner circle as Beria, Molotov, Malenkov, and Voroshilov. Stalin encouraged such dissension among his lieutenants. An anecdote by V. V. Kolotov, one of Nikolai Voznesensky's aides, is revealing:

> Late one night I received a package from Beria addressed to Voznesensky. As usual, I opened the package and took out a thick bundle of papers fastened together. On the first sheet was printed: "List of people subject to . . ." In my hands was a long list of people condemned to be shot. . . . At the end of the list, diagonally, Beria, Shkiryatov, and Malenkov had signed their names.
>
> The list had been sent to Voznesensky for his approval. This was a first in my long years of working in the Kremlin. Till that day nothing of the sort had ever come to Voznesensky. I went at once to Nikolai Alekseevich's office and gave him the list that was burning my fingers. Voznesensky began to read it attentively. He would read a page or two, stop, think for a while, return to the page he had read, and read further. When he had finished reading the list, looking at the signatures underneath, Nikolai Alekseevich said indignantly: "Return this list by courier to where you got it and inform the proper person by telephone that I will never sign such lists. I am not a judge and don't know whether the people on the list need to be shot. And tell them never to send such lists to me again."
>
> Beria could not help but remember Voznesensky's categorical refusal to endorse these death sentences for "enemies of the people."[3]

In the first years following the war the influence of these younger officials, who had distinguished themselves during the war, increased markedly. Voznesensky, for example, was made first deputy chairman of the USSR Council of Ministers. Stalin, although chairman, did not like to attend government meetings and let Voznesensky fill in for him. This offended the vanity of men like Voroshilov, Molotov, Beria, and Kaganovich. A. A. Kuznetsov, rising to a secretaryship in the apparatus of the Central Committee, was given the job of checking the activity of the security organs. The young leaders were threatened from another direction as well. The rigid framework of Stalin's cult was too confining for the most capable of them. Sooner or later some of them were bound to become a nuisance to Stalin, as people who might diminish his own authority. That is how death came to Voznesensky, after he had been in charge of Gosplan for eleven years, since December 1937.

3. Kolotov's book on Voznesensky has been published in two editions, but the passage quoted here does not appear in either. It was apparently removed by the censors or the editors. [See V. V. Kolotov and G. A. Petrovichev, *N. A. Voznesenskii (1903–1950). Biograficheskii ocherk* (Moscow, 1963). —G. S.]

A major factor creating a conflict with Stalin was Voznesensky's book on the war economy of the Soviet Union, which was issued in 1947.[4] Its detailed analysis was based on much new factual material, and despite certain mistakes, it soon became popular among economists, who began to cite it on the same level as Stalin's works. Although Stalin had read the manuscript in 1947 and had even signed the authorization for publication, the book was suddenly declared to be anti-Marxist and was withdrawn. At the beginning of 1949 Stalin removed Voznesensky from all his posts, including membership in the Central Committee. Stalin also refused to see his former aide and hear him out.

Voznesensky remained at liberty for several months following his "disgrace." Apparently there was not even a pretext for his arrest. Beria tried to create one—an excuse for decimating the Gosplan leadership—by concocting a case about the loss of some secret papers in Gosplan. Not only the chairman of Gosplan but two deputy chairmen, A. D. Panov and A. V. Kuptsov, and several other officials were brought to trial. Voznesensky spoiled the show by flatly denying the charges and exposing the provocative nature of the trial in his first statement. Fearing further exposure, Beria ordered that Voznesensky appear in court no more and that the other defendants be condemned.

This was only a postponement for Voznesensky. Yet even then, out of office, with Beria after him, he did not lose faith in Stalin. His wife relates that he repeatedly phoned Poskrebyshev, Stalin's secretary, asking him to send over a courier, with whom he sent back memoranda pleading for work and assuring Stalin of his devotion and honesty. But he did not get an answer. He believed that there was some sort of misunderstanding. "While Stalin is getting to the bottom of this," he told his family, "I must not lose time." He continued to work on a new book, "The Political Economy of Communism," which he had begun in 1948, but it remained unfinished. In 1950 he was arrested and shot.[5] Before being executed, Voznesensky, Rodionov, and Kuznetsov were subjected to especially refined tortures under the personal supervision of Beria.

In the postwar period the Soviet intelligentsia was struck some particularly hard blows. Instead of serious, dispassionate analysis of both the achievements and certain errors of Soviet writers, composers, theater

4. Voznesensky, *Voennaia ekonomika SSSR v period Otechestvennoi voiny* (Moscow, 1947). [There is an English translation (New York, 1948).—D. J.]

5. See *Literaturnaya gazeta*, November 30, 1963; and *Voprosy istorii KPSS*, 1963, no. 6, p. 98.

people, and so on, Stalin and Zhdanov launched pogrom-style campaigns of denunciation, one after another, which severely damaged Soviet culture at home and its prestige abroad. The persecution began in 1946–1947 with a series of speeches by Zhdanov, resulting in the expulsion of Mikhail Zoshchenko and Anna Akhmatova from the Union of Writers. Other artists were subjected to mudslinging:

Boris Pasternak, Dmitri Shostakovich, V. I. Muradeli, Sergei Prokofiev, Aram Khachaturyan, Sergei Eisenstein, Vsevolod I. Pudovkin, V. Ya. Shebalin, N. Ya. Myaskovsky, Nikolai Pogodin, Ilya Selvinsky, V. Kirsanov, Vasily Grossman, Olga Bergolts, and Aleksandr Gladkov.

Soon the arrests began. Among the many writers, poets, and critics arrested in 1948–1950 were:

Aleksandr Gladkov, Perets Markish, D. Bergelson, B. D. Chetverikov, S. Galkin, D. Gofshtein, Lev Kvitko, Itsik Fefer, Boris Dyakov, and Yaroslav Smelyakov.

A major literary scholar, G. A. Gukovsky, died in confinement, and two other experts in literature, A. Isbakh and I. M. Musinov, were hit by the repression.

The Jewish theater was in fact destroyed by the security police, the MGB (Ministry of State Security). Many leading actors of this theater were arrested, including V. L. Zuskin, a director and outstanding performer. The head of the theater, Solomon Mikhoels, a prominent public figure as well as a great actor, was killed. Emmanuel d'Astier de la Vigerie[6] tells how Stalin, on Kaganovich's advice, invited Mikhoels to play the role of King Lear for him in 1946. This remarkable actor was repeatedly invited to give private performances of Shakespearean roles for Stalin. Each time Stalin thanked Mikhoels and praised his acting. But in 1948, with Stalin's knowledge, if not on his initiative, Beria's agents killed Mikhoels in Minsk, then made up the story that he died in an auto accident. A few years later he was posthumously labeled a spy for Anglo-American intelligence.

Those were also the years of an ugly campaign against "cosmopolitanism" and "worship of things foreign," bringing dozens of arrests and thousands of dismissals. It was dangerous even to quote foreign sources, to say nothing of corresponding with foreign scholars. Among those driven from their work were:

6. *Sur Staline* (Paris, 1964).

I. I. Yuzovsky, a major theatrical and literary critic; I. S. Zvavich, a publicist; I. L. Altman, A. S. Gurvich, B. Dairedzhiev, and S. M. Mokulsky.

After the meetings of the Agricultural Academy and the Academy of Medical Sciences in 1948 and 1950 the medical and biological sciences were subjected to unprecedented devastation. Dozens of leading scientists were repressed and thousands were fired or demoted. Among those arrested were Academician V. V. Parin and the prominent geneticist V. P. Efroimson. Among the academicians fired or demoted were:

L. A. Orbeli, N. P. Dubinin, M. M. Zavadovsky, I. I. Shmalgauzen, P. N. Konstantinov, P. K. Anokhin, and I. S. Beritashvili.

Many years of persecution finally drove D. A. Sabinin, the leading Russian plant physiologist, to suicide.

Repression touched other sciences as well as biology. Among those arrested were Doctor of Technical Sciences and General of Artillery P. A. Gelvikh; Professor S. S. Yudin, an outstanding physician, and originator of many operative techniques; and the historian Ye. L. Shteinberg.

Attached to prisoners' dossiers were coded initials describing their "crimes"—for example, KRTD meaning "counter revolutionary Trotskyist activity." In the postwar period new initials appeared: VAT for "praising American technology"; VAD, "praising American democracy"; and PZ, "kowtowing to the West."

In the years 1946–1949 many émigrés who had returned to the Soviet Union after the war were arrested. An intensive campaign for return to the homeland had begun in 1945–1946 among émigrés living in Western Europe and Manchuria. Several thousand people responded to these appeals, of whom most were by this time children of the émigrés of the early twenties. Yet there were some former Russian officers as well. Most of the arrests before 1950 were on the standard charges of "espionage" or "anti-Soviet activity while in residence abroad." Among those arrested was the Old Bolshevik Gabriel Myasnikov, who had spoken out for freedom of the press in the Soviet Union in 1921. In 1922 he had been expelled from the party and had tried to form the oppositional "Workers' Group," which not surprisingly was branded a "counterrevolutionary organization." Myasnikov escaped across the border and for more than twenty years worked as a simple laborer in a French factory. Although the Soviet embassy had promised him complete safety in the Soviet Union, he was arrested immediately upon returning home. Also arrested was I. A. Krivoshein, son of one of the leaders of the White movement. Krivoshein had been active in the French Resistance, and had even become one of that movement's inner circle. He was given back his Soviet citizenship, but after two years was arrested and sentenced to ten years' imprisonment.

In late 1949 the MGB cooked up a story about the existence of a "pro-American Jewish conspiracy" in the Soviet Union, which was followed by the arrests of leading officials and public figures of Jewish origin. Solomon Lozovsky (Dridzo), who had just turned seventy-four, an Old Bolshevik member of the Central Committee and deputy minister of foreign affairs, was arrested and shot. Almost all the members of the Jewish Antifascist Committee were arrested, and most were shot. (Academician Lena Shtern was exiled.) In the summer of 1952 a large group of Jewish poets and writers who had been arrested earlier were also shot.

Early in 1949 Mikhail Borodin was arrested and soon shot. In the twenties he had been the Soviet Communist Party's chief political adviser to the Kuomintang revolutionary nationalist movement in China and a personal friend of Sun Yat-sen. From 1941 to 1949 Borodin had worked as editor in chief of the English-language newspaper *Moscow News* as well as chief editor of the Soviet Information Bureau. Almost the entire editorial staff of *Moscow News* was arrested with Lozovsky, including the American journalist Anna Louise Strong, who was accused of espionage and expelled from the Soviet Union.

The repression of former political prisoners in 1948 and 1949 deserves special attention. While the war was on, they remained in confinement, even those whose terms ended in 1942–1945. The great victory, one would think, should have relieved the tension and permitted a general amnesty. It was expected, and an amnesty was in fact declared—but not for "enemies of the people." On the contrary, in the first years after the war a wave of terror swept through the camps. A vast number of prisoners received illegal extensions of their sentences by five, eight, or ten years. Many politicals were transferred from general to special camps with an "intensified regime." On completion of their sentences some were released from the camps but condemned to "eternal settlement" in northern areas, in the Kolyma region, Siberia, and Kazakhstan. A very few received permission to return to European Russia, but not, as a rule, to the big cities. In the summer of 1947 I met one of these "lucky ones," I. P. Gavrilov, who had found work as chief agronomist at a state farm near Moscow. He had been a friend of my father's. Although the "lucky ones" were relatively few, almost all were rearrested in 1948–1949. They were sent back to prisons and camps, often without any concrete charges, simply for preventive custody, as it was called. Those few who by some oversight were not rearrested found themselves in a terrible position. No one would hire them or register their right to live anywhere; they often wandered through the country for months and years without roofs over their heads. Some were so desperate they committed suicide; others became beggars; there were even some who returned to "their" camps, hoping to find work as wage laborers.

On November 26, 1948, the Presidium of the USSR Supreme Soviet passed a decree that stated: "Those exiled during the Great Patriotic War to remote districts of the Soviet Union on suspicion of treason, Germans, Chechens, Ingush, Crimean Tatars, . . . are to remain in those places forever, and in the case of flight from their place of registration will be sentenced to twenty years hard labor."

In late 1951 the MGB issued an order which placed all exiles and resettled persons, regardless of how or why they had come to be in that situation, under the terms of the decree of November 26, 1948. The period of exile for all was made permanent, so that those convicted for political reasons during the Stalin years had no hope of ever returning to their families or home towns.

I have been discussing arrests and executions of completely innocent persons, but I shall also take note of a special trend in the postwar years —the emergence of small conspiratorial groups among young people in Leningrad, Moscow, and Georgia whose aim was to fight the cult of Stalin and his dictatorship and to promote the "revival of Leninism." Sometimes group members took on theoretical tasks, such as writing a true history of the party or a critique of Stalin's philosophical and political statements. But in some cases the possibility of Stalin's or Beria's assassination was considered. In Moscow, for example, there was a group of sixteen students who called themselves the "Union of Struggle for the Cause of Revolution" (SBDR—Soyuz Borby za Delo Revoliutsii). Aleksandr Voronel, who emigrated to Israel in the seventies, wrote later that he heard about the existence in Moscow alone of dozens of similar circles and was personally acquainted with representatives of nine anti-Stalinist youth groups. As a rule, these groups had strictly Marxist programs; sometimes they put out journals and composed manifestos. Voronel himself was first arrested as part of a case against one such group.

Under conditions of mass terror, all-embracing surveillance, and the universal cult of Stalin these groups were usually quickly discovered and their members arrested. Although matters had never gone beyond plans and discussions and the drafting of programs with any of these groups, the sentences handed down at closed trials were very severe. Three leaders of the SBDR group, B. V. Slutsky, V. L. Furman, and Ye. Z. Gurevich, who were only nineteen or twenty years old, were shot. The other members of the group were sentenced to twenty-five years imprisonment. They were freed only after the Twentieth Party Congress.

Some writers and Old Bolsheviks also spoke out clandestinely against the crimes of the Stalinist dictatorship. In 1940 Lydia Chukovskaya wrote a story ("The Deserted House") which contained a protest against mass repression. Anna Akhmatova produced her renowned "Requiem." The Old Bolshevik A. P. Spunde, a member of the first Soviet government and the Central Executive Committee, who was expelled from the party and worked as a bookkeeper in the Moscow Trading Company, wrote his memoirs in 1947–1949. He tried to give an accurate history of the party and to expose the myths of Stalinist propaganda. His comments on Stalin's *Short Course* were particularly sharp. Another Communist Party member of more recent vintage, B. A. Gryaznykh, while in a camp, wrote a pamphlet entitled "Stalinist Socialism in the Light of Leninism," which was circulated in manuscript copies in the mining areas of the southern department of Dalstroi. The pamphlet, as its author later admitted,[7] contained many exaggerations and mistaken assertions, since at that time through no fault of his own Gryaznykh was able to see Soviet life only from its most unattractive side. However, a number of the pamphlet's charges against Stalin and his administration are fully justified.

The Leningrad Communist Yelena Vladimirova wrote the long narrative poem "Kolyma" while in prison, along with many shorter verses sharply protesting the inhumanity of Stalin's camps. Anti-Stalinist poetry was also written in Moscow by the young poet Mandel (Naum Korzhavin). Yevtushenko later commented:

I don't know if Mandel's name will be remembered in the history of Russian poets but it will certainly be remembered in the history of Russian social thought. He was the only poet who openly wrote and recited verse against Stalin while Stalin was alive.[8]

7. Statement of August 12, 1956, by B. A. Gryaznykh to the commission of the USSR Supreme Soviet visiting the Magadan region. A copy of Gryaznykh's statement is in my archives. His subsequent fate is unknown to me.

8. [The English wording is from Yevtushenko, *Precocious Autobiography* (New York,

All such uncoordinated individual protests could not of course disturb the foundations of Stalin's despotism in the slightest.

■ 2

REPRESSION IN THE "PEOPLE'S DEMOCRACIES"

As a result of the Soviet victory in the Great Patriotic War, governments were established in Eastern and Southeastern Europe forming a bloc of allied countries (dependent on the USSR) which in the Soviet press were usually called "people's democracies." The postwar history of these countries is rich in events that require special study and analysis. But in the limits of this work I cannot discuss the history of those countries from 1944 to 1948, a history that included many examples of unlawful political repression, the suppression of opposition movements, and violation of democratic freedoms.

By 1948 Stalin's policy toward those countries, in Ernst Henri's telling phrase, was one of "socialist Caesarism." Stalin regarded the leaders of the new socialist countries as his vassals, obliged to carry out all his instructions without demur. He saw the extension of the socialist camp as the extension of his personal domain. And if the interests of some country, even the national interests of the Soviet Union, came into conflict with his vainglorious pretensions, he unhesitatingly gave priority to his pretensions. Considering himself the absolute master and supreme arbiter in the socialist camp, Stalin intervened unceremoniously in the internal affairs of the East European Communist parties, imposing his own decisions, which were often completely stereotyped, and treating the leaders of those parties with extreme rudeness. Ignoring the political and economic individuality of each East European country, their specific interests and needs, he tried to convert them into protectorates rather than independent, friendly allies of the Soviet Union.

Discontent was the unavoidable result, not only among the petty-bourgeois masses, who were very sensitive to national restrictions, but also among the working class and the Communist parties. In the context of the Stalin cult, which was implanted in all the socialist countries, this policy was bound to produce conflicts both within those countries and in relations between governments.

1963), p. 76. Medvedev quotes from the unpublished Russian text, a copy of which is in his archives. Excerpts from Vladimirova's "Kolyma" may be found in *An End to Silence* (New York, 1982), pp. 95–96. —G. S.]

The inevitable conflict was most acute in relations with Yugoslavia, which from 1945 to 1947 was considered the most advanced of the "people's democracies." It was in Yugoslavia that the armed struggle against Nazi occupation acquired the greatest scope during the war, with the leading role unquestionably played by the Communist Party. It was the country that immediately after liberation introduced the most radical democratic and socialist changes, including agrarian reform and nationalization of industry. This vanguard role, both in fighting the fascist occupation and in effecting a socialist transformation, enhanced the popularity of the Yugoslav Communist leaders at home and in the other people's democracies. No one could say that the Yugoslav government was imposed by the Soviet Army or as a result of Soviet intervention.

Any attempt to judge whether all of Tito's foreign and domestic policies were correct is beyond the scope of this book. The essential point here is the source of Stalin's fury. He was enraged not by Tito's mistakes, whether real or imaginary, but by the Yugoslav leader's growing popularity and independence of judgment. Tito and the other Yugoslav Communist leaders were reluctant to accept all of Stalin's recommendations on the economic and political development of Yugoslavia. They refused to always follow the Soviet model. This striving for autonomy, in foreign as well as internal policy finally led to a complete break between the USSR and Yugoslavia, and Stalin was chiefly responsible. The Yugoslav Communist leaders were branded "a gang of Trotskyite-Bukharinite murderers" and "agents of imperialism." For several years, at Stalin's insistence, the world Communist press joined in a campaign of unrestrained slander, calling this socialist country a terrorist fascist dictatorship, a center for British and American intelligence and anti-Communist propaganda. Stalin broke off economic relations with Yugoslavia, Soviet troops were moved up to the Yugoslav borders, and the Soviet press literally called for civil war in Yugoslavia.

For a while Stalin seriously considered plans for invading Yugoslavia with the Soviet army, but in the end could not bring himself to take such a risky step. He placed his main bets on the formation of underground groups inside Yugoslavia to organize Tito's assassination. Tito was well protected, however, and almost all the terrorists sent to Yugoslavia were apprehended. Stalin was dissatisfied with the MGB's "poor performance" and several times said to Beria, "What are you dragging it out for?"— referring to Tito's assassination.

After Stalin's death a note from Tito was found in Stalin's desk among other important papers. The note read, "Comrade Stalin, I ask you to stop sending terrorists to Yugoslavia to murder me. We have already caught seven. . . . If this doesn't stop, I will send one man to Moscow, and there will be no need to send a second."

After the break with Yugoslavia collectivization and industrialization were accelerated in all the people's democracies, without consideration for the concrete conditions in the various countries or their readiness for such changes. Many countries were subjected to a stereotyped, instead of a creative, application of Soviet experience. As a result the standard of living of the populace at large deteriorated. Yet Stalin and his obedient servants, such as Mátyás Rákosi in Hungary, Boleslaw Beirut in Poland, Viko Chervenkov in Bulgaria, Klement Gottwald in Czechoslovakia, and Enver Hoxha in Albania, responded to criticism with mass repression. They resurrected Stalin's argument that class struggle in socialist countries grows more intense as socialism develops. On this basis they created tales of counterrevolutionary, Titoist underground organizations, directed from Belgrade, Washington, and London.

From 1948 to 1952, with "methodological guidance" being provided by the Soviet punitive agencies, "enemies of the people" were discovered among the party rank and file and the leaders in Hungary, Bulgaria, Romania, Poland, Czechoslovakia, and Albania. In almost all the people's democracies show trials were staged, clearly imitating the Soviet originals of 1936–1938. Even the preparations for these trials were partly carried out in the Soviet Union, with the prisoners brought there from the other countries. Vladimir Prison, according to V. V. Zurabov, who was there in the early fifties, was filled with Communists from the people's democracies.

Most of the accused were brought by torture to make obedient confessions of monstrous crimes. Lászlo Rajk, for example, the former minister of foreign affairs and of internal affairs in the Hungarian People's Republic and long before that a leader of the Hungarian workers' movement and of the resistance to Admiral Horthy's fascist regime, confessed that he had been an agent provocateur of that regime. From 1931 on he had allegedly betrayed more than two hundred Communists to the police. He declared that he was in the service of Yugoslav and British intelligence services, that he was not a Hungarian Jew but a German, and so on.

The same kind of ridiculous fabrications were recited in Sofia, Bulgaria, where a show trial was held in the first half of December 1949. On the defendants' bench were eleven Communists who had held various government posts, including some of the highest. The main defendant was Traicho Kostov, a member of the Politburo of the Bulgarian Communist Party and a Central Committee member of that party since 1924. He was considered the second most important and authoritative figure in the Bulgarian party after Georgi Dimitrov. Yet he was accused of countless crimes committed while Dimitrov was still alive and with Dimitrov's consent. Kostov was the only defendant who flatly denied the charges against him and continued throughout the trial to assert his innocence and try to expose the whole shameful production. Peter Semerdzhiev gives the following description of the way Kostov conducted himself on the last day of the trial:

> The three main defendants were allowed a final speech after the others. Traicho Kostov was called after Nikola Pavlov and before Ivan Stefanov. Straightening himself up between two state security agents arrayed in ordinary police uniforms, he managed to say:
> "In my last speech before the esteemed court, I owe it to my conscience to declare to them and to the Bulgarian public that I have never served in the British intelligence, never participated in the criminal plans of Tito and his clique . . ."
> The chairman of the court tried to interrupt him to prevent any further statement from being heard, but Kostov hastened to finish:
> "I always regarded the Soviet Union with respect and esteem . . ."
> The courtroom grew noisy. The court personnel and the numerous state security representatives were embarrassed. The select audience was filled with commotion. The agents guarding Traicho Kostov grabbed hold of him, to force him to sit down. Only those standing nearby heard him declare:
> "Let the Bulgarian people know that I am innocent!" These were the last words Traicho Kostov spoke in the courtroom. The two guards, holding his coattails, managed to seat themselves on the bench and dragged him down after them. Heavily he sank between them. The audience and several foreign correspondents watched the shameful scene with astonishment as it played out in the setting of a military club that had been turned into a courtroom.[9]

The sentence of the Bulgarian Supreme Court in "the case of the treasonous espionage gang of Traicho Kostov" condemned all the accused "to death by execution, deprived forever of all rights, in accordance with Article 30 of the Criminal Code." Before the sentence was carried out, Traicho Kostov was subjected to two days and nights of uninterrupted

9. Peter Semerdzhiev, *Sudebnyi protsess Traicho Kostova v Bolgarii (7–12 dekabria 1949 g.)* (Jerusalem, 1980), pp. 97–98.

torture after the trial. Later a statement appeared in the Bulgarian press supposedly signed by Kostov:

I confess that I am guilty of the charges made against me by the court and fully confirm the testimony I gave during the preliminary investigation. . . . The sentence of the Supreme Court is absolutely justified and in keeping with the interests of Bulgaria in its true and peaceful development and in its struggle against the Anglo-American imperialists and the encroachments of their agents— Tito and his gang, the traitors to socialism—upon the territorial integrity and sovereignty of Bulgaria.

In Poland the show trials involved a "diversionist and espionage organization" allegedly operating within the Polish Army. The defendants were military leaders, headed by Marian Spychalski, minister of defense. After Spychalski's arrest his surprise replacement as defense minister was Soviet Marshal Konstantin Rokossovsky, of Polish nationality. Polish First Secretary Wladyslaw Gomulka was arrested. Stalin insisted on Gomulka's trial, but Bierut postponed it under various pretexts, fearing the negative reaction of the Polish people.

In Czechoslovakia in 1949–1951 many leaders were jailed, among them Vladimir Clementis, Gustav Husak, Josef Smrkovsky, Eduard Goldstücker, Maria Svermova, Josef Goldman, Eugen Loebl, and Arthur London. General Ludvik Svoboda, one of the main organizers of the Czechoslovak People's Army, was removed from all government posts and sent to a village to be chairman of an agricultural cooperative. This repression was carried out under pressure from Stalin and Beria, with the cooperation of Klement Gottwald. Taking active roles were both Antonin Novotný, a leading member of the Central Committee who was later installed as president of Czechoslovakia, and Rudolf Slanský, general secretary of the party. In 1951 Slanský himself was removed from his post and arrested soon afterward.

The mechanics of the preparation and conduct of the Slanský trial, presumably similar to other trials of that period, were disclosed in many publications in the Czechoslovak press during 1968 and in books and articles published by Czechoslovak Communists who left the country after the suppression of the Prague Spring. Several articles, for example, were published in Prague in the spring of 1968 by Eugen Loebl, who had been deputy minister of foreign trade at the time of his arrest in 1949.[10] Loebl was a defendant in the Slanský trial in 1952 and survived

10. [Cf. Eugen Loebl and Dusan Pokorny, *Die Revolution rehabililtiert ihre Kinder*.

to be fully rehabilitated in 1963. According to his account, the trial was a long time in preparation, and the defendants were subjected to the most refined methods of torture. At first, Loebl was identified as an "agent of Tito." But times changed, and in the early fifties it was decided that the trial should take on an "anti-Semitic" flavor, in light of Slanský's Jewish background. So Loebl came to be an "agent of international Zionism" and a "member of the underground Slanský committee." For several months before the trial, according to Loebl, the participants in the "conspiracy" were forced to rehearse the evidence over and over, both individually and as a group. If someone forgot his lines, he was yelled at. Better food was given for good performances. "Dress rehearsals" were conducted without the judges or prosecutor, but under the investigators' direction. In this way inconsistencies were eliminated. All testimony was simultaneously translated for the Soviet security officials who attended these rehearsals. These Soviet "teachers" made observations and corrections which were immediately written into the record and memorized by the prisoners. The presence of the defendants inhibited no one.

The Slanský trial began on November 20, 1952. A prompter sat close to each defendant. The accused were well-fed and well dressed. Doctor Sommer anxiously looked after their well-being. The judges asked only those questions that had been rehearsed. Most of the accused were sentenced to death, but Loebl was given life imprisonment.

The Slanský trial was described in detail in a book by one other surviving participant of the proceedings—*The Confession* by Arthur London.[11] According to London, during the pretrial investigations Soviet security agents compiled a "file" of slanderous materials against Jaques Duclos, Luigi Longo, Raymond Guillaut, and other prominent leaders of Western Communist parties.

These trials in the socialist countries were accompanied by a wave of mass repression among Communists and non-party members, leaders of the peasant and petty-bourgeois movements, and so on. In Hungary, for example, more than 150,000 political prisoners were in camps and prisons in early 1953. In Czechoslovakia, according to information published in Prague in 1968, there were more than 100,000 political prisoners in

---

Hinter den Kulissen des Slansky-Prozesses (Vienna, 1968). Translated into English as *Stalinism in Prague* (New York), 1969. — D. J.]

11. [London's *Confession* (New York, 1970) was also made into a film of the same name, directed by Costa Gavras. — G. S.]

1953, while between 1948 and 1953 over 25,000 were either executed or died in prison. Tens of thousands were in prison in Poland and Bulgaria.

In Romania, Antonescu Lucretiu Patranascu, general secretary of the Romanian Party during the underground and organizer of the revolt, was arrested and killed, along with V. Luca, deputy chairman of the Romanian Council of Ministers, Ana Pauker, Romanian minister of foreign affairs and distinguished figure in the international Communist movement, and many others.

In Albania many Communists also perished, including Kotchi Dzodze (Koci Xoxe), a secretary of the Central Committee.

■ 3

WEAKENING OF THE WORKER-PEASANT ALLIANCE

The dramatic events, distortions, and illegalities of collectivization from 1929 to 1933 have been discussed in an earlier chapter. The consequences of those events continued to be felt for many years. In 1937, although it was announced that the grain harvest had reached 7.3 billion poods, in fact the gross yield was only 5.9 billion and the average yearly harvest during the second five-year plan was only 4.45 billion, lower than in 1913 [1 pood = 36.113 lbs.]. Food rationing ended, to be sure, but agricultural abundance was still a distant dream.

The third five-year plan projected further progress, which was not realized. In 1938 and 1939 agricultural output fell below the 1937 level; in 1940 that level was surpassed by only 5 to 6 percent. Instead of the planned yearly grain harvest of 8 billion poods, the average for 1938–1940 was 4.756 billion poods. An enormous gap had developed by the end of the thirties between the rapid development of industry and the slow development of agriculture. This prevented the establishment of normal relations between the city and the countryside, between the working class and the peasantry.

The heart of the problem was the forced transfer, or "pumping," of funds from agriculture to industry. In the twenties agriculture produced more than half the gross national product of the Soviet Union, while hardly any wealth was being accumulated by state industry, which was still very weak. For that reason the transfer of privately accumulated wealth from agriculture to industry was a justified measure, even though forced. The "scissors" effect (the disparity between agricultural and industrial prices), the "supertax" on agricultural goods, and the forced transfer of values from industry to agriculture were all discussed openly at that time. At a Central Committee plenum in 1929, for example, Stalin quite frankly acknowledged that a "supertax," "something like tribute," was being extracted from the peasantry. He promised that this emergency measure would soon be stopped.[12] The promise was not kept. Nor were the notorious "scissors" eliminated. In the late thirties the prices paid to collective and state farms remained very low, while those farms continued to be overcharged for manufactured goods and for the services of the Machine Tractor Stations. Thus the forced transfer of funds from the countryside to the city continued.

The war threw Soviet agriculture even further back. Agriculture suffered greater losses than any other branch of the national economy. In 1945 agricultural output was only a little more than 80 percent of the 1913 level. The number of farm machines had decreased severalfold, and labor was in short supply (because of the millions killed in the war). Many collective farms were staffed only by women, old men, and boys. In other words, the effort to improve agriculture had to start all over again.

In 1946 the fourth five-year plan began, with ambitious goals for agriculture. Not one of them was reached. It was only with difficulty, in fact, that the 1940 level was reached. Though the number of horned cattle rose to 58.1 million, this was still lower than in 1916 and 1928. As for hogs, the number remained below the prewar level. In 1951 the fifth five-year plan began. In 1953 gross agricultural output had increased by only 5 percent. The average yearly grain harvest in 1949–1953 was around 81 million tons. Per capita grain production in 1953 was 19 percent lower than in 1913. It is hardly surprising that virtually no grain was available for fodder or export. The average yield of most crops was lower in 1949–1953 than in 1913. The targets of a widely publicized three-year plan from 1949 to 1952 for increased livestock raising by the state farms and collective farms also were not met.

The main reason for the postwar stagnation in agriculture was the Soviet government's violation of the principle that farmers need personal material incentives. Although industry was already accumulating significant surpluses, the "pumping" of funds from the countryside to the cities continued to increase in the last years of Stalin's life. Procurement prices

12. Stalin, *Sochineniia*, 12:49ff.

—the prices paid by the Soviet government for obligatory deliveries of agricultural products by the collective farms—remained at the prewar level at a time when the real value of money was sharply declining. The collective farms had to sell the bulk of their produce at prices much lower than the cost of production. In 1953 a centner of grain [100 kilograms] brought 90 kopecks—four to five times less than the average cost of production. One ruble was paid for a centner of sugar beets—little more than half the average cost of production. The price of potatoes did not even cover the cost of transporting them to the state procurement centers. Most of the marketable meat was surrendered by the collective farms as payment in kind for the work of Machine Tractor Stations or at procurement prices equal to only a few percentage points of the retail price on meat.

At the same time retail and wholesale prices for industrial goods increased severalfold. In 1940, in order to earn enough to purchase a ZIS-5 truck, a collective farm in the Ukraine had to sell 99 tons of wheat; in 1948, 124 tons; and in 1949, 238 tons.[13]

Moreover, in the last years under Stalin a perverse system of planning state procurements was established, which assigned to collective farms a total sum of deliveries exceeding both the overall state plans and the capabilities of many collective farms. The result was a huge accumulation of arrears, while grain procurements took on the character of forced confiscations.[14] In many areas, especially outside the black-earth (chernozem) zone, virtually all the farms' surplus was being pumped out of the countryside and even a part of their subsistence requirements. If farming in these regions was not entirely ruined by this perverse policy but sometimes even made a little progress, it was only because millions upon millions of collective farmers were working without pay—working not for money or for produce but for marks (palochki) in their labor books. As for means of subsistence, they had to be obtained not by collective-farm work but by work on the household plots, which were less encumbered by taxes and obligatory deliveries. Without their private plots the collective farmers simply could not have survived; in return for their collective-farm labor days they did not receive even the minimum necessities of life. Frequently it was their desire to keep the household plots that forced the peasants to work on the collective-farm fields, since only

13. *Kommunist* (1968), no. 4, p. 68.
14. [*Prodrazverstka*, Medvedev's word here, was the term used to describe grain requisitioning during the civil war. —D. J.]

members of collective farms had the right to those plots. In other words, unpaid labor on the collective-farm fields was turned into a strange payment the peasant made for the right to use his own little plot of land, without which his family could not live. Instead of developing truly collective and socialist relations in the countryside, this system preserved and intensified the commitment to private property. It is valid to ask whether one could regard as socialist a collective farm whose members received virtually nothing for their labor on the collectively owned fields and survived only because of the earnings from their private plots.

On top of all this, precisely in the postwar years there was a continual increase in taxation of the private plots. Every head of livestock, every fruit tree was subjected to tax or to obligatory deliveries. After nearly destroying the incentive to collective-farm work, Stalin was weakening the incentive to work on the private plot. Some peasant families quit raising livestock and even chopped down the fruit trees in their gardens. Many found themselves in a truly hopeless situation; they did not get enough to live on either from the collective farm or from their own plot. Want became their constant companion. Many were also prevented from quitting agriculture and moving to the city. The passport system set up under Stalin withheld passports from many collective farmers, who therefore could not leave their villages without permission. At the same time traditional peasant crafts began to be restricted and banned, which made the situation even worse, especially in the non-black-earth region.[15]

According to Yu. Chernichenko, Vyshinsky had a hand in the elimination of many rural cottage industries. In one instance he discovered a collective farm that was mining coal from an old abandoned mine and reported it to Stalin. As early as October 1938 the Council of People's Commissars issued a decree prohibiting collective farms from "the organization of industrial operations not related to agricultural production." This decree declared subsidiary private labor by collective farmers to be illegal, placing such activity under surveillance by the Procuracy. Many extremely important traditional village industries were thus proclaimed to be crimes against the state. Local officials of the Procuracy were told to investigate such activity and bring violators to justice. Special instructions were soon issued by the commissariats of agriculture and finance, transferring to government agencies those collective farm operations

15. [Cottage industry provided an important supplement to agricultural income for peasants in non-*chernozem* areas. — D. J.]

which were "not related to agriculture and whose products were being sold on the side."[16]

Did Stalin know about the extreme impoverishment of the peasants, whom he had promised in the mid-thirties to make "well to do"? According to Khrushchev and several others close to Stalin, the dictator judged the situation from the false, rosy-hued picture presented in such propaganda works of "socialist realism" as the film *Kuban Cossacks* or Semyon Babayevsky's novel *The Cavalier of the Gold Star.*

Zverev, the minister of finance under Stalin, tells of an episode when Stalin proposed a further increase in rural taxation. Stalin was convinced that all rural inhabitants were really quite well off. When Zverev objected Stalin accused his minister of being inadequately informed about the material situation of the collective farmers. Zverev writes:

> Once he said to me, half joking and half serious: "It's enough for a peasant to sell one chicken in order to keep the Ministry of Finance happy."
> "Unfortunately, Comrade Stalin," I replied, "things are far from being that way. Some collective farmers wouldn't be able to pay their taxes even if they sold a cow."[17]

The agricultural system that developed under Stalin completely contradicted the basic principles of socialist economics and disrupted the alliance between the working class and the peasantry. Stalin tried to base agriculture not on personal material incentives and not even on enthusiasm, but above all on orders, on compulsion. Moreover, the "pumping" of funds from agriculture to industry, which did not contribute very much to the growth of industry, had long since ceased to make up for the enormous losses suffered by the economy as a whole because of the slow rate of growth in agriculture and the consequent shortage of food for the population and of raw materials for light industry. This vicious cycle became the main source of the stagnation that affected the entire Soviet economy.

Stalin did not see that a crisis was developing in the economy. His ignorance of conditions reached the point where almost any intervention he made in economic affairs resulted in serious losses and difficulties. Stalin's "great construction projects," the "great Stalin plan for the transformation of nature,"[18] the erection of tall buildings in Moscow, the

16. *Novy mir* (1966), no. 8, pp. 154–155.
17. A. G. Zverev, *Zapiski ministra* (Moscow, 1973), p. 244.
18. [A plan to change the climate by planting millions of hectares of trees and changing the flow of rivers. —D. J.]

beginning of the Turkmen canal or the Salekhard-Igarka railway line, the dozens of ostentatious and expensive pavilions at the Agricultural Exhibition in Moscow—these are a few examples of Stalin's blunders. They were intended to be grandiose monuments of his epoch, but they were utterly at variance with the real needs and resources of the Soviet Union at the time. On the other hand, the construction of new housing was almost at a standstill, although the urban population was markedly increasing. In general, Stalin followed a labor policy that was also based on compulsion. Workers were forbidden to change jobs and were punished severely for the smallest infractions, such as lateness. The role of the trade unions was weakened, and there was no workers' participation in management whatsoever.

■ 4
OFFICIAL ANTI-SEMITISM

In the previous chapter I discussed the deportation of several nationalities from the Volga region, the Northern Caucasus, Crimea, and Transcaucasia, the destruction of their national culture, and the dissolution of their autonomous districts or republics. The Baltic nations were also given no small cause for grievance against Stalin and his regime. In addition, in the postwar period the Abkhazian people had their national rights restricted and an attempt was made to assimilate them forcibly into the Georgian Soviet Republic. Many injustices were committed against the Armenians too. For example, Armenian families living in Georgia were discriminated against, and thousands of Armenian families were simply deported from Georgia. In 1949 Beria made up a story about the existence of a Dashnak counterrevolutionary underground in Armenia and with Stalin's approval deported thousands of Armenian families, especially from Yerevan, to the Altai region. The deportation was carried out by security police and local forces in one day, without any advance notice. Among those deported were many Armenians who after the war had returned to their homeland from other countries with the permission of the Soviet government.

In general, exaggerated attention was paid to a person's nationality in the Stalin era. Great importance was attributed to the information about nationality that appeared on passports and applications. Signs of great-power chauvinism in Stalin's policies grew constantly stronger. The Russian element in the USSR was stressed to the point that a cult of the

Russian nation was created. From the heights of the Kremlin Stalin himself proclaimed it "the most outstanding nation of all the nations that make up the USSR." The Russian nation was invariably referred to as "the leading nation," "the first among equals," "the elder brother," and so on. Orienting himself toward surviving Great Russian prejudices, Stalin increasingly replaced internationalism by a nationalist outlook. A symbol of the time was the absence in Moscow of a monument to Marx, to Engels, or even to Lenin, while a statue of Yury Dolgoruky, a stupid and cruel twelfth-century prince, went up on Soviet Square, replacing the Obelisk of Freedom that had been erected at Lenin's suggestion.[19]

At the same time the rights of the union republics were increasingly curtailed. As a reaction to this policy there was a revival of local nationalist feelings, which had almost vanished in the thirties. In the Caucasus and Central Asia manifestations of national dissension reappeared.

Especially great damage was done to the Soviet Union's international reputation by the anti-Semitism promoted by Stalin and his retinue.

In 1931 Stalin had declared that anti-Semitism, as an extreme form of racial chauvinism, was a dangerous survival of cannibalism.

Anti-Semitism is dangerous for the workers as a false path, leading them off the correct road and taking them into the jungle. Therefore Communists, as consistent internationalists, cannot but be consistent and sworn enemies of anti-Semitism.[20]

Stalin soon forgot his own words. As early as 1936–1938 specifically Jewish organizations were hit by the mass terror. Repression struck almost all the leaders of the Jewish Autonomous Region (in Birobidzhan) as well as chairmen of Jewish collective farms in that region and in the Kuban and the Crimea. In Belorussia in 1936 a case was concocted on the false charges that a Jewish "fascist organization" had formed around the Yiddish-language magazine *Stern*. Some former leaders of the left wing of the Bund (M. Litvinov, E. Frumkina, Vainshtein), who had joined the Bolshevik Party after the October revolution, were alleged to have organized a Jewish underground throughout the Soviet Union. Every such fabrication was accompanied by the arrests of hundreds. In fact in Belorussia and the Ukraine even before the war Jewish cultural organizations were ravaged and the number of Jewish secondary and vocational schools and Yiddish or Hebrew publications was reduced.

19. It was during the reign of Yuri Dolgoruky as prince of Vladimir that the first historical mention of Moscow appeared, in 1147. Thus he is referred to as "the founder of Moscow."
20. Stalin, *Sochineniia*, 13:28.

During the war Stalin insisted on a number of measures that restricted the rights of Soviet Jews. After the war he began to exclude all Jews from the party and government apparatus, covering his actions with talk about the counterrevolutionary activities of international Zionist organizations, ignoring the existence in foreign parts of many White Guard Russian, Ukrainian, Georgian, and other nationalist organizations. In 1948, as we have seen, almost the entire staff of the Jewish Antifascist Committee was arrested, though it had been set up during the war on the initiative of the Central Committee. Of course the members of this committee had had various contacts with Jewish nationalist organizations abroad. But there was nothing illegal about that; the committee had been set up to establish such contacts.

After the arrest of the committee members, anti-Jewish measures increased. As a "prophylactic measure," a limit was placed on the admission of children of Jews to many departments at universities and to many other institutions of higher education. Jews were barred from the diplomatic service and were gradually squeezed out of the courts and the procuratorial agencies, except as defense lawyers. In most higher educational institutions, in scientific institutes, even in many factories a secret quota was introduced for Jews, like the one that the tsarist government established at Pobedonostsev's request.[21] Even in the defense of academic dissertations Jews were admitted only as a certain percentage of Russians and other nationalities. Though Jews had played a great role in the revolution, civil war, and first decade of Soviet power, under Stalin in the forties and early fifties there was hardly a single Jew even among raikom secretaries. Anti-Semitism was also plainly evident in the campaign against "cosmopolitanism," which was used to close down Jewish schools, theaters, newspapers, and magazines.

Most anti-Jewish measures were not given publicity; they were usually carried out on oral instructions. But the anti-Semitic feelings of Stalin and his retinue, including Kaganovich, a Jew, were no secret to the party apparatus. And then, in the last years of his life, Stalin cast aside almost all ideological screens and made anti-Semitism an open, obvious part of official government policy. Everything indicated that he was beginning preparations for a mass deportation of Jews to remote districts, as had been done with the Volga Germans, Crimean Tatars, and others. The

21. [Konstantin Pobedonostsev, chief bureaucrat of the Russian Orthodox Church and adviser to the last two tsars, was generally regarded as the *ne plus ultra* of Russian reactionaries. — D. J.]

Jews were to become one more scapegoat for his despotic system, which constantly sought ways of shifting the blame for its deficiencies.

In late 1952, not without Stalin's knowledge, the "doctors' case" was organized. Lydia Timashuk, a radiologist in the Kremlin Hospital and a secret agent of the Ministry of State Security (MGB), wrote Stalin an obviously inspired letter, saying that she had observed many eminent doctors applying wrong methods of treatment. Her letter displeased Beria and alarmed some MGB officials, who feared that they might be accused of insufficient vigilance. V. S. Abakumov, the minister of state security, ordered the head of the MGB's investigation department, M. D. Ryumin, not to investigate the letter and even arrested him. But Stalin ordered Ryumin's release, dismissed Abakumov, and appointed S. D. Ignatyev minister of state security. Moreover, Stalin took personal charge of the investigation of the Kremlin doctors' case, summoning and instructing the agents. "If you don't get the doctors' confessions," he told Ignatyev, "you'll lose your head."

After that warning the MGB went to work in earnest on the doctors. On January 13, 1953, the central newspapers reported the "unmasking" of an organization of wrecking doctors, including such major physicians as V. N. Vinogradov,[22] M. S. Vovsi, M. Kogan, B. Klin, P. I. Yegorov, A. Feldman, A. Grinshtein, Ya. Etinger, and G. Maiorov. They had allegedly murdered Zhdanov, shortened the life of Shcherbakov, and tried to do the same to many admirals and marshals. The MGB communique about the "plot" charged that the doctors were hired agents of foreign intelligence and that most of them were also connected with the international Jewish nationalist organization Joint, whose chief representative in the Soviet Union was the actor and director Solomon Mikhoels, who, as we have seen, had been murdered in Minsk in 1948.[23]

This slanderous report marked the beginning of an anti-Semitic campaign that should have been unimaginable in the Soviet system. In medical schools, hospitals, and many other institutions thousands of Jewish specialists were expelled as a "prophylactic measure." Many university departments, hospitals, and laboratories lost as much as half their staffs. Many books by Jews were removed from the forthcoming lists of publishing houses. Even some medicines developed by the arrested doctors were banned, although they had won general recognition. In

22. According to Svetlana Alliluyeva, Vinogradov had been Stalin's personal physician for more than twenty years.

23. ["Joint" was the Joint Distribution Agency, a charitable organization. —D. J.]

some places hooligan elements beat up Jews. This anti-Semitic campaign, reminiscent of the pogroms, aroused sharp protests abroad and disturbed the friends of the Soviet Union. Two leaders of the World Peace Council, Frederic Joliot-Curie and Paul Robeson, were reported to have flown to Moscow to meet with Stalin, but he refused to see them.

Some Soviet historians still deny Stalin's anti-Semitism. Khrushchev tried to deny it. But hundreds of facts prove the contrary. The archives of the Old Bolshevik Yevgeny Frolov contain a document entitled "The Anti-Semitism of J. V. Stalin," a compilation of the most obvious manifestations. Here is that list:

Repeated statements that there were many Jews in the opposition groups. An attempt to represent the "united opposition" of Trotsky, Kamenev, and Zinoviev as a conspiracy of "three dissatisfied Jewish intellectuals" against the party.

Making his daughter, Svetlana, divorce her husband, Grigory Moroz, a Jew, and making his son Vasily divorce his Jewish wife.

His rejection at the beginning of the war of a list of editors for front-line and army newspapers on the ground that many of the nominees were Jews.

The termination of the only Jewish-language magazine published in Moscow.

The closing of the Soviet-Polish border to Jews fleeing from the Nazis, and their death in the Warsaw ghetto.

The termination of the Jewish newspaper *Emes* [Truth, Pravda] at the end of 1948.

The termination of a Jewish paper in Birobidzhan.

The closing of the Jewish theater.

The liquidation of the Jewish Antifascist Committee at the end of 1948, and the arrest of its leaders.

The arrest of Jewish poets and prose writers who used Yiddish—Perets Markish, Kvitko, Fefer, Bergelson, et al.

The murder of Mikhoels, and the ban on an investigation.

The creation of the Lozovsky case, and Lozovsky's arrest.

The campaign against cosmopolitanism.

The doctors' case.

The preparation for resettlement of Jews in a ghetto: the building of barracks, the preparation of an Appeal to the Jewish People by Ivan Mints, the collection of signatures for the appeal by Ya. S. Khavinson, a meeting at the Stalingrad Tractor Factory, and the adoption of a resolution to resettle the Jews.

The arrest of the leading Jewish officials in the Dynamo Factory on the charge of belonging to a Jewish counterrevolutionary organization.

The arrest of a group of leading Jewish officials in the Likhachev Factory and in the Metro Administration.

The purge of Jews from the Central Committee, the Moscow Committee, the Moscow City Committee, the raion committees, the newspaper *Pravda*, the MVD, the Procurator's office, the courts, military organizations, the Ministry of

Foreign Affairs, the Soviet Information Bureau, the Radio Committee, and other organizations.

The discharge of most Jewish political officials in the army in the second half of the war.

The arrest of Jews who declared a desire to go to Israel.

The fabrication of the Slanský case on the charge of contacts with a Zionist organization.

Pogrom-type articles in *Kultura i Zhizn, Meditsinsky rabotnik, Pravda, Izvestia,* and other central newspapers.

An anti-Semitic cover on *Krokodil* (Romm reading André Gide).[24]

The exposé of "rootless cosmopolitans" hiding under pseudonyms.[25]

Konstantin Simonov's article against the campaign, and Sholokhov's article in defense of the campaign.

The fabrication of the "case" of the anti-party group of theater critics (A. Gurvich, Yuzovsky, et al.) in January 1949.

The fabrication of the "case" of Jewish poets and film directors.

Percentage quotas for Jews entering institutions of higher education.

Restricted registration of Jews in big cities.

Denial of jobs to Jews.

The organization of pogroms in the Ukraine.

The list is far from complete. But it is enough to show that Stalin himself took the path that, in his own words, could lead only back to the jungle.

24. [In the Cyrillic alphabet the name Gide is identical with *zhid,* a pejorative for Jew. Mikhail Romm is a leading Soviet film director of Jewish background. — D. J.]

25. [Frolov is referring to attacks on Jewish writers who used non-Jewish pen names. — D. J.]

14

THE IMPACT OF STALINISM ON SCIENCE AND ART

■ 1
THE SOCIAL SCIENCES

The Stalinist system destroyed thousands of creative people, but its disastrous consequences in science and culture went beyond that. Rational forms and methods in the government's dealings with science and culture were perverted. Bureaucratism, worship of rank, dictatorial methods, and monopolistic practices were entrenched in these highly specialized areas of public life. High-handed interference by Stalin and his associates directly affected fundamental aspects of many extremely important branches of science and culture.

The social sciences were especially vulnerable. As the nineteenth-century Arab thinker Abd al-Rahman al-Kawakibi has written:

Yes, a despot's knees do shake, but [only] from fear of [the kind of] learning that is connected with real life, such as theoretical thought, rationalist philosophy, the study of the rights of nations, the rights of the people, civics, the detailed study of history, the art of oratory, and so on. . . . A despot invariably feels wretched in the presence of a man who knows more than he, the despot. Therefore he does not tolerate the presence of a talented scholar and, if he must have [the services of a scholar] . . . , he chooses a cringing flatterer.[1]

In most of the social sciences Stalin alone had the right to make discoveries and draw major conclusions; everyone else was assigned the role of a popularizer or commentator. There was no room for free discussion and the contest of various opinions. Instead, dogmatism, rote learning *(nachetnichestvo)*, stagnation, and inertia prevailed. The truth was not what corresponded to facts, to empirical research, but what Comrade Stalin had declared to be true, and to a lesser degree, Lenin, Marx, and Engels. Quotations from "the classics of Marxism-Leninism" and above all from the newly canonized classics of Stalin became the main proof that a given proposition was true. Inconvenient facts were juggled, distorted, or simply ignored.

The study of history in general, and the history of the CPSU in particular, fell on especially bad times. Between 1946 and 1952 alone, no less than six hundred books and pamphlets, in a total printing of twenty million copies, were devoted to Stalin's speeches and articles, which of course were praised to the skies. As a prominent Soviet historian has noted:

Toward the mid-thirties the possibility of scholarly investigation of contemporary history was reduced to a minimum. The increasingly limited amount of publishable information no longer permitted a scholarly analysis of industrial and agricultural development. Critical verification of this information became impossible. The investigator was deprived of information about the standard of living in the city and the countryside, the social structure, and many other aspects of sociopolitical life. The accessible area of archival sources was sharply limited. At the same time the fight against "vulgar sociologism," "the antihistorical school" of M. N. Pokrovsky, conditioned the historian against independent theoretical work. Theoretical analysis and generalization became the monopoly of one man —J. V. Stalin. . . .

The biggest event in the development of the historiography of Soviet society was the publication in 1936 of the *History of the CPSU: Short Course.* The extremely one-sided and schematic conception of this book was subordinated in the final analysis to the task of exalting and glorifying Stalin, validating and justifying all his actions. . . . The truly outstanding triumphs and achievements

1. *Priroda despotizma i gibel 'nost' poraboshcheniia* (Moscow, 1964), pp. 24–25.

of the Soviet people, of the Communist Party, were recounted in a panegyrical spirit, were represented as one undiluted triumph, with difficulties, mistakes, and shortcomings virtually excluded. The narrative itself . . . was accomplished by stringing together quotations from Stalin's works or paraphrases of them. . . . The final chapters of the *Short Course*, which reflect most fully the characteristic features of the ideology of Stalin's cult, are a monstrous blend of whitewashing and mudslinging, of panegyrics and slander. Since this book was not meant to give a scholarly elucidation and explanation of the historical process, it was written in the form of expounding axioms, which required no proof and did not have to be understood but memorized, learned by heart. The moment the *Short Course* appeared it was proclaimed "an encyclopedia of basic knowledge in the field of Marxism-Leninism," "a means of heightening political vigilance," . . . the sole and official "guide to party history," "permitting no willful interpretations." . . . Historical science was denied the opportunity to examine the phenomena of social life, to analyze facts creatively. The loss of many historians in the mass repression of the thirties and the postwar period also left its mark. . . . The result of all this was a sharp drop in the number of works on the history of Soviet society, and a shift from scholarly research to mass agitation, at best to works of popularization.[2]

All the achievements of Soviet historians during the first twenty years of Soviet rule were canceled out. Party and government figures who had fallen victim to repression were referred to only as "spies" or "enemies of the people" if they were mentioned at all. All books and other writings by arrested historians or others in the social sciences were removed from circulation. The crudest kind of falsification in works on general history and the history of the party became the rule rather than the exception. For example, the *Short Course* declared that the slogan "Make all collective farmers prosperous," which Stalin formulated in 1933, was realized by 1937.

The short biography of Stalin published after the war was an equally glaring example of fraudulence. Indeed, it is impossible to list all the distortions contained in that little book. In the postwar period the entire history of the deported nationalities was also crudely distorted, including the liberation struggle of the peoples of the Caucasus in the nineteenth century.

Many other instances of brazen falsification of history could be cited. I

2. Unfortunately, I cannot yet give the name of the historian quoted here. To what he said I may add that in the first ten years after the appearance of the *Short Course*, it was published in 30 million copies—despite four years of war, economic difficulties, and shortages of paper. I should also add that in 1938 all important archives came under the control of the NKVD, and the publication of documents on the history of Soviet society virtually ended.

have already mentioned that Stalin was said to have founded the famous Baku underground press, although he was not even in Baku at the time. Some photographs allegedly portraying Stalin's life were pure montage —a photograph in *Pravda* August 8, 1932, for example, showing Lenin and Stalin standing together. Genuinely historical photos were subjected to careful retouching, so that inconvenient people would disappear (for example, the well-known photo "Lenin and Stalin at Gorki in 1922"). Some figures were even removed from negatives. All the mistakes Stalin made in 1917 were concealed or attributed to Kamenev alone. Stalin's mistakes on the national question were also kept quiet, such as his plan for "autonomization." Instead he was exalted as the supposed founder of the USSR. Stalin was also portrayed, contrary to the truth, not only as Lenin's best and closest disciple but as his intimate friend. Stalin's relationship with Lenin was transformed into a tale that "surpasses all the most touching fables of the ancients concerning human friendship."[3]

Economics was also in deep trouble. During the first ten years of Soviet rule that science had grown and prospered, but growth was replaced by backward motion in the thirties and forties, when the central problems of this discipline, especially the economics of socialism, were hardly worked on at all. The publication of books on specific issues was sharply curtailed, many research institutes were closed, scholarly discussions were stopped. For twenty years the Soviet Union had no textbook on political economy. Agricultural economics was particularly degraded. Almost no work was done on such fundamental topics as agricultural costs and prices, accounting *(khozraschet)* and profitability *(rentabelnost)*, increasing the marketed proportion *(tovarnost)* of agricultural output, payment of labor, differential land rent, and so on. Such a vital branch of economics as the science of management was neglected, while the administration of the economy became increasingly petrified, overcentralized, bureaucratic, and bogged down by paper work. The factories and managers that performed best were not encouraged, and systems to encourage workers by material incentives were poorly developed. Research centers founded in the twenties to study the scientific organization of labor were closed, although several of them had been started on Lenin's initiative and with his help.[4] Genuine scientific research in economics was often impossible, and it was cut off from the natural sciences, from concrete planning work, and from statistics. A great deal of statisti-

3. The Old Bolshevik S. Petrov wrote this in *Pravda*, April 24, 1950.
4. For example, the Central Institute of Labor.

cal material was classified as top secret. In many cases statistical information was simply not gathered any longer, resulting in the near total collapse of statistics as a science.

Jurisprudence also deteriorated, with Vyshinsky as the dictatorial plenipotentiary. It was he who established the principles that a court cannot aspire to absolute truth and must accordingly be satisfied with some degree of probability; that evaluation of evidence is based only on inner conviction; that the law is an algebraic formula, which is corrected in the process of application by the judge. Vyshinsky even suggested that the law should not be applied at all, if it has "lagged behind life." "We must remember Stalin's teaching," he told a March 1937 meeting of party members active in the Procuracy, "that there are periods, there are moments in the life of a society, particularly our society, when laws turn out to be obsolete and must be set aside."[5] It was Vyshinsky who established that an accomplice must bear responsibility for all the activity of the group he belongs to, even though he had nothing to do with the commission of a crime and did not give his consent to it. In cases involving crimes against the state Vyshinsky held that the confession of the accused was sufficient proof. He cynically declared that a prisoner who denied his guilt had to prove himself innocent. Completely ignoring the educative and organizing function of the law, he reduced it to mere compulsion. In the same way he gave "scientific" justification to the new regime in the camps and prisons.

Thus the science that should have defended legality was converted into a pseudoscientific defense of Stalinist willfulness. It must also be borne in mind that Stalin not only ignored the basic laws of the state, including the Constitution. The system of legislation was itself perverted. At Stalin's first suggestion the legislators would pass any law, even if it contradicted the fundamental norms of socialist society.

Marxist philosophy also declined. Nothing can be said about other philosophical systems, since only adherents of Marxism could teach, work at research institutes, and publish their writings.

Stalin's pamphlet *Dialectical and Historical Materialism* (Moscow, 1938) was proclaimed the ultimate in philosophical thinking, when in fact it held back the development of real philosophical inquiry for many years. Problems in materialist dialectics, the theory of knowledge, logic, and the methodology of science were hardly studied by Soviet philosophers.

5. Quoted in *Voprosy istorii KPSS*, 1964, no. 2, p. 19.

Not progress but regress was the rule in many areas of the history of philosophy, particularly in the study of classical German philosophy. A certain contempt was even displayed toward some of Lenin's writings in philosophy. His well-known *Philosophical Notebooks* was excluded from his collected works.[6]

During the thirties and forties the real processes and contradictions at work in Soviet society were not studied. Concrete sociological investigations were halted in favor of expounding general theoretical schemes. Philosophers did not analyze the data of science; they usually limited themselves to the rehearsal of examples and illustrations chosen to fit predetermined stereotypes.

The concept of a union between philosophy and natural science was violated. Many Soviet philosophers perverted this concept and arbitrarily branded certain theories that they found inconvenient or simply incomprehensible as "idealistic" or "metaphysical." This pasting of derogatory labels on concrete scientific trends did great harm not only to philosophy but also to natural science. Many scientists were automatically classified as proponents of reactionary ideology. Major scientists were driven out of science and even physically destroyed. Some leading philosophers pasted the label of "idealistic philosophy" on the theory of relativity, the study of genes, the chemical theory of resonance, cybernetics, and mathematical logic. All this did enormous harm to the economic and technological development of the Soviet Union.

Pedagogy also suffered during the cult. P. V. Rudnev, Krupskaya's secretary and a former official in the Commissariat of Education, has described the real state of affairs:

In essence an entire period in the history of Soviet pedagogy was being canceled out—the period of its formation, when the basic principles of Communist education were worked out, a Soviet system of preschool education and polytechnical schools joining labor and learning. . . . That was a period when the Communist children's movement was created, when enormous political and educational work was done among the teachers, when old specialists were drawn into the building of a new system, when a rapprochement was effected between them and the Soviet regime, and the great mass of bourgeois and petty-bourgeois pedagogical theories was reevaluated in the light of Marxist theory. It was a period of bold creativity . . . , of passionate arguments . . . , of training new

6. In 1952 V. Kruzhkov reported to Stalin the plan for completing the fourth edition of Lenin's *Collected Works*. When Stalin saw the *Philosophical Notebooks* in the plan he remarked with irritation: "Don't stretch it too far; don't stretch the Leninist heritage too far." Kruzhkov took the hint.

young pedagogical cadres, of boldly promoting the best representatives of the teachers to leading posts in administration and teacher training. It was the period . . . of Lunacharsky, Krupskaya, Bubnov, Skrypnik . . . , of the founding of pedagogical journals not only in Moscow, Leningrad, and Kharkov but also in the provinces (Novosibirsk, Sverdlovsk, Gorky, Rostov, Ivanovo, and so on), when there was a large methodological literature, not only of a didactic nature but also describing the actual experience of Soviet schoolwork in the period 1918–36.

The assessment of this period's pedagogy in the Central Committee resolution of 1936 promoted distortions concerning educational theory and practice that are of more than historical importance to us.[7]

In the mid-thirties under the pretext of a struggle against "excesses" some prominent figures in Stalin's entourage began to cancel out and negate the positive achievements of the Soviet school system and pedagogical theory in the twenties. The 1936 Central Committee resolution on "pedology" gave a tendentious and mistaken assessment of the state of pedagogical science. Less and less attention was paid in the schools to problems of polytechnical education, to the concept of combining instruction and training with productive labor. The teaching of natural science was divorced from life and labor; all links between school and workplace were lost. Eventually even the modest shops in the schools were closed, and labor training was dropped from school curricula.

Krupskaya vigorously protested this trend. She reminded the Central Committee in a letter that Marx and Lenin had insisted on the union of mental and physical labor in the educational process.

On this issue we fought with teachers of the old gymnasia, who scorn labor. . . . In recent years the teaching of labor in the schools has been reduced to nothing. Some sort of handicraft "labor processes" are taught; labor is isolated from study more than ever. . . . In a few days the question of abolishing the teaching of labor in the schools, of closing down school shops, will be voted on in the Central Committee. Not the reorganization of labor, but its liquidation. This question was not discussed with engineers, agronomists, workers, collective farmers, young people. Only old teachers, instructors of various subjects, have been consulted.[8]

Stalin and Zhdanov ignored Krupskaya's letter. Under their leadership the schools were gradually transformed into "Soviet gymnasia." Not only were vocational training and instruction abolished but many long-forgot-

---

7. Rudnev, "Iz istorii sovetskoi shkoly," unpublished manuscript, a copy of which is in my archive. [The Central Committee resolution of 1936 refers to a decree of July 4 condemning "pedology." See *Direktivy i postanovleniia sovetskogo pravitel'stva o narodnom obrazovanii* (Moscow, 1947), 1: 190–193.—D. J.]

8. *Uchitel'skaia gazeta*, February 21, 1962.

ten features of the old gymnasium were revived, such as the teaching of Latin and separate schools for boys and girls. Thus basic principles of Communist education were perverted, and a scornful attitude was fostered toward physical labor and working people.

■ 2

THE BELITTLING OF LENIN'S ROLE

In discussing the impact of Stalinism on the social sciences, I must also mention the belittling of Lenin's role in the history of the party and the Soviet state. Lenin's role was downgraded surreptitiously, bit by bit, at the same time that he was being praised beyond all measure. Yet the process of downgrading was very wide-ranging and thorough.

In an interview with the German writer Emil Ludwig, Stalin said, "I am only a pupil of Lenin, and the goal of my life is to be a worthy pupil of him."[9] Such statements merely expressed Stalin's customary hypocrisy. In reality Stalin was envious of Lenin's place in history and tried to appropriate it for himself.

As early as 1920, while speaking at the celebration of Lenin's fiftieth birthday, Stalin unexpectedly remarked—"no one," he said, "has yet spoken" about this—that "at times, in matters of great importance, Comrade Lenin admitted his failings." He portrayed Lenin as a theorist with a poor idea of what was going on in the country, who gave the party incorrect instructions at the most critical moment before the October revolution. Twisting the facts, Stalin claimed that the "practical leaders" of the Central Committee (implying himself of course) had seen more clearly than Lenin the "pitfalls, gullies, and ravines along our way." He made it seem that Lenin, who was hiding in the fall of 1917, had left the armed insurrection to the "practical leaders," presumably Stalin above all. He pictured Lenin as saying "Yes, you were right," when he emerged from hiding to greet the victorious Congress of Soviets.

The reader can see from my account in the first chapter of this book how far Stalin's assertions are from the truth. Yet it is indicative that twenty-six years later, in editing this speech for inclusion in his collected works, Stalin made the wording of this very part of his speech significantly stronger, stressing Lenin's "mistakes" more than ever. The Soviet writer B. V. Yakovlev has counted more than a hundred changes that

9. Stalin, *Sochineniia*, 13:105.

Stalin made in the text.[10] For example, he inserted this extremely mis-leading remark: "Despite all Lenin's demands, we did not listen to him; we kept to the path of strengthening the Soviets and arrived at the Congress of Soviets on October 25, at a successful insurrection." One might think that Lenin was opposed to strengthening the soviets, that it was not Lenin but Stalin and his "faction" (the very word Stalin used twice in his 1920 speech) who prepared the party to carry out the armed insurrection.

Lenin's role was further downplayed by promoting the idea that there had been two main leaders of the October revolution, sometimes called the theory of the "two chiefs." In the mid-twenties Stalin himself scoffed at this theory every way he could because at that time Trotsky was generally referred to as leader number two. In the thirties, however, the theory became official, for now Stalin was portrayed as the "second chief" of the revolution. Sometimes he was even placed in the foreground. On the twentieth anniversary of the revolution *Pravda* asserted that the armed insurrection in Petrograd was prepared by the Central Commit-tee, "headed by Stalin." A contemporaneous historical journal spelled out this fable in detail and assigned Stalin a role in the civil war far more important than Lenin's.[11]

After 1945 the fable of the two chiefs was extended to all the periods of party history, beginning with the revolution of 1905. A number of au-thors even claimed that Stalin, together with Lenin, had created the party, had always shared the leadership with him, and that Lenin, in the last years of his life, was greatly influenced by Stalin. Kalinin, to take a notable example, wrote: "Comrade Stalin together with Lenin created, built, and strengthened our party. With Lenin he led the party, the revolutionary movement, and the October armed insurrection."[12]

Stalin arbitrarily decided what could be published not only about Lenin but even by him. The current *Polnoe sobranie sochinenii* (suppos-edly the "Complete Collected Works of Lenin")—the fifth edition—contains many "new" documents, letters, and articles that had been lying

10. See Stalin, *Sochineniia*, 4:317. The original version appeared in *50-letie V. I. Lenina* (Moscow, 1920).

11. See *Istoricheskii zhurnal*, 1937, no. 10, especially pp. 24–26, 66, the articles by A. Fokht and M. Lurye. For the belittling of Lenin's role in the civil war and the enhancement of Stalin's, see Stalin's "Otvet t. Razinu," *Bolshevik*, 1947, no. 3, and *I. V. Stalin, Kratkaia biografiia* (Moscow, 1947), pp. 82–83.

12. M. I. Kalinin, *K 60-letiiu so dnia rozhdeniia tovarishcha Stalina* (Moscow, 1939), p. 89.

in the safes of the Institute of Marxism-Leninism and sometimes in Stalin's personal files. Some items that had been included in the second or third editions, published in the twenties and thirties, were excluded from the fourth edition, published in the forties and fifties. One example is an extremely interesting item in both tone and content: "In Memory of Comrade Proshyan."[13]

In almost every work about Lenin published in the postwar period more than half the text was devoted not to Lenin but to Stalin. Even in the thirties the Lenin Prize for outstanding achievements in art and science was dropped. After a few years the Stalin Prize was inaugurated. Artificial barriers prevented the writing of a scholarly biography of Lenin. Special Central Committee resolutions forebade publication of Marietta Shaginyan's novel about the Ulyanov family and the book "Six Years with Lenin" by S. Gil', Lenin's chauffeur. These orders were rescinded only after the Twentieth Party Congress.[14]

Libraries were obliged to get rid of reminiscences not only by Bolsheviks who had been proclaimed "enemies of the people"—such as Vladimir Nevsky, Antonov-Ovseyenko, and G. I. Lomov—but also by Krupskaya, V. D. Bonch-Bruevich, and Lunacharsky. Lenin's plan for the building of socialism in the Soviet Union was renamed Stalin's plan. The famous GOELRO plan, the first attempt at a Soviet economic plan, drawn up by the State Committee on Electrification at Lenin's initiative, was attributed to Stalin in a long poem published in *Komsomolskaya pravda* in the early fifties. Kaganovich was especially zealous in this process of elevating Stalin over Lenin. "We all say Leninism, Leninism," he remarked one day at Stalin's dacha, "but Lenin has been gone for a long time. Stalin has done more than Lenin and we should talk about 'Stalinism.' We've had enough about Leninism." It is also noteworthy that the number of books by Stalin was ten times greater than those by Marx and Engels and two and half times more than Lenin's.

Along with the belittling of Lenin the cult of Stalin continued to grow, reaching unheard-of proportions, with Stalin encouraging the unabashed glorification of his own person. In the early thirties Stalin objected to a proposal for a biography of himself made by Yaroslavsky and some other sycophant historians. "The time has not yet come to write such a biography," was his oracular remark. But here too he was playing the hypocrite. He was simply looking for a more "reputable" author. Pressure was

13. Lenin, *Sobranie sochinenii*, 3d ed., 23:438–439.
14. See *Spravochnik partiinogo rabotnika* (Moscow, 1957), p. 364.

put on Maxim Gorky, who even began work on a Stalin biography but soon gave it up. The search spread to distinguished Western authors. In early 1936 a biography of Stalin by the prominent French writer Henri Barbusse was published as a serial in the large-circulation periodical *Roman-gazeta*. Barbusse received all the material he needed for this book directly from the party's Central Committee. However, within a year the book was removed from all libraries because it referred to dozens of Stalin's "comrades-in-arms" who had been arrested soon after the book appeared.

In 1937, when the Children's Publishing House (Detgiz) produced a book of "Stories about Stalin's Childhood" and sent it to Stalin for approval, he sent Detgiz the following letter:

> February 16, 1938
> I am strongly opposed to the publication of "Stories about Stalin's Childhood." The book is filled with a mass of factual distortions, untruths, exaggerations, and undeserved encomia. The author has been misled by lovers of fairy tales—by liars (perhaps "honest liars") and timeservers. A pity for the author, but facts remain facts. But that isn't the main thing. The main thing is that the book has the tendency to inculcate in Soviet people (and people in general) the cult of the personality of chiefs and infallible heroes. That is dangerous, harmful. The theory of "heroes and the mob" is not Bolshevik but Socialist Revolutionary. The Socialist Revolutionaries say the "Heroes make a people, turn it from a mob into a people." "The people makes heroes," reply the Bolsheviks. This book is grist for the Socialist Revolutionaries' mill; it will harm our general Bolshevik cause. My advice is to burn the book.
>
> J. Stalin[15]

On the occasion of Stalin's sixtieth birthday his short biography was printed in three issues of *Pravda*, December 21–23, 1939, but he had not yet decided to bring it out as a separate booklet.

In the postwar period Stalin abandoned such hypocritical hesitations. In the late forties he not only endorsed the proposal for a biography of himself but closely followed the writing of it, inserting many handwritten remarks in the manuscript, especially where he found insufficient praise for himself. Some of these tributes to himself were read to the Twentieth Party Congress by Khrushchev in his "secret speech." The most astonishing was the solemn declaration that "Stalin did not permit himself a trace of self-importance, conceit, or vanity." This was written about himself by the same Stalin who commented on proposals by a certain Colonel Razin:

15. *Voprosy istorii*, 1953, no. 11, p. 21.

"The dithyrambs addressed to Stalin hurt one's ears. It is simply embarrassing to read them."[16]

Stalin's seventieth birthday was celebrated with unbelievable pomp. One major writer declared that people of the future would call Stalin's time "the epoch of justice" and might choose his birthday as the beginning of a new calendar, calling it "the Day of Thanksgiving" of the Year One.[17] Two months later another writer put these reverent words in the same newspaper:

If you meet with difficulties in your work or suddenly doubt your abilities, think of him, of Stalin, and you will find the confidence you need. If you feel tired in an hour when you should not—think of him, of Stalin, and your work will go well. If you are seeking a correct decision, think of him, of Stalin, and you will find that decision. . . . "Stalin said"—that means the people think so. "The People said"—that means Stalin thought so.[18]

Stalin himself, the Twentieth Party Congress was told, chose the text of the Soviet national anthem, which said not a word about the Communist Party but contained a paean to Stalin: "Stalin has trained us to faith in the people; to labor, to great deeds he has inspired us." For a long time the Museum of the Revolution in Moscow was turned into a museum of gifts to Stalin.

While he was still alive new monuments were constantly being raised to him all over the country. On July 2, 1951, Stalin signed a decree of the Council of Ministers providing for the erection of a monumental statue of himself on the Volga-Don Canal, and on September 4 of the same year he ordered thirty-three tons of bronze for it. His megalomania grew along with his power and glory. In the thirties he demonstratively wore a simple soldier's coat; in the fifties he never parted with a marshal's uniform. He even took the title Generalissimo, previously borne by only four men in Russian history: A. S. Shein, who led the Russian troops in Peter the Great's first campaigns; Peter the Great's favorite, Alexander Menshikov; Prince Anton Ulrich, the consort of Empress Anna; and Alexander Suvorov. In foreign countries during Stalin's lifetime only Chiang Kai-shek and Francisco Franco assumed such a title.

16. *Bolshevik,* 1947, no. 3, p. 8.
17. *Pravda,* December 18, 1949.
18. *Pravda,* February 17, 1950.

■ 3

STALIN'S THEORETICAL LEGACY

Although Stalin wished to be recognized as a great Marxist theoretician, he was obviously unable to cope with the tasks that arose on the theoretical plane for Marxists and the international Communist movement from 1924 to 1953. The list of theoretical problems that he helped to solve is small. On the other hand, there is a long list of important problems that should have been solved in the Stalin era but were not.

Stalin's theoretical works can be divided into three main groups. The first consists of his popularizations, such as *Foundations of Leninism.* Largely commentary on quotations from the writings of Marx, Engels, and Lenin, these works contain little that was original. In them Stalin presented many ideas from the classical works of Marxism in an oversimplified way, reducing their content to the most elementary formulas. It can be argued that Stalin was a master at constructing simplified schemas. He constantly promoted slogans that would appeal to the poorly educated masses, without caring whether those slogans corresponded to reality. In this respect Stalin acted as a skilled demagogue, one of the main reasons for his success. All "great" demagogues have used similar methods. Hitler once said: "Political problems are complicated and confused. . . . I . . . simplified them and reduced them to the simplest terms. The masses understood that and followed me." [19]

It is also noteworthy that Stalin borrowed much of his commentary— without acknowledgment. His prerevolutionary article on the national question is a good example. Endlessly acclaimed during the years of the cult as the fundamental work on the national question, it is in fact merely part of a body of Marxist writings on the problem. Lenin had positive comments on Stalin's article, but he spoke just as highly of a number of other articles and pamphlets on the national question in that period— those of O. N. Lola (Stepanyuk) and P. I. Stuchka (Vetern), for example. A lively discussion on the national question was going on among Marxists at the time, with Lenin himself writing much on the subject. Against that background Stalin's contribution does not seem especially original, including his highly touted definition of "a nation." The characteristics by which Stalin defined "a nation" were obviously borrowed, without acknowledgment, from Karl Kautsky and Otto Bauer. Kautsky gave the

19. Yu. A. Levada, *Sotsial'naia priroda religii* (Moscow, 1965), p. 235.

first three characteristics of a nation as a common language, common territory, and common economic ties. Stalin gave the same three, in the same order, adding a fourth from Otto Bauer—a common national character, although Stalin used different wording: "a psychological cast of mind *(sklad)* manifesting itself in a common culture *(obshchnost kultury)*."[20]

The origins of Stalin's *Foundations of Leninism* are even more revealing. Delivered as lectures at Sverdlovsk University in early April 1924, they appeared in *Pravda* during April and May of the same year. At that very time Stalin had the manuscript of Filipp A. Ksenofontov's treatise *Lenin's Doctrine of Revolution.* Ksenofontov, who had been helping Stalin in theoretical matters, was sent to work in Tashkent soon after Stalin read his manuscript. Rumors circulated that Ksenofontov was protesting Stalin's appropriation of many formulations. These rumors were soon substantiated by the appearance of Ksenofontov's book. The author took pains in the preface to specify the exact date and place of writing:

Sverdlov University, October–November 1923. The comparatively late publication [1925] is due to the fact that the manuscript was first reviewed by M. N. Lyadov and then was in the possession of Comrade Stalin for final review (April–June).[21]

The preface was dated January 1925, and to drive home the fact of priority, the date of completion of the main text was put at the end of the book: March 13, 1924.

A simple collation of Stalin's and Ksenofontov's book shows their great similarity in organization, in exposition of central ideas, in basic definitions. Ksenofontov rejected the notion that Leninism is simply "Marxism in practice," or "the Marxism of Russian reality." He insisted that Leninism is much more: "the science of the revolutionary politics of the working class in conditions of imperialism, i.e., the theory and practice of the proletarian revolution."[22] Stalin rejected the same notions and came to the same conclusion:

Leninism is Marxism of the era of imperialism and of the proletarian revolution. More precisely, Leninism is the theory and tactics of the proletarian revolution

20. These questions are discussed in more detail in a manuscript by Yu. M. Semenov, *Iz istorii teoreticheskoi razrabotkoi problemy natsii v marksistskoi literature,* a copy of which is in my archive.

21. Ksenofontov, *Uchenie Lenina o revoliutsii* (Moscow, 1925).

22. Ibid., p. 16.

in general, the theory and tactics of the dictatorship of the proletariat in particular.[23]

Stalin also echoed Ksenofontov on the connection between the national question in colonial countries and the proletarian revolution in advanced countries.[24] Their analyses of the dictatorship of the proletariat are also strikingly similar. In a private letter to Ksenofontov in July 1924, Stalin gave him some credit for helping prepare *Foundations of Leninism*. But in 1926, when Ksenofontov asked for Stalin's permission to cite the letter, Stalin refused.[25] This disagreement over priority ended in the typical Stalin manner: Ksenofontov was arrested in 1937 and killed during interrogation.

The second group of Stalin's works deals with concrete problems of socialist construction and with theoretical issues that had not previously confronted Marxism. Here again, originality is notably absent. Propositions that were hailed as great discoveries by propagandists of the cult were actually trivial platitudes. But it must be granted that Stalin was a master at making these platitudes seem important. And once again many of these supposedly new insights were unacknowledged borrowings. For example, he was long credited with the comprehensive criticism of mechanistic and idealistic distortions of Marxist philosophy. In fact he merely appended a highly oversimplified summary to a prolonged discussion. Likewise his famous six conditions of economic construction were merely a summation of the debates at a June 1931 conference of business managers. All six conditions had been presented both separately and together by many managers, both at the conference and in a number of preliminary documents.

The same was true of Stalin's "discovery" of socialist realism. About forty-five writers and critics met at Gorky's house on October 26, 1932, and talked about the method of Soviet literature. Stalin, who spoke at the end of the meeting, was simply repeating what many had already said when he called this method "socialist realism." The term had also appeared in earlier publications. Thus Stalin was by no means the first formulator of this aesthetic category.[26] An obvious lack of originality also marked Stalin's overdue criticism of N. Ya. Marr's school of linguistics. Long before 1950, when Stalin published his articles on linguistics, the

23. Stalin, *Sochineniia*, 6:70–71.
24. Compare pp. 82–83 of Ksenofontov with Stalin, *Sochineniia*, 6:141–143.
25. Stalin, *Sochineniia*, 9:152.
26. See Yu. Borev, *Vvedenie v estetiku* (Moscow, 1965), pp. 231–232.

ideas he endorsed had been repeatedly argued by Marr's opponents, including Academician V. V. Vinogradov and Professor A. S. Chikobava, who gave Stalin much help in preparing the articles.

Of course Stalin did not simply repeat material prepared for him by the Central Committee apparatus. He worked up or rewrote the material himself after consulting widely with specialists and reviewing printed materials. For example, in producing his last work, *Economic Problems of Socialism* (1952), Stalin drew on materials from a conference of leading Soviet economists held in November 1951 and consulted with Academician Yevgeny Varga. Similarly, although the *History of the CPSU: Short Course* was written by a special brigade, it was endlessly referred to as one of Stalin's works. In 1938 M. Samoilov, director of the Museum of the Revolution and a former Bolshevik deputy to the tsarist Duma, wrote to Stalin requesting some pages of the *Short Course* manuscript for display in the museum. Stalin returned the letter with the following reply scrawled across it:

Comrade Samoilov, I didn't think that in your old age you would occupy yourself with such trifles. If the book is already published in millions of copies, why do you want the manuscript? To put your mind at rest, I burned all the manuscripts.

J. Stalin

Neither was Stalin the author of the Constitution, though it was called the "Stalin Constitution." A large collective worked it up, including Bukharin and Radek, who were subsequently killed. A commission also worked on the Model Charter for collective farms, which was called the "Stalin Charter." Numerous other examples could be given.

The third group of Stalin's works do contain some original thoughts. He has far less to his credit than other eminent colleagues of Lenin, and most of that was written before 1930. Of course it would be wrong to reject these works just because they belong to Stalin. (By the same token, the many valuable theoretical works of Bukharin and other former leaders of the opposition should not be rejected.) But it must be said that Stalin's few original works contain more incorrect than correct views. The list of his theoretical achievements is short; the list of his theoretical errors is long.

A common source of Stalin's theoretical errors was his basic limitations: poor theoretical background, inadequate knowledge, and his innate penchant for the schematization of reality. He frequently took some view of

Lenin's, which was valid in a bygone historical setting, and turned it into an absolute law for all times.

Only a few examples of Stalin's mistakes in theory can be given here, and even those without the detailed analysis they deserve.

For one example, in 1936, when the Soviet Union still lagged far behind the capitalist countries economically, Stalin declared that the economic base for a socialist society had already been built. Only "a much easier task" remained, he said—to crown this base with the appropriate superstructures. In fact the creation of socialist superstructures is an exceptionally long and difficult job, much more so than the founders of the Soviet state imagined. Yet only three years later Stalin told the Eighteenth Party Congress that socialism had already been completely built.

Similarly, in a 1936 interview with the American newspaper publisher Roy Howard Stalin said that classes had been eliminated in the Soviet Union. On the other hand, he constantly insisted that the class struggle would intensify as the country moved toward the complete triumph of socialism. In fact, it was to be expected that the class struggle, as it had previously been known, would subside.

The stages and functions of the Soviet state were all mixed up by Stalin. From all of Lenin's comments on the dictatorship of the proletariat Stalin singled out the mistaken formula that the "term 'dictatorship' means nothing more nor less than authority untrammeled by any laws, absolutely unrestricted by any rules whatever, and based directly on force."[27] From this definition it is possible to extract the mistaken idea that "the end justifies the means." Yet Lenin himself always stressed the necessity of unwavering adherence to the new Soviet laws, which were meant to support the proletariat in its struggle with its enemies.[28] During most of the twenties and in the thirties the Soviet Union was not at war; it lived under peacetime conditions. Yet Stalin never felt bound by any laws or restricted by any rules whatever.

In *Economic Problems of Socialism* Stalin made the mistaken assertion that the problem of overcoming the division between mental and manual labor was "a new problem" posed by the practical experience of building socialism in the Soviet Union, as though that problem had never been discussed in classical Marxist writings. He also presented the question of polytechnical education in a very one-sided way.

27. Lenin, PSS, 41:383; CW, 31:353.
28. Lenin, PSS, 39:156.

Stalin interpreted Lenin's theory of the socialist revolution in a mistaken way, reducing it to nothing more than the idea that the victory of socialism was possible in a single country.

In other ways too the history of Marxism was blighted. Stalin voiced doubt about the existence of Communist ideals before Marx and expressed great scorn for utopian socialism, which in fact was one of the most important sources of Marxism. He also gave a distorted evaluation of the Russian populists (the Narodniks). The *History of the CPSU: Short Course* labeled them all "opponents of Marxism," even though the first populists were active before Marxism appeared in Russia. Only their faults were brought out, which was completely at variance with the assessments made by Marx, Engels, and Lenin. The *Short Course* declared that the "People's Will"[29] brought nothing but harm to the revolutionary movement in Russia.

Stalin mistakenly asserted that the Bolshevik Party in 1917 was mainly a "national force," of importance only to Russia. Similarly, he was wrong in claiming that as both a political tendency and a party Bolshevism had existed only since 1912, after the Prague Conference (which, incidentally, coopted Stalin to the CC). Lenin of course dated the origins of Bolshevism from 1903.[30]

Stalin's assessment of collectivization—as a revolution equal in importance to the October revolution—was also mistaken.

Stalin made a totally wrong assessment of the Social Democratic movement in general and its left wing in particular; hence his incorrect views of such left socialist figures as Rosa Luxemburg. He presented it as axiomatic that opportunism completely dominated the Second International, thus contradicting Lenin's position that the Second International had done "extraordinarily important and useful work in spreading socialism and in the preliminary, basic work of organizing the forces of socialism."[31]

In the field of Russian history, Stalin not only completely justified Ivan the Terrible and his *oprichnina;* he even considered Malyuta Skuratov a great, progressive statesman.[32] Under Stalin's influence, works of history and art glorified many other tsars and princes, who were portrayed in an

29. [The revolutionary organization that assassinated Alexander II in 1881.—D. J.]
30. [1903 was the year of the Second Congress of the RSDLP, at which the split between Bolsheviks and Mensheviks first occurred.—G. S.]
31. Lenin, PSS, 26:103.
32. [Skuratov was a particularly violent official of the oprichnina, Ivan's agency of terror. —D. J.]

extremely distorted fashion. Thus the legend of Alexander Nevsky was revived. The tsars and the Orthodox Church had accounted him a divine protector of the imperial throne, hushing up the fact that he called the Tatars into Novgorod to suppress a popular rebellion. Many of the tsarist wars of conquest were justified in Stalinist historiography, including Nicholas I's wars in the Caucasus. At the same time Shamil, the hero of the national liberation struggle of the Caucasian peoples, was depicted as an agent of British imperialism and of the Ottoman Empire.

Finally, I must note Stalin's misinterpretation of the feudal and slave-holding social formations. Stalin simply identified the feudal formation with one of its variants—serfdom. He ignored the diversity in forms of land use and landownership under feudalism in favor of simplistic generalities about the feudal lords' monopoly of landownership and their proprietary relationship to peasants. It was also wrong to insist that slaves in revolt struck the fatal blow at the slaveholding social formation.

In philosophy Stalin was at best a dilettante. He lacked both systematic training and genuine self-education. His philosophical writings, marked by primitivism, oversimplification, superficiality, and dogmatic schematization, impoverished dialectical materialism. He was badly mistaken in his attitude toward German classical philosophy in general and Hegel in particular (his absurd formula dismissed Hegelian philosophy as an aristocratic reaction to the French Revolution.) He also propounded numerous mistaken views in the realm of historical materialism.

Economic theory also felt the impact of Stalin's ignorant willfulness. He misinterpreted the operation of the law of value in a socialist society. He denied the commodity character of production in the USSR, maintaining that under socialism the law of value did not apply to the means of production. Thus the principle of equivalence in funding the expenses of production was violated, which further obstructed the operation of material incentives. According to Stalin, in a socialist society the law of value operates merely in the sphere of circulation and only "influences" production. He also completely ignored differential rent in agricultural production. He noted with satisfaction that consumer purchasing power was growing faster than production, thereby transforming shortages and queues into a law of life. He even denied the existence of a surplus product[33] under socialism.

He asserted that the collective property of the *kolkhozy* held back the

33. [Marx's term for the difference between the worker's wage and the amount of value he produces. —D. J.]

development of agricultural production. He urged the transformation of such property to public ownership by means of an accelerated replacement of commodity circulation by a system of direct exchange of products. He excluded the basic means of production from *kolkhoz* property and opposed the sale of agricultural machinery to the *kolkhozy*. He declared that collective and state farms could make do with a minimum of profit, even none at all. In fact state farms that made no profit covered their losses at the expense of the state budget, which had the effect, among others, of obstructing the improvement of the farms. As for the collective farms, which could not tap the state budget, they shifted their financial difficulties onto their members. And of course Stalin's principle of "higher profitability" (*rentabelnost*), according to which all *kolkhozy* were profitable in some higher sense of the word, although they suffered losses individually, was not much help to those farms and their members. In general, Stalin's view of agriculture concentrated on the fulfillment of obligatory deliveries, not on raising productivity and profitability.

On the development of capitalist economies, Stalin was confused and superficial. He failed to perceive the increasing role of the state—see, for example, his interview with H. G. Wells—and believed that capitalism would keep sliding downhill through successive crises. Only in his last years did he take note of the economic functions of the capitalist state, but greatly oversimplified the relations between state and economy with his formula that the machinery of government was totally subordinated to the monopolies. He insisted on the absolute impoverishment of the workers under capitalism, although the facts did not fit this theory, and he gave an incorrect explanation for the underutilization of industrial capacity that was so characteristic of the capitalist economy in the thirties and forties.

Stalin made quite a few important theoretical errors in his analysis of the national question and problems of the national liberation movement.

Many of the concepts he advanced in the areas of jurisprudence and military science were likewise mistaken.

These are only some of the theoretical errors made by Stalin that have been criticized in the Soviet press. He did not advance the theory of scientific socialism. If it is possible to speak of a Stalinist stage in the theoretical field, it is one of decline and stagnation.

■ 4

THE NATURAL SCIENCES

All the natural sciences were hampered by the Stalin cult, in some cases directly through Stalin's personal intervention, in others indirectly through the bureaucratic system that prevailed in most scientific institutions. Stalin told geologists where and how to look for oil, instructed biologists on problems of heredity, advised doctors on their specialties.[34] His example was often followed by other members of the Politburo.

Progress in the sciences was slowed by such ugly features of the bureaucratic system as the coarse and uncomradely tone of scientific discussions, the constant attempt to politicize science, and the tendency to separate it into Soviet and bourgeois camps. These conditions guaranteed the rise of adventurers and careerists, who used the support of powerful but incompetent administrators.

It is well known that biology was in a particularly bad position during the years of the cult; Stalin considered himself practically a specialist in the field.[35] The tragic history of this science and of the thirty-year discussion in biology and agronomy has been presented in detail in Zhores A. Medvedev's book, "Essays in the History of the Biological-Agronomical Discussion," to which I refer the reader.[36] It was with Stalin's support that Lysenko and his circle conducted one after another of several pogroms in biology and held back the development of that science for thirty years.[37] Under the influence of the cult of Stalin and the cult of Lysenko many experimentally established natural laws were ignored in biology, and various ignorant ideas received official recognition.

As a result Soviet agriculture, biology, and agricultural chemistry suffered great damage. For example, a special resolution supported by Lysenko was adopted on Stalin's initiative, with the result that V. R.

34. See *Novy mir*, 1966, no. 8, p. 282.

35. In an article on Stalin's seventieth birthday his personal secretary, Poskrebyshev, wrote that Stalin was supposedly a specialist in several narrow spheres of biology and agriculture. Not only was he said to be the organizer of citrus cultivation in the Black Sea district but the researcher who investigated the possibility of such cultivation and that of eucalyptus trees in Moscow, the breeding of branched wheat, etc. (*Pravda*, December 1949.)

36. Zhores Medvedev's book was circulated in manuscript copies in the USSR and was published in many countries under the title *The Rise and Fall of T. D. Lysenko* (e.g., New York, 1969). [Cf. D. Joravsky, *The Lysenko Affair* (Cambridge, Ma., 1970), pp. 184–185, for the publication history. — D. J.]

37. Lysenko continued to enjoy support in the 1950s and 1960s.

Williams' grassland system of crop rotation was imposed uniformly and unimaginatively on all agriculture zones of the country.[38] Also with Stalin's support, the ignorant conceptions of O. B. Lepeshinskaya (such as the rejection of cytology) were firmly established in science for many years.

Medical science also suffered from methods of work modeled on Lysenko's. The "Pavlovian doctrine" was proclaimed to be the sole correct approach in medical science, with only one aspect of Ivan Pavlov's rich heritage being dogmatically enthroned—his theory of higher nervous activity. As S. Mordashev, a member of the Soviet Academy of Medical Sciences, has pointed out, certain scientists assumed the role of infallible interpreters of Pavlov's work, his only direct heirs. All trends in physiology other than theirs—various ways of studying the nervous system, evolutionary physiology, cellular physiology, endocrinology—were banned. Even Pavlov's work on the physiology of digestion, for which he was awarded the Nobel Prize, was neglected, which in the end adversely affected the study of diseases of the digestive organs, their diagnosis and treatment. Instead of developing Pavlov's fruitful legacy, these dogmatic physiologists ruined it.[39]

The uncompromising attitude characteristic of every cult showed itself during the cult of Stalin in the destruction of an enormous number of books disagreeable to his regime. The books were not burned in town squares; rather, tens of millions of them were burned at night at dumps or shipped to paper mills as pulp. Not only were all books by "enemies of the people" removed but also all books that merely referred in a favorable way to these "enemies." Even old magazines and newspapers were destroyed or put away in "special collections" (*spetskhraneniia*)— that is, restricted to a few people. Extremely important scientific works were taken out of scholarly circulation, and the continuity of development in scientific ideas was broken.

The struggle to establish priority in scientific and technical discoveries took on an extremely distorted character in the postwar period. The question of priority was examined from the point of view of national rivalry, and the claims of discoveries and inventions by many people in other nations were unjustifiably disputed.

Most communication between Soviet scientists and those of other

38. [For an explanation, see Zhores Medvedev, *The Rise and Fall of T. D. Lysenko*, pp. 86–99, and Joravsky, *The Lysenko Affair* pp. 293–305. —D. J.]

39. *Pravda*, June 11, 1965.

countries was interrupted. Soviet scientists for the most part did not participate in international meetings and symposia. This kind of isolation did great harm to the Soviet Union. Soviet science began to lag significantly behind world science and could not take advantage of world scientific potential for the benefit of the Soviet people.

■ 5
ART AND LITERATURE

Despite imperfections Soviet literature and art made rather quick progress in the twenties and early thirties. One indication of this was the First Congress of Soviet Writers in 1934, where a spirit of optimism prevailed. But the mass repression of the late thirties decimated the arts, destroying not only people but their works. For those not directly affected by the political terror the conditions for cultural creativity suffered disastrous change.

It would not be difficult to demonstrate that from 1936 to 1953, despite the terror, many important works were still created in Soviet art and literature; but it would be wrong to list the important works of those years and ignore the fact that cultural development slowed down markedly, while one-sidedness became the characteristic feature of the Soviet arts.

The pernicious influence of Stalinism was felt in many ways. A notable example was the triumph of a primitive interpretation of the concept "socialist realism." Many major works by Soviet artists and writers could hardly be made to fit that rigid mold. Senseless restrictions were imposed not only on the content but also on the form of any work of art.

Analogous narrowness and distortion were imposed on Lenin's concept of *partiinost* (party spirit, or party-mindedness) in literature and art. When Lenin advanced this concept he by no means excluded the possibility of different literary and artistic methods and trends or "schools." In the Stalin era *partiinost* was taken to mean subordination of writers and artists to the decisions of various party officials. Artists were supposed to be only "soldiers of the party," in the most primitive sense of the word. They were deprived of the chance to discover reality independently; they were told not only what but how to create. A great many products of creative endeavor that could not be considered "party" works simply went unpublished. Examples include many of the writings of Mikhail

Bulgakov, Anna Akhmatova, Boris Pasternak, and Andrei Platonov that have since been published in the Soviet Union.

Incompetent but powerful officials interfered at will with literature and art. Forgotten was the June 1925 resolution of the Central Committee, which noted that literary matters must be handled with

> great tact, caution, and patience, banishing the tone of literary command, all pretentious, semi-literate and complacent Communist conceit. . . . The party must utterly extirpate attempts at crude, incompetent administrative interference in literary matters.[40]

In the party bosses' actual dealings with literary people there was no tact, caution, or patience. A complex bureaucratic hierarchy was set up to choose and approve works of art. Many censors and administrators, most of them incompetent, handled a book before it might reach Stalin, who was quite ready to intervene in the crudest possible ways.

Yemelyan Yaroslavsky, in his book *On Comrade Stalin,* reported that the great man not only liked to read belles-lettres; in his youth he had written "very good poems," which were printed in the paper *Iveria* over the pseudonym "Soselo." Fortunately, Stalin was not, like Mao Tse-tung, proclaimed the greatest poet of modern times. But he did have a considerable impact on Soviet literature and art. In many cases his comments determined the fate of a creative work—sometimes of the creator as well. For example, he forbade the performance of A. M. Afinogenov's play *The Lie,* which was in rehearsal at three hundred theaters. Stalin did not like the way the heroine condemned the falsehood that had crept into Soviet lives.[41] Then there was the case of Bulgakov's play *Flight.* Gorky wrote of it: "This is a superb comedy, with deeply hidden satirical content. I am firmly convinced that *Flight* will be a triumph when the Moscow Art Theater puts it on, a tremendous success." But Stalin expressed a negative opinion and in a letter to V. Bill-Belotserkovsky asserted that the success of Bulgakov's play *Days of the Turbins* had been undeserved. As a result, *Flight* and most of Bulgakov's other plays were banned from the stage.[42] Stalin's personal interference cut off Shostakovich's opera *Katerina Izmailova (The Lady Macbeth of the Mtsensk District),* which had been playing successfully in a number of theaters for two years. For some reason Stalin did not like the music. Stalin also

40. *O partiinoi i sovetskoi pechati. Sbornik dokumentov* (Moscow, 1954), pp. 346–347.
41. See *Znamya,* 1963, no. 1, p. 211.
42. See M. Bulgakov, *Izbrannaia proza* (Moscow, 1966), pp. 29–30.

banned many classics. Just before the Moscow Art Theater went on tour to Paris, it was forbidden to perform Pushkin's *Boris Godunov*. The director of the theater, M. Arkadyev, wrote Stalin a "letter of repentance" in July 1937, after he had been fired. He listed the "dubious" elements in Pushkin's tragedy, which had been pointed out to him "from above." Noble Poland was contrasted with poor Russia. The False Dmitry was not "presented by Pushkin for what he really was—an agent of foreign intervention."[43]

It was in the years of the cult that the political censor acquired enormous power, the ultimate say-so, in any publishing house. In an earlier chapter I quoted Lunacharsky on the necessity for censorship in Soviet Russia, but in the twenties he had also called for a different arrangement:

> We need a flourishing, diversified literature. Obviously the censor should not allow clearly counterrevolutionary stuff to pass. But apart from that, everything that shows talent should have free access to the book market. Only when we have such a broad literature will we have a genuine loudspeaker into which all strata and groups of our enormous country will speak; only then will we have sufficient material, both in the subjective statements of these writers as representatives of these groups and in objective observations of our reality seen from various points of view.[44]

No one in the censorship organs of Stalin's time followed Lunacharsky's sensible advice. In the 1936–1937 season ten out of nineteen new plays in major theaters were taken off the stage, including the ballet *The Bright Stream*, with music by Shostakovich. In that same season more than ten theaters were closed down in Moscow alone and ten others in Leningrad. In the 1937–1938 season fifty-six plays were removed from the repertoire and banned, including all the works of Vladimir Kirshon, Bruno Jasienski, I. Mikitenko, and other arrested playwrights.

The same arbitrary rule governed the film industry. In 1935 thirty-four films were stopped in production, in 1936 fifty-five, and in 1937, when the number of movies permitted to start production had sharply dropped, thirteen were still stopped in midcourse. During the same years more than twenty films were taken out of circulation after they had already been shown. It is therefore understandable why no more than ten feature films were released in any one of the postwar years, despite an abundance of studios.[45]

43. From materials in the possession of the literary and cultural historian L. M. Zak.
44. *Literaturnoe nasledstvo*, no. 74, (Moscow, 1965), p. 31.
45. Based on data gathered by L. M. Zak.

That was the time, incidentally, when Stalin encouraged biographical films, not about revolutionaries but about Russian tsars, princes, and military leaders. He ordered color films about Ivan the Terrible, Peter the Great, Alexander Nevsky, generals Suvorov and Kutuzov, and Admiral Ushakov. He reviewed the scenarios and even chose the directors. The famous director M. I. Romm has aptly described the resulting stereotype, using his own film, *Admiral Ushakov*, as an example. The people were depicted as a faceless mass, clay in the omnipotent hands of the flawless hero—and the hero, too, ultimately lacked individuality, since he had no inner contradictions and therefore no development of character.[46]

Artistic and literary criticism were on a very low level during the cult. From the mid-thirties on, one noisy assault followed another. Vicious campaigns were waged against "Meyerholdism," against "formalism" in music, against the film director Sergei Eisenstein, and against certain "artistic daubers."

Verbal beatings of this sort became especially common in the postwar period. I have already mentioned Zhdanov's speech concerning the journals *Zvezda* and *Leningrad*, which set off attacks on various writers. Indiscriminate assaults were also made on the works of leading composers. A 1948 campaign against a small group of theater critics turned into a major pogrom against "cosmopolitans," with very serious consequences.

Most striking of all was the monotony of the literature resulting from such pressures. The best works published in the thirties were devoted for the most part to civil war themes, and in the forties the major works dealt with the Great Patriotic War. Other themes were simply ignored or white-washed. Lawlessness and repression, bureaucracy and the degeneration of a part of the apparatus were forbidden topics. The embellishment of reality became the hallmark of many writers. Writing about collective farms was especially prone to this vice. A typical product was Babaevsky's novel *Cavalier of the Gold Star*, which received the Stalin Prize. For a typical cinematic embellishment of rural life, there was *Cossacks of the Kuban*.

Another favored genre of late Stalinist art was the panegyric exalting Stalin himself. Toward his sixtieth and seventieth birthdays (1939 and 1949) the press was full of sham folk epistles in verse, on "the Father of

46. *Pravda*, April 17, 1962.

the Peoples" and the like. Painting and sculpture became pompous, overdecorated portraiture. Ostentatious facades and utterly useless decoration dominated architecture.

Konstantin Simonov has written that postwar Soviet writers did not produce outright lies, but to a considerable extent wrote half-truths about contemporary Soviet life, "and half-truths are the enemy of art."[47] These protestations are true only in part. Soviet literature and art, like its historiography, presented not only half-truths but often plain distortions and falsifications. Suffice it to recall O. Maltsev's book *The Yugoslav Tragedy,* which depicted the leaders of the Yugoslav Communist Party as spies and traitors. As for the historical novel, recall V. Kostylev's trilogy, *Ivan the Terrible,* which portrayed its hero not only as a just and wise ruler but even as an affable and affectionate man in his relations with common people. The author justified Ivan's executions and even sympathized with him, saying, "it was rather hard for the sovereign-father!" And Malyuta Skuratov, that bloody executioner, emerges "staid, businesslike, an impartial public servant, an avid partisan of the middle and petty gentry." Skuratov had "a humane, Russian heart"; "in his life and death he was a model of love for the homeland." The same brazen falsification of history can be seen in V. Yazvitsky's five-volume novel *Ivan III, Lord of All Rus,* and in many other books, plays, and films on historical subjects.

Deliberate distortions were especially numerous in works on revolutionary subjects, such as Aleksei Tolstoy's novel *Bread* and such films as *The Vow, Unforgettable 1919, The Great Citizen,* and *Lenin in October.* In *Lenin in 1918* the director Romm and the lead actor Shchukin achieved a remarkable portrait of Lenin, but his constant adviser and friend was— Stalin. As for Bukharin, Zinoviev, and Lenin's other colleagues, they were depicted as agents of bourgeois intelligence services even in 1918, dreaming with the Left SRs of murdering Lenin.

In his book *Far from Moscow,* V. Azhaev concealed the fact that almost all the workers building the oil pipeline on Sakhalin were prisoners, while the directors of the project were commanders of the Far Eastern concentration camps. (The character of Batmanov is based on V. A. Barabanov, formerly chief of Vorkuta.) Similarly in books on the building of Komsomolsk on the Amur, nothing was said of the thousands of prisoners who often performed the most laborious work.

47. *Novy mir,* 1956, no. 12, pp. 242–243.

Increasing cultural isolation was another feature of the postwar period. The Soviet people knew less and less about cultural developments outside the socialist countries. Under the guise of struggling against cosmopolitanism and "foreign fads," Soviet writers were fenced off from the progressive intelligentsia of the West. For example, in 1949 Soviet newspapers called Hemingway "a snob who has lost his conscience"; the antifascist writer Lion Feuchtwanger was identified as a "literary huckster"; while Sinclair Lewis was said to have "a dirty little soul."

Finally the suppression of democracy in cultural organizations must be noted. Congresses of writers were no longer held on the union level, for example, and no new elections were held for the board of directors of the Writers' Union.

15

SOCIALISM AND PSEUDOSOCIALISM

THE DOMINANCE OF BUREAUCRACY

Socialism, even the ideal conception of it, does not guarantee full equality of material possibilities or an equal position in society to everyone, because people differ individually. Socialism must, however, ensure substantial progress toward equality in the most important sense—equality of rights and obligations, just treatment of all, and equal opportunity for all to discover and develop their talents and abilities. It must reduce the flagrant material inequality that exists under capitalism, eliminating both excessive wealth and humiliating poverty. Stalin's bureaucratic socialism was little concerned about the achievement of such goals.

Degeneration and the rise of bureaucratism in the twenties and early thirties at all levels of party and government administration have already been discussed. The savage terror and the Stalin cult intensified these antisocialist and antidemocratic tendencies.

All remnants of independence were lost by the trade unions, which were originally supposed to be a bulwark of democracy, defending workers against the bureaucratic encroachments of the government apparatus. Opposing the view that the unions should be made part of the state, Lenin wrote: "Our state right now is such that the whole organized proletariat must defend itself against it." The trade unions, he said, cannot lose

such a basic function as nonclass "economic struggle," in the sense of struggle against bureaucratic perversions in the Soviet apparatus, in the sense of protecting the material and spiritual interests of the toiling masses by ways and means not available to that apparatus.[1]

What is more, Lenin suggested that in fifteen or twenty years the trade unions would take on a major share of management. But nothing of the sort happened. Stalin did not try even as an experiment to introduce elements of workers' participation in management. The trade unions were for all practical purposes made part of the state. They were transformed into a simple appendage of party and economic agencies. From 1932 to 1947 no trade union congresses were held in the Soviet Union.

The character, function, and structure of the soviets were also changed. Originally organs of democracy and direct instruments of the people's rule, Stalin retained them in form, but in reality they "were plunged into a lethargic sleep."[2] Both at the center and in the provinces they became mere appendages of party committees, mute executors of directives coming from party agencies.

The Constitution of 1936 did not arrest this process. To be sure, elections to the soviets became more democratic from a formal point of view. Deputies to local soviets had been elected by open voting in factories and other institutions; after 1936 they were elected in polling places scattered through territorial districts, with the entire adult population casting secret ballots. Before the voters elected deputies directly only to the local soviets, the local soviets elected deputies to the next higher soviets, and so on. After 1936 all elections became direct, and the voters of each district elected deputies to the local soviet, the city soviet,

1. Lenin, PSS, 42: 297.
2. *Problemy mira i sotsializma*, (1963), no. 5, p. 60.

the oblast soviet, the republic soviet, and the Supreme Soviet of the USSR. But in reality this system, which copied procedures in bourgeois democracies with their multiparty systems, was hardly a step forward for the Soviet state. The change from open voting to a secret ballot was the only genuine progress. Otherwise the new system was even regressive. Factories and other institutions lost the chance to influence the soviets. Interaction between deputies and voters was considerably weakened, and it became much harder for the voters to follow the activities of a deputy or to recall him. When elections were held directly at factories and other institutions, voters could discuss the relative merits of various candidates and choose the best one. Now voters had no choice but the one name presented for each office.

All this decreased the deputies' responsibility to their constituents, and the voters also lost a sense of responsibility—many of them quickly forgot whom they had voted for in the last elections. The interdependence of soviets on different levels also declined. Formerly, when local soviets elected higher ones, the lower had some claim to control the higher; under the new system control passed only from the top down. Many workers and peasants continued to be elected as deputies, but this meant little, for the work of government was done more and more by the soviets' executive committees, which carried out directives from the center and paid little attention to local initiative. The soviets were not convened regularly. The supreme soviets of the republics generally met only to ratify the budgets and the decrees issued by their presidiums. Even the ratification of the budget was secured, as a rule, only several months after the budget had gone into effect. Legislation originated only in the executive arm or most often in the party's Central Committee, not among the deputies. The Supreme Soviet almost never engaged in real discussion of the bills presented to it for discussion. Deputies never criticized the bills—until the executive organs proposed the revocation of bills that had been passed without a murmur.

The party also suffered from violations of democracy during these years. Stalin's disregard for the Central Committee and for party congresses has been discussed. On the republic, oblast, and local levels also, regular meetings of plenary organizations were not convened. Instead, all basic questions were decided by party bureaus or by the first secretary of a party unit. Party leaders were in fact appointed "from above" after being hand-picked by higher party bodies. Naturally party leaders appointed in such a way considered themselves responsible not to those below them but only to those above them. Gradually many of them turned into simple executors of instructions, into *chinovniki*, as functionaries were called under the old regime.

Thus, while a democratic system was preserved in form, in fact a bureaucratic hierarchy arose, with privileges for the *chinovniki* increasing at each higher level, including privileged access to information. The top levels of the hierarchy were distinguished from the lower ones not so much by the talents and abilities of the officials as by the degree to which they were initiated into the "mysteries" of the system. Wladyslaw Gomulka, in a speech to the Eighth Plenum of the Central Committee of the Polish United Workers Party (Communist Party) on October 20, 1956, gave the following well-informed description of the Stalinist bureaucratic hierarchy:

The cult of personality cannot be reduced merely to the person of Stalin. The cult of personality is a certain system which prevailed in the Soviet Union and which was transplanted to probably all of the Communist parties, as well as to the countries of the socialist camp, including Poland.

The essence of this system consisted in the fact that a hierarchic ladder of cults was created. In the bloc of socialist states it was Stalin who stood at the top of this hierarchic ladder. All those who stood on lower rungs of the ladder bowed their heads to him. Those who bowed their heads were not only other leaders of the CPSU and leaders of the Soviet Union but also the leaders of the Communist and Workers parties of the socialist countries. These leaders occupied the second rung on the ladder of the cult of personality. They in turn donned the robes of infallibility and wisdom. But their cult was effective only on the territory of the countries where they stood at the top of the national cult ladder. This cult could be called a reflected brilliance, a borrowed light. It shone as the moon does. Nevertheless within its own sphere of action it was all-powerful.

The chief figure in a cult of personality understood everything, knew everything, decided everything, and directed everything in his field of activity. He was the most intelligent person, regardless of his actual knowledge, abilities, and personal qualities. It was not so bad when a reasonable and modest man was arrayed in the garment of a cult. Such a man usually felt bad in such attire. It can be said that he was ashamed and did not want to wear it, though he could not entirely take it off. . . .

Matters were worse or even quite bad when a limited man, a stupid agent for someone else, or a rotten careerist, got power, i.e., the right to a cult. Such people buried socialism, unthinkingly but surely. Given the system of the cult, the party as a whole could act independently only within the framework of subordination to the chief cult. If anyone tried to get outside this framework, he was threatened with anathema by his comrades. If an entire party was involved, then the other parties anathemized it. . . .

The system of the cult of personality shaped the minds, shaped the mode of thinking of party leaders and members. Some believed and were convinced that the only infallible interpreter of Marxist science, the only person who was developing and enriching it correctly, showing the only correct road to socialism, was Stalin. It followed that everything that did not correspond to his ideas and orders was harmful, was bound to entail abandonment of Marxism-Leninsim, was a heresy. Others, who had their doubts, were also convinced that any attempt to express their thoughts in public not only would change nothing but would end with unpleasant consequences for themselves. Still others were indifferent to everything except the path that would take them to a soft chair and guarantee that chair. . . .

This system violated democratic principles and the rule of law. Under this system the characters and consciences of men were broken, people were trampled underfoot and their honor was besmirched. Slandering, falsehood, lies, even provocation served as instruments in the exercise of power. . . .

Terror and demoralization were spread far and wide. On the soil of the cult of personality phenomena arose which violated and even nullified the most profound meaning of people's power.[3]

Lenin often made the point that the workers' state derived its strength from the consciousness of the masses. It was strong when the masses knew everything, could pass judgment on everything, and do everything consciously. Of course such consciousness does not come by itself; it can only be the result of prolonged education of the people to independence and a sense of responsibility, to conscious discipline, to democracy and love of freedom, to hatred of injustice and arbitrary rule. Unfortunately the Soviet people did not have the chance to go through more than the beginning stages of such an education. Under the Stalin cult they were educated in another, unproletarian spirit, in the spirit of blind subjection to the authority of the chiefs, above all Stalin.

Stalin mistrusted and despised the people. He belonged to a workers' party but did not respect workers. He said of a man from a working-class milieu: "This one's from under his machine. What's he doing mixing in?" He never visited factories or spent time among workers. As for the peasants, his trip to Siberia in early 1928 was his last visit to a village.

Marx and Engels, who foresaw the possibility of the bureaucratic degeneration of a proletarian state, thought two measures would provide effective protection: the right to universal election and to recall all officials; and a level of salaries for officials not exceeding workers' wages. The evolution of the Soviet state in the Stalin era showed that such

3. W. Gomulka, *Rech' na VIII plenume TsK PORP* (Warsaw, 1956), pp. 39–41. [An English version of Gomulka's remarks on "the cult of personality" is in *National Communism and Popular Revolt in Eastern Europe* (New York, 1956), pp. 228–231. —G. S.]

measures were utopian. The right to recall officials, like the right of free democratic elections, became a fiction; it ceased to exist, for in the Soviet social mechanism there were no means, no organizations, no political institutions, to guarantee the exercise of the people's democratic rights.

The restrictions on official salaries also turned out to be a weak protection against degeneration. The Soviet regime did not blindly imitate the Paris Commune; the Council of People's Commisars, following the socialist principle of payment according to work performed, set the minimum monthly wages of workers' helpers at 120 rubles, while the chairman of the council received 600 rubles. Thus, the ratio between the lowest worker's wages and the highest official's salary was 1 to 5. In the ensuing civil war and economic collapse, real wages dropped far below the subsistence minimum. For a long time manual and white-collar workers were obliged to deny themselves necessities, to live half-starved. On the other hand, specialists, most of whom were of the bourgeois intelligentsia, could not be drawn into the service of the young Soviet state without salaries that were fairly high for the time.

With respect to Communists, even those who held the highest posts, Lenin demanded moderation. He showed concern for their health and food and living accommodations, but insisted that their salaries, his own included, be kept within certain limits. No luxuries were allowed. In general, Lenin opposed both the equalization of all wages and excessively high salaries, especially for party members. This policy resulted in the so-called party maximum—a wage ceiling for all Communists. Lenin considered any excessive inequality in pay or living conditions "a source of corruption within the party and a factor reducing the authority of Communists."[4]

Numerous party resolutions called for the prohibition or reduction of unjustifiable privileges for highly placed officials. In October 1923 the Central Committee and the Central Control Commission sent all party organizations and party members a special circular concerning misappropriation of state funds and goods. In particular the circular ordered a halt to the furnishing of apartments and private dachas at state expense. Grants of goods to party members were to be tapered off; the standard of living appropriate to responsible officials was to be achieved by raising salaries, which would be subject to strict accounting, as grants of goods were not.[5]

4. *VKP(b) v rezoliutsiiakh* . . . , 1936, 1: 358–359, 361–362.
5. See *Spravochnik partrabotnika*, issue no. 3, (Moscow, 1923), pp. 95–96; also, "O

For the most part the party maximum was an operative rule until the end of the twenties and early thirties. Then it began to be undermined, primarily by the decline in the real wages of most workers. The limited increase in money wages did not cover the rapid rise in prices; a considerable number of workers found their income sinking below the subsistence minimum. The small circle of high officials began to be protected as early as the first five-year plan by the creation of a system of special stores, distributing centers, and dining rooms, where goods could be obtained at fixed prices. Gradually they acquired other privileges too: their own hospitals, free vacation homes, dachas, and so on. In the same period a peculiar habit began to appear: the active party membership began to receive expensive gifts for holidays, congresses, and conferences. On February 8, 1932, the party maximum was formally abolished, bringing a new increase in the real income of leading officials.

When the economic situation improved, permitting the abolition of rationing in 1935 and a steady increase in real wages, the privileges of high officials were not terminated. On the contrary, they were increased. A system of representatives' subsidies *(predstavitelskie dotatsii)* was established for all officials at the level of the chairman of a city soviet and higher. Moreover, the direct salaries of higher officials rose much faster than wages of ordinary workers. Many officials increased their salaries even more through a system of combining jobs *(sovmestitelstvo)*; that is, one man held several offices, receiving full pay for each. Thus the 1-to-5 ratio between an average worker's salary and that of the highest official, which Lenin evidently considered optimal, was violated even before the war.

Subsequently the ratio grew still greater. During the war and the first postwar years, when the real wages of ordinary workers were falling once again, the salaries of the highest officials (those in the Nomenklatura) continued to rise. That was the period when the disgraceful system of "packets" *(pakety)* was introduced in the higher state and party institutions. Each month almost every high official would receive an envelope or packet containing a large sum, often much higher than the salary formally designated for his post. These payments passed through special financial channels, were not subject to taxes, and were kept secret from the rank-and-file officials of the institution.

---

bor'be s izlishestvami i prestupnym ispol' zovaniem sluzhebnogo polozheniia chlenami partii," circular no. 58 of the Central Committee and Central Control Commission, October 19, 1923.

In the postwar years the ratio between the real wages of an average worker and the salary of the highest official became scandalously large. (I will not even bring into comparison the very lowest wages, twenty-seven to thirty rubles in present prices, which was three to four times less than the subsistence minimum.) If we estimate not only formal direct money salary but the whole system of payments, then the ratio was 1 to 40, 1 to 50, and for some officials even 1 to 100.

As for members of the Politburo and Stalin himself, the cost of keeping them does not submit to calculation. The numerous dachas and apartments, the huge domestic staffs, the expenses for their staffs and guards rose to millions of rubles yearly. As for the cost of maintaining Stalin, that nearly defies calculation.

Among party leaders in the twenties Stalin was known for the ascetic simplicity of his personal life, and echoes of that lifestyle persisted. For example, at his dacha in Kuntsevo there was hardly any furniture in the rooms he used for leisure or sleep. There was a clothes closet, a shelf with a small number of books (his main library was at his Kremlin apartment), a plain lamp without a shade, and a bed. Yet on the whole Stalin's was a large and complex "household," with a huge staff and a large bodyguard. In addition to his "nearby" dacha at Kuntsevo there was a "further" dacha, to which he did not go very often but which was maintained with a staff and bodyguard just as if he were there all the time. Vacation houses were also built for Stalin near Sochi, near Sukhumi, at Novy Afon, on Lake Ritsa, and higher up in the mountains. In the Crimea, besides his dacha, rooms were kept in readiness for him at some of the old tsarist palaces. In the late forties a house was built for Stalin on Lake Valdai near Novgorod. All these houses and dachas were staffed and guarded year round with a huge number of highly paid personnel. At the head of this vast assemblage was General N. S. Vlasik.[6]

It is said that Stalin once asked Vlasik to calculate the cost to the state of maintaining his, Stalin's, person. With the help of specialists Vlasik made extremely careful calculations and came up with a figure so astronomical that even Stalin was not only astonished but upset. "It cannot be," he told Vlasik. "That's a lie." Beria immediately assured Stalin that Vlasik's calculations were nonsense, and Vlasik was fired. I do not know whether this story is true, but if it is, we can be sure Vlasik was closer to the truth than Beria.

6. Stalin's daughter gives a cutting description of Vlasik in *Twenty Letters to a Friend* (New York, 1967), pp. 138–139.

The political passivity of the masses, the absence of real democracy, including freedom of criticism and opposition, the high salaries and "packets," the extreme centralization and lack of any popular control over officials—all this generated an amazingly rapid growth of bureaucracy. A bureaucrat is not simply a government functionary who sits in an office and directs certain affairs. A bureaucrat is a privileged functionary, cut off from real life, from the people, from the needs and interests of common folk. Bureaucrats are interested in their jobs as positions to be preserved and improved not as tasks to be done. They will knowingly do something unnecessary or even harmful for the people if it will preserve their positions. Careerism and subservience, red tape and protocol are their constant companions. Basic ignorance, especially of cultural achievements, emotional dullness, and a limited intellect are, as Yevgeny Gnedin rightly remarks, typical characteristics of the bureaucrat.[7]

Bureaucracy was not only a product of the personality cult; it provided fertile soil for its continued growth. Marx put it very well:

Bureaucracy considers itself the ultimate purpose of the state. . . . The higher circles rely on the lower in everything involving a knowledge of particulars; the lower circles trust the upper in everything involving an understanding of the universal, and thus they lead each other into delusions. . . . The universal spirit of bureaucracy is mystery, sacrament. Observance of this sacrament is ensured from within by hierarchal organization, and with relation to the outside world by its closed corporative character. Authority is therefore the criterion of knowledge, and the deification of authority is its manner of thought.[8]

The lack of effective controls, the passivity of the masses, and bureaucracy inevitably generated corruption. The venality of many officials during the cult of personality reached such proportions that the countermeasures taken since Stalin's death have not been sufficiently effective. Extreme measures had to be used; in 1962 the death penalty was authorized for certain cases of bribe-taking.

Bureaucracy and corruption during the cult of personality destroyed the masses' belief that they, the simple people, were the real masters of their country. Under these conditions it was impossible to effectively instill in people a communist attitude toward labor.

Not all the leaders during the cult were corrupt bureaucrats. As has been pointed out, the mid-thirties witnessed the rise of a whole new generation of able and dedicated young officials. But the conditions of

7. Gnedin, "Biurokratiia XX-go veka," *Novy mir* (1966), no. 2, p. 199.
8. Marx and Engels, *Sochineniia*, 2nd ed., 1:271–272.

the cult militated against their rise to the top. Cruel and unprincipled careerists could best adapt to the situation. Under Stalin's dictatorship the disciplined, imperious leader was the most likely to succeed, intolerant of criticism from below, saying one thing and doing another, incapable even of talking with the common people, relying on force and intimidation in dealings with them.[9]

A Stalinist was usually a careerist who combined arrogance and conceit with political instability and hypocrisy. Many of these "Communists" wanted not only power but ostentatious luxury, a clear demonstration of their elevation above the people. The majority of Stalinists did not hesitate to put their hands in the public till, to use state property as their own. Observing the life-style and ways of thinking of these Stalinist bureaucrats, some Western theorists and Soviet contributors to *samizdat* have argued that a new class arose in the Soviet Union, the Nomenklatura class, a class of bourgeoisified officials. In fact, part of the leading cadres did degenerate, but the process did not go so far as to create a new class. On the other hand, the possibility of such a result cannot be ruled out. During the long years of the Stalinist dictatorship clearly defined elements of a bureaucratic oligarchy and a caste system arose in the higher and middle levels of leadership; a clearly defined part of these leaders began to consider their position and privileges a right that must be defended by any means.

After Stalin's death, authors such as Vladimir Dudintsev exposed the ugly truth about such leaders. His 1956 novel *Not by Bread Alone* portrayed the typical Stalinist official in the figure of Drozdov, the chief villain of the novel. The writer Konstantin Paustovsky, at a discussion of Dudintsev's novel made the following comments on this type of official.

The new caste of Drozdovs is still with us, . . . there are still thousands and thousands of them. . . . Recently I took a trip around Europe on the steamer *Pobeda*. In the second and third classes there were workers, engineers, artists, musicians, writers; in the first class were the Drozdovs. I need not tell you that they had and could have absolutely no contact with the second and third classes. They revealed hostility to everything except their position; they astounded us by their ignorance. They and we had completely different ideas about what constituted the prestige and honor of our country. One of the Drozdovs, standing before *The Last Judgment*, asked: "Is that the judgment of Mussolini?" Another, looking at the Acropolis, said: "How could the proletariat allow the Acropolis to be built?" A third, overhearing a comment on the amazing color of the Mediter-

9. For an effective contrast between the Leninist and Stalinist types of leaders, see A. Metchenko, *Kommunist* (1964), no. 12.

ranean, asked severely: "And is our water back home worse?" These predators, proprietors, cynics, and obscurantists openly, without fear or embarrassment, carried on anti-Semitic conversations worthy of true Nazis. They were jobbers, quite, quite indifferent to anything else. . . . Where did they come from, these bootlickers and traitors, who think they have the right to speak in the name of the people? Where did they originate? They are the consequence of the cult; the situation trained them to regard the people as dung to fertilize their career. Intrigues, slander, moral assassination, and just plain assassination—these are their weapons, as a result of which Meyerhold, Babel, Artem Vesely are not in this hall with us today. The Drozdovs destroyed them. The cause that moved them was their own prosperity. Dudintsev has given one example of their terrible work. . . . We must fight the corruption that can ruin the country. The behavior of these Drozdovs is encased in slogans; they give blasphemous speeches, saying that they are acting for the good of the people. Who gave them the right to represent the people? Dudintsev has only begun the battle; the task of our literature is to fight it to the end.[10]

The fresh stream that flowed into Soviet life after the Twentieth and Twenty-Second congresses swept a great many of these Stalinists into the dustbin of history. But not all of them retired to cut roses at their dachas. Many adapted to the new situation and gave their backing to a new generation of bureaucrats who are more cautious but no less dangerous to the development of Soviet society toward socialism.

■ 2
POLITICAL SECTARIANISM

While dogmatism and rote learning reigned in ideology, political life was afflicted with sectarianism. Sectarianism has always been one of the most widespread and dangerous diseases of the revolutionary and socialist movement. I cannot say that Marx and Engels were always models of patience, but they understood very well the harm caused by sectarianism and fought against sectarian deformities in revolutionary organizations and in individual revolutionaries. Lenin, too, was no model of patience, but he also opposed sectarian narrowness and closed-mindedness in the revolutionary movement. In working toward the revolution and in founding the first workers' state in the world, Lenin sought to rally around the party all those who could be won for the revolution. His nonsectarian policy toward bourgeois specialists and his refusal to excommunicate comrades who erred have been noted.

10. A copy of Paustovsky's speech is in my archives.

Indeed, Lenin could pay eloquent tribute to people with whom he had had many sharp disagreements, such as Plekhanov and Kautsky. In both cases Lenin insisted that their works be published in full and studied by all Communists.[11] The obituary he wrote on the Left SR, P. P. Proshyan, is remarkably revealing. "Comrade Proshyan," as Lenin did not hesitate to call him, "did more before July 1918 to strengthen the Soviet regime than he did in July 1918 to damage it."[12] Lenin knew very well that Proshyan had been sentenced to three years in prison for taking part in the Left SR insurrection against the Soviet regime, that he had not served his sentence but had gone into hiding with a false passport, and that he had died in a dilapidated hospital.[13]

Lenin's attitude toward N. N. Nakoryakov (Nazar Uralsky) provides another illuminating example. An Old Bolshevik, Nakoryakov had done much revolutionary work in various Russian cities and abroad. In 1916, however, he took a defensist position (that is, supported the Russian war effort), and after the February revolution he supported the Provisional Government. In 1919–1920 he served in Denikin's army, but became disillusioned with the White Guard movement, left it, and entered the service of the Soviet government. Lenin followed his political evolution closely, considering him a valuable official of the Soviet regime. In November 1921 Lenin arranged a meeting with Nakoryakov, and on January 4, 1922, he wrote to Preobrazhensky: "Please drop me a few lines about Nazar Nakoryakov. Has he got a job? What are his political feelings—have they changed lately or are they the same as before?"[14] Preobrazhensky replied that the conversation with Lenin had made a great impression on Nakoryakov, but his political evolution was very slow and he was working in an unimportant job in the Trade Union Council. In 1922, with Lenin's influence, Nakoryakov was appointed director of the State Publishing House of Artistic Literature. In 1925 he joined the Bolshevik Party once again.[15]

Stalin's way was utterly different. Sectarianism and indiscriminate mistrust were characteristic of him from the start. I have already described his refusal to trust any of the military specialists during the civil war, in

11. See Lenin, PPS, 25:22; 33:104; 42:290.
12. Lenin, PPS, 37:384–385.
13. See the magazine *Katorga i ssylka* (1924), no. 2, pp. 222–223.
14. Lenin, PSS, 54:107.
15. Under Stalin, Nakoryakov was arrested but managed to survive and at the time of the Twentieth Congress was rehabilitated. He died in 1970, having reached the age of almost ninety.

spite of the party's clearly expressed policy. In the late twenties and early thirties he showed the same unjustified mistrust toward almost all the bourgeois specialists, many of whom fell victim to lawless repression. As for party comrades who made mistakes, Stalin never forgot or forgave. They were forced to make repeated declarations of repentance, and if they were destroyed, the historical record was changed to make all their past activity seem an unbroken chain of crimes and blunders.

Worse yet, from the end of the thirties huge groups of Soviet people were placed under suspicion regardless of their actual behavior, on the basis of completely arbitrary and subjective criteria. It was then, when Stalin's despotism was utterly unlimited, that sectarianism became one of the most important elements of party and state policy. Talking about "prophylactic measures" against an alleged intensification of the class struggle, Stalin divided all citizens into two categories: the politically reliable and the politically unreliable. "Unreliables" were barred from any responsible positions and confined to routine jobs regardless of their abilities.

Who were classified as "unreliable"? (Former capitalists and counter-revolutionaries are not considered; only a few of them remained in the country.) First, there were children and close relatives of "enemies of the people"—numbering in the millions. Then there were children, even grandchildren, of former kulaks and other members of the exploiting classes—again millions of people. There were millions more who had relatives abroad. After the war almost all former prisoners of war and repatriated people, their children and close relatives were put into this category. The tens of millions who spent the war in territory occupied by the Germans were also suspect, their rights and opportunities restricted.

A final peculiarity of this sectarianism must be noted. As far as Stalin and his entourage were concerned, it was not the result of anxiety about the purity of the party or the leading agencies of the state. They made many exceptions for themselves and for people who suited their purposes. Relatives of "enemies of the people," former oppositionists, former Mensheviks, and so on could be found at the highest levels. No agency was stricter in selection of personnel than the NKVD, yet that agency had the most alien elements, people who had once been expelled from the party, people with criminal records and dubious political histories. Thus for the Stalinists sectarianism was only another means of preserving their own rights and privileges.

■ 3
HYPOCRISY

The ideology and practice of the personality cult flagrantly contradicted the principles of Marxism, of scientific socialism. This contradiction engendered one of the most characteristic and dangerous features of the Stalinist system and the Stalin era—the profound disparity between word and deed.

Many examples have been given of Stalin's shockingly cynical double dealing, his habit of saying one thing and doing exactly the opposite. He spoke of collective leadership and made decisions on his own. He said the alliance between the workers and peasants should be strengthened at the very time when he was destroying that alliance. He advocated voluntary collectivization and sanctioned force. In 1932, having authorized the deportation of entire Cossack villages from the Kuban region to the far north, he declared:

> We need not look to the peasants for the cause of the difficulties in grain collection, but to ourselves, our own ranks. For we are in power. We have the resources of the state at our disposal. It is up to us to direct the collective farms, and we must bear full responsibility for work in the countryside.[16]

While systematically falsifying history and contemporary events, he sanctimoniously exclaimed: "God forbid that we should be infected with the disease of fearing the truth. The Bolsheviks differ from all other parties in that they do not fear the truth, are not afraid to look truth in the eye, however bitter it may be."[17]

He said that a son is not answerable for his father; yet oral instructions were disseminated everywhere imposing all sorts of restrictions on the rights of children whose fathers had fallen victim to his repression. While belittling Lenin, Stalin often said, "How could anyone equate me with Lenin!"[18] Accusing hundreds of thousands of innocent citizens of plotting against the Soviet regime, Stalin himself carried out a plot to usurp power in the party and state.

Persecuting the intelligentsia, Stalin denounced Makhaevshchina[19] and

16. Stalin, *Sochineniia*, 13:233.
17. Ibid., 12:9.
18. Ibid., 13:260.
19. A left-wing form of anti-intellectualism. The Polish radical Jan Machajski urged the exclusion of intellectuals from the proletarian movement.

called the intelligentsia the salt of the Soviet earth. "Write the truth!" was his cogent pronouncement at a meeting with Soviet writers, who had asked him what they should write about first of all. Yet he himself promoted lies and the varnishing of reality in literature.

While sanctioning the arrest of millions and the execution of hundreds of thousands of innocent Soviet citizens, while observing the mass terror with equanimity, even with pleasure, Stalin spoke of concern for people. "Every capable and understanding official must be looked after carefully, cared for and cultivated. People must be cultivated with as much care as a gardener cultivates a select type of fruit tree. . . . It must be understood at last that of all the most precious capital that exists in the world the most precious and the most crucial is people, cadres."[20]

Stalin even denounced the cult of personality. In 1932, when the Society of Old Bolsheviks asked for permission to open an exhibition of documents concerning his life and activity, he refused. "I am against it because such enterprises lead to the establishment of a 'cult of personality,' which is harmful and incompatible with the spirit of the party."[21] A few years later the Society of Old Bolsheviks was abolished, while hundreds, even thousands of exhibitions celebrated "the greatest genius of modern times." In 1930 he wrote a letter to a certain Shatunovsky, urging him not to speak of devotion to Stalin or to any individual. "That is not a Bolshevik principle. Have devotion to the working class, to its party, to its state, but don't mix that up with devotion to individuals, which is an inane and unnecessary toy of the intelligentsia."[22] This letter was first published in 1951, at a time when every newspaper and every speech expressed personal devotion to Stalin much more frequently than devotion to the party, the working class, or the Soviet state.

In a 1928 speech Stalin uttered the following words, which of course were belied by his own actions:

> The fact that the chiefs rising to the top become separated from the masses, while the masses begin to look up at them from below, not daring to criticize them—this fact cannot but create a certain danger of isolation and estrangement between the chiefs and the masses. This danger may reach the point where the chiefs get conceited and consider themselves infallible. And what good can come

20. *Pravda*, May 6, 1935.

21. Central Party Archives of the Institute of Marxism-Leninism, collection 558, section 1, file 4572, sheet 1.

22. Stalin, *Sochineniia*, 13:19. (Stalin's works lack a scholarly apparatus, so that as a rule the first names or initials of those he addressed are not given. Probably the person Stalin was writing to in this instance was Ya. M. Shatunovsky, an economist and lecturer.)

of the leaders on top growing conceited and beginning to look down on the masses from above? Clearly nothing but disaster for the party can come from this.[23]

A profound connoisseur of human failings, a brilliant master of bureaucratic psychology, Stalin systematically inculcated respect for rank in every field of life. All sorts of tables of ranks were worked out, and promotion was accompanied by privileges, rigorously defined for each rank, as well as by increased responsibility and pay. Special uniforms and insignia were worn not only in the army but by railway workers, juridical officials, and diplomats. For himself Stalin devised the special rank of Generalissimo. Yet he declared, "For the most part I am not an admirer of those who worship rank."[24]

And how many times did Stalin call for criticism and self-criticism! For example:

Sometimes people say that self-criticism is a good thing for a party that has not yet come to power and has "nothing to lose," but self-criticism is dangerous and harmful for a party that has come to power, that is surrounded by hostile forces, against which enemies can use exposure of its weaknesses. . . .

That is completely untrue! On the contrary, it is precisely because the Bolsheviks have come to power, precisely because the Bolsheviks may get conceited about their achievements, precisely because the Bolsheviks may not notice their weaknesses, and thus may make the enemy's work easier, precisely for these reasons self-criticism is especially necessary now, after the taking of power.

The purpose of self-criticism is to reveal and eliminate our weaknesses. Is it not clear that self-criticism in a dictatorship of the proletariat can only facilitate the Bolsheviks' struggle against the enemies of the working class? . . .

To put off self-criticism is to make things easier for our enemies, to aggravate our weaknesses and mistakes. But to do all this is impossible without . . . involving the working class and the peasantry in the elimination of our weaknesses, our mistakes.[25]

Fine preaching, and often quoted in the years of the cult, but not practiced, for the author did not practice it.

And how sharply Stalin denounced arbitrary rule in the party! "I am absolutely against a policy of expelling all dissident (*inakomysliashchie*) comrades," he wrote to a German Communist.

I am against such a policy not because I feel sorry for dissidents but because such a policy generates in the party a regime of intimidation, a regime of fright,

23. Stalin, *Sochineniia*, 11:31.
24. Ibid., 12:114.
25. Ibid., 11:128–130.

a regime that kills the spirit of self-criticism and initiative. It is not good if the party chiefs are feared but not respected.[26]

Any comment here would be superfluous.

The disparity between word and deed penetrated every sphere of party and government activity in the Stalin years. "Stalin's school was a very rough school," A. V. Snegov told the All-Union Conference of Historians in 1962. "Besides destroying honorable people, he corrupted those who remained alive. He forced people to carry out dirty missions, and on the ideological front taught them to lie."[27] All of the mass media embellished reality, ignoring difficulties, conflicts, injustices, and arbitrary acts. On the other hand, many good decisions were made; they were simply never carried out. The incongruity between words and deeds consisted not only in saying one thing and doing another but in saying nothing about much that was done.

"Workers cannot have faith in leaders," Stalin once said, "where words are not backed up by deeds, where leaders say one thing and do another." Here again comment would be superfluous.

■ 4
PSEUDOSOCIALISM

Socialism means not only that social ownership replaces private ownership in the means of production and not only a change in the relationship of man to machine but also a change in relations between people, which is not an automatic consequence of the change in property relations. The oppression and exploitation of some by others can occur not only through the institution of private property but also through the institution of state power as well as other forms of management and control. True socialism, as it was conceived by its best adherents in the past, was meant to exclude any form of exploitation or oppression; it was conceived of as a profoundly humane system, created for the happiness of all people.

As early as February 1845 Friedrich Engels remarked in reflections on the historical mission of the working class that the essence of socialism consists in "the creation for all people of such conditions that all will have the chance to develop their human nature freely, to live in human relationships with their neighbors, without fear of violent destruction of

26. Ibid., 7:44–50.
27. *Vsesoiuznoe soveshchanie istorikov. Stenogramma* (Moscow, 1964), p. 270.

their well-being."[28] The definition of a communist society given in *The Communist Manifesto* is this: "An association in which the free development of each is the condition for the free development of all."[29] This definition is one of the most fundamental in the doctrine of scientific socialism.

The goal of the party founded by Lenin was to create a genuinely socialist society. After the October revolution quite a lot was done toward that goal through the efforts of the party and the people. The October revolution made the factories the property of the workers' state and gave land to the peasants, thereby laying the economic foundation for a truly socialist democracy. The workers won extensive social rights and freedoms, women received equal rights with men, the road to culture and education was opened to the masses, and the way to abolition of national and class antagonisms was cleared. It would be wrong to deny these achievements by referring to the deformities of the Stalinist period. In place of relationships of enmity, rivalry, and exploitation those of friendship and cooperation came into existence more and more. This process was significantly retarded, however, under the conditions of Stalin's dictatorship.

The development of socialism and socialist relations cannot be viewed one-sidedly, however, as nothing more than the struggle between socialist elements, on the one hand, and, on the other, surviving elements of capitalism, feudalism, and other precapitalist exploitative societies. Historical experience has shown that capitalism and feudalism do not always appear in their traditional, open form; they often veil themselves in outwardly attractive camouflage. A typical example of such social mimicry is the "Guarani republic" created by the Jesuits in Paraguay in 1610 and lasting for more than 150 years. Tens of thousands of Guarani Indians lived in special settlements, organized by Jesuit missionaries, under conditions of regimentation and complete lack of personal freedom. Yet the Jesuits declared that this was a "Christian Communist Republic."

There have been many such pseudocommunist or pseudosocialist projects. In a work entitled "The Marxist Tradition of Struggle Against 'Barracks Communism,' " the Soviet philosopher Yuri Karyakin has made an original analysis of Marx and Engels' comments on such "crude," "primitive," "leveling," "unreasoned," "ascetic," "barrack" types of socialism. (All the adjectives are Marx's or Engels's.) They all involve the

28. Marx and Engels, *Sochineniia*, 2d ed., 2:554.
29. Ibid., 4:447.

transformation of a very limited perception into a world view. Repudiation of the individual is the beginning and the end of this ideology. Repudiation of the individual generates envy, a striving to level, the rule of universal grayness, mediocrity, militant ignorance, blind hatred of "educated people," the transformation of the great democratic demand for equality into the reduction of all "ordinary people" to the lowest or the mean level, willful instead of scientific politics, a peculiar secular religion in which "truth" is presented to the faitfhul as a revelation from above, as a miraculous gift, but more often as a command requiring unquestioning obedience. Talk about democracy is turned into organized enthusiasm for these commandments. The relations between shepherds and sheep is actually a case of the blind leading the blind. Jesuitry, at first spontaneous and unconscious, develops, improves, and may attain a degree of self-consciousness. The proclaimed goals may gradually fade into the background and become only a means to realize the one genuine goal: to seize and hold personal power.[30]

Despite the spread of Marxism and the triumph of the October revolution, pseudosocialism has not disappeared in the twentieth century but has actually gained ground. That is not surprising. Pseudosocialism is a weed that is very hard to extirpate, for it spreads together with genuine socialism, always changing its appearance. By no means all ideologists and politicians who are essentially bourgeois express open hostility to socialism and communism. Many try to take advantage of the ideas and slogans of socialism, which are popular among the masses. Leaders of petty-bourgeois movements are especially given to this tactic. German fascism, for example, masked its archreactionary content with the term "National Socialism." Of course there was not a grain of socialism in either the "Christian Communist Republic" in Paraguay or the "National Socialist" state in Germany. But many social systems and states have arisen in recent decades that combine features of real and sham socialism. And that was the case in the USSR in the period of Stalin's cult.

According to Marxist-Leninist theory, socialism is the first, incomplete phase or stage in the evolution toward a fully communist society.[31] In the stage of socialism elements of communism appear in society—public

30. Karyakin, "Marksistskaia traditsiia bor'by protiv 'kazarmennogo kommunizma.' " A copy of this unpublished manuscript is in my archives.

31. [Marx's *Critique of the Gotha Program,* which described the new society as bearing the "birthmarks" of the old, distinguished a lower stage of socialism from a higher one. Lenin, and after him many Soviet Marxists, termed the higher stage communism and the lower one socialism. —G. S.]

ownership of the means of production, a communist attitude toward labor, and communist morality. Many of what Marx called the "birthmarks of capitalism" also persist in this first stage. In changed and weakened form phenomena and social relations typical of capitalism continue to exist—for example, money, commodity production, inequality in distribution and consumption, giving rise to inequality of possibilities for individual development, and of course the state and other forms of political coercion. Such phenomena and social relations took shape over the course of centuries. They can be changed and placed at the service of the people, but they cannot be eliminated overnight. Several decades or even centuries are needed for that. However, it is not these that constitute pseudosocialism. They are characteristic features of the stage of socialism. They are what distinguishes the lower socialist phase from the more advanced forms of communist society, which do not yet exist in reality.

In the socialist phase there also exist social evils that have nothing to do with socialism; they represent remnants and vestiges of previous class societies in their previously repulsive form. Stealing and bribe-taking are obvious examples. These are also "birthmarks of the past," which socialist society must fight against as elements that are alien and hostile to itself. Many defective institutions and social relations left over from previous social formations persist under socialism essentially unchanged but in a new form that is outwardly camouflaged as "socialist." The defenders of such institutions and relations hide behind socialist terminology and claim to be building socialism but in fact are destroying it, undermining its foundations. That is what I mean by pseudosocialism. These "birthmarks" left over from capitalism and feudalism do not stand out in socialist society like stains on a white tablecloth. They are often indistinguishable from the surrounding social reality. Only profound analysis (or juridical investigation) can reveal the true nature of these "spots." A vacation resort for highly placed officials of some government department might be organized, for example, but in fact it would function as a brothel. That is an example from the realm of "rest and recreation." An example in the realm of public administration would be the formation of a leadership group or clique, bound together by ties of personal loyalty in the interests of mutual advancement and mutual protection, and the concealment of this feudal type of vassal relationship under declarations about "selection of cadres on the basis of political principle and practical efficiency." This is a much more dangerous form of pseudosocialism.

We can see, unfortunately, that many pseudosocialist forms of social relations were implanted after the revolution not by representatives of the former ruling classes but by former revolutionaries, who had come from the working class and peasantry.

Eighteenth-century philosophers argued about the interaction of social environment and human nature. "Man must be reeducated," some would say, "and then the social environment will change." "The social environment must be reshaped," said others, "and then people will change." Marxism sought to synthesize these opposing views. As Marx said, "Revolution is necessary not only because there is no other possible way to overthrow the ruling class but also because it is only in and through a revolution that the insurgent class can free itself from all the old crap and become capable of building society on a new basis."[32]

The decades since the October revolution have confirmed Marx's conclusion, although with certain important corrections. Not only in Russia but in many other countries the old economic and political institutions were drastically changed. The old distinctions of class and property were erased. In the process people also changed, especially those who took part in the revolution. But for one thing, not all of them changed for the better, and for another, the changes in the nature and character of people proceeded much more slowly than the economic and political transformations. It is therefore hardly surprising that many defects of the old society appeared in the new setting, often in a new form.

The analysis of these processes is crucial to an understanding of Soviet society. We cannot overlook the fact that along with the genuine thing sham socialism, or barracks socialism, actively aided by Stalin and the Stalinists, became part of Soviet reality. The distinguishing feature of Stalinist pseudosocialism was the gross violation of humane principles, under cover of lying talk about love for the people and socialist ideals. There was of course nothing socialist in mass arrests and murders of innocent people, in the huge machine of terror, the system of prisons and camps with their semislave labor. Other features of pseudosocialism can be perceived outside the institutions of terror: in the countryside, where many collective farmers received next to nothing for their labor on the communal land and could live only off the produce of their household plots. Pseudosocialism is evident in official indifference and nastiness to ordinary people, in disregard for their needs, in bureaucracy

32. Marx and Engels, *Sochineniia,* 2nd ed. 3:70. [Retranslated from the Russian.— G. S.]

and sectarianism. Laws that made criminals of people who were late to work or quit their jobs, even teenagers and women who had just miscarried, that sent kolkhoz women to Siberian exile for taking a bit of grain (*za koloski*)—all these are examples of Stalinist pseudosocialism. Another pseudosocialist institution was established in almost all workplaces under Stalin—workers were searched as they left their jobs. This system had existed in tsarist Russia before the 1905 revolution. Among the chief slogans of the workers' movement during that revolution was the abolition of such searches.

A precise description of Stalinist pseudosocialism has been provided by the Soviet economist Elkon Georgievich Leikin:

In broad historical perspective the Stalinist system can be regarded as a zigzag away from socialism on the USSR's path toward socialism. . . . But it was not simply a zigzag, not simply an unsuccessful variant of the movement toward socialism. In many essential features it was an abandonment of socialism. The great economic and cultural achievements won by the talent, labor, and heroism of our people for the sake of socialism were not placed in the service of socialism by the Stalinist system, with its ignorant, bureaucratic, and antihuman methods borrowed from the terrorist forms of capitalism and even from feudalism. . . .

But as the Stalinist system took our country, which was growing economically and culturally, with growing opportunities and growing demands, further and further away from socialism, the people were led to believe that they were not only building but had already built a socialist society. Thus, little by little, inevitably, the notion was fixed in people's minds that everything that constituted the political, ideological, and moral basis of Soviet society under Stalin was socialism: the cult of the state and worship of rank, the irresponsibility of those who hold power and the population's lack of rights, the hierarchy of privileges and the canonization of hypocrisy, the barrack system of social and intellectual life, the suppression of the individual and the destruction of independent thought, the environment of terror and suspicion, the atomization of people and the notorious "vigilance," the uncontrolled violence and the legalized cruelty. All of this was taken to be socialism.

But that is precisely how socialist society has been lampooned by ideologists of capitalism ever since the socialist movement appeared. The Stalinist system converted this hostile slander into reality. It could do this only by parasitizing the great works of our people, which was roused by October to the construction of socialism, by parasitizing its great faith in the final triumph of Leninist socialism and its great readiness to endure everything for the sake of that triumph. . . . The greatest tragedy of proletarian socialism, perhaps the greatest in its entire history, was the debasement and discrediting of socialism under the banner and in the name of socialism, in the epoch when mankind had begun the socialist revolution, in the very country that first began it and was called to serve as an example for other countries, and in the name of Lenin, a name connected by all people everywhere with the ideals of the socialist revolution. Without doubt this is Stalin's greatest crime, this besmirching, this betrayal of the cause of revolutionary socialism, the socialism of Marx and Lenin. This was a service to world capitalism unequalled by any enemies of socialism.[33]

Thus alongside of truly socialist relations, state-capitalist and semifeudal relations could be found, concealed under a pseudosocialist mask. To this can be added, with reference to the Gulag system of forced labor camps, state slaveholding relations.

The task of Soviet historians, sociologists, philosophers, and economists is to disentangle the diverse elements of the Stalinist system. There should be neither exaggeration nor minimization of these elements of pseudosocialism. Many people, both counterrevolutionary enemies and also Social Democrats, have pointed out the pseudosocialist features of Soviet society, sometimes with considerable accuracy. But they usually reduce the whole political and economic system to forms of pseudosocialism, and therefore they have been unable to see the true nature of the Soviet social system, its sources of strength and prospects for development. The Nazi leaders must have fed on such one-sided analyses when they shouted that Russia was a colossus with feet of clay, that Russia would collapse like a house of cards with the first Red Army defeat.

Among Soviet citizens and friends of the Soviet Union abroad the opposite error could often be found. Observing the many achievements of the Soviet Union and the many elements of truly socialist relationships, they did not see and did not want to see the many manifestations of pseudosocialism. As a result they could not understand the nature of the complex social and political processes in the Soviet Union, and therefore the exposure of the cult of Stalin's personality took them by surprise. It is impossible to comprehend Soviet society if one recognizes only the features of barracks pseudosocialism that were established in the Stalin era and in some cases even earlier. But it is also impossible if one sees only the truly socialist relationships.

The distinguishing characteristic of the Stalin era and the succeeding period has been not only the struggle between socialism and capitalism in their open manifestations but also the struggle between socialism and

33. The quotation is from an unpublished essay by Leikin, who died recently in his eighties. A copy of the manuscript is in my archives. In the 1970s Leikin began to publish some of his writings outside the Soviet Union under the pseudonym "Zimin." Although the authorities knew about this, they took no action against the old man. In the same way they did not touch the late Yevgeny Gnedin, who also began publishing abroad at the age of eighty.

barracks pseudosocialism. Some form of that struggle was unavoidable. But the particularly savage forms and the temporary triumph of pseudosocialism were avoidable. With different leadership there could have been very different results in the development of the Soviet Union not only up to the early fifties, when the Stalin era ended, but also up to the eighties.

CONCLUSION

■ 1
STALIN'S LAST YEARS

Decrepitude marked the last years of Stalin's life. The old despot became more and more suspicious. He stayed at his dachas most of the time, hardly ever living in his Kremlin apartment, not even visiting Moscow for weeks on end. The woods surrounding his dachas were filled with traps and mines. The corps of guards, under his direct command, grew constantly larger. Everyone summoned to meet with him was carefully searched. No one could be sure how such a meeting would end: with the visitor's arrest or a safe return home. For the most part Stalin lived in complete isolation. As in the past, he feared air travel; not once in his life did he take a plane. When his train went south, all other train traffic on his route was stopped, and MVD troops were posted every 100 or 150 meters along the way. Two or three separate, but short, trains—with Stalin in one of them—would make the trip, traveling nonstop but never after dark. When he was in the south he sometimes went for walks along the shore but never entered the water: he did not know how to swim.

He disliked going to the Kremlin through the then narrow streets of the Arbat district. The decision was therefore made to construct a special "upper line" of the Moscow subway, from the Kalinin station to Stalin's dacha at Kuntsevo, in addition to the "lower line," for public use, which had stops at four stations—Revolution Square, Arbat, Smolensk, and Kiev. The "upper line" was in operation as far as the Kiev station even before the war. Muscovites were supposed to make use of the ornately decorated "lower line" while the "upper line" was to be reserved exclusively for official use. This plan was not completed before Stalin's death in 1953.

Until the late twenties Stalin liked to walk around within the Kremlin; fairly often in the evenings he would also go for walks in the poorly lit streets outside the Kremlin but near it. In his later years he no longer went out into the streets. Several long underground passageways were built, apparently during the war, from the Kremlin to the Central Committee building on Nogin Square and to some other buildings in the center of Moscow, such as the Bolshoi Theater and the House of Trade Unions, so that top government and military leaders could go from one to the other without using the street. The guards in these "communication ways" were MVD troops, not members of Stalin's personal bodyguard, a fact that aroused Stalin's suspicious ire. Admiral Isakov recalls the following incident in his memoirs:

Stalin and I were walking through the long passageways under the Kremlin. At each crossing stood guards, who according to the code of procedure, fixed their gaze on each approaching person and followed him with their eyes until they could "pass him on" mentally to the next guard. I had barely noticed and begun to think about this when Stalin, seeming to read my thoughts, said with venomous hatred: "They're on guard, sure. . . . But you just watch—they'll shoot you in the back themselves."[1]

In the last years of his life Stalin was often ill and took very little part in the affairs of state. He occupied his time with various amusements. He liked to cut out colored pictures and photos in magazines, make

1. I. S. Isakov, "Iz vospominanii," unpublished manuscript.

montages of them, and paste them up on the walls of his bedroom and office. Guests were often invited to play chess with Stalin, but warned never to win. He enjoyed watching the Russian game *gorodki* and played it himself in earlier years, though poorly. Most of all he liked to play billiards and had a large pool table at each of his dachas. Sergei Shtemenko, who was chief of the General Staff from 1948 to 1952, often visited Stalin at Kuntsevo and describes him as follows:

Aside from holiday concerts and performances, which were usually arranged after official ceremonies, Stalin never went anywhere. For him "theater at home" consisted in listening to records or music on the radio. He personally gave a test hearing to most of the new records, which were regularly delivered to him, and would pass judgment on them right then and there. Notations in Stalin's hand would appear on the records: Good, Fair, Poor, or Trash. In the chest and on the end tables on either side of the massive record player, a gift to Stalin from the Americans in 1945, only the records with the first two inscriptions were kept. The rest were thrown out. Next to the phonograph was a gramophone of domestic make with a hand crank. Its owner took it with him wherever necessary. . . .

Not far from the house [the reference is to Stalin's "nearby" dacha at Kuntsevo, where he stayed most often] were several hollow tree trunks—without twigs or branches—in which nests for birds and squirrels had been contrived. This was a veritable songbirds' paradise. In front of this tree-hollow town were little feeding trays. Almost every day Stalin came here to feed his feathered friends. . . .

In the corner of the porch to the left of the main door was an iron spade with a wooden handle shiny from use; other garden tools were kept in a large cabinet. Stalin loved to look after his roses and apple trees, planted along the edge of the pond; he tended a small grove of lemon trees as well, and even . . . raised watermelons.[2]

In these years Stalin's suspicions extended to such devoted aides as Molotov, Kaganovich, Voroshilov, and Mikoyan. Molotov's wife was arrested and exiled, and Kaganovich's brother was driven to suicide. More and more these four top aides were excluded from important decision making. They were no longer summoned to Politburo meetings. Shortly before the Nineteenth Party Congress of 1952 Stalin publicly called Molotov and Voroshilov British spies and Mikoyan a Turkish spy. At a dinner with literary people Stalin also called Aleksei Tolstoy, Ilya Ehrenburg, and Pyotr Pavlenko international spies.[3] None of these people was arrested. At the Nineteenth Congress Molotov, Kaganovich, Voroshilov,

2. S. M. Shtemenko, *General'ny shtab v gody voiny* (Moscow, 1974), 2:39–40, 384.

3. Aleksandr Fadeev, who was at the dinner, reported the comment to his friend, N. K. Ilyukhov. [Tolstoy, Ehrenburg, and Pavlenko were very successful writers in the Stalin era. So was Fadeev, who became an alcoholic and committed suicide in 1956. — D. J.]

and Mikoyan were reelected to the Politburo, which was renamed the Presidium and swamped with new members. For the moment Stalin was probably concerned not so much with destroying his aides as with scaring them. Similarly, Stalin's personal secretary, Poskrebyshev, who had attended him for nearly twenty years, was barred from the Kremlin, and his wife was arrested. He himself spent the last months before Stalin's death at his dacha awaiting arrest. Likewise, General Vlasik, the head of Stalin's bodyguard, disappeared without a trace.

The émigré author Abdurrakhman Avtorkhanov has tried to make the case that in 1952 Stalin was actually deprived of power, which passed to Malenkov and Beria. He claims that these two men, who controlled the party apparatus and the machinery of repression, were powerful enough not only to disregard Stalin's opinions but even to act against his will. According to Avtorkhanov's version of events, Malenkov gave the main report at the Nineteenth Congress without Stalin's consent and against his will. Beria and Malenkov allegedly drew up a list of future members of the Central Committee Presidium, including Molotov, Kaganovich, Voroshilov, and Mikoyan, even though Stalin wished to expel them from the party leadership. Avtorkhanov even claims that at the postcongress plenum of the Central Committee Stalin submitted his resignation and the plenum accepted it.[4]

All this is obviously the fruit of Avtorkhanov's imagination. Despite Stalin's illness and age, he still kept the reins of power firmly in his hands. He often treated his assistants rudely and unceremoniously, referring to them contemptuously as "blind kittens." It is true that at the plenum after the Nineteenth Party Congress Stalin unexpectedly asked to be relieved of his duties, citing his age and the disloyalty of Molotov, Voroshilov, and several others. But the plenum refused to accept Stalin's resignation; indeed, virtually on its knees, it begged him to stay. Stalin "agreed" and immediately proposed a new Presidium and Secretariat, based on a list he had drawn up in advance. The list, in addition to the members of the then existing Poliburo, included the names of many who until then had enjoyed no special influence in the party. Such an "enlarged" Presidium obviously signaled forthcoming changes in the party leadership. During those last months Malenkov remained in Stalin's favor, but the same could not be said of Beria. The "doctor's plot" and the so-called Mingrelian case, which provided a pretext for the arrest of

4. Avtorkhanov, *Zagadka smerti Stalina* (Frankfort, 1976), p. 161.

many of Beria's cronies in Georgia,[5] caused Beria himself to be banished from Stalin's presence. During the questioning of Abakumov, the former minister of state security, the interrogators tried to force him to confess that Beria had ties with foreign intelligence.

The press began to stress once again the thesis that class struggle intensifies as the country moves closer to socialism. On January 13, 1953, *Pravda* denounced "right opportunists . . . who take the anti-Marxist position that class struggle is dying out. . . . The more we progress, the more intense will be the struggle of enemies of the people." On January 31 and February 6 *Pravda* repeated the charge, this time describing people who were allegedly creating new, widespread counterrevolutionary organizations:

> Fragments of the shattered exploiting classes, . . . masked epigones of defeated anti-Soviet groups—Mensheviks, SRs, Trotskyites, Bukharinites, bourgeois nationalists . . . all sorts of degenerate elements—people who kowtow to all things foreign, pilferers of socialist property. . . . The Anglo-American imperialists are now placing their bets on such people.[6]

All the signs pointed to another 1937. Only Stalin's death at the beginning of March 1953 prevented a renewal of mass repression.

Within several months after Stalin's death the most absurd rumors began to circulate in Georgia about its causes. Stalin's son Vasily frequently added credence to these rumors. As early as 1953, he began shouting during his drunken orgies that his father had been murdered. In the seventies Avtorkhanov collected a large number of such fantastic rumors and published them in his book. Citing Stalin's alleged good health, Avtorkhanov assures the reader that in all likelihood Stalin was murdered, the murderer being none other than Beria. In the preface to his book Avtorkhanov writes:

> If every member of Stalin's last Politburo has died or will die a peaceful death, that is thanks to the man they killed: Beria. If a second Great Purge, far more terrible than the Yezhovshchina did not happen, if hundreds of thousands were saved from Cheka bullets and millions from the prison camps, it is most likely that the country owes Beria a debt of gratitude for this too. It was not his intention, but he did perform this unwitting service. . . . Beria knew too much about both Stalin and the fate of his own predecessors to indulge in illusions. [He

5. See *Ocherki po istorii KP Gruzii* (Tbilisi, 1963), p. 248. [For the doctors' case, see above, chapter 13. The Mingrelians, a subgroup of the Georgian nationality, were charged with nationalism in 1951.—D. J.]

6. *Pravda*, February 6, 1953.

knew that] Stalin wanted his head. Beria had no other way of saving his own life than to take Stalin's. Thus Beria's plot against Stalin was organized, one that was incomparably difficult but quite brilliant in its manner of execution. The organizer of this plot demonstrated that he excelled Stalin in an area in which Stalin considered himself the master—the art of political murder.[7]

Although Avtorkhanov goes on for three hundred pages in an attempt to prove his assertions, he does not make them believable. For example, Stalin was by no means in "good health." Boris Bazhanov, whose memoirs I discussed in part 2, described Stalin's health as follows:

> His was a sedentary and extremely unhealthy way of life. He never took up sports or did any physical labor. He smoked a pipe and drank, preferring Kakhetian wine. During the second half of his reign he spent every evening at the table, eating and drinking in the company of his Politburo. With this kind of life it is amazing that he lived to be seventy-three.[8]

In fact Stalin was never noted for good health. Even in late 1933 and early 1934 arterial spasms and serious heart disturbances were noted, an illness that was then called "quinsy." Today doctors describe these as symptoms of the serious illness of angina pectoris or coronary thrombosis. Stalin had trouble breathing and severe pains in the left side of his chest and all over his rib cage. The main cause of this illness was not only his unhealthy sedentary life but his smoking habit.

In late 1933 and early 1934 Stalin's condition was so serious that the Politburo considered it necessary to name a possible successor (Kirov). Stalin recovered, but not completely. He continued to have high blood pressure, and attacks of angina occurred again, more than once. He suffered an especially long and serious attack in late 1948. Not only his smoking habit but the tremendous stress of the war years was telling on him by then. He was sick for nearly half a year, and the doctors were seriously concerned about the prognosis.

Stalin's seventieth birthday found him a severely ill man. The fact that he sat in silence at his own birthday celebration, listening to the speeches and greetings without making even a short speech of acknowledgment, gave rise to various and contradictory interpretations. I happen to know, however, that in December 1949, before he had fully recovered from his angina attack, Stalin was suffering from disturbances of his normal ability to speak. That was the main reason why he did not make even a brief

---

7. Avtorkhanov, *Zagadka smerti Stalina*, pp. 1–2.
8. Bazhanov, *Vospominaniia sekretaria Stalina* (Paris[?], 1980), pp. 145–146.

speech at his birthday celebration. It was partly because of Stalin's illness that talks with a delegation from the new Chinese Communist government of Mao Tse-tung lasted an unusually long time. The state of Stalin's health was also one of the reasons why he could not make the major report at the Nineteenth Party Congress, entrusting that task instead to Malenkov and limiting himself to brief summary remarks. In the last months of his life Stalin suffered from painful attacks of high blood pressure. He was tormented by frequent headaches, although he stubbornly refused to submit to systematic treatment or even a medical examination.

Thus I have no grounds to question the medical report on the causes of Stalin's death that was signed by A. Tretyakov, the minister of health, I. Kuperin, head of the Kremlin medical services, and a large group of leading physicians.[9]

Stalin had a severe brain hemorrhage in one of his dachas near Moscow in the late evening of March 1 or early morning of March 2. He usually spent his evenings in complete isolation. The fact that he did not ask for his dinner at the usual time that evening worried his guards. The woman who cleaned Stalin's rooms, and who therefore had the right to enter the room where he was resting, peeked in and saw that he was lying on the rug with his clothes on. The guards could not bring themselves to go in, but instead called the Presidium. Not until the morning of March 2 did doctors arrive and take the first electocardiogram. From that time on members of the Presidium remained by Stalin's side, taking turns two at a time, as Stalin was given intensive care. Details of these events are given in Khrushchev's memoirs and Svetlana Alliluyeva's *Twenty Letters to a Friend.* Alliluyeva writes:

My father died a difficult and terrible death. . . . For the last twelve hours the lack of oxygen was acute. His face altered and became dark. His lips turned black and the features became unrecognizable. The last hours were nothing but a slow strangulation. The death agony was horrible. He literally choked to death as we watched. At what seemed like the very last moment he suddenly opened his eyes and cast a glance over everyone in the room. It was a terrible glance, insane or perhaps angry and full of the fear of death and the unfamiliar faces of the doctors bent over him. The glance swept over everyone in a second. Then something incomprehensible and awesome happened that to this day I can't forget and don't understand. He suddenly lifted his left hand as though he were pointing to

9. *Izvestia,* March 7, 1953.

something above or bringing down a curse on us all. The gesture was incomprehensible but full of menace, and no one could say to whom or at what it might be directed.[10]

Stalin's death was indirectly the cause of one more tragedy. During the time he lay in state millions of people crowded into central Moscow to pay their last respects to this man whom they knew so little, whom they had trusted so long. Because of the authorities' incompetent organization, the crowd got out of hand. Hundreds, perhaps thousands, of Soviet citizens were crushed or trampled to death by other Soviet citizens, blinded by the cult of Stalin's person. In those same days the NKVD arrested hundreds of people in Moscow alone, as part of the "mobilization plan" of preventive arrests, designed for war or any serious domestic or foreign complications. This plan was put into partial effect while Stalin lay in state. But those were probably the last tragedies connected with Stalin's name. There began a new era, which requires separate study and analysis.

■ 2

THE PROBLEM OF ASSESSING STALIN'S RECORD

The evaluation of Stalin's record as a whole has attracted many historians and commentators. Even among people who are not hostile to socialism or communism one often encounters the view that Stalin loyally continued Lenin's cause, was the most important recent leader of the Communist movement, and transformed the face of Russia and of the whole world. While acknowledging and condemning Stalin's crimes, these historians try to make the case that the building of socialism in a country like Russia could not have been accomplished without barbarism, cruelty, and the creation of a despotic totalitarian state. In any case, they argue, Stalin's name is inseparable from Lenin's and from the program and methods of the Communist Party in general.

Some official Soviet historians and certain bourgeois commentators hold similar views. For example, the West German newspaper *Die Welt* ran a big article on the tenth anniversary of Stalin's death, declaring that Stalin had transformed Russia from a backward agrarian country into a mighty industrial power capable of resisting Hitler's invasion, as tsarist

10. Svetlana Alliluyeva, *Twenty Letters to a Friend* (New York, 1967), p. 10.

Russia could never have done. To the question whether the misery and destruction of millions were really necessary for Russia to keep its independence, *Die Welt* had no answer. That question was left as "one of the many enigmas" of history.[11]

Approximately the same approach was taken by one of Stalin's best-known biographers, Isaac Deutscher.[12] Telling the story of industrialization and collectivization, Deutscher contended that Stalin could be considered one of the greatest reformers of all times and nations. In Deutscher's opinion Lenin and Trotsky led the October revolution and gave the Soviet people the ideas of socialism, but only Stalin put these ideas into effect. The price was very high, but Deutscher saw in that fact merely proof of the difficulty of the task.

I cannot agree with the reasoning of *Die Welt* or Deutscher. It was not Stalin who taught the Soviet people to read and write, as the article in *Die Welt* claims. It was the October revolution that opened the road to education and culture for the Soviet people. Our country would have traveled that road far more quickly if Stalin had not destroyed hundreds of thousands of the intelligentsia, both old and new. Prisoners in Stalin's concentration camps accomplished a great deal, building almost all the canals and hydroelectric stations in the USSR, many railways, factories, pipelines, even tall buildings in Moscow. But industry would have developed faster if these millions of innocent people had been employed as free workers. Likewise, Stalin's use of force against the peasantry slowed down the growth rate of agriculture with painful effects on the whole Soviet economy to the present day. He did not speed up but rather slowed down the overall rate of development that our country might have enjoyed. The "price" our people paid, its sacrifices, underline not the difficulty of the task but Stalin's cruel recklessness. The price was so great that even today we continue to pay for much that was done by Stalin. Too much of what Deutscher calls "victories" turned out in fact to be defeats for socialism.

Many right-wing socialists also make an incorrect and tendentious assessment of Stalin's work. For example, Pietro Nenni asks what en-

11. *Die Welt*, March 5, 1963.

12. [Medvedev cites a 1962 Stuttgart edition of Deutscher's *Stalin: A Political Biography*. He seems unaware of Deutscher's ideological position, which places him among the "socialists and revisionists of various persuasions." He was a Polish Jewish Communist, expelled in 1932 for Trotskyism, who kept the faith that democratic socialism would someday triumph over Stalinism in the Soviet Union. —D. J.]

abled Stalin to win and hold power, then answers: "More than any other Bolshevik leader he had absorbed 'Russian reality.' "[13] Intent on escaping from the notion that one man was responsible for the multitude of events and processes associated with Stalin's name, Nenni simply identifies Stalinism with "the Communism of three decades, from the death of Lenin to the death of Stalin."

This approach of equating Stalinism with socialism and Leninism is taken even more persistently by opponents of Marxism and socialism in general or by those who once supported socialism but now oppose it. Solzhenitsyn asserts, for example, that Stalin was never a major political figure and that there never was a distinct phenomenon that could be called "Stalinism"; there was only Marxism and Leninism. Stalin "followed exactly in Lenin's footsteps," he says, "acting as a blind and superficial force carrying out someone else's will."[14]

Milovan Djilas takes a different tack in his *Conversations with Stalin*. He calls Stalin "the greatest criminal in history," yet warns against injustice in the final appraisal:

> What he wished to accomplish, and even that which he did accomplish, could not be accomplished in any other way. The forces that swept him forward and that he led, with their absolute ideals, could have had no other kind of leader but him, given that level of Russian and world relations, nor could they have been served by different methods. The creator of a closed social system, he was at the same time its instrument and, in changed circumstances and all too late, he became its victim. Unsurpassed in violence and crime, Stalin was no less the leader and organizer of a certain social system.[15]

The main point of such arguments is clear: if the socialist system in the USSR could not have been created in any other way than by monstrous crimes, it follows that no more such experiments should be made; if Stalin's lawlessness flows from the very nature of socialism, Marxism, and Leninism, then those doctrines too should be renounced.

Dogmatists and Stalinists in the socialist camp do not of course draw such far-reaching conclusions, although they too try to show that there was total continuity from Lenin to Stalin. Some of the dogmatists avoid

13. [Nenni, *Le prospettive dei socialismo dopo la destalinizzazione* (Turin, 1962). Medvedev quotes a Russian translation, *Perspektivy sotsializma posle destalinizatsii*, (Moscow, 1963), p. 16.—D. J.]

14. See Aleksander Solzhenitsyn, *Arkhipelag-Gulag*, Bk. 1, (Paris, 1973), p. 80; and an interview with Solzhenitsyn in Stockholm in *Russkaia mysl'* (Paris), January 16, 1975.

15. Milovan Djilas, *Conversations with Stalin* (New York, 1962), pp. 187, 190, 191.

the term "crime," preferring "mistake." Molotov in his day wrote that way about Stalin.[16] And the Chinese Communist newspaper *Jenmin Jibao* was equally lenient in 1956 and 1957 articles on Stalin, referring only to his "serious mistakes."[17] Another series of articles in the Chinese press between 1963 and 1965 was even more lenient. An editorial in *Jenmin Jibao* in 1963 said:

Stalin's mistakes should serve as a historical lesson and a warning to Soviet Communists and Communists of other countries not to repeat such mistakes or to make fewer mistakes. And this would be beneficial. Positive as well as negative historical experiences, if they are correctly . . . generalized, are useful for all Communists.[18]

The newspaper goes on to recommend Lenin's attitude toward Rosa Luxemburg and August Bebel. Although they made quite a few mistakes in their fight against counterrevolution—so the argument goes—that did not prevent Lenin from respecting them as great revolutionaries and learning from their mistakes.

Such analogies are not appropriate to Stalin, because his repressive actions in the thirties were not directed against counterrevolutionaries. The main tendency of the mass repression was to exterminate the prorevolutionary cadres of the party, the army, and the intelligentsia. "In the seventeen years I spent in Stalinist prisons and camps," A. V. Snegov writes in his "Open Letter to Mao Tse-tung," "I saw no counterrevolutionaries."[19] The memoirs of Ya. I. Drobinsky, former secretary of the party's Mogilev city committee, include a bitterly ironical episode. A real Polish spy, an officer in the intelligence section of the Polish General Staff, was suddenly put in a cell in Minsk Prison that was full of party activists and Soviet commanders from the border areas. The entire cell, especially the army men, took a hostile attitude toward the Pole. At one point the Pole got angry and asked one of the commanders:

What do you want from me? Why are you so hostile toward me? After all, I am a Polish citizen, a Polish nationalist, an officer and a patriot, in a Soviet prison. That is normal; that is absolutely normal. But why are you, a Soviet patriot and Communist, in a Soviet prison? That is completely incomprehensible to me, and not at all normal. Can you explain it to me?

16. *Pravda*, April 22, 1957.
17. *Narodnyi Kitai*, 1957, no. 2, supplement, p. 7.
18. *Jenmin Jibao*, September 13, 1963.
19. A copy of Snegov's open letter is in my archives.

Naturally no one could. Subsequently the Polish officer was exchanged for a Soviet intelligence agent, while most of the Soviet officers from the same cell were shot.[20]

Another totally unacceptable theory is one that could be called "balancing." Stalin's crimes are placed on one side of the scales and his achievements on the other. In both the Soviet press and the Chinese press "calculations" have been made, purporting to show that Stalin's record consisted of 30 percent crime and 70 percent accomplishment. However, the rendering of great services by a political leader to his country and party does not absolve him from all sins or give him the right to commit crimes with impunity. Besides, when such "calculations" are made the items placed on the scale to counterbalance Stalin's crimes are usually victories gained by the Soviet people, not by Stalin, and often they were gained *in spite of* Stalin's mistakes and crimes.

Stalin was a leader in hard times. For many years he enjoyed the confidence of a majority of the party and the people. During those years the nation he led made considerable progress culturally and economically and gained victory in the Great Patriotic War. But would those successes not have been greater still if the terror of the thirties had not occurred? Could we not have won the war much faster and with fewer losses if Stalin had not destroyed the best military leaders before the war and if he had conducted a more sensible foreign policy? What do we really have to thank Stalin for? For the fact that he did not bring our country and army to total disaster?

It is a fact that Stalin was Lenin's heir as leader of the Soviet Communist Party and the world Communist movement. But he was the kind of heir who squandered rather than increased his inheritance. Therefore we cannot equate Stalinism with socialism, Marxism, or Leninism—no matter how imperfect those doctrines might be in some respects. Stalinism is the sum total of the perversions Stalin introduced into the theory and practice of scientific socialism. It is a phenomenon profoundly alien to Marxism and Leninism.

Many great figures of the past, in whom all humanity takes pride, also had weaknesses and shortcomings. To their contemporaries such shortcomings sometimes seemed quite significant, but we hardly remember such things in comparison to the main accomplishments of those people. Stalin's lawlessness and arbitrary rule will never be forgotten. The things

20. From the memoirs of Ya. I. Drobinsky.

that Stalin did belong to history, and his name will always be part of history, but humanity can never take pride in him. "Evil rulers," says an Oriental proverb, "find no refuge even in the grave. Posterity pursues their memory, and twenty centuries cannot wipe the disgrace from them."

Of course Stalin did teach some lessons to those who came after him. We now know that socialism—although it does not automatically produce lawlessness, as its enemies maintain—is in itself no guarantee against lawlessness and the abuse of power. If socialism is not combined with democracy, it can become a breeding ground for new crimes. Under Stalin the Soviet Union was afflicted by a serious disease and lost many of its finest sons and daughters. Important steps have been made toward recovery, but not everything connected with the Stalin cult and Stalinism is behind us, by no means everything. The process of cleansing socialism and the Communist movement, of washing out all the layers of Stalinist filth, is not yet finished. Firmly and consistently the process must be carried through to the end.

GLOSSARY

Bukharinist Supporter of the policies or theories of Nikolai Bukharin, or of the "right deviation" (the opposition to Stalin from the right, within the Soviet Communist Party); sometimes termed pejoratively "Bukharinite."

Central Committee or CC The chief policy making body of the Communist Party of the Soviet Union during periods between congresses. It convenes usually two or three times a year at a plenary session, or "plenum." Between plenums policy is made by the Politburo, which is technically a body elected by the CC.

Central Executive Committee or CEC From 1917 to 1936 the chief policy making body of the Soviet government, nominally elected by and responsible to a Congress of Soviets. In 1936 it was replaced by the Presidium of the Supreme Soviet.

Cheka *See* State Security Agencies. This Soviet acronym was taken from the initials of the organization Chrezvychainaya Komissia (Extraordinary Commission), established by the new Soviet government in December 1917 to combat counterrevolution and sabotage.

Chekist A member of the Soviet security police. Originally it meant "agent of the Cheka," but the term continued to be used for any operative of the security police agencies that succeeded the Cheka.

Communist Party of the Soviet Union or CPSU Since 1917, the ruling party of the Soviet Union and, since the early twenties, the only legal political party in that country. It was originally the Bolshevik faction, led by Lenin, within the Russian Social Democratic Labor Party, but changed its name to Russian Communist Party (Bolshevik) in 1918, then to All-Union Communist Party (Bolshevik) in 1925. The present name was adopted in 1952, with the parenthetical reference to the Bolsheviks being dropped. In this book, unless otherwise specified, "the party" refers to this organization.

Council of People's Commissars (Russian acronym, Sovnarkom) Highest government body in the USSR, equivalent to a cabinet in Western governmental structure. In 1946, the term "people's commissar" was dropped in favor of the more traditional term "minister," and this body became the present Council of Ministers. The chairman of the Council has a position roughly equivalent to that of prime minister in Western countries.

Gorkom (plural, gorkomy) The party committee of a city or town *(gorod)*.

GPU *See* State Security Agencies. The initials stand for State Political Administration (Gosudarstvennoe Politicheskoe Upravlenie).

Great Patriotic War The Soviet term for the war waged by the USSR against Nazi Germany and its allies, from Hitler's invasion of the USSR in June 1941 through the Soviet occupation of Berlin and the unconditional surrender of Germany in May 1945 and of Japan in August. Hitler's invasion brought the Soviet Union into World War II, but the Soviet war effort is officially regarded as a separate component of the world war, not synonymous with it.

Kolkhoz (plural, kolkhozes) A collective farm (owned collectively by its members, like a cooperative, but usually obliged to deliver a certain quantity of agricultural goods to the Soviet government each year); the term is not italicized in the text.

Kolkhoznik Collective farmer.

Komsomol The youth organization of the Soviet Communist movement, for ages fourteen through twenty-eight, the only officially permitted political organization for young people.

Krai Sometimes translated as "territory"; a large administrative unit, usually in an outlying part of the USSR near a past or present border.

Kraikom (plural, kraikomy) The party committee of a *krai*.

Machine and Tractor Station (or MTS) A government-owned depot of agricultural machinery for use by kolkhozes; an instrument for reinforcing government control of the collective farms.

MGB *See* State Security Agencies.

MTS *See* Machine and Tractor Station.

MVD *See* State Security Agencies.

NKVD *See* State Security Agencies.

Nomenklatura Literally, a list of official positions in the Soviet system that may be filled by appointment only, from above; by extension, the holders of such positions, especially the highly placed party and government leaders, who are perceived as the chief beneficiaries and controllers of the system.

Obkom (plural, obkomy) The party committee of an *oblast*.

Oblast (plural, oblasti) Sometimes translated as "province"; a large administrative unit, consisting of a number of *raiony*.

OGPU Same as GPU.

Okrug (plural, okrugi) Usually occurring with the adjective *voenny* and translated as "military district." Not the same as a *raion*, which is also translated as "district."

Old Bolshevik Term used for veteran revolutionaries who had been with the Bolshevik movement most of their lives, usually since before the revolution.

Oprichnik Member of the *oprichnina*.

Oprichnina In sixteenth-century Russia, Ivan the Terrible's special police force, which carried out his reign of terror.

Pioneers The Soviet Communist organization for schoolchildren, ages ten to fifteen.

Politburo The Political Bureau of the Central Committee of the CPSU, its chief policy making body between CC plenums.

Presidium of the Central Committee The name of the Politburo from 1952 to 1966.

Presidium of the Supreme Soviet *See* Central Executive Committee.

Raikom (plural, raikomy) The party committee of a *raion*.

Raion (plural, raiony) Usually translated as "district," it is a smaller unit, a number of which make up an *oblast;* a city may also have several *raiony*.

RSFSR (Russian Soviet Federated Socialist Republic) The largest and most central of the fifteen republics constituting the Union of Soviet Socialist Republics (USSR). Often referred to briefly as the Russian Republic.

Sovkhoz (plural, sovkhozes) A state farm (wholly owned by the government).

State Security Agencies The Cheka, 1917–1922, was succeeded by the GPU (also called OGPU), which in turn was reorganized in 1934 as the NKVD (People's Commissariat of Internal Affairs). In 1941 a separate NKGB (People's Commissariat of State Security) was established, while police duties not directly involving "state security" were left to the NKVD. In 1946 the NKVD was changed to the MVD (Ministry of Internal Affairs) and the NKGB to the MGB (Ministry of State Security). In 1954, after Stalin's death, the MGB was reorganized as the KGB (Committee of State Security) under the Council of Ministers; that is, it was reduced in status from a ministry to a "committee," while still remaining very powerful. See also the author's account of the history of these agencies in chapter 11, section 8.

Troika (plural, troiki) In Russian, a general term meaning "threesome"; specifically, in the Stalin era, a three-member board with special powers to sentence people without following normal legal procedure.

Trotskyist, "Trotskyite" The term Trotskyist refers to a supporter of the program and positions of Leon Trotsky as leader of the Left Opposition in the Soviet Communist Party, the International Left Opposition of the late twenties and early thirties, or the Fourth International (from the mid-thirties on). Often termed pejoratively "Trotskyite." In English-speaking countries, especially in the thirties, when the pro-Stalinist Communist parties were a strong influence, the term "Trotskyite" was widely used. Official Soviet publications, translated into English, such as the texts of the Moscow trials, commonly contained such phrases as "Trotskyite mad dogs." In the present translation "Trotskyite" is used only when quoting from or referring to Stalinist accusations or diatribes. Otherwise, the form used is "Trotskyist." (In Russian, there is only one form—*trotskist* [or, for a female, *trotskistka*]—and the movement or doctrine is *trotskizm*.)

Zinovievist Supporter of the theories or policies of Grigory Zinoviev as head of the "New Opposition" in 1925 and after. Sometimes termed pejoratively "Zinovievite."

INDEX